THE ESSENTIAL GUIDE TO ENTERTAINMENT LAW

DEALMAKING

Edited by

Jay Shanker
Kirk Schroder

with a foreword by Peter Dekom

EG2EL, LLC

> Questions about this Publication
>
> For assistance with shipments, billing or other customer service matters, please call our Customer Services Department at:
>
> 1 - (323) 570-1380
>
> To obtain a copy of EG2EL: Dealmaking, please visit: www.EG2EL.com
>
> See our web page about this book:
>
> www.EG2EL.com

COPYRIGHT © 2021
by EG2EL, LLC

All rights reserved. No part of this publication may be reproduced in any form or by any electronic or mechanical means including information storage and retrieval systems without permission in writing from the publisher.

First Paperback Edition
Printed in the United States of America.
ISBN 978-1-7361695-0-6

EG2EL, LLC
2310 West Main Street
Suite 208
Richmond, VA 23220
www.EG2EL.com

— SUMMARY CONTENTS —

Contents v
Foreword by Peter Dekom xxix
Preface by Jay Shanker xxxiii
Preface by Kirk Schroder xxxvii
About the Editors/Authors xxxix
Disclaimer lv

CHAPTER 1
Motion Picture Development and Production 1
Greg Snodgrass

CHAPTER 2
Motion Picture Distribution 47
Stephen Monas

CHAPTER 3
Motion Picture Finance 93
Robert Williams

CHAPTER 4
Introduction to Television 165
Ken Basin

CHAPTER 5
Unscripted Television 187
Justin B. Wineburgh

CHAPTER 6
Scripted Television 237
Ken Basin

CHAPTER 7
Music Industry Law: A 360° View 373
Henry Root

Chapter 8
Music Publishing Industry 455
Jeffrey Brabec, Todd Brabec

Chapter 9
Theater Law Victoria 507
Victoria Traube, Hailey Ferber

Chapter 10
Literary Publishing 547
Gail Ross

Chapter 11
Video Games, Interactive Media and Dealmaking 583
Andrew Boortz

Chapter 12
A Guide to Structuring and Taxation in the Entertainment Industry 669
Brad Cohen, Shane Nix

Chapter 13
Recurring Contracting Concerns: Some Further Thoughts 753
Jay Shanker

Chapter 14
Fundamentals of Entertainment Talent Representation by Agents and Managers 773
Kirk Schroder, Jay Shanker

Chapter 15
Developing an Entertainment Law Practice 819
Kirk Schroder, Jay Shanker

Glossary of Terms 853
Illustrative Forms List 917
Index 923

— CONTENTS —

Foreword by Peter Dekom xxix
Preface by Jay Shanker xxxiii
Preface by Kirk Schroder xxxvii
About the Editors/Authors xxxix
Disclaimer lv

CHAPTER 1
Motion Picture Development and Production
Greg Snodgrass

1.1. Motion Picture Development and Production:
     An Overview 1
1.2. Underlying Rights 3
     1.2.1. Chain of Title 6
     1.2.2. Securing Underlying Rights 10
1.3. Development 17
     1.3.1. Writer Agreements 18
     1.3.2. Line Producers 20
     1.3.3. Producer Agreements 21
     1.3.4. Director Agreements 24
     1.3.5. Actor Agreements 27
     1.3.6. (What the Heck Is) Pay or Play? 33
     1.3.7. Contingent Compensation 35
           1.3.7.1. Box Office Bonuses 35
           1.3.7.2. Gross Participations 37
           1.3.7.3. Deferments 37
           1.3.7.4. Net Participations 38
1.4. Production 39
     1.4.1. Below the Line 39
     1.4.2. (In Praise of) the Boilerplate 41
     1.4.3. A Word about Music 42
     1.4.4. Clearances 43
     1.4.5. Insurance 43
     1.4.6. Locations 44
     1.4.7. Production Service and Effects Agreements 45
1.5. About the Forms 45

Chapter 2
Motion Picture Distribution
Stephen Monas

2.1. Introduction: Art, Meet Commerce 47
2.2. Parties: What Is a "Distributor"? 52
2.3. Picture Specifications and Approvals 55
    2.3.1. Screenplay, Director, Cast, Budget 56
    2.3.2. Essential Elements 56
    2.3.3. Advertising Rights 57
    2.3.4. Production Cost 57
    2.3.5. Approvals 58
    2.3.6. Other Specifications 58
2.4. Term and Territory 60
    2.4.1. Term 60
    2.4.2. Territory 61
    2.4.3. Territorial Definitions 62
    2.4.4. European Union 63
2.5. Rights 64
    2.5.1. Copyright Basics 64
    2.5.2. Definition of Rights 65
        2.5.2.1. Exploitation Rights 65
        2.5.2.2. Advertising Rights 67
        2.5.2.3. Ancillary Rights 67
        2.5.2.4. Derivative Rights 68
2.6. Holdbacks and Windows 69
2.7. Minimum Guarantees 71
    2.7.1. Payment Terms 72
        2.7.1.1. Domestic Distribution 72
        2.7.1.2. Foreign Distribution 72
        2.7.1.3. License Agreement 73
    2.7.2. Interparty Agreements and NOAs 73
    2.7.3. Sales Agents and Intermediaries 74
2.8. Application of Gross Receipts 74
    2.8.1. Gross Receipts 75
    2.8.2. Distribution Fees 77
    2.8.3. Distribution Expenses 79
    2.8.4. Recoupment of Minimum Guarantee 80
    2.8.5. Box Office Bonuses; VOD Bonuses 81
2.9. Delivery 84
2.10. Security Interests 85
    2.10.1. UCC Financing Statement 86

          2.10.2. Copyright Mortgage 87
          2.10.3. State and Federal Law Conflicts 87
   2.11. Theatrical Release Commitments 89
   2.12. Piracy 90
   2.13. Remedies 91
   2.14. Other Provisions 91

CHAPTER 3
Motion Picture Finance
Robert Williams

3.1. Introduction 93
3.2. The Parties 96
     3.2.1. The Distributors 97
     3.2.2. The Sales Agent 98
     3.2.3. The Production SPV/Borrower/Licensor 99
     3.2.4. The Financiers 101
     3.2.5. The Completion Guarantor 106
     3.2.6. The Laboratory 108
     3.2.7. The Guilds 109
     3.2.8. The Collection Agent 110
     3.2.9. Other Parties 110
3.3. The Finance Agreements 111
     3.3.1. Development Finance 111
     3.3.2. Pre-Production Finance: The Budget, Strike Price
            and Finance Plan 113
     3.3.3. Pre-production Finance: The Pre-production Facility 117
     3.3.4. Production Finance: The Mezzanine Loan 120
            3.3.4.1. The Mezzanine Term Sheet for Production
                     Financing 121
            3.3.4.2. The Mezzanine Loan Agreement 124
            3.3.4.3. Production Finance: The Senior Loan
                     Documents 131
            3.3.4.4. Production Finance: The Equity 132
            3.3.4.5. Securities Laws and Equity Investments 135
                     a. Regulation D 136
                     b. Regulation S 140
                     c. Crowdfunding as an Alternative Equity
                        Model for Lower Budget Films 140
3.4. Security 142
     3.4.1. Security Agreements 142
     3.4.2. Cross-Border Security Issues 145

		3.4.3.	The Creation of a Security Interest in the United States..149
		3.4.4.	Perfection of a Security Interest under Article 9..150
		3.4.5.	Perfection of Security Interests in U.S. Copyright: The Copyright Mortgage........................152
	3.4.6.	Stock and LLC Membership Pledge Agreements....................153	
	3.4.7.	Notices of Assignment, Interparty and Intercreditor Security Documentation...155	
		3.4.7.1.	Notices of Assignment...155
		3.4.7.2.	The Sales Agent Interparty Agreement 157
		3.4.7.3.	Intercreditor Agreements...159
	3.4.8.	The Completion Guaranty...160	
	3.4.9.	Laboratory Pledgeholder Agreements......................................161	
	3.4.10.	The Collection Account Management Agreement...................161	
3.5.	Conclusion..163		

CHAPTER 4
Introduction to Television
Ken Basin

4.1.	An Overview..165	
4.2.	Who Are the Players (and How Do They Interact)?..............................166	
	4.2.1	Service Providers (Talent) 167
	4.2.2.	Studios 169
	4.2.3.	Networks...171
	4.2.4.	MVPDs 173
	4.2.5.	Broadcast Stations..174
	4.2.6.	Advertisers 175
4.3.	Online Video Distribution...177	
	4.3.1.	Types of Online Video Distribution..177
		4.3.1.1. SVOD 178
		4.3.1.2. AVOD 178
		4.3.1.3. TVOD 179
		4.3.1.4. FVOD 179
		4.3.1.5. VOD 179
	4.3.2.	Other Key Distinctions 180
	4.3.3.	The Roles of Digital Content Companies 181

CHAPTER 5
Unscripted Television
Justin B. Wineburgh

5.1. Introduction – Dealmaking in the "Unscripted" Television Industry 187
5.2. Option, Co-Production and Joint Venture Agreement 189
    5.2.1. Term, Tail, and Freeze Period 190
    5.2.2. Fees and Payments 191
    5.2.3. Control 192
    5.2.4. Credit 192
    5.2.5. Post Term Rights and Obligations 193
5.3. Talent Attachment 193
    5.3.1. Before the Sale – The Talent Attachment 194
        5.3.1.1. Length of the Attachment 194
        5.3.1.2. The Non-Compete Provision 195
        5.3.1.3. Development Services 196
        5.3.1.4. Compensation 197
    5.3.2. After the Sale – The Talent Agreement 197
        5.3.2.1. Participation 197
            a. Fixed Compensation 197
            b. Contingent Compensation 198
            c. Pre-Prodution/Production of the Program 199
            d. Access 199
            e. Locations 200
            f. On-Camera Services 201
            g. Post-production Participation 201
            h. Additional Participation 201
            i. Promotional Appearances 202
        5.3.2.2. Grant of Rights 203
        5.3.2.3. Additional Common Provisions of Talent Agreements 205
            a. Restrictions on Use of Trademark 205
            b. Termination 205
            c. Remedies 205
            d. Unions/Guilds 205
            e. Employment Relationship 206
            f. Assignment 206
            g. Representations 206
            h. Mediation/Arbitration 207
5.4. Distribution Agreements 207
    5.4.1. Granted Rights 208

	5.4.2.	Territory	208
	5.4.3.	Production Budgets, License Fees and Payment	209
	5.4.4.	Guidelines and Approvals	211
	5.4.5.	Editing and Delivery	211
	5.4.6.	Promotion of the Series	212
5.5.	Independent Contractor Agreement	212
	5.5.1.	Introduction	212
	5.5.2.	Services and Length of Term	213
	5.5.3.	Consideration, Expenses, Benefits and Credit	214
	5.5.4.	Contractor Status	214
	5.5.5.	Work for Hire	215
	5.5.6.	Name and Likeness	215
	5.5.7.	Assignment	216
	5.5.8.	Confidentiality	216
5.6.	Release, Consents and Location Agreement	217
	5.6.1.	Location Agreement	218
		5.6.1.1. Grant of Rights	218
		5.6.1.2. Length of Term	219
		5.6.1.3. Compensation	220
		5.6.1.4. Confidentiality	220
	5.6.2.	Standard Appearance Release	220
		5.6.2.1. Grant of Rights	220
		5.6.2.2. Compensation	221
		5.6.2.3. Confidentiality	222
		5.6.2.4. Third Party Releases	222
		5.6.2.5. Authorization for Release of Medical Information	222
	5.6.3.	Ultra-Hazardous Activities and Assumption of Risk	222
	5.6.4.	Appearance Release for a Minor	223
	5.6.5.	Acquired Footage/Still Photograph License	224
	5.6.6.	Authorization to Use Names, Products and Logos	225
	5.6.7.	Public Filming Notice	225
5.7.	Product and Service Placement Agreements	225
	5.7.1.	Introduction	225
	5.7.2.	Placement of the Product and Failure to Place	228
	5.7.3.	The Manner of Display	228
	5.7.4.	Fees and Payments	229
	5.7.5.	Representations, Warranties and Indemnity Provisions	229
5.8.	Composer Agreements and Music Licenses	230
	5.8.1.	Introduction	230
	5.8.2.	Composer Agreement	231
		5.8.2.1. Fees	231
		5.8.2.2. Ownership Rights	232
		5.8.2.3. Credit	233

	5.8.3.	Music Licensing Agreement 233
		5.8.3.1. Grant of Rights 233
		5.8.3.2. Compensation 234
		5.8.3.3. Warranties and Indemnification Provisions...............234
5.9.	Conclusion	234

CHAPTER 6
Scripted Television
Ken Basin

6.1.	An Introduction to Scripted Television...237
	6.1.1. Scripted Television from the Perspective of Studio Business Affairs..237
	6.1.2. Scripted Television as a Medium..238
	6.1.3. The Life Cycle of a Scripted Television Series 240
	6.1.3.1. From Idea to Production 240
	a. Packaging and Studio Rights Acquisition............240
	b. Pitching and Set-Up...242
	c. Script Development...244
	d. Pilot 245
	e. Upfronts 247
	f. Staffing and Writing 248
	6.1.3.2. Production..249
	6.1.3.3. Distribution...252
	a. Media 252
	b. Territory 254
	c. Time 256
	6.1.4. The Power of Tax Incentives 256
6.2.	Underlying Rights Agreements 260
	6.2.1. Books and Articles..261
	6.2.1.1. Option Fees and Terms...261
	6.2.1.2. Purchase Price 262
	6.2.1.3. Royalties...263
	6.2.1.4. Backend 263
	6.2.1.5. Bonuses 264
	6.2.1.6. Granted Rights...264
	6.2.1.7. Reserved and Frozen Rights 265
	6.2.1.8. Consulting Services 267
	6.2.1.9. Credit..267
	6.2.1.10. Subsequent Productions 268
	6.2.1.11. Reversion 269
	6.2.1.12. A Note on Non-Fiction Pieces 270

CONTENTS

- 6.2.2. Life Rights 271
- 6.2.3. Format Rights 272
- 6.3. Talent Agreements 273
  - 6.3.1. Writing/Writer-Producer Agreements 273
    - 6.3.1.1. Writing and Spec Acquisition 274
    - 6.3.1.2. Producing Fees 276
    - 6.3.1.3. Years/Locks 277
    - 6.3.1.4. Services and Exclusivity 279
    - 6.3.1.5. Preexisting Commitments 280
    - 6.3.1.6. Consulting 281
    - 6.3.1.7. Royalties 282
    - 6.3.1.8. Bonuses 283
    - 6.3.1.9. Backend 284
    - 6.3.1.10. Credit 286
    - 6.3.1.11. Perks 287
    - 6.3.1.12. Subsequent Productions 288
  - 6.3.2. Non-Writing Producer Agreements 289
    - 6.3.2.1. Development Fees 290
    - 6.3.2.2. Producing Fees 290
    - 6.3.2.3. Locks 291
    - 6.3.2.4. Services and Exclusivity 291
    - 6.3.2.5. Royalties 292
    - 6.3.2.6. Bonuses 292
    - 6.3.2.7. Consulting 292
    - 6.3.2.8. Backend 293
    - 6.3.2.9. Credit 293
    - 6.3.2.10. Perks 293
    - 6.3.2.11. Subsequent Productions 294
  - 6.3.3. Pilot Director Agreements 294
    - 6.3.3.1. Services 295
    - 6.3.3.2. Directing Fees 296
    - 6.3.3.3. Executive Producing 296
    - 6.3.3.4. Royalties 297
    - 6.3.3.5. Bonuses 297
    - 6.3.3.6. Backend 298
    - 6.3.3.7. Credit 298
    - 6.3.3.8. Perks 298
    - 6.3.3.9. Subsequent Productions 299
  - 6.3.4. Actor Agreements 299
    - 6.3.4.1. Test Options 301
    - 6.3.4.2. Pilot Services 302
    - 6.3.4.3. Pilot and Series Fees 303
    - 6.3.4.4. Series Options 304

CONTENTS

	6.3.4.5. Series Guarantees	307
	6.3.4.6. Credit/Billing	308
	6.3.4.7. Dressing Room	309
	6.3.4.8. Photo/Likeness/Biography Approvals	310
	6.3.4.9. Merchandising Rights	311
	6.3.4.10. Other Approvals/Consultations	312
	6.3.4.11. Travel/Relocation	313
	6.3.4.12. Exclusivity	314
	6.3.4.13. Publicity/Promotion	315
6.3.5.	Staffing Writer Agreements	316
	6.3.5.1. Term/Options	316
	6.3.5.2. Credit	317
	6.3.5.3. Fees	318
	6.3.5.4. Guarantees	319
	6.3.5.5. Episodic Scripts	320
	6.3.5.6. Exclusivity	320
	6.3.5.7. Showrunners	321
6.3.6.	Agency Package Commissions	322
6.3.7.	Other Key Agreements	323
6.4. Backend		326
6.4.1.	Gross Receipts	328
6.4.2.	Distribution Fees	332
6.4.3.	Distribution Expenses	334
6.4.4.	Overhead	335
6.4.5.	Interest	336
6.4.6.	Cost of Production	336
6.4.7.	Third-Party Participations	337
6.4.8.	Treatment of Tax Incentives	338
6.5. License and Co-Production Agreements		340
6.5.1.	Network License Agreements	341
	6.5.1.1. Development Contributions	342
	6.5.1.2. Pilot and Series Options	342
	6.5.1.3. Series Term	343
	6.5.1.4. Pilot and Series License Fees	344
	a. *Initial License Fees*	345
	b. *Breakage*	348
	c. *Later Season License Fees*	349
	d. *Success Bonuses*	349
	6.5.1.5. Minimum Orders	350
	6.5.1.6. Licensed Rights	351
	a. *Network Exhibition and Runs*	351
	b. *Digital Rights (Traditional Licensees)*	353
	c. *Digital Righs (Digital Platforms)*	356

    6.5.1.7. License Territory and Term 357
    6.5.1.8. Network Exclusivity 358
    6.5.1.9. Revenue Backstops 361
    6.5.1.10. Subsequent Seasons and Derivative
        Productions 361
    6.5.1.11. Network Approvals 362
    6.5.1.12. Network Promotional Rights 363
    6.5.1.13. Contingent Compensation 364
  6.5.2. Co-Production Agreements 364
    6.5.2.1. Lead Studio 366
    6.5.2.2. Distribution Rights 367
    6.5.2.3. Allocation of Revenues 368
       a. Gross Receipts 368
       b. Distribution Fees 369
       c. Distribution Expenses 369
       d. Deficit 370
       e. Unapproved Overages 370
       f. Lead Studio Overhead 371
       g. Third-Party Participations 371
       h. Studio Net Proceeds 372
6.6. Conclusion 372

CHAPTER 7
Music Industry Law: A 360° View
Henry Root

7.1 An Introduction to Music Industry Law 373
7.2. Performance and Touring 377
  7.2.1. The Concert Performer as a Business 378
    7.2.1.1. Names and Trademarks 379
    7.2.1.2. Selection of the Business Form 381
  7.2.2. Repertoire 382
  7.2.3. Touring 384
7.3. The Personal Appearance Contract 389
  7.3.1. Conditions of Performance 389
    7.3.1.1. Hotel 390
    7.3.1.2. Ground Transportation 391
    7.3.1.3. Security 391
    7.3.1.4. Dressing Room 391
    7.3.1.5. Food 392
  7.3.2. Technical Conditions 392

CONTENTS

	7.3.2.1. Stage Crew	392
	7.3.2.2. Stage Requirement	393
	7.3.2.3. Electricity	393
	7.3.2.4. Equipment	393
	7.3.2.5. Performance Personnel	393
	7.3.2.6. Safety Requirements	394
	7.3.2.7. Venue Licensing	394
7.3.3.	Presentation Conditions	395
7.3.4.	Compensation Derived from Performances	396
	7.3.4.1. Performance Fees	396
	7.3.4.2. Sponsorship and Underwriting Fees (Tour Support)	397
	7.3.4.3. Ancillary Market Income	398
	7.3.4.4. Merchandising Income	401
	7.3.4.5. Fan Clubs and VIP Ticket Packages	404
7.4. Recording Agreements		409
7.4.1.	Types of Recording Agreements	412
	7.4.1.1. Exclusive Artist's Agreement	412
	7.4.1.2. Production Agreement	412
	7.4.1.3. Master Purchase Agreement	413
7.4.2.	Scope of Services	414
	7.4.2.1. Recording Commitment	414
	7.4.2.2. Scope of Services to Be Delivered	415
	7.4.2.3. Excluded Services	417
7.4.3.	Scope of Rights Granted	418
	7.4.3.1. In the Recording	418
	a. In General	418
	b. DAT Home Recording.	419
	c. Digital Broadcasting	420
	7.4.3.2. Rights in the Composition: Publishing	423
	a. Publishing	423
	b. The Controlled Compositions Clause	424
	c. Rerecording Restriction	425
	7.4.3.3. Publicity Rights	425
	7.4.3.4. Merchandising Rights	426
	7.4.3.5. Web Site Rights	426
7.4.4.	Production Agreements	428
	7.4.4.1. Production Company's Services	428
	7.4.4.2. Performer's Services	429
	7.4.4.3. Rights Granted	429
7.4.5.	Master Purchase/Master License	430
7.4.6.	Delivery and Control	430
	7.4.6.1. Control	431

                7.4.6.2. Delivery 432
        7.4.7. Royalties 434
                7.4.7.1. Advances and Recording Costs 436
                7.4.7.2. Calculation of Royalties 438
                        a. *Artist's Royalties* 438
                                1. Basic Royalty Rate..439
                                2. Adjustments 440
                                        A. *Free goods* 440
                                        B. *Ancillary distribution* 440
                                        C. *New "media" formats* 441
                                        D. *Packaging deduction* 441
                                3. Statutory Royalties...441
                                4. Digital Phonogram Distribution....................442
                                5. Alternate Royalties 442
                        b. *Mechanical Royalties* 443
                7.4.7.3. Merchandising Income 445
                7.4.7.4. Music Publishing Royalties 445
                7.4.7.5. Music Videos/Videograms 446
                7.4.7.6. Collateral Entertainment Activities 447
        7.4.8. Accounting..450
                7.4.8.1. Accounting Periods..450
                7.4.8.2. Reserves against Returns..450
                7.4.8.3. Recoupment and Cross-Collateralization 451
                7.4.8.4. Audit Rights...452
        7.4.9. Bankruptcy..453

CHAPTER 8
Music Publishing Law
Jeffrey Brabec, Todd Brabec

8.1. Music Publishing and Copyright 455
        8.1.1. Exclusive Rights of Copyright...455
        8.1.2. The Role of the Music Publisher..457
        8.1.3. Sources of Income 457
8.2. Common Music Publishing Industry Agreements 458
        8.2.1. The Single Song Agreement 459
        8.2.2. The Exclusive Songwriter Agreement 459
                8.2.2.1. Minimum Delivery Commitments...........................460
                8.2.2.2. Album per Contract Period Commitment................462
                8.2.2.3. Option Pickups 462
                8.2.2.4. Royalties 463
                8.2.2.5. Advances 463

	8.2.2.6. Approvals	464
	8.2.2.7. Reversion and Retention	465
8.2.3.	Co-Publishing Agreements	466
	8.2.3.1. Copyright Ownership of Compositions	466
	8.2.3.2. Administration	467
	8.2.3.3. Sharing of Income	467
	8.2.3.4. Advances	468
	8.2.3.5. Approvals	470
	8.2.3.6. Reversion and Retention of Rights	470
	8.2.3.7. First Negotiation and Matching Rights	471
8.2.4.	Participation Agreements	472
8.2.5.	Administration Agreements	472
	8.2.5.1. Role of the Administrator	473
	8.2.5.2. Term	473
	8.2.5.3. Controlled Compositions	473
	8.2.5.4. Royalties/Fees	473
	8.2.5.5. Advances	474
	8.2.5.6. Reversion and Rights to Accrued Royalties	474
	8.2.5.7. Retention of Certain Rights	475
	8.2.5.8. Payment of Songwriters	475
8.2.6.	Co-Administration Agreements	475
8.2.7.	Foreign Subpublishing Agreements	476
	8.2.7.1. Term	477
	8.2.7.2. Compositions Controlled	477
	8.2.7.3. Rights Granted	477
	8.2.7.4. Royalties	477
	8.2.7.5. Advances	478
	8.2.7.6. Retention of Rights	478
8.2.8.	Joint Venture Agreements	478
	8.2.8.1. Writers to Be Signed	479
	8.2.8.2. Exclusivity as to Potential Signings	479
	8.2.8.3. Preparation of Songwriter Agreements	479
	8.2.8.4. Payment of Advances to the Signed Writers	480
	8.2.8.5. Signing Fund	480
	8.2.8.6. Advance Payments to Writers in Option Years	481
	8.2.8.7. How Options Are Exercised	481
	8.2.8.8. Additional Advances to the Joint Venture Party	481
	8.2.8.9. Overhead	482
	8.2.8.10. Sharing of Income	482
	8.2.8.11. Sharing of Income Percentages	483

		8.2.8.12. Term 483
		8.2.8.13. Reversion of Administration Rights 483
	8.2.9.	Acquisition Agreements...484
		8.2.9.1. Non-disclosure Agreement 485
		8.2.9.2. The Prospectus..485
		8.2.9.3. Acquisition Proposal...................................486
		8.2.9.4. Letter of Intent..486
		8.2.9.5. Due Diligence...487
		a. Legal Due Diligence..............................487
		b. Financial Due Diligence......................488
		8.2.9.6. The Purchase Price 489
		8.2.9.7. The Long Form Acquisition Agreement...489
8.3.	Music Licensing..490	
	8.3.1.	Mechanical Licenses..490
	8.3.2.	The Performance Right..493
	8.3.3.	Overview of the Field 494
	8.3.4.	Revenue 495
	8.3.5.	Types of License Agreements.....................................496
	8.3.6.	Consent Decrees 498
	8.3.7.	Synchronization Licenses 500
		8.3.7.1. Motion Pictures: 500
		8.3.7.2. Television 501
	8.3.8.	Basic Licensing Principles..501
	8.3.9.	Video Games..502
	8.3.10.	Musical Theatre Licenses 504
		8.3.10.1. Dramatists Guild of America Approved
		Production Contract..................................504
		8.3.19.2. Royalty Pools: 505
		8.3.10.3. Fixed Dollar Shows 506
	8.3.11.	Additional Types of Licenses 506

CHAPTER 9
Theater Law
Victoria Traube, Hailey Ferber

9.1.	Introduction: Dramatis Personae...507
9.2.	Production Rights 509
	9.2.1. Musicals and Plays...509
	9.2.2. First Class and Other Productions................................509
	9.2.3. Profit and Non-Profit Theatre 511
9.3.	Underlying Rights...512
	9.3.1. Kinds of Underlying Material 512

	9.3.2.	What Rights Need to Be Acquired?..512
	9.3.3.	Terms of Underlying Rights Agreements 515
		9.3.3.1. Option Periods 515
		9.3.3.2. Option Exercise 516
		9.3.3.3. Merger 516
		9.3.3.4. Option Payments; Royalties and Net Profits 517
		9.3.3.5. Credit 518
		9.3.3.6. Special Issues with Studios.......................................518
		9.3.3.7. Right to Use Pre-Existing Musical Compositions..518
9.4.	Collaboration Agreements..519
9.5.	Dramatists Guild Approved Production Contract..................................521
	9.5.1.	Option Periods and Payments; Advance Payments..................523
	9.5.2.	Royalties 524
	9.5.3.	Subsidiary Rights...525
	9.5.4.	Additional Production Rights 526
	9.5.5.	Travel Expenses...526
	9.5.6.	Billing 527
	9.5.7.	Commercial Use Products..527
	9.5.8.	Cast Albums...528
9.6.	Development...528
	9.6.1.	Enhancement Agreements 529
	9.6.2.	Enhancement Funds...530
	9.6.3.	Control 530
	9.6.4.	Financial Participation 530
	9.6.5.	Credit 531
	9.6.6.	Physical Production 532
9.7.	Financing..532
9.8.	Creative and Cast Agreements..534
	9.8.1.	Director and Choreographer Contracts 534
	9.8.2.	Actor's Agreement...538
		9.8.2.1. Minimum Basic Agreements 538
		9.8.2.2. Star Contract...539
		9.8.2.3. Designer Contracts 540
		9.8.2.4. Orchestrator and Arranger Contracts........................540
9.9.	Touring 541
9.10.	Licensing 543
9.11.	Revivals..544

CHAPTER 10
Literary Publishing
Gail Ross

10.1. Introduction: The Nature of the Industry 547
    10.1.1. Categories of Publications 547
        10.1.1.1. Trade Books 548
        10.1.1.2. Reference and Educational Publications 549
        10.1.1.3. Newspapers and General Circulation Periodicals 550
        10.1.1.4. General Circulation Journals 551
        10.1.1.5. Professional Publications 551
10.2. Trade Books 551
    10.2.1. Getting a Deal 551
    10.2.2. Analyzing the Terms of an Author Agreement 553
        10.2.2.1. Opening Provisions 554
        10.2.2.2. The Work and/or the Description of the Work 555
        10.2.2.3. The Grant of Rights 556
        10.2.2.4. Delivery 559
        10.2.2.5. Acceptance of Manuscript 560
        10.2.2.6. Compensation 562
            a. Advances against Royalties 562
            b. Royalties 564
            c. Subsidiary Rights 566
        10.2.2.7. Warranties and Representations and Indemnification 569
        10.2.2.8. Next Works 570
        10.2.2.9. Out of Print 571
        10.2.2.10. Revisions 572
        10.2.2.11. Copyright 573
        10.2.2.12. Accounting Statement and Inspections 573
        10.2.2.13. Competing Works 574
        10.2.2.14. Agency Provision 575
10.3. Self-Publishing 575
10.4. Freelance Periodical Agreements 577
    10.4.1. The Subject of the Work 577
    10.4.2. The Grant of Rights 577
    10.4.3. Warranties and Representations 578
    10.4.4. Payments and Expenses 578
10.5. Scholarly / Professional Journal Publication 579
10.6. Agency Agreements 580

CHAPTER 11
Video Games, Interactive Media and Dealmaking
Andrew Boortz

11.1. Introduction / Nomenclature 583
    11.1.1. What Is Covered Today by The Term "Video Games"? 584
    11.1.2. Platforms 584
        11.1.2.1. PC Games 584
        11.1.2.2. Console Games 585
        11.1.2.3. Mobile Games 586
        11.1.2.4. Social Network Games 586
        11.1.2.5. New Platforms 587
    11.1.3. Game Types and Genres 587
        11.1.3.1. Action 588
        11.1.3.2. Adventure 588
        11.1.3.3. Action-Adventure 588
        11.1.3.4. Role Playing 588
        11.1.3.5. Simulation 588
        11.1.3.6. Sports 589
        11.1.3.7. Strategy 589
        11.1.3.8. Casual Games 589
    11.1.4. Business Models 589
        11.1.4.1. Premium Purchase Price 590
        11.1.4.2. Subscription 590
        11.1.4.3. Free to Play 591
11.2. Industry Entities and Their Roles 592
    11.2.1. Developers 592
    11.2.2. Publishers 592
    11.2.3. Distributors and Console Manufacturers 593
    11.2.4. Licensors and Middleware Providers 594
11.3. Financing the Creation of Video Games 594
    11.3.1. Self-Funding 595
    11.3.2. Publisher-Funded Games 596
        11.3.2.1. Work-for-Hire 597
        11.3.2.2. Traditional Publishing (Publisher
                   Recoupment) Deal 600
        11.3.2.3. Prototype Deal 601
        11.3.2.4. Equity Funding 602
        11.3.2.5. End-User Assisted Funding 604
                a. *Crowdfunding* 604
                b. *Early Access Sales* 605

                c. Issues with End User-Assisted Funding............606
           11.3.2.6. Tax Credits..607
11.4. Getting a Game from Concept to the Consumer......................................608
    11.4.1. Concepting and Pitch Decks 609
           11.4.1.1. World Narrative 609
           11.4.1.2. Design Pillars..610
           11.4.1.3. Gameplay Loop..610
           11.4.1.4. Market Analysis 611
           11.4.1.5. Budget...611
           11.4.1.6. Other Materials 612
    11.4.2. Pitching Financiers..612
    11.4.3. Negotiating the Publishing Deal 613
           11.4.3.1. Important Definitions..613
                a. Gross and Net Revenue 614
                b. Developer Proprietary Technology..................614
                c. Platform 614
                d. Publisher Materials 615
                e. Term 615
                f. Territory...616
           11.4.3.2. Funding 617
                a. Project Finance Funds......................................617
                b. License Fees and Minimum Guarantees 618
                c. Recoupable versus. Non-Recoupable
                    Funds 618
           11.4.3.3. License Grants 619
                a. Right to Operate and Commercially
                    Exploit the Game..619
                b. Right to Market the Game 621
                c. Exclusive versus. Non-Exclusive Rights 622
           11.4.3.4. Representations and Warranties..............................623
                a. Integration of Third Party Software,
                    Tools and Technologies 623
                b. Material Compliance with Agreed
                    Upon Specifications 623
                c. Open Source Software.......................................623
                d. Viruses, Trojan Horses, and Similar
                    Malicious Code 624
                e. Easter Eggs 624
           11.4.3.5. Ownership..625
                a. The Game..625
                b. Marketing Materials 626
                c. Billing and User Databases 627

		d.	Development and Operational Responsibilities 627
			1. Developer Responsibilities 627
			2. Creative Control... 628
			3. Outsourcing and Sublicensing Development... 628
			4. Key Personnel 629
			5. Bug Correction... 629
			6. Ongoing Content Creation 630
		e.	Publisher Responsibilities................................ 630
			1. Milestone Review and Approvals............. 630
			2. Quality Assurance and Certification 631
			3. Technical Infrastructure and Operation 633
			4. Localizations.. 633
			5. Websites and Social Media Channels 634
			6. Customer Support 634
	11.4.3.6.	Royalties and Audits... 635
		a.	*Royalty Terms* 635
		b.	*Recoupment of Development Advances* 636
		c.	*Record Keeping and Audits*.............................. 636
		d.	*Payment Terms* 637
	11.4.3.7.	Expiration, Termination and Wind Down.............. 638
		a.	*Expiration* 638
		b.	*Termination for Cause* 639
		c.	*Termination for Convenience*........................... 640
		d.	*Other Terminations*.. 640
		e.	*Wind-Up*... 641
	11.4.3.8.	Downstream and Additional Rights 641
		a.	*Rights in Future Works* 641
		b.	*Ancillary Products* 643
11.4.4.	Commercializing the Game and Operational Agreements 644
	11.4.4.1.	Relationships with the Console Manufacturers... 644
		a.	*Initial Due Diligence: Developers and Publishers* 644
		b.	*Developer-Console Manufacturer Agreements*... 645
		c.	*Publisher-Console Manufacturer Agreement* 645
	11.4.4.2.	Licenses for IP 646
	11.4.4.3.	Marketing Support 646

xxiv　　　　　　　　　　　　　CONTENTS

        a. *User Acquisition*..647
        b. *Brand Awareness* 648
     11.4.4.4. Customer Support 648
     11.4.4.5. Payment Gateways and Payment
          Processors 649
11.5. Regulation of Video Games..650
  11.5.1. Data Privacy 651
     11.5.1.1. United States Data Protection 651
     11.5.1.2. European Union Data Protection 653
     11.5.1.3. Data Protection Best Practices..............................654
  11.5.2. Consumer Protection 655
     11.5.2.1. COPPA 655
     11.5.2.2. Subscription Pricing...657
  11.5.3. Video Games, Violent Imagery and the First
     Amendment..658
  11.5.4. Right of Publicity 659
11.6. Looking into the Future 660
  11.6.1. eSports...660
  11.6.2. Virtual Reality and Augmented Reality 661
11.7. Conclusion 663
Appendix 1 ESRB Ratings 665
Appendix 2 PEGI Ratings 666

CHAPTER 12
A Guide to Structuring and Taxation in the Entertainment Industry
Brad Cohen, Shane Nix

12.1. General Tax Principles..670
  12.1.1. Income...670
  12.1.2. Methods of Accounting 671
     12.1.2.1. Cash Method of Accounting 673
         a. *Qualified Personal Services
          Corporation* 674
         b. *Gross Receipts Test*..675
     12.1.2.2. Accrual Method of Accounting.............................676
         a. *Fixed Liability*..677
         b. *Liability Determinable with Reasonable
          Accuracy* 677
         c. *Economic Performance* 678
  12.1.3. Minimizing Tax Liability 678
     12.1.3.1. Tax Deductions...678

		a.	Compensation for Personal Services 679
		b.	Traveling Expenses 682
		c.	Meals and Entertainment 684
		d.	Depreciation and Amortization Deductions 685
		e.	Production Costs for Certain Qualified Film, Television and Live Theatrical Productions 685
		f.	Pass-Through Deduction under the Tax Act and Jobs Act...685
	12.1.3.2.	Tax Credits..687
	12.1.3.3.	Loss Limitations 687
		a.	Passive Activity Losses 687
		b.	Pass-Through Loss Limitation under Tax Cuts and Jobs Act......................................688
		c.	Net Operating Losses 689
	12.1.3.4.	Character of Income...690
	12.1.3.5.	Writer's Share – Musical Works..............................690
12.1.4.	Tax Deferral 691
	12.1.4.1.	Deferral Method for Advance Payments................692
12.1.5.	Agency Theory: Exception to Gross Income 695
12.1.6.	Taxable Years 696
	12.1.6.1.	Fiscal Year 697
	12.1.6.2.	Required Tax Years 698
	12.1.6.3.	Section 444 Election 699
	12.1.6.4.	Calendar Year 703

12.2. Considerations for Choice of Entity 703
    12.2.1. C-corporation 704
    12.2.2. S-Corporation...705
    12.2.3. Tax Partnerships; LLCs..707
    12.2.4. Qualified Personal Service Company ("QPSC") 708
    12.2.5. Personal Holding Company 710
    12.2.6. Accumulated Earnings Tax 712
    12.2.7. State Entity Level Taxes 713
        12.2.7.1. California Gross Receipts Tax 713
        12.2.7.2. California Net Income Tax on S-corporations...714

12.3. Employee versus Independent Contractor 714
12.4. Structuring Entertainment Transactions (Formation and Operations) 715
    12.4.1. Loanout Companies 715
        12.4.1.1. General Benefits 716
        12.4.1.2. Work-for-Hire Relationship...................................719

           12.4.1.3. Employment Agreement 719
           12.4.1.4. Non-Qualified Deferred Compensation
                     ("409A") 720
   12.4.2. Motion Pictures and Television...721
   12.4.3. Music...721
           12.4.3.1. General Structuring Considerations 721
           12.4.3.2. Tax Benefits to Separating Intellectual
                     Property..722
           12.4.3.3. Shareholder Agreements 723
   12.4.4. Production Companies 723
           12.4.4.1. Back-to-Back Loanout Structures..........................723
           12.4.4.2. Structuring Collection Account Management
                     Agreements..724
           12.4.4.3. Capitalizing Production Costs................................725
           12.4.4.4 Income Forecast Method...728
           12.4.4.5. Section 181 Election/Bonus Depreciation 729
                     a. Code Section 181 730
                     b. Bonus Depreciation 731
                     c. Summary of Key Distinctions between
                        Current and Prior Law 732
           12.4.4.6. Crowd Funding 733
           12.4.4.7. Overhead Accounts / Planning................................734
   12.4.5. State Tax Incentives 735
12.5 Taxation of Intellectual Property in the Entertainment
Industry...738
   12.5.1. Copyrights...738
   12.5.2. Trademarks...739
12.6. Estate and Tax Planning for Rights of Publicity.....................................740

CHAPTER 13
Recurring Contract Concerns:
Some Further Thoughts
Jay Shanker

13.1. Billing Credit 754
   13.1.1. Title Billing Credits...756
           13.1.1.1. Talent's Perspective 756
           13.1.1.2. Marketer's Perspective...757
                     a. Marketing 757
                     b. Audience Inducement.......................................758
                     c. Talent Inducement..758
   13.1.2. Advertising and Publicity Credits 759

		13.1.2.1. Talent's Perspective..759
		13.1.2.2. Marketer's Perspective...759
	13.1.3.	Merchandising and Commercial Tie-Ins...............................760
		13.1.3.1. Talent's Perspective..761
		13.1.3.2. Marketer's Perspective...762
	13.1.4.	Artist's Refusal of Credit 762
13.2. Enforcement of Personal Performance Obligations.............................764
13.3. Arbitration 767
13.4. The Challenge of Defining Profits..769

CHAPTER 14
Fundamentals of Entertainment Talent Representation by Agents and Managers
Kirk Schroder, Jay Shanker

14.1. Introduction: Understanding the Roles of Agents and Managers...773
14.2. Agents..776
    14.2.1. Evaluating a Proposed Artist – Agent Relationship 777
    14.2.2. Talent Agencies versus Independent Agent Representation..781
    14.2.3. Agent/Agency Representation Agreements 785
        14.2.3.1. Duration 789
        14.2.3.2. Areas of Representation...790
        14.2.3.3. Commissions..791
        14.2.3.4. Collection Rights and Payment Obligations 797
        14.2.3.5. Performance Goals...798
        14.2.3.6. Documenting Adjustments to the Standard Agency Agreement 799
14.3. Personal Managers..800
14.4. Business Managers/Accountants 807
14.5. Conflicts of Interest 808
    14.5.1. Self-Dealing 810
    14.5.2. Representation of Competing Clients......................................811
    14.5.3. Leveraging 812
    14.5.4. Self-Promoting 814
14.6. Conclusion 816

CHAPTER 15
Developing an Entertainment Law Practice
Kirk Schroder, Jay Shanker

15.1. Introduction	819
15.2. Defining Entertainment Law	820
15.2.1. Drawing upon Tenets of Other Legal Disciplines	821
15.2.2. State Statutes and Regulations	822
15.2.3. Collective Bargaining Agreements	823
15.2.4. Economic Models and Business Practices	825
15.3. Understanding the Market for Clients	828
15.3.1. Practicing in the Primary Markets	834
15.3.2. Practicing in the Secondary Markets	834
15.4. Effectively Representing an Entertainment Industry Client	837
15.4.1. Lawyers Acting in Non-Lawyer Roles	843
15.4.2. Engagement Letters	844
15.4.3. Professional Liability Insurance	847
15.4.4. Determining Fees	848
15.5. Conclusion	850
Glossary of Terms	853
Illustrative Forms List	917
Index	923

— FOREWORD —

Peter Dekom

I've been practicing entertainment law for over four decades in virtually every facet of the industry covered by these volumes (and more). I've had the good fortune of working with clients at the highest levels of the business during this period, many of whom I started working with as they graduated from film school or launched their first projects, while others came to me for representation at the height of their success – and I've seen a lot. It would have been nice to have had the benefit of access to a resource like *The Essential Guide to Entertainment Law* as I began my legal career in the industry in the 1970s. Fortunately, you now have that opportunity with the publication of this two-volume resource detailing the ins and outs of law practice and dealmaking in the entertainment industries.

Over the years I've been continually surprised by how many people think they are gifted enough to compete creatively with Hollywood (that generic "*Hollywood*" which identifies an industry and culture more than a place, and now describes a global industry with professional roots all over the United States and across the world). They are creatives, critics, marketing whizzes and others who will tell you all the things that Hollywood gets wrong or doesn't get at all. There's a tad of truth in some of this, but juxtaposed to all of these critiques and creative yearnings are the triumphs and tribulations of those who in the past took the risks – and made it. They are the professionals. God bless those risk-takers, but…

As much as creativity within film, music, books, plays, electronic gaming and television is a pinnacle for artistic expressions and reflection of our culture, it is also a rather significant part of our commercial and legal landscape. It is unquestionably big business – no, make that "huge business." And where there is that much money and power at stake, playing the game without knowing the rules, the players, and the risks of engagement is deeply unwise – even if your goal is breaking or challenging the system at some level. These books can help serious creatives, entrepreneurs, executives and legal professionals navigate these landscapes.

The legal underpinnings of these entertainment industry enterprises start with Article I, Section 8, Clause 8 of the U.S. Constitution – the so-called "copyright" clause. They extend up through the mass of legal regulations and restrictions on raising financing and trundling through piles of customs and practices in every phase of entertainment. Then there are the barriers which have been erected by insiders to keep the unaware out, establishing (and maintaining) the hurdles that have historically determined what content goes into (or is excluded from) theaters, store shelves, the airwaves and Internet. Many of these policies and practices have been established and long maintained by the industry goliaths that have succeeded, repeatedly, in turning mere ideas into gold and that still have significant sway over who gets in and who is kept out of the innermost workings of these businesses. Then there is the gatekeeping role of numerous government entities, some offering subsidies for production, others offering sticky taxing fingers, and those in many foreign territories determining what products can be distributed generally. Then there are the primary talent and labor guilds that monitor many higher-end industry productions (film, television, theater and even musical projects) through agreements with studios and producers that go on for literally thousands of pages of fine print. Navigating all of this toward success can be daunting and is not for the fainthearted. So let's just say, "It's complicated." Add into the mix globalization and the digital transformations that are reshaping our communications, entertainment, and knowledge universes, and you get "complicated on steroids."

Experienced entertainment lawyers Jay Shanker and Kirk Schroder with *The Essential Guide to Entertainment Law: Dealmaking*, and Shanker, Paul Supnik and Jonathan Reichman with *The Essential Guide to Entertainment Law: Intellectual Property*, have taken on the herculean task of explaining this complexity to those newcomers to the field who really and seriously "want in" as well as to active professionals in the field already "in," but in need of a refresher on issues they may not have encountered in a while, or perhaps at all. I know and have worked with both of these types of readers, and *The Essential Guide to Entertainment Law* delivers abundant knowledge on a broad spectrum of legal and business practices in the entertainment industries to both audiences. This book series encompasses pragmatics – from broad deal parameters to the essential little details that can kill you if neglected. The authors/editors of this project have recruited the insights of more than a dozen additional experts, many of whom I also know well and each having decades of relevant experience to explain, teach, and warn about the intel they have accumulated in the course of their careers.

Be assured this two-volume series on the practice of entertainment industry law – comprising as it does an impressively deep survey of (i) dealmaking strategies, custom and practice and (ii) intellectual property law and other formal legal essentials, is a magnificent assemblage that can benefit anyone engaged in the industry, from neophyte to seasoned entertainment professional. Read what you care about in these volumes, in any order and level of depth you please, and you can't go wrong. Treat these books as the basis of a course in entertainment law and deal-making, or use them as a frequent reference source to get a handle on some or all of the wide range of entertainment law subjects covered here – most of which, I assure you, will arise on a recurring basis in your professional practice or careers in Entertainment.

Enjoy the read, and the ride!

— Preface —

Jay Shanker

Welcome to *The Essential Guide to Entertainment Law*.

This two-volume project has two primary objectives:

The first is to explore the basics of dealmaking in the principal entertainment industry transactional sectors (film, TV, music, theater, book publishing, electronic gaming and entertainment industry taxation), all addressed in EG2EL:Dealmaking.

The second is to similarly examine the fundamental intellectual property law principles and issues of copyright, trademark, unfair competition, rights of publicity and publicity which are the foundation for a substantial part of the industry's functioning, and which we address in EG2EL: Intellectual Property.

We encourage readers to acquire both volumes, and to also partake of the wealth of information contained in the illustrative form agreements that accompany the Dealmaking book available online to those who have purchased EG2EL:Dealmaking or the two-volume set. (For more on obtaining these forms and accessing other online resources of this project, please visit www.EG2EL.com and www.jurispub.com.)

The information delivered in these volumes has been assembled by a "dream team" of nearly 20 entertainment industry legal experts who work in and with leading law firms and entertainment companies on behalf of many of the most prominent creative artists, companies and projects in the business.

With EG2EL: Dealmaking my co-editor Kirk Schroder and I recruited fourteen of these highly regarded lawyer contributors to cover the landscape of industry dealmaking, bringing with them decades of high-level experience and insight to the many subjects addressed in this volume. Each guides you, the reader, through the fundamentals of deal structuring in their industry sectors and practices. We believe you will find their respective voices as distinctive as their approaches to their legal practices.

Likewise, my EG2EL: Intellectual Property co-authors Paul Supnik and Jonathan Reichman and I have sought to provide a concise yet comprehensive roadmap to the IP landscape by discussing those IP issues most relevant to entertainment industry transactions in the U.S.

Understanding those issues will help establish the parameters of underlying rights – knowledge essential to securing most industry project financing and distribution. Paul and Jonathan are among the most experienced and admired practitioners in the entertainment IP fields.

These two volumes and the available E2GEL illustrative forms are intended as hands-on desk top references for both the experienced and aspiring entertainment lawyer, for industry executives and creatives, for investors in entertainment projects, and for law and business students, each of whom will be able to navigate these volumes in useful ways.

For experienced entertainment lawyers, EG2EL can offer a "checklist" on projects in which you are active, or can provide an overview of a sector or issue in which you have less experience or require a concentrated "refresher."

The volumes can also serve as a primer for lawyers for whom "entertainment" is not a primary practice focus (or perhaps is just an "aspiration"). For this audience, EG2EL may help you level the playing field in transactions with more experienced counsel, or may simply enable you to confidently recruit and effectively service new clients.

It is also our intent that EG2EL will prove equally valuable to entertainment industry business executives and professionals, "creatives," investors, MBA and entertainment industry sector pre-professional students, and others seeking a broad overview of the legal and business underpinnings of the industry. Whether as a frequent or occasional FAQ resource, EG2EL can help these readers better navigate fundamental questions which can make that initial call to a lawyer more productive (and cost-effective). Additionally, EG2EL can help readers get a fuller grasp of their lawyer's prescriptions for a transaction after the consultation has occurred or when the paperwork arrives. Packed as these volumes are with the knowledge of so many noted figures in the industry, we believe EG2EL delivers a range and quality of information that can generally only be obtained by years of active experience in the industries covered by these volumes. (If our lawyer readers recommend these books to clients to strengthen their clients' understanding of the entertainment industry's business and legal frameworks so they in turn understand the value of a competent lawyer's guidance in the service of the clients' success – we'll feel a large part of our mission with EG2EL has been fulfilled.)

Notes of gratitude are in order to those who have made this project and my involvement in it possible.

PREFACE

First, to David Guinn and the late Harold Orenstein, whose *Entertainment Law & Business: A Guide to the Law and Business Practices of the Entertainment Industry*, first published in 1989, informs the structure and many of the chapters in these volumes. I came on board that project as a co-author in 2004 at the request of our publisher, Juris, and nearly 15 years later EL&B guides the spirit of EG2EL.

Next, to Michael Kitzen and Cynthia Nieves at Juris, who have patiently encouraged and supported the long gestation of these two new volumes and now bring this work to new audiences.

To gifted lawyers and mentors Alan Latman, Gabriel Perle and Richard Sherwood, who live in my memory and who each were instrumental in illuminating my path to a career in entertainment law, and Peter Dekom, Tom Rowan and John Hermes who, in turn, opened doors to signature opportunities in my professional career. I am forever indebted to each of these gentlemen.

To my co-editor Kirk Schroder and co-authors Paul Supnik and Jonathan Reichman, whose exemplary work and insights on these volumes on which we collaborated have helped insure that EG2EL will provide invaluable legal and business tools for a new generation of entertainment industry readers.

To the other exceptional author-contributors whose work is embodied in the transactional volume Kirk and I have edited, you comprise a dream team I am honored to be associated with. Assembled under one roof you'd constitute one of the most formidable entertainment law firms in the industry.

Needless to say, it has been a pleasure and privilege to work with and learn from each of the distinguished professionals who have contributed to the the construction of these volumes.

To Zach Oubre and Steven Cole of McAfee &Taft, and to Blake Johnson, Cullen Sweeney, Nancy Seeley and the rest of my entertainment law practice group team at Crowe & Dunlevy, my heartfelt thanks for your support and input to these volumes as this project has and will continue to evolve.

I also wish to express my gratitude to my clients and other professional colleagues of the past 35 years who have helped make my practice of law in the fields which are the subject of these volumes so stimulating and rewarding. To my parents, Ben and Shirley Shanker, who have amazed and inspired me each day in my life, and to my wife

Sara Jane and our children Jorja, Rachel and Eliot, who (even more than my clients) wondrously insure that no two days in my life are alike – my love and appreciation know no bounds.

In closing, a reflection with roots in my law school years. I shopped a couple of times a year at Syms Discount Clothiers in Manhattan for the suits and ties that got me through law firm interviews and summer clerkships. As some of you may remember, Syms' ads declared, "An Educated Consumer Is Our Best Customer,™" and this slogan, a prescription for turning quality service to customer loyalty, stuck with me. My most rewarding professional relationships over the years, whether in private practice or in-house for several dynamic entertainment companies, have been with clients who did their homework, asked good questions, and appreciated the value that knowledgeable and efficient lawyering can bring to the table in support of the strategic and dealmaking opportunities and challenges of client projects and careers.

It is my hope that these two volumes of *The Essential Guide to Entertainment Law* will support each of us (lawyers and non-lawyers alike) in our quest to provide more responsive and effective counsel to our clients and their projects in the Entertainment Industry, while at the same time enabling our clients to become better "educated consumers" of our guidance and services – and in turn our "best customers."

— Preface —

Kirk T. Schroder

One of my favorite newspaper columnists was Warren T. Brookes, who passed away many years ago. In one of his columns, published on Thanksgiving Day and titled "The Power of Thanksgiving," he observed, "There seems to be a metaphysical law that just as the appearance of good in our lives elicits gratitude, gratitude itself, unconditional and pure, seems to elicit more good."

Brookes' observation of this universal law of life best describes my journey as Co-Editor of *The Essential Guide to Entertainment Law*. Why? Well, none of it would have happened but for the goodness I received along this path. First and foremost, I thank the goodness of my Co-Editor, Jay Shanker, without whose efforts, this book would not be possible. He was gracious in accommodating several events in my life which introduced twists and turns to my involvement with this book. Besides being an outstanding entertainment lawyer and first-rate editor, Jay is a wonderful person and as they say a "good soul." I am grateful that he invited me to join him on this project, but more importantly, I am truly grateful for his friendship.

I also thank the goodness of our contributing authors, many of whom I've known for years. They not only agreed to contribute their legal wisdom to this book, but did so in a manner that I know will be of great value and assistance to our readers. Make no mistake, putting a book together of this scope and depth was a massive undertaking. Our contributing authors took great pride and attention in sharing their expertise in the specific entertainment industries covered in this book. They were all great to work with and I hope this book lives up to the vision that Jay and I shared with them at the start of this path.

In my editing and writing duties for this book, I had help along the way. Tyler Kellerman was invaluable in assisting on various research and writing assignments. I also want to thank Nicole Grunow and Austin Chandler for their important contributions to this book.

I am also blessed with a lot of love from my family. As such, I want to acknowledge my daughter, Sarina, and my parents, Ted and Gloria, and my brother Greg, and my twin sister Janine. I love you dearly.

As someone who bootstrapped an entertainment law career in a secondary entertainment market, this book is something that I had always hoped for when I first started that career. But it's something that I also currently want as a seasoned lawyer looking for deeper insight, instead of a basic cursory review of the legal aspects of the entertainment industry.

May those who read this book benefit greatly from its good and may that good elicit even more good for those who worked on this book and for those who explore its pages.

— ABOUT THE EDITORS / AUTHORS —

- **Jay Shanker**

Jay Shanker is a veteran entertainment industry attorney whose practice encompasses a wide array of film, television, theater, music, live entertainment, new media, fine arts, publishing and sports industry transactions for individual and corporate clients, including both public and private companies, across the U.S. and abroad. His clients and their projects have over the years garnered prestigious international awards in every major creative media, including Oscar, Emmy, Grammy and Clio nominations and awards. A graduate of Yale and the NYU School of Law, Mr. Shanker has practiced law in Los Angeles since 1981, and in 2005 relocated his practice to Oklahoma City, where he now serves as a director at Crowe & Dunlevy, a national law firm based in Oklahoma City, with additional offices in Dallas and Tulsa. He is co-author of *Entertainment Law & Business*, the third edition of which was published by Juris in 2013. He was also a contributing editor for *Entertainment Industry Contracts*, published by Matthew Bender in 1996 and co-editor of *Law and the Television of the '80s*, published by Oceana in 1982. He has taught courses on entertainment law at the University of Oklahoma and Oklahoma City University, and has lectured on entertainment industry legal matters at UCLA, USC and the American Film Institute (AFI) in Los Angeles and New York, for the Producers Guild of America, and for the American Bar Association and other leading continuing legal education forums on entertainment law topics. Mr. Shanker has served on the advisory committee of the AFI's Third Decade Council and was a founding board member of the Academy of Interactive Arts and Sciences. His achievements have earned him repeated inclusion in *The Best Lawyers in America* (Entertainment Law – Motion Pictures and Television; Entertainment Law – Music). He is admitted to practice in California, Oklahoma and the District of Columbia. For more information about Jay Shanker and his firm please visit www.crowedunlevy.com

- **Kirk Schroder**

Kirk Schroder, a founding partner of the Richmond, Virginia Law Firm, Schroder Davis, PLC, has an extensive entertainment and arts law practice. Kirk Schroder is named in the current edition of *The Best Lawyers in America®* for the field of entertainment law. He is also rated an "AV"* lawyer by Martindale - Hubbell, its highest rating for lawyers. He was elected by his national peers in the entertainment and sports law profession to serve as the Chair of the American Bar Association Entertainment & Sports Law section (2008 –10). His law practice in all involves transactional work in all major entertainment fields, and draws entertainment and arts-related clients from all over the United States and the world.

He holds BA and BSBA degrees from the University of Richmond, where he also earned his law degree. He additionally holds a Ph.D. in Education from the University of Virginia.

Mr. Schroder has written extensively on a wide range of entertainment law topics, and is a frequent panelist and lecturer on entertainment industry and legal topics throughout the U.S. For more on Kirk Schroder and his firm please visit www.schroderdavis.com.

About the Contributing Authors:

- **Ken Basin**

Ken Basin currently works as Senior Vice President, Business Affairs for Paramount Television, where he is responsible for dealmaking with talent, producers, and licensees in support of Paramount's broad slate of television programming (including scripted, unscripted, network, basic cable, premium cable, first-run syndicated, and first-run digital programming). Prior to joining Paramount, Ken Basin was a Vice President of Business Affairs at Sony Television, where he served as the lead business affairs executive for the development and production of series such as *$100,000 Pyramid* (ABC), *S.T.R.O.N.G.* (NBC), *The Briefcase* (CBS), *Sneaky Pete* (Amazon), *Good Girls Revolt* (Amazon), and *The Dr. Oz Show* (first-run syndication).

He also previously served as the Co-Head of Business Affairs at Amazon Studios, where he supervised all aspects of dealmaking, business strategy, and business development in connection with the development, financing, production, distribution, marketing, and ancillary exploitation of Amazon's slate of original programming, including primetime television drama, primetime television comedy, children's television, and theatrical motion pictures. The second Business Affairs executive ever hired by Amazon Studios, Ken Basin created and implemented numerous new company forms and policies, developed new business models and negotiated complex co-production and license agreements with major and mini-major traditional media studio partners, and helped to launch the studio's debut slate of original television pilots and series for first-run exhibition on Amazon Prime Instant Video. Before joining Amazon, he was an associate at the Century City law firm of Greenberg Glusker Fields Claman & Machtinger, LLP, where he developed a hybrid practice of entertainment transactions and entertainment litigation, and served as the Associate Chair of the firm's Entertainment Department (the first associate ever promoted to a formal department leadership role in the 50-year history of the firm).

Ken Basin is also a published scholar, as well as a long-time speaker and commentator, on entertainment and intellectual property legal matters. Since 2014, he has been a Lecturer on Law at Harvard Law School (where he teaches Entertainment and Media Law), and an Adjunct Professor at UCLA School of Law (where he teaches Television Law) and Southwestern Law School (where he teaches Motion Picture Production Law). He has also lectured widely on entertainment and intellectual property-related issues, including to classes and audiences at Pepperdine University School of Law, Stanford Law School, University of Virginia Law School, USC Gould School of Law, USC School of Cinematic Arts University of Tennessee College of Law, UCLA Anderson School of Management, and UCLA Extension School. While at Greenberg Glusker, Mr. Basin co-founded and served as Editor in Chief of the firm's award-winning Law Land Blog, a self-described "lawyer's look at the weird, wacky, wonderful world of the entertainment industry" that tackled complex entertainment news and legal issues with humor, insight, and a fair dose of hi trademark snark.

In 2011, *Variety* named Ken Basin one "the best and the brightest … attorneys that stand above the crowd and represent the next generation of sharp legal minds in the entertainment business" in its "Hollywood Law: Up Next" feature, and in 2012, the magazine profiled him as one of a small crop of rising "legal eagles" in its "Hollywood's New Leaders" feature.

- **Andrew Boortz**

Andrew Boortz is the Managing Vice President for Western Business and Corporate Development for Nexon Group, Korea's largest gaming company, having previously served as General Counsel for Nexon America, Inc. and Nexon M, Inc., its subsidiaries. Nexon specializes in free to play PC, mobile and social games. As General Counsel for Nexon America and Nexon M, Mr. Boortz oversaw all legal, regulatory, litigation and public policy activities of the Nexon group in North America, South America and Oceana. Prior to joining Nexon, Mr. Boortz practiced law as an associate with

Reed Smith LLP. He holds a B.S. degree from Cornell, and received his law degree from Georgetown.

- **Jeff Brabec**

    Jeff Brabec is Vice President of Business Affairs for BMG Chrysalis (representing the catalogues of Bruno Mars, John Legend, Kurt Cobain, ZZ Top, Buddy Holly, Hal David, Burt Bacharach, Roger Waters, Chuck Berry, Blondie, David Bowie, Paul Anka, Billy Idol, Jethro Tull, Yeah Yeah Yeahs, A3 (The Sopranos television theme) and Ray LaMontagne). He specializes in evaluating, analyzing, projecting income and negotiating music publishing catalogue acquisitions as well as songwriter, co-publishing, participation, administration, subpublishing and joint venture agreements. He has negotiated more than 1,000 movie, television, video, new technology and advertising commercial agreements for chart writers, writer-recording artists and writer-producers. He is also a recipient of the Deems Taylor Award for Excellence in Music Journalism.

    Previously, he was Vice President of Business Affairs for The PolyGram Music Group and Director of Business Affairs for both The Welk Music Group and Arista-Interworld Music Group where he represented the catalogues of Elton John, Henry Mancini, Van Morrison, Jimi Hendrix, Hall & Oates, Jerome Kern, and Oscar Hammerstein II, among others. A graduate of New York University School of Law, he was also formerly a government legal services attorney.

    College, university and law school guest lecturing and teaching include USC, NYU, University of Miami, Berklee College of Music, Belmont University, Loyola New Orleans, UCLA, and Southwestern Law, University of Colorado among many others.

ABOUT THE EDITORS / AUTHORS

- **Todd Brabec**

Todd Brabec, as Executive Vice President and Worldwide Director of Membership for ASCAP (the American Society of Composers, Authors and Publishers – the world's largest music licensing organization) for well over 3 decades, was in charge of all ASCAP Membership operations throughout the world with offices in Los Angeles, New York, Nashville, London, Miami, Chicago and Puerto Rico, all writer and publisher payment formula recommendations, changes and implementation, all advances, loans and other member financial arrangements, all competitive payments and systems analysis and was responsible for signing most of ASCAP's successful songwriters and writer/artists including James Taylor, Marvin Gaye, Metallica, Green Day, Smokey Robinson, Joni Mitchell, Neil Young, Journey, the Jimi Hendrix catalogue, Earth, Wind & Fire, Bob McDill, Jeff Lynne, Tom Petty, Sting, Marc Anthony, ZZ Top, Motley Crue, Billy Joel, Donna Summer, Foreigner, Bryan Adams, Steely Dan and Jimmy Jam and Terry Lewis as well as the blockbuster film and television composers James Horner(*Avatar* and *Titanic*-the two top- grossing films of all time), Alan Silvestri (Marvel's *The Avengers*), Hans Zimmer (*Pirates of the Caribbean* films), James Newton Howard (*Dark Knight*), Michael Giacchino (*Up*, *Medal of Honor* video games) and Randy Newman (*Toy Story* films), among many others.

Through his leadership, direction and efforts over 37 years, ASCAP grew from 60 million dollars to 1 billion dollars in annual revenues, from 30,000 members to 350,000 writers and publishers and from a 20% overall market share to market share dominance in radio, television, feature films and all other major media. In addition, he was able, during his long career, to eliminate all ASCAP payment policies, provisions, formulas and rules which were not in the best interests of songwriters and composers, as well as significantly increasing the payments for film and television scores, theme songs, and hit songs on radio.

He is former Governing Committee Member as well as Music Chair and Budget Chair of the American Bar Association Forum on the Entertainment and Sports Industries, and is a recipient of the Deems Taylor Award for Excellence in Music Journalism, the MEIEA

Educational Leadership Award, and the Texas Star Award from the State Bar of Texas for Outstanding Contribution and Achievement in the field of Entertainment Law.

- **Brad Cohen**

Brad Cohen is a partner in the Century City office of Jeffers Mangels Butler & Mitchell, LLP. His practice emphasizes business planning related to complex corporate and partnership transactions, including mergers and acquisitions, financing and business succession planning, income tax planning, and estate tax planning, all on an integrated basis. Mr. Cohen is best known for his business and tax advice related to the motion picture, television, music, emerging media and sports industries. One of the focuses of his practice is coordinating the relationships among the entertainment, advertising and nonprofit industries. He has incorporated his personal commitment to philanthropy into a key element of his legal practice, providing multi-faceted counsel to clients regarding their involvement in charitable endeavors, including developing strategic plans, outlining the associated tax benefits and identifying the appropriate corporate brands and sponsorships. Brad Cohen acted as principal counsel representing the lead donor who financed the acquisition, delivery and permanent exhibition of the Space Shuttle Endeavour located at the California Science Center in Los Angeles. He also advises clients on tax controversy, executive compensation (including deferred compensation) and tax aspects of marital settlement negotiations. He currently represents a production icon in the creation and operation of the Compton Performing Arts Center. He was also a lobbyist before the United States Congress for the Tax Reform Research Group. He is also an Ironman Triathlon finisher.

Mr. Cohen's clients include ultra-high net worth individuals and their closely-held businesses. He has also represented studios, record companies, production companies and sports teams, as well as high-profile performing artists and behind-the-scenes individuals. His clients have also included former presidents of the United States and a United States senator.

He is a Director of the Motion Picture Tax Institute and a past Chair of the Entertainment-Tax Subcommittee of the Tax Section of the Los Angeles County Bar Association. He was a delegate to the Los Angeles County Bar Association Tax Section Washington, DC Delegation and a former Chairperson of the Taxation Section of the Century City Bar Association. He is on the planning committee for the Cal CPA Education Foundation's Entertainment Industry Conference.

Mr. Cohen earned his LL.M., Taxation from New York University, 1981, his J.D. at Hofstra University School of Law, 1979, and his B.S. from Northeastern University, 1976 *cum laude*. For more on Brad Cohen and his law firm, please visit http://www.jmbm.com.

- **Peter J. Dekom**

Peter J. Dekom practices law in Los Angeles. Mr. Dekom is currently Vice-Chairman of Dick Cook Studios, partnered with former Walt Disney Studios Chairman, Richard Cook. He was formerly Of counsel with Weissmann Wolff Bergman Coleman Grodin & Evall and a partner in the firm of Bloom, Dekom, Hergott and Cook. Mr. Dekom's clients include or have included such Hollywood notables as George Lucas, Paul Haggis, Keenen Ivory Wayans, John Travolta, Ron Howard, Rob Reiner, Andy Davis, Robert Towne and Larry Gordon among many others, as well as corporate clients such as Sears, Roebuck and Co., Pacific Telesis and Japan Victor Corporation (JVC). He has been listed in Forbes among the top 100 lawyers in the United States and in Premiere Magazine as one of the 50 most powerful people in Hollywood.

Mr. Dekom has been a management/marketing consultant, and entrepreneur in the fields of entertainment, Internet, and telecommunications. As a consultant to the state of New Mexico for almost a decade, he was instrumental in creating, writing and implementing legislation to encourage film and television production in the state and supervised the film loan program portion of that incentive structure until the spring of 2011.

Mr. Dekom served on the board of directors of Imagine Films Entertainment while the company remained publicly traded and was a board member of Will Vinton Studios and Cinebase Software, among others, leaving upon change of ownership. He has also served as a member of the Academy of Television Arts and Sciences and Academy Foundation, Board of Directors, Chairman (now Emeritus) of the American Cinematheque, and on the Advisory Board of the Shanghai International Film Festival. He serves on the Governing Committee for the America Bar Assn.'s Sports and Entertainment Law Section, where he often authored articles, delivered lectures and continues to be an active participant.

In 2012, the American Bar Association, through its Forum on Sports and Entertainment Law, honored Mr. Dekom with its highest recognition for entertainment lawyers, the Ed Rubin Service Award. Author of dozens of scholarly articles, Mr. Dekom also is the co-author of Not on My Watch; Hollywood vs. the Future (New Millennium Publishing, 2003) with Peter Sealey and author of Next: Reinventing Media, Marketing and Entertainment (HekaRose Publishing Group 2014). He has served as an adjunct professor in the UCLA Film School, a lecturer (entertainment marketing) at the University of California, Berkeley Haas School of Business as well as being a featured speaker at film festivals, corporations, universities and bar associations all over the world.

In addition to his professional pursuits, Mr. Dekom is author of the seminal public policy blog Unshred America (http://unshred.blogspot.com/).

- **Hailey Ferber**

Hailey Ferber, Senior Vice President of Business and Legal Affairs at The Araca Group, a renowned theatrical production and brand management company, came to work in the theater industry after studying with Manny Azenberg at Duke University. Prior to joining the Araca Group she was an Associate at Levine Plotkin & Menin, LLP where she was a production attorney for the Broadway shows *Hamilton: An American Musical*, *It's Only A Play*, *Something Rotten!*, and *On Your Feet!*, among others. For more on Hailey Ferber, please visit www.araca.com.

ABOUT THE EDITORS / AUTHORS

- **Steve Monas**

Stephen Monas is an experienced lawyer and executive with over thirty years in the entertainment industry. He founded Business Affairs, Inc. in July of 1999. Since that time, Steve Monas and the attorneys of BAI have built a client list of many of the most respected names in the independent motion picture and television industries. He has represented producers, distributors, bond companies, sales agents, and financiers in every aspect of the entertainment business. He is a frequent lecturer, moderator, and panelist at seminars on the entertainment industry. Before founding BAI, he served as Executive Vice President and head of Business Affairs for MDP Worldwide, President of Vision International, Vice President of Business Affairs with Vestron Pictures, and as an associate with New York law firms Frankfurt Garbus Klein & Selz, Pavia & Harcourt, and Brown & Wood. He received his J.D. from Columbia University in 1981, and is admitted to practice in both New York and California. You can find more about Steve Monas and Business Affairs, Inc. at www.bizaffairs.com.

- **Shane Nix**

Shane Nix, Counsel to the law firm Venable LLP, advises companies and individuals on various business transactions with an emphasis on transactional tax matters relating to the acquisition, disposition and restructuring of businesses, corporations and partnerships. He has a broad range of experience in corporate, international and partnership taxation. At Venable, he advises clients in many different industries, including technology, real estate, hospitality, media and entertainment. He has significant experience advising actors, actresses, musicians, producers, directors and financers on a wide range of individual, corporate, and partnership tax issues specific to the entertainment industry, as well as advising executives in connection with equity compensation matters.

ABOUT THE EDITORS / AUTHORS xlix

Prior to joining Venable, Shane Nix was an associate tax attorney at a global *American Lawyer 100* firm in Silicon Valley where he represented both sell-side and buy-side clients in M&A transactions and advised technology and media companies with respect to choice of entity formation and various tax matters.

Mr. Nix began his career at PricewaterhouseCoopers in New York City where he advised public and private companies and private equity firms on international and domestic aspects of restructurings, divestures and various stages of mergers and acquisitions, including due diligence, structuring and post-merger integration. He also worked at Deloitte Tax LLP in Chicago as a tax consultant focusing on R&D tax credit substantiation.

In addition to scholarly publications, Shane Nix has contributed to publications in the *Journal of Taxation* covering bad debt deductions and worthless stock losses.

He currently serves on the Executive Committee for the USC Tax Institute as Chairman of the Individual Taxation Subcommittee, and on the Planning Committee for the CalCPA Entertainment Industry Conference. He is also a member of the Motion Picture and Television Tax Institute and frequently speaks on matters pertaining to the entertainment and media industries. More information on Shane Nix and his firm may be found at www.venable.com

- **Henry Root**

  Henry W. Root is a partner in the entertainment media firm of Lapidus, Root, Franklin & Sacharow, LLP. He has over 35 years of legal and business affairs experience in the music, television and media industries. He began his legal career at MCA Records, Inc. after several years of working as a concert producer and subsequently as a tour manager and lighting designer for internationally renowned musical performers. Mr. Root has represented recording artists signed to nearly every major label, as well as award-winning songwriters and producers, independent music publishers, record labels, book authors, and the principal cast members of several reality TV series. Henry Root has also overseen business and legal affairs for the production and delivery of programming to every major network as well as for distribution on the Internet, and provides counsel in transactions for the valuation, purchase and sale of music publishing assets and to banks in connection with lending activities in the entertainment industry.

He was presented with the 2017 Ed Rubin Award by The American Bar Association Forum on the Entertainment and Sports Industries. The Ed Rubin Award is the forum's highest honor and is given in recognition of outstanding leadership and service. He served for six years as Chair of the Music & Personal Appearances Division of the forum and presently sits on the Governing Committee of that organization. He is an adjunct professor of music law at the University of Miami School of Law. He has been repeatedly selected by his peers for inclusion in *Super Lawyers* and has been named in *Top Attorneys in North America*. He also is a noted author and frequent lecturer and panelist.

For more on Henry Root and his firm, please visit http://www.lrfslaw.com.

- **Gail Ross**

Gail Ross is a partner at Trister, Ross, Schadler & Gold, PLLC in Washington D.C. where she has focused on the legal aspects of publishing and media law for the last 25 years. Gail Ross writes and lectures frequently on publishing issues. She teaches CLE courses on publishing law for the D.C. Bar and the Practicing Law Institute. She is the author of *The Writer's Lawyer* (Times Books, 1989) and has also been named numerous times as one of the *Best Lawyers in America* and *Washingtonian's* Best Lawyers for entertainment law.

She is also the president of the Ross Yoon Agency, representing important commercial nonfiction in a variety of areas. Ross Yoon clients include top doctors, CEOs, prize-winning journalists, and historians, and experts in a variety of fields. She and her team work closely with their authors and have earned a reputation in the industry for providing rigorous, enthusiastic editorial guidance at all stages of the publishing process. In the last year alone, close to a dozen of her books have been *New York Times* bestsellers.

For more information about Gail Ross's legal practice and literary agency, please visit www.tristerross.com or www.rossyoon.com.

ABOUT THE EDITORS / AUTHORS   li

- **Greg Snodgrass**

  Greg Snodgrass is an in-house attorney at Universal Pictures, where he drafts and negotiates above-the-line motion picture development and production agreements. Prior to joining the studio, Mr. Snodgrass was an attorney at the transactional entertainment law firm Business Affairs, Inc., where he represented studios, financiers and producers and negotiated and drafted agreements relating to every step of the motion picture development, financing, production and distribution process. He also reviewed and resolved complex chain of title histories and handled various music licensing issues on behalf of the firm's clients. He is a graduate from the University of North Carolina at Chapel Hill and the Indiana University – Bloomington School of Law.

- **Victoria Traube**

  Victoria Traube is Senior Vice President/ Business Affairs and General Counsel of Concord Music Publishing, with responsibility for the business and legal affairs of The Rodgers & Hammerstein Organization, Boosey & Hawkes in New York and Imagem Music in New York. She was previously Vice President and Head of New York Motion Picture and Theatre Business Affairs for International Creative Management, Inc., where she worked with Sam Cohn. Before that she was Senior Counsel and Director of Business Affairs for Home Box Office, Inc. and an associate at the New York law firm of Paul Weiss Rifkind Wharton & Garrison. She is a Trustee of The God Bless America Fund. She served as Theatre Chair of the American Bar Association's Forum on the Sports and Entertainment Industries and Chair of the Entertainment Law Committee of the Association of The Bar of The City of New York. She is a graduate of the University of Pennsylvania Law School, where she was a member of The Law Review, and Radcliffe College. For more on Victoria Traube and her company, please visit http://concord.com/music-publishing/

- **Robert Williams**

Robert Williams founded RW Law to expand his entertainment and media practice after over a decade of experience as an attorney at Skadden, Arps, Slate, Meagher & Flom, LLP and Dechert LLP. He brings a wealth of knowledge to each deal, leveraging his hands-on experience with complex transactions. He focuses on: film and television development, finance and distribution; licensing of intellectual property and copyright; secured transactions; and general corporate matters. Mr. Williams is an executive producer of *Z for Zachariah*, a Craig Zobel film starring Chris Pine, Margot Robbie and Chiwetel Ejiofor.

Mr. Williams has lectured multiple times at Bucerius Law School, Hamburg, and is published in the *Virginia Law & Business Review* as well as in the *Virginia Tax Review*. At the University of Virginia School of Law he served as Articles Review Editor for both the *Virginia Tax Review* and the *Virginia Journal of International Law*, two of the most acclaimed and influential law journals in their respective fields. For more information about Robert Williams and his practice, please visit www.r-wlaw.com.

- **Justin B. Wineburgh**

Justin Wineburgh is the President and CEO of Alkemy X, a creative media company with more than 250 employees and contractors located in Philadelphia and New York City. From traditional commercials to original content to social/digital campaigns, Alkemy X produces content for all platforms, working with brand, advertising and entertainment clients. Clients include HBO, Nickelodeon, AMC, TruTV, FOX, CBS, ABC, Food Network, Discovery Channel, MTV, and National Geographic, among many others. Under Wineburgh's leadership, Alkemy X developed and implemented a strategic vision, which has led to significant year over year company-wide growth.

Before joining Alkemy X, Mr. Wineburgh spent 16 years at Cozen O'Connor, an international law firm with more than 700 attorneys, where he built and headed the firm's media, entertainment and sports law practice. During his tenure as a partner at the firm, Mr. Wineburgh established himself as a "Super Lawyer" in the practice of Entertainment and Sports Law. American Lawyer Media once called him a "true pioneer in the entertainment industry," where he served as a production counsel to dozens of films and hundreds of television shows. He has also acted as outside counsel to numerous media and entertainment companies. Mr. Wineburgh repeatedly represented clients at the Sundance, Cannes, CineVegas, and Toronto International Film Festivals, as well as at the American Film Market, and the Comic-Con International Convention.

Mr. Wineburgh is frequently interviewed and cited in the media regarding business and legal matters of the entertainment industry. A regular lecturer worldwide, he is an advisory board member and adjunct professor of Entertainment Law for Drexel University's Entertainment & Arts Management program, as well as the School of Film and Media Arts at Temple University.

Mr. Wineburgh also sits on the Advisory Board of the Philadelphia Volunteer Lawyers for the Arts, as well as the Executive Boards of the Philadelphia Film Society, and the Pennsylvania Film Industry Association. He is a member of the Entertainment, Arts and Sports Law Committees of the Pennsylvania and Florida Bar Associations.

For more on Justin Wineburgh and his company, please visit http://www.alkemy-x.com/.

— DISCLAIMER —

The Presentations in These Volumes Do Not Constitute Legal Advice.

The materials contained herein represent the opinions of the authors and/or the editors, and should not be construed to be the views or opinions of the law firms or companies with whom such persons are in partnership, by whom they are employed, with whom they are otherwise associated, nor of Juris Publishing.

Nothing contained in this book is to be considered as the rendering of legal advice for specific cases or transactions, and readers are responsible for obtaining such advice from their own legal counsel. This book and its contents (including any legal forms or sample agreements included for reference) are intended for educational and informational purposes only.

— CHAPTER 1 —

MOTION PICTURE DEVELOPMENT AND PRODUCTION

Greg Snodgrass*

1.1. Motion Picture Development and Production: An Overview
1.2. Underlying Rights
1.3. Development
1.4. Production
1.5. About the Forms

1.1. MOTION PICTURE DEVELOPMENT AND PRODUCTION: AN OVERVIEW

Every year at the Academy Awards, the motion picture industry congratulates itself on various aspects of achievement in film production – directors, actors, writers and many other artists are awarded for being the "best" across dozens of categories. The winner in each individual category, e.g., the best director, the best cinematographer, and the best supporting actor, is invited on stage and has an opportunity to say a few words before being not-so-subtly played off by the orchestra. The most prominent award – for best picture – is saved until the end of the ceremony. Unlike all the preceding awards, which are given to specific individuals, it is not so obvious who should accept the award for best picture, which is meant to recognize the achievement of the picture as a whole. So who is it that we see on stage, desperately trying to squeeze in their last few thank-yous before the network cedes the telecast to the local news? It is the producer.

What does a producer do? Sometimes, producers have very little to do with the actual production of a film (see more about "baggage producers" later in the chapter). More often, the producer is the one most responsible for ensuring all the individual components of the motion picture development, financing and production process come

---

* **Greg Snodgrass** is Senior Counsel, Legal Affairs at Universal Pictures. The author expresses his gratitude to Steve Monas for his help in conceptualizing this chapter, and for the six-year education that preceded its writing.

together to form a cohesive whole. The Producers Guild of America (PGA) describes the producer as the one who "initiates, coordinates, supervises and controls, either on his/her own authority, or subject to the authority of an employer, all aspects of the motion-picture and/or television production process, including creative, financial, technological and administrative. A Producer is involved throughout all phases of production from inception to completion, including coordination, supervision and control of all other talents and crafts, subject to the provisions of their collective bargaining agreements and personal service contracts."[1] Put simply, a producer's job is to nurture the creative process, champion the project, and solve the manifold problems that threaten to prevent that original germ of an idea from becoming a critically acclaimed and financially successful motion picture. Even though "producer" is a single title, this job requires wearing many hats, and is usually fulfilled by more than one person on a given project.

Because the producer is involved from beginning to end, his or her experience can serve as a nice through-line for understanding the motion picture development and production process. Accordingly, this chapter is written from the perspective of a producer's attorney, and attempts to provide a detailed overview of the entire process without getting lost in the weeds in any one topic. In some places, specific negotiating positions are recommended – always from the production attorney's orientation – because this process is essentially one long negotiation among a multitude of parties, and it simplifies the explanation if a side is picked. (It also may have something to do with the fact that the author has spent his career as a production attorney.)

This chapter begins with a discussion of the various kinds of underlying rights that serve as the basis for motion pictures – it explains what these rights are, how to acquire them, and how to ensure third parties actually have the rights they are purporting to grant. Then, the chapter will outline the various personal service agreements that are entered into during development and production, first by looking at specific roles, then by discussing some of the common issues to all of these agreements. Finally, the chapter concludes with a brief look at some of the other aspects of production not previously covered.

---

[1] http://www.producersguild.org/?page=faq.

1.2. UNDERLYING RIGHTS

Every film is based on underlying rights of one sort or another. These rights may be manifested in the form of a published novel (*The Godfather*) or autobiography (*Raging Bull*), an unpublished stage play (*Casablanca*), a pre-existing film (*Ocean's Eleven*) or television series (*Mission Impossible*), a person's life story (*Gandhi*), a song (*Frosty the Snowman*), a graphic novel (*Batman*), a toy (*The Lego Movie*), a board game (*Clue*), a video game (*Tomb Raider*), or, these days, even a mobile phone app (*The Angry Birds Movie*). Some films are based on the rarest of all forms of underlying rights: an original idea. Of course, that original idea may be set within the context of historical events, either loosely (*Singin' in the Rain*) or more directly (*Chinatown*), and might also be inspired by actual people from history (*Citizen Kane*).

In broad strokes, the underlying rights being acquired as the basis of a motion picture could be based in copyright, trademark, personal rights or implied contract. You will likely encounter some combination of all of these on every project.

Under the Copyright Act of 1976, "copyright protection subsists...in original works of authorship fixed in any tangible medium of expression...[including] the following categories: (1) literary works; (2) musical works, including any accompanying words; (3) dramatic works, including any accompanying music; (4) pantomimes and choreographic works; (5) pictorial, graphic, and sculptural works; (6) motion pictures and other audiovisual works; (7) sound recordings; and (8) architectural works."[2] As a result, almost all works of art and entertainment are protected by copyright, and, unless the term of copyright has expired or one of the exceptions to exclusivity applies (e.g., fair use),[3] a license or grant of rights will need to be obtained before a film can be made based in whole or in part upon the copyrightable elements of the underlying work. This is not limited to works as a whole; if an individual has contributed copyrightable elements to a larger work – for example, if a writer makes changes to a script that are incorporated into the motion picture – then a grant of rights must be obtained from the individual.

When it comes to underlying rights, trademark issues tend to come up less frequently than copyright issues do, but they are no less

---

[2] 17 U.S.C. § 102.
[3] 17 U.S.C. § 107 *et seq.*

important to resolve when they occur. In the United States, the Lanham Act[4] is the primary source of trademark protection (though state and common law trademark should not be ignored). Under the Lanham Act, the trademark registrant is given a civil cause of action against any person who uses the registrant's mark (which is defined as any word, name, symbol or device used to identify and distinguish goods or services[5]) in commerce without authorization.[6] Of course, the First Amendment provides broad protection for filmmakers, but this protection usually will not extend to the use of someone else's trademarks in a way that would lead to consumer confusion as to the source of the film. Titles are not typically protected under trademark law, since they are only used to describe a single work, but if the title is used as a source identifier (i.e., brand), then trademark protection would apply. For instance, the popular *Encyclopedia Brown* children's book franchise wasn't protected by trademark when the first book was released in 1963, but now that twenty-nine books have been published, all with *Encyclopedia Brown* in the title, that name has become a source identifier, and, after an initial rejection by the United States Patent and Trademark Office,[7] has been registered for federal trademark protection.[8] Even though this mark is registered in the class designated for books, and motion pictures are in a different class, it would be problematic to use the *Encyclopedia Brown* mark in a film title without the mark owner's consent.

Personal rights can be divided into two categories: rights of privacy and publicity. In his landmark treatise on the right of privacy,[9] William Prosser outlines four different categories of privacy invasion: intrusion, public disclosure of private facts, false light in the public eye, and appropriation. On the other hand, the right of publicity is generally regarded as a property right (not based in tort, like the privacy rights outlined above), whereby an individual can control the use of his or her name and likeness for commercial purposes. The First Amendment virtually eliminates right of publicity concerns in connection with motion pictures, since mass media is fundamentally

---

[4] 15 U.S.C. §§ 1051-1127.
[5] 15 U.S.C. § 1127.
[6] 15 U.S.C. § 1114(1).
[7] http://tinyurl.com/j5kcsbc.
[8] http://tinyurl.com/zrnhbay.
[9] William L. Prosser, *Privacy*, 48 Cal. L. Rev. 383 (1960).

deemed a form of expression – but rights of privacy and publicity are particularly complicated due to the fact that they are based in common law and/or on state law, with lots of variance across jurisdictions. It would not be practical to delve into all the nuances here, but at the most elemental level, the filmmaker should avoid depicting a real, presently-living person (including as a composite character) in a manner that could be deemed defamatory or an invasion of privacy. People often refer to "life story rights," but this is a misnomer – they do not constitute a property right like copyright does, but rather a release and covenant by the "owner" of such rights, in exchange for some negotiated (usually financial) consideration, not to sue for defamation, invasion of privacy or a similar claim. It is also important to consider the non-legal issues relating to a project based on real people – for instance, even if it is determined that a signed release is not necessary because the subject to be depicted is no longer living, surviving family members are often sensitive to the manner in which the subject is depicted, and may threaten legal action or complain in the press about the project – either of which would have a real economic impact on the project. Conversely, even if a signed release is not necessary, having a family "on board" with a project can lend it an air of authenticity and a stamp of approval that might be economically advantageous.

While ideas in themselves are not protectable under copyright[10] or any other branch of intellectual property law, they have been accorded indirect protection via contract law. The definitive case on this issue (at least in California) is *Desny v. Wilder*.[11] In that case, the plaintiff had relayed an idea to famed director Billy Wilder's assistant, and then after relaying the idea, had explained that he would expect to be compensated if Billy Wilder used the idea, to which the assistant evidently said, "naturally we will pay you for it" if the idea is used.[12] Less than a year later, the plaintiff became aware of a project to be directed by Wilder based on the same idea the plaintiff had relayed to Wilder's assistant, and filed suit against Wilder. The plaintiff argued that this established a contract between the parties for compensation if the story were used, but Wilder's defense was that the idea was conveyed prior to any promise of compensation, and therefore there

---

[10] 17 U.S.C. § 102(b).
[11] 46 Cal.2d 715 (1956).
[12] Ibid. at 727.

was no contract due to failure of consideration. The court's response was simple: it doesn't matter whether the promise to pay was made before or after disclosure, as long as the promise was made, and as an alternative, even if no promise was ever expressly made, the plaintiff can prevail if "the circumstances preceding and attending disclosure, together with the conduct of the offered acting with knowledge of the circumstances, show a promise of the type usually referred to as 'implied' or 'implied-in-fact.'"[13] In light of this, if a motion picture is based on an idea that has been submitted to the producers, it would be advisable to enter into a written agreement with the person who submitted the idea, even if copyright or other property rights do not seem to be attached to the idea.

1.2.1. Chain of Title

Chain of title review should be a component of any acquisition of underlying rights. At its essence, this means identifying the genesis of the idea upon which the motion picture is based, then tracing each link in the chain of ownership to ensure that the rights were properly transferred and are not subject to any restrictions or encumbrances that would impair the producers' ability to produce and exploit the picture. Since it is impossible to prove a negative, it will never be possible to prove that a project's chain of title is clear, but there are certain steps that have become industry standard for ensuring that due diligence has been undertaken.

The first step is identifying the source of the project – where did the idea come from? It could be a completely original concept dreamed up by a producer or pitched by a writer, or it might be an original take on a published work of media, art or entertainment. Either way, it would be advisable to enter into an agreement with the originator of the idea, and if the project is based on preexisting intellectual property, then permission will also need to be obtained from the owner of that property. Furthermore, if the preexisting intellectual property is based on the lives of real people, then, to the extent those people are going to be depicted in the motion picture, a signed release will need to be obtained from them. There are exceptions to needing a signed release, but the safest course of action is to always get a signed release. If

---

[13] Ibid. at 738.

falling back on some other legal theory as to why a release is not necessary, proceed with caution, and rely on the advice of an attorney specializing in the applicable field of law.

We will review the development process in more detail later in the chapter,[14] but it is of paramount importance to build a solid chain of title throughout development. As a part of the acquisition of any underlying written material (e.g., acquiring the film rights to a book or existing screenplay), steps should be taken to ensure that all written material has been registered for copyright with the United States Copyright Office, and that all transfers of rights in such written material are confirmed in a signed writing. If there is no screenplay at the time of rights acquisition, then once the screenplay has been written, it should be registered for copyright; however, as a matter of policy, some studios and production companies do not register screenplays until the picture has been greenlit, since a component of registration is providing a "deposit copy" of the screenplay to the Library of Congress, which theoretically is made available to the public. The decision about when to register is a business decision to be made by the client – since copyright vests in a screenplay at the moment of creation, there is less urgency to register immediately, but there are certain advantages conferred by copyright registration (including a public record of the claimed ownership, and the availability of statutory damages if the work is registered prior to the infringement). In any event, once the screenplay has been registered for copyright, it is unnecessary to register subsequent drafts. Since the United States Copyright Office tends to take months to process applications (generally eight to fourteen months at the time of this writing,[15] but it once took the author over five years to register a screenplay copyright), it will be necessary to maintain records of the application that was submitted, as well as a receipt documenting payment of the application fee and documentation showing that the deposit copy has been submitted (and the United States Copyright Office has a convenient online registration system that allows you to upload a deposit copy of the screenplay in PDF format). This collection of submission documents will serve as interim proof that the copyright

---

[14] *See* section 1.3 below.
[15] http://www.copyright.gov/eco/; *See* also Chapter 1 of Volume II of this series on copyright issues in the practice of entertainment law.

registration is in process, and can be replaced by a copy of the copyright registration certificate once it has been received.

Once the motion picture has been completed, the motion picture itself should also be registered for copyright. As with the screenplay, copies of the submission documentation should be retained until the registration certificate has been received. At the time of copyright registration, the United States Copyright Office requires the registrant to submit one physical copy of the "best edition" of the work to the Library of Congress.[16] For an unpublished screenplay, a PDF version is acceptable as the best edition, but for a completed motion picture (especially if the picture has been released by the time the examiner reviews the application), the examiner will require a film print of the picture as a deposit copy, or if the picture has never been printed to film, then the examiner will require a deposit copy in the best possible video format. This can easily cost hundreds or, in the case of film prints, thousands of dollars, and will be an unpleasant surprise for the producer who fails to budget for this item.

If your client is not acquiring the rights in the underlying work directly from the author, then you will need to obtain documentation of each intervening assignment. Each link in this chain needs to contain a clear written grant of the rights that your client needs in order to produce the picture at hand, and also needs to include language allowing those rights to be assigned to third parties. The intervening assignments also need to include a waiver of the right to seek termination or injunctive relief in connection with any exploitation of the rights being assigned. If the underlying work was produced under the jurisdiction of the Writers Guild of America (WGA), then a WGA Literary Material Assumption Agreement needs to be obtained.

To the extent an assignment requires payment as part of the transaction, it will also be necessary to sufficiently document proof that such payment has actually been made. This is usually required even when a contract doesn't explicitly condition the assignment upon payment. Each studio, production company, investor and/or bond company has their own standards for acceptable proof of payment (and for chain of title generally), but a copy of a canceled check is generally regarded as sufficient proof of payment, as is a signed acknowledgment of receipt of payment from the assigning party.

---

[16] http://www.copyright.gov/circs/circ07b.pdf.

Generally speaking, a copy of an email from the assigning party or their representative acknowledging receipt of payment, or a copy of a wire transfer confirmation, or a copy of the check and cover letter sent to the assigning party with proof of delivery, would be treated as an acceptable form of proof of payment.

If the underlying work is a book, then you will typically find that the author retained the copyright in the book and the ability to license motion picture rights to third parties (i.e., to your client, the producer). However, on occasion, the book publisher is granted the full copyright in the book, or at least the right to negotiate film and television deals on the author's behalf, in which case you and your client will need to negotiate with the publisher instead of the author. Either way, you should obtain a copy of the publishing agreement and verify that you and your client are dealing with the correct party. When rights are acquired directly from the author or author's estate, you will also need to obtain a release from the publisher confirming that they do not control the rights that are being granted to your client.

If the underlying work is based on real people or events, then you will need to obtain from the author an annotated copy of the work, outlining which events and characters are real, which are fictionalized, and which are a hybrid of real and fictionalized people and events. Depending on the results of the annotation, you may also need to obtain signed releases from any living people who are depicted in the work in a manner that might infringe on their personal rights (or, alternatively, you may need to advise your client to exclude certain characters or events from the picture).

If your client is not the first producer involved with the underlying rights in question, it is possible that the prior studio or producer has commissioned a screenplay based on the underlying rights, and the prior studio/producer will typically own this script outright as a work made for hire (as opposed to the underlying rights, which may have been optioned, but never purchased, by the prior producer). As a derivative work, this "sterile script" cannot be produced without first obtaining the rights in the underlying work (since producing the sterile script would be an infringement of the copyright in the underlying work). On the other hand, if your client obtains rights in the underlying work, they cannot use the material that is unique to the sterile script without also obtaining the rights to the sterile script. Thus, the new producer must decide whether to acquire the sterile script from the prior producer or steer clear of the unique material in the sterile script so that there is no substantial similarity. The latter course is fairly risky, and often requires obtaining a legal opinion from an attorney recognized by insurance providers as an expert in the field, as well as several additional procedures to prevent the new writers from seeing the material commissioned by the prior producers. It is usually easier (and certainly less risky) to negotiate an agreement to purchase the sterile script from the prior producers. If the sterile script was written under the jurisdiction of the Writers Guild of America, then the prior writer may also be able to avail himself or herself of the re-acquisition provisions of the WGA Basic Agreement; it is a complicated process, but under certain conditions, the writer can buy the sterile script from the commissioning studio, then sell it to a new producer under certain terms and conditions.

1.2.2. Securing Underlying Rights

Once you've conducted the necessary chain of title analysis and determined which rights need to be acquired, you need to construct a deal to acquire those rights. There is, of course, an infinite number of ways to construct these deals, but for purposes of this chapter, we will simply look at the most typical structure: the option/purchase agreement. At its essence, an option is a grant of the exclusive right to purchase specified rights from the seller for a specified period of time on specified terms. For instance, a producer might pay a book author US$5,000 for an eighteen-month exclusive window wherein the producer may purchase all motion picture and television rights in the book by paying the author an amount equal to 2.5% of the budget of the picture (perhaps subject to a negotiated minimum and/or maximum amount, often referred to as a "floor" and a "ceiling"), less the option fee already paid. The producer might also negotiate for the right to extend the initial option period for an additional twelve to eighteen months in exchange for an additional US$5,000 payment, which might not count towards the purchase price. Additional terms to be negotiated could include credit, a participation in the profits of the film, the first opportunity to render writing services on this project or on sequels and remakes and other derivative works, a reversion of rights if principal photography is not commenced within a certain amount of time after the option is exercised, premiere tickets, royalties payable to the author if derivative works are exploited, a DVD or Blu-ray copy of the picture, and the author reserving certain rights (e.g., book publication or live stage rights) subject to a holdback and/or right of first negotiation and last refusal (or alternatively, first refusal) for the producer.

The option period typically commences on the date that all the principal business terms of the option were agreed, even if a long form agreement has not been signed yet. The initial option period typically runs until eighteen months after the long form agreement has been signed and chain of title for the underlying work has been approved. Even though your producer client may wish to agree to an initial option period shorter than eighteen months, he or she should be counseled against this – it almost always takes longer than expected to bring the talent and financing together on a project, and the producer also usually needs time to develop the screenplay. Even if the property being optioned is already a screenplay, it is rare that this will be the draft of the script that ends up being produced.

The amount of the initial option fee varies depending on the popularity of the underlying work, the popularity of the author, and the length of the initial option period. Under WGA rules, the option fee must be at least 10% of the applicable minimum purchase price,[17] and "10% of the purchase price" has emerged as a (highly flexible) rule of thumb for determining option fees, even when the purchase price is higher than the WGA minimum, or in circumstances where WGA rules don't apply. Under normal circumstances, the initial option fee will be treated as applicable against the purchase price, meaning that if the option is exercised and the purchase price is paid, the producer can deduct from the purchase price the initial option fee that the producer has already paid.

At the time the initial deal is being negotiated, it would be advisable to negotiate for the right to extend the initial option period once or even twice for an additional payment for each such extension. This way, if the producer is nearing the end of the initial option period, he or she need not open up new negotiations with the owner of the property, but instead can simply pay an additional fee to extend the option period unilaterally. Typically, this extension period would run for an additional twelve to eighteen months, and the required payment

---

[17] WGA 2014 Theatrical and Television Minimum Basic Agreement Article 13 A.

is often the same amount as the initial option fee. Whereas the initial option fee is usually applicable against the purchase price, it is not unusual for producers to agree that the extension payment is not applicable against the purchase price.

As with the option fee, the amount of the purchase price will vary based on a number of factors. The purchase price might be a flat dollar amount, or it might be a percentage of the budget of the picture; the latter structure becomes more appealing to both parties if the budget of the picture is not readily ascertained at the time the option is being negotiated (e.g., the same horror script might be made for $1 million or $55 million, depending on cast, special effects, and other factors). If the purchase price is determined based on the budget of the picture, it would be advisable to negotiate a ceiling so that the purchase price doesn't balloon out of control on a high budget production. Presumably, the owner of the property will also ask you for a floor on the purchase price, so they are guaranteed a minimum amount even if the budget is exceedingly low (and, to an extent, a purchase price floor may prevent your client from making a low budget picture in the first place). Also, the following items should be expressly excluded from the calculation: financing costs, insurance premiums, legal and completion guarantor fees, contingency reserve, and the purchase price itself. As a compromise, you might agree that the purchase price floor will be included in the budget calculation, but the balance of these items should always be excluded.

To exercise the option and purchase the rights, the mechanics of the contract should not require any steps of the producer other than to notify the owner that the option is exercised and pay the purchase price. Any required steps beyond this (e.g., negotiating additional terms in good faith) will undermine the purpose of the option agreement, and should be avoided. The long form agreement should clearly specify the person or entity to be paid (and the allocation among parties if there are multiple owners), the manner of payment (check, wire transfer, etc.), and where the payment should be sent. Otherwise, the producer may find himself or herself in a situation where he or she is unable to exercise the option and pay the purchase price, not for a lack of funds, but for a lack of payment instructions. Extending and exercising options tends to happen at the last minute, and not discovering this problem until the deadline is days (or hours) away could be disastrous. The producer also does not want to be in a situation where the purchase terms weren't fully negotiated up front, and it subsequently becomes impossible for the producer to finalize those terms with the property owner – whether due to a falling out between the parties, or due to the death of the property owner (the producer's chain of title becomes much more complicated – sometimes insurmountably so – if the producer has to negotiate with an estate).

Some property owners may seek to condition the producer's ability to extend or exercise the option upon certain development milestones being achieved (for example, a screenplay adaptation being commissioned or completed, a director or star attached, etc.), but these kinds of conditions should be avoided. The conditions are often cast in subjective terms – e.g., what does it mean to say that an actor is "attached," and do your client and the property owner (or you and your client, for that matter) answer this question the same way? Even if the requested conditions are clear and non-subjective, they may make it more difficult for third parties to ascertain whether the producer had the right to extend or exercise the option – e.g., if the right to extend the option is conditioned on a draft screenplay having been completed during the initial option period, what would be sufficient documentation to establish that the writer finished their draft before the option period expired, and will the third party financier that your client is trying to attract to the project feel the same way? If the property owner is looking for a way to ensure that your client only extends the option if they are "serious" about the project, it would be far more preferable to negotiate an elevated extension fee.

In terms of credit, it is customary to accord source material credit to the author of the underlying work (e.g., "based on the book by" credit). This credit usually appears on a separate card in the main titles of the picture, and also in the billing block of paid advertising for the picture. You might also agree to accord credit in the billing block of any excluded advertising (i.e., advertising that the distributor considers – because of size or medium – exempt from the usual paid ad credit requirements) where the writer of the screenplay is accorded credit (except for award, congratulatory or similar ads only naming the person being honored). However, if the underlying work being optioned is a screenplay, then you should simply agree that all matters relating to credit will be determined pursuant to WGA rules. The guild has a comprehensive set of rules regarding what credit to accord and where to accord it; agreeing to anything to the contrary will likely put your contract at odds with guild rules. Even if the project is not currently being developed under the jurisdiction of the WGA, it is possible that at some point in the future your client or your client's assignee will want to hire a WGA writer, in which case it will be important that the contracts for all preceding writers provide for credit pursuant to WGA rules. (It should be noted that the parties may independently agree to abide by these rules, even if the writers are not WGA members and their production contract is consequently not subject to the WGA agreement.) Regardless, all credit should be subject to any applicable guild rules and the customary exclusions of the distributor(s) of the picture. Otherwise, you may be forced to choose between breaching a guild agreement or your option agreement; neither choice is appealing. The contract should also recite that all other matters relating to credit will be determined in the producer's sole discretion, so there is some leeway to make changes as long as they conform to the specific provisions contained in the option agreement.

Ordinarily, the owner of the underlying rights will negotiate for some kind of participation in the revenues of the picture. If the underlying property is a book, a life story or some other non-screenplay material, you might agree to a participation in the net profits of somewhere between 2.5% and 5%. If the underlying work is a screenplay, you might agree to a 5% net participation if the writer ends up receiving sole credit, or a 2.5% net participation if the writer ends up receiving shared credit. Of course, there are many other forms of backend participation, as well as deferments, box office bonuses, and other forms of contingent compensation. These variations are beyond the scope of this chapter, but one word of caution: before agreeing to any form of contingent compensation, you should confirm with your producer/financier client that they will be in a position to pay the compensation when due – for example, if your client is an independent producer and no distribution is in place when the option agreement is being negotiated, it would not be advisable to agree to box office bonuses unless your client has sufficient cash on hand to pay the bonuses out of pocket (since box office bonuses are payable soon after the applicable threshold is reached, but the box office revenues do not reach the independent producer until months later).

Depending on the nature of the underlying work, the writer might negotiate to reserve certain rights in the work. For example, if the work is a book, the author will expect to reserve publication rights (including electronic publication rights) so he or she can continue to publish the book and keep the revenues from such exploitation, and the author will also want to reserve the right to write and publish sequels to the original book. The book author will also want to reserve radio, live television and live stage rights. In decades past, these were not controversial rights for the author to reserve, but with the recent success of live stage productions based on film properties, and the even more recent revival of interest in and success of live television programs based on prior films and/or books, producers have grown more reluctant to allow the author to reserve these rights (not without a fight, anyway). If they do allow the writer to reserve rights, then those rights (other than publication rights in the book and any sequel books) should be subject to a holdback for a minimum period of time after the producers' release of the picture, usually five years (or for seven years after the option is exercised, if earlier). After the holdback has expired, the producer should have a right of first negotiation and last refusal (meaning a matching right for any third party offers) in connection with any exploitation of the reserved rights (other than publication rights in the book and any sequels). If the underlying work is a screenplay, then all rights in the script should be granted to the producer, and no rights should be reserved.

If a writer receives sole writing credit on a picture (i.e., "screenplay by" or "written by"), it is not unusual for the producer to agree, subject to certain terms and conditions, that the writer is entitled to a right of first negotiation to render writing services on sequels, remakes and certain other productions based on the original picture. This right of first negotiation should be limited to a certain number of years after the initial commercial release of the original picture (usually five to ten years), and will often require that the writer must still then be an active professional writer in the industry. Occasionally, when your client is optioning a screenplay, the writer's representatives will also want the writer to have the first opportunity to make any revisions to the current script before any third party writer can make changes (and, in fact, WGA rules require this if the screenplay being optioned was an original screenplay).[18]

---

[18] WGA Article 16.A.3.c. and d.

It is also not unusual to agree that the writer will receive certain royalties if derivative works are made based on the picture. If the material being optioned is a screenplay, these passive payments should be conditioned on the writer receiving "separated rights" under the WGA agreement (or you might agree that the writer is entitled to 50% of the specified royalty if the writer receives shared separation of rights). Separated rights are certain economic and creative rights accorded by the WGA to the professional writer who is most responsible for the original material (e.g., a story, characters, motivational drivers, unique settings, etc.) that ends up in the completed picture. A writer who wrote the first draft of the screenplay is more likely to receive separated rights than a writer who wrote a mere polish near the end of the development process. If the material being optioned is not a screenplay, you might agree that the passive royalties are not conditioned on separation of rights at all.

A writer will also typically ask that the material being optioned automatically revert to the writer if the option is exercised, but principal photography doesn't subsequently commence within a certain number of years (usually five to ten years). If the producer agrees to this, the reversion should be subject to a lien for all of the producer's development costs (or, at a minimum, all amounts paid to the writer by the producer). Studios are usually reluctant to agree to reversions, but the WGA does allow writers to buy back their literary material under certain conditions.[19] For an independent producer, reversions are less problematic, as an independent producer would almost never exercise the option until principal photography actually commences, in which case the reversion would be a moot point. If a reversion is triggered, then that means some kind of disaster scenario must have befallen the producer, and it is hard to imagine the producer wouldn't be happy for someone else to make the picture if it meant the producer would be repaid all the amounts paid to the writer (or more). There are a couple of points to be careful about when negotiating reversion provisions. The first is to make clear when the producer is entitled to repayment – it could be payable as soon as the project is set up with a third party, or it could be payable on subsequent commencement of principal photography. In the latter case, you are essentially agreeing that the third party gets a free option on your reverted material, since the third

---

[19] WGA Article 16.A.8.

party doesn't have to pay anything unless and until the picture actually commences. It is not necessarily a problem to agree to this, but it is an area where you should seek clear direction from your client so there are not any surprises later. Another point to be wary of is what material reverts to the writer. Unless specifically agreed as a business point by your client, the only material that should revert is the material that is being optioned – the rights in any screenplay drafts commissioned by your client as a work made for hire (whether written by the writer of the underlying work or a third party) should not be included in the reverting material. Finally, it is important to clarify what amounts must be repaid if the material reverts – the producer would prefer that all expenses incurred to date in connection with the project are recoupable, whereas the writer would generally prefer that only amounts paid to the writer be required for refund. In my experience, the writer usually ends up winning this argument. In any event, the WGA requires under their reacquisition provisions that the writer only has to repay the amounts they have previously been paid in order to buy the material back from the commissioning producer, but before the writer can subsequently assign that reclaimed material to a third party, the original commissioning producer must be repaid all costs in connection with the literary material. There are many conditions and exceptions to the WGA reacquisition provisions that are not covered here,[20] so proceed with caution if your client is interested in going down this road.

1.3. DEVELOPMENT

Acquiring the underlying rights and clearing chain of title is merely the beginning of a project's development process. Your client will next want to create a screenplay that has creative merit and is feasible to produce within the target budget. Typically, the first step will be to hire a writer to create an original screenplay (or rewrite the existing screenplay, if the underlying material includes a screenplay that your client wants to use as a starting point). As with the initial chain of title clearance, you will want to ensure that all rights and material generated during the development phase can and will pass to the production (whether undertaken by the developing entity or by

---

[20] WGA Article 16.A.8.

assignment to a separate production company or financier). Anyone who renders services during this phase, including both writers and anyone who is supervising and giving notes to the writers (e.g., producers and directors) should all have a signed agreement before they begin rendering services (or, at a minimum, a brief "certificate of engagement" that confirms the results and proceeds of their services are a work made for hire for the production, that any material they contribute will be original and free of claims, and that the person is waiving the right to seek an injunction against the production). It cannot be overstated how important this will become once the project proceeds to production – if the people who have worked on the script haven't already signed away their rights to the production, your client will be at risk of a copyright claim and will have very little leverage in the negotiation of compensation, etc., for these parties.

In addition to the continuing obligation to keep the chain of title clear, you will also want to ensure that the agreements with people and companies who are rendering services during the development phase outline the terms and conditions of the engagement. The business points for each agreement will be covered below.

1.3.1. Writer Agreements

The first question when your client is hiring a writer is whether the writer is a member of the Writers Guild of America (WGA). If not, then anything goes – your client and the writer are free to negotiate any kind of arrangement they'd like (though the WGA rules, including the WGA minimum fees, often serve as a guide during negotiations, even with a non-guild member). If your client wants to hire a writer who is a WGA member, then your client will be required to become signatory to the WGA Basic Agreement, and both sides will be governed by WGA rules.

While it is possible to hire writers on a weekly basis under WGA rules, it is much more common in the theatrical feature world for writers to be hired on a "step" basis, where they are paid for each pass of writing they make on a script. The WGA has divided those steps into the following forms: a treatment, first draft screenplay, final draft screenplay (often called a "set" or a "set of revisions"), rewrite and polish. The WGA has also set minimum "scale" amounts that its members must be paid for each of these forms, which varies depending on whether the step is guaranteed or is at the producer's option, and also depending on the budget of the project. (The scale goes up once the budget increases beyond $5 million, for example, and if the budget is extremely low, the scale might be reduced or it might even be possible to defer a portion of the required payment.[21])

Once your client has determined the number and form of the steps they want the writer to perform, the fixed compensation for each step (and amount of time given for the writer to complete each step) needs to be negotiated. You and your client also need to negotiate whether any of the steps will be optional – for instance, if your client is commissioning an original screenplay, do they want to guarantee a set of revisions now, or make the revisions an optional step that the producer can exercise once they have seen the writer's first draft? The advantage if the former approach is WGA scale is lower if the revisions are guaranteed up front, while the advantage of the latter approach is the producer can avoid being obligated to pay for revisions if the producer is so displeased with the writer's first draft that the producer doesn't want to throw good money after bad by paying for the set of revisions. You or your client will also need to negotiate the timing of each stage in this process – when the writer has commenced on the first step, how long the writer is given to complete each step, how long the producer has to review and provide notes to each draft turned in by the writer, and how long the producer has to decide whether to exercise any optional steps provided in the agreement.

In addition to the fixed compensation for each step, the writer will try to negotiate for some kind of bonus based on credit. The typical structure provides for a fixed amount to be paid if the writer receives sole credit on the picture (which should always be determined by WGA rules, even if the contract is non-guild), reducible by all prior amounts paid to the writer (i.e., the fixed compensation for each writing step actually paid), plus a backend participation equal to 5% of the net profits of the picture. In the event a writer receives shared credit (again, as determined by WGA rules), they are most often entitled to receive an amount equal to half of what the sole credit bonus would have been (i.e., first deduct prior sums paid from the sole credit bonus amount, then divide the result by two), plus a participation equal to 2.5% of the net profits of the picture. Occasionally, the shared credit

---

[21] http://www.wga.org/uploadedFiles/writers_resources/LBA-Filings.pdf.

bonus is a fixed dollar amount instead of the foregoing formula. There are various other bells and whistles – for example, a "production bonus" paid on commencement of principal photography of the picture, regardless of whether the writer is entitled to credit, but possibly depending on whether the writer is the "last writer" hired before principal photography commences (excluding the customary polish done by the director of the picture).

As covered above in connection with optioning a screenplay, the writer will likely ask for the first opportunity to render writing services on sequels, remakes and other derivative works (including television series, especially if the writer has prior television experience), and for the right to receive passive royalties if they are not engaged to render services on such derivative productions. These demands are customarily fine with the producer, but the first opportunity right should always be conditioned on the writer receiving sole credit on the first picture (otherwise, your client could end up owing the first opportunity to more than one writer, which wouldn't work), that the additional writing obligation expires a reasonable number of years following the work on the first picture (i.e., so the commitment cannot be claimed decades later), and the passive royalties should always be conditioned on the writer being accorded separation of rights under the WGA rules.

1.3.2. Line Producers

In order to raise financing for the picture (or to comply with the producer's internal greenlight process), it will become necessary at some point to create a budget and schedule based on the current draft of the script, even though none of these documents will be final at this point. The main producer will typically hire an experienced line producer to prepare these documents, usually with an eye to hiring the same line producer to oversee the production later (in hopes that the line producer is able to deliver the production according to the budget and schedule he or she initially prepared, though numerous factors beyond the line producer's control may lead to budget increases and schedule delays).

As a result, the line producer's deal is often worked out as a flat fee for the initial budget and schedule work, with an optional component if the picture proceeds to production. If the production is DGA signatory, then it will be required to hire a unit production manager (UPM), and the line producing and UPM roles are often fulfilled by the same person under a single, hybrid contract that provides for a UPM fee to be paid on a weekly basis, plus a separate line producing fee, which might be an additional weekly rate or might be a flat fee payable on a 20/60/10/10 basis as outlined in the producer section below. The balance of a line producer's contract will typically follow the same structure as other producer contracts – see the following section for more detail.

1.3.3. Producer Agreements

Producer agreements are not governed by any guild (the Producers Guild of America governs the assignment of the "p.g.a" mark in credits, but they do not govern any terms or conditions of the employment of producers as a collective bargaining unit), so these agreements are in some ways easier and in some ways more difficult to negotiate than writer, director and actor agreements. On the one hand, there is no overriding set of guild rules of which you need to be aware, but on the other hand, the lack of overriding guild rules means more needs to be negotiated.

One of the most important – and often overlooked – aspects of a producer deal is the scope of services. At one extreme is the main producer of the project, who should be rendering services on a non-exclusive but first priority basis during development (by supervising script development and assisting with the casting and crew hires), then on an exclusive basis through principal photography, and finally on a non-exclusive but first priority basis again until the picture is completed and delivered to the distributor. At the other extreme on the services spectrum is the "baggage" producer. This is someone who won't really be rendering producing services on the project (at least not on a going forward basis), but has been attached to the project as a condition to some underlying rights or other talent deal (e.g., your client wants to hire an A-list actor, but the actor won't sign on to the project unless you give her manager an executive producer credit). We might even add a category called "barrel" producers: these are people who helped during script development without signing a certificate of engagement or other document confirming their results and proceeds are a work for hire for the production. As a result, they have your client over a barrel, and often require some kind of producing credit, compensation and backend as an inducement to sign the work for hire agreement. In between the main producers and the baggage producers are other people who render services to varying degrees on the project – some of these people may have rendered creative producing services during development, others might be line producers or assistant directors who have precedent for producer credit or who render services at a discounted rate (i.e., below their usual quote) during production, and others might be people who assist with (or provide) the financing for the production. *Lee Daniels' The Butler* famously had forty-one producers and executive producers, which is in itself a great illustration of how difficult it can be to assemble the talent and financing necessary to make an independent film.

Generally speaking, a producer's fixed compensation comes in the form of a flat fee that covers the entire engagement, regardless of duration (line producers are an occasional exception – they sometimes work for a weekly fee). Typically, the first 20% of this fixed fee is paid in equal weekly installments during pre-production, the next 60% is paid in equal weekly installments over the course of principal photography, the next 10% is paid in lump sum on delivery of the director's cut, or alternately some other step in the post-production process like completion of dubbing and scoring, and the final 10% is paid in lump sum on delivery of the answer print of the picture. This installment formula is designed to ensure the producer remains incentivized to fulfill all production obligations. However, if the producer is baggage, the fee might be paid in one lump sum on commencement of principal photography.

There are a variety of types of producer credit. In film, the simple producer credit is the highest ranking (with "produced by" credit sometimes reserved for the primary producer(s), and "producer" credit given to the other producers), while the executive producer credit is the second most desirable credit, followed by co-producer, then associate producer. In addition to agreeing to the type of credit, your client and the producer will need to agree on the relative position of the credit among other credits of the same type, and where the credit will appear (e.g., in the main title sequence, the billing block of paid advertising, the billing block of excluded advertising where other individual producers are accorded credit, etc.). Occasionally, an assistant director or baggage producer might agree to their producer credit being included in the end title scroll of the picture only, but usually anyone with a producer-type credit will negotiate for that credit to appear in the main titles. The producer will push for the credit to appear on a separate card by itself, but your client will need to be mindful of the number of producer-type credits being granted. If the list of producers and executive producers is fairly limited, then it is less of a problem to agree to separate card credits, but your client still may want to put any producers or executive producers who worked as a team on a shared card. On a production with a plethora of producer-type credits, it will be impossible to agree to a separate card credit for every producer and executive producer, so you will need to ensure that a shared card can be used for most or all of them. It would also be best to avoid guaranteeing separate card credit for any associate producers or co-producers. The same concerns apply for the billing block of print and print equivalent advertising, including in billboards, posters, newspapers, magazines, and television or online ads. It would be a bit unusual not to agree that a producer or executive producer credit will appear in the billing block, but your client would do well to limit the list of producers and executive producers to the extent possible. It is also not unusual to agree that the producer-type credit will appear in the billing block of excluded advertising where anyone else receiving the same producer-type credit is credited, but if there are many producers and executive producers, it would again be wise to resist this.

Depending on the producer's role, they may seek a participation in the profits of the picture. This will be entirely dependent on the nature of the services being rendered and the relative bargaining power of the parties. Unlike writers, actors and directors, the producers' participation might be subject to reduction by some or all other third party talent/creative participants (as distinguished from financier participations). This occurs because the producer is often hired before the cast and director have been hired, and so your client (i.e., in this instance the financier or primary production company) and the producer do not know how many backend points will need to be allocated to the other talent. To protect the producer's backend from being eliminated entirely, they may negotiate for a "soft floor" where any further reductions must be made in lockstep with reductions in the financier's (or some other party's) backend participation, and then at a certain point, a "hard floor" kicks in, and the producer's percentage cannot be reduced below this number. This structure might not be tenable for the minor producers on the project, but this structure does hold appeal for the main producer – he or she will be entitled to "whatever's left" after the other participants have been paid, but there will be incentive for the producer (and anyone sharing the reductions below the soft floor) to limit any participations to third parties. The typical rule of thumb is 50% of the profits is reserved for the financier(s) as a group, and 50% is reserved for allocation among all creative contributors, including the producers.[22]

For the main producers, you should also make sure a list of the important picture specifications are included in the agreement, including the allowable Motion Picture Association of America (MPAA) rating (e.g., "G", "PG", "PG-13", "R"), running time, and budget. Your client will want to be able to hold the main producers accountable for keeping the production on track for delivery to the distributor.

1.3.4. Director Agreements

Whereas the producer's engagement is completely negotiable, if the picture is produced under the Directors Guild of America (DGA) Basic Agreement, there are a number of overriding guild rules covering the director's engagement (including his or her creative rights and credit). For purposes of this discussion, it is worth noting that many if not most of these guidelines may for convenience be incorporated by reference in contracts for independent films produced outside of DGA jurisdiction, too.

Unlike the producer agreement, you pretty much know what you're going to get in terms of services. The director will be involved in the development of the screenplay, and will probably write his or her own polish of the script right before principal photography commences. The director will also oversee the hiring of the key crew members and be responsible for the initial cut of the picture.

Specifically, "the Director's function is to contribute to all of the creative elements of a film and to participate in molding and integrating them into one cohesive dramatic and aesthetic whole."[23] As a result, prior to the director's employment, the producer is obligated to inform the director about the material creative elements of the

---

[22] *See* further discussion regarding net proceeds in section 1.3.7.4 below.
[23] DGA Basic Agreement of 2014 7-101.

project.[24] Once the director is hired and until the director delivers the "director's cut" of the picture, the producer must consult with the director of any proposed changes to the elements of the project (e.g., script, budget, cast, locations, crew, third party approval rights).[25]

Once a director has directed at least 90% of the scheduled principal photography of the project, the director's post-production rights under the DGA will be vested.[26] The primary post-production right of the director is the right to create his or her own cut of the picture (and for this to be the first cut prepared by anyone), free of interference from any producers.[27] The director must be given a specific period of time to complete the director's cut; this varies depending on the budget of the picture, but often lasts ten weeks after the editor(s) complete the assembly of the picture (i.e., when the footage has been roughly arranged in the same order as the screenplay describes).[28] Once the director's cut is completed, the director is entitled to one "preview" of the director's cut – this is a public or large private screening where an audience can view the picture and provide feedback.

Of course, the director's cut and preview (often referred to in shorthand as "one cut and one preview") is only the minimum amount required by the DGA. A director can negotiate for two or three cuts and previews, or even to have "final cut" over the picture (which is exceedingly rare). Even if your producer client is willing to give final cut approval to the director (perhaps because of the director's stature, or material involvement in the assembly of rights and talent for the production of the picture), it would be wise to counsel your client against giving it, or at least to include certain protections and exceptions. For instance, the final cut right should be conditioned on the picture being on time and within the budget (and any editing periods guaranteed to the director will need to be budgeted). Also, if distribution for the picture has not been finalized at the time the director agreement is being negotiated, then your client is in the difficult position of not knowing what the currently-unknown distributor(s) will require in terms of editing rights. At a minimum, your client's distributors will require the ability to edit to create

---

[24] DGA Basic Agreement of 2014 7-201.
[25] DGA Basic Agreement of 2014 7-202.
[26] DGA Basic Agreement of 2014 7-503.
[27] DGA Basic Agreement of 2014 7-504.
[28] DGA Basic Agreement of 2014 7-505.

television and airline versions of the picture, to achieve a desired rating, and to accommodate any government censorship requirements in that distributor's territory. Even if your client gives final cut rights to the director, these rights should be extinguished once the picture is delivered to the distributor (i.e., the distributor will be free to edit the picture as they see fit). You might also agree to use commercially reasonable efforts to cause the distributor not to edit the picture without the director's approval, but you would want to make clear that any lack of success on this front would not be deemed a breach of the director's agreement. If the project is a negative pickup, then your job becomes simpler (though not necessarily easier), in that you can simply ask the distributor whether they're willing to allow the director to have final cut of the picture (if your producer client is even willing to give it), and if the distributor doesn't agree, then you can tell the director no and blame it on the distributor.

There are other variations on the director's cutting rights, like the "bake-off," where the director and producer can each prepare their own cuts and preview them at recruited screenings, and the version that scores higher with the audience becomes the definitive version. However, there usually is not enough money in the budget of an independent production to take advantage of these kinds of creative solutions. The other side of this coin, though, is you won't usually find your client hiring a director with precedent for final cutting authority on low budget independent productions.

At lower budget levels, the director's fixed compensation is often a weekly rate. However, as the budget increases, it becomes more likely that the director's fee is a flat amount payable on the same 20/60/10/10 basis as outlined in the producer section above. A director is also usually entitled to a participation in the revenues of the picture. The amount varies depending on the stature of the director and whether the director gave a discount on fixed compensation in order to keep the budget down, but something in the neighborhood of 7.5% to 10% of revenues after the cost of production has been recouped would not be unusual.

Just like producers, directors will expect to receive credit on a separate card in the main titles, as well as in the billing block of paid advertising and in the billing block of any excluded advertising where any other non-cast is credited. Indeed, DGA rules outline a fairly stringent set of credit requirements with respect to the director. In addition to the DGA-mandated individual credits, a director will often seek a possessory (also known as "film by" credit) on the picture. The WGA frowns on this credit, as they feel it minimizes the writer's contribution to the picture, but there is no explicit prohibition against according it to the director. Some production companies will only agree to a possessory credit if the director also wrote the original draft of the screenplay, or if the director has precedent for receiving a possessory credit.

1.3.5. Actor Agreements

In some ways, actor agreements are the most difficult to negotiate, as almost everything is negotiable. Assuming the production is signatory to the Screen Actors Guild (SAG) – and this is a safe assumption, since many projects are not signatory to the DGA or WGA, but very few are not signatory to SAG – then the first question will be whether the actor is guaranteed $65,000 or more in total compensation for acting services. If so, then the actor will fall under "Schedule F" of the SAG Basic Agreement and your client will be free to negotiate many employment provisions that would otherwise be set in stone by the guild – including overtime and meal breaks, scheduling, minimum daily or weekly compensation, etc. For the rest of this section, we'll refer to those above the $65,000 threshold as Schedule F actors, and those below the threshold as daily/weekly actors.

The two most important deal points when hiring a Schedule F actor are the fixed compensation and the scheduling. Nobody forgets to negotiate the compensation, but it is surprising how often the schedule is overlooked. It is helpful to think of an actor as someone selling his or her time – they won't want to make a binding commitment to block out time for your client's production (and therefore pass on other opportunities) unless they are guaranteed payment even if you end up not using them.[29] They also can't make an indefinite commitment to your production; unless your client is paying a sizable sum in guaranteed compensation, the actor will expect some kind of guaranteed date after which he or she can accept new work without having to get your client's approval first. So, as you are negotiating the actor deal, make sure to specify two things with clarity: the total

---

[29] *See* more on this point in the pay or play section 1.3.6 of this chapter.

number of days or weeks that you will need the actor to actually render services (rehearsal and shooting days, etc.), and the window of time in which you need the actor to be available to you (e.g., three consecutive weeks of services, commencing within two weeks before or after a specific date, within which the services will be rendered).

Your client would be ill advised to agree to a duration and window for exactly the amount of time your client is planning on using the actor. Production schedules change frequently, especially on independent productions and/or if the director is relatively inexperienced. To allow for this, you should negotiate for some additional "free" days that can be used consecutively with principal photography, as well as some "free" days non-consecutive to principal photography where you can bring the actor back for post-production work (e.g., dialogue replacement, dubbing). It is okay to agree that these post-production free days are subject to the actor's prior professional commitments, but you should avoid agreeing to this restriction with respect to the free principal photography days (or risk the ire of the line producer and assistant director, who will have a scheduling nightmare on their hands). The actor's representatives will probably require that after the scheduled days and free days are exhausted, the actor be entitled to "overage" compensation at the same rate as the fixed compensation represents in relation to the originally scheduled period of services. In other words, if an actor was paid $100,000 for ten days of scheduled work, and they agreed to two free days, but the production required five days beyond the originally scheduled ten, then the actor would be entitled to $30,000 in overages.

On the other hand, you also need to negotiate the window in which your client may require the actor to render services to the production (this is sometimes referred to as the actor being in "first position" to the production). Because an actor is selling time slots, he or she is not going to want to give you a large cushion in which to get your work done – instead, he or she will try to collapse the window to what the schedule currently allows, so that he or she remains available for other projects outside of this narrowed window. Even if you are not able to negotiate for many "free" days, the production should still be able to require the actor to continue rendering services through the completion of principal photography of the picture – the overages may be expensive, but at least you won't lose the actor entirely. Agreeing to any kind of stop date for the actor (i.e., the production guarantees the actor will be released by a certain date, or agrees the production will be in "second position" to another production starting on a certain date) is problematic and should not be agreed unless approved by the line producer, your client, the cast insurance provider and the completion guarantor (if any).

If you're hiring a daily or weekly actor, you can continue to employ them as long as you continue paying them at the negotiated daily/weekly rate, provided that the actor has not negotiated a specific stop date or something similar. The costs add up, but at least you will be able to keep the actor in first position to the production if need be. With daily and weekly actors, there are several nuances with regard to hours worked in a day, days worked in a week, and the production's ability to "drop and pick up" the actor if they only need the actor for a day or two now, then have a gap of a week or two before needing to use the actor again for a week or more – ; a good line producer will know these rules inside and out, and will be able to take maximum advantage of them for the benefit of the production.

Fixed compensation is usually the first deal point discussed. For Schedule F actors, it is usually a fixed amount payable in equal weekly installments over the scheduled period of the actor's services, with overages payable at the same rate for any services required beyond the originally scheduled days and any agreed free days. For daily/weekly actors, the fixed compensation is set at a daily/weekly rate, and the actor is paid at that rate (plus overtime and other SAG-mandated amounts/penalties) for the duration of employment. In the case of a daily or weekly actor, the agent might negotiate for a guaranteed minimum number of weeks of employment, in which case the actor must be paid the full amount for the guaranteed period, unless they are terminated for cause. This guarantee functions in a similar manner to "pay or play" to protect the actor from passing up on other opportunities only to be terminated by the production for creative (or other) reasons.

The actor's agent will often negotiate for the fixed compensation to be put in escrow with the agency to ensure the production actually has the ability to pay the agreed amount (if the actor begins working and then the production misses payroll, the actor is put in an impossibly awkward situation, so the actor's reps will often insist that independent producers put money in escrow in an agency or law firm trust account before the actor even travels). If escrow is agreed by your client, then you will need to enter into an escrow agreement with the agency – this can be a brief document drafted by the agency, but you need to ensure the agency is required to obey your instructions with regard to suspending payments in the event the actor is suspended or terminated pursuant to the terms of the actor agreement. Ideally, your client won't be required to deposit the actor's fee in escrow until the acting and escrow agreements are fully executed, or at least the agent won't be allowed to disburse money from escrow to the actor until the acting and escrow agreements are fully executed.

Contingent compensation is covered in another section of this chapter,[30] but you will typically find actors entitled to the lion's share of the contingent compensation on a project. Since they're usually the driving factor in terms of distribution revenues on a picture, they have the bargaining power to negotiate for the most in up-front and contingent compensation. The actor's representatives will often try to require that you create a collection account for the project and make the actor a party to the collection account management agreement. While it is fine (even ideal) for the actor to be a beneficiary of the collection account (i.e., someone the collection account manager pays directly), it is not a good idea for the actor to be a party to the collection agreement. Actors' representatives can be extremely slow to review the agreement and there is often money sitting in the account, waiting to be disbursed until the agreement is signed by all parties. You could always agree to provide a copy of the waterfall exhibit from the collection agreement, which shows how all revenues are to be disbursed. This would give the actor's representatives comfort that they will be accounted to properly without grinding the collection agreement negotiations to a halt.

The next issue when negotiating actor agreements is credit. The relative position of actor credits is determined by negotiation, but usually depends on the size of the role and the stature of the actors. So, if a project has two main characters, the bigger "star" will often get first position credit and the other actor will be in second position. Supporting cast will generally be placed behind the lead cast, though a big star in a supporting role might be credited at the very end of the cast credits, with "with" or "and" in front of their name. When negotiating position of actor credits, it is important to phrase as "no

---

[30] *See* section 1.3.7 below.

less favorable than _____ position among the cast credits" or something similar, so that your client can move the actor up in the list without having to amend the agreement or otherwise get the actor's approval.

The actor's representatives will also want to specify that the actor's credit will appear on a separate card in the main titles (as opposed to a shared card or in the end titles only). These are mostly creative decisions for your client to make, but putting every name on a separate card in the main titles could stretch the main titles to an unacceptable duration, so it would be best to limit the list of separate card credits as much as possible. One compromise position that sometimes works is to agree that if any actor other than _____ (with the "blank" to be filled in with a list of the actors ahead of this actor in credit order) is given a separate card credit, then this actor will be accorded credit on a separate card as well. For the actors on shared cards, their representatives might negotiate the number of other actors that can be on the same card and the actor's relative position on the card (e.g., first, or no less than second), and this would be a creative decision for your client to make. Representatives of top-level actors might also negotiate to have their name appear before the title in the main titles – this should only be guaranteed if the actor is truly a star and also one of the lead cast. For lead cast who are not top stars, it might be okay to agree their credit will come before the title if any other cast is credited before the title, but anything more favorable than a tie to other actors should be avoided.

For the main cast agreements, it is okay to agree that the actor will be accorded credit in the billing block of paid advertising for the picture, but this needs to be subject to the customary exclusions of the distributor of the picture. As with the main titles, it is okay to agree top-level stars will be accorded credit above the title in the billing block (as their identification may be a desirable part of the picture's "sell"), or perhaps to agree to an above-the-title tie for an actor who is not a star but is in the one or two most principal roles. The actor's representatives will often ask for exceptions to the excluded ad policy (e.g., for soundtrack albums, home video packaging, etc.), but you should never agree to this unless you know who the distributor will be and what specific exclusions they require. It is safest to just keep the blanket "subject to customary exclusions" language as controlling, though it is okay for the lead cast to agree that if any other actor is accorded credit in excluded advertising, then he or she will be accorded credit in that excluded advertising, as well (except for award-type advertising naming only the person being honored – e.g., a "for your consideration" advertisement for a specific cast member). Anything beyond an excluded ad tie to the other cast can create problems later, and the distributor might require you to go back and amend the actor's agreement, which the actor might not be willing to agree to (this would be the proverbial rock and hard place).

Actors will often ask for credit above the artwork title in the key artwork (i.e., the main image used in advertising). This should never be guaranteed, and even a tie to other cast should only be given sparingly. The distributor of the picture will have very specific opinions about who needs to be used for marketing purposes to help sell the picture, and if you have agreed to an entangling mess of guarantees and/or ties in connection with the artwork title, it can make life extremely difficult for the distributor's marketing department (which, in turn, means that life will be difficult for you). These are ultimately business decisions for your client to make, but you would do well to counsel them to give on this point only sparingly, especially in light of the fact that the distributor will almost certainly have a different opinion from your client as to which cast members will be most beneficial in marketing the picture and maximizing its revenues.

In addition to being credited above the title in key art, actors will also ask for a likeness tie, meaning that if any other actor's likeness appears recognizably in the key art, then this actor's likeness must appear in the key art, as well. If this is agreed, then the actor will also ask for a size tie, meaning that the size of their likeness cannot be any smaller than any other actor's likeness appearing in the key art, taking into account the relative "real life" size differences of the actors and the difficulty of measuring. As with artwork title credit, a likeness tie should be given only sparingly, and a likeness size tie should be given even more cautiously.

It is customary to agree that an actor will have the right to approve the still photographs that will be used in the marketing of the picture (with the actor required to approve at least 50% of stills in which they appear alone or 75% of stills in which they appear with others who have approval rights). On independent films, it is also customary to agree that an actor will have the right to approve non-photographic likenesses of the actor (i.e., drawings) used in marketing materials, with no more than a couple of rounds of back-and-forth between the actor and the production company. It is also normal to agree that the actor has a right of approval over any blooper footage (SAG requires this anyway) or behind the scenes footage in which the actor appears that the production company is going to use in the marketing of the film or in the added value materials for the home video release of the picture (e.g., DVD extras). Subject to the above, the producer should have the right to use the actor's name, voice and likeness in connection with the marketing and promotion of the picture. Sometimes an actor will ask for the right to approve use of name, voice and likeness in merchandising or commercial tie-ins – studios are reluctant to agree to this, but independent producers often do not have the leverage to resist giving this (and merchandising and commercial tie-in rights are less likely to actually be exploited on independent pictures, anyway). Under SAG rules, actors have a right of prior written approval over any scenes that require them (or their double) to appear nude or as engaging in sexual conduct – this is the case regardless what the acting contract says, but actors' representatives will often ask that the contract spell this out explicitly (including specific descriptions of the scenes being filmed, and limitations on what can and cannot be shot).

1.3.6. (What the Heck Is) Pay or Play?

"Pay or play" is a concept created to protect above-the-line talent from being terminated without receiving their full fixed fee. The parties will agree that at a certain point in the production process (often well before principal photography commences), the talent becomes "pay or play," and if they are subsequently terminated without cause, they will be entitled to their entire fixed fee, regardless of whether it has accrued at the moment of termination. Since the talent has blocked out their schedule for this production, they want to ensure they will be compensated for that time even if the producer decides to go a different direction or the production does not move forward. The contract will recite that the talent can be terminated at any time, for any reason, with or without cause, but if the talent has become "pay or play" and is then terminated for any reason other than force majeure and/or the talent's default or disability, the talent will be entitled to their full fee. For instance, if an actor is made "pay or play" and then a project is abandoned because the financing didn't come through, the person or entity that made the "pay or play" commitment to the actor will still be on the hook to pay the actor. Typically, a contract will say that talent becomes "pay or play" on the earlier of commencement of principal photography, or the hiring company electing to proceed to production of the picture with the talent in the specified role. Electing to proceed is usually defined as either written notice from the hiring party that they are proceeding to production, or the script, budget and schedule have been set (including a firm start date), and all (or sometimes just one) of the other cast and the director have been made "pay or play." While the "pay or play" provision does help protect the talent, it also provides a clear way for the producer to terminate the talent's services, even without cause – the producer can merely pay the balance of compensation owed and send the talent packing (subject to any applicable guild rules).

Contrast this with "pay and play," where the talent – usually, the director – is not only guaranteed his or her compensation, but also the right to render services without being suspended or terminated (unless for cause) for a specified period of time. A director might ask to be "pay and play" for the first two weeks of principal photography – this means the director cannot be fired without cause (however "cause" is defined) during these two weeks, and the director has a window of time in which to get his or her bearings before the producer can step in and fire the director.

Any "pay or play" (or "pay and play") provision should be subject to the talent signing their agreement first – otherwise, your client could be in the unenviable position of the talent becoming "pay or play" before you know exactly what you're getting from them (and what it is costing you). If you are also agreeing to give the talent any approval rights relating to the production (e.g., giving the director approval over the principal cast, or vice versa), then you should ensure the approval rights convert to meaningful consultation (or at least mutual approval with your client holding the tiebreaker) once the talent has become "pay or play" – otherwise, the talent could refuse to approve an element of the picture, thus making it impossible for the project to move forward, but your client still would have to pay the talent's full fee.

1.3.7. Contingent Compensation

For an attorney inexperienced in the film business, no part of the contract is more intimidating than the section governing contingent compensation. I've divided these into four different broad categories below, with a brief description of each and consideration of the issues each introduces.

1.3.7.1. Box Office Bonuses

Box office bonuses are straightforward contingent bonuses based on the theatrical performance of the picture – if the picture reaches certain theatrical revenue thresholds, then certain bonuses become payable. The thresholds might be keyed to United States box office (or perhaps US and Canadian box office), worldwide box office, or both, in which case the threshold is typically formulated as "the earlier to occur of $X million in USBO (or domestic box office if Canadian receipts are included) and $2X million in WWBO." The bonuses might cease after a certain level of revenues, or they might continue indefinitely at every specified increment of box office receipts. Box office bonuses are appealing to talent, because box office numbers are widely reported and there are no complicated accounting calculations involved (unless the thresholds are based on the budget of the picture, as outlined below). While it may be tempting for your client to say, "If the picture is so successful that these box office bonuses are triggered, I will be happy to pay them," it is worth bearing in mind that the box office bonuses will become payable long before your client ever actually sees a dime from the revenues of the picture. The box office thresholds will likely be reached within the first couple weeks of release, but your client is not likely to receive an accounting or payment from the distributor until a month or two after the first calendar quarter of the picture's release (e.g., if the picture is released in January, your client won't be paid by the distributor until May at the earliest). If the distributor spent significant funds on a minimum guarantee and/or prints and advertising, then it might take several months for them to recoup, even if the picture is wildly successful. Meanwhile, your client will be forced to either breach the talent agreements if there are no funds available (including if, for example, an advance was paid by the distributor but used in the production of the film) or pay the box office bonuses out of pocket. Either way, your client will probably be asking you why you let them agree to box office bonuses. Talent reps will also probably ask you to require the distributor of the picture to assume the box office bonuses and pay them directly to the talent, but this can be problematic for a couple of reasons. First of all, rights are often split out by territory on independent productions, with one distributor handling the United States (and possibly Canada), and one or many distributors handling the rest of the world. In this scenario, a U.S. distributor is not going to assume box office bonuses that might be triggered based on worldwide box office, even if the picture doesn't perform as well domestically. Also, assuming the obligation to pay box office bonuses affects the financial models of the distributor, and so the distributor may refuse to assume them, or if they pay them on behalf of the producer/financier they may offset this "cost" by increases in distribution fees or other charges to the producer. If you do not know who the distributor will be at the time the talent agreements are being negotiated, you are not in a position to guarantee to the talent that you will be able to cause the distributor to assume the bonuses directly, outside of a "good faith" effort undertaking, which is unlikely to satisfy talent demanding this level of participation.

One variation on box office bonuses leaves them triggered at variable thresholds depending on the budget of the picture. For instance, you might negotiate that the first bonus threshold is when box office revenues equal double the negative cost of the picture plus marketing expenses. Since the distributor and exhibitor typically split box office revenues 50/50, the "doubling" ensures the distributor will have received an amount equal to the negative cost plus marketing expenses, at which point the distributor will be at or beyond breakeven (depending on whether there was an advance from the distributor and the size of the advance in relation to the negative cost). If you use a formula like this for the first bonus threshold, a distributor will be much more likely to assume the box office bonus obligations directly (but they still might not agree to do so), and the talent is also less likely to begin receiving box office bonuses before your client is in the black with the distributor. To the extent the talent is entitled to a profit participation in addition to the box office bonuses, any box office bonus(es) paid should be treated as an advance applicable against the talent's other contingent participation.

1.3.7.2. Gross Participations

As with box office bonuses, a participation in the gross revenues of the picture is appealing to talent, because it doesn't require the cost of production to be calculated or recouped. Instead, the talent is entitled to a percentage of every dollar that the producer receives (after the distributor and/or sales agents deduct their fees, costs and expenses "off the top"). However, the investors on an independent production may be unwilling to share the picture revenues until they have recouped their entire investment – most likely, they are only going to approve a gross participation (with the window for any defined level of revenues or profits often called a "corridor") for a top-level star who is going to drive sales of the picture. Studios often agree to escalate the gross participation percentage at certain artificial "break points" (e.g., when "X" or "Y" milestone(s) occur in the picture's economic performance), but on independent films, it usually makes more sense to agree to a stable percentage payable from the producer's first dollar in gross receipts (i.e., the waterfall stage following deduction of distribution fees and expenses but before negative and financing costs are recouped) until the production has reached "net" profits.

1.3.7.3. Deferments

Deferments can vary wildly, but they tend to be a fixed dollar amount payable out of a pool at a defined point in the revenue waterfall (with each stage in the waterfall representing a different level of fee or cost/expense recoupment or profitability of the picture). The most generic deferment pool would be paid at the time immediately prior to net profits – after the distributors, sales agents and collection account managers have taken their fees and expenses off the top, the production has recouped the negative cost of the picture (which may include interest on loans and/or a premium return on equity investments), and any gross participations and/or box office bonuses have been paid. If multiple people have been granted deferments, they might be paid on a *pari passu* basis, which would mean on a dollar-for-dollar basis until each respective deferment has been paid in full (e.g., if there are three people receiving deferments of $1, $2, and $3, respectively, then the first $3 of revenue would be divided equally among the three deferees, at which point the first deferment would be paid in full, then the next

$2 would be divided equally among the remaining two deferees, at which point the second deferment would be paid in full, and the next $1 would be paid to the final remaining deferee). Alternatively, the deferment pool could be paid on a *pro rata pari passu* basis, which takes into account the relative size of the deferments when allocating revenues (e.g., using the same deferment pool in the prior example, the first dollar of revenue would be divided 1/6 to the first deferee, 1/3 to the second deferee, and 1/2 to the third deferee, and every subsequent dollar of revenue would be divided in the same manner until all three deferments are simultaneously paid in full). If the talent is working for a discounted up-front rate, then talent reps will often ask to make up the difference, usually with a further premium, via deferments in an amount equal to the talent's studio "quote" (i.e., the amount the talent has received from studios in the past for rendering similar services). The fixed compensation might be treated as an advance against the deferment, but generally a deferment is not applicable against a net participation.

1.3.7.4. Net Participations

A net participation is the last – and therefore least likely – form of contingent compensation to be paid. It is simply the amount that remains after all of the production's other costs, expenses and contingent participations (e.g., box office bonuses, gross participations and deferments) have been deducted, recouped and paid. Generally speaking, productions will divide the net profits equally – half to the equity investors on a pro rata basis according to their relative investments, and half to be divided among the talent according to their contracts. And the independent producer's reward for his or her hard work on the project (probably after deferring all or a portion of his or her fee) is whatever few percentage points of net profits remain after all the other talent has been awarded their points. For this reason, it is not unusual to find the main producer and the other talent at odds over how to allocate the backend. On the one hand, the producer is usually the person who has been involved with the project the longest, and often for little or no up-front compensation, but on the other hand, the talent may add tremendous marketing value to a film, despite having spent as little as a week or two working on the project. This can become a source of friction during negotiations; talent representatives often view net participations as easy for the producer to give away, since it requires no financial risk on the part of the producer (since it is only paid when received), but for the main producer, the net participation may be their only source of (potential) financial compensation for the film.

Typically, an independent producer will hire a collection account management company to collect and administer all of the revenues on the project, and so the collection account manager will be responsible for allocating and paying the applicable participations and deferments.

1.4. PRODUCTION

Although some, and sometimes many, of the preceding considerations will not come into play until a project is "greenlit" for actual production, the following issues are generally not addressed until a project is fully funded and active preproduction is about to commence or is in some instances (music acquisition, for example) well underway. The subjects addressed in this section are important aspects of virtually every motion picture production, whether dramatic, documentary, animated or effects-driven, and related agreements will be negotiated and documented with varying levels of complexity and precision depending on the respective production and the lawyers/producers involved.[31]

1.4.1. Below the Line

The personnel involved with a production are often divided into two categories – above-the-line and below-the-line. This terminology has its roots in the typical format of the first page of a film budget, which contains a dividing line between the principal cast, director, producer(s) and writer(s) on a project, on the one hand, and all the other personnel on a project, on the other hand. Above-the-line costs tend to vary wildly depending on the specific talent being hired, whereas below-the-line costs tend to fall within a narrower range, regardless of the talent hired. This isn't to say that the below-the-line budget on an effects-laden superhero movie will be the same as the below-the-line

---

[31] The discussion of "boilerplate" provisions in section 1.4.2 will be equally relevant to the agreements referenced in the chapter's section 1.3 pertaining to motion picture development.

budget on a relationship drama set in the modern day, but rather that the compensation difference between Gaffer A and Gaffer B tends to vary much less than the compensation difference between Director A and Director B.

The line producer, unit production manager, assistant directors, casting director, composer, costume designer, editor, production designer and director of photography (and all of their employees) typically fall within the below-the-line budget, though the line producer might end up above the line depending on the fee and credit being given. Usually, these "heads of department" will be selected by the director and/or the line producer, and the line producer will often negotiate the principal deal terms for these personnel. On independent productions, the production attorney might negotiate the long form agreements for the heads of department, and then the other below-the-line crew will sign a more basic crew deal memo. On studio productions, there is typically a separate department of attorneys who handle all the below-the-line agreements on a project (which would include agreements for locations, rentals, crew, etc.).

For the heads of department, it is not unusual for the production to pay a weekly rate, plus some kind of "kit rental" fee on top of the weekly rate to cover the use of their personally-owned materials on the production (e.g., for a director of photography to use their lenses on a production, or a line producer to use their laptop on a production). Heads of department will also usually ask for some kind of guarantee on their compensation – this functions in a similar manner to "pay or play" for above-the-line talent by guaranteeing that the person will be paid a negotiated number of weeks' salary, even if they are terminated earlier than expected for a reason other than force majeure or their default or disability. The heads of department will also typically negotiate to receive credit on a separate card in the main titles, and in the billing block of certain paid advertising for the picture (perhaps with a tie to other heads of department). Other than a few other bells and whistles, the balance of a below-the-line crew contract will be standard boilerplate language contained in all agreements for personal services on film productions.

1.4.2. *(In Praise of) the Boilerplate*

Attorneys often refer to the standard terms and conditions of a contract as "boilerplate." Over the years, entertainment contracts have evolved to include a number of standard terms and conditions that do not vary much from contract to contract, and this boilerplate often gets a bad rap, as it makes the agreements longer and more cumbersome for both sides to negotiate. However, much like rules, contractual provisions can all trace their origin to a time when a producer was stuck in a situation not covered by the contract, and so a new provision was added to the boilerplate of the producer's contracts for their new deals/projects going forward. In other words, most of the boilerplate will rarely make a difference in real life, but on those occasions when it does, both the client and the attorney (and the private attorney's malpractice insurance carrier) will be happy it is there. Of course, there is no reason to make contracts unnecessarily long, and the entertainment attorney would do well to avoid stating the same thing multiple times in a contract, or using overwrought language when plain English will suffice.

The sample representative contracts accompanying this book provide examples of the kind of boilerplate language that should be included in personal service contracts for motion pictures (as well as service contracts across the entertainment industry generally), but it is particularly important to include the following provisions: (a) a recital that the results and proceeds of all services are a work for hire; (b) representations and warranties that the results and proceeds will be original to the person rendering services, and won't infringe on any third party rights; (c) a waiver of the individual's right to seek an injunction if the production breaches the agreement; (d) a waiver of "moral rights" or the equivalent (i.e., a waiver of any restrictions on the producer's or others' right to alter or amend the employee's contributions); (e) an express right of the production to suspend or terminate its obligations to the individual if the individual breaches the agreement, is disabled, or if an event beyond the production's control (i.e., an event of force majeure) occurs; (f) a grant of the right to use the individual's name, voice and likeness in connection with the marketing and exploitation of the picture (including in "added value" materials included in the home video release of the picture); and (g) an explicit right for the production to assign the agreement (and the results and proceeds of the individual's services) to a third party. This is just an illustrative, and by no means exhaustive, list of considerations which should appear or be incorporated by reference in well-considered industry agreements.

1.4.3. A Word about Music

The specifics of music law are beyond the scope of this chapter, but it bears mentioning that any music included in the picture is subject to the same copyright clearance concerns outlined elsewhere in this chapter, and will need to be either licensed from the owner of the song (the composition) and the owner of the sound recording of the song (the master), or commissioned as a work made for hire for the production by the songwriter or composer. Typically, the composed music is commissioned as a work made for hire (increasingly, on a "package" basis, where the composer agrees to an all-in fee and is responsible for all the creation and recording costs for the score). Usually, any other music to be incorporated into the picture is licensed via a synchronization license for the composition, entered into with the songwriter or the publishing company designated by the songwriter, and a master use license for the pre-existing sound recording, entered into with the performer, producer or record label that owns/controls the recording.

Music can be incredibly expensive to commission and/or license, so your client should clear everything in advance before incorporating it into the picture – especially music that is part of the scene in which it is included (e.g., music playing on a television or radio in the background, or a song sung by a member of the principal cast). Since it would be almost impossible to cut this "diegetic" music without doing severe damage to the scene, the picture can be compromised if the music has not been cleared in advance of the scene being shot. If, for example, one of the characters is singing an un-cleared song at a key plot point, and your client is subsequently unable to agree to a synchronization fee with the owner of the song (or even worse, the song owner refuses to license the song altogether), then your client will be forced to either cut the scene from the movie, or re-shoot the scene without the song in question. Either option will cost money and likely also damage the picture from a creative perspective.

1.4.4. Clearances

Any item that appears on screen or in the soundtrack of the picture – whether a poster appearing in the background, a dialogue reference to a brand, or a depiction of a real-life person doing or saying something on screen – needs to be cleared by the production attorney, and often a signed release will be required. The analysis is essentially the same as that outlined in the chain of title section of this chapter – any item subject to copyright or trademark needs to be cleared in some fashion, and any action, dialogue or other reference that might implicate an individual's personal rights also needs to be cleared. For specific guidance, you should consult with an attorney experienced in this area.

1.4.5. Insurance

Insurance requirements will vary from production to production; the financiers, distributors and completion guarantors will all have slightly different requirements for the project, depending on the budget, release plan, and any number of other factors. The production will probably be required to obtain several different insurance policies to protect against various risks – cast insurance in case the disability or death of a cast member causes production delays, essential element insurance if completion of services by a particular cast member or director is a condition for distributors to pay license fees or minimum guarantees, general liability insurance for injuries on set and the like, currency insurance to hedge against fluctuations in the exchange rate, and errors and omissions insurance to protect against third party claims relating to copyright, trademark or personality/publicity rights. A completion bond is not really insurance, but it bears mentioning in this section – it is a guarantee (by the bond company to the picture's financiers) that the picture will be completed and delivered to the picture's distributors according to certain pre-negotiated parameters and deadlines. All of these options can be overwhelming and expensive. However, proceeding without adequate protection could lead to disaster, so your client should consult with several experienced professionals when navigating this process – the line producer, bond company, production attorney, and a trusted insurance broker can all be valuable resources.

1.4.6. Locations

Location agreements are often difficult to negotiate, not due to the complexity of the terms, but rather due to the colliding worlds of film production and commercial real estate. There is often a "battle of the forms" where the location will want to use its form contract, and the production attorney will want to use his or her form. Attorneys representing locations are often less familiar with entertainment contracts, and some of the more standard terms in entertainment contracts might seem alarming (e.g., the waiver of injunctive relief). The inverse is also true – entertainment attorneys may not be as familiar with commercial real estate agreements. Finally, location fees do not typically serve as a primary revenue source for locations, so they are more likely to use a "take it or leave it" approach, since they may view renting their location to a production as not worth the trouble; on the other hand, the director and/or location scout have probably identified this location as the only location that will suffice for creative reasons, and so there will be a lot of pressure from the production for you to "take it" and not "leave it."

Negotiating these agreements tends to become an exercise in risk management – you will try to convince the location to change problematic provisions, they will agree to some changes and refuse others, and you will have to advise your client of the risks in proceeding despite the problematic provisions (and it's important to keep in mind who your client is – just because the location manager says a provision is acceptable does not make it so). In particular, locations will sometimes require that nothing objectionable be filmed on the premises, or that the location have the right to eject the production from the premises if the filming creates a disturbance (which is often nebulously defined and gives broad discretion to the location), or the location might not allow the production to reschedule the shoot day if production needs change (e.g., due to weather). At a minimum, the location agreement ought to include an acknowledgment that the production will own the footage it shoots, and will have the right to use that footage worldwide in perpetuity in all media. Additionally, the location needs to agree to waive the right to seek an injunction against the advertising and exploitation of the picture, and the agreement should include a joint inspection procedure where representatives from the location and the production walk through the property immediately after the production vacates the premises, and any damage not noted at that time will not be the production's responsibility. Location agreements will often include insurance requirements – you will want to point these out to your client so they can ensure the production insurance complies with the minimum coverage requirements of the location agreement.

1.4.7. Production Service and Effects Agreements

If a third party entity is hired to render significant services during production of the picture (services beyond that of a simple vendor who has no management responsibilities on the production), then a production service agreement (PSA) is often utilized. PSAs are also often used for financing and tax reasons – for instance, the company that is providing the financing for a picture might "hire" a subsidiary or affiliated entity to produce the picture. (Thus, the financing entity owns the picture, but might not assume all of the underlying obligations of the production entity.) Depending on the nature of the project, it may also be necessary to hire one or more effects companies to add visual or sound effects to the picture. (This is true even on productions that do not contain obvious CGI.) In either case, these agreements should provide that all work done by the third party company is a work made for hire for the production, and also appropriate representations and warranties about the originality and non-infringing nature of the work, as well as a right of takeover by the production if the third party is in breach of the agreement. For effects agreements, there should also be an exhibit or schedule outlining the specific work that is to be done by the effects house, with pricing for each line item (or some other way of accounting for work that is inevitably added to or removed from the original schedule).

1.5. ABOUT THE FORMS

Several film production forms accompany the full edition of this volume. These are intended to serve as a sample of common language used in film contracts, and so – in the interest of concision – many of the more esoteric and/or complicated provisions (some favoring the producer and some favoring talent) have been intentionally omitted. Also, since these contracts tend to be negotiated a bit like trench warfare, it is common to include less favorable language in the first draft so you have "something left to give" in subsequent drafts. These forms are intended to fall somewhere in the middle of the negotiation, so the language is not entirely stacked in the producer's favor, but it also does not include every last available "give." This seems like the most helpful point in the process to view the contract, even though there are many additions and deletions that could be made to enhance the contract for talent and/or protect the producer.

MOTION PICTURE PRODUCTION – ILLUSTRATIVE FORMS:

- Literary Rights Option-Purchase Actor Agreement
- Motion Picture Screenwriter Agreement
- Director Agreement
- Actor Agreement
- Producer Agreement
- Head of Department / Crew Agreement
- Services/Rights Agreements – Standard Terms and Conditions

── CHAPTER 2 ──

MOTION PICTURE DISTRIBUTION

Stephen Monas[*]

2.1. Introduction: Art, Meet Commerce
2.2. Parties: What Is a "Distributor"?
2.3. Picture Specifications and Approvals
2.4. Term and Territory
2.5. Rights
2.6. Holdbacks and Windows
2.7. Minimum Guarantees
2.8. Application of Gross Receipts
2.9. Delivery
2.10. Security Interests
2.11. Theatrical Release Commitments
2.12. Piracy
2.13. Remedies
2.14. Other Provisions

2.1. INTRODUCTION: ART, MEET COMMERCE

You know the question: "If a tree falls in the forest, does it make a sound?" In other words, can sound exist without an ear to hear it? Does an event actually happen if there is no one to observe it? And is there any point, creatively or financially, in producing a movie unless an audience can see it?

This chapter examines the commercial transaction that makes it possible to bring a movie to its audience: The Motion Picture Distribution Agreement, in some of its myriad forms. The negotiation of this Agreement is the nexus at which Art meets Commerce: On the one hand, we are dealing here with a specific art form, the full length "feature film" that was originally developed to be exhibited as the main nightly event in motion picture theatres, and still drives much (though not all) entertainment content; and on the other, a business that has evolved in the past hundred plus years to support, commercialize and ultimately exploit that content for financial gain.

---

[*] **Stephen Monas** is a founding partner of Business Affairs, Inc.

In the following discussion we will identify a number of the basic features of typical Motion Picture Distribution Agreements, and examine some of the issues that arise in the course of drafting and negotiating them. We begin with the parties and their roles in the distribution process, the product to be distributed, and the place(s) and time for distribution; then we look at the media that will be exploited, the division of money to be earned, up front and on the back end, and ultimately the balancing of rights of the various parties. The goal is to give you a general, if not definitive, sense of how this agreement works, and to introduce you to some of the issues that have arisen as the motion picture business evolves.

A Brief Word about Forms

Throughout this chapter I will be referring to the following Exhibits in the electronic materials available to those who purchase *The Essential Guide to Entertainment Law*. These are provided both to illustrate the range of terms that are negotiated in distribution agreements, and to allow the reader to become familiar with the language, form and substance of the agreements. Included among these representative reference forms are the following:

- Acquisition Agreement: This is a form that might be used by a U.S.-based distributor to acquire rights in all (or many) media in the United States and, often, Canada, the so-called "domestic" territory. Many of the provisions in this agreement reflect the leverage that U.S. distributors have by virtue of the importance of the domestic territory, both because of its size and the usual leading role U.S. release takes in marketing English-language pictures worldwide.

- IFTA Distribution Agreement: This is a form provided by the Independent Film and Television Alliance, the self-described "global trade association for the independent motion picture and television industry." This Distribution Agreement is used, in many variations, primarily by foreign sales agents (see below for a discussion of their function) when licensing motion picture rights to foreign territorial distributors. "Independent" as used in this context means simply not affiliated with the distribution arms of the major studios (also described below). Many of the differences between this agreement and the Acquisition Agreement serve to illustrate the relatively weaker leverage of typical foreign distributors, excluding of course those in major foreign territories such as China, the UK, France, Japan, etc.

- Negative Pickup Agreement: The name of this agreement is, one suspects, deliberately obscure and misleading, especially today when so few pictures are shot on film, and there is literally no film "negative" to "pick up." However, the title and concept have survived: The distributor, primarily U.S.-based and probably a major studio, agrees before a picture is produced to pay the entire cost of production of the picture upon delivery, in return for the copyright and all other rights to the picture worldwide and in perpetuity. This agreement is in many ways an extreme version of the Acquisition Agreement, which, in turn, is a more aggressive version of the IFTA Distribution Agreement.

- Sales Agency Agreement: In this agreement, no distribution rights are granted to the sales agent, so this is not really a distribution agreement at all: The agent is engaged by the copyright owner/filmmaker to find, negotiate and enter into distribution agreements on behalf of the filmmaker as its exclusive agent. In this agreement, the approvals and controls shift to the filmmaker, and the sales agent typically provides no advance or minimum guarantee to the filmmaker. Sales agents often play a significant role in helping a filmmaker finance its picture through pre-sales.

War Stories: Platoon

In 1986 I was five years out of law school, and got my first "in house" job as a junior Business Affairs executive at what was then the largest home video distributor in the world: Vestron Video, now long defunct. In those days, it was possible to buy the right to distribute feature films in home video (meaning videocassettes; DVD had not been invented yet) separately from any other rights, because the major studios had not yet figured out that this was the gold mine that would save their businesses, at least until VOD came along. Vestron was at the forefront of this business, and had just raised $200 million in the public markets when I joined.

At the time, Vestron was in the business, among other things, of "pre-buying" the right to distribute feature films in North America, and in 1986 they had pre-bought video rights to Oliver Stone's second feature film *Platoon* from the producer Hemdale (also now long defunct), for a Minimum Guarantee I can't remember, payable on delivery and video "availability" (i.e., after a theatrical holdback of six months from the picture's release in movie theatres). As the new Business Affairs guy, I was given as my first assignment the task of drafting the Home Video Distribution Agreements for these two pictures, and I was thrilled.

Luckily, I didn't have to draft anything from scratch; there was a 40+ page form, and all I had to do was fill in the relevant information: the identity of the parties, the name of the picture and the various elements (stars, Director etc.), amount of the minimum guarantee (MG) and (most importantly, as it turned out) the payment schedule, and back end terms and so on, all under the supervision of a senior Business Affairs executive.

As it turned out, *Platoon* was a sensation at the 1986 Cannes Film Festival, and everyone was convinced it was going to be a huge hit (which it was, grossing $138 million at the domestic box office, the equivalent of a gazillion dollars today). Vestron management was so excited they organized a screening of the film for employees, and the entire company was galvanized. Then one day the Chairman got a call from Hemdale to the following effect: Yes, we know we have an agreement, but if you want us to deliver *Platoon*, you will have to pay us double the MG we previously agreed to, because it's very good and you are going to make a lot of money.

Much litigation ensued: Hemdale's entire case rested on their interpretation of the payment schedule that I had drafted, which said something to the effect of: $_____, payable: (i) __% on delivery of the picture to Vestron; (ii) __% on video availability; and (iii) the balance three months later. Hemdale's argument was that since clause (ii) did not say "conditional on delivery" or "__ months following delivery," that the second payment was due *whether or not* the producers ever delivered the picture, which, of course, was not the intent and certainly not the deal.

As was the practice in those days, Vestron filed for an injunction in California state court, alleging that Hemdale had breached their distribution agreement, and that Vestron would suffer various kinds of irreparable harm if Hemdale were allowed to proceed to license the video rights to Vestron's arch-rival HBO Video (also now defunct, though of course the pay TV platform lives on). The state court judge was not impressed, and refused to grant the injunction, apparently believing either that Hemdale's tortured reading of my drafting was possibly correct, or that Vestron could be compensated by money damages even if we were right.

Undeterred, Vestron's new attorneys filed suit in Federal court, claiming that Hemdale and HBO Video were preparing to infringe Vestron's rights under copyright, on the then novel theory that the grant of distribution rights was a grant of copyright, and that under the 1976 Copyright Act, an exclusive licensee of even a portion of the copyright of a protected work had the same rights as the author or copyright proprietor. As a copyright claimant, the attorneys argued, Vestron had a presumptive right to an injunction for this infringement.

And they lost: The District Court held that there was no federal claim involved, that this was purely a contract case that should be decided in state court. However, on appeal the Federal 9th Circuit Court of Appeals agreed with Vestron that there was a copyright claim involved, and instructed the District Court to reconsider the case. (*Vestron, Inc. v. Home Box Office, Inc.*, 839 F.2d 1380 (9th Cir.1988)). At which point, the District Court promptly granted Vestron an injunction, and we settled with HBO and Hemdale just in time for HBO Video to sell 350,000 units at a "retail" price of $99.95 apiece (do the math: at 40% off, the wholesale value of the cassettes was $21 Million).[1]

There are many lessons here: First, every stupid provision of every mind-numbing distribution agreement counts. A close (and obviously deviously wrong) reading of the most innocuous provision of the distribution agreement you are negotiating might convince a judge that the other side at least has an argument worth hearing. Second, there is a complex interplay of contract, copyright, agency, trust and other legal concepts throughout these deals; hopefully, you will never have to deal with them. Third, there is a reason that after *Platoon* every U.S. distributor requires and gets a security interest in the distribution rights they have been granted (not to mention a waiver of the right to terminate and/or sue for injunctive relief): Theoretically, this provides them with an extra-judicial means of enforcing their rights under the distribution agreement, so that the distributor does not have to worry about whether a state or federal judge will grant them an injunction in a similar situation. Finally, the distribution business is changing all the time: Not only do these players no longer exist, their entire business disappeared when the major studios and independents realized that they could rely on the "safety net" of home video to make up for the vagaries of the theatrical marketplace; and then just as suddenly, the safety net broke. If you haven't noticed, nobody sells 350,000 video units of any film at $60 each today.

2.2. PARTIES: WHAT IS A "DISTRIBUTOR"?

Like any contract, it takes at least two parties to make a motion picture distribution agreement: Throughout this chapter, for simplicity's sake we will call those parties the "Owner" and the "Distributor." The Owner should ideally be the entity that owns the distribution rights; this sounds simple and obvious enough, but is sometimes an elusive concept – not everyone understands the importance of chain of title. All too often, a Distributor will find itself dealing with a "producer" who neither owns nor controls the distribution rights. As in so many transactions, *caveat emptor* is the rule for Distributors to follow.

---

[1] *See* "Platoon's' Video Battle Over," Los Angeles Times, January 19, 1988 at http://articles.latimes.com/1988-01-19/entertainment/ca-37018_1_home-video-rights.

Of equal importance, the Owner in this transaction needs to know what kind of an *emptor* they are dealing with: Like producers, there are many different kinds of entities that go by the name "distributor," but they do not all have the same function or structure. That function or structure is important for any Owner to understand, as it will determine, among other things, the resources of the distributor, their business practices, and how many different parties are taking pieces of the revenues generated by the Owner's picture before any of it will come back to them.

If you go to www.imdbpro.com (the pay version of the Internet Movie Database, owned by Amazon), and open the Companies dropdown menu to click on Distributors, you will find what appears to be an almost infinite number of companies, literally thousands of entities in the entertainment business that define themselves as "distributors." Since the IMDb rankings are based on how many people are looking at a particular company at the time you click, the list is constantly changing; however, among the top 25 entities as of this writing, we find the following:

- Warner Bros., Paramount, Universal – together with Disney, Fox and Sony Pictures, the "majors," the "studios" or the "major studios." Structurally, as distributors the majors are distinguished by their size, which translates as their ability to distribute directly (including via subsidiaries or affiliates) throughout (most of) the world, and their superior clout in the marketplace. Their size also typically makes the majors less flexible in their agreements, more likely to rely on precedent, and more concerned with their liability as the deep-pocketed party in any transaction. The "majors" as majors, are also increasingly preoccupied with the release of "major" pictures, and with few exceptions tend to be the exclusive distributors of films in the highest (i.e., $100 Million plus) budget range.

- Lionsgate, The Weinstein Company, STX, Broad Green –These are "independent" distributors, sometimes inconsistently referred to as "mini-majors"– by the time you read this chapter, there may be more prominent independents, and the entities named here may have ceased to exist; given the amount of capital needed to sustain these operations, and the fickle realities of the motion picture marketplace, this is a constantly shifting landscape. Structurally, at least in the United States, these companies maintain their own theatrical distribution (i.e., license their pictures to movie theatres and collect their share of box office receipts from theatres), home video distribution (although physical distribution of DVDs may be serviced by a major), and license directly to VOD and television. Outside the United States, these companies typically license their pictures territory by territory to local distributors, although some, like Lionsgate, may also have ownership interests in one or more of those foreign distributors as well.

- Focus, Screen Gems, Fox Searchlight, New Line – These companies, which may also be referred to by some as "mini-majors," are divisions of the majors, with their own personalities and histories. In the U.S., they have access to their parent companies' distribution operations, but typically administer their own marketing; in the foreign market they may be able to utilize the parent company output deals and other distribution advantages, and/or act as a foreign sales agent, licensing territory by territory.

- FilmNation, XYZ Films – These companies are examples of sales agents, so technically not distributors at all, in that they do not generally own the copyrights/distribution rights in the pictures that they license. Sales agents are typically engaged by the producer/copyright owner to market their picture to foreign distributors, to negotiate territorial agreements with those distributors, often on a "pre-buy" basis before the picture is produced, and to deliver the picture to the distributors when it is completed, all on behalf of the copyright owner as their exclusive agent. Often, however, the producers dealing with sales agents, and even the sales agents themselves, may not appreciate the difference between being a distributor – the owner, even if for a limited territory or time, of the distribution rights – and an agent, i.e., the alter ego and fiduciary of the distributor.[2]

---

[2] For a description of the role of the sales agent, the evolution of the sales agency business, and the legal differences between distributors and sales agents, *see* Clements, Grace, "A Fistful of Dynamite: How Independent Film's Cowboy Culture

- Participant, RatPac, Legendary – These are all listed on IMDB as "distributors" when in fact they are financiers and production companies; of course, some significant production companies maintain the in-house capability to also directly license the pictures they produce to (foreign) territorial distributors, like a foreign sales agent; however, for our purposes they are unlikely to be entering into an agreement as the Distributor.

- Netflix, Amazon Studios – Obviously major players in the production and distribution area, these companies are better characterized as end users rather than distributors in the various territories in which they operate. Their distribution agreements, more properly characterized as "digital licenses," are distinguished primarily by the fact that there is no division of revenues involved – Netflix, in particular, is not sharing the subscription fees it receives. Thus, even when Netflix acquires all worldwide rights in perpetuity to a motion picture prior to production, and bills it as a "Netflix Original," they agree to make a fixed "buyout" payment, with no additional net profits, royalties or other accountings.

2.3. PICTURE SPECIFICATIONS AND APPROVALS

As in any good contract, the first function of the Distribution Agreement is to identify the commodity that the Distributor is purchasing or licensing. If the Picture that is the subject of the agreement is a finished film that the Distributor has already seen, this job is relatively easy: It may be possible to describe the Picture by as little as its title, and the date screened by the Distributor.

Often, however, and more typically with commercial, higher budget pictures, a Distributor may be acquiring distribution rights to a Picture that is somewhere earlier in the process of production, which could theoretically be anywhere from an idea summarized in one written line or paragraph, to a film in the last stages of editing. The "pre-buy" transaction typically occurs when enough elements have been defined – screenplay, budget, cast, director – for the Distributor to

---

Creates Unstable Sales Agency Agreements," Journal of International Media and Entertainment Law, April 24, 2014.

make a commercial judgment regarding the likely value of the Picture when finished.

In the context of a Negative Pickup Agreement, the transaction may occur even earlier in the life of a picture: The typical scenario, though not the only one, would be that a screenplay developed by a producer, either in tandem with the studio or independently, was ready to be further packaged, budgeted and set up for production, but the studio for whatever reason wanted the production to take place at arm's length, and be financed by a bank or other financier by discounting the studio's obligation to "pick up" the picture for the full budget cost when it is completed.[3] In the past those reasons have included a production that the studio wanted someone else (typically a bond company) to control and guarantee completion and delivery of; or that the studio wanted the financing to not appear on their balance sheet; or that Guild issues prevented the studio from producing at the optimum budget.

Following are the picture specifications and approvable elements that customarily appear in Distribution and Negative Pickup Agreements.

2.3.1. Screenplay, Director, Cast, Budget

These four elements are the building blocks of any feature film production, and are usually put together in more or less that order. In a pre-buy Distribution Agreement, the screenplay will be identified by the date of the specific draft that is being pre-approved, often with a specified page count, and the Distributor will have the right to approve any changes to that draft, subject to minor changes resulting from exigencies of production.

2.3.2. Essential Elements

Some pictures may be sold on the basis of screenplay and genre alone, regardless of who the director is, or who is in the principal cast. More often, the value of pictures sold on a pre-buy basis is determined by the attachment of star actors or less frequently a star director. Director and cast may be specifically identified, or the parties may agree on a pre-approved list (which in this author's experience almost

---

[3] See this book's section on Film Finance (Chapter 3).

never includes the actor(s) or director who are ultimately engaged). If the principal actor(s) or director are already attached, and are truly (in the judgment of the Distributor) essential to the value of the Picture, the Distribution Agreement may specify that one or more such individuals are "Essential Elements," meaning if the actor does not appear in the picture in the specified role, or the director does not direct the picture through principal photography, the Distributor may refuse to accept delivery of the picture, and may terminate the Agreement without paying the agreed advance.

If the producer is banking the pre-buy Distribution Agreement in order to finance production, the financier and/or bond company will require that additional insurance beyond the customary cast insurance be obtained with respect to any such individual identified as an Essential Element. Because the consequences of illness or other disability of an Essential Element will result in greater loss to the insurer than replacement of a non-essential cast member, the insurer will require special medical examinations for any Essential Elements to determine if there are any special medical conditions to take into account.

2.3.3. Advertising Rights

In addition to an Essential Element appearing in the final picture, distributors will want the right to advertise the picture using the name and likeness of that individual. While this may seem obvious, there are numerous instances in which the actor and his or her representatives may want to restrict such use, if for instance a major star is playing a secondary role or even a brief cameo, and does not want to dilute his or her "brand." Thus, the Distribution Agreement (and most commonly the domestic Distribution Agreement) may specify that the Essential Element's name and likeness may appear in the advertising artwork, how many other individuals must appear and/or be credited alongside the Essential Element, and the position that the Essential Element's credit may appear in relative to the other individuals.

2.3.4. Production Cost

The Distribution Agreement may also specify the amount of the production budget of the subject picture, as this amount is a measure of both the anticipated production values of the finished picture, and the portion of the production cost that the particular distributor is covering with their advance. While the percentage value of particular territories is a constantly shifting target, distributors and good sales agents are generally aware of the range of values in particular territories at any particular time.

2.3.5. Approvals

As you review the various Agreements in this chapter's supplemental materials, you will see that the approvals of the respective distributor or agent range from almost none in the Sales Agency Agreement (unless the agent is providing an advance) to some in the IFTA form, more in the domestic Distribution Agreement, and virtually total control of every production element and the respective agreements relating to those elements in the Negative Pickup Agreement. Conversely, the approvals accorded to the producer/licensor in each of those agreements with respect to the marketing and distribution of the picture are far greater in the Sales Agency Agreement, and will generally include the right of the producer to approve all distribution agreements, marketing materials, expenses and other matters (after all, this is an *agency* relationship); the IFTA Agreement will provide for the licensor's approval over release dates, marketing campaigns, and similar matters; the domestic Distribution Agreement may include minor approvals or consultation for the licensor; and the Negative Pickup Agreement will not.

2.3.6. Other Specifications

Finally, the Distribution Agreement and attached Delivery Schedule will contain other specifications that are important to the Distributor's ability to distribute, including the promised rating (usually formulated with reference to the Motion Picture Association of America (MPAA) categories,[4] but sometimes including local rating designations as well), length (generally between 85 minutes not counting main and end titles and 120 minutes including titles, unless the distributor is buying an art film), and technical specifications relating to whether the picture is being shot on film or, more commonly, in digital HD.

---

[4] *See* http://www.mpaa.org/film-ratings/ and also see http://filmratings.com/how.html (the website of the MPAA's Film Classification and Ratings Administration, or CARA).

Selling the Sizzle

Lest all of this sound too predictable, Adam Smith's rational consumers making informed decisions in a competitive marketplace, please remember: It's the Film Business, where "nobody knows anything," in William Goldman's famous words.

So, another war story: When I first went to the Cannes Film Festival in 1989, I took a meeting with a well-known sales agent, Mark Damon, the reputed "King of Cannes," who later became my employer.[5] Mark had previously had great success in the foreign market with *9½ Weeks* (released in 1986), a picture that had not done well with U.S. audiences, but performed spectacularly abroad, which proved Mark's basic thesis that producers would always be better off uncrossing their rights so that they could reap the benefits of big success in some territories without worrying about covering losses in others. (See the discussion of "cross-collateralization" in Section.2.4.2 below).

When I walked into Mark's sales office in Cannes, he had one large black and white poster prominently displayed, featuring a scantily clad model with a sleep mask over her eyes, sprawled on a bed, with only a title and the name of the director – Zalman King, one of the writers of *9½ Weeks* – in the artwork. Expressing interest in the project, I asked Mark who was in the movie (well, no one yet), what the budget was (who knows?) and who wrote the script (there was none).

But this being Cannes, and Mark's great skills being what they were, he had managed to pre-sell rights to this non-existent "picture" in most of the world, and in the process raised enough money to commission a screenplay, hire cast and crew, shoot the picture and still have a couple million dollars left over – all without a U.S. deal.

Whether anyone, including Mark, could repeat that particular performance in today's marketplace is questionable; foreign distributors have reputedly become more savvy, the irrational exuberance of the markets has cooled, and too many pictures have not lived up to their pre-buy hype. But in the end, it's still the Film Business, in which trading on the unreasonable expectations of distributors and the fickle taste of the consuming public are the keys to survival.

---

[5] For more on Mark Damon, *see* Damon, Mark and Schreyer, Linda, *From Cowboy to Mogul to Monster: The Neverending Story of Film Pioneer Mark Damon*, AuthorHouse 2008.

2.4. TERM AND TERRITORY

2.4.1. Term

The duration of copyright protection for a work made for hire (which a motion picture almost always is) under the United States Copyright Act of 1976 is the earlier of 95 years from first publication or 120 years from creation.[6] For works created before 1978, and for works created in certain foreign jurisdictions, different and more complex rules apply. However, 95 years is a good useful life for a motion picture; the vast majority of films in distribution today are of much more recent vintage. With digital technology making the preservation and restoration (not to mention the production and delivery) of motion pictures easier, however, the future is likely to be awash in century-old films.

The duration, or term, of Distribution Agreements varies with the size and leverage of the specific territory. Pictures are generally licensed for distribution in smaller foreign territories for a period of 7 years from delivery of the picture to the distributor. However, in larger territories, including the United States, the distribution term may extend for 15, 25 or more years, and not uncommonly in the U.S., in "perpetuity," by which point, of course, the picture has been in the public domain for a very long time, and the contractual term is virtually meaningless.

The term of Sales Agency Agreements, because they are essentially service agreements, may be much shorter: It is not unheard of to engage a sales agent to sell a motion picture for one or two years, at which point they will presumably have sold all the territories they are capable of selling. In addition, a Sales Agency Agreement may provide that the producer may terminate the agreement if the agent has not achieved a specified level of sales in the first and/or second year. The duration and survival of the distribution agreements that the agent has entered into before the termination of the agency will, of course, be longer, and will not (along with, typically, the agents' commissions for these sales) be affected by the termination. Sales agents naturally resist such shorter terms, as they will seek to build a "library" of pictures that they control the sales of, and will try to earn additional fees by selling the second cycle of distribution rights available after the initial distribution agreements they have negotiated terminate.

---

[6] 17 U.S. Code 302.

2.4.2. Territory

For the most part in this chapter we avoid the Big Picture, the historical, political, and social context of motion picture distribution, and focus on the transactional realities of the Distribution Agreement. However, in thinking about territories and territorial definitions, it may help to step back and survey the landscape. In 2018, the known universe includes 206 sovereign states, according to Wikipedia, each with their own unique systems of law and governance. The rules governing distribution of motion pictures into each of these states theoretically varies according to local laws and policy concerning copyright, contracts and commercial transactions generally.

In the beginning, one can imagine that defining exclusive territories was simple, from a legal point of view: Motion pictures were reproduced on film that was contained in canisters, and exhibited in motion picture theatres to paying audiences. The notion of territorial distribution was therefore relatively straightforward, and circumscribed by describable boundaries. The advent of television posed some challenges to that notion because of the ability to broadcast signals across national boundaries; from a practical point of view, however, broadcast "spillover" was limited and could be dealt with as a relatively insignificant exception to territorial exclusivity. Even home video distribution could be dealt with using territorial models based on the recorded music business, with a couple of extra impediments (language and different video formats) thrown in.

However, the advent of the Internet and the resulting explosion of on demand digital media have completely disrupted this business model for motion pictures, as they have for so many other businesses: Or have they? The territorial provisions in sample agreements accompanying this chapter actually look very much like their counterparts from 30 or even 50 years ago, although the fonts are nicer and some of the names of the territories have changed. Given the vested commercial interests of distributors and rights owners in the territorial system of distribution, this aspect of the business has been slow to adapt.

But you know it must: As in the music business, the expectation of consumers that all content will be instantly available everywhere has created enormous pressure on the motion picture industry that initially expresses itself at the consumer level as "piracy," i.e., unauthorized access to and reproduction of motion pictures, regardless of territory, and on the slower-to-adapt legislative side as regulations such as those under consideration in the European Union requiring "cross-border portability" of online access to content.[7] Even language and certainly technical formats are no longer obstacles to distribution, as both recording and distribution of multi-language versions of pictures has become cheaper and quicker to accomplish digitally.

The independent film business of selling distribution rights territory by territory has long been touted by its proponents as a way of maximizing the value of a motion picture by "uncrossing" the revenues of the various territories (i.e., by not applying the losses incurred in one territory where the film did not work against the profits in another territory where it did). In a traditional studio worldwide distribution deal, all revenues are "cross-collateralized" against all expenses, including distribution expenses and fees, as well as all production expenses and interest.[8] Thus a film could be a hit in one territory, but still be in a loss position overall if it performed poorly in other territories. In the independent model, the local distributor in a territory where the film did not perform well would have to absorb any losses, while the unrelated distributor in a territory where the film was a hit would share its profits with the producer. This is the pitch on which the foreign sales business of the IFTA members was built – however, whether it can survive in the world of universal online access remains to be seen.

2.4.3. Territorial Definitions

IFTA publishes a useful Schedule of Territory Definitions, which is attached to the form IFTA Distribution Agreement accompanying this chapter. Study it and you will know the next time someone mentions "DOM/TOM" that they are referring to the French "departments d'outre-mer" and "territoires d'outre-mer," former colonies with varying legal status. The Schedule provides a guide to how motion picture territories are divided up by country, region and language. You will note, however, that the definition of territory in the "domestic" Acquisition Agreement adds several jurisdictions that you might not think of as being part of the United States or Canada, namely

---

[7] See section 2.4.4 European Union, below.
[8] See section 2.8 Application of Gross Receipts, below.

Bermuda, the Bahamas, and the Turks and Caicos Islands. This territorial expansion is not so much the result of imperialist ambition as business reality: The satellite television "footprint" as well as online Video on Demand services from the U.S. now reach those English-language (or in some cases mixed language) territories, so they have been effectively annexed to the U.S. The definition of the United States in the very back of the Acquisition Agreement also specifies that it includes "all military bases, ships, aircraft and oil rigs flying the flag of or serviced from the United States or whose principal offices are located in the United States (regardless of the country of the "flag flown" or registry), diplomatic posts and camps, installations and reservations of the Armed Forces of the United States, including the USO, Veteran's Administration, Red Cross and similar organizations, as well as maritime facilities and other commercial and/or industrial installations wherever located." These additional provisions often conflict with other distribution agreements the producer or its agent may have entered into, commonly for instance an airlines deal (since so many airlines are serviced out of the United States) or Pan-Latin American satellite television deals, which customarily include the same Caribbean islands. These conflicts, once noted, are generally negotiated out by restricting the airlines to those flying the American flag, and providing that non-English language distribution in the Caribbean is on a non-exclusive basis.

2.4.4. European Union

As noted above, as of this writing the European Commission has proposed Regulations concerning "cross-border portability" of online content services[9] in the 28 (soon, post-Brexit, to be 27) states comprising the European Union. Predictably enough, IFTA has responded with concern regarding the continuing viability of the territorial distribution system, "the core of independent production financing, marketing and distribution."[10]

---

[9] *See* https://ec.europa.eu/transparency/regdoc/rep/1/2015/EN/1-2015-627-EN-F1-1.PDF.

[10] *See IFTA Files Comments with the U.K. Government regarding the European Commission's Proposed Legislation for the Portability of Online Content in the EU*, February 12, 2016, http://www.ifta-online.org/recent-filings-updates.

The concept of "cross-border portability," that is, the ability of a resident of (say) France to access Canal Plus online while vacationing in Malaga, or while on business in Bucharest, is of course totally compatible with the policy of the European Union to provide freedom of access to information and services within the "internal market" of the EU. A resident of California would rightly be irritated if they could not access HBO Now on their iPad while gambling in Las Vegas; why shouldn't a resident of the EU have the same freedom? Unfortunately for the existing independent film business structure, this inevitable erosion of territorial boundaries will ultimately chip away at IFTA's "core of independent . . . distribution"; and what will replace it is likely to be larger, pan-EU distributor(s) with more leverage and the ability to cross-collateralize its expenses against revenue from all 27 Member states.

2.5. RIGHTS

2.5.1. Copyright Basics

The United States Copyright Act provides that copyright owners have the following six exclusive rights (17 USC 106):

a. To reproduce the work, i.e., to make copies;

b. To prepare "derivative works" based on the work;

c. To distribute copies of the work "by sale or other transfer of ownership, or by rental, lease, or lending";

d. To perform the work publicly;

e. To display the work publicly;

f. To digitally transmit sound recordings.

In other words, the owner of copyright holds a "bundle" of exclusive rights, each of which may be separately alienated (licensed, sold, granted) or reserved. Distribution of a motion picture will typically include all of the above, other than preparation of derivative works (although this may be dealt with separately) and digital transmission of sound recordings. Each of the rights enumerated may be further divided by term and by territory, as we have seen above; and they may be further divided by specifying the medium of distribution.

The Copyright Act further provides that any of the above exclusive rights may be transferred and owned separately; and that the transferee/owner of any particular right is entitled to all of the protection and remedies of a copyright owner to the extent of that right (17 USC 201(d)(2)). Thus, upon execution of a Distribution Agreement which contains a grant of rights, the Distributor becomes an owner of copyright, "to the extent of" those rights.

2.5.2. Definition of Rights

In return for a share of the revenues to be generated from distribution and exploitation of a motion picture, and often in return for an advance against such share, the Owner grants Distributor certain rights "under copyright and otherwise" with respect to the motion picture. The Copyright Act's minimalist description of the right to distribute works "by sale or other transfer of ownership, or by rental, lease, or lending" doesn't begin to describe the smorgasbord of rights defined in the typical Distribution Agreement. Essentially the rights break down into four categories: Exploitation rights, advertising rights, ancillary rights, and derivative rights.

2.5.2.1 Exploitation Rights

The evolution of the motion picture business has been to create new media for exploitation of the same content, while new media at the same time require the evolution of content (e.g., the evolution of television series, talk shows, and webisodes). The advent of television, at first, created consternation in the courts as to whether television was even a different medium from theatrical distribution.[11] Given the subsequent proliferation of media, you could now make yourself crazy trying to define and differentiate all media that exist at any moment in time for the exploitation even of the traditional feature film: The IFTA Definitions in the accompanying materials list seven categories of rights, broken down conveniently into three subdivisions each; the Acquisitions Agreement currently defines seventeen separate media, with an additional fourteen categories included in those media, and seventeen separate delivery categories for television alone; and

---

[11] *See* Ettore v. Philco Television Broadcasting Corporation, 229 F. 2d 481, and the cases cited.

arguably neither of these agreements definitively encompasses all available media.

Given this plethora of defined media, you have to ask what the point is of even trying to differentiate. As noted early in this chapter in connection with the "Platoon" case, "split rights" distribution was once an important piece of the puzzle for financing independent motion pictures: Just as the foreign sales agent could promise uncrossed revenue streams by selling multiple territories to separate buyers, the home video distributor could promise an advance and a revenue stream from a single medium or related media that was not reduced by the cost of theatrical release in the same territory. However, that distribution deal lasted only as long as it took the major content creators, i.e., the studios, to build their own home video distribution systems; the independent video distribution business arguably was already on its way to extinction by the time *Platoon* was released.

In addition, the rising cost of marketing the theatrical release of motion pictures, anachronistically known as "P&A," for "prints and advertising," means that virtually no distributor, studio or independent, can afford to release a picture in theatres without the additional revenue from home video and other media to recoup the expenses incurred in theatrical distribution. In the distant past it was a rarity that a picture did not recoup at least its P&A out of theatrical revenues; today it is the rare picture that does recoup.

A similar trajectory is taking place today with the major SVOD platforms, treading the path blazed by pay television networks: Netflix, Amazon, Hulu began by licensing specific distribution rights from producers for their subscribers and customers, which became a potentially uncrossed source of revenue for producers; however, in order to differentiate themselves from competitors in the battle for new subscribers (and to retain existing subscribers), all have moved in the direction of "original" programming for which they typically own distribution rights in all media.

Increasingly then the formulation of distribution rights in Distribution Agreements is "all rights whether now known or hereafter [not 'hereinafter,' as we see all too often] invented," with common carveouts for/reservation of rights in certain ancillary and derivative rights as noted below. The Negative Pickup Agreement in its "pure" form as a grant of all rights worldwide and in perpetuity to the studio would have no reservation of rights at all.

2.5.2.2. Advertising Rights

Critical to the right of exploitation, of course, is the right to advertise and promote the motion picture to the public. If a distributor has for some reason acquired exploitation rights in fewer than all media, the advertising rights may need to specify the right to advertise in specific media otherwise controlled by other distributors. In addition, as noted above under Specifications, the Distributor will often specify how and where the name and likeness of the principal cast may be used in advertising, and the Owner will be responsible for making sure that the talent agreements delivered to the Distributor are consistent with those requirements. The right to use a cast member's name and likeness to advertise a picture involves rights of privacy and publicity that are distinguishable from (and generally given greater protection than) the right to use that person's name, likeness and performance in the picture itself, and so need to be specifically granted, both in the services agreement for the performer and generally in the Distribution Agreement itself.

2.5.2.3. Ancillary Rights

Whichever side of the Distribution Agreement negotiation you are on, you should use care in throwing the term "Ancillary Rights" around: There does not appear to be any broad consensus on what constitutes an "ancillary right" in a motion picture. The IFTA definitions specify that ancillary rights include only the right to exhibit a picture on airlines, ships and in hotels; the Acquisition Agreement does not include any of those in its definition, but says the term includes, without limitation, "Merchandising Rights, commercial tie-in rights, Print Publishing Rights, Soundtrack Album Rights, Master Rights, Music Publishing Rights, Music Performance Rights, Clip Rights and Electronic Publishing Rights." And a random search of the Internet leads to the following on a website created by Columbia Law School: "Ancillary right, in relation to entertainment law, is a contractual agreement in which a percentage of the profits are received and derived from the sale of action figures, posters, CDs, books, T-shirts, etc. relating to a film or motion picture,"[12] which may mean merchandising, publishing and soundtrack album rights.

---

[12] *See* http://web.law.columbia.edu/keep-your-copyrights/glossary/ancillary-rights.

If we fall back on a common understanding of ancillary as secondary or subsidiary, then the broader category contained in the Acquisition Agreement makes the most sense of the three cited above. The right to create action figures and T-shirts (i.e., Merchandising), screenplays, synopses and novelizations (Print Publishing), and to license use of the score and other musical compositions written for the picture (Music Publishing), all involve the identification and exploitation of elements contained in the picture that are separately protectable under copyright, and are secondary in the sense that the means of exploitation of these items are separate and distinct from exploitation of the picture itself.

Perhaps for this reason it is not uncommon for Distributors to agree that Owners may reserve and separately license one or more ancillary rights: Independent distributors in particular are more likely to be focused on the marketing and distribution of the picture itself in theatrical, VOD, DVD, television and related media, and less likely to have the personnel and specific expertise to also exploit these "secondary" markets, which for many pictures generate little or no income in any case.

2.5.2.4. Derivative Rights

As noted above, one of the exclusive rights belonging to the Owner of copyright in a work is the right to create "derivative works" based upon that work. The Copyright Act goes on to define "derivative work" as a "work based upon one or more preexisting works, such as a . . . motion picture version. . ."[13] For motion pictures the familiar derivative works include sequels, prequels, remakes and television series.

The typical Distribution Agreement (including the Acquisition Agreement and IFTA Agreement included in this chapter's forms) will provide that the Owner reserves all rights with respect to such derivative works; in larger territories, including the U.S., the agreement will also provide that the Distributor has a right of first negotiation and last refusal, or sometimes a more limited right of first refusal, to distribute a sequel, prequel or remake in its territory as well. In this context, a right of last refusal means that if the parties cannot reach an agreement after a specified period of negotiation (usually 30 days), the

---

[13] 17 USC §101.

Owner is free to license the rights to a third party, provided that they must offer the rights again to Owner on the same terms that they are willing to accept from such third party. A right of first refusal will only require the Owner to offer such rights to the Distributor on the terms they are willing to accept from a third party if the third party offer is less favorable to or equal to (or in some cases only marginally, e.g., 20%, better than) the last deal offered by the Distributor.

A Distributor looking for a more secure hold on rights to sequels may include instead of a first negotiation and refusal requirement an option to acquire the rights to any sequel at a specified price; logically, the price for the sequel would be more than that of the first picture, as the assumption is that a sequel will only be made if the first picture is successful. As a result, among other things the fees paid to actors, director and writers tend to increase for a sequel, and the budgets increase. The sequel option may also be on a "rolling" basis, i.e., the Distributor has an option to acquire rights to a number of sequels, but will lose that right if it did not acquire the prior sequel.

Since the distribution of television series is a different business from distribution of feature films, these rights will not typically be included in either a first negotiation or first refusal provision, unless the distributor happens to have a particular interest in those rights given the specific project, and/or is already in that business. There are enough examples of television series that far outlived and out-earned the pictures they were based on (e.g., *Buffy the Vampire Slayer*, *M.A.S.H.*), that Distributors may be motivated to preserve some future rights in any picture they acquire.

Of course, the same logic would apply to video games, mobile apps and other works and media that have yet to be invented – these are derivative works whose exploitation today may be secondary or "ancillary" to the exploitation of the picture they are derived from, but have the potential to outperform the original.

2.6. HOLDBACKS AND WINDOWS

The theatrical exhibition business, which, of course, for many years was the only medium of exploitation of motion pictures, still relies commercially in this country and elsewhere on being the first, and generally during the initial release period the only, place that "theatrical" motion pictures can be seen. While the advent of "day and date" limited theatrical and VOD release of pictures in the United States has challenged that model, theatre owners, and particularly the large chains, have pushed back against screening pictures in any significant numbers that are available in any other medium at the same time. In addition, the dominance of the U.S. both as a source of motion pictures and as the world's largest market for entertainment has meant that the rest of the world (the "ROW") has generally had to wait until motion pictures were first released in the U.S. before they were made available for foreign audiences, with major studios/distributor tent-pole pictures being the general exception.

For a time, the sequence of media in which a feature film could be released was relatively uniform, and that sequence was reflected in the contractual holdbacks and windowing in Distribution Agreements (as well as by law in certain territories, notably France). But given the ever-multiplying new distribution media noted above, the rise of China and other territories as significant markets for entertainment, and the technological ability to "legitimately" release pictures simultaneously worldwide, as well as the accompanying technological ability to immediately access copies of those same pictures everywhere illegally, the traditional distribution holdbacks and windows have morphed into a constantly shifting and hotly contested area of negotiation.

Having said all that, you can see in the Acquisition Agreement the more or less state of the art (as of this writing) in "standard" holdbacks: "The Picture shall not be commercially released anywhere in the world in any media until [the earlier of: (a)] the date the Picture is initially released commercially in the Territory [; and (b) [ten] [six] months following the date Complete Delivery is effected]." The expectation of a holdback of ten months, or even six, may be wishful thinking, as foreign distributors and sales agents increasingly maintain that there should be no more than a four-month lag. If the Picture is released theatrically, as indicated in the accompanying materials, the Agreement seeks to have foreign release in any other medium (really VOD, which is the culprit behind virtually all piracy today) withheld until the domestic Distributor releases in home video. The IFTA form Agreement is much more specific, with windows for each medium that hearken back to an earlier time, but remain variable depending on the territory.

Unfortunately, there is a logistical and legal problem at the heart of any territorial holdback provision: The Distribution Agreement for any one territory (e.g., the United States) is typically between two parties, the Owner and the Distributor, neither of whom actually controls the release of the picture in any other territory. The best the domestic Distributor can require is that the Owner contractually prohibit, or at least not authorize, the release of the picture in any foreign territory prior to release (in the same media, if you have the leverage) in the United States. But this provision does not give the U.S. Distributor the ability to actually prevent any such other release from occurring; the Distributor has no contractual privity with the foreign distributors, so even if the Owner has included appropriate holdbacks in its foreign distribution agreements, and the foreign distributor is in breach, the best argument that the U.S. Distributor has is that it is a third party beneficiary of the foreign distributor's holdback agreement, or that somehow the foreign distributor is infringing the U.S. Distributor's exclusive distribution rights. And frankly the situation is no better if the Owner or (more commonly) its foreign sales agent has not included appropriate holdbacks in the foreign agreements, and is therefore in breach of its contractual obligations to the U.S. Distributor; you can sue the Owner and try to prove that the early release will decrease your revenues, a speculative exercise at best, but that won't stop the foreign release from going forward.

2.7. MINIMUM GUARANTEES

The Minimum Guarantee ("MG" herein), also known as the Advance, is the amount payable by the Distributor to the Owner as an advance against the Owner's share of distribution revenues. As noted in the **Motion Picture Finance** chapter, this obligation is the basis for much of independent motion picture financing, as lenders will loan a discounted amount against the aggregate minimum guarantees already secured by the Owner or its agent, as well as in many cases the additional projected minimum guarantees that the Owner's sales agent is projecting to secure. The amount of the MG is, of course, hotly negotiated with the Distributor either by the Owner or its sales agent, or both, and is obviously a bet by the Distributor on the ultimate performance of a picture in its specific territory, which bet in a pre-buy situation may be based on nothing more than faith in the script or other elements then known to the Distributor (see "Picture Specifications and Approvals" above). In a Negative Pickup Agreement, the Minimum

72 ESSENTIAL GUIDE TO ENTERTAINMENT LAW: DEALMAKING

Guarantee will logically (but not always) be equal to the final production cost of the picture, since the Distributor is "picking up" the entire "negative," i.e., all rights to the picture worldwide and in perpetuity.

2.7.1 Payment Terms

As is the case with respect to virtually all of the terms discussed in this chapter, the actual payment terms of any particular Distribution Agreement may be varied by negotiation,[14] but as a starting point, the forms in the accompanying contract materials show the following:

2.7.1.1 Domestic Distribution

The typical domestic Acquisition Agreement and the Negative Pickup Agreement each provide for payment of the MG in full upon completion of delivery,[15] generally a long and, for most Owners, onerous process that requires the Owner to provide all relevant legal documentation as well as all physical elements necessary for release of the Picture in the territory. Occasionally a domestic Distributor will provide for payment of a small portion of the MG against initial delivery of basic chain of title documentation and physical materials necessary for creation of marketing materials so that the Distributor may prepare the marketing campaign before the final picture is ready for delivery; and in situations where the domestic Distributor's obligation to pay the MG is being loaned against by a bank of other lender, the Distributor will agree to pay most of the MG against limited "mandatory" delivery (see "Interparty Agreements and NOAs" below).

2.7.1.2. Foreign Distribution

The payment terms of a typical foreign Distribution Agreement, as you can see in the IFTA Form, are more generous to the Owner, which is an indication of both the historically weaker position of the foreign distributor, and the relatively lower importance of delivery in most foreign territories. Foreign distributors, other than in the largest territories, will typically pay 20% of the negotiated MG upon

---

[14] *See* the practice commentary "It's All Non-negotiable," in section 2.8.5 below.
[15] *See* section 2.9 Delivery, below).

execution of a long form agreement, with the balance payable upon receipt of a "Notice of Delivery," which is just a notice from the sales agent or Owner that required materials are available for delivery. The Distributor then pays the MG, and orders and pays for materials from the sales agent before it has anything that can actually be released. The delivery risk in these agreements is completely on the Distributor, unlike its domestic counterpart. In a time when pictures were shot on film, the sale of 35mm prints at a hefty markup was also a separate profit center for sales agents; with the advent of digital distribution and delivery, that profit center has largely disappeared.

2.7.1.3. License Agreement

You may note in the SVOD License Agreement that the payment terms are even more extended than in the Acquisition Agreement: The license fee is payable on a calendar quarter basis over three years, commencing after delivery and "availability," i.e., the expiration of any exclusive windows that would prohibit SVOD rights from being exploited. The license fee is not an MG in the sense that the Owner does not share in any additional revenues generated by the SVOD licensee, so there is nothing more for the licensee to advance against.

2.7.2. Interparty Agreements and NOAs

Interparty Agreements and their shorter foreign cousin the Notice and Acceptance of Assignment ("NOA") are financing documents that affect the payment of MGs by: (a) assigning payment from the Owner to a financier; (b) waiving any conditions to payment (such as approvals, counterclaims, offsets) other than delivery, or in the case of the NOA, Notice of Delivery; and (c) limiting the number of items that must be delivered (typically characterized as "mandatory" delivery items) to those that a completion guarantor will guarantee. These factors are covered more thoroughly in the Finance chapter; however, they are worth noting here for two reasons.

First, it is common for an Owner's attorney to require in negotiating a domestic Distribution Agreement that a majority of the MG be payable on mandatory or "essential" delivery. Most Distributors will resist this, acknowledging that they would make such a concession to a bank or even other financier, but not to a production company. Second, if a Distributor does enter into an Interparty Agreement or otherwise agrees to pay the MG against essential or mandatory delivery, they will typically hold back an amount sufficient to guarantee that the Owner will be motivated to complete the balance of complete delivery.

2.7.3. Sales Agents and Intermediaries

As noted above, Sales Agency Agreements typically do not include MGs. If the Agreement does provide for payment of an MG, it will likely be payable much like a domestic Distribution Agreement against complete delivery.

Sales Agency Agreements will however typically include an agreed-on schedule of "asks" and "takes", i.e., projections on a territory-by-territory basis of the anticipated MGs that the Sales Agent will be able to secure for the Owner, with a high end (asks) and low end (takes). These schedules serve as a pre-approval for the Sales Agent to conclude Distribution Agreements at the minimum take level; any agreement providing for an MG below that level will require additional consent from the Owner. In addition, the Sales Agent may agree to terminate the agreement if a certain level of sales or percentage of "takes" is not achieved within a specified period.

The MGs secured by Sales Agents in those foreign Distribution Agreements are often subject to foreign withholding taxes applicable to royalty payments, since the MG by definition is an advance against the copyright owner's share of revenues; while the U.S. has a fairly extensive network of treaties with other countries that reduce or eliminate those withholding taxes, there are other jurisdictions that may have more extensive networks and/or better withholding rates. Thus, for certain territories there may be two Distribution Agreements: One between the Owner or Sales Agent and the Tax Intermediary located in a tax-favorable jurisdiction, and a second "mirror" Distribution Agreement between the Tax Intermediary and the Distributor.

2.8. APPLICATION OF GROSS RECEIPTS

Motion picture accounting is a notoriously complex subject, full of arcane traps for the unwary and more twists and turns than the famous Monte Carlo Grand Prix; the subject deserves its own book(s), and there are a number of them on the market.[16] All of which is to say that we can't possibly examine this subject in the kind of detail that may in fact be warranted. At the same time, the details of these accounting provisions are the least likely to be negotiated by the Distributor and its attorneys, in house or out, for reasons noted elsewhere.[17] However, for our purposes the application of gross receipts in a "typical" Distribution Agreement can be simply outlined as (1) Gross Receipts, less (2) Distribution Fees, less (3) Distribution Expenses, less (4) the Minimum Guarantee, equals (5) Net (all capitalized terms being subject to their contractual definitions), all of which may be fair game in a negotiation.

2.8.1 Gross Receipts

This is where it is very important that you understand what kind of Distributor you are actually dealing with. Looking back at the list in Section 2.2 above, we identified six categories of entities that define themselves as distributors, only four of which purport to share distribution revenues with Owners: Major Studios; Mini-majors; Divisions of Majors; and Sales Agents (the other two were production companies, which are Owners, and digital licensees, which don't generally report or share).

"Gross Receipts" means for each of these entities at least the amounts, the revenues, the monies actually received by (or credited to the account of) the Distributor, less in some cases "off the top" deduction of certain limited expenses such as collection costs and bank fees. But the number of intervening parties who have taken a cut of revenues before they reach the Distributor is not the same for the Major Studio as for the Mini-major, Sales Agent or even for the divisions of the Majors. A Major Studio is more likely to be collecting revenues in more territories "at the source," meaning directly from motion picture theatres, VOD licensees, DVD wholesalers and television broadcasters (each of which is of course collecting those monies a little closer to the

---

[16] Examples include Daniels, Bill; Leedy, David; and Sills, Steven, *Movie Money: Understanding Hollywood's (Creative) Accounting Practices*, 2nd ed., Silman-James Press, 2006; Vogel, Harold L., *Entertainment Industry Economics: A Guide for Financial Analysis*, Cambridge University Press, 1986-2015; Epstein, Edward J., *The Hollywood Economist 2.0: The Hidden Financial Reality behind the Movies*, Melville House, 2012.

[17] *See* practice commentary "It's All Non-negotiable..." in section 2.8.5 below.

actual "source," the consumer). The Mini-major (in our IMDb examples, Lionsgate, The Weinstein Company, STX, Broad Green) may be able to collect from some or all of the same entities in the United States, but typically license foreign rights to territorial distributors, who may collect "at the source" in their territory, and then take out their own Distribution Fees and Distribution Expenses before remitting to the Mini-major. The same is true of the Sales Agents (e.g., FilmNation, XYZ) and may also be true of Divisions of Majors (e.g., Focus, Screen Gems, Fox Searchlight, New Line).

All of this would seem to suggest that distribution through a Major will always result in greater Gross Receipts being reported to the Owner than will distribution through a Mini-major, Sales Agent or Division of Major. However, this would ignore the fact that the latter entities generate the majority of their income through collecting Minimum Guarantees from foreign distributors, which may in some cases be equal to or greater than the ultimate "at the source" revenues reported to the Majors. This also means that the usual contractual provision excluding advances and guarantees from Gross Receipts "until earned" has much greater significance in non-Major Studio Distribution Agreements. The Owner in a deal with a Sales Agent or Mini-major will not want to (and shouldn't have to) wait until a Minimum Guarantee collected from a foreign distributor is actually "earned" (i.e., the picture is released and generates enough revenue for that distributor to recoup the MG) in order to get paid – that could be a year down the road, or never.

Home video gross receipts, from the beginning of time (i.e., the 1980s), have been reported by the Majors and most Mini-majors on a "royalty" basis, meaning that instead of reporting all actual amounts received less Distribution Fee and Distribution Expenses, home video receipts have been reported as a percentage (usually 20% for "rental" home video, and often less for "sell through," which is now virtually all of the home video market) of the "at source" wholesale amount, theoretically without deduction of associated manufacturing and shipping expenses. This practice was adopted early on from the music business, where (believe it or not) recorded music was sold exclusively in the form of packaged goods, i.e., vinyl LPs, and later CDs, before downloading and streaming were possible. Studios would then typically deduct a distribution fee from the royalty, with the justification that historically (i.e., before the 1980s) the Studios did not do their own video distribution.

Given the dwindling significance of the home video market, the negotiation of home video royalties is a less hotly contested topic than it once was. However, many Distribution Agreements will still provide for home video accounting on a royalty basis, and even more include VOD in the definition of home video, even though the underlying parallels to the packaged music business obviously do not apply to VOD. Thus a distributor receiving say 70% of the fees generated from streaming a motion picture on a VOD outlet may credit 20% of that 70% to recoupment of Distribution Expenses and MG, and keep the balance to defray its virtual "costs."

2.8.2. Distribution Fees

The first item typically deducted by Distributors from Gross Receipts (other than the "off the top" costs) is the Distribution Fee (or Sales Fee, in a Sales Agency Agreement), formulated as a percentage of Gross Receipts. These fees vary widely, but in a domestic Distribution Agreement for a theatrical motion picture in which it is anticipated or required that the Distributor release the picture theatrically and advance the resulting P&A expenses as well as a Minimum Guarantee, the "full" theatrical fee will be 30% to 35% of the Gross Receipts derived from theatrical distribution, and fees with respect to receipts from other media will range from 30% to as much as 50%. At the other end of the spectrum, if the Owner is not looking for a Minimum Guarantee, and/or is able to finance the theatrical releasing costs itself, fees for all media may be as low as 7.5% to 15% in all media, reflecting the diminished costs/risks to the distributor to enter the deal.

The ostensible purpose of the Distribution Fee is to cover the Distributor's cost of doing business, plus presumably a profit margin in a moderate to large success. Since the relative size and function of distributors varies widely, as does the relative performance of pictures in the marketplace, it would be hard to say where overhead ends and profit begins in any particular negotiation (and if you are the attorney drafting or negotiating the agreement, it's probably not your call anyway). However, assuming (i) the overhead cost and profit target are more or less equal from picture to picture, and (ii) that the distributor or sales agent negotiating its distribution fee is doing so on the basis of its projections of gross receipts, a picture expected to generate $5 million or $6 million in gross will bear a higher distribution fee than one expected to generate $15 million or $20 million. In other words, to the distributor or agent a fee of 30% on a $5 million gross will have the same bottom line result as a 10% fee on a $15 million gross. Another way to attack the same issue which arguably incentivizes the distributor to keep its costs down and maximize profits is to negotiate a lower distribution fee but include a share of profits following recoupment of expenses and MG.

Of course "Gross Receipts" does not mean the same thing for every Distributor. As noted above, Mini-majors, Sales Agents and Divisions of Majors, after recoupment of the Minimum Guarantees paid by foreign distributors (one form of Gross Receipts), are typically receiving distribution revenues after a local distributor that they have licensed deducts its fees and expenses (also Gross Receipts). However, in the latter case the Owner is facing the prospect of having its share of Gross Receipts reduced not just by the Distributor or Sales Agent it is dealing with, but by the fees of one or more local subdistributors in the long chain of distribution between Owner and the consumer; added to which is the sense that it is not fair for a Distributor to charge a 30% fee for the simple act of licensing rights to another distributor, and that Distributors should be incentivized to keep the fees of subdistributors as low as possible. One popular subject of negotiation therefore is whether and to what extent the "full" fees noted above are inclusive of the fees of subdistributors.

There are two typical ways this fee issue is resolved by Mini-majors and Divisions of Majors: In the first, Gross Receipts and the negotiated full Distribution Fee are calculated at the subdistributor level, without deduction of the sub's fee, when reported to the Owner; in the second, Gross Receipts are reported at the Distributor level, net of the sub's fee, and a lower "override" is deducted, usually in the area of 10% of Gross Receipts. So either the full fee is being charged for the "full" distribution function, at the sub level, or the reduced fee is being charged for the act of licensing to a sub, and calculated at the master Distributor level. In some Distribution Agreements the Distributor will have the right to decide, on a case-by-case basis, which accounting method to elect. For a Sales Agent, there is no such choice, as their entire function is to license distributors territory by territory; as a result, the Sales Agent fee is always calculated as an override, net of all amounts deducted by the local distributor, and will rarely be as high as the fees of a full-service Distributor. Again, it should be remembered that the Mini-majors, Divisions and Sales Agents will generate the majority of their foreign revenues by collecting Minimum Guarantees from distributors; thus, this particular negotiation only matters once those Minimum Guarantees have been recouped by the local distributors, and overages are generated from their territories. This eventuality is also known by some cynics as a Cold Day in Hell; but it does happen.

2.8.3. Distribution Expenses

The single largest expense typically incurred by Distributors is the cost of theatrical release in the United States. Given the widespread use of digital distribution (as of 2015, the MPAA estimates that 93% of theatres worldwide are digital[18]), the cost of reproducing and transporting pictures to theatres is virtually nothing; the main expense, as it has been for a long time, is buying advertising – particularly for television, but also for print, radio and online outlets. In addition, the Distributor will incur significant expense in creating and testing the marketing campaign, including at least trailers for use online and in theatres, television spots, "key art" for online and print posters, as well as screenings, premieres and other publicity events relating to the release. For those distributors and sales agents licensing the picture territory by territory, there is the additional sometimes considerable expense of attending film markets/festivals (currently at least Cannes, Toronto, AFM (i.e., IFTA's American Film Market in Santa Monica) and Berlin).

Other more miscellaneous categories of Distribution Expenses may include residuals that are advanced by the Distributor pursuant to a Distributor's Assumption Agreement with the talent guilds; box office bonuses or other "pre-break" participations assumed by the Distributor; and legal expenses incurred in pursuing claims against parties infringing the copyright in the picture (typically by downloading pirated copies) or defending claims for which the Owner has agreed to indemnify the Distributor.

---

[18] *See* MPAA Theatrical Market Statistics 2015 (http://www.mpaa.org/wp-content/uploads/2016/04/MPAA-Theatrical-Market-Statistics-2015_Final.pdf)

Typical negotiations around Distribution Expenses focus on overhead, interest and overall limits on expenditures. The basic concern of Owners is to what extent the amounts deducted from revenues as Distribution Expenses are the actual (or to be redundant, "direct, third party, out of pocket") costs of the Distributor, as opposed to the internal expenses of running its business (such as salaries, rent and travel) that the Distribution Fee is supposed to cover. This is not always an immediately obvious distinction – if a Distributor hires an in-house lawyer to draft and negotiate its Distribution Agreements, as opposed to paying an outside law firm for this work, is that overhead? – and largely rests on notions of what the "traditional" in-house functions of a Distributor are.

One solution from the Major Studio point of view is to tack on advertising overhead fees equal to 5% to 10% of their out-of-pocket expenses, on the basis that they have hired in-house personnel to create marketing campaigns and place advertising, instead of hiring outside companies to do so. Mini-majors, depending on their size, may add on such costs as well, although they may also choose to go to outside vendors. The Distribution Expense provisions may also allow for the deduction of interest on expenses, typically in the area of prime plus 2%, leading to the erudite-sounding comment from producers' counsel that there be "no interest on overhead, and no overhead on interest."

Sales agents will usually agree to a limit on deductible out-of-pocket expenses, with exclusions for the creation of delivery materials or advertising materials that the Owner has promised to provide. And it is now common practice for sales agents to charge a flat fee of $75,000 to $125,000 for the cost of attending the various sales markets, which you might think was one of the basic overhead expenses of running a sales agency business, but from the agent's perspective represents the continuing increase in costs of selling films in an increasingly competitive market environment.

2.8.4. Recoupment of Minimum Guarantee

Following deduction of Distribution Fees and Distribution Expenses, the balance of Gross Receipts is applied to recoupment of the Minimum Guarantee. In domestic Distribution Agreements, as in the Acquisition Agreement example in the accompanying contractual form materials, the Distributor will often be entitled to a percentage of the Gross Receipts remaining after fees and expenses, as an upside reward (sometimes negotiated for a reduction in Distribution Fees) for their labors. Some Distribution Agreements in this category will provide that the Minimum Guarantee, which after all is an advance against the Owner's share of revenues, is recouped out of the Owner's share; others may provide that the MG is recouped out of 100% of Gross Receipts after Distribution Fees and Distribution Expenses, and the Distributor and Owner then share in the balance.

2.8.5. Box Office Bonuses; VOD Bonuses

The concept of a "Box Office Bonus," i.e., a fixed payment due when the reported amount of box office receipts reaches a specified level, evolved as an alternative to talent participation accounting, which at its worst rested on arcane and non-negotiable net profit definitions which are difficult to monitor and expensive to audit, and at its best relied on straight reporting of gross receipts by Distributors. The beauty of a Box Office Bonus (a/k/a BOB) from the participant's point of view is that box office grosses are published weekly in several sources (the usual standard still being *Variety*),[19] and that the bonuses do not depend on recoupment by producers or distributors of fees, expenses, production costs, etc.; they are gross participations in the purest sense.

Box Office Bonuses began showing up in Distribution Agreements as Distributors' assumption of the Owners' obligations to pay BOBs to talent; however, producers soon caught on to the concept as well, and began negotiating Box Office Bonuses that exceeded the amounts they had agreed to pay talent. Today BOBs are often formulated as $_____ payable upon the earlier of reported Domestic Box Office (DBO) reaching X times the Negative Cost (or sometimes combined Negative Cost and theatrical releasing costs, or P&A) of a picture, or reported Worldwide Box Office (WWBO) reaching double the DBO number; still a gross participation, but obviously now also dependent on the Distributor's accounting and reporting of Negative Cost and Distribution Expenses.

---

[19] But a number of online sources have joined the fray; *See*, for example www.boxofficemojo.com , www.boxofficeguru.com.

Of course, box office grosses are an imperfect measure of the success of a particular picture from the Distributor's point of view: Distributors in the U.S. will ultimately collect 50% (for Majors) or less (for independents) of the gross figures from theatres; and given the amount of P&A spent, and the time that it actually takes to collect from theatres, the Distributor may be a long way from profitability at the same time that it is writing checks for BOBs. However, box office grosses continue to be the most widely available measure of a film's ultimate performance, and so BOBs are likely to continue to be a common source of compensation.

The inclusion of box office grosses from China in WWBO calculations has presented a couple of additional issues for non-Chinese distributors: First, the Chinese government limits not only the number of foreign films that may be distributed in China in any year, but also limits the percentage of theatrical revenues that foreign distributors may collect. Thus, virtually every WWBO formula today includes the qualification that only one-third to one-half of the box office grosses from China is included in calculating worldwide gross. A slightly different issue is the reported inflation of Chinese box office numbers,[20] which may result in further reduction of the amounts credited to worldwide gross.

With the increasing importance of so-called "day and date" releases in the U.S., i.e., simultaneous limited theatrical and premium-priced Video On Demand release of a picture, Owners (like talent) are also negotiating VOD bonuses in Distribution Agreements. These are structured, like Box Office Bonuses, as specific payments based on the number of premium VOD sales (defined based on price point and/or the initial period of VOD availability); so again, this represents a gross participation that is not dependent on recoupment of costs and fees, but less transparent than Box Office Bonuses, as there is currently no centralized public reporting of VOD numbers.[21]

---

[20] *See* "China Box Office: 'IP Man 3' Opens to $75M Amid Fraud Allegations," Hollywood Reporter March 6, 2016, http://www.hollywoodreporter.com/news/china-box-office-ip-man-873060 ; *see also* "China Film Execs Claim 'Terminator' a Victim of Box-Office Fraud to Boost Propaganda Movie,' Hollywood Reporter September 7, 2015, http://www.hollywoodreporter.com/news/china-film-execs-claim-terminator-820874.

[21] For more on this topic, *see* "How to Read the Numbers for 'The Interview,'" http://birthmoviesdeath.com/2015/01/07.

It's All Non-negotiable; but Some Things Are More Non-negotiable than Others

Negotiation of a Distribution Agreement is usually a variation on the "David and Goliath" story: the scrappy little individual production company Owner versus the behemoth institutional Distributor. Of course, the actual relative size and leverage of the Owner and Distributor may vary greatly from deal to deal; but the psychology tends to be pretty consistent. One reason is that small as well as large Distributors need to have a "standard" way of doing business, so that they can hope to manage the marketing, distribution and accounting relating to multiple pictures with what is always an insufficient number of over-burdened employees; so their attitude in negotiations tends to be shaped by this institutional frame of reference. Another reason, generally ignored by Owners and their counsel, is that the motion picture distribution business is a high risk, low margin affair; from the Distributor's point of view, it's a miracle that they survive at all, and most, other than the Majors, don't survive long.

As a result, the attitude of most attorneys and others negotiating on behalf of Distributors tends to be fairly inflexible: Both institutional policy and institutional memory limit the extent to which the Distributor's attorney will be ready or able to unleash his or her creative powers on a Distribution Agreement; from his or her point of view, the starting point is that the Agreement is essentially non-negotiable. The Owner's attorney, in contrast, is representing a *sui generis* creature, a unique motion picture that at its best breaks all traditional rules, and has the potential for virtually limitless profit; so of course everything is negotiable. And thus the clash of the unstoppable force and the immovable object begins.

Remember, there isn't a definitive list somewhere of which items can be negotiated, and what the outcome of the negotiation of those items "should" be (there are plenty of lists that purport to do so – they should mostly be ignored). What may be crucial for one producer/financier may be relatively unimportant to another. We can only give the same advice to both David and Goliath: Pick your battles, and keep any eye out for that little stone.

2.9. DELIVERY

There is relatively little controversy over the requirements of Distribution Agreements regarding "physical" delivery of pictures, i.e., the delivery to Distributors of the technical items that will enable the Distributor to carry out the actual distribution of a picture. Smaller territories may have to pay for the creation of duplicate copies, or take greater risk by paying Minimum Guarantees first and taking delivery later, as noted above; but especially with the advent of digital theatrical distribution, there just isn't that much to argue about with respect to physical delivery.

"Legal" delivery is another matter. The Major Studios, Mini-majors and other domestic distributors all typically require that Owners deliver complete evidence of chain of title, including copyright reports and signed copies of all underlying documents (which must include specific provisions regarding grants of rights, waiver of injunctive relief) and proof of required payments; signed agreements with all principal cast members (also with required provisions), the director, heads of department; errors and omissions insurance applications, policies and certificates; memos regarding credits, name and likeness restrictions, profit participations; music licenses and cue sheets; guild affiliations and approvals; minor court confirmations; and much, much more. From the Owner's point of view, these requirements are onerous and sometimes impossible to fulfill, and may appear to be just another excuse for the Distributor to delay or refuse payment, sometimes until well after the actual release of the picture. How important can these mere paper items be, if the Distributor is willing to take a risk and release the picture anyway?

From the domestic Distributor's point of view, of course, these "mere paper" items may contain fatal or at least expensive pitfalls: In recent years there have been dramatic instances of Major Studios being threatened with injunction because of gaps in the chain of title to finished pictures (notably the *Watchmen* and *Dukes of Hazzard* features at Warner Bros),[22] or failure to secure clearances with respect

---

[22] For a taste of what can be at stake in these battles, see for example http://deadline.com/2008/08/urgent-warners-watchmen-in-legal-peril-6734/; https://www.lawyersandsettlements.com/settlements/03949/dukes_of_hazzard.html.

to use of protected material (in *12 Monkeys*[23] and *Devil's Advocate*,[24] to name a couple). Less dramatically, as noted above, restrictions regarding use of actors' names and likeness may scuttle marketing plans or reduce the anticipated value of a picture in the marketplace; music licenses may turn out to require additional payments, be limited in time or limit "out of context" use in trailers and advertising; minor actors may disaffirm their contracts and withdraw their grant of rights once they reach majority; and a host of other potential horribles may lurk in the documentation (or lack thereof) of a motion picture.

Judging from the IFTA Distribution Agreement delivery requirements, foreign distributors, especially in smaller territories, evidently are typically not worried about these issues. A variety of reasons have been advanced for this. First, the U.S. is typically (although not always) the first market for release, so the domestic distributor may be the canary in the coal mine for detecting unknown issues when it releases a picture. Second, the U.S. is still the largest distribution market, so the revenues generated here make the distributor a more attractive (and often more deeply-pocketed) initial target. Third, the U.S. is reputedly a more litigious society than most, with armies of under-employed attorneys ready to take on glamorous entertainment litigation. And fourth, there is a collective institutional memory that starts with the Studios regarding every possible legal thing that has ever gone wrong in the history of the motion picture business. That institutional memory affects the thinking and practices even of non-Studio distributors because Studio practices are the traditional "gold standard" for distributor behavior, at least in the administrative/legal world, and many of the attorneys and paralegals working in the non-Studio independent distribution world have Studio background and training. Besides, you don't have to be a Studio to be sued.

2.10. SECURITY INTERESTS

At the beginning of this Chapter there is a Sidebar about the *Platoon* case that seeks to both entertain and instruct you as to the origin of the common industry practice in the United States of Distributors taking security interests in the rights that they have been

---

[23] *See*, "12 Monkeys": *Woods v. Universal City Studios, Inc.* et al. 920 F.Supp 62 (S.D.N.Y 1996).

[24] http://variety.com/1998/film/news/settlement-reached-in-devil-s-advocate-case-1117467814/.

granted. If you haven't read it already, please do so. Essentially, by taking and perfecting a security interest Distributors are trying to create a means to enforce performance of the Owner's obligations without having to go to court for equitable relief (i.e., an injunction) and at the same time putting the world (including potential poachers and innocent buyers) on notice of their rights by filing a UCC Financing Statement in the appropriate jurisdiction, and recording a Copyright Mortgage with the U.S. Copyright Office. In addition, the Distributor by properly perfecting its security interest preserves the advantages of a secured creditor in the event of a bankruptcy filing by the debtor/Owner.[25]

2.10.1. UCC Financing Statement

The Uniform Commercial Code, or UCC, is State law that is (more or less) uniform throughout the 50 United States, Article 9 of which is designed among other things to allow creditors to create, "perfect" (i.e., make enforceable) and enforce security interests in various kinds of property. A security interest, as defined in the UCC, is simply "an interest in personal property or fixtures which secures payment or performance of an obligation."[26] That property as it relates to motion pictures may include tangible items (e.g., cameras, props, sets, equipment) and intangibles (accounts, contract rights, proceeds, copyrights). In the event there are multiple creditors with security interests in the same property, the UCC also provides rules for determining whose security interests are senior and will prevail in a dispute; generally the first party to file is the first in line, and may institute foreclosure actions that wipe out the interests of junior creditors. In order to perfect the security interest granted in a Distribution Agreement that is subject to the law of one of the United States, the first step is to file a UCC Financing Statement (usually designated as a UCC-1) in the state where the Owner is located; the Owner's signature is not required on the Financing Statement, but a separate written authorization to acknowledge the Distributor's authority to so file is generally provided for in the Distribution Agreement.

---

[25] *See*, 11 USC §544(a)(1994); there is also an in-depth discussion of security interests as they relate to the financing of motion pictures in the **Motion Picture Finance** chapter in this volume.

[26] *See*, UCC §1201 (b)(35).

2.10.2. Copyright Mortgage

U.S. Copyright Law is federal law, unlike the UCC, and since at least January 1, 1978 generally preempts all state law with respect to legal rights that fall "within the general scope of copyright."[27] In addition, Article 9 of the UCC specifically does not apply to the extent that a statute of the United States preempts it.[28] It is therefore essential that in order to perfect a security interest in the copyright (i.e., in the distribution rights of the picture that have been granted to the Distributor), a Copyright Mortgage must be executed and filed with the U.S. Copyright Office. In addition, in order to comply with the Copyright Act provisions regarding the recordation of copyright transfers (which by definition includes copyright mortgages), the copyright in the picture must be registered.[29]

2.10.3. State and Federal Law Conflicts

Whether federal law so completely preempts state law in this area that the UCC filing is unnecessary, whether federal law requires or merely permits the recordation or security interests, and the question of who wins the battle between a creditor with a perfected first priority interest under the UCC and a creditor with a first-recorded Copyright Mortgage, are fascinating questions that have concerned prominent jurists[30] and inspired countless law review articles.[31] For better or worse, given the largely unsettled law in this area, the transactional attorney representing a Distributor will follow the "belt and suspenders" practice derided by Judge Kosinski in *National Peregrine* (see footnote 29, above), record her/his client's security interest at both state and federal levels, and hope for the best.

---

[27] *See*, 17 USC §301(a).
[28] *See*, UCC § 109(c).
[29] *See*, 17 USC §205(c).
[30] *See*, in particular, Judge Kosinski in *National Peregrine, Inc. v. Capitol Fed. Sav. & Loan Ass'n*, 116 B.R. 194, 199 (C.D. Cal. 1990).
[31] *See*, for example, Peter L. Choate, *Belts, Suspenders, and the Perfection of Security Interests in Copyrights: The Undressing of the Contemporary Creditor*, 31 Loy. L.A. L. Rev. 1415 (1998); Robert H. Rotstein, *Paul Heald's "Resolving Priority Disputes in Intellectual Property Collateral": A Comment*, 1 J. Intell. Prop. L. 167 (1993), and the many articles cited.

"Legal" Knowledge and Contract Negotiation

There are some advantages to being a lawyer when you are negotiating a distribution agreement: You can (usually) charge more per hour than non-lawyers, if that's how you are getting paid; you can (usually) make it from one end of the contract to the other without falling asleep; and if the party you are dealing with on the other side is not a lawyer, you can (usually) bully them with your unstated but tacitly understood secret knowledge of how things really work (that one never ceases to surprise me).

But when both parties to a distribution agreement negotiation are attorneys, the legal knowledge that we use tends to be pretty superficial, and probably wrong in most cases: We always cross out "best efforts," and replace it with "commercially reasonable" or "good faith" efforts, because we vaguely remember from law school that "best efforts" means you would have to spend money, litigate, and/or cross a moat filled with alligators to accomplish whatever it is that you are being asked to try to do. Is this still true? Does it matter? I don't know.

The lawyer who didn't draft the agreement always inserts "material" and "reasonable" wherever they can think of it, and adds "not to be unreasonably withheld" wherever the word "approval" appears. This creates a quandary for the drafter; we all consider ourselves reasonable people (we went to Law School, didn't we? If we had been unreasonable, we would have told our parents to shove it, and pursued being a rock star/dancer/director ourselves), but if we meant "reasonable, material" we would have put it in the agreement in the first place; plus it feels like we are giving up some moral high ground. And maybe it made a difference somewhere in some legal decision, who knows? Facing these questions/risks, the prudent lawyer will insert a boilerplate provision in most contracts reciting that the agreement is to be interpreted as if "jointly drafted" by the parties, but if the term is eventually deemed ambiguous, even this "cover" for the draftsperson will offer small solace.

It is only when negotiations fall apart that the "real" lawyer in most of us is called upon: Our client, whoever it may be, inevitably wants to know whether there is an enforceable agreement – is there a deal? Can we (they) get out of it? What do you mean, material terms? Don't you need a signed agreement? What's an obligation to negotiate in good faith? At which point, most of us use our legal knowledge to call a litigator.

2.11. THEATRICAL RELEASE COMMITMENTS

Despite the onslaught of new and more convenient media in which to view feature films, traditional motion picture theatrical release, and specifically (though not always) wide theatrical release in the United States, seemingly remains the Holy Grail of many filmmakers, sought after for the prestige, exposure and potential financial bonanza that they believe their picture and their career deserve. In addition, for more purely commercial reasons, the financiers and producers of a picture may have pre-sold foreign distribution rights on the basis and/or explicit promise of a U.S. theatrical release, in order to get larger foreign Minimum Guarantees, or may have entered into SVOD and/or pay television licenses on the same basis. Thus while the general (and generally "non-negotiable") rule of the Distribution Agreement is that the Distributor has absolute discretion over how, when and in which media to release a picture, a domestic theatrical release commitment, including the outside release date, the number of screens (either in the first weekend or during the course of release) and the amount of P&A (often broken down to a specific release budget) is often a hotly-negotiated provision.

In a pre-buy context, domestic Distributors may be understandably reluctant to commit to a wide theatrical release, at least if they are funding the releasing costs, or relying on a third party (other than the Owner) to do so. One variation of this commitment then may be to provide that if for any reason the picture is not released theatrically, or is released but does not meet the minimum release requirements, the Distributor will pay a larger MG, to make up for decreased license fees from other rights and territories. Another less common variation is to agree that if the Distributor does not commit to a wide theatrical release following a screening of the picture (which may include a recruited screening and minimum audience research numbers), the Owner has a specified period of time in which to find a qualified distributor that agrees to release the picture theatrically, and may repurchase the rights for a premium. While many Distributors instinctively resist the idea of providing Owners such a convenient "backstop," given the amount of time invested in, financial models based on, and publicity released about their upcoming slate of pictures, it is sometimes a face-saving device for Owners, and far less risky than an unconditional commitment to release.

Occasionally an independent film producer may have access to additional investor funds for print and advertising expenditures for festival or even limited theatrical release in order to attract commercial distribution, and in some cases this funding might be made available to the distributor to supplement its own marketing expenditures as leverage in securing that commercial distribution or improving the terms (usually in the form of reduced distribution fees) of the distribution deal itself.

2.12. PIRACY

Not so long ago, the entire film business watched in horror as its close relative, the music business, was decimated and ultimately forever changed by "peer to peer" filesharing, i.e., massive copyright "piracy" on the Internet starting in 1999. While DVDs have not been as completely replaced by streaming and downloading as CDs have been (as the size of digital video files makes this a bit more challenging for consumers/ pirates), the film business as a whole has made a dramatic shift to online exhibition: A March 2016 study by SNL Kagan found that 98% of "premium" films (defined as box office hits released from 2002 to 2015, "all time" box office hits, the top 100 AFI Films and the top 60 independent films 2013 to 2015) were available on at least one of 47 online services surveyed, and 95% were available on at least five such services.[32]

Another study issued by the Advisory Committee on Enforcement of WIPO, the World Intellectual Property Organization, notes that "although DVD/VHS sales were increasing from 2000 to 2003, after the introduction and widespread adoption of the BitTorrent filesharing protocol, these sales dropped by 27% from 2004 to 2008."[33] With online availability, massive worldwide piracy poses a threat to the ability of Distributors to control and monetize the distribution of pictures.

In addition to engaging personnel and software to hunt down illegal sites and issue takedown notices, Distributors have sought to contractually require Owners to institute security procedures with

---

[32] *See*, SNL Kagan, *U.S. Availability of Films and TV Titles in the Digital Age*, available on the MPAA website at www.mpaa.org.

[33] *See*, various authors, Copyright Enforcement in the Digital Age: Empirical Economic Evidence and Conclusions, WIPO 2015.

respect to protection of film materials during production, at screenings of the picture at various stages, in creation and distribution of marketing materials, and to allow the Distributors to institute anti-piracy actions both inside and outside their contractual territory.

2.13. REMEDIES

Looking back at the touchstone with which we started this chapter, it is clear that one of the provisions most lacking from the *Platoon* agreement in 1986 was a waiver by the Owner of the right to terminate the agreement, or to seek an injunction or other equitable relief. This standard and truly non-negotiable provision in every domestic Distribution Agreement limits the Owner in the event of any alleged breach or default of agreement to legal action for payment of damages only, in order to spare the Distributor the nightmare scenario of having to pull a theatrical, online or DVD release that is already in process – often with booked expenses, including P&A, exceeding the cost of the underlying picture – because of a dispute with the Owner. Because the Owner's typical concern is that they will be left with no effective remedy in the event a Distributor fails or refuses to pay, the waiver of injunctive relief is sometimes qualified as being effective only after payment of the MG, or the first installment of the MG obligation.

This ubiquitous provision may create a serious problem for the Owner in the event a Distributor files for a Chapter 7 or Chapter 11 Bankruptcy: While the Bankruptcy Trustee has the right to "reject" a Distribution Agreement on behalf of a Distributor, and avoid paying the MG or performing any other executory obligations, rejection in Bankruptcy is not the same as termination: In essence, the rejection is treated as a breach of the Distribution Agreement, and the Owner's remedies are limited by the terms of the Agreement, leaving Owners in the position of having not only no remedy in equity (i.e., termination) or at law, since the Bankruptcy suspends all such actions.

2.14. OTHER PROVISIONS

Of course, we could go on. As you can see, the Distribution Agreements in the supplemental materials include volumes of Representations and Warranties (primarily from Owner to Distributor),

Notices, Choice of Law and Jurisdiction and more. We aren't saying these aren't important, and read them if you dare. But remember when forging these agreements, while everything is "non-negotiable" – some things are just more non-negotiable than others.

MOTION PICTURE DISTRIBUTION – ILLUSTRATIVE FORMS:

- Acquisition Agreement
- Negative Pickup Distribution Agreement
- IFTA Form Sales Agency Agreement
- IFTA Multiple Rights Distribution Agreement

— Chapter 3 —

Motion Picture Finance

Robert Williams[*]

3.1. Introduction
3.2. The Parties
3.3. The Finance Agreements
3.4. Security
3.5. Conclusion

3.1. INTRODUCTION

Motion picture finance is best understood as a type of project finance. The leveraged financing structures used to produce independent films often resemble the structures used to finance brick-and-mortar projects. When a new strip mall or power plant is built, the financing required to complete the project is secured before the foundation is laid. The project developer procures the necessary financing by pledging valuable contractual commitments entered into with respect to the completed project. These promises usually take the form of rents or sales and assure a source of debt repayment. To give financiers comfort that the underlying promises will become enforceable, the completion and delivery of the project to specification will be bonded.

Similarly, when a film is independently financed the cameras generally start rolling only after all the funds necessary to complete and deliver the film have been committed. In the place of architects and blueprints, writers draft a screenplay. In the place of tenants who pay rent or power purchasers who buy kilowatt-hours, distributors commit to pay license fees. And in the place of a construction bond, a completion guarantor guarantees that the invested sums will be used to complete and deliver the film to the distributors who have agreed to pay for it.

And yet, unlike megawatts or square feet, the demand for a completed motion picture is grounded in intangible and often unpredictable qualities, like the desire to find meaning or humor outside of the daily routine, to experience vicariously a new and different story or simply to be entertained. The evanescent and

---

[*] **Robert Williams** is the founder and principal of RW Law (Munich, Germany).

variable nature of this demand, coupled with increasing competition from the myriad of growing alternative entertainment products, brings extra challenges to film financing.

It is no secret that the film industry is facing new challenges as people change the ways they consume film. Once reliable formulas for capturing box office receipts are proving inadequate. No amount of marketing or prints and advertising (P&A) spending, can guarantee a successful opening weekend at the box office in an age where information is disseminated across the world in minutes through social media. Gen Zers have never known a time without wireless technology. According to research from London based EY, more than 90 percent of teenagers today have access to a smartphone, 60 percent use a tablet, and 90 percent watch YouTube daily.[1]

These technological changes have increased impulse viewing on wireless devices and changed the way film (and television, for that matter) are now being consumed. Electronic consumption on Internet-based streaming services by way of download ("electronic sell-through" or EST), transactional purchase ("transactional video on demand" or TVOD), subscription service ("subscription video on demand" or SVOD) or ad-driven online viewing ("advertising video on demand" or AVOD) has created a new and growing media market (often referred to as the "Over the top" or OTT market). The OTT market strongly competes with traditional forms of media consumption while offering new forms of content like web-series that attract high viewership and first-class talent. These competing modes of consumption and content have increased domestic box office risk for independent feature-length theatrical films that do not carry a blockbuster brand to draw an audience through the door. As a result, domestic widescreen releases are more difficult for independent producers to secure, which in turn puts pressure on international sales valuations, and it is the international market that essentially enables the production of first-class independent films.[2] While the current environment has presented challenges to traditional forms of

---

[1] See Chris Tribbey. *Study: Gen Z Changing Media, Entertainment Business Practices*, available at http://www.broadcastingcable.com/news/technology/study-gen-z-changing-media-entertainment-business-practices/155476 (last viewed July 9, 2016).

[2] See MPAA 2015 Theatrical Statistics Summary, *available at* http://www.mpaa.org/wp-content/uploads/2016/04/MPAA-Theatrical-Market-Statistics-2015_Final.pdf. (international box office revenues of $27.2 billion were two-and-a-half times domestic revenues in 2015, and held steady in 2016).

independent film financing, it has also opened doors to new sources of finance and revenue. Premier SVOD services like Netflix and Amazon are now engaged in financing significant independent theatrical film projects. In addition, demand for film in China continues to boom, and Chinese investors are playing an increasingly important role in financing both studio and major independent "Hollywood" films.[3]

To manage these divergent and powerful forces, producers scour the world for creative sources of finance, which are often found in foreign tax credit and other soft money production incentives. The use of tax credit schemes generally requires production funds to be spent locally as part of a co-production or through the use of local production services. As more "Hollywood" productions adopt foreign funding and producing structures, the financial structures used to produce independent film have become increasingly diverse, and the legal elements have become more complex. Financing an independent film production is often a cross-border exercise with parties represented from all over the world.

This chapter provides an introduction to the legal elements necessary to successfully manage and close a typical independent film finance transaction, taking an inside look at the legal architecture, primarily from a U.S. federal and state law perspective. The various legal disciplines utilized in a film finance transaction include leveraged finance, commercial law, secured transactions and intellectual property. U.S. law often applies to the production finance, license and commissioning agreements if the licensing entity and lead producers are located in the United States. Nevertheless, the global reach of many independently produced films adds cross border elements that often require the advice of special foreign counsel. Even if the licensing entity that commissions the film and borrows the production finance is a U.S. entity, foreign law may apply to the use of foreign production elements, intermediary licensors and financiers. This chapter addresses the interplay between different legal systems that may be involved in larger independent film finance transactions.

The first part of this chapter introduces the roles of the parties involved in closing a typical independent film finance transaction. An understanding of the respective interests and obligations of these parties sets the stage for understanding the financial structuring. The second part discusses the concept of the budget and the loan and equity

---

[3] *See id.* The Chinese box office grew 8% in 2015.

finance agreements relevant to the various stages of development and production of an independently produced film. The third part concludes by discussing the elements essential to securing the lenders' investments in the project, which are critical to closing the finance package.

3.2. THE PARTIES

The producers, the sales agent, the financiers and the completion guarantor are typically the core parties who work together to configure the structure for commissioning and licensing an independently financed film and for borrowing the production funds to create it. These parties create a finance plan that takes into account the film's production budget, cash flow schedule and delivery schedule in light of projected revenues and the cost of finance. Tax credit and soft money incentives, which are usually tied to the location(s) of principal photography and post-production, are also usually necessary to complete the finance plan. In addition, production financiers generally require the finance plan to be proved up by pre-sale commitments from distributors before they dedicate funds to the production. The diagram below presents a simple structure of an independently financed film. The relationships are discussed in the subsections that follow.

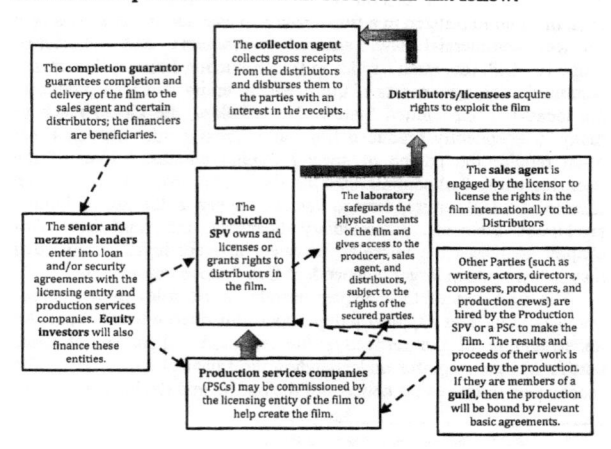

The **collection agent** collects gross receipts from the distributors and disburses them to the parties with an interest in the receipts.

The **completion guarantor** guarantees completion and delivery of the film to the sales agent and certain distributors; the financiers are beneficiaries.

Distributors/licensees acquire rights to exploit the film

The **laboratory** safeguards the physical elements of the film and gives access to the producers, sales agent, and distributors, subject to the rights of the secured parties.

The **Production SPV** owns and licenses or grants rights to distributors in the film.

The **sales agent** is engaged by the licensor to license the rights in the film internationally to the Distributors

The **senior and mezzanine lenders** enter into loan and/or security agreements with the licensing entity and production services companies. **Equity investors** will also finance these entities.

Other Parties (such as writers, actors, directors, composers, producers, and production crews) are hired by the Production SPV or a PSC to make the film. The results and proceeds of their work is owned by the production. If they are members of a **guild**, then the production will be bound by relevant basic agreements.

Production services companies (PSCs) may be commissioned by the licensing entity of the film to help create the film.

3.2.1. The Distributors

The financing of independent film begins and ends with the obligations of distributors. Financiers will put tens of millions of dollars on the line to produce a film if the project is backed by creditworthy distributors who agree to acquire rights in the completed film once it is delivered according to agreed specifications.

Film financing is typically structured in a way that limits a lender's recourse to the rights in a film, and revenues derived therefrom, if the production loans are not repaid. Accordingly, the worldwide monetization of the rights in the film through distribution provides the value that lenders rely on to recoup their investment. Film financiers generally wait until the film's value can be gauged with a measure of acceptability before they irrevocably commit to extend financing. An unproduced motion picture has a highly uncertain value until distributors agree to buy it. The price at which a handful of distributors ultimately license the film will verify the film's sales estimates, which in turn determines the size of the financing package and the size of the film's budget.

The first step to monetize an independently financed film usually takes the form of "pre-sale" distribution agreements under which international distributors promise to pay minimum license fees (often referred to as "minimum guarantees") upon completion and delivery of the film in exchange for certain exclusive rights to exploit the film in a defined territory for a specific term. Pre-sale distribution agreements are agreed before the production finance is closed and generally before principal photography begins. The sum total of the pre-sales, discounted for counterparty risk, plus the estimated value of future sales in unsold territories around the world, plus soft-money production incentives, typically comprise the entire value of most independently produced films. Financiers lend against this value, which sustains the finance plan for production and delivery of the film. In a studio production finance and distribution deal, the pre-sales concept generally does not apply, because the studio agrees to cash flow the production in exchange for worldwide distribution rights and significant creative control. Nevertheless, the studio will run an internal sales analysis with respect to its own distribution network.

3.2.2. The Sales Agent

Producers of an independent film project often engage a sales agent to gain access to distributors. The sales agent typically gets the exclusive right to market and sell the film in certain territories (usually the world excluding North America) for a term of years. The sales agent's estimates of the prices at which the film will be sold, namely its "ask" and "take" price list for various territories around the world, build the initial foundation for the film's finance plan. The "ask" price represents the high-end of the estimate and the "take" price the low-end, and taken together, they should represent a reasonable prognosis for the value that the completed film will command in the international marketplace according to the sales agent's internal modeling. The financial model for any given film mostly depends on the key elements attached to the film (i.e., the writer(s), director, principal cast, and the producers).

Depending on the strength of initial pre-sales at film markets around the world, revisions to the estimates may be required. The sales estimates for the unsold territories (often referred to as the "gap" territories) form a critical piece of the finance plan, because the lender that finances the gap territories (often referred to as the "mezzanine" or "gap" lender) relies on such estimates to determine the size of its production loan and its risk exposure. Ideally, the mezzanine loan will plug the gap in financing left by the difference between the size of the film's budget and the amount of senior financing secured by soft money production incentives and the pre-sold territories that are under license at the time the production loan package is closed.

The sales agent typically retains a commission from gross receipts of the film's sales in an amount between ten and thirty percent. Smaller budget films are typically subject to larger commissions. If the budget is large enough, it is customary for the sales agent to defer or restructure a portion of its entitlements until the lenders' loans, plus an agreed return, have been paid from gross receipts. If the sales agent does not successfully sell a certain number of territories at or above the estimated "take" prices by a certain date, then the lenders may have a right to terminate the sales agency agreement. In such cases, the sales agent typically continues to receive a commission on receipts from the territories that it has sold. In addition to selling the film, the sales agent typically assembles the physical materials and paperwork that each international distributor requires to complete delivery of the film.

There are a handful of leading sales agents that have deep contacts in the industry. They often work closely with the major talent agencies like Creative Artists Agency (CAA), William Morris/Endeavor (WME) and United Talent Agency (UTA). If a script is particularly strong, or the project has attracted "Class A" talent or a director that has achieved international recognition, and the producers themselves have not already packaged the film, a well-connected sales agent might assist in packaging the film with internationally recognized talent. The goal is to increase the commerciality of the film and the market price that distributors are willing to commit in advance to pay, based on the film's packaged elements of script, actors, director and producers, coupled in some cases with an assured U.S. theatrical release of the film, which in turn elevates eventual international revenue realization.

The pre-sold territories and the estimated value of the unsold "gap" territories form the core collateral that supports the production finance package. Regardless of the level of talent involved, ultimately the commitments from distributors determine the budget and quality of an independently produced film. Unlike independently produced films, the studios have their own distribution networks. If a film is financed by a studio, unless rights in certain territories are reserved to the production company, generally no sales agent will be appointed in connection with the picture.

3.2.3. The Production SPV / Borrower / Licensor

To prepare to sell and finance a film, producers will assign, or cause to be assigned, to a newly formed special purpose vehicle (SPV) all rights, titles and interests in and to the film. Often such assignment will take the form of a single picture license, pursuant to which the production SPV is granted the exclusive right to produce and exploit a single feature length motion picture. By structuring the license in this manner, producers reserve the right to make sequels, prequels and spin-offs in an entity outside the reach of production liens and lender security interests.

The production SPV will be formed in a country that is party to the international copyright treaties and conventions administered by the World Intellectual Property Organization (WIPO). A host of additional factors will determine the actual location of the SPV's formation, such as the location of the producers who will own and operate the licensing vehicle, the location of the financiers, the requirements of any soft money financing and the desired choice of law. If the film is produced by U.S. producers, often a U.S. production SPV will be formed. However, because of attractive foreign tax-optimized finance plans, many films with well-known "Hollywood" producers are made by foreign production companies, funded by foreign financiers and foreign soft money. For example, in recent years many production companies with U.S. producers have been formed in and operated out of the United Kingdom to utilize that country's attractive tax-advantaged enterprise investment scheme, referred to as E.I.S. This incentive program requires the film to be commissioned by a U.K. entity. There also is an emergent perception of London, BREXIT notwithstanding, as the hub of a growing international film industry. Foreign sales drive the profit margins of the theatrical motion picture business, and important industry players have moved significant parts of their business from L.A. to London in recognition of this trend.

The production SPV generally will acquire all rights in the film, including the copyright and rights under copyright, either by commissioning the production or receiving an assignment of rights. If the film is a co-production, however, a local production entity may be required to hold the local copyright to take advantage of local soft money incentives. In certain circumstances, the rights licensed to a foreign distributor will flow through an intermediary licensor in a foreign territory. This optimizes the withholding taxes owed with respect to gross receipts that eventually flow to the ultimate licensing entity (net of the intermediary licensor's fees).

The production SPV typically borrows the production finance, although loans may be provided at different levels in the production and licensing structure. The film's financiers will analyze the film's chain of title to ensure that the proper licensing entities have acquired the requisite rights under copyright in the film, whether they be a production SPV, a co-production entity, or another entity formed to produce or license the film. Each entity in the production and licensing structure will be required to grant a security interest in the film collateral to secure the production finance; the lenders will ensure that their security extends over all film assets.

3.2.4. The Financiers

Film is an alternative investment asset that continues to attract a wide range of investors, from banks to private equity funds to private wealth management and family offices to individuals with an emotional connection to a project. This Chapter focuses on the leveraged financing of independently produced films.

While the film industry is sensitive to overall economic conditions, particularly those that affect the liquidity of potential financiers, the correlation between the investment performance of film assets and the performance of the overall capital markets is non-linear. Film financing is distinguished from other asset-backed financing by the nature of the collateral. When a lender evaluates an investment in an operating company, it can generate a relatively clear picture of the potential risks involved based on metrics like operating margins, earnings, product development, growth trajectory, product demand and the competitive landscape. An unproduced film has no directly comparable metrics. Lenders rely instead on an opaque demand for a product that showcases known actors, directors, writers and producers, as is reflected by pre-sale distribution agreements and sales estimates. Ultimately, the film's budget will depend on the nature and strength of the production package and its ability to attract sales.

The monetary policy of central banks around the world in recent years has driven high quality debt investments up in price and down in yield, and this has pushed investors out the risk curve in an effort to realize performance on investment. While the merits of this policy are questionable, the impact on investment in film has been clear: higher-yielding alternative asset classes like film have benefited from an influx of cash as increased liquidity chases limited product. Studio and major production company courtship of and by Chinese financiers has also helped push other resources normally embraced and absorbed by studio projects into the independent market. At the same time, film has benefitted from increased demand to fill premium and exclusive pay TV and OTT windows, while falling box office revenues have strained the traditional independent financing model. In light of these developments, premium content is in higher demand than ever, but the financing landscape has become much more competitive.

Generally speaking, there are three tranches of financing that together make up the budget for an independently financed film: a senior tranche, a mezzanine tranche (so-called because it sits between the senior tranche and the equity) and the equity. There is, however, no limit to the permutations of how films get financed. A single financier might finance the entire film, or there may be hundreds if a crowd-funding model is utilized. Whether there be one or a hundred financiers, the critical factor to assess risk is what kind of collateral is backing the investment, and how many other parties have access to revenues from that collateral and at what time. Sometimes financing may be provided by parties who furnish or directly finance a film's music or their own production services by way of a "sweat equity investment" or credit tied to these services, or in the form of a fully or partially deferred fee for these services with a premium over their standard rates built into the deferment. An in-kind investment of services is also common among visual effects and post-production houses. This Chapter focuses on the senior, mezzanine and equity tranches, which form the core of the film financing structure.

The senior lender finances the pre-sale receivables, or so-called "minimum guarantees," owed to the Production SPV or other licensing vehicle under the pre-sale distribution agreements that have already been executed at the time the senior loan is made to the production company. The senior lender may also finance tax credits or other soft money production incentives, which typically become payable only after the production can prove that budgeted costs were spent in accordance with governmental requirements. The senior lender typically also takes a second lien in all other film collateral. The senior lender of an independently produced film is often a bank.

The senior lender will not extend financing to the production unless the pre-sale minimum guarantees have become "bankable." To become bankable, an independent, reputable completion guarantor must guarantee the completion and delivery of the film to the pre-sale distributors, giving the senior lender comfort that the pre-sale distributors' respective obligations to acquire and pay for the film upon delivery will be enforceable. The role of the completion guarantor is discussed in greater detail below.

By obtaining the completion guaranty, the senior lender reduces its completion or delivery risk but retains the credit risk of the pre-sale distributors. If a distributor is reputable, or has secured a letter of credit, a bank may finance the minimum guarantee at 90 to 100 percent of the face value of such receivables, net of bank charges and an interest and fee reserve. Currently, such loans bear interest at historically low rates. If a distributor's creditworthiness or reputation for timely payment has suffered in the industry, then in the absence of a letter-of-credit a senior lender will only lend a fraction against the minimum guarantee that the distributor has promised to pay upon delivery of the film. In extreme cases, the discount can reach as high as 100 percent, in which case the proceeds of the pre-sale distribution agreement would serve as the senior lender's collateral, but the lender would not lend even a dollar against it.

The mezzanine, or "gap," lender finances the unsold rights in the film and may also finance the tax credits or other production incentives if another lender does not finance them. Like the senior lender, the mezzanine lender takes a second lien in all other film collateral. The mezzanine lender might be the same bank that provides the senior tranche (although a bank will typically refuse to finance gap exposure in excess of 15 percent of the budget), or it could be a private equity or hedge fund or other consortium of investors.

The mezzanine lender's primary concern is to approximate correctly the value of the film in the unsold "gap" territories. Because the mezzanine lender relies on the estimated "take" prices generated by the sales agent to determine the amount of credit to lend to the production, the lender must have a high degree of confidence in the sales agent's valuation process. To gain a level of comfort with such estimates, a mezzanine lender will often require as a condition to lending that certain significant territories are sold at or above the "take" estimates and that a certain percentage of the budget (usually at least 60 percent) has been financed by pre-sales at or above the "take" prices together with soft money production incentives. Key international territories include Germany and the United Kingdom. Italy, Spain and France remain important markets, but in the current economic environment, sales forecasts for these territories can be overly optimistic, so a mezzanine lender may require as a condition to lending that one of these territories be sold at or above the "take" price to indicate that the film is commercial.

The mezzanine loan often will be discounted to approximately 50 percent of the estimated "take" value of the aggregate unsold territories. This discount may vary depending upon forecast sales commissions, collection agent fees, any unbudgeted guild residuals and the size of the interest and fee reserve (which will depend on the anticipated duration of the loan). Further discounts may be necessary to take into account that a sale will not be concluded at the "take" estimate in any given territory.

Distributor payments are the lenders' primary security, so lenders will require the licensor of the film to assign to the lender all of its rights, titles and interests in and to each distribution agreement by way of security, and the distributors will be required to acknowledge each such assignment. These notices and acknowledgments are referred to in the industry as NOAs, and they form a critical part of the lenders' (and completion guarantor's) security package. In addition, typically the mezzanine lender will insist on the right to approve any distribution agreement executed with respect to the "gap" collateral if its loan remains outstanding or is not fully collateralized by approved sales.

Under the senior and mezzanine tranches sits the equity. The equity is the riskiest piece of financing and is the hardest to attract. An equity financier generally sits behind the lenders' rights to worldwide receipts from the sold (i.e., the pre-sales) and unsold (i.e., the gap) territories and the tax credit proceeds that collateralize the debt. To recoup and make a return, an equity investor typically relies on the film being sold promptly at or above the "take" estimates or producing substantial overages and backend participations for the production. As noted above, the gap estimates are usually subject to steep financing discounts, resulting in a significant margin between the "take" price and the amount of gap lending. This margin is typically larger than the margin between the pre-sale minimum guarantees and the amount of senior debt. For this reason, if there are too many pre-sales, and too little gap, the ability to attract an equity investor declines. The discount applied to the gap estimates is the play that attracts an equity investor willing to make a bet on strong demand for the film in the unsold territories. In addition, an equity investor may be offered first position in one or two unsold territories to mitigate its risk; even so, to avoid complications with licensing and intercreditor issues, the equity should remain unsecured, or have a secured position only in proceeds from the sale of rights in the territory in which it has negotiated priority.

Often the equity tranche is funded by the producers or their affiliates or other individuals who have a vested interest in making the film. Recoupment of the equity tranche usually requires that the demand for the film meet or exceed its expectations. Unless the film does well enough to see the lenders repaid in full, or unless the equity has negotiated a priority position with respect to receipts in one or more territories, the equity will not see any of its investment recouped, let alone a return on it. In exchange for this high level of risk, the equity investors receive a substantial premium (often 20 percent per annum) and a material share of the right to net profits or backend participation in the film.

As a rule of thumb, financiers are entitled to 50 percent of the net profits or backend participation from an independently produced film. The senior lender usually receives no share of net profits, and the mezzanine lender will usually take between 5 percent and 20 percent, depending on how early such lender boarded the project, the strength of its collateral position and the competitive landscape for alternative financing. The equity will take the balance of the financiers' share. The other 50 percent of the film's net profits are paid to the producers and talent pool. The financiers might concede some of their backend points to the talent pool if necessary to secure multiple Class A actors or a renowned director, which could materially increase the value of the film.

The use of "senior," "mezzanine" and "equity" labels in film financing can be misleading. In a typical asset-backed, leveraged finance transaction outside the film industry, a "mezzanine" lender takes a subordinated second or third lien in the relevant collateral. In independent film financing, contrary to the connotation that the title brings, the mezzanine lender is in fact senior with respect to its primary collateral (i.e., the unsold territories). Indeed, any other senior lender to the film production will be required to subordinate to the mezzanine lender its right to payment from, and its lien on, all film collateral in the unsold territories that comprise the mezzanine lender's primary collateral.

Moreover, it is important to understand that labels like "senior," "mezzanine" and "equity" can be relatively meaningless when it comes to assessing repayment risk. The risk curve for any of these tranches depends as much, if not more, on the strength of the underlying collateral measured against the size of the budget for the film than on the relative positioning of the financiers (although position is of course critical). In a financing structure where a film has strong pre-sales and significant overages estimated in the gap territories relative to the budget, the equity can be far more assured of recoupment than even a mezzanine lender in a similar financing structure where the pre-sales are having trouble hitting the "take" prices. The value of the sales is ultimately paramount.

There is no magical finance structure that is guaranteed to work for any given film. For many smaller independent films, all financing may be provided in the form of equity, with investors hoping the finished film will find distributor interest following production through sales agents or exposure via festivals. The financing process is fluid and depends upon many shifting variables, including the relationships among the producers, financiers and sales agents and the relevant experience of the parties. No matter how large the budget, one can expect to find a perpetual shortfall of cash. Nevertheless, generally speaking, if a reputable sales agent is attached to the film and has provided estimates that are supported by credible pre-sales, and the budget works according to such estimates, there is a high likelihood that the film will be financed and produced.

3.2.5. The Completion Guarantor

A customary, first class independently produced and financed film enlisting Class A talent and a renowned director typically has a direct cost budget between $8 million and $40 million. There are outliers both to the upside and downside. The financing necessary to produce the film is required up front, secured by distributor obligations that only become enforceable after the film is produced and delivered to specification and by soft money tax credits or rebates that become effective only after certain services are performed during production. Because abandoned films rarely make their money back, it is critical to the financing parties, and a condition precedent to their funding obligations, that a reliable and independent third party guarantees the completion and delivery of the film.

This party is known as the completion guarantor. The completion guarantor provides the financiers a warranty that the film will be completed and delivered on time and on budget. The completion guarantor simultaneously enters into a completion agreement with the production SPV, under which it will have the right to take over production of the film in the event that circumstances arise that result in an exposure under its guaranty.

Financiers are not the only parties that may require a completion bond. In a studio turnaround deal, in which a studio has sold rights in a project that it developed, the studio typically retains a net profits interest and may defer allocable overhead. To protect its contingent interest in the film, which may be substantial, the studio will require the production and delivery to be bonded by a completion guarantor. Additionally, sometimes a studio finance, distribution and production agreement will require a completion guaranty to ensure that the producers complete the project on budget and on time. This is particularly the case where the studio has not developed the project internally.

Before issuing the bond that guarantees the completion and delivery of the film, the completion guarantor will closely review and approve the material elements of the film, its final budget, and the cash flow schedule required to shoot, edit and deliver the film, all in light of the requirements of the script. The funds necessary to meet this budget are referred to as the "strike price" for the film. Prior to the effectiveness of the completion guaranty, the completion guarantor usually will require the financiers to escrow, or in the case of a bank to irrevocably commit to fund, the entire strike price, or ensure that all deferrals necessary to meet a shortfall in the strike price have been agreed.

Further, the completion guarantor will require that all currency risk is hedged, all rights to produce the film have been or will be acquired as a first day payment, all services that are essential for production and delivery of the film according to specification are subject to inducement letters under which the principal cast, director and producers agree to perform services in accordance with the budget and production schedule, all required insurance is in place, and that its security interest in all relevant film collateral has been perfected. In this sense the completion guarantor serves as a type of hub – and a helpful guide – for monitoring the pre-production activities and requirements necessary to reach the financial close and start of principal photography of an independently produced film.

The completion bond fee will depend on the size of the budget and the completion guarantor's assessment of the risks of the project. Typically, the fee is 2 percent to 4 percent of the strike price net of the bond fee and contingency. Producers with a strong track record of on time and on budget delivery will be at the lower end of the range. To mitigate risk, the completion guarantor will require that a contingency be funded as part of the strike price. The contingency is usually 10% of the direct production costs, but it may be higher or lower depending on the risk. For example, a higher contingency may be required if the film involves significant visual effects or a director with a track record for breaking the budget. The contingency might be lower for smaller budget films where execution is straightforward, and the producers and director have stellar track records. The contingency may be used by the production only with the permission of the completion guarantor. Any remaining contingency will be used to repay outstanding production debt or deferred production costs. If the bond fee is high due to a high-risk production, the completion guarantor may agree to refund 10 to 50 percent of the fee if the film is completed and delivered on time and on budget, though these rebates occur less frequently than in former times.

If the completion guarantor advances funds to complete and deliver the film under its guaranty, it will recoup those funds in a position that is subordinated to the lenders. An intercreditor agreement will set forth the respective rights of all secured parties in the common film collateral, and the completion guarantor will recoup any out-of-pocket investment in the film after the secured lenders are fully repaid.

3.2.6. The Laboratory

The production SPV typically owns the film and all its elements, and the lenders and the completion guarantor have a security interest in all of the production SPV's rights and interest in the film, including the physical elements. In order to ensure that the physical elements of the film are securely maintained, the secured parties will require the production SPV and any other production services company to deposit all physical elements with a film laboratory or post-production house where storage and disposal are strictly regulated pursuant to a laboratory pledgeholder agreement.

The laboratory and its permitted assigns will serve as the custodian of all physical elements of the film, including all negatives, digital camera files, duplicates, prints, soundtracks, recordings and special effects, in whatever stage of completion. Absent a default in the loan documents, the laboratory holds the physical elements to the order of the production and the sales agent to enable completion and delivery of the film to the sales agent and the distributors. However, under the laboratory pledgeholder agreement, the production lenders will ensure that in the event of a default the laboratory will take instruction solely from the secured lenders regarding access to and disposal of the film's physical elements.

3.2.7. The Guilds

The most important guilds to take into account for purposes of creating a film's finance plan are the Writers Guild of America East and West (WGA), the Directors Guild of America, Inc., (DGA) the Screen Actors Guild, and the American Federation of Radio and Television Artists (SAG-AFTRA). If the writer(s), actors or director of the film are members of any of these guilds, then the production will be subject to the collective bargaining agreements of the respective guilds whose members are involved in the film. These agreements lock the production into specific, non-negotiable obligations, including minimum payments for specified services, financial assurances, limits on work hours, reservation of rights in certain work product, credit allocation, and ultimately use obligations, which include the right to receive payment from gross receipts from exploitation of the film in various media and territories.

While a discussion of the collective bargaining agreements remains outside the scope of this Chapter, it is important to bear in mind that a properly structured finance plan must take into account the payments required to be made to the respective guilds for use of the film. Known as "residuals," these payment obligations apply to worldwide, first-dollar gross receipts. Specifically, a percentage of the budget should be allocated to establish a reserve for residuals owed on the minimum guarantees paid by the distributors. The residuals under the WGA and DGA basic agreements currently range from 1.2 percent to 1.8 percent of certain gross receipts. Residuals are more than double that under the SAG-AFTRA basic agreement. A typical residuals reserve for a film involving all three guilds is 9.8 percent of the gross receipts owed from the pre-sold territories.

If a residuals reserve is not budgeted, or if a residuals reserve is established but then exhausted, the guilds will collect their residuals upon deposit of the minimum guarantees into the collection account appointed for the picture proceeds. The finance plan must take into account the deduction from gross receipts resulting from payment of the residuals off the top of such gross receipts, because this money will not be available to repay the lenders, or any other party involved in the production. Additionally, the guilds will require a security interest in the film to protect their right to such proceeds. It is therefore in the interests of the financiers to ensure that the residuals owed on pre-sale minimum guarantees, and possibly on estimated minimum guarantees in unsold territories, are budgeted with a reserve paid to the guilds in respect of such obligations. The guilds will typically agree to subordinate to other secured creditors their security interest and right to payment from proceeds of the film with respect to which a residuals reserve has been established. Any overages from the territories yielding residuals in excess of the reserve will be subject to an off-the top reduction to fill up a new residuals reserve.

3.2.8. The Collection Agent

The complexity of the financing structures and the myriad of rights and interests in the proceeds of the film that are held by the various parties involved in producing the film generally induces the parties (particularly those with a deferred or subordinated position) to require the engagement of a collection account manager to collect and administer all gross receipts payable to the production SPV or other licensing vehicle. The sole exception to this rule relates to proceeds payable to a bank that acts as the senior lender (provided that a residuals reserve is established, and the bank agrees to pay the sales agent any sales commission owed on such proceeds). For all other proceeds, a collection account is managed and controlled by the collection account manager, or CAM, who holds the proceeds in trust for the beneficiaries of such funds, to be disbursed as agreed by the parties in interest under the collection account management agreement, or CAMA. The CAMA will require the sales agent to include a provision in the license agreements under which the distributors or licensees of the film will pay all gross receipts owed to the licensor into the collection account. Additionally, each party to the CAMA will be required to forward any gross receipts that it receives into the collection account. The CAM will calculate the respective parties' entitlements to such receipts and disburse such receipts net of its expenses and fees according to the agreed waterfall in the CAMA.

3.2.9. Other Parties

The financial close of an independently financed film requires the commitments of a host of other parties including the director, principal actors, individual producers, the production services companies, visual effects companies, possibly a tax credit consultant and lawyers. A discussion of these other parties is beyond the scope of this Chapter. The parties discussed above, together with the individual producers and their representatives, forge the finance plan to greenlight production. This process usually kicks off with a financing term sheet.

3.3. THE FINANCE AGREEMENTS

Film financiers fund film projects at almost any stage of development or production. Naturally, the deal terms vary depending on the point of entry and scope of financing. The earlier a financier commits to finance the production of a film, the more conditions to funding and the more upside it will require.

The recoupment of development financing, pre-production financing and/or production financing each relies on a finance plan under which the film's budget works in relation to the value of discounted future gross receipts from exploitation of the film. The financing required for the development of a film and its production, completion and delivery are often split apart, with development financing being recouped as a first day payment upon the funding of the production loans. Pre-production financing might be included in the development financing or in the production loan package or it might be shared among them. Below, each step of the financing process is addressed in turn.

3.3.1. Development Finance

Development finance is the earliest money funded for a motion picture project. It is used to kick-start the project and to advance it towards production. The sources for inspiration for a film's development are endless, whether it be an original idea, an article in a newspaper or magazine, a novel, a memoir, a play, a treatment, or simply a log line. To unlock development finance the project developer must capture the imagination of the financier in a manner that plays to a theatrical film. James Cameron has said that *Titanic* was born from a six-word pitch: "Romeo and Juliette on that ship."[4]

---

[4] *See Reflections on* Titanic, Part 1, *a documentary* (2012) *produced by* Thomas C. Grane and Laurent Bouzereau.

Development money is used build the project to the stage at which it can be green-lit. This involves optioning the literary rights upon which the screenplay will be based, such as a novel or an existing script, hiring writing services to write and polish the screenplay, establishing the production team and financing structure, attaching key talent and a director, and funding ancillary costs such as legal fees for negotiating the required agreements. Development finance might also include funding for budgeting, location scouting and other pre-production spending – which may even include deposits against lead actor services.

Development often requires hundreds of thousands of dollars. In cases where a script must be commissioned, the development financier should be prepared to fund more than a first draft; multiple rewrites and polishes are usually necessary to bring the script to a level that can attract the director and talent needed to support a multi-million dollar budget. This in turn requires time, and to the extent a script is developed based on rights under option, multiple option extensions may be necessary. The return of the development financier's investment literally turns on a hope that the screenwriter(s) will churn out something commercial, and there is a material risk that after having spent hundreds of thousands of dollars over the course of a few years, the project will attract no interest at the level that would permit recoupment of the investment. For projects based on an already completed screenplay, the initial risk hinges on whether the commercial package can be assembled from the screenplay, and at what cost, before full financing may be secured.

Independent development financing is often funded by producers or a studio. For small independent films, development funding typically hinges on the passion and persuasiveness of the producer's vision for the film, and solicitation of support. If a star or an exceptional writer or producer is provisionally attached to the concept, third-party development funding will be easier to attract. The development financier will usually insist on holding the rights to the intellectual property that it finances. The development financier will also insist on having the determining vote in the event of deadlock on matters with respect to how its funds are being used.

Development financing deals are often closed solely on a detailed term sheet that provides (i) a description of the project, including the approved writers and producers, (ii) the development budget with a scheduled use of proceeds, (iii) a finance plan – with one model for set-up with a studio and one model for independent production, (iv) the conditions under which the rights in the project will be assigned from the development financier to a studio or to a production SPV, such as the set-up of the project with a studio or the sale of a certain number of pre-sales at or above the "take" prices, coupled with a perfected security interest if financial obligations to the development financier remain outstanding at the time of such assignment, (v) the premium (often referred to as a VIG, from the Russian word *vigorish,* meaning "winnings") or other return on the investment, (vi) any entitlement of the investor to onscreen credits and (vii) determination of who has control over the development and production of the project and its creative and financial elements. If the project is successfully developed and greenlit, the development financier will be cashed out, with a full return on its investment from early, if not first, proceeds of the production loans. For this reason, it is unusual for the development financier to be offered more than a few percentage points in the backend participation in net or adjusted gross proceeds from exploitation of the film.

A prodigious amount of sweat equity is involved in any development project. It is therefore important to work with knowledgeable and trustworthy people during the development phase of a project with whom the likelihood of serious conflict is minimal – regardless of what powers are granted under contract. In instances where these concerns are not fully anticipated and addressed, it is not uncommon for disputes to encumber a project so substantially that its ultimate production may be delayed if not abandoned.

3.3.2. Pre-Production Finance: The Budget, Strike Price and Finance Plan

Whether or not a film moves beyond development and into production turns on the finance plan, the validity of which depends on the size of the film's budget in relation to the value of the collateral capable of supporting the film's financing, production, and delivery costs. The budget plays a vital role in pinpointing and categorizing the costs necessary to produce, complete and deliver the film. It is the lynchpin around which the entire finance plan revolves. Once the final budget is approved and bonded, few changes may be made to it without the approval of the financiers or the completion guarantor.

The term "budget" brings with it significant room for ambiguity, because many costs incurred in connection with the production and delivery of a film are not part of its negative cost (i.e., they don't show up on the screen), but those additional costs must be taken into account when analyzing the amount of money that the financiers are willing to lend the production to create the film.

Under a workable finance plan, the film's collateral must be sufficient to cover both (i) the negative cost of the film, which is the cash amount required to produce and deliver the film according to specification (this is also referred to as the "direct cost" or "going in" budget) plus (ii) all further charges, fees and expenses of the various parties involved in financing, producing, marketing and delivering the film that are payable from gross receipts due or that otherwise reduce the license fees or advances payable to the production (such additional fees and expenses, when added to the direct cost budget, generally comprise the "all-in" budget for the film).

The direct cost budget is an important metric often used to establish rights acquisition fees, overages and caps, because it closely reflects the costs that show up on the screen. It includes the above-the-line costs for the story and script rights, the director, the principal cast and the producers and the below-the-line costs for cast and crew, music, editing, insurance, marketing and delivery. The further costs that are not technically required to complete and deliver the film, but that are charged to the production, are also included in the all-in budget. These additional costs include: the residuals reserve; the sales agent marketing allowances or advances on commissions; any budgeted producer overhead; financing fees, interest, premiums and expenses; legal fees; and the bond fee and bond contingency. The all-in budget does not include the cost to release the film, including theatrical P&A. Such costs are paid by the distributors and are taken into account when negotiating the licenses for the completed film. P&A costs are distinguishable from production marketing and publicity costs associated with licensing the film. Production marketing and publicity costs generally are incurred by the sales agent and are included in the all-in budget because they are either funded from the direct cost budget or recouped off the top from exploitation proceeds (thereby reducing the financiers' recoupment).

The strike price represents the sum that the completion guarantor requires to be indefeasibly funded (often in escrow) for the production and delivery of the film before it will issue the completion guaranty. The completion guarantor monitors the spending of the strike price to ensure that the film is completed and delivered to specification as required under the completion guaranty and in accordance with the bonded budget and production cash flow schedule. At the insistence of the lenders the strike price generally reflects a sum that is close to the all-in budget for the film. As such, financing fees, an interest reserve, a sum for sales agent marketing expenses, the bond fee and contingency and certain legal costs are generally included in the strike price. However, there are no hard and fast rules for what is ultimately included in the final, approved, bonded budget beyond the amount of funding required to produce and deliver the film and pay the bond fee and contingency.

Many costs associated with production are non-cash items that are paid with debt and recouped from gross receipts. Financing fees, for example, may be due and payable to the lenders on the date of funding, but are generally funded by debt (i.e., via a cashless transaction effected through the loan reserve that reduces financing available to the production under the credit line). Likewise, any interest due during the course of the term of the production loans will be capitalized and paid by reserved debt. In addition, expenses incurred by the financing parties but that are reimbursable by the production will be funded from the loan reserve or an additional advance under the loan agreement.

The extent to which such costs are included in the approved, all-in budget for the film is mostly irrelevant to the production: one way or the other these costs will come out of gross receipts. As noted earlier, production loans are typically secured only by the film project collateral. Therefore, financiers must recoup both their loans for the negative cost of the production and their loans for fees, interest and other expenses from the film's gross receipts. The value of the film collateral (i.e., gross receipts from the film's worldwide exploitation) must adequately cover not only the negative cost of the motion picture but all of the production-related expenses in order for the finance plan to hold up. In this sense, the all-in budget provides a helpful look at the actual cost of the film.

As discussed above, the guilds charge residuals on first dollar worldwide gross receipts from all but the initial theatrical release of a feature length film. These charges are made on revenues derived from use of the film, not on profits from such use. Residuals accrue prior to the recoupment of the negative cost of the film, and they reduce the lenders' recoupment. If residuals are reserved as part of the strike price, then the guilds will usually agree to subordinate to the secured lenders their right to payment from the gross receipts on which such reserve has been calculated, subject to there being a CAMA in place to govern their priority position with respect to later receipts. The residuals reserve is a cash reserve paid to the guilds from the production funding source, and as such, it will accrue interest, which the finance plan must take into account.

Any residuals reserve will typically apply to international receipts only, because the domestic distributor for the film usually assumes the liability to pay residuals on domestic receipts. In such cases, residuals that are owed on domestic receipts will not reduce the minimum guarantee paid by the domestic distributor, and the finance plan remains unaffected by such obligations. The international distributors on the other hand refuse to accept liability for residuals owed on gross receipts. As a result, residuals become due and payable by the licensor on the minimum guarantees paid to the licensor by international distributors. These obligations impact the finance plan, because they reduce the recoupment available to repay the financiers.

Bearing this in mind, the all-in budget is the most useful tool to evaluate the strength of the finance plan in light of the risks embedded in the collateral structure. The all-in budget informs the finance plan because it contains the broadest measure of all of the costs advanced, whether in cash or as a cashless advance from the loan reserve, or as an added expense that increases the credit line. All such costs must be recouped from the film's gross receipts – sometimes, as in the case of residuals and non-deferred sales commissions and expenses, before the lenders are repaid, and in any case, before the backend participations in net or adjusted gross receipts apply.

To ensure the integrity of the finance plan, lenders only approve a "budget" that reflects the all-in budget. The financing fees, an adequate interest reserve, a residuals reserve and other costs chargeable to the production and recoupable from gross receipts must be taken into account. Any expenses incurred by the lenders (or other parties) that are chargeable to the production and not included in the final approved budget stresses the available collateral, particularly if such expenses are payable ahead of the lenders' recoupment, like collection agent fees, non-deferred sales commissions, unanticipated delivery costs, sales expenses or residuals that have not been reserved. While budgeted expenses will bear interest that is reserved, unbudgeted expenses (for example heavy legal charges incurred on a complicated closing) will bear interest that is not reserved. Because all such expenses must be recouped from gross receipts along with the budgeted fees and interest, to the extent any charges are not included in the final approved budget, lenders account for them in their own financial plan for the film, relying on their collateral buffer to be repaid.

The film's collateral, which is comprised of the pre-sold territories plus the "take price" estimates in the unsold territories plus the soft-money incentives, must exceed the all-in budget (with a buffer to take into account counterparty and gap risk) plus any additional unbudgeted fees or expenses payable from the film's estimated gross receipts. Before closing the financing of the production loans, the financiers will scrutinize all of the costs, fees, expenses and any other rights to recoupment from gross receipts, whether or not budgeted, in light of their own recoupment position to ensure that the finance plan holds up.

The lenders usually ensure their right to recoupment is ahead of all other parties with the exception of the fees of the collection agent, the sales agent's non-deferred commissions and the residuals owed to the guilds. It is important to keep in mind that while deferring items in the direct cost budget to a recoupment position from gross receipts can reduce the negative cost of the film, it cannot increase the collateral available to pay such deferred expenses, and any such deferments are usually subordinated to the financiers' right to collect from gross receipts. If the collateral or bargaining power is sufficient, a corridor into gross receipts might be offered alongside the financiers with respect to such deferments, but this is rare.

Once the all-in budget is sketched out, the feasibility of the finance plan takes shape in light of pre-sales. The all-in budget will take final form as the film enters pre-production.

3.3.3. Pre-production Finance: The Pre-production Facility

Pre-production finance is often provided by the development financier or the equity. Alternatively, if the production loan package can be agreed early enough, and the relevant conditions are satisfied, pre-production expenses may be financed by the mezzanine or senior lender as part of the production advances. Often significant pre-production costs loom on the horizon before producers have arranged pre-production financing or closed the production finance package. The pressure to begin pre-production may come from a variety of sources. For example, the timing of the close of the pre-production or production financing that is used to pay the option exercise price must coincide with the option period or any extension of the option period. Additionally, the director and the principal cast may be available only during certain windows, necessitating a fixed principal photography start date as well as deposits toward their services.

Meanwhile, issues often remain outstanding that prevent the strike price from being fully funded. Recall that the strike price is the amount of money required by the completion guarantor to complete and deliver the film. Until the strike price is escrowed or fully committed, the completion guarantor will not issue the completion bond. Without the completion bond, the senior and mezzanine lenders generally will not advance their production loans, which might have been used to fund pre-production expenses. Potential culprits for delays in funding the strike price include pre-sale distributors who have failed to pay their initial deposits, the failure to timely hedge currency exposure for production spending in a foreign currency coupled with an unfavorable shift in the relevant exchange rate, the failure to finalize production documentation required to close the production loans, such as security agreements with foreign production services companies or notices of assignment with pre-sale distributors, and the failure to reduce the budget or agree deferrals at the level required to support the finance plan.

A pre-production facility provides bridge financing to enable the production to keep the lights on when a project is greenlit before the completion bond is effective and the production loans are funded. Once a lender commits to finance pre-production expenses under these circumstances, it is forced to take completion risk, which it generally goes to great lengths to avoid. Whatever issues prevented a timely issuance of the completion bond and financial close of the production loans might continue indefinitely. In such cases the pre-production lender must advance millions to the production for weeks into principal photography or else face abandonment and possibly a total loss of the funded investment. The entire film project therefore potentially becomes the pre-production lender's liability notwithstanding the fact that the lender may have capped its pre-production commitment. To account for this risk, a pre-production lender will require the right to take over the production and/or advance additional funds to prevent the production from defaulting on its commitments or abandoning the film.

Pre-production finance of this kind is expensive, often demanding a high flat return accompanied by heavy default penalties. The pricing reflects in part the high risk of the loan and in part the reluctance of lenders to fund stressed situations where significant uncertainties abound regarding other lenders' financial commitments to the film and whether a completion guaranty will become effective. If a pre-production facility is required, it is usually provided by one of the production lenders who is already familiar with the finance plan and the status of the film's collateral. The pre-production facility is generally refinanced by the senior and mezzanine production loans when the strike price is funded and the completion guaranty becomes effective. The failure to close the production financing by a fixed maturity date will result in a high rate of default interest on the pre-production facility, which is designed to incentivize a quick close of the production financing and to prevent the pre-production facility from turning into a production facility.

Due to the nature of the completion risk accepted by a pre-production lender, a host of conditions precedent and conditions subsequent will be required in the pre-production loan agreement to ensure that the production stays on track. Prior to lending, a pre-production financier generally will require (i) approval of the chain of title and the motion picture project licensing and lending structure, (ii) approval of the all-in budget, the director, the principal cast and a detailed production cash flow schedule that includes the pre-production spending, (iii) acknowledgment by the completion guarantor that each line item in the production cash flow schedule will qualify towards meeting the strike price, and (iv) a first lien security package that has been granted and perfected under which all film collateral is made available to the pre-production lender to secure the loan.

The satisfaction of other important production elements will be conditions precedent or become conditions subsequent to funding depending on their status at the time the pre-production facility is arranged. For example, if elements of the budget or the screenplay are not definitively agreed, or any producer, talent or director agreements have not been executed or any production services agreements have not been entered into, but which are required for production, the lender will set reasonable outside dates to execute such agreements as conditions subsequent to the extension of credit.

The pre-production lender will have the right to take over and complete the film upon a default that is not cured in a timely manner or that cannot be cured. Events of default include a breach of the conditions subsequent, defects in the representations and warranties given by the production SPV and other events that materially threaten the value of the film or its collateral. While no lender wants to take over a film, given that completion and delivery of the film is the only means of generating revenue out of the project, the lender must be in a position to do so to protect its investment.

To preserve bargaining power after funding the pre-production facility, the pre-production lender will generally require that all material production loan documents, including the sales agent interparty agreement, are in forms approved by the lender by an outside date. The production should require that such forms be consistent with the lender's past precedent and ideally agree to the forms prior to the execution of the pre-production facility.

In light of the foregoing, time management – particularly by the producers and the sales agent – is critical in the window leading up to pre-production. Proper time management may avert a situation where emergency pre-production funding is required at high cost to the production or if such funding is necessary avoid an expensive default under the pre-production facility.

3.3.4. Production Finance: The Mezzanine Loan

Usually it is not a protracted negotiation of the production financing agreements that creates the need for a pre-production bridge facility, but rather the failure to meet the conditions to lend under the production loan agreements. The material terms of the production loan package are often agreed many months (or even in years) prior to the start of principal photography. Indeed, the most coveted film financing commitment is the one under which a financier guarantees to finance the production of a film before the producers have even agreed any material licensing deals. The term sheet that governs such a commitment provides a road map to close the financing package for the entire motion picture project.

3.3.4.1 The Mezzanine Term Sheet for Production Financing

Producers attempt to secure a financial commitment from a lender to finance their motion picture as early in the development process as possible, and many lenders are willing to make conditional production financing commitments in exchange for the exclusive right to finance the film. Unless the lender has also financed the film's development, such a deal generally becomes attractive only after there is a package in place like a script, a preliminary budget, a noted director, a member of the principal cast, and/or a respected producer known to attract high level talent. It is also likely that a sales agent will have provided sales estimates for the film.

Recall that the mezzanine lender finances the portion of the budget that is not advanced by the senior lender. Because the mezzanine lender is willing to step into this "gap" and lend against the estimated value of the film in unsold territories, it is also the natural party to underwrite the film from an early stage in the production process. Once an elemental package is in place, the producer and lender often reach agreement on the material terms of financing the production of the film in a term sheet.

The term sheet under which the mezzanine financing is agreed is often executed immediately before one of the major film markets, because the ability to attract sales increases significantly if a lender is committed to finance the project. The financing term sheet memorializes the essential terms of the lender's early-stage commitment and its corresponding entitlements. In the term sheet the parties generally seek to:

- approve a selection of agreed creative elements such as the script and the director or principal cast;
- establish a range for the all-in budget and specify the elements to be included in it with a caveat that the final budget will be subject to the lender's approval;
- approve the individual producers and the sales agent;

- confirm the structure(s) for holding the rights in the film;
- agree the approach to maximizing soft money and tax credits;
- loosely define the pricing and recoupment structure for the production loan and net profits;
- define the gap commitment;
- provide for a provisional grant of security and other material conditions to lend; and
- generally, set the tone for the progress to production, determining the areas over which the lender has approval rights and specifically identifying known action items.

Due to the early stage commitment, the lender will require an exclusive right to finance the film and to select or approve any third-party financiers. The lender may also require control over the rights in the film.

Even if all relevant creative elements are agreed with specificity, few lenders will provide an unqualified financial commitment at an early stage of production; lenders typically do not accept completion and delivery risk on independent productions, and before committing to fund the strike price they require evidence that the film is commercial at the approved budget. Therefore, a focal element of the term sheet negotiation will be the nature and extent of the pre-sales that the producers must obtain prior to the extension of the financial commitment. A lender will generally require as a pre-condition to funding that sold territories account for at least 50 percent of the approved budget at or above the "take prices." Lenders may require a higher threshold, particularly if they agree to finance at an early stage in the production process. The "take prices" for the balance of unsold territories, when added to the pre-sales and soft-money incentives, will be required to equal or exceed the all-in budget for the film. The "take price" sales estimates will be required to be prepared in good faith by a lender-approved sales agent.

In addition, the term sheet should provide for the manner of calculating the amount of financing available with respect to the unsold territories. Recall from the above discussion of the budget that the gross receipts from the licensing agreements must sufficiently cover the negative cost of the film and all other costs charged to the production. This will be reflected in the financial commitment, represented by the "take prices" less:

- residuals payable according to the take estimates;
- the collection agent fees and expenses;
- any talent corridors into gross receipts;
- the estimated sales commissions and expenses;
- an interest reserve and a reserve for other financing fees paid with debt on the financial close;
- a reserve for estimated withholding taxes, to the extent applicable; and
- any further discount required by the lender in light of its credit analysis of the relevant licensee.

Further conditions on funding might include securing a tax credit opinion that tax credits will be available to fund at least 20 percent of the approved budget.

The mezzanine financing term sheet will condition funding on fulfillment of the lender's standard conditions precedent in its long-form loan agreement, which will include approval of the chain of title, the distribution agreements entered into with respect to the unsold territories and the effectiveness of the completion bond. The lender may also insist at this stage on the right to approve the final cut of the film unless its loan is fully collateralized or repaid at the time such determination is made. Additionally, the waterfall of gross receipts, including the backend participation of the financier, will be agreed in broad brush strokes. A financier that has conditionally guaranteed the production financing of a film at an early stage, even on a qualified basis, will expect an allocation of 50 percent of 100 percent of the film's adjusted gross receipts, also referred to as "defined net proceeds" or "net profits."

Net profits from an independent film are the gross receipts paid to the licensor from the worldwide exploitation of the film after deducting residuals, CAM fees, sales agent fees and expenses, recoupment of the financiers' investments (including interest, premiums and financing fees), the recoupment of the completion guarantor, if applicable, the payment of any talent corridors and the recoupment of any deferrals of the producers, the director and talent.

The lender's 50 percent stake, which is often referred to as the "financiers' share," will be used to pay the backend participations of all financial investors; provided that if the development financier has a backend stake, it should be paid out of the talent share. Whereas the senior lender generally has no interest in net profits, any equity investor will receive a sizable share, all depending on the size and risk of the investment. The other 50 percent stake, referred to as the "talent's share" or "producer's share" is reserved to the production company, from which the backend participations of principal cast, the director, the writers, the producers and other non-financing parties are paid. The exact nature of the split is often the subject of intense negotiation with the final allocation being determined by the level of anticipated talent participations, the strength of the collateral and competitiveness of the financing.

Having obtained an early financing commitment, producers benefit from a strong position to market the film and close key talent and director deals. Most experienced directors and Class A talent have "pay or play" provisions in their contracts, meaning that, conditioned only on the start of principal photography or the effectiveness of a completion guaranty the directing or acting fee is payable whether or not the services are ultimately required (e.g., in the event the film is abandoned). A financier who is willing to back such a "pay or play" offer provides a strong help to the production when it negotiates the director and principal cast deals.

3.3.4.2. The Mezzanine Loan Agreement

If the pre-sales and the estimates for the unsold territories are on target, then the final budget will be approved, the long-form mezzanine loan agreement will be negotiated in conformance with the mezzanine financing term sheet, and the parties will work to close the senior loan, fund the strike price and begin production.

The essential terms of the mezzanine lender's loan agreement can be broken down into distinct parts that address, respectively:

- the credit extension and its repayment;
- the conditions to funding;

- the production specifications, completion and delivery of the film and the application of proceeds from the collateral;
- the grant of security;
- borrower's representations and warranties;
- borrower's affirmative and negative covenants;
- events of default; remedies; and
- boilerplate.

The loan agreement is usually entered into with the production SPV, which holds the copyright in the film and licenses the worldwide rights. Sometimes other entities in the production structure borrow the funds to meet specific production incentive requirements, in which case the security structure must align defaults and remedies across all relevant production entities.

The mezzanine loan agreement establishes the credit limit, or the maximum amount that may be requested to be borrowed under the loan agreement, which will include a reserve for financing fees and interest over the life of the loan, and the terms of repayment. Interest, costs, fees and expenses chargeable to the reserve will be added to the unpaid principal balance of the loans as and when charged. Any production lender will insist on its right to fund in excess of the agreed credit limit to take into account expenses chargeable to the lender that are in excess of the reserve, or as may be necessary to restructure the loan documents or to take over, complete and deliver the film following an event of default. A maturity date will be set somewhere between 18 months and 36 months after funding, depending on the funding date, the number of unsold territories and the outside bonded delivery date agreed with the distributors.

Pricing for the mezzanine loan tranche varies by project but often approximates 10 percent per annum with an arrangement fee of 5-10 percent of the credit extension. The structuring of interest pricing and net return may vary according to the lender's jurisdiction of organization and operation. For example, U.S. tax treaties with certain foreign jurisdictions exempt qualified portfolio interest income from withholding taxes, whereas a premium or the portion of original issue discount allocated to capital gains upon early repayment of principal may be subject to withholding tax. It is worthwhile consulting a U.S.

tax expert on these matters with respect to any foreign funding of a U.S. production loan, particularly because the loan agreement will likely require a tax gross up by the production company to increase the lender's entitlements by the amount of any income that is withheld.

The mezzanine loan agreement will condition any advances on the execution of all relevant loan documentation and on the strike price being fully funded but for such lender's own contribution. The senior lender will require all other financiers to fund first, usually by means of an escrow arrangement. To fully fund the strike price usually requires all distributor deposits then due to have been paid into the production account, or other parties must defer their right to payment under the budget to the extent such funds are missing. The closing loan documents include the completion guaranty, the sales agent interparty agreement, all existing distribution agreements and the related notices of assignment providing for payment directly to the lender or the collection account of the relevant minimum guarantees, the laboratory pledgeholder agreement and the security agreements and related documentation like UCC financing statements, powers of attorney, powers of sale, copyright mortgages, bank account control agreements and any accommodation security.

Further closing deliverables include the executed sales agency agreement, incumbency and officers certificates certifying the corporate or limited liability company resolutions authorizing the loan documentation and related transaction documents, as well as certificates of good standing and certified copies of the organizational documents of the borrower. The lender may ask for a legal opinion regarding the legal status of the borrower, and chain-of-title will need to have been approved by counsel. As is the case with virtually all loan agreements, the representations and warranties made by the borrower as of the date of execution are brought down to the funding date and must be true and correct as of such date (except to the extent they relate expressly to a different date), and the borrower must be solvent and not in default under the loan agreement or any of the other transaction documents.

Additionally, prior to releasing funds, the mezzanine lender will require that the production documentation is fully complete, including the approved budget, approved screenplay, approved cash flow and production schedules, and a title report and a copyright report by an approved provider, such as Thomson Compumark or Dennis Angel.

The production will have obtained all required insurance, and the lender will have been named as a loss payee or additional insured under the relevant policies. Production insurances generally include:

- protection with respect to the director and key cast (including any applicable essential element insurance);
- negative and faulty stock insurance;
- prop and equipment insurance;
- third party liability, property and damage insurance; and
- errors and omissions, or E&O, insurance commencing on or prior to the first day of principal photography of the film and ending no earlier than three years from commencement of principal photography.

Major distributors will require extensions of the E&O policy.

A section of the loan agreement will be devoted to production specifications and will forbid the production company to deviate from the specifications without prior approval by the lender or the completion guarantor. In addition, the borrower, which is typically the licensing entity and owner of the film, will assign and grant to the lender a security interest in all of its rights, title and interest in the film and all related property. If such entity is an SPV, as is typically the case, the security interest typically will cover all of its personal property. There may be specific carve-outs agreed on a case-by-case basis to take into account named collateral that is entirely outside the lender's security, such as tax credit rights and proceeds that are financed by another party. A separate intercreditor agreement will allocate the collateral proceeds among the lenders and regulate their overlapping security interests in the film collateral.

The borrower will make representations and warranties that are found in most loan agreements regarding its formation and existence, due authorization and execution of the loan transaction documents, compliance with laws, priority and perfection of the lender's security interest, the nature of the deposit accounts and record keeping, its rights in the collateral and the absence of conflicts, claims, defaults and material adverse effect. Likewise, most affirmative covenants of the borrower will be similar to covenants made in loan and security agreements outside the film industry, including the borrower's duty to maintain its legal existence, properties and insurance, to reimburse the lender for its costs and expenses incurred in connection with negotiating and enforcing the loan agreement, to pay and discharge its tax liabilities in a timely manner, to properly keep its books and records and maintain a system of accounting principles administered in accordance with Generally Accepted Accounting Principles consistently applied, to give timely notice of default or the commencement of any proceeding potentially adverse to any aspect of the transaction, to indemnify the lender for damages resulting from breach, to maintain the priority of the lender's security interest and to register its copyrights and trademarks in the collateral.

Certain affirmative covenants specific to film finance transactions address the care for and inspection of the film collateral. The use of proceeds will be limited to approved production costs and the payment of approved financing fees and expenses. The lender will be granted the right to inspect the film collateral and require that upon request the licensor furnish all information related to the film, including reports on the location and status of the physical elements. Further, the borrower will covenant to deposit all physical properties relating to the delivery of the film with an approved laboratory, subject to a laboratory pledgeholder agreement.

The mezzanine lender will require that all loans be repaid mandatorily by all collateral proceeds as and when such proceeds are collected (including any insurance proceeds, product placement revenues, no claims bonuses and any balance remaining in the production account after delivery of the film to the sales agent). The senior lender's loan agreement will contain the same provision. The sales agent interparty agreement will regulate the application of collateral proceeds among the transaction parties and prevail in the event of conflict with the terms of the loan agreement. As discussed above, the claims of the guilds for residuals must be taken into account if the film has been exploited at the time such proceeds are available for distribution.

The loan agreement may also entitle the lender to exercise any of borrower's rights to terminate the sales agency agreement upon a default or event of default under the loan agreement. The lender will forbid the borrower from amending any approved distribution agreements without the lender's consent and require the borrower to maintain only the scheduled production bank accounts until the termination of the loan agreement. The borrower will further agree that prior to the repayment of the loan it will only enter into new or replacement distribution agreements that are approved by the lender. The loan agreement may further require the borrower to enter into any distribution agreement approved by the lender above a set valuation tied to the "take" prices, and if sales have not been closed by a certain time, then at any price in the lender's discretion. If the licensor of the film is not the borrower, then identical covenants will be made in a security agreement entered into with the licensing entity.

Because the business of the borrowing entity is almost always limited to the production of the film, the negative covenants are broad and sweeping, generally locking the borrower down to observance of the relevant transaction documents. No material contracts apart from the approved loan, and security and distribution agreements may be entered into without the lender's prior written approval, and no further indebtedness may be incurred without the lender's prior written approval. Additionally, there will be a blanket prohibition on all liens that are not specifically permitted. The intercreditor agreement will regulate the provision of loans by other lenders to the production and the grant of liens to secure them.

The borrower's breach of any representation, warranty or covenant will give rise to a default under the loan agreement and each related security agreement, as will the borrower's default or a relevant third party's default under material transaction documents, such as any other loan or security agreement, the sales agency agreement, distribution agreements, notices of assignment, intercreditor agreements, the sales agent interparty agreement, the completion agreement and the completion guaranty. If the default can be cured, then an appropriate amount of time to cure is typically granted.

The extent to which defaults under third party agreements are capable of accelerating outstanding indebtedness is often a point that is heavily negotiated. For example, if a distributor causes an event of default, in some cases a lender may agree that only that part of the debt secured by the defaulting distributor's minimum guarantee accelerates and becomes subject to default interest. Likewise, an event of default in relation to the sales agent (e.g., insolvency of the sales agent) might give rise to remedies and accelerate repayment only to the extent the mezzanine loan is not fully collateralized at the time of default. However, such concessions will be part of an overall security package under which the lender is comfortable that it can protect its position. If it becomes obvious that a distributor's default may cause further losses (for example the default of a U.S. distributor upon whose theatrical release commitment the enforceability of other distribution agreements relies), no such relief will be granted.

Following an event of default, essentially all remedies at law and equity will be made available to the mezzanine lender. Further, the specific forms of power of attorney and power of sale that are executed in connection with the financial close will become exercisable, subject to the terms of the intercreditor agreement agreed to with the senior lender.

The final terms of the loan agreement are usually bespoke, as each film has its unique issues. The final form of loan agreement will also reflect the experience and relative bargaining power of the respective parties and their counsel, the competitiveness of the film project, and how the deal is situated in light of the relationships among the parties involved. To reach the financial close, the legal rights and obligations of numerous parties must work together. If each loan document were to acknowledge the interacting and, in some cases, overriding legal obligations of the other transaction parties, the agreements would become so cumbersome as to render them entirely unwieldy. As such, the contractual rights agreed by the borrowing entities and other entities providing security to the lenders will often provide for rights in the collateral that conflict with the rights granted to other parties. For example, generally, the senior lender will have priority liens in the film assets in the pre-sold territories, and the mezzanine lender will have priority liens in the unsold territories, and each lender will be subrogated to the other lender, meaning it will step into the shoes of the other lender, as soon as the other lender's loan obligations are indefeasibly repaid. Notwithstanding the foregoing, the respective loan agreements and security documentation will grant each lender full rights and remedies with respect to all of the film collateral and with respect to the mandatory use of collateral proceeds to repay the debt. The particular rights and remedies available to the respective lenders as to the collateral will be agreed between the lenders in an intercreditor agreement.

3.3.4.3. Production Finance: The Senior Loan Documents

The senior finance tranche is the last money funded, and pre-sale financing is usually obtained without undue difficulty as long as the chain of title is clear, and the licensees are creditworthy. A mezzanine lender with the exclusive right to finance the film under the terms of a mezzanine finance term sheet (see above) often will arrange the senior financing, which is usually provided by a bank. Once a bank is involved, it typically drives the process into the financial close, working closely with the mezzanine lender and the production. Any overages from the senior pre-sale collateral will be available to pay down the mezzanine lender's outstanding indebtedness, just as any overages from the mezzanine collateral will be available to pay down the senior lender's outstanding indebtedness.

Like the mezzanine production loan, the senior production loan usually kicks off with a term sheet. This term sheet is usually agreed shortly before drafting the long-form senior loan agreement; it drills down into the finance plan and generally establishes the pricing, conditions precedent to funding and terms of recoupment. Because the senior lender finances the pre-sold territories that are subject to binding commitments with fixed outside delivery dates, the senior loan typically has a shorter duration than the mezzanine lender's loan.

The senior lender's term sheet will also include a schedule of all the pre-sale distribution agreements and their respective minimum guarantee and deposit commitments. These distributors will be categorized and assigned a degree of credit quality in the term sheet. For example, the senior lender might agree to advance 100 percent of the minimum guarantees owed by creditworthy distributors in the "A" bucket of distributors, but only 50 percent of the minimum guarantees owed by distributors of dubious credit quality in the "C" bucket, with a range in the "B" bucket. The aggregate advance commitments available to the production will be net of the senior lender's budgeted financing fees, residuals, sales commission, senior lender legal costs, an interest reserve (and perhaps the tax consultant fee if the senior lender is financing tax credits) and the credit risk discount, if any, applicable to the relevant distributor. Because the senior lender typically instructs payment by the pre-sale distributors directly to its account through relevant notices of assignment, there are no collection agent fees to deduct from gross receipts payable to the senior lender.

The senior loan agreement is similar to the mezzanine loan agreement in its essential terms.

3.3.4.4. Production Finance: The Equity

The equity is typically the most challenging financing to find due to the risk. The term "equity" is used to refer to all forms of unsecured financing for the film, including investments by production service providers in the form of deferrals, as discussed in greater detail above in section 3.2. – The Parties. Equity investors generally structure their entitlement in the form of recoupment from a share of adjusted gross receipts after the lenders have been repaid in full.

Because most production SPVs are pass-through vehicles for tax treatment, and an ownership stake in a production vehicle can have burdensome reporting consequences for investors, the equity investment is generally structured as an economic interest in a share of adjusted gross receipts in the film. A collection account management agreement will be required by the equity investor to ensure its right to such proceeds is properly accounted for. However, investments that utilize a crowdfunding model – which would also rightly be called "equity" – are made directly into the production and licensing vehicle. Crowdfunding is discussed below.

An investment agreement, the sales agent interparty agreement, the collection account management agreement and a completion guaranty are often the only closing documents required by an equity investor, whose investment is usually entirely unsecured. The equity financing agreement, which may take the form of a term sheet, will ensure that the film:

- will conform to the approved screenplay, subject to incidental changes that do not materially alter the plot, story, characters or setting;
- be directed by an approved director;
- star an approved principal cast;
- be produced in general accordance with the approved direct cost budget, subject to changes as exigencies of production arise;

- be produced in a manner to meet the delivery requirements of the sales agency agreement and distribution agreements;
- provide for at least one executive producer credit if the investment is substantial; and
- be subject to a completion guaranty of which the equity investor is a beneficiary.

Equity investors will generally be granted meaningful consultation rights and have the right to sit on panels that approve changes to the approved cast or director, but the equity investors will defer to the secured lenders or the completion guarantor if there is a material change in the cast or director and there is disagreement regarding the replacement.

The sales agent interparty agreement, which is executed by the production SPV, the financiers and the sales agent, usually sets forth the respective funding obligations of the parties. The lenders will require an equity investor to escrow its financing commitment prior to the closing of the production finance loans. The equity investor will in turn typically require that its investment cannot be used by the production without its consent until all production financing is in place and the completion bond is effective.

On occasion, to sweeten an equity deal, a first-place recoupment position in one or more unsold territories may be offered to an equity investor. An equity investor's success in obtaining a recoupment window into specified gross receipts depends largely on the risk it takes against other collateral, and of course a required negotiation with the secured creditors. In addition, the equity may seek to have a right to proceeds from exploitation of the film after the lenders have recouped their initial expected return, which may not fully retire all obligations owed to the lenders, particularly if the gap has not sold on time or there have been cost overruns, delays or surprise legal issues. By capping a lender's return, the equity can be assured that if the debt exceeds the amount set forth in the finance plan due to higher-than-anticipated expenses, accumulated default interest or the extension of additional production financing, the equity investor is not wiped out. For the equity to achieve such a concession from the secured lenders is unusual. The secured lenders will push back vigorously with the argument that such a risk precisely reflects the nature of equity and its associated risk-reward profile. In particular, senior creditors, who in principle do not assume material collateral risk and usually are not involved in window-dressing the film, reject such demands flat out. Mezzanine lenders who are deeply involved in the financial structuring and who have a vested interest seeing the strike price funded with the help of equity may be open to accommodating such an equity recoupment window into specific (and narrowly defined) collateral, but only if they have recouped all out-of-pocket expenses (e.g., any additional legal fees, etc.) in addition to their initial principal commitment and initial expected return on investment.

Sometimes equity investors will request a lien on film collateral. For example, this circumstance might arise in a turnaround scenario where rights are acquired from a studio that has already invested heavily in the project but has decided to abandon its further development, charge back a material portion of its direct development costs to the new production team and retain a contingent interest in adjusted gross receipts from any resulting production. In such a case, the studio will request a lien to protect its contingent interest in adjusted gross receipts subordinated to the production lenders' recoupment position. In other cases, the equity investor may request to receive security in any territory in which it is offered a corridor for recoupment. For practical purposes, a blanket lien securing an equity stake should be avoided at all costs, because the protection granted to the equity from such security does not outweigh the significant transaction costs that will arise from having to include the equity investors on every interparty and intercreditor agreement relevant to the film collateral. It is, however, possible to grant the equity investor a lien in proceeds only.

Because the equity investor is not a secured party, a breach by the production SPV of its obligations to the equity investor under the equity financing agreement may turn out to be unenforceable following a bankruptcy of the production SPV. Without the power to dispose of the underlying collateral, the equity investors' stake is protected through (i) the sales agent interparty agreement, which regulates the funding procedures and sets forth the recoupment waterfall for picture proceeds among the sales agent and financiers, and (ii) the collection account management agreement, or CAMA, which requires the most significant transaction parties, including the mezzanine lender, to forward without deduction all proceeds from exploitation of the collateral that are in such party's possession into the collection account for distribution.

3.3.4.5. Securities Laws and Equity Investments

If an interest in the film project constitutes a "security" within the meaning of federal securities laws, then generally both the offer and the sale of such interest will be subject to the disclosure and registration requirements of Section 5 of the Securities Act of 1933, as amended (the "Securities Act"), the antifraud prohibitions of Section 17 of the Securities Act, the disclosure-based civil remedies under Sections 11 and 12(a)(2) of the Securities Act, and the antifraud provisions of Section 10 and Rule 10b-5 under the Securities Exchange Act of 1934, as amended (the "Exchange Act").

To the extent that producers solicit investment by offering a net profits interest in adjusted gross receipts from exploitation of a film, such an interest would be a "security" unless the purchaser of the interest meaningfully contributes to the creation or distribution of the film. This may be the case even if no shares or limited liability interests in the production or licensing entity are sold to such investor. The U.S. Supreme Court has held that Congress "enacted a definition of 'security' sufficiently broad to encompass virtually any instrument that might be sold as an investment."[5] The relevant test as to whether federal securities laws apply to an offer or sale of any interest in a film project looks at the nature of the interest. Generally speaking, an offer of an interest in the profits of a film that is produced by the efforts of third parties would be an offer of an "investment contract," which is a type of "security" regulated under U.S. federal securities laws.[6]

Federal securities laws generally do not apply to commercial loan agreements (although there can be concern around syndications), because loans made for commercial or consumer purposes are not "securities." Any determination must be made on a case-by-case basis. If the loan is structured to resemble an equity investment, then the transaction may be a securities transaction. For example, if a net profits participation is conveyed to a lender, this conveyance begins to look more like an equity investment, which would be subject to U.S. state and federal securities laws. For this reason, the equity participation granted

---

[5] See Reves v. Ernst & Young, 494 U.S. 56 (1990).

[6] See, e.g., SEC v. W.J. Howey Co., 328 U.S. 293 (1946) (holding that an offer of plots of land planted with orange trees that were subject to service contracts under the control of the promotor for the cultivation, harvest and marketing of the crops constituted an offer of an "investment contract").

to a lender should be made in an agreement that is separate from the loan agreement.

If an investment in a film is subject to federal securities laws, then the issuer of the security (e.g., the production SPV or other entity that raises production funds) is required to register the offering with the U.S. Securities and Exchange Commission, or SEC, or find a lawful exemption from registration. Registration is a prolonged and expensive process that is impractical for single picture independent financing. An exemption from registration may be found under Regulation D of the Securities Act, which exempts certain private offerings, under Regulation S if the offer and sale is made outside the United States to persons who are not resident in the United States, and under new Section 4(a)(6) of the Securities Act and related Regulation Crowdfunding.

a. Regulation D

For decades, the standard safe harbor exemption for offers and sales of securities in the United States from the disclosure and registration requirements of Section 5 has been Rule 506 of Regulation D. Rule 506 is a safe harbor for private offerings. There is no limit applicable to the amount of money that can be raised in a Rule 506 offering. If the requirements of Rule 506 are met, the SEC takes the view that the offering is exempt under Section 4(a)(2) of the Securities Act. Regulation D sets forth two further offering categories that are exempt "small issues" under Section 3(b) of the Securities Act. Rule 504 exempts offers and sales if during the preceding 12-month period aggregate sales utilizing a Section 3(b) exemption do not exceed $1,000,000, and Rule 505 exempts offers and sales if during the preceding 12-month period aggregate sales utilizing a Section 3(b) exemption do not exceed $5,000,000. Both Rule 504 and Rule 505 utilize the exemption under Section 3(b), so an offering under either Rule will count for the limitations on amounts sold under both Rule 504 and Rule 505 during the 12-month period preceding any offering under either rule.

To qualify under any Regulation D exemption, the offer and sale may not involve general solicitation. General solicitation includes any advertisement, article, notice or other communication published in any newspaper, magazine, or similar media or broadcast over television or radio, as well as the use of an unrestricted publicly available website.[7] Public dissemination of factual business information that is not presented in a manner that constitutes an offer of securities does not constitute general solicitation and is permissible.[8]

Rule 504 and 506 provide for specific cases in which general solicitation may be used to offer and sell the securities. Under Rule 504(b), general solicitation is permitted if substantive disclosure documents are delivered to the investors or the securities are registered with at least one state in which the offering is made and the required disclosure is delivered to each purchaser, or if each investor is an "accredited investor"[9] and state law exempts the offering from registration and permits general solicitation. Under Rule 506(c), general solicitation is permitted as long as the offering is made to "accredited investors" and the issuer has taken reasonable steps to verify that the purchasers are "accredited investors."

Verification under Rule 506(c) may be made by any reasonable means, but must conform to a "principles based approach" that takes into account the nature of the offering (e.g., any minimum investment amounts), the nature of the purchaser, the information available about

---

[7] *See* Regulation D, Rule 502(c); *SEC Compliance and Disclosure Interpretations*, 256.23, available at https://www.sec.gov/divisions/corpfin/guidance/securitiesactrules-interps.htm#256.23. *See also, SEC Interpretation: Use of Electronic Media*, Release No. 33-7856 available at https://www.sec.gov/rules/interp/34-42728.htm.

[8] *Id.* at 256.24 – 256.25 ("Information not involving an offer of securities may be disseminated widely without violating Rule 502(c). For example, factual business information that does not condition the public mind or arouse public interest in a securities offering is not an offer and may be disseminated widely. Information that involves an offer of securities through any form of general solicitation would contravene Rule 502(c)").

[9] Regulations D, Rule 501(a) defines "accredited investor." The definition includes (i) certain financial institutions, such as banks, brokers or dealers registered with the SEC, investment companies registered with the SEC, business development companies and SBICs, insurance companies and certain employee benefit plans, (ii) charitable organizations with more than $5 million in assets, (iii) directors, executive officers and general partners of the issuer of the securities, (iv) a natural person with (A) a net worth or joint net worth with that person's spouse exceeding $1,000,000 (excluding the primary residence) or (B) individual income in excess of $200,000 in each of the two most recent years or joint income with a spouse in excess of $300,000 and with a reasonable expectation of reaching the same income level in the current year, (v) trusts with assets in excess of $5,000,000 that were not formed for purpose of the investment and (vi) any entity in which all of the equity owners are accredited investors.

the purchaser, and the manner in which the purchaser was solicited.[10] Rule 506(c) provides examples of how verification may be undertaken, such as by reviewing tax declarations to verify income, together with a representation that the purchaser has a reasonable expectation of reaching the same income level during the current year, reviewing bank statements and nationwide credit reports to verify net worth, or obtaining written confirmation from a registered broker dealer, registered investment adviser, an attorney in good standing or a certified public accountant who has taken reasonable steps to verify in the last three months that such purchaser is an accredited investor.[11]

An offering under Rule 505 or 506 may not be made to more than 35 persons who are not "accredited investors," and under Rule 506 the issuer must reasonably believe that each non-accredited investor has the financial and business sophistication to understand the merits and risks of the investment. The number of accredited investors is unlimited in any Regulation D offering. The issuer must comply with specific disclosure requirements in each Rule 505 offering or in a Rule 506 offering that is made to non-accredited investors. If disclosure is required, the issuer must provide specified business and financial information a reasonable time before the sale.[12] The precise nature of the disclosure depends on the organizational nature of the issuer, the size of the offering, and whether the issuer is subject to the reporting requirements of the Exchange Act.[13] There are no specific disclosure requirements applicable to a Rule 504 offering unless the offering uses a form of general solicitation, as discussed above. Neither Rule 505 nor Rule 504 offerings require the issuer to determine whether any investor has the sophistication required to assess the risks and merits of the investment; but whereas Rule 505 limits the number of non-accredited investors and permits general solicitation if certain disclosure requirements are met, Rule 504 does not.

One advantage of a Regulation D offering is that civil liability under Section 12(a)(2) of the Securities Act, which makes issuers liable for certain material misstatements and omissions in a prospectus,

---

[10] *See Eliminating the Prohibition against General Solicitation and General Advertising in Rule 506 and Rule 144A*, Release No. 33-9415, *available at* https://www.sec.gov/rules/final/2013/33-9415.pdf.
[11] *See* Regulation D, Rule 506(c)(2)(ii).
[12] *See* Regulation D, Rule 502(b)(1).
[13] *See* Regulation D, Rule 502(b)(2).

does not apply to private offerings. In *Gustafson v. Alloyd Co.*, the U.S. Supreme Court held that the liability provisions of Section 12(a)(2) do not apply to private sales.[14] Accordingly, investors in Regulation D offerings generally may assert federal securities law claims only under section 10(b) and Rule 10b-5 under the Exchange Act.[15] Rule 10b-5 liability requires a showing of intent to defraud or reckless indifference to the truth, which is a higher burden than the reasonable care standard of Section 12(a)(2).

For each offering under Regulation D, the issuer must provide the SEC a notice of sale by filing the information required by Form D within 15 days after the first sale. In addition, U.S. state securities laws (or "Blue Sky Laws") apply to the offer of sale of securities to investors in the relevant state, unless the securities are "covered securities" under Section 18(b)(4) of the Securities Act. Securities offered under Rule 506 qualify as "covered securities" of the Securities Act and are therefore exempt from state registration requirements. However, almost every state in which a Rule 506 offering or sale is made requires a notice filing and payment of a filing fee, even if the transactions are exempt from state regulation.[16] Usually the states accept Form D in satisfaction of the notice filing, although some states require a supplemental form. Note that securities offered and sold under Rules 504 and 505 are not "covered securities," and are therefore not exempt from state securities law regulations.

Finally, issuers should exercise reasonable care to assure that securities sold under Regulation D are not sold to an underwriter within the meaning of Section 2(a)(11) of the Securities Act (i.e., a purchase with a view to distribution). An exemption applies to offerings made under Rule 504 if the same requirements are met that apply to Rule 504 offerings that use general solicitation.[17]

---

[14] 513 U.S. 561 (1995).

[15] Note that a widely circulated private offering memorandum might not qualify as a "private offering." *See* Sloane Overseas Fund, Ltd. v. Sapiens International Corp. 941 F. Supp. 1369 (S.D.N.Y. 1996).

[16] Note that some attorneys take the view that in New York State private offerings are exempt from notice requirements.

[17] *See* Regulations D, Rule 502(d); *see supra* at 64.

b. Regulation S

Film investors are located in many jurisdictions around the world. Regulation S offers a useful exemption from the U.S. securities registration requirements to offerings that are conducted outside the United States. Such offerings must be made to persons outside the United States without any directed selling efforts in the United States. If the issuer is a U.S. entity or if there is U.S. market interest in the securities, then additional offering restrictions apply.[18]

c. Crowdfunding as an Alternative Equity Model for Lower Budget Films

Until the spring of 2016, crowdfunding took the form of donations. No return of or on a crowdfunding "investment" was offered so as to avoid the legal consequences of offering an investment contract. A few high profile films were partially financed in this manner, including *Wish I Was Here* by Zach Braff, which raised over $3,000,000 on Kickstarter. In lieu of a financial return, "backers" who contributed money received various privileges based on the size of the donation, including access to inside material, messages from stars, invitations to screenings of the film and other promotions. Effective May 16, 2016, Congress and the SEC have provided a means of crowdfunding to sell securities, provided that offers and sales comply with newly added Section 4(a)(6) of the Securities Act and Regulation Crowdfunding.

Crowdfunding offerings under Section 4(a)(6) may not exceed $1,000,000 during the 12-month period preceding the date of sale. In addition, the aggregate amount sold to any investor under Section 4(a)(6) during the 12-month period preceding the transaction cannot exceed a specified sum, which is tied to the annual income or net worth of the investor.[19] Further, to take advantage of the exemption, the issuer must be organized in the United States and cannot be an Exchange Act reporting company, an investment company under the Investment Company Act of 1940 or an excluded investment company under Section 3(b) or 3(c) of the Investment Company Act.

---

[18] *See* Regulation S, Rules 901-905.

[19] If either the annual income or net worth of such investor is less than $100,000, then the aggregate sales in the 12-month period may not exceed the greater of the greater of $2,000 or 5 percent of the annual income or net worth of such investor. If the annual income or net worth is $100,000 or more, then aggregate sales in the 12-month period cannot exceed 10 percent of such investor's annual income or net worth, capped at $100,000.

Regulation Crowdfunding also requires certain disclosures by issuers to investors and the filing of Form C with the SEC.[20] Issuers are also required to update the offering document during the offering period to disclose material changes and provide information on the issuer's progress towards reaching the target-offering amount. In addition, issuers relying on the Regulation Crowdfunding exemption are required to file an annual report with the Commission and provide it to investors.[21]

Regulation Crowdfunding requires the offering to be conducted through a registered broker-dealer or "funding portal," which is a new type of SEC registrant. The relevant intermediary must facilitate the offer and sale of the crowdfunded securities, provide communication channels to permit discussions about offerings on its platform, make available information about the issuer and the offering, provide investors with educational materials, and take measures to reduce the risk of fraud.[22] Meanwhile, the intermediaries are prohibited from offering investment advice or making recommendations, soliciting purchases or sales of securities offered on its platform, and handling investor funds.[23]

Given the limited amount of capital that can be raised under Regulation Crowdfunding, coupled with the disclosure obligations and the required use of a registered broker-dealer or funding platform to carry out the offering, it remains to be seen whether issuers will embrace the new crowdfunding exemption as a cost-effective means of raising capital for film productions.

---

[20] *See Crowdfunding*, Release No. 33-9974, *available at* https://www.sec.gov/rules/final/2015/33-9974.pdf. Disclosures required by the final rule include: (i) Information about officers and directors and owners of 20 percent or more of the issuer; (ii) A description of the issuer's business and the use of proceeds from the offering; (iii) The price to the public of the securities or the method for determining the price; (iv) The target offering amount, the deadline to reach the target offering amount, and whether the issuer will accept investments in excess of the target offering amount; (v) Certain related-party transactions; (vi) A discussion of the issuer's financial condition; and (vii) Financial statements of the issuer that are, depending on the amount offered and sold during a 12-month period, accompanied by information from the issuer's tax returns, reviewed by an independent public accountant, or audited by an independent auditor. An issuer relying on these rules for the first time would be permitted to provide reviewed rather than audited financial statements, unless financial statements of the issuer are available that have been audited by an independent auditor.

[21] *See id.*
[22] *See id.*
[23] *See id.*

3.4. SECURITY

The lenders' security package is a critical part of independent film financing. Generally, if the borrower of the production funds cannot repay the production loans, the lenders' recourse is limited to the collateral that comprises the producing and licensing structure of the film. Rarely do lenders have general recourse to a producer's assets unrelated to the film, although such recourse may arise on low budget projects when no completion bond is in effect. In such a case, producers may be required to bond the film with personal liability for overspend or the failure to complete and deliver the film on time. In any case, virtually no financing from a secured lender will be forthcoming until the lender is satisfied that its interest in the film collateral is secured and perfected according to its rights in and to the film collateral.

Each lender's security package is generally comprised of (i) security agreements with the borrower, intermediary licensing entities and production services companies that have commissioned any part of the production of the film or otherwise hold rights in the film, (ii) stock or membership interest pledge agreements with the borrower and/or licensor of the film and (iii) documentation necessary to perfect, protect and enforce the foregoing rights, such as UCC-1 financing statements and authorizations to file security, copyright mortgages, powers of attorney, powers of sale, deposit account control agreements, the sales agent interparty agreement, laboratory pledgeholder agreements, intercreditor agreements and licensee interparty agreements and notices of assignment. The principal elements of the security package are discussed below.

3.4.1. Security Agreements

The core of a lender's security package are the security agreements. The essential purpose of the security agreement is to grant the film financier a security interest in and lien on the film and its related property to secure the repayment of the money advanced under the loan agreements. A security interest is a property interest that gives the grantee the right to take possession of and license, sell or otherwise turn to account in an extra-judicial process the property that is subject to such interest following an uncured event of default with respect to a secured obligation. Generally, development financiers, pre-production lenders, mezzanine lenders and senior lenders are secured parties, while equity investors are unsecured.

Naturally, the borrower of the production money will execute a security agreement for the benefit of the respective lenders. Out of concern for hidden liabilities that could interfere with the lenders' rights in the film collateral, film financing structures are typically set up with a newly formed production SPV that borrows the production funds to produce or commission the production of the film and whose sole property will be the film project.

Multiple additional security agreements are usually necessary to create a comprehensive security package because property interests in the film may be owned on different levels of the film's commissioning and licensing structure. Any entity in the production and licensing structure of the film with a property interest in the film other than distributors will be required to grant a security interest in its film-related assets to the secured lenders. For example, often tax incentives that support the film's budget require production funds to be spent by a production company that is organized under the laws of the local jurisdiction that provides such incentives; meanwhile, the licensing entity may sit in different jurisdiction.

Regardless of where the rights sit, or the jurisdiction in which production, post-production or co-production services are performed, each entity with a role in commissioning, producing or licensing the film will enter into a security agreement with each of the secured lenders. The collective security induces the lenders to make the production loans by granting them a security interest in the assets necessary to complete, deliver and license the film in the event of a borrower default.

Security agreements are also the means by which lenders obtain critical affirmative and negative covenants from production services companies that are not otherwise in contractual privity with them. These production services companies are beneficiaries of the lenders' advances to the production, but without a security agreement, the lenders lack assurance that their claims to the film assets following an event of default under the loan agreements would prevail over the claims of the production services companies to the same assets. In the security agreement, lenders require the subordination of the production services company's rights in the film assets, together with a standstill guarantee vis-à-vis the lender's exercise of its rights in the film assets.

Further, the lender's security agreement with a production services company that is commissioned to create a portion of the film will provide that such company will:

- produce the film in strict accordance with the production services agreement and in accordance with the approved budget, screenplay and production schedule;
- not grant any person an interest in collateral proceeds that is not approved by the lender;
- perform its services as a work for hire and stipulate that it has no copyright interest in the film or lien on any of the film assets, and agree that if it is found to have any such copyright interest that it assigns all such rights to the commissioning entity;
- deliver all pre-print materials to the laboratory approved by the lender; and
- not exhibit the film for anyone not involved in the production of the film.

Additionally, the security agreement will provide that an event of default under the loan agreement will cause a default under the security agreement and permit the lender to exercise all available remedies with respect to the collateral.

If the licensing entity for the film does not also borrow the production loans, then the licensing entity will enter into a security agreement with the lenders in which it will grant a security interest in the film collateral and make relevant representations, warranties and covenants. Such representations, warranties and covenants would typically be found in the loan agreement if the licensor is also the borrower of the production funds. For example, the licensor of the film will agree not to make or permit to be made any modification to the elements of the film that are agreed under the sales agency agreement, the licensing intermediary agreements, the distribution agreements, or the completion guaranty without the prior written consent of the lender, or to license the film on terms other than those approved by the relevant lender or to make unauthorized modifications to any distribution agreements.

3.4.2. Cross-Border Security Issues

Of paramount importance to a secured film financier is the ability to enforce its security interest, not only against the debtor, but also against third parties seeking satisfaction of their own claims against the same debtor. Because the film collateral and the respective parties who grant security interests in the film collateral may be located in different jurisdictions, care should be taken to ensure that the respective security agreements comply with the applicable law of the jurisdiction in which the interests will need to be enforced.

A security interest is a property interest; only lawful interests in property are enforceable. To be lawful, the interest must comply with the law of the jurisdiction in which enforcement of the security interest is sought, which often involves a complicated application of principles of conflicts of law. The manner in which a security interest is created and perfected varies from country to country. In many jurisdictions around the world, including the Unites States, a secured party can only achieve a priority security interest by "perfecting" the security interest ahead of other creditors through compliance with the requirements of a national registration or recording system. Because interests in property are typically governed by the law of the jurisdiction of the situs of the property, the law applicable to the security agreement and the creation of the security interests must be compatible with the law of the territory in which such security interest ultimately will need to be enforced. If the laws in these jurisdictions differ, a second set of local law security agreements should be agreed to ensure the interest is locally enforceable and that conflicts of law principles do not result in the application of law with which the lender has not complied.

Accordingly, lenders must identify foreign entities with a potential interest in the film, evaluate the nature and location of that interest and consider how to create and perfect a security interest in the relevant property. This typically requires an evaluation of the local law of the jurisdiction in which a production services company or other entity involved in the creation or licensing of the film is located. Of particular concern is how such local jurisdiction would apply its conflicts of law principles to the local enforcement of a security interest created under foreign law, or to enforcement of a foreign judgment or arbitral award.

Absent a violation of fundamental public policy or mandatory law, and assuming local jurisdictional requirements are met, courts generally will apply the choice of law of the parties under contract (*lex contractus*) to interpret the substantive provisions of contract as long as there is a reasonable relationship between the choice of law and the parties.[24] However, notwithstanding the general application of lex contractus, mandatory local law may apply to the use or enforcement of local interests in property – particularly in intellectual property, such as copyright. Therefore, enforcement of the terms of a security agreement governing foreign property in a foreign jurisdiction may result in the application of foreign law to substantive elements of the security contract, such as whether an enforceable interest exists, and the nature of the remedies that may be had following a breach, while other elements purely concerning the contract like its interpretation and validity would be governed by the lex contractus.[25]

The manner of creating an enforceable security interest, particularly in copyright, differs across countries. Copyright in a single original work is governed by the respective substantive laws of each country around the world on a territorial basis. For example, the proper recordation with the U.S. Copyright Office of a copyright mortgage over the global copyright in a film has no direct bearing on the enforcement of the foreign copyrights in foreign lands unless a treaty or the conflict of law provisions of that foreign land recognizes the application of U.S. copyright law.[26]

---

[24] *See, e.g.,* Welsbach Elec. v. MasTec N. Am., 7 N.Y.3d 624, 629 (2006) ("Generally, courts will enforce a choice-of-law clause so long as the chosen law bears a reasonable relationship to the parties or the transaction").

[25] *See* The Final Report to the Study on Intellectual Property and the Conflict of Laws (2000), a study commissioned by the European Commission discussing the laws applicable to intellectual property and contract in various countries around the world *available at* http://ec.europa.eu/internal_market/copyright/docs/studies/etd1999b53000 e16_en.pdf.

[26] The fact that a foreign forum might not apply U.S. law to the provisions of an agreement governed by U.S. law that transfers a security interest in global copyright as a matter of practice should not cause the exclusion of foreign copyright from such agreement (broader assignments are as a rule better than narrower assignments). Indeed, the grant may still be effective under applicable foreign law, and in some cases U.S. courts will provide remedies for breaches in foreign territories where the primary infringement occurs is the United States. *See, e.g.,* Update Art Inc. v. Modiin Pubs., 843 F.2d 1061 (2d Cit. 1988); Gaste v. Kaisermann, 863 F.2d 1061 (2d Cir. 1988). Nevertheless, if the film is commissioned or produced abroad, research should be done to ensure that requirements of the relevant foreign law are met to create an enforceable and perfected security interest in the foreign copyright.

The extent to which a forum country's law will be applied to enforce an interest in copyright (or any other property interest) in the forum country will depend on the private international law of the forum country. The law applicable in one country may be the forum in which protection is sought (*lex loci protectionis*), in another country it may be the law of the country where the damaging act has been committed (*lex delicti*), in another country it may be the law of the country where the work is originally published (*lex originis*), and still yet in a few countries that have not acceded to the Berne Convention, the Universal Copyright Convention or another international copyright convention or treaty, the interest might not be recognized at all.

An examination of private international law is beyond the scope of this Chapter, but it is critical to understand that its application can vary widely around the world and can result in very different outcomes. To the extent that countries are members of the Berne Convention, Article 5(2) has generally been interpreted to require the application of the law of the country in which protection is claimed.[27] This is the principal of national treatment, which is in keeping with Article 9(2)(a), and which provides, "ownership of copyright in a cinematographic work shall be a matter for legislation in the country where protection is claimed." The extent to which a local forum would permit parties to deviate from this principle by mutual agreement and recognize the application of a different foreign law with respect to assignment of property interests that arise under local law should be evaluated by qualified local counsel – both in the jurisdiction that is chosen to govern the assignment of the copyright and in the jurisdiction where the copyright would need to be protected.

---

[27] Article 5(2) of the Berne Convention provides in relevant part, "...apart from the provisions of this Convention, the extent of protection, as well as the means of redress afforded to the author to protect his rights, shall be governed exclusively by the laws of the country where protection is claimed." Noted copyright scholars have concluded that the application of the law of the country in which enforcement is sought complies with the principles of the Berne Convention. *See* The Final Report to the Study on Intellectual Property and the Conflict of Laws (2000), a study commissioned by the European Commission *available at* http://ec.europa.eu/internal_market/ copyright/docs/studies/ etd1999b53000e16_en.pdf; *but see* Graeme B. Dinwoodie, Conflicts and International Copyright Litigation: The Role of International Norms *available at* http://www.kentlaw. edu/depts/ipp/publications/MaxPlanck2004-05.pdf (stating that copyright scholars have held it is by no means clear that Article 5 of the Berne Convention requires a particular choice of law rule).

In addition to copyright, private international law may recognize the creation of an enforceable security interest under foreign law in tangible and other personal property in a local forum, even if the nature of the security and manner of attachment differs from local law. However, generally such interest would only be recognized to the extent (i) the provisions of the foreign law are not contrary to mandatory local law, (ii) are deemed to be substantive and not procedural and (iii) do not violate the fundamental public policy of the local forum. The risk of inadvertently impairing or voiding a security interest that was properly attached and perfected under the law of one country (e.g., the United States) by failing to comply with the mandatory law, public policy or procedure in another country (e.g., the United Kingdom) in which the security interest must be enforced can only be adequately assessed by special foreign counsel.

To ensure that an enforceable security interest is granted over an ownership interest in the film arising in a different country, typically a U.S. secured film financier will require a security agreement and copyright mortgage under U.S. law with a U.S. forum in addition to counterpart security agreements under the local law of each jurisdiction in which any other entity with a property interest in the film is operating. This "belt-and-suspenders" approach maximizes the potential remedies and enforcement venues for the lenders that must rely on an enforceable security interest to protect their investment. Addressing the foreign legal issues surrounding security can add a significant strain to the budget and should be evaluated when considering where to shoot and edit the film.

To the extent that domestic law is chosen to govern a security agreement with a foreign counterparty and both jurisdictions are signatories to the New York Convention (i.e., the United Nations Commission on International Trade Law's Convention on the Recognition and Enforcement of Foreign Arbitral Awards (New York, 1958) (the "New York Convention"), it is prudent to consider arbitration as a means of resolving any disputes arising in connection with the security agreement. Foreign arbitral awards are judicially recognized and enforced more efficiently than foreign judgments in jurisdictions that are signatories to the New York Convention. In such case, the forum for the arbitration should be in the country whose law governs the security agreement. All relevant treaties and bilateral agreements should be considered before determining the applicable law and forum for arbitration.

3.4.3. The Creation of a Security Interest in the United States

Under Article 9 of the Uniform Commercial Code, which has been substantially adopted by all 50 U.S. states, a security interest attaches to specific collateral when it becomes enforceable.[28] A security interest becomes enforceable under Article 9 by the convergence of three legal criteria.

First, the security interest should be memorialized in a written record and authenticated (i.e., signed) by the "debtor," which is the party granting the security interest.[29] An executed security agreement satisfies this requirement. The collateral must be described in sufficient detail to reasonably identify it.[30] A broad description such as "all assets whether now existing or hereafter acquired and all accessions thereto and proceeds therefrom" might be used to describe the collateral of a production SPV whose universe of property is the film collateral. If, however, the film collateral constitutes only a portion of the debtor's property, then the UCC definitions of property as related to the identified film project are often used to sufficiently describe the collateral.

Second, value must be given by the secured party.[31] Value need not be given directly to the debtor to give effect to the debtor's grant of security interest; for example, a production services company that grants a security interest to a production lender might receive payment for its services from the production SPV's borrowed funds as opposed to receiving funds directly from the lender.[32] The recitals of the

---

[28] *See* U.C.C. §9-203(b). Unless otherwise noted, this Chapter addresses the law as embodied in the amended Uniform Commercial Code (2010) and not as actually implemented by the separate states.

[29] A security interest may also attach to certain property through possession or control. For this reason the laboratories that hold the physical elements of the film acknowledge in the laboratory pledgeholder agreement that they hold such elements for the benefit of the lenders (*see* U.C.C. §9-13(c)).

[30] *See* U.C.C. §9-108.

[31] *See* U.C.C. §9-203(b).

[32] *See, e.g.,* In Re Valle Feed of Farmington, Inc. 80 B.R. 150, 152-153 (Bankr. E.D. Mo. 1987) ("It is true that under Missouri law, a security interest cannot attach unless value has been given.... It is not true, however, that the entity whose assets are pledged must receive the consideration for doing so; for in Missouri, 'a person gives `value' for rights if he acquires them . . . in return for any consideration sufficient to support a simple contract'").

relevant security agreement should contain statements detailing how the value given by the lender is related to the collateral in which the lender receives a security interest from the debtor. If the link is tenuous, then the grant of security should be made by accommodation.

Third, the debtor must have the right, or the power to transfer the right, in the collateral.[33] The grant of a security interest is a conveyance of a property interest; the debtor can only convey property that it has the legal power to convey. Regardless of how the collateral is described in the security agreement, the secured party will only take an interest in the underlying collateral to the extent the debtor has power to convey it. For this reason, in addition to the representations and warranties of the debtor with respect to the collateral, the vetting of the chain of title in the film is a crucial element of lender due diligence.

Once these three requirements are met, the security interest attaches and becomes effective.

3.4.4. Perfection of a Security Interest under Article 9

Under Article 9 of the UCC, the attachment of a security interest establishes the creditor's interest in the property, but it does not establish priority over other creditors with a competing security interest in the same property. For a secured film financier to establish a priority interest in the film collateral it must "perfect" its security interest ahead of other creditors or it must contractually subordinate other interests in the collateral by means of an intercreditor or interparty agreement. Additionally, by perfecting a security interest the lender can preserve its lien in the collateral if the debtor enters bankruptcy protection.

Under Article 9, the manner of perfecting a security interest is determined by the nature of the underlying personal property in which the security interest is attached. A secured lender should perfect its security interest in the film collateral governed by Article 9 of the UCC by (i) filing a financing statement with respect to all personal property related to the film, (ii) taking "control" over deposit accounts by means of a deposit account control agreement, which is the sole means of perfecting a security interest in a deposit account, and (iii) notifying insurance policy holders of the grant of the security interest, which is

---

[33] *See* U.C.C. §9-203(b).

the sole means of perfecting a security interest in proceeds under a policy of insurance that is not a health care insurance receivable.[34]

A secured lender must file the financing statement in the jurisdiction where the debtor is located to properly perfect under Article 9.[35] For this purpose, entities registered under the laws of any U.S. state (like a production SPV in the form of a limited liability company or corporation) are deemed to be located in the state in which they are formed.[36]

If a debtor resides abroad or maintains its sole place of business or its chief executive office outside the United States (like a foreign production services company), compliance with the registration and recording procedures of the law of the debtor's jurisdiction may be required to perfect the security interest governed by Article 9. Article 9 requires compliance with foreign recording procedures if the laws of the foreign jurisdiction "generally require" information concerning a non-possessory security interest to be made "generally available" in a filing, recording or registration system in order to establish priority over another lien creditor.[37]

In many foreign jurisdictions, such as Germany, there is no counterpart to the system of recording provided within the meaning of UCC §9-307(b). In such cases, to properly perfect under Article 9, the foreign debtor is deemed to be located in Washington, D.C.[38] Because the criteria for mandatory foreign filing procedures are somewhat

---

[34] See UCC §§ 9-308 – 316. For purposes of Article 9, film assets are generally comprised of: goods (the physical elements of the film and related materials, which will be held to order by a laboratory); accounts (the right to amounts payable under license agreements and insurance policies); deposit accounts; letter-of-credit rights (to the extent such supporting obligations exist); general intangibles (the intellectual property and rights to receive payment under the financing documentation), and the proceeds of such collateral.

[35] Note that if the debtor signs an authorization to file a financing statement such authorization is an "authenticated record" within the meaning of UCC §9-509(a)(1), which coupled with UCC §9-502(d) entitles a lender to file a financing statement *before* the security interest has attached. For purposes of priority, the date of filing or perfection is relevant, not the date of attachment (see UCC §322(a)(1)). Accordingly, to protect and enhance a secured position against competing secured claimants, lenders often obtain authorization from the debtor to file the financing statement before the security interest attaches as a matter of law (e.g., before the release of the production loans).

[36] See UCC §9-307(e).
[37] See UCC § 9-307(b).
[38] See id.

vague, to perfect a security interest governed by Article 9 in the property of a foreign debtor, a secured film financier should file a financing statement in the District of Columbia in addition to any potentially required foreign registrations. As discussed above, it is important to note that compliance with U.S. law does not mean that the security interest will be enforceable against collateral located in a foreign jurisdiction. If the debtor has few or no assets in the United States, or if the primary collateral is in a foreign territory, it becomes important to evaluate the enforceability of the security interest in the applicable foreign jurisdiction.

Not all relevant film collateral is subject to Article 9. While Article 9 covers an interest in insurance proceeds, it does not cover an interest in the underlying insurance policies that might be used to insure the production. To perfect an interest in such insurance policies, a film financier must be added to the policy as a loss payee or additional insured. Additionally, U.S. copyright is governed exclusively by federal law.

3.4.5. Perfection of Security Interests in U.S. Copyright: The Copyright Mortgage

With respect to undertakings commenced after January 1, 1978, all legal and equitable rights that fall within the scope of federal copyright are exclusively governed by federal law.[39] Additionally, courts have ruled that interests closely tied to copyright fall within the exclusive parameter of federal law.[40] To perfect a security interest in rights under U.S. copyright, secured parties must comply with federal law to the extent there is applicable federal legislation.

Federal statute governs the recordation of transfers of U.S. copyright ownership.[41] Under federal law a transfer of copyright ownership includes mortgages and other hypothecations, like the grant of a security interest. Federal law does not, however, legislate with respect to the grant and attachment of a security interest in rights under copyright. The UCC, as implemented by the various states, or such

---

[39] See 17 U.S.C. §301.
[40] See, e.g.,, National Peregrine, Inc. v. Capitol Fed. Sav. & Loan Ass'n, 116 B.R. 194, 199 (C.D. Cal. 1990); In re Avalon Software, Inc., 209 B.R. 517, 521 (Bankr. D. Ariz. 1997).
[41] See 17 U.S.C. § 205.

other law as is applicable to the transfer of the security interest, governs how a security interest in copyright is transferred and created. Federal law governs the manner in which a security interest in U.S. copyright is recorded and perfected.[42]

Film financiers that take a security interest in U.S. copyright in a film and its underlying works should follow the UCC (as adopted in the state of the debtor's location) with respect to meeting the requirements necessary to attach a security interest in U.S. copyright and follow federal law with respect to the registration and recording procedures required to perfect the security interest. Case law on this topic is not uniform, however, so secured parties should perfect their interests in rights under copyright by filing a UCC-1 financing statement in the jurisdiction where the debtor is located and by recording the transfer with the U.S. Copyright Office.

A copyright mortgage is a document that creates a lien on and a security interest in U.S. copyright. Federal copyright law provides that recordation of a document in the U.S. Copyright Office gives all persons constructive notice of the facts stated in the recorded document if two conditions are satisfied. First, the document must specifically identify the work to which it pertains so that a reasonable search under the title or registration number of the work would reveal the interest after it is recorded. Second, the relevant work must also be registered.[43]

As between two copyright mortgages recorded with an interest in the same work, the one that was executed first prevails if it was duly recorded within one month after its execution in the United States or within two months after its execution outside the United States, or at any later time before recordation of the later transfer.[44] The later transfer will prevail (subject to the foregoing rules) if it is recorded first in the proper manner, in good faith and for valuable consideration (or on the basis of a binding promise to pay royalties) without notice of the earlier transfer.[45]

3.4.6. Stock and LLC Membership Pledge Agreements

Often lenders will require that they be the beneficiary of a stock or limited liability company membership pledge agreement (or similar pledge agreement), pursuant to which the owners of the licensing entity

---

[42] *See* In Re Avalon Software, Inc. 209 B.R. 517, 520 (Bankr.D.Ariz 1997).
[43] *See* 17 U.S.C. 205(c).
[44] *See* 17 U.S.C. 205(d).
[45] *See id.*

of the film will assign their interests in the licensing entity to the lenders as security for the repayment of the production loans. There are a number of issues worth mentioning with respect to these agreements.

First, if the beneficiary of the pledge is a foreign entity without a U.S. trade or business, it should carefully examine the tax consequences of foreclosure on any such pledge. If the pledged interests are in a pass-through tax vehicle, like a limited liability company, a foreign person's control over such interests may result in the operation of a U.S. trade or business, which can have unfavorable U.S. tax consequences for the foreign secured party. Any such issues should be reviewed by special tax counsel.

Second, because control takes precedence over filing with respect to a security interest in securities, to perfect a security interest in investment property, the secured party will require the securities to be certificated, endorsed and delivered. Specific procedures should be followed in order to meet the statutory definition of control, as specified in Article 8 of the UCC. In order to ensure that delivery is valid, if the issuer is a limited liability company, the organizational documents of the issuer of the security should provide that (i) each of its limited liability interests are a "security" within the meaning of Article 8 of the UCC and will be governed by the Article 8 of the UCC and (ii) so long as any pledge of any membership interests is in effect, such section will not be amended until all security interests granted in any membership interest of the debtor have been terminated.

Finally, it is worth noting that after an event of default, lenders who exercise a high degree of control over a borrower through exercise of pledged ownership interests should consider the potential application of the doctrine of equitable subordination that could arise in a bankruptcy proceeding of such entity. The doctrine of equitable subordination applies to a lender that takes a high degree of control over a borrower, requiring the lender to also assume fiduciary duties that officers and directors would owe to the entity, such as the exercise of reasonable care. Failure to exercise such care may result in the equitable subordination, or stripping, of the secured party's priority liens in a bankruptcy proceeding of the borrower. If a lender forecloses on pledged securities of the borrower and exercises voting rights in the borrower, the lender should ensure that the day-to-day affairs and business decisions of the issuer remain in the exclusive domain of the appointed managers, who maintain their independent judgment.[46]

3.4.7. Notices of Assignment, Interparty and Intercreditor Security Documentation

Perfected and enforceable security interests are requisite to the release of the production loans, but standing alone they may be insufficient to protect the lenders' interests in the film. Under Article 9, a provision in a security agreement that prevents the unauthorized transfer of rights in the film will not prevent a license or sale that is contrary to such restriction (though it would result in a default under the agreement).[47] Moreover, it is impractical and cost-prohibitive for lenders to perfect a security interest in the intangible assets of the film in each territory in which it might be licensed, and even so, such perfection might not secure the interest against bona fide licensees. The lenders and the completion guarantor may therefore require other additional documentation to further protect their rights in the collateral.

3.4.7.1. Notices of Assignment

Lenders require the licensing entity, sales agent, distributors and the completion guarantor to enter into notices and acknowledgments of assignment, or "NOAs," with respect to rights licensed or granted under distribution agreements in order to secure their loans, which are collateralized by the distribution agreements. NOAs serve to put distributors on notice of the secured parties' interests in the licensor's rights under the distribution agreements. In addition, the NOAs will specify:

- when the receipts promised under the distribution agreement become due and payable (notwithstanding any difference in terms provided for under the distribution agreement);

---

[46] *See* Citibank 828 F.2d 686 (11th Cir. 1987), *cert. denied*, 484 U.S. 1062 (1988) ("[W]hen the pledged stock represents a controlling interest and the pledgee becomes involved in the management of the company . . . its duty of reasonable care follows it and attaches to all its activities.") *citing* Empire Life Ins. Co. of America v. Valdak Corp., 468 F.2d 330, 335 (5th Cir.1972).

[47] See U.C.C. §9-401(b) ("An agreement between the debtor and secured party which prohibits a transfer of the debtor's rights in collateral or makes the transfer a default does not prevent the transfer from taking effect").

- when the secured parties will release or subordinate their security interests in the rights licensed under the distribution agreement to the rights of the distributor;

- that such receipts are payable directly to the lender or the collection account and may only be satisfied by payment in such manner; and

- that certain risks associated with potential defaults by the licensor under the relevant license agreements are allocated to the distributor.

Specifically, the NOA must address certain concepts to render the receipts owed under the relevant distribution agreement "bankable," or capable of being bonded and re-financed. To be "bankable," a distributor must agree to pay the minimum guarantee when the licensor effects "delivery" of a film that meets basic agreed specifications, such as its length, duration, rating, aspect ratio, and any essential elements, such as a principal cast member or the director, all of which must have been bonded.

Under the NOA, a distributor may not refuse to accept delivery or pay the minimum guarantee if the film is "delivered" by the outside delivery date according to the agreed specifications, notwithstanding any other requirements that were agreed concerning the film under the distribution agreement. Typically, "delivery" is defined in the NOA as receipt by the distributor of a "notice of delivery" stating that the specifications are met, and the delivery materials are available to be ordered by the distributor. However, U.S. and large international distributors that pay significant minimum guarantees will only agree to pay the minimum guarantee once they have received and proofed whether the film's technical elements are of first class quality. In such case, the completion guarantor specifies which elements are sufficient to be accepted by the distributor to effect "delivery," notwithstanding the list of delivery materials required to be delivered under the distribution agreement.

Under the NOA, the provision of such bonded delivery materials will trigger payment of 90 to 95 percent of the minimum guarantee, and the balance of the minimum guarantee will become due once "complete delivery" of the remaining materials that were not bonded for "delivery" under the NOA are delivered to the distributor.

Further, to be bankable the NOA must provide clear protocol regarding the delivery procedures and the resolution of any disputes as to whether "delivery" has been duly effected. The completion guarantor will approve these procedures. If delivery fails under the NOA, as determined by an arbitrator in the event of a dispute, the completion guarantor will be required to pay the loss resulting from the failure to complete delivery in accordance with the terms of the completion guaranty.

The NOA will also include waiver language making it clear that the secured parties take only an assignment of rights and do not assume any liabilities in connection with the assigned rights. To further protect the secured parties' interests, the NOA typically specifies that notwithstanding anything to the contrary in the distribution agreement, the rights in the film will not vest in the distributor until the minimum guarantee owed thereunder is paid in full, and the distributor may not release the film until the minimum guarantee is paid in full. Such terms will be heavily negotiated with major U.S. distributors, who generally require that the rights granted under the distribution agreement vest upon execution of the distribution agreement. Such distributors also press for the ability to release the film once the bonded delivery payment is made (which, as noted above, typically comprises 90 to 95 percent of the minimum guarantee).

The terms of the NOA will modify the terms of the distribution agreement as between the secured parties and the distributor to the extent there is a conflict between the NOA and the terms of the distribution agreement, but the distributor will reserve its rights under the distribution agreement as against the licensor for any breaches of the distribution agreement. As a secured party, the completion guarantor will be a beneficiary of the NOA in a position subordinated to the lenders. Because lenders do not take delivery risk, the acceptance and agreement of the terms of such NOAs by the distributors form a critical piece of their security package for the film. As such, the pre-sale distributors will be required to execute NOAs as a condition to the closing of the production loans.

3.4.7.2. The Sales Agent Interparty Agreement

As discussed above, the production SPV/borrower, the sales agent, the financiers and the completion guarantor each have varying obligations and rights with respect to the film. For the benefit of the secured parties, a sales agent interparty agreement is agreed to regulate the areas in which respective interests overlap and potentially conflict. The sales agent interparty agreement modifies and amends the terms of the sales agency agreement to the extent there is conflict with the terms in the sales agent interparty agreement.

First, to avoid any uncertainty regarding the specifications of the film that are relevant to the finance plan and the completion bond, the parties will agree on the final version of the screenplay and production schedule, any essential elements and the criteria and procedures for replacement of principle cast and/or the director.

Second, to ensure that the parties are in agreement as to how the strike price will be funded and as to the respective parties' rights to cash generated from deposits and sales of the film, the agreement will set forth the order in which parties with the obligation to fund the film release their funds and the manner in which cash proceeds received from exploiting the rights in the film (such as distributor deposits and product placement revenue) will be directed. In addition, any deferral of the sales agent's rights to payment under the sales agency agreement as may be necessary to meet the strike price will be set forth in this agreement, as will the manner of recoupment.

Third, the agreement will ensure that the sales agency agreement will not be modified or terminated except under specific conditions. Usually the sales agent effects delivery to the distributors, which triggers the duty of the distributors to pay the minimum guarantees. Those receipts repay the debt used to produce, complete and deliver the film, which makes the concept of delivery of ultimate importance to the financing structure. Accordingly, the sales agent interparty agreement will provide a dispute resolution mechanism for disagreements that arise as to whether the film has been properly "delivered" to the sales agent. The sales agent will not be permitted to terminate the sales agency agreement unless delivery cannot be effected by a specified outside date. Additionally, the sales agent will acknowledge its approval of the film's chain-of-title so that it will not be able to refuse delivery on account of any deficiency with the chain-of-title of the film. The sales agent interparty agreement typically grants the controlling lender the right to terminate the sales agent upon the occurrence of specified events, such as the insolvency or default of the sales agent or the inability of the sales agent to sell a certain number of territories at or above the "take" price by an outside date.

Finally, the sales agent interparty agreement will address the parties' rights in the film and the relevant collateral. Notwithstanding the sales agent's rights to license or transfer rights in the film on behalf of the licensor under the sales agency agreement, the controlling lenders will be granted approval rights over the terms of distribution agreements and notices of assignment entered into by the sales agent with distributors in the territories comprising the controlling lenders' respective collateral. Further, the sales agent will be obligated to notify the lenders of any distributor defaults, pursue collections and provide the lenders upon request with financial information relating to the exploitation of the film. The sales agent's expenses incurred in carrying out these duties are generally recouped off the top of gross receipts after the residuals are paid, which will be memorialized in the collection account management agreement. However, the sales agent interparty agreement will provide for the subordination of the rights held by the completion guarantor and sales agent in the film to the lenders' priority interests in such rights.

3.4.7.3. Intercreditor Agreements

Often more than one lender will provide production finance secured by the same collateral. In addition, the completion guarantor will have a perfected security interest in the film collateral to secure any obligations arising under the completion guarantee. In order to regulate the rights of the respective creditors in the film collateral, these secured parties will enter into an intercreditor agreement under which their interests and priorities in the respective collateral are agreed (notwithstanding the order in which any such party may have perfected its interests therein). The creditors will also make covenants concerning the actions that each party may take, or agrees not to take, in the event of a default with respect to the collateral. The completion guarantor will subordinate its liens and right of payment to the film financiers.

If the guilds (e.g., SAG, WGA or DGA in the U.S., or their equivalents in other countries) are involved, they also will have a security interest in the film collateral in order to secure the obligations of the production to make the required residuals payments on worldwide, first-dollar gross receipts (excluding theatrical receipts). Each guild has a standard form of intercreditor and subordination agreement that it will require the financiers to sign unless an adequate residuals reserve has been budgeted and paid. From a lender's perspective, managing the guilds and residuals payments is a critical part of ensuring a workable finance plan. If a residuals reserve is budgeted, it may be possible to reverse the tables and have the guilds subordinate their rights in the collateral to the lender up to the extent of such reserve.

3.4.8. The Completion Guaranty

As noted previously in this Chapter, when financing the production of a film, the financiers generally do not take completion and delivery risk. In addition to requiring the execution of notices of assignment, lenders almost universally require the production and delivery of the film to be bonded by a reputable completion guarantor. The completion guarantor agrees to complete and deliver the film by an outside delivery date or pay to the beneficiary of the completion guaranty an agreed sum. Typically, the financiers will be entitled to receive the amount of their initial investment with interest, premia or financing fees in the event the film cannot be completed and delivered to specification. If the completion guarantor is required to make any such payment, then the completion guarantor will be subrogated to the rights of the financiers in the film. The completion guarantor will have the right to take over the film if necessary to complete delivery on time or ensure that the film stays on budget.

As a preliminary matter, the completion guarantor will not agree to provide a completion bond for a film until it has approved the chain of title, the budget, the script, the finance plan and the production schedule. The completion guarantor will also require inducement letters from the director and lead cast in which each represents that he or she has reviewed the script, the budget and the production schedule and can perform his or her required services on time and within the budget.

Prior to releasing the completion guaranty, the completion guarantor's fee must be paid and the strike price for the film must be fully funded. The strike price is the budgeted sum necessary to complete and deliver the film according to specification. Because the completion guarantor is paid to take completion risk, it can serve a valuable function by identifying potential issues that create risk for the production and focusing the producers' attention on elements necessary to meet the strike price and close the financing for the production. The completion guarantor will take a security interest and copyright mortgage in the film collateral and subordinate its lien and right to payment to the secured lenders.

3.4.9. Laboratory Pledgeholder Agreements

The physical elements of the film will be kept in the custody of a film laboratory or post production house to prevent piracy and damage and to ensure that access is granted only to those persons who have a right to access the film materials.

Because the custodian laboratory has physical possession of valuable film collateral, the lenders require that it enter into a laboratory pledgeholder agreement with the lenders, any production services companies commissioned to help create the film, the sales agent and the completion guarantor. The laboratory pledgeholder agreement will specify where the physical elements may be stored, acknowledge the lenders' priority interests in the physical elements of the film, agree that the controlling lender has the right to give instructions to the laboratory concerning its collateral upon delivery to the laboratory of an "exclusive control notice," and agree who may otherwise have access to the physical elements of the film.

Under the laboratory pledgeholder agreement the producers, the sales agent and approved distributors generally have access to the physical elements of the film unless and until the laboratory receives an exclusive control notice from one of the secured parties. An exclusive control notice would be delivered as part of a foreclosure on collateral following an event of default, or following a payment by the completion guarantor under the completion guarantee. After such time, the laboratory will take exclusive instruction from the issuer of such notice, or if there be two or more lenders, each of which has first ranking security with respect to specific film collateral, then from each such lender. The lenders' respective rights in the physical elements will be regulated under an intercreditor agreement.

3.4.10. The Collection Account Management Agreement

The collection account management agreement, or "CAMA," is the agreement under which the collection account manager, or "CAM," agrees to receive and hold in trust for distribution the gross receipts to which the licensor of the film is entitled. The CAM processes and distributes the receipts as agreed in the waterfall appended to the CAMA. The CAMA is a critical document designed to avoid disputes regarding entitlements to cash flows from the exploitation of the film.

Typically, the CAM will receive its fee (usually about 1% of gross receipts) off the top, followed by the sales agent's non-deferred commissions. The secured lenders will then recoup their investment and return, and the equity will follow. Once the equity has recouped its investment and return, the parties that deferred their fees for services will recoup their deferments with an agreed return. Once all deferred parties are recouped, the film begins to see a profit, and the parties with a backend position are paid according to their share of backend.

The variations on the foregoing schedule are limitless. Gross corridors may be added at different levels or with respect to different sources of receipts (such as domestic receipts only), and the CAMA will reflect alterations to the parties' respective recoupment positions that may have been agreed at the last minute to close the production financing. If the completion guarantor is required to pay money to complete and deliver the film, it will collect its loss after the obligations owed to the financiers have been paid in full.

The CAMA will also set forth how "net profits" are defined and distributed. Net profits payable with respect to an independent film are fairly straightforward. Unlike a studio definition, the net profits of an independent production are calculated based on the "gross receipts to production" that have already been reduced by all distributor reimbursable expenses and licensing or distribution fees. Further, there is generally no need to address calculations for recoupment of the negative cost and marketing. In the waterfall of gross receipts to the production, a line that references the financiers' and sales agent entitlements suffices to achieve this purpose. If a studio is financing a film, the defined entitlements of back-end participants in adjusted gross receipts is far more involved, because the starting point for the calculation is worldwide first dollar gross receipts, from which must be deducted the global distribution fees and expenses as well as the negative cost of the film, plus studio overhead and financing costs.

3.5. CONCLUSION

Film financing is challenging and immensely rewarding for those who appreciate being part of an artistic vision capable of impacting millions of people. Perhaps no other industry has an international reach of such depth while crossing so many legal disciplines. The ability to anticipate the legal issues that arise in connection with a film project is a valuable skill necessary to keep these complex projects on track, and a sound understanding of the legal mechanics and the various interests of the parties involved provides a solid foundation for arriving at a successful financial close. It is the hope of this author that this Chapter has helped to provide that understanding.

MOTION PICTURE FINANCE – ILLUSTRATIVE FORMS

- Gap-Senior Lender Loan and Security Agreement
- Mezzanine Financing Term Sheet Agreement (Early Stage)
- Notice of Assignment

— CHAPTER 4 —

INTRODUCTION TO TELEVISION

Ken Basin[*]

4.1. An Overview
4.2. Who Are the Players (and How Do They Interact)?
4.3. Online Video Distribution

4.1. AN OVERVIEW

Making television entertainment is a team sport. The process of developing, producing, and distributing original television programming is a collaboration among literally hundreds of individuals – producers, directors, writers, actors, artisans, craftspeople, drivers, and more. And behind those individuals are a series of executive teams employed by the studios and networks behind those shows – creative development executives who help craft the story and creative direction of a proposed series; creative current executives who foster the show's creative direction once in production; production executives who help set and manage budgets and translate a creative vision into a physical production plan; lawyers who help document agreements and identify and manage risks; accountants and finance executives who measure and manage money flows; research, marketing, and programming executives who help the show find an audience; distribution executives who monetize the produced show in other markets; and others.

Appreciating the roles played by the many individuals who contribute to the television industry (and the web of business and legal relationships that bind them) requires first understanding the overarching structure of the television industry. And, as a threshold matter, understanding that overarching structure starts with one key fact: that television, as a business, relies on a dual revenue model. In general, entertainment economics can be divided into two categories – "direct pay" and "advertiser-supported." The classic "direct pay" system is the theatrical feature film, in which viewers go to a movie

---

[*] **Ken Basin** is Sr. Vice President, Business Affairs for Paramount Television

theater and pay for a ticket in order to gain access to the product, with a one-to-one relationship between viewers and tickets. The classic "advertiser-supported" model is exemplified by terrestrial radio, in which entertainment is made freely available over the airwaves and collecting user fees is virtually impossible, so the money that makes the industry run comes from advertisers, who pay for the opportunity to convey their messages to customers.[1] The modern television ecosystem, however, features a combination of "direct pay" (in the form of transaction and subscription fees from viewers) and "ad support" (with advertising remaining a dominant presence on most television platforms). In the long term, regardless of its initial distribution platform, virtually every piece of television content produced today is made viable through a combination of "direct pay" and "ad-supported" revenues.

With that fact established, we can now turn our attention to the broad framework of the television industry, and the general categories of individuals and entities that comprise it.

4.2. WHO ARE THE PLAYERS (AND HOW DO THEY INTERACT)?

Who made the successful television series, *House of Cards*?

If you answered "Netflix," you would be wrong. Netflix exhibits *House of Cards* in the United States (and several other territories), but the show was actually produced (and owned) by a company called Media Rights Capital, which is known primarily for its feature films such as raunchy talking-bear comedy *Ted* (2012) and science fiction epic *Elysium* (2013). For *House of Cards*, Netflix acts in the role of a "network," while Media Rights Capital functions as a "studio" and "production company." This distinction is one of the centerpieces to understanding how television is created and monetized.

Like many other industries, the television industry is comprised of a series of independent actors with specialized roles who engage in

---

[1] The classic, pre-cable broadcast television industry of the mid-twentieth century United States was similarly a fully advertiser-supported business. An alternative model can be found in the United Kingdom, where the government taxes television owners to support public broadcasting services. However, this public taxation system does not amount to a traditional "direct pay" system, in that television owners are taxed equally based on television ownership, without regard for the specific programming (or volume of programming) those device owners actually consume.

transactions by which, collectively, they develop, produce, market, and distribute a product to consumers around the world. And, as in many other industries, the precise role played by all of the players is sometimes opaque to the consuming public. The following chart visualizes the major categories of entities in the television industry, and the essential types of agreements that bind them to one another:

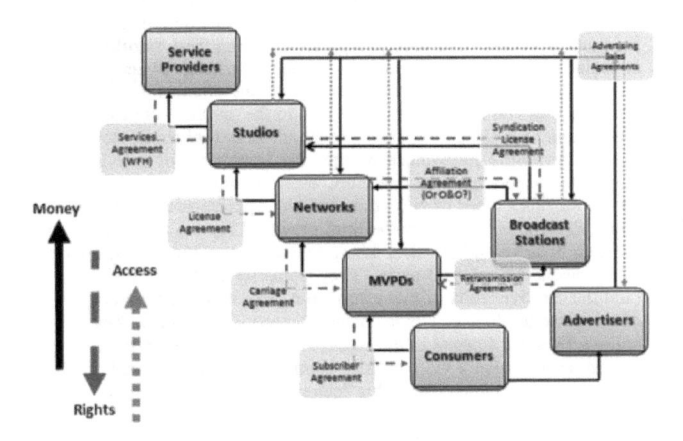

Chapter 4 – Chart One

In the chart above, money generally flows upwards (via the solid black lines); intellectual property rights generally flow downwards (via the dark grey dashed lines); and access to the consumer (both via traditional advertising and more contemporary methods, such as product integration) is provided to advertisers (via the light grey dotted lines).

4.2.1. Service Providers (Talent)

Actors, writers, directors, producers, and other service providers – which, for purposes of this chapter, will be referred to collectively as "talent"[2] – are the day-to-day workers of the television industry. While the names and/or faces of the most prominent of these individuals may be familiar to viewers at home, most of these individuals are largely unknown to the general public (though, of course, many aspire to greater recognition and acclaim).

The day-to-day work of developing and producing television content is generally performed by dozens or hundreds of freelance workers who are engaged to lend their expertise and labor to the production process. The most recognizable among these "workers" are so-called "above-the-line" talent – actors, writers, directors, and producers who centrally influence and guide the creative process, and whose names and images may be central to the public's interest in and recognition of a piece of content. In broad, structural terms, however, these high-profile individuals occupy the same type of role as that played by editors, camera operators, electricians, carpenters, and the dozens of other types of crew members who participate in production (generally known as "below-the-line" crew). They are hired and paid for their creative and physical labor, generally on a show-by-show (or even episode-by-episode) basis. They primarily contribute their effort (and the creative fruits of that effort) to a project, without making any direct personal financial investment. Consequently, while they may enjoy a financial interest in the success of a project (i.e., "backend" or "profit participation") via a defined contingent compensation formula, they generally have no ownership interest in the final product (even if they personally came up with the idea for it).

This category includes not only individual service providers, but also a variety of corporate actors, from physical asset vendors (such as caterers and equipment rental companies) to creative services vendors (such as visual effects companies) to so-called "production companies." Within this last category, companies may focus primarily on physical production (meaning the day-to-day management of all of the human and physical resources that go into the production process) or creative development (identifying, developing, and selling ideas or

---

[2] In the entertainment industry, the term "talent" is sometimes used to refer more narrowly to actors, and "talent agents and managers" to refer to agents or managers who specialize in representing actors, as distinguished from "literary agents and managers," who specialize in representing writers and directors. Unless specifically noted, this chapter will use "talent" to refer more broadly to any high-level creative service provider, including writer/producers, non-writing producers, directors, and actors.

intellectual property as the basis for production). In many instances, such creative production companies are closely aligned with, or may even be a mere "vanity shingle" for, prominent individual members of the talent community – for instance, Amblin Entertainment is the production company founded and controlled by director Steven Spielberg, Smokehouse Productions by multi-hyphenate George Clooney, and Appian Way by actor Leonardo DiCaprio. Other prominent production companies such as Anonymous Content, 3Arts, and Brillstein Entertainment Partners are primarily talent management companies with deep rosters of successful writers as clients, which often results in these companies (and/or their principals) becoming attached as producers to their clients' projects. Although these companies may invest a limited amount of capital in their own salaries/overhead, or in preliminary development activity, they seldom provide direct at-risk production financing for projects, and often lay off their overhead costs onto studio partners (as an element of exclusive overall or first look deals entered into between studios and such companies) while recouping development costs from production budgets when projects actually proceed to production.

These parties are generally in direct contractual relationships with studios, and although the details of these deals vary depending on the role these parties play in the development and production process, the unifying thread is that the studio that engages and pays a service provider is the owner of the results and proceeds of the service provider's efforts, as a work-made-for-hire under copyright law.[3]

4.2.2. Studios

Studios may be the most important players in the television industry that consumers know little or nothing about. These companies are at the center of the development and production of television content – sourcing ideas for shows from the talent marketplace, hiring and paying service providers, financing and managing production of

---

[3] The "work-for-hire" or "work-made-for-hire" is a concept arising under U.S. copyright law, which designates the employer of a party or parties creating intellectual property (e.g., writers, directors, and actors) to be the legal author and owner, from inception, of the copyright (and other intellectual property rights) of the employees' work. This concept is sometimes abbreviated as "WFH" (which abbreviation appears in Chart One above).

shows, and generally owning the resulting intellectual property – but cultivate little relationship directly with consumers.

Studios operate a high risk/high reward business. Although much of the labor of production is outsourced to service providers who are engaged for active projects, rather than retained on salary, studios nevertheless operate a high-overhead business, employing significant numbers of full-time executives and support staff. Studios finance or co-finance development expenses for a large volume of projects, only a small percentage of which are ever likely to make it to production of a pilot, let alone a series. This is, in part, because studios depend on networks to order projects to production, and the vast majority of development projects will never cross that hurdle (and therefore never see a return on the studio's investments). Even projects which make it to production may cause the studio millions or even tens of millions of dollars in losses if they fail to find an audience and are quickly canceled by the commissioning network. But with a major hit such as *Friends*, *Seinfeld*, or the *CSI* franchise, the studio's profits can easily reach hundreds of millions of dollars – and these major successes are necessary to subsidize the higher volume of projects that fail while the studio is in search of that next big hit.

Studios are an essentially "B2B" (or "business-to-business") business, engaging in numerous vital transactions with more visible players in the television industry (such as talent, on the one hand, and networks, on the other hand), while often operating more or less invisibly to the general public. For most television series, the only outward identification of the studio is a two- to five-second logo at the conclusion of the end credits. Few television viewers could likely identify the studios behind hits such as *House of Cards*, *Breaking Bad*, or *The Big Bang Theory* (Media Rights Capital, Sony Pictures Television, and Warner Bros. Television, respectively), yet it is the studios that, in the long-term, will likely reap the greatest economic rewards of their shows' successes. Because most studios have little branding relationship with the general public, they will often seek to develop and produce a wide variety of very diverse shows, across a variety of networks/platforms, without necessarily forming a "house brand."[4]

---

[4] It is important to note that, just because a studio may not have a "house brand" from the perspective of the viewing public, it probably has a reputation within the industry itself – generated by the studio's own history of successes and failures in

The precise elements of the contractual relationship between a studio and a network for a given television series will vary depending on a number of factors, including the type of network involved (e.g., broadcast vs. cable vs. digital), the type of show (e.g., thirty-minute comedy vs. sixty-minute drama), and the relationship between the studio and network (e.g., independent third-party studio vs. affiliated company). In general, however, the relationship between studio and network is based on a license agreement, by which the studio grants the network specified, limited rights in the series.

4.2.3. Networks

Networks are the first players in the television industry's chain of rights transfers who tend to maintain a direct relationship with the consumer. They function as aggregators and distributors, collecting a variety of television series produced by different studios but generally consistent with a network "brand," and then marketing – and, in some cases, directly delivering – that content to consumers.

Networks work hard (and spend heavily on marketing) to create a "brand" and to market that brand to viewers as a signifier of a certain style or quality of content, often embodied in a pithy advertising slogan, such as HBO's "It's not TV. It's HBO." Although consumers may not be able to put the perception into words, they generally associate networks with a specific type or style of series. A network's slate is, in the current television environment, generally a mix of content that it has acquired via license agreements with third-party studios/content owners, and content which it has generated in-house through a subsidiary studio or acquired via license from an affiliated studio entity.

The business models of networks have historically emphasized either the "direct pay" or the "ad-supported" revenue model, although modern trends have pushed networks to embrace a hybrid of the two. On one end of the spectrum are the broadcast networks (i.e., ABC, CBS, Fox, and NBC), which are freely accessible to customers across the country through their over-the-air broadcast signals. These networks primarily support themselves financially by selling advertising against their content, the value of which is tied to the volume and demographics

---

various formats and genres – as an effective/reliable or ineffective/unreliable producer of specific types of television programming.

of the network's viewership. Roughly speaking, the difference between the network's total advertising revenue, on the one hand, and the network's total content licensing costs, marketing expenses, and operational overhead, on the other hand, traditionally constituted the network's profits.[5] On the other end of the spectrum are "premium pay networks" such as Showtime and Starz, which generate 100% of their revenue from customer subscription fees, and promote their lack of advertising as a major attractive feature of their services. In between are conventional cable networks, such as FX and AMC, which generate revenue through a combination of advertising sold against their programming and carriage fees received from cable and satellite providers.

Although a branding relationship with the customer is a ubiquitous aspect of the network's place in the television industry, networks may or may not maintain a direct economic relationship with their customers. Just as Apple takes advantage of its status as a powerhouse consumer brand to operate its own Apple retail stores, certain networks maintain disintermediated subscription relationships directly with their customers, as Netflix has from inception, or as HBO began to do when, in 2015, it debuted HBO Now, a direct-to-consumer HBO subscription service that did not rely on cable or satellite television providers to offer customers access to the network.

However, as in the retail world, most brands (networks) market to consumers but, in their day-to-day sales activity, actually function as

---

[5] Even broadcast networks, however, have begun to hybridize their business model. Broadcast networks generate ever increasing portions of their aggregate revenue through "retransmission consent fees" paid by cable and satellite providers (and financed by those providers through subscriber fees) in exchange for the right to carry and reproduce local broadcast stations' signals as part of the cable/satellite providers' subscription packages. In addition, all of the broadcast networks have either flirted with or actively launched Internet-based services, such as CBS's All Access, by which customers can access both local broadcast station streams and network library content over the Internet, through dedicated apps, by paying subscription fees directly to the network. In 2016, CBS made headlines when it announced that its new *Star Trek* television series would premiere on the CBS broadcast network, but thereafter be available exclusively through the CBS All Access subscription service. (However, CBS's focus on CBS All Access can be best understood not as a diversification of revenue streams, but a reaction to evolving consumer habits, which, in the twenty-first century, have moved away from traditional in-home, subscription-driven viewing experiences [a shift often referred to as "cord cutting"], and toward mobile and digital viewing experiences.)

wholesalers, selling their products to retailers who, in turn, sell those products through to the actual consumers. For most television networks, this means entering into carriage agreements with multichannel video primary distributors, or MVPDs, such as cable and satellite television providers, who in turn bundle and actually deliver these networks into viewers' homes. Although the details of such carriage agreements are extremely complex and generally beyond the scope of this chapter, in general, these agreements provide for the MVPDs to pay the network some portion of the fees received from each subscriber to the MVPD's service in exchange for the MVPD's right to include the network as part of its channel offering to subscribers.

4.2.4. MVPDs

Multichannel video primary distributors (MVPDs) such as Spectrum (formerly Time Warner Cable), Comcast, DirecTV, and Verizon FIOS are the television industry players that maintain the closest economic relationship with the customer, actually representing the point of sale where customers exchange their dollars for access to television programming.

Although the technical means they use vary from service to service (e.g., coaxial cable for cable providers; microwave transmissions for satellite providers; fiber optic cable for telecommunications providers), MVPDs all provide essentially the same service to customers – a bundle of networks, delivered directly into the viewer's home. MVPDs maintain subscription relationships with customers, collecting the monthly fees which, alongside the advertising revenue infused into the system at multiple levels, represent the essential economic fuel that flows through all of the other participants in the chain of television production and distribution.

Like brick-and-mortar retailers of traditional physical goods, who have to spend heavily on real estate or other physical overhead expenses, MVPDs invest significantly in the costly infrastructure needed to actually deliver access to television programming in viewers' homes. Like many retailers, they generally provide customers with access to very similar collections of products (i.e., networks), but compete with one another based on price, reliability, customer service, and overall customer experience. In marketing to consumers, they advertise both themselves and the products (i.e., networks) that they offer.

4.2.5. Broadcast Stations

Broadcast stations are usually closely affiliated with broadcast networks (i.e., ABC, CBS, Fox, and NBC), but are technically separate entities. Every broadcast station in every geographic market – e.g., KABC7 in Los Angeles, CA, or WNBC4 in New York, NY – is a distinct business and a distinct corporate entity. In many major media markets, such as Los Angeles and New York, the broadcast networks actually own the local stations which carry their programming. Such stations are known as "owned and operated" or "O&O" stations. Other broadcast stations, particularly in smaller markets, may be owned and operated independently of the major networks, and enter into so-called "affiliation agreements" to gain access to such networks' programming. Many of these so-called "independent" stations, however, are still parts of large "station groups" collectively owned by major media companies such as Tribune Broadcasting and Sinclair Communications.

Network-affiliated broadcast stations are generally provided with programming by their affiliated network for broadcast during morning and evening primetime hours. They fill the rest of the broadcast day (and unaffiliated stations fill the entire broadcast day) with a combination of original self-produced programming (most commonly local news); licensed reruns of television shows which were previously broadcast by a television network (so-called "second-run syndication licenses," usually for beloved half-hour comedies); licensed broadcasts of movies or other previously exploited programming; and licensed broadcasts of first-run original content produced by third parties (so-called "first-run syndication," typically in connection with daytime talk shows, such as *Ellen* or *The Dr. Oz Show*, or daytime game shows, such as *Jeopardy!* and *Wheel of Fortune*).

Broadcast stations are also subject to an overlapping pair of regulatory structures, administered by the Federal Communications Commission (or FCC)[6], known as "must carry" and "retransmission consent."[7] By virtue of this regulatory framework, smaller broadcast

---

[6] More broadly, broadcast stations are uniquely subject to regulation by the FCC, which regulatory scheme is generally outside the scope of this chapter, but which dramatically impact all aspects of the operation of these businesses.

[7] Historically, prior to the advent of consumer satellite television services in the 1980s and telecommunications-based television services in the 1990s, a handful of cable providers maintained nearly monopolistic control over the market for

stations (such as public television stations and other stations without a major network affiliation) generally compel MVPDs to offer their channels to local subscribers in their markets for no compensation (based on the premise that the public benefits from the broad availability of such broadcast stations), while larger broadcast stations (in particular, those affiliated with major networks) receive significant fees from these MVPDs, via so-called "retransmission agreements," in exchange for allowing the MVPDs to include their stations in packages for local subscribers. These retransmission fees are typically split between the broadcast station and its affiliated network (an arrangement known as "reverse retransmission"), and represent an increasingly vital source of revenue for both broadcast stations and networks.[8]

4.2.6. Advertisers

As described at the beginning of this chapter, one of the contemporary television industry's defining characteristics is that, as a business, it relies on a dual revenue model, which combines traditional "direct pay" (best exemplified by theatrical feature film exhibition) and "advertiser-supported" (best exemplified by terrestrial radio) business models. The "direct pay" revenue in this system originates with consumers, who pay subscription fees to MVPDs (such as Comcast, DirecTV, and Verizon FIOS) and direct-to-consumer "over-the-top" subscription services (such as Netflix, Amazon Prime Video, and Hulu, described in further detail in section 4.3.3. below). These fees filter

---

multichannel television subscriptions, often engaging in minimal (if any) competition with one another on a geographic market-by-market basis. The prohibitively expensive cost of building cable wiring infrastructure posed a significant barrier to entry for would-be market challengers. The FCC's "must carry" and "retransmission consent" system was implemented as part of the 1992 United States Cable Television Consumer Protection and Competition Act, and offered broadcast networks and stations special protection in the face of the superior market power enjoyed by cable providers during this era. These rules are embodied in 7 U.S.C. Part II, and were upheld by the U.S. Supreme Court in *Turner Broadcasting v. Federal Communications Commission*, 520 U.S. 180 (1997). In the intervening years, however, the pace of regulatory evolution has been slow, while the cable industry's market power has steadily eroded in the face of challenges from satellite and telecommunications-based television providers.

[8] Between 2006 and 2014, aggregate broadcast station retransmission fees grew from $200 million per year to $4.6 billion per year, with analysts estimating that they could grow as high as $10 to $20 billion annually in the years ahead.

upward through the television ecosystem through the series of intermediary contractual relationships described above (in the form of per-subscriber fees paid by MVPDs to the networks they carry and license fees paid by networks to the studios that provide their content).

Advertisers, on the other hand, channel money into the television ecosystem at virtually every stage of the process. On average, approximately 25% of broadcast time on advertiser-supported television networks – eight minutes of each half-hour program, or sixteen minutes of each one-hour program – is dedicated to advertising. Although national networks – which offer the broadest reach to the biggest advertisers – realize much of this revenue, the available advertising inventory (and associated advertising revenue) is allocated amongst all of the players in the system, with MVPDs, networks, and studios all acting as sellers of advertising time.

For instance, carriage agreements divide available advertising minutes between MVPDs (who often sell their available advertising minutes to local advertisers on a market-by-market basis) and networks (who sell their available advertising minutes primarily to national advertisers).[9] Similarly, affiliation agreements between local broadcast stations and national networks allocate available advertising minutes during the day to each of the parties, with the national network controlling most or all of the advertising inventory tied to the network's nationally-distributed programming, while the station controls most or all of the advertising presented alongside the station's self-produced or licensed syndicated programming.[10] In the world of first-run syndication (which is dominated by daytime talk shows and daytime game shows), licensee stations typically compensate the studios with a mix of cash license fees and "barter" advertising time – in other words, allowing the studio that produces and distributes a show to sell, for its own benefit, some portion of the available advertising time during the program.

In general, creative and production service providers are effectively shut out of the television advertising sales market, with

---

[9] This allocation of advertising inventory explains why viewers of national cable networks may still be presented with advertisements for local businesses.

[10] For this reason, local news programming – for which broadcast stations control the entire available advertising inventory – is especially vital to the economic well-being of broadcast stations. Local stations also make a disproportionate amount of their revenue during election years, when political advertisers – who usually target specific, narrow geographic markets – buy advertising time in great quantities.

studios and networks expressly prohibiting writers, producers, and other providers from accepting compensation from advertisers without the studio and/or network's explicit consent or control over the transaction[11]

4.3. ONLINE VIDEO DISTRIBUTION

The emergence of online video distribution – the FCC's preferred regulatory term for the market most people refer to as "streaming" or "digital video" – over the last ten years has presented the television industry with its greatest market challenges and its greatest market opportunities of recent history. Online video distribution represents, all at once, the death of some classic markets (having largely cannibalized the physical home video business), the birth of a new one (providing a valuable new medium/window for downstream distribution of traditional television programming), and the exciting new frontier in original content (with the major players investing heavily in original programming and emerging as vital buyers for new television content). As these emerging businesses have looked to find their footing in the broader entertainment industry, they have both heavily influenced and been heavily influenced by, traditional television businesses and structures.

4.3.1. Types of Online Video Distribution

Online video distribution can generally be broken down into a series of acronyms, which differentiate among these various business models by their method of monetization. Content licenses often distinguish explicitly among these forms of distribution; services, on the other hand, may expressly rely on a combination of one or more of these means of monetization. Digital buyers of content consider the prior streaming history of a television series in determining that series' market value, and prior exhibition via the same streaming model (e.g., subscription-based, ad-supported, etc.) is generally considered to have a stronger downward impact on the licensing value of content,

---

[11] Federal regulations, particularly in the broadcast television world (which is subject to FCC oversight), also require that broadcasters disclose payments made by advertisers in exchange for having their products used, depicted, or mentioned on television.

compared to prior exhibition via a different streaming model. Although ongoing technological change will inevitably force further consideration of these labels in the future, for the time being, the world of online video distribution can be fairly reliably divided as follows:

4.3.1.1. SVOD

"SVOD" refers to "Subscription Video On Demand" – authenticated access for paying subscribers to a library of on-demand streaming content. The most recognizable providers of premium television content online, such as Netflix and Amazon Prime Instant Video, generally follow a primarily SVOD-based model. SVOD constitutes a "direct pay" form of monetization, in that customers must pay for access to content, rather than receiving it for free in exchange for exposure to advertisements. However, it is an attenuated form of direct pay, in that customers pay for blanket access to a library of content, without regard to whether they are watching any specific piece, or any particularly quantity, of content (analogous to a customer paying for a subscription to a traditional pay television network like HBO, even if they may not watch every individual piece of content on that network).

4.3.1.2. AVOD

"AVOD" refers to "Advertising-Supported Video On Demand" – customer access to one or more pieces of on-demand streaming content, which is provided at no charge to the customer but is accompanied by advertisements (which may be "pre-roll" [i.e., before the content itself], "mid-roll" [i.e., in the middle of the content, like a commercial break], and/or "post-roll" [after the content is complete]). The Google-owned YouTube is currently the dominant market examples of a pure AVOD service, although more recently, the company has sought to diversify its business model by offering an SVOD variant called YouTube Red. Until 2016, Hulu also offered a subscription-less AVOD service, sometimes referred to as "Hulu Classic" (as distinguished from the company's subscription-based "Hulu Plus" service), although the company eventually merged its service tiers into a single SVOD/AVOD hybrid (i.e., a subscription-based service that also generates revenue by serving ads with its content)

4.3.1.3. TVOD

"TVOD" refers to "Transactional Video On Demand" – paid access to content online, with purchase and/or rental fees paid on a specific product-by-product basis (rather than for a blanket subscription to a library of content). TVOD can be further subdivided into "EST" (or "Electronic Sell-Through," referring to permanent downloads of episodes or series, akin to the purchase of a traditional physical DVD or Blu-ray that the customer gets to keep[12]) and "ERT" (or "Electronic Rental," referring to a temporary time-limited download/viewing right, akin to the rental of a traditional physical DVD or Blu-ray), although it bears noting that there is currently little or no active "ERT" market in connection with television (as opposed to theatrical feature film) distribution. Major TVOD services include digital marketplaces such as Apple's iTunes, Google Play, and Amazon Instant Video. TVOD is largely viewed as a successor to, and replacement for, the traditional home video market. Alongside traditional home video, it represents the purest expression of theatrical-style "direct pay" distribution/ consumption in the television industry.

4.3.1.4. FVOD

"FVOD" refers to "Free Video On Demand" – access to digital content without a direct charge, subscription charge, or requirement of viewing ads. Because it is essentially a non-monetized business, FVOD has little practical role in the professionalized television industry, and typically appears, if at all, in the context of promotional exhibition of special feature-type secondary content (though even this type of content is often advertising-supported).

4.3.1.5. VOD

"VOD" stands simply for "Video On Demand," and although the term is often used, it is essentially ambiguous and should be interpreted with care. VOD may act as a blanket term, which encompasses all of

---

[12] As a technical matter, some companies take the legal position that there is no such thing as a "sale" of digital content, and that even "EST" is merely a perpetual license to the consumer, not a "sale" as such. This fine legal parsing can have consequences for revenue accounting and piracy enforcement, but as a practical matter, is something of a legal fiction.

the above forms of Video On Demand exhibition. It may be used as a synonym for ERT, or may refer more narrowly to a free or ad-supported form of ERT which is offered through MVPD set-top boxes in connection with the customer's subscription to a television network included in his or her cable/satellite package. Of all of the acronyms involved in the alphabet soup of online video distribution, "VOD" can be the most ambiguous, particularly when used without a clear context.

4.3.2. Other Key Distinctions

In addition to identifying the method of monetization of digital content, licenses for digital exhibition generally must take into account a few other key factors in defining the scope of such licenses (and therefore defining the scope of rights which are reserved and may be sold to another buyer).

First, streaming rights may be granted on a standalone basis, or solely a companion basis. "Standalone" rights are those granted to services which are inherently streaming-based, such as Netflix and Hulu. "Companion" rights are granted to traditional linear network licensees, who want to provide their customers (often subscribers, in the case of basic cable or premium pay television networks) with concurrent web-based access to the shows on their linear streams. These rights may be exploited through directly-branded websites (such as ABC.com); directly-branded mobile applications (such as HBO Go and FX Now); affiliated streaming services (such as Hulu, which is a joint venture of ABC, Fox, Comcast/NBCUniversal, and – most recently, as of late 2016 – Time Warner); or the MVPDs that carry a network (through set-top box on-demand offerings, which are tied to the customer's actual channel subscription package).

Second, the status of "permanent downloads" is an important subject of current negotiation between content owners and digital content platforms. SVOD (as well as AVOD) services have generally been presumed to offer their content on a streaming basis – technically, this means that the customer never permanently downloads the content to the hard drive of one of their own devices, but accesses it through the Internet on a real-time basis (and therefore must be actively connected to the Internet in order to access the content). However, to manage bandwidth usage and improve customer experience, streaming services such as Netflix and Amazon have explored changing their technological model to allow subscribers to download content for permanent or semi-permanent access off-line so long as customers maintain active subscriptions (akin to Spotify's strategy in the mobile music marketplace). Future generations of licenses will contain explicit terms governing this form of hybrid SVOD/TVOD exploitation. However, existing licenses which did not contemplate such exhibition must now be reinterpreted to account for such a practice, with licensees taking the position that subscription-authentication renders it subject to and included within their SVOD licenses, and licensors taking the position that the move toward downloading rather than streaming is outside the scope of the original licenses, requiring a renegotiation with (and further license fees from) the licensee.

Third, there exists a growing marketplace – entirely separate from those introduced above – of linear digital services. "Linear" services are those which provide a continuous pre-programmed stream of content, via one or more channels, which is accessed by the customer by dipping into the stream at any given time. Such video services are digital and streaming, but are not "on demand," in the sense that the customer does not have on-demand control over what he or she watches and when. To date, there has been limited activity in this space – which also occupies an arguably nebulous legal and regulatory position with respect to elements of copyright and communications law which govern linear broadcast that are delivered to customers via more traditional technological means.[13] However, as the regulatory landscape clears up in the years ahead, it seems likely that linear (as opposed to on-demand) digital licensing will emerge as another market opportunity for owners of television content.

4.3.3. The Roles of Digital Content Companies

In understanding the role of digital content platforms in the marketplace, it is helpful to refer back to our previous visualization of

---

[13] Litigation involving Aereo, a service that allowed subscribers to view live and time-shifted streams of over-the-air broadcast television stations on Internet-connected devices, reached the U.S. Supreme Court in 2014, challenging the boundaries of copyright and communications law. An adverse Supreme Court ruling led the company to suspend business operations in June 2014, and declare bankruptcy in November 2014.

the television industry, at Chart One above. Most every major digital content company can be understood as occupying a specific position in Chart One – and most every position in Chart One has been taken up by at least one major digital content company.

Most well-known digital platforms function primarily as networks; Netflix, Amazon Prime Instant Video, and Hulu all function essentially as pay television networks in the mold of HBO and Showtime, charging subscription fees for access to their entire services (albeit without the intermediation of an MVPD).[14] Streaming service Crackle is the leading fully advertising-supported streaming service, resembling a traditional broadcast network which makes its content available to users at no direct charge and derives its income primarily through advertising revenue.

At the same time, the evolution of Netflix, Amazon Prime Instant Video, and Hulu looks a lot like the evolution, one to two decades before, of prominent basic cable networks such as AMC[15] and FX[16], which evolved over time from offering only second-run content that had already appeared in theaters or on television, to original content produced by third-party studios, to a mix of content produced by third-

---

[14] The demands of this subscription-based model help contextualize and explain the strategic decisions of such SVOD services. Operating a subscription-based business means persuading customers to not only initiate a subscription, but just as importantly, to pay out-of-pocket fees, month after month, to maintain their access to the service. This requires the service to offer customers a sufficiently compelling value proposition to justify the monthly expense. One important way to create value for the customer is to offer a wide and diverse selection of content accessible via the subscription. Even more important, however, is offering the customer compelling content *that they cannot find/access anywhere else*. This premium on exclusivity helps explain the natural trajectory of subscription services toward increasing focuses on exclusive, premium, first-run content.

[15] In its early days, when "AMC" stood for "American Movie Classics," AMC was known for airing classic Hollywood films. It broke into original programming with shows like Sony Pictures Television's *Breaking Bad* and Lionsgate Television's *Mad Men*. More recent hits, such as megafranchise *The Walking Dead* and its spinoff *Fear the Walking Dead*, have been drawn from the affiliated AMC Studios.

[16] For years, FX's programming day was comprised primary of reruns of broadcast network shows, such as *Dharma & Greg*, *Married... with Children*, and *Fear Factor*. It moved into original programming with shows like Sony Pictures Television's *The Shield* and Warner Bros. Television's *Nip/Tuck*. More recent hits like *American Crime Story* and *The League* have come from studio arm FX Productions, and the network has continued to lean heavily on studio affiliates 20th Century Fox Television (*American Horror Story*) and Fox 21 Studios (*Tyrant*), which recently merged with sister studio Fox Television Studios.

party studios and content produced by their own in-house/affiliated studio arms.[17] All three services' streaming offerings began with a focus on second-run licensing of content that had previously appeared on other networks – essentially, cable syndication licenses in a digital context. Netflix and Amazon relied on arms-length licensing deals with outside studios, while Hulu enjoyed a pipeline of content from its owner-affiliates, broadcast networks ABC, Fox, and NBC. In response to increasing competition from one another and rising content licensing costs for second-run programming, all three services eventually expanded into original content. Netflix was first to market with its original content, debuting Norwegian series *Lilyhammer* in 2012 and breakout hit *House of Cards* in 2013, and initially relied entirely on outside studios to provide its content (*House of Cards* from Media Rights Capital; *Hemlock Grove* from Gaumont International Television; *Orange Is the New Black* from Lionsgate Television; *Arrested Development* from 20th Century Fox Television; etc.). More recently, Netflix has moved toward acting as a studio and producing its own content through its studio arm, allowing it to own and control all rights in its programming, such as its daily talk show *Chelsea* and hit drama *Stranger Things*.[18] Amazon trailed Netflix in entering the market for original content, debuting its series *Alpha House* and *Betas* in 2013; however, unlike Netflix, Amazon embraced a position as a studio as well as a network from inception, with both of its debut series being produced through Amazon Studios. Since then, Amazon's slate has represented a mix of in-house Amazon Studios shows (such as *Transparent* and *Man in the High Castle*) and shows licensed from

---

[17] It bears noting that, over the years, the broadcast networks have developed a similar preference for content which they (or their affiliated sister studios) own in whole or in part. In the case of the broadcast networks, however, this shift in business practice emerged as a result of significant regulatory change. In 1970, the FCC adopted a set of rules known as the "Financial Interest and Syndication Rules," or "fin-syn rules," which effectively prohibited the broadcast networks from owning the programming that they broadcast. These rules were somewhat relaxed during the 1980s, before being abolished entirely in 1993. The repeal of the fin-syn regulatory scheme precipitated a major shift by the broadcast networks toward ownership of their own programming, and with it, a substantial contraction in the marketplace of independent television studios (which found it increasingly difficult to compete with network-affiliated studios for scarce broadcast time, in light of the networks' significant financial incentives to favor their affiliated studios).

[18] Economic factors driving this move are explored in greater detail in Chapter 6 of this volume on scripted television.

outside studios (such as Fabrik Entertainment's *Bosch* and Sony Pictures Television's *Good Girls Revolt* and *Sneaky Pete*). Among the three major streaming companies, only Hulu has, to date, continued to rely exclusively on original content from outside studios (such as Warner Bros. Television's *11.22.63*, Lionsgate Television's *Casual*, and Universal Television's *The Path*), although in many cases, Hulu's supplying studios (such as Universal Television) are themselves corporate affiliates of Hulu's parent companies. All three services also tend to take co-production positions in programming licensed from third-party studios.

In light of the foregoing, when it comes to original content produced for digital services, these platforms can be understood essentially not as *sui generis* players, but as a subset of networks, albeit with unique licensing requirements specific to the technological and economic models underlying their services.

The market also reflects a number of emerging digital MVPDs, such as Google's Google Fiber, Sony's Playstation Vue, and Dish Network's Sling TV, all of which provide traditional-looking (if somewhat downsized) packages of linear channels, delivered via broadband Internet rather than through traditional coaxial, fiber-optic, or satellite equipment. YouTube, in offering a variety of "channels" curated by third parties on its service, also arguably serves as a digital MVPD[19] (though it may alternatively interpreted as an ad-supported

---

[19] In this analogy, multichannel networks which have sprung up within the YouTube ecosystem (and primarily target and serve YouTube's millennial audience), such as Fullscreen, Maker, Machinima, and AwesomenessTV, can be understood as the "networks," while the producers and creators they work with function as the "service providers" and "studios," often retaining most or all of the rights in their content. These businesses, however, are undergoing a period of rapid transformation in their business models, looking to reduce their dependence on YouTube as a platform and expand their revenue streams. For instance, in 2015, AwesomenessTV struck a deal with Verizon to provide more than 200 hours of original programming for Verizon's upcoming Go90 subscription service; the next year, Verizon acquired a significant stake in AwesomenessTV, looking to use the company to further bolster its exclusive content offerings on Go90. Around the same time period, in 2014, competing MCN Fullscreen was acquired by a joint venture called Otter Media which was funded in part by AT&T, and shortly thereafter announced that it would debut its own Fullscreen-branded SVOD service, which launched in 2016. This ecosystem of short-form content, which was largely born and nurtured on YouTube before expanding to a number of proprietary services with major investment from conglomerates like Verizon, AT&T, and Comcast, warrants its own chapter (if not book).

network on its main service, and a subscription-supported network through its curated YouTube Red service).

Finally, TVOD retailers, such as Apple's iTunes and Google Play, do not fit neatly into the above chart, but occupy a spot traditionally held by retailers and renters of physical home video products, such as Target, Best Buy, and now-defunct rental house Blockbuster Video.

— CHAPTER 5 —

UNSCRIPTED TELEVISION

Justin B. Wineburgh[*]

5.1. Introduction: Dealmaking in the "Unscripted" Television Industry
5.2. Option, Co-Production and Joint Venture Agreements
5.3. Talent Attachment
5.4. Distribution Agreements
5.5. Independent Contractor Agreement
5.6. Release, Consents and Location Agreement
5.7. Product and Service Placement Agreements
5.8. Composer Agreements and Music Licenses
5.9. Conclusion

5.1. INTRODUCTION: DEALMAKING IN THE "UNSCRIPTED" TELEVISION INDUSTRY

For years, reality television, or unscripted programming, has been the fastest growing segment of the entertainment industry. While its popularity exploded in the early 2000s, a time largely regarded as the birth of reality television, its history actually goes back much further. Why? Because "reality television" is nothing more than the integration and portrayal of real life on television. Indeed, for decades, television has been peering into the lives of "regular people" in many ways – from dating, to contests, to pranks.

The 1940s saw the birth of one of the most famous reality television shows of all time – *Candid Camera*, in which humorous pranks were played on unknowing "participants." The show was a massive success, airing for years and leaving an indelible mark on our television landscape. For certain, "prank-style" shows have remained tremendously popular, from *America's Funniest Home Video*, to *Punk'd* and its progeny, to the regular repertoire of pranks played out each night on our daily late night talk shows.

---

[*] **Justin B. Wineburgh** is President and CEO of Alkemy X.

The decade after the birth of prank programming saw the launch of contest shows in the 1950s with the first airing of the *Miss America Pageant*. In the decades that followed, contests became, and still remain, one of the largest themes of reality programming, from the wildly popular traditional game shows, such as *Jeopardy* and *Wheel of Fortune*, to the contests portrayed on *Survivor* and *Amazing Race*. And, ultimately, we reached reality programming contests of individual talent, with shows such as *Star Search* initially, to *American Idol*, and then onto the countless competition cooking shows including *Top Chef* and *Chopped*. And, of course, the list goes on and on and on....

The entertainment vehicle we know as reality television has become a common, and wildly successful, programming recipe for two simple reasons working hand-in-hand. It allows an "Average Joe" the opportunity to achieve fifteen minutes of fame (and oftentimes more), while giving the viewer an opportunity to be a voyeur and get an insider, behind-the-scenes look into a situation they would not otherwise have access to see. Reality television plays perfectly into human nature, and our fascination with the lives and interactions of regular people doing seemingly regular things, while interacting with each other and the world. Our lives are a constant inquiry into why and how certain things happen, and what happens behind the scenes. We have always been interested in seeing everyday people argue, fight, cry, make up, struggle, succeed, laugh, date, fall in love, work, lose and win. Television responded to that interest, all in the name of entertainment, and to the delight of generations of television audiences.

Of course, it also does not hurt that reality television is often far less costly to produce than a scripted program of similar length. As a result, unscripted programming provides networks with a compelling bang for the buck with programming that has the ability to generate loyal viewers and the associated advertising dollars, as compared against more expensive scripted content, but with a safer hedge against the unfortunate consequence of equivalent (and even lesser) ratings performance.

And, thus, the unscripted industry thrives, with no end for growth in sight.

5.2. OPTION, CO-PRODUCTION AND JOINT VENTURE AGREEMENTS[1]

The singular goal of any creator of unscripted, reality or *cinema-verité* television or digital content is to sell a project. However, there is no one particular manner in which this goal can be achieved. The steps that lead up to the sale of a project can take any number of paths. While established, well-known producers of reality content may be able to sell a concept directly to a network or end-user, less experienced creators may have a harder course to chart, but many options exist nonetheless.

All creators of reality content, experienced or not, may seek and obtain a development deal whereby the network or another buyer provides the producer with support to further develop the project. Generally, the development deal includes some level of financial support, as well as creative guidance, to refine the project. Naturally, the development deal is for projects that show favorable potential early on. In turn, networks reach the conclusion that there will be the reasonable likelihood of a return after initial investment.

Many times, however, a budding reality television creator may seek to partner with a well-established production company that has a proven track record. In doing so, the parties may seek any number of contractual arrangements. The first is to enter into an option or "shopping" agreement (whereby the more established producer obtains the right, but not the obligation, to buy, sell, develop, "pitch" to potential buyers), or obtain specific rights in the reality television project for an agreed-upon price at some time in the future, all with the ultimate goal of getting a project in the hands of the end-user, the viewing audience. Such an arrangement benefits both the established and inexperienced party. The experienced producer has the opportunity to profit from the inexperienced producer's concept, while the inexperienced producer benefits from working with an established, reputable company that will increase the chances of getting the project sold.

Nonetheless, it is not always about experience and reputation. Sometimes, each party brings a unique contribution to a project.

---

[1] The commentary and concepts discussed in this section of the chapter are further illustrated in "co-production" and "joint venture" forms accompanying this volume.

Although a single contribution is not sufficient to reach the intended goal, when the contributions and skills of many are combined and taken in the aggregate, a sale of the show can occur. One party may have access to the subject matter, while the other has the financial resources to bring a product to fruition. Again, the touchstone is that each party can benefit in some way from the other, and each recognizes the value of working together. Under such circumstances, the parties may choose to enter into a Co-Production or Joint Venture Agreement. In doing so, the parties will clearly define their relationship, as well as the role, obligations and rights of each in connection with the project.

Options, Co-Production and Joint Venture Agreements exist in many forms, from simple one-page letters to comprehensive, meticulous documents complete with copyright assignments. Irrespective of which form is used, however, it is critical for the parties to clearly identify the rights, responsibilities and obligations of each. The following is an outline of the key provisions that appear in all of these various agreements, along with issues to consider during the negotiation of such an arrangement.

5.2.1. Term, Tail and Freeze Period

These provisions identify the length of time pursuant to which the parties are bound to each other. This could be the period during which the more established producer in an Option Agreement may exercise the right to acquire the reality project for further development or production (called the "Option Period"), or the period during which one party is authorized to "pitch" someone else's project to financiers, networks, distributors or others for further development or production, or the length of time that the parties to a Co-Production or Joint Venture Agreement agree to otherwise work together. The standard option term is generally one (1) year to eighteen (18) months, with the term of shopping agreements typically six (6) to twelve (12) months, with variations of each arising under certain circumstances. While the initial inclination may be to keep the term short, it is important to leave the term long enough so that each party has the ability to do what has to be done to develop the project, and ultimately complete its sale.

Although the length of the term is clearly stated, there will almost always be an option for an extension. In the event that there are ongoing, bona fide discussions to sell the project at the end of the term, a "tail period" provision will extend the term for a finite period of time to enable the parties to conclude such discussions. Both the initial term and length of an extension are subject to negotiation, but be careful. While a longer term may give the impression that the parties are more likely to find a buyer, a shorter term may have the same intended result. After all, there is no better motivator than a ticking clock with a firm expiration date.

In addition, it is not uncommon to include a "freeze period" after the expiration of the term. This provision keeps the parties honest by deterring either from deliberately stifling a sale as the expiration of the term approaches in order to move forward with the project elsewhere without the involvement of the other. The terms of this "freeze period" are negotiable, but the intent is clear – if a sale does not happen by the end of the term, the party to whom rights revert is then precluded from selling the project to an entity previously approached without the involvement of the other for a period of time that is generally long enough to make the project go stale before such acquiror(s) can be "re"-approached.

5.2.2. Fees and Payments

As expected, fees and payments vary greatly and depend on a number of factors, including the value of the concept, the budget for its production, the stature of each party, the bargaining strength of the party's representatives, and the rights that a party seeks or the obligations it is willing to undertake. Fees can be a set dollar amount, or tied to a percentage of the actual budget of the project on its sale, or a negotiated portion of the fees of the stronger, lead partner in the collaboration. Additionally, fees may be different depending on where the show is sold – i.e., to a major television network, other broadcast or cable platforms (in view of the often wide range of possible production budgets across these outlets). The fees may be a recoupable advance against the sale price if the project proceeds. However, in many cases where no studio, network, or major financing entity is involved at the outset, no actual cash compensation is exchanged when the agreement is signed. Instead, what is tendered as consideration are promises to use commercially reasonable efforts to further develop, produce and seek to sell the project.

5.2.3. Control

The parties must decide how to control the development, production and sale of the project. There are many areas of reality television development that require decision making and can be controlled, ranging from the creative direction, to financing opportunities, to those required in connection with the distribution and sale of the project. As expected, each are subject to negotiation and, while many of the usual respective bargaining power considerations come into play, the natural course of how the party's relationship came to be may be the best guide. Generally, a party with prior production credits and network relationships will likely demand control of the project. In some instances, the party that had the relationship with the talent central to the project may be best suited to determine its creative course, while yet in other instances, the party making the financial commitment should dictate the financial and business considerations. Importantly, as with any collaborative process, it is not uncommon to offer meaningful consultation rights to the non-controlling party. In the end, it is important to realize that, once the sale of a project occurs, it is usually the financier or network that has full and complete control and decision-making; as such, the control decisions between two collaborating parties are generally only applicable prior to a sale or other disposition of the project.

5.2.4. Credit

Undeniably, on-screen credit is one of the most fundamental aspects of the entertainment business. Credit is often more important than the compensation to be paid. Everyone wants prominent recognition for his or her contribution to the project, no matter how trivial the work may have been. Reality television is no different. From the highest ranking credit of executive producer on down, credits are subject to much jockeying from the earliest stages of the project. Each credit may be shared (i.e., co-executive producer), and then move down in stature. So, the ball rolls downhill to the producer, co-producer, associate producer, co-associate producer, field producer, development producer, and so on and so forth. And, then, each category of credits may be shared with those similarly situated, with the parties negotiating over whose credit will be listed first. But the negotiations do not stop at the order to which the credits are listed. The size, placement, and duration of time on the screen also come into play. In the end, upon airing of the show, each credit is subject to the network's final approval anyway so, at best, an argument over credits at the outset is nothing more than setting the field for what the parties are entitled to seek to be accorded.

5.2.5. Post Term Rights and Obligations

It is equally important to take into consideration the end of the term if the parties have not been successful in selling the project, such as what happens to the project, and how each party's contributions during the term of the relationship are to be handled. While the parties may not want to have anything to do with each other after the term, each may separately want to continue to try to sell the project (or prevent the other from doing so). As such, it is important to recognize that the separately identifiable and protectable intellectual property that each party brought into the project at the beginning generally will revert to its original contributor. Either party shall then be free to pitch, sell and produce a reality television program similar to the project (or not, if the party that originated the concept can secure such a covenant from the other party); however, it is absolutely critical to ensure that neither party violates the copyright or other intellectual property rights of the other in connection with such subsequent activities. Certainly, an imprecise handling of the post-term rights and obligations of each party will lead to a cloud over the project, potentially freezing it from further exploitation and sale permanently.

5.3. TALENT ATTACHMENT[2]

Reality programming has become a staple of modern day television. Indeed, the unscripted franchises are as popular, if not more popular, than their scripted counterparts. While many of these unscripted shows depend on one person to lead the "cast," others depend on a specific group of people, while others are based on the existence of a specific entity, such as a business. Attaching the key person, group of people, or business to a reality concept at the earliest stages is critical for a variety of reasons.

---

[2] For further illustration of these concepts, please refer to this chapter's talent agreement forms accompanying this volume.

First, as soon as a concept is born, the creator needs to ensure that the people or business upon which the show will be based is/are aligned and committed to the production. This connection to the concept protects the creator, tying him or her to the talent or business, and offering the security and protection that the concept, which the creator has worked so hard to develop, will not be stolen. Moreover, this tie signifies to potential purchasers of the show, i.e., the networks, that if and when it buys a show, the talent or business involved is bona fide, real and committed, and will not back out. Indeed, what good would it be for a creator of a reality show to develop and pitch a concept if the talent or business could change course and back out on a whim? Similarly, why would a purchaser of the potential show commit time and resources if the talent could walk away? The Talent Attachment Agreement (sometimes also called a Holding or Shopping Agreement with the same intended effect) serves a simple, critical purpose – to tie the talent or business to the show that is being created, protecting the creator and assuring the purchaser that the talent or business is committed to the project.

This agreement allows a creator to present and sell a reality television show concept for some period of time with the essential creative elements – i.e., talent or a business – contractually tied to the project. It can be a simple one-page memorandum permitting the creator to attempt to sell a concept with a particular individual, group of individuals or business as part of the show, or a significant, comprehensive agreement with numerous addenda, detailing the scope of all rights and any limitations between the show and the talent. However the intended purpose is clear – upon disposition and sale of the reality show, many of each party's material rights and obligations have been spelled out in advance. Below, we will examine some of the essential elements of attaching talent or a business to a reality production.

5.3.1. Before the Sale – The Talent Attachment

5.3.1.1. Length of the Attachment

As indicated, the term specifies the length of time the producer has to develop, pitch and sell the reality concept with the talent or business attached to the project. Most often, the term is exclusive, and the talent agrees that for the period of the attachment, no other individual or entity will be permitted to develop or sell a show with the talent or business involved. Like everything else, all of this is negotiable. The talent likely wants the period to be short, while the producer wants as much time as possible. However, as is often the case, development and sale of the project takes time – therefore, making the period too short does not allow for sufficient development efforts to take place, merely setting the concept up for failure before it even becomes a show. For planning purposes, the average term of an attachment is nine (9) months to one (1) year.

Although talent attachment contracts clearly define how long the parties are bound to each other, there is generally also a provision to allow for an extension. This provision protects the producer at the end of the term, and allows for a brief extension of time to enable the parties to conclude any active, bona fide negotiation for the set up or sale of a reality project then underway. Without this provision, the talent is able to walk away from the project immediately when the term expires, without any regard for the practicality of the situation. This extension forces a reality show creator and purchaser involved in an ongoing negotiation to conclude their business, without tying up the attached talent indefinitely. Of course, the negotiations must be active and real, and this extension cannot be invoked merely out of convenience to allow the creator to stall and belatedly try to sell the project with talent exclusively attached.

5.3.1.2. The Non-Compete Provision

First and foremost, this provision provides the creator with exclusivity during the term of the attachment, and prohibits the talent or business from participating in any other reality show that competes with the show that is being developed. Moreover, this provision gives the creator assurance that talent will not stifle the creator's efforts to sell the show as the term nears its expiration. Specifically, should the creator be unsuccessful in selling the reality show before the attachment expires, this provision prohibits the talent or business from immediately being involved in another show with the same or substantially similar premise (think intellectual property infringement law, in this regard) once the attachment expires. Indeed, it protects against the unscrupulous seller who may lie in wait, for one reason or another, only to pitch or sell an identical reality show after the attachment expires, yet without the original creator involved. (This will likewise discourage a buyer to whom the project was presented from circumventing the creator with an immediate overture to talent once they believe the creator or packager's rights have expired.) With this post-term freeze period, the original creator is protected and has the security that, for some period of time, any active negotiations can be concluded. The term of this restrictive period varies, and can be from weeks, to months, or longer. The provision may also provide for a further "non-circumvention" restriction on talent from approaching a buyer or production company to which the project was submitted for a period of time following the term, typically a six (6) months to twelve (12) months duration, even if talent is free to approach other networks to which no prior overture was made.

5.3.1.3. Development Services

Often, the talent is required to assist in the creation of the pitch materials for a developing reality show, as well as pitching the project, obtaining permission and clearances from others, and filming a trailer (the so-called "sizzle tape") of the project for potential purchasers. This provision is critical to ensure that the creator obtains the support and involvement of the talent early on in the project's development. This provision may also include approval and controls over the development of the project. Indeed, while the creator of the reality show may want complete creative control, the input of the talent is not only desirable in most instances, it may be critical to the success of the project in others (where, for example, talent has unique expertise or experience relevant to the execution of the concept). However, the input of the talent should not be absolute (e.g., meaningful consultation may be fine, but the creator should have the right to exercise final creative control), and should be limited to creative elements of the show only; unless the creator of the show is looking for a business partner, the talent should not be empowered to make any financial or business decisions related to the project, or anything regarding its sale or disposition. The bottom line here is that any creative control afforded to talent must be limited because, when the show is sold, all final creative decisions will likely be made by the financier, network, or buyer.

5.3.1.4. Compensation

Unless the talent is established and noteworthy in the public eye, or has some other superior bargaining power, talent is usually attached to the potential project for free. Furthermore, the attachment makes clear that the talent agrees to negotiate compensation, including ancillary revenue, merchandising and royalties, in good faith, subject to the budget of the show, as well as any precedent applicable to similarly situated talent, should the reality project be sold for distribution and exploitation.

5.3.2. After the Sale – The Talent Agreement

A more formal Talent Agreement, with its many addenda, follows the Talent Attachment Agreement, and determines the scope and extent of the rights and obligations of the talent once the reality television program is sold and going to proceed. Beyond the rights granted to the production, it sets forth numerous representations and warranties that talent must generally make about physical and mental well-being, television and other media exclusivity, limitations as to other outside personal and professional activities, and specifies strict confidentiality provisions. The talent must concurrently sign comprehensive waivers, releases of liability, and assumption of risk agreements, which are especially important for the creators of shows where the risk of significant personal injury, or other harm, is presented. The following are the key provisions of the long form, post-sale Talent Agreement.

5.3.2.1. Participation

As its name implies, the participation provision in a reality television program ("Program") establishes the compensation to be paid to the talent, sets forth the talent's rights, and determines the extent of the talent's obligations, and generally includes the following:

a. Fixed Compensation

As expected, this is usually the most heavily negotiated and scrutinized portion of the Talent Agreement. First, there is a basic fee paid to the talent, usually on a per-episode basis, as compensation for participating on-camera in the show. Like all matters of respective bargaining power, the fee to be paid is driven by the talent's stature and fame, as well as precedent (both for the talent in question, as well as for similarly situated talent), balanced against the budget of the show. This episodic fee can range from just a few thousand dollars for unknown talent on the first season of a new show with a limited budget (i.e., $200,000 or less per episode) on a "small" cable network, to $50,000 to $100,000 per episode (and even higher) for well-known talent after multiple seasons of a highly successful show with a significant budget (i.e., $750,000 per episode plus) on a major broadcast network. The negotiation and calculation of available fees will also depend on whether the talent is the primary focus of the series, or one person in a larger ensemble of primary or secondary "characters", who all must ultimately share in a fixed pool of funds budgeted for talent attachment. And, of course, it is frequently common to ensure that the talent receives an increase (generally 5%) with each new cycle of series episodes.

Talent should also seek to be compensated for the exploitation of content that is a sequel, prequel or spin-off of the show for which the talent has been cast, regardless of whether or not the talent is actually included in the cast of that additional show. Usually, this is a percentage of the talent's fee on the initial show, likely twenty-five (25%) to fifty percent (50%), and compensates the talent for the participation in the first show which leads to the successful sale of more shows.

b. Contingent Compensation

There are a series of additional revenue streams that may increase the "profits" of a reality production, and the talent should seek to participate in and be paid a percentage of those profits. As is frequently the case in the entertainment industry, this is a complicated matter, and must take into account the total gross revenue generated by the show from all possible avenues (i.e., including potential off-network exploitation, and soundtrack and merchandise sales), the deductions to that revenue for the various fees, costs and expenses associated with producing the show, and then a determination of the show's bottom line net profit. Be careful, as the net profits for a new (and even long running) show are frequently small, if anything, so the skilled negotiator must recognize which pot the profit participation is taken from (i.e., adjusted gross, first net, net after further deductions, etc.), and then understand all of the deductions that will be made to reach that point. As such, while the numerical percentage of a talent profit participation payment may seem large, if taken from the lowest net profit category (or even worse!), the talent will likely be left with no additional profit payment.

c. Pre-Production/Production of the Program

The talent agrees to participate in connection with the pre-production and production of the Program as and to the extent required on such dates as the producer may reasonably designate. The talent must acknowledge that due to the documentary or cinema-verité nature of the Program as a reality production, the producer cannot anticipate day-to-day changes to the production schedule and, therefore, the talent agrees to cooperate with the producer in good faith with respect to changes in the production schedule. In addition, the talent agrees to meet with and be interviewed both on-camera and off-camera, at reasonable times and places in connection with the Project. Certainly, while pre-production and production activities are extensive, expectations of reasonableness and good faith behavior from both parties apply – talent should be protected against any unreasonable, unannounced intrusion during development or production that may interfere with talent's customary and normal personal commitments and professional obligations.

d. Access

The talent also grants the producer the right to videotape, film, portray, photograph and otherwise record the talent, the talent's actions and voice on a basis up to 24-hours-a-day, 7-days-a-week in the course of the talent's life, whether by microphone or otherwise. The talent must agree that during the filming of the Program, cameras and other audio and/or video recording devices may be placed in and around any and all private, semi-public and public areas to which the talent may have access, and that these cameras and other recording devices may record events, conversations, actions, reactions and/or other information which would otherwise be private, personal and confidential in nature. The talent must explicitly acknowledge and understand that in connection with the taping of the Program, the talent waives and shall not have an expectation of privacy – such a waiver is absolutely critical to protect the producer from the litany of claims that these recordings may present.

Importantly, however, this access is not without limits, and talent should seek to protect legitimate and reasonable expectations of privacy. For example, talent may wish to restrict access to intimate or personal matters, or otherwise limit exposure to anything which may be considered embarrassing, and such requests are routine and usually accommodated (unless they would undermine the general theme of the program). Similarly, access to photographs, documents, and business records that are of an intimate, personal, proprietary and confidential nature must be protected, so long as such restriction does not impact the creative direction of the show. Finally, talent should be careful to protect against access to situations or circumstances which could portray the talent in a lewd, negative or unfavorable manner, or interfere with the talent's name or reputation. As expected, any restrictions to the broad and unlimited access reality productions seek will be closely scrutinized and negotiated; however, reasonable restrictions that do not significantly impact the creative direction of the show are frequently granted.

e. Locations

The talent must also explicitly acknowledge and understand that the filming of the Program may take place at various locations and that, to the extent that the talent has the right to grant access to and control those locations, it must grant the producer the right to enter and occupy these locations, and place cameras, temporary structures and other audio and/or visual recording devices for the purpose of capturing material for the Program. Of course, consideration must be given to areas that are sensitive or private, such as bedrooms, bathrooms, or other areas where there may be a heightened expectation of privacy, like a physician's office. Moreover, if the talent does not control the areas in which the producer wishes to record, the talent is required to use reasonable efforts to assist the producer in securing the permission of the owner or authorized representative of the location to allow the producer to gain desired access.

Location access is not without limits either, and talent will often raise legitimate concerns as to "space" to be protected against during production. Indeed, unfettered intrusion into personal or intimate areas, such as bedrooms, bathrooms, and children' areas, should be guarded against. Moreover, a business premises should be protected against filming activities that may interrupt the normal and customary operation of the talent's business, as well as from an intrusion that could result in the disclosure of sensitive, proprietary or confidential information regarding the business or its operation.

f. On-Camera Services

The talent must agree that the producer may film, tape and otherwise record the talent's name, likeness, voice, personality, personal identification, and conversations, statements, performances, and activities during and in connection with the Program, as well as personal experiences, biographical data, incidents, situations, actions, reactions and events which have occurred or will occur in connection with the Program. The talent must understand that the producer may require the talent to wear a microphone, or that recording devices may otherwise be placed at various locations, concealed or otherwise and, finally, that the talent may be accompanied by the filming crew for certain enumerated periods during the Program. While talent may seek to approve any final use or appearance of the recorded activities, especially to avoid a negative portrayal, such requests are often difficult to accommodate and, certainly, never absolute. Indeed, to limit, temper or modify what may ultimately be portrayed would undermine the "reality" of the Program, not to mention create an administrative nightmare for the producer required to seek and obtain such approvals, perhaps from multiple parties, under tight production and delivery timetables.

g. Post-production Participation

The talent must also agree to be available, on request, for any additional taping or post-production activities that may be needed after the end of taping of the Program. This participation should include, but not necessarily be limited to pre-records, wrap-arounds, interviews, as well as appearances on final episodes, reunion episodes, and recap episodes.

h. Additional Participation

This is a "catch-all" provision where the talent is generally required to provide further services to the reality show. These services are performed at an additional rate from a few hundred dollars for limited Internet-based or social media activity, to thousands of dollars for more extensive work. Such additional participation is generally in connection with the production of: (i) enhancement materials including, without limitation, host wraparounds, on-screen commentary, voiceover materials, mini-episodes; (ii) promotional spots, trailers and in-store sales tapes; (iii) gaming content including, but not limited to, voiceover and image/motion capture materials; (iv) graphics/wallpaper content (e.g., talent photos) and audio content (e.g., voice tone/voice ring-back content); (v) any television special (e.g., launch or finale specials, reunion specials, or "where are they now?"/ update specials), compilation (e.g. so-called "cram sessions," recap episodes or other clip shows), reunion or "best-of" programs; and/or extended episode content (e.g., to create so-called "super-sized" versions of episodes) in connection with the Program; (vi) virtual reality environments and community applications, websites, webpages or weblogs to be written and/or maintained by the talent under the producer's guidance or direction (of course subject to the producer's right to edit and/or otherwise approve any and all elements thereof); (vii) additional footage relating to the talent that is not primarily intended for incorporation into the Program, but which may be used for other purposes; and (viii) other similar materials.

l. Promotional Appearances

The talent may also be requested to be available to participate as, when and where the producer, network or even sponsors of the Program may require in connection with the promotion, marketing, advertising, publicity, interviews and similar matters, and make other appearances including photographic or commercial production sessions as well as event appearances for institutional advertising and promotions for the producer and/or the television network(s) that broadcast the Program, as well as the Program itself. This provision is, as expected, subject to extensive negotiation, including the extent of the appearances that may be required, expenses tied to travel that may be required, and the associated compensation that will be paid, if separate, apart from and in addition to the compensation being paid to the talent for participation in the Program. While it is reasonable and expected that some promotional activities will be included in the base compensation, there is certainly a reasonable limit to such requirements, beyond which any further promotional efforts should be at a compensated rate.

5.3.2.2. Grant of Rights

In addition to securing the talent's participation, and subject to reasonableness and the various negotiable points outlined above, it is critically important for the creator and producer of a reality production to secure a litany of rights from the talent which, when bundled together, allows the creator to distribute the show without fear of lawsuits or repercussion. The rights granted include the following:

Everything related to the talent's participation in or contribution to the Program, including any performance, life story elements, interviews, ideas, suggestions, themes, plots, stories, characters, dialogue, text, designs, graphics, titles, drawings, artwork, digital works, songs, music, photography, video, film and any other material. It is equally important as part of this broad scope of rights to identify any and all of the talent's contributions as a works-made-for-hire specially ordered or commissioned for the Program to not run afoul of copyright law.

The grant must also include the ability to use, develop, market, sell, manufacture, exhibit, distribute, broadcast, license and/or otherwise exploit all of the rights. The scope and extent is a point to be negotiated, from limited territories and formats, to something as broad as the entire universe, in perpetuity, in any and all media, platforms and formats, whether known or devised at a later date.

The producer must also have the right to change, add to, take from, translate, reformat or reprocess the Program, and the talent's appearance therein, as the producer may determine in its sole discretion. Again, this provision is often heavily negotiated – the producer will want free reign to edit as deemed appropriate, while the talent will certainly want to limit the "creative license" to prevent any appearance that may be unfavorable or otherwise undermines the talent's reputation or goodwill.

Importantly, the producer must also have the right to use, and authorize others to use, all of the rights granted by the talent, and those rights must extend to advertising, publicity, marketing, promotional and commercial tie-in purposes of the Program. Again, the scope and extent of these additional rights are to be heavily negotiated.

Sometimes, the talent will sing or perform original musical works in the Program. Accordingly, musical rights have to be addressed, and the producer needs to secure synchronization rights in the music publishing of each composition used in the Program (whether the compositions are composed, owned and controlled by talent, or are controlled by third party publishers from whom rights have to be obtained), as well as ancillary uses thereof, in perpetuity. As expected, especially for preexisting musical works, these rights are non-exclusive.

The producer must be granted the right to use and license the talent's name and likeness for the purpose of, and in connection with, the sale of third party products, goods and services that may appear on or in the Program. As expected, this aspect of the rights, as well as any associated compensation therewith, is heavily negotiated.

Often, the talent or business featured in a reality production has a developing, or even vibrant, business endeavor. It is not uncommon for a production company of (and even the network airing) a reality program to participate in the additional success of such commercial activities generated as a result of being featured on the reality show. While the terms of the profit participation are negotiable, and the methods of calculation vary widely, the concept remains the same – how successful were the business activities prior to the reality show, what are the baseline financial metrics (i.e., revenue, profitability, etc.), and what is the increase as a result of the publicity from the show? Once that is determined, the percentages vary, but are usually in the range of ten to twenty-five percent (10–25%) of the increase realized following airing.

Moreover, great lengths are taken to protect the child and, as such, there are frequently also provisions whereby the parent or guardian relinquishes the earnings of a minor, covenants to not interfere with the performance of the minor's services, and conversely in certain circumstances, guarantees the performance obligations of the minor. Further, in some jurisdictions, application must be made to a court to review and approve the terms of the minor's contract.

5.3.2.3. Additional Common Provisions of Talent Agreements

a. Restrictions on Use of Trademark

The networks closely protect intellectual property and good will, aggressively protecting against the talent using the names, logos, trade names or trademarks of the network or any production company involved in the Program. Talent (whether individuals or businesses) with established brands and trademarks may seek some similar protection from use by the network, production company or sponsors of the Program not directly associated with its advertising and promotion.

b. Termination

The producer needs the right to terminate a reality production. This termination right can be invoked for any reason or no reason at all, can be tied to an event of force majeure, or be the result of some other trigger. In any case, the producer will seek to secure the right to suspend or terminate production, and be released from any further obligations to the talent if and when this occurs.

c. Remedies

The producer needs to ensure that all legal and equitable remedies are reserved to protect against an actual or threatened breach of contract by the talent. However, in the event it may have claims against the production company or network, the talent is limited to only recover monetary damages for actual harm caused by an action of the producer. To be certain, absent some unusual circumstance, the talent is required to broadly waive any right to equitable relief, or the right to enjoin, restrain or interfere with the Program, or any granted rights, in any manner.

d. Unions/Guilds

Most reality productions are non-union, and the talent must specifically acknowledge and understand that participation in the reality production does not fall under the jurisdiction of SAG, AFTRA or any other guild, union or other collective bargaining agreement (even if the talent might be eligible as a guild member to work under a guild umbrella if the Program were a movie or other scripted production).

e. Employment Relationship

While the talent agreement indicates that the relationship between the production company and reality show talent does not constitute an employment relationship, joint venture or partnership between them, and that the talent is not to be deemed or considered the producer's agent for any purpose, that is not the end of the analysis. In fact, a reality show participant will likely qualify as an "employee" of the production company, as three key elements are met: 1) the participant is acting to "serve the interests" of the production company; 2) the production company consents, and indeed requests, those "services;" and 3) the production company controls the manner and means by which the services are performed. The first two elements are readily met. The third aspect of control is met too, despite the concept of "reality." Indeed, once production starts, the production company controls the entire production, from requiring the talent's services to be performed around the clock, with breaks set by the production company, to locations being determined by the production company, to affording the talent little input on the creative direction of the Program. As such, the talent is legally considered an employee of the production company, affording the talent the protections afforded in the usual employment relationship.

f. Assignment

The assignment provision is unexpectedly critical, and is an explicit acknowledgment that the producer may transfer all of the rights in connection with the Program as deemed necessary, such as to a network or distributor, while the talent is specifically prohibited from assigning any obligations, such as the obligation to appear and participate in the Program. Certainly, the producer's third-party assignment rights are freely exercisable, while the talent's assignment of obligations is strictly limited.

g. Representations

To avoid any legal defenses that could potentially be used to void the agreement with disastrous consequences, the talent is asked to make a variety of representations and warranties, including that the talent has provided all documentation and information requested or required by the producer in connection with any statutory record-keeping obligations such as the talent's full legal name (as well as any previous names, aliases, stage names, professional names and/or nicknames), current address, and date of birth. Most productions will do extensive background checks on talent, including driving record searches, as well as bankruptcy, civil and criminal litigation checks, to insure that the representations and warranties are accurate, and that there are no circumstances involving talent's past or present activities that could be considered detrimental to the Program, the network and its sponsors.

h. Mediation/Arbitration

The election of remedies varies greatly, with some networks requiring a jury trial, others relying on basic arbitration clauses, and others requiring comprehensive alternative binding dispute resolution procedures, including mediation.

5.4. DISTRIBUTION AGREEMENTS[3]

Distribution is the ultimate goal of all reality television creators – the sale or licensing of their creation for exhibition. As expected, distribution comes with a long, detailed agreement which defines the rights and obligations of each party. This agreement outlines in great detail the terms of distribution, and the associated issues of ownership, delivery obligations and broadcasting. Negotiating a distribution agreement for a reality television program is a complex task.

While distributors, broadcasters and end-users of content are well-versed in the terms and conditions of agreements to acquire content for exploitation, producers and creators rarely have sufficient knowledge of the intricacies of these dealings. Therefore, as substantial matters of rights and obligations are involved, producers often hire a third party representative to sell the project to a distributor, and then negotiate the terms of these agreements.

---

[3] This section provides commentary to concepts more fully illustrated in the supplemental distribution agreements to this chapter.

As part of the representation process, the creator must clearly define for the representative the range of rights that the creator is willing (or able) to grant for distribution. As new distribution platforms continue to emerge, distribution companies have become more specialized. As a result, the producer's representative needs to ensure that the distributor has the necessary market expertise and contacts to distribute the series in the preferred medium(s).

An analysis of the general provisions of a standard distribution agreement, and the potential issues that may arise in structuring these agreements, follows.

5.4.1. Granted Rights

The granted rights provision specifies the markets and media in which the distributor is able to exhibit or exploit the Program. The rights granted under this provision will determine the content of further provisions under the agreement, especially the amount paid to the producer. A distributor may be granted all rights to distribute the series as it sees fit, or limited to a very small market and one medium of distribution, and/or for a limited or long(er) period of exhibition.

This provision also outlines the obligations of the producer with regard to the number and length of the episodes it must deliver. Distribution agreements granting all rights to a series will generally contain language for the network's option to order and receive rights to future seasons of the show.

Distribution agreements must also have clearly defined language regarding copyright claims to the series. Pursuant to the U.S. Copyright Act, a traditional "all rights" distribution agreement will contain language naming the distributor the "sole author" and worldwide owner of all ideas, concepts, and work relating to the series.

5.4.2. Territory

Many distribution contracts for reality television describe the scope of territory as "worldwide" or "the universe" without any limitations. However, some agreements limit the distributor's geographic scope to circulate the series. This can become increasingly complicated if the distributor has online distribution rights such as VOD (Video-On-Demand) or SVOD (Subscription-Video-On-Demand). Should this instance arise, the distributor will likely be required to use geo-filtering technology, which allows the distributor to restrict online access to viewers based on geographic location.

5.4.3. Production Budgets, License Fees and Payment

There are a variety of paths that unscripted content may take to evolve to a series, each with different financing. Of course, each depends on the network, and how that network wants to "test" the concept.

First, networks may request a development reel or presentation of the concept. This is generally a shortened version of an entire episode, while longer and more detailed than the usual three to five minute sizzle tape that is commonly used to pitch the project in the first place. This presentation invariably features the talent that will carry the show, or flesh out the format that the concept entails. For this work, networks may offer a payment generally in the range of $10,000 to $25,000, or slightly more. It is important to note that this payment does not usually include a production fee or profit, and it behooves the wise production company to put all of the financial resources onto the screen at this early stage – for a strong presentation or development reel can sway a network to order a show, or otherwise push a show that is on the cusp into production and save it from an early creative death.

Once the decision has been made to proceed past the development stage, and to an episode that will be airable, there are a number of choices. The network may order a pilot, or a pilot plus a specified number of episodes, or a partial season of six, eight or ten episodes, or a series of thirteen episodes, all the way up to an order of twenty-six episodes. Obviously, the more episodes that are ordered plays into the network's confidence that the show will be a success. At this point, the network wants to get the greatest return on its investment, and knows that it will have to spend production dollars to realize advertising revenue. For shows that will appear on major broadcast networks, reality shows in primetime will generally command episodic budgets between $250,000 and $2 million per hour, depending on the concept and format. Conversely, for reality shows to be broadcast on a cable network, production budgets range from about $75,000 to $350,000 per hour episode. And, of course, the production budgets increase with each season that the show is successful.

For the production company, reality shows are far from a financial boon. The production company can anticipate a gross fee of about ten percent of the episodic budget, which may be capped by the network at a dollar ceiling. After all, the network wants the budget to end up in the finished product that appears on screen, and not go into the production company's pocket. And, of course, this production company fee may then be split between multiple parties if there is a group responsible for bringing the show or concept to the screen.

Sadly, the first two seasons are rough for the production company. The production budget is tight, the production company fee is predetermined, and the network will invariably demand changes as the production evolves, with little additional compensation to the production company. Of course, the production company still has its fixed costs and associated business expenses, making the first two seasons of any show a risky proposition for any producer. But, once the third season arrives, a milestone that the vast majority of shows do not ever see, budgets (and consequently the margins) and ancillary licensing of products and merchandise generally increase, leading to fifty percent or more in the margins.

Whatever the ultimate series budget, distributors can pay producers for the right to distribute works in a variety of methods. While some parties agree upon a flat rate per episode paid by the distributor, with a payment schedule tied to various production dates and milestones, another (albeit less common) method of payment may be based on an advance tied to the success of a show. In the latter case, the producer receives a payment upfront, usually upon the signing of the agreement, and does not receive another payment until the distributor has received that payment back, plus some fee on top of that amount, and then the parties agree upon a revenue share of the resultant distribution receipts. Of course, the producer will prefer as big of an advance as possible, entitling the distributor to a higher fee and larger royalty percentage due to the increased risk of the distributor not recouping its initial payment. The distributor is counting on a top-flight program from its supplier on a tight budget, while the producer is counting on the distributor/ network's commitment (and ability) to successfully position and market the series.

5.4.4. Guidelines and Approvals

A distribution agreement is not just a contract to sell a series, but it also creates and sets the terms and conditions of an ongoing business and working relationship between the parties during the production of the series, which in success may be years-long. Distributing networks, whether they are streaming companies, broadcast or cable television networks, have specific company standards and practices that require strict conformity. As a result, the producer must consult regularly with the distributor to comply with a myriad of standards. Undoubtedly, the network will invariably have the final say over the major elements of production, including creative direction, executive producers, show runner, talent, credits, and the inclusion of any third party product or service into the show. Of course, depending on precedent and stature, the production company may be afforded meaningful consultation rights, or may be given pre-approval of certain aspects of the production in advance.

5.4.5. Editing and Delivery

The rights to final edit in a Program can be a contentious negotiating point between the producer and the distributor. The distributor will want the autonomy to prepare significant notes and comments to the production before airing, and the ability to make all final edits at its sole and absolute discretion. Conversely, the producer will want the creative vision to remain intact, and will not want the network or final end user to be able to modify any aspect of the series without consent. Should the agreement be an "all rights" contract, it is likely that the majority of these issues will be decided in favor of the distributor retaining broad final control over the production.

Additionally, this provision details the format and specifications covering technical delivery of each episode to the distributor or network. In the event that the producer fails to deliver all of the requisite materials in the manner agreed upon, the distributor may have the right to create those materials itself and charge the expenses back to the producer. Should the payment method be in the form of an advance, the distributor could also withhold a portion of the advance against final acceptance of all delivery elements, and use the funds to create the necessary delivery elements if and as required.

5.4.6. Promotion of the Series

The distributor will negotiate for, and usually retain, complete control over the marketing, promotion and advertising of the series. Further, the distributor will likely have the right to authorize a third party to publicize the show without the producer's consent. Finally, the producer will often be required to receive the prior written consent of the distributor before being able to promote the program, or its involvement in the program, in any manner, until and unless authorized to do so by the distributor.

5.5. INDEPENDENT CONTRACTOR AGREEMENT[4]

5.5.1. Introduction

Creating and producing reality television requires a number of people performing a variety of diverse tasks. Instead of hiring everyone working on the project as an employee, producers generally engage workers as independent contractors. But what are the advantages, and risks, of a production company contracting out work instead of hiring actual employees for the various jobs?

The primary benefit that a production company gains from hiring independent contractors is a substantial savings on taxes and payroll. Producing a reality television is costly, so companies take advantage of every opportunity to deliver the reality show on time, and on budget. Additionally, the production company reduces its liability when contracting out work as opposed to hiring an employee to do the task. Should a true independent contractor sustain an injury while performing a task on set, the production company would not be responsible for paying any workers' compensation benefits.

Of course, there are restrictions on whether a worker can be classified as an independent contractor, as opposed to an employee, which will be discussed in greater detail below. Without such guidelines, the production company would undoubtedly list the entire crew as independent contractors as a cost-saving measure, blatantly improper conduct, and subjecting the production company to significant penalties and fines. However, the production company is

---

[4] This section provides commentary to concepts more fully illustrated in the accompanying independent contractor forms.

able to avoid many of these restrictions by utilizing a "loan-out" company to staff many parts of the production crew. A loan-out company is an independent contractor held responsible for engaging much of the production staff, including: editors, camerapersons, composers, designers, and other individuals. This arrangement allows the production company to avoid paying employer payroll taxes, insurance, and other costs associated with having full time employees. Certainly, there is a fine line between employee versus an independent contractor, and the production company should consult tax and labor law professionals with expertise in the state(s) in which production will occur to avoid any employee misclassification issues. The following provides an overview of the general components of an independent contractor agreement, as well as the potential issues that may arise.

5.5.2. Services and Length of Term

It is critical that the independent contractor agreement precisely define the services to be rendered, and the length of the period over which those services will be performed. Of course, the services, and level of detail required in defining those services, will vary depending on the role. It is important to clearly define all of the services to be provided by the contractor in order to avoid misunderstandings and disputes in the future; indeed, the parties will often include a schedule, or "scope of work," explicitly outlining the work to be performed by the contractor.

The length of the term for which the services will be rendered may also vary greatly. Some services have a clearly delineated start and end date, while others are open-ended, and may run until the defined services are completed, or the production has concluded. Moreover, the actual hours of services required may vary, from exclusive, full-time duties during active production, to part-time, or even completely free during other periods. This flexibility will enable the production to engage, and pay, the contractor only as needed, avoiding the need to pay a full time employee. Of course, the independent contractor may resist, as the contractor may encounter difficulty managing workload to ensure sufficient work and income without a gap in schedule or pay. For this reason, often the contractor will render services non-exclusively, allowing the freedom to work elsewhere when not needed during any given period of the production.

5.5.3. Consideration, Expenses, Benefits and Credit

Contractors are usually paid on either a flat rate or a periodic basis. A variety of factors affect the amount of compensation that the independent contractor will receive, such as the reputation of the contractor, the type of service being provided, and the size of the production budget. Additionally, the location of the production will affect the contractor's pay, especially if the agreement is covered under a union contract. When negotiating the engagement of the contractor, it is important to understand a particular region's range of compensation for the service provided by a similarly qualified individual. If the contractor is working a non-union job, there is the potential for the compensation to be less than the established guild minimums.

In addition, the parties should negotiate how costs and expenses, such as airfare and travel, lodging, and equipment purchases will be reimbursed, if at all. The contract should also unambiguously state that the production company is not responsible for any additional benefits such as health care, disability, life insurance, workers' compensation, and retirement plans, all usually offered in a traditional employer-employee relationship.

As is frequent in the entertainment industry, credit attribution is often the most contentious aspect of the negotiation of an independent contractor agreement. As expected, the contractor will negotiate for the best credit position possible, as the credit accorded a contractor goes a long way in future career success. The contractor will seek a credit position close to the main body of the program, as well as credit in the associated advertising and promotional activity.

5.5.4. Contractor Status

This provision is intended to unequivocally define the independent contractor relationship. The rules regarding classification of one as independent contractor or as an employee depend on the jurisdiction, and the penalties for misclassification can be severe. Regulatory authorities consider a number of factors in making this determination, including day-to-day supervision of the individual and control by the company; times and places of work designated by the company; exclusivity or non-exclusivity of services to the company; whether the individual's or company's tools, materials, facilities and equipment are being utilized; whether the individual is either creating new materials for the company or providing preexisting materials he or she has previously created; and so on. This list is not exhaustive, and different jurisdictions (and even different examiners within the same jurisdiction) may put more emphasis on one factor over another. Being that the factors associated with whether a worker is to be considered an independent contractor or an employee are ambiguous, this section should provide definitive language in an attempt to avoid any issue of misclassifying the worker as an employee. The provision should also reiterate that the independent contractor is solely responsible for handling taxes associated with compensation. As mentioned above, the popularity of loan-out companies are on the rise, as this arrangement eliminates any confusion as to whether the worker is an employee or an independent contractor.

5.5.5. Work for Hire

The inclusion of a work-for-hire provision is critical to the independent contractor agreement, as it ensures that copyright ownership in the creative work is vested with the production company. Without such a written provision, evolving from the U.S. Copyright Act, the contractor could claim ownership in the work and results and proceeds thereof. This provision ensures that the contractor's compensation includes not only payment for the services rendered, but also for a transfer of all rights in the creative work to the production company, and a relinquishment of any rights of the contractor in the results and the proceeds of the creative services rendered.

5.5.6. Name and Likeness

Although it is rare that a production company would use the name and likeness of an independent contractor to promote itself or the Program, it is still an important right to negotiate. Should the contractor win any prestigious awards for the work on a production, or any previous awards for exceptional work, or be involved in another hit series, the production company will want to exploit such a positive achievement to bolster advertising of the show. Of course, contractors are usually open to this type of agreement, as touting a contractor's accomplishments only increases the contractor's value and drives demand for future services.

5.5.7. Assignment

Related to a work for hire, an assignment provision is customary in the reality television industry to enable the production company to grant its rights in the production, and the agreements of those rendering services in connection with the production, to a third party, such as a network. The assignment of rights is critical, as it allows for the production to be transferred to a network, distributor or other end-user without restriction or issues in the chain of title. The production company may choose to concurrently assign its obligations, and seek to be relieved of any liability. Here, the contractor may be willing to agree to an assignment of obligations, as the third party (such as a network) may be in a better position or more readily able to indemnify the contractor should any harm or loss occur; of course, the contractor, if shrewd, will insist that all assignments be in writing, include assumption of the production company's obligations to the contractor, provide for notice of assignment to the contractor, and stipulate that the production company remain secondarily liable, even if the assignment of obligations is agreed to.

Conversely, the production company will prohibit the contractor from assigning obligations to a third party. The production company specifically hired the contractor due to a particular skill set to render a specific task. It would be counterproductive to the production company if that contactor would then be able to delegate obligations to some third party.

5.5.8. Confidentiality

A confidentiality provision, or non-disclosure agreement, should be included in every independent contractor agreement. Being that a contractor will have direct access to confidential information related to the project (whether concerning the production, production company, the network, talent, events depicted in the series – including outcomes of competitions, dramatic "cliffhangers" in cinema-verité-styled productions, etc.), and is not an employee of the production company, the company has an increased risk, and must take precautionary measures to secure proper protection for its intellectual property and the production. The language in this provision should be abundantly clear that all work and information – written and oral – related to the project is the sole property of the production company. The contractor has no right to disclose any of this information to a third party without written consent from the production company. And, finally, it must be clear that any unauthorized disclosure of this protected information by the contractor will be a material breach of the contract, entitling the production company to legal and equitable relief, including an injunction to prevent further or ongoing confidentiality breaches and a right to pursue liquidated damages.

5.6. RELEASES, CONSENTS AND LOCATION AGREEMENT[5]

The litany of claims that arise out of a reality television production are endless. As such, producers must err on the side of abundant caution with respect to obtaining the necessary releases and consents. Releases, consents and authorizations allow producers to legally use and exploit whatever footage that is obtained during shooting, while also containing an explicit and broad waiver of claims, including those related to defamation, privacy, publicity and copyright claims, but extending to claims of personal injury and property damage. To avoid lawsuits and liability, written consent forms and releases should be obtained for all participants or those who appear in a show, locations used and accessed, and products, logos or other materials depicted. Release and consent forms, coupled with an effective liability insurance policy, broadly shield the producer from various liabilities and lawsuits, so long as the waivers are not obtained by any means of misrepresentation, deception, fraud or undue influence.

In reality television programming, most non-featured participants are not compensated for appearing in the production; however, comprehensive written releases and consents are still required. Producers are not required by law to obtain the written consent of all participants on a show, and the laws pertaining to the rights of privacy and publicity, as well as the exceptions to the enforcement of these rights, provide guidance. Moreover, the producer has broad delivery obligations for clearing all materials to be used in the production in advance and, further, a liability insurer will not provide coverage for the production absent written release agreements.

The necessary release and consent provisions vary case by case. Some releases may include an acknowledgment that the individual may

---

[5] This section provides commentary to concepts more fully illustrated in accompanying release, consent and location agreement forms.

be subject to a host of physical or psychological peril, such as the dangers presented in various physical makeover shows (e.g., those involving weight loss or surgery). Others may include an acknowledgement that the producers may engage in intentional acts, or intentionally place the participant in a dangerous situation that would otherwise constitute tortious conduct, such as those presented in physical competition shows. Release and consent agreements may even require the participant to release the producers from liability for the harmful, physical consequences that may result after intimate encounters with other participants. It is imperative that a producer have an experienced attorney review all the release and consent forms to make sure that all of the necessary protections are satisfied. And, finally, as described in depth later in this chapter, participants may be required to sign an additional release protecting against liability for the participation in ultra-hazardous or dangerous activities, such as stunts, sports, or extreme physical activity, where a "garden variety" release and limitation of liability would not be sufficient.

5.6.1. Location Agreement

Most reality shows are not filmed in a studio. The show could take place at a privately-owned business, in a private home, or on privately-owned land. In these cases, producers must obtain the appropriate documentation to legally film the show prior to the start of production. The owner of the land or building may receive a rental fee for allowing access to and the use of private property. Additionally, the owner may also require that the producer obtain specific insurance for the duration of the use of the property. The producer might also be required to obtain releases from neighboring premises or permits from the local government if any filming will take place on public property. Location agreements vary in length, depending on the duration of the rental, the manner in which the location will be used, and the value of the property being used. Below are the main provisions contained in a location agreement, as well as issues that frequently arise during negotiations.

5.6.1.1. Grant of Rights

The extent of the permissible use of the property is defined under this provision. Depending on the type of show being filmed, some producers may want complete exclusivity of the property for the entire duration of access to the property. The producer might also negotiate for exclusivity of the property to keep the content of the show private. Additionally, the producer could negotiate for language prohibiting the owner from renting out the property for another production project to prevent the location from being seen in a competitor's show.

The producer's control over the premises should also be clearly defined. It is common for the production of a show to require renovations of a rented location. This could include swapping out furniture, paintings, or even re-construction of the property's layout. The agreement may then also contain terms requiring that the producer return the location to its original state upon the completion of the filming, reasonable wear and tear excepted. Any renovation details must be clearly defined beforehand.

Responsibilities for damage that may occur on the premises during the production of the show can cause issues between the parties. The producer will want to limit responsibility for any damage that may occur, while the owner will want to hold the producer completely liable.

The producer will also likely want to have complete autonomy over the final edits of the show and portrayal of the premises. The consent agreement should contain language that prohibits the producer from displaying the premises in a negative light. If the use of the premises is minimal, the producer should also negotiate for language that does not obligate the use of any footage made on the property.

5.6.1.2. Length of Term

The producer must be careful when negotiating the length of the access to the location. It could be expensive to extend the use of a location beyond its original limit should filming not be timely completed. Likewise, the producer should also negotiate the right to delay the final payment until after filming of the series is complete, especially if filming may be delayed.

A "force majeure" provision is important to include in a location agreement, particularly if the weather could cause delays in filming. Any unforeseeable circumstance beyond the producer's control that would hamper the production while on the premises would constitute an event of force majeure. This provision enables the producer to extend the length of the term equal to the time that was lost from the event without additional cost.

5.6.1.3. Compensation

The length of the term and exclusivity of the use of the premises (which relates to costs to the owner of being deprived access to the premises, or preventing others from having access, in whole or in part) are key factors in determining the amount that the producer will have to pay. Compensation can either be an agreed-upon flat rate, or a daily fee. The owner of the premises will likely also require the producer to obtain and pay for sufficient insurance to cover any accidents that occur during the production on the property. In some instances, additional costs may be included, such as utilities, insurances, extra security that may be required during production, and cleaning and property repair.

5.6.1.4. Confidentiality

The producer should require that the owner of the property, and any employees associated with the property, be prohibited from disclosing any information learned or seen while filming is taking place at the location.

5.6.2. Standard Appearance Release

5.6.2.1. Grant of Rights

The producer will want extremely broad appearance releases to minimize any possible restrictions during the filming of the show. These considerations apply to both featured talent expected to appear in all episodes of the series, as well as an individual whose incidental appearance may only be seen in one or a couple of episodes. This provision will define how expansive the producer's rights are to use an individual's name and likeness in connection with the show, and the producer will likely seek unconditional, unlimited consent to use an individual's name and likeness. Furthermore, this consent authority will extend to any advertising and promotional efforts relating to the show. However, participants will sometimes try to limit the producer's merchandising and product rights, with a payment to be made for more expansive rights, or for approval rights before certain merchandising is permitted to occur. However, as the producer has an overwhelming advantage in bargaining power, most evident prior to shooting, most agreements grant the producer the right to use the participant's name and likeness as deemed appropriate.

The section will also detail the amount of access that the producer will have to the individual. Depending on the show, the access to film an individual could be limited to a specific location or time, or it could be unlimited for an agreed-upon period of time. Further, this provision will likely grant the producer the right, but not the obligation, to distribute, reproduce, sublicense, sell, and edit the footage without any limitations, including the possible licensing of film clips for inclusion in other productions.

Most importantly, this provision will clearly state that the appearance on the show is for hire. By doing so, an individual gives up any potential copyright and ownership rights for his or her appearance on the show.

5.6.2.2. Compensation

Often, individuals appearing on reality shows will receive no monetary compensation for appearing on a show. This is particularly true of an individual who will be briefly featured, incidental to the Program, or non-essential to the production. Moreover, an individual will gladly appear in a show in exchange for self-promotion or free advertising of a business, or in the hope of becoming famous. However, some reality shows will compensate certain individuals who visibly appear. Certainly, the payment is always driven by the budget of the show, as well as the distributor, be it a broadcast or cable network or digital platform. As described elsewhere in this chapter, payment could be in the form of an agreed-upon amount per appearance (per week of production or per episode in which the individual appears), or built into the show as a prize for winning a competition, and may also include additional payment for profits, ancillary revenue, merchandising, music and the like. Producers of a reality show that is filmed at a specific location for an extended period of time will almost always pay the participant for travel and lodging expenses.

5.6.2.3. Confidentiality

As noted elsewhere with respect to all individuals contributing services to the production of non-scripted programming, a confidentiality provision is essential in a standard appearance release form. The clause shall state that the individual is prohibited from disclosing any information directly or indirectly related to the show. This provision becomes increasingly important in reality shows that contain competitions where individuals may be eliminated before the show airs, or that contain a "reveal" of a renovation.

5.6.2.4. Third Party Releases

The producer may require an individual to use reasonable efforts, at no cost to the individual (or the producer), to assist the producer in obtaining releases from additional individuals who may be critical to a reality production, such as current or former members of the individual's family and friends, dependents, heirs, boyfriends, ex-boyfriends, girlfriends, ex-girlfriends, clients, co-workers, doctors, therapists, nurses, etc. The extent of this cooperation, of course, is always subject to negotiation and limits.

5.6.2.5. Authorization for Release of Medical Information

The participant authorizes the producer to obtain and use any and all of his or her medical records and health plan information, including, without limitation, those records pertaining to physical, emotional, psychological and mental health, and records including HIV-related information. The producer is authorized to release all such records including, but not limited to, records concerning medical and health-related services rendered to the participant, as well as claims and enrollment information.

5.6.3. Ultra-Hazardous Activities and Assumption of Risk

Some reality shows involve individuals taking part in extremely dangerous activities where there is the risk of severe injury, or even death. The producer must be aware of the severe legal ramifications that could occur as a result of any injury that may be suffered by participating in such dangerous activity. Since some activities involve a serious risk of harm that cannot be eliminated even with the utmost care, the abnormally dangerous activity falls into a category of strict liability. Due to the abnormally dangerous activity being performed, the producer will require a separate, ultra-hazardous assumption of the risk release form to protect all the parties associated with the show from lawsuits arising out of such dangerous activity.

By signing this additional release, an individual acknowledges the risk involved, and is freely and voluntarily taking part in the activity without any coercion, pressure, or undue influence from any other party. There is a full and complete waiver of the right to assert any claims against the producer, a network, or any other party involved with the show. There will likely be language warranting that the individual is in good physical and mental health, and without any medical condition that may affect the ability to perform or take part in the dangerous activity. Additionally, the individual will confirm adequate health insurance to cover any potential cost that would result from an unforeseen and unfortunate accident or injury.

The participant may in turn require that such hazardous activities will be supervised by competent stunt coordinators, that adequate emergency medical personnel will be on scene for emergencies, and that emergency medical care will be authorized by the participant. As a general matter, it is prudent for the production company to make these arrangements and take such precautions for its own protection as additional "insurance" toward its exposure, if an injury, or worse, should occur during production.

5.6.4. Appearance Release for a Minor

Producers should take extra precautions with respect to featuring any minor in the production. Generally, only the parent or legal guardian has the authority to consent for a minor to appear. Indeed, consent from a temporary guardian who is in custody of the child will not be valid. Further, the producer must be aware of the specific laws regarding the engagement of minors in the jurisdiction where filming is being conducted. Some jurisdictions hold that even if a parent or legal guardian provides the appropriate consent for the minor's appearance in a show, the minor can revoke that consent upon reaching the age of majority. In some states, the producers are required to make an application to a court for the minor's contract to be reviewed and approved by a judge, with the producer certifying that the minor's payment is placed into a trust. And, finally, to ensure further protection of minors, it is not unusual for a production to be required to file what is commonly referred to as a "Pence Certification" with the Office of the United States Attorney General confirming that no minors will be involved in the filming of sexually explicit material. Importantly, these agreements are enforceable against the minor's parents only.

The release used for a minor will otherwise have many of the same provisions that are in a standard appearance release form. There will be provisions regarding the producer's rights to use the minor's name and likeness, confidentiality, compensation, work for hire and ownership rights, and medical information. Although a lot of these provisions touch on the same topics, special consideration must be given to the fact that a minor is involved. For example, depending on the child's age and the laws in the jurisdiction where the show is being filmed, issues regarding child labor laws must be addressed.

5.6.5. Acquired Footage/Still Photograph License

In this release, the owner of preexisting material grants the producer and the network the irrevocable right, but not the obligation, to incorporate certain film or video footage, or still photography, into the production. In addition, the owner grants the right to use and authorize others to use the licensed materials in the distribution, sale, licensing, marketing, advertising, promotion, exhibition and other exploitation of the reality television program, in all markets and media, throughout the universe, in perpetuity.

The owner also warrants and represents ownership of the materials, as well as the right to grant the use of the materials without infringing on the rights of any third party. And, of course, the owner will indemnify and hold harmless any party from and against any and all claims, damages, liabilities, costs and expenses arising out of any breach of warranty.

5.6.6. Authorization to Use Names, Products and Logos

In this release, the owner grants the right to photograph, record, reproduce or otherwise use product(s), and any related names, trademarks, service marks, trade names, logos, copyrighted material and/or other materials, in the production, exhibition, exploitation, and promotion of the reality program, in all forms of media. Moreover, the owner represents that no other consent is required to enable such usage.

5.6.7. Public Filming Notice

When a reality television production occurs in public, and some individuals may briefly appear in the background, a signed release is generally not required. However, to avoid any potential invasion of privacy claims, producers should do one of two things. First, obtain a simple appearance release from anyone appearing more than incidentally or, alternatively, post at least one, and preferably two, prominent public filming notices (e.g., signage at the entrance to a store, restaurant or public lobby, or at either end of a street or sidewalk where filming may be occurring), which warns people that, if they voluntarily proceed past the notice, they may appear incidentally in a production that will be broadcast to the public.

5.7. PRODUCT AND SERVICE PLACEMENT AGREEMENTS[6]

5.7.1. Introduction

In reality television, viewers often see a product with its trademarked name and logo prominently displayed. It is highly unlikely that this occurrence was a mere coincidence. This intentional, subtle advertising, known as "product placement," is used to promote a product or brand during the course of a reality show. However, this advertising technique is not limited to the inclusion of a product into reality programming; it also extends to the incorporation of services. A

---

[6] This section provides commentary to concepts more fully illustrated in accompanying porduct placement and servicing form agreements.

supplier company can infuse its trademarked brand, product, and/or service into a reality show in three main ways: 1) a product is placed into a show where its trademarked logo is prominently featured; 2) products are donated for direct use in a show, such as materials for a makeover series; and 3) services are provided free of charge in exchange for promotional purposes or verbal mentions.

Many modern reality shows would not be feasible without product placement or the donation of products and services. Any makeover show perfectly illustrates the need for, and pervasive use of, product and service placement in reality television production. The basic premise of a makeover show calls for the complete reconstruction, renovation or transformation of a person, a home, or a business. But who is paying for all of the services required, or materials used, to accomplish the makeover task at hand? And, as importantly, who is liable and responsible for any negligence during the performance of the services, or defects in the workmanship or products, that may arise? All of these issues are negotiated and decided before the production commences, and are set forth in the appropriate product or service placement agreement.

The supplier will enter into a product or service placement agreement to fulfill one intended purpose: the ability to advertise to a potential paying consumer. This becomes more important with today's fast-paced age of technology. With the exponential growth of on-demand viewing, many viewers can fast-forward through traditional commercials. Therefore, suppliers needed to develop new methods to reach the widest possible audience. To accomplish this goal, suppliers have learned how to persuade a production company to insert products into a production; indeed, a simple gratis donation of a product or service guarantees placement, if even fleeting. Importantly, the use of product or services placement allows a manufacturer or supplier to target a specific audience demographic known to watch a particular reality show.

Concurrently, a production company may benefit from the inclusion of donated products and services to a reality show, and will actively seek such arrangements. In the competitive state of today's production environment, companies must look for new and creative ways to deliver the best possible show with a challenged budget (e.g., a production can obtain a necessary prop or tool or wardrobe for free that it would otherwise have to pay for, and can realize a fee for such placement, whether the product would have been necessary to the production or not). With a well-negotiated agreement, a product or service placement can provide a financial benefit to a production, as well as the use of a product in the background of a scene. Not only could there be a hefty payment for a product or service to be prominently featured, but it may provide a show creator with a basis for an entire show to revolve around the products or services of one unique company.

The parties must be aware of network-related issues before entering into a product or service placement agreement. Some networks will have detailed "Standards and Practices" that restrict the broadcasting and promotion of potentially controversial products, such as guns and alcohol. Also, the production company must be sure to avoid conflicts with any paid advertisers of the network, or talent on the network, that could be a direct competitor of the supplier or product being utilized.

There are a few government regulations pertaining to product or services placement that the parties must be aware of, as well. Most notably, the Federal Communications Commission (FCC) regulates programming under the Communications Act of 1934, and considers product placement to be "advertising" which requires the public disclosure of all paid placements in a program. Indeed, if a program receives anything of value in exchange for causing material to be broadcast, the sponsorship and identity of the sponsor must be disclosed. However, the exceptions to required disclosures are broad. For example, disclosure is not required if the supplier donates the product or service, the charge for exposure is nominal, or if the placement is used for a realistic effect.

Depending on the type of product or service and the extent of its placement, the applicable agreements may vary from a simple one-page contract to a long, detailed document. It is imperative to identify and agree upon the rights, responsibilities, and obligations of each party, which should be detailed in the agreement. A failure to do so could lead to a disastrous outcome, as a disappointed supplier could file a claim against the production company (or even worse, the network) before the show even airs; alternatively, a failure to comply with an obligation may prevent the production company from receiving full payment for the placement. This section provides an overview of the general components of these agreements, as well as issues that may arise during the negotiation process.

5.7.2. Placement of the Product and Failure to Place

The placement provision of an agreement between a supplier and production company defines the means of placement of the product or service in a reality show. Placement may consist of visual exposure to the product or service, as well as a verbal referral to the supplier's name, product or service being provided. The placement provision also describes the extent of the obligation of the production company to display the product or service. Due to the unpredictable nature of reality show production, the production company will want to protect itself by not providing any assurances as to the size, style, length, nature, or duration of the placement of the product or service.

Additionally the parties should agree upon a "failure to place" provision. This provision clearly defines the consequences of not including the product in the reality show if the product ends up on the "cutting room floor." Common consequences include paying the full value of the service or product provided or, if possible, returning the product to the supplier. The parties may also agree to continue their arrangement with the promise that the product will be placed in a later episode.

5.7.3. The Manner of Display

In a product or service placement agreement, the supplier will either pay the production company or donate the product or service in exchange for marketing and exposure of its product or service. Therefore, it would be disadvantageous to the supplier if the product or service is shown as defective or in a negative light. While the production company will negotiate for complete creative autonomy over the precise manner in which the product is used or displayed, there will likely be language in the agreement prohibiting the product or service from being displayed negatively, or in any way that tends to undermine the goodwill of the manufacturer or supplier. The supplier will want language requiring the production company to obtain written consent prior to displaying the product or service in any way other than its intended purpose.

5.7.4. Fees and Payments

The form and amount of payment for a product or service is another provision that may greatly vary. The supplier's fee ranges from a simple donation of the product or service to the production company, to several hundred thousand dollars if the product or service has a prominent role in the reality show. Furthermore, agreed-upon fees may be re-opened for negotiation as the editing process continues, depending on the final usage of the product or service. Finally, as is often common in the entertainment industry, another compensation formula involves the payment being dependent on the success of the show. In doing so, a show that is successful and lends itself to a lot of reruns could allow the parties to agree that the supplier pay more due to the increased advertising exposure for their company (while on the other hand, some suppliers may see little value in their current product being featured in reruns years after release). The fees and payment section should unambiguously define the exact type of payment that will occur between the two parties to avoid any arbitration and lawsuits.

Successful reality shows that include a product or service placement will undoubtedly also negotiate future marketing campaigns tied to the product or service. These deals may include a series of future advertisements, such as commercials or printed ads, which display the supplier's connection to the show. Again, all of this is subject to a substantial negotiation and takes into account not only rights for the inclusion of the product or service but, also, the rights of anyone who may be using or benefitting from the usage.

5.7.5. Representations, Warranties and Indemnity Provisions

Representations and warranties are binding statements and promises concerning the status of a party or its business. By offering a warranty, the promisor is guaranteeing the truthfulness of the statement. In general, a party offering a representation or warranty seeks to make minimal promises, and offer limited remedies, along with broad disclaimers. Conversely, the recipient of the promises will seek extremely specific and objective language, attempting to get the broadest possible protection and assurance.

With a representation and warranty from a product supplier or service provider, the production company gets significant protection. First, there is the assurance that the provider has the full right and authority to enter into the agreement and to provide the product or service sought. Moreover, the supplier is guaranteeing that it has the right, title and interest to any trademarks, copyrights, trade dress or service marks attached to and associated with the product or service. Finally, the recipient of the warranty obtains the usual protections afforded any consumer of a good, product or service, such as the warranty of merchantability and good and workmanship performance.

Concurrently, the production company will represent and warrant to the supplier or service provider that it will use the product or service in its intended manner and purpose. Further, the production company gives the assurance that the depiction of the product or service will not subject the supplier or provider to any trademark, copyright, patent or other property right claims, anything considered defamatory, or that undermines the reputation or goodwill of the product, supplier or provider.

5.8. COMPOSER AGREEMENTS AND MUSIC LICENSES[7]

5.8.1. Introduction

Music can play a crucial role in enhancing the experience and impact of any audiovisual content, and especially in the production of a reality television show. There is strong interplay between visual effects, character dialogue, and music to lure the viewer into the story. The use of music ranges from a catchy theme song so that the program resonates with the viewer long after the show has been watched, to the enhancement of an intense, emotional moment. And, of course, the use of popular music may give rise to another revenue stream for the show completely.

But, the use of music in a reality program is much more complicated and expensive than it first appears, as producers are tasked with obtaining a whole host of rights to ensure that intellectual property rights in both recordings and underlying compositions are not violated. Generally speaking, there are two contracts largely utilized to

---

[7] This section provides commentary to concepts more fully illustrated in accompanying composer engagement and music licensing forms.

enable the cleared usage of music in a reality television show: 1) Music Licensing Agreements; and 2) Composer Agreements. A music licensing agreement grants a producer the right to use music that has already been recorded and copyrighted by another person or organization in timed synchronization with the audiovisual recording, while a composer agreement is a contract with a composer to prepare original music for the show. Each agreement will be discussed below, in turn.

5.8.2. Composer Agreement

5.8.2.1. Fees

Cost is a critical factor when a producer is debating between using existing music versus hiring a composer to write a new musical composition, as engaging a relatively unknown, yet talented, composer to write original music for a show is likely more affordable than licensing copyrighted music.

Composer agreements generally outline basic compensation methods. The producer will pay the composer an agreed-upon flat fee for the production and delivery of a recorded musical composition. The cost to produce the music – such as studio time, equipment rentals, and staff costs – can either be built into the total payment to the composer or paid for directly by the producer. The agreement will typically specify the producer's orchestration requirements (e.g., all synthesizer and samples from the composer's studio, or requiring acoustic or electronic instrumental and/or vocal performances by the composer/musician or an ensemble of session players), and if other arrangers, mixers. If the cost of production is built into the flat fee, the composer must be careful to only accept a fee that will adequately cover the cost of producing the music and fair compensation.

Composers should keep in mind issues of ownership rights to the music when negotiating compensation. Most composer agreements grant full and complete ownership to the producer, meaning that the only form of compensation the composer will likely receive for his or her work is the flat fee. However, there are two other possibilities for the composer to receive additional compensation in the future. The first option is to retain rights to the "writer's share" of public performance royalties; i.e., whenever the show is played on a broadcast medium, the broadcaster is legally bound to pay public performance royalties for the music it contains. This royalty is split 50/50 between the publisher and the writer. The producer owning the copyright to the music receives the publisher's share, while the composer receives the writer's entire share. Alternatively, the second possibility is for the producer to pay the composer if a soundtrack or album of the show is created. This option is more of a rarity in the context of reality shows and, thus, the parties will likely agree to fairly negotiate such compensation terms in good faith at a later time.

5.8.2.2. Ownership Rights

The ownership rights provision is the most crucial aspect of any composer agreement because it unambiguously details which party has the rights to the music outside of its use in the show. Typically, the producer will be granted complete ownership rights over the work in a composer agreement by labeling the composer's work as a "work for hire." Under copyright law, a work for hire agreement deems the employer as the author of the work created. Additionally, the producer should include language stating that the composer transfers all rights in and to the music to the producer. This language protects the producer's rights to the music should the music recorded not be considered a "work for hire" under federal copyright law.

The producer owns rights to the music under a work-for-hire agreement. The producer will have final edits to the work, as well as the ability to use the music in marketing, advertising and promotional efforts of the program without the composer's consent. Furthermore, the producer has the ability to license the music to a third-party. For example, should a third party completely unrelated to the show later want to use the musical composition created by the composer and acquired by the production company, the only required consent would be that of the producer. Accordingly, the producer then receives all of the financial benefits from licensing out the music, except for any writer's share royalties payable to the composer or subject to an agreement with the composer to negotiate for a separate soundtrack release. However, these ownership and compensation rights are all negotiable, and a producer working with a limited budget may choose to grant the composer a percentage of additional ownership income or a percentage of the publisher's share of royalties – or even some sort of non-exclusive license to utilize the music and recordings delivered, rather than outright ownership – in exchange for a lower initial flat rate fee.

5.8.2.3. Credit

The composer has strong incentives, much like the rest of the production staff, to receive prominent credit for the work created. A favorable credit position is a great way for the composer to obtain future work and command higher fees. Well-known composers will invariably attempt to negotiate for a "single card" credit for the composer's name to be the only one displayed on-screen.

5.8.3. Music Licensing Agreement

5.8.3.1. Grant of Rights

Where the production company opts to acquire rights to preexisting musical compositions and recordings, the grant of rights section must unambiguously explain the rights in the copyrighted music being obtained by the producer, including any rights to edit an existing recording or to rerecord an existing composition, as well as the limits on any rights in connection with the distribution, advertising, exclusivity, and scope that the music may be used. The producer will likely negotiate for the right to 1) edit and adapt the song to the specific needs of the production (which may for example include the right to perform and record a "cover" version of the song in a musical competition show); 2) reproduce and distribute work related to the show that contains the copyrighted song without any restrictions; and 3) freely use the name and likeness of the musician that created the work. The licensing of these rights are generally embodied in a "synchronization license" covering rights to the underlying composition, entered into with the song's publisher, and a "master use" license with the owner of the preexisting recorded version of the song the producer intends to include in the series generally (e.g., theme music) or in a single series episode. Sometimes the proprietor of the recording and publishing rights may be the same party, in which case these agreements can be merged into one. The author of the work should make sure there is non-exclusive language pertaining to the producer's right to the music being licensed. If the producer has exclusive rights to the song, the author will not be able to license the song to other vendors for a specified period of time. Of course, the payment to be made is directly related to the manner, use and extent of the music that the production company seeks. As expected, the broader the usage sought, the higher the license fee to be charged.

Importantly, unlike the composer agreement, the rights provision of a license agreement makes it explicitly clear that the copyright in the music being licensed remains with the musician, who will retain full and complete ownership of the work. Concurrently, the license agreement will be equally clear that, even with the inclusion of the owned music in the program, the musician licensing the music acknowledges no copyright ownership in the program itself.

5.8.3.2. Compensation

A producer's right to license popular pre-recorded music can be quite expensive. The method for payment is likely a flat rate for the license to use the song. Should there be an option to extend or expand the license, that fee will also likely be addressed. While the producer will attempt to include language providing that the author of the music has no rights to any additional fees or royalties, even this can be eroded.

5.8.3.3. Warranties and Indemnification Provisions

It is essential for the producer to receive a guarantee from the author of the song as to full and complete copyright ownership of the song, and that the author does not need any approval to grant the license of use to the producer. Furthermore, the author will indemnify the producer from any potential legal liability relating to a copyright claim for use of the song from a third party.

5.9. CONCLUSION

There can be no doubt that reality television's place is and will remain at the forefront of programming. We are all drawn in due to an inexplicable force. We become attached to the individuals portrayed, loving them, just as often hating them, but always connecting with them on a first-name, personal basis. We know how they live, what they eat, when they sleep, who they love, who they hate. Reality television has been dubbed a "guilty pleasure," giving us a glimpse into someone else's life, as we bite our nails and watch their choices and risks play out in real time. It provides an escape from our own lives and reality, to look at others who have issues, problems and more at stake. Yet still relatable, it keeps us returning each week for the next episode. Indeed, a reality show can succeed overnight, instantly connecting to its audience, spurring conversations at the "water cooler" the next morning.

In an industry driven by our gaze and marketing dollars, reality programming is one of the entertainment industry's most powerful tools. Viewers are the key target for marketing dollars, and a reality show that draws a consistent, unified audience, is mission critical. In a society with an insatiable appetite for content, reality television is always searching for that next big hit, whatever is bigger and better than what we already have seen. There is truth in the saying that "art imitates life," and in a world where someone else's reality can provide us with an escape from our own, reality television has provided, and always will provide, that much needed vacation.

It is absolutely impossible to predict what the next reality television sensation will be until after the production dollars have been spent, the show has aired, and the audience has spoken. We can take a lesson from *Candid Camera* and *The Miss America Pageant* and know that, so long as interesting characters with unique experiences and compelling situations continue to present themselves, from wherever they may come, reality television is here to stay.

UNSCRIPTED TELEVISION – ILLUSTRATIVE FORMS:

- Acquired Footage Still Photograph Form
- Authorization to Use Name, Product, Logo Release
- Composer Agreement Form
- Co-Production Option Agreement Form
- Distribution Agreement Form
- Independent Contractor Agreement Form

- Joint Venture Agreement Form
- Location Agreement
- Merchandise and Product Placement License Agreement
- Minor Release
- Master Recording and Music Synchronization License Agreement
- Public Filming Notice
- Release of Liability and Assumption of Risk Form
- Release for Ultrahazardous Activity
- Standard Appearance Release
- Talent Agreement (long form)
- Talent Attachment Agreement (short form)

— CHAPTER 6 —

SCRIPTED TELEVISION

Ken Basin[*]

6.1. An Introduction to Scripted Television
6.2. Underlying Rights Agreements
6.3. Talent Agreements
6.4. Backend
6.5. License and Co-Production Agreements
6.6. Conclusion

6.1. AN INTRODUCTION TO SCRIPTED TELEVISION

6.1.1. Scripted Television from the Perspective of Studio Business Affairs

This chapter is written primarily from the perspective of the scripted television[1] studio business affairs executive – a negotiator, usually (but not always) a lawyer, who negotiates the substantive terms of all of the agreements to engage, acquire, or otherwise incorporate the major elements that transform a show from a nascent idea to a produced series debuting on a television network. In the simplest terms, when a creative executive points at something – a book to adapt, a script to develop, an actor to hire, a network to sell to – and says "I want that," the business affairs executive's job is to get it for them on commercially sensible terms. Yet this description understates the role of the business affairs executive, who, in successful practice, is not only a dealmaker but also a problem solver, who must use a combination of business and legal acumen to reconcile the needs and desires of competing (and sometimes single-minded) constituencies into something resembling a feasible course of action. While business

---

[*] **Ken Basin** is Sr. Vice President, Business Affairs for Paramount Television.
[1] While there is naturally some overlap between scripted and unscripted television, unscripted television presents a host of distinct business and legal issues. These are explored in greater detail in Chapter 5 of this book. While much of the information contained in this chapter may be instructive, in part or by analogy, for unscripted television, it should not be considered a directly adaptable guide.

affairs, as a function, is sometimes combined with an explicitly legal role (i.e., "business and legal affairs"), the "business affairs" viewpoint is conceptually distinct from that of "legal affairs" (which is concerned primarily with the drafting and negotiation of paperwork reflecting previously negotiated substantive terms) or of "counsel" (which, to the extent separate and distinct from "legal affairs," concerns itself with other risk management and legal compliance issues).

This primary perspective is of value for a variety of reasons (beyond the fact that, self-servingly, the author is a studio business affairs executive). While the essential legal principles of contracts, tort, intellectual property, and other blackletter legal areas apply consistently in television as they do in other fields, the key substantive business deal structures are largely unique to the industry, and are driven by the particular characteristics of the television medium. This drives this chapter's focus on conventionally "business affairs," rather than "legal affairs," issues, even in a collection on "Entertainment Law." Moreover, as described in the general introduction to the television industry in chapter 4, the studio is uniquely at the crux of television dealmaking, both up the chain of development (with rightsholders and service providers) and down the other side (with co-producing studios and network licensees) – hence the focus on the unique role of the studio business affairs executive (rather than the network executive or talent representative). The studio's key "hub" position in the industry's dealmaking chain makes it an ideal perspective from which to evaluate the industry overall.

6.1.2. Scripted Television as a Medium

There are two key consistent characteristics of scripted television (which, for purposes of this chapter, will be further referred to simply as "television") programming which are essential to understanding the web of deal structures that bind the scripted television industry together.

First, television is a writer-driven medium. To understand the meaning of this statement, it is helpful to compare the role of the writer in television to that of the writer in the theatrical feature film industry. In television, in the vast majority of cases, the lead creative force behind a series (the "showrunner") is a writer. This is in contrast to feature films, where the director is typically the "auteur" creative force behind a production. In television, most of the credited producers of a series are writers, who shepherd the project throughout its life-cycle. In feature films, on the other hand, the writer's role is generally performed entirely during the pre-production phase, and writers have little or no ongoing role in the actual production of their scripts. In television, a pilot script is usually (though not always) written by a single individual or writing team, who conceptualizes the world of the series and takes the studio and network's notes throughout the series development process. This, too, is at odds with the feature world, particularly that of big-budget studio films, where writing is often effectively done by committee, with new writers commonly being hired to rewrite the work of previous writers, without working in direct collaboration with one another. Finally, in television, a pilot – and sometimes even a series – is typically greenlit to production on the strength of a pilot script and the reliability of the writers and producers, with actors and directors being hired after the threshold decision to proceed to production has been made. This is also a major difference from feature films, where the attachment of one or more key actors (and typically a director, as well) is virtually always the necessary component that pushes a film project from development into production. The dominant role played by writers in the television industry manifests itself in the process, and the deals, that bring a series to life.

Second, television is a serialized medium. This may or may not be the case in a creative sense – some dramas, such as AMC's *Breaking Bad* or HBO's *Game of Thrones*, involve complex, arced storylines which unfurl over a period of years (and require that the viewer watch from the beginning of the series to truly follow along), while other types of shows, such as game shows, talk shows, multi-camera comedies (e.g., *Two and a Half Men*), and procedural dramas (e.g., "cop shows" such as *Law and Order*) integrate some serialized character or situational development, but can generally be understood and enjoyed in single-episode viewings. But from a production perspective, a successful television series is always an ongoing project, which requires creative and production continuity over a period of years (as distinct from a theatrical feature film, in which cast and crew together come together once, usually over a continuous or semi-continuous period of time, to produce a single closed-ended project). Consequently, the dealmaking framework of television protects the ability of parties to maintain continuity of production and distribution over a period of years.

6.1.3. The Life Cycle of a Scripted Television Series

6.1.3.1. From Idea to Production

The process of getting a television series from an idea (which may not even be committed to paper yet) to series production can be essentially divided into six stages. In the area of broadcast network television, which is organized around a principal "broadcast season" that runs from September of each year to June of the following year, the development process is so well-established (and has remained so consistent over the decades) that it can be reliably mapped to the calendar. On other platforms (such as cable, premium cable, and digital platforms), the process is largely the same, but can start or end at any time of year, due to such platforms' tendency to debut new programming year round, without reliance on the traditional broadcast calendar. These six stages are as follows:

a. Packaging and Studio Rights Acquisition

Every television series starts with an idea. This idea may be "original," i.e., a fresh invention from someone (usually a writer)'s mind, or "non-original," i.e., based on some underlying piece of intellectual property (such as a book, article, film, foreign television format, or true life story). The process begins as that idea is expanded and surrounded with additional key elements.[2]

The earliest stages of this process may take place solely among the development-stage "service providers" and their agencies. Independent writers, producers, and/or rightsholders may find one another, either directly or through their agencies (which often represent multiple parties in a single creative "package"), and agree to jointly "pitch" (i.e., try to sell to) studios with a project. Parties may informally agree to work with each other without entering into an explicit agreement, or may enter into a more formal "shopping agreement." In a shopping agreement, the parties agree to jointly develop and market a project, and agree that neither party will enter into a further agreement with a studio in connection with the project unless the other party also successfully negotiates a deal. In such a case, in order to proceed with the project, the studio acquiring rights

---

[2] This process goes on year round, but for broadcast network television projects, the studio dealmaking process is typically at its peak in late summer through early autumn.

will usually have to enter into agreements with all of the principals who have come together during this pre-packaging process.[3]

The formal dealmaking process generally begins as a studio acquires rights to the idea, script, underlying property, or combination of these elements that will someday become a TV show. If the idea is original, the studio will enter into an agreement with the writer. If the writer is sufficiently senior and experienced, then the writer will usually sell a verbal pitch of his or her idea, without having committed it to paper. In addition, the presumption is typically that a senior, experienced writer will go on to "showrun" the eventual series, if it is produced. If the writer is more junior, he or she may have to write out a draft of their idea "on spec" (i.e., independently and without compensation) in order to convince a studio to develop the project. The junior writer/creator should also expect that, at some point, he or she will be paired with a more experienced writer who will serve in the showrunner role. If the project is also based on an underlying piece of intellectual property (e.g., book, life story, etc.), the studio will concurrently enter into an option-purchase agreement with the owner of this intellectual property.

The studio may, at this time, also make deals with multiple elements that have been pre-packaged (as described above) as a threshold to developing the project at all. Alternatively, the studio may make deals solely with a key writer or rightsholder, with the intention of independently choosing and hiring further elements down the line. Often, the studio will seek to incorporate a writer and/or producer with whom it has entered into an exclusive "overall deal" (which provides for that individual to render services exclusively for a single studio for a given period of time, in exchange for a significant guaranteed annual compensation which is recouped against fees as earned).

Over the course of this process, the studio will work with the individuals involved to craft and improve the idea, and make strategic decisions about what key elements – underlying rights (essential, if applicable), writer/creator/producer (essential), showrunner (common but non-essential, if not the writer/creator), non-writing producer(s) (usually at least one, sometimes more), and perhaps pilot director (rarer) and/or one or at most two actor(s) (rarer still, but increasingly common) – it wants to attach to the project prior to the next phase: the network pitch.[4]

---

[3] Deals made at this stage of the process are described in further detail in sections 6.2 and 6.3 below.

[4] In some cases, the service providers who initiate a project may elect to directly pitch one or more networks, without first approaching a studio. Where a network is

b. Pitching and Set-Up

Once the pitch is ready and the studio has reached agreement on key terms with all of the necessary elements, the producers and studio executives collectively pitch one or more networks, seeking to "sell" the project to a network.[5] The studio, having already made deals with all of the elements and obtained control of the necessary rights, makes a deal with an interested network to continue the development and/or production of the project. Although the term "sale" refers to successfully making any deal with a network by which the development of the project is continued, the type of commitment actually obtained may vary widely, depending on the strength of the package and pitch, the interest level of the network, and the competitiveness of the bidding among multiple interested networks.

Most initial network deals are for development only, with the network agreeing to bear a portion of writing and other development expenses, in exchange for the studio granting the network the exclusive right, for some specified period of time, to order the production of a pilot and/or series. The studio and network may negotiate over, among other issues, the amount of expense covered by the network (at entry levels, 50% network coverage is typical, sometimes subject to a specified cap [e.g., $75,000]; though it may be as high as 100%); the number of development steps committed to (or available at the option of) the network (e.g., "backup scripts" for further episodes; series "bibles" or formats; etc.); the amount of time the network has to commit to production of a pilot or series; and whether the network has the right to order production of a pilot, versus being forced to choose to produce a series or nothing at all. The parties may also negotiate regarding what rights, economic or otherwise, the network retains with respect to the material in the event that it declines to order a pilot or series – typically, rights revert to the studio, subject to a lien in favor of the network for its share of development expenses (potentially with interest) and possibly a modest passive participation (with both fixed and contingent compensation) payable to the network if the series is

---

pitched directly and is interested in proceeding, it typically refers the project and its elements to a studio of the network's choosing – usually a studio with which the network is affiliated – which will proceed with development of the project pursuant to a development agreement between the network and studio.

[5] For broadcast network television projects, this typically takes place throughout autumn.

ultimately produced elsewhere. At higher levels, particularly in competitive situations involving broadcast networks, the network may commit to pay a specified penalty to the studio – which may range in value from five figures to seven figures – in the event that the network elects not to proceed to production of a pilot, and/or a further penalty if a pilot is produced but the network does not proceed to production of a series.[6]

Some networks require that, in order to proceed with development of a project, a license agreement be negotiated in full at this time, at least as to substantive principal terms.[7] Other networks will proceed with development on the basis of a mutual obligation to negotiate a license agreement in good faith at the time the network wishes to order production of a pilot and/or series, with a specified mechanism for what happens if the parties are unable to reach an agreement at that time – typically, a reversion to the studio, finite holdback against exploitation elsewhere, and lien for the network's costs if the project is produced elsewhere. In addition, a network with an affiliated studio may negotiate, at this time, for its sister studio to be granted a co-production position in the project.[8]

For very strong packages, and/or in highly competitive situations, the studio may obtain from the network a "pilot commitment," meaning a commitment by the network to order (and pay its share) for the production of a pilot. As a technical matter, the network is never actually committed to *do* anything, and can scrap production of the pilot at any time, or never proceed to production at all. However, this pilot commitment is typically expressed as a press release announcing the pilot order (which publicly commits the network to the project) and a pilot penalty equal to most or all of the full license fee that the network would have paid for a pilot (payable whether or not the pilot is actually produced).

Finally, at the highest, most competitive levels, the network may make a "straight-to-series" order – or even, in the rarest cases, a

---

[6] Curiously, the terminology of "penalties" is dominant, even in negotiation among experienced legal professionals in the television industry, despite the blackletter rule from contract law that contractual penalties are unenforceable. Presumably, the tight-knit, repeat-business nature of the entertainment industry is responsible for the fact that no network has ever mounted a full legal challenge to its obligation to pay such a penalty.

[7] Such license agreements are described in further detail in section 6.5.1 below.

[8] *See* section 6.5.2 below.

multiple-season order from inception. Again, because a network is never actually contractually committed to *do* anything – only to pay as if it did – as a technical matter, this "series commitment" is expressed as a press release and a commitment to pay the minimum number of episodic license fees, based on the minimum episodic order negotiated as part of the applicable license agreement. However, in practice, it is exceptionally unusual, and very costly, for a network to back away from a series commitment.

Because the majority of "sales" to networks are for development only, without a pilot or series commitment, the following steps contemplate a further development and piloting process.

c. Script Development

During the script development stage, the studio,[9] network, writer, and producers work together to further develop a project. If the project was sold on the basis of a pitch alone, the writer prepares a complete draft of a pilot script, and then writes subsequent drafts taking into account the notes of network and studio executives. If the project was based on a "spec script" already written by the writer, the writer goes straight to working on rewrites, again based on the notes of network and studio executives. Typically, these drafts are reviewed and commented on by other producers prior to formal submission to the studio and/or network.

For the most part, there is little dealmaking activity during this period. It is possible that the studio and network may jointly elect to attach further elements to the project at this stage, or to engage a subsequent, independent writer or writing team to further revise the pilot script (although this would be somewhat unusual in television development). In addition, if necessary, the studio may negotiate for and commission additional writing steps from the writer, to the extent required by the network but not otherwise provided for in the writer's existing deal. For the most part, however, this period is dominated by creative development activity, which will determine which projects reach the next stage of the process – the pilot.

---

[9] For broadcast network television projects, this phase generally takes place from mid-autumn through January of the following year.

d. Pilot

A television pilot is assembled over a period of intense creative, production, and dealmaking activity, during which the key team behind a project is solidified, and the words on a page are translated into a full audiovisual product. Networks typically order pilots in batches, so that they can choose among a group of pilots, side-by-side, in determining which projects will make it to series production.[10] Although it is difficult to make precise estimates, and figures will vary depending on the year, the network/platform, and the overall health of the marketplace, approximately 10% to 20% of developed projects may expect to earn a pilot order (and, of these pilots, approximately 20% to 40% may expect to earn series orders).

For those projects that are not ordered to pilot production, the process may be dead, or it may simply reset to an earlier stage. In most cases, networks have "two bites" to order production of a pilot based on a developed script; meaning that if a network initially declines to order a pilot, it may continue to develop the project and reevaluate that decision during its next window for pilot orders. (In cable, where the development and production calendar is less consistent, the network's option window is typically defined in months rather than "bites.") During this development period, the network may commission further revisions of the pilot script, or additional written materials (such as proposed scripts for episodes after the pilot, or a series format or bible which describes the proposed series) to assist the network in further evaluating the project. If the network's option has expired, or if it agrees to waive its rights and terminate its option early, the studio may seek a new network to take over development of the project, or perhaps proceed immediately to pilot production. For instance, AMC's *Breaking Bad* was originally developed for FX network; when FX declined to order a pilot, studio Sony Pictures Television made a new deal with AMC to keep the project alive, and the rest is history.

For those projects that are ordered to pilot production, the sprint is on. The first steps are typically to engage casting directors (who will assist in identifying and casting actors), line producers (who will assist in recruiting and engaging a production crew, and creating and managing a production budget), and a pilot director (who will help

---

[10] For broadcast network television projects, pilots are typically ordered in January and February, and produced between February and May.

set the stylistic template of the proposed series, in the form of the pilot, and work with the producers to identify and hire key members of the crew).[11] In addition, the studio and network will reengage in negotiating any major elements of the studio-network license agreement which had been left to future good faith negotiation (although even at this stage, they may elect to reserve finalization of the thorniest issues until after the pilot has been produced). Production executives and producers will work furiously to generate and refine a production budget, while the pilot script is continuously tweaked to respond to the demands of the budget (and vice versa).

The casting process for "series regular" actors (a classification explained in greater detail in Section 6.3.4 below, but which generally identifies the most significant principal actors in a series) involves a mix of so-called "straight offers" and "test options." "Straight offers" are firm offers to actors to be engaged on the pilot (with options to be hired for a series, if ordered), and are generally reserved for highly experienced actors with significant stature and/or name recognition, usually in lead roles. Such offers may be conditioned on a meeting with producers and/or a "reading" by the actor of lines from the pilot script (for further evaluation by producers and executives), though many high-level actors refuse to audition for parts in any way and will only consider and negotiate an offer with no creative contingencies attached.[12] Customarily, only one straight offer, to one desired actor, can be outstanding for a role at any given time.

Most major roles, however, are cast via a series of test option deals, by which the studio simultaneously enters into agreements with multiple actors who are competing for a single part. The candidates have been vetted by casting directors and producers but are typically precluded from formally auditioning for studio or network executives (whether in person or via taped audition) until they have not only closed a substantive deal, but signed paperwork which gives the studio the option to engage them for the pilot upon prenegotiated terms. Usually, two to four actors at a time may compete for a role, although often none of the candidates are selected and a new batch is identified for a subsequent test. Consequently, for a single tricky role, ten or

---

[11] Again, the key deals are described in further detail in sections 6.2 and 6.3 below.

[12] The offer may nevertheless be subject to specified business contingencies, such as the studio concluding its license agreement negotiations with the network, if still outstanding.

more separate deals could be made and negotiated to signature – often in windows of only 24 hours or less. Because of the volume and time pressures of this process, the negotiation of both deal terms and paperwork often relies extensively on non-negotiable terms and pre-negotiated cut-through paperwork forms.

Particularly during broadcast network pilot season, when literally dozens of pilots are in concurrent preproduction and production across the country, the competition for the best talent in every role is high, which further contributes to the need for the dealmaking process to proceed swiftly and decisively. For any given pilot, this process may continue at a frenzied pace until the very eve of commencement of photography (and, for lesser roles/elements which are not needed until later, into the period of pilot production). Eventually, however, a pilot is completed and delivered to the network, and the studio and talent wait to see if the network elects to order a series based on the pilot.

e. Upfronts

The term "upfront" refers to an event held by a television network, attended by talent, press, and major advertisers, during which the network announces its newest series for the upcoming season.[13] In some cases, the network has already committed to production of a series, and the upfront is merely the public announcement and celebration of that decision.

In other cases, however, a network may be on the fence about ordering (or "picking up") a series, or may be deciding among various competing prospective series, and will use the upfront period to gauge advertiser interest before making a final decision. In this climate of uncertainty, with much at stake in the form of a series order, the upfront period may include a frenzy of eleventh-hour dealmaking and renegotiation, during which networks and studios may revisit key terms of their agreements (or finally conclude negotiation on any issues which had been left unresolved up to that point) as they hash out at last which shows will make it to series production.

As at the pilot stage, a project which is not immediately ordered to series production may be dead, or it may simply be on hold or sent back a step. As with the pilot order, networks typically have "two

---

[13] Broadcast television networks generally hold their annual upfronts in New York City in late May, in rapid succession to one another.

bites" (or a negotiated period of months following delivery of the pilot) to order production of a series based on a pilot. An unsuccessful pilot may be subject to further development with the original commissioning network, which may include rewrites of the pilot script, recasting of the actors, and/or engagement of additional or replacement writers, producers, or pilot directors. In addition, if a network decisively passes on an unsuccessful pilot (sometimes referred to as a "broken pilot"), the studio – often in a race against the clock of expiring actor option dates – may look to entice a different network to take over the project. For instance, Amazon's *Sneaky Pete* was initially developed and produced as a pilot for CBS, before CBS passed on the project and Amazon elected to commission reshoots of the originally produced pilot, eventually committing to production of a series based on that revised pilot.

For those shows which are ordered to production, the process swiftly (and sometimes even semi-concurrently) moves into the final pre-production stage: staffing and writing.

f. Staffing and Writing

Although a television pilot is almost always the product of the mind of a single writer (or writing team), a television series is inevitably a collaboration among a team of writers. The next stage of the process is to engage a "writer's room"[14] – a group of writers and writer/producers who, together, will not only determine the story and write the scripts for the coming season, but serve as key lieutenants to the showrunner and help creatively lead the production of the newborn television series.[15] As with network pilot season, immediately during and after broadcast network upfronts, there are a significant number of new series launching at the same time, which creates significant competition for desirable talent in these roles, and drives a hot pace of dealmaking.

In addition to writer/producers, studios may look to engage producer/directors (who will be expected to direct multiple episodes of the series, and to work with other episodic directors to maintain a consistent look and feel for the series). At this time, the studio will

---

[14] For broadcast network television projects, the staffing process typically begins in May or June, with writing commencing immediately in anticipation of series production beginning in late summer.

[15] The relevant deals are described in further detail in section 6.3.5 below.

also hire replacements for any key elements engaged for the pilot (e.g., actors, line producers, casting directors) who, for whatever reason (perhaps because they had been engaged for the pilot only, or because the studio and/or network elected to replace them), are not returning for the production of the series.

Over this period, the principal creative and production team will be locked in. Meanwhile, the "writer's room" will come together to "break the season" (i.e., to determine the overarching narrative and character arcs for the season), before the individual writers and writing teams are assigned specific episodes to write. As the show takes creative shape, the line producer and his or her team will determine a series production plan that takes into account a studio-determined budget as well as the creative content of the scripts being generated by the writers. The episodic writing of a series will usually still be in progress (hopefully with a significant head start) when, at last, the show moves into its mature creative phase – series production.

6.1.3.2. Production

Television series production involves a coordinated effort to generate a significant amount of content within a relatively short period of time. A full season of a broadcast network television series is at least thirteen, usually twenty-two, and potentially up to twenty-six episodes. In cable (including premium digital services, such as Netflix, Hulu, and Amazon), a full season order is usually thirteen episodes, although some platforms tend toward shorter orders of ten or even eight episodes, while others (often in the final season of a successful series) may order a "super-sized" season of sixteen to twenty episodes.

In order to meet the exhibition calendars of traditional broadcast and cable television networks (particularly broadcast networks), series typically enter into production after only the first few episodes have been written. Writing of later episodes occurs concurrently with production of earlier episodes, and earlier episodes begin airing on television while later episodes are still in production. For premium digital providers, which have largely adopted a "binge viewing" release strategy (i.e., all episodes of a series are made available concurrently), production still typically begins while writing is ongoing, but exhibition must be delayed until all episodes have been fully produced and delivered.

The series production process generally relies on a rolling production schedule, with overlapping episodic production periods. For instance, episode #2 of a season enters pre-production as episode #1 is filming. When episode #1 completes filming, it immediately goes into post-production, while episode #2 begins filming. But at the same time, while episode #2 begins filming, episode #3 enters pre-production. In other words, at any given moment during the middle of a production season, three episodes are likely in some phase of production at the same time – one in pre-production, one in production, and one in post-production. (And a fourth, earlier episode may, at the same time, be airing on television that week!)

This intense, overlapping production calendar involves very short production periods, particularly relative to theatrical feature film production, which typically takes at least several weeks, and often several months (or even years for complex, effects-driven films), to yield a two-hour product. Multi-camera half-hour comedies (which generally film before a live studio audience) typically involve two days of pre-production and five days of production (of which two days are dedicated to filming, and three days to rehearsal, blocking, and other preparatory work). Single-camera half-hour comedies (which generally film over multiple takes without an audience present) also usually require two days of pre-production and five days of production, all of which are dedicated to filming. One-hour dramas are typically allowed seven days of pre-production and eight days of photography (although for premium digital platforms, which often feature longer episodic running times [due to lack of commercials] and binge viewing releases, the production calendar may be extended to nine or even ten days or more of photography per episode). Because of the tight, overlapping production and exhibition calendars, going overschedule is seldom an acceptable option. The critical necessity of on-time, on-budget delivery drives the television industry's particularly strong preference for proven, experienced writers and producers leading every production.

The principal cast and crew of a television series are engaged at the outset of production for the season, and, for the most part, stay with the show through the completion of production of that season. Shows often also attempt to maintain crew continuity from season to season, although only the highest-level "above the line" personnel (actors, writers, producers) are actually subject to contractual studio options for their services in subsequent seasons. While there may be further high-level dealmaking activity over the course of production of a season, most deals at this stage are negotiated by the high-level series staff that have already been hired by the studio, in accordance with the studio-approved budget – for instance, line producers negotiate most deals for crew department heads, who in turn negotiate deals for the members of their teams; production managers and coordinators engaged by the senior producers negotiate location and lease agreements; casting directors negotiate deals for guest and recurring actors; etc. Studio business affairs executives may be called upon throughout this process to assist the production team, coordinate necessary approvals from co-production partners and/or network licensees, and obtain additional financial contributions from network licensees to offset unusual major expenses designed to enhance the show (such as large acting fees for major guest performers, or additional production costs for large-scale, major event episodes).

High-level dealmaking activity may ramp up between seasons, as major new elements in various capacities are added (such as new actors), replaced (such as mid-level writer/producers or producers/directors), or have their contracts renewed prior to or upon expiration (particularly showrunners, whose initial agreements usually expire after two seasons have been produced). In addition, when a series is especially successful, studios will often entertain renegotiation of terms with actors who are still under contract, by which the actors may increase their episodic fees or acquire (or expand) a share of profits from the series – even if the actors are still technically under contract for years to come. For instance, in 2012, the adult cast of ABC's *Modern Family* famously banded together to renegotiate their agreements prior to production of the series' fourth season (a typical window for such renegotiations), going so far as to jointly sue studio 20th Century Fox Television to void their contracts when negotiations stalemated. (The parties settled and the actors returned to the show with substantial raises.) Backend participants may also seek to receive advances against their contingent compensation (also referred to more casually as "profit participation"), if the show has proven successful enough that it seems certain to show profits under the defined formula. In short, when a television series succeeds, the principal contributors to that success will seek to be rewarded for that success as the series matures, and the studio must balance the growing cost pressure created by those rewards.

6.1.3.3. Distribution

It is often said that a copyright is a "bundle of rights," whose divisibility is limited only by the availability of markets and the creativity of lawyers. This divisibility provides the foundation of the distribution and profit-making strategy of the television studio. For each project, the studio owns a single key asset – a television series, whose property value is embodied in the copyright of that series and each episode thereof. The business of a television studio is to sell that same product over and over, enough times to enough buyers, to recoup its investment in the cost of production and finally make a profit. In other words, a television studio makes money by using the divisibility of its copyrights to maximize revenue across media, territory, and time.

a. Media

The initial network on which a television series first airs is the show's first exhibition medium, but in success, it is never the show's last. As technology and business models evolve, new opportunities emerge.

The classic secondary medium for a television show is simply elsewhere in television – exploitation that is generally referred to as "off-network" or "syndication." Syndication licenses for content that has already appeared on a network can involve a variety of buyers, and a variety of modes of exhibition. A license may provide for once-a-week exhibition of episodes by the licensee, or multiple-times-a-week (or "strip") exhibition. The licensee may be a cable network, or one or more broadcast stations. Conventional wisdom holds that the syndication market is most robust for: (1) half-hour shows (which are easier to schedule than one-hour shows); (2) episodic, non-serialized comedies (which are easier to watch and enjoy on a one-off basis than serialized shows with continuing plotlines); (3) shows which originally aired on broadcast television (which are both more familiar to viewers and would be all-new to the cable market, compared to cable series); and (4) shows with at least 100 episodes (which can fill a five-times-a-week exhibition schedule without dipping into repeats for at least twenty weeks).[16] Classic syndication success stories include multi-

---

[16] The historical minimum "magic number" for series to access syndication was three seasons of twenty-two episodes each – i.e., a total of sixty-six episodes – which

camera comedies such as *Seinfeld, Friends,* and *The Big Bang Theory.* However, procedural dramas (such as CBS's *CSI* and *NCIS* franchises and NBC's *Law and Order* franchise) have also enjoyed successful cable syndication runs, as have some more serialized comedies with more limited runs, such as HBO's *Entourage* and *Sex and the City.* Due to a combination of contractual holdbacks in the initial network license and the need to stockpile a sufficient quantity of episodes, exploitation of a series in syndication typically begins three years (i.e., sixty-six episodes) to four years (i.e., eighty-eight episodes) after the series' premiere on its original network.

Although its overall importance in the industry has diminished in recent years, home video remains a significant downstream market for television distribution. Physical home video distribution (these days, in the form of DVDs or Blu-ray discs) typically occurs, on a season-by-season basis, following the end of the broadcast season during which the featured episodes were initially exhibited, with the precise timing of the release often coordinated to coincide with and support the launch of the following season. In more recent years, permanent digital downloads of television episodes (so-called electronic sell-through, or "EST"), through online retailers such as iTunes (which launched its video download services for television series in 2005), Google Play, and Amazon, has largely supplanted the traditional home video market. In fact, EST licenses are often handled by the same distribution executives who manage traditional home video, and are accounted for as home video transactions. Although EST exploitation may also be held back until the end of a given season's run on its home network, individual episodes are often made available for paid download only hours after their network premieres.

The most important new market to emerge in the television industry in recent years is digital streaming, exemplified by so-called "over-the-top"[17] services such as Netflix, Amazon Prime Video, and Hulu. These services offer customers the ability to stream episodes of a variety of television series which were originally exhibited on

---

enables thirteen weeks of reruns at the rate of five exhibitions per week, before episodes are repeated.

[17] The term "over-the-top" refers to these services' technological capacity to reach users through their general-purpose Internet subscriptions, without relying on a separate, service-specific technological system (such as the coaxial cables that underlie cable television, or fiber optic cables used by telecommunications-based television and Internet providers).

traditional television networks.[18] Competition among the three major streaming providers has led to a sharp increase, in recent years, in streaming license fees, particularly for valuable exclusive licenses. In addition, variation among streaming providers in their specific business models (e.g., subscription-based vs. ad-supported) has allowed licensors to narrowly define the scope of streaming licenses, in hopes of facilitating multiple streaming sales. Conventional wisdom holds that the streaming market is most robust for serialized, one-hour dramas – programming that is prone to "binge viewing" sessions in which customers consume several episodes in a single sitting in order to keep up with an engrossing ongoing story. Although, in the early days of the streaming market, the applicable holdbacks against streaming exhibition often mirrored the holdbacks against "off-network" or syndicated television exhibition, the more common recent practice is for each season of a television series to become available on a streaming service shortly before the debut of the subsequent season, a strategy which has proven valuable in attracting new audiences for the show (and its original network).[19]

b. Territory

Although local entertainment industries have emerged throughout the world, the United States remains the number one producer and exporter of entertainment content worldwide, and the U.S.'s

---

[18] They have also all made significant pushes into commissioning their own original, exclusive first-run content. Issues related to such series are discussed in greater detail in 6.5.1 below.

[19] The classic second-window streaming success story is AMC's *Breaking Bad*. Although it is now one of the most successful and celebrated television series of all time, for its first three seasons, the show was a critical darling with a very limited audience. The show narrowly avoided cancellation after its third season, and shortly before the fourth season's premiere, the first three seasons were made available for streaming on Netflix, where it was soon discovered – and hungrily consumed en masse – by a new, younger audience. That audience eventually followed the show to its home network, where ratings for the fourth and fifth seasons soared on the strength of the viewers who had discovered the show on Netflix (where audiences were able to immerse themselves in three seasons of backstory in time for the network premiere of the show's fourth season). This complementary relationship between the show's exhibitions on AMC and Netflix helped redefine the industry's prevailing assumptions about the impact of streaming services on traditional television markets, and the ultimate success of *Breaking Bad* was vital in defining and enhancing AMC's brand as a new destination for premium original content.

entertainment exports are a cornerstone of the country's cultural and economic power across the globe. A successful American television series will be licensed for exhibition in dozens of territories, both English-speaking and non-English-speaking (where shows may be distributed with subtitles or dubbed into the local language). Most networks operate specifically in a single country, especially in North America and Western Europe (although there are a number of regional networks that serve multiple countries in Latin America, Africa, and Southeast Asia), and most content licenses define a limited exhibition territory. Consequently, a single television series can be sold dozens of times to buyers across the world, and the pattern of multiple sales across media and time can, in success, be replicated on a country-by-country basis. U.S. networks are typically guaranteed worldwide premiere rights with respect to each episode of a television series, but international exhibition may otherwise be nearly concurrent with American exhibition.

Conventional wisdom holds that the international market is most robust for one-hour dramas, especially action-oriented and procedural dramas, which are most universally appreciated across cultural and linguistic lines.[20] However, physical comedy can also find a substantial audience abroad.[21] The value of international licenses can vary dramatically depending on the population sizes, economic capacities, and interest levels of various territories, but in general, the most valuable international markets for American television series are the United Kingdom and Germany. Canada, France, Spain, and Australia may also be economically significant, and China continues to emerge as an increasingly important market (despite high levels of intellectual property piracy there). The financial prospects of a series in international markets is heavily influenced by the identity of the

---

[20] The viability of dramas in the international market, combined with their success in the streaming market, and the ability to access these markets without necessarily needing to produce a high volume of episodes, has made the one-hour drama a favorite of smaller, independent (and often more risk-averse) television studios.

[21] In addition, while situation comedies (or "sitcoms") often "translate" badly into foreign languages and cultures, television "formats" may successfully traverse international borders, becoming the basis for local adaptations (reflecting local sensibilities) of successful comedies from the United States (or for American adaptations of successful comedies from other countries). Such international format licenses can prove highly lucrative for the producers of the original series. *See* section 6.2.3 below.

commissioning American network, with shows that are exhibited on U.S. broadcast networks generally commanding the highest international license fees.

c. Time

With few exceptions, every license is finite, providing for the licensee to enjoy rights for a limited number of runs on a particular media platform or platforms, or a specified period of time. In every territory, in every media, a successful television series may be licensed again and again over time, with multiple successive licenses over a span of years in the various exhibition media. This long tail for revenue generation creates significant asset value in successful library television series, and contributes to the industry's structural reliance on a small number of mega-hits which, over time, subsidize the development and production of a large volume of unsuccessful or only marginally successful series.

6.1.4. The Power of Tax Incentives

An ongoing television series production is a large business, which employees not only traditional "talents" such as writers, directors, actors, and producers, but also literally hundreds of tradesman and craftspeople, from carpenters to caterers, for months at a time. In addition, beyond the jobs created by the production itself, the cast and crew who descend upon a location to participate in the production of a television series spend significant dollars with local businesses. As a result, in order to incentivize studios to produce television shows (as well as other filmed productions) in their jurisdictions, government authorities at all levels – municipal, state/provincial, and national – employ a variety of incentive programs, usually in the form of tax credits or tax-based benefits, designed to lure producers with the promise of costs savings and economic efficiencies.[22] In turn, such incentive programs dramatically impact studio decision-making with respect to where to produce a series, and how much to spend on its production.

---

[22] The actual efficacy of these programs, in terms of the level of job creation and economic stimulus versus the direct economic cost to the governments, is hotly disputed.

Production incentive programs take a variety of forms, and vary widely from jurisdiction to jurisdiction (both within the U.S., and, increasingly, around the world). Common incentive programs include:

- Production rebates, by which a government authority directly reimburses a studio for some percentage of the studio's production expenditures within the jurisdiction;

- Tax credits, by which a government authority credits against a studio's local tax obligations some percentage of the studio's production expenditures within the jurisdiction. These tax credits may be transferrable (meaning that the studio can sell the tax credit to a third party who may be better able realize it) or non-transferrable (meaning that the studio cannot sell the tax credit, and therefore must have enough direct income tax liability in the jurisdiction in order to be able to realize the credit's benefits for itself);

- Tax rebates, by which a government authority refunds to a studio some portion of the studio's income, sales, value added, or other taxes, after such taxes have already been paid by the studio;

- Tax exemptions, by which a government authority exempts a studio, *ex ante*, from paying taxes (typically sales or value added taxes), which would otherwise by due in connection with the studio's activities in the jurisdiction;

- Direct government financing, by which a government authority actually contributes funds toward the production of a series;

- Subsidized production resources, such as production stages and warehouses, owned by the government authority and leased to productions at favorable rates; and

- Film commissions and film offices, by which a government authority provides logistical support services to studios short of direct economics subsidies (such as assistance with obtaining film permits, scouting locations, and hiring local crew), in order to make it easier for the studios to do business within the jurisdictions.

Such programs are often subject to extremely specific conditions, including:

- Limitations on the types of eligible productions (e.g., theatrical feature films vs. television series; scripted vs. unscripted productions; dramas vs. comedies);
- Budget requirements (both floors and ceilings), which may be designed to appeal particularly to smaller or larger productions, according to the policy goals of the authority operating the program;
- Local expenditure requirements, which have the effect of requiring a production to spend a meaningful portion of its total budget within the local jurisdiction in order to access an incentive program (thereby limiting the value of such credits to productions which make only token investments in the local economy);
- Local content requirements (such as local story, character, and location elements), which are common in direct government financing programs operated at the national level, and designed to promote the cultural goals of the authority operating the program;
- Local talent requirements, which require a production to make significant efforts to engage local cast and crew in production, rather than importing cast and crew from outside areas; and
- Local content ownership, in order to promote the further development of meaningful local film and television industries.

Government authorities may offer any one of the above programs, or a combination of multiple such programs, in order to lure studios to produce projects within their jurisdictions. Each program may be subject to specific and varying conditions. Depending on where it is produced, a production may concurrently enjoy access to multiple incentive programs offered at various levels of government – a municipal film commission office, a state or provincial tax credit, and a national production grant. For instance, a television production in Vancouver may simultaneously enjoy benefits from the Vancouver municipal government, the provincial British Columbia government, and the national Canadian government.

Perhaps the most prominent and impactful form of production incentives are tax credits, which are typically valued at between 20% and 35% of the studio's production expenditures within the jurisdiction. The studio is required to maintain exhaustive records of its expenses in order to support the claimed value of its tax credit, and the value of the credit may be capped based on the studio's ingoing production budget, as reflected in the studio's initial application for the credit. Where tax credits are transferable, secondary markets have emerged to facilitate the transfer of tax credits from the originating studios (who often have too little local tax liability to fully realize such credits) to local businesses or high net-worth individuals (who can save thousands or even millions of dollars by purchasing such credits at 85 to 95 cents on the dollar, pocketing the difference). Tax credit agents act as middlemen, connecting buyers and sellers in exchange for a percentage (usually two to three percent) of the value of the credits. Some jurisdictions, such as Louisiana, offer direct buy-back programs, essentially allowing studios to more quickly and easily monetize their tax credits by selling them back to the state for 88 to 90 cents on the dollar (depending on market conditions). In any event, though, between the application, recordkeeping, and reporting processes, as well as the annualized tax cycle in each jurisdiction, studios must typically wait several months, or sometimes even years, to realize the benefit of these tax credits.[23]

Some jurisdictions offer tax incentives on an unlimited basis, to as many productions as are qualified and willing to avail themselves of the programs. Other programs – particularly those instituted in the states of New York and California (traditional centers of entertainment production) in order to staunch the exodus of productions induced by the availability of favorable incentive programs elsewhere – are subject to annual caps which are insufficient to meet the total theoretical demand from producers, and are therefore allocated based on lotteries or other application processes used to distribute these scarce resources.

---

[23] Larger producers can cover production expenses from available cash and withstand the wait for these credits to pay off in due course. Smaller producers with more immediate cash flow needs may obtain bank loans, secured against the tax credits (and with value carved out to cover the interest and fees on these loans), to monetize the credits immediately, and apply the proceeds against the studio's cost of production in real time.

Successful tax incentive programs in states such as New Mexico, Georgia, Louisiana, Pennsylvania, and Virginia have had the effect of building up meaningful local production economies and resources in areas that were previously devoid of substantial production activity. In addition, significant government subsidies from countries such as Canada and France, in the form of both tax credits and direct government financing, have helped turn these countries into major centers of film and television production. But because the overall value of these programs to the sponsoring jurisdictions – weighing loss of tax revenues against the gains from local economic stimulus and job creation – is hotly debated, governments may rescind existing incentive programs with little or no notice, and with few protections for studios that depended on those programs in deciding where to produce a series. As a result, studios often skeptically consider the long-term stability of tax incentive programs in deciding where to produce their series.

In determining the economic risk and profit potential of a television production, major studios pay close attention to the availability, security, and value of tax credits and other incentive programs. Budgets are typically generated to reflect both "gross" and "net" spends, and these "net budgets" are often the basis of calculating license fees and modeling a series' economic prospects.[24] Based on its business projections, a studio may determine a maximum "net" spend it is willing to commit to a production, and the overall gross cost (and, accordingly, production value) of the series may therefore vary substantially depending on whether or not the studio can obtain a tax credit to offset its production costs. These calculations can prove determinative of not only where a series is physically produced, but also of the creative content of a series, as well as the threshold decision of whether it is produced at all.[25]

6.2. UNDERLYING RIGHTS AGREEMENTS

With the basic structural landscape of the television industry established, we can now turn our attention to the key deals in the life

---

[24] *See* section 6.5 below.

[25] For instance, AMC's *Breaking Bad* was, in its early development, set in California's Inland Empire, east of Los Angeles. When attractive tax incentives lured the production to New Mexico, the show was creatively reset in Albuquerque in order to preserve the verisimilitude of the setting.

cycle of television development, production, and exhibition. The first category of such agreements goes to underlying rights – the acquisition of preexisting intellectual property for adaptation into a television series. In an increasingly crowded television landscape, buyers increasingly look to preexisting intellectual property for a long-term creative plan – and a built-in audience. Major hits such as HBO's *Game of Thrones* (adapted from an ongoing series of fantasy novels by George R.R. Martin) and AMC's *The Walking Dead* (adapted from an ongoing series of comic books by Robert Kirkman) speak to the power of underlying rights in the marketplace. Although virtually any type of content can be treated as intellectual property and thus made subject to an option/purchase agreement – short-lived CBS sitcom *$h*! My Dad Says* was based on a popular Twitter feed of (almost) the same name – the most common properties on which television series are based (other than fully original series concepts) are published books and articles; life rights; and format rights.

6.2.1. Books and Articles.[26]

6.2.1.1. Option Fees and Terms

When optioning a book or article, an initial option period of twelve months to eighteen months is typical, reflecting the window of time necessary to develop, write, and solicit an order of a television series based on the underlying property. Initial option fees typically range between $2,500 and $10,000, and are applicable against the purchase price, though higher option fees can be found on highly desirable properties and/or in competitive dealmaking situations. An initial option fee in the range of 10% of the negotiated purchase price is typical.

Most option/purchase agreements also include a studio option to extend the option period by an additional nine to eighteen months, usually for the same price as the initial option fee (or proportionate to the size of the option period), but non-applicable against the purchase price. In some cases, option extension periods may be shorter than initial option periods, or may be conditioned on "active development" or certain development milestones, such as a writer having been

---

[26] A sample book rights agreement is included among this chapter's supplemental forms.

engaged to write a pilot teleplay or a network agreeing to develop the project (though such conditions are more common when the optioning party is an independent producer rather than a major studio, which usually resist such conditions).

6.2.1.2. Purchase Price

The purchase price is the amount paid by the optioning party to acquire the rights under option. It is typically paid upon production of a pilot, though a studio whose option is about to expire (and which does not hold any contractual option extensions) may elect to purchase the rights prior to the expiration of the studio's option in order to retain the rights. On the other hand, in rare instances, the payment of the purchase price may be deferred to production of a series based on the rights.

A typical purchase price for a book or article may range between $30,000 and $100,000, though again, the prominence of the property (in terms of audience, sales, or other metrics), the scope of the property (e.g., a book series versus a short story or short-form article), and the presence or absence of a competitive dealmaking situation may drive purchase prices as high as $500,000 (and recently, even higher). If a project may be developed as either an ongoing episodic series, or a closed-ended television movie or mini-series, there may be different purchase prices negotiated for each form of initial production (with television movies and limited series coming with a higher price tag). If theatrical feature film rights are subject to the option, they will also often be subject to a separately negotiated purchase price – usually higher than the corresponding television purchase price, and often denominated as a percentage of the film's ingoing production budget (2% to 3%) with a floor and a ceiling (with ranges that could span from $100,000 to as much as $2,000,000 for a bestselling blockbuster property).[27]

---

[27] Often, a studio acquires rights for television and motion picture productions simultaneously, potentially without knowing what medium the studio will initially pursue for adaptation.

6.2.1.3. Royalties

Where the applicable production is an ongoing episodic television series (as opposed to a television movie or mini-series), in addition to the purchase price, the deal will also include a negotiated episodic royalty, which is payable to the rightsholder for the life of the series' production. These royalties typically range from $1,500 per episode to $10,000 per episode (excluding the pilot), and may be tiered depending on the platform for which the series is produced.[28] In addition, rightsholders may negotiate to receive further royalties for reruns of each such episode, though this is not as commonly granted for underlying rightsholders as for pilot script writers,[29] and this right may be granted for broadcast network television series but not for cable series (where heavy reruns are more common) or digital series (where on-demand streaming renders the concept of a "rerun" a non sequitur).

6.2.1.4. Backend

In addition to a purchase price and royalty, the seller of television rights will expect to receive a share of the "backend" or contingent compensation from the series.[30] Depending on the stature and nature of the underlying property, this share tends to range between 1.5% and 5% of modified adjusted gross receipts ("MAGR") or the corresponding principal defined form of contingent compensation used by the applicable studio, with the majority of properties drawing 2.5%

---

[28] For instance, because budgets for broadcast television series tend to be higher than for cable television series, the deal may specify a higher episodic royalty if the applicable series is produced for broadcast than if it is produced for cable. Some studios may also allow this higher tier to include premium pay cable networks (such as HBO, Showtime, and Starz), while other studios may employ a three-tier system, with broadcast networks occupying the highest tier, premium pay cable networks occupying a middle tier, and basic cable networks occupying the bottom tier. Premium digital services such as Netflix and Amazon, whose budgets on their most prominent series frequently exceed those of broadcast network series, are usually included in these higher tiers. Precise categorization often varies according to the particular policies and practices of each studio. Henceforth, where this chapter refers to "tiering" of entitlements according to networks/platforms, the foregoing breakdown may be assumed to apply.

[29] *See* section 6.3.1 below.

[30] The definition and accounting for contingent compensation is discussed in greater detail in section 6.4 below.

of MAGR in backend. (A single percentage point of MAGR is sometimes referred to as a "point.") Because it is based on the adaptation of existing intellectual property, as opposed to the ongoing rendering of services, the share of backend accorded in respect of the underlying source material is typically considered fully vested from inception.

6.2.1.5. Bonuses

Additional bonuses are a common, but not ubiquitous, economic element of underlying rights deals. The most common bonuses are for the ordering of a series (as opposed to merely a pilot) based on the underlying rights; these typically range from $10,000 to $50,000, most frequently set at $25,000, with proration based on the number of episodes actually ordered and broadcast. Where a property is more valuable, or a rightsholder has essentially granted a discount on the initial purchase price, there may be additional bonuses (sometimes of comparable value; sometimes of escalating value) built into the deal for subsequent seasons of the series. If the initial option is obtained by a small independent producer (especially if that initial option is granted for free), there may be "set-up" bonuses triggered by the development of the project with a major studio or a network.

6.2.1.6. Granted Rights

Every option/purchase agreement must specify the rights which are being optioned, and are therefore subject to purchase, by the studio. Major studios typically define their rights acquisition as encompassing all rights in the underlying property, other than those which are expressly reserved (i.e., starting from 100% of rights, and working their way down). Smaller producers and studios may settle for acquiring only specified rights (e.g., "all motion picture and television rights"), with all rights not expressly enumerated being reserved by the seller (i.e., starting from 0% of rights, and working their way up). Although television rights are the obvious rights subject to such deals, rights deals must also encompass so-called "allied and ancillary" or "subsidiary" rights, such as merchandising, music publishing, soundtrack, live stage, theme park, and subsequent/derivative productions. In addition, where the rightsholder claims trademark rights in any elements of those properties, it may be necessary to negotiate terms around the transfer, co-registration, or other coordination of such rights, particularly where the buyer wishes to integrate such trademarks into the title of the contemplated series and/or engage in merchandising and other licensing activity around the series.

6.2.1.7. Reserved and Frozen Rights

Because most major studios' rights deals operate on the (non-negotiable) model of acquiring all rights in the underlying property other than explicitly reserved rights, much of the negotiation of these rights agreements focuses on reserved, rather than granted rights.

The author or rightsholder of a book or article is essentially always permitted to reserve the ongoing right to publish the original work, and to publish or authorize the publication of author-written prequel or sequel books (although there may be negotiated limitations on "enhanced books" which incorporate audiovisual elements, and/or negotiation about the pre-acquisition of corresponding motion picture and television rights in such author-written sequels). The status of comic books and graphic novel adaptations may also be subject to negotiation – rights grantors seek to reserve these rights as a form of publishing, while grantees seek to acquire them as a form of merchandising.

Other rights which are typically reserved by the author without controversy include radio rights (i.e., dramatic radio adaptations); live recital rights (i.e., public readings); and possibly live television rights (i.e., live telecast of a dramatic performance).

Authors often seek to reserve merchandising rights in their works, though this is seldom agreed by studios. There may be a distinction drawn between "classic merchandise" (i.e., merchandise which is based solely on the underlying work) and "series merchandise" (i.e., merchandise which recognizably incorporates logos, actor likenesses, or other unique elements of the television adaptation), though typically, this is only entertained by the acquiring studio where there is a meaningful preexisting merchandising program in place for the property. Otherwise, most television studios have a strong expectation that they will control merchandising, and, at best, may agree to a "separate pot" royalty granting the rightsholder a share of merchandising revenue which is not cross-collateralized with series production expenses and distribution revenues.

Major negotiation may take place around theatrical feature film rights and live stage rights, which may have significant value. The acquirer's ability to obtain such rights may depend on the relative bargaining power of the parties, and on the buyer's ability to make the case that it is positioned to effectively exploit such rights (e.g., through an affiliated motion picture production and distribution arm).

Rights which are reserved by the author, other than publishing rights for the initial work and author-written sequels and live recital rights, are typically subject to holdbacks which prevent the owner from exploiting such reserved rights for a defined period of time. Many television studios employ a framework from feature deals known as the "5/7 holdback" – reserved rights are held back until the earlier of five years following the initial exhibition of a production based on the property, or seven years following the execution of the rights agreement. However, because of television's ongoing serialized production and distribution model, a more common holdback structure would be clocked to the initial exhibition of the last episode of a series or the expiration of a network's option to order more seasons of the series, with the actual length of the holdback (usually one to three years) potentially telescoping depending on how many seasons of the series were actually produced. These reserved rights may also be subject to a right of first negotiation and/or a right of first or last refusal in favor of the purchaser of the granted rights, as that party would have a natural interest in acquiring such reserved rights at some future time. And again, each of these rights (particularly, e.g., theatrical motion picture rights) may have a separate purchase price and/or backend structure assigned to it.

Where parties cannot reach agreement on the granting or reservation of rights – again, most commonly with respect to theatrical feature film rights and/or live stage rights – they may agree to freeze these rights, essentially rendering these rights permanently unexploitable by both the buyer and the seller unless they are able to reach some future agreement on the terms for the "unfreezing" and exploitation of these rights.

6.2.1.8. Consulting Services

Rights agreements may include a services agreement element, by which the author of the underlying work agrees to render ongoing consulting services to assist the studio with developing and producing the series based on his or her work. For the seller, this is a way to draw more financial benefit from the deal; for the buyer, the author's perspective may be useful to the writers and producers of the series, particularly where the underlying work is autobiographical or heavily research-based. Consulting fees typically range between $1,500 and $10,000 per episode, and may be committed for a single season, two or three seasons, or for the life of the series. Unlike a royalty, these fees are not passive and require the author to be available to render a reasonable amount of services when called for, though in practice, the level of commitment is often very low, and authors often relish the opportunity to have an ongoing impact on the television series based on their work. At higher levels, particularly where the author has some personal experience in television, such consulting deals may escalate to full-fledged non-writing producing deals.[31]

6.2.1.9. Credit

Source credit is typically accorded to the underlying work from which a series is adapted. A typical form would be "Based on the novel by [AUTHOR]" if the series has the same title as the underlying work, or "Based on the novel [TITLE] by [AUTHOR]" if the series has a different title. For non-fiction works, "Inspired by" credit is more common than "Based on," typically for risk management reasons – television series based in whole or in part on true life events must often emphasize their fictionalization in order to reduce the risk of right of publicity and/or defamation claims from the individuals connected to the works.[32] Rightsholders typically seek to negotiate for these source credits to appear in the main or opening titles,[33] rather than the end

---

[31] *See* section 6.3.2 below.
[32] *See* section 6.2.2 below.
[33] Although these terms are used somewhat inconsistently and interchangeably, to be precise, "main titles" refers to an opening title sequence which precedes the actual action of the episode (and may be elaborately animated or produced, as in the case for well-known, Emmy-winning main title sequences for HBO's *True Detective* and *Game of Thrones*), while "opening titles" refers to credits which appear at the beginning of

credits, of a series. In addition, rightsholders may push for such credits to appear in paid advertising for the series (with placement often tied to credits accorded to writers and creators).

In addition, if there is a consulting services component to the rights deal, there is usually a separate credit granted to the author for such services. "Executive Consultant" is a standard lower-level credit, usually granted in the end titles; "Consulting Producer" would be considered a higher-level credit, and may be granted in the main or opening titles (where other major producers are credited). If more substantial credits are accorded (such as "Co-Executive Producer" or "Executive Producer"), these services agreements have typically been expanded into full-fledged producing deals, as noted in section 6.2.1.8 above.[34]

6.2.1.10. Subsequent Productions

Because the rights granted in these agreements typically include the right to produce future productions (whether remakes, sequels, prequels, or spinoffs of the original series), there are usually negotiated economic terms that relate to such subsequent productions.

Payments for subsequent series may include additional purchase prices, royalties, bonuses, and backend; the buyer will typically seek to limit the variety of repeated payments (e.g., royalties and backend only), while the seller will seek to have all of the various forms of payment obligation revived for subsequent series.

---

the episode, with text superimposed over the actual filmed action of the episode. There is significant flexibility (and inconsistency) in what credits appear in the main titles vs. the opening titles, nor does every series necessarily include both main and opening titles. In general, main titles contain, at a minimum, the name of the series, and often the series' "Created By" credit (which is described in greater detail in section 6.3.1.10 below). Some main title sequences also incorporate the credits for series regular actors (whose deals are described in greater detail in section 6.3.4 below). Longer main title sequences may also include credits for producers, episodic directors, and episodic writers, though these are more often included in the opening titles. In general, credits for individuals of like functions (e.g., all series regulars, all producers above a given seniority level, etc.) are grouped together within one of these two title sequences. But creative variations abound; for instance, some shows include neither main titles nor opening titles, and credit even senior cast and crew at the end of the episode (a format which is sometimes referred to as "main-on-end").

[34] The WGA discourages crediting individuals as "Creative Consultants," and requires studios to obtain a special waiver from the guild in order to accord credit to an individual in this particular form.

A low-level rights agreement might provide for 50% of the applicable negotiated payments for the initial series to be made for any generic spinoffs (definitions vary, but typically meaning a spinoff which includes as a principal character one or more principal characters who appear in the original series or the underlying work) or sequels/prequels, 33% of the applicable negotiated payments to be made for any remakes, and 25% for any planted spinoffs (spinoffs which follow a character which is introduced anew into the original series in order to set such characters up for their own series, e.g., the character of Mork from Ork, played by Robin Williams, who appeared in a single episode of *Happy Days* before being spun off into the series *Mork & Mindy*). At higher levels, generic spinoffs, sequels/prequels, and remakes may be subject to rights payments up to 100% of the payments owed for the original series, and planted spinoffs paid at up to 50%.

6.2.1.11. Reversion

Rightsholders will often negotiate for the rights granted in an option/purchase agreement to automatically return to the grantor after a specified period of time, depending on whether, or the extent to which, programming has actually been produced based on the granted rights. Such "reversion" is a subtle but often hotly contested deal issue.

Reversion is typically allowed without objection when rights are purchased but no pilot is ever produced, or if a pilot is produced but no series episodes are produced. (A typical reversion may kick in if no pilot is produced within a year of rights purchase, or no series is produced within a year of completion of the pilot.) However, the issue is more contested where the rightsholder looks to reclaim rights even after a series is produced. Buyers will want their purchase of rights to vest permanently if any series episodes are produced; sellers will want rights to eventually return to them no matter how many series episodes are produced, once continuous production of a series has ended. Typical compromises involve rights which vest permanently with the buyer if a threshold number of episodes or seasons of the series are produced (often two to three seasons or seasons' worth of episodes), but which are subject to reversion if those thresholds are not met. The reversion typically occurs one to three years after the last episode of a series is exhibited (or after the network's option to order more seasons expires), and, as with the holdback on reserved rights, this time period may increase or decrease depending on how many episodes/seasons have actually been produced before cancellation. For the most part, unless the property under option is extremely well-known or valuable, the studio will insist that, at some point, its rights vest permanently.

Reversion is typically subject to a lien for the buyer's purchase price and its unreimbursed development expenses (if no pilot or series was ever produced), or at least for its purchase price (if a pilot or series was produced). The buyer may also seek a passive participation in any new productions based on the rights it had previously acquired, the right to and size of which may also be tied to how many episodes/seasons had actually been produced (if any) prior to reversion, and which typically range from $2,500 to $5,000 per episode in royalties and 2.5% to 5% of MAGR in backend.

6.2.1.12. A Note on Non-Fiction Pieces

Under U.S. copyright law, it is said, facts are free – while a non-fiction work is subject to copyright protection, the facts contained within a non-fiction work are not. Therefore, in most cases, it may not be strictly necessary, as a matter of law, to obtain rights to a non-fiction work which is intended as the foundation of a television series. Moreover, if a non-fiction work concerns one or more living individuals, it may be necessary to obtain the life rights of the individuals depicted in the work, whether or not a studio obtains the rights to the work itself.

In spite of these elements of blackletter law, producers of television content will nevertheless often obtain rights in non-fiction works as a starting point for the development of a series. This decision can be motivated by a number of factors. If there is only one available source for the facts on which the series is to be based, obtaining rights in that source can be a sensible act of risk mitigation, helping to avoid the hassle and expense of defending a lawsuit from the author (even if the suit itself is not meritorious). Making a rights deal may discourage a competing studio or network from pursuing a similar project, or provide access to valuable consulting services from the author, which can be a resource as the series moves forward. Sometimes, the creative team just wants to use the specific title of the non-fiction work for their series, which could by itself be deemed to justify the cost of the rights deal (particularly if that title is already well-known to the public). Even if not strictly necessary, underlying intellectual property may also prove valuable in attracting interest from network licensees. In light of these factors, rights deals for non-fiction works are surprisingly common, although the economics of such deals tend to be somewhat more modest than those of deals for fictional works.

6.2.2. Life Rights

Where a television series is inspired by or based on the life of a real, living human being, the studio will typically enter into a "life rights" agreement with one or more of the individuals at the heart of the story. The overall structure of such an agreement is generally identical to that of an option/purchase agreement for rights in a book, article, or other published work, although these deals tend toward the lower end of the economic range described in Section 6.2.1 above.

Strictly speaking, there is no such thing as a "life right" under any form of property law in the United States. A grant of "life rights" is actually a promise by the grantor not to sue the grantee under any one of several legal theories which could potentially support a lawsuit arising out of the depiction of that person and his or her life (e.g., right of publicity, defamation, false light, public disclosure of private facts, intentional infliction of emotional distress, etc.). Consequently, the hallmark feature of a "life rights" agreement is a broad waiver of claims.

Because, under U.S. law, defamation and privacy-based torts can only be pursued by living plaintiffs, and the First Amendment otherwise offers a strong defense against right of publicity claims, life rights are usually obtained only from living individuals, and not from estates. That being said, the same factors which would cause a studio to obtain rights from the author of a non-fiction work may motivate a studio to obtain life rights even from a deceased individual's estate (particularly if the studio may face problems with potential infringement of trademarks owned by the estate if it proceeds without the estate's consent). Moreover, even if the primary subject of a television series is deceased, friends, colleagues, and family members of that individual (who could be readily identifiable by their relationship to the primary subject) could still be alive, and therefore pose a risk of claims. Consequently, open-ended series (as opposed to closed-ended television movies or mini-series) that are closely and recognizably based on true stories are relatively uncommon, and are usually subject to extensive legal vetting throughout the production process.

The buyer of "life rights" generally demands that the rights and waivers it receives under the deal are granted exclusively (so as to prevent any competing "authorized" projects about the same individual), and that the subject cooperates with the buyer going forward (for example, by providing access to personal notes and memorabilia, or assisting in obtaining releases from friends and family members). Specific negotiation may take place concerning the scope of the rights granted (e.g., for a television series only vs. for other entertainment products such as films and stage plays, carveouts for news or documentary programming, etc.); limitations on the portions of an individual's life which are subject to the rights grant/claim waiver (e.g., limiting the grant to a certain time period in the individual's life); specific objective restrictions on how the individual may be portrayed (e.g., prohibiting the individual from being portrayed as committing a crime or engaging in an extramarital affair); and rules governing whether the real names of the subject (or the subject's family members) may be used in the actual series.

6.2.3. Format Rights

Another increasingly rich source of television inspiration is, simply, television: formats of television series from foreign countries. Game shows and other unscripted series have long been exported across national boundaries and adapted into local versions. More recently, scripted series have become subject to the same process of international adaptation: NBC's long-running hit *The Office* was based on a British television series of the same name; Showtime's *Homeland* is based on an Israeli series called *Prisoners of War*; NBC's short-lived *Game of Silence* was based on Turkish series *Suskunlar*. Formats also travel in the opposite direction, out of the United States: Fox's first major comedy hit, *Married... with Children*, has been adapted to local versions in at least a dozen countries, while AMC's hit *Breaking Bad* was recently recreated for the Latin American market as *Metastasis*.

Format rights agreements also largely track the structure and economic parameters of option/purchase agreements for print publications – option fees and periods, purchase price, royalties, bonuses, backend, subsequent productions, reversion. Negotiation around the granted and reserved rights focuses on territory (addressing both the geographic source of an adaptation, and the buyer's right to distribute that adaption more broadly; for instance, a U.S. buyer probably only needs to obtain English-language U.S. adaptation rights, but will want to preserve the right to distribute its U.S. version worldwide); restrictions on the distribution of the original series or other versions in the buyer's territory (U.S. networks generally will want to limit the availability of other versions, particularly other English-language versions, of a format they have taken to market in the U.S.); and the right to use other specific elements of the original series, such as music or specific episodic stories or teleplays, in the local version.

In addition, because international format rights are generally held by the individual producers of those foreign formats, and because these individuals are usually experienced television professionals, format rights deals are almost always accompanied by non-writing executive producer deals for the individuals (or principals of the company) who control the format.

6.3. TALENT AGREEMENTS

6.3.1. Writing/Writer-Producer Agreements[35]

Because television is a writer-driven medium, the writer-producer agreement is often the most significant deal in the development process. At the development/pilot stage, there is seldom any such thing as a writing deal by itself – nearly every agreement for the writing or acquisition of a pilot script will include negotiated terms for the writer's ongoing participation in the production of the series as a producer (usually an "Executive Producer," the highest-level credit in television). An experienced creator will be expected to serve as the "showrunner" of the series, the lead creative manager of the production process. This job requires a complete television production skill set consisting not only of the ability to write great scripts, but also to generate story arcs, lead large teams of writers and other production

---

[35] A sample writing/writer-producer agreement is included among this chapter's supplemental forms.

personnel, understand and manage budgets and schedules, and otherwise coordinate with studio and network executives. Less-experienced writers will still usually be engaged as senior-level producers, and will enjoy a meaningful and central creative role in the series going forward, but will be paired with (and ultimately subordinate to) more experienced producers who are brought on to run the show, if produced (and who may actually join at a very early stage and help supervise the actual pilot writing process).[36]

6.3.1.1. Writing and Spec Acquisition

When a writer "sells" a show to a studio, he or she may be approaching the studio with a verbalized idea for a new series (a "pitch"), or with a previously written pilot script embodying that idea (a "spec script"). Less experienced writers must generally write out their ideas, independently and without initial compensation, into a "spec script" in order to attract attention and interest; more experienced writers seldom put pen to paper until they have a firm deal in place based on their pitch.

A "pitch" may be purchased on one of three basic structures – if/come, firm, or blind. An "if/come" deal relates to a specific idea that the writer has pitched to a studio. The studio negotiates writing and producing terms for the writer to develop the idea, but the entire agreement (and all financial commitments) are contingent on the studio, in turn, selling that idea to a third-party network licensee (which will contribute to the development costs of the project). A "firm" deal is reserved for higher-level writers, and involves a commitment to pay for the writer to write the project, whether or not a network deal can be put into place. A "blind" deal is sometimes used synonymously with a firm deal, but more precisely refers to a firm deal that is not tied to a specific predetermined show idea; it may commit the studio to pay for a script from the writer, but require the writer to pitch multiple concepts before the studio approves one of them to proceed to writing. Sometimes, these deal structures can be combined; for instance, a studio may make an "if/come" deal with a writer for a

---

[36] Often, these originating but initially subordinate writers will find their producer status elevated in later seasons, as showrunners move on to other projects, and other key creative personnel for the series move up the producing ladder. *See* section 6.3.1.10 below.

specific concept, with the understanding that if that idea does not sell to a network and the if/come deal is therefore never triggered, the deal automatically converts to a blind script deal.

Where a writer walks in with a pre-written spec script, the deal is based on an option/purchase structure (but, again, with a negotiated producing deal as part of the agreement). A writer may grant a free "if/come" option to the studio to immediately shop the spec script to network buyers; a network's commitment to develop the project could then trigger either a paid option fee (and specified option window), or the payment of the whole purchase price. Alternatively, particularly if the studio does not intend to pitch the spec script to networks in its current form, the studio may immediately pay for an option on the script (which, again, usually costs about 10% of the purchase price, and in any event must be no less than 10% of the Writers Guild of America [WGA] scale minimum price for the pilot script). Again, the parties may negotiate as to whether payment of the purchase price is triggered merely by a network's agreement to develop the project, or only when the studio elects to purchase the rights (or, at latest, upon commencement of production of a pilot based upon the script). Larger studios are apt to pay the purchase price based on earlier triggers, in order to attract writers with more immediate paydays and maintain tighter control of rights; smaller studios may seek to defer large payment obligations as long as possible (ideally until a major studio or network brings its checkbook to the table).

A script deal typically buys out five writing steps – a story (or outline), first draft, two sets of revisions, and a polish (although creative executives and non-writing producers will often informally manage the writing process and, in practice, obtain more drafts from writers than are formally reflected in this structure). Where a spec script is acquired, the purchase price typically buys out the initial story and draft reflected in the existing script, and pre-pays for the two sets of revisions and the polish by the writer.

As of 2018, WGA scale minimum for a network primetime thirty-minute pilot script (story and teleplay) is approximately $39,000, and for a network primetime sixty-minute pilot script (story and teleplay) is approximately $58,000. For non-network primetime (e.g., cable), the applicable scale numbers are approximately $22,000 for a thirty-minute script, and approximately $41,000 for a sixty-minute script. Larger studios, as a matter of policy, tend to pay at least the "upset price" for a pilot script. The "upset price" is a WGA-determined minimum – as of 2018, approximately $55,000 for thirty-minute pilot scripts and approximately $80,000 for sixty-minute scripts – which allows the studio to buy out certain "separated rights" (including stage, theatrical, publication, and merchandising rights) which are otherwise automatically reserved to the writer/creator of an original television series under the WGA Basic Agreement.[37] Independent studios may negotiate separate writing fees or purchase prices, depending on whether the project sells to a broadcast network (or other high-budget platform, such as Netflix or HBO) or a cable network. Where a deal is based on WGA scale minimum fees, the parties may sometimes negotiate to add a 10% premium on applicable WGA scale amounts, in order to cover the agency commissions payable by the writer on his or her fees.

The actual writing fee/purchase price negotiated may vary wildly depending on the "quotes" (i.e., past deals) of the writer; the contemplated budget of the project; the nature of the contemplated distribution platform; the policies of the studios and networks involved; and applicable WGA scale. For major broadcast, cable, and premium digital television production, writing fees/script purchase prices tend to range between approximately $75,000 and $250,000, with most scripts costing between $100,000 and $200,000, and some outliers on either end. WGA scale minimums may or may not be applicable to productions which are written for new media (digital) exhibition, depending on the budgets of the productions and the number of subscribers to the service; on smaller platforms and for short-form productions, prices are freely negotiated, and are typically significantly lower than for traditional television development (e.g., approximately $10,000).

6.3.1.2. Producing Fees

Producing fees for writer/producers who create a series are a function of a number of factors, including the quotes of the writer; the contemplated budget of the project; the nature of the contemplated

---

[37] Although the WGA Basic Agreement technically requires a "separate negotiation" in a "separate document" and for a "separate consideration" for the studio to acquire such separated rights, studios generally manage this via a small separate form included with the writer agreement, and a nominal separate fee (e.g., $100), both of which are effectively non-negotiable.

distribution platform; the policies of the studios and networks involved; and whether or not the writer/producer is expected to serve as the showrunner. It is generally understood that broadcast networks, premium pay television networks, and premium digital platforms support higher overall budgets – and therefore higher fees to executive producers. When it is unknown, at the time a project is initially put into development, what platform it will sell to, the deal may provide for tiered executive producer fees depending on the identity of the network buyers. In addition, many studios require that total ingoing executive producer fees on any given project be capped; consequently, a writer/producer who is working as part of a large team of collaborating producers may be expected to work for lower fees than if that same writer/producer was involved in a package with fewer high-level collaborators.

Executive producer fees for writer/creators generally range from $15,000 per episode to $60,000 per episode, depending on the various factors set forth above (though again, there are outliers on either end with experienced creators-showrunners on high-budget projects commanding closer to $100,000 per episode). Pilot fees may be identical to the negotiated episodic fee for the first season, or slightly elevated. 5% cumulative annual bumps in episodic fees are typical, but variations abound; some studios insist on lower (e.g., 4% bumps), while others may be willing to offer larger, round increases between the first and second season's episodic rates (e.g., an increase of $2,500 or $5,000 per episode), particularly where the executive producer is perceived to have allowed some form of "discount" on the initial fee.

6.3.1.3. Years/Locks

Most deals for producing services by a writer/creator cover a pilot and two seasons of production (although inexperienced, lower-level writers may sometimes be forced to accept three-year deals). Because of the central role that writers (as creators, showrunners, or both) play in the creative process, writers generally prefer such short-term deals for at least two reasons: first, because of the expectation that, in success, they will be able to negotiate a more favorable deal to return to a show in its third season (or thereafter); and second, to allow themselves greater freedom/opportunity to move on to their next creative endeavor at that time.

While a two-year deal may often be presumed for a writer/producer creator, the "lock" under the deal may be more heavily negotiated. In television, the presumption in every deal is that a studio never actually has to *use* the services of an individual it has engaged, but it may have to pay for those services even if they are unused. This is the concept of "pay-or-play" – a guarantee that an artist will be paid some specified amount, whether or not the artist's services are actually required by the hiring party. "Pay-or-play" protects artists by providing for some amount of their fees to be guaranteed; but it also protects studios by preserving the studio's unfettered right to terminate anyone, at any time, with or without cause, as long as it is willing to deal with the financial consequences (if any) of that decision.

The "lock" under a writer/producer deal refers to the period of time for which the writer/producer's fees are guaranteed, if the series is actually produced for that long, whether or not the writer's services are actually used. A "one-year lock" would guarantee the payment of episodic fees for the pilot and all episodes produced for the first season of the series. A "two-year lock" would guarantee the payment of episodic fees for the pilot and all episodes produced for the first two seasons of the series. A "modified two-year lock," also known as a "two-year Warner lock," is effectively an initial one-year lock, which automatically expands to cover the second season of the series if the studio fails to exercise its "pay-or-play" right (i.e., termination without cause) prior to the completion of the individual's services on the first season.

The vast majority of deals for writer/producers who function as series creators provide for two-year Warner locks. Higher level deals for more experienced writers may provide for a firm two-year lock. At the very highest levels, a creator with major bargaining power may negotiate for a "life lock" – i.e., to be guaranteed the payment of the artist's episodic fees for all episodes produced for the entire run of the series – with an option (held by the individual) to "drop down" to a lower level of services[38] at some point during the term of the deal. This provides the writer/producer with a maximum amount of protection and flexibility – he or she cannot be divested of his or her fees for the life of the series without cause, but can still force a subsequent renegotiation (in his or her own favor) by threatening to

---

[38] *See* section 6.3.1.6 below.

exercise the "drop down" right and effectively walk away from the obligation to continue to work on the show in a full-time showrunning capacity.

Locks for writer/producers are generally credit-contingent. Because the WGA credit determination process[39] has not taken place at the time a pilot is order to production, the writer/producer's lock for pilot services is usually contingent on the individual having been the sole writer of the pilot script, as produced (perhaps excluding production polishes). If the individual was not the sole writer, his or her services are usually at the studio's option. Similarly, a writer/producer's series lock is usually contingent upon the writer obtaining sole "created by" credit on the series according to the WGA's determination; if the writer does not obtain sole "created by" credit, again, his or her services are usually at the studio's option. However, if writers are assigned to work together, or for writers who are brought in to rewrite a preexisting script, it is typically agreed that shared "created by" with concurrent or preexisting writer(s) will suffice to satisfy such a condition.

6.3.1.4. Services and Exclusivity

When rendering services as executive producers, writer/producers generally work on a full-time basis on a single series, and provide services to their studio on an exclusive basis during production periods of that series. However, there are several nuances and exceptions to this general presumption.

Writers at all levels often want the right to continue to develop projects for third parties, and/or to write for feature films, even while one of their series is ongoing. This is generally agreed as a matter of course for hiatus periods (i.e., when the individual's ongoing series is not in active production), and the right to develop (but not produce) for third parties is often permitted (on a part-time, "second position," non-interfering basis) even during production periods (though sometimes such third-party development is not allowed during production of the critical first season of a series).

Extremely experienced and prolific writer/producers may insist on the right to render even production services on more than one series at

---

[39] *See* section 6.3.1.10 below.

the same time (often with the benefit of a strong "number two" writer/producer working beneath them[40]). Typically, if this is agreed, it is in a context where all of those series are being produced by a single studio, which can coordinate closely with the writer/producer to manage his or her schedule across various commitments. For instance, during 2013, showrunner Chuck Lorre worked on four different broadcast network comedies – *Two and a Half Men*, *Mike & Molly*, *The Big Bang Theory*, and *Mom* – for studio Warner Bros. Television and network CBS at the same time.

6.3.1.5. Preexisting Commitments

Because of the large and steep funnel of television development (many development projects, which yield few pilots, which yield even fewer series), successful writers often have multiple projects in development at any given time. These concurrent deals, which may be made with separate studios for projects that are developed at separate networks, require managing the "priority" or "position" of the writer's various commitments.

In general, the television industry subscribes to a presumption of "first in time, first in line" – services on any project are usually subject to any preexisting contractual commitments. If a writer's higher-priority project goes into production, he or she is usually rendered unavailable to render ongoing services on a lower-priority project. If a lower-priority project goes into production while a higher-priority project is still in development, the studio behind the lower-priority project faces a risk that the writer may be forced to walk away in order to work on the higher-priority project if it is subsequently ordered to production as well. For this reason, studios will often consider a writer who is subject to a higher-priority preexisting commitment to a third party to be effectively unavailable unless that writer obtains a waiver from the other employer of its right to pull that writer away.

If a writer/producer is subject to higher-priority preexisting commitments at the time a script deal is entered into, the negotiated script price is usually discounted somewhat (e.g., by around 15% to 25% compared to what the writer would command for a first-position deal), to account for the risk of the writer's unavailability at the time a

---

[40] *See* section 6.3.5 below.

pilot or series may be produced. If the writing services themselves are interfered with by a preexisting commitment, the studio usually has the right to "roll" the deal (i.e., to postpone writing by up to twelve months, into the next development season), or to terminate the agreement. If the writer/producer cannot render executive producer services on the pilot due to a prior commitment, series services are usually then at the studio's option.

Usually, if a preexisting commitment goes away (because the project dies in development without ever being produced), subsequent existing commitments automatically move up in "position" or "priority." In some instances, however, aggressive representatives with prolific, in-demand clients (or whose clients are accepting substantially lower-than-market script fees) may seek to make "no position" deals (i.e., deals that do not enjoy priority over subsequent development projects until a production is actually ordered), or to otherwise reserve the right to book additional projects in higher priority than a current deal.

Finally, higher-level writers who are stacking multiple concurrent development projects may make two-tier deals, such that, if the writer/producer is unavailable to render services at a full, "Tier 1" exclusive executive producer level (as described in Section 6.3.1.4 above), they may still be locked to render services (and collect fees) at a less-demanding (and lower-paid) non-exclusive "Tier 2" level of services (though often still with an executive producer credit).

6.3.1.6. Consulting

Most writer/producer agreements provide that, at the end of the individual's initial two-year term as an executive producer (assuming that the term of executive producer services is not extended), the individual is locked for an additional two years to render services as a consultant. This is referred to as a "consulting one-for-one," as in one year of consulting services for each year of executive producer services rendered. Consultant-level services are non-exclusive, only occasionally (if ever) in-person, and typically non-writing. Although the studio may require active services to be rendered in exchange for the consulting fees ascribed to such services, as a matter of practice, a former executive producer's stint as a consultant is often nearly or entirely passive (often because the executive producer's successor as showrunner wants to establish and preserve his or her own creative stewardship of the series going forward).

A consulting lock is typically conditioned on the writer/producer having received sole "created by" credit on the series, having rendered two years of executive producer services without being "pay-or-played" (i.e., terminated without cause), and otherwise not being in breach of his or her agreement. The applicable fee is usually $7,500 or $10,000 per episode produced during the two years of the consulting lock (non-escalating), though it may be as low as $5,000 per episode, as high as $15,000 per episode, or stated as a fraction (e.g., one-third or, rarely, one-half) of the individual's last-earned executive producer fee. At very high levels, the consulting lock that follows the period of executive producer services may be for the life of the series, rather than on a "one-for-one" basis, though this is rare.

6.3.1.7. Royalties

In addition to any applicable executive producing and/or consulting fees, the creator of a television series is almost always entitled to a passive episodic royalty for the life of the series, excluding only the pilot (which royalty is cumulative with any services fees or other bonuses payable to the individual). These royalties typically range from $2,500 per episode to $6,000 per episode for a writer who receives sole "created by" credit (as always, with outliers on either side), and are reducible if the writer receives shared "created by" credit to an amount between 50% and 75% of the applicable royalty for sole "created by" credit. The reduction for shared "created by" credit may be automatic to the reduced level indicated above, or on a dollar-for-dollar basis (to the negotiated floor) based on royalties payable to other credited writer(s). And, as with other economic terms, the applicable royalty may be tiered, depending on the platform for which the series is produced. Finally, on broadcast network shows, it is typical for the writer to receive an additional "100/5" royalty – that is, a further royalty payment equal to 20% of the initial royalty amount, payable for each of the first five reruns of the applicable episode.[41]

---

[41] For cable programming, some (but not all) studios agree to a "100/12" royalty – that is, a further royalty payment equal to 8.33% of the initial royalty amount, payable for each of the first twelve reruns of the applicable episode by the program's cable

6.3.1.8. Bonuses

Virtually every writer/producer deal for a series creator also provides for a series sales bonus, payable to the writer if the project makes it past the pilot stage and a series is actually produced. The vast majority of such bonuses are for $25,000 for a writer who receives sole "created by" credit, reducible (either automatically or on a dollar-for-dollar basis by bonuses paid to other writers) if the writer receives shared "created by" credit to $12,500. However, the applicable "sole credit" bonus may, in some instances, be reduced to $20,000 (e.g., if the series is produced for lower-budget cable, or for very low-stature writers), or increased to as high as $50,000 (for very prominent creators). On rare occasions, series sales bonuses may also be payable for one or more subsequent seasons of a series, but such an agreement is unusual, and typically a negotiated response to unique circumstances.

Usually, such series sales bonuses are subject to proration based on the number of series episodes actually produced. For broadcast network series, the standard is for the full bonus to be payable based on the production of twelve series episodes (excluding the pilot), with proration downward for smaller production runs, and no bonus payable for fewer than six episodes produced. In cable, the negotiated proration may be more favorable (e.g., 100% payable based on ten episodes produced, inclusive of pilot), less favorable (e.g., 100% payable based on 20 episodes produced, inclusive of pilot), or identical to the standard "12/6 proration" for broadcast network deals, depending on the identities, policies, and order patterns of the studios and networks involved.

In rarer cases, particularly where a writer has agreed to a lower-than-market pilot script writing fee, the deal may also provide for a pilot production bonus (which often serves to get the writer to where they wanted to be economically for the script alone, in the successful scenario of a pilot being produced).

---

licensee. For first-run programming on streaming services, for which the concept of a "rerun" is a non sequitur, no such rerun royalties are generally due.

6.3.1.9. Backend[42]

As with other entitlements under writer/producer deals, the amount of backend accorded to a writer under his or her deal is typically tied to the share of "creation by" credit received by the writer, with a base entitlement that is laid out if the writer receives sole "created by" credit, and various applicable reductions from that base entitlement. Backend entitlements are, like other deal terms, heavily driven by the stature and quotes of the writer, and in particular, whether it is contemplated that the writer will render showrunning services in series, or whether a third-party showrunner will have to be engaged to help produce the series, once ordered. However, because most studios have rigid policies capping the total contingent compensation granted in connection with any given series (for most studios, 35% of the MAGR or the corresponding form of contingent compensation used by the applicable studio), backend reductions are commonly negotiated for heavily-packaged projects that involve many prominent elements who are entitled to contingent compensation.

It is common for a writer/producer's backend entitlement to be stated as involving an artificially high ceiling (again, conditioned on the writer receiving sole "created by" credit on the series). This ceiling is usually reducible, to some extent, by participations granted by the studio to third parties (i.e., other producers, writers, actors, and other participants) in connection with the same series,[43] and may be further reducible if total backend entitlements on the series, for all participants, exceed a maximum threshold (usually 35% or 30% in the aggregate, without regard for differences in definition). The writer's backend will be further reducible (if not automatically reduced) if the writer receives shared "created by" credit on the series, with, in most cases, no backend actually due for a writer who does not receive even a share of "created by" credit (though such a circumstance is rare, and, when it arises, usually specifically negotiated around). In some cases, where a writer's status as a potential showrunner is uncertain at the time the

---

[42] Again, to best understand these terms, it may be best to first consult the more detailed discussion of contingent compensation contained in section 6.4 below.

[43] It is essentially inevitable that *some* third-party participations will be granted in connection with the series, and therefore, that this initial reduction will be triggered. Consequently, the initial "ceiling" figure in a backend deal term is often essentially cosmetic and virtually impossible for the participant to achieve, and the floors more relevant in determining the writer's practical, real-life entitlement.

deal is made, the backend terms may reflect tiering or further reducibility if the writer is not the sole showrunner, and the studio is forced to provide backend to a third-party showrunner.

To illustrate, a substantial writer/producer deal, for a writer who is expected to showrun his or her series, may provide that the writer receives 17.5% of MAGR if he or she receives sole "created by" credit, reducible on a dollar-for-dollar basis by all participations granted to third parties to 15% of MAGR, further reducible on a dollar-for-dollar basis to the extent that aggregate participations granted on the series exceed 35% of MAGR to a floor for the writer of 12.5% of MAGR, further reducible if the writer receives shared "created by" credit to a floor of 7.5% of MAGR. (This may be stated, in shorthand, as "17.5% → 15% → >35% to 12.5% → for shared to 7.5%.")

At the lowest entry level, floors of 5% to 7.5% for sole "created by" credit, and 2.5% to 5% for shared "created by" credit, are common. At middle levels, floors of 10% to 12.5% for sole credit, and 7.5% for shared credit, are typical. At high levels, one might expect to floors of 15% to 17.5% for sole credit, and up to 12.5% for shared credit. The applicable ceilings under such deals may range from 10% (at low levels) to 20% (at high levels) to as high as 35% (at the highest, rarest of levels, 35% representing the full pool of backend most studios will allow on any given project); again, however, the structure of reducibility built into these terms, and the practical necessity of granting participations to parties other than the writer/producer, renders such ceilings largely symbolic and cosmetic.

For writer/creators, contingent compensation virtually always vests in quarters – one-quarter upon completion of the writer's pilot writing services, one-quarter upon completion of pilot producing services, one-quarter upon completion of series producing services for the first season, and one-quarter upon completion of series producing services for the second season. Some studios may allow (particularly for higher level writers) for *pro rata* vesting of the final two quarters – in other words, if a writer is terminated after half of the episodes of the second season have been produced, he or she will vest for one-half of the final one-quarter of the writer's backend, i.e., for a total of 87.5% of the writer's total backend entitlement. Sometimes, such *pro rata* vesting may require that the writer complete services on at least half the episodes of the season in order to receive any share of vesting for that season.

6.3.1.10. Credit

There are three main credit issues in play in writer/producer deals for show creators: producing credit, logo or company credit, and creation credit.[44]

Pilot writers are virtually always accorded Co-Executive Producer or Executive Producer credit.[45] Some studios offer Executive Producer credit to all creators, regardless of stature; others restrict lower-level creators to Co-Executive Producer credit, or, at worst, Supervising Producer credit, though this is rare. If a junior writer starts with Co-Executive Producer credit for the pilot and first season of the series, it is common for the deal to provide for the writer to graduate to Executive Producer credit in the second season of the series. Such credits are virtually always granted on separate cards (or, for bona fide writing teams, on cards shared only between the members of the team), in the main or opening titles of the series.

Higher-level writers, particularly those with showrunning experience, may also be accorded a "logo credit" or "company credit," in the form of a logo which appears after the end credits at the end of each episode. This logo card typically bears the name of the writer's "production company," though for the vast majority of writers, this is essentially a vanity company name that serves as a calling card for the writer him or herself, and does not signify a meaningful full-fledged production company operation. Negotiated issues around such logo credits include conditions (e.g., requiring that the writer receive sole "created by" credit, and/or that he or she be rendering sole or co-showrunning services); whether such logo must be static or may be animated; and whether such logo must appear on a separate card or may be on a shared card with another logo (which is a function of both the writer's stature and the availability of such logo cards, which are limited in number by virtually all networks to no more than three or four cards per episode).

Finally, deals must address "created by" credit (which, as discussed throughout this section, is a condition for most of the

---

[44] In television, all credits for all roles are customarily made subject to the approval of the applicable network, including the negotiated credits for writer/producers, other than guild-determined and mandated credits.

[45] The hierarchy of television producing credits is discussed in further detail in section 6.3.5.2 below.

entitlements under a writer/producer deal). This usually actually requires little negotiation, because most major scripted television production is subject to the jurisdiction of the WGA, which has exclusive control over the determination of writing and series creation credits for WGA-covered series. As a general rule, whatever writer(s) receive(s) "written by" (or, if the story and teleplay for the pilot were written by separate individuals or teams, "story by" and "teleplay by" credit) on the pilot episode of the series also receive(s) "created by" credit on that series. This credit determination (which is made by the WGA) then becomes the basis of satisfying various conditions on the writer's benefits under his or her deal. However, where the pilot script is based on underlying material (such as a book, article, movie, or preexisting television format), "written by" and "created by" credits are generally unavailable under the WGA's credit determination standards. In such circumstances, it is common to negotiate for "created by" and "written by"-based credit conditions (for purposes of writer benefits) to be deemed satisfied if the writer receives "developed by" and "teleplay by" credit, respectively. Studios also usually agree to submit any writer who solely wrote a pilot script for "developed by" credit from the WGA, if the WGA determines that "created by" credit is unavailable.[46]

Other aspects of writing credit (including the determination of episodic writing credits in series, and the placement of such credits) are also generally determined and governed by the WGA, and therefore not expressly negotiated.[47]

6.3.1.11. Perks

There are a small number of "perks" which may be negotiated as part of a writer/producer deal. Most writer/producers are accorded a right to an office, assistant, and parking during production periods of a series; for showrunners, the office and assistant must usually be

---

[46] The WGA technically allows for studios to contractually accord "created by" credit, outside of the WGA credit determination process, where a pilot/series is based on underlying material. Some studios use creative alternatives, such as "Created for television by." However, such contractual entitlements are extremely rare.

[47] In many respects, credits are so fleeting and non-obvious to viewers as to be largely meaningless. Nevertheless, such credits can be extremely significant for the professional resumes of the parties, and provide valuable precedents that substantially influence the parties' entitlements in subsequently negotiated deals.

exclusive (rather than shared with other series staffers). Showrunners are typically entitled to meaningful consultation with respect to key creative issues on the show, befitting their role as the primary creative stewards of the series, but full-blown contractual approval rights over any creative or business elements are extremely rare to the point of being virtually nonexistent. If a writer is required to travel as part of his or her services (e.g., to a distant location to supervise physical production of an episode the writer has written), the writer is typically provided with business class travel, first-class hotel accommodations, ground transportation, and a per diem (minimum terms for which are prescribed by the WGA Basic Agreement, where applicable).[48]

6.3.1.12. Subsequent Productions

Finally, a writer/producer deal will typically provide the writer with the first opportunity to negotiate to render pilot writing and pilot/series executive producing services on certain subsequent productions based on the original television series. This right is often limited to television spinoffs, although for higher-level writers and writers with bona fide theatrical writing experience, it may extend to cover theatrical derivatives as well.

This first opportunity is subject to various customary conditions, including some or all of the following: the writer receiving sole "created by" credit on the original series; the writer rendering at least two years of executive producing services on the original series without being "pay-or-played"; the writer not being in breach of his or her original deal; the writer being professionally available when required by the studio; approval of any applicable network (which the studio must generally use good faith efforts to obtain); the writer then being active in the industry; and time limits (e.g., the derivative being produced within five or seven years, measured from the production of the pilot, the production or exhibition of the last episode of the series on which the individual actually rendered executive producer services,

---

[48] In some cases (particularly when a series films in Los Angeles, though sometimes for New York, as well), the writing team (led by the showrunner) lives and works in the same city where production takes place. However, for series that shoot outside of Los Angeles and New York, it is common for the writers (including the showrunner) to be based in Los Angeles, while other producers and series staffers manage day-to-day affairs at the production location, subject to periodic set visits by the showrunner and/or by the writers of specific episodes as they are actually produced.

or the production or exhibition of the last episode of the original series). The first opportunity right may be initially be limited to the first spinoff of the original series, but automatically "roll" for (i.e., apply to) subsequent spinoffs, if the same conditions continue to be satisfied for each successive spinoff.

Often, the first opportunity clause will provide that, for comparable productions (e.g., television spinoffs to a television series), the writer's deal for the original series serves as a floor for the negotiation of a new deal for the spinoff. Commonly, such clauses will further provide that, if no deal is reached or if certain conditions (such as availability or network approval) of the first opportunity right are not satisfied, the creator of the original series is entitled to a passive participation on the spinoff. This usually amounts to 50% of the royalty and backend (but, usually, not the executive producer fees) of the original series for any generic spinoffs or sequels/prequels/remakes, or 25% to 33% of the royalty and backend (but, usually, not the executive producer fees) of the original series for any planted spinoffs.

6.3.2. Non-Writing Producer Agreements

Non-writing producers serve a variety of roles on television series. Many effectively serve as an outsourced labor force for a studio's development activities, scouting the marketplace for interesting pitches from writers and underlying properties to adapt and bringing them to the attention of studios. Many non-writing producers enjoy close relationships with writers, actors, or other key talent, and can play a vital role in the packaging of a product; others focus on close relationships with studio and network executives and decision-makers, which can be vital to getting traction for a project. Some play an active role in casting, crafting the visual look and feel of a series, or other key creative tasks which are not directly related to writing, while others actively engage directly with writers (albeit without ever putting pen to paper themselves). Many series have an executive producer who serves as producer/director, personally directing multiple episodes of the series while working closely with the line producer and other episodic directors to manage physical production and maintain a consistent look and feel to the series.[49] And some non-writing

---

[49] Unless the producer/director is actively involved in setting up a project with a studio and developing it before the pilot stage, however, such deals usually bear more

producers are simply the managers and close confidantes and creative supporters of writers, rightsholders, star actors or other elements of the creative process, who manage to insinuate themselves as producers of their friends' or clients' projects.

In general, non-writing producer deals are subject to the same basic structure as writer/producer deals (with the obvious exception of pilot-writing services, which are non-applicable to such deals). Consequently, the summary set forth in Section 6.3.1 above can generally be understood to apply to non-writing producers, as well, with the following caveats and modifications.

6.3.2.1. Development Fees

Although non-writing producers do not personally write the pilot screenplay, they are often actively engaged in that process, working closely with the writer to craft the initial story, and providing notes on the writer's drafts. For the most part, such services are rendered by the non-executive producer for no initial charge, in exchange for the promise of episodic fees and backend if a pilot or series is ever actually produced. But in some rare instances, a non-writing producer may be able to extract from the studio a development fee (which may be an advance against future fees owed to that producer for services on the pilot/series). Where applicable, such fees typically range between $10,000 and $50,000, with $25,000 being most common (but again, all such development fees are relatively uncommon, and usually reserved for high-level producers in unique circumstances).

6.3.2.2. Producing Fees

The range of producing fees for non-writing producers, and the structure of fee bumps in subsequent seasons, is typically comparable for non-writing producers as for writing producers (i.e., between $15,000 and $50,000 per episode), though for non-writing producers,

---

resemblance to staffing deals (described in section 6.3.5 below) than to other non-writing producer deals. Similarly, high-level line producers may be accorded Co-Executive Producer or Executive Producer credit, but also render exclusive full-time services which are structured more like staffing writer deals than other non-writing producer deals. Indeed, although the term "non-writing producer" is a technically correct description of an EP-credited producer/director or line producer, the term would not generally be used in reference to such roles.

fees near the top of this range are substantially rarer than for high-level writing producers. Where a studio employs hard caps on aggregate executive producer fees on any given series, non-writing producers are more likely than writer/producers to reduce their fees to accommodate a package of many high-level collaborators. In addition, unlike writer/producers, non-writing producers are typically not in a position to substantially renegotiate their fees upward in future seasons, even on a successful series.

6.3.2.3. Locks

Although the variety of locks applicable to non-writing producers is identical to those applicable to writer/producers, the norms for such locks are different. Non-writing producer deals may be based on two-year Warner locks at lower levels, or life locks at higher levels; however, the majority of non-writing producer deals feature firm two-year locks. In addition, because non-writing producers do not receive story, teleplay, writing, or series creation credit, the credit-based conditions for locks under writer/producer deals are not applicable to writer-producer deals. Instead, series locks are typically conditioned only on the individual not being in breach and completing pilot producer services without being "pay-or-played." Finally, because non-writing producers typically play a more vital role in the development and pilot stages of a television series, and a less vital role in its ongoing production, they have less leverage than writer/producers to negotiate more favorable terms to stay with a successful series in later seasons. Consequently, unlike writer/producers (who generally favor two-year deals), non-writing producers all seek to be locked for the life of a series (particularly since, as explained below, their exclusivity is rarely if ever a condition of their attachment).

6.3.2.4. Services and Exclusivity

Unlike writer/producers, whose services for a series are usually substantially exclusive and full-time, the services obligation of non-writing producers is usually non-exclusive, with services for third parties not to materially interfere. Some studios may insist that particularly key non-writing producers render services on a non-exclusive, first-priority basis (or require that at least one of the members of a two-person producing team be designated to do so), but this is relatively rare; and, with the exception of producer/directors, requiring full-time exclusive services from non-writing producers is virtually unheard of. This comparatively low standard of services allows non-writing producers to concurrently work on multiple projects at any given time, and the most successful and prolific such producers routinely render services on multiple series simultaneously.

6.3.2.5. Royalties

Non-writing producing deals generally do not provide for the producer to receive any form of passive royalty (as distinguished from "backend" participations, as described in Section 6.3.2.8 below), under any circumstances. Fees for non-writing producers essentially always require some level of services to be rendered (though the actual level of services required by the studio or provided by the producer may vary widely from person to person and from project to project).

6.3.2.6. Bonuses

Series sales bonuses for non-writing producers may be given from time to time (and are certainly more common than royalties), but are substantially rarer than for writer/producers (for whom they are essentially ubiquitous). When provided for a non-writing producer, the parameters are generally the same as for writer/producers, although again, credit conditions are not applicable.

6.3.2.7. Consulting

Non-writing producers who are not locked for the life of a series may also be entitled to a "consulting one-for-one." As with some of the other terms for non-writing producers, this entitlement is not necessarily as automatic and ubiquitous as it is for writer/producers, but it is relatively common. In addition, a life lock as a consultant (which commences after the initial lock as an executive producer has expired) is a more common accommodation to non-writing producers, as a step short of the desired life lock as executive producer.[50]

---

[50] Significantly, a studio may elect to continue to engage a non-writing producer as an executive producer (rather than as a consultant), even after the individual's "lock" as executive producer has expired. In fact, this is fairly common where the

6.3.2.8. Backend

In general, the backend entitlements for non-writing producers are comparable to those applicable to writer/producers, with a few key distinctions. First, again, credit contingencies do not apply, so the backend entitlement simply vests over the period of the producer's services without regard for credit. Second, rather than vesting in quarters, the backend for a non-writing producer typically vests in thirds – one-third upon completion of pilot producing services, one-third upon completion of series producing services for the first season, and one-third upon completion of series producing services for the second season (with similar variations around *pro rata* vesting). (Again, this is because the first quarter vest for writer/producers, based on the completion of pilot script writing services, is not applicable to the non-writing producer context.) Third, the range of backend granted to non-writing producers varies more widely depending on stature than for writer/producers, with backend floors that may range from 2.5% of MAGR to 17.5% of MAGR.

6.3.2.9. Credit

The vast majority of negotiated credits for non-writing producers are as Executive Producer, though high-level non-writing producers may also negotiate for lesser credits (such as Co-Executive Producer or Producer) for their own development executives. High-level non-writing producers also seek and receive logo/company credits, subject to the same variations and parameters described for writer/producers (but again, absent any credit or showrunning-based conditions). But again, issues related to pilot teleplay and series creation credit simply do not apply to non-writing producers.

6.3.2.10. Perks

The perks accorded to non-writing producers are comparable to those provided for writer/producers, although exclusive offices and exclusive assistants are rarer, given the comparatively part-time, non-

---

relationship between the non-writing producer and the studio and other members of the creative team is positive. However, studios naturally prefer preserving their flexibility to make this decision to contractually committing themselves from inception to paying executive producer fees for the life of a series.

exclusive nature of the role. Some non-writing producers may also negotiate for a guarantee that the studio will pay for their travel to the production location of the pilot and/or series at least once (or once per season), in order to assure their ongoing creative involvement with the production, though studios generally reserve such decisions about the necessity and propriety of in-person on-set services to their own judgment, rather than making contractual commitments.

6.3.2.11. Subsequent Productions

Like writer/producers, non-writing producers typically seek to be attached to subsequent productions based on the original television series they have developed. First opportunities for subsequent productions, comparable to those accorded to writer/producers (but again, excluding credit conditions which are not applicable to non-writing producers), are sometimes accorded to non-writing producers, as well. Some studios grant such entitlements freely, while others tend to reserve them only for higher-level producers or those who have some special articulable history with a property or project. This is in contrast to writer/producers, for whom first opportunity rights, at least for subsequent television series, are generally granted freely (albeit subject to the sole "created by" credit condition). In addition, while writer/producers may expect to receive some form of passive participation if no deal is reached on the subsequent production, passives for non-writing producers are relatively rare (and, where granted, typically limited to a share of backend; again, 50% of the share from the original series for generic spinoffs, sequels, prequels, and remakes, and 25% to 33% for planted spinoffs).

6.3.3. Pilot Director Agreements[51]

Although the role of the director is comparatively diminished in television relative to the significance of the director in the theatrical motion picture industry, the pilot director still has a very important role to play in setting the stylistic, tonal, and visual template of the series to come. He or she also usually coordinates closely with the executive producers and creative executives of the project in connection with the

---

[51] A sample pilot director agreement is included in this Chapter's supplemental forms.

casting process. Even where a series is ordered directly to production without a pilot, the director of the first episode is chosen with particular care, and has a comparable creative impact on the series. Pilot directors are usually engaged after a pilot has been ordered to production, in close coordination with the network, although the current trend in television development favors packaging of multiple elements early in the process, and it is not uncommon for pilot directors to be attached to a project during the development phase (although the director's ultimate right to actually direct the pilot is then typically subject to network approval, which the studio will use good faith efforts to obtain). In addition, as the television medium has continued to grow in prestige and attract more and more theatrical talent, major directors have taken an increasingly active role in sourcing and developing new television projects, even before these proposed series are pitched to a studio.

6.3.3.1 Services

The services of a pilot director are typically rendered on an exclusive basis during formal pre-production (a period of about six to eight weeks) and production (about two to four weeks) of the pilot, and on a non-exclusive but first-priority basis during post-production of the pilot, until delivery of the director's cut. Between the delivery of the director's cut and final delivery, the director's services may be fully non-exclusive and subject to such individual's professional availability. The actual level of activity by the director during this late post-production stage varies widely in actual practice, with directors who are also engaged and credited as executive producers tending to play a more active role during these late stages.

If the pilot director is attached at the development stage, when the actual production period for the pilot is totally unknown (and totally speculative), the director's obligations are usually subject to his or her professional availability at the time the pilot is ordered. If the director is unavailable at that time, he or she may be entirely divested from the project without any further obligations owed; or, more commonly, entitled to some more limited (and less lucrative) ongoing attachment as a non-exclusive, non-writing executive producer.

6.3.3.2. Directing Fees

The fees paid to pilot directors vary widely depending on the length of the pilot (i.e., thirty-minute vs. sixty-minute) and the identities and policies of the applicable studios and networks. Some smaller cable networks and their affiliated studios never pay more than more than applicable DGA (Directors Guild of America) scale minimums for pilot directors[52] – as of 2018, approximately $77,000 for thirty-minute broadcast network pilots; approximately $102,000 for sixty-minute broadcast network pilots; approximately $46,000 for thirty-minute basic cable pilots; and approximately $61,000 for sixty-minute basic cable pilots.[53] At most studios, pilot directing fees range from approximately $100,000 to $250,000, depending on the nature of the production, the platform, and the director's quotes and stature, although highly sought-after feature directors may, on rare occasions, command even higher fees. The DGA Basic Agreement also permits any portions of the pilot directing fee in excess of 200% of applicable scale for the days worked to be credited against residuals[54], if explicitly agreed by the studio and director; consequently, deals featuring high directing fees often include a residual crediting component.

6.3.3.3. Executive Producing

Directors who participated in the development of the project are usually also attached as executive producers for the resulting series. In general, the terms of this attachment follow the structure described in Section 6.3.2 above for non-exclusive non-writing producers, though in some rare cases, the pilot director may stay with the series as a full-time, exclusive producer/director.

---

[52] Virtually all director engagements in the United States, at least with respect to scripted television, are subject to DGA jurisdiction, irrespective of network/platform and budget.

[53] Like WGA-governed script fees, applicable DGA minimums for directors of projects on digital platforms may be tied to the corresponding broadcast network or basic cable minimums, or may be freely negotiable without any minimum, depending on the budget of the production and the number of subscribers of the relevant digital platform.

[54] The term "residuals" refers to payments payable to talent, as a percentage of revenues received by a studio from international and other secondary exploitation of a series, pursuant to applicable union collective bargaining agreements. All three of the principal talent collective bargaining agreements – with SAG/AFTRA, WGA, and DGA – provide for residual payments to union-covered service providers.

Where a director has not participated in the development of the project and was only engaged after the pilot was ordered to production, he or she may be still credited as an executive producer – although in such circumstances, usually only for the pilot, without being attached to the series on an ongoing basis. The function of a pilot-only executive producer role may vary. The credit may signify a heightened level of creative leadership and responsibility, particularly if other executive producers on the pilot are relatively inexperienced. It may be a mere vanity gift to satisfy the director's desire to be credited more prominently. It may serve as cover for the studio on the financials of the deal, allowing the studio to pay the director a relative lower pilot directing fee, but supplement it with a separately-stated executive producer fee (which may range from $10,000 to $50,000, and which fee the studio may or may not elect to treat as part of the budgeted fee pool for all executive producers).

6.3.3.4. Royalties

The director of a pilot is usually entitled to a passive royalty for the life of the resulting series, if it is ordered. This royalty generally ranges from approximately $3,000 per episode to $6,000 per episode (with, as always, outliers on either side), usually falling somewhere in that range in proportion to the level of the other terms of the deal. Tiering, rerun royalties, and other structural elements of this entitlement are generally akin to those applicable under writer/producer deals (with the condition of being the sole pilot director replacing any applicable writing-credit based conditions).

6.3.3.5. Bonuses

Independent of the ongoing episodic royalty, the director of a pilot which is ordered to series is also typically entitled to a series sales bonus. In every respect, these bonuses are generally identical to the corresponding entitlement for writer/producers – $25,000 being considered standard (with lower or higher amounts possible according to stature), proration according to the number of episodes actually produced, and potential tiering or other differentiation depending on the network for which the series is ultimately produced.

6.3.3.6. Backend

The majority of pilot directors receive 2.5% of MAGR in backend from series that are produced based on their pilots, which contingent compensation vests 100% based on the director's pilot services. Inexperienced pilot directors may receive somewhat less backend (e.g., 2% of MAGR, or, in very rare cases, as low as 1.5% of MAGR), while highly successful and experienced pilot directors may command 3% to 4% of MAGR, and A-list theatrical directors and the most prolific pilot directors may, in rare instances, receive up to 5% of MAGR for pilot directing services alone.

In addition, if the director is engaged as a non-writing executive producer in series, there may be additional points allocated to those services, which would vest consistently with how such points may vest for any non-writing executive producer (e.g., in thirds, across the pilot and first two seasons of series services; although sometimes, the executive producing backend will simply vest in halves, across the first two seasons of services, because the director has already vested for a share of contingent compensation based on his or her pilot directing services alone).

6.3.3.7. Credit

Credit for pilot directors is generally governed by the DGA Agreement (including matters of determination, form, and placement) and therefore not expressly negotiated. However, executive producer credit, where applicable, must be negotiated, and is subject to the same issues applicable to other non-writing executive producers. (Additionally, as noted in Section 6.3.3.3 above, the director's engagement and crediting as an executive producer may be limited to the pilot only, or may extend into series.)

6.3.3.8. Perks

The "perks" accorded to a pilot director are generally comparable to those accorded to a showrunning executive producer – travel (business class transportation, first-class hotel accommodations, ground transportation or rental car, and per diem, with certain minimums for these perquisites prescribed by the DGA Basic

Agreement), parking, and office and assistant (usually exclusive to the director). Many directors look to have their own personal assistants put on the payroll of the production for the duration of their services, a request which is usually accommodated, though this may become more expensive (and therefore more problematic) if the director (and therefore the assistant) needs to travel for the pilot production.

6.3.3.9. Subsequent Productions

Many pilot directors seek a first opportunity to be engaged to direct the pilot of any spinoffs of the series for which they are currently engaged. Where granted, the conditions applicable to such a first opportunity are generally equivalent to those applicable to a writer/producer's first opportunity to write and executive produce the spinoff. However, first opportunities for pilot directors are exceedingly rare and generally reserved for the highest-level directors (unlike first opportunities for writer/producers, which are usually given as a matter of course).

6.3.4. Actor Agreements[55]

If writer/producer agreements most potently illustrate television's status as a writer-driven medium, then actor agreements reflect television's status as a serialized medium.[56]

Unlike a motion picture – which, in even the most extreme circumstances, seldom requires more than a year of the actors' time to produce, and usually significantly less (i.e., months or even weeks), a successful television series will be in production for five to eight months a year, every year, for five, seven, ten, or even more years. And for viewers, actors are the (literal) faces of these series. Actor agreements must therefore strike a balance between, on the one hand, the actors' desires to preserve the opportunity to develop their careers and accept work outside of their primary television series; and, on the other hand, the needs of the studio and network to protect series continuity over a period of years.

---

[55] A sample series regular actor agreement is included in this chapter's supplemental forms.

[56] *See* section 6.1.2 above.

The terms below relate to agreements for "series regulars" – the six to ten lead actors (although the list tends to grow in later seasons of a series) who are most central to the show's creative content. These actors enter into complex, multi-year deals which firmly establish the television series as their primary employment, and their primary obligation, for as long as the studio and network wish to continue to employ them. Such deals are distinguishable from "recurring guest" deals – deals which contemplate the actor appearing in multiple episodes of a series, often over long story arcs, but without binding the actor to the series long-term to the same extent.[57]

To the viewer, it may be difficult to distinguish which cast members of a series are series regulars and which are recurring guests. Typically, series regulars are credited in a series' main or opening titles, while guests are credited elsewhere under the heading "Guest Starring" or "Special Guest," but in some cases, guests may successfully negotiate to be credited among series regulars. In any given episode, the role of a guest star may be of equal or greater prominence to that of any given series regular. Usually, recurring guest stars appear on a series sporadically or for specific finite runs, but this, too, is not always the case – actors Grizzwald "Grizz" Chapman and Kevin "Dot Com" Brown appeared on over eighty episodes of NBC's hit series *30 Rock* as recurring guests, rather than series regulars. Actors who start out as recurring guests may eventually be promoted to series regulars, as was the case for Jim Rash, who played Dean Craig Pelton on NBC's *Community*; other actors may turn down the opportunity to move from a recurring to a regular role, as was reportedly the case with Alison Brie, who played Trudy Campbell on AMC's *Mad Men*.

Rather, the major difference between series regulars and recurring guests is not discernible on-screen, but off-screen, in the actors' contracts. The primary distinguishing features of a series regular agreement, compared to a recurring guest agreement, are threefold – term, priority, and exclusivity. With respect to term, series regulars make an open-ended commitment for multiple seasons, as may be required in the future by the studio and network; recurring guest stars contract for a specified, committed number of episodes at any given

---

[57] In addition, one may consider a "guest actor" deal – a deal for an actor to appears in only one or two episodes of a series – as a third category of television acting agreement.

time, and only after the studio and network have resolved to actually produce those episodes. With respect to priority, series regulars generally must preserve their availability to work as, when, and where required by the studio and network as the series proceeds; recurring guest stars can fill their schedules freely with other work unless and until they are firmly engaged, with guaranteed compensation and specified dates, to work on their episodes. With respect to exclusivity, series regulars generally agree (for the benefit of the network that airs their series) to severely curtail their right to take outside work in television; recurring guest stars generally do not submit to any such exclusivity. The same actor may work for vastly different episodic rates, depending on whether he or she is engaged as a series regular or a recurring guest star; indeed, while the willingness of actors to take discounts on their highest-negotiated fees varies from actor to actor, it is not unusual for an actor to charge anywhere from two to ten times as much per episode to appear as a series regular, versus being engaged as a guest star or recurring guest. In effect, a significant portion of the episodic fee payable to actors under series regular deals compensates them not only for working for the studio, but also for *not* working for third parties.

6.3.4.1. Test Options

For actors who must test for a role, as opposed to receiving a straight offer, the studio must negotiate specific terms for its initial option.[58] There are actually typically two "tests" for actors who are going through the casting process – a studio test (where the studio's executives consider options which have been curated by a show's producers and casting directors), and a network test (where the network's executives consider options that have been deemed acceptable by the studio's executives to show to the network). For the most part, in the modern industry, the actor's "test performance" is actually pre-recorded by the casting directors, and simply shown to studio and/or network executives at the appointed date and time. Studio executives generally will not consider, and in no event will present to a network, an actor whose deal is not fully negotiated and executed by the actor prior to the date and time of the test. This policy

---

[58] The "test option" process is explained in section 6.1.3.1.d above.

contributes to the "fire drill" pace of dealmaking for test options, especially during broadcast network pilot season, when there is an extensive amount of simultaneous casting activity going on within the television community. Casting decisions are usually made by consensus among network, studio, producers, and casting directors, although network approval is mandatory – and, in the event of a disagreement, the network's will tends to prevail.

The studio takes an option to engage the actor for pilot (or, if there is no pilot, first season) services, which is exercisable within a specified period following the test – usually five business days, often reducible to three business days if the actor receives a bona fide outside offer for another engagement. During the height of pilot season, and in highly competitive situations, the option period may be shorter. If there are separate tests scheduled at the studio and network levels, the deal must specify which test triggers the option period, and whether the option period automatically shifts or extends if the test date and time changes.

The actor's engagement may be subject to further conditions, such as the conclusion of negotiations between the studio and network of a license agreement, or the satisfaction of other conditions imposed by the studio or network on the unconditional greenlight of the pilot production. Outstanding conditions which are outside of the actor's control may cause some actors to hesitate to commit to a test option agreement, and often, deals will provide that all conditions must be waived or acknowledged satisfied within a specified time, or the actor is free to walk away from the deal.[59]

6.3.4.2. Pilot Services

The pilot component of a series regular deal typically buys out a specified number of days of services for pre-production (e.g., rehearsal, wardrobe fittings, etc.), production, and post-production (including retakes, added scenes, and audio dubbing/looping work), which is usually specifically tailored to the pilot production schedule, with a

---

[59] Because acting engagements are often contingent in this fashion, an actor (and his or her representatives) may pursue multiple series opportunities during a single casting cycle, by arranging the various offers in precise contractual "priority" relative to one another. Of course, the studio/network may consequently elect to pass on an actor whose availability is uncertain when time is of the essence for a casting decision.

few buffer days. This buyout will usually cover some small number (e.g., two to four) of post-production days which may be non-consecutive with the principal period of pilot production, although nonconsecutive services days are usually subject to the actor's professional availability. Services in excess of the pre-bought days may be paid at the applicable SAG/AFTRA (Screen Actors Guild/American Federation of Television and Radio Artists) scale minimum rate, though, where an actor's initial compensation exceeds the applicable SAG/AFTRA scale rate (as is typical for series regular engagements), it is more common for overage days to be paid at a *pro rata* daily rate, based on the negotiated pilot fee divided by the number of bought-out work days under the actor's pilot deal.

6.3.4.3. Pilot and Series Fees

The fees paid to a series regular actor are a function of many factors, including the stature and quotes of the actor; the prominence of the role in the series; the overall budget of the series and the cast budget in particular; and the amount of budget available for the studio to spend following commitments of the balance of the cast budget to previously-engaged actors. Actors and their representatives will generally expect to make no less than the amount negotiated for their most recent deal, and will seek to improve upon such quotes to the greatest extent possible, especially where the quote was "earned" (i.e., the actor was actually cast in the role, and performed in a pilot and/or series). However, some actors and their representatives will accept slightly lower fees for "straight offers" than for "test options," because they are freed from having to further compete to win the role.

Typically, the actor's episodic rate for the first season of a series will be the same as his or her pilot fee, though pilot fees may sometimes be slightly above or below the applicable first season fee, depending on negotiating needs and policies. The majority of studios and networks recognize five percent cumulative annual bumps in this episodic rate (i.e., on a season-by-season basis), though some studios, as a matter of policy, limit such increases to four percent. Some studios will consider granting actors an unusually high fee bump between the first and second seasons, particularly if the actor's negotiated fee for the pilot and/or first season are below the actor's quote or otherwise unusually low; however, most major studios tend to avoid this. Fees may be tied to program length (i.e., thirty-minute episodes, sixty-minute episodes, etc., taking into consideration that shorter episodes generally have smaller budgets and take less time to produce), with negotiated increases (which may or may not be on a *pro rata* basis) for episodes whose running times exceed the presumed program length under the deal.

Finally, the parties may negotiate to deem some portion of the actor's negotiated pilot and episodic fee – which portion may be denominated as a specific dollar amount or a percentage, often 10% to 20%, of the actor's fee – to be an advance against residuals which may be due to the actor, pursuant to the requirements of the SAG Basic Agreement, for the studio's foreign or off-network exploitation of the series.

In kids programming, child stars typically make about $7,500 to $12,500 per episode for the pilot and first season, with escalations thereafter. Child actors on adult primetime programs usually start at between $10,000 and $20,000 per episode. Inexperienced adult actors with no preexisting quotes as a series regular usually earn between $17,500 and $22,500 per episode to start. The vast majority of steadily working television actors make between $25,000 and $75,000 per episode, with major stars who have appeared in numerous series or who have significant film experience commanding between $75,000 and $125,000 per episode. In more recent years, as premium cable and digital platforms have sought to lure A-list movie stars to the small screen, fees for the highest-level actors have climbed north of $125,000 with the biggest names and highest earners reportedly commanding up to $1 million per episode on series for these platforms.

6.3.4.4. Series Options

An actor's pilot fee buys out an initial option to engage the actor to render services on a series (if ordered). During this option period, the actor is precluded from accepting any third-party engagements which would prevent him or her from rendering series services as required by the studio.[60] The initial series option date may be set based on a

---

[60] To be clear, the studio is virtually never obligated to engage an actor to render services, even if the series is ordered; CBS chief Les Moonves famously demanded that *Big Bang Theory* pilot actress Amanda Walsh be replaced for the series, leading to the subsequent casting of star Kaley Cuoco.

concrete calendar date (which is typical for broadcast network pilots, which are produced in early spring with initial series option dates set to June 30 of that year), or a specified amount of time following the delivery of the pilot (which is typical for cable pilots which produce year-round, and is usually set to three to six months following the pilot delivery).

Studios also typically build in contractual extensions for such initial options (often to accommodate the right of a network licensee to place a later series order in anticipation of a mid-season launch). The historical standard for such extensions is six months (on a broadcast network pilot, to December 31 of that year), subject to payment to the actor of an additional pilot fee. More recently, studios and networks have experimented with variations such as breaking up the six-month extension into two three-month extensions for a half-pilot fee each, and/or making extension fees applicable in whole or in part against subsequent series fees. Extensions may prove particularly controversial or difficult to negotiate if they have the effect of keeping an actor off the market for a subsequent pilot season (as may be the case for cable pilots which are initially produced later in the year). For the most part, all series regulars engaged for a given pilot are accorded equivalent treatment (with extension fees scaled according to their respective pilot fees) in the option structures under their deals.

In addition, the series regular deal must specify option periods for the studio to exercise its option to engage the actor for subsequent seasons of the series. Again, these subsequent season option dates may be defined based on calendar dates (again typical for broadcast network pilots; usually June 30 annually), or a specified amount of time following the delivery or exhibition of the last episode of the prior season (again typical for cable; commonly set to the earlier of six to seven months following the final delivery, or nine to ten months following the initial exhibition, of the last episode of the prior season). Subsequent season option dates may also be annualized to the calendar date of the initial series option deadline. In any event, the subsequent season options must be set with sufficient spacing to allow the studio and network adequate time to produce and exhibit enough of the prior season for them to be prepared to make decisions about whether a show will be renewed, and whether any given actor will be required to return. Some studios and networks also negotiate for the ability to pay for one-time extensions and/or re-annualizations of subsequent season option dates, in order to account for potential delays or exigencies of production or exhibition that may make it difficult for them to be ready to render decisions within the default option period. Again, all series regulars engaged for a given series are generally accorded equivalent treatment in such option structures.

The vast majority or series regular deals bind the actor to the studio for six years.[61] This practice derives from California law, under which the so-called "seven years rule" renders personal services contracts with terms longer than seven years unenforceable.[62] In rare instances – in particular, deals with extremely high-level and active film actors (who are reluctant to sign extremely long-term deals), and deals for closed-ended limited or anthology series (which do not require season-to-season continuity of characters) – studios may agree to accept shorter-term deals (e.g., three or four years). Prominent feature actors tend to demand this. However, deviations from six-year deals are still unusual, and even where a character is specifically contemplated to require only a one- or two-year story arc before being written out of the series, the preferred studio practice is to obtain a six-year deal on a blanket, non-negotiable basis.[63] In addition, studios behind successful series often, as a matter of courtesy and custom, entertain renegotiations of actors' deals following the fourth season of a series,

---

[61] Deals for broadcast network series are often for "six and a half years," with the "half year" allowing for six full seasons that follow a shortened (e.g., eight to thirteen episodes) first season which is ordered to production for a "mid-season start" – i.e., premiering during January to April, rather than September or October, of the applicable broadcast year. For reference, "broadcast years" are typically understood to run from September of any given calendar year until August of the following year.

[62] During the contentious cast renegotiation, also discussed in section .C.2 above, the actors' lawyers sought leverage in their negotiation by suing for a declaration that the actors' contracts were altogether void, due to an alleged error in the dating and structuring of the actors' deals, which had the effect of extending their terms to more than seven years (and therefore caused the contracts to violate California's "seven years rule."

[63] Such conservatism in deal-making can often prove extremely important in hindsight. For instance, it has been widely reported that the character of Jesse Pinkman (played by Aaron Paul) was initially intended to die before the end of the first season of *Breaking Bad*, but series creator Vince Gilligan was so impressed with Paul's performance in the series that he decided to change his creative plan, making the character of Jesse Pinkman central to the show's full five-season run. Had studio Sony Pictures Television made a one-year deal with Paul from the outset because of Gilligan's initial creative plan, it would have been forced to negotiate a new (and potentially significantly more expensive) deal to extend Paul's run on the show after the first season.

as described in Section 6.1.3.2 above (although actors' representatives may push for renegotiations even earlier, where a show is particularly successful, and/or the show is especially important to its network, and/or the actor was somehow underpaid from the outset). Such renegotiations may be conditioned on the actor's agreement to extend the deal by adding further series options.

6.3.4.5. Series Guarantees

A series regular deal will also specify a guaranteed number of episodes-per-year for the actor. The majority of series regulars are guaranteed to receive their episodic fees for all episodes produced during any season for which they are engaged (whether or not they actually appear in every episode). Actors in smaller roles may receive "fractional guarantees" – the usual variations for broadcast network series are 7/13 or 10/13,[64] and for cable series is 7/10. Such guarantees are generally driven by the creative needs and expectations of the series creator and producers, but sometimes, the decision-making may flow in the opposite direction: a major actor who is negotiating to play a character which is contemplated for a fractional guarantee may insist on being guaranteed all episodes produced, effectively forcing the studio and creative team to alter their ingoing creative plan and enhance the character's significance, or to take on dead-weight financial obligations (paying an actor for all episodes produced, whether or not the actor is actually used in all such episodes), in order to successfully close the deal with the desired actor. In addition, it is not uncommon for a role with a fractional guarantee in the first season of a series to escalate to "all episodes produced" by the second or third year of the deal.

In addition to stating a series guarantee as a percentage (7/10, 7/13, 10/13, or all) of episodes produced, a series regular deal will also typically provide for a per-season numerical number of guaranteed

---

[64] This reflects the fact that, until recently, most broadcast series were ordered in increments of no less than thirteen episodes, and a full season usually consisted of twenty-six episodes. In recent years, a "full order" for a broadcast network is usually twenty-two episodes rather than twenty-six (though particularly successful series may still be ordered for twenty-three to twenty-six episodes in a given season).

episodic fees.[65] The majority of deals, whether for broadcast or cable, guarantee actors a minimum of seven episodic fees for the first season of the series, reducible to a minimum of six episodic fees if the initial order is for six or fewer episodes. In subsequent years, the annual guarantee will increase somewhat, usually to thirteen episodes for broadcast network series, and to anywhere from ten to thirteen episodes in cable (but in any event no more than the expected actual number of episodes per season).

In some instances, actors' representatives may seek to negotiate maximums as well as minimums on their clients' episodic services. This issue typically arises when a high-level film actor is tentative about committing to long annual television production periods, or when a show is being produced for a newer platform with a relatively unestablished order pattern (making it difficult for the actors and their representatives to measure and predict the level of commitment they are undertaking). Studios and networks are both typically extremely resistant to such maximums – for studios, more episodes generally corresponds to more revenue, while networks naturally want to maximize the available number of episodes of their most successful series. Consequently, studios generally resist making any accommodations with respect to series maximums, though they may sometimes agree that production of more than a specified number of episodes per season automatically triggers an annual fee bump. In addition, in the rare instance where a studio actually agrees to limit the number of episodes for which an actor may be required to render services in any given season, that studio will nevertheless reserve the right to produce as many episodes per season as the studio (and/or its commissioning network) desires (albeit without paying the actor for unworked episodes in excess of the negotiated maximum).

6.3.4.6. Credit/Billing

Series regulars are generally guaranteed that their screen credits will appear in the series' main or opening titles, grouped with other series regulars, and in a size and style which is no less favorable than

---

[65] This is driven by the SAG Basic Agreement, which requires that actor be guaranteed no less than seven episodic fees per season in order for the studio to maintain its exclusive option on the actor's services.

the credit accorded to any other series regular actors.[66] Duration ties are also common, but less universal. Series regulars' credits typically appear on every episode of the series, whether or not the actor actually appears, although some studios and networks revise the credits for each episode to reflect only actors who actually appear in that episode.[67]

Higher-level actors, or actors who know that they are negotiating for a particularly prominent role, will negotiate for guaranteed credit position (in other words, a requirement that their credit will appear first [or in some other numerical position] among all credited series regulars). Credit position is usually a creative decision, combining considerations of the prominence of the actor and the prominence of the role in the series. Position guarantees are generally styled as "no less than ___ position," to allow the studio to accord even more favorable credit position in its own discretion. Higher-level actors in smaller supporting roles often negotiate to receive the final credit among series regulars, with the word "and" in front of their names; if this credit has already been committed to an actor, a subsequent actor in a similar position may negotiate for credit in penultimate position, with the word "with" preceding his or her name. Early in the casting process, a studio negotiating with a prominent actor may negotiate for credit position options that it may choose among in its discretion (e.g., a credit which will appear in no less than second position, or in penultimate/"with" position, or in last/"and" position, at the studio's discretion). Alternatively, a studio may preserve its right to credit all series regular actors in alphabetical order.

6.3.4.7. Dressing Room

The type of dressing room accorded to an actor during production of the series is generally considered a material substantive term of the actor's deal, as actors will spend a considerable part of each shooting day prepping (or waiting) for their calls off-set. When a show is filmed on a studio stage location (as is common for multi-camera comedies), actors are generally provided with private dressing rooms within the

---

[66] By contrast, "Guest Star" credits almost always appear in the end titles of each episode.

[67] For instance, this is the case on HBO's *Game of Thrones*, which sports a particularly massive cast of series regulars, none of whom consistently appear in every single episode of the series.

studio facility. However, when a show is filming on location, actors will be provided with spaces in dressing room trailers, and may negotiate fiercely for favorable accommodations. Single "star" trailers (which have a single compartment, for a single actor) are fairly uncommon in television production, and, because of cost considerations, many studios have strict policies against providing such dressing rooms. Most series regulars (as well as high-level guest stars) are accorded one compartment in a so-called "double banger" (i.e., a 40+ foot trailer with two separate side-by-side private compartments). Lower-level series regulars (and most guest stars) may be accorded one compartment in a so-called "triple banger" (i.e., a trailer with three smaller side-by-side-by-side private compartments). Triple bangers are especially common for shows which film on location in New York City, where space constraints are a major production consideration. Nearly every actor will seek (though not every actor will receive) contractual assurances that his or her dressing facility will be no less favorable in any material respect than that accorded to any other actor on the series.[68]

6.3.4.8. Photo/Likeness/Biography Approvals

Most series regulars will negotiate for approval rights over still images, non-photographic likenesses, and biographical information depicting or concerning the actor that are used in publicity for the series. Studios have widely disparate policies with respect to the granting of such rights; some studios accord them to series regulars as a matter of course, while others steadfastly reserve such rights only for higher-level actors (sometimes by requiring, as a matter of policy, that an actor must receive higher than a threshold fee in order to qualify to receive such approval rights).

When an approval over still photographs is granted, it may be granted solely as to photographs in which the actor appears alone, or extended to photographs in which the actor appears with others (or

---

[68] It is difficult to overstate how important dressing room issues can become for some actors, and therefore, for the negotiation of some actor deals. For instance, many actors negotiate for extremely specific dressing room furnishings and amenities. Moreover, while such details are never negotiated contractually, the most particular actors may insist on being assigned whatever trailer (or trailer compartment) is physically nearest to the actual filming area, as a way of reflecting that actor's superior importance to the production.

with others possessing comparable approval rights). Actors must typically approve no less than 50% of photographs in which they appear alone, and, if applicable, no less than 75% of photographs in which they appear with others, and must exercise such approvals (typically through their representatives) within short time windows or those approvals are deemed granted. For non-photographic likenesses, the actor negotiates for how many rounds of comments (or "passes") he or she is permitted to make on a proposed rendering before it is deemed approved – usually one pass, and almost never more than two passes, being the standard.

Vitally, while a studio may agree to accord such approval rights to an actor, networks – which are the entities that actually control the majority of advertising activity around a series – virtually never agree to assume the corresponding obligation and honor such approval rights. Consequently, such restrictions are almost always limited to advertising materials which are created by or under the direct control of the studio (and therefore may have somewhat limited practical effect).

6.3.4.9. Merchandising Rights

Actors often seek a right of approval over the use of their names, voices, and/or likenesses in merchandising, though such approvals are seldom granted to series regulars (whose significant guaranteed compensation is generally understood to include compensation for exclusivity, likeness rights, and the like), as opposed to high-level guests (who may appear in as little as one episode, for what may be a modest fee, and therefore have greater basis to resist granting such rights). More commonly, actors are granted a limited right of approval over the use of their names or likenesses in specified restricted categories (e.g., firearms, alcohol, tobacco, pharmaceuticals, personal hygiene products, etc., as well as product categories which directly compete with the actor's preexisting branding and endorsement obligations for third-party brands).[69] In addition, a studio will generally agree to pay actors a percentage of the studio's revenues from

---

[69] One contested but highly valuable category is gambling. Although some actors may be sensitive about the use of their names or likenesses in lottery games, slot machines, and comparable contexts, these rights can be extremely valuable to the studio (and, by extension, to the actor who receives a royalty for the use of his or her likeness).

merchandising featuring that actor's likeness. The standard royalty rate is 5% of the studio's "net merchandising receipts" (the studio's merchandising receipts, less distribution fees for the studio or its subdistributors, and out-of-pocket expenses), reducible by royalties granted to other actors featured on the same piece of merchandise to a floor of 2.5% of the studio's "net merchandising receipts" from each such product.[70]

6.3.4.10. Other Approvals/Consultations

There are a small number of approval and consultation rights for which actors may negotiate in series regular deals. Actual contractual approval rights are exceedingly rare, and, when such requests are accommodated, it is almost always in the form of a contractual consultation (rather than approval) right. In addition, as for many of the deal points discussed throughout this section, the according of such rights depends on the stature and bargaining power of the actor.

Very high-level actors who are attached at the development stage of a project, when the details of the creative team and content are not yet certain, may seek and receive consultation rights over the pilot screenplay, the pilot writer, the pilot director, principal filming location, and/or the showrunner, to the extent that such elements have not already been determined as of the time the actor makes his or her deal. Any such rights would be considered exceptional.

More commonly, series regulars have a contractual right to consult with producers with respect to the look and feel of their hair, makeup, and wardrobe for the series. Higher levels, actors with particular sensitivities may also receive contractual consultation or approval rights over the actual personnel engaged to render hair, makeup, and wardrobe services. Approval over the distribution of bloopers featuring the actor is relatively common, though approval of non-blooper behind-the-scenes or deleted scenes footage is often sought but seldom granted.

---

[70] In some instances, however, studios may seek further reducibility of their royalty obligations from products which feature a large number of (royalty-earning) cast members from an ensemble cast.

6.3.4.11. Travel/Relocation

If an actor is to render services on a pilot which is produced more than 50 or 75 miles from his or her principal residence, as a matter of course, the actor will be provided with a standard travel package – business class transportation, first-class hotel accommodations, ground transportation, and a per diem (minimum terms for which are prescribed by the SAG Basic Agreement, where applicable).[71] High-level actors often negotiate for first-class transportation and/or companion tickets, though these are seldom provided in television (as opposed to feature films, where they are more common accommodations).[72]

For series, however, studios generally presume that an actor will actually relocate permanently (or at least for the life of the series) to the filming location of the series.[73] Consequently, in lieu of providing transportation and accommodations, the deal will typically provide for a flat, one-time relocation package for the actor, applicable for the first season only – usually comprised of one or two business-class tickets, and a non-accountable allowance of around $7,500 to $10,000, per season. At higher levels, an actor may be provided with as many as four business class tickets (which the actor may use to travel back and forth to his or her permanent home, or to provide transportation for friends or family members), and a relocation fee as high as $25,000, though such enhanced packages are reserved only for extremely high-level, hotly-negotiated deals.

Because many actors are sensitive to where they live and work – and the pursuit of cost-saving tax incentives has attracted production away from traditional entertainment industry centers like Los Angeles and New York (and toward places such as Toronto, Vancouver, New

---

[71] This basic travel package is also the norm for guest stars who must travel for filming.

[72] For many years, the SAG Basic Agreement actually required that all actors on SAG productions be flown first-class, a costly perk which was pared back to a business class guarantee during the collective bargaining that led to the 2011 amendment and extension of the SAG Basic Agreement.

[73] This presumption may hold less water for shorter-order cable series, which produce ten to thirteen episodes over five to six-month production periods per year, compared to broadcast network series, which usually produce twenty-two episodes over an eight-month production period per year. Nevertheless, even if fictional, this assumption is a hallmark of most series regular deals.

Orleans, Pittsburgh, Atlanta, and Albuquerque)[74] – high-level actors will often negotiate for the right to opt out of their obligations altogether if the studio moves principal production of the series away from one of a negotiated list of production locations that the actor deems acceptable. Unusually lucrative relocation packages are often a product of a studio's efforts to persuade an actor to entertain alternative production locations.

6.3.4.12. Exclusivity

As noted in the preface to this section, exclusivity is one of the key elements that distinguish a series regular deal from a guest star deal. Most networks have a somewhat proprietary attitude toward talent that appear on their shows[75]; consequently, networks usually require that studios obtain significant exclusivity (within television) over actors' services as a condition of engaging such actors as series regulars. Deviations from such exclusivity requirements are extremely rare, and require the network's approval in every instance.

Series regulars' services are generally fully exclusive (in all media) during production periods, exclusive in television (subject to limited carveouts) at all times, and always first-priority with respect to production services (which means that the studio has first call on the actor's time, and can call on the actor to render production services whenever necessary, unless the studio has specifically agreed to waive such priority for specified dates on which the actor wishes to take other work).[76] The exclusivity in television typically includes carveouts for non-recurring/non-regular guest appearances for third parties (which are often limited to no more than three appearances every thirteen

---

[74] *See* section 6.1.4 above.

[75] This attitude – which was born in era with three broadcast networks and no cable networks – is arguably anachronistic in the modern marketplace, which features literally dozens of competing television networks and digital platforms, and actors who jump regularly between feature film and television work. But it is nevertheless ubiquitous, particularly among broadcast networks, which often work hard to create a brand association in viewers' minds between a given star and their own network.

[76] Depending on the network, genre, and level of compensation, lesser exclusivity may be considered – for instance, performers on unscripted series are generally subject to far more limited exclusivity requirements, such as exclusivity solely in unscripted programming, or in programming of a comparable genre or theme. However, again, such compromise is rare for actors on scripted series, who generally submit to full exclusivity in television (subject to the carveouts described here).

weeks), and unlimited appearances in talk, news, radio, game, panel, or variety-type programs. Guest appearances for third parties may also be subject to "time period" protection – i.e., the actor may not agree to make a guest appearance for a series which is likely to be broadcast on the same date and time of the week as the actor's primary series. Some studios also prohibit actors from rendering behind-camera (e.g., writing, directing, or producing) services for outside television series (though this is more commonly a studio, rather than network, prerogative).

Series regulars are also typically restricted or prohibited from entering into commercial endorsement agreements (and, in particular, from entering into commercial endorsement agreements with competitors of a series' major sponsors) during the term of their agreements for a series. Actors with preexisting endorsement relationships must typically disclose these up-front, and obtain specific contractual carveouts to allow these relationships to continue.

6.3.4.13. Publicity/Promotion

For a series to succeed, it is vital that it be promoted aggressively, and actors have a unique and critical role to play in the publicity and promotion of a television series. Consequently, series regular deals usually include explicit terms setting forth the actor's obligation to render publicity services, as directed by the studio and/or the network, to support the series.

Generally, publicity services may be freely required of the actor during series production periods, while publicity services which are to be rendered outside of production periods are subject to the actor's professional availability, and to the studio or network's obligation to provide transportation, accommodations, and expenses if the actor must travel in connection with such promotional services. However, studios and networks generally require that the actor remain available to render publicity services, on a first-priority basis, in connection with key annual promotional events, whether or not these events fall during production periods. Such lists of first-priority promotional obligations are hotly negotiated, particularly for feature actors who want to preserve their ability to work freely outside of series production periods. At a minimum, studios and networks require their actors to remain available to appear at the network's annual Upfronts event, and at the network's presentation at annual Television Critics Association events (or "TCAs"), which are a key part of the network's promotional cycle. In addition, studios and networks may seek to guarantee the actor's availability for other key events (such as major national and international sales and distribution conferences [such as MIPCOM in Cannes], Comic-Con, or series or season premiere events), or time periods (such as the one or two weeks immediately preceding the scheduled premiere of a series or season).

6.3.5. Staffing Writer Agreements

"Staffing writing agreements" (or simply "staffing agreements") are those for the writers and writer/producers (other than the creator) who will populate the "writer's room" for the series. Depending on the creative needs of the series, the nature of the distribution platform, and the number of episodes being produced, a series will typically employ between four and eight "staffing" writers per season. Writers are generally selected by consensus among the showrunning executive producer, studio executives, and network executives. These individuals may contribute generally to episodic ideas (e.g., dialogue, scenes, or entire storylines), write full original teleplays for the series, or punch up or rewrite episodic teleplays prepared initially or primarily by other writers. Often, writers are identified based on the preexisting relationships and preferences of senior writers and executives, although on ongoing existing series, a new junior writer may earn a spot on the writing staff by submitting a "spec script" which demonstrates the individual's creative command of the series' characters and tone. If the showrunner of a series is not the writer/creator of the pilot, the showrunner's agreement is essentially a variation of a staffing agreement (the particulars of which are discussed in Section 6.3.5.7 below).

6.3.5.1. Term/Options

The vast majority of staffing agreements are three-year deals, covering the immediately upcoming production season of a series, with studio options to engage the writer, season-by-season, for up to two additional seasons thereafter. This default may be discarded in favor of a one or two-year deal for particularly high-level writers, or writers who are engaged to work on a part-time or consulting basis.

6.3.5.2. Credit

The majority of producer-type credits on any given television series belong to writer/producers (whose primary responsibility is in the writer's room), and there is a well-established hierarchy of credits for writers (which, like other credits, are subject to network approval).[77] The most junior and inexperienced writers begin as Staff Writers, with a promotion track that goes to Story Editor, then Executive Story Editor, then Co-Producer, then Producer, then Supervising Producer, then Co-Executive Producer, and finally Executive Producer.[78] In addition, writers who are working part-time or otherwise below their usual rank or pay may be accorded Consulting Producer credit, which occupies a less obvious position within the above hierarchy. As writers grow to higher and higher ranks, they are generally expected to assume more duties in connection with the production, as well as writing, of series episodes. Lower-ranked writers may be released from their services once writing of a season has been completed, while higher-ranked writers may be expected to work until the completion of photography for the season (which may be several weeks after writing is completed).

Writers must generally work for one to two complete seasons (of ten to twenty-two episodes each) at any given title level before being promoted to the next title, with the promotion track moving more slowly between more senior ranks. In early seasons, a writer's room will typically feature writers of widely varied titles and experience levels. In later seasons of a series, staff titles tend to be more top-heavy, as staffers who have remained with a show for many seasons have crawled up the ranks, and escalating production budgets on a successful series can support more expensive staff.

---

[77] As discussed in section 6.3.2 above, most shows also employ one or more non-writing Executive Producers, who often played a key role in the packaging and development of a project, and may employ a producer/director who is also credited as an Executive Producer (or, if less experienced, perhaps Co-Executive Producer). "Produced by" (as opposed to "Producer") credit is generally accorded to line producers (discussed in section 6.3.7 below), although higher-level line producers may instead receive credit as Co-Executive Producer or even Executive Producer, as well. "Co-Producer," "Associate Producer," or "Producer" credit may also be accorded to lower-level non-writing producers (such as the development executives who serve credited Executive Producers).

[78] Executive Producer credit for writers who are neither creators nor showrunners is relatively rare, and usually accorded only for strong "second-in-command" types with close personal relationships with the showrunner.

6.3.5.3. Fees

Writers who are engaged as Staff Writers are almost always paid the WGA-mandated scale minimum for term writers, which varies depending on the number of weeks guaranteed to the writer under his or her deal. As of 2018, this amount ranges between approximately $3,700 per week and $4,700 per week, with the most common minimum guarantee, of 20 weeks, requiring a minimum rate of approximately $4,100 per week. Writers who are working for a second season as Staff Writers may expect to make 110% of WGA scale.

Writers who are engaged as Story Editors are almost always paid the so-called "Article 14" scale minimum (referring to the WGA Basic Agreement section governing "Writers Employed in Additional Capacities"). As with Staff Writers, the applicable scale minimum depends on the number of weeks guaranteed to the writer under his or her deal, and as of 2018, the rate for a 20-week guarantee is approximately $6,600 per week. Executive Story Editors usually receive between Article 14 scale and 110% of Article 14 scale.

Starting at the co-producer level, writers are generally engaged on the basis of episodic, rather than weekly, fees. Expected fees climb with titles, and range from $12,000 to $15,000 per episode for Co-Producers, to $16,000 to $19,000 per episode for Supervising Producers. In each subsequent year of a multi-year deal, the writer may expect to see a fee bump between $500 and $2,500 per episode, even if he or she is not being promoted in title (though title escalations often involve more substantial fee bumps). At the Co-Executive Producer and Executive Producer levels, episodic fees can climb substantially higher (according to experience and quotes), though the showrunner always remains the highest-paid writer/producer on a series.

Although fees for Co-Producers and more senior writer/producers are typically denominated episodically, the engagement of such writers remains subject to the applicable WGA Article 14 weekly scale minimum rate. Regardless of the negotiated episodic fee, writers cannot be paid less than this scale amount, once their fee is amortized over the number of weeks they actually work. In addition, for deals entered into after May 2018, the episodic fees paid to a writer earning less than $350,000 per year buy out no more than 2.4 weeks of services per episodic fee, with average compensation paid at the rate of one additional episodic fee per further 2.4 weeks worked (prorated for average periods under 2.4 weeks).

This backstop proves especially significant for cable and digital series which produce fewer episodes than broadcast series, but whose production periods are not shortened in the same proportion as the number of episodes produced.

6.3.5.4. Guarantees

Weekly engagements (i.e., for Staff Writers, Story Editors and Executive Story Editors) usually guarantee a minimum number of weeks, depending on the needs of the production schedule and the studio's desire to qualify for more favorable scale minimum weekly rates. As discussed in Section 6.3.5.3 above, 20-week guarantees are common, with the studios retaining options to extend the writer's services for as many additional weeks as are necessary for the writer to complete his or her duties for the season.

Episodic engagements for the first season of a series typically cover the initial network order, with the studio retaining a further option to extend the writer's engagement for any backorder of additional episodes by the network. Even in later seasons of a series (particularly for broadcast network series), for a writer's first year on staff, the applicable guarantee will usually cover only an initial chunk of episodes (e.g., thirteen out of twenty-two), as a hedge for the studio is in its new relationship with the writer, with the studio holding an option to extend the writer's guarantee and services for the balance of episodes produced. In subsequent years of a writer's deal, the applicable guarantee will cover all episodes produced for the applicable season. Unlike in series regular actor deals, there is typically no episodic minimum attached to the "all episodes produced" guarantee (as the WGA Basic Agreement, unlike the SAG Basic Agreement, does not require any such minimum guarantee in order for a studio to retain its exclusive options on a writer's services), although writers nevertheless at all times enjoy the backstop of the applicable WGA Article 14 scale minimum for weeks actually worked by the writer.

6.3.5.5. Episodic Scripts

Scripts for individual episodes of a series are generally assigned to writers at the discretion of the showrunner, with the approval of the studio and network. Such episodic scripts are always paid at the applicable WGA scale minimum rate – as of 2018, approximately $39,000 for a sixty-minute broadcast network episode; approximately $26,000 for a thirty-minute broadcast network episode; approximately $27,000 for a sixty-minute cable episode; and approximately $15,000 for a thirty-minute cable episode. As with other WGA and DGA scale minimum amounts, the applicable minimums (if any) for digital productions depends on the subscriber base of the digital platform and the budget of the series, and, depending on these variables, may be pegged to the corresponding broadcast network minimum, the corresponding cable minimum, or freely negotiable.[79] For Staff Writers – and sometimes, though not usually, for Story Editors and Executive Story Editors – episodic script fees are applicable against the writer's weekly fees. For most Story Editors and Executive Story Editors, and all writers more senior than that, episodic script fees are paid on top of the writer's negotiated weekly or episodic fees.

6.3.5.6. Exclusivity

Most staffing writers render services on a fully exclusive basis – or, at a minimum, on an exclusive basis with respect to television services, with no other services to materially interfere – during production periods. Writers will seek the right to develop (i.e., write and develop pilot scripts) for third parties during the term of this engagement. This is typically permitted during hiatus periods of a writer's primary series, and often allowed on a second-priority/non-interfering basis during production periods of the second and third seasons under his or her deal, but most studios prohibit staffed writers from developing during their first production season on a show (particularly if that is also the show's first season). The right to write and render development services for theatrical feature films (again, on a second-priority/non-interfering basis) is usually more freely given throughout the term of a writer's deal.

---

[79] Most series produced for Amazon and Netflix, and some series produced for Hulu, are sufficiently high-budget to qualify for broadcast network minimums. Some smaller series on these platforms are subject to cable minimums.

Writers will also often negotiate for the right to opt out of their staffing deals in the event that a project they have created and developed is ordered to production of a pilot or series. Usually, this request is accommodated with respect to development projects which predate the staffing deal itself, although typically, the studio only permits the writer to opt out between seasons (or to decline an engagement for an upcoming season), and not to leave a production season midstream. However, even though studios seldom grant a contractual right to opt out mid-season (and, when they do, usually require significant notice and coordination to avoid disruption to the series), when a writer's development project is ordered to production, many studios will, as a courtesy, agree to release the writer from his or her obligations, so as not to deprive the writer the opportunity to work on his or her own series.

Finally, particularly at junior and mid-range levels, many studios will require writers who have staffed onto one of their shows to accord the studio a "first look" at any proposed development projects during the term of the writer's staffing deal, giving the studio the opportunity to negotiate with the writer to develop any such project before the writer is permitted to present it to third-party studios.

6.3.5.7. Showrunners

Deals for showrunners who did not create a series (but were attached later, perhaps because the writer/creator of the pilot was too junior to lead the series through production) largely resemble other staffing deals. Such agreements usually have two-year (rather than three-year) terms, and the applicable credit is always "Executive Producer." If a showrunner joins a series prior to its third season, he or she will typically demand a share of backend from the series, the size of which will depend on the showrunner's stature and quotes, as well as the timing of the showrunner's attachment (with showrunners who are attached at earlier stages, such as during development or pilot production, usually commanding more substantial contingent compensation than those attached after one or more seasons have been produced). Typical backend allotments for such showrunners range from 1% of MAGR to 5% of MAGR (and, in rare cases, up to 7.5% or even 10% of MAGR, especially for showrunners who are attached at the development stage of the project and supervise the more junior writer/creator's work on the pilot script).

6.3.6. Agency Package Commissions

Most people understand agency economics to be based on percentage commissions – indeed, agencies are sometimes colloquially referred to in industry trade publications as "tenpercenteries," referring to the standard 10% commission charged by talent agencies on all revenues earned by their clients. In fact, however, the major Hollywood agencies – currently, William Morris Endeavor ("WME"), Creative Artists Agency ("CAA"), United Talent Agency ("UTA"), and International Creative Management ("ICM"), with a second tier of "mini-major" agencies in Paradigm Talent Agency and The Gersh Agency – make the majority of their money from so-called "agency package commissions" paid directly to the agencies by television studios.

One of the ways the agencies can create opportunities for their clients is by connecting them to one another, putting together compelling groups of talented individuals who can more effectively attract the attention and interest of studios and networks than any one of the clients could alone. Starting in the early 1990s, agencies began seeking payment from the studios for the services rendered by the agency in effectively doing, on the studio's behalf, the job of putting together (i.e., "packaging") the major creative elements of a project. In exchange for this fee, in addition to having brought together the initial key creative elements, the agency promises to continue servicing the project's future creative needs, providing from its client base a steady pipeline of staffing writers, actors, and other mid-level and lower-level contributors the show will need to thrive in the future. If two major agencies combine to provide the key elements for a series, they may agree with the studio and amongst themselves to split a packaging fee, which each agency receiving a so-called "half package." (Splits in thirds are also sometimes negotiated, but are less common.) The agency's entitlement to a package commission on a project, also known as its "package position," is typically negotiated at the time development deals are first entered into between the studio and the major creative elements. These days, nearly every major scripted television series includes at least a partial package commission that has been committed to one or more agencies in connection with the project. Moreover, although the term "package" is universally used to refer to the fees paid to agencies in such circumstances, increasingly, agencies demand and receive partial or even full package positions on the basis of a single major agency-represented element (such as a writer/creator who is qualified to showrun his or her own series, or a particularly prolific and well-established non-writing producer; in either case referred to as a "packageable element").

The standard agency package commission in scripted television is known as a "3/3/10 package" – a studio that agrees to pay a "full package" pays the agency (a) an up-front fee equal to 3% of the license fee received from the initial domestic network licensee[80]; (b) an additional fee, equal to the first 3% fee, which is deferred and payable (if ever) out of the Net Proceeds of the series[81]; and (c) a backend equal to 10% of MAGR (generally on the same definition as the most favorable definition accorded by the studio to any of the agency's clients on the project, but with no third-party participations of any kind taken off the top). Most studios and networks impose an episodic cap on the value of the 3%-of-license-fee upfront fee, usually between $15,000 and $75,000 (depending on show length, total budget level, applicable network, etc.), with episodic package fees in the $40,000 to $50,000 range being especially common.

6.3.7. Other Key Agreements

While there are a number of other key contributors to the creative success and smooth physical production of a television series, the deals for such individuals tend to be simpler, and warrant only more general discussion here.

Every show needs a line producer (whose role is explained in greater detail in Section 6.1.3.1.d above), and usually, line producers engaged for the pilot are subject to options for the studio to continue to

---

[80] This up-front fee is accounted for as a production cost of the show, and is reflected in its production budget.

[81] A series' "Net Proceeds" are calculated very similarly to its "Modified Adjusted Gross Receipts," using essentially the same formula, but with the studio deducting higher distribution fees and overhead charges. Because of the extremely high deductions taken by the studio, even the most successful television series are extremely unlikely to ever "break even" under a "Net Proceeds" definition. Again, these backend formulae are more fully addressed in section 6.4, below.

engage the line producer for the series (with the deals usually covering up to three seasons of services). Line producer pilot fees typically range from $50,000 to $70,000, while episodic fees range from $20,000 to $35,000 for the first season, with negotiated bumps (usually 4% to 5%) for subsequent seasons. Line producers of complex premium cable or streaming series with long production schedules but few episodes may receive $60,000 to $75,000 per episode. The base credit accorded to such line producers is "Produced by," though more experienced line producers may command Co-Executive Producer or (at the highest levels and/or in later years of a series) Executive Producer credit. Some producers also work as unit production managers (or UPMs), a DGA-covered class of services (which enables the individuals to access DGA health, welfare, and pension plans), and a portion of the line producer's fees may be allocated to such additional services (without increasing his or her aggregate compensation). Line producers may also negotiate for reimbursement of expenses (particularly if they loan the production key equipment which they own). In addition, unlike many other producers (including showrunners), line producers must generally work from the production location, and will therefore negotiate more extensive travel and relocation expense packages (often on the basis of flat monthly allowances, where appropriate).

Casting directors are another essential part of the team, mandatory at the pilot, and usually continuing with the series if ordered. The initial engagement of a casting director (or team of casting directors) for a pilot will usually cover ten weeks of services, at a fee between $45,000 and $70,000, with additional weeks paid at a *pro rata* weekly rate. The studio will agree to cover the cost of a junior casting associate or casting assistant (or, on particularly expansive or challenging pilots, both), and to provide or reimburse the casting directors for office and other business expenses. As with line producers, studios typically retain options to engage the casting directors, season-by-season, for up to three seasons, at an episodic rate which often closely corresponds to the applicable weekly rate from the pilot. In other words, a casting director who works for ten weeks on a pilot for $50,000 will often render series casting services (which are less intensive than pilot casting services) for $5,000 per episode during the first season, with negotiated bumps – again, usually 4% to 5% – for subsequent seasons. High-level casting directors may seek to be credited in the main or opening (rather than end) titles, though such accommodations may depend on network and studio policies. Casting directors who work on a pilot may also receive a modest bonus (e.g., $5,000) if the pilot is picked up to series, and to receive additional fees (again, usually $5,000) for any additional series regular roles that the casting directors cast (or recast) during production of the series.

Episodic directors are generally hired on an episode-by-episode basis, for a finite number of days corresponding to the pre-production, photography, and post-production periods for each episode. Compensation is almost always set to the applicable DGA scale minimum rate – as of 2018, approximately $46,000 for a sixty-minute broadcast network episode; approximately $27,000 for a thirty-minute broadcast network episode; between approximately $24,000 and approximately $34,000 for a sixty-minute cable episode (depending on the episodic budget and which season the series is in); and between approximately $12,000 and approximately $17,000 for a thirty-minute cable episode (depending on the episodic budget and which season the series is in), although the fees may grow based on a daily rate if production requires more than the DGA-specified number of days covered by these scale amounts. Pre-production and photography services are rendered exclusively on location, and post-production services are rendered on a non-exclusive basis, often in the city where the writer's room is based (e.g., Los Angeles or New York) rather than at the principal production location. In later seasons of successful series, lead actors may be rewarded with episodic directing assignments.

As noted in Section 6.3.4 above, non-series regular acting deals are typically very simple, and require negotiating only episodes, dates, role, trailer, and fee (although complications may arise if a studio wishes to extend an actor's story arc, and representatives may seek escalating fees as an actor appears in more episodes). Nearly every other crew member – including vital department heads such as the editor, director of photography, production designer, and costume designer – is engaged on a weekly basis, with deals often negotiated directly by the line producer or UPM in accordance with the budget, with or without the direct involvement and participation of the studio (other than to approve the identities of the individuals engaged).

6.4. BACKEND

As discussed throughout Sections 6.2 and 6.3 above, contingent compensation (or "profit participation" or "backend") is a key component of numerous agreements with the key creative talent and underlying rightsholders behind a television series. Backend represents the talent's opportunity to share in the upside of a truly successful television series. When a series succeeds in a big way, the value of even a modest share of backend will easily prove far more valuable to the profit participant than whatever upfront fees he or she may have collected from the budget of the series over the course of the production.

As referenced in various sections above, to control the total amount of participations granted for any given series, most studios employ a rigid and non-negotiable policy of limiting the contingent compensation granted on any given series to no more than 35% of MAGR. (Some studios attempt to employ caps as low as 30% of MAGR, or as high as 40% of MAGR, but both would be considered somewhat exceptional, particularly the higher cap.) Although differences in backend definitions can make one participant's 1% of MAGR worth substantially more or less than another's, for purposes of ease and rough justice, this 35% cap is generally applied without regard to differences in definition. The rigidity of this policy has proven especially important in the modern era of television development, which emphasizes the packaging of numerous high-level elements as a way to help projects break through the noise of a crowded marketplace. The hard 35% cap requires participants in series with many profit participants to accept lower backend floors than they may otherwise be inclined to accept, or to renegotiate their existing entitlements in order to make points available for the studio to allocate to a newly-added element on the series (such as an actor or showrunner attached late in the development and production process).

Profit participants receive regular statements (typically quarterly or semi-annually) and enjoy audit rights, which allow them to review the studio's records of revenues and expenses in order to scrutinize the studio's calculations and accountings to the participant. Such audit rights are subject to incontestability provisions, which require that a participant commence an audit (or a lawsuit based upon an audit) within a specified period of time following his or her receipt of accounting statements (usually two to three years), or else those accounting statements are deemed final and binding upon the participant. However, most studios freely agree to toll such deadlines at the participant's request, which allows a participant's audit to cover more accounting periods at once (making the audit process more efficient for studio and participant alike). In addition, some studios require that any disputes arising out of an audit or accounting issue be submitted to binding arbitration, rather than being litigated in open court. This helps the studio avoid unfavorable publicity arising out of an audit dispute with a profit participant, while also minimizing the risk that an adverse judgment opens up the floodgates for other claims.[82] For those studios that prefer arbitration to litigation, such arbitration clauses are usually non-negotiable in concept, and scarcely negotiable in detail.

The details of contingent compensation can vary in numerous ways between studios. Different studios employ different terminology; this chapter universally uses the term "Modified Adjusted Gross Receipts" (or "MAGR"), which is common, but some studios refer to their defined form of contingent compensation as "Modified Adjusted Gross" ("MAG"), "Modified Gross Receipts" ("MGR"), "Adjusted Defined Receipts" ("ADR"), "Contingent Proceeds" ("CP"), or by other terms still. Some studios use relatively plain-language backend definitions which are as few as three pages long, while others rely on complex and detailed definitions which can run for literally dozens of pages. And different studios have different policies as to various key aspects of these definitions, with each studio prioritizing the issues important to it, and no one studio systematically offering participants the most or least favorable available definition in every respect.

Despite such variation, however, at the end of the day, every television contingent compensation definition is a mostly similar formula, whose main variables are simply the dollars earned by the studio from all forms of exploitation of a series, and the expenses incurred by the studio in all aspects of production, marketing, and distribution. As a series goes through its life cycle of ongoing production and development, this formula is regularly calculated and

---

[82] Such studios may also require that non-accounting disputes arising out of their agreements with talent be submitted to arbitration, though even studios which do not require arbitration of non-accounting disputes may demand it for accounting disputes in particular.

recalculated to account for revenues and expenses, as they each mount; although over time and in success, it is fair to expect revenues to accrue faster (and for a longer period of time) than expenses.

The basic television contingent compensation formula (sometimes referred to as a "waterfall") can be articulated as follows:

> Gross Receipts
> — Distribution Fees
> — Distribution Expenses
> — Overhead
> — Interest
> — Cost of Production
> — Third-Party Participations
>
> = Modified Adjusted Gross Receipts

What follows is a deeper examination of each of the elements of this formula.

6.4.1. Gross Receipts

"Gross receipts" refers to all revenue received by (or credited to) a studio from its exploitation of a television series and all rights therein, from all sources. For the most part, this is a straightforward concept. There are, however, some important nuances.

First, it may be necessary to clarify at what level (or, to put it another way, from the receipts of which entity) gross receipts are determined. For instance, if a studio intends to use a subdistributor to distribute any of its rights in a series, the gross receipts should generally be measured as those collected by the subdistributor (as opposed to those remitted to the studio after the subdistributor retains its fees and expenses), although the proper treatment of this issue also depends on how distribution fees are assessed on such revenues. (E.g., if gross receipts are defined at the subdistributor level, then it is appropriate for the studio to assess distribution fees on them; if gross receipts are defined net of the subdistributor's withholdings, then a distribution fee should not be charged.) In addition, many studios use special purpose production entities to produce (and enter into contracts) in connection with a series[83]; in such cases, gross receipts should be defined as those received by that special purpose entity or any of its affiliates, to ensure that the studio's real receipts are properly accounted for. On the other hand, to the extent that a studio is part of a major horizontally integrated conglomerate (such as ABC Studios, a Disney company, or Universal Television, a Comcast/NBCUniversal company), and affiliates of the studio engage in distribution activities which are customarily performed by third-party licensees, then the definition may need to identify appropriate revenues *of the studio, as a studio*, and to wall off revenues from affiliates who are acting in the capacity of bona fide third party distribution partners. This issue commonly arises with respect to revenues from the exploitation of ancillary rights, such as music publishing, soundtracks, and merchandising.[84]

Second, "all revenue from all sources" may not necessarily mean "*all* revenue from *all* sources," and a definition may be drafted to expressly exclude certain revenues from gross receipts. For instance, although derivatives rights – e.g., the right to produce spinoffs, sequels, theatrical feature adaptations, etc. – are among the "all rights therein" for a television series, most backend definitions expressly exclude revenues (and expenses) from these separate productions. The one exception may be license fees received from third parties for the right to create local language adaptations of a series, which may be accountable as gross receipts. Some studios may seek to exclude

---

[83] Studios may favor such "special purpose vehicles" for reasons of liability management and/or tax and accounting preferences, among other considerations.

[84] To illustrate, imagine a television series produced by ABC Studios (a Disney company), which spawns a toy that is produced by a Disney-owned consumer products company, which is in turn sold to a customer at a Disney retail store. Although the Disney retail store is owned by an affiliate of ABC Studios, the studio would not account to a profit participant for the money collected at the point of sale by the Disney Store as "gross receipts." Rather, it would rely on a formula to translate the Disney Store's retail revenues into the Disney-owned consumer products company's wholesale revenues, and in turn translate those into ABC Studios' licensing revenues (which would then be deemed ABC Studios' "gross receipts" from that merchandising transaction). This mathematical process essentially simulates the revenues ABC Studios would have realized if it were an independent company that operated solely in the business of television production and distribution, and had licensed merchandising rights to a third-party licensee, which in turn placed its merchandise on the shelves of a third-party retailer.

ratings and other bonuses received from their licensees, or revenues received in connection with product placements or integrations. Such exclusions, where sought at all, are often negotiable.

Third, nearly all backend definitions include special accounting provisions related to home video revenues, treating as accountable "gross receipts" an amount equal to 20% of the receipts actually received by the studio or its affiliated company from home video distribution.[85] This unusual royalty-based accounting is a function of the history of home video distribution in the film and television industry. In the 1980s, when the home video market was first emerging for feature films (and was altogether nonexistent for television series), most film studios relied on small outside companies to exploit these rights, which were not perceived as particularly valuable. The film studios entered into deals with these outside home video subdistributors by which the studios received a 20% royalty from the subdistributors (who absorbed all duplication and manufacturing expenses from their 80% shares). These royalties, in turn, became the gross receipts that were accounted to profit participants in the films. Eventually, however, the major studios (such as Fox, Disney, Paramount, Universal, Columbia, and Warner Bros.) realized two crucial facts: first, that home video was quickly developing into a huge business[86]; and second, that the home video subdistributors' costs only amounted to approximately 40% of their revenues, allowing those subdistributors a huge profit margin even after accounting to the studios for their 20% royalties. The studios quickly developed in-house home video distribution arms, effectively increasing their share of wholesale revenue from home video sales from 20% to 60% (while forcing many smaller, independent home video subdistributors out of the business). When the studios did so, however, they decided to retain for themselves the full benefit of that additional 40% margin, by redefining their theatrical contingent compensation definitions to continue to account for home video revenues at a 20% royalty rate (as if the studios were still receiving 20% royalties from real third-party home video distributors). By the time profit participants and their

---

[85] At higher levels, this royalty rate may be negotiated up to approximately 35% or 40%, but this is rare for all studios, and seldom if ever granted by major studios.

[86] Indeed, home video receipts (initially based on VHS tapes, and later DVDs and Blu-rays) were critical in economically buoying the entire film industry through the 1990s and early 2000s.

representatives realized the economic impact of this move, the practice was firmly established, and the studios were able to maintain it through sheer stubbornness and superior bargaining power. The 20% royalty rates for home video revenues were eventually imported into the backend definitions of television studios, and by the 2000s, a robust home video/DVD market for television programming had emerged as well. This 20% royalty accounting for home video revenues remains the standard to this day.

Fourth, the historical quirk of royalty accounting for home video receipts has impacted the accounting (and negotiation) around receipts received from digital licensees of television (and other) content, such as Netflix, Amazon, and Hulu. When these digital platforms first emerged and began pouring license fees into the studios, backend definitions that had been drafted years before were silent as to the treatment of revenues from such sources. Citing the precipitous collapse of the home video market that coincided with the emergence of these new digital platforms (which had begun rendering physical home video effectively obsolete), the studios initially reasoned that the new digital platforms were effectively successors to the home video market, and therefore that revenues received from digital platforms should be treated as home video revenue – at a 20% royalty rate. They took this position despite the fact that the actual physical manufacturing and distribution costs associated with traditional home video distribution (which had been absorbed within the 80% of home video revenues withheld from the profit participant) were virtually nonexistent when it came to the distribution of digital content, in 1s and 0s, to the new platforms. Profit participants and their representatives (including the talent guilds) across the film and television industries revolted against this reasoning, and currently, the majority of studios account for revenues received from SVOD and AVOD-type licensees as television revenue (which is accounted for based on 100% of revenues received), although most studios continue to treat revenue from TVOD/EST-type licensees (which more closely resemble traditional home video distribution) as home video (and therefore account for it at a 20% royalty rate).

Finally, where a studio licenses a television series to its affiliated network (e.g., AMC Studios producing a show for AMC network, or CBS Studios producing a show for the CBS broadcast network), the studio's backend definition will include an "imputed license fee," a contractually defined amount that represents the revenues received by the studio from its sister network. This is because sister studios and networks generally do not engage in arms-length negotiations to determine the precise scope of rights granted to, and license fees paid by, the broadcasting network, nor is real money necessarily transferred from the account of the network to the studio. In lieu of such a negotiation and payment, the studio's backend definition will identify an amount that the studio is deemed to have received from its sister network for its license (and the studio will continue to account to the participant for revenues received from third-party sources, as actually received). As with arms-length negotiated license fees,[87] the applicable imputed license fee may be denominated as a flat dollar amount (or series of flat dollar amounts) or as a percentage of the production budget (with or without caps) according to the preferences and policies of the entities involved. In order to induce participants to accept these definitions, the applicable imputed license fees are generally structured and valued to resemble license fees that may have been obtained in a real arms-length negotiation, and the license fee generally buys out a specified scope of exploitation by the network. Often, the applicable imputed license fee is non-negotiable by the participant, or negotiable only within a narrow range and only for high-level participants. In general, however, participants can expect that such imputed license fees will be somewhat less substantial than the license fees that the studio would extract from an unaffiliated network licensee in a bona fide arms-length negotiation. For licensing transactions with affiliated entities other than the initial network license, participants may negotiate for an express contractual requirement that such transactions be conducted on an arms-length basis.

6.4.2. Distribution Fees

In calculating MAGR, the studio will first deduct, off-the-top, a percentage of revenues received from nearly all sources. This distribution fee represents compensation to the studio for its investment of time, effort, overhead, and other resources in the distribution process.

---

[87] *See* section 6.5.1.4 below.

The distribution fees charged by a studio are one of the most critical, and most hotly negotiated, elements of a backend definition. They generally range from 10% to 25%, with some variation among studios regarding the lowest fees they will agree to, and the circumstances under which they will agree to their most favorable available distribution fees. A 15% distribution fee is relatively common, with 10% being considered "A-level." Some studios distinguish among various revenue sources in defining the applicable distribution fee – for instance, charging a higher distribution fee on revenues from foreign distribution than from domestic, or on revenues received from the exploitation of ancillary rights rather than traditional linear licensing of series episodes (based on the argument that such sales require more effort to generate substantial revenue). Other studios simply charge a flat distribution fee, as negotiated, on revenues from all sources. Across the board, however, studios will generally agree to forego charging distribution fees on revenues received in respect of the initial domestic license for a television series, on the rationale that a television series is never produced in the first place without the initial commission from the domestic licensee, and therefore no distribution resources or separate efforts were actually expended to obtain these revenues. In addition, some studios will agree not to charge a distribution fee on home video receipts (because those receipts are already being accounted for on a 20% royalty basis, rather than based on 100% of revenues actually received).

Most studios freely agree that, to the extent they rely on subdistributors to exploit rights in certain media or territories, the applicable distribution fees charged by the studio (which are charged based on the gross receipts received by the subdistributor, as opposed to those received by the studio after the subdistributor withholds its share[88]) are inclusive of any distribution fees charged and retained by the subdistributor. If the fee charged by the subdistributor is less than the fee charged by the studio, the studio retains the difference as its own fee (with studios justifying this margin by reference to the amount of effort and resources it takes to engage, manage, and generally police subdistributors). Where the distribution fee charged by a subdistributor is greater than the distribution fee that would

---

[88] *See* section 6.4.1 above.

otherwise be charged by the studio, the backend definition may expressly provide that the higher distribution fee applies (so that the studio is not forced to economically absorb the difference between the distribution fee charged by the subdistributor and that otherwise applicable to the participant in the backend accounting). Where the distribution fee charged by a subdistributor is equal to or greater than that charged by the studio, the studio may provide for its own right to take an "override" on such distribution fee, meaning a distribution fee charged on the subdistributor's receipts, over and above that charged by the subdistributor (again, citing the effort and expense of managing and monitoring the subdistributor). Such overrides have become rare in more recent years, and generally do not exceed 5% of gross receipts.

6.4.3. Distribution Expenses

After retaining distribution fees, studios will next reimburse themselves, off-the-top, for all actual expenses incurred in the process of distribution. Such expenses may include, without limitation, advertising and marketing expenses; costs for subtitling or dubbing of foreign versions; the expense of duplicating and transporting physical materials to licensees; clearance fees which have not otherwise been accounted for as production costs; residuals and reuse fees payable to talent pursuant to applicable union collective bargaining agreements; costs of enforcement (including intellectual property and audit litigation); and other so-called "off-the-tops" (referring to checking, collection, currency conversion, and certain tax [but not income tax] expenses). If negotiated, many studios will agree not to deduct some or all distribution expenses attributable directly to home video distribution, because they are already accounting for the resulting revenues on a 20% royalty basis. While participants sometimes may attempt to negotiate for a cap on deductible distribution expenses (e.g., that they may not exceed 5% of gross receipts), studios seldom agree to such caps for profit participants (due to the risk that legitimate out-of-pocket expenses may, in fact, exceed such limits).

In general, studios recoup their actual, third-party, out-of-pocket distribution expenses. However, larger studios which maintain (whether directly or through an affiliated entity) certain in-house creative services facilities (e.g., to assist in advertising and marketing) may assess fair-market charges for such services, as though they had been obtained and paid for from third parties. Some studios may also attempt, particularly in definitions for low-level profit participants, to charge "advertising overhead" (i.e., a 5% to 15% surcharge on advertising expenses); however, this is rare, and often waived in negotiation, as the rationale for such a surcharge is essentially duplicative with the rationale for the studio's distribution fees. In addition, some studios may seek to assess and recoup interest on their distribution expenses, but this is also relatively uncommon. Many studios will agree to clarify, for the benefit of participants, that expenses which are charged as production costs may not also be recouped as distribution expenses, and vice versa.[89]

6.4.4. Overhead

After deducting distribution fees and distribution expenses, the studio will next recoup an overhead charge, which compensates the studio for the in-house salaries, offices, and other overhead expenses used in the studio's production business. This overhead charge is calculated as a percentage of the actual cost of production of the series, and generally ranges between 10% and 15%. Like distribution fees, the percentage amount of the overhead charge is heavily negotiated, and has a significant impact on the value of an individual's contingent compensation – a participant in revenues from a hit series who is entitled to 10% of MAGR with a 10% distribution fee and 10% overhead charge may earn literally millions more dollars than another participant in the same series who is entitled to 10% of MAGR with a 15% distribution fee and 15% overhead charge.

In scripted television (which is based on a deficit financing model[90]), studios generally do not assess production fees (or other fees for in-house executives or staff) within the budget of the show itself.[91]

---

[89] In general, where an expense may be reasonably justified as a production charge or a distribution expense, the studio will opt to treat it as the former, to take advantage of applicable overhead and interest charges (which, as noted here, apply to production expenses but not to distribution expenses).

[90] *See* section 6.5.1.4.a below.

[91] This is not the case in unscripted television, in which the license fee paid by the network is generally equal to the full cost of production, and the studio or production company typically receives a fee within the budget of the series equal to 10% of the

Consequently, many studios will freely agree not to charge participants for any production company or supervisory fees, other than the negotiated percentage-based overhead charge. In addition, studios will generally agree not to calculate an overhead charge on interest assessed against the production cost,[92] or on contingent compensation paid to third-party participants.

6.4.5. Interest

The studio will next charge and recoup interest on the actual expenses it incurred in producing a television series. This interest is generally recouped from gross receipts after the studio has deducted its distribution fees, distribution expenses, and overhead, but before revenue is applied against the cost of production (effectively increasing the amount of time that interest runs on the underlying production costs). Such interest is assessed whether or not the studio actually relies on outside financing to cover its costs of production, as compensation to the studio for its loss of use of the funds (which could have been applied to other production or corporate purposes).

If the studio does rely on outside financing, the applicable interest deduction is likely equal to the studio's actual cost of financing; if the studio relies on its own cash reserves to finance production, interest is usually assessed at a rate between 1% and 2% above the then-current prime interest rate. Studios will generally agree not to charge interest on the overhead charge assessed by the studio, or on contingent compensation paid to third-party participants, or on the interest itself (in other words, the interest rate is simple, not compound).

6.4.6. Cost of Production

Next, the studio will recoup its actual cost of production of the series. As with distribution expenses, these are generally actual, out-

---

hard production costs of the series (perhaps subject to a cap). For such programs, studios usually also assess profit participants an overhead charge as part of their backend definitions, but may agree to not to calculate such overhead charges on the production company fees retained by the studio from the budget of the series, or even (at higher levels) to reduce such overhead charges in the backend definition on a dollar-for-dollar basis by the production company fees retained by the studio from the budget of the series.

[92] *See* section 6.4.5 below.

of-pocket, third-party costs that had been paid out by the studio. However, to the extent the studio relied on some of its own facilities (or those of an affiliated entity) in connection with the production, it may also record and assess charges for such resources at fair-market rates. Some profit participants are wary of definitions which may allow for the assessment of "overbudget penalties," i.e., percentage multipliers of any costs of production in excess of the ingoing budget for the series. However, such penalties are very rare in television contingent compensation definitions (as distinct from feature film profit participation definitions, where they are common, particularly for participations granted to producers and directors, who have a direct responsibility for controlling budgets).

6.4.7. Third-Party Participations

Finally, after recouping the cost of production, some studios also deduct from profit participants, off-the-top, contingent compensation paid by the studio to some or all other profit participants on the same show. In other words, if a Participant A is entitled to receive 10% of MAGR, but the studio retains the right to deduct third-party participants off-the-top and has granted 25% of MAGR to Participant B, then Participant A's 10% is effectively 10% of 75% of MAGR, or 7.5% of 100%. At the same time, Participant B has Participant A's participation deducted off-the-top of Participant B's definition, so Participant B really receives 25% of 90% of MAGR, or 22.5% of 100% of MAGR. When third parties are prohibited from being deducted off-the-top in calculating MAGR, a participant's backend entitlement is usually explicitly styled as being "of 100% of MAGR" – in other words, "10% of 100% of MAGR," rather than simply "10% of MAGR."

Some studios grant "of 100%" participations to all participants, regardless of stature. Some grant "of 100%" participations on a discretionary basis, depending on the stature and negotiating leverage of the participant. Some studios will grant "of 100%" participations only to those receiving relatively low participations, such as 5% or under, because denying this accommodation would cause such a massive dilution of that individual's backend as a result of the large volume of participations granted to third parties. Studios that reserve the right to deduct third-party participations off-the-top will generally not deduct third-party participations both "off-the-top" *and* "off-the-bottom." In other words, if Participant A is entitled to receive 15% of MAGR, reducible on a dollar-for-dollar basis by all participations granted to third parties to a floor of 10% of MAGR, the studio will usually at least agree that those third-party participations which have the effect of reducing Participant A from 15% to 10% of MAGR may not also be deducted off-the-top in calculating the value of each percentage point of MAGR.

Even those studios which expressly agree not to deduct third-party participations off-the-top in calculating MAGR universally reserve the right to deduct, off-the-top, contingent compensation paid to talent agencies in respect of their "packages" on the show.[93] Such agency packages are actually usually recouped as distribution expenses, immediately after the studio retains its distribution fees from gross receipts. In addition, even studios which generally agree not to deduct third-party participations off-the-top may also reserve the right to treat advances on participations granted to third parties as production costs (with or without the right to assess interest and/or overhead on such advances) until such advances have actually been earned, thereby delaying the "break point" at which other participants will begin to see fresh cash from their contingent compensation formula. Finally, some studios retain the right to deduct participations granted to network licensees[94], if any, off-the-top. Those studios which agree not to deduct network/licensee participations off-the-top generally require that such participations fit within their standard 35% cap on aggregate third-party participations.

Whether and to what extent third-party participations may be deducted off-the-top in calculating MAGR is, together with the percentage values of distribution fees and overhead, one of the most impactful negotiated variables determining the value of a participant's contingent compensation.

6.4.8. Treatment of Tax Incentives[95]

Although tax incentives are not expressly addressed in the waterfall described above, how a studio accounts for them (if at all) is

---

[93] *See* section 6.3.6 above.
[94] *See* section 6.5.1.8 below.
[95] More on tax incentives can be found in Chapter 12 of this volume.

arguably the fourth major driver of the value of a contingent compensation definition. As described in Section 6.1.4 above, tax incentives significantly impact not only whether and where a television series is produced, but how much the studio is willing to invest (in gross dollars) in the show's production. The significant financial impact of tax incentives affects not only a studio's economic situation, but that of profit participants, as well.

As was the case with the emergence, in the 2000s, of digital platforms as a source of television licensing revenue, when state production incentives rose to prominence in the 1990s, most studio backend definitions were silent as to their impact on the calculation of MAGR. In this vacuum, many studios initially declined to account for tax incentives at all when calculating contingent compensation for talent participants. Enjoying the subsidy provided by these tax incentives, the studios increased their gross spending on production. This increased spending, combined with the non-acknowledgment of tax incentives, had the effect of diminishing the value of participants' contingent compensation by making it more difficult for the show to achieve breakeven or profit, according to the applicable MAGR definitions. When this practice was eventually discovered by participants and their representatives, a wave of contentious audit claims and litigation ensued.

These days, studios almost always account for tax incentives in their backend calculations in some fashion. Talent representatives consistently negotiate for tax incentives to be recorded as a reduction in the production cost of the series. Such a characterization is simple and intuitive, and generally consistent with how studios model their own production costs for series – defining expenses based on net (as in, net of applicable tax incentives), rather than gross, spends. As a practical matter, treating tax incentives in this manner both reduces the amount of production costs which must be recouped for the MAGR definition to first show profit (or "break"), and reduces the principal base on which overhead and interest charges are calculated. This substantially accelerates the point at which profit participants would expect to see their backends pay off. However, studios seldom accord such treatment to tax incentives.

Instead, most studios treat tax incentives, in whole or in part (and net of any actual third-party costs of obtaining, accessing, or otherwise monetizing such incentives) as gross receipts. This has the effect of preserving a higher principal base for production cost, which preserves a higher overhead charge and interest charge that must be recouped from revenues before participants first see payments under their backend definitions. In addition, the classification of tax incentive monies as gross receipts, rather than reductions in production costs, allows the studio to charge a distribution fee on the applicable amounts (although talent representatives who accept the classification of tax incentives as gross receipts may negotiate to prohibit the studio from charging its distribution fee on these amounts). Studios justify this practice by reference to the amount of time and effort required for the studio to get the benefit of these tax incentive programs. As described in Section 6.1.4 above, these programs are complex and vary widely from state to state, requiring considerable expertise from studio production and tax executives in order to maximize them. Obtaining a tax credit is far from automatic; it requires meticulous, sometimes burdensome recordkeeping, reporting, and filing with state authorities. Moreover, while a tax credit can be fairly reliably estimated, it may take months or even years to actually receive the financial benefits from such programs, during which time the studio is actually out-of-pocket on the full gross production spend for the series. In short, while most studios have come around to giving participants the benefit of tax incentives in some fashion, for purposes of profit participation definitions, the major studios have been mostly consistent in treating such incentives as gross receipts rather than reductions in cost.

6.5. LICENSE AND CO-PRODUCTION AGREEMENTS

Sections 6.2 through 6.4 of this chapter have focused on the relationships between studios and the various categories of rightsholders and service providers which sit up the chain from studios. The chart below, examined in chapter 4, section 4.1, of this book, nicely provides a visual representation of the television industry.

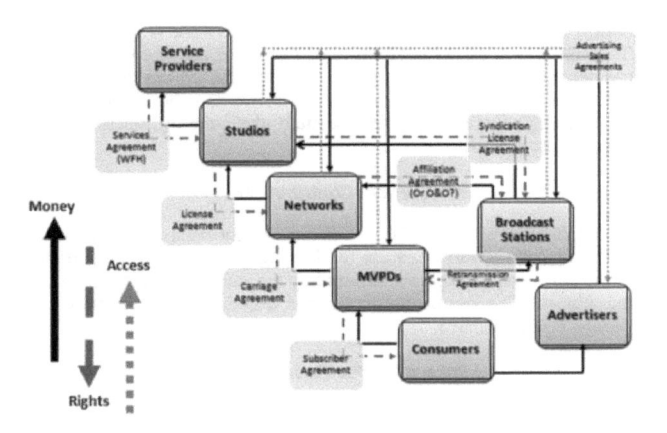

[Figure: Diagram showing relationships between Service Providers, Studios, Networks, MVPDs, Broadcast Stations, Advertisers, and Consumers, with various agreements (Services Agreement (WFH), License Agreement, Affiliation Agreement (O&O?), Syndication License Agreement, Carriage Agreement, Retransmission Agreement, Subscriber Agreement, Advertising Sales Agreements) connecting them. A legend indicates Money, Access, and Rights flows.]

We now turn our attention to the next linkage in the chain, between studios and networks, as well as a further relationship not directly reflected in the visualization above: co-production agreements between two studios – one of which is often affiliated with the commissioning network – to jointly own, finance, and produce a series.

6.5.1. Network License Agreements

No single agreement has a greater effect on the ultimate profitability of a television series to its studio than the initial network license agreement, the deal under which a television series is first commissioned and exhibited by an American licensee. If, as described in Section 6.1.3.3 above, "a television studio makes money by using the divisibility of its copyrights to maximize revenue across media, territory, and time," then the goal of a studio in negotiating a network license agreement is to grant the network as few rights, in as few territories, for as brief a term, and for as much money, as possible, retaining for itself as much freedom as possible to further license the same series to additional licensees across various platforms, countries, and time windows. The particulars of these agreements vary widely depending on whether the network at issue is a broadcast network, a basic cable network, a premium pay cable network (e.g., HBO or Showtime), or a digital platform (e.g., Netflix or Amazon) – and this chapter will endeavor to summarize some key differences that emerge in license deals across various types of networks – but the essential issues being negotiated remain essentially the same regardless of the nature of the licensee.

6.5.1.1. Development Contributions

At the time a series is first set up with a network for development, the studio and network negotiate for the network to cover some portion of the development expenses incurred by the studio in connection with the project. The key parameters of this negotiation are discussed in Section 6.1.3.1.b above.

6.5.1.2. Pilot and Series Options

When a studio sets up a project with a network for development, it grants that network the exclusive option to order a pilot and/or series episodes of the project.

Broadcast networks generally insist on "two bites," meaning two opportunities to order a pilot or series to production. At the pilot phase, the "bites" refer to the network's customary annual "pilot seasons," with pilot production orders placed by February 28 of the applicable year; at the series phase, broadcast networks must generally order production of a series for a fall start no later than May 31 of the applicable year, or for a mid-season start no later than December 15 of the applicable year. However, when a project is set up with a broadcast network in a competitive situation, the studio will often negotiate for the network to have only "one bite" for pilot and/or series, making it easier (and faster) for the studio to solicit interest from a competing network if the original network declines to proceed with the project.

For non-broadcast network licensees who often order pilots and series without regard for the traditional, rigid annual calendar employed by the broadcast networks, pilot option periods are defined based on a certain number of months (usually three to six) following the delivery of the final pilot script writing step commissioned by the network. For such licensees, the initial series option period is also based on a certain number of months (again, usually three to six) following the studio's delivery of the completed pilot.

In addition, the parties must negotiate the timing of the network's options to order subsequent seasons of the series. For broadcast networks, the applicable option must generally be exercised by May 31 annually. For other networks, the season-to-season option date may be annualized based on the option exercise date or option exercise deadline for the initial series option (in other words, if the initial series option was exercisable by October 31 of a given year, the option for subsequent seasons must be exercised by October 31 each year); fixed to a certain number of weeks prior to the expiration of the annual cast option dates[96]; or set based on a certain number of months following the final delivery and/or initial exhibition of the final episode of the prior season (typically, the earlier of six months following initial exhibition, or nine months following final delivery, of the last episode of the prior season).

6.5.1.3. Series Term

The "series term" of a network license agreement identifies the number of consecutive, dependent options held by the network to order additional seasons.

Traditionally, most broadcast network license agreements had four-year (or four-and-a-half-year[97]) terms, meaning that the network had the ability to order a pilot and up to four seasons under its original license agreement, before the network would be forced to negotiate a new license agreement with the studio covering additional seasons. In success, a network would be highly motivated to retain the ability to continue ordering and exhibiting new seasons of the series, and the studio would be able to extract a substantial improvement in its license terms commencing with the fifth season of the series. From the studio's perspective, a traditional 4/4.5-year term license agreement is preferable, and remains achievable for especially desirable projects, particularly when networks are competing with one another for the opportunity to develop such projects.

---

[96] *See* section 6.3.4.4 above.

[97] Again, the half-year refers to a first season of a series with a mid-season start, which will entail a reduced number of episodes (typically, thirteen) than a full season with a fall start (which is usually comprised of twenty-two episodes). This same "half-year" concept is incorporated into the term of series regular actor agreements for broadcast network series. *See* section 6.3.4.4 above.

However, for less competitive projects, broadcast networks have increasingly begun to insist on so-called "extended term" license agreements, which provide for seven-year (or seven-and-a-half-year) terms, thereby delaying the point at which the network may face a costly renegotiation with the studio to a point that few series have the longevity to achieve. Although these extended term license agreements include prenegotiated improvements in the license fee structure that kick in with the fifth season of the series[98], and may include a premium even on the license fees for the first four years which the network pays in respect of receiving the extended term, these negotiated improvements are often less substantial than those the studio would expect to negotiate for a successful series entering its fifth season following the expiration of a traditional 4/4.5-year term deal.

Outside of the broadcast network context, most networks insist on even longer, "perpetual term" license agreements, which grant the network unlimited successive, consecutive, dependent options to continue ordering new seasons of the series, for as long as they wish to do so. Like extended term deals, perpetual term license agreements provide for studio-friendly escalations in the economic terms that are prenegotiated at the inception of the deal, when the studio has less leverage than it would enjoy if the network faced the prospect of losing a successful series to a competing network due to an expiring license agreement.

6.5.1.4. Pilot and Series License Fees

The fundamental economic term of a license agreement is the license fee paid by the network in exchange for the rights granted to it under the deal. The size of the license fee commanded by the studio is a function of numerous factors, including the desirability of the project and its elements and the competitiveness of bidding amongst multiple networks; the budget of the series; the scope of the rights (in terms of media, territory, and time) obtained by the network licensee; the series term of the license agreement; and the extent of the network-imposed holdbacks on the studio's reserved rights in the series. The license fee negotiation is, like all television industry negotiation, heavily influenced by the policies and precedents of the parties. However, it is

---

[98] *See* sections 6.5.1.4.c and d below.

also often driven by complex financial modeling by both parties, with the studio attempting to determine the extent to which its network license agreement will allow it to effectively monetize the series with third parties (and whether these financial opportunities, alongside the network's license fee, will generate an appropriate return on the studio's investment), and the network attempting to determine what types of ratings (and resulting advertising sales) would be necessary to recoup its investment in the series (in the form of both license fees and marketing expenses) and show a profit of its own.

a. Initial License Fees

Scripted television is based on a deficit model, meaning that the initial license fee that a domestic network pays to a studio to commission a series is less than the full cost of production. That difference between cost and initial license fee is known as the "deficit," and it represents the studio's at-risk investment in the series (and the hole that the studio must climb out, with revenues from media, territories, and exhibition windows beyond the initial network license, to show a profit).

The license fee for a series may be stated as a fixed dollar amount, or as a percentage of budget (although even when the license fee is a fixed dollar amount, that figure is negotiated with explicit consideration for the probable budget of the series). Broadcast networks tend to prefer to negotiate license fees in terms of dollars, while cable networks (including premium pay cable) and digital platforms are more likely to favor percentage-based license fees.

For reference, the following budget ranges (exclusive of applicable tax credits) may be considered typical, although as always, the final number depends on the creative and financial appetite of the commissioning network (with the highest budgets usually found on broadcast network television, premium pay cable, and digital platforms, and the lowest budgets on basic cable), as well as the creative demands of the subject matter of the show (e.g., major effects-driven science fiction/fantasy vs. small-scale character and dialogue-driven comedy) and the number of episodes produced (with larger orders allowing fixed startup and construction costs to be amortized across a higher number of episodes).

SHOW TYPE	PILOT BUDGET	SERIES BUDGET[99]
30-minute comedy	$1 million – $4 million	$500,000 – $3 million[100]
60-minute drama	$5 million – $12 million	$2 million – $6 million[101]

Of course, there are (as always) outliers on all sides, with large-scale projects like Netflix's *The Get Down* and HBO's *Vinyl* featuring reported production budgets well above the foregoing benchmarks.

For a broadcast network comedy, the expected license fee would fall between $1 million and $1.75 million for pilot (likely representing 30% to 40% of the production cost), and between $750,000 and $1.25 million per episode for series (likely representing 50% to 60% of the production cost). For a broadcast network drama, the expected license fee would be between $3.5 million and $4 million for pilot (again, likely representing 30% to 40% of the production cost), and between $1,500,000 and $2,000,000 per episode for series (likely representing 40% to 50% of the production cost).

Because the secondary market value of a cable (even pay premium cable) series is generally expected to be less than that of a broadcast network series,[102] the market generally provides for lower deficits on cable productions. Depending on the extent of the rights granted and the holdbacks imposed on other exploitation, the expected license fee

---

[99] A television season production budget typically consists of an "amortization budget" (which covers fixed costs associated with the season, such as principal set construction, which do not increase or decrease depending on the number of episodes produced) and a "pattern budget" (which covers episode-by-episode costs, based on assumed production parameters, such as the number of speaking parts in each episode and the number of days of on location production vs. in-studio production). The total episodic budget is the pattern budget plus the amortization budget, amortized over the number of episodes actually produced, which is why the average per-episode expense goes down if more episodes are ordered and produced.

[100] As of this writing, most comedies would fall in the $1 million to $2 million per episode range.

[101] As of this writing, most dramas would fall into the $3 million to $4 million per episode range.

[102] This diminution in value is a function of multiple factors, including reduced license fees from international broadcasters relative to those commanded for network series, and the probable unavailability of a cable syndication deal for a show that was exhibited, from inception, on cable.

from the U.S. cable network is likely between 65% and 85% of budget (potentially subject to a cap that corresponds to a probable budget number). Additional license fees may also be prenegotiated if the network insists on acquiring expansive digital rights.[103] Usually, the percentage license fee is calculated on the "net budget" (i.e., the budget, net of tax incentives or rebates obtained by the studio in connection with the production), although in some cases, it may be negotiated based on the "gross budget" (i.e., the budget without regard for tax incentives, in which case any tax incentives realized would directly and exclusively benefit the studio). For a cable comedy, the applicable license fee may be even higher, approaching 100% of the budget (again, because of the diminished off-network revenue-generating opportunities for cable comedies, in particular).

Scripted series produced for digital platforms such as Netflix and Amazon generally do not have deficits. These digital services have extensive international territorial footprints, and an internal mandate to acquire sufficient rights to make their shows available across all or substantially all territories served by the platforms. In addition, these platforms tend to have long license terms and expansive exclusivity requirements, and make it difficult or functionally impossible for outside studios to license their shows to competing digital platforms, thereby diminishing or eliminating an important revenue source for each series. In negotiating license agreements with these digital platforms as initial licensees, studios seek to extract from the network sufficient value to make up for the licensing opportunities in international territories and secondary markets which will be diminished or destroyed by the commissioning platform's license requirements. As a result, the applicable license fees obtained by studios from platforms such as Netflix and Amazon are typically substantially greater than 100% of the cost of production series (which amount may represent nearly all of the revenue the studio reasonably expects to earn from the show for the life of the series).[104] The amount of license fee above the cost of production, known as the "premium,"

---

[103] *See* section 6.5.1.6.b below.
[104] For purposes of determining residuals obligations, applicability of distribution fees against revenues in backend calculation, and other accounting-related purposes, there is typically an internal allocation of this license fee between domestic and international rights.

may be stated as a percentage of budget or in flat dollar terms. These are sometimes referred to as "cost-plus" deals.[105]

b. Breakage

The network may agree to supplement its initial negotiated license fee with additional payments, which are meant to subsidize and incentivize the studio to enhance the production value and marketability of the series – for instance, by hiring well-known and sought-after actors, or producing flashy event episodes, at costs that exceed the pattern budget for the series. Such supplemental amounts are referred to as "breakage."

Breakage may be prenegotiated, or addressed by the studio and network on an ongoing basis as proposed production enhancements arise. For instance, many network license agreements include a prenegotiated "cast breakage" formula, by which the network agrees to pay, on top of its license fee, anywhere from 50% to 100% of incremental costs of the episodic series regular budget over a threshold amount. A typical formulation would be "50/50 over $250,000," meaning that, for every dollar in episodic series regular fees committed by the studio in excess of $250,000 per episode, the network will automatically enhance its initial license fee by 50 cents. In addition, for internal recordkeeping or precedential reasons, some networks choose to internally allocate a portion of the negotiated license fee to "breakage," even though it is fixed and negotiated from inception; such characterizations are largely cosmetic. More often, however, the studio and network will discuss production enhancements on a case-by-case basis, with networks covering anywhere from 50% to 100% of the proposed incremental expense, depending on the perceived value to the network of the enhancement.

---

[105] It is important to note that these high license fees – again, typically a substantial percentage above the cost of production – have driven Netflix and Amazon to invest increasingly heavily in developing and producing their own shows, without relying on outside studios. Acting as networks, they must pay more than 100% of the cost of any given series simply to obtain the minimum subset of rights they need to feed their businesses worldwide. Acting as studios, they can control 100% of the rights in a series, worldwide, for the cost of production. Economically, it is obviously hugely advantageous to these platforms to produce and own their own content, rather than relying on outside suppliers. However, competition for the best programming from the best creative talent keeps these platforms in business with outside studios, despite the attendant costs – at least for the time being.

c. Later Season License Fees

Although the practice is not completely ubiquitous, in most "extended term" (i.e., longer than 4/4.5 years, usually 7/7.5 years[106]) or "perpetual term" licenses, the network's license fee automatically increases, commencing in the fifth season of the series (or sixth, if the first season was a mid-season start), to the studio's full cost of production. In other words, starting in the fifth season of a series, the studio moves to a zero-deficit production model, and its revenues from other sources are effectively pure profit. At this stage, the network reviews and approves the annual budgets for the series, and the studio remains responsible for any overages incurred relative to the ingoing approved budget (other than those also paid by the network as breakage), but the network bears 100% of the ingoing budgeted costs. This makes the fifth season an important benchmark for the studio to reach in terms of maximizing the profitability of a series (although the significant financial impact to the network of ordering a fifth season may prove an impediment to shows which are already at risk of cancellation at the end of their fourth seasons). In some cases, an "extended term" or "perpetual term" license agreement may provide for further escalations in the license fee in even later seasons, to some multiple or amount in excess of cost of production, though such escalations are not as common as the move to a "cost of production" in the fifth season.

d. Success Bonuses

In addition to the license fee increase to cost of production in the fifth year, there are two main ways that license agreements (especially extended or perpetual term deals, which must compensate the studio for lost renegotiation opportunity) reward a studio for the success of a series: ratings/rankings bonuses, and deficit recoupment.

Ratings and rankings bonuses are additional payments from the network to the studio (often, but not always, on a per-episode basis) which are triggered by a series achieving certain average viewership benchmarks, as measured and published by the Nielsen Company

---

[106] As explained in section 6.3.4.4 above, the notion of "half years" refers to series whose first season is ordered to production for a "mid-season start" – i.e., premiering during January to April, rather than September or October, of the applicable broadcast year.

(whose publications remain the standard in the television industry). Such bonuses may be triggered by a series achieving minimum ratings figures, minimum rankings relative to other primetime television series, or both. They are often tiered, with bonuses that escalate as successively higher ratings or rankings thresholds are achieved. These bonuses may be payable starting in the fifth season of a series, or, in some cases, a studio may be able to negotiate for ratings/rankings bonuses which are accessible starting in the second or third season of a series. In addition, if a series hits specified ratings/rankings thresholds, the network may agree to automatic enhancements in the license fees payable for repeat broadcasts.[107]

"Deficit recoupment" refers to the network's reimbursement to the studio, typically in the fifth (or fifth and sixth) seasons of a series, of the studio's production deficits from the first four production seasons of the show. This mechanism simulates a common demand of studios when negotiating a license renewal/extension for a highly successful series entering its fifth season under a traditional 4/4.5 year term deal. Like the aforementioned bonuses, deficit recoupment may be conditioned, in whole or in part, on the show achieving specified Nielsen ratings or rankings. Because a network cannot directly control the deficits a studio chooses to undertake during the first four production seasons, deficit reimbursement may also be subject to negotiated episodic caps.

6.5.1.5. Minimum Orders

The network's right, pursuant to the license agreement, to order production of a season of a series is subject to a minimum episodic order.[108] For broadcast network shows, the standard is as follows: (a)

---

[107] *See* section 6.5.1.6.a below.

[108] Such minimums are important to the studio because the number of episodes produced can substantially impact the economics of a series. As discussed in section 6.5.1.4.a above, the per-episode cost of a series goes down as the episodic order goes up, because certain fixed production costs can be amortized over a greater number of episodes. In addition, license fees are typically negotiated on a per-episode basis, so more episodes produced necessarily equates to more aggregate revenue. Consequently, although the studio carries a higher aggregate deficit on a larger order, the episodic deficit is lower and easier to overcome. However, even with these minimum order requirements, networks often reserve the right to reduce their order, subject to paying certain shut-down/diminished amortization costs. In such cases, the studio would remain obligated to produce and deliver the reduced number

for the first season, thirteen episodes (inclusive of the pilot), with an option to order a "back nine" of episodes if the show has a fall (rather than mid-season) start; (b) for the second season, twenty-two episodes if the first season had a fall start, or thirteen episodes (with another "back nine" option) if the first season had a mid-season start; and (c) for the third and subsequent seasons, twenty-two episodes. For cable and digital platforms, the applicable minimum orders are more specifically negotiated, according to the general exhibition patterns of the commissioning network and the financial demands on the studio for the specific project. Most studios seek to require at least twelve or thirteen-episode annual orders (inclusive of the pilot for the first season), though many non-broadcast networks have moved increasingly toward shorter seasons, often ten episodes annually, and sometimes as few as eight episodes per season. Because of the worsened amortization and diminished outside revenue prospects associated with such short orders, studios may demand particularly premium episodic license fees to compensate.

6.5.1.6. Licensed Rights

Any intellectual property license must define the scope of the rights being licensed, and network license agreements for television programs are no different. Network license agreements grant networks only specific enumerated rights, with all rights not covered by the grant of rights reserved by the studio (although potentially encumbered by a holdback[109]). For the most part, networks define the scope of the rights being granted according to the needs of their particular businesses, and studios adjust the pricing of the license fee accordingly, although every year brings a fresh push-and-pull between studios and networks, with networks seeking ever more expansive grants of rights while looking to avoid any associated increase in the license fees they must pay for such rights.

a. Network Exhibition and Runs

Most obviously, the network must obtain the right to exhibit the series on its own network, in every way that network is delivered to

---

of episodes (although the shortened order would render void the network's contractual options to order further seasons).

[109] *See* section 6.5.1.8 below.

customers. For broadcast networks, this means the over-the-air broadcast signals of affiliate stations, as well as authorized retransmissions by MVPDs; for cable networks, this primarily means MVPD carriage. As distribution technologies have evolved, however, the contractual definitions of "network exhibition" have grown more expansive, so as to cover any newly-emerged technical delivery mechanisms on which a network may rely.[110] In general, regardless of technological means, in order to qualify as "network exhibition," the service must always bear certain characteristics based on the primary traditional network – for instance, the stream to the customer must be preprogrammed and linear (as opposed to "on demand"), and must be offered to the customer on the same basis as the primary network distribution (i.e., free for broadcast networks; subscription-supported and authenticated for cable networks, etc.). Separate from defining "network exhibition" with regard to their own networks, some networks also negotiate for the right to "repurpose" some of their permitted runs by exhibiting series episodes through affiliated sister networks (often for primarily promotional purposes).

Networks are generally limited to a finite number of "runs" (i.e., distinct, scheduled exhibitions) of the licensed episode of a series, and must pay additional license fees (on the order of $25,000 to $50,000 per run) for repeats beyond a negotiated threshold. Some networks base the number of permitted runs, and the threshold for triggering repeat fees, on an episode-by-episode basis. Others define these limits and thresholds based on multiples of the total number of episodes ordered by the network in each season, with a sub-limit on repeats for any given episode. For broadcast networks, the limit usually amounts, by one of these means of calculation, to a cap of three to four runs per episode under the initial network license; for cable networks, the

---

[110] For example, some cable networks are now available not only through traditional MVPDs such as cable, satellite, and telecommunications providers, but also through Internet-based subscription services such as Sling TV and PlayStation Vue. For technological reasons, these "virtual MVPD" or "VMVPD" services do not meet the traditional technical or regulatory definitions of "MVPD," but offer functionally and substantively identical services to traditional MVPDs. Some networks also make their linear streams accessible to customers through their websites or dedicated mobile apps, as long as the customers authenticate themselves with confirmed MVPD subscriptions. Networks must take care to define "network exhibition" so as to ensure their ability to avail themselves of such new distribution opportunities, without losing access to the content they carry on their traditional streams.

maximum number of runs is usually much higher (e.g., up to twelve runs), or even unlimited. In any event, at a minimum, the network is generally responsible for reimbursing the studio for any residuals obligations arising out of the network's repeat exhibition of series episodes, and repeat fees to the studio generally escalate the more reruns the network takes.

b. Digital Rights (Traditional Licensees)

For the most part, network license agreements – particularly broadcast network license agreements – evolve seldom and slowly. Budgets, and therefore license fees, have crawled up over time (though not necessarily at the same rate), but little else has changed much over the years. Networks and studios that regularly do business together often simply duplicate their recently negotiated license agreements, plug in fresh numbers on a show-by-show basis, make a few incremental changes, and proceed. The huge exception to this trend, however, has been with respect to digital rights, which arguably represent the fastest-changing – and most economically impactful – area of constant negotiation (and renegotiation) between studios and networks.

In this context, "digital rights" refers to exploitation and distribution of a series to customers via the Internet, typically on an "on demand" (rather than preprogrammed/linear) basis, that does not fall within the definition of "network exhibition."[111] Digital rights may be exploited through various technological platforms – for instance, a network may make episodes of a series available to its customers on demand through the network's website (such as ABC.com), or through a dedicated mobile app (such as HBO Go or FX Now). Digital rights may also be exploited through an MVPD, rather than by the network directly; indeed, most MVPDs provide on-demand access to a significant number of shows that are exhibited by networks covered by the customer's MVPD subscription. This right (which is very valuable to the MVPD) must be granted to the MVPD by the network; and in turn, the network must obtain the applicable rights from the studio in order to pass them on to the MVPD. In general, the studio's grant of digital rights to the network explicitly requires that the digital rights be exploited on a platform that is owned and/or branded by the network,

---

[111] *See* section 6.5.1.6.6.a above.

or by an MVPD that carries the network; thus, for instance, a network would not be permitted to obtain digital rights and sublicense them, for a fee, to Netflix. The primary exception to this requirement is that ABC, Fox, and NBC, which jointly own Hulu, regularly obtain the right to exercise their digital rights through Hulu (even though the Hulu service does not expressly carry ABC, Fox, or NBC branding).

For many years, the standard for digital rights was the so-called "rolling five" deal – the right to make available to customers, on an on-demand basis, up to five episodes of the series at a time, to enable customers who fall behind on a series to catch up on recent episodes. Under a "rolling five" deal, as any new episode after the fifth is made available to customers, an older one must be taken offline. In addition, typically, if the network licensee is ad-supported (which is essentially true of all television networks, other than premium pay channels like HBO), the network's streaming of its "rolling five" episodes would have to be ad-supported as well. These rights were regarded by studios and networks alike as "companion rights" to the primary network license, and granted without additional charge by the studio.

More recently, however, the battle has been over "stacking rights" – the right to make every episode of a given season of a series, without numerical limit, available to customers for "on demand" streaming while that season is ongoing. In order to meet growing customer demand for "on demand" viewing of their favorite television shows, networks have become increasingly aggressive in demanding in-season stacking rights for virtually all new series that they order to production. Although such stacking rights remain subject to the same branding requirements as traditional "rolling five" licenses (i.e., the rights must be exploited through a digital platform that expressly carries the branding of the licensee network [e.g., CBS All Access] or one of its partner MVPDs [e.g., TWC TV], other than special exceptions for Hulu), and are still considered "companion rights" to the primary network license, studios have succeeded in demanding supplemental license fees in exchange for these stacking rights. That said, the studios have also been largely dissatisfied with the license fees that networks – particularly broadcast networks – have been willing to assign to such rights.

Premium cable networks such as HBO and Showtime, who embraced digital exploitation more rapidly than broadcast networks and have offered subscription-authenticated companion applications such as HBO Go and Showtime Anytime for several years, have been licensing extensive digital rights alongside their network exhibition rights for years. The digital rights obtained by premium pay cable networks typically include not only in-season stacking rights, but also full out-of-season streaming rights (which may be granted on an exclusive or non-exclusive basis, and which are priced out by the studio and network accordingly). As a result, these networks have been able to offer their subscribers library access to virtually every episode of every original series they have ever commissioned.

Digital rights have proven especially problematic to negotiate because of the unique challenges they represent for studios and networks alike. From the networks' perspective, the networks' efforts to reach their customers are constantly evolving, and networks are under significant market pressure to ensure that they can offer all of their programming to customers on as wide-ranging and consistent a basis as possible (even though that programming may be licensed from numerous studio partners with different, separately negotiated deals). Because networks can exploit only those rights which are expressly licensed to them, any change in their business model or distribution scheme can reveal major gaps in the rights they control, and studios can make these gaps extremely costly to fill.[112] On the other hand, from the studios' perspective, selling digital rights to third-party, second-window licensees has become a critical component of the overall business of making and distributing a television series. But the more expansively an initial network has exploited a series digitally, the less the studio can expect to earn in license fees from third-party digital licensees, who feel that the value of their rights has been diminished by the prior availability of the series on an on-demand basis. Because

---

[112] One major example of such an unanticipated rights gap, arising out of a change in business model, is that of Hulu, and its parents, the ABC, Fox, and NBC broadcast networks. As discussed here, studios have traditionally required that, where an ad-supported network obtains digital rights, it must exploit those digital rights on an ad-supported basis as well. For many years, networks had little problem abiding by this requirement, even when the networks made shows available on Hulu (whose paid subscription service was also ad-supported, even while the company simultaneously offered a free ad-supported service, which was phased out in 2016). More recently, however, Hulu has sought to make its subscription offering more appealing to consumers by moving the service toward an ad-free experience. For this reason, these networks have begun to reject the traditional requirement that their digital rights must be exploited on an ad-supported basis.

digital buyers of content consider the prior streaming history of a television series in determining the license fees they are willing to pay for such series, studios often complain that network acquisition of stacking rights severely diminishes the license fees the studios can obtain from subsequent digital licensees (and that the supplemental license fees paid by networks for such stacking rights are too low to fully compensate the studios for that loss).[113] This significantly impacts the long-term profitability of the series.

With new technologies and business models emerging on a seemingly daily basis, digital rights promise to remain one of the most hotly-negotiated elements of network license agreements in the years to come.

c. Digital Rights (Digital Platforms)

The foregoing discussion contemplates digital rights as "companion rights" to a traditional network television license. However, the parameters for digital rights are fundamentally different when the initial, first-run licensee is, itself, a digital platform.[114]

In such cases, the traditional notions of "network exhibition," or of finite "runs" and "repeats," are, by definition, not applicable. The primary rights being granted are the digital rights. Therefore, there are certainly no limits as to how many episodes the licensee may exhibit at any given time. Branding requirements for first-run digital licensees may be relaxed somewhat[115], although restrictions on sublicensing remain common. The license may also expressly prohibit or require the series to be offered on a subscription and/or ad-supported basis, and in general, studios – seeking to protect even speculative outside revenue generation opportunities – prefer to grant digital rights that are

---

[113] Whether this alleged diminution in value to the third-party licensee from the initial network's exploitation of digital rights is factually true is debatable, but this is actually somewhat beside the point. The third-party licensees take the position that it is true, and reduce their spending accordingly, so the studio feels the impact of the alleged diminution regardless of the factual reality.

[114] In such a case, the digital rights being granted may be referred to as "standalone" rights (because they are not tied to an underlying network television license).

[115] For instance, from 2011 to 2014, Amazon operated its streaming business in the United Kingdom and Germany through an acquired subsidiary called LOVEFiLM, before finally folding the service into its self-branded Amazon Instant Video service in February 2014.

as narrow and specific to their licensee's then-current distribution model as possible. That said, the major digital platforms have sought to negotiate for flexibility to evolve their business models over time without losing the ability to continue to exhibit their original series.[116]

6.5.1.7. License Territory and Term

All intellectual property licenses must specifically identify the territories and time periods that are within the scope of the license, and again, network license agreements are no exception.

For most U.S. networks, the applicable territory is simply the United States, its territories and possessions.[117] Puerto Rico and Bermuda are often included as part of the United States, and Puerto Rican and Bermudan rights may be subdivided between English-language rights (which are often included as part of a U.S. license) and Spanish-language rights (which are often excluded from U.S. licenses or granted only on a non-exclusive basis, so as to allow the studio to also include these rights in pan-Latin American licenses).

Some cable networks are also made available in a limited number of territories outside of the United States (most often Canada, but sometimes in Europe). Usually, the foreign version of a network is affiliated with and carries much of the same content as its American sibling, but is technically separately programmed and not on an identical concurrent linear stream as the American network. Sometimes, a network which is offered on one technological/economic basis in the United States (e.g., a premium pay cable network) is offered on a different technological/economic basis in other territories (e.g., as a standalone streaming service). In any event, when an American network has a foreign operation to sustain, it often concurrently obtains the rights for the international territories it needs, with additional license fees negotiated according to the prevailing economic terms for such territories.

The major shift in territorial negotiation in recent years has been reflected, again, in licenses with digital platforms such as Netflix, Amazon, and Hulu. As of 2018 both Netflix and Amazon Prime Video are available in approximately 200 countries, including all major

---

[116] Again, consider Hulu's decision to strip ads from its paid subscription service.
[117] Every territory also typically includes its military bases, and airlines and cruise ships which fly the flag of that country.

territories other than China. Hulu has made periodic overtures toward the international market, though its international expansion plan has been less decisive than that of its competitors. Although all of these services engage in licensing activity on a country-by-country basis, for their original, first-run programming, they generally require that studios grant them rights covering all territories that they serve and/or have plans to serve in the immediate future (which, for all intents and purposes with Netflix and Amazon, means the entire world). As discussed in section 6.5.1.4.a above, these platforms' extensive geographic licensing mandates force them to pay high, cost-plus license fees to acquire original content from outside studios (which high license fees are, in turn, driving them to reduce their dependence on outside content providers and increase their capacities as studios as well as networks).

Finally, studios impose time limits on how long network licensees may exhibit series episodes. For broadcast networks, the exhibition term is typically coextensive with the series term: as soon as the network allows its option to order a new season to expire unexercised, it no longer has the right to broadcast old episodes of the series (although any negotiated holdbacks on outside exploitation[118] remain in full effect). For cable and digital platforms, the exhibition term typically extends for several years after the network's initial exhibition of the last original episode produced (with older seasons functionally being subject to a longer exhibition term than newer seasons, and the license for all seasons expiring at the same time). The precise number of years varies from network to network, and the license fee demands of the studio increase (albeit non-linearly) with the length of the term.

6.5.1.8. Network Exclusivity

In general, a studio reserves for itself all rights that it has not granted to its network licensee. These reserved rights become the basis of the studio's efforts to realize a profit by maximizing revenue-generating opportunities across media, territory, and time. However, the original network licensee has a significant interest in protecting its investment in a series (which investment amounts to a substantial percentage of the show's cost of production) by ensuring that, at least

---

[118] *See* section 6.5.1.8 below.

for some time, the network is the exclusive home of the content that its viewers want to consume. Consequently, every network license agreement includes a set of holdbacks, which restrict the timing on which a studio may exercise its reserved rights in a series.

In general, a studio may engage in non-primetime "off-network" or "syndication" licensing of a broadcast television series on a once-a-week basis commencing three years after the debut of the series, and on a more-than-once-a-week basis commencing four years after the debut of the series. Such licenses may be granted to cable network licensees, or to broadcast station licensees. For a cable series, comparable syndication windows generally apply, but only allowing for licensing to broadcast stations, not to competing cable networks during the term of the agreement. Similar holdbacks may be (but are not always) applicable to any linear television exhibition of a series which is initially produced for a digital platform.

In the early days of digital platforms such as Netflix and Amazon, off-network second-run exploitation of a conventional television series via SVOD or other digital platforms was subject to the same holdback window as traditionally applied to off-network linear television/syndication licensing. In more recent years, however, studios have been able to make the case that the availability of recent seasons of ongoing television series on streaming services is complementary, rather than cannibalistic, to the home network where new episodes debut.[119] Such concurrent availability presents opportunities for both series and viewers, allowing shows to find new audiences, while enabling new viewers to discover and quickly "catch up" with established, ongoing series without missing a beat. As a result – particularly in connection with heavily serialized (and therefore "binge-worthy") dramas – many networks now permit studios to make old seasons available through third-party streaming services as soon as thirty days before the subsequent season is set to premiere on the primary network. However, the willingness of a network to allow such "early SVOD" licensing may also depend on the extent to which the network maintains and relies on its own digital platform or service.[120]

---

[119] *See* section 6.1.3.3.a above.

[120] For instance, for many years, HBO – which actively promotes the availability of its complete television library on its companion HBO Go digital service (and eventually launched its standalone HBO Now digital service with the same offering) – declined to make any of its shows available through third-party digital platforms. As

Home video availability of a television series serves a similar "catch up" function for viewers (and, in any event, is not practical for a studio to pursue, on a season-by-season basis, until each season has been exhibited in full by its premiere network). Consequently, many networks (particularly cable networks) also permit studios to exploit home video rights (which include contemporary technologies such as DVD and Blu-ray), on a season-by-season basis, as soon as one to three months before the debut of the following season of the series. Distribution of individual series episodes via electronic sell-through ("EST") – the closest digital counterpart to traditional home video distribution – may be permitted even faster, as soon as a few hours after the initial network premiere of each episode. However, broadcast networks sometimes prefer to fully prohibit the studio from pursuing home video distribution of a series until after the network has ceased to order new seasons.

Studios are generally free to exhibit any episode of a television series internationally, at any time, subject only to the U.S. network's right to make the initial worldwide premiere of each episode, on an episode-by-episode basis. "Ancillary rights," such as licensing and merchandising, soundtrack, and publishing rights can also generally be exploited by the studio freely, without holdback or reservation. The one exception to the foregoing statement about "ancillary rights" may be in connection with "derivative rights" (i.e., the right to produce or authorize the production of spinoff or sequel television series, theatrical motion pictures, stage plays, or other new productions), which are often frozen during the series term of the license agreement. In other words, as long as the network licensee continues ordering new seasons of the series, the studio may not exploit such derivative rights without the network's approval (which, in the case of derivative television series, would generally be granted by the network only if it were also the network licensee for the new series).[121]

---

of 2014, HBO announced a deal to make many of its classic, no-longer-current series available through Amazon Prime, but the network continues to jealously protect its exclusive digital distribution of current and more recent HBO series.

[121] Such rights may also remain encumbered post-term, as explained in section 6.5.1.10 below.

6.5.1.9. Revenue Backstops

Depending on the extent to which a network obtains unusually extensive rights, or imposes holdbacks or other restrictions on the studio's exploitation of its reserved rights under the network license agreement,[122] the studio may demand that the network guarantee a minimum level of revenue to the studio from the studio's exercise of the rights it has retained.

For instance, if a commissioning network obtains unusually extensive digital rights as part of its license, the studio will be concerned that its revenue from future domestic digital licenses will decrease. Similarly, if a network seeks to bolster the exclusivity under its deal by precluding the studio from making second-window syndication or digital licenses within the network's territory for an unusually long period of time, the studio may complain that such a holdback depresses the value of the studio's retained rights under the licensee.

The studio may condition its agreement to such terms on the network providing the studio with an economic "backstop," by which the network agrees to reimburse the studio for any shortfall between, on the one hand, its actual domestic distribution revenues, and, on the other hand, the revenues the studio would have expected to achieve absent the unusual license terms. (The benchmark for this "expected revenue" figure would be highly negotiated between the parties.) Studios may also seek such backstops from newer or less established networks, from which the studio's revenue prospects for international or second-window domestic licensing are uncertain due to the initial licensee's lack of stature or unestablished value in the marketplace.

6.5.1.10. Subsequent Seasons and Derivative Productions

From the perspective of a studio, preserving the ability to seek out a new network licensee once the initial licensee has lost interest in the series is vital to maximizing the long-term economic prospects of a project.[123] Similarly, a studio may realize major additional value from

---

[122] *See* sections 6.5.1.6.b and 6.5.1.8 above.

[123] Studios have been able to extend the life cycles of numerous prominent series by finding them new homes after they were canceled by their original networks. For

a successful series by producing spinoffs, or even converting a series into a franchise with multiple iterations (such as *Law & Order* [NBC], *CSI* [CBS], or *NCIS* [CBS]). On the other hand, a network wants to take care to preserve its ability to retain control of future seasons of a successful series, even after the initial term of the license agreement has expired, and to establish itself as the natural home for any derivative productions of a successful series, even if that original series is no longer on the air.

Typically, these competing interests are resolved through post-term first negotiation and first refusal (or, occasionally, last refusal) rights. These procedural safeguards offer a network a meaningful advantage over competing networks when it comes to obtaining rights in subsequent seasons or derivative productions of a successful series, while at the same time protecting the studio's ability to monetize and maximize valuable rights if a show's original home network is uninterested in proceeding (or if the parties are unable to negotiate a deal).

6.5.1.11. Network Approvals

Networks enjoy broad (and broadly stated) creative approval rights in connection with the series they commission. Such approval rights extend not only to the creative content of the show (including filming locations, production drafts of episodic scripts, and final cuts of produced episodes), but also to the hiring (and firing) of key personnel engaged in connection with the series (including executive producers, directors, writers, series regular and major recurring guest actors). In addition, as discussed in various sections above, networks generally maintain exclusive authority over the granting of credits for series that appear on their air.

The final creative content of a series is a result of an ongoing process of push and pull among producers/service providers, studio executives, and network executives. As between the service providers

---

instance, Sony Pictures Television was able to extend the lives of series such as *Community* (canceled after five seasons on NBC; renewed for a sixth season by Yahoo!) and *Damages* (canceled after three seasons on FX; renewed for fourth and fifth seasons by DirecTV). Touchstone Television did the same for *Scrubs* (canceled after seven seasons on NBC; renewed for eighth and ninth seasons by ABC), while Warner Bros. Television did so for *Southland* (canceled after one season by NBC; renewed for four additional seasons by TNT).

and the studio, in the event of a disagreement, the former must adhere to the directions of the latter. But as between the studio and the network, the parties must generally reach mutual understanding (or at least accommodation) which respect to all key creative matters, with neither side having the right to unilaterally designate or force creative choices against the other side's will – although in many cases, creative decisions may be forced (or creative disagreements effectively resolved) by the demands of budget, schedule, or other production exigencies.

6.5.1.12. Network Promotional Rights

Because one of the network's key roles in the television industry is to market its shows (and itself as a content destination) to the viewing public, the studio typically accords its network licensee broad rights to promote the availability of a series on the network's service, and, in connection with such promotion, to create (at the network's own expense) marketing materials (such as commercials, trailers, and print advertisements) which are technically built from and derivative of the underlying elements of the series. In addition, the network generally requires that the studio take reasonable steps, in its agreements with actors, writers, and other key service providers, to obtain the right to use such individuals' names and likenesses in the promotion of the series, and to require them to participate in publicity activities, as required by the network.[124]

Networks often directly finance, outside of the budget and license fees for the series, the creation of key marketing materials (such as series posters/key art and electronic press kits). In turn, studios often agree to cost-sharing arrangements with the networks, by which the studios reimburse the networks for a portion of these expenses in exchange for the right to use (and to authorize the studio's other international and downstream licensees to use) such network-financed/created marketing materials.

---

[124] *See* section 6.3.4.13. above.

6.5.1.13. Contingent Compensation

Assuming there is no co-production relationship between a network's affiliated studio and the lead production studio for a series,[125] the position of the network is that of licensee, and the studio remains the sole owner of the series (and, therefore, primary beneficiary of the upside in the series' success). Nevertheless, some networks – particularly cable networks – feel that they should be compensated for providing the initial platform (and financing most of the initial marketing/promotional expenses) that launch a series to success. Such networks may negotiate for a share of contingent compensation from the series, which allows them to share in the "profits" of the series in much the same way as the backend-earning rightsholders and talent/service providers (with contingent compensation that is calculated comparably).[126] The studio may require that such participations accorded to a network licensee fit within its typical cap (usually 35%) on total third-party participations, or that the network's participation be deducted "off the top" in calculating the talent's participations.[127]

6.5.2. Co-Production Agreements

Two studios may join forces to jointly own and produce a television series. Such an arrangement is known as a co-production.

In the U.S. television market, co-productions generally arise in two scenarios: when two different studios control separate elements (in the form of underlying rights, or writers, directors, or other talent who are subject to exclusive overall agreements by which they commit their services to a single studio for a term of years) which they wish to join together to create a series; and when a studio seeks to license a series to a network with an affiliated studio arm. The latter scenario is the most common. Although a co-production is not legally a partnership, the two parties to a co-production agreement are commonly referred to as "co-production partners."

As discussed in section 4.3.3. of the "Introduction to Television" chapter, over time, most networks have developed a preference for

---

[125] *See* section 6.5.2 below.
[126] *See* section 6.4 above.
[127] *See* section 6.4.7 above.

owning their own content (either directly or through an affiliated entity).[128] In addition, as discussed in Section 6.5.1.13. above, most networks reason that, because it is their initial investment in promoting a series and bringing it to market that sets up a show for success, they should reap the long-term financial rewards of that success. Consequently, many networks will require, as a condition of licensing a series from a third-party television studio, that they be allowed (via their studio arms) to become a co-owner of the project – indeed, some cable networks require this on a blanket basis, refusing to order production of any series in which they do not have at least a partial ownership interest. In such circumstances, to avoid a conflict of interest, the independent studio has unilateral authority to negotiate the license agreement with the network on behalf of the co-production.

The applicable co-production/ownership split may vary, but a 50/50 split is typical (and, going forward, this section will assume a 50/50 co-production in describing the applicable terms). A 50/50 co-producer generally pays 50% of the deficit, bears 50% of the risk, owns 50% of the copyright, and enjoys 50% of the upside from the production. A co-production is an inherently risk mitigating structure (which logically means that it is therefore an upside-capping structure, as well). From the perspective of a network-affiliated studio, however, acquiring a co-production stake in somebody else's project is often a particularly good investment[129] – and, depending on the timing of the co-production arrangement, may be a particularly effective risk

---

[128] As discussed above, from the network's perspective, paying 100% of the cost of production to own 100% of the rights in a series is preferable to paying a license fee which represents a substantial portion of the cost of production in exchange for a limited subset of rights.

[129] Applying even rough math, the economic efficiency to a network of obtaining a co-production position quickly becomes clear. As discussed in section 6.5.1.4.a, the initial licensee fee for a project will often equal approximately 50% of its budget (with the remaining 50% constituting the series deficit). For that 50% contribution, the network will be a pure licensee, enjoying little or no upside in the ultimate success of the series across other territories and platforms. However, by paying an incremental 25% of 100% of the budget (i.e., 50% of the 50% deficit), the network (via its affiliated studio) can effectively obtain a 50% stake in the upside of the series. This economic efficiency becomes only more obvious for cable networks that ordinarily pay higher license fees, in the range of 75% of the initial series budget. For these networks, obtaining a 50% co-production position means covering an incremental 12.5% of 100% of the budget (i.e., 50% of the 25% deficit) – in other words, paying approximately 16.67% more money than the bare license fee (i.e., 87.6% vs. 75%), in exchange for a 50% stake in the series' success.

mitigation strategy. For instance, some networks will initially agree to develop a project with an outside studio on a pure license basis, but subsequently insist on entering into a co-production prior to ordering a pilot or series. In a world where few development projects are ordered to pilot and few pilots or ordered to series,[130] this effectively shifts 100% of the risk of development and/or pilot production onto the third-party studio, while allowing the network-affiliated studio to reap 50% of the upside once its sister network has decided it wants to move forward with a series. In addition, because how long a series remains on the air directly correlates to how much money it makes or loses for its studio, a network may be more likely to continue ordering a series that it owns in whole or in part than a series in which it has no ownership interest.

There are two primary categories of duties which must be allocated in a co-production agreement: which studio is responsible for leading physical production of the series, and which studio (or studios) control the distribution rights in the series. In addition, there are a number of economic terms related to these roles which must be negotiated in order to determine the flow of revenues from the series.

6.5.2.1. Lead Studio

The "lead studio" in a co-production is the studio that is responsible for managing physical production of the series. For the most part, the lead studio manages the production process as it would if it were the sole studio, but along the way, it must obtain the approval of its co-production partner of all budgets (and enhancements thereto) and key creative decisions (such as the casting of actors and hiring of writers and directors). Because of the way co-production revenues are allocated, studios consider it desirable to be the lead studio. Where two studios enter into a co-production agreement after one of them has independently developed the project or otherwise engaged all of the key talent, the studio that commenced the development process generally gets to be the lead studio. Where two studios enter into a co-production arrangement at the very outset of the development process, the choice of lead studio may be hotly negotiated, with the role generally going to the larger studio with superior bargaining power (or,

---

[130] *See* section 6.1.3.1 above.

in the event of an effective tie in that regard, to whichever studio contributes more – or the more important – elements to the production).

6.5.2.2. Distribution Rights

The parties to a co-production agreement must allocate series distribution rights. In some cases, a single studio – often but not necessarily the lead studio – will control all of the distribution rights in the series, with the co-production partner's economic interest in the project essentially being passive. In many cases, however, distribution rights are divided between the co-production partners, typically on the basis of territory, with one partner controlling all distribution rights in the United States and/or Canada, and the other partner controlling all distribution rights throughout the rest of the world.[131] As explained in section 6.1.3.3 above, conventional wisdom holds that the domestic market (and, in particular, the prospect of significant syndication revenue) is most valuable for comedies, while the international market is most valuable for dramas, and this assumption generally informs the positions two studios will take when negotiating for which studio controls which territory. However, a network-affiliated studio has an extra incentive to control domestic distribution rights, so that it can manage the amount of local distribution that may directly compete with its sister network's exhibition of a series. In order to induce the other side to give up distribution rights which one co-production partner wishes to control, that party may guarantee the other a minimum amount of revenue from the rights (which minimum may escalate depending on the number of seasons produced).

One unique area of negotiation concerns derivative rights. In some co-production agreements, the co-producers agree to effectively freeze the right to produce spinoff television series, theatrical feature films, or other separate productions based on the original television series, requiring the consent of both parties to proceed. Other co-production agreements permit one or both parties – usually the lead studio – to unilaterally force the development and production of a derivative project, with the other party having an option to participate as a co-producer, either on the same terms applicable to the original co-

---

[131] Ancillary rights such as soundtrack, music publishing, and merchandising, may be controlled by one of the co-production partners worldwide, or split between them according to their territorial controls over the general distribution of the series.

production or on new terms to be negotiated in good faith. If one of the parties to a co-production elects not to proceed as a partner in any new derivative production, it typically receives some passive participation in such derivative.

6.5.2.3. Allocation of Revenues

The waterfall of revenues between co-production partners resembles that enshrined in a profit participation definition. In the simplest terms, it can be articulated as follows:

      Gross Receipts
— Distribution Fees
— Distribution Expenses
— Deficit
— Unapproved Overages
— Lead Studio Overhead
— Third-Party Participations

= Studio Net Proceeds

In practice, however, the revenue participation enjoyed by a co-production partner is simpler and cleaner than that applied to a profit participant. The counterintuitive deductions and exclusions that characterize a talent backend definition[132] (which are sometimes derisively referred to as "Hollywood Accounting") are largely stripped out of a co-production waterfall.

What follows is a deeper examination of each of the elements of this co-production waterfall.

a. Gross Receipts

As with a talent backend definition, "gross receipts" refers to all revenue received by (or credited to) a studio from its exploitation of a television series and all rights therein, from all sources. Unlike a talent backend definition, however, in a co-production agreement, "all means all." Even if distribution rights are divided between the co-production partners, all revenues flow through a single joint waterfall. There are no artificially depressed imputed license fees. Home video revenues

---

[132] *See* section 6.4. above.

are accounted for at 100% of revenues received, rather than on a royalty basis (and any applicable distribution costs for such home video exploitation are deducted, at actual cost, as distribution expenses). To the extent that any revenues are excluded from "gross receipts" for purposes of the co-production waterfall, they are still accounted for in other ways. For instance, revenues from product placements/ integrations, tax incentives, and copyright enforcement recoveries may be applied directly against the deficit (without either side deducting distribution fees or applying these amounts against distribution expenses), or otherwise distributed to the co-production partners outside of the waterfall according to their respective shares. Revenues from derivative productions may be excluded from gross receipts, but the parties will have otherwise negotiated controls, co-production rights, or passive participations applicable to such productions. Although issues may still arise when a co-production partner who controls certain distribution rights enters into licensing transactions with its affiliated entities, or foregoes licensing opportunities in order to protect the interests of its sister network, for the most part, the accounting for gross receipts between co-production partners is clean.

b. Distribution Fees

As it does when accounting to profit participants, the studio that controls distribution rights deducts a distribution fee, off-the-top, from all revenues generated from the exploitation of rights under its control. If distribution rights are divided between co-production partners, each partner retains distribution fees from the revenues it generates from its own rights, and the distribution fee applicable to each side is usually the same. Between co-production partners, distribution fees range between 5% and 20%, with 10% being typical.

c. Distribution Expenses

Deductions for distribution expenses operate more or less identically under a co-production agreement as under a profit participation definition. If distribution rights are divided between the co-production partners, each partner recoups its distribution expenses from the revenues it generates from its own exploitation of rights, (including guild-mandated residuals) and remits the balance to flow through the rest of the waterfall on a fully cross-collateralized basis. Co-production partners may negotiate more successfully for caps on the other studio's distribution expenses; if such caps are agreed, they are typically set to 5% to 10% of the studio's gross receipts, excluding from such cap residuals and music clearance costs.

d. Deficit

As explained in Section 6.5.1.4.a above, the "deficit" is the difference between the cost of production of the series and the initial network license fee. Each of the co-production partners initially pays for a share of the deficit equal to its percentage interest in the co-production (again, usually 50/50), and, once distribution fees and distribution expenses have been deducted, each partner recovers its share of the deficit from gross receipts on a *pro rata pari passu* basis. This distribution continues until each side has fully recovered its investment in the cost of production, although the recoupment of deficit contributions for each side is capped based on the ingoing production budgets of the series (subject to any further mutually-approved budget enhancements).

e. Unapproved Overages

Because the co-production partners' deficit recoupment is capped based on the ingoing production budgets of the series, to the extent the lead studio (which is responsible for managing production) overspent and incurred unapproved overages, it does not recover such expenses as part of the deficit recoupment phase of the waterfall. However, after each side has fully recouped its respective share of the deficit, the lead studio may next recover the unapproved overages which it initially bore during production of the series. Such recovery of unapproved overages is usually capped at an amount equal to 2% to 3% of the ingoing production budget of the series.[133] To the extent that the lead studio faces a runaway production and incurs overages in excess of this cap, it will be forced to bear such expenses solely out of its own share of revenues from the waterfall.

---

[133] Anytime any deal term is specified as a percentage of the ingoing production budget, the parties must specify whether this percentage is calculated based on the budget net of applicable tax incentives (a lower number), or the gross budget without accounting for such incentives (a higher number).

f. Lead Studio Overhead

After the lead studio recoups its unapproved overages (if any) from the waterfall, it is entitled to retain 100% of revenues, up to a specified percentage of the budget, as an overhead charge. This overhead charge represents the lead studio's compensation for its investment of time, effort, and overhead in managing the production, as well as its assumption of the risk of production overages (which it could only recoup from revenues in a later order of priority, and subject to cap). In co-production agreements, the lead studio's overhead charge is generally 5% or 7.5%, though in rare cases, may be as high as 10%. Sometimes, this percentage is subject to an artificial negotiated cap, or may be set based on a percentage of the first season's budget, with flat increases for subsequent seasons that are not tied to the actual budgets of subsequent season (which will likely grow faster than such flat increases would provide). Note that, in a co-production definition, the studio deducts its overhead charge *after* the co-production partners have recovered their contributions to the cost of production, while in a talent profit participation definition, the overhead charge is deducted *before* the studio recovers its cost of production. In addition, while a co-production waterfall does provide for an overhead deduction by the lead studio, neither of the partners in the co-production generally charge the other interest on their respective contributions to production or distribution expenses.

g. Third-Party Participations

Finally, revenues from the series go to paying third-party participants – specifically talent and agency profit participants, whose backend interests are calculated on the basis described in Section 6.4 above. Effectively, the fact of the co-production does not impact the calculation or accounting of participations to talent, who will see the same backend payments they would have seen had there been no co-production. The backend definition used by the lead studio, which engages all of the talent, controls for the talent and agency participations on the series. In effect, the co-production partners bear the cost of these participations in proportion to their respective co-production shares (so, most likely, 50/50).

h. *Studio Net Proceeds*

Finally, whatever remains of gross receipts after all of the foregoing deductions constitutes the "studio net proceeds" of the series, and these are again divided between the co-production partners in proportion to their respective co-production shares (so, most likely, 50/50).

6.6. CONCLUSION

In today's rapidly evolving business and creative landscape, any detailed description of the business, legal, or creative norms of television is likely to prove semi-obsolete in the time it takes for a manuscript to reach publication. This chapter's description of the nuts and bolts of the scripted television production industry must, and will, evolve in the years ahead, as the medium of television itself continues to evolve. But the broad description of the television business provided here, and the portrait it paints of a challenging and dynamic industry, should remain true – and, hopefully, useful – for years to come.

SCRIPTED TELEVISION – ILLUSTRATIVE FORMS:

- Book Rights Agreement
- Writing/Writer-Producer Agreement
- Pilot Director Agreement
- Series Regular Actor Agreement

— CHAPTER 7 —

MUSIC INDUSTRY LAW: A 360° VIEW

Henry Root[*]

7.1. An Introduction to Music Industry Law
7.2. Performance and Touring
7.3. The Personal Appearance Contract
7.4. Recording Agreements

7.1. AN INTRODUCTION TO MUSIC INDUSTRY LAW

It is August of 2017 as I write this Chapter. The transactional basis upon which the material financial terms of music industry contracts (particularly in the recording and music publishing arena) are predicted, the income streams upon which the material financial terms of recording and other music industry agreements are derived and the case law and statutory law affecting the music industry are all in a state of constant flux.

In the recording industry, as revenues from physical disc and download sales continue to decline and revenues from digital performances of sound recordings through streaming services increase, recording agreements more and more resemble "net profits"/"net receipts" deals, where certain costs come "off the top" and the remaining income is shared between the record label and the artist – rather than the long recognized standard methodology of applying a royalty "base rate" against the wholesale or retail price of a record after allowance for artificial deductions from the wholesale or retail price, such as, by way of example, "free goods" allowances and "packaging deductions."

In 2016, SoundExchange (the independent nonprofit collective management organization that collects and distributes digital performance royalties to featured artists who perform on, and to the

---

[*] **Henry Root** is a founding partner of Lapidus, Root, Franklin & Sacharow, LLP. The author wishes to acknowledge and thank Stan Soocher, Esq., Kelly Vallon, Esq., and Leigh Zeichick, Esq. for their contributions to the preparation of this chapter.

copyright holders of, sound recordings)[1] paid out more than a quarter of a billion dollars to record music rights holders – its biggest three-month distribution in two years. According to the US company's latest data, it delivered $263.5 million dollars to labels and artists in the three month period ending September, 2016[,] up 29.2% from the previous year.[2]

And the SoundExchange digital performance revenues derived from non-interactive streaming of sound recordings are only the tip of the iceberg, when compared to revenues derived from interactive performance services such as Pandora and Spotify, along with the Apple and Amazon music streaming services.

Just a short five years ago, who would have predicted the recent surge in vinyl record sales, which by the way, is having the ancillary effect of driving sales of consumer electronics, turntables, amplifiers, speakers and related audio play back equipment. "According to a game-smashing prediction released in the summer of 2017, sales of vinyl records are set to again become a billion dollar industry. Specifically, sales of records themselves will reach the $800-900 million-mark, with turntables and other accessories likely throwing things into 9-figures.... The prediction was outlined in Deloitte's ... 'TMT Predictions' report."[3]

Could this be a return to the era when retail stores stocked and sold 45 rpm singles and top line 33 1/3rd rpm disc albums at a price lower than the cost of purchase by the stores in order to attract consumer foot traffic into the store in order to sell consumer electronics which carry a higher profit margin? And who could have predicted five short years ago that one of the biggest piracy issues to confront the recording industry would have been the distribution of counterfeit CDs through online store purchases through Amazon and its competitors?[4]

In the live concert performance industry, bold efforts were completed to halt or diminish ticket scalping. The ticket resale market

---

[1] SoundExchange administers the statutory license, which allows services to stream artistic content while paying a fixed rate for each play. SoundExchange collects and distributes royalties for the featured artist and the sound recording copyright owner when content is played on a non-interactive digital source. https://www.soundexchange.com/about/general-faq/

[2] http://www.musicbusinessworldwide.com/soundexchange-paid-263-5m-q3-biggest-quarter-two-years/

[3] http://www.digitalmusicnews.com/2017/01/11/vinyl-records-billion-dollar-industry/

[4] http://www.wsj.com/articles/boost-in-online-pirated-cd-sales-deal-another-blow-to-music-industry-1477867243.

is estimated at $5 billion a year in the United States alone.[5] President Obama signed the Better Online Ticket Sales Act of 2016 (the "BOTS Act") into law. "The BOTS Act prohibits circumventing a website's security measures to acquire event tickets. It also restricts the reselling of tickets when the seller knows or should have known they were acquired through circumvention. Importantly, it empowers the Federal Trade Commission and the States to enforce the law, but does not provide a private right of action to consumers."[6] In 2016 as well, New York Governor Andrew Cuomo signed a bill into law criminalizing the use of ticket bots in the city, making it a class A misdemeanor that could result in a fine of up to $1,000 or twice an individual's gain from a crime as well as one year in jail.[7]

In the so-called "Blurred Lines" case, a federal jury in Los Angeles found that Robin Thicke and Pharrell Williams committed copyright infringement, and awarded more than $7.3 million to Mr. Gaye's family in concluding that Robin Thicke and Pharrell Williams copied elements of Gaye's 1977 song "Got to Give It Up" without permission when writing the hit song "Blurred Lines."[8] The holding on that case is now on appeal, and 212 recording artists and songwriters (including members of Train, Linkin Park, Earth, Wind & Fire, The Black Crowes, Fall Out Boy, Tool and Tears for Fears as well as Rivers Cuomo of Weezer, John Oates of Hall & Oates, R. Kelly, Hans Zimmer, Jennifer Hudson, Jean Baptiste, Evan Bogart and Brian Burton (Danger Mouse) have filed an amicus brief with the 9th Circuit Court of Appeals in support of the appeal by Robin Thicke and Pharrell Williams (and rapper T.I. (aka Clifford Harris Jr.)) to overturn the trial court judgment).[9]

In June of 2016, the so-called "Stairway to Heaven" case was decided, with a jury determining that the iconic guitar riff in "Stairway to Heaven" was not copied from Spirit's 1968 instrumental "Taurus."[10]

---

[5] https://www.bloomberg.com/view/articles/2016-12-09/how-to-end-ticket-scalping.

[6] http://www.adlawaccess.com/2016/12/articles/better-online-ticket-sales-act-of-2016/.

[7] http://www.theverge.com/2016/11/28/13770774/new-york-criminalizes-ticket-scalping-bots.

[8] https://www.nytimes.com/2015/03/11/business/media/blurred-lines-infringed-on-marvin-gaye-copyright-jury-rules.html?_r=0.

[9] http://www.hollywoodreporter.com/thr-esq/blurred-lines-appeal-gets-support-924213.

[10] http://www.hollywoodreporter.com/thr-esq/led-zeppelin-wins-stairway-heaven-905866.

In the music publishing industry, the controversy over "100% licensing" a/k/a "fractional licensing" and/or "full works licensing" continues. "The difference between fractionalized licensing and full-works licensing is that in the former case a licensee must obtain a license from each copyright owner of a song – no matter how many authors it may have – in order for the user, say radio, to play that song. The music publishing industry says that fractionalized licensing is the way it has worked for decades. In full-works licensing, a licensee or music user would need a license from only one of the songwriters – and licensees claim that's the way they have been operating too for decades." In 2016 the Department of Justice issued a ruling regarding the anti-trust consent decrees that govern ASCAP and BMI, the two major U.S. performance rights organizations (PROs), interpreting the consent decrees requires ASCAP and BMI to grant public performance licenses covering 100 percent of compositions (so-called "full works licensing").[11] Judge Louis Stanton ruled against the Dept. of Justice's controversial decision.[12] [13]The Department of Justice has appealed Judge Stanton's decision.[14] The ASCAP rate court has yet to rule on the issue.

In the legislation arena, the "Fair Play Fair Pay Act of 2015"[15] was introduced, which, "if passed, would require terrestrial radio stations to join satellite and [I]nternet radio […] in making payments to performers for their broadcast on radio. In addition, the act would also require all forms of radio to pay master recordings royalties on music made prior to 1972, and do away with any grandfathering under the Digital Millennium Copyright Act which allowed certain older digital services to pay discounted rates. (That grandfathering clause is currently the subject of a lawsuit from SoundExchange against Mood Media.)"[16]

---

[11] http://www.billboard.com/articles/business/7573537/doj-appeal-bmi-consent-decree-de http://www.billboard.com/articles/news/7511194/bmi-rate-court-judge-rules-against-dept-of-justices-100-percent-licensingcision-fractional-licensing.

[12] Id.

[13] U.S. v. Broadcast Music Inc., case number 16-3830, in the U.S. Court of Appeals for the Second Circuit.

[14] http://www.billboard.com/articles/business/7573537/doj-appeal-bmi-consent-decree-decision-fractional-licensing.

[15] H. R. 1733, intended to amend title 17, United States Code, to provide fair treatment of radio stations and artists for the use of sound recordings, and for other purposes, introduced 4/13/15; see also http://www.newyorker.com/news/daily-comment/congresss-chance-to-be-fair-to-musicians.

[16] http://www.billboard.com/articles/business/6531693/fair-play-fair-pay-act-performance-royalty-radio.

As of this writing, Donald Trump is halfway through his first year as President of the United States. How will his administration approach copyright law and potential reforms? Core copyright industries contribute approximately $1.2 trillion to the U.S. economy annually, and employ over 5.5 million American workers.[17] "As an entertainment personality, he first became known as an author, writing: *Trump: The Art of the Deal*, first published in 1987. Trump has written other books since, but he became most widely known for his starring role as the host of the reality TV series, *The Apprentice*. Trump recently tweeted that he conceived of the idea of *The Apprentice* with producer Mark Burnett, and he will continue to receive Executive Producer credit on the show even after he is sworn in as President. Trump also owned the Miss Universe beauty pageant from 1996 until 2015. All in all, Trump has over 30 copyrights to his name, not including any owned by his companies."[18]

Long gone are the days when the practice of music law was as simple as "Term, Territory, Advance, Royalty Rates, Marketing Restrictions – let's have lunch." Music law is quite arguably the most complicated area of intellectual property law. To be a competent practitioner, one must stay abreast of not only financial and economic trends, knowledge which is acquired slowly and over time from practice, experience, one-on-one contact with persons of position, influence and power, reading articles, treatises and trade publication voraciously, but also from closely following developments in case and statutory law.

The purpose of this chapter is to provide the practitioner and non-practitioner alike a useful resource to reference when confronted by an issue in a music area with which they may not be familiar. This introduction will at the same time serve as an admonition that established patterns of practice in the music law arena are constantly subject to supplementation and change.

7.2. PERFORMANCE AND TOURING

To understand the performance aspect of the music industry one must first appreciate the diversity of music performances – from performances of the Metropolitan Opera, the Cleveland Orchestra, or

---

[17] http://www.ipwatchdog.com/2016/12/18/trump-administration-copyright-law-copyright-reforms/id=75793/ (last visited 01/17/17).
[18] *Id.*

the San Francisco Ballet Company to those of Bruce Springsteen, U2, and Celine Dion; from the small nonprofit programs affiliated with schools or other institutions, to the spectacularly profit-oriented productions of superstars, whether country, classical, rock, hip-hop or pop, in supersized arenas and stadiums.

Although orchestral performance has its place in the music market, a specific analysis of opera, musical theater or ballet would exceed the limited scope of this chapter. Nonetheless, the legal and practical aspects of managing a symphony orchestra, although specialized, are generally similar to management practices in other areas previously discussed, such as opera and ballet, which follow the practices of the theater industry.[19]

Instead, this section focuses on concert promotion and the concert artist. In this area we need not distinguish between the classical and contemporary music scenes because they become ever more similar. How can one distinguish the reception and activities of a Placido Domingo or a Yo-Yo Ma from those of a Paul McCartney or a Bruce Springsteen when their performances move from concert halls to arenas or even stadium venues? Moreover, although the specifics of a recording studio musician's career differ from those of an orchestral musician's or a soloist's career, most attempt to model their careers on that of the concert performer (in terms of both live and recorded performances).

7.2.1. The Concert Performer as a Business

The first, and perhaps one of the most difficult, concepts for performers of commercial music to accept is that they are not only involved in an industry (as opposed to an art), but that they in themselves may also be required to function as a business within that industry. They differ from performers in other fields of entertainment in that they often collaborate in their enterprises (such as in performing groups) and often themselves produce the programs that promoters book (and frequently as we will discuss later in this chapter, the recordings that contained their songs and performances). They function through true business entities as opposed to being employees of a producer or promoter. They possess assets (such as valuable names/trademarks/service marks, very expensive musical equipment, and often copyrights), employ numerous individuals (such as agents,

---

[19] See infra Chapter 9.

managers, supporting musicians and tour personnel), and (if all goes well) earn substantial income.

By accepting the premise of performers as business entities, it is easier to identify areas of legal concern with respect to the organization of an artist's career.

7.2.1.1 Names and Trademarks

The professional name that an artist elects to use has great economic potential. When the name is simply the given name of the individual, its protection may principally arise under the laws of publicity/privacy[20] and unfair competition.[21] A person is, as a rule, entitled to the use of his or her name.[22] Therefore, the use of that name will not automatically require an analysis of additional forms of protection, but undertaking a trademark search to identify any potential conflicts would be prudent. It is possible, if in fact advisable, for an individual who records, performs and/or exploits merchandise using his/her own name to secure trademark and service mark protection for their name. The adoption of a fictitious name by an individual or group should in all cases be reviewed by counsel to ensure that it poses no potential conflict with similar names and to facilitate the registration of the name as a trademark and/or service mark[23] for activities in the music and/or other industries.[24]

---

[20] See Chapter 4 on this topic in Volume II of this series.

[21] See Chapter 3 on this topic in Volume II of this series.

[22] Although that may require clarification as to an existing user's contractually permitted exploitation of the name. See, e.g., Warren *Miller Entertainment Inc. (WME) v. Level 1 Productions Inc.*, 09-02254 (D.Colo. 2009), which involved an exclusive license snowboard and ski filmmaker Warren Miller gave to a production company, in perpetuity, in all media, to the name, the personal endorsement, use of voice, and the likeness of Warren Miller, only when used with its existing business, and the fruits of its related efforts." The agreement further stated: "The intention of this Agreement is also to clarify and agree that Warren A. Miller is free to use his own name however he desires so long as he does not infringe upon the exclusive rights [herein]."

[23] A service mark (or service mark) is a word, phrase, symbol or logo that is used to brand, identify, and distinguish a service, such as the entertainment services of an individual or group as, e.g., a performing artist. This is in contrast to a trademark, which is a word, phrase, symbol or logo that is used to brand, identify, and distinguish a product, such as records and merchandising items that bear the name of the individual or group. See https://secureyourtrademark.com/blog/trademark-or-service-mark-whats-the-difference (last visited September 15, 2016)

[24] See Chapter 3 on this topic in Volume II of this series.

A group name and related trademarks and service marks also become an asset of the group and have commercial value.[25] The value of the name can survive the replacement of some or even all of its original members,[26] but without an agreement governing disposition of the name following the withdrawal of one or more members,[27] the value of the name may be destroyed[28] or the departing[29] or remaining members may be precluded from using it.[30] The failure to adequately address the "how and when" members and former members of a group have the right to use the group name, trademark and service mark and the terms upon which such use during and after a member's association with the group in connection with the group's partnership (or other governing) agreement, as more specifically discussed in 7.2.1.2 below, can lead to extensive, expensive and contentious litigation.[31] Witness for example, the litigation commenced by the surviving members of Lynyrd Skynrd against the group's former drummer, Artimus Pyle, and Cleopatra Records, to halt the production of a motion picture by Cleopatra Records portraying the 1977 airplane crash in which Ronnie Van Zant, the group's original lead singer perished, claiming that such a production by Artimus Pyle and Cleopatra Records violated a 1988 consent order governing the use of the band's name.[32] Moreover, the name itself can be created or acquired by a non-performer, such as a manager, and controlled irrespective of the subsequent role played by the performers who worked under that name and established its recognition value.[33]

---

[25] *Id. See also* Five Platters, Inc. v. Purdie, 419 F. Supp. 372 (D. Md. 1976).
[26] *Id.*
[27] Such agreements being held effective in Gutkowski v. Jackell, N.Y.L.J., Nov. 25, 1968, at 16, col. 4.
[28] *See* Fuqua v. Watson, 107 U.S.P.Q. 251, 1955 WL6611 (N.Y. Sup.Ct. Nov. 10, 1955).
[29] *See* Marshak v. Green, 505 F. Supp. 1054 (S.D.N.Y. 1981).
[30] *See* Noone v. Banner Talent Assocs. Inc., 398 F. Supp. 260 (S.D.N.Y. 1975).
[31] See for example, Rare Earth, (Rare Earth, Inc. v. Hoorelbeke, 401 F. Supp. 26 (S.D.N.Y. 1975)); The Drifters, (Marshak v. Sheppard, 666 E Supp. 590 (S.D.N.Y. 1987)); Lynyrd Skynyrd, (Grondin v. Rossington, 690 F. Supp. 200 (S.D.N.Y. 1988)); The Beach Boys, (Brother Records, Inc. v. Jardine, 432 F.3d 939 (9th Cir. 2005)); and The Doors, (Densmore v. Manzarek, 2008 WL 2209993 (Cal. App. 2008)).
[32] Ronnie Van Zant Inc. et al v. Pyle et al, U.S. District Court, Southern District of New York, No. 17-03360. See also http://www.reuters.com/article/us-music-lynyrdskynyrd-lawsuit-idUSKBN19A2L9.
[33] *See* Marshak v. Treadwell, 240 F.3d 184 (3d Cir. 2001).

This latter result seems to violate the normal trademark rationale that trademark law is designed to protect consumers by facilitating the identification of the source of goods and services. Because music fans are primarily concerned with the artists who make up that group and they undoubtedly identify those individuals (or at least the featured performers) as the source of the music that they like, it appears anomalous to assert that the name of that group can be owned by a non-performer (or an entity providing the services of those identifiable individuals making up the group). In what sense is it misleading for members of the original group "The Drifters" who recorded the group's best known works to bill themselves as "The Drifters" or the "Original Drifters"? Nonetheless, because they do not own the name, they can be precluded from its use.[34] In response, *Truth in Music Advertising* laws that have now been passed, in one form or another, in a number of states,[35] may preclude some so-called "tribute" acts from too closely emulating the names and logos of the bands they imitate in their performances on the basis of "misleading advertising," but such statutes may not provide protection where one or more original group members are involved in such performances and/or the tribute act or its presenter is the current trademark proprietor.

7.2.1.2. Selection of the Business Form

Because the decision whether to operate as a proprietorship or corporation is based on financial and tax-planning considerations, it should be made in consultation with a qualified accountant or tax advisor.

Where the performer consists of a group of individuals, there should be an agreement among the members setting forth the key aspects of ownership and operation. Whether this takes the form of a partnership agreement, a corporate shareholders (S-corporation) agreement, or a limited liability company (LLC) membership operating agreement, the existence of such an agreement is vital to the preservation of group assets (such as the name)[36] or the ability of the group to continue in the event of the death, disability, or withdrawal of one or more of its

---

[34] *Id.*

[35] Such laws have been passed in 34 states, including CA, CT, CO, DE, FL, IL, IN, KS, MA, MD, MI, MO, ME, MN, NJ, ND, NV, NH, NY, NC, OK, OH, OR, PA, RI, SC, TN, TX, UT, VA, VE, WA, and WI, and bills are pending in several other states as of the publication of this edition.

[36] *See supra* §7.2.1.1.

members. Moreover, the drafting of such an agreement provides an ideal opportunity for members of the group to review formally their method of operations, which often evolves casually but that may eventually prove inadequate to meet the demands of growth and commercial success.[37] Such an agreement may not guarantee complete harmony or success, but having the group members calmly discuss many of these issues before they arise often effectively counters the stresses and demands the agreement is drawn to address. In this way, it is possible to avoid conflicts brought on by momentary business or personal crises (which may ironically include coping with certain aspects of success) that might otherwise disrupt the group. It is not unusual for performers to have multiple business entities, such as, by way of example, one corporation to lend the performer's personal services as musicians and entertainers in connection with tours and other personal appearances, another to furnish the performer's recording services, another to operate tours or merchandise licensing and sales, and still another to hold title to the performer's copyrighted musical compositions. There is no "one size fits all" and each situation must be considered on its own merits in consultation with the performer's corporate and tax advisors. [38]

7.2.2. Repertoire

What comprises a performer's repertoire will depend on whether he or she is a writer/performer who performs only or mostly his or her own work or uses material written by others. For the writers/performers who record and perform their own works exclusively, there are few legal or business problems that exist outside of those to which they directly obligate themselves (e.g., the engagement of an arranger to arrange a musical composition created by the performer).

Performers who record and/or perform the works of others face a number of different challenges relating to what they are going to perform on stage and on recordings. First is the determination of what to perform. The selection of repertoire is usually done in consultation with the personal manager and/or an A&R (artist and repertory) executive at the record company to which that performer may be

---

[37] *See* form Band Partnership Agreement Checklist provided among this chapter's online supplemental forms.

[38] *See* Form of Entity Schedule from "Music Law for the General Practitioner" by Thomas R. Leavens, provided among this chapter's online supplemental forms.

contracted. In many cases, the repertoire to be recorded is to be selected by mutual agreement with the record company, but invariably the record company has the final say in that it may choose not to release a record it does not like. A successful performer, his or her manager, as well as the record company's A&R person are deluged with suggested material for the performer to record by music publishers and by both new and successful songwriters. Where the performer is also a lyric writer or composer, it is recommended that the performer and his/her personal representatives avoid involvement in the review or acceptance of unsolicited material unless accompanied by a signed legal release from the submitting party insulating the artist from the risk of frivolous infringement claims.

Once the material owned by others is chosen, the right to use the material must be obtained along with the assurance that it can be adapted to suit the style or needs of the performer. If the chosen work is in the public domain, of course, there are no restrictions on its use. If a musical composition is to be performed before live audiences, the right to perform the music live is available through ASCAP, BMI, SESAC, or Global Rights Management ("GMR") in the United States and affiliated societies abroad (the license for which is generally issued to the establishment where the performance will take place or by the promoter of the personal appearance with the validity of the license ideally subject to a requirement in the performer's personal appearance contract). The right to record the composition is available from the copyright proprietor directly in the instance of its first commercial recording, and if the composition has previously been recorded and released, then through a statutory license under the copyright law, or directly from the copyright proprietor if a license fee less than the statutory rate is to be sought.[39]

Many music publishers and other copyright proprietors choose to affiliate with and use the services and resources of the Harry Fox Agency, which was established in 1927 by the National Music Publishers' Association (NMPA) as an agency to license, collect, and distribute royalties on behalf of musical copyright owners and which provides rights management, licensing, and royalty services for its affiliates.[40] HFA issues mechanical licenses for products manufactured and distributed in the United States. A mechanical license grants the rights to reproduce and distribute copyrighted musical compositions

---

[39] 17 U.S.C. §115 (2012).
[40] https://www.harryfox.com/publishers/what_does_hfa_do.html.

(songs) for use on CDs, records, tapes, ringtones, permanent digital downloads, interactive streams and other digital formats supporting various business models, including locker-based music services and bundled music offerings.

The right to adapt (i.e., *arrange*) the music to suit the performer's style is somewhat problematic. First, absent the express consent of the owner authorizing such adaptation (and assuming that the arrangement would satisfy the originality requirement of copyrightability)[41] the adaptation itself would not be copyrightable.[42] Moreover, although the compulsory license provision of the copyright act "includes the privilege of making a musical arrangement of the work to the extent necessary to conform it to the style or manner of interpretation of the performance involved,"[43] no such privilege is granted by law to make arrangements for public performances of arrangements. Moreover, where the BMI agreement with its members authorizes BMI to grant arrangement rights,[44] the ASCAP agreement does not.[45] It is, nonetheless, the custom of the popular music industry to make such arrangements.

As previously noted, although the small performing rights with respect to a composition never before recorded are available through ASCAP[46] and BMI,[47] there is no compulsory license provision under U.S. Copyright law allowing the performer to record it.[48] Such permission may be acquired only from the copyright owner.

7.2.3. Touring

Touring is generally essential for all performers to develop their craft and to grow and sustain their audiences, but it is not itself

---

[41] *See* The Essential Guide to Entertainment Law: Intellectual Property (Vol. II of this Series) §1.2.2.

[42] *See* 17 U.S.C. §§103, 115 (2012).

[43] 17 U.S.C. §115(a) (2) (2012) (codifying prior judicial interpretations of the compulsory license provisions of the 1909 Act §1(e). TeeVee Toons, Inc. v. DM Records, Inc., 05 Civ. 5602 (S.D.N.Y. 2007). (The U.S. District Court for the Southern District of New York ruled that a genuine issue of material fact existed as to whether a record-distribution agreement included the right to make derivative works from the underlying compositions.)

[44] BMI Affiliation Agreement ¶ Third C.

[45] *See* ASCAP Membership Agreement.

[46] ASCAP Membership Agreement VI.

[47] BMI Affiliation Agreement ¶ Second.

[48] §115 applies only *after* phonorecords of the nondramatic musical work have been distributed to the public with the consent of the owner.

necessarily profitable. Nonetheless, for superstars and successful (whether by creative and/or business standards) solo or small-ensemble performers, touring can be highly lucrative.[49] Touring can be particularly remunerative for so-called legacy artists, whose royalty income from record sales and song writing activities likely have declined over the years since the height of their recording careers. For example, Guns N' Roses are reported to have grossed $116.8 million during the North American leg of its June 23 – August 22, 2016 North American "Not in This Lifetime..." tour, which was attended by more than one million fans at 25 performances.[50]

Pollstar, a service that monitors live performance/touring statistics, reports that live concert ticket sales for the 100 biggest tours of 2015 generated over $4.7 billion in revenues, a figure up approximately eleven percent from the prior year.[51] Ticket prices in 2015 decreased by 4 percent from the previous year; however the total number of tickets sold increased by 16 percent.[52]

For middle-level performers, such as those whose popularity crested a decade or two ago and who are now touring middle-size theatres and casino-venues, touring may nonetheless not only be profitable but may be their principal source of income as income from record sales decline. But for almost all new performers – and for many star performers who carry very large productions of sound, lights, and personnel – touring may at best be a breakeven proposition and at worst generate losses.

One of the principal reasons for touring, for all but the middle category of performers, is that the tour helps promote record and merchandising sales and builds the stature of the performer. For this reason, most "non-legacy" performers will schedule tours to coincide with the launch of a new record album release.

---

[49] In 2015, the top 20 touring acts accounted for over $1.5 billion in revenue, with the top two acts accounting for over $200 million each (Taylor Swift – $217.4 million; One Direction – $208 million), and three more with over $100 each (U2 – $133.6 million; The Rolling Stones – $131.5 million; Kenny Chesney – $114 million). *See* Hugh McIntyre, *The Highest-Grossing Tours of 2015*, FORBES (Jan. 12, 2016, 8:40 AM), http://www.forbes.com/sites/hughmcintyre/2016/01/12/these-were-the-highest-grossing-tours-of-2015/#3132e4b7e0e5.

[50] http://www.billboard.com/articles/columns/chart-beat/7503431/guns-n-roses-tour-117-million-bruce-

[51] POLLSTAR, 2015 POLLSTAR YEAR END BUSINESS ANALYSIS (2016), http://www.pollstarpro.com/files/charts2015/2015YearEndBusinessAnalysis.pdf.

[52] *See id.*

Record companies in the 1960s and early 1970s helped underwrite the costs of tours by their artists, but following the recession in the 1970s, again during the label retrenchment of the 1990s, and again since the tightening economic conditions besetting the industry in 2008 to 2009, this practice has diminished considerably. In the wake of further record industry restructuring in response to declining sales of recorded music in the past decade, many labels have begun to demand a participation in some or all of artist concert touring, merchandising endorsement, publishing and other entertainment-related income streams as part of so-called "360 Deals" (so-called, because the label seeks participation in the full "360 degrees" of artist commercial activities) or "Multiple Rights Deals" to help offset the risks of investment in record production and release. The major record labels[53] (which represent the majority of the music sold, making up as much as 80 percent of the music market or more depending on the year [54]) take the position that their marketing and release of an artist's recordings are a primary engine for the artist's success in and throughout all fields of the artist's entertainment endeavours, including the artist's touring "fortunes" and, as such, the label should also participate directly as a partner/investor – particularly in a period in which touring and associated merchandising rights may eclipse income generated from record sales. Where record labels, major and independent alike, may have once viewed tour support as an unavoidable if not indispensable marketing cost of record sales, now the recording and its promotion are understood to be marketing vehicles for all artist entertainment industry related revenues from which the labels uniformly seek a participation, and, depending on the status and leverage of the artist, the labels may be willing to increase their support (financial and otherwise) for artists who agree to grant the label an economic participation in most, if not all, fields of the artist's entertainment career, including tour income.

Other than for superstar tours, the reduction in tour support resulted in a downsizing of shows (i.e., reducing the technical equipment, number of personnel, and other "perks" on the road) and

---

[53] Major labels since 2012 (Big Three) include Universal Music Group (with most of EMI's recorded music division absorbed into UMG), Sony Music Entertainment (EMI Music Publishing absorbed into Sony/ATV Music Publishing), and Warner Music Group (EMI's Parlophone and EMI/Virgin Classics labels absorbed into WMG on 1 July 2013)[12] *https://en.wikipedia.org/wiki/Record_label.*

[54] https://www.thebalance.com/big-three-record-labels-2460743.

required performers to appear in smaller venues with lower costs and less risks in the event that they did not sell out. However, recognizing the promotional value of touring, performers sought other ways to finance tours.

Star performers may enter into a comprehensive tour agreement with a national promoter or even international promoter (e.g., Live Nation or AEG) that guarantees a minimum fee against a percentage of ticket sales and merchandising grosses, and, in turn, assumes all other production and venue arrangements, which likely will include the right to solicit tour sponsorship. Rights typically granted in such comprehensive tour agreements might include not only the right to solicit tour sponsorship (with the artist generally having the right to reasonably approve the identity of the sponsor, the right to preclude potential tour sponsors whose goods or service would conflict or compete with those of already existing artist sponsors or those who are inconsistent with the artist's "identity," and any sponsor benefits or "deliverables" requested by a tour sponsor that require active participation by the artist, such as "meet and greets," concert streaming, etc.). They may also include the right to promote and present all live performances by the artist, the right to control the sales and allocation of all ticket inventories through all sales and distribution channels, the right to implement revenue maximizing services including but not limited to "first class" seating, VIP packages, and the right to book private personal appearances (which are not advertised and for which tickets are not sold to the general public).

The insurance provisions of touring agreements are also the subject of extensive negotiation. Whether the artist is a "baby band" just undertaking a touring career or an international superstar, obtaining, at a minimum, general liability insurance and, at higher levels, non-appearance and tour cancellation insurance are critical considerations for the performer. Commonly tour agreements provide that if any concert is cancelled by reason of a force majeure event, the artist and promoter will use their commercially reasonable efforts to reschedule such concert to a mutually approved date or replace such concert with a mutually approved substitute, contiguous to the current itinerary for the tour. Beyond that, if any cancelled concert cannot be rescheduled or replaced, then the promoter will generally not be required to make the per show guarantee payment for that concert (which should be covered by the artist's tour cancellation insurance). However, if any concert cancellation is due solely to the fault of the artist, then the artist is liable to the promoter for all direct, out of pocket, verified expenses directly related to the applicable cancelled concert (with the promoter generally required to use its commercially reasonable efforts to mitigate the resulting costs promptly after any such cancellation).

While star performers may arrange commercial sponsorships, new performers are often left to find an "angel" or to self-finance their tours. With respect to such sponsorship, whether for an arena act or a new band touring small clubs, a corporate sponsor provides money to mount and finance the tour in exchange for the right to have its corporate logo or logo for its product(s) included in the advertising or promotion of all of the tour dates, or perhaps to use the artist's music, name, trademarks, service marks and likeness in its independent advertising and promotion. Beyond this, the sponsor may agree to pay for advertisements, agree to purchase a guaranteed number of tickets at each venue, agree to pay a promotional fee in addition to costs, the sponsor may also elect to enter into a separate advertising agreement with the performer in which the performer may appear as a spokesperson for the company (or at least permit use of the artist's approved name, approved likeness(es) and perhaps music) in a commercial print, television and/or radio advertising campaign that coincides with the tour. In all aspects of the artist's career, it is important for the artist to control they manner in which the artist is portrayed and the artist ordinarily will have the right to approve before use all of the "Artist's Identifications" to be used by the tour promoter and any sponsors, including artist's personal and professional names, any nickname, likeness (including caricatures), photographs, video/film footage, voice, twitter feed, facsimile signature, trademarks, service marks, biographical information, artwork, designs, logos, graphics, and the like and any reproduction or simulation of the foregoing.

Typical sponsorship arrangements made by managers, agents, or intermediary companies will involve rights to merchandising, including T-shirts, sweatshirts, and other memorabilia imprinted with the name of the artists and the sponsor, coinciding with the tour or for a separate term, with the costs and proceeds divided in a manner reflecting the strengths of the negotiating parties. Where the artist is recording pursuant to a 360 Deal, the label may be participating actively in one or more of the merchandising or promotional capacities, and will in any case likely share passively in the pool of sponsorship and merchandising revenues.

In negotiating the concert tour agreement with the tour promoter, the artist must also arrive at terms to set aside and make available a sufficient number of preferred seats for members of the artist's fan club and other VIP ticket sales endeavours, which topic is addressed more fully in section 7.3.4.5 below.

7.3. THE PERSONAL APPEARANCE CONTRACT

In negotiating a personal appearance contract, one must bear in mind the nature of the enterprise. First, it involves the services of a person or group who must be concerned with the conditions under which he or she (or they will be performing. Performers often create and design their own productions, and may insist upon approval over technical elements and working conditions that surround their performance, as well as the right to control all creative aspects of their performance, such as choice and order of material to be performed, and the identity of the opening artist(s) who appear before the "headliner's" performance.

Technical details are normally addressed in an artist's rider[55] attached to a standard performance contract (with the key business terms of the engagement, including identity of the promoter, venue, date, length of performance and fees, appearing in the principal section of the agreement, sometimes referred to as the "face page").[56]

7.3.1. Conditions of Performance

Much of a performer's career – and, indeed, their life – is given to touring. For weeks at a time the performer literally lives out of a suitcase, travels in commercial airplanes or tour buses for a van, and occupies myriad dressing rooms, hotel rooms (or, depending on the artist's stature, friends' couches) of varying degrees of comfort and cleanliness.

Recognizing the chaos of the touring life, performers try to control some of their working conditions. In some areas of entertainment, unions may prescribe minimum conditions; in others they are a negotiable part of the employment agreement. Such control is needed

---

[55] *See* sample form Booking Agreement and Rider included with this chapter's form materials.

[56] See sample form Personal Appearance Agreement included in this chapter's forms.

so that performances will not be impaired. Although provisions in a performance agreement prescribing personal living conditions might seem trivial (and are not without abuse, as with contract rider instructions about the stocking of liquor cabinets or the acceptable colors of candies to be provided in a dressing room), they may also be genuinely material to the well-being of the performing artist who can spend a good part of their working life on the road, and whose comfort can have a direct effect on the calibre of their performance day in and "night" out. Of particular importance to the performer's tour personnel is the "tour manager" or "road manager", whose duties include undertaking the "show advance" with the prompter's (or venue's) production manager in order to ascertain that all technical and living requirements of the performance agreement and technical rider will be available or, if adjustments are necessitated, agree upon what accommodations can be substituted. It is common for larger tours to have a "road manager" whose principal job is to ensure the comfort of the performer(s) (who may travel separately from the road crew), including making certain that the performer arrive on time for any press and promotional activities, rehearsals and the show as well as a tour manager to whom the other members of the tour staff report. Some common areas of concern follow.[57]

7.3.1.1 Hotel

Most promoters establish relationships with local hotels or chains that allow them to book rooms at substantially reduced rates and with preferential service. Most performers do not know the availability, price, or quality of the local hotel market. Rather than waste time and effort investigating it, they require that they be supplied with a sufficient number of first-class rooms to house themselves and the touring staff. If the performer has played in a particular venue before, they may specify which hotels are acceptable. On larger tours the performers will frequently stay at a different, higher class of service hotel than the tour staff.

---

[57] David Lee Roth, CRAZY FROM THE HEART (Hyperion, 1997) pp. 97-98, in which Roth describes the colored candy requirements not as a symbol of band excess, but as a canary in a coal mine indicator of whether the promoters were paying attention to contract riders, which also contained myriad technical terms which could affect band member as well as audience safety, etc.

7.3.1.2. Ground Transportation

Artists who tour by commercial aviation generally require that the promoter provide a car, cargo van (for bags and personal equipment) and drivers to and from the airport, the hotel, the venue, any press appearances, or even round the clock. This is not luxury. A performer generally works on a tight schedule that includes technical rehearsals at the venue, resting before performances, and fulfilling public relations obligations.

7.3.1.3. Security

All well-known performers must be concerned with security. For some, this may mean limiting the number of visitors backstage who might interrupt the performer's preparations for performance or physical recovery or preparation for departure after performance. But there is also concern about the security of the expensive lighting and sound equipment carried on tour (and safety of performers, crew and "civilians" near such equipment). For superstars, full-time security patrols and guards may reasonably be required to protect the artist from their frenzied fans and paparazzi. On larger tours, the performer's own security travels with the performer and supplement security is provided by the local promoter at the venue. In general, the performer will have control over who has what level of access to the stage and backstage areas (including dressing rooms) and issues its own access credentials and/or approves those to be issued by the venue and local promoter.

7.3.1.4. Dressing Room

The size and amenities provided in the dressing room are important to a performer. A dressing room is generally more than a room in which to change clothes and get "made-up" before and after a performance. In some locales, distance from hotel to performance venue may mean the artist can spend hours in a dressing room between sound check and performance. Accommodations for press interviews, entertaining local VIP guests or even a massage or nap can be important. The artist may reasonably seek assurance that the size, location, and amenities of the rooms should, if possible, fulfill these needs.

7.3.1.5. Food

In order to check sound equipment at the concert venue, performers arrive several hours before the performance and stay several hours after the concert signing autographs for fans or greeting friends who attended the performance. Their technical and support staff often arrives earlier and stays later than the performer. Therefore, having food supplied by the promoter for both the performer and his/her crew at a venue is standard. Moreover, to ensure the quality and quantity of the food supplied, many touring artists provide menus specifying the type of food and drinks they are to be served (requirements that may address legitimate health or performance issues, such as a guitarist's understandable aversion to greasy finger food immediately before hitting the stage).

7.3.2. Technical Conditions

Details of physical production are identified in a technical rider attached to the principle performance agreement or "face page".[58] Physical production elements vary, as does the determination of who supplies them. For example, a concert pianist normally does not transport an acoustic grand piano from city to city. Because the feel or action of pianos varies from brand to brand, the pianist may specify that the promoter supply a particular type and brand of piano (i.e., a Steinway) and identify the standard to which that piano must be tuned (i.e., "440 = A/tune to perfect fourths").

On the other hand, many rock groups tour with enormous productions, including sound and lights carried in one or more tractor-trailer trucks. The technical rider for such a touring entity identifies the following kinds of elements.[59]

7.3.2.1. Stage Crew

The technical rider identifies the number of individuals needed to load and unload, hang, operate, and strike the production according to

---

[58] Note that most performance personal appearance contracts are standardized, union-drafted agreements issued by agents.

[59] Presented here are the characteristic provisions of an *artist's technical rider*. It should be noted that many venues issue their own technical riders as to what equipment and/or production elements they will provide.

function (so that if the venue is unionized the appropriate categories of workers are called) and duration of call (i.e., how long each function takes to finish). Unions, such as IATSE (the International Alliance of Theatrical Stage Employees), often provide minimum staffing requirements (commonly identified as being submitted on the card or yellow card calls) for certain types or sizes of shows that may exceed those required by the performer.

7.3.2.2. Stage Requirement

Particularly massive productions, such as those designed for arenas or stadiums, may require the construction and installation of special stage platforms, sound reinforcement and lighting arrays. Here, the rider specifies size, load tolerance, and layout with respect to the equipment to be set up.

7.3.2.3. Electricity

Rock bands that tour with enormous amounts of electrical sound equipment, lights, and lasers require that a venue supply sufficient electrical capacity. The technical rider identifies the number and location of circuits to be supplied along with their required amperage.

7.3.2.4. Equipment

The rider specifies the equipment to be supplied by the promoter, such as a tuned piano, locally obtainable lighting equipment, loading equipment, etc. In many cases, established touring musical acts may travel with personal musical instruments, but require the local promoter to secure and provide amplifiers, microphones, stage monitors, PA systems and stage lighting to the band's reasonable specifications (so-called "backline rentals"), and most major markets have professional sound companies in the business of catering to these requirements.

7.3.2.5. Performance Personnel

The rider may also require additional performance personnel to be supplied by the promoter. This may include locally contracted supporting musicians for a backup ensemble or orchestra who will be expected to have rehearsed the headlining artist's charts/arrangements prior to scheduled performance, supplemented by only a brief rehearsal with the headline performer(s) prior to show time.

7.3.2.6. Safety Requirements

A component of a production that is considered routine in many venues may represent significant safety hazards in others. The use of pyrotechnics, increasingly common in rock concerts, sporting events, and other situations, presents the most obvious safety hazard – as evidenced by two 2003 tragedies, one in a Rhode Island nightclub where ninety-seven people died as a result of fireworks misused in a rock band's stage performance, and another that occurred only a week later in which twenty-one people died trying to escape a fire in a Chicago nightclub. Moreover, the use of hazardous elements (such as pyrotechnics) may require special licensing. The presence of wild animals, laser lighting effects or rigging to "fly" performers on or off stage might also be at issue. In such situations, the performance rider should identify the hazardous performance element and require that the promoter provide a facility that is safe for such use (or conversely that the artist will agree to exclude the feature from a scheduled performance).

7.3.2.7. Venue Licensing

It is commonly assumed that a performance venue will be comply with all applicable ordinances and maintain all necessary licenses for public performances, whether on the basis of physical code and public safety requirements contemplated in the preceding section, public health code requirements, or other business licensing requirements relating to noise, alcoholic beverage sales, and music public performance licenses through ASCAP, BMI, SESAC, and GMR (collectively known as Performing Rights Organizations or "PRO"s). However, the fact is that the venue itself may or may not be properly licensed. For example, nightclubs and similar venues are more likely than not to have annual "blanket" performance license agreements with the PRO's. But larger venues that are leased to promoters for the purpose of presentations of concerts typically impose the obligation to secure the necessary public performance licenses on the promoter under the terms of the venue lease for the show(s) concerned. Because the performers could be held responsible for failure to obtain such a safety related license or the performance date could be threatened by a promoter's failure to obtain these or other licenses, the rider should require that the promoter obtain and provide for advance review copies of all necessary licenses, including the public performance licenses.

7.3.3. Presentation Conditions

Performers are concerned with the manner in which they are presented to the public. Their reputations and public personas are valuable assets that may garner intangible rewards, such as critical or public attention, or tangible rewards such as endorsement contracts or employment in other media. Performers' agreements with the promoters typically provide for the performer to retain 100 percent creative control over all aspects of the artist's performance, such as selection and order of material to be performance, manner of presentation of the performances, staging, lighting and sound design and the like. The ways in which promoters promote their concerts affect this potential and accordingly performers exercise control over certain aspects of the marketing, advertising, and promotion of their concerts in order to protect the performer's brand and maximize its goodwill value.

Therefore, performers specify (often in the form of a credit or billing rider) how they (individually or as a band) are to be credited, including location, size, and prominence of the credit line and in what media the credit is to appear (i.e., billboards, posters, print, radio, television and online advertising and publicity, etc.). The performer may supply photographs, logos, or likenesses that may be used for promotion and may require approval of material to be created by the promoter.[60] The performer also may supply television or radio commercials and may insist that they be used in an advertising plan approved by them.

The performer may specify certain conditions regarding public relations activities in which he or she will participate. For example, the performer may agree to personal interviews on local television or radio but not for local newspapers (or vice versa), or to appear at a local event for one charity but not another.

Finally, the performer may choose to bring along an "opening act" or have one supplied by the promoter. Some may alternatively identify the opening act to be supplied, or reserve approval over one to be furnished by the local promoter.

---

[60] *See supra* §7.2.3 for discussion of further Artist approval rights in these contexts.

7.3.4. Compensation Derived from Performances

In addition to revenues from recording (and in the case of singer/songwriters, from music publishing), artists rely on four principal sources of income relating to their appearances: performance fees (single booking and touring), underwriting fees (tour sponsorship), ancillary market income, and merchandising income.

7.3.4.1. Performance Fees

The performance fee is what the promoter or other tour underwriter pays the artist for each performance, with provision for added fees for each additional performance. Fees may be set as a flat sum, as a guarantee against a share of the gross receipts, or as a fixed amount with a share of gross receipts over break-even costs (i.e., the cost of presenting the concert, including any fix advance paid the artist).

On execution of the agreement, the promoter is generally required to pay a deposit of 50 percent of the fee with the balance to be paid on the artist's appearance at the venue immediately before the performance, with any overage (i.e., a share of the gross ticket sales in excess of the guarantee) paid by the end of the performance and accompanied by a box office statement. If the performance is to be presented outside the United States, or the promoter is not one with a pre-existing known and positive reputation in the industry in general, and if the performance is a "private engagement" not publicized to the general public, 100 percent of the fee will be payable in advance. These deposits are typically paid to the performer's booking agent, which will retain the deposits in an escrow account until the performance has been completed.

Where the promoter is a national promoter e.g.,, Live Nation or AEG) who has secured the exclusive right to present an entire tour comprised of a series of consecutive engagements, a negotiated portion of 80 – 90 percent of the overall tour guarantee will be paid on signing of the tour agreement, and the balance paid out as earned per show (less all applicable withholding tax, night of show cash draws, any other agreed upon deductions, and a reserve to be liquidated in the tour settlement statement). The successful artist appearing in larger venues will generally have a designated representative (tour manager or tour accountant) involved in reconciling attendance, ticket sales and artist fees with the promoter at the conclusion of each night's performance.

Under a traditional national (or international) tour structure: (a) The promoter is contracting for a specific number of performances over a specific period in markets and venues consistent with a mutually agreed set of criteria, etc., which performances collectively constitute the "tour"; (b) The promoter pays the artist (or the artist's touring company) the following: (i) one or more loans prior to the first show of the tour (in large part to cover start-up production costs in launching the tour), which are then recouped out of some portion of the per show guarantee (for example, 50 percent or less of the loan(s) get repaid to promoter out of each per show guarantee, such that the loans are paid in full once the artist has played all of the shows on the tour); (ii) a per show guarantee, which is commonly an equal amount for each show (provided, however, a per show guarantee may be increased for a stadium show if the tour is primarily booked in arena –sized venues, or conversely reduced for a theater or club show), with the aggregate of all of the per show guarantees is the "Guarantee."; and (iii) A percentage of "Net Pot Revenue"(i.e., the net profits constituting tour revenue less show costs, with the artist bearing production costs) to the extent this amount is in excess of the Guarantee.[61] Commonly Net Pot Revenues are allocated 90 percent to the artist and 10 percent to the promoter and once the Guarantee has been recouped (i.e., the Net Pot Revenues have reached the Guarantee divided by the artist's percentage of Net Pot Revenue (commonly referred to as "breakeven" or the "split point"), then the artist's share of additional Net Pot Revenue escalates to 95 percent. In negotiating these provisions, especially in the case of the "new and developing artists", note that most opening acts do not make enough to cover their production costs; they tour as an opening act for the promotional value of such appearances, and care must be taken in budgeting where a portion of the fee being paid to the artist will go to repaying loans made for start-up production costs.[62]

7.3.4.2. Sponsorship and Underwriting Fees (Tour Support)

Additional underwriting fees are received by the performer to pay for the costs of touring. One form of underwriting fee may be exacted

---

[61] Note, it remains to be seen how quickly the phrase "Net Pot Revenues" will be replaced by "Net Proceeds" or some other term in contracts in the increasing number of states which are licensing marijuana sales and consumption.

[62] The author thanks Marion Gonzalez, Esq. for his insights on Tour Agreements.

from the promoter either by requiring the promoter to provide travel, lodging, and equipment or a "sound and light" fee separate from the performance fee.

Another form of underwriting occurs when the performer enters into a relationship with a corporate sponsor that agrees to cover the cost of the tour in exchange for the benefits of exposure the association with the artist may bring its brand or products.[63] In a corporate underwritten tour, one must make sure that there are no local promoter-sponsorship conflicts. Some local promoters enter into corporate-sponsorship agreements to underwrite their own costs. For understandable reasons, a performer's corporate sponsor (generally a national sponsor) contractually precludes an underwritten performer from appearing in a locally promoted event underwritten by a local competitor (e. g., where competing signage or credits may appear on stage, otherwise in or at the venue, in promotional advertising, etc.). Similar conflicts may arise between a tour sponsor's requirements and a sponsorship obligation of the performance venue (e.g., where one mobile phone company is the tour sponsor, and the tour is booked in an arena or amphitheatre "named" for a competing company, or in which a tour is sponsored by a particular beverage company and a competing company has exclusive rights to serve its beverages at the venue).

And as previously noted, some artists with substantial traditional record company deals may still be the beneficiaries of label tour support as part of their overall recording agreements.

7.3.4.3. Ancillary Market Income

Many promoters (festival promoters in particular) try to co-promote the artist's live performances with live television or live streaming or, occasionally but with less frequency, as DVD's become less relevant, to permanently fix the performance for sale to television, home video, Internet and other media. Additionally, in the case of live concert streaming, the promoter may also seek to archive a certain number of the artist's live performance of a certain number of songs (3-5 being typical) for subsequent on demand streaming (which would also require the consent of the music publisher of the archived songs in the form of synchronization licenses, the public performance rights for the website from which the live and archived performances would have

---

[63] See supra §7.2.3.

to be obtained from those publishers or from the PRO's ASCAP, BMI, SESAC and GMR (and from the PRO's of all other territories in which the streaming will be made available), and, more likely than not, a "waiver of exclusivity" will need to be obtained from the artist's record company).

Assuming that the performer is contractually free to grant such rights, the performer usually seeks a separate fee for each aspect of their performance (i.e., a live performance fee *plus* a production fee for the program) and in most cases, performers will also seek a share of profits from the distribution of the program in various media (whether in the form of a royalty based upon the license fees for broadcast of the program and/or for unit sales if the program is sold to the public as a DVD, or alternatively a net proceeds participation when revenue from such exploitation exceeds a renegotiated breakpoint calculated on the basis of production and marketing costs).

In the case of live and archived internet streaming, the artist's compensation may or may not be included in the artist's fees for the concert performance (i.e., the obligation to permit the recording and streaming may be a condition of the artist's engagement for the concert), but the music publishers of the songs performed will need to be paid for the synchronization rights, the license fees to the PRO's will need to be remitted and, almost without exception, the artist's record company will not only want to be paid to "waive its exclusivity", but also will want to own the recordings with the right to exploit them by, through and in any and all manners, means and methods, in perpetuity following the expiration of the archived streaming on demand window (which rarely exceeds six (6) months). The ownership and exploitation of the concert recordings will be qualified by whatever creative and marketing controls the artist has negotiated in the recording agreement and, if the artist has consented to the exploitation of the recordings by this record company, the artist will receive the royalties that have been provided for in the recording agreement (or otherwise as may be negotiated in connection with the "waiver of exclusivity").

Problems in exploiting these ancillary market opportunities arise principally through conflicts with prior contractual obligations of the performer. For example, the performer may have a recording contract with one company that would either preclude the performer from making a home video or other audio- or videorecordings for any other company, from re-recording compositions embodied on records previously released within a five-year period,[64] or from participating in more than[65] a specified number of featured or guest appearances on such ancillary productions in a given time frame, absent label approval

---

[64] This is known as a "re-recording restriction."

[65] References in this chapter to "record" should be understood by the reader in the sense customarily understood in the Unites States recorded music industry and not as references to recordings in physical disc formats, such as CDs and vinyl discs alone. The definition of "Record" from an exclusive recording agreement with major US record distributor might read as a "'Record'" means any form of reproduction, distribution, transmission or communication of Recordings (whether or not in physical form) now or hereafter known (including reproductions of sound alone or together with visual images) which is manufactured, distributed, transmitted or communicated primarily for personal use, home use, institutional (e.g., library or school) use, jukebox use, or use in means of transportation, including any computer-assisted media (e.g., CD-ROM, DVD Audio, CD Extra, Enhanced CD) or use as a so-called 'ringtone' in any form (e.g., as so-called 'master ringtones,' 'polyphonic ringtones' and 'MIDI ringtones')."

A "Recording" means "any recording of sound or data used in the production of sound, whether or not coupled with a visual image, by any method and on any substance or material, whether now or hereafter known, which is used or useful in the recording, production and/or manufacture of Records or for any other exploitation of sound.

The reader may wish to also contract the foregoing definitions with the following definitions from the US Copyright Act, noting that a "digital phonorecord delivery" as defined below is commonly understood as a "download", which is also subsumed in the recording industry definition of "Record" above:

"Phonorecords" are material objects in which sounds, other than those accompanying a motion picture or other audiovisual work, are fixed by any method now known or later developed, and from which the sounds can be perceived, reproduced, or otherwise communicated, either directly or with the aid of a machine or device. The term "phonorecords" includes the material object in which the sounds are first fixed. (17 U.S.C. § 101).

"Sound recordings" are works that result from the fixation of a series of musical, spoken, or other sounds, but not including the sounds accompanying a motion picture or other audiovisual work, regardless of the nature of the material objects, such as disks, tapes, or other phonorecords, in which they are embodied. (17 U.S.C. § 101)

A "digital phonorecord delivery" is each individual delivery of a phonorecord by digital transmission of a sound recording which results in a specifically identifiable reproduction by or for any transmission recipient of a phonorecord of that sound recording, regardless of whether the digital transmission is also a public performance of the sound recording or any nondramatic musical work embodied therein. A digital phonorecord delivery does not result from a real-time, nonintegrated subscription transmission of a sound recording where no reproduction of the sound recording or the musical work embodied therein is made from the inception of the transmission through to its receipt by the transmission recipient in order to make the sound recording audible. (17 U.S.C. § 115(d).)

(or the approval of a third party video distributor who may be holding rights to another recent project featuring the artist).

Additional concerns develop in clearing the rights to use musical material in a new medium. Although the public performing rights for live concerts are obtainable pursuant to blanket licenses from the performing-rights societies,[66] and for a live audio recording of the performance of compositions not composed by the featured performer through statutory compulsory licenses under copyright law, such licenses do not grant audiovisual synchronization rights that must be obtained directly from the copyright proprietors over whom the performer may be unable to exert any real control.[67] There is no statutory compulsory licensing privilege for audiovisual synchronization rights as there is for mechanical rights.[68] It is the legal responsibility of the promoter/producer to clear these rights. The producer of these concert films generally seeks the performer's cooperation and may even require the performer to alter the program when it includes compositions that, for one reason or another, the copyright proprietor simply refuses to license (or at least to perform enough readily cleared material to ensure a performance video can be edited so as satisfy commercial requirements).

7.3.4.4. Merchandising Income

The sale of T-shirts, buttons, posters, records, or other memorabilia at concerts generates substantial profits, which for many performers can dramatically exceed record and performance income.[69] The principal beneficiary of this business (i. e., the artist, the label, the licensor, etc.) depends on the strength of the negotiators.

---

[66] *See* the Brabec's §8.3, *infra*, explanation of Performing Rights Societies and their functions in music publishing licensing.

[67] The performing rights to a "live" performance simultaneously transmitted over television or the broadcast of a taped program would be governed by that station's blanket license.

[68] 17 U.S.C. §115 (2012). *See also infra* §8.3.

[69] It has been estimated, for example, that the group New Kids on the Block grossed over $640 million from merchandise sales alone in 1990. Zimmerman, *New Kids Crowned Kings of Merchandise*, VARIETY (Aug. 8, 1990) p.53. More recently, Kanye West sold $780,000 in merchandise in a single evening at concert at Madison Square Garden. *See* Olivia Waring, *Kanye West has sold more merchandise than the Pope*, METRO UK (Sep. 11, 2016, 5:07 PM), http://metro.co.uk/2016/09/11/kanye-west-has-sold-more-merchandise-than-the-pope-6121925/.

Many successful performers license merchandising rights to companies that then produce the goods, distribute them to stores, and/or tour with the performer as concessionaire. On such a tour, the company may supply the goods and people to sell them, with a percentage of the sales going to the performer. Alternatively, the performer may carry a supply of goods on the tour that they have purchased or commissioned for manufacture and that they desire to sell.

However, many venues (theaters and stadiums) have contracts with vendors who have the exclusive right to operate food, beverage, and other concessions within the venue. Allowing other sellers within the venue would violate this exclusivity. A promoter may argue that its promotion efforts brought in the audience that makes up the market for these goods and so the promoter should have the right to sell to this specific audience.

A common compromise calls for the performer or the performer's merchandising company to supply the goods to the promoter or the promoter's concessionaire and to receive a percentage of any sales, with the remainder divided between the promoter and the venue concessionaire. It is also the promoter's obligation to ensure that no pirated or unlicensed merchandise is sold at the venue or in its environs.

One common method of determining the performer's tour merchandise royalties is on a "Net Tour Profits" basis. From one hundred percent (100%) of all "gross tour merchandise proceeds" from sales of Artist Products at the Artist's live performance engagements are deduced (i) venue costs (including, without limitation, hall fees, sales tax, credit card service fees and venue security), and (ii) any value-added tax or its equivalent, if applicable to arrive at the amount of "Net Tour Sales." To arrive at "Net Tour Profits, the following are typically deducted from Net Tour Sales":

> All direct, actual, out-of-pocket, customary "road expenses" paid by the tour merchandiser in connection with the manufacture, distribution, sale and transportation of merchandise, including, without limitation, road expenses (including, without limitation, staff costs, travel, shipping, per diems), import duties, anti-bootleg security, vending expenses and the costs of goods produced. Road expenses would include (A) lodging (including bus bunk space) for the tour merchandiser's vending personnel, compensation to the tour

merchandise vending staff, costs of travel for the vending staff, costs of shipping the merchandise, per diems paid to the vending staff, import duties, anti-bootleg security, vending expenses and the costs of goods produced. Depending on the leverage of the performer, the tour merchandiser may also deducted an administration fee or overhead charge of between five percent (5%) and ten percent (10%) of the Net Tour Sales.

Another method of computing tour merchandise royalties is to calculate on a "Net Tour Sales Basis" (as opposed to the above "Net Tour Profits" basis). Where tour merchandisers compute on a "Net Tour Sales" basis, the costs to be deducted from gross tour merchandise revenues are generally limited to deduction of taxes and credit card processing charges off the top to arrive at "net tour merchandise revenues" after which venue fees (approximately twenty-five percent (25%)) and costs of merchandise artwork creation and design are deducted. From the remaining "Net Tour Sales", the performer receives between seventy-five percent (75%) and eighty percent (80%) of such Net Tour Revenues.

In the final analysis, whether the performer will receive a percentage of Net Tour Profits or Net Tour Sales will be established by the business policies of the tour merchandiser, with the performer receiving a lower percentage of Net Tour Sales, which are determined on a more favourable basis given fewer expenses are deducted in arriving at the amount to be distributed, than the performer would receive if the royalties are to be computed on a "Net Tour Profits" basis.

Very roughly speaking, (i) taxes will vary jurisdiction to jurisdiction, but seven percent (7%) might be a reasonable average, (ii) venue fees will run between twenty-five percent (25%) and thirty-five percent (35%), (ii) artwork design and creation costs might run two and one-half percent (2.5%) to five percent (5%), (iii) road expenses could be estimated at eight percent (8%) to ten percent (10%), (iv) freight and shipping costs might run from three percent (3%) to five percent (5%), (v) service fees from two percent (2%) to four percent (4%) and (vi) excess inventory costs from one percent (1%) to four percent (4%).

7.3.4.5. Fan Clubs and VIP Ticket Packages

Operation of fan clubs, which themselves may include so-called "VIP concert ticket" packages and "backstage" fan engagement opportunities for touring artists present significant income sources.[70] A notable recent example was a Beyoncé "Beyfirst Package", priced at $1,505, which included: a reserved front-row seat; a pre-show reception featuring free booze and food, as well as fan-favorite Beyoncé hits and "themed decor," a souvenir seat-back cover; your own parking spot; "crowd-free" merchandise shopping; and an exclusive "merchandise item". A recent Nick Jonas and Demi Lovato tour offered "The Ultimate VIP Dressing Room Package", priced at $10,000, entitling a fan and three friends to a dressing room backstage, including their own rider; with a personal visit by the artists to the "fan's" dressing room to "say hi," autograph items and take photos; access to a stage-side lounge; poster hand-signed by Jonas and Lovato; and dinner in "tour catering." [71]

Generally speaking, fan clubs are run by third party services which are engaged either by the artists themselves or by the record labels with which the artists have exclusive recording and/or exclusive distribution agreements. Under so-called "360 Recording Agreements" the record labels with which the artists are signed will most likely be entitled to receive a percentage of income derived from the artist's fan club offerings or, in accordance with the policies and practices of some record labels, the label may obtain the exclusive right to operate the artist's fan club.

The artist will typically have reasonable approval rights over all aspects of, and fan engagement opportunities provided by, any fan club service operator. Fundamental services a fan club operator should, at a minimum, provide to the artist include development and management of the fan club; creating and hosting the official artist fan club website; collecting and managing revenue and costs of membership sales; creation and fulfilment of fan club membership packages; responding to fan club member's emails; providing customer service support for fan club issues; posting and distributing announcements about the artist's tour schedule, contests, and special promotions; maintaining a

---

[70] See < http://www.nytimes.com/2010/05/23/arts/music/23VIP.html>
[71] See < http://www.rollingstone.com/music/pictures/are-summers-biggest-tour-vip-packages-worth-it-20160512>.

current database of fan club members; providing ticketing services, travel packages, and other fan club member experiences; developing fan club merchandise (to be sold through the fan club website); conducting fan club activities which may include, but not be limited to, email blasts to fan club members; online seeding activities, contests, and promotions; renewal reminders to current members; refer-a-friend programs; on-site membership acquisition through VIP parties, fliers, etc.; special offers with purchase of membership; and providing credit card, accounting and processing services, and developing payment, delivery and refund policies to fulfill all orders of fan club merchandise to members.

The fan club operator will often have the right to manufacture merchandise, subject to any third party rights artist has with a third party merchandiser(s) requiring the operator to purchase merchandise through such licensee(s), but the fan club service will control the exclusive right to sell fan club merchandise through the fan club website. The artist, fan club operator and the artist's third party merchandiser will frequently collaborate with one another in the creation of merchandise to be available for distribution to and/or purchase by the artist's fan club members. Alternately, in negotiation of the artist's exclusive merchandising agreement with a third party, the artist may withhold rights to create and sell "fan club merchandise" from the scope of the exclusive merchandising agreement in connection with designs and products which will be made available on a limited basis solely to paid members of the artist's fan club (and not to retail establishments, other forms of ecommerce or online sales or in connection with concert tours). If arrangements are made for sales of artist's merchandise manufactured by the artist's third party merchandiser to the artist's fan club members, the fan club operator will pay the third party merchandiser the wholesale cost of goods, less the amount of the artist's royalty under the third party merchandiser (and the artist will not be paid any royalties under the third party merchandise agreement; rather, the artist will be paid for such sales under the terms of the fan club agreement.

The artist's agreement with the fan club operator may or may not permit the fan club operator to run the artist's VIP concert ticket sales operation and other fan engagement activities conducted in connection with the artist's concert tours. Again, all aspects of the artist's VIP concert ticket sales operations and other fan engagement activities and offerings are subject to the artist's specific rights of approval. If the artist's fan club operator does not obtain the right to conduct VIP ticket sales and tour fan engagement opportunities, there are services which specialize in those endeavours with which the artist might enter into an agreement or, in some instances, the tour promoter with which the artist has entered into a tour agreement may obtain the right to pursue those endeavours.

The party providing VIP ticket sales management services will obtain the right (and obligation) to sell concert tickets prior to and during public on-sale dates, and manage preferred seating, VIP ticketing and other perks to purchasers at tour venues and other appearances (sometimes referred to as "ticket packages"), and make the necessary arrangements to sell, ship to the purchaser or leave at will call ticket packages that include mutually agreed upon benefits. The price of ticket packages shall include cost of ticket plus any merchandise item, convenience fee, and shipping. In negotiating the tour agreement the artist will use reasonable commercial efforts to secure as many premier tickets for the ticket packages as possible and put such premier tickets on sale through the fan club website prior to tickets going on sale to the general public.[72] The artist and the party providing VIP ticket sales management services mutually agree upon the price per person and the number of premiere tickets to be sold to each fan club member prior to each concert tour.

The party providing VIP ticket sales management services shall sell and manage fan engagement packages to include mutually agreed upon benefits (which can include, for example, "front row" / preferred seating, a pre-show backstage tour, a pre-or-post show meet and greet and/or photo opportunity with the artist, "after parties", and the like). In negotiations between the artist and the tour promoter, it is incumbent upon the artist to attempt to secure as many VIP / preferred seating tickets as possible for deployment in connection with engagement packages and put such engagement packages on sale through the fan club website prior to tickets going on sale to the general public. The agreement with the VIP ticket sales management service will obligate the artist to make a minimum percentage of a venue's tickets available for sale for the fan club ticketing and fan engagement packages, and will provide, for example, that those preferred seats shall be "P1

---

[72] See Bands and Ticketmaster Wrangle Over Rules for Fan Club Sales" <https://www.nytimes.com/2015/10/05/business/media/bands-and-ticketmaster-wrangle-over-rules-for-fan-club-sales.html?_r=0 >

tickets", sufficient in quantity and allocated in the front row sections to fulfill specific orders for the VIP fan club packages. "P1" tickets are for seats located closest to the stage, and/or in the "pit", which tickets labelled as being "P2", "P3", "P4" and so on being farther away from the stage (e.g., beyond the first 10-20 rows on the floor, concourse level, etc.). The price per person for engagement packages and the number sold to fan club members are mutually agreed upon between the artist and the VIP ticket sales management service prior to each concert tour.

VIP ticket sales and fan engagement packages may also include travel packages offered to fan club members for the artist's concert tours and may include benefits such as hotel rooms located near venue, bus transportation, parties, meet and greet and/or photo opportunities with the artist, the pricing for which and the number to be made available to also be mutually agreed upon between the artist and the VIP ticket sales management service prior to each concert tour.

The fan club service and/or VIP ticket sales management service agreements will provide for the artist to receive an advance against the artist's share of "Net Profits" under the agreement concerned. The artist's share of Net Profits is in the neighbourhood of fifty percent (50%) to seventy-five percent (75%). "Net Profits" are usually considered to gross revenues actually received or credited from all sales less "costs". "Costs" are considered to be as all actual direct out-of-pocket non-overhead costs of goods, manufacturing, production, creation and/or sourcing of marketing packages, fan club membership packages, promotional giveaways and/or fan club merchandise; any artist pre-approved marketing costs including Internet seeding campaigns, email blasts, and membership drives; in-bound freight charges; shipping and handling charges that are not passed on to the purchaser; third party fulfilment fees; fees and costs for any VIP ticket sales management service representation being provided on-site at concert events; specific out-of-pocket costs associated with servicing the fan club, including artist approval of specific online marketing company engagement servicing the club, technical licenses for the fan club Website; warehouse, storage, and shipment fees; any credits for cancellations and inventory write-offs and obsolescence charges; sales, use and value-added taxes; and in the case of VIP ticket sales benefits with onsite activations, hall and vending fees, hall security fees, the cost of obtaining and enforcing bootleg injunctions, fees incurred for the acceptance of credit cards, cost of goods, freight, security, vendor salaries, hotel accommodations, per diems, and road costs. The fan club operator and/or VIP ticket management service is usually also entitled to an "administration fee" of three percent (3%) to five percent (5%) of the gross revenues actually received or credited. The artist should seek to have approval over costs and/or receive a cost estimate (and a "profit & loss" projection, showing low, medium and high profits projections) and be meaningfully consulted regarding all costs before being incurred.

Since the artist's advance under any VIP ticket management service is predicated upon, among other factors, the number of concert dates to be performed on the tour concerned, and the seating capacity of the venues at which the artist will perform, and in view of the fact that significant "upfront" start-up expenses will be incurred be the VIP ticket management service before the tour commences, the VIP ticket management service agreement will contain provisions for failure to timely commence the tour (or failure to commence it at all) (in which case the artist will be obligated to repay the advance and any costs incurred to VIP ticket management service), cancellation (in which case if the cancellation is of a negotiated percentage of the scheduled concert dates (e.g., thirty percent (30%) or more), the VIP ticket management service shall have the right to demand a refund of a pro rata portion of the advance based on the percentage of such dates not performed (not to exceed the then-unrecouped balance of the advance), plus the amount of unrecouped costs having been incurred by the VIP ticket management service.

Postponement of a tour leg, or a postponement of one or more individual concert performance dates if the tour has already commenced, or a cancellation of an entire tour when not followed by either a resumption of the tour and/or by the rebooking of such tour leg or of the individually cancelled events within a specified, negotiated-for period of time (usually within *sixty (60) to one hundred twenty (120)) days following the first postponed performance)* will be deemed to be a "cancellation" under the contract of the applicable tour leg, individual concert performance dates or of the tour as a whole, in which event the VIP ticket management service will ordinarily have the right to demand all or a pro-rata repayment of all or any portion of the unrecouped advance plus the amount of unrecouped costs having been incurred by the VIP ticket management service in accordance with the immediately preceding paragraph.

Although all of these considerations may seem of little relevance to the nascent band or solo artist struggling to merely make ends meet on the road, many of these concepts are in fact scalable to a small but steady artist following, and bits and pieces of these "big act" strategies can be assembled in support of even small club and house concert tours to develop and expand fan allegiance and artist-fan rapport. There are a number of fan club management services available to the independent recording and touring artist which provide merchandise, E-commerce, ticketing/VIP tickets and fan engagement activities, consumer analytics and other services, such as fanclubhouse.com, omgvip.com., and artistarena.com, that last of which is operated by the Warner Music Group and is "built to partner with artists to focus on their brand and how they connect with their fans."[73]

7.4. RECORDING AGREEMENTS

The most important contract any new musical performer can sign is a recording contract. And in the current recording industry environment, where 360 Deals are now the norm, there little doubt that the artist will be obligated to concurrently enter into a so-called "collateral entertainment activities agreement" (a "CEA Agreement"), the terms of which may or may not be within the four walls of the recording agreement, under which the recording company will control and/or have an economic participation interest in all of the artist's non-record entertainment industry endeavours.[74] For the unknown artist, a recording contract with its promised release and promotion of records is the artist's introduction to a larger public – a first step toward fame and fortune. For the middle-level performer, it is one element of a multifaceted career that in itself may represent significant income but that, often more importantly, contributes public exposure and publicity values toward the performer's activities in concerts, television commercials, acting, and writing. For superstar performers, a deal with a major record company can produce enormous income and consequent industry influence.[75]

---

[73] *See* < http://www.artistarena.com>
[74] *See* §7.4.1.1 below for a discussion of CEA Agreements.
[75] It has been estimated that Michael Jackson, prior to his death, sold from 50 to over 100 million copies of his 1982 album *Thriller*, and earned over $75 million from the album and associated videos.

The acceleration of technological changes relating to music delivery in the last 25 years (digital recording, the internet and resulting popularity of file sharing, downloads, and now streaming as alternatives to conventional LP and CD distribution, the explosive market penetration of portable digital music devices and smartphones, etc.) has left the record industry reeling. A series of consolidations among the major record labels leaves three predominant companies in the marketplace: Sony Music Entertainment, Universal Music Group, and Warner Music Group. These labels, through their direct releases and those of their subsidiary companies (e.g., Sony's Columbia Records, WMG's Atlantic and/or Universal Music Group's Geffen or Interscope labels), account for more than 62 percent of worldwide recorded music sales annually, including, by some estimates, more than 80 percent of streaming royalties[76]

Independent labels have emerged as a major force for the introduction of new artists and new music during the last quarter century. Independent labels brought in an estimated $5.6 billion worldwide in 2015, including nearly $1 billion in streaming revenues.[77]

Independent labels are typically companies to which the majors provide distribution services, offering access to the major's mainstream retail and online marketplaces for an off the top distribution fee and expenses, while enabling the independent label to retain ownership or creative control over their product. Alternatively, indie labels and individual artists may sell through a spectrum of large and small record distribution companies (in the old, physical – product days known as " rack jobbers") that while not labels themselves aggregate the distribution of independent product on a purchase order or consignment basis and make these recordings available through national wholesale and retail channels (from big box stores to the remaining independent specialty record retailers), as well as through digital services. Finally, independent labels and even individual artists now increasingly sell directly to these outlets and via the internet to reach audiences, foregoing the inventory and overhead expenses inherent in working with corporate intermediaries – whether major labels or distributors. Given the relative ease with which an artist can "self-release" records in the present marketplace, directly to the

---

[76] Paul Resnikoff, *Two-Thirds of All Music Sold Comes from Just 3 Companies*, DIGITAL MUSIC NEWS (Aug. 3, 2016), http://www.digitalmusicnews.com/2016/08/03/two-thirds-music-sales-come-three-major-labels/.

[77] *See id.*

consumer, or through one of the many "aggregators" (for example, CD Baby, The Orchard, TuneCore, SongFlow),[78] when considering whether to pursue an agreement with an independent record label, it is critical to ascertain (and if possible to do so, obtain a contractual guarantee) that the label will prepare and execute a marketing plan and budget; otherwise the artist may just as well continue with "self-release"/ "self-distribution" until a label or distribution willing and prepared to make guaranteed release, marketing and promotional commitments surfaces.

Tracing industry trends has also become more complex with the shift from a physical to a digital marketplace. On the one hand, traditional "sales" of music have fallen precipitously. Industry analysts reported that in 2015 U.S. sales of albums (CDs and full album digital downloads of music) totalled 208.3 million units, down nearly 20 percent from 2014 (257 million units), and down over 50 percent from 2010 (443 million units).[79] In fact, 2015 sales are down across nearly all formats – physical CDs (down 3.8 percent or roughly 300,000 fewer CDs sold), digital albums (down 3.5 percent or roughly 3.9 million fewer digital albums sold), and digital songs (down 11.3 percent or roughly 124 million fewer digital songs sold) – with vinyl being the only format showing an increase in sales (up 53.8 percent or roughly 2.1 million more vinyl units sold) to nearly 10 million units, enjoying a consistent pattern of growth for ten consecutive years, but still only accounting for 5 percent of all music sales).[80]

On the other hand, this overall fall in sales is counterbalanced by the rise of digital "streaming" services like Spotify, Tidal, and Apple Music, which allow music consumers to access music through a paid subscription instead of individual purchases. Streaming services saw sharp increases in 2015 over 2014, whether measured by total streams (up 96 percent), audio streams (up 97 percent), or video streams (up 95 percent).

---

[78] *See* http://www.hypebot.com/hypebot/2013/11/the-indie-musicians-guide-to-digital-distribution.html for an excellent overview of aggregators and calculation of royalties each pays. (last visited August 13, 2017); also *see* https://www.forbes.com/sites/hughmcintyre/2016/01/08/vinyl-sales-surged-30-percent-in-2015-led-by-adele-and-taylor-swift/#5de65f7b6d6b regarding continuing trends in "vinyl" sales growth.

[79] *Compare* 2015 BUZZANGLE MUSIC U.S. INDUSTRY SNAPSHOT, http://www/buzz anglemusic.com/2015industrysnapshot *with* Daniel Kreps, *Streaming, Vinyl Rises Amid Declining Album Sales in Nielsen's 2014 Report*, ROLLING STONE (Jan. 8, 2015), http://www.rollingstone.com/music/news/streaming-vinyl-rises-amid-declining-album-sales-in-nielsens-2014-report-20150108.

[80] 2015 BUZZANGLE MUSIC U.S. INDUSTRY SNAPSHOT, http://www/buzzangle music.com/2015industrysnapshot

The advent of streaming has affected how success in the industry is measured, with the definition of "album sales" broadening to capture the digital trends, and in the process creating a new yardstick: the "equivalent album unit."[81] Under this new scheme, 10 digital track downloads sold or 1,500 tracks streamed can each equal an "equivalent album unit," and will be treated the same in accountings as a traditional album sale.[82]

Under this new broader view, the industry's future looks very different from the discouraging decline in traditional album sales seen above: 2015 saw 509.8 million equivalent album units sold, a 19.5 percent increase from 2014.

7.4.1. Types of Recording Agreements

There are essentially three types of recording agreements in common use: exclusive artist's agreements (including the so-called 360 Deal), production agreements, and master purchase agreements.

7.4.1.1. Exclusive Artist's Agreement

An exclusive artist's agreement is entered into directly by a record label or production company with a performing artist for his or her services as a recording artist during the term[83] of the agreement. Concurrently with entering the recording agreement, the artist will likely be required to enter into a separate CEA Agreement (on occasion the CEA income participation terms may be contained in the recording agreement itself).

7.4.1.2. Production Agreement

A production agreement is entered into between a recording company and a production entity (either a company or other business organization) for the production of and delivery to the record company of recorded masters[84] suitable for release as phonorecords. A

---

[81] *See* Randall Roberts, *A New Spin on No. 1 Records*, LOS ANGELES TIMES (Aug. 31, 2016).
[82] *See id.*
[83] *See infra* §7.4.2.1.
[84] A record master is commonly defined as a final mixed and edited tape of an individual composition having a set minimum duration (e.g., three minutes) suitable as the basis for creating elements needed to manufacture phonorecords. An album is made

production agreement is generally tied to a specific artist. It may, however, involve a specific record producer who then contracts with one or more recording artists the producer seeks to develop. In its most common form, it involves a recording artist who, in order to exert greater artistic control over the recordings, has formed a business entity to produce them. The artist who enters into an exclusive recording agreement with the production company will typically grant the production company CEA income participation rights, and the artist attorney had best heed that, in the likely event that the distributor with which the production company enters an agreement for the release of the artist's recordings insists upon a CEA income participation as well, the CEA participation owed to the production company is reduced by the participation of the distributor (often to a "floor" of 3 percent to 5 percent of the artist's non-record income). By way of example, if, with respect to the artist's merchandise income under the artist's recording agreement with the production company, the production company is entitled to an income participation equal to ten percent of the artist's merchandising income and the distributor insists upon the same percentage of that income, the merchandise income to the production company would be reduced to 3 percent to 5 percent, and the result would be that that artist ends up granting 13 percent to15 percent of the merchandise income in the aggregate between the production company and the distributor. Additionally, it is typical that when the production company secures distribution for the artist's recordings, the artist will be required to execute an inducement letter providing, in general, that the artist will perform services (and grant CEA income participation rights) directly to the distributor in the event of a default by the production company to do so.

7.4.1.3. Master Purchase Agreement

In a master purchase agreement, a record company buys previously produced masters[85] and the copyrights in these masters[86] for purposes of manufacture and distribution of phonorecords. As an alternative to purchasing the masters outright, the record company may license the use

---

up of a number of masters. A phonorecord is any physical analog or digital transcription of the master (e.g., record, tape, CD or digital file).

[85] *Id.*

[86] A sound recording is separately copyrightable from the composition embodied on it. *See* §1.2.1 in the Intellectual Property volume to this Series discussing the subject matter of Copyright. *See also* 17 U.S.C. §102 (2012).

of the masters and their copyrights for a limited period of time. This form of agreement is typically utilized when a label wishes to acquire a completed, independently produced recording (which may already have been commercially released on a limited basis by the artist or a smaller label), or occasionally to "re-release" an older recording.

7.4.2. Scope of Services

The rights obtained by the record company vary both according to the type of recording agreement involved and the specific terms negotiated for that agreement. Nonetheless, the standard terms of an exclusive artist's agreement commonly serve as a template for the other two types of agreements.

Moreover, the rights conveyed under an exclusive artist's agreement are in turn of two types: the rights to the performer's services and the rights to the products of those services.

The typical exclusive recording agreement will provide that the artist will render exclusive services for the making of "Recordings" embodying the artist's performances, and the term "Recordings" is generally defined broadly as "any recording of sound or data used in the production of sound, whether or not coupled with a visual image, by any method and on any substance or material, whether now or hereafter known, which is used or useful in the recording, production and/or manufacture of records or for any other exploitation of sound."

7.4.2.1 Recording Commitment

A key element is the term of the agreement, i.e., how long the label has access to the artist's exclusive services for the production of one or more "albums" or individual masters.[87]

The recording commitment establishes the number of masters and/or albums to be delivered under the agreement. Generally, record companies will require one album for each year of the term (i.e., the date of the commencement of the initial term or option running through nine months after the delivery of the required masters or album) plus an option on the part of the record company to require a second album

---

[87] Although recorded music is increasing released and consumed as "singles", the reference to "albums" remains a common fixture of recording agreements to designate the quantity of material an artist may be required to produce and deliver to a producer or label during a given time period, and typically denotes a requirement of ten, and sometimes more, masters to be considered as a commercial package.

during each year of the term. Note, however, that the term may of necessity be extended to cover the time necessary to record the album.

The standard initial term for an exclusive agreement is one year from the date of execution or nine months from delivery of the masters, whichever is later. This is usually coupled with additional option terms (generally four to seven options of one year or nine months from delivery) exercisable solely by the record company.

The argument for additional options is that each recording represents a sizeable outlay of funds for both recording and promotion, all of which is of a direct benefit to the performer. A record company seeks to take advantage of the artist's success by continuing its exclusivity. Conversely, because the record company made the initial investment in the recordings and the promotion of the artist's records, if the releases are not economically successful, the record company should have the right to attempt to recoup that investment through the exercise of options to continue the term and cause the delivery of further recordings.

It should be noted that although the record company typically controls all of the options in the agreement (i.e., deciding whether to exercise them or not), the recording commitment should require that the company record the minimum commitment in order to exercise its next option and to release what has been recorded if it is commercially satisfactory. In many cases, the record company may provide that it satisfies its obligation to record by paying the artist union scale or some other negotiated fee in lieu of recording, a solution that is likely to be unsatisfactory from the artist's point of view.

Although ideally the artist may wish to treat each recording separately, if required to enter into this type of arrangement he or she should seek to (1) limit the number of options beyond the initial project, and/or make their exercise contingent on defined sales performance milestones for prior albums, and (2) make certain that the recording company will in fact not only record but also meaningfully release those recordings during the period in which the performer is exclusive to the company.

7.4.2.2. Scope of Services to Be Delivered

The agreement must provide the parameters of the services that the performer is to render, including when, what, and how those services are to be performed.

These are exclusive services agreements, so the performer cannot record for anyone else during the term. The rationale for this prohibition and the alternate durations (i.e., one year or nine months) is that a record company can promote only a limited number of records at a time and does not want to release a record by an individual artist or group that would compete with other records by the same artist or group already in release, i.e., it does not it wish to release a new record by the performer if the previous recording is still on the charts and selling well. Nevertheless, it does want commitment from the performer to replenish its inventory of recordings in the event the performer should be unavailable to record at some future date. In today's 360 Deal environment, the rationale extending the exclusivity to virtually all forms of media in which the artist may render services or create properties derived from the results and proceeds of the artist's services is that, having made the investments in the artist's career by financing the recording and marketing costs, the record company should either control or have the right to participate in the artist's income in all areas of the entertainment industry.

The agreement provides that "the performer is *employed*[88] as a recording artist, musician and/or vocalist for the purposes of making master recordings from which phonorecords may be produced embodying the recorded performances of the performer and for such purposes as are normally incidental thereto." Although the foregoing description of the performer's services (as it commonly appears in these types of agreements) may appear straightforward, there are some nuances that may expand what may first appear to be a limited scope. First, although the term *phonorecord* has a statutory meaning under copyright law,[89] it may have a *different* meaning under the contract. For example, it is commonly defined in the recording agreement to include audiovisual devices designed primarily for home use. Thus the record company may hold the exclusive right, whether exercised or not, to that performer's services for the making of a music video. Also, as theatrical motion pictures, broadcast and cable television programs are produced with the home video market as an anticipated secondary market and revenue source, the labels may seek to impose this broader

---

[88] This term is significant in that these recordings are generally defined as works made for hire for purposes of copyright. *See* §1.7.3 in the Intellectual Property Law (Volume II) companion to this book.

[89] 17 U.S.C. §101 (2012).

definition of phonorecord so that a performer may be precluded from performing in these other media absent the label's consent.

Incidental services include publicity and promotional activities, posing for album cover photos, or appearing at press conferences and at industry conventions.

The agreement also requires that the performer's recording services be rendered exclusively for the benefit of the record company (unless otherwise agreed) during the term of the agreement, that the services are to be rendered to the best of performer's ability, and that they be performed under the direction and supervision of the company. In the context of the 360 Deal, this requirement will extend to live performance and promotional services, in addition to services in the recording studio.

7.4.2.3. Excluded Services

Most performers seek to limit the scope of the agreement's exclusivity so that it does not preclude them from participation in areas they deem significant to their careers. For example, a performer who is also an actor or actress, or a writer of non-musical works (e.g., poetry or fiction), or who also does work as a composer on film scores (with their potential for sound track album spinoffs) would need an agreement that allows an exclusion for such activity(s). Where the performer desires to record for others (e.g., for a festival promoter to enable the live streaming and/or on demand archived viewing of the performer's concert appearance, for television awards shows such as the Grammys, television talk shows, and the like), a "waiver of exclusivity" must be obtained from the performer's record company by the producer desiring to obtain the services of the performer.[90] These "waivers of exclusivity" tend to be heavily negotiated and the common result is that the record company owns the recordings made by the producer, with the right to exploit them without financial compensation to the producer (and the performer's approval and income participation rights to be as provided for in his/her recording agreement) with the producer obtaining a limited right or license to produce the recordings and telecast or stream them for a relatively limited period of time and only within a limited territory.

---

[90] *See supra* §7.2.4.3 for a discussion of label waivers.

7.4.3. Scope of Rights Granted

7.4.3.1. In the Recording

a. In General

(i) Under the United States Copyright Act, a *sound recording* is defined as a work that "result[s] from the fixation of a series of musical ... sounds"[91] with all rights in the recording limited to the protection of only the actual sounds fixed in that recording.[92] The record company generally seeks to acquire all rights in the sound recording (and, as noted above, all other forms of recordings of the artist's performances in other than sound alone media) as the employer/author of the recordings under the works-made-for-hire doctrine.[93] In support of this, the agreement identifies the sound recording as a work made for hire as required under the statute[94] and then sets forth all of the label's rights in the recordings. This is done both for the sake of caution (i.e., in case a court decides that the performer was not an employee) and in order to convey rights that may exist other than copyright. These additional rights include those governed by the law of unfair competition[95] and/or the rights of publicity/privacy.[96] The rights specified in the agreement as being conveyed will include the right to manufacture and distribute the recordings in any form (such as tapes or CDs or digital files on a thumbdrive or digital downloads), the right to edit and revise the recordings,[97] the right to couple the recordings with recordings by other artists, and the right to use or license the reuse of the recordings in any medium (such as films or television).

(ii) Though of decreasing relevance (and more difficult to obtain during the course of negotiations in view of declining record industry revenues resulting the record companies being less inclined to cede control to the artist), depending on the leverage of the artist, the artist may be able to negotiate for limitations on the record company's exploitation rights through what are commonly referred to as

---

[91] 17 U.S.C. §101 (2012).
[92] *Id.* §124. *See* §1.4 in the Intellectual Property Law Volume.
[93] *See id* §1.7.3. *See also* 17 U.S.C. §201(b).
[94] 17 U.S.C. §101 (2012).
[95] *See* §3.10 in the Intellectual Property Law Volume.
[96] *See id* Chapter 4.
[97] A possible infringement of the right against unfair competition. *See* id §2.10. *See also* Gilliam v. Am. Broad. Cos. 538 F.2d 14 (2d Cir. 1976).

"marketing restrictions", examples of which include restrictions on the record company's rights to (i) license for coupling any artist recording on any particular record that embodies recordings by performers other than artist (e.g. motion picture soundtrack records containing recordings by multiple artists); (ii) release any album as a reduced price (mid-line or budget) record prior to twelve (12) months to eighteen (18) months following the date of initial United States release of that album; (iii) sell copies of any album as "cut-outs" or as overstock (rapidly disappearing in the download/streaming era); (iv) initially release an album other than on one of the company's then-current top line labels; (v) commercially release any record embodying "Outtakes" (meaning preliminary or unfinished versions of recordings); (vi) re-sequence any album, except to the extent necessary with respect to compact disc or other configurations for timing purposes; (ix) require the artist to deliver any so-called "live" recordings; (x) license the artist's recordings for use as so-called "samples"; (xi) require the artist to perform with other artists for any recording; or (xii) release any album containing more than ten (10) masters, unless such album was delivered by the artist with a greater number of masters. All of these types of restrictions may be limited as to territory (e.g., the United States), term (e.g., they may not apply after the term of the recording agreement ends), and/or the recouped position of the artist's royalty account (e.g., the record company's rights may not be limited if the artist's account is in an unrecouped position, or, in that event, the record company may only be obligated to consult with the artist before proceeding with the otherwise restricted activity).

The artist with leverage may also be able to obtain a provision requiring the record company to consult with the artist with respect to the record company's initial overall marketing plan (and budget) for the initial commercial release of each album in the United States.

b. DAT Home Recording

Although now eclipsed in significance by new technologies and practices, The Audio Home Recording Act, through the enactment of Chapter 10 of the copyright law in 1992,[98] created a statutory license for the private copying of phonograms (and other works) by means of

---

[98] *Compare* 17 U.S.C. §§1001-03, 1005, 1008-09 (1992) *with* 17 U.S.C. §§1004, 1006, 1007, 1010 (2004).

the new digital audio tape (DAT) technology. As a part of this statutory licensing scheme, the owners of phonograms, and performers, are entitled to compensation for the copying of their protected phonograms through devices and media primarily dedicated to digital audio recording (DAT tapes and later blank CDs). The statute notably excluded computing devices that could be used for general copying of "non-musical literary works, including computer programs and databases, and failed to address issues that would arise with the growth of the internet. While the law provides that the statutory royalty is to be allocated between producers and performers according to a formula established in the law (38.41 percent to 25.60 percent, respectively)[99] a number of record labels and producers have attempted to capture the featured performer's royalties as well under the terms of their recording agreements with artists. The growth of the internet as a means of exploitation of recordings through downloads and streaming services has rendered the significance of the Audio Home Recording Act nearly moot today.

c. Digital Broadcasting[100]

Since the enactment Digital Performance Right in Sound Recordings Act of 1995 ("DPRA"), owners of a copyright in sound recordings have the exclusive right "to perform the copyrighted work publicly by means of a digital audio transmission." A statutory compulsory license is available to service providers of non-interactive digital audio performance services under sections 112 and 114 of the Copyright Act. The section 114 statutory license covers public performances by four classes of digital music services: eligible nonsubscription services (i.e., noninteractive webcasters and simulcasters that charge no fees), preexisting subscription services (i.e., residential subscription services which began providing music over digital cable or satellite television before July 1998), new subscription services (i.e., noninteractive webcasters and simulcasters that charge a fee, as well as residential subscription services providing music over digital cable or satellite television since July 1998), and preexisting

---

[99] *Id.* at §1006(2) (a) (2012).
[100] *See* "Streaming Revenue: Music Rights Owners and Agents Experience Unprecedented Speed, Transparency and Efficiency with Digital Services" by Bill Colitre for an excellent discussion of audio streaming services from "California Lawyer", May, 2017

satellite digital audio radio services (i.e., SiriusXM Radio). Currently, SoundExchange is the only entity authorized by Congress to administer the statutory licenses described in sections 112 and 114, and consequently collects and distributes royalties for the featured artist, non-featured artists and the sound recording copyright owner when content is played on a non-interactive digital source SoundExchange has paid out more than $3.5 billion in royalties since its first distribution. Under the law, 45 percent of digital performance royalties are paid directly to the featured artists on a recording, and 5 percent are paid to a fund for non-featured artists (of which 2½ percent to the American Federation of Musicians for distribution to non-feature musicians who have performed on sound recordings and 2½ percent to the American Federation of Television and Radio Artists for distribution to non-featured vocalists). The other 50 percent of the performance royalties are paid to the rights owner of the sound recording.

Noninteractive services are very generally defined as those in which the user experience mimics a radio broadcast: that is, the users may not choose the specific track or artist they wish to hear, but are provided a pre-programmed or semi-random combination of tracks, the specific selection and order of which remain unknown to the listener (i.e. no pre-published playlist). For services which provide an interactive service or on-demand access to certain tracks or artists (e.g., YouTube or Spotify), the statutory license does not apply, and a direct license must be obtained from the copyright holder.

While the performer receives his/her digital performance royalties directly from SoundExchange for the types of non-interactive services described above, with respect to interactive digital audio transmission services (i.e., where the subscriber selects the particular music to be played), the record company (which is typically the owner of the sound recordings under the recording agreement with the performer) has exclusive right to license these types of performing rights and is entitled to negotiate a "voluntary license" (as opposed to the compulsory license available to non-interactive services) with the service provider. In this instance, royalties to the performer are paid according to the terms of the recording (or distribution) agreement between the performer and the producer. Digital performances of recordings by means of interactive service are sometimes described in recording agreements as "Electronic Transmissions" for which the royalty rate is typically equal to the royalty rate that applies to the album on which the applicable recording was originally released. Means of electronic transmission include but are not limited to, "cybercasts", "webcasts", "streaming audio", "streaming audio/visual", "digital downloads", direct broadcast satellite, point-to-multipoint satellite, multipoint distribution service, point-to-point distribution service, cable system, telephone system, broadcast station, transmission of Recordings via a subscription service, and any other forms of transmission now known or hereafter devised) whether or not such transmission is made on-demand or near on-demand, whether or not a direct or indirect charge is made to receive the transmission and whether or not such transmission results in a specifically identifiable reproduction by or for any transmission recipient, and downloading.

A couple of important points regarding the treatment of interactive "electronic" transmissions under recording agreements are worth noting here.

First, unlike performance royalties for non-interactive services which are collected and administrated by SoundExchange and for which the performer is paid his/her 45 percent share of compulsory license income directly, as described above (and, as such does not get credited to recoupment of advances or other costs under the recording agreement, as it is not collected by the record company as the owner of the recording), as interactive performance royalties are paid to the record company (as the owner of the recordings under the recording agreement), the performer's share under the recording agreement is credited against outstanding advances or other costs as a conventional finished good royalty as would be the royalty for CDs and vinyl records.

Second, after much controversy in the early digital distribution years as to whether the royalty to the performer under a recording agreement would be treated as a "net receipt" (as are flat fee licenses, from which performers are generally credited with a royalty equal to 50 percent of amounts received by the record company), or instead as "net sales" from which a royalty based upon the wholesale or retail price of the record (subject to further adjustment under the calculation provisions of the recording agreement), the industry has settled on crediting the performer's royalty account with a royalty equal to the royalty rate which applies to the album on which the applicable recording was originally released (even for so-called "singles" and transmissions).

Third, because several provisions of the typical recording agreement provide for the performer to benefit by receiving higher "escalated" record and mechanical royalty rates by reason of attaining negotiated for sales plateaus, it is important to take sales by means of electronic transmission into account when negotiation those provisions For example, if a royalty rate will be prospectively increased, on an album-by-album basis, in connection with album sales in excess of 500,000 units and one million units, respectively[101], then track equivalent albums, where one might negotiate that 10 individual track downloads be agreed to equal one album sale and streaming equivalent albums, where one might negotiation that 1500 on-demand streams from paid subscription streaming services may equal one album sale or similar negotiated for plateaus should be sought during negotiations.

7.4.3.2   Rights in the Composition: Publishing

a. Publishing

Rarely in the major label system will the record company seek to acquire an interest in the copyrights in the compositions being recorded when written by the recording artist. Where the major or independent record company does so, it may do this by obtaining co-publishing rights to the compositions under a separate agreement where typically 50 percent ownership together with the exclusive administration rights are acquired and then administered by the label's music publishing division. However, rather than obtaining the co-publishing rights in this fashion, it is now more common for a record company to provide an incentive to the songwriting artist by including a clause in the recording agreement providing that if the artist enters into a publishing agreement with the record company's publishing affiliate, the record company will pay the artist mechanical royalties for the artist-written compositions embodied on the records at the then current full minimum statutory mechanical license rate, rather than at a lesser "controlled composition" rate provided for in the recording agreement (typically resulting in a 25 percent royalty improvement for the artist/songwriter).[102] Additionally, under the terms of a 360 Deal or

---

[101] These are milestones achieved by a very select number or artists/recordings annually in the current market.

[102] In 2008, the Copyright Royalty Board (CRB) set mechanical rates for the period 2008-2012 for the sale of physical recordings and permanent digital downloads, at 9.1¢ per song sold on a physical recording or digital download. In 2012, NMPA, RIAA and DIMA entered into an industry-wide rate agreement which covered the years 2013 to 2017; a consensus agreement that was approved by the Copyright

CEA Agreement, whereby the record company obtains an income participation in the artist's music publishing income, the record company will waive the right to participate in the music publishing income if the artist enters into a publishing agreement with the music publishing affiliate of the record company.

b. The Controlled Compositions Clause

It is standard for recording agreements to contain a grant of a mechanical license for the use of each composition written in whole or part by the artist at less than the statutory rate,[103] while typically capping the number of tracks per recording for which such royalties will be paid to 10 per album, seeking as low as possible a total mechanical royalty for all masters contained in an album as possible and specifying that any excess cost (i.e., for higher than a discounted three-quarter rate and/or for more than the maximum number of allowed track licenses) will be deducted from the artist's royalty. The theory behind such requirements is that the artist generally picks the songs he or she intends to records, and if the mechanical royalty breaks the licensing budget the artist should pay for the overage. This license will also cover sales via digital phonorecord distribution, though because of the requirements of the statute, the structure of the controlled composition language may be a little different to accommodate those statutory requirements. The typical controlled composition clause obligates the artist to obtain the mechanical (and promo video synchronization) rights from others to all compositions the performer desires to record, although this may be secured by the label's lawyers on the artist's behalf, at the label's discretion.[104] Two additional important observations (i) though record companies may seek to reduce mechanical royalty rates by contract, the U.S. Copyright Act specifically requires the full statutory rate be paid on downloads (defined in the Act as "digital phonorecord deliveries") in view of the fact that the record company incurs no manufacturing or

---

Royalty Judges. The 2008 rates and configurations were continued download with a rate of 1.75¢ per minute if the recording was over 5 minutes. *Royalties in the Age of the Internet / 2016 by Todd Brabec and Jeff Brabec*. More on this can be found in the Brabecs' Chapter 8 on Music Publishing Law in this volume.

[103] *See supra* §7.1. *See also* 17 U.S.C. §115 (2012).

[104] *See* the *controlled compositions* clause in the Recording Agreement included with this chapter's forms.

packaging costs in connection with the distribution of downloads; [105] and (ii) The National Music Publishers' Association, the Nashville Songwriters Association International, Warner Music Group Universal Music Group and Sony Music Entertainment have all submitted a joint agreement to the Copyright Royalty Board that will settle ongoing disagreements over the proposed new statutory mechanical royalty rates from 2018-2022, which new agreement includes a roll-forward of rates covering physical products, digital downloads, and ringtones.[106]

c. Rerecording Restriction

In order to preserve its exclusivity in the recordings (which benefit it possesses only because of its rights in the actual sounds embodied on that recording),[107] and to provide the record company with a reasonable period of time within which to recover all of the recording, marketing, promotion and other costs invested by the record company -- and hopefully to profit from that investment -- the record company normally requires the performer to agree not to rerecord (either in a studio or as "live" versions) any of the compositions recorded for a period of five years following the release of its recordings or three years after the artist's contract with the record company terminates, whichever is longer, so that multiple versions of a song recorded by the same artist do not concurrently find their way to the market absent label approval.

7.4.3.3. Publicity Rights

Promoting the sale of records involves advertising and directly touches on a performer's rights of publicity and/or privacy.[108] Therefore, the agreement specifically grants the record company the right to use and permit others to use the performer's name (i.e., that of an individual or a group), likeness, biography, and signature, along with any trademarks

---

[105] 17 USC 115(c) (3) (E) (i) provides that its provisions shall apply over "contrary royalty rates specified in a contract pursuant to which a recording artist who is the author of a nondramatic musical work grants a license under that person's exclusive rights" in the musical work, or which "commits another person", such as the publisher of the musical works written by the artist to grant a license in that musical work.

[106] See https://musicrow.com/2016/10/nmpa-nsai-sony-resolve-issues-with-copyright-royalty-board

[107] 17 U.S.C. §114 (2012).

[108] See Chapter 4 in this book's Intellectual Property Law companion Volume II.

that may be associated with the artist (i.e., a brand name and logo) for advertising and trade purpose. This right can generally be restricted by the performer to uses made only in connection with the manufacture, distribution, sale, and exploitation of the recordings or in the institutional advertising of the company, and the performer can typically limit the record company's rights to use only likenesses and biographical materials that have been pre-approved by the performer.

7.4.3.4. Merchandising Rights

At least within the major label system, the days when the major labels owned affiliated merchandising companies are behind us and record companies for the most party no longer seek to control the performer's commercial merchandising rights. However, the record company's participation in merchandising rights and revenues is an important component of the new 360 Deal, providing the recording company with a participation in a negotiated percentage of merchandising revenues (customarily gross merchandise revenues less only all actual, bonafide, direct, out-of-pocket costs incurred or costs which have been previously deducted by a third party manufacturer and/or fulfilment entity in connection with manufacturing and distribution of the merchandise concerned). Normally, the record company obtains only the negotiated-for income participation, and the performer's merchandise revenues are not treated as part of the gross receipts from which recording and marketing costs are recovered in the calculation of artist record royalties and payments due. Additionally, these merchandising revenues and costs are not typically further not cross-collateralized with other costs and income under the recording agreement.

7.4.3.5. Web Site Rights

The Internet has evolved from being a powerful threat to the traditional record industry's sales, initially facilitating an enormous level of piracy,[109] to become an equally powerful marketing and

---

[109] Industry sources estimate that music piracy in 2015 increased nearly 20% over 2014. *See* Tim Ingham, *Global Music Piracy Downloads Grew Almost a Fifth in 2015*, MUSIC BUSINESS WORLDWIDE (Jan. 21, 2016), http://www.musicbusinessworldwide.com/global-music-piracy-downloads-grew-by-almost-a-fifth-in-2015.

distribution tool for artists, record companies, and the industry as a whole. One aspect of that marketing is the creation of web sites and similar online destinations designed to promote particular groups or individuals, whether they utilize unique artist domain names, or are presented as part of a Facebook, YouTube or similar service. An official web site for a particular performer can serve a number of functions. First, it preempts others from using a domain name to either trade upon the good will of the performer or to post content the web site to criticize or attack the performer. An official site with the domain name or names most likely to be associated with the performer will appear first on search engines, thus pre-empting "rogue" sites unfavorable to the performer.[110] Second the site can be used to support fan clubs and others interested in the performer, by providing them with background information on the performer(s), allowing the fans to create bulletin boards, and promoting the commercial activities of the performer (including live performances and the sale of music, video and merchandise by mail or online downloads).

Typically, the recording agreement will grant the record company the exclusive right to maintain and host the performer's "official website" having a URL based on or containing the performer's professional name during the term of the recording agreement, and a non-exclusive right to host a website dedicated to the performer after the term in order to continue promoting the recordings produced and released during the term. The performer normally has the right to approve the so-called "look and feel", including the musical material and the content embodied, on the official website. Following the term of the recording agreement, the recording company should be obligated to transfer its rights in the official site (back) to the performer.

One area of heavy negotiation regarding website rights under a recording agreement concerns who owns the consumer data collected by the record company from the operation of the official website. The record company may require the performer to provide the record company with information obtained by the performer about users of and/or visitors to any sites which the performer controls, including e-mail lists obtained or derived from any such site, and the performer may obligate the record company to conversely provide him/her with information it obtains about users of and/or visitors to the official website.

---

[110] *See* Ricker, *"All You Need Is Hate" Prompts a Legal Refrain* at www.lawnewsnet.com/stories/A2265-1999Jun11.html.

Finally, the record company should be obligated to be responsible cover all costs for establishment, registration and maintenance of the official website as its sole non-recoupable expense.

7.4.4. Production Agreements

The rights conveyed under a production agreement include the services of the production company, the services of the performer, and the rights to the products of those services.

7.4.4.1. Production Company's Services

In a production agreement the production company agrees to produce and deliver recordings to the record company. Because records are not sold based on who produced them (as opposed to who performs on them), based on competition of product there is no need for the exclusive services[111] of a production company. Nonetheless, a record company may engage a production company to secure a key creative talent (such as a particular producer or musical director), and the agreement will require that the key talent participate in all recordings made under the supervision of the production company. Moreover, if that key talent is important enough, the agreement may provide that the record company receive the right to utilize the services of the production company over a certain period of time (to insure continued availability of that key talent). Further, the agreement may require that the record company engage the production company to record a certain number of masters within a time period (a recording commitment[112] with the production company). Many major artists act as their own "producers" in this regard (some even maintaining comprehensive home or commercial recording facilities for their recording activities), and will prefer to record through a "production deal" to leverage financial advantage and creative control. In other instances, independent producers may have desirable promising or established artists under contract (thereby functioning as indie "A&R" conduits for the label) and may advance considerable sums and energy in "demo" work for the artists in the process of gaining label attention. In such instances the producer may insist on a "production deal" involving him/herself

---

[111] See supra §7.4.1.
[112] See supra §7.4.2.1.

and/or his/her company in the production of the recording as a quid pro quo for the development effort and expenditures so undertaken.

7.4.4.2. Performer's Services

Sometimes a production company is engaged to produce recordings of a performer provided by the record company. In such a situation, the services of the performer are controlled by the agreement between the performer and record company (usually in the form of an exclusive artist's agreement).

However, many production companies may be owned by a performer who insists on controlling his or her own production, or the production company may have an exclusive artist's agreement with a performer before he or she (or the production company) comes to the record company. In either case, the record company seeks to benefit from the services of the performer, emulating the terms of a direct engagement as closely as possible.

To accomplish this, the production company is required to deliver the services of the performer that the performer would be required to render directly to the recording company under an exclusive artist's agreement. Next, the record company requires the performer to confirm a provision in which the performer agrees to comply directly with the terms of the agreement if for some reason the entity acting as intermediary (i.e., the independent production company) fails for any reason to do so. Finally, to protect itself against the possible loss of the performer's services (e.g., by possible defaults of the producer in its obligations to the artist, or by dissolution of the production company), the recording company may require that both performer and/or production company give it notice of such defaults or dissolution so that the record company may intervene and assume the responsibilities of the production company. In such an event, the record company becomes the producer while leaving the others to resolve the differences among themselves.

7.4.4.3. Rights Granted

A production agreement is entered into prior to the creation of the recordings, and the production company is often defined by the agreement as an employee of the record company for purposes of copyright in the performance and recordings, with all the recordings being works made for hire for purposes of the record company's copyright ownership.[113] Nonetheless, as in the case of the exclusive artist's agreement, the production agreement defines all of the rights being transferred including the rights in the recordings,[114] the compositions,[115] publicity rights,[116] and merchandising rights.[117]

7.4.5. Master Purchase/Master License

A master purchase/master license agreement is substantially different from either an exclusive artist's agreement or a production agreement. In a master purchase/master license agreement, a record company is buying the rights to recordings previously made and independently owned, whether by the artist, the production company, or even another label. No prospective services are involved, as the recording is complete by the time the transaction occurs. A limited exclusivity is created by causing the seller to agree not to compete with the record company by rerecording the compositions being transferred. Therefore, the focus of the agreement rests on the rights conveyed.

A master purchase/master license agreement may involve an outright and absolute sale of the masters, or it may involve a license for a limited (or unlimited) term within a limited (or unlimited) territory. It may involve a transfer of limited rights (such as "only for the manufacture and distribution of phonorecords") or unlimited rights (such as "for use in any and all media now known or hereinafter devised").

In negotiating such an agreement, the record company seeks all the same rights it obtains under its standard exclusive artist's agreement, including options for future recordings. The master owner, in contrast, seeks to retain as much ownership and control as possible.

7.4.6. Delivery and Control

The issues of delivery and control relate primarily to the recording process, i.e., who controls what is recorded, how it is recorded, and what is to be delivered. (Where a recording is acquired through a master purchase/license agreement, only the last consideration will apply.)

---

[113] *See supra* §7.4.2.2.
[114] *See supra* §7.4.3.1.
[115] *See supra* §7.4.3.2.
[116] *See supra* §7.4.3.3.
[117] *See supra* §7.4.3.4.

7.4.6.1. Control

The artist/performer is ordinarily the party most responsible for the sound and substance of the recordings that the public buys (although arguably in some new musical genres, including techno, hip-hop and rap, the producer is in effect the artist, primarily responsible for achieving a recordings signature sound). Moreover, although a recording represents a single product to a record company, it may represent an important milestone in the career of that performer through public exposure for the performer's output and performing style. For these reasons, performers seek to exert a significant amount of control over their recordings, including the selection of repertoire, recording personnel, and technical decisions.

Although the ultimate control over a recording (i.e., whether or not it is released to the public) is exercised by the recording company,[118] the recording process represents a considerable investment that the recording company seeks in every way possible to protect. In addition to bringing its resources, relationships and the experience of its personnel to the recording process, a successful recording company can presumably contribute marketing expertise that can be invaluable in guiding the emerging performer toward success in the marketplace.[119]

Conflicts may be resolved by compromises allowing the performer to propose the form, manner, and content of the recording, with the company exercising the right of approval over what is proposed. If the record company believes that the performer needs guidance in creating a more commercial sound, it may suggest that the recordings be produced by a particular record producer (who exercises primary control over the actual recordings). Unless the artist is recording pursuant to an "all in" recording fund[120] the budgets for any recordings inevitably are controlled by the company, which does not authorize the recording to commence without first approving the budget.

Unless the artist has a very high degree of leverage, which is generally attained by reason of a history of sales success attributable to the artist's previous recordings, recording agreements will require that the recordings delivered by the artist to the record company be

---

[118] It should be noted that although some superstars may be able to force a company to release their recordings, no one can force a company to be enthusiastic about that release.

[119] Control over the marketing is invariably reserved to the recording company.

[120] See supra §7.3.3.2.

"technically and commercially satisfactory." Whether a recording meets the "commercially satisfactory" standard is obviously a subjective judgement. One way to approach the issue is to negotiate that a recording that is of the same caliber and style as the recordings previously delivered to and released by the record company (or, if as to the first record under a recording agreement, then of the same caliber and style of songs and performance that induced the record company to enter into the recording contract). Artists with leverage are able to limit the delivery standard to "technically satisfactory" recordings.

While the record company makes the ultimate decision whether to release a record, the wise artist attorney should be able to negotiate a provision for a "release commitment", which obligates the record company to actually release records delivered by the artist which comply with the delivery standard called for under the recording agreement. A typical release commitment provides that the record company will distribute an album delivered by the artist in the United States within one hundred twenty (120) days after delivery and, if the record company fails to do so, the artist's sole remedy for non-release is the right to notify the record company, within sixty (60) days after the end of the one hundred twenty (120) day period concerned, that the artist intends to terminate the term of the recording agreement unless the record company releases such album within sixty (60) days after receipt of the artist's notice, failing which the artist may terminate the term of the recording upon further notice. Obtaining commitments to release records outside of the United States is more complicated and generally tied to the album attaining a level of commercial success (sales or chart position) in the United States.

7.4.6.2. Delivery

The delivery requirements specifically identify what physical materials, including technical recording elements and paperwork, must be delivered to the recording company in order to satisfy the recording commitment.[121] This "delivery" signals the end of the recording process, and allows for the computation of recording costs for which the performer will be charged.[122] If the recording process is totally under the control of the record company, delivery is nothing more than

---

[121] *See supra* §7.4.2.1.
[122] *See id.*

the performer's appearing to record at a time and place specified by the company, and then doing so to the best of his or her ability. To the extent that the performer has any control over recording and editing, the agreement states that delivery involves submission of a fully mixed audio and mastered multi-track[123] digital audio tape or its equivalent (e.g., digital files on a hard drive recorder) suitable for the creation of CDs and, with increasing rarity, metal masters used in the pressing of vinyl records (now primarily for DJ production of dance music and for audiophile buyers or hard core fans of an artist, only. The recorded music industry today is enjoying explosive growth in sales of vinyl records. For example, each year the record industry promotes an annual "Record Store Day", the 10th installment of which fell in April 22, 2017, during which vinyl album sales grew 213 percent to 547,000 sold (across all retailers, not just indies), making it the biggest non-Christmas season week for vinyl albums since Nielsen began electronically tracking point-of-sale music purchases in 1991. Specifically, at indie retailers, there were 409,000 vinyl albums sold in the week ending April 27, 2017 (up 484 percent).[124]

Delivery provisions have been complicated in recent years by the practice of "sampling" (i.e., the taking of excerpts from preexisting phonograms and including them within a new work). Because sampling generally, though not always, involves taking only a small amount of another composition and then altering it through processes of editing, remixing, and digital manipulation, many artists perceive this practice as defensible without a license from the owner of a copyrighted underlying work (fair use being a "defense", and not a "right")[125]. However, because some courts have determined that such use is not permissible,[126] record companies (who frequently have been

---

[123] A recording may embody as many as twenty-four or thirty-two (or more) tracks – that is, it can be composed of that many parts (i.e., violins on one track [mono] or two tracks [stereo]; percussion on another, etc.). Nonetheless, these multiple tracks are generally mixed down (balanced for tone, volume, prominence, etc.) to two tracks (left and right), or to 5.1 or 7.1 channel "surround" sound configurations, with the ".1" signifying bass to subwoofer channel processing, and remaining channels denoting center/left/right/rear placement in theatre, including increasingly home theatre, installations.

[124] *See* http://www.billboard.com/articles/columns/chart-beat/7783467/record-store-day-2017-top-selling-vinyl-albums-singles (last visited August 13, 2017)

[125] *See* §1.5 of this book's Intellectual Property Law companion volume.

[126] *See* Bridgeport Music, Inc. v. Dimension Films, 410 F.3d 792 (6th Cir. 2005), where the court refused to accept a de minimis defense and instead held the use of even

left with significant financial responsibility for these infringements on their artist's releases) are responding with increasingly complex and detailed delivery requirements specifying that if a recording is to incorporate sampled music, the sampled music must be licensed for use prior to the composition embodying that sampled use being mastered (thus avoiding mastering costs if the sample cannot be cleared). The company will also require detailed reporting of what music is being sampled, chronological sequencing, artist information, recording dates, and other sample data. Finally, because clearing samples is a time-consuming and often expensive task, the delivery and release schedules can be significantly delayed if clearances are not secured early on.

7.4.7. Royalties

Before considering the structure of royalty arrangements for recording artist and songwriter participations in record sales, a brief overview of the economics of generating record revenue in the current marketplace is in order.

The Record Industry Association of America (RIAA) reports that only ten percent of recordings released by the major labels in recent years are likely to be profitable. The wholesale revenue to a label on a $16.00 to $20.00 (at retail) CD release is $10 and the online digital download revenue from the sale of an album over iTunes or the other major online music retailers at $10 to $12.50 ($1.00 to $1.25 per single) will be closer to $5.00 or $6.00 (i.e., 50 percent to 60 percent of the online list price of the album or single). Moreover, download sales are predominantly single song transactions rather than album sales. Thus, an album length recording that sells 100,000 units via CD and paid downloads (which in the current marketplace will be considered a "hit" recording) may generate in the range of $750,000 in *gross* revenues to the record company or distributor (when online sales are factored in). After recoupment of manufacturing costs of $ 0.50 to $ 0.55 a unit for CDs manufactured in large quantities (independent distributor costs for smaller manufacturing runs can be significantly

---

3 notes lasting 2 seconds from one sound recording, incorporated without authorization as a repeating loop in another, constituted infringement. But see VMG Salsoul, LLC v. Ciccone, 824 F.3d 871 (9th Cir. 2016), in which the Ninth Circuit accepted a de minimis defense in a suit over an unlicensed sound recording sample that was used in Madonna's "Vogue."

higher), packaging costs calculated by the labels at as much as twenty five percent of gross, advertising and promotional costs of twenty percent of gross, and artist royalties of ten percent to fourteen percent (which generally will not result in additional payments to the artist until record production costs and interest are recouped from the artist royalty participation), the label is left with a "profit" of approximately $250,000 for a modest "hit" before factoring into its corporate revenue the costs of its own overhead and operations, including the cost of artist development for projects that may never be released or if released may never be profitable. Although million-selling records may bring record companies and recording artists profits 10 times or more greater than that for a 100,000 unit-selling project, each successful project must support losses of another nine unsuccessful releases, which may be considerable if recording and preliminary marketing costs for such projects are high. And with unauthorized downloads and other duplication of music exceeding the number of purchased records for many artists and genres, not to mention high volumes of low-paying streams bringing relatively modest compensation to artists and labels versus the traditional physical sales, these numbers bring the challenges facing record companies and recording artists into sharp perspective.

Royalty provisions in a typical recording contract can take up as much as half of the entire document. They are extremely complex and are often tailored to the particular distribution, sale, and accounts-collection business models of the respective record company, which can themselves very substantially. While these provisions may change with each selling season, they are influenced by changes in the competitive landscape, as well as by the commercial implications of emerging technological innovations. The record companies today characterize the basis upon which royalties are computed as "transparent." Gone now are the days when, for example, it was common to pay a royalty on 90 percent of the records sold, for the antiquated reason that when records were first being manufactured and distributed, they were made out of shellac, which was breakable during shipping. Hence a so-called "breakage" allowance was incorporated into artist agreements for technical reasons that no longer exist. Similarly, gone now are "packaging charges" calculated as a percentage of a recording's wholesale pricing and originally based on audio cassette and CD plastic jewel-box cases and packaging (which are now being increasingly replaced by less expensive paper sleeve containers, if not by package-free downloads) which formerly appeared as a standard deductible expense of the label.

7.4.7.1. Advances and Recording Costs

All recording costs and certain other costs incurred in the production, manufacture and marketing of records are treated as advances against (and recoupable from) the performer's royalty. Recording costs generally include wages, fees, advances and payments of any nature to or in respect of all musicians, vocalists, conductors, arrangers, orchestrators, engineers, producers, copyists; payments to a trustee or fund based on wages to the extent required by any agreement between the record company and any labor organization or trustee; union session scale fees payable to the performer and other musicians and vocalists; studio, tape, editing, mixing, re-mixing, mastering and engineering costs; artist development costs including physical training, vocal conditioning, cosmetic enhancement and other similar costs, authoring costs; all costs of travel, per diems, rehearsal halls, non-studio facilities and equipment, dubdown, rental and transportation of instruments; all costs occasioned by the cancellation of any scheduled recording session; all amounts paid in connection with the production, conversion, authoring, mastering and delivery of audiovisual materials prepared for or embodied on records; all expenses of clearing and licensing any samples embodied on recordings; and all other costs and expenses incurred in the production, but not the manufacture, of records or otherwise which are then customarily recognized as recording costs in the recording industry.

Examples of other costs chargeable against and recoupable from the performer's royalty may include, without limitation, costs of artwork in excess of the record company's standard costs, and mechanical royalties in excess of the "ceiling" or "cap" set under the "controlled composition clause of the recording agreement.[127]

Recording agreements provide for advances to the performer typically structured in one of two different ways: First, the performer may receive an "in pocket" advance in specified installments, payable on execution of a recording agreement, commencement of recording, and delivery of the record (50 percent on execution of the recording agreement or commencement of recording of the applicable record, 25

---

[127] See supra §7.4.3.2.b.

percent on commencement of mixing and 25 percent less any costs incurred in excess of the mutually approved recording budget upon delivery and acceptance of the record by the record company being a typical payment schedule). Under this formula, the record company will additionally pay the recording costs (as additional recoupable royalty advances) pursuant to a mutually approved budget (as to which, if the performer delivers the recordings under budget, the underage is retained by the record company and if the performer exceeds the budget, the record company may have recourse against the performer's mechanical royalties or against the performer as a direct debt owed to the record company. Alternatively, the performer may be given an "all in recording fund" in a specified dollar amount, a portion of which (typically 10 percent to 20 percent) is paid to the performer as an "in pocket advance" upon execution of the recording agreement or commencement of recording the applicable record. All subsequent and approved costs of production are paid from this "recording fund" during recording, and the remaining balance is paid to the performer upon delivery and acceptance of the record by the record company. The "in pocket" advances are intended to cover the performer's living expenses during the recording process as well as fees incurred by the performer in entering into the agreement payable to the performer's attorney, accountant, manager and other members of the team.

Nonetheless, on the theory that it is best for the artist to obtain as much money as possible upfront, it is common practice for artists' representatives to seek large advances for each recording under the terms of the contract. Although the artist will be expected to pay actual recording costs out of these advances (or more accurately, in common practice, the record producer will retain and pay out recording costs according to an agreed upon schedule with the artist), what is left over after payment of actual recording costs is generally retained by the artist as an advance royalty. While in some cases these advances will be arbitrarily set at the outset according to what one may expect actual recording costs to be, one way to link these advances to the performance of prior recording released by that artist is to state that the advance for the next recording will be a certain percentage (i.e., 50 to 150 percent) of royalties earned by the preceding released record as of a certain date prior to or up to the time when the company is exercising its option for a new recording. In such cases, the intent is clearly to obtain not only recording costs but advances for the direct benefit of the artist, which usually represents a large part of an artist's livelihood from release to release. It is important to note, however, that advances are almost universally recoupable from the artist's subsequent royalty entitlements, so that where advances on a prior project remain unrecouped, the label will usually seek the right to roll those deficits onto the artist's account for future recordings. Consequently, the artist and representative should carefully consider whether advances for recording or living costs might be better spent on marketing or other promotional efforts that could increase the likelihood of a recording's success, and thus leverage future income, and cover personal expenses through other means when possible.

Before addressing strategies for obtaining and managing sales advances in the artist negotiation, it must be noted that fewer and fewer artists can command the significant six- and even seven-figure advances that were for many years a hallmark of the industry. For one, the cost of recording has diminished significantly as a function of new technology. And of course, for another, label profitability has diminished as fans have gravitated away from purchasing music, have shifted their buying from albums to singles when they do purchase music – consequently rendering million-selling records the province of only a few new and legacy acts, where not long ago gold and platinum record sales were almost commonplace.

7.4.7.2. Calculation of Royalties

Royalties, or sums paid to artists, producers and a limited number of other creative contractors for the sale of their records, no matter how denominated, are divided into two categories: an artist's royalty payable to the performer as a performer, and the mechanical royalty payable to the copyright owner of the compositions) whether that is the performer or some third party).

a. Artist's Royalties

An artist's royalties clause in a conventional recording agreement first states the percentage royalty that the company will pay the performer (the base rate), and then explains how that royalty will be adjusted.

1. **Basic Royalty Rate.** Depending on the policy of the record company, the artist's royalty base rate (the "Basic U.S. Rate") is a certain percentage of the "Royalty Base Price," which may, depending on the practices of the record company concerned, be based upon (i) the suggested retail list price ("SRLP"), (ii) the wholesale price ("WSP"), (iii) or "posted price to distributors" ("PPD") of the recordings in a phonorecord/disc and download formats (usually ranging from 10 percent to 20 percent of the SRLP, with royalty percentages calculated against wholesale prices proportionately higher in view of the reduced wholesale price of the recording). The SRLP may be defined as an artificial uplift (e.g., 130 percent) of the record company's lowest wholesale price in the configurational category concerned. The Basic U.S. Rate is computed on sales in the United States of top-line, top-price records sold through normal retail and permanent download channels in the album configuration, and is reduced both for sales outside the United States and with respect to sales of records that are other than full-priced records sold in the album configuration. Royalties for new artists generally start in the lower end of the 10 percent to 20 percent range, and for top-selling artists will start in the mid- to upper end of this range. These royalty percentages are in turn calculated against a percentage of all records sold. This percentage of records sold is negotiable up to 100 percent (with labels typically paying on 90 percent of physical goods shipped, less returns), and the royalty percentage may be subject to escalation based on sales performance of the album for which the royalty rate is being computed, and/or for each subsequent recording if the preceding recording was released under the contract.

With the rapidly increasing decline in sales of records in the physical disc configuration, two new trends for royalty definition have emerged in recent years: With one, the Royalty Base Price is determined on the WSP or PPD for the record concerned, which eliminates taking into account many of the old school artificial royalty reductions that no longer have relevance in the digital era, such as packaging/container charges and free goods deductions. In another, exploitations of records via digital platforms, such as downloads and streams and in other than album configurations, are taken into account in determining whether the threshold for sales-based royalty escalations have been attained. Not unsurprisingly, these new so-called "transparent" royalty calculations result in the same number of pennies per album being paid as were payable and paid under the old formulas, despite the fact that the rationales for the old artificial reductions (such as container charges and free goods allowances no longer make sense in the digital era). In negotiating the royalty escalation provisions of a contemporary recording agreement, one could negotiate that the Basic U.S. Rate will increase on the basis of album units to include digital downloads of albums, with sales of ten (10) digital download singles equalling one (1) album for purposes of reaching the threshold for rate increase, and/or that number of streams that will equate to one single or one album sale.

2. **Adjustments.** The effective Basic U.S. Rate may be modified by certain charges, exclusions and/or deductions, which have become fairly standard in major label agreements, but may be susceptible to some negotiation.

A. *Free goods.* Free goods (copies given away for promotion purposes to music journalists and critics, to radio stations for prizes, etc., and to retailers based on volume of units sold, effectively reducing the nest wholesale price of goods to the retailer) are always excluded from the payment of royalties on the theory that the record company receives no payment for them. However, because some free goods are used by record companies to promote newly released recordings by granting retailers additional "free" CDs based on the volume they order for sale and which they may in turn sell (in effect, discounting the wholesale price of the units purchased), one may argue that there should be a limit on the amount of recordings used for these purposes. Such a limit is generally addressed by limiting all free goods to a certain percentage of the total records sold at full price. If the applicable Royalty Base Rate is based on PPD, there likely will not be an adjustment for free goods as records are no longer given away for promotional purposes. In any case, there is no justification for container charge and/or free goods reductions for record sales in digital configurations.

B. *Ancillary distribution.* In the past record companies heavily distributed records through nonrecord store outlets with sales prices set at substantial discounts to those paid by record stores. These outlets included record clubs, military post exchanges, and wholesale sales of large stocks to exporters. For each of these, the record company would pay a reduced royalty, usually calculated as a certain percentage (50 percent to 75 percent) of the base royalty. Although sales through such channels have diminished markedly, and for some labels almost entirely, these provisions still appear in many standard agreements.

C. "New" media formats. When tapes and CDs were originally introduced, because start-up costs were so great and the cost of production was so much higher than the conventional phonographic disc recording, record companies negotiated a special reduced royalty. This royalty generally stated that the record company would pay the artist the same royalty for a tape or CD as was paid for a disc, despite the fact the tape or CD bore a higher wholesale and retail price. This special royalty has now been largely dropped, in part due to the demise of the vinyl LP and even audio cassette as popular consumer formats, and royalties are now commonly paid based upon the actual selling price of the CD (save for certain special situations in foreign countries). However, learning from this, record producers are now including a special royalty for new media that sets the royalty for that new media (regardless of its actual selling price) at a certain percentage of the royalty paid for the same recording in CD format, even if the costs of such distribution, as with digital downloads, bear little relation to the costs of selling the physical phonogram product. The "new media" reduction no longer applies to sales of records in digital configurations (including sales by download as well as streaming transmissions).

D. Packaging deduction. A certain percentage of the selling price is allocated to pay for the cost of packaging, which is deductible from the base royalty-sales price. Although most record sales are now in CD and digital download formats, provisions for vinyl and tape products still appear in most contracts, and most major labels remain reluctant to forego their "packaging" charges for even non-physical digital sales. Common deductions are 10 percent of the SRLP for all disc albums, mini-LPs and 12-inch singles; 15 percent of the SRLP for all disc records packaged in multi-fold containers or with special inserts or attachments; 20 percent of the SRLP for tapes; and 25 percent of the SRLP for CD and other new formats. For the most part, the packaging deduction no longer applies to reduce royalties on sales of records in digital configurations.

3. Statutory Royalties. With the emergence of new statutory performers' rights royalties, initially in such areas as DAT home recording and now for digital download and other transmission services,[128] provision should be made to assure that the performer actually receives these royalties. As previously noted, record producers

---

[128] *See, supra* §7.4.3.1.b.

in the early days of these technologies attempted to retain these royalties for their own benefit. Moreover, as these rights accrue they will join other international arrangements where there may be opportunities for performers to benefit from performing rights income arising in countries other than their native country, through participation in some international collective rights organizations.[129]

4. Digital Phonogram Distribution.[130] The statutory recognition of digital record distribution does not create a new right insofar as the performer is concerned. It is intended to protect songwriters. Nonetheless, it emphasized the potential of this market as a new and alternate form of distribution, an expectation borne out since the law's enactment. As the cost of digital phonorecord distribution is significantly less than the cost of physical phonogram (i.e., CD) distribution, efforts should be made to negotiate significantly higher royalties on digital sales for artists and a waiver of such adjustments as the deduction for the cost of the "package." Record companies will, of course, try to resist this and treat such distribution as subject to basic rate (often reflected as packaging fee allowances of 25 percent of gross revenues, or manufacturing/packaging charges).

5. Alternate Royalties. All income from licensing of master recordings, as well as from all sources that are not otherwise specified in the agreement, should be shared on a 50-50 basis.[131]

---

[129] See D. Sinacore-Guinn, COLLECTIVE ADMINISTRATION OF COPYRIGHTS AND NEIGHBORING RIGHTS: INTERNATIONAL PRACTICES, PROCEDURES AND ORGANIZATIONS, §§18.0 et. seq.

[130] See, supra §7.4.3.1.a.

[131] It should be noted that some artists have secured revenue share agreements with independent and foreign labels, particularly in the 360 Deal arena, in which the parties split profits 50/50 or on the basis of some other negotiated proportion after the label recoups direct costs of recording and marketing a record, including artist advances. Such arrangements are characterized by labels as more of a partnership than employment arrangement, and may be advantageous to artists whose projects perform at a "break even" or better level and who are in a position to properly monitor and audit actual label costs. More importantly the Detroit music producers who launched the career of Marshall Mathers (aka "Eminem") and have an exclusive recording agreement with him in 2010 in 2010 persuaded the 9th Circuit (on appeal) that sales of Eminem's recordings via iTunes and other digital services should be treated as "masters licensed" rather than as "records sold", resulting in a 50/50 revenue split between label and artist of net download revenues, rather than 12% to 20% of the SRLP of the sales (the latter position having been taken by Eminem's label in its prior accountings). The difference to the artist was estimated as $1.00 to $2.00 per album ($ 0.10 to $ 0.20 per single), which in the case of a best-selling artist like Eminem will

b. Mechanical Royalties

In addition to the royalties payable to the performer, the record company is obligated to pay a royalty to the copyright owner of any compositions used in the recording.[132] To the extent that a record company owns the compositions in question or exerts complete control over their selection,[133] there should be no reason to address this issue in the performer's agreement. However, because most performers have some degree of initial control over their repertoire, a record company sets the parameters of mechanical royalties that it is willing to pay and states that if the performer elects to record compositions that necessitate paying royalties to the copyright owners greater than those budgeted by the record company, then the performer will have the difference deducted from the artist's royalties. A standard mechanical royalty provision often limits payment to "three-quarters of the statutory rate" (commonly referred to as the controlled composition rate)[134] up to a fixed maximum amount per album (e.g., ten times the controlled composition rate, assuming a typical "album" contains 10 songs).

In dealing with standard statutory rates, one possible area of confusion arises when the compositions being licensed exceed five minutes. Under the terms of the current statutory license,[135] the minimum statutory rate is based on a mixed minimum and long-form rate system where every composition, regardless of length, is subject to a standard "flat" minimum royalty, while longer compositions (i.e., those exceeding five minutes), are to receive a royalty calculated on a per minute basis (i.e., a seven-minute composition would receive a royalty of seven times the one-minute figure). In order to limit their royalty obligations, record companies commonly seek to define the "statutory rate" as the flat minimum rate, while writers seek the more generous per minute, long-format rate. Unless it can otherwise be specifically negotiated and set forth in the agreement, current practice tends to favor the record company's interpretation, particularly where the phrase "minimum statutory rate" is clearly set forth.

---

consequently result in adjusted royalties in favor of the artist of millions of dollars. *See* F.B.T. Productions, LLC; Em2M, LLC v Aftermath Records; UMG Recording, Inc.; Ary, Inc., 621 F.3rd 958 (9th Cir. 2010), *cert. denied*, 562 U.S. 1268 (2011).

[132] *See, supra* §7.3.3.2.
[133] *See, supra* §§7.4.7.2, 7.4.6.
[134] *See, supra* §7.4.3.1.
[135] 17 U.S.C. §115 (2012); 37 C.F.R. §307.3 (2015).

Most compositions are now licensed at 3/4 of the statutory rate (commonly referred to as the "3/4 Rate"). It is also common for recording contracts to incorporate provisions to establish the maximum amount of mechanical royalties payable on an album (typically 10 but on rare occasions 11 or 12) even if the recording delivered by the artist or production company actually contains more than that stated. It would appear that the law should respect the contract as to the number of compositions covered in such a clause, but require that producers pay full statutory royalties for any additional compositions. This protection not only benefits the artist who is also a songwriter, but also non-writing artists seeking access to top-flight material by other writers for their recordings.

In negotiating the controlled composition rate, most recording companies will be very firm in demanding the adjustment to 75 percent of the statutory rate. An artist with some bargaining strength may be able to demand "bumps" in the rate so that the minimum is increased for each subsequent recording made under that agreement (e.g., First Album – 75 percent; Second album – 85 percent; Third Album – 95 percent; Fourth through Seventh – 100 percent) or bumps based upon sales of the album (e.g., 1-249,999 – 75 percent; 250,000-499,999 – 87.5 percent; 500,000+ – 100 percent).

The more problematic element of the controlled composition clause is the per album rate. An artist who records a significant number of compositions written and/or owned by other people (i.e. one half or more of the total compositions) risks the possibility that mechanical royalties payable to other creators will result in the artist receiving no royalties for his or her own compositions included on that album or, even worse, that mechanical royalties in excess of the per album rate will be deducted from the artist's record royalties. In theory, an artist has some control over which compositions to record. However, record companies generally exercise final "approval" rights over the artist's selections and unless it is quite certain that the artist will be recording almost exclusively self-controlled compositions, some effort should be made to tie the decisions of the record company's repertoire choices to a payment scheme for those choices which will not penalize the recording artist (if for example, the label presses for covers rather than the artist's original compositions, or to include 12 or more compositions on a recording when the artist is comfortable with 10).

7.4.7.3. Merchandising Income

Where formerly record companies would seek to obtain commercial merchandising rights from the artist, either under the terms of the recording agreement or by means of a separate merchandising agreement, the near universal trend is that the artist retains those rights subject to the grant to the record company of an income participation with respect to the exercise of the artist's merchandise under the 360 Deal provisions of the recording agreement (or, in many cases, under a separate "collateral entertainment activities agreement" relating to the artist's non-record entertainment activities entered into concurrently with the recording agreement). Under the older model, a common payment agreement provides that the record company will share equally the net merchandising income it earned by licensing merchandising rights, after deduction of all expenses and an administration fee calculated as a percentage of the gross merchandising income. The record company itself would often license these rights to an outside merchandising specialist, whose fees for marketing and administrative services are typically 50 percent of gross license fees for merchandising rights (where the label or the specialist is not also engaged in the manufacture and distribution of such merchandising products for sale). Where the label is merely acting as an agent to engage a third party licensing representative to manage merchandising in exchange for a fee of typically half of revenues generated, the artist should push aggressively to reduce the label's percentage participation in resulting net revenues.

7.4.7.4. Music Publishing Royalties

In almost all instances in which the performer assigns music publishing rights to the record company (or more frequently to a music publishing company affiliate of the record company), the rights granted and royalties for those rights are governed by a separate music publishing agreement with all the standard royalties applicable thereto.[136] That being said, a label offering an artist a 360 Deal may seek to incorporate publishing rights into a single agreement which also addresses participation in touring and merchandising, as well as recording rights and revenue sharing of the artist's "publisher" revenue interests (although the "composer share" interest will remain excluded).[137]

---

[136] *See* the Brabecs' Chapter 8 on Music Publishing Law in this volume.
[137] *See infra* Chapter 8.

7.4.7.5. Music Videos/Videograms

While it is still true that most artist music videos are very expensive commercials used to promote that artist's newest recording, the market for music videos in various formats and in various media has grown to the point that for many artists significant income may be generated from the licensing and sale of music videos, or from any collateral advertising revenues which such videos may generate from online sources and social media, including YouTube and Facebook. Recording companies commonly acquire music video rights within the recording agreement, in a form modeled after the recording agreement itself (becoming a kind of mini-video recording agreement within the agreement). The company will acquire the right to produce one or more music videos taken from compositions included on a record produced under the same agreement and to distribute those videos in the form of videograms. As was the case with the recordings themselves, the videos are produced using money "advanced" by the recording company and recoupable out of the artist's total royalties (for both phonograms and videograms), and consequently the artist's representative should take care to advise their clients that budgets for these projects should be reasonable in relation to the promotional value and revenues they are likely to support. While closely resembling the "recording costs" advance system for phonograms, the one difference here is that the recording company may agree to charge the artist's account only one-half of the actual recording costs, or alternatively to charge the artist's account only one-half of the amount and reserve the right to recoup the balance out of videogram royalties only. However, the increasing success of e-mail and web-driven "guerrilla" marketing using video and audio materials to promote touring and recordings (e.g., via YouTube, FaceBook and a number of other social networking channels which have effectively supplanted MTV, record stores and radio as the "places" young people go to listen to new music) may enable artists to forego highly produced video projects (which may have been essential when MTV was the primary marketing tool for new music) for more creative (and inexpensive) conceptual projects that can satisfy or exceed audience expectations and attract viral distribution by old and new fans online.

When the resulting music videos are in fact sold for home video use, the record company will pay the artist a royalty based upon the suggested retail list price (10 to 15 percent SRLP), subject to standard adjustments for alternative means of distribution (e.g., consumer downloads) and discounting practices. Where the videos are streamed online, advertiser- supported web sites or mobile and other services from which the label derives revenue, the artist should seek to obtain some royalty participation based in this ad revenue as well. Where the videograms are licensed for use of television, cable, or other media, the record company will commonly deduct a distribution fee (around 25 percent of gross income), all costs and expenses of distribution, all third-party payments (e.g., union fees, royalties to other parties), and taxes and then, out of the remainder (the adjusted gross income) it will commonly pay the artist a fixed percentage (usually 25 to 50 percent of the adjusted gross income).

7.4.7.6. Collateral Entertainment Activities

In the present "360 degree era,, contemporaneously with the entering into of any recording agreement, the artist will likely be required to enter into an agreement (a "CEA" Agreement), covering the artist's "collateral entertainment activities," which typically include the artist's endeavours in the areas of (i) merchandising, (ii) touring, (iii) music publishing (iv) the artist's activities in and throughout the entertainment industry, as a singer, musician, publisher, lyricist, producer, mixer, re-mixer) and the exploitation of all rights related to such activities); (v) the artist's activities as a personality, presenter, celebrity, spokesperson or in connection with the sponsorship or endorsements of products or services (and the exploitation of all rights related to such activities); (vi) the use of artist identifications such as name(s), photos/likenesses, logos and trademarks in connection with the establishment of any artist-based or subscription-based web sites offering varying levels of content (sometimes referred to as "Fan Club Sites") (and the exploitation of all rights related to such activities); and (vii) any other entertainment activities engaged in by the artist. As a result of the negotiation of these CEA Agreements, excluded endeavours might include the artist's appearance in television (scripted or non-scripted), film or other non-musical audio-visual recordings or other modes of distribution and merchandising sponsorships and endorsements in connection therewith or the promotion thereof, and other music activities not related to writing, recording, touring in support of his or her own projects (i.e., a "day-job" in another area of the music or entertainment industry, or perhaps producing for other artists). The CEA terms may be contained within the four walls of the recording agreement or may be contained in a separate CEA Agreement. The CEA terms may provide that the record company is actually in control of some or all of the artist's collateral entertainment activities (so-called "active participation"), in which case the record company (or one of its affiliates) would act as the artist's music publisher and have the right to furnish the artist's services to others in the areas of touring, sponsorships, endorsements and/or to reproduce or license the Artist's Identifications to others in connection with tour and retail merchandise. In other cases (so-called "passive participation") the record company may not control the artist's collateral entertainment activities, but rather be entitled to an income participation on the artist's earnings in those areas. Whether the record company is an active or passive participant in the artist's collateral entertainment activities, the artist's earnings streams are typically not cross-collateralized with each other or with artist's recording related income.

Where the record company has a "passive participation" in the artist's non-record income, the artist may be obligated to account for and pay to the record company (or the record company may be entitled to collect directly and keep for its own account) an income participation in the range of five percent (5 percent) to twenty percent (20 percent) of the artist's non-record income. This participation percentage can vary greatly depending on the type of income to which the participation is being applied (e.g., 20 percent as to publishing, sponsorships, acting and endorsements and 10 percent as to touring and merchandising). The participation percentage may be prospectively reduced after the record company's participation receipts attain a certain level (e.g., from 10 percent to 7.5 percent once the record company has received one million dollars ($1,000,000) in non-record income. percentages amount equal to seven and one-half percent (7.5 percent). The amount of the "gross non-record income" against which the participation is being determined may be less up to thirty five percent (35 percent) of such gross to the extent that such amount is actually paid to the artist's managers, attorneys, business managers and/or booking agents. If the artist enters into a publishing agreement with the record company's music publishing entity, then the record company will typically not be entitled to participate in the artist's publishing income prospectively after the publishing agreement is entered into with the record company affiliate.

In addition to the typical "off the top" deductions from "gross" for the artist's professional representatives discussed above, each type of non-record income in which the record company participates will likely have its own category of deductions from "gross" in arriving at the "net" to which the participation will apply (e.g., costs of artwork creation, manufacture and distribution in respect of merchandise, mechanical royalties payable to the artist under the controlled compositions clause of the recording agreement, and the actual costs of "sound and lights" and costs of opening acts charged to the artist and certain other "show expenses" in connection with touring). The negotiation of tour participations is the most complex, and in some cases may result in an "X percent of gross less specified expenses with a floor of y percent of gross" calculation. It may be possible as well, particularly with a "new and developing artist" to negotiate that personal appearance revenues relating to a particular live performance for which the artist receives a less than a certain amount (e.g., appearance fees of less than ten thousand dollars ($10,000) are excluded from the record company participation).

The period of time for which the record company is entitled to its non-record income participation is the subject of negotiation as well, and typically exceeds the term of the recording agreement. Furthermore, the CEA agreement may provide that the record company has the right to receive its participation with respect to non-record income derived from any agreement or opportunity which arises or is substantially negotiated during the term of the recording agreement and that is entered into within some negotiated period of time thereafter. Additionally, the record company may have the right to receive its participation in connection with any concert (or series of concerts) entered into (or commenced) during the term of the recording agreement until its completion, notwithstanding the earlier termination or expiration of the term of the recording agreement.

Where the record company is an "active participant" in the artist's non-record entertainment activities, each applicable non-record agreement (e.g., concert touring, music publishing, fan club website, merchandising, etc.) is separately negotiated on an arm's length basis on the terms generally applicable to the type of agreement being entered, although it can be argued that the transactions are less than "arm's length" given the fact that the artist is being required to enter the applicable agreement as a condition of entering into the recording agreement.

7.4.8. Accounting

The accounting provisions of the recording agreement set forth when and how royalties are to be paid.

7.4.8.1. Accounting Periods

Performers' royalties are normally paid on a semi-annual basis, while mechanical royalties are paid on a quarterly basis. Payment is made forty-five to ninety days following the sales or accounting period being reported and are accompanied by statements indicating sales occurring during the period. Statements will vary in detail from company to company, and consequently the level of detail to be contained in the statements can be an additional issue worthy of negotiation.

7.4.8.2. Reserves against Returns

As with book publishers,[138] a record company sells records to distributors and record stores subject to a right of the distributor/store to return unsold copies. Thus a record can be sold during one accounting period and can be "unsold" or returned during the next. Rather than obligating the record company to pay all royalties during the first period and then, if subsequent sales do not offset these returns, requiring the performers to repay royalties in later periods (which they may not be in a financial position to do), record companies impose a reserve against returns policy, enabling them to withhold artist's royalties otherwise due and payable until such time as any prior overpayments (based on the rate of returns) can be settled. The artist in such circumstances should always insist that reserves be liquidated if not actually offset by returns within a fixed number of accounting periods after they are initially withheld. For established artists, limitations on reserves can be negotiated based on prior commercial performance. New artists will generally be at the label's mercy on this issue, because sales results (and the prospective volume of returns) are nearly impossible to predict for a first recording. There should be no

---

[138] See Gail Ross' Chapter 11 on Literary Publishing Law in this volume.

reserves held with respect to income derived from downloads or streams (or other forms of digital distribution) inasmuch as those formats are not subject to a privilege of return.

7.4.8.3. Recoupment and Cross-Collateralization

As previously indicated, recording contracts charge the total cost of producing the recordings (and any advances paid to the performer) against the performer's royalty account.[139] Under this procedure, the record company first applies all of the performer's earned royalties toward recovery of its recording costs and certain other permitted costs (i.e., recoupment) and only then becomes obligated to pay royalties to the performer.

This concept is enlarged when the company obtains the right to apply royalties earned from one recording to repay recording costs of another under a single multiyear/multi-album recording agreement. In some instances, under a 360 Deal the record company may offset certain costs/revenues between not only individual recordings, but also against income derived from the artist's collateral entertainment activities. This cross-collateralization occurs most frequently in multirecord agreements under which the recording costs of all masters made under the agreement may be recouped prior to the company paying the performer any royalties. It should be noted, however, that such cross-collateralization might occur even where these grants of rights are governed by separate agreements. The result, of course, is that an artist's potential upside from a breakthrough hit album midway through a multiyear contract may go to pay off prior label deficits and put little or nothing in the artist's pocket -- other than indirectly, through increases in the artist's touring, merchandising and/or publishing income (if publishing is not likewise made part of a cross-collateralization formula with the label) driven by a record's popularity. It should be noted that, even in the present "360 Degree" era, cross-collateralization of the artist's record and non-record income is not common. An unusually large advance which has been forecast against projected earnings to be derived from all of the artist's record and non-record activities might justify some requirement of cross-collateralization, however.

---

[139] See supra §7.4.7.1.

7.4.8.4. Audit Rights

Despite computers, sophisticated accounting software, and often a battery of accountants and attorneys, few large organizations are absolutely free of errors in their accounting practices. Performers must have the right to audit a record company's books and records with respect to an agreement. Although this right is found in all agreements, variations in its scope and terms of implementation are numerous and a number of restrictions limit the audit right. For example, reasonable notice of the intent to audit must be given (so that arrangements may be made to provide company personnel to supervise the audit). Notice may also enable the record company to "clean up its act" before audit scrutiny illuminates practices that may be intentional rather than inadvertent. Contracts will typically provide that the audit must occur during normal business hours and at the company's place of business, or where its business records are customarily maintained (which may be in an accountant's office, or perhaps the offices of a parent company in another city or even country). The company may restrict who may perform the audit – usually a certified public accountant not currently or recently engaged in performing an audit of the company's books and records in another dispute. This latter requirement is designed to dissuade accountants, who are auditing for one client, from notifying other performers whose accounts are or may be in error, so as to in effect solicit additional audit work or to use information obtained in the settlement of one audit against the company in another. The company often restricts audits to a frequency of no more than once per year and may declare that any statement to which the performer fails to object within twelve to twenty-four months of its issuance is deemed binding on the artist. Finally, if objection is made to an accounting and a settlement is not reached, the performer may be given only one year to eighteen months to commence litigation or be forever barred therefrom (a self-serving statute of limitations). As an "incentive" for the record company to insure the accuracy of its reporting, the artist may seek an interest charge on delayed or under-reported payments, along with the recovery of all or some portion of his or her audit costs, where a judgment or settlement in excess of, for example, 10 percent of any (under-) reported royalty is established. Note that audits which identify bona fide discrepancies are often settled by compromise between the record company royalty recipients. Where settlement is not achieved, the artist may be forced to initiate a claim against the record company which can be exceedingly expensive and time-consuming (and which may serve to upset the balance of the relationship between artist and record company. Consequently, addressing dispute resolution mechanisms upfront in the recording agreement can be of real significance down the road.

7.4.9. Bankruptcy

Given the complex financial nature of a recording agreement with its provision of paying royalties and collecting identified expenses, it is possible for a recording company to make money from a particular agreement while the artist makes little or nothing from that same agreement. Where the artist is charged for significant production expenses and any advance paid against subsequent royalties (usually for living expenses), it is easy to understand why so few recording artists see real earnings from their projects. In response to this, some artists have sought to reject unprofitable contracts (which may require additional recordings even where the artist has seen little or no royalty overages on prior contractual albums) under the bankruptcy laws, but with limited and mixed results.[140] In order to prevail in terminating or reforming a recording contract, the performer will have to prove that the contract is causing the performer grievous financial distress and that he or she needs to be released in order to start afresh.[141] Yet even if this is accomplished, it is an open question as to whether the court will allow the performer to enter into a recording agreement with a competing company.[142]

While recording agreements will certainly not allow performers a termination right in the event of artist bankruptcy, the threat of bankruptcy can be considered in the (re)negotiation of terms to assure fairness in artist/ label dealings. Conversely, the artist will want to

---

[140] Stuart J. Wald, *Bankruptcy and Personal Services Contracts: What Works, What Doesn't, and Why*, 16(1) ENT & SPORTS LAWYER 3-10 (1998).

[141] *See* Kokoszka v. Belford, 417 U.S. 642, 644-45 (1974).

[142] *See* Wald, *Bankruptcy and Personal Services Contracts: What Works, What Doesn't, and Why*, 16(1) ENT & SPORTS LAWYER 3-10, at 10 (1998).

insure that his or her agreements with the label permit the artist to terminate the agreement, or recapture some or all rights granted by the artist under the agreement, if the label itself enters voluntary or involuntary bankruptcy proceedings, creating a risk if not likelihood that the company will be unable to fulfill its executory obligations (whether for lack of funds, or from the prospect that the artist's contacts with the company will be "out," and new management may have little personal or creative interest in artist's projects.

MUSIC INDUSTRY LAW – ILLUSTRATIVE FORMS:

- 360 Collateral Entertainment Agreement – Merchandising
- Administration Agreement
- Artist Management Agreement
- Band Partnership Agreement
- Booking Agreement and Rider
- Distribution Agreement
- Exclusive Songwriter Agreement
- Label Services Agreement
- Master (Sampling) Agreement
- Master Use License (Television)
- Merchandise Agreement
- Musician Session Release
- Net Profits Definition
- Publishing / Sample Interpolation Agreement
- Recording Agreement
- Single Song Recording Agreement
- Songwriter Split Agreement
- Sponsorship Agreement (Events)
- Sponsorship Agreement (Products)
- Tour Promoter Agreement
- Touring (Band) Member Agreement

── CHAPTER 8 ──

MUSIC PUBLISHING LAW

Jeffrey Brabec,* Todd Brabec[†]

8.1. Music Publishing and Copyright
8.2. Common Music Publishing Industry Agreements
8.3. Music Licensing

8.1. MUSIC PUBLISHING AND COPYRIGHT

The primary basis of the Music Publishing business is the United States Copyright Act which provides protection to original works of authorship including musical works and any accompanying words, dramatic works, including any accompanying music, and motion pictures and other audio-visual works and sound recordings into which music is incorporated, among other categories of works.

Copyright is a worldwide concept set forth in the national laws of most countries, in international copyright treaties and conventions, as well as in bilateral agreements between the United States and other countries. It is important to note that the protections offered under each country's laws can and do vary as to the specific rights involved as well as the provisions affecting those rights including, among others, the duration of protection, the types of works protected and the exceptions and limitations on those rights.

8.1.1 Exclusive Rights of Copyright

The exclusive nature of the rights of copyright under the United States Copyright Act forms the basis of most compensation due

---

* **Jeffrey Brabec** is Vice President of Business Affairs for BMG.

† **Todd Brabec** is an Entertainment Law attorney and former Executive Vice President and Worldwide Director of Membership for ASCAP.

The authors extend their thanks to all of the very fine people with whom they have worked over the years and to the many songwriters, writers/artists, and film and television composers responsible for the creative efforts at the heart of the Entertainment Business...

musical works. These rights are set forth in 17 U.S.C. Section 106 of the law. Specifically, they are:

i. "The right to reproduce the copyrighted work in copies or phonorecords." This right includes the ability to authorize copies of a work that are fixed in practically any form, including tapes, records, CDs, digital audio files and sheet music.

ii. "The right to prepare derivative works based upon the copyrighted work." This right allows a copyright owner to authorize motion picture adaptations, arrangements, abridgements, translations, sound recordings and other uses that are based on the original work.

iii. "The right to distribute copies or phonorecords of the copyrighted work to the public by sale or other transfer of ownership, or by rental, lease or lending." This right gives the copyright owner control over the first authorized record or copy of the work. After the first "copy" is authorized, anyone else may record the work by complying with the compulsory licensing provisions of the Act.

iv. "The right to perform the work publicly." This right forms the basis of all performing rights organization licensing activities and royalties throughout the world (ASCAP, BMI, SESAC, GMR, etc.).

v. "The right to display the copyrighted work publicly." This right authorizes individual images of a work such as posting lyrics on a website.

vi. "In the case of sound recordings, to perform the work publicly by means of a digital audio transmission." This right is similar to the public performance right for musical compositions but is very limited in its scope and applies primarily to non-interactive music streaming services, satellite radio and music subscription services. Interactive (on-demand) services are not covered.

It is important to note that the Act also contains certain limitations on these exclusive rights including "fair use," specific types of reproductions and distributions by libraries and archives, certain educational uses in the course of face-to-face teaching activities, certain types of secondary transmissions of broadcast programming by cable and performances in the course of religious services (but not if the service is broadcast to the public at large), among others.

8.1.2. The Role of the Music Publisher

As opposed to record companies which represent master recordings and recording artists, *music publishers* represent musical compositions which include music, lyrics and scores, and the songwriters, lyricists and/or composers who create them, which are, in turn, embodied in master recordings and live and other recorded performances. In their role as representative of the composition and writer, their responsibilities include registration of their compositions with the U.S. domestic licensing and collection organizations (e.g., ASCAP, BMI, SESAC, Global Music Rights, Harry Fox Agency, etc.), and the United States Copyright Office, along with registration of their compositions with performing right and mechanical right societies outside the United States via subpublishers. Publishers also manage the enforcement of rights against infringers, the promotion of compositions to secure new uses (such as television, motion pictures, advertising commercials, video games, apps, etc.), the licensing of all types of music users and the collection of income. Their role also includes responding to licensing and other inquiries relating to the compositions, monitoring music users to ensure receipt of correct royalty and/or fee accountings, auditing licensees to make sure that under accountings have not occurred and will not occur, developing strategies for licensing new media, staying abreast of legislative or legal proceedings affecting copyright, funding demo recordings, setting up collaborations with other writers and providing travel funds, if necessary, and, in the case of many songwriters, advancing them monies and providing financial support to make sure, among other reasons, that they can concentrate on writing and have the right equipment to do such.

8.1.3. Sources of Income

Because music publishing refers to the representation of musical compositions, lyrics and scores, the potential sources of income are much more varied than for the representation of master recordings due to the fact the composition is more than an individual recording artist performance on a specific master that may be requested by a potential music user (e.g., think of the many thousands of compositions which have been recorded by dozens of different performing artists, often in the course of multiple decades of popularity). In fact, in many cases, there is no pre-existing master at all in the licensed use (i.e., where the licensee intends to commercially "premiere" the composition in their own original recorded version). In both cases, however, the music publisher will be involved directly or indirectly in the licensing process and negotiation of fees whereas the record company will only be involved if the specific master recording that it owns is being licensed for the particular use requested.

Examples of just some of the many income-generating media and means in which music can be used are television (broadcast over-the-air, cable, video-on-demand, Internet), terrestrial radio, motion pictures, electronic and mobile video games and apps, CDs, vinyl, tape and downloads, advertising commercials, Broadway, off-Broadway, road and amateur theatrical productions, printed lyrics or music, karaoke, streaming services, slot machines, digital and non-digital jukeboxes, interactive dolls and toys, e-cards, physical greeting cards (including printed lyrics or music performed via embedded chips), theatrical trailers, television promos, online lyric sites, ringtones, ringbacks, sampling, lyrics on clothing, "how to play" lessons, DVDs, holograms and subscription services, to name just a few.

8.2. COMMON MUSIC PUBLISHING INDUSTRY AGREEMENTS

The primary agreements that will be encountered in the music publishing area are:

- The Single-Song Agreement
- The Exclusive Songwriter Agreement
- The Co-Publishing Agreement
- The Participation Agreement
- The Administration Agreement
- The Co-Administration Agreement
- The Foreign Subpublishing Agreement
- The Joint Venture Agreement
- The Acquisition Agreement

The following sections will concentrate on the more essential provisions of these agreements, providing insights and perspective as to how each is generally deployed and implemented.

8.2.1. The Single Song Agreement

If the music publisher is interested in one (1) of a songwriter's compositions (or a selected few) but does not want to enter into an exclusive arrangement for an entire catalog, including works written in the future, the writer may be offered a single song agreement. Under this type of agreement, the songwriter will assign either one hundred percent (100%) or fifty percent (50%) of the copyright plus full worldwide administration rights to the publisher. The "term" (i.e., the duration of the agreement) is usually the life of the copyright in the composition(s), with possible partial or full reversion at some stated time in the future if certain negotiated milestones are not satisfied. There will usually be an advance paid which will be recoupable from future royalties derived from exploitation of the composition.

In many cases, the publisher will also offer to return all rights in and to the composition to the writer if a commercial recording or other negotiated licensed use (for example, placement in a motion picture or television series) does not occur within a stated period of time after the signing of the agreement. If an advance was paid to the writer, the reversion is usually conditioned on the repayment of the advance. In addition, if a professional studio demo recording was financed by the publisher as a means of securing licensing interests, its costs will, in most cases, have to be repaid prior to the ownership of the demo being assigned to the songwriter (although the publisher may not otherwise have the right to commercially exploit the demo recording).

8.2.2. The Exclusive Songwriter Agreement

This agreement is one of the primary contractual relationships between songwriters and music publishers. Under this type of agreement, songwriters agree to create musical compositions exclusively for a music publisher during a set period of time which is negotiated between the parties. The songwriter grants the exclusive right to own or co-own all the compositions written by the songwriter during the period (with exceptions when a writer is hired to compose the music or creates the lyrics for a motion picture or television series and a waiver of exclusivity is granted). In exchange, the songwriter will receive monetary advances for publishing rights in the compositions to be created and assigned, either on a monthly, quarterly or yearly basis, as well as other benefits such as the publisher's administration of the copyrights, collection of income for uses, promotion and protection and enforcement of rights.

As with the single song agreement, the copyright in the compositions will be assigned and transferred to the music publisher either on a one hundred percent (100%) basis or fifty percent (50%) basis if a co-publishing agreement is entered into between the songwriter's publishing entity and the major publisher (i.e., the songwriter retains a half interest in the copyright). The music publisher will also be given the right to administer the compositions throughout the world.

8.2.2.1. Minimum Delivery Commitments

Under virtually all exclusive songwriter agreements, there is an obligation on the part of the songwriter to deliver a minimum number of newly-written compositions (a "Minimum Delivery Commitment") during each contract period of the Term (e.g., a year, 18-months, 2-years, etc.) and, depending on whether the songwriter is also a recording artist or record producer, a certain number of recorded and commercially-released compositions (a "Minimum Release Commitment").

If the commitment is limited to newly written compositions, there is usually a requirement that a composition must be suitable for commercial exploitation in the publisher's reasonable opinion. If it is not, then the composition will not count toward the Minimum Delivery Commitment. In many agreements, there will be a provision that allows such a rejected composition to be excluded from the agreement and returned to the songwriter. Since many compositions may be co-written with other songwriters, the agreement will virtually always provide for fractional equivalents to count toward fulfillment of the Minimum Delivery Commitment. For example, if the Minimum Delivery Commitment is seven (7) wholly-written compositions, there will be language stating "or the equivalent thereof." Thus, if a songwriter delivered fourteen (14) co-written compositions in which the writers' interests are fifty percent (50%) each, this would fulfill the seven (7) full-composition requirement.

Depending on the contract and company, there may be requirements as to how compositions are delivered before they are deemed accepted by the publisher. For example, the publisher will usually ask for a professional quality demo recording (in at least MP3 (320 kbps) quality format), full details of writer(s) and composer(s) and their respective percentage contributions to the compositions, third party publisher information if applicable, plus a lyric sheet of each composition being delivered.

If the Minimum Delivery Commitment has a release requirement, the fulfillment requirement becomes much more complex, depending on, in most cases, whether the songwriter is a recording artist or record producer. For example, if the songwriter or writers are also performing artists with a record deal, the contract may take the form of an album-based agreement in which there is a commitment for the commercial release of a newly recorded album (or its equivalent) during each contract period of the term of the agreement. If the songwriter is a record producer or a non-recording artist, the deal may instead take shape as an individual track release agreement in which there will be a commitment for the commercial release of a number of individual compositions regardless of whether they are on one album or on releases by a number of different recording artists. In both cases, however, there is usually a delivery commitment of a specified number of unreleased, newly-written compositions and a separate commercial release commitment with, generally, a smaller numerical requirement. For example, an agreement might require ten (10) newly-written compositions as the Minimum Delivery Commitment but require that only four (4) of those compositions must be released. Other agreements might leave the number the same so that the Minimum Delivery Commitment and Minimum Release Commitment are identical.

It should be noted that the numbers mentioned represent the minimum requirement for a particular contract period. If the writer delivers more than the minimum, some agreements allow for a portion of the excess (at least in the case of the Minimum Release Commitment) to be used toward the next contract period and others treat the excess as additional compositions during the period of delivery or release.

Suffice it to say, there are many variations in this area depending upon the bargaining power of the parties and the amount of advances being paid for the minimum number of compositions required for delivery. Obviously, the larger the advance figure, the higher the release commitment; the lower the advance, the lower the delivery and/or release commitment.

8.2.2.2. Album per Contract Period Commitment

In most album-based agreements, there is a commitment by the writer/recording artist to have one (1) album commercially released during each contract period of the agreement. For example, the term of a representative publishing agreement might be for the longer of one (1) year or until the commercial release of an album, with the publisher having additional options to extend the agreement for additional contact periods each of which will have a release commitment of one (1) additional newly recorded studio album, or an equivalent number of master tracks (e.g., ten).

8.2.2.3. Option Pickups

In most album-based publishing agreements, the current contract period extends through the commercial release of the album which fulfills the commitment for that period until a number of days after the delivery of the next newly-recorded album to the artist's record company. Thirty (30) days is a representative figure in many agreements. In effect, the publisher is given the right to listen to the new album as well as secure information as to the number of compositions and shares controlled by its writer (versus those controlled by other collaborators) and the mechanical royalty rate being paid for that album before it has to decide whether or not to exercise its option to move into the next option period that will control that album. If the option is exercised, the publisher will control the delivered album. If the publisher decides to not exercise the option, the term of the album-based agreement will expire and the writer/artist will be able to offer the album to another publisher or to self-publish the compositions contained in the album.

There are a number of issues which may occur if the publisher does not exercise the option, foremost being what happens to the compositions that have been written since the release of the last accepted album which are not contained on the album for which the option was not exercised. The result depends on negotiation with some scenarios resulting in all such compositions being returned to the songwriter with another being any compositions which have not been commercially exploited by the publisher (for example, if the publisher had secured a video game license of such a composition it would be retained) being returned to the songwriter.

8.2.2.4. Royalties

The royalty split between songwriter and music publisher is an equal sharing of non-performance income. For example, if $10,000 is received for a digital download mechanical or television synchronization license, the publisher will generally agree to pay the songwriter fifty percent (50%) of these monies and retain the other fifty percent (50%). Since the songwriter usually receives his or her writer's share of performance income directly from their performing rights organization (e.g., ASCAP, BMI, SESAC or GMR), the writer would not be entitled to receive anything on the basis of the publisher's share of performance income unless the writer and publisher have entered into a co-publishing agreement.

8.2.2.5. Advances

Advances are non-returnable payments to the songwriter which are recoupable from future royalties due the writer under the publishing agreement. In virtually all cases, the writer's share of performance income is not used by the publisher to recoup advances since performing rights organizations pay the writer's share of performance income directly to the songwriter. In some cases, the publisher might be able to use this source of income to help recoup advances but this is usually when the advances are very substantial and the songwriter is willing to agree to such terms so as to secure the advance.

The amount of advances depends on a number of factors including whether the writer is bringing an existing royalty earning back catalogue or new material with strong potential into the agreement, the current and past activity of the writer, the future projects that the writer might be committed to, whether there is competition between publishers for the services of the writer, the excitement and confidence in the songwriter and his/her potential by the creative department of the publisher, whether the songwriter is a recording artist or has the potential of signing a record deal, whether the writer is an established or up and coming producer, among many, many other factors.

Advances can be paid on a yearly basis, on a monthly basis or on a weekly basis. Additionally, advances may be paid when certain delivery criteria are achieved (such as $____ on delivery of five (5) newly written compositions), and certain release criteria are achieved (for example $____ when two (2) compositions have been commercially released in the United States by a major or indie record company). There also may be advances paid when a writer's compositions reach certain trade chart levels (for example Top 10 on the Billboard Singles Chart), or certain threshold income or sales levels (for example 100,000 United States Soundscan digital units sold).

There are many possible variations for these arrangements and all are dependent upon the bargaining power of the parties.

8.2.2.6. Approvals

Depending upon the bargaining power of the songwriter, there may be a number of restrictions placed upon the music publisher with respect to its ability to license the compositions without the approval of the writer. For example, some agreements (although not that common) give the songwriter almost total control of how the compositions are licensed. Other agreements establish general categories of potential uses which require writer pre-approval, such as advertising commercials, political announcements, or NC-17 rated motion pictures. Others can establish very specific exclusions, such as advertising commercials for personal hygiene products or alcohol, scenes in a film or television series which incorporate nudity or violent activity, etc. And others may just refer to a type of use limitation, such as a featured visual vocal sung by a character in a motion picture, television show or video game, as opposed to a background vocal or instrumental use which may be permitted.

The list of uses that need the songwriter's approval can be extensive and, as mentioned above, can be very general or very specific in nature. In cases where there are approval rights provided for in the agreement, the writer usually negotiates for a certain period of time in which to respond to a request from the music publisher for approval or disapproval, and if there is no response within the time allotted, the use is, in most cases, deemed approved. For example, a representative clause might state that if the songwriter (or his or her authorized representative) does not respond within five (5) days of the written request from the publisher, the use is deemed approved. For information purposes, since television series requests usually require quick responses because of the shooting schedule of the series or episode in which the composition is being used, the publisher will try to shorten the time period for the writer to respond (for example, one (1) or two (2) business days for television license requests). Resolution of these issues, however, depends on the bargaining power of the parties negotiating the agreement as well as the policies of the particular publishing company.

As a practical matter, having too many restrictions on a publishing agreement can tie the hands of a publisher which seeks to trade in clearable and licensable compositions. In fact, many publishers maintain lists of compositions that are not constrained by approval rights (other than by the publisher) and they communicate those lists to the many clearance personnel, music supervisors and potential users of music as a service whose requirements may not be limited to a particular song, genre or style, and whose turnaround time for completing a music cue requires immediate confirmation of a song's availability and terms of use.

8.2.2.7. Reversion and Retention

Many agreements are for the life of copyright in the compositions subject, of course, to the provisions of the U.S. Copyright Law with respect to statutory terminations (i.e., Sections 304 (c) and 203 of Title 17, U.S.C. of the Copyright Act). Depending upon the parties' bargaining power, full or partial contractual reversions can be negotiated. There will be more specifics as to this subject in the following section on Co-Publishing Agreements, but virtually all reversion provisions (other than statutory copyright reversions) are subject to the music publisher having recouped (or having been repaid) all or a percentage of all unearned advances, which have been paid to the songwriter.

8.2.3. Co-Publishing Agreements

The co-publishing agreement is one of the more prevalent contractual agreements between songwriters and music publishers. In most cases, it is part of an exclusive songwriter agreement, but it can be a stand-alone contractual arrangement which applies to one or more musical compositions without being tied to a future active songwriter agreement.

A co-publishing agreement assumes that a writer already has an existing publishing company or is about to form one. When a songwriter creates a musical composition, that writer is in reality the copyright owner of that work and in theory is also the publisher of that composition – assuming, of course, that the songwriter is not signed to another publishing company or some other entity claiming ownership rights. At this point, the writer must decide on the form of his or her publishing company – e.g., a single proprietorship, a partnership or an LLC or S-Corp corporate entity – clear a name and join a performing right organization. The ASCAP and BMI application process normally has a one-time administration fee as well as minimum performance eligibility requirements to join. In the case of SESAC, there are no dues or fees but one has to be invited to join. The same is true with Global Music Rights. With ASCAP and SESAC, one must be a publisher member/affiliate to receive publisher performance monies (50% of all distributions) whereas BMI will pay the writer the publisher share for a performance if the writer does not have an existing BMI publishing company.

8.2.3.1. Copyright Ownership of Compositions

In most cases, the major music publisher (i.e., the established commercial music publisher which will act as the dominant "executive" partner with control over the subsequent exploitation of publishing rights in the compositions) and the writer's publishing company will share the copyright ownership of the composition controlled by the agreement on a 50/50 basis. In this regard, the songwriter will assign fifty percent (50%) of the copyright to the major publisher and assign or retain the remaining fifty percent (50%) for the writer's publishing company. There are other percentage sharing arrangements but this formula is the most common. This interest is of course independent of the songwriter's fifty percent (50%) revenue share to which the writer is separately entitled (i.e., the publisher's share is 50% and the writer's share is 50% – and if a co-publisher is granted half the "publisher share", it is in effect entitled to 25% of all revenues associated with the exploitation of the composition).

8.2.3.2. Administration

The major publisher (rather than the songwriter's publishing company will act as the administrator and undertake the dominant responsibilities of registration, protection, promotion and licensing of the compositions. Since this is ostensibly the primary focus of a full service major publishing company, if not full-time business, it is arguably in a position to manage these tasks more successfully than the songwriter/publisher, whose more important contribution to the relationship may require focus on writing, recording and performing.

8.2.3.3. Sharing of Income

Income is shared on an equal basis between the major publisher and writer's publishing company after a number of deductions. In virtually all cases, this sharing is of the net income and not the gross income received in the United States. The income sharing can take one of two forms. One method is for the administrating publisher to pay the songwriter his or her fifty percent (50%) of income received and then pay the songwriter's music publishing company fifty percent (50%) of the remainder. For example, if $10,000 were earned, the writer would be paid $5,000 as the songwriter and the major publisher and writer's company would each share the remaining $5,000 ($2,500 apiece). This results in the songwriter and the writer's company receiving $7,500 of the $10,000 (a 75/25 split). Publisher performance income would be paid differently because the songwriter's share of performance income is usually paid directly to the songwriter by the writer's performing rights organization (or by the publisher if such rights have been licensed directly). The so-called publisher's share of performance income is paid directly to the administering publisher who then shares such royalties on a 50/50 basis with the songwriter's company.

The other method of royalty accounting is to just combine the songwriter share and writer's co publisher's share of non-performance monies into one payment, which would result in a royalty payout to the writer of seventy-five (75%) of non-performance income and fifty percent (50%) of the publisher's share of performance income. In either case, the result would be the same monetarily.

8.2.3.4. Advances

Advances can be paid as provided for in the exclusive songwriter agreement and can also be based upon other factors depending on whether the agreement is (i) an album release based agreement (one that is more appropriate for a writer/recording artist who has an existing recording artist agreement with a record label or is about to sign such an agreement),(ii) a producer-writer release based agreement (one that recognizes the reality of a producer being used by a number of different recording artists to produce their recordings with the delivery emphasis being on the commercial release of individual tracks rather than one album featuring one recording artist), or (iii) a writer-centric deal (i.e., an agreement that focuses on the songwriter's ability to create and regularly deliver new musical compositions either solely or in collaboration with others for recording by third party artists).

If the agreement is based on the delivery and commercial release of albums (which is standard if the writer is a recording artist), advances are structured in a number of ways with the following being two of the more common:

- a percentage of the advance will be paid when the album is delivered and accepted by the record company with the remaining portion paid when the album is actually released; or
- the entire advance will be paid on the commercial release of the album.

There are a number of variations in this area, but the actual amount of the advance will almost always depend on the number of compositions written by the songwriter which are embodied on the album as well as the amount of mechanical royalties that will be payable to the major publisher for its own account, that of the songwriter and the songwriter's publishing company. To illustrate, the co-publishing agreement might condition the full amount of the advance upon the songwriter/artist writing at least seventy percent (70%) of the album, with the aggregate mechanical royalties being paid to the publisher at the statutory rate being no less than 64 cents (e.g., if seven (7) of ten (10) songs comprising a ten-song album are licensed at the statutory rate of 0.091 cents per song, the resulting cumulative royalty is 63.7 cents). Another variation, among many, is to calculate the full advance based on the writer having written one hundred percent (100%) of the album with the mechanical royalties that are payable being at least ten (10) times statutory (where the label caps the number of licenses it will pay for per album at ten (10) tracks, even if 11 or 12 tracks appear on the recording). If either or both of these criteria are not met, then the advance will be reduced proportionately. This is a very important calculation since the controlled composition clauses which, in many respects, only relate primarily to physical product for the territory of the United States can be very complicated and can have a very substantive impact on the calculation and recoupment of the advance monies which are payable.

Recognizing the changing environment of how recordings are released (for example, increasing emphasis on EPs and singles, etc.), advances can be structured in a number of other ways, including less moneys for individual track releases, or bonus advances based on achieving agreed upon sales or streaming criteria with a smaller album release base advance (if a full album release eventually occurs), with advances possibly reduced by or recalculated because of monies already paid for previously released compositions that appear on the album.

The type of record company releasing the album (major vs. indie), the territory of release and the configuration of the release (physical and digital, versus digital only) are also very important, material factors in determining whether the full or reduced advance will be paid (e.g., different amounts might be paid depending on whether the release is on a major or an indie record label).

How the parties define what constitutes an "acceptable" recording company for purposes of satisfying this royalty requirement is a very important issue to consider, as it may determine whether the artist will be entitled to receive an advance. "Acceptable" may be tied to gross revenues, number of annual releases, total sales, number of releases that "chart", etc., quantified over a one-year or two-year prior period. Often the issue is addressed by attaching a schedule of acceptable record companies (major and indie). If an album is released on a record label that does not fit within the agreed criteria, the release may not trigger the payment. Consequently, the term may be suspended and extended until another "album" is released in a manner satisfying the requirement.

The size of an advance might also vary based on whether an album is released on a major record label or an indie. For example, a sample clause might provide for an advance if the album is released by a major record company with such advance being reduced if the release is by an indie. In some cases, advances may be payable for foreign release in territories outside the U.S. if there is no U.S. commercial release. Additionally, the amount of an advance may be based on whether it is a digital only release or a digital plus physical release.

Advances are also based on a number of other factors, including whether the songwriter also has a recording agreement as a performing artist (and is thus in position to record and promote his/her own music), if not whether there is interest in signing the writer by a record company (taking into account the reputation of the company), whether the writer has a track record of past success as a songwriter and/or recording artist, the belief by the publisher in the quality of compositions being written, and the types of projects in which the writer is currently involved.

In contrast to the album based advance type agreement, in the writer/producer type of co-publishing agreement the advances may be based on the commercial release of a set number of individual tracks, with advances paid as these tracks are sequentially released (for example, no payments occur until the release of a minimum of four (4) tracks out of a required twelve (12) or more in the contract period). Additional advances can be paid as other release criteria are achieved (for example, another advance when eight (8) aggregate releases occur during the then current contract period, etc.).

8.2.3.5. Approvals

Approvals are similar to those mentioned in the section on exclusive songwriting agreements. To reiterate, approval rights may vary widely depending on the sensibilities of the songwriter involved, the company's policies, and the bargaining power of the parties.

8.2.3.6. Reversion and Retention of Rights

The majority of co-publishing agreements are for the life of copyright. Nonetheless depending upon the bargaining power of the parties and the policies of the major publisher, many agreements do provide for reversion of some or all rights at a certain negotiated time in the future if certain milestones have not been achieved (e.g., after ___ years if there's been no commercial placement of a particular composition(s), if the composition has failed to generate a certain minimum amount of publishing revenue, etc.)..

For example, a publisher might agree to re-assign to the writer's publishing company administration rights to the songwriter's and the songwriter's co-publisher's share of all compositions a number of years after the expiration of the agreement, with proviso that such reversion will not occur until all advances have been recouped or repaid. If this scenario occurs, the major publisher will continue to own and control its rights and the parties may then enter a co-administration agreement to establish how the compositions will be jointly licensed and administered in the future.

Other agreements may provide for a full reversion of all rights at some negotiated point in time in the future (for example, all rights to revert at the later of twenty (20) years after expiration of the term or recoupment of all advances paid to the writer and/or the writer's publishing company).

It should be noted that the effective date of many of these reversion clauses will be at the start of the next calendar quarter or semi-annual calendar period after the actual reversion date to coincide with the end of a royalty accounting period, either from the publisher or the collection societies.

8.2.3.7. First Negotiation and Matching Rights

Many co-publishing agreements have provisions dealing with first negotiation and matching rights. A first negotiation provision is usually triggered when a co-publisher either decides to sell its interests in the compositions or receives an offer from a third party to acquire the co-publishing interest. This type of clause will give the major publisher an exclusive right to negotiate with the co-publisher for a period of time (for example, thirty (30) days) to try to negotiate an agreement for the rights being sold.

In the matching right scenario, the major publisher is given a "first refusal" right to match the terms of the offer from the third party. There is always a time limit placed upon such right. In addition, there is usually language contained in the provision that gives the major publisher a "last refusal" right to match any revised substantive offer that is made by a third party if the major publisher elected not to match the initial offer.

8.2.4. Participation Agreements

The participation agreement is almost identical to the co-publishing agreement with the primary difference being that the writer's publishing company is not a copyright owner since the copyright to the compositions will be exclusively assigned to (or owned on a work for hire basis by) the administering publisher. The royalty split will, in most cases, be the same as the co-publishing agreement (75/25 of non-performance income and 50/50 of the publisher's share of performance income) but can be negotiated differently. This type of agreement is utilized primarily in situations where the songwriter has not established a publishing entity.

8.2.5. Administration Agreements

An administration agreement may provide a reasonable alternative to a co-publishing agreement, whereby the administrator receives a fee or royalty share in exchange for the administration of licensing and collections for certain songs or catalogues (acting in effect as an "agent" for the compositions, rather than as their "owner"). Administration agreements are, in many respects, similar to co-publishing agreements in format but with some major differences. The first is that the term of the agreement is much shorter. The second is that the copyright in and to the compositions is not transferred to the administering publisher; an exception being the assignment of a small copyright percentage for the purpose of qualifying for awards from performing rights organizations. The third is that the fees retained by the administrating publisher are less than those retained in a co-publishing agreement. The fourth is that the reversion of rights occurs at a sooner time than in a co-publishing agreement since, depending on the terms of the agreement and the recoupment of advances as well as the continued right to collect royalties which were earned prior to the expiration of the term, reversion of rights can happen upon expiration of the term with the original copyright owner being able to immediately assign the administration rights to another publisher on a prospective basis.

8.2.5.1. Role of the Administrator

The role of the administrator is to make sure that the catalogue represented is registered properly, that royalties are collected from all users of the compositions, that users are audited if royalties have been underpaid, that the compositions are protected from infringement, that the compositions are marketed and promoted, and that licenses to users are issued and monitored.

8.2.5.2. Term

The term of these agreements is normally between three (3) and five (5) years but can be negotiated for a longer period if the parties agree. In cases where an advance or advances have been paid, the term will usually last for the longer of the specified year-based term or the recoupment of all advances paid. The administered party will virtually always have the right to repay any unrecouped advance balance (many times at between one hundred percent (100%) to one hundred fifteen percent (115%) of the amount) to effect recoupment, and, subject to the other terms of the agreement, thereby terminate the agreement and recapture the song(s) and/or catalogue at the end of the period if advances are otherwise still in the "red."

8.2.5.3. Controlled Compositions

The agreement can cover one composition, a set catalogue of existing compositions, compositions newly created during the term, compositions contained on a particular album or albums, or any combination thereof and more.

8.2.5.4. Royalties/Fees

The administering publisher will charge from ten percent (10%) to fifteen percent (15%) of the income it collects for its services. Depending on bargaining power, the fees can be as low as five percent (5%), but this is not the norm. The fees are usually based on income received in the United States after the fees of subpublishers in foreign territories have been deducted (if the territory includes countries outside the United States). Depending on the agreement between the parties, those foreign publisher fees can be capped at a certain percentage of income received (for example, no foreign subpublisher can charge more than ten percent (10%) for its services) or can be eliminated entirely (for example, the overall fee being charged by the U.S. administrator would include all fees being charged by subpublishers in territories outside the United States). As to the capping of foreign subpublishing fees, on occasion there will be different fee caps depending on whether the foreign subpublisher is an independent third party or is an affiliate of the U.S. administrator.

8.2.5.5. Advances

In the case of catalogues with consistent earnings or the potential for future earnings, advances will vary. There might be an overall catalogue advance at the commencement of the agreement, the amount of which is based on past earnings. There may be additional advances paid during the term if the initial advance (or subsequent advances) have been recouped ("rollover advances"). There may be further advances payable upon the commercial release of an album or a certain number of tracks as well as many other variations which may occur during the term of the agreement.

8.2.5.6. Reversion and Rights to Accrued Royalties

In most cases, once the term of the administration agreement has expired, all rights to administer the compositions will revert to the copyright owner, so that if the term of the agreement expires on December 31 of any year, the copyright owner can select a new administrator (or instead enter into a new third-party publishing or co-publishing agreement if it so chooses) as of January 1 of the next year.

In the majority of cases, the current administrator will be entitled to continue to collect royalties and charge a fee for uses which were licensed during the term (for example, mechanical royalties for digital downloads or for a broadcast of a television episode containing a composition which occurred during the term) regardless of the fact that those royalties will be paid after the expiration of the term. There is usually a time limit placed on such "collection of accrued royalty" rights. For example, a twelve (12)-month period for the United States generated income and eighteen (18) months for foreign generated income is not uncommon.

Sometimes in cases where the administrator is allowed to collect income that accrued prior to the commencement of the term, there may be a total cut-off as to the administrator's right to collect income that accrued during the term but is paid after the term has expired. There are some agreements that allow both, depending on the types of income covered.

8.2.5.7. Retention of Certain Rights

Certain agreements contain provisions which will reward the administrator for achieving certain negotiated milestones. A typical example is for the administrator to continue to represent a composition for a negotiated number of additional years after expiration of the term if the administrator was able to secure a new recording(s) of one or more compositions which reached a certain position on the music industry trade paper charts or achieved a certain plateau on the sales charts.

8.2.5.8. Payment of Songwriters

If the catalogue being administered has a number of writers signed to it, the administrator may be asked to handle the preparation of statements and payment of royalties to each specific songwriter and/or co-publisher in relation to its ownership interests. On the other hand, if the catalogue is owned by one writer, the administrator will usually take its fee and remit one statement and remittance to the songwriter or the songwriter's publishing designee.

8.2.6. Co-Administration Agreements

Co-administration agreements are used to define the rights and activities of publishers when there are two (2) or more copyright owners on a composition (where there is joint ownership). These agreements define how the parties can license their shares of the composition and, in some cases, the entire composition on behalf of all writers and publishers who have an interest.

Many agreements dictate that each party can only license its share of the composition, with any licensee (such as a film producer, advertising agency, television production company, etc., seeking to utilize the composition) being able to license the entire composition only if all the copyright owners agree. In fact, there is normally language inserted which advises the potential licensee that it must seek and secure a separate license from all parties who have an interest in the composition. Other agreements provide that any one party can enter into an agreement on behalf of all the others provided the license is non-exclusive, the rates are statutory or otherwise customary (e.g., a negotiated "three-quarter" rate for physical product), and that the licensee pays all of the copyright owners their proportionate share of the fee or royalties directly.

8.2.7. Foreign Subpublishing Agreements

Since the music and entertainment business is worldwide, music publishers in the United States will enter into agreements with publishers in foreign countries to ensure that their compositions are effectively represented by parties who know the local customs, regulations and business practices of – as well as the prominent licensees in – their respective territories. These contractual arrangements are referred to as subpublishing agreements.

The subpublishing agreement, in many respects, is very similar to an administration agreement with the major difference being that the territory is for one or more foreign countries outside of the United States. As with administration agreements, the reasons for selecting one's representative vary from the need for making sure that royalties are properly collected and compositions are correctly registered with the licensing and collection societies in that territory, to promoting the catalogue for uses in locally produced projects such as commercials, film, television, video games and local language recordings.

In this regard, certain global publishing companies have wholly owned or co-owned affiliates in most, if not all, of the major territories of the world and will use their network of such companies to represent the United States originating catalogue.

Some publishers have affiliates in certain major territories which will represent them, but in others will use independent third parties. And many independent publishers will select independent unaffiliated companies to represent their catalogues in all foreign territories, depending on their needs and expectations.

8.2.7.1. Term

The term for subpublishing agreements is, in most cases, three (3) years, at the conclusion of which the agreement will either expire or be extended via further agreement. Some agreements have a set term with automatic renewals unless notice to the contrary is given by either party prior to the expiration date. For example, there might be automatic one (1) year renewals unless the U.S. publisher gives notice to the contrary not less than thirty (30) days before expiration of the then current contract period. If there is an advance paid and the advance is still unrecouped at the end of the term, the term is usually extended until the later of recoupment or repayment.

8.2.7.2. Compositions Controlled

These agreements can control one composition, a catalogue of compositions, newly written compositions during the term, and/or the compositions contained on an album, among other possible formulae.

8.2.7.3. Rights Granted

The subpublisher will be granted all the rights that it needs to effectively represent the compositions in its territory, including the right to register and license the compositions, collect monies from users and protect the compositions in the case of infringement. The copyright to the compositions will remain with the original publisher/copyright owner and not be transferred to the subpublisher. Certain rights such as grand rights, merchandising rights and advertising commercial uses may either be excluded or included only with the consent of the original publisher on a case-by-case basis. In the grant of synchronization rights, the local subpublisher is almost always allowed to enter into a worldwide synchronization license with a motion picture or television series producer if the project originates in the subpublisher's territory.

8.2.7.4. Royalties

Subpublisher fees are totally negotiable but usually range from ten percent (10%) to fifteen percent (15%), with percentages increasing for new cover recordings by local artists or synchronization uses which have been directly initiated and/or secured by the subpublisher.

8.2.7.5. Advances

Depending on the earning power of the catalogue, advances are definitely part of the equation. There may be an advance paid by the subpublisher to the controlling publisher upon the signing of the agreement with additional advances payable either on the anniversary or anniversaries of the commencement of the term or upon previous advances being recouped or, in some cases, when a percentage of prior advances have been recouped.

8.2.7.6. Retention of Rights

Many current agreements allow the subpublisher to retain its rights to a particular composition (or local version of a composition) if it has created, through its efforts, a new income producing opportunity in its market. For example, the subpublisher might retain the composition on a local language cover recording that it was responsible for securing for an additional period of time after expiration of the term as a reward for its efforts. There are many variations in this area and the above is just an example of how the concept might work.

8.2.8. Joint Venture Agreements

A number of writer-artists and writer-producers (usually through their self-owned publishing companies) have joint venture agreements with larger music publishers as a way to build a catalogue or develop other writers with the financial assistance of the other party. The value to the major publisher of the joint venture versus the other structures we've examined is that it can utilize the creative services of the successful writer as a talent scout to identify and recruit other new songwriters that the successful writer wants to develop and that the major publisher may not have access to.

These joint venture agreements, like the other publishing exploitation structures discussed in this chapter, take many forms depending on the bargaining power, needs and expectations of the parties. The following represent the major structural areas of such a relationship.

8.2.8.1. Writers to Be Signed

One of the major issues to be resolved is the type of leeway the writer-venture party will have in signing other songwriters. One approach is to have signings occur only with the mutual approval of both parties. Another approach is to allow the venture writer to sign a certain number of songwriters without the approval of the major publisher provided the terms of these agreements adhere to certain agreed upon parameters (for example, up to two writers will be allowed to be signed without preapproval if the yearly advances are not in excess of $50,000, the delivery commitment is not less than ten (10) compositions each, the release commitment is not less than two (2) compositions each, there will be a minimum of three (3) option periods and that the retention of rights is not less than twenty (20) years, etc.).

8.2.8.2. Exclusivity as to Potential Signings

Some agreements provide for the joint venture party to give the major publisher an exclusive first look at and the right to sign every songwriter that it is interested in signing, with the major publisher having the right to sign each such writer pursuant to the joint venture. In these types of arrangements, there are usually guaranteed advances and other benefits provided to the joint venture party such as contributions to overhead since every writer who is signable has to be first presented to the major publisher before they can be offered to any other company.

Other agreements are of a non-exclusive nature in which the joint venture party has the right but not the obligation to submit every possible signing to the major publisher. This scenario is more common when there are no advances being paid to the venture party or when the parties have a preexisting good working relationship and just want to continue a successful arrangement without specified contractual commitments.

8.2.8.3. Preparation of Songwriter Agreements

In virtually all cases, the major music publisher will provide the services of its in-house lawyer to draft and negotiate agreements with writers who are being signed to the joint venture. These negotiations will always be in consultation with the venture party, with the value of such services (which can be substantial in terms of both cost and expertise) being part of the benefits provided. The major publisher will also handle all licensing and other agreements relating to the compositions controlled by the joint venture; in some cases with respect to licensing with the consultation and/or approval of the venture party.

8.2.8.4. Payment of Advances to the Signed Writers

Many agreements provide that the major publisher will be responsible for the payment of all advances to the songwriters signed to the joint venture. Other agreements will have both of the venture parties sharing in the payment of advances either on an equal basis or one which is a bit more favorable to the venture party (such as a 60/40 split of advance responsibility). A third possibility entails the venture party paying all the advances and using the administrative and/or promotion services of the major publisher.

8.2.8.5. Signing Fund

Some agreements have what are known as signing funds or available signing funds which guarantee the joint venture party that there will be a certain specified aggregate dollar amount that will be available during the term of the joint venture agreement for making new deals. Sometimes this is stated as a per year figure (for example $100,000 per year during the three (3)-year term, etc.) or as an aggregate overall term amount (for example $100,000 in the aggregate during the entire three (3)-year period of the term). If the figure is based on a yearly guaranteed available advance fund and the entire fund is not utilized during a particular one (1)-year period, then the excess can either be extinguished or carried forward to be used in the next contract period.

When there is such a guaranteed signing fund, the agreements which fall under this type of provision have to come within certain agreed upon parameters (such as committed advances on a deal by deal basis cannot exceed "___" dollars, the royalty splits cannot be more favorable to the signed writer than "___," etc.), these signings are referred to as "puts." In addition, there will be a cap on the number of puts that can be committed during any contract period to prevent the overall guaranteed advance amount from being prematurely exhausted.

8.2.8.6. Advance Payments to Writers in Option Years

Some agreements provide that the major publisher will continue to pay the advances to writers signed to the venture during the option periods of their agreements. Other agreements will provide that if the options are exercised, both parties have to contribute to the advances and, if one party elects not to pay its share, then that party will not be able to share in the compositions written during that option period as well as any income related thereto. In addition, the party who has elected not to pay its share of advances during one option period will have no further rights in and to compositions written during any future option period.

8.2.8.7. How Options Are Exercised

In most cases, there will need to be mutual approval between the parties for an option to be exercised. As an option date for a particular songwriter agreement is approaching, the major publisher and the joint venture party will discuss their views. In the event that both parties agree to proceed, then the option will be exercised and the songwriter agreement will move forward into the next contract period. In some cases, the parties will share the payment of advances, and in others the major publisher will continue to pay.

In the event that one of the parties elects not to exercise the option, the other party will have the right to do so on its own behalf. The party exercising the option will take over responsibility for paying all advances due the writer for that exercised contract period and will control all the compositions separately outside of the joint venture agreement. The party which elected not to exercise the option will still participate in all compositions written during prior periods under the terms of the joint venture agreement but will have no rights in and to any of the compositions written during the exercised option period or future option periods, if any.

8.2.8.8. Additional Advances to the Joint Venture Party

In a number of agreements, the major publisher will pay a separate advance or advances to the joint venture party. Such will be recoupable from the net publisher royalties that will be due the venture party's share of publishing income. For example, if the joint venture parties were sharing on a 50/50 equal basis and $1,000 was received as the publisher's share of performance income from the applicable performing rights organization and the joint venture publishing companies were each entitled to fifty percent (50%) of that gross amount in the aggregate (i.e., because the songwriter's publishing company was entitled to the other fifty percent (50%) pursuant to a co-publishing arrangement), the joint venture party would be entitled to $250 (i.e., one-half of the $500 remaining after the third party songwriter's publishing company was credited with its fifty percent (50%) share). The major publisher would then credit the venture partner with its fifty percent (50%) share of the remaining publishing income and if the advance to the venture partner was unrecouped, the major music publisher would deduct any unrecouped advance balance from the share of royalties owed the venture party.

8.2.8.9. Overhead

On occasion, all or a portion of the venture party's overhead will be picked up by the major publisher, generally on a recoupable advance basis.

8.2.8.10. Sharing of Income

If the major music publisher has been responsible for paying the advances to the songwriters signed to the joint venture, the joint venture party will be entitled to receive its share of the net publishing income prospectively after all advances have been recouped. Certain agreements handle this aspect on an agreement by agreement basis. For example, publishing royalties will flow to the venture party as each specific writer deal recoups with no royalties being paid for income related to the writer agreements which remain unrecouped.

Other agreements provide that the venture party will start receiving its share of publishing royalties only when all advances to all writers signed under the joint venture agreement have been recouped in the aggregate (i.e., on a "cross collateralized" basis across the catalogue).

8.2.8.11. Sharing of Income Percentages

In most cases, the major music publisher and the joint venture party agree to share the net income after payment of songwriter/co-publishing royalties to the writers signed and other agreed upon costs on an equal 50/50 basis. Depending on the bargaining power of the parties, the responsibilities being undertaken by each of the parties (payment of advances to songwriters, administrative and promotion services, copyright registration fees, etc.), as well as the structure of the agreement (exclusive vs. non-exclusive, short term vs. long term, minimum signing fund vs. optional fund, etc.), the percentage sharing may vary, sometimes in favor of the major publisher and sometimes in favor of the venture party. These percentages can also be modified or revised depending upon the relative success of the venture in hitting certain financial or other milestones contained in the original agreement, as amended from time to time.

8.2.8.12. Term

The active term of these agreements can be from one (1) to three (3) years or can be for a different specified period (such as one (1) year with two (2) one (1)-year options). Since many of the songwriter agreements will last longer than the active term of the joint venture, the terms of the joint venture agreement will remain in effect with respect to songwriter agreements signed during the active term which extend in turn beyond the expiration of the duration of the underlying venture agreement (with provisions for the control of new songs and the responsibility for advances, etc., being dictated by the contractual understandings contained in the joint venture agreement).

8.2.8.13. Reversion of Administration Rights

Since the major publisher is the party who is administering the writers and compositions controlled by the venture, including the writer's share of non-performance income derived from these compositions, one important clause in these agreements relates to the venture party's ability to administer its share of the catalogue. In this regard, there is usually an exclusive administration period which lasts during the term of the exclusive songwriter agreements that have been entered into by the venture. During this period, the major publisher will not only administer the catalogue on a worldwide basis but will also be responsible for all the contractual obligations to the various writers who have been signed, including the payment of songwriter and/or co-publishing royalties.

Once the exclusive administration period is over, however, the venture party's share of the publishing will be reassigned so that it will be able to license its respective share and collect royalties directly from the societies and users of the compositions. Under this scenario, the major publisher will continue to license and administer its publisher share as well as the songwriter's share of the compositions (and continue its obligation to account to the songwriters) since the only thing that the venture party would be entitled to would be its retained proportional share of the publishing.

It should be noted that if the venture party has received advances from the major publisher, reversion of publishing rights will generally be subject to the prior recoupment of the advances and will not occur if there is an unrecouped advance balance.

Additionally, certain venture agreements provide that the major publisher will continue to be the administrator of the joint venture without any reassignment of the venture party's share of the publishing. Alternatively, the agreements may provide that such reassignment will only take place if the songwriters signed by the joint venture have recouped all advances paid to them.

8.2.9. Acquisition Agreements

Whether it's buying one song, a catalogue of compositions, or songwriter royalties, the acquisition of musical assets continues to be a primary focus for investment in the music business, alongside touring and recording. There are two basic acquisition type agreements. A common structure for such investments has the acquiring party (usually a music publishing company but it can be an investment or other entertainment focused company as well) buying the actual corporate or other legal entity which owns the musical assets. The other is an acquisition of the assets only (i.e., a catalogue of musical compositions themselves and the agreements under which the compositions were initially acquired by the seller, which may represent the full or only a partial catalogue of the seller's compositions). This latter type of agreement is referred to as an asset sale and is usually the preferred vehicle for the buyer.

This section will concentrate on the asset sale, but it should be noted that when the transaction involves the acquisition of a legal entity due diligence must be undertaken not only as to the underlying catalog assets but also the structure, history and unrelated contractual obligations and liabilities of the company, as well. For example, the buyer has to not only investigate the assets but also has to research areas such as the terms and outstanding obligations tied to lines of credit, loan or other financing agreements, employee contracts, including guaranteed bonus or other incentive payments, tax returns, trademark, service mark and trade name registration issues, compensation and severance issues, insurance policies, past and projected budgets, minutes of shareholder meetings, certificates of organization, formation and bylaws, to name just a few.

8.2.9.1. Non-disclosure Agreement

The asset sale transaction, in almost all cases, begins with the seller requesting the potential buyer (or buyers) to sign a non-disclosure/confidentiality agreement before the seller will provide the buyer with the information necessary for the buyer to make a reasoned offer or proposal. This agreement is usually referred to as an "NDA" or confidentiality agreement. Since the buyer will be providing the seller with confidential information as to its rights in and to the assets being acquired, plus underlying agreements under which it gained its rights as well as detailed financial information pertaining to income and expenses, the buyer will dictate that, as a condition to receiving such information, the potential buyer will agree to keep all such information confidential for a prescribed period of time. There are exceptions to this rule with respect to information that is readily available to the public or which the buyer is able to develop on its own, but this document is usually the essential preliminary agreement that allows the due diligence and negotiation process to move forward.

8.2.9.2. The Prospectus

After the NDA has been signed (but sometimes before) the seller will send a prospectus of the catalogue being offered for sale to the prospective buyers. The prospectus can take many forms and vary from just a few pages to highlight some interesting aspects of the catalogue (for example, chart activity of the compositions, the names and accomplishments of the songwriters signed, upcoming committed or potential income generating projects, etc.) or can be a very substantial document of twenty (20) to over one hundred (100) pages containing very comprehensive and high level information broadly covering the legal and financial aspects of the catalogue or rights being sold.

Obviously, the more detailed the information provided, the quicker and easier the due diligence can be, enabling the buyer to concentrate on confirmation of the substantive facts presented by the seller rather than on rudimentary information-gathering. On the other hand, the less information contained in the prospectus (which occurs many times with parties just trying to secure initial interest from a number of potential bidders), the more due diligence will subsequently need to be done to get at the real issues that are important to any acquisition; an approach which can often delay the acquisition. The seller may wish to provide less information if its intentions are merely exploratory, or more if it hopes to conclude the transaction with a bona fide potential buyer more expeditiously.

8.2.9.3. Acquisition Proposal

Once the potential buyer has had an opportunity to review the information provided by the seller with respect to the legal, business and financial aspects of the assets being acquired, (this information often, being provided via an Internet data room which is password-protected), the parties will then, if a deal is desired, move to a letter of intent.

8.2.9.4. Letter of Intent

The letter of intent (LOI), or memorandum of understanding (MOU) as it is sometimes called, is intended to be a legally binding document which solidifies the key terms of the contractual relationship of the buyer and seller prior to a long form acquisition agreement being negotiated. In it the parties will include all the substantive terms of the agreement between the buyer and seller. Included will be a description of the assets being acquired, the purchase price, including a schedule of continuing payments if not all paid at the signing of the long form agreement, a recitation of the earnings on which the purchase price is based, warranties by the seller as to its rights and representations (legal, contractual and financial), any unique provisions such as earn outs, holdbacks, price reduction or termination clauses if due diligence uncovers substantive variations and/or problems with representations of the seller, an income cutoff date on or after which the buyer will receive the benefit of income generated by the catalogue or asset as well as any other important aspects mutually agreed to by the parties.

8.2.9.5. Due Diligence

In order for a potential buyer to make a responsible offer to acquire a catalogue or other musical asset, such as the songwriter's share of royalties (non-performance income, performance income, or both), the buyer will undertake a due diligence investigation into the assets being acquired. There is legal due diligence and financial due diligence (often performed by several individuals or teams with different expertise in collaboration), with these two types of due diligence usually conducted simultaneously.

a. Legal Due Diligence

The primary focus of the legal due diligence undertaking relates to copyright, contractual chain of title, terms of the underlying agreements through which the seller secured its rights, third party contractual commitments (rights and obligations), potential termination issues and possible third-party encumbrances and/or claims.

Some of the major elements of the legal inquiry include a search in the U.S. Copyright Office records of the catalogues important (i.e., higher grossing or otherwise most prominent) compositions to confirm the registrations and chain of title, reviewing the relevant songwriter and other agreements with respect to the term of rights, the ability to assign the agreements, whether there are any exploitation and/or licensing restrictions, whether there are any key person clauses (i.e., requirements of direct participation by a particular member of the target company executive team as a condition of the underlying publishing deal(s)) which could restrict the sale and whether there exist reversion provisions in any of the contracts. In addition, there will be a review of all foreign subpublishing agreements to determine when they can be either terminated or re-negotiated. And there will be a review of any U.S. Copyright Law termination issues (i.e., the right of authors or their statutory heirs to terminate copyright grants for the territory of the U.S.) with respect to the individual compositions in the catalogue being acquired.

If the catalogue includes active songwriter agreements, the review will also summarize what the future financial and contractual commitments are since the buyer will, on completing the purchase, become the party who will be responsible for fulfilling the terms of these agreements.

b. Financial Due Diligence

The initial financial inquiry will test the validity of the financial information contained in the seller's prospectus or data room disclosures. Included in this analysis is a review of royalty statements and remittances received by the seller from licensees, such as record companies and audio-visual productions (e.g., television, motion picture, advertising commercials and video game producers, as well as the performing rights organizations). The next exercise is to match the income received with the monies paid as royalty obligations to songwriters and co-publishers to make sure that all third parties were paid correctly and that the calculation of retained net income is accurate, since that is the figure which is most important to the buyer.

Additional inquiries will be made to see if third-party licensees such as subpublishers have been paying the seller correctly, whether there are any audit claims outstanding and, if so, their validity (which will also be analyzed as part of the legal due diligence), whether there are any substantial one-time non-reoccurring income events included in the income figures which may not happen again such as an audit recovery, performing right organization bonuses for radio and streaming chart activity, long term catalogue performance activity or top rated viewership/ Nielsen television ratings, a positive litigation settlement as well as any other items that would result in an over statement of sustainable income by the seller. Likewise, the analysis will determine if there are any substantial contingent "expense" events (e.g., milestone or extension bonuses) which would have a material adverse impact on the net revenue disclosures.

8.2.9.6. The Purchase Price

In an asset sale, the purchase price is almost always based on an analysis of past income as the basis for projecting future income In some cases, the prospective buyer will review the past five (5) years of income statements, in others, the past two (2) or three (3) years. Analysis will be by income type (e.g., performances, mechanicals, synchronizations, and other revenue sources). Since it is an asset sale, and accurate determination of the net publisher's share of income ("NPS") or publisher retained income is the key to determining value (i.e., gross income received less all third party royalty and expense obligations, which in simplest terms involves a calculation of payments due songwriters, copublishers, administrators, recording demo costs, etc.).

After arriving at a representative annual average NPS, the prospective buyer will do a projection of future income based on the catalogue's prior performance and the buyer's (often proprietary) model of calculating the catalogue's continuing performance into the future, typically taking into account its own assessment of waning and emerging demand for music rights due to new technologies or its own unique strategic resources. The buyer will, in many transactions but not all, then introduce a multiple on the NPS figure to arrive at the final purchase price. Among some of the many factors that are introduced into the equation are potential loss of rights to compositions in the future due to contractual reversions and the potential or actual copyright terminations, whether the compositions are easily licensable as well as current and future industry trends with respect to the increase or decrease in value of the primary income types which comprise the financial worth of the catalogue.

8.2.9.7. The Long Form Acquisition Agreement

After the due diligence procedures are complete and the negotiations finalized, a long form agreement will be signed which will describe the assets being sold, detail how the purchase price is to be paid, detail any holdback amounts and conditions for their release, and provide for an effective income cut-off date for the seller and commencement date for the buyer – all of which will be consistent with the provisions of the term sheet unless due diligence has established problems with the deal as originally contemplated. It will also include warranty and liability provisions, provisions for reduction of the purchase price if there is a breach of representations and rights are consequently lost, confidentiality and restrictions on issuance of a press release language, copyright assignments and letters of direction which will be sent to all payees and licensees (including the performing rights organizations) to notify them of the change of ownership and that all monies should be sent to (or will henceforth be paid by) the new copyright owner.

8.3. MUSIC LICENSING

In its representation of songwriters and their musical compositions that it controls, there are a number of typical licensing agreements that are negotiated and entered into by music publishers. The primary transactions they relate to being:

- Mechanical licenses
- Performance licenses
- Synchronization licenses
- Motion Picture licenses
- Television licenses
- Video Game licenses
- Musical Theatre licenses

8.3.1. Mechanical Licenses

The mechanical license is used to allow a record company or other entity to manufacture and distribute musical compositions on physical product (such as CDs, tapes and vinyl records, etc.), via digital audio downloads or ringtones, and via other digital transmission processes such as inter-active streams, time-out, limited or non-permanent downloads related primarily to subscription services and locker services, to name just a few.

To secure a mechanical license in the United States, a record company, recording artist or producer will either go to the Harry Fox Agency or directly to the music publisher who owns or controls the composition being recorded and distributed. It should be mentioned that if a composition has been previously released in the United States with the permission of the copyright owner, any artist and record company can record and commercially release a newly recorded version of that composition (generally referred to as a "cover" recording) pursuant to the compulsory license provisions of the United States Copyright Act (Section 115) by paying the statutory mechanical rate (addressed in greater detail below) for each recording of a composition that is manufactured and distributed.

The Harry Fox Agency (which was acquired by the performing rights organization SESAC from the National Music Publishers Association in 2015) is the primary mechanical rights organization in the United States, representing a large number of independent music publishers in the licensing of compositions and other musical works for CDs, permanent digital downloads, records, audio tapes, vinyl, interactive streams and locker services, among other audio digital formats. In addition to licensing mechanical rights, another important Harry Fox Agency service is the auditing of record companies and other licensees to ensure proper royalty accounting. The current commission rate is 11.5% for most of its licensing administration services (i.e., a fee it adds to the costs of the licensing rates for the recordings it processes). It should be noted that many if not most of the large publishers license mechanical rights directly to producers or labels on big projects with some electing to simultaneously license directly as well as through the Fox Agency, depending on the catalogue being represented.

The current mechanical compulsory license rate structure in the United States is 9.1 cents per each composition contained on a recording of five (5) minutes or less in duration, and 1.75 cents per minute for recordings longer than five (5) minutes. The statutory rate for ringtones is 24 cents. The rates for these configurations (referred to as "Subpart A Configurations") were extended by the Copyright Royalty Judges for a five (5)-year period when they published the final regulations in the Federal Register on May 28, 2017.

The statutory rates for the many types of inter-active streaming services (which currently include interactive streaming, limited downloads, paid locker services, purchased content lockers, mixed service bundles, limited offerings and music bundles) are somewhat complex and vary depending on the type of activity being offered and whether the service is based on a subscription or ad-supported model.

As a general rule, they involve a percentage of the service's revenue, a percentage of the royalties the service pays to record companies, ("Total Content Costs" or "TCC"), with minimums if there are subscribers less, the amounts paid to performing right organizations. The Copyright Royalty Board's statutory "all in" (mechanical and performance rights) royalty rates for these services in 2018 are the greater of 11.4% of a service's revenue or 22% of TCC with increases on an annual basis for five years until 2022 when the rates will be the greater of 15% of service revenue or 26.2% of TCC.

The mechanical license agreement is usually no more than a two (2)-page agreement plus a schedule containing the pertinent information on the composition being licensed, which will normally indicate the license number, the title of the composition, the writer(s), the publisher(s), the title of the release, the recording artist, the record label, the catalogue number for the recording, the format, the release date, the duration of the recording, the ISRC number (which is used to identify a particular sound recording) and the royalty rate.

With respect to permanent digital downloads ("DPDs"), the mechanical rate is virtually always statutory although there are some exceptions. As to physical product, however, the per-composition mechanical rates can vary (especially if the writer is either the recording artist or producer) depending on the agreement with the record company and what is known as the "controlled composition" clause. This is the provision of the recording agreement or record company/producer agreement which dictates how the mechanical royalty rate is calculated for compositions contained on the album which are written or controlled by the writer/artist or writer/producer.

There are many variations in these controlled composition clauses but virtually all have the effect of reducing the per composition mechanical royalty rate paid by the label. For example, there may be an aggregate royalty cap on the album (for example, $1.00) with any overage reducing the mechanical royalties due for the compositions written by the writer/artist or writer/producer. There might be a provision that mechanical royalties will be paid at a seventy-five percent (75%) of statutory rate (the so-called and quite commonly negotiated "three-quarter" rate for physical product) rather than the full 9.1 cents statutory rate. These are just a few of the variations that may be negotiated in the proposed agreement with the record company releasing the physical product album. It should be noted that these reduction of mechanical royalty clauses do not, in almost all cases, apply to sales in countries outside of the United States.

Other provisions include accounting provisions (with reports and royalties usually due forty-five (45) days after each calendar quarter), transmission of electronic data-formatted royalty statements and royalties, audit rights, termination of the license for failure to pay, conditions upon assignment, as well as language stating that the version contained in the recording cannot change the basic melody or character of the work and that the copyright in any arrangement will vest in the copyright owners of the composition upon creation of the arrangement.

Since all countries of the world have different formulas for the calculation of mechanical rates for sales in their respective territories (many are based on a percentage of the wholesale or retail price), one must have a grasp of this market as well since, in many cases, there might be more cumulative income generated outside the United States than within it. Appreciation of such rates is many times monitored by a publishing company's subpublishers in the various territories, but a grasp of at least the basics should be continually researched to understand current rates as well as potential future changes dictated by legislation, court decisions, directives or other factors.

8.3.2. The Performance Right

One of the most important rights of copyright throughout the world is the musical composition performance right. This right applies to practically every type of music use, whether it's music on television, in feature films, on the radio, in a college or university setting, a hotel, concert hall, bar, restaurant, auditorium, arena or stadium, outdoor festival venues, or online streaming services, among other types of uses and locations where music is performed live or via recordings. Basically, the right requires that a music user acquire a license from the musical work's copyright holder to publicly perform the compositions. Some form of compensation to the copyright owner will normally be part of the deal. The issuance of such a license avoids the statutory penalties for copyright infringement, which can be substantial, especially if the infringement is willful. For most songwriters, composers and music publishers, the performance right is their primary source of continuing royalty income throughout the copyright term of the work.

In the United States, writers and publishers join or affiliate with collective licensing organizations which negotiate license agreements with all manner of enterprises that host or transmit live and recorded musical performances, collect and administer the license fees and then distribute them to their writer and publisher members or affiliates who have performances in the specific area or media being licensed. Writers and publishers grant to these organizations the non-exclusive right to license the non-dramatic public performance of their works (a performance of a live Broadway musical would be considered a dramatic or grand right and therefore would not be covered by such a license). The three primary performing rights organizations (PROs) in the United States are the American Society of Composers, Authors and Publishers (ASCAP), a non-profit membership association founded in 1914 by writers and publishers, Broadcast Music Inc. (BMI), a non-profit corporation organized by the broadcasting industry in 1939, and SESAC (originally known as the Society of European Stage, Authors and Composers), a private, family-owned business formed in 1930 which was sold in 1992 to a group of investors, resulting in a change of its business structure to a for-profit corporation, then again in 2013 to Ritzi Traverse Management, a private equity firm, and finally in 2016 to the investment firm, The Blackstone Group. In 2013, an additional competitor for music licensing, Global Music Rights (GMR), entered the field as a for-profit competitor to ASCAP, BMI and SESAC.

8.3.3. Overview of the Field

The choice as to which PRO a writer joins or affiliates with can be a complex one, as all four U.S. PROs are entirely different in practically every aspect of their operations and royalty payment structures. They each have different membership and affiliation contracts, length of agreements, royalty formulas, methodologies and payment categories, resignation and termination rules, dates and procedures, withdrawal of works provisions, organizational structures and governing documents, dispute resolution procedures, bonus and financial reward practices for successful songs, theme songs and underscore (e.g., hit songs on radio or streaming services, songs with a significant past history of performances, compositions contained in high viewership or top rated Nielsen television shows, etc.), payment/distribution dates, performance surveys and foreign country collection procedures, among other items. In addition, each organization can change its payment policies and rules without notice to its writers and publishers. Finally, a writer can be a member (ASCAP), affiliate (BMI, SESAC), or a client (GMR) of only one organization at any given time. As the U.S. PROs are in competition with each other as to members and license fees, a significant number of successful writers have switched from one PRO to another during their careers due to differences in respective royalty payments, monetary advances and loans, financial guarantees, personal relationships, philosophical or organizational preferences or for other reasons, as the PRO practices and policies, including royalty calculation methodologies, may change over time to the detriment of a particular songwriter's or composer's catalogue or career interests.

For many music publishers, it is common to have multiple companies with each belonging to at least three of the PROs as the publisher has to follow the writer's membership or affiliation. For instance, if a publisher signed an ASCAP writer, that writer's works would have to be placed into an ASCAP publishing company in order for the publisher to be paid. Similarly, if an ASCAP and BMI writer co-write a composition, the BMI writer's share would be placed with a BMI publisher and the ASCAP writer's share would be placed with an ASCAP publisher. As previously noted, fifty percent (50%) of all PRO royalty distributions for a specific performance go to the writers of the work with the remaining fifty percent (50%) distributed to the music publishers of the composition, with each "basket" in turn allocated among one or several writers and publishers for each composition when so required by contractual co-writer and/or co-publisher agreements.

8.3.4. Revenue

The starting point for the calculation of the writer and publisher royalties for any type of performance in any media is the license fees that have been negotiated in the specific area of performance. In the United States, performing rights organizations collect in excess of two billion dollars annually and distribute approximately eighty-seven percent (87%) of those fees back to writers and publishers. ASCAP and BMI represent close to ninety percent (90%) of the collections in this field, with the remainder shared by the other PROs. License fees can vary each year based on the specific negotiation of license fees with the user, the term of the license, the type of license agreement agreed to, whether there have been major shifts of repertory from one PRO to another and whether the license fee was a market rate voluntary negotiation, a court-set interim fee or was established by a final judgment, among other factors. Some of the license fee formulas utilized include factors such as an agreed upon annual or multiple year flat-dollar amount, a percentage of gross revenue, the intensity of music use (e.g., different percentages for music intensive, general entertainment, and sports and news programs in cable television), an industry-wide, negotiated, non-revenue- based deal, a per-subscriber fee, annual expenditures for all entertainment, an escalating percentage over the course of the deal, seating capacity of a venue, percentage of advertising gross receipts, gross ticket revenue, admission charge, square feet of the establishment, use of live or mechanical music or a jukebox, annual CPI increases, among many others.

The main sources of performing rights organization revenue are broadcast, network and cable television, terrestrial and satellite radio, general licensing (live concerts, hotels, bars, clubs, universities, etc.) and all forms of online music use (audio and audio-visual streaming services, primarily) sometimes referred to as New Media. In addition, approximately 700 million dollars of the over 2 billion dollars being collected by U.S. PROs comes in from foreign country collecting societies for U.S. works being performed in foreign territories. Most of the incoming foreign money is earmarked for distribution to writers, as most publishers collect their respective shares directly from foreign societies through subpublishers or via direct membership in foreign country societies.

8.3.5. Types of License Agreements

License agreements in this field are either negotiated or court-prescribed (as more fully explained below), and can take many forms. The most common type of license is the blanket license which allows a user the right to perform any and all works in a PRO's repertory during the term of the license in its particular setting or service, for a specific negotiated or court-set fee. A variation of this type of license is the "carve out" or "adjustable fee blanket license" which is a blanket license subject to the carve outs for any negotiated direct licenses for selected music that may be utilized/performed at (e.g., a business location) or by (e.g., a broadcaster) the user. A per-program license is where a station pays a license fee only for each program using ASCAP, BMI or SESAC music that is not otherwise licensed directly or at the source with the fee dependent on the advertising revenue the program has generated for the station. This license also provides for an "incidental" music use fee to compensate writers and publishers for performances in announcements and for so-called "ambient" uses.

Additional types of licenses are the "per segment" license and the "through-to-the-audience" license. The "per segment" license is a non-exclusive license that authorizes a music user to perform any and all works in the PRO repertory in all segments of the music user's activities in a single industry. The "through-to-the-audience" license allows broadcasters, digital services and background/foreground music services to cover with one license all public performances along the chain of transmission, so long as the fee paid reflects the value of all performances made pursuant to the license. In addition, there has to be an economic relationship between the music users in the chain as to the delivery or transmittal of the musical content. It is important to note that the consent decrees do not prevent ASCAP or BMI and a user from agreeing on any other form of license.

All ASCAP, BMI and SESAC membership and affiliation agreements with writers and publishers are non-exclusive, meaning that a copyright owner member or affiliate can issue, directly or through an agent other than a performing rights organization, non-exclusive licenses to music users for rights of public performance. In light of the non-exclusive nature of these agreements, it is important to understand two additional types of license agreements as they relate directly to this non-exclusivity: the "direct" and the "source" license. A direct license is an agreement between an ASCAP, BMI or SESAC member or affiliate and a music user that grants the user the right to publicly perform the copyright owner's music contained in the PRO catalogue. A source license is an agreement between a copyright owner and an entity that produces and supplies programs containing its music granting the right to authorize others to publicly perform the music, which may be desirable for a user that does not have or wish to seek a PRO license for reasons of cost or other considerations.

Both of these types of agreements bypass the ASCAP, BMI and SESAC licensing structures and their negotiation requires knowledge of the entire field of "back end royalties" as well as their negotiation. For example, some of the questions that should be asked when negotiating a direct license is whether the direct or source license provides some form of continuing royalty payments as would occur under a standard PRO license, whether the license is worldwide or limited to the United States and Canada, is the license for all media, selective media or a single medium, what is the duration of the license, and how is the fee to be split between writers and publishers, among others.

8.3.6. Consent Decrees

Both ASCAP and BMI are governed by consent decrees with the U.S. Department of Justice. These decrees were entered into in 1941 due to alleged violations of federal anti-trust laws and restrict, to a certain degree, both organizations' operations. These decrees have been modified in the case of ASCAP in 1950, 1960 and in 2001 (Second Amended Final Judgment referred to as AFJ2) and with BMI in 1966 and 1994.

Some of the primary provisions of these decrees establish prohibitions against the following:

Interference with a writer or publisher's right to license works directly; discrimination in setting different license fees or other terms and conditions between licensees "similarly situated"; granting a license in excess of five (5) years duration; not granting a music user, upon written request, a license to perform all of the works in the PRO's repertory, licensing movie theaters the right of public performance for music synchronized with motion pictures (i.e., no such license is currently required for the United States); and, in the case of ASCAP only the licensing of any musical composition right other than the right of public performance on a non-exclusive basis.

The issue of what happens when a user or user group (e.g., the terrestrial radio industry, music streaming services, etc.) cannot come to an agreement with ASCAP or BMI as to what "reasonable fees" should be for the use of music in their business has been a contentious one from inception. The consent decrees dealt with this issue by designating a separate "rate court" for both ASCAP (1950) and BMI (1994) whereby judicial determination would come into play if ASCAP or BMI could not reach a negotiated agreement with a user. The decree allows any party to apply to the U.S. District Court for the Southern District of New York to fix interim fees pending the negotiation or litigation of "reasonable" final fees. These decisions are appealable to the 2nd Circuit Court of Appeals. Over the years, these courts have conducted trials concerning most type of media, including network, local and cable television, the terrestrial radio industry as well as the online music streaming area.

An additional review of the decrees by the Department of Justice with a view toward certain modifications was commenced in 2014 with comments elicited from all segments of the music and user communities as well as the general public. Among the issues being considered was the ability of a PRO to bundle and negotiate multiple rights (performance, mechanical, etc.) instead of just the performance right, the ability of music publishers to withdraw partial rights from a PRO (e.g., withdraw digital rights for direct licensing purposes and keep traditional media licensing with the PROs) and the replacement of the "rate courts" with a system of mandatory arbitration, among other changes. An additional issue involved the DOJ's position that ASCAP and BMI be required to offer "full work" licenses as opposed to the "fractional" licenses that they had always offered to music users. A "full work" license allows one PRO to license all shares of a work co-written by writers of different PROs whereas under a "fractional" license, the PRO can only license its share of a work. The BMI rate Court judge ruled that "fractional" licenses were allowed under the decree with the 2nd Circuit Court of Appeals affirming that decision.

SESAC is not governed by a consent decree nor does it have a "rate court" mechanism similar to ASCAP and BMI to resolve the determination of fees for the use of SESAC music. Anti-trust litigation was commenced against SESAC by the Television Music License Committee (local television stations) and the Radio Music Licensing Committee (terrestrial radio) in 2009 and 2012 respectively, both of which were resolved through settlements. In both cases, SESAC agreed that in the future the parties would participate in binding arbitration to set reasonable license fees if voluntary agreements could not be reached on industry rates. In addition, SESAC agreed not to interfere with the efforts of any writer or publisher affiliate to directly license their works to a user.

Global Music Rights (GMR), a music rights management company and the newest PRO under discussion, is completely unregulated as of this writing and is not currently subject to a rate court, mandatory arbitration or rate-setting procedure; leaving all terms of its licensing, including exclusivity terms, open to negotiation.

8.3.7. Synchronization Licenses

These are the licenses which are utilized when a musical work is used in a television program, motion picture, video game or any other type of audio-visual project. In the United States, the terms of these licenses, with few exceptions, are totally negotiable since there are virtually no statutory schemes in this area. The following sections will review some of the major points of licensing music in a number of the more important media.

8.3.7.1. Motion Pictures

The motion picture synchronization license, which is obtained directly from a composition's publisher, is in many respects a very straightforward document when one is licensing pre-existing compositions which were not written for the film. This license embodies a broad rights license as it is usually for life of copyright, very wide in its scope and covers virtually all distribution media now known or hereafter devised. It should be noted that the grant of rights does include home and personal video and there are normally no additional royalties payable for these uses. Occasionally small film projects will license rights for a more limited time frame, media or territory to reduce costs until the full scope of likely distribution can be determined.

The primary issues in this area for the licensor/publisher are the securing of a scene description so that the licensor knows how its composition is being used, the type of use involved (for example, visual vocal sung by a character on-screen, background instrumental, closing credits, opening credits, etc.), the duration of the use (for example, 30 seconds, 2 minutes, etc.) and whether there are multiple uses in different scenes. In addition, factors such as whether it is a major motion picture, indie production or documentary as well as the music budget all come into play in the negotiation of the final fee, in addition to the scope of rights granted.

It is also essential that the film's producer be required to create a music cue sheet which details all the music in the motion picture, how the composition was used, the timing of the use and authorship/ownership and PRO information as part of the terms of the synchronization license, since this document is the cornerstone of being paid post-theatrical release songwriter, composer and publisher performance royalties for theatrical distribution outside the United States and for broadcast television, cable, satellite and online performances of the film worldwide.

8.3.7.2. Television

Considering the wide range of distribution media and platforms in this area (for example network television, local broadcast stations, pay television, video-on-demand, Internet streaming services, commercials, etc.) licensing negotiations can be complex depending on the rights being requested by the program's producer, either on a guaranteed or optional basis.

With this in mind, some of the basic licensing principles will be outlined.

8.3.8. Basic Licensing Principles

When you are licensing pre-existing musical compositions to a dramatic series, the primary type of synchronization license for successful shows is what is known as an "all-media excluding theatrical" license. In effect, once the composition is put into a scene in a series episode, the producer can distribute that episode to any and all media now known or hereafter devised with the only exception being that it cannot be shown in motion picture theatres. The grant of rights will, in virtually all cases, include home and personal video and will be a life of copyright license with the territory being the world or universe.

Two other types of synchronization licenses that are used in this area are an "all television with a home/personal video option" (i.e., a separate fee is paid if the video option is exercised) and an "all television including home/personal video" agreement where the fee for both rights is paid at the time the license is signed.

If the series is music or dance-centric (such as *The Voice*, *Dancing with the Stars*, etc.), the licenses are much different as the territory is initially very limited and the term much shorter than a dramatic series. There are usually a number of options in these types of licenses which can extend the term, enlarge the territory and increase the rights being granted, all at the election of the producer (typically reducing up-front licensing fees, but generally increasing the aggregate license fees for all media, worldwide, for the life of copyright, if and when eventually required if the series' distribution is extended for, by way of example, syndication or international territories). By way of further example, some of the options might relate to ringtones, ringbacks, downloads (both audio and audio-visual), etc. In most licenses, the exercise of the option by the producer has to be done within a set period of time (for example, within two (2) years after the initial broadcast of the episode or end of a particular season for a series).

Some of the primary issues in negotiating a television license are the territory of distribution, the term, the use in the episode or series, the rights being requested and the music budget for the series. As with motion pictures, it is important that the licensor secures a copy of the music cue sheet from the producer to make sure all the information concerning the actual use is correct and the licensor can effectively police the use for subsequent performance-royalty purposes worldwide.

8.3.9. Video Games

There are two (2) primary types of synchronization licenses when negotiating the right to use a pre-existing song in a video game. For most genres of games (adventure, action, sports, games based on feature films or television series, etc.), the license is similar to a feature film "synch" license with certain variations. The license will contain the title of the composition, songwriter and publisher information, a use description (e.g., background vocal), the duration of the use (e.g., up to a full use, multiple uses, etc.), the territory (normally a non-exclusive worldwide license as games are sold in many countries) and the term (many games have short term licenses as the shelf life of most games is limited, e.g. for five (5) years or ten (10) years from release date, etc.).

The Grant of Rights and Media clause will be extensive and will normally cover "all gaming platforms, operating systems, devices or methods of distribution pursuant to which interactive entertainment software may be used by or delivered to end users, whether now existing or hereafter created." Another variation might read "Any and all entertainment platforms whether tangible or intangible, including

Play Station, Xbox, Nintendo, handheld and mobile wireless formats, all cellular phones and PDAs, online services and online social networking sites and any of the foregoing's successors and predecessors."

As to payments, there will be a one-time fee with no additional compensation based on the sales success of the game. The use of master recordings will normally be on a most-favored-nations basis with the license fee paid for the underlying musical composition.

When dealing with music-centric games though (for example, *Guitar Hero, Dance Central, Rock Band, Just Dance*, etc.), an entirely different form of license is utilized where additional monies can be generated based on the success of the particular game. Most of the license clauses will be the same as a normal "synch" license with the exception of the fee and payment clause. Some of the writer/publisher formulas used in these types of games are a per unit royalty (e.g., three (3) cents per composition per unit, which may be reduced to a lower floor to take into account a reduction in the wholesale price of the game at some point in its life cycle), an escalating per unit royalty with increased payments based on the game's success and a sales plateau criteria formula where additional monetary payments are made when the game reaches certain sales levels. Advances will many times also be negotiated which are recoupable against future royalties, and a "most –favored-nations" clause may be demanded if the master recording is used (e.g., the fee for the composition will be no less than the license fee paid for the inclusion in the game soundtrack of the master recording, versus some new cover recording produced expressly for use in the game.)

Even if a musical composition is not included in the original game, monies can still be earned for outside compositions which are chosen as downloadable content (DLC). These are songs and master recordings that are allowed to be downloaded into a game subsequent to a game's release. The royalty rates for DLC compositions are normally a percentage of the per-download net sales price or revenue (e.g., fifteen percent (15%)) coupled with an advance against future royalties. If the composition is part of a multiple song purchased bundle or pack, the per-song royalty percent would be a pro-rata share of the bundle's net sales. DLC normally has a most-favored-nations clause with the master recording and vice versa.

Many of the licenses allow the use of the song in menus and game scenes, the right to use and display the title and lyrics in the game, specific in-context marketing and promotional uses and, in some cases, the ability for the consumer to record their gaming experience (e.g., dance and karaoke games) and share the resulting videos on social media sites.

8.3.10. Musical Theatre Licenses

Broadway and touring stage productions can provide substantial writer and publisher royalties for pre-existing musical compositions used in a dramatic context. Successful shows that use pre-existing songs have generated millions of dollars to investors and writers and publishers. Licenses in this area are directly negotiated by the music publisher/copyright owner with the show's producer and are normally referred to as "Grand Rights Song Licenses." It is important to note that these types of live theatre uses are not covered by the blanket licenses issued by performing rights organizations (ASCAP, BMI, SESAC, etc.).

The most common types of license agreements in this area are the Dramatists Guild of America Approved Production Contract for Musical Plays (DGA/APC), the Royalty Pool agreement and the "Fixed Dollar" show. For "catalogue musicals" (e.g., *Jersey Boys*, *Mamma Mia!*, *Beautiful: the Carole King Musical*, *Rock of Ages*, *Motown: The Musical*, etc.), the most common royalty agreement is the royalty pool or a combination of the royalty pool with the fixed dollar show.

8.3.10.1. Dramatists Guild of America Approved Production Contract

The DGA/APC contract is a model contract which covers most aspects of a live stage production from start to finish. This contract requires certain minimum payments as well as specific royalty payments to the book writer, composer and lyricist of any musical. The contract also provides minimum option payments that are paid by a producer prior to any Broadway opening as well as the royalty formulas in effect prior to investor recoupment as well as post investor recoupment. Additional areas covered include approvals, producer rights, subsidiary rights, amateur, ancillary and revival performances, and motion picture rights, among many other issues.

As to royalties, the book writer (librettist), composer and lyricist (jointly the "Author") share four and one-half percent (4.5%) of the

Gross Weekly Box Office Receipts (GWBOR) prior to investor recoupment with an increase to six percent (6%) once full investor recoupment is achieved (normally one hundred ten percent (110%) of the total invested). As opposed to the feature film and television area where most works written specifically for those media are work-for-hire agreements where the producer becomes the author and copyright owner, the practice in the theatre is that the composer, lyricist and book writer retain their copyrights in their creations. In the case of pre-existing compositions owned or co-owned by a music publisher, the copyrights remain with the original copyright owner subject to the payment of contractual royalties to the songwriter.

8.3.10.2. Royalty Pools

The royalty pool arrangement is an agreement in which all royalty participants share in an agreed upon percentage of the weekly operating profits of a show. The royalty participants can include many parties including the composer, lyricist, book writer, choreographer, primary actors or cast, underlying rights owner (a book or film), the publisher and writer of pre-existing compositions, etc. The basic computations for this pool involve the Gross Weekly Box Office Receipts (GWBOR) of the show and the weekly costs of running the show. For example, if a Broadway show was grossing 1.5 million dollars a week and its weekly operating costs were $750,000, the weekly operating profit would be $750,000. If the royalty pool was thirty-five percent (35%), the pool monies to be distributed to all participants would be $262,500; with the remaining sixty-five percent (65%) of profits ($487,500) being applied to investor recoupment. Each of the participants in the pool is assigned points with distributions made on the number of points each participant has. Many times, there will be a minimum weekly royalty that must be paid for each point in the pool regardless of the weekly operating profit or loss of the show. These "minimum" payments can be waived by the parties if necessary. For example, participants might waive the fees if a show was losing money or in danger of closing.

8.3.10.3. Fixed Dollar Shows

For pre-existing compositions being used in these type of shows, a per-song weekly fee will be negotiated by the music publisher with the fee remaining constant regardless of the success (or failure) and box office of the show. In the case of some "catalogue musicals," you may have a combination of a royalty pool arrangement for the primary songs and a weekly fixed-dollar amount arrangement being applied to the lesser known or less important songs being used.

8.3.11. Additional Types of Licenses

Because of the many different types of music use being encountered in today's world, the licensing structure of any agreement needs to be reviewed in light of the technology involved, the rights being requested and the basic concepts found in many of the primary types of licenses we have just covered. Agreements are constantly evolving, reflecting the changing challenges, opportunities and solutions to which a songwriter, publisher and those advising them must be tenaciously sensitive and attuned.

MUSIC PUBLISHING – ILLUSTRATIVE FORMS:

- Music Composition Interpolation (Sample) License
- Music Publishing Catalog Administration Agreement (short form)
- Songwriter Co-Publishing Agreement (short form)
- Synchronization License

— CHAPTER 9 —

THEATER LAW

Victoria Traube,* Hailey Ferber†

9.1. Introduction: Dramatis Personae
9.2. Production Rights
9.3. Underlying Rights
9.4. Collaboration Agreements
9.5. Dramatists Guild Approved Production Contract
9.6. Development
9.7. Financing
9.8. Creative and Cast Agreements
9.9. Touring
9.10. Licensing
9.11. Revivals

9.1. INTRODUCTION: DRAMATIS PERSONAE

"My curse on plays that have to be set up in fifty ways," wrote William Butler Yeats.[1] The work of setting up stage productions falls to producers, general managers, theatre owners, and creative and technical personnel, represented by lawyers, agents, and unions. Here is a brief description of the cast of characters who appear in this chapter.

Producers are responsible for the financing, management, and marketing of their shows. Oscar Hammerstein II said, "A producer is a rare, paradoxical genius – hard-headed, soft-hearted, cautious, reckless, a hopeful innocent in fair weather, a stern pilot in stormy weather, a mathematician who prefers to ignore the laws of mathematics and trust intuition, an idealist, a realist, a practical dreamer, a sophisticated gambler, a stage-struck child. That's a producer."[2]

---

* **Victoria Traube** is Senior Vice President/Business Affairs and General Counsel of Concord Music Publishing, North America.

† **Hailey Ferber** is Senior Vice President of Business and Legal Affairs at the Araca Group.

[1] Yates, William Butler. "The Fascination of What's Difficult," Responsibilities and Other Poems. New York. 1916. 7 Aug. 2016 <http://www.bartleby.com/147/41.html>.

[2] Ostrow, Stuart. *Present at the Creation, Leaping in the Dark, and Going against the Grain: 1776, Pippin, M. Butterfly, La Bete, & Other Broadway Adventures.* Milwaukee: Applause Theatre & Cinema, 2005.

General Managers are the producer's right hand in making deals and managing the enterprise.

Theatre owners are the industry's landlords. Their ownership of the real estate gives them great power. In New York, the primary theatre owners are The Shubert Organization with seventeen Broadway theatres, The Nederlander Organization with ten, and Jujamcyn Theaters with five.[3]

Theatre owners and producers belong to The Broadway League, the national trade association for the Broadway theatre industry, to which presenters and general managers also belong. The League bargains with the theatrical unions on behalf of its members.

The theatrical unions include Actors' Equity Association ("Equity"), Stage Directors and Choreographers Society ("SDC"), American Federation of Musicians ("AFM"), United Scenic Artists ("USA"), International Alliance of Theatrical Stage Employees ("IATSE"), and Association of Theatrical Press Agents and Managers ("ATPAM").[4]

Agents represent playwrights, composers, lyricists, bookwriters, directors, choreographers, actors, and other creative personnel. Agents sometimes "package" a production, representing playwright, director, and stars. Many creative personnel have both agents and lawyers, who work as a team.

The producer's lawyer drafts the financing documents, supervises compliance with securities laws, and drafts and negotiates the rights agreement with the authors as well as any underlying rights agreement. The production attorney may also assist the general manager with the agreements with actors, directors, and other creative personnel. The lawyer for creative personnel works in tandem with the agent and, typically, is responsible for the production contract with the authors, while the agent takes primary responsibility for contracts with directors, designers, and actors.

---

[3] The not-for-profit Roundabout Theatre Company has three Broadway theatres, Ambassador Theatre Group has two, the not-for-profits Second Stage Theater, Manhattan Theatre Club, and Lincoln Center Theater each have one, Disney Theatrical Group has one, and one is independently owned. "Broadway Theatre." *Wikipedia*. Wikimedia Foundation, 6 Aug. 2016. Web. 07 Aug. 2016.

[4] The Dramatists Guild, Inc. ("Guild") is a trade organization, not a union.

9.2. PRODUCTION RIGHTS

9.2.1. Musicals and Plays

Whether the work is a musical or a straight play, the kind of production contemplated determines the substance of the agreement between the producer and author or authors, which is referred to as the Production Agreement or the Author Agreement.[5] A play usually has one author (although there are exceptions like the teams of Howard Lindsay and Russel Crouse or George S. Kaufman and Moss Hart). A musical is a collaborative work, with a bookwriter, composer, and lyricist contributing to the whole. Occasionally, they are all the same person such as Jonathan Larson, the creator of *Rent* or Lin-Manuel Miranda, the creator of *Hamilton*.[6]

9.2.2. First Class and Other Productions

There are various kinds of theatrical productions, ranging from first class to second class to stock and amateur, and including both tours and sit-down productions. A first class production is, according to the Guild's Approved Production Contract (commonly known as the "APC"), presented "in a first class theatre in a first class manner, with a first class cast and a first class director."[7] Productions in Broadway and West End theatres are universally acknowledged to be first class, as are those in theatres in various cities in the United States and Canada that have traditionally presented first class tours of shows that typically originate on Broadway (e.g., the Hollywood Pantages

---

[5] The Dramatists Guild, Inc. Approved Production Contract is the Production Agreement most commonly used for Broadway productions.

[6] Multiple authors are common; for example, composer and bookwriter/lyricist (THE KING AND I and other works by Richard Rodgers and Oscar Hammerstein II, MY FAIR LADY and other works by Frederick Loewe and Alan Jay Lerner) or composer/lyricist and bookwriter (INTO THE WOODS, and other works by Stephen Sondheim and James Lapine, PACIFIC OVERTURES and other works by Mr. Sondheim and John Weidman) or composer, lyricist and bookwriter (ANNIE by Charles Strouse, Martin Charnin, and Thomas Meehan, WEST SIDE STORY by Leonard Bernstein, Stephen Sondheim, and Arthur Laurents).

[7] Dramatists Guild, Inc. Approved Production Contract for Musical Plays. Section 1.01.

Theatre, which is owned by the Nederlander Organization). There is, however, no clear-cut definition of "first class."

Off-Broadway productions take place in theatres in New York City so classified by Equity. Off-Broadway theatres range in size from 99 to 499 seats.[8] Some Off-Broadway theatres are commercial (e.g., New World Stages and Westside Theatre) and others are non-profit (e.g., Playwrights Horizons and Second Stage Theater). Off-Off-Broadway Theatres have up to 99 seats. Outside New York City, stock productions are also defined by and take place under the applicable Equity contract. Amateur productions are distinguished by their unpaid performers and are presented by schools, colleges, and community groups. Second class productions are defined under the APC as all productions other than first class, Off-Broadway, and stock and amateur productions.

A production either "sits down" in one theatre or tours from city to city and sometimes even country to country. Broadway, Off-Broadway, West End or regional theatre engagements are all examples of "sit downs." Another kind of sit down takes place when additional productions of a Broadway success have open-ended runs in cities like Los Angeles or Chicago, where large enthusiastic audiences can support a long engagement. Starting after, or even during, a successful Broadway engagement, a show will tour from one city to another, playing anywhere from a week to a month or more in each city. The first tour after Broadway is almost always a first class tour. Subsequent tours may be second class, which typically play shorter engagements, often in smaller cities, although some cities support both first and second class tour engagements.

Rights for stock and amateur productions are available through several licensing agencies (Musical Theatre International, Tams-Witmark, Samuel French, R & H Theatricals, Theatrical Rights Worldwide, Dramatists Play Service, and Broadway Play Publishing), which issue standard license agreements and provide production materials for their libraries of existing plays and musicals. The licensing agencies acquire rights to new works that have been presented on Broadway, Off-Broadway or sometimes in one or more regional theatres.

---

[8] Viagas, Robert. "Several members have written asking for a definition of the difference among Broadway, Off-Broadway and Off-Off-Broadway" *Playbill*. N.p., 04 Jan. 1998. Web. 28 Dec. 2016. <http://www.playbill.com/article/how-to-tell-broadway-from-off-broadway-from-com-110450>

While this chapter focuses primarily on first class productions, many of the same issues and concerns addressed here apply to all productions, whether first class or second class, commercial or non-commercial in nature. Of primary importance is obtaining the necessary rights from the author and any underlying rights owners. For stock and amateur productions, this process is straightforward; for professional productions, there is an added layer of complexity, which is described in detail below.

9.2.3. Profit and Non-Profit Theatre

The hallmark of non-profit theatre is that all income must go back into the operation of the business.[9] There is no rule against making money, but there are limitations on how it is spent.

At one time, Broadway theatre was resolutely commercial, with producers and investors investing in the hope of a handsome return. Today, however, profit and non-profit enterprises are intertwined. Lincoln Center Theater, a non-profit, has one theatre that is a Tony Award-eligible Broadway house (the Vivian Beaumont) and two Off-Broadway houses (the Mitzi E. Newhouse and the Claire Tow). The Roundabout Theatre Company, also a non-profit, has three Tony-eligible houses (the American Airlines Theatre, the Stephen Sondheim Theatre and Studio 54, an Off-Broadway theatre (The Laura Pels) and an experimental theatre (the Roundabout Underground Black Box Theatre). Another non-profit, the Manhattan Theatre Club, has a Broadway house (the Samuel J. Friedman Theatre) and two Off-Broadway houses (Stage I and Stage II at New York City Center), as does Second Stage Theater (on Broadway, the Helen Hayes Theatre; and Off-Broadway the Tony Kiser Theatre and the McGinn/Cazale Theatre). Of the major non-profits in New York City, only the Public Theatre lacks a Broadway house. Shows like *Fun Home* and *Hamilton* were produced at the Public with enhancement money from commercial producers and transferred to commercial Broadway houses.

Touring is a commercial business, but otherwise most theatre outside New York is done by non-profits. Regional theatres produce

---

[9] "The Complicated Relationship between Commercial and Not-for-Profit Theatres." American Theatre. N.p., 13 Mar. 2014. Web. 28 Dec. 2016. <http://www.americantheatre.org/2014/03/13/relationship-between-commercial-not-for-profit-theatres/>

their own seasons, sometimes including a production headed to Broadway with enhancement funding provided by hopeful Broadway producers. The League of Resident Theatres ("LORT") has 75 member theatres in 30 states and the District of Columbia. These theatres are typically referred to interchangeably as "Regional," "Resident" and "LORT Theatres."

9.3. UNDERLYING RIGHTS

9.3.1. Kinds of Underlying Material

Broadway musicals are usually based on underlying material, such as a movie, a play or sometimes a life story; straight plays are more likely to be original and not based on underlying material. In the spring of 2016, there were 28 musicals on Broadway; eight were based on motion pictures (in two cases with an underlying novel or play as well as a movie), 13 were based on books or plays, three were based on life stories using existing songs by the subjects of the shows, one was a jukebox musical using existing songs with an original book, one was a Cirque du Soleil show, and only three were original works.

9.3.2. What Rights Need to Be Acquired?

The process of acquiring underlying rights may begin in several ways. Sometimes the authors themselves will obtain the necessary rights for a show they are developing "on spec," without the involvement of a producer. More often, a producer will engage a writing team and also acquire the underlying rights.

The actual task of acquiring any necessary rights will generally fall to the production counsel. The first step is to determine what underlying rights are needed and make a plan to acquire them, taking into account both the cost of the rights and the time frame for obtaining them. Usually, the source of the underlying material is clear. A typical situation involves a stage musical based on a non-musical motion picture or a novel. One of the stickiest questions is what rights are necessary for a musical where the story was initially told in a novel, which was then made into a movie. The answer depends on whether the musical's story can be told using only material from the novel without incorporating any elements from the movie, such as specific dialogue, new characters, and different events. In recent examples, *The Bridges of Madison County* and *American Psycho* were each based only on the novel and not the subsequent motion picture, while the revival of *The Color Purple* was based on both the novel and the motion picture. A particularly complex case was the stage musical *Mary Poppins*, which was based on both the Disney musical motion picture *Mary Poppins* and the children's books by P.L. Travers. The stage rights to the Travers book were controlled by Cameron Mackintosh, which led to an unusual producing partnership between Disney Theatrical Group and Mr. Mackintosh, both historic sole producers, first in the West End and then on Broadway. Another familiar model is the stage musical based on a film musical, like the Disney stage productions *Beauty and the Beast, The Lion King, The Little Mermaid* and *Aladdin*, which were based on animated Disney musical motion pictures.

Additionally, the production counsel needs to be aware of the possibility of "separated rights" held by the writer of a movie or television program that is not based on pre-existing underlying material under the Theatrical and Television Basic Agreement ("MBA") of the Writers Guild of America ("WGA").[10] The WGA defines Separated Rights as "a group of rights that the MBA provides to writers of original material. They are derived from Copyright... The WGA negotiated for certain of the copyright rights to be separated out and conveyed instead to the writer [rather than to the producer of the motion picture.]... The special rights differ for television and for theatrical motion pictures."[11] These are complex provisions, requiring counsel familiar with the details of the MBA.

The answer to whether the producer must acquire the rights to both the novel and the motion picture may not be obvious and cautious lawyers, producers, and authors will give serious consideration as to whether a musical can be written using only elements of the novel. By relying solely on a novel, the producer and authors avoid the additional expense and creative encumbrances of a studio deal. However, one declines to make a deal with the studio at one's peril, since at least a

---

[10] "2014 Writers Guild of America - Alliance of Motion Picture and Television Producers Theatrical and Television Basic Agreement." (n.d.): Article 16.A.3.b. Writers Guild of America, 2 May 2014. Web. 7 Aug. 2016. <http://www.wga.org/uploadedFiles/writers_resources/contracts/MBA14.pdf>

[11] "Understanding Separated Rights." (n.d.): Writers Guild of America. Web. 7 Aug. 2016. <http://www.wga.org/contracts/know-your-rights/understanding-separated-rights>

cease and desist letter, if not a lawsuit, will typically ensue. In *Canal+ Image UK Ltd. v. Lutvak*,[12] the authors declined to deal with the studio and prevailed on a motion to dismiss. Canal+ sued the authors of the musical *A Gentleman's Guide to Love and Murder* for copyright infringement and breach of contract relating to Canal+'s motion picture *Kind Hearts and Coronets*. The authors had entered into an agreement with the studio to adapt the motion picture into a musical. After Canal+ decided not to produce the musical, the authors learned that the film was based on a novel in the public domain entitled *Israel Rank*. The authors revised their musical to follow the plot of the novel, removing all elements contained only in the film, but kept the film's dramatic device of having a single actor play the eight murder victims.[13] In deciding the defendants' motion to dismiss, the court held that there was no copyright infringement and that the breach of contract claim was preempted by the Copyright Act. The court determined that very few elements of the movie were actually protectable and that there were no substantial similarities between the protectable elements of the movie and the musical.[14] The court found that the use of a single actor to play multiple roles was "a standard convention... not protectable in itself because there is nothing original about the device."[15] Finally, the court held that "the total concept and feel of the Film is a dark comedy drama about a disinherited heir who murders his relatives to obtain the baronetcy, while that of the Musical is a bawdy, over-the-top send-up of the same (unprotectable) plot."[16]

It is worth noting the possibility that a play or musical may be a parody of an underlying work and, as such, entitled to protection under the fair use doctrine. However, litigation may well be necessary to maintain this position, with attendant expense and uncertainty. In *Adjmi v. DLT Entertainment Ltd.*,[17] the playwright sought a declaratory judgment that his play *3C* did not infringe the defendants' copyright in the 1970s sitcom, *Three's Company*. The play had run Off-Broadway, despite DLT Entertainment's cease and desist demand asserting that *3C* infringed the copyright in the sitcom, and the playwright wanted to

---

[12] 773 F. Supp. 2d 419 (S.D.N.Y. 2011).
[13] *Id.* at 425-26.
[14] *Id.* at 429-30.
[15] *Id.* at 433.
[16] *Id.* at 439.
[17] 97 F. Supp. 3rd 512 (S.D.N.Y. 2015).

publish the play and license future productions.[18] The parties acknowledged that the play "copies the plot premise, characters, sets and certain scenes from [the television series]."[19] According to the court, the series was "happy, light-hearted, run-of-the-mill, sometimes almost slapstick situation comedy," accompanied by a laugh track, while, in contrast, *3C* "assumes a heavy tone from the outset" with dialogue "sometimes disjointed and rapidly shifting in tone and topic"; it "turns *Three's Company's* sunny 1970s Santa Monica into an upside-down, dark version of itself."[20] The court held that *3C* was a "highly transformative parody"[21] of *Three's Company*, posing minimal risk to the market for *Three's Company*, and entered a declaratory judgment in plaintiff's favor.

9.3.3. Terms of Underlying Rights Agreements

9.3.3.1 Option Periods

A helpful way to look at any entertainment law contract is to consider the elements of time, money, credit, and creative control. For underlying rights, the first timing issue is the duration of the option. A year is typical (occasionally, 18 months), which is usually extendable for a second period and, sometimes, a third period, each of the same length. During the option period(s), the producer will have the right to engage in development, including to commission the book and score, and will simultaneously look to attach a director and stars, secure a theatre, and solicit financing for developmental and production purposes. If the rightsholder is a studio or a well-known writer, the producer will likely be required to provide progress to production updates, in order to receive extensions of the option period. Progress to production elements may include engagement of bookwriter, composer, and lyricist, receipt of a first or subsequent draft of the book and musical compositions, a deal with a director, a deal with a star, a developmental production, or a deal for a Broadway theatre.

---

[18] *Id.* at 515.
[19] *Id.* at 522.
[20] *Id.* at 531-32, 522-23, 530.
[21] *Id.* at 532.

9.3.3.2. Option Exercise

Option exercise typically occurs with the first paid public performance of the work on Broadway or in the West End within the contractually specified period. Depending on the plans for production, the contract may specify that the option exercise occurs with the first Off-Broadway performance. It would be possible to provide by contract for earlier exercise of the option, for example, upon the opening of a developmental production, but this would almost certainly be premature since many steps remain in the life of a show from that time.

9.3.3.3. Merger

Another key date is when "merger" occurs. Merger means that the rights in the underlying work merge with the book, music, and lyrics, so that the individual elements are treated as one and are controlled solely by the authors (following the expiration of the producer's production rights) for licensing purposes. The merged rights may belong to a studio if the underlying work is a motion picture or to the author of a novel or owner of a life story that constitutes the underlying work. Merger clauses in the 1940s and 50s were very broad, excluding only publication rights in the underlying material; all other rights merged into the musical, including motion picture and television rights, so that the dramatists could exploit the musical in all media. Contemporary merger clauses are much less sweeping. A merger clause in a rights agreement with a movie studio will provide for merger only of live stage rights in the motion picture and the musical. The merger clause may even apply only to musical stage rights, with the studio reserving the right to authorize a non-musical stage version of the movie, subject to a holdback of these rights for some specified period.

Merger will typically occur if the production runs on Broadway or in the West End for at least 21 paid public performances, including an official press opening and no more than eight previews. However, if the underlying work is an important novel or a motion picture, the period required for merger may be 208 performances (six months of eight performances a week) or some other substantial number of performances. When representing a rightsholder, be careful not to allow premature merger, such as merger occurring during a second class or developmental engagement. The goal is to avoid tying up the underlying rights before the producer has successfully mounted a first class production.

The merger may initially be non-exclusive,[22] becoming exclusive only after some significant number of performances. The merger will continue to be exclusive for some period and then become non-exclusive if the studio has not received a specified threshold amount averaged over a specified number of years. The process of becoming non-exclusive is known as "demerger" at which point the rightsholder is able to license the rights for a completely new musical based on the underlying work. In practice, this may be hard for the underlying rightsholder to do if the original musical has achieved any meaningful reputation prior to demerger. Sometimes, the producer and the authors are able to negotiate with the studio to waive "demerger" in return for "topping off," which is the payment of the difference between the threshold amount and the lesser amount actually received by the studio during the applicable period.

9.3.3.4. Option Payments; Royalties and Net Profits

Option payments can vary from $5,000 to $30,000 for each option period, depending on the underlying material, and are generally recoupable from initial royalties otherwise payable to the rightsholder. Compensation for exercise of the option is paid as royalties and (particularly where a studio is involved) net profits. When royalties are paid based on weekly operating profits, a studio will generally require advances and royalties equal to one third of the total paid to the authors of the book, music and lyrics; the amount is slightly higher when royalties are calculated on gross. The studio will also receive a participation in subsidiary rights proceeds (a concept explained in detail below) equal to 25% of the total paid to the rightsholder and the authors of the book, music and lyrics. In addition, a studio will require somewhere between 2% and 5% of 100% of net profits. If the rightsholder is the writer of a successful novel, he or she will receive terms comparable to those received by a studio. All of these amounts are subject to negotiation and will vary based on the nature and prior success of the underlying property and the negotiating power of the

---

[22] Non-exclusive merger means that the authors have the right to exploit the musical after expiration of the producer's rights, but the rightsholder retains the right to authorize another theatrical work based on the underlying property. As a practical matter, non-exclusive merger does not take the producer or the authors very far, since the threat of a competing musical stage work remains.

respective parties. If the rightsholder is not a movie studio or the author of an important book, all of these amounts may be reduced, while conversely, if the underlying material is a "blockbuster," they may be substantially increased.

9.3.3.5. Credit

Where the underlying work is a motion picture, credit is generally in the form "Based upon the [Studio] Motion Picture [title of film if different from title of play or musical]" wherever the authors are billed, with certain negotiated exceptions. If the underlying work is a novel or a life story, appropriate substitutions should be made.

9.3.3.6. Special Issues with Studios

Rather than granting full rights backed by representations, warranties and indemnification (which are expected if not required from the individual authors of an original work), studios will only "quitclaim" rights to use their properties. The quitclaim covers only such rights as the studio may actually have, (i.e., "we grant you such rights as we may have," without specifying the rights being granted,) and the representations and warranties are limited to the right to enter into and perform the agreement, lack of knowledge of any assignment, hypothecation or disposition of the quitclaimed rights to any third party, and lack of knowledge of any pending or threatened claims that would conflict with the quitclaimed rights. A studio granting underlying rights will often have the right to approve the bookwriter, composer, lyricist and director. The studio may even obtain approval rights over the book and score. It will also have the right of first refusal to invest some portion of the capitalization of the production, and may insist on being a producer of the show.

9.3.3.7. Right to Use Pre-Existing Musical Compositions

The jukebox musical uses previously released popular songs as its score, often from a single composer, band or singer. *Beautiful* (Carole King), *Jersey Boys* (The Four Seasons), and *On Your Feet!* (Emilio and Gloria Estefan) are examples, based on the life stories of the songwriters. These shows require clearances, often done by a specialized music clearance house, for the rights to the musical compositions from the music publishers. Music publishers can be as insistent on lucrative deal terms as movie studios (where they perceive that their catalogue is essential to the production and likely to attract audiences) and will require at least some level of approval over how their songs are used and some limitations on the duration of the rights granted. The music publisher may not want to grant stock and amateur rights or motion picture rights at the time the stage deal is made, which leaves the authors in the position of having to negotiate a new deal for those rights at a later stage; rights for a cast album are also essential to a production. Another issue is whether the rights to the songs are non-exclusive to the production. Where a life story is being told, exclusivity is very important to the producer and writers. In clearing music rights, the best hope is that the producer is willing to be flexible about which songs she or he will choose to include.

9.4. COLLABORATION AGREEMENTS

Works written by multiple authors require a collaboration agreement to define the rights, responsibilities and obligations of the collaborators. In the absence of a collaboration agreement or in the case of a badly drafted one, any dispute arising among the collaborators will be much more difficult to resolve. As with other entertainment agreements, the key issues are money, credit and control. The collaboration agreement should be prepared at the start of, or at least early in, the collaborative process.

The division of money is relatively clear-cut. For musicals, the bookwriter, composer and lyricist almost always share advances, royalties and other proceeds equally, in thirds. This includes not only money from the initial stage production, but also all subsequent productions and the exploitation of other rights, such as motion pictures or television programs. It is possible to imagine a situation where the contribution of one collaborator could command a premium; such a negotiation might well be contentious. Where two authors create all three elements, one-third will generally be allocated to each element, although a 50-50 split between the two collaborators sometimes occurs. The customary exceptions to the basic split are the publication of the book and lyrics where the composer will probably not share and the exploitation of the small rights in the music and lyrics, which will be shared solely by the composer and lyricist. Small rights to musical compositions are acquired by music publishing companies, ranging from the majors (i.e., Universal Music Publishing Group, Sony/ATV Music Publishing, Warner/Chappell Music) and independent music publishers, which may be large or small.

Billing is straightforward and usually accorded in the order of book, music, lyrics. There are occasional exceptions such as the case of Rodgers & Hammerstein, where Richard Rodgers always received first position for the music. The collaboration agreement should specify that, if one author receives billing, so will all other authors, and that type size and style will be the same for all authors. The exact size and placement of the authors' credits are provided in the agreement with the producer, not the collaboration agreement.

The more complicated issues relate to business and creative decision-making. Business decisions include such matters as the choice of producer, the terms of the production contract, the choice of a stock and amateur licensing agent, and the terms of a movie sale. Creative decisions involve approvals, such as the director, designers, and principal cast. Certain creative approvals belong to the creator of the element at issue; the bookwriter approves changes in the book and the composer and lyricist approve changes in the music or lyrics. The composer will have approval over the musical elements like musical director, conductor, orchestrator, arranger(s), orchestrations and arrangements. The default position in the APC is that each of the book, music and lyrics has one vote on creative approvals and the majority of elements rules, without regard to the actual number of collaborators. The collaborators, however, may choose to provide otherwise in the collaboration agreement. As a practical matter, if there are only two collaborators, the authors often agree that decisions will be unanimous; the alternative is to give the author of two elements ultimate control over decisions. If there are three collaborators, the question is whether to require a majority or unanimity. All of these alternatives have advantages and disadvantages in practice. Most of the issues relating to approval rights within the author team must be determined by the collaborators themselves, and the lawyer's task is to provide guidance. As between the author team and the producer, approvals are addressed in the APC.[23]

In addition to underlying rights, the concept of merger also applies to the book, music and lyrics of a musical. The collaboration agreement should provide that, when certain specified conditions are satisfied, the book, music and lyrics will merge into a single work that can only be exploited as a whole. If the conditions for merger are not satisfied, each author will have the right to use the element or elements she or he created for other purposes, for example, the song in another musical or the lyrics with another tune. Merger for these purposes will occur as agreed by the authors after a certain number of performances of a specified kind of production, such as after the first paid public performance or after 21 performances on Broadway. Certain rights, notably the so-called "small" or "music publishing" rights to perform, record or otherwise use a musical composition other than in the context of the dramatico-musical work (for example, to grant recording rights to individual artists or use in film, television or commercials if unrelated to the "grand rights" granted to the stage production), do not merge and are retained by the composer and lyricist.

9.5. DRAMATISTS GUILD APPROVED PRODUCTION CONTRACT

With over 7,000 members nationwide, it is likely that a show's author (or at least one member of the author team) will be a member of the Dramatists Guild of America. American dramatists were originally members of the Authors League of America founded in 1912. By 1921, the Authors League of America had split into two distinct branches: the Authors Guild and the Dramatists Guild. Today, the Guild is the only national organization that represents the interests of playwrights, bookwriters, composers, and lyricists writing for the theatre. In order to qualify as a full "member" of the Guild, a writer must have had a work produced at the professional level or published by an "established" publisher.

Unlike film and television writers (who are employees of the studios and write on a work-for-hire basis), dramatists are independent contractors and own their work in perpetuity. Consequently, the Guild is a trade association, not a union, and its members do not receive the

---

[23] *See* Dramatists Guild, Inc. Approved Production Contract for Musical Plays. Section 8.01(a).

protections of the National Labor Relations Act. As a result, Guild members are not permitted to bargain collectively. This fact has historically been the source of considerable disagreement among producers, the Guild, and Guild members. The 1941 version of the Guild's Minimum Basic Agreement was challenged in a decision by the United States Court of Appeals for the Second Circuit in *Ring v. Spina*.[24] The *Ring* court found the 1941 Minimum Basic Agreement to be in violation of Section 1 of the Sherman Act by virtue of its compulsory arbitration provision, its closed shop requirement, and its effect upon price. The 1946 version of the Minimum Basic Agreement eliminated the provisions found unlawful in *Ring*, and the playwrights and producers maintained a détente of sorts utilizing the same royalty terms for playwright compensation that had been agreed upon in the 1936 Minimum Basic Agreement.[25]

In 1983, Richard Barr, the president of the League of New York Theaters and Producers, sued the Guild and three of its members alleging that they "conspired to fix the minimum prices and other terms on which they will deal with producers and have agreed among themselves that they will not license a play to producers except upon the minimum terms incorporated in a standard form contract the Minimum Basic Production Contract ("MBPC") promulgated by the Guild."[26] The Guild countersued the League, alleging that the producers had conspired among themselves through the mechanism of the MBPC, and fixed, stabilized and/or maintained at artificially low and non-competitive levels the compensation received by playwrights.[27] The parties settled out of court and producers and the Guild ultimately came to a compromise in the form of the APC, which replaced the MBPC.[28]

---

[24] 148 F. 2d 647 (2d Cir. 1945).
[25] Sevush, Ralph. "RE: APC Section." Message to Victoria G. Traube. 18 July 2016. E-mail.
[26] "Plaintiff Barr seeks a declaration that the alleged conspiracy is violative of Section 1 of the Sherman Act, 15 U.S.C. § 1, and an injunction against the "use of contracts containing minimum terms and conditions for the production of any author's work as a legitimate theatrical attraction." Barr v. Dramatists Guild, Inc., 573 F. Supp. 555 (S.D.N.Y. 1983), 557.
[27] Sevush, Ralph. "RE: APC Section." Message to Victoria G. Traube. 18 July 2016. E-mail.
[28] Breglio, John. "The Approved Production Contract." *I Wanna Be a Producer: How to Make a Killing on Broadway ... or Get Killed*. Milwaukee: Applause Theatre & Cinema, 2016. 115.

Articles I through XXI of the APC contain the minimum terms accepted by the Guild; however, the parties may modify terms with a rider attached as Article XXII. Once agreed upon by the author and the producer, the APC, including Article XXII (which alone is often 20 to 30 pages), is subject to certification by the Guild. The current APC addresses the following key issues:

9.5.1. Option Periods and Payments; Advance Payments

The option periods and payments set forth in Article II of the APC are often heavily modified in Article XXII. For authors who are Broadway veterans, option payments can be in the tens of thousands of dollars. Producers will often ask for an extension or tolling of the option period of up to six months or a year to accommodate the availability of a director, theatre, or star. In the event the producer presents Second Class Performances or Developmental Productions (as each such term is defined in the APC), the option periods are tolled for the duration of these productions, plus 60 days.[29]

The advance payments set forth in Article III of the APC are tied to the capitalization of the production, with a cap of $35,000 for plays and $60,000 for musicals.[30] Under Section 6.01, certain option payments may be deducted from the advance payments,[31] and, in accordance with Section 6.01, all of the option and advance payments paid to the authors are deductible from the royalties earned by the author, at the rate of up to 50% of royalties per performance week, following the recoupment of production expenses. In the event the option payments or advance payments are in excess of the APC's minimum amounts, the producer may negotiate to have the excess amounts recouped from first royalties, rather than post-recoupment.

---

[29] Dramatists Guild, Inc. Approved Production Contract for Musical Plays. Section 2.04.

[30] Since these figures were negotiated in 1985, the advances are often now treated as minimums rather than caps.

[31] For plays, only the payment for the third option period is deductible; however, for musicals, payments made for all but the first option period are deductible from the advance payments. *See* Dramatists Guild, Inc. Approved Production Contract for Plays. Section 6.01.

9.5.2. Royalties

Traditionally, authors were always paid royalties based on gross weekly box office receipts ("GWBOR").[32] For Broadway musicals, payment on GWBOR typically means 4.5% increasing to 6% following recoupment, in accordance with the Guild minimum standard.[33] Over time, as the average capitalization of shows increased and weekly operating costs continued to rise, it became increasingly difficult for investors to recoup their investment, while royalty participants received payment in full.[34] To take a simplified example, if a musical generates $600,000 of GWBOR and has fixed weekly operating expenses of $530,000, there will be $70,000 in weekly operating profit; however, if the weekly royalties payable to the percentage royalty participants total 15% of GWBOR (i.e., $90,000), the show will end up losing $20,000 that week. Under this scenario, for each week the show is running, the investors will receive nothing, while the royalty participants will receive significant contractual royalty payments.

To solve this problem and better address the investors' interests, the industry developed the "royalty pool." The royalty pool is a profit-sharing model that repays the investors at the same time it pays the percentage royalty participants (which includes the lead producers), by dividing the weekly operating profit between the investors and the royalty participants.[35] Royalty pools are sometimes expressed as the percentage of weekly operating profits payable to all of the percentage royalty participants, for example, 35% increasing to 40% at recoupment. The royalty participants share in a percentage of weekly operating profits on a pro rata basis in proportion to each participant's gross royalty percentage. Generally, the author's royalty is expressed as a percentage of the entire weekly operating profit, not just the author's share of the

---

[32] GWBOR is the total received by the production from ticket sales for that performance week. That amount is then reduced to the so-called "net gross" by the deduction of certain taxes and fees such as the restoration fee paid to the theatre. See Dramatists Guild, Inc. Approved Production Contract for Musical Plays. Section 4.03.

[33] These percentages are typically divided equally among the three departments with the book, music, and lyrics each receiving 1.5% increasing to 2% after recoupment.

[34] It is not uncommon for a Broadway musical to have a capitalization of anywhere from 12 to 18 million dollars.

[35] The percentage split between the investors and the royalty participants is a negotiated point.

royalty pool. The standard percentage of weekly operating profits payable to a musical's author team for a first class production is 15.56% of 100% of weekly operating profits prior to recoupment and 17.78% of 100% of weekly operating profits following recoupment.[36]

Most shows today pay royalties on the basis of weekly operating profits instead of on gross. Typically, once a show elects to pay royalties on the gross, the show must continue to calculate royalties that way for the duration of the run. Another royalty issue that is often addressed in Article XXII is payment to the author on the basis of company share, which is relevant for touring productions.

An additional concept, amortization, was introduced to help productions reach recoupment faster. The producer is able to treat a fixed amount (typically, 2% of the capitalization with a negotiated cap) as an additional weekly expense for purposes of calculating the show's operating expenses. This weekly amount goes toward recoupment by the investors. For the royalty participants, amortization reduces weekly operating profit and therefore royalties. In consideration for accepting this reduction in royalties, the author team will often receive an additional advance, additional guaranteed weekly minimums, as well as an additional deferred royalty post-recoupment until 110% of the author's deferred royalties are paid back, and sometimes even a share of net profits.

9.5.3. Subsidiary Rights

The APC defines the term "Subsidiary Rights" as the rights in the play or musical relating to seven different methods of exploitation: Media Productions, Audio-Visual Productions, Commercial Use Products, Stock Performances, Amateur Performances, Ancillary Performances, and Revival Performances.[37] In short, subsidiary rights relate to exploitation of the show other than by the original producer. The stock and amateur deal or even the motion picture deal will often be made while the original producer's rights are still in effect. A producer may even agree to a limited exploitation of stock and amateur rights, like allowing high school productions of *School of Rock* during

---

[36] Whether this increase takes place in the week following recoupment or following 110% of recoupment is subject to negotiation.

[37] These seven terms are each defined in Section 11.01 of the Dramatists Guild, Inc. Approved Production Contract for Musical Plays.

the Broadway run.[38] For a show that is not a financial success during its initial commercial run, subsidiary rights will determine whether the investors will ever recoup their investments.

For a producer, there are three primary questions regarding subsidiary rights: when does the producer become entitled to share, for how long, and in what manner? The first question is addressed in Section 11.02 of the APC; the producer is entitled to share in subsidiary rights only after she or he has "vested." There are many ways in which the producer can vest; the most common, under the APC, is by presenting 10 preview performances, plus an official opening in New York City. Section 11.03(c) offers three different alternatives (the "Producer's Alternatives"), which specify how the producer will share in subsidiary rights.[39] Article XXII may also provide the producer with the additional option to share under the MBPC formula.[40] Each of the Producer's Alternatives, as well as the MBPC formula, also specifies how long the producer will share in each method of exploitation. The producer's subsidiary rights election will depend on the nature of the property and is often made with input from the general manager and production counsel.

9.5.4. Additional Production Rights

In addition to sharing in subsidiary rights, once the producer vests she or he also obtains the right to produce Off-Broadway productions and productions in what are referred to as the "Additional Territories" – the British Isles, Australia, and New Zealand. For a new show, Article XXII will outline the producer's rights in the rest of the world, including advances, time allowed to produce, and the royalty.

9.5.5. Travel Expenses

Expenses are addressed generally in Section 8.04 of the APC and, in respect of the Additional Territories, in Section 9.08. Specifics, such as reimbursement for rental cars, class of airfare, the extent to

---

[38] "School Of Rock." Rodgers & Hammerstein. N.p., n.d. Web. 21 Aug. 2016. <http://www.rnh.com/show/383/School-Of-Rock>.

[39] For plays, there are four Producer's Alternatives.

[40] If Article XXII provides for the MBPC formula, it should also expressly allow the producer to share in Revival Performances, which is not a provision of the MBPC.

which private ground transportation will be provided, and the amount of the author's per diem in various major cities throughout the world, are all negotiated points included in Article XXII. Not only do these individual expenses add up over time (e.g., if a bookwriter who lives in Los Angeles is required by the producer to travel to New York multiple times, the difference in price between economy class airfare and first class airfare will make a difference), but other members of the creative team, such as the director, will often tie their travel expenses to those of the author.

9.5.6. Billing

Section 8.10 of the APC guarantees the author billing whenever the producer or the director receives billing; however, this is generally a starting point. Article XXII will go into detail regarding the size of the author's billing in relation to the show's title and who else, if anyone, is entitled to receive billing as large as or larger than the author's billing. Equally important, Article XXII will specify where the producer is and is not required to accord the author billing. Production counsel should always include language which provides that casual or inadvertent failure to comply with the billing provisions will not constitute a breach of the agreement by the producer, so long as the producer rectifies the mistake upon notice of the error, prospectively, as soon as practicable.

9.5.7. Commercial Use Products

The APC addresses merchandise derived from the play or musical (i.e., "Commercial Use Products") two different ways. While the producer has production rights, he or she also has the right to create, manufacture, and sell Commercial Use Products, subject to sharing the proceeds with the author. When such sales are on theatre premises, the author is entitled to a sum equal to 10% of the gross retail sales (less taxes) not to exceed 50% of the producer's license fee. With respect to all other sales, the author has a right to 50% of the producer's net receipts.[41]

---

[41] Dramatists Guild, Inc. Approved Production Contract for Musical Plays. Section 11.05.

Once the producer's production rights have expired, all of the rights in Commercial Use Products revert to the author, and the producer is entitled to share passively in income derived from dispositions by the author for a period of 40 years following the close of the last performance presented by the producer.

9.5.8. Cast Albums

Record companies used to bid for the rights to Broadway hits; cast albums were often best sellers. Times have changed. Although the occasional smash like *Hamilton* is also a best-selling album, original cast albums are rarely profitable. Today, almost every Broadway musical is recorded, but more often by newcomers like Sh-K-Boom and PS Classics than the major labels. Cast album costs are paid by the producers, sometimes with help from the authors. While profit solely from sales of the album is unlikely, the album documents the musical and serves as a marketing tool for the Broadway production, as well as subsequent touring productions, and stock and amateur licensing.[42] Net proceeds received from the disposition of a cast album (including all royalties and advances) are divided 60% to the author (and the underlying rights owner, if any) and 40% to the producer.

9.6. DEVELOPMENT

As the author develops the play or musical, the producer, whether a commercial producer or a not-for-profit theatre that commissioned the work, will want to try the material out with actors in front of an invited audience. Presenting the show at various stages of development accomplishes two different objectives – it allows the entire creative team to see what is working and what is not, and it gives the producer the opportunity to gauge the level of interest within the industry and determine how difficult it will be to raise money and obtain a theatre. Equity allows its members to participate in three different development levels: readings, labs, and workshops.

---

[42] Green, Jesse. "Why Does Nearly Every Broadway Show Still Release a Cast Album?" *New York Magazine* 6 Oct. 2015: n. page. Web. <http://www.vulture.com/2015/10/broadway-shows-cast-albums.html>

9.6.1. Enhancement Agreements

Until the late 1970s, it was common for new works to have one or more commercial engagements out of town in cities like Boston and Philadelphia prior to opening in New York City. Safe from the lights (and critics) of Broadway, the creative team could try out material in front of a live audience, replace musical numbers that were not working, and even make changes to the cast. With production expenses continuing to climb, it is increasingly rare for musicals, and all but unheard of for plays, to have commercial out-of-town tryouts. In order to contain costs and continue to receive feedback from live audiences before arriving on Broadway, many commercial producers now work with not-for-profit theatres, such as the 5th Avenue Theatre in Seattle, the Old Globe in San Diego, and the Paper Mill Playhouse in Milburn, New Jersey to present so-called "developmental productions" of their musicals. Unlike readings, labs, and workshops, a developmental production is fully-staged with sets and costumes, and, most importantly, is open to the paying public.

The so-called "enhancement agreement" between the not-for-profit theatre and the commercial producer will vary, depending on the scale of the production, the size of the not-for-profit, and the commercial potential of the show. Often, the commercial producer will license its exclusive right to produce a developmental production of the musical (which it obtained in the original grant of rights from the authors) to the not-for-profit theatre. The theatre will then mount its own production of the work for a limited run as part of its season, and the commercial producer will have the opportunity to see how a live audience reacts – all for a fraction of what a first class production outside New York City would otherwise cost.

Of primary interest to the not-for-profit theatre is the opportunity to further its mission by producing a high caliber work for its audience, which is usually made up of subscribers. In addition, there is the potential for new sources of revenue in the form of ongoing financial participation, should the show have a life after the not-for-profit theatre's production. For the commercial producer, the focus is on testing the material and the cast while limiting financial risk.[43] With these interests

---

[43] Baruch, Jason P. "The Arranged Marriage between Not-For-Profit Theater Companies and Commercial Producers." *Sendroff & Baruch, LLP*. N.p., n.d. Web. 10 Apr. 2016. <http://sendroffbaruch.com/the-arranged-marriage-between-not-for-profit-theater-companies-and-commercial-producers/>

in mind, the not-for-profit theatre and the commercial producer will often go back and forth on the following key points in the enhancement agreement.

9.6.2. Enhancement Funds

Generally, the not-for-profit will require that the commercial producer provide funding to "enhance" the theatre's production of the work. For example, a not-for-profit theatre may reasonably believe that its production of the commercial producer's musical will cost $1.2 million; however, the theatre only has a budget of $800,000 to spend on each musical it produces in a season. The commercial producer will provide so-called "enhancement funds" in the amount of $400,000 to make up the difference in cost, and the theatre will be able to present a higher quality production, in furtherance of its mission, without going over budget. The commercial producer will want to keep the enhancement funds as low as possible, and will often raise this money from third parties in order to limit her or his exposure.

9.6.3. Control

The issue of control is a particularly interesting one; the theatre alone must control the production or it risks losing its status as a not-for-profit entity.[44] For this reason, it is essential that a not-profit-theatre consult a tax specialist, before entering into an enhancement agreement with a commercial producer. Nevertheless, the commercial producer may be entitled to certain mutual decision-making rights in respect of budget, casting, etc. and may even have the right to share in net adjusted gross box office receipts ("NAGBOR"), provided that the commercial producer never receives a benefit that is in excess of what is accorded to the not-for-profit.

9.6.4. Financial Participation

In consideration of the not-profit-theatre's contributions to the development of the musical, it is customary for the not-profit theatre to receive a royalty and, in many cases, a share of net profits from the

---

[44] Ibid.

initial commercial production.[45] This passive income can make a considerable difference to a not-profit-theatre, should the commercial production ultimately prove to be commercially successful. Commercial producers often try to make the not-for-profit's right to share in these revenue streams contingent upon the first preview of the initial commercial production occurring within a certain period following the not-for-profit theatre's staging of the work, since the value of the not-for-profit's production to the show's overall development diminishes over time. Similarly, in the event the commercial producer determines that a second developmental production is necessary for the musical's progress, the commercial producer will want the two not-for-profits to share any royalty and net profits, in order to avoid overburdening any subsequent commercial production.

In reality, not all shows leave a not-for-profit theatre and go straight to Broadway (if to Broadway at all); however, this does not mean that the work will be a financial failure, thanks to revenue earned from subsidiary rights. In order to ensure some form of ongoing income in the event royalties and net profits never materialize, not-for-profit theatres will often enter into a separate agreement directly with the author for a percentage of the author's share of revenue generated from dispositions of subsidiary rights. The commercial producer will then provide in the enhancement agreement that, once the commercial producer "vests," the not-for-profit theatre must waive (or assign to the commercial producer) this share of subsidiary rights revenue in return for receiving the royalty and net profit participation discussed above. If the commercial producer never vests, the not-for-profit retains its share of subsidiary rights.

9.6.5. Credit

Not-for-profit theatres are almost always entitled to receive credit in connection with the commercial producer's productions in the form of either "in association with" or "World premiere at." Credit allows the not-for-profit to raise its profile on a national level (potentially catching the eye of future subscribers and commercial producers alike) and is therefore important to the ongoing success of the theatre.

---

[45] Whether the not-for-profit theatre's ongoing financial participation is limited to the initial first (or second) class production produced by the commercial producer, applies to all productions under the commercial producer's license or control, or something in between (such as limiting participation to the Broadway and West End productions, and the initial first class tour) is always a heavily negotiated point.

9.6.6. Physical Production

At the conclusion of the not-for-profit's production, the commercial producer will typically have the right, for nominal consideration, to take ownership of the physical elements of the production, such as projections, sets, costumes, props, wigs, and other assets that were purchased specifically for the production and not taken from the not-for-profit's reusable items.

9.7. FINANCING

As the development process continues, commercial producers may elect to self-finance various readings and perhaps even a lab or workshop. Major media conglomerates often elect to fund the entire project through opening night. Typically, however, the money for a show's initial development phase is raised from a limited number of investors. In addition to readings, labs and workshops, these funds are used to pay for legal and accounting expenses, advances to the author team, and payments to underlying rightsholders, among other expenses. Due to the high-risk nature of their investments, since a show in development may never actually reach production, early-stage investors are usually entitled to additional consideration. Such benefits may include the right to increase the amount of the investment when the producers are ready to mount a commercial production, a share of adjusted net profits payable from the producer's share (as explained below), and, in the event a commercial production is ultimately produced, tickets to opening night and access to house seats. A producer should confer with a securities expert, before preparing to raise this initial round of funding.

When the producer has committed to mounting a commercial production, she or he will form the production entity, which is typically either a limited partnership or a limited liability company.[46] The production entity will eventually hold the rights granted by the underlying rightsholder, if there is one, and the authors, and the production entity's investors will ultimately share in the revenue derived from the exploitation of those rights. The most common approach to financing commercial productions in the U.S. is through

---

[46] The producer should consult with a tax specialist, when determining what type of entity to use as the production entity.

the sale of interests in the production entity to investors. This sale of interests to third parties constitutes a sale of securities, adding an additional layer of complexity to the fundraising process.[47] Any producer contemplating offering securities must consider all state and federal regulations and, if applicable, the Arts and Cultural Affairs Laws of the State of New York. Most securities offerings in the theatrical industry are made pursuant to Regulation D of the Securities Act of 1933.[48] Regulation D contains three rules, 504, 505 and 506, each of which provides an exemption from the SEC's registration requirements. All three rules make a distinction between "accredited investors" and "non-accredited investors." An accredited investor is a natural person, trust, or entity that satisfies one of the requirements under Rule 501(a) of Regulation D of the Securities Act of 1933. The primary reason for this distinction is to limit the purchase of unregistered securities to those who can withstand the risk of such an investment.[49]

In the world of theatrical financing, Rule 506 is the rule most often elected, since it permits those relying on it to raise unlimited funds. In 2013, the SEC adopted amendments to Rule 506, in order to implement certain requirements of the Jumpstart Our Business Startups Act (or JOBS Act). As a result of the amendments, there are now two distinct exemptions under Rule 506: Rule 506(b) and Rule 506(c). Under Rule 506(b), the issuer is not permitted to use general solicitation or advertising to market the securities. In contrast, Rule 506(c) permits broad solicitation and general advertising of the offering, subject to very stringent requirements, among other significant distinctions.

If production counsel is not a securities lawyer, it is imperative that she or he consult with a securities expert throughout the offering process, since failure to comply with federal securities laws or blue sky laws could potentially expose the producer to considerable civil and, in some cases, criminal liability and may stall the project or halt its advancement entirely.[50]

---

[47] Brown, Elliot H., and Daniel M. Wasser. "A Practical Guide to Theatrical Financing." *FWRV Law Firm*. N.p., 1 Sept. 1998. Web. 10 Apr. 2016. <http://fwrv.com/ articles/100642-a-practical-guide-to-theatrical-financing.html>.

[48] Farber, Donald C. "Raising Money – Necessary Filings – The Securities and Exchange Commission and Attorney General." *Producing Theatre: A Comprehensive Legal and Business Guide*. New York: Drama Book, 1981. 93.

[49] Securities and Exchange Commission: The Office of Investor Education and Advocacy. (2013). *Accredited Investors* (SEC Pub. No. 158).

[50] Farber 87-88.

The standard structure in the U.S. theatrical industry provides that the production entity's cash flow is used to pay back the investors' capital contributions until the point of recoupment. Once all production expenses (less bonds, security deposits, and other recoverable items) have been recouped by the production entity, net profits may be paid to underlying rightsholders, a non-profit theatre that produced a developmental production, the director, if she or he is particularly sought after, and, in some rare instances, the producer, who may take a share of net profits as so-called "torchbearer points" in consideration for rendering developmental services. After these off-the-top payments, the remaining net profits, which are referred to as "adjusted net profits," are customarily divided equally between the general partners or managers of the entity (i.e., the "producer's share") and the investors. Each investor will receive a pro rata share of the investors' share. For example, if an investor contributed $1 million to the production entity and all capital contributions are $10 million, in the aggregate, that investor would receive 10% of the investors' share.

Depending on the size of the production entity's capitalization and the level of interest from investors, some producers may provide those making significant investments (such investors are often referred to as "co-producers") with a share of adjusted net profits payable solely from the producer's share, in addition to the pro rata portion of the investors' share to which that co-producer is entitled as an investor. Other benefits that producers often give to co-producers include billing above the title of the show, a biography in the program, the right to invest in future productions that are separately financed, access to house seats, and tickets to the opening night performance along with passes to the opening night party.

9.8. CREATIVE AND CAST AGREEMENTS

9.8.1. Director and Choreographer Contracts

Before rehearsals begin and continuing through previews, the director works with the authors to develop and revise the musical. The director is usually not a writer; the task is to guide and suggest.[51] The director also collaborates with the designers of the physical production,

---

[51] Occasionally, the bookwriter is also the director.

which must reflect the director's vision of the show and staging plans. The director supervises the rehearsal process, during which the actors come to inhabit their characters. There is an ancient theatrical joke in which an actor asks the director for his motivation to cross stage left and the director replies, "Because I told you to." The modern directorial process is considerably more complex. The task of the director is not to prescribe, but to elicit and then edit, criticize and shape the actors' performances.

The SDC establishes minimum fees, advances, royalties, billing and deals with artistic and intellectual property issues. Since its formation in 1959, the SDC has sought to strengthen the artistic approvals and intellectual property rights of the director, a stance that has long been the source of conflict between the union and the Guild. With respect to artistic rights, Article XIX of the SDC Broadway Collective Bargaining Agreement ("SDC Broadway CBA") provides that "If the Director is available, and subject to the prior approval of the author and the final approval of the Producer, the Director shall have approval, not to be unreasonably withheld or delayed, of cast, replacements, understudies, designers and designs, production stage manager, and director of other companies." The director's approval rights under the union agreement are both subject to and more limited than the author's approval rights; however, the approvals (like all rights under any collective bargaining agreement) are minimums, and an established director can negotiate for broader approval rights. What is not negotiable, however, is the collaborative nature of the approval process. The director cannot dictate, but must reach agreement with the author and the producer.

Article XVIII of the SDC Broadway CBA relating to property rights is worth quoting at length. Note the care with which this provision avoids impinging on the rights of the authors:

> In order to facilitate the Director and/or the Choreographer's ability to prevent the unauthorized re-creation of direction and or choreography, the Producer and the Director and/or Choreographer agree that, as between themselves, all rights in the Direction and Choreography... shall be, upon its creation, and will remain the sole and exclusive property of the Director and/or Choreographer respectively, [subject, however to the irrevocable license of the producer to use the direction or choreography in the producer's own or licensed subsequent

productions for which the director or choreographer is entitled to payment]... The foregoing is not intended to alter, diminish or affect, in any way, any of the Author's rights in the play.

In 1976, Congress added "choreographic works" to 17 U.S.C. Section 102 (a) (4), protecting the choreographer's work from infringement if the requirements of fixation in a tangible form and sufficient originality are satisfied.[52] Fixation may be by video recording, notation or computer technology.[53]

Whether direction is protected under the Copyright Act is far less certain; despite numerous law review articles and notes,[54] no court has ruled directly on the issue. The first question is factual: What is direction? Is it the blocking, which is the movement of the actors on stage, or more broadly, the stage pictures created by the director; the director's contributions to the script; the director's concept, which is embodied in the physical production (copyright in which is held by the designers), and the performances of the actors; or is it all of these? The legal issues are also complex. Does direction have sufficient originality and is it subject to fixation in a tangible form (both of which are necessary to meet the requirements for copyright protection under 17 U.S.C. Section 102 (a))?

---

[52] See Arcomano, Nicholas. "THE COPYRIGHT LAW AND DANCE." *The New York Times*. 10 Jan. 1981. Web. 17 Aug. 2016. <http://www.nytimes.com/1981/01/11/arts/the-copyright-law-and-dance.html>

[53] See Lakes, Joi Michelle. "A PAS DE DEUX FOR CHOREOGRAPHY AND COPYRIGHT." New York University Law Review 80 (2005): 1829-861. Web. 5 May 2016. <http://www.nyulawreview.org/sites/default/files/pdf/NYULawReview-80-6-Lakes.pdf>.

[54] See Livingston, Margit. "Inspiration or Imitation: Copyright Protection for Stage Directions," 50 Boston College Law Review 427 (2009); Leichtman, Dav*id*. "Most Unhappy Collaborators: An Argument Against the Recognition of Property Ownership in Stage Directions," 20 Colum.-VLA J.L. & Arts 683 (1996); Litman, Jessica. "Copyright in the Stage Direction of a Broadway Musical," 7 Colum-VLA J.L. & Arts 309 (1983); Yellin, Talia. "New Directions for Copyright: The Property Rights of Stage Directors," 24 Colum-VLA J.L. & Arts 317 (2001); Karaoke, Elvis. "Shakespeare and the Search for Copyrightable Stage Direction," 43 Ariz. L. Rev 677 (2001); Freemal, Beth. "Theatre, Stage Directions & Copyright Law," 71 Chi-Kent L. Rev 1017 (1996); Maxwell, Jennifer J. "Making a Federal Case for Copyrighting Stage Directions: Einhorn v. Mergatroyd Productions," 77 Marshall Rev. Intell. Prop. L.393 ((2008); Stein, Deana S. "Every Move That She Makes: Copyright Protection for Stage Directions and the Fictional Character Standard," 34 Cardozo Law Review 1571 (2013).

Directors have brought a number of lawsuits claiming that their rights in their direction were infringed by subsequent productions. In a 1994 lawsuit, director Gerald Gutierrez claimed that his stage direction of *The Most Happy Fella* by Frank Loesser at the Goodspeed Opera (and subsequently on Broadway) was infringed by a subsequent production in Chicago. The producer of the Chicago production had viewed a videotape of Mr. Gutierrez's production at the Theatre on Film and Tape Archive of the New York Public Library, rented the sets from that production, and hired its lead actor. The case was settled by payment of an undisclosed sum and an apology by the producer in an ad in Variety. In 1996, director Joe Mantello sued Caldwell Theatre in connection with its production under a license issued by Dramatists Play Service, for violation of the Lanham Act and infringement of Mantello's copyright in his direction of the Off-Broadway and Broadway productions of *Love! Valour! Compassion!* Mr. Mantello asserted that the Caldwell production was "a 90 to 95% replication" of his Broadway production, including the staging of the opening and the use of a dollhouse on a green mound as a significant prop.[55] The case was dismissed for lack of personal jurisdiction but refiled in Florida, and ultimately settled for $7,000 and defendants' acknowledgment that "the theatre had inadvertently used [Mantello's] work without his permission."[56] In 2006, an Off-Off Broadway director claimed breach of contract and copyright infringement based on his dismissal from a production that opened using his work. The court held that his claims survived a motion to dismiss and after trial granted the director $800 in damages. Although not addressing the copyright claim directly, the judge noted that "The claimed (blocking and choreography script) consisted of movements of actors and positioning of actors. There is a very lively question, I suppose, as to whether that is an appropriate subject of the copyright as to which I express no opinion. If it is, however, the deposit copy certainly didn't cover it because it is impossible to discern with precision from the deposit copy just exactly what the [stage] movements were and what the [stage] positioning was."[57]

---

[55] *See* Green, Jesse. "Exit, Pursued by a Lawyer," *New York Times*, 29 January 29 2006. <http://www.nytimes.com/2006/01/29/theater/newsandfeatures/exit-pursued-by-a-lawyer.html>.

[56] Marks, Peter. "Love, Valour, Déjà Vu," *New York Times*, 29 March 1996. <http://www.nytimes.com/1996/03/29/theater/on-stage-and-off.html>.

[57] McClernan, Nancy. "The Strange Case of EDWARD EINHORN V. MERGATROYD PRODUCTIONS." Editorial. *THE DRAMATIST* Sept. 2006: n. page.

Although the law is not clear, directors have had some success in defending their interests in court. There is a lesson in the previous history for lawyers who represent regional and amateur theatres: Warn your clients of the possible exposure created by too literal use of elements from a previous Broadway or touring production, to the extent these elements are not specified by the author.

Without regard to the copyrightability of the director's work, another approach to compensation for the use of direction in subsequent productions is a share of the net proceeds from the authors' disposition of subsidiary rights. The SDC has long argued for such a participation under its collective bargaining agreements, so far without success.[58] Nevertheless, a successful director, or one who has made a contribution that the authors acknowledge as unique, may negotiate successfully with the authors for a participation in subsidiary rights as a matter of contract.[59]

9.8.2. Actor's Agreement

9.8.2.1. Minimum Basic Agreements

Equity negotiates and administers more than 30 national and regional contracts with theatrical employers (described on Equity's website), which provide "minimum salaries, benefits, job security and numerous other protections to ensure a safe and dignified work environment."[60] These contracts are all minimum basic agreements, which prohibit engagement of an actor on less favorable terms, but allow the negotiation of more favorable terms. Salary, credit, dressing room conditions and amenities, term of services, and the right to leave the show for a motion picture or television job are among the terms

---

The Strange Case of EDWARD EINHORN V. MERGATROYD PRODUCTIONS. Web. 21 Aug. 2016. <http://mcclernan.com/strangecase/>.

[58] The current SDC CBA provides that if The League of American Theatres and Producers ever grants "subsidiary rights to any other Union... then the SDC shall have the right to reopen the [Collective Bargaining] Agreement for the sole purpose of negotiating subsidiary rights for Directors and Choreographers."

[59] *See* McKinley, Jesse. "Suit! Anger! Agreement!" *New York Times*, 26 March 1999. <http://www.nytimes.com/1999/03/26/movies/on-stage-and-off.html>.

[60] "Actorsequity.org | About Equity's Contracts and Codes." *Actors' Equity Association*. N.p., n.d. Web. 13 April. 2016.<http://www.actorsequity.org/AboutEquity/contracts.asp>.

frequently negotiated. What can be obtained through negotiation is, of course, a function of the actor's stature and experience.

9.8.2.2. Star Contract

The contract of a star has the most room for negotiation. Typically, the star contract will be negotiated by the general manager with the star's agent in consultation with the star's lawyer. Compensation is the first issue: weekly salary, percentage of gross (starting at breakeven or some other predetermined level of gross, in rare cases from first dollar), bonuses for a Tony award nomination and a Tony award win. A star may also receive a percentage of net profits for originating a role. The Equity bond guarantees two weeks' salary, but, for a star, there should be a guarantee of four to eight weeks salary.

The next key issue is the term of the deal. For musicals, producers want stars to commit for a full year, at least from the start of rehearsal, but the star may only want a six-month commitment. This is an important issue, because the loss of a star too early in the run can damage the show at the box office. It is important to establish outside dates for the start of performances out of town, if any, the start of previews and the official press opening. The star may also want an "out" clause for a theatrical or television movie or TV pilot.

Credit matters, but there is usually little controversy about the appropriate credit for a star. The only difficulty arises when there are two stars who are both arguably entitled to first position. A motion picture solution is so-called "Towering Inferno" billing, where the two names go on a diagonal, with one name lower left and the other name upper right.[61] This is perhaps best suggested as a "simple proposal" that will make both actors realize that there must be a better solution.[62] The star should have billing in all advertising and publicity, including ABC ads. The fallback position is billing in all ads of a specified size or larger. The star must also have billing in all ads in which another performer's name appears, except award, nomination or congratulatory ads. A major star will be billed on the marquee and will appear on the

---

[61] Wolf, Matt. "The Billing Debate with Two Great Stars." *The Guardian*. 12 Oct. 2002. <https://www.theguardian.com/theobserver/2002/oct/13/featuresreview.review1>.

[62] One of the authors of this chapter once seriously annoyed an actor by suggesting that he take second position to his co-star on the basis of "ladies first"; this is not recommended.

cover of the Playbill. Photo and likeness approval is essential to the star and rarely controversial.

A large part of the negotiation for a star will be devoted to perks and approvals. Transportation to and from the theatre is essential, generally by car and driver; a dinner stop at producer's expense is also desirable. The star will have a dresser and may also require a hairdresser. Likewise, the wigmaker, if any, may be subject to the star's approval. The star should have first choice of dressing room, which should be freshly painted and decorated. The star may also require a massage therapist, vocal coach or trainer, the expense of which may be justified by the physical requirements of the role. Security protection on arrival at and departure from the theatre is worth considering and in some cases essential. If the star comes from out of town, she or he must have hotel and per diem or, more likely, an apartment approved by the star and paid for by the producer, plus first class transportation. The star should also have the option to do the first class tour, and, possibly, the production in the West End and any sit-down production in Los Angeles, with the terms subject to good faith negotiation. Interviews and publicity services should also be subject to the star's approval.

9.8.2.3. Designer Contracts

There are four main categories of designers: sets, costumes, lighting and sound.[63] The USA, the designers union, has approximately forty collective bargaining agreements with employers in various fields, which establish fees, royalties and other minimum terms and conditions. Designers own the copyrights in their designs. They receive credit on the title page of the program and in certain advertisements. Their contracts are typically negotiated by their agents with the general manager.

9.8.2.4. Orchestrator and Arranger Contracts

The composer provides a piano-vocal version of the songs, which the orchestrator arranges for performance by the orchestra. Prior to orchestration, the arrangers arrange the music for specific purposes; there are vocal arrangements, dance arrangements and sometimes

---

[63] Other categories include projection designer, computer artist, graphic artists and categories for assistants.

incidental arrangements. The melody and harmonies as written by the composer constitute a vocal arrangement in its simplest form. Vocal arrangements also adapt the music as written by the composer for specific performers and combinations of performers.[64] Dance arrangements are created from the musical compositions written by the composer of the show after the choreographer and dancers have been hired and require close collaboration between the choreographer and the dance arranger.[65] Orchestrators and arrangers are engaged as employees for hire with the copyright vesting in the composer. Reuse of orchestrations and arrangements for any purpose is subject to payments for the new use under the applicable agreement of the American Federation of Musicians.[66] These uses include cast albums and stock and amateur rental of the materials.

9.9. TOURING

In the original grant of rights from the authors, one of the most important rights acquired by the producer is the right to produce and present first and second class touring productions of the play or musical featuring a traveling company of actors performing in various cities. Touring productions offer producers and rightsholders an opportunity to reach a wider audience. These productions also afford investors the potential opportunity to offset losses from Broadway.[67]

---

[64] *See* Suskin, Steven. *The Sound of Broadway Music: A Book of Orchestrators and Orchestrations*. New York: Oxford University Press, 2009. 187-191, which includes wonderful descriptions of the creation of the vocal arrangements for "Sing for Your Supper" by Richard Rodgers and Lorenz Hart and "Oklahoma" by Richard Rodgers and Oscar Hammerstein II.

[65] Suskin 187.

[66] *See* Collective Bargaining Agreement between The Broadway League, Inc., Disney Theatrical Productions Inc. and Association Musicians of Greater New York, Local 802, Schedule B, Section C. Note that "rental publication [for stock and amateur use of orchestrations and arrangements]" will be paid at the rate of 80% of the minimum Local 802 scale for material used for rental publication. However, if Employer-Producer elects within 90 days from the official opening to pre-pay for such rental publication, said rate shall be reduced to 25%. Under Schedule B, these payments are the obligation of the Producer or the Composer; however, who pays the rental reuse payment is subject to negotiation by the Producer, the Composer and the stock or amateur licensing agent.

[67] Healy, Patrick. "On the Road, Actors Seek Higher Pay." *The New York Times*. 26 Jan. 2014. Web. 11 Sept. 2016. <http://www.nytimes.com/2014/01/27/theater/on-the-road-actors-seek-higher-pay.html>.

The producer and the presenter, along with the booking agent, are the primary players behind touring productions. The producer is responsible for capitalizing the tour (which is usually done through a separate offering of interests by a new production entity[68]), putting together the company of actors, and setting the guarantee required to be paid by the local presenter to the producer for the engagement. The booking agent is the party that "sells" the show to the presenter and negotiates the terms of the engagement.[69] The presenter covers the presenting costs (e.g., theatre rent and cleaning costs, administrative costs, utilities, etc.) and is responsible for advertising and selling the show. The presenter will determine how best to price each engagement and will enter into agreements with the ticketing platforms such as Ticketmaster.

One important factor presenters consider when evaluating a show is the guarantee. The amount is set by the producer (based on the show's budget), and covers the production costs (which are amortized for the duration of the tour) and the weekly running costs.[70] The guarantee may simply be a fixed amount, but usually also includes a percentage of NAGBOR.[71] The terms of the guarantee will influence how many weeks a presenter will want to book a particular show. The larger the guarantee, the greater the risk to the presenter, since the presenter must pay the guarantee no matter how the show is selling. If presenters ultimately determine that the guarantee is too high and, therefore, that the tour is not economically feasible, the producer may decide to reevaluate the budget, in order to increase the number of weeks that presenters will bring to the table.[72]

---

[68] The new production entity will receive a license to produce the touring production from the original production entity (the so-called "mother company"), in consideration for which the mother company will receive some kind of compensation such as a weekly fee and a share of net profits.

[69] Stein, Tobie S., and Jessica Bathurst. *Performing Arts Management: A Handbook of Professional Practices.* New York: Allworth, 2008. 402.

[70] The production costs, reflected in the production budget, covers everything up to the first performance (including sets, costumes, fees, rehearsal salaries, pre-opening advertising, administrative charges, advances against royalties). The weekly operating budget includes the running costs of the show beginning with the first performance (including salaries, department operating expenses, weekly advertising and promotion, theatre rental, front of house and house crew expenses, fixed fees, administrative and general expenses, and royalties).

[71] i.e., the gross, less taxes, fees, and commissions.

[72] Stein and Bathurst.

The producer also receives a percentage of overage, which is what remains of NAGBOR after the presenter's expenses, the producer's guarantee, and any "middle money," which is a negotiated sum paid after the presenter's expenses and the producer's guarantee. Overage is typically divided 60% to the producer and 40% to the presenter.

An alternative to the guarantee-based arrangement is the "four-wall deal" in which the producer, in essence, rents the theatre (i.e., "four walls") from the presenter. In this arrangement, the presenter receives its fixed costs, ticket commissions, and possibly a small percent of overage. The producer pays all show expenses that would otherwise be covered by a guarantee, plus advertising and stagehand and musician costs. The producer bears the majority of the risk, since there is no guaranteed income; however, for those shows that are likely to be very successful outside of New York City, this model allows the producer to capture a larger portion of the upside.[73]

9.10. LICENSING

After a new show has toured, the rights are made available for professional and amateur licensing by licensing agencies that issue standard agreements and provide production materials.[74] This option is not just available for Broadway hits; shows that have lost money on Broadway often have a lucrative second life in stock and amateur licensing, generating substantial income for authors, producers and investors.[75]

The most important term in the stock and amateur licensing agreement is the advance against royalties negotiated by the agent for the authors, which can be anywhere from $25,000 to multiples of $1,000,000 for a Broadway hit. Royalties are set by the licensing

---

[73] Vogel, Frederic B., and Ben Hodges. *The Commercial Theater Institute Guide to Producing Plays and Musicals*. New York: Applause Theatre & Cinema, 2006. 169.

[74] The most prominent licensing houses are Musical Theatre International, Tams Witmark, Samuel French, R & H Theatricals, Theatrical Rights Worldwide, Dramatists Play Service, and Broadway Play Publishing.

[75] *See* Hofler, Robert. "Life after Death on Broadway." *Variety*. N.p., 20 Nov. 2009. Web. 11 Sept. 2016. <http://variety.com/2009/legit/news/life-after-death-on-broadway-1118011669/>. ("Community theaters and high school productions don't generate the instant big bucks of Broadway and tours, but the royalties paid to creatives, producers and investors are pure profit, and a behemoth show can bring in $1 million to $3 million a year for decades.")

house and are not negotiable. The licensing house receives a standard commission of 10% on professional productions and 20% on amateur productions, which pay lower royalties (often a flat fee), and the first class agents for the authors of the show typically receive one quarter of this commission. The term of the license may be anywhere from ten years to the copyright term. There is also negotiation about the countries included in the territory.

The theatre is a cyclical business. After a show has had a stock and amateur life, successful or otherwise intriguing titles are revived on Broadway or as tours – sometimes within a few years but often decades later. While the revival is playing, stock and amateur performances will be restricted, at least in some cities. After the revival has closed, the cycle begins again as the show goes back into stock and amateur licensing.[76]

9.11. REVIVALS

Not all Broadway production contracts are APCs; contracts for revivals present their own issues. As a general matter, the authors of a classic musical or play (or their estates) have leverage not available to the authors of a new work. For example, the producer of a revival does not automatically receive a subsidiary rights participation. If a subsidiary rights participation is granted, it will be for a smaller percentage and a shorter time than the producer's participation on a new show. Moreover, the participation is often limited to a percentage of the amount by which the show's post-revival earnings exceed the average earnings for the five-year period before the revival.

Advances and royalties for a revival may be higher than under the APC; however, as for most new productions, the royalties will be paid in a pool and not on gross. The authors of a revival (or their estates) will resist amortization and will require a net profit participation in success.

In addition, the terms for the vesting of touring rights will probably be more restrictive for a revival than for a new show, requiring a run of

---

[76] An example is Rodgers & Hammerstein's THE KING AND I, which opened on Broadway in 1951 and ran for three years. The show was revived in 1977, 1985, 1996 and 2015. In between first class revivals, productions were licensed by R & H Theatricals, the stock and amateur licensing arm of the Rodgers & Hammerstein Organization.

three to six months or more on Broadway. Additional territories for a revival are also the subject for negotiation. As an example, although a new revival of *Fiddler on the Roof* opened on Broadway in the 2015-2016 season, a different production of *Fiddler* played at the same time in Australia. Classic shows are in demand throughout the world, and producers accustomed to getting rights in many countries for new shows may find that there are limits on what territories are available for revivals and the window of time in which they must open a revival in these territories.

THEATER LAW – ILLUSTRATIVE AGREEMENTS:

- Dramatists Guild Music Collaboration Agreement
- Theatrical Play Commission Agreement
- Underlying Rights Agreement for Dramatico-Musical Work (Movie Studio Form for adaptation from screenplay)
- Dramatico-Musical Production Contract – Off-Broadway
- Rider for Approved Production Contract for Musical Plays (Specimen)
- Professional Production Agreement between Agent for Dramatist and Producer of (straight) Play
- Director's Agreement (Broadway)
- Choreographer's Agreement (Broadway)
- General Management Agreement for Musical
- Agreement to a Single Engagement by a Presenter
- Underlying Rights Agreement (Broadway Revival)

— CHAPTER 10 —

LITERARY PUBLISHING

Gail Ross[*]

10.1. Introduction: The Nature of the Industry
10.2. Trade Books
10.3. Self-Publishing
10.4. Freelance Periodical Agreements
10.5. Scholarly / Professional Journal Publication
10.6. Agency Agreements

10.1. INTRODUCTION: NATURE OF THE INDUSTRY

Like most sectors of the entertainment industry, literary publishing operates under a set of sometimes arcane conventions, and knowledge of the nature of the industry is consequently key to assessing its deals and contracts. Some of these conventions have been in place for a lifetime or more. For example, one of its key economic drivers — the fact that unsold print copies of books are fully returnable to publishers by retailers — is a vestige of the Great Depression, when it was determined that bookstores should receive added economic incentives to remain open. Others are more recent — the digital revolution has brought stunning changes, including a dynamic electronic books business and data on readers' interests, whereabouts, and price sensitivities.

10.1.1. Categories of Publications

This chapter will examine the most common types of publications: (1) trade books (fiction and non-fiction books for the general public), (2) reference and educational publications, (3) newspapers and popular periodicals, (4) general circulation journals, and (5) professional publications. In most cases, these publications appear in print and electronic form. However, there are a growing number of electronic-

---

[*] **Gail Ross** is President of the Ross Yoon Agency, and partner at Trister, Ross, Schadler & Gold, PLLC.

only publications, and even when print and e-book editions are published simultaneously, the electronic versions may differ from their print counterparts. Blogs updated throughout the day, banner ads related to ever changing content, and breaking news reported as it occurs are now standard features for new media publications in several of these categories.

10.1.1.1 Trade Books

There's an old joke in the industry that the phrase "publishing business" is an oxymoron. But the trade book business is alive and well despite constant talk of its demise. In both 2015 and 2016, print unit sales posted annual gains. Retail accounts include independent and chain bookstores, Amazon, and large mass merchandizers like Walmart and Target.[1] The increases were in fiction and non-fiction, with the highest gains in the latter. The increase in print fiction sales marks the first time since 2010, when the e-book market became a major factor in book industry revenues, that fiction print units increased. According to the American Association of Publishers, in 2015 there was a 10% drop in overall digital sales, including self-published titles, but digital audio grew significantly.[2] In contrast, in 2016, total print sales hit 674 million units, marking the third-straight year of growth, according to Nielsen BookScan, which tracks about 80% of print sales in the US.[3] The digital revolution has allowed authors rejected by traditional publishers or enamored of the speed and control afforded by self-publication to sell their books[4] through an array of self-publishing platforms including Amazon and Smashwords. *Publishers Weekly* launched its own section devoted to trends in the growing world of self-publishing. According to Bowker, the company and research group that assigns ISBNs to books (including self-published works), the number of self-published titles grew 17% in 2013. The indicators suggest that it is a maturing industry evolving from "a frantic, Wild West–style space to a more serious business."[5] While every year sees major self-published success stories,

---

[1] *Publishers Weekly* 1-1-16, 1-6-17.
[2] Association of American Publishers StetShot (March 22, 2016).
[3] Jonathan Segura "Print Book Sales Rose Again in 2016" *Publishers Weekly* (January 06, 2017).
[4] Mathew Ingram, "Here's Why the Antitrust Claim against Amazon by Authors Groups Is Doomed" *Fortune* (August 21, 2015).
[5] "Self-Publishing Publications Counts Report," Bowker (2014).

particularly in genre fiction, self-published titles rarely appear in bookstores, nor are they reviewed or publicized by major media outlets.

The growth and market share of Amazon continues to affect trade books. According to a May 2014 study by the Codex group, Amazon had a 64% market share of e-book sales and a 41% market share of all new book sales — print and e-book. In July of 2015, Authors United, a group of authors, with the support of the American Booksellers Association, which represents independently-owned bookstores, asked the US Department of Justice to examine Amazon's business practices. The coalition of authors and indie stores voiced concerns about predatory selling, abuse of monopoly power over publishers, and a closed e-book system centered on Amazon's proprietary Kindle, among other concerns.

The Authors United complaint is only the latest skirmish involving the publishing world and the Justice Department. In 2012 the Justice Department brought a lawsuit against Apple and the five largest publishers, who Amazon claims colluded in raising the price of e-books.[6] The lawsuit resulted in a settlement where the Federal District Court for the Southern District of New York found that there was a conspiracy among five top US publishers (Hachette, HarperCollins, Macmillan, Penguin and Simon & Schuster) and Apple to fix and raise the retail prices of e-books.

10.1.1.2. Reference and Educational Publications

Reference publications include dictionaries, thesauruses, and encyclopedias. Educational publications are school textbooks from K–12 to college. These works are labor-intensive and tend to be controlled by textbook publishers who make them available directly to educational institutions for distribution or sale to students. Because textbooks are subject to state and local curriculum standards, textbook publishers provide more resources to their creation and management than to those of trade books. Textbooks have long shelf lives, and publishers need to keep them revised and updated to correspond with education market demands. Even if they are written by non-staff authors, the contracts typically grant all rights to the publisher because of this need.

---

[6] *See* David Streitfeld "Accusing Amazon of Antitrust Violation, Authors and Booksellers Demand Inquiry," *NY Times* (July 14, 2015).

10.1.1.3. Newspapers and General Circulation Periodicals

Daily newspapers (e.g., the *New York Times*, *Wall Street Journal* and *USA Today*) and the vast array of magazines (e.g., *The New Yorker*, *People*, and the *Atlantic*) make up this category. While traditionally called periodicals because they published periodically in print either daily, weekly or monthly, these outlets' online versions are often updated constantly. Many staffs are bifurcated between the print and online editions, with separate design, sales, and advertising departments. Major staff writers' work will generally appear in both versions, but digital platforms often hire dedicated online writers as well.

Advertising dollars continue to be the primary source of income for these publications. Newsstand and subscription sales are secondary, the latter often offered at a discount in an effort to increase readership and thus drive up ad prices. Advertisers buy ad space according to rate cards that establish prices based on the demographics of the readership. Those demographics include the size of the readership and its characteristics, such as gender, age, education level, and home ownership. Online advertising rates began at much lower rates, but with growing readership and "eyeballs," as a publication's reach has come be known, those rates are increasing.

The consumer magazine industry generated $24.6 billion from advertising and subscriptions in 2015. According to a recent study that dollar number will likely remain flat over the next four years.[7] The newspaper world faces different challenges. Traditionally advertising from classified ads for homes, automobiles and jobs supported local newspapers. Today the advent of Craigslist and other employment, automotive and homebuyer websites across the country has forever changed newspaper classified ad revenue. Moreover, as non-subscription news websites proliferate, the newspapers that are surviving (and in some instances still continue to grow like national publications such as *The New York Times* and *The Washington Post*) are working arduously to produce distinct print and digital editorial products that they hope readers (and advertisers) will continue to pay for in some form.

---

[7] Michael Sebastian, Magazine Revenue to Climb Slightly as Newspaper Decline Continues Advertising Age (June 2, 2015).

10.1.1.4. General Circulation Journals

These journals are often referred to as "special interest publications," and count among them titles such as *Foreign Affairs* and *The Partisan Review*. They regularly feature long, in-depth pieces on the journal's particular subject matter commissioned from experts or well-known writers in their given area. While advertising is important to their revenues, these journals rely heavily on higher subscription rates from loyal readers who find them required reading in their area of expertise. Like all media concerns, their online editions will add extra content and may only be available to subscribers.

10.1.1.5. Professional Publications

This category includes commercial publications that are focused on an industry but are run like the general circulation publications discussed above. They may be entertaining for readers outside of the industry, but their marketing and sales efforts are focused on members of the industry. For people in the entertainment industry, publications like *Publisher's Weekly*, *Publisher's Marketplace*, *Variety*, and *Billboard* are widely popular.

Professional journals published by non-profit organizations, including universities and professional associations, have limited professional staffs and commission articles from freelance writers or academics. Academic journals rarely pay fees to contributors, who are often professors or students seeking professional prestige and exposure for their ideas rather than remuneration.

10.2. TRADE BOOKS

10.2.1. Getting a Deal

Prior to receiving a book contract, most authors receive a written offer from one or more publishers wishing to publish the book. The offer, based on a book proposal or a partial or complete manuscript generally solicited by the publisher from or submitted to the publisher by the author's agent, includes basic deal terms: the grant of rights the publishers seeks, the advance and royalties, the due date, and any special provisions unique to that deal. In the trade publishing world, agents often send an author's proposal to several publishers at the same time. This process is known as a *multiple submission*. It is considered professional courtesy to inform the various publishers that others are considering the submission; naming the publishers is not done unless a particular media conglomerate requires that each of its publishing imprints be informed when one of its sister imprints is interested too.

If there is interest from multiple publishers, the agent will determine how best to seek offers from appropriate editors at various publishing houses. A very interested editor who has worked quickly to garner great enthusiasm from editorial, publicity, sales and marketing departments may attempt make what is known as a *preemptive bid*. The idea behind the preempt is to entice the author with early and considerable interest while avoiding a bidding war. A preempt offer is rarely left on the table more than 24 hours. If a preempt is accepted, the other publishers are informed and the deal is done. If the preempt is put forth by a publisher which is clear author favorite and the agent determines it is a fair offer, it can be a win-win for author and publisher.

Alternatively, if the agent and author want to see how the marketplace values the book, the agent will send out a closing memo to all interested parties with specific rules for *auctioning* the book. The rules state the time and date the auction will begin, the grant of rights being offered, and often a request for any unique marketing ideas supplementing any subsequent offer. Most auctions fall into one of two categories: (1) rolling or rounds or (2) best bids. Auctions can last for hours or days and are handled by phone and email. In a rounds auction, each publisher makes an initial advance bid, and once all bids are received, the agent orders them lowest to highest. The lowest bidder in the first round can stay in the auction by entering a second-round bid higher than the top bid from round one. If a publisher fails to do so, it drops from the auction and the rounds continue, with the lowest bidder starting each new round improving on the highest bid from the last one. In a best bids auction, each publisher bids once. In either case, the auction memo should state that the author is not required to go with the highest bidder, since other considerations such as the experience of the editor, a more favorable advance payout schedule, or an especially promising marketing plan may outweigh an advance differential.

Some deals are done less formally, with agents talking deal points over a couple of days with a small number of publishers. Others have employed unique variations on the best bids and rounds auctions as agents feel are necessary for a given project. When there is only one interested party, the agent's job still is to make the best deal possible for her client, even without pressure of competition. It is also worth noting the auction strategy is best deployed for authors whose projects have some inherent *heat*, as it may be tough to recover from a failed auction in which there are no bidders, or in which bids fall below levels acceptable to the author and agent.

10.2.2. Analyzing the Terms of an Author Agreement

All publishing companies have author agreements with standard boilerplate contracts, typically close to twenty pages (but often considerably longer), with dozens of provisions detailing every aspect of the book's life. From creation to copyright, editing to the cover, pricing, publicity, and promotion, this often intimidating document lays out the delicate balance between the needs of the publisher and the author. In theory, both parties seek the same thing: a brilliant book that is a critical and commercial success. In reality, authors and publishers may see success differently. Moreover, not every book published is as good as anticipated, nor is every great book a commercial success.

Most publishing houses have several versions of their so-called "standard" author agreements. An author offered an author agreement *without* the aid of an established literary agent will need a careful analysis of the boilerplate by a knowledgeable publishing lawyer to adapt the boilerplate as much as possible to his or her needs. In such cases, the publishing lawyer is best served by finding other "pre-negotiated" forms and keeping a library for reference purposes.

Publishers who regularly deal with particular literary agencies will adapt their "standard" boilerplate provisions in their proposed author agreements and provide those agencies' authors with an author agreement containing so-called "pre-negotiated" boilerplate provisions. In this sense, "pre-negotiated" means that the specific legal form of the publisher's author agreement sent via the particular literary agencies already contains revisions (such as language stricken as well as added language and provisions) already indicated in the "pre-negotiated" form before a publishing agreement negotiation commences. This allows the publishing agreement negotiation to be focused on the key terms and particulars of the current deal instead of asking for revisions that a publisher is already inclined to give to an author. After articulating the identities of the parties, the boilerplate refers to them throughout the contract by their role (e.g., Author, Publisher, the Work), and the discussion of contracts below will follow that convention. Literary agencies review the revised boilerplate in their "pre-negotiated" author agreements regularly to make changes required by an ever-evolving publishing business, such as, for example, updating the provisions for e-books and digital audio rights.

This section will explain the provisions of a typical author agreement or trade book contract, making note of the variations among scholarly or specialized presses as appropriate. The listing of provisions below are not necessarily in the same order as a publishing lawyer will find in an author agreement depending on the publisher's specific form of an author agreement. In such instances, the publishing lawyer will want to make certain that the concepts below are properly addressed in the author agreement.

10.2.2.1 Opening Provisions

The opening provisions of an author agreement naming the parties and provisionally identifying the title of the literary work may seem deceptively simple. Deciding whether the contracting party is the author or the author's loan-out company (e.g., a personal services company) is critical. Because the agreement requires licensing of rights, the contracting party must indeed control those rights. Moreover, it is not uncommon for authors to create their literary work through a business entity for tax planning purposes, liability and other business purposes. If an author writes and creates literary works through a business entity like a limited liability company or a corporation that business entity will need to be the contracting party with the publisher. In this instance, the publishing lawyer will need to confirm and/or document the business entity's good standing and ownership in the literary work, in addition to, among other tasks, verifying warranties and representations in the author agreement. When a business entity is the contracting party in an author agreement, publishers typically require a so-called "inducement letter" (e.g. an inducement for the publisher to enter into the agreement with the business entity in lieu of the author) whereby the individual author or authors make certain personal guarantees on behalf of the business entity that the author(s) will personally abide by the author agreement. Further, if the opening provisions indicate that the literary work, at the time of signing the author agreement, has a "working title" or a "provisional title", then it will be important to add a provision that the determination of the book's final title shall be mutually agreed by the parties.

10.2.2.2. The Work and/or the Description of the Work

In these provisions, an author agrees to deliver to the publisher the book that is the subject of the author agreement, which is then often referred to throughout the remainder of the author agreement as the "Work". Prior to agreeing to publication, the editor and author will have agreed upon both the projected word count (usually a target range with a minimum word count and a maximum word count) for the Work and the photographs or illustrations required for the Work to be accepted. These items will be delineated here. In circumstances where photographs, illustrations and/or other materials have yet to be agreed upon the author will want mutual agreement on those items (especially for items added by the publisher which the author's consent will not be unreasonably withheld). Since publishing boilerplate requires an author to deliver illustrations and photographs with permissions at the author's expense, this clause must be carefully analyzed. When working with an author on a heavily illustrated book, it is wise to determine these costs and responsibilities and discuss an allocation of those costs and responsibilities with the publisher well before the contract arrives. One significant responsibility related to photographs, illustrations and other materials added to the Work, will be the publisher's requirement that the author be responsible, at the author's own expense, for obtaining the necessary written permissions and/or release to use such items in the book. After assessing the scope of the specific responsibilities and after any agreed upon re-allocation of some of them, if possible, to the publisher, the author will want the publisher to provide an approved form of permission or release for the author to use or at the very least, for the publisher to pre-approve (and provide comment where applicable) the form the author desires to use in obtaining such permissions and/or releases. In general trade-book publishing, most novelists are offered contracts after a full draft of the novel is reviewed by a publisher, and thus a description of the work is a simple matter. For a non-fiction literary work, an author has typically only prepared a detailed book proposal with a sample chapter or two. In the year or more many authors toil from contract to finished manuscript, outlines change. It is critical that the description of the book be both accurate and general enough to allow for such flexibility. Ideally the author and editor will be working closely enough that there will be no surprises, but editors leave, and publishers' interests change. Publishers shouldn't have to accept books that are completely different than what was proposed. Nor should authors be forced to plead for the acceptability of the work (see section 10.2.3 below) if the final manuscript is reasonably different from the book proposal.

10.2.2.3. The Grant of Rights

The grant of rights from the author to the publisher is a major provision in an author agreement. Since these provisions tend be very broad in the scope of rights that are being granted, it is very important for the author's representatives to closely review the specific grants to make sure they conform to market practices, the publisher's capacity to exploit such rights and the author's defined objectives. Every type of publishing contract grants to the publisher *exclusive* publication rights (e.g. to print, publish and sell) during some or all of the full term of copyright applicable to the work in each country and or territory covered by the agreement. Authors work closely with their representatives to decide which of three territorial grants to make to the US publisher:

(1) Exclusively throughout the world in all languages;

(2) Exclusively throughout the world in the English language only; or

(3) Exclusively throughout the United States, including all US territories, dependencies, military bases, wherever located; the Philippines; and Canada in the English language.[8]

---

[8] Due to the growth of the market for titles in the US in the Spanish language, several major publishers are requesting the right to publish in Spanish. Any publisher for the title in Spain or Latin America will thus have to be made aware of any resulting

Regardless of the choice, the grant of rights provision will typically include a non-exclusive grant for English language rights in the parts of the world known as the Open Market. The Open Market comprises countries where U.S. and British Commonwealth publishers have agreed that both the American and British English-language versions of a title can be sold. Each publisher will list the countries in the Open Market in an appendix to the publishing agreement. This appendix must be carefully reviewed, as some boilerplate definitions of the Open Market in US publishing agreements may include territories with some connection to the current or former English Commonwealth, like India and Singapore, which publishers in the United Kingdom require as part of any exclusive grant.

In addition to the various types of print rights that will be granted to a publisher (more of them will be explained further below in the Subsidiary Rights section 10.2.2.6. c. below), all types of publishing agreements will address the following additional rights:

- **Audio Rights.** The sound recording of the author's book being read or so-called "audio books" is an important right with commercial possibilities for both author and publisher. And not all books are made into audio books. An author may want to reserve audio book rights altogether if the publisher does not intend to produce or license rights the production of audio books — or at the very least ask the publisher for audio book rights to revert back to the author if an audio book is not created and made available for sale after a certain time period (1 year to 3 years are suggested starting points) from the initial public sale of the print edition.

- **Merchandising Rights.** The book may have commercial possibilities for products like mugs, games, t-shirts, dolls and other merchandise based on the book's characters, storylines and other components of the book. It is very rare to grant these merchandising or so-called "commercial" rights to a publisher, but when they are granted attention must be paid to how they will dovetail with the rights that may subsequently be required for a movie or television deal, if the book successfully migrates to such media.

---

grant of rights or consequent restrictions on import/export of Spanish language editions to or from the US.

- **Performance Rights.** So-called "performance rights" typically cover television, motion picture, radio, live stage, dramatic renditions and even theme park rights. Like merchandising rights it is very rare for an author to give a publisher such rights (or even a percentage of such rights as noted in the Subsidiary Rights section below). There are many reasons for an author not to give away such rights to a publisher, besides it being customary not to do so. First, the publisher is typically not in the business of producing films, TV programs, live stage performances, etc., and would merely be collecting an unearned windfall upon the placement of such rights, as the likelihood of exploiting any performance rights is small and the process of soliciting a film or television deal for a book or unpublished manuscript is a whole other process largely unrelated to the publishing of the book (although a publisher will argue that "but for the book..."). Second, most literary agents have existing relationships with other agents who handle the sale of specific performance rights and while the author will bear that additional costs in agent fees and in negotiating further development deals for the book (if such is even possible for the book in question) these rights are an important additional source of potential revenue for the author. Thus, it's possible that an author may not have any income beyond the initial advance of the book because the publisher's recoupment has not occurred; but the author may have the opportunity for additional income due to the sale or licensing of one or more performance rights, and these calculations may influence the terms of the publication deal itself.

- **Electronic or "E-Book" Rights and "Enhanced E-Books" or "Multimedia Books" Rights.** Given the increase in books being made available in digital or electronic form, addressing these rights is essential for both publisher and author. Such provisions will permit the publisher to publish (and transmit) the book in various electronic and/or digital formats (many of which continue to emerge as new platforms and formats are created in the entertainment industry). Generally, electronic or "e-books" pertain to so-called "display rights" in such mediums, whereby the words of the book are transcribed or otherwise reproduced in a digital display format. On the other hand, so-called "enhanced e-books" or "multimedia books" give the book additional audio, video and interactive content that go beyond the printed words of the book and give the reader an enhanced experience of the book. It is important that the enhanced e-book or multimedia rights granted to the publisher not diminish the author's reserved performance rights discussed above, and that the two format rights can overlap.

- **Reservation of Rights.** All publishing agreements should have a broad reservation of rights by the author for any and all rights not expressly granted to the publisher in the agreement. Even in light of such a provision in favor of the author, publishers will include language that will include some form of "all other rights" or all "rights in future mediums or media, whether now known or hereinafter devised" to be granted to the publisher. These types of provisions contradict the purpose of an author's reservation of rights – specifically to allow the author to benefit from new income streams for new formats of rights yet unknown. Thus, such provisions should be stricken from the publishing agreement and if the publisher insists on such language there must be a "catch-all" compensation provision that will require the publisher to negotiate with the author for the compensation of such new right before a publisher is permitted to exploit such rights. Otherwise, as such rights come into existence an author could lose revenue for such future format rights that are exploited by a publisher because the compensation to the author is not specified in the publishing agreement.

10.2.2.4. Delivery

Prior to contract, the author and the editor agree upon an anticipated delivery date for the manuscript itself and any required deliverables defined as the Work. Some agreements will include earlier dates for "progress materials."

An author's failure to meet delivery dates can result in the publisher choosing to cancel the contract and require immediate repayment of any advance monies already paid (as the publisher may have a certain plan window in mind for publication of the topical book, have capacity for only a limited number of books in a particular publishing cycle, and/or may simply lose confidence that the author will complete the work at all). Publishers also insist that in the case of a work terminated for non-delivery, "the Author shall not, for a period of one year, self-publish the Work or submit the Work or anything substantially similar to it, in whole or in part to another publisher without resubmitting it to the initial Publisher." This precludes authors who have second thoughts about the publishing deal they entered into from simply choosing to not deliver their contracted manuscript in favor of a new offer from another publisher, perhaps for more money. Whenever possible, a grace period should be added to this clause so that a publisher may not terminate for non-delivery until 30 or 60 days after the due date, once agreed.

10.2.2.5. Acceptance of Manuscript

As part of its Fair Contract Initiative to educate authors on fair publishing contracts, the Author's Guild lays out eight principles for fair contracts, including the precept that "Delivery and acceptance provisions shouldn't give publishers a way out of publishing the book."[9]

Of course, in rare cases, an author might fail to deliver an acceptable manuscript, delivering instead an incomplete or substandard manuscript or – especially in the nonfiction world, where works are sold on proposal rather than from a complete manuscript – a work substantially different than the one originally agreed upon. This clause balances the right of the publisher to reject work that does not meet expectations with the right of the author to be compensated for work product meeting the contractual criteria.

All publishing contracts include a provision stipulating publishers may determine whether the finished manuscript is satisfactory to the publisher, in the publisher's sole discretion, before paying the acceptance portion of the advance, and most publishers' boilerplate gives all the discretion to the publisher. In such circumstances, the publisher's discretion can be based on commercial changes in the market in addition to editorial discretion. In situations where the finished manuscript is not accepted due to the publisher's perceived changes in the marketplace, a provision in the publishing agreement should permit the author to keep any monies advanced already under

---

[9] https://www.authorsguild.org/wp-content/uploads/2015/05/Fair-Contract-Initiative_mission_Final_6.pdf

the publishing agreement, as well as permit the author to shop the finished manuscript to other publishers. In circumstances where the finished manuscript is rejected for editorial reasons, the author is usually required to return the advance back to the publisher, but many publishing agreements now permit the author to shop the finished manuscript to another publishing house and then give the author a grace period of up to a year to return such advance payments. However, most major publishers will permit several limits on this discretion. First, the publisher must tell the author in writing why it found the manuscript unacceptable and provide a reasonable time for the author to make edits if editorial concerns exist. Second, an unacceptability determination has to be about the work itself and whether it meets the criteria originally agreed upon. If possible, the author should insist on contractual language that ensures that a rejection of a finished manuscript cannot be used as a way for a publisher to change its mind about the deal or determine that market conditions have changed to avoid its commitment. This will be obvious if the author is sending portions of the work to an editor before completion of the finished manuscript and receiving editorial direction and approval during that process. To go a step further, an author should insist on a provision that obligates the publisher to provide reasonable editorial assistance to the author before the manuscript is finished. However, because courts have held that publishers have a good faith duty to provide authors with editorial assistance in order to make the finished manuscript "acceptable",[10] some publishers will include in their boilerplate provisions language that relieves the publisher of any duty to assist the author editorially or to make any good-faith effort to help the author complete the manuscript in a manner that would lead to its acceptance. Thus, these concepts must be closely analyzed and negotiated by the author's representatives.

---

[10] See *Harcourt Brace Jovanovich, Inc. v. Goldwater*, 532 F.Supp. 619 (S.D.N.Y. 1982) ("there is an implied obligation in a contract of this kind for the publisher to engage in appropriate editorial work with the author") and *Dell Publishing Co. v. Wheldon*, 577 F.Supp. 1459 (S.D.N.Y. 1984) (including a duty of the publisher to give an author an opportunity to make a revision).

10.2.2.6. Compensation

A typical publishing contract will describe the author's compensation in three separate clauses dealing with (1) an advance, (2) royalties, and (3) income from subsidiary rights agreements.

a. Advances against Royalties

Advances are just that: money the publisher pays in advance of royalties or subsidiary rights income that will otherwise become due the author from the actual exploitation of the work. It represents the publisher's best guess of what an author might earn in the first year or two following the work's publication. Advances are the publisher's guaranteed investment in the work, excluding physical printing costs and advertising and marketing expenditures (which generally won't be established until after delivery and evaluation of the completed manuscript). Should the author not "earn out" his or her advance from book sales or other income, as is the case with many trade books, the publisher hopes that its profit margins on that title or other more successful titles will cover its overvaluation on that book. This is why you will often hear that advances are recoupable, but not refundable. Understandably, specialized and university presses cannot afford to speculate significant sums of money in this manner, so advances are small (and take advantage of the fact many of their authors are salaried faculty at institutions for whom writing and publishing is part of the regular research/teaching salary equation). Because most professional writers live off their advances for the years between signing an agreement and publishing a book, the size and payout schedule of the advance are considered two of the most important deal points in any negotiation.

From an author's perspective, the ideal advance is paid out in only two payments: the first on signing and the remainder on the publisher's acceptance of the manuscript. For very small advances, the two-step payment may be acceptable. Typically, though, in trade book contracts with five-, six-, and even seven-figure advances, the payouts are in 3 installments: one each at signing, acceptance, and first publication. Many publishers now add a fourth payment that falls one year after initial publication of the hardcover edition or upon paperback publication. Paperback publication, which typically follows hardcover publication by 12 months, was the milestone for this last payment in prior years, but in today's marketplace, with the discounting of hardcovers and the availability of e-book editions, many books are no longer published in paperback at all. While the boilerplate for these payouts suggest equal payments, it is possible in a negotiation to receive payouts that allow for larger payments, for example, at the outset, when the need is the greatest. In some cases an author may choose a lower advance if the payout schedule is significantly more attractive.[11]

Determining whether an advance is good for a given title requires a fair amount of knowledge of the publishing business. One publisher once shared privately, "it's not the publisher's responsibility to replace a writer's salary while he writes his book, but rather to determine an economically sensible investment based on a variety of factors." Publishers prepare profit and loss projections (a "P&L") for each title. Prior to filling out the house's standard form, acquiring editors collect information from throughout the company. First they determine the ideal physical size for the book and include the costs for paper, printing and binding. They factor in a budget for publicity and marketing as well as overhead. The returns discussed later in this chapter are considered too. The sales department estimates sales projections based on the author's previous sales or those of similar works. The P&L is then shared with the publisher, which authorizes a maximum advance offer based on the projections. While this exercise suggests a certain rigor to the process, some estimate that 60 to 70% of books do not earn back their advances, typically due to unmet sales expectations.

In analyzing provisions regarding advances, it's important for the author to be aware of all circumstances where the author may be required to return the advance. As a general rule, advances are non-refundable. However, as noted earlier in this chapter, nearly all publishing agreements provide for advances to be returned to the publishers where (1) the manuscript is not delivered on time, (2) the manuscript is rejected and/or (3) if author permits the publisher to reject the manuscript because of changes in the marketplace where the publisher no longer believes the publication of the book has commercial viability. Likewise, some publishers will permit the author to keep advances paid to date if the publisher no longer believes the book project to be commercially viable. An author not only to wants to

---

[11] Michael Meyer, "About that Book Advance," *New York Times* (April 10, 2009).

pay close attention to the circumstances of how an advance may be returned to the publisher but also, as discussed in Section 10.2.2.3 above ("Acceptance of Manuscript"), how and when the advance will be paid back to the publisher. While no author ever wants to be in such circumstances, it is important to negotiate and address these contract provisions with the publisher.

b. Royalties

The fundamental basis of compensation to authors in publishing agreements is the payment of a percentage of defined revenue streams from the commercial exploitation of the book which are known as "royalties". The defined structure and the computation of royalties in publishing agreements for major publishing houses are largely standard, but depending on factors like the author's prior track record and popularity, the nature of the book and other circumstances meriting the publisher's strong interest in the book, there are key points to royalties contract provisions that are negotiated by the author and his or her representatives.

Publishers pay to authors, or credit to authors' accounts (when the advance is not yet "earned out") royalties based on (1) the "Suggested Retail Price", often indicated on the cover or dust-jacket of the book or by the publisher in its catalogue, or (2) the "Amount Received" or the "Actual Receipts", constituting monies actually received by the publisher after discounts, return allowances and applicable taxes, only. The royalty is for each book unit sold and not returned and the royalty percentage varies according to the edition (i.e., for hardcover, trade paperback, mass market paperback, and large print editions). Although the rates below may vary for well-established authors, for most major publishers the standard royalties based on percentages of suggested retail price are as follows:

- Hardcover: 10% on the first 5,000; 12.5% on the next 5,000; and 15% on all copies thereafter.

- Trade Paperback: 7.5% or sometime in two tiers of 6% up to 10,000 units (or a higher number) and then 7.5% for all units thereafter.

- Mass Market Paperback: 8% on the first 150,000 units; 10% on all copies thereafter.

- Large Print: 10% for any hardcover and 7.5% for any paperback edition.
- Canadian Sales Made by the US Publisher: Two thirds (2/3) of the prevailing US rate for each respective edition based on cover price.

Royalties based on the "Amount Received" by the publisher apply to the following categories: export, promotional and special sales, premiums, book clubs, and direct mail. Two significant sources of income for authors also fall into this category: audio works and digital book-based editions, commonly referred to as e-books. The typical royalty rates for these categories of publication are as follows:

- Audio Work if sold throughout regular wholesale, retail or library channels: 10% of the Amount Received.
- Audio Work delivered by means of digital download or "streaming": 25% of the Amount Received.
- E-Book or Electronic or Digital Editions. 25% of the US suggested retail price. Given the popularity of, revenues from, and still evolving distribution patterns for books in electronic formats, it is customary for publishing agreements to also include a provision that if the publisher gives a higher rate for e-books or Electronic Editions to other authors during the term, then the author's royalty rate will likewise be increased to that new rate.

University presses and small independent publishers often account to the author on the basis of the total amounts received by the publisher for individual book sales without deduction, or what's often called a net royalty. Often a straight 10% net royalty for all editions is offered. Bookstores pay publishers a wholesale price for each book that ranges from 40% to 55% off the suggested retail price. For a $20 book, if the publisher receives $11, the author's resulting net royalty is $1.10. This is of course substantially lower than the Suggested List Price royalty of $2.00 at the same 10% royalty rate, but the formula is justified by independent and academic publishers on the basis of generally lower sales volume projections and higher relative unit costs of operations than those which can be realized by larger commercial publishers moving more and potentially better-selling titles.

c. Subsidiary Rights

Depending on the grant of rights licensed to the publisher, it may be entitled to sublicense the work to third parties for exploitation in media other than books. Given the globalization and consolidation of entertainment companies (including their publishing divisions), the publisher may seek (or be obliged) to license these rights to an affiliated entity. It is therefore important to make sure that the licensing of subsidiary rights is conducted on a bona fide third party, arms-length basis when the buyer or licensee is another division of the same entertainment conglomerate posing a potential risk (if not likelihood) that the fees agreed upon may be other than arms-length, and thus potentially detrimental to the author's interest. This requirement may, however, be a difficult point to achieve depending on the leverage an author has in the negotiation. In any case, in subsidiary licensing arrangements third parties assume the functions of a publisher in creating, producing, marketing, and disseminating their own branded editions of all or part of the work. It is common to ask for the publisher to obtain an author's prior consent for such licensing with the proviso that the author will not unreasonably withhold consent (but again, the publisher may seek "preapproval" as to affiliate licensees as a matter of policy). While it will be rare that an author will withhold such consent this approval process allows an author to keep informed of the various types of commercial exploitation occurring with the work. The publisher pays or credits to the author's account at the time of the next regular accounting a receipt as follows:

Publisher / Author

First Serial (use of serializations or excerpts, in newspapers, magazines or other periodicals before publication of the Work)	10%	90%
Second Serial (use of serializations or excerpts, in newspapers, magazines or other periodicals after publication of the Work, and condensations, digests and anthologies)	50%	50%
Book Club	50%	50%
Permissions	50%	50%
Trade or Mass-Market Paperback	50%	50%
Other Book Publication (including, but not limited to, hardcover, large-type editions, mail order, premium and other special editions and schoolbook and book fair editions licenses)	50%	50%
British Commonwealth (which may include any of the rights granted elsewhere in this Agreement, including First Serial and Audio Recording rights, even when such rights are not granted to the Publisher in the Exclusive Territories)	20%	80%
Translation (which may include any of the rights granted elsewhere in this Agreement, including First Serial and Audio Recording rights, even when such rights are not granted to the Publisher in the English language)	25%	75%
Digital or E-Book Edition or Enhanced E-Book Edition (e.g. where the Publisher is licensing these rights to a third party, which is not common in today's market)	50%	50%
Audio Recording (when this right is being licensed to a third party)	50%	50%
Paper Products (such as journals, note cards and calendars)	50%	50%
Commercial and Merchandising (derivative products such as the use of a title or character for clothing, toys, board games or video games). NOTE: THESE RIGHTS ARE NOT COMMONLY GRANTED TO PUBLISHERS AND THE AUTHOR SHOULD BE VERY CAUTIOUS IN GRANTING COMMERCIAL AND MERCHANDISING RIGHTS.	50%	50%
Performance (motion picture, television, home video, video on demand and all other forms of audio-visual, radio, live stage, soundtrack and music publishing, and all allied merchandising rights derived therefrom. NOTE THESE RIGHTS ARE RARELY GRANTED TO PUBLISHERS AND THE PERCENTAGES LISTED ARE ONLY IN CIRCUMSTANCES WHERE THE AUTHOR HAS DECIDED TO PERMIT THE PUBLISHER TO HAVE A SMALL PORTION OF SUCH REVENUE.	10%	90%

As previously discussed, if the author has only granted US and Canada or World English rights, the subsidiary chart above will read differently. If the author works as a journalist (as an employee or freelancer), holding on to the first serial rights may make sense. Since the days of a hefty check for a magazine publication of book excerpt or serialization, which might often be heralded on the cover of *TIME* or *Newsweek*, are long over, agents often let the subsidiary rights department of the publishing house solicit these excerpt deals. Excerpts in magazines today are primarily valuable for publicizing the book, but rarely make a significant dent in the author's unearned advance. Moreover, as previously noted, authors' agents will seek (and generally succeed) to hold onto the potentially lucrative commercial/merchandising and performance rights. Performance rights include motion picture, documentary, television, DVD, video on demand, and all other forms of audiovisual, radio, live stage, soundtrack, and music publishing, all allied merchandising rights. University and independent presses tend to offer authors a 50-50 share in most of these categories. Ideally, the author will be able to approve all subsidiary rights licenses. Publishers may in turn insist that such approvals "will not be unreasonably withheld or delayed." Where the author's agent may be more adept at exploiting these rights than the staff or representatives of such publishers, or simply based on the fact the author will likely be more motivated and diligent in pursuing these deals, the author should seek to retain control of these rights even if some split cannot be avoided.

With respect to Performance rights, a contract should state that the publisher "shall grant the Purchaser of those rights the privilege to publish excerpts of the Work not exceed 7,500 words or (10% of the total Work, whichever is less, for advertising and promoting those rights." The publisher will generally require the author use his or her best efforts to secure in the agreement for the sale of performance rights permission for the publisher to use photographic stills from and the title of the authorized production in any tie-in edition of the work the publisher may seek to release to capitalize on the marketing and promotion of the licensed film, television or stage production (e.g., for the once ubiquitous "Now a major motion picture" book cover and advertising banner designed to stir additional book sales).

10.2.2.7. Warranties and Representations and Indemnification

Every publishing contract contains detailed clauses specifying the warranties the author must make about the material, followed by the author's indemnification of the publisher should a third party bring an action against the publisher arising from the author's alleged breach of one or more of the warranties. The warranties generally state that (1) the Author is the sole author of the work; (2) the Author has the full power to enter into the agreement; (3) the Author is sole owner of the rights granted to the Publisher in the Agreement; (4) if the Work is nonfiction, all statements asserted as facts are based on the Author's careful investigation and research; (4) no material in the Work violates any contract of the Author; (5) the rights granted are not otherwise encumbered; (6) no material in the Work is confidential or subject to a non-disclosure agreement; (7) the Work is original except materials for which the Author has permissions to include or which is in the public domain; (8) the material has been lawfully obtained; (9) the Work contains no libelous matter nor infringes the right of privacy, trademark, right of publicity, statutory or common law copyright, or any other personal or property rights of any third party; and (10) any recipe, formula or instruction contained in the work is accurate and is not injurious to the user.

Most authors will much prefer that these warranties be prefaced with the phrase "to the best of my knowledge", but few publishers will permit the change. In fact, the major publishers who cover each author under the standard errors and omission or media perils insurance policies severely limit the changes authors and agents can make to this clause. Standard indemnity provisions in these agreements state that if the author and publisher should be sued by a third party making claims against the work (e.g., for copyright infringement, libel or invasion of privacy, topics explored more fully in the Intellectual Property volume in this series), the author will indemnify or reimburse the publisher for any costs, including attorney fees, caused by this litigation. Authors should understand the nature and scope of a publisher's insurance coverage as it applies both to the defense of such claims and payment of any award of damages or other recovery to which third party claimants may become entitled. With smaller publishers who don't offer to include authors as additional insureds or don't have policies at all, ideally ameliorative language that limits the author's responsibility to situations where he or she is ultimately found at fault in a proceeding reduced to judgment – and not merely alleged to be at fault – is preferred. The requested change should limit the author's responsibility to claims that are sustained in the court of last resort only. These requirements appear in almost all commercial legal contracts, but can be particularly burdensome for an author with limited means when the indemnity obligation can significantly exceed the authors upside from the sale of the work. The negotiation of indemnity obligations should also address the allocation of costs where a publisher seeks to settle a claim which the author believes would be adjudicated more favorably. In these instances the author may seek reasonable prospective settlement consultation and approval rights. The Author's Guild[12] also has begun to offer to its individual author members media perils insurance for these circumstances.

Many publishing agreements will have one-way indemnification agreements (e.g. the author is the only party providing an indemnification). In such cases, at the very least, depending on the circumstances of the nature of the literary material, an author can seek from the publisher contract language where the publisher indemnifies the author for claims relating to: (1) any added materials supplied by the publisher, (2) the publisher's breach of the agreement, and (3) any other exploitation of the work by the publisher, which claims do not arise from the author's breach or default. Indemnification provisions not only provide for the payment of damages but also for costs and expenses, most notably attorney fees (which is likely an important issue for an author to enforce rights under the publishing agreement). If a publisher refuses to provide an indemnification provision for the author for the publisher's breach of the agreement, another possible provision is to permit attorney fees and costs to be awarded to either party prevailing in any legal dispute over the publishing agreement.

10.2.2.8. Next Works

Publishers want to protect their investments in authors and titles. They do this through the acceptability clause discussed above and often through a clause dealing with the author's future works. Authors are

---

[12] Information relating to Authors Guild membership eligibility, services and benefits may be found at https://www.authorsguild.org/

required to agree that the contracted work will be the author's next published work, whether alone or in collaboration with anyone else. In what is known as a competitive works clause, the author will stipulate that he or she will not publish or authorize publication of any work in print or digital form containing similar material, if in the publisher's judgment it would injure the publisher's ability to sell the work itself. Depending on the author's expertise and output, the definition of "similar material" and the broad discretion of the publisher's judgment should be addressed. In many respects, the publisher and author share the same goal on these issues: maximizing book sales. However, since the proscription lasts for the life of the work, an author with a given expertise may be ready to publish a new book with some similar subjects, themes and material before this clause would lapse.

Furthermore, publishers often require that they receive the exclusive "option" on the author's next work. Publishers' boilerplate typically states that the author must show a full manuscript to the publisher before showing it elsewhere. The boilerplate may additionally state that if the publisher does not wish to proceed or makes an offer that the author finds unacceptable, the author may not accept an offer from another publisher without giving the original publisher a chance to match the offer. Author representatives have successfully modified these clauses to allow for the option to be exercised on a detailed book proposal with two sample chapters, 90 days following acceptance of the first work and without the matching provision. If the author anticipates creating future works unrelated to the contracted work (e.g., a novel when the contracted work is non-fiction or vice versa, or a new non-fiction work on a substantially different topic than that contracted for), the author may seek to limit the publisher's rights in this regard – particularly if the publisher does not generally publish the sort of work that may follow (e.g., a work of literary criticism at a publisher dedicated to contemporary fiction).

10.2.2.9. Out of Print

The out-of-print clause, otherwise known as the reversion of rights clause, allows the author to ask the publisher to revert back to the author rights to a work once the work is no longer available for sale, or in common parlance, is no longer "in print." While in decades past the issue was how to define "in print" for purposes of this clause in terms of numbers of physical copies sold or in the publisher's warehouse and available for physical sale, the advent of the e-book and print-on-demand technology rendered that battle moot. Titles would forever be in print electronically unless another solution was found to assess whether a title was selling. Thus, it is important for the author to ensure that e-book, digital versions of the book and other similar technology formats like print-on-demand versions are not determinative of whether or not the book is "in print". One common solution is to base the "in print" standard on the number of overall sales for a determined consecutive number of accounting periods. The major publishers have agreed to a clause that reads something like: "The Work shall be considered in print if it is available for purchase in the US in a full-length English-language edition and is listed in Publisher's re-order form and has generated at least three hundred (300) aggregate sales in any format over the two (2) accounting periods immediately preceding the Author's notice to the Publisher."

10.2.2.10. Revisions

Most boilerplate contracts contain a revisions clause. In a large majority of cases, these clauses are not necessary and may be stricken. Novels or works of history or biography, for example, will not be revised. However, in some cases involving work on current topical themes, the publisher will ask an author to add a new chapter or refresh the work prior to publication in paperback. That is not considered a revision in the traditional sense of the clause, and will be up to the parties to negotiate.

In contrast, revisions *are* regularly made in reference books or textbooks with long anticipated shelf lives because ongoing updates represent significant streams of revenue for both publisher and author (e.g., a state school system's adoption of a particular science text, which could extend for many years). Thus, these clauses should be carefully considered. Issues arise if the publisher believes a revision is necessary by a particular date and the author is unable or unwilling to do the work at that time, if at all. In these instances, publishers will want the ability to bring in another author and deduct that reviser's fee from the original author's royalties. In cases where the original author of a textbook, for example, is well-known in the field and remains the lead author despite not doing the revisions, that author will often want to choose the reviser and ensure that his or her royalties never drop below a 50% floor.

10.2.2.11. Copyright

Generally publishing contracts state that the copyright is owned by the author. Though some smaller publishers and university presses have boilerplate that states the copyright shall be in the name of the publisher, most will modify the clause in favor of the author's retention of copyright if pressed to do so. The distinction is important, in no small measure, because the US Copyright Act extends copyright for new works to the author's life plus 70 years, or even longer for works "made for hire" by a contracting employer.[13] In any case, the clause will state that notice of copyright in the work will appear in each copy of the work and copies of any of the publisher's licensees, too. The US Copyright Act grants certain statutory rights to works registered at the copyright office within 90 days of initial publication. Usually publishers will do this for all its titles, and this clause will state so.

10.2.2.12. Accounting Statement and Inspections

While some small publishers and university presses account to the author only once a year, major trade houses account semi-annually. The most surprising aspect of the standard publishing agreement for authors in this regard is that, despite the prevalence of automation in sales data retrieval today, the statements and payments generally not arrive per the contract until up to four (4) months following the end of the respective reporting period (e.g., April 31 for the period ending December 31). While many major publishers have instituted author portals whereby an author can receive real-time information about sales, monies owed from royalties and amounts received from the disposition of subsidiary rights licenses are delayed for those four

---

[13] For Works Created on or after January 1, 1978, The law automatically protects a work that is created and fixed in a tangible medium of expression on or after January 1, 1978, from the moment of its creation and gives it a term lasting for the author's life plus an additional 70 years. For a "joint work prepared by two or more authors who did not work for hire," the term lasts for 70 years after the last surviving author's death. For works made for hire and anonymous and pseudonymous works, the duration of copyright is 95 years from first publication or 120 years from creation, whichever is shorter (unless the author's identity is later revealed in Copyright Office records, in which case the term becomes the author's life plus 70 years). For more information about works made for hire, see Circular 9, Works Made for Hire under the 1976 Copyright Act.

months. The publisher's rationale for such late reporting is that it can take this much time to consolidate offsetting expenses and charges allocable against the income reported, and that an accelerated calculation and payment obligation will result in frequent overpayment which may not readily be recoverable by the Publisher in subsequent cycles, and if recoverable will then take another year to process.

While royalty statements are notoriously difficult to decipher, most author representatives are sufficiently knowledgeable to answer most author questions or find the answers from the royalty managers at the publishing houses. Ideally the statements would include: the number of physical copies printed, shipped, sold and returned in the period (and cumulatively during the term of the agreement); the reserve against returns; digital sales sources and revenues; and the details of subsidiary rights sales. The reserve against returns represents the amount of royalties a publisher holds back to cover physical copies shipped to wholesalers or retailers but later returned unsold from these accounts. Publishers often agree to limit use of a reserve to the first four royalty periods, based on the assumption that by then the publisher will understand the market needs for that title. Contractual reserves should not exceed 15-20% of total reported sales, and should be liquidated periodically as the volume of sales and rate of returns diminishes.

Every publisher should permit authors to inspect the publisher's books and records relating to their work during regular business hours and in accordance with customary accounting procedures. Clauses codifying that right usually say that the inspections cannot occur more than once a year, shall be conducted by the author or author's designated representative, and may not take place more than two or three years after receipt of the royalty statement in question. Author representatives should further include a clause stating that if errors in accounting amounting to 5% or more of the total amount due the author are found to the author's disadvantage, the publisher shall pay the shortfall and the reasonable cost of the audit (with a cap on audit expenses equal to the established shortfall often being an agreed middle ground on this issue), plus interest on these amounts until paid.

10.2.2.13. Competing Works

Nearly all publishing agreements have provisions that prohibit an author from exercising any rights where the nature of such rights are related to the book (for example, subject matter, similar characters, themes, plots and storylines) while the book is being developed and for a period time after the book is released for public sale. These provisions must be carefully analyzed by the author to make certain that they are reasonable and that they do not prevent the author from other forms of publishing or exercising reserved rights important to the author's career (for example, an academic scholar) or valuable other revenue streams. An author should expect the first draft of this provision to be broadly crafted to seem that the author can't do anything connected to the book during the specified period. The author then must suggest language to narrow the scope of such provision. Where possible the author should specify specific activities of the author that are permitted and will not violate the competing works provision.

10.2.2.14. Agency Provision

When the author is represented by an agent the publishing agreement will contain an agency clause that will authorize the publisher to send the author's agent all payments due to the author. The agent then will deduct the agent's fee and then distribute the balance to the author. The agency clause is generally revocable by the author (although to do so will likely put the author in breach of the author's agreement with the agent) unless the provision states that the agency clause and the agent's right to receive the payments on behalf of the author is "coupled with an interest". Such language is intended to give the agent a separate property right beyond the contractual obligation.

10.3. SELF-PUBLISHING

As noted at the beginning of the chapter, the world of self-publishing in both print and digital formats has grown immensely in recent years. Authors may choose this option over a conventional publishing relationship for a variety of reasons. It is no longer seen as merely a route to readers for those who could not find a trade publisher. In fact, some authors choose this route at the outset for reasons of speed, control, and even profitability.[14] An array of

---

[14] Self-published authors may receive as much as double what trade book authors receive from online booksellers because they are not sharing revenue with a major publisher. On the other hand, they have received no advance, nor the editing and marketing services that come with being published by a general trade publisher. The Chapter on " Self-Publishing Options" in *The Writer's Legal Guide* by Key Murray and Tad Crawford (Allworth Press 2013) offers a great overview on these contracts.

reputable firms publish works in digital and/or print formats on a "for hire" or similar basis. They offer packages of services to choose from that include editing, copyediting, formatting, cover creation, assigning an ISBN, listings on wholesale and retail websites, distribution, marketing, and payment collection and disbursement. The simplest services may do nothing more than convert a manuscript into an e-book format (and different e-book platforms may require delivery of slightly varying coded formats), offer it for sale on several sites, and collect and pay out monies remitted by these sites (after deducting its additional services fees or commissions). Producing and distributing print copies of a given title is surely more expensive than doing so with e-books, but several of these companies offer what is known as "print on demand" services making print copies available to the author or book sellers, in addition to e-books.

The contracts for self-publishing are very different than trade book contracts. First off, some contracts appear on the digital publishing company website and require a mere click to accept the terms. Others leave room for more negotiation. The basic items to address are: the grant of rights, upfront fees to the publisher for work performed (as there will rarely be author advances in these deals), reporting and payment, royalties, and termination.

Unlike traditional publishing agreements, these contracts are more similar to a service agreement than to a broad grant of rights. In most cases, the publisher only needs the non-exclusive rights to create, sell, and market the work in print-on-demand and/or e-book form. If the publisher's responsibilities include collecting and remitting the authors monies, the agreement should specify monthly or quarterly reporting and payments and permit access to real-time account information on its website for the author, as well as the audit provisions applicable to more traditional publishing agreements. If royalties are based on net proceeds, a reasonable definition of net would include deductions for costs of conversion from print to required digital formats, and encryption to prevent wholesale duplication of the works without compensation to the publisher and author. Often, though, the conversion is paid for separately by the author upfront, as is the cost for other negotiated services like cover design, editing and marketing. Author representatives should help clients determine their needs and the reasonableness of the costs for services.

The termination clause is very important in any self-publishing agreement. Thirty days' notice of termination is ideal. For those authors who still hope to interest a traditional trade publisher in the work by showing its initial e-book sales, and in those cases in which a "self-publishing" services company's performance is unsatisfactory, a short notice provision allows maximum flexibility and should be mutually acceptable where the author has essentially covered the publisher's costs and some profit upfront on a fee basis.

This fast-evolving segment of the industry is expanding with many competitors for an author's business. This means ongoing assessment of an author's needs, a given publisher's capabilities and reputation, and a simple, non-restrictive agreement.

10.4. FREELANCE PERIODICAL AGREEMENTS

Print and online media organizations often hire freelance writers as independent contractors, rather than employees, for articles, columns, blog posts or any combination. These contracts are generally a few pages and cover the subject of the work, delivery date, grant of rights, warranties and representations, expenses, and fees.

10.4.1. The Subject of the Work

The agreement or work order should contain a brief description of the proposed assignment. If the assignment is based on a query or pitch letter, this can be attached to the contract when describing the work. Typically any such contract will include a word count and denote any other special requirements.

10.4.2. The Grant of Rights

When it comes to the grant of rights clause, contracts today typically call for a grant of all rights or acknowledgment that the assignment will be deemed work made for hire conveying copyright to the publication as author. Years ago, writers would only grant First North American Serial Rights for these assignments such that the publication would have the right to be first in North America to publish; after a specified time, the author is free to publish the work in its original or an expanded form elsewhere. The digital marketplace and the Supreme Court decision in the *Tasini*[15] case has complicated this issue. Publishers want to control all print and digital uses in all territories simultaneously. Thus, writers are advised to negotiate their fees with the loss of other income from such repurposing opportunity in mind. Depending on the publication, however, writers' representatives may claw back certain rights, including television and film rights and the right to write books based in whole or in part on the article's subject matter.

10.4.3. Warranties and Representations

Like all publishing contracts, writers make representations and warranties that their work is original, not previously published, and will not defame, invade the privacy of, or be injurious to any third party; will not violate any law; and will not infringe upon the personal or proprietary rights of or give rise to any claim by a third party. Monthly magazines with long lead times for their articles often have counsel review these articles before publication, but these days, only a few magazines are known to have fact checkers on staff. Generally, publications rely on the author's reputation and on these "reps and warranties." Author advocates will often try to limit the reps and warranties to "to the best of author's knowledge" or grant coverage for the freelancer under the publication's errors and omissions policy. These efforts may meet with varying publisher accommodations for the same reasons discussed earlier with respect to indemnity carve-outs in book deals.

10.4.4. Payments and Expenses

Fees vary from publication to publication. Some freelancers will sign an agreement to be paid monthly for a certain number of articles and blog posts. Others will be paid by the word for a given article or a number of articles over a period of time. Some offer an additional percentage of the fee for any subsidiary income, such as foreign licenses. Many of these contracts will include what's known as a cancellation or "kill fee," which is the amount the author receives if the assignment is either unacceptable or not published for any reason. In the event an

---

[15] N.Y. Times Co. v. Tasini, 533 U.S. 483 (2001), in which a database is determined to be a new collective work; *compare with* Greenberg v. Nat'l Geographic, 244 F.3d 1267 (11th Cir. 2001), in which CD-ROM duplication of original magazine editions containing freelance photographs was found to be consistent with underlying "print" collective work license.

assignment is canceled or the work is rejected, the rights must clearly revert to the author as well, so that the work might be published elsewhere. Thirty percent of the assignment fee is a typical kill fee. Some assignments require significant travel or research expenses. Any required approvals, limits, and the method for payment of such expenses should be specified in the agreement, and/or factored into the kill fee if the author is bearing these expenses against a final anticipated payment for the work.

10.5. SCHOLARLY/PROFESSIONAL JOURNAL PUBLICATION

Academics and other scholars are often faced with the need to "publish or perish" – that is, they must have research published in specialized journals to enhance or maintain their careers. All writers like to earn money for their work, but with these publications, often affiliated with nonprofit organizations or universities, a long tradition dictates that "consideration" for their efforts be measured by prestige and exposure rather than dollars and cents.

The publication will usually provide a contract after it has read the complete work and has had it approved by a peer-review process. The journal editor will select two to three other experts in the field to respond to the work with written assessments and recommendations before publication. While this is standard operation procedure, the time-associated lags can be frustrating, and may sometimes undermine the authors desire to have cutting-edge work reported before a competing researcher or institution does so.

These contracts often ask for the assignment of the entire copyright in the work. This allows the journals to use the articles in databases and research services that combine decades of scholarship. It is common that a reservation of rights clause be included that ensures the journal has no rights to the underlying research and that the author can freely use the article in his or her own books and author website. Often the journal will require an acknowledgement that the piece was first published in the journal, which is not a burdensome responsibility.

Academics are not given fees for these articles; however, many journals will agree to share any licensing fees received from the repurposing the article in other publications and/or from the licensing of reprint permissions from services like Copyright Clearance Center. These payments typically are made annually to the author.

10.6. AGENCY AGREEMENTS

The vast majority of trade publishing contracts are negotiated by the author's agent. Currently the Association of Author Representatives, the membership organization based in New York City, has close to 400 members nationwide. Most literary agencies provide boilerplate contracts for authors to sign when initiating a representation relationship with the agent or agency that should be carefully reviewed. Some simply rely on the agency clause in the publishing contract. A standard agency clause in a book contract designates the agent the author's sole and exclusive representative in connection with the contract and related matters, and affirms that any written communications with the agent is binding upon the author. It also dictates that all statements, payments and other communications should be sent to the agent, that payments be made payable in the name of the agent, and that receipt of payments and communications by the agent constitutes receipt by the author for the publisher's purposes.

Agency agreements should include the scope of the agreement, a clear term, applicable commissions, payment/expense and accounting provisions, and delineation of the agent's duties. Most agreements will state that the agent handle a client's literary rights for a particular property or for all works created during the term of the agreement. Whether the agreement includes an author's freelance work in magazines and other publications should be specified, as well as the agent's entitlement to commission film and television revenues from the disposition of these rights in a work that the agent sold to a publisher, if the agent is not directly involved in the film or television deal on behalf of the author.

Today, reputable agents do not charge reading fees to evaluate potential properties. It is considered a cost of doing business, and such payments are verboten. The general fee for literary agents is 15% of the author's receipts from the US publisher and from exploitation of film and television rights. The percentage may climb to 20% or 25% of receipts arising from contracts with foreign publishers, since the US agents are typically dividing this fee with literary agents in each territory. Agencies that do not have film and television agents in-house typically partner with film and TV agents for these deals and divide the 15%. However, on larger deals, entertainment lawyers specializing in TV and film (generally based in Los Angeles) may be necessary facilitators, charging hourly fees for negotiating and contract review services or alternatively working on a contingency basis typically in the range of an additional 5% of eventual author advances, fees (where, for example, an author may be attached to consult on, write or produce the adaptation) and royalties. If an agency is charging expenses, they should be limited to reasonable and necessary out-of-pocket expenses, and any agreement should specify dollar amounts that require approval before exceeded.

Some agents are more communicative than others. Authors deserve to know where a book proposal or manuscript is submitted and see copies of any written responses. This requirement can be added to the agreement.

Agents prefer long-term agreements. However, these are very personal relationships that require a shared vision of the project and shared work effort. Whenever possible the agreements should be terminable at either party's request. That said, if the author has signed a publishing contract, the agent's rights to ongoing money and responsibilities to advance the author's interests throughout the publishing process continue intact. Some issues arise when an author uses another agent for his next book and the author prefers the new agent to handle any issues that arise with the older title. This happens often with unsold foreign rights to the older book, which may become more attractive upon the release of a successful follow-up title or alternatively if far down the road the publisher of the first book wants the author to create new material for a new edition. As in much of the rest of the publishing business, relations among agents are generally collegial, and these things are sorted out by a phone call. Some agency agreements stipulate that upon termination, if the author obtains a publishing contract from a publisher originally contacted by the terminated agent, that agent is entitled to the commission. The theory that undergirds this position is that the author terminated before the agent was really finished with its solicitation of particular publishers. Surely if the first agent is close to closing on a deal, the second agent shouldn't receive the commission. To avoid any disputes over commissions for deals in progress upon termination, the agent and the author should determine if there are any open offers or active negotiations underway near the agreement's end date, or provide a "tail" period to the representation term to enable such solicitations to fully play out.

Rarely do lawsuits occur over agency agreements in the literary arena. However, one case in the last few years got some attention. The Peter Lampack Agency, which had represented bestselling mystery writer Martha Grimes on several books, claimed a commission on one of her novels published by Penguin, her then-publisher, because the option clause giving Penguin the first look at the new novel was negotiated by that agency even though she had terminated the agency relationship before Penguin exercised its option and came to terms with Grimes.[16] In November 2010, a New York Supreme Court judge dismissed the lawsuit.[17]

For additional readings on trends and industry developments pertaining to representing authors, agents and publishers in the literary publishing fields, the following online resources may be of further interest and value:

1. www.Publishersmarketplace.com
2. The Shatzkin Files (www.idealog.com/blog)
3. www.Janefriedman.com
4. www.Publishingtrends.com
5. www.Publishersweekly.com
6. www.Digitalbookworld.com
7. http://lunch.publishersmarketplace.com/
8. www.Authorsguild.org
9. www.publishingtrends.com
10. Association of American Publishers - www.publishers.org
11. Association of Authors' Representatives – www.aaronline.org

LITERARY PUBLISHING - ILLUSTRATIVE FORMS:

- Literary Publishing Agreement
- Foreign Rights Publishing Agreement
- Self- Publishing Agreement
- Collaboration (Co-Writer) Agreement
- Collaboration (Ghostwriter) Agreement

---

[16] Grimes's book, *The Way of All Flesh*, is a satire of the publishing business that opens with a pair of hit men spraying bullets across the aquarium in the Clownfish café, where conniving agent L. Bass Hess is eating lunch.

[17] Peter Lampack Agency, Inc. v. Grimes, 2012 NY Slip Op 01576 [93 AD3d 430].

— **CHAPTER 11** —

VIDEO GAMES, INTERACTIVE MEDIA AND DEALMAKING

Andrew Boortz[*]

11.1. Introduction / Nomenclature
11.2. Industry Entities and Their Roles
11.3. Financing the Creation of Video Games
11.4. Getting a Game from Concept to the Consumer
11.5. Regulation of Video Games
11.6. Looking into the Future
11.7. Conclusion

11.1 INTRODUCTION / NOMENCLATURE

Video games and interactive media, though perhaps the newest of the entertainment genres covered in this book, are nonetheless a sector of the entertainment industry rife with legal complexities that can seem bewildering to both novice practitioners and seasoned advocates alike. The video game industry, and accordingly the practice of law built up to support it, have norms, jargon and practices that are unique to it, just as the movie, TV, music and live performance industries do. Thus, the purpose of this chapter is to introduce attorneys and dealmakers to the world of video games and interactive media, and provide a high level overview of the various issues and solutions that one may encounter in dealmaking within the video game industry.

Importantly, this chapter does not cover all issues that may arise in the course of game development, production and distribution, nor does it address litigation strategy and procedure as it may pertain to contractual and other disputes in the video game industry. Instead, this

---

[*] **Andrew Boortz** is the Managing Vice President for Western Business and Corporate Development for the NEXON Group. Prior to that he was General Counsel for Nexon's western business entities. The author would like to express his indebtedness to his family, friends, co-workers, law firm colleagues, clients, assistants, researchers, students and adversaries who each taught him lessons about life, the law, and pursuing his passions in the entertainment industry. He extends his deepest love and gratitude to them all.

section is for dealmakers and counselors, and is written with them primarily in mind.

11.1.1. What Is Covered Today by the Term "Video Games"?

"Video games" can be used generically to refer to any interactive software product that is built for the primary purpose of entertaining the person who interacts with that software. This includes everything from small games contained on one's smartphone or tablet device to large games played on computers or dedicated console systems. What "video games" does not refer to, and what should be kept conceptually separate, is any interactive software used for the primary purpose of gambling. Gambling-related software is, perhaps somewhat confusingly, referred to as "gaming" within that industry, and those unfamiliar with the differences between "video games" and "gaming" can find themselves in a quandary by confusing these two.

In this chapter we focus strictly on video games, and we do that by first classifying video games by platform, then by genre and type, and finally by the specific business model the game developer/publisher may choose to embrace for its exploitation. Each of these come with their own unique technology requirements and revenue assumptions, so it is important for the practitioner to readily identify both their similarities and differences to provide appropriate advice to clients in all phases of this business.

11.1.2. Platforms

To begin the classification, "platforms" refer to the device, system or media on which the game is played or experienced. There are (as of the writing of this book) five broad types of platforms: personal computer or "PC," consoles (stand-alone devices build for playing games, mobile, social, and developing platforms such as virtual reality and augmented reality.

11.1.2.1. PC Games

Personal computers are where many people first experienced video games. In fact, the case could be made that PC was the original video game console, with games such as OXO (an adaptation of tic-tac-toe) being made for the EDSAC mainframe in 1952.[1] Yet PC gaming did not really take off until the late 1970's and early 1980's when the explosion of personal computing power put PCs into homes all across the world. The increase in computer availability led to an increase in games being made and distributed for those devices, whether as printed code in magazines, on floppy disks or as "shareware" or "freeware" in chat rooms and on BBS (online billboards, and early precursors of services such as AOL). While PC gaming's popularity slowed in the 1990's as other platforms – particularly consoles – became available, PC gaming is enjoying a resurgence today and is an important platform in the video game ecosystem.

PC gaming can include both games that are primarily contained within a particular media (a CD or Blu-ray disc, a download to a particular computer hard drive, etc.), or an online game where the majority of the game resides on servers outside of the device which a person uses to play the game.

Today, some of the most popular games in the world are PC games: *League of Legends*, *World of Warcraft*, and *Counter Strike* to name but a few, with the most successful of these games boasting installed user/player communities in excess of tens, if not hundreds, of million fans each.

11.1.2.2. Console Games

Consoles refer to systems that are purpose-built for video games (and today, the console systems – which are relative "super computers" compared to the machines which launched the earliest days of video gaming – do many things other than simply play games). While many consoles have come and gone over the years, the three most notable console manufacturers today are Sony (PlayStation), Microsoft (Xbox) and Nintendo (with their variety of consoles, the most recent of which is the Nintendo Switch). The term "console" may mean the generic grouping of devices, a particular brand within that grouping, or a particular model or device from a brand.

Traditionally, console devices relied upon disks, cartridges or other media on which the game resided as a means of distribution. Players would purchase that media in order to obtain the game, and would need

---

[1] Wilkes, M.V. (January 1997). "Arithmetic on the EDSAC." IEEE Annals of the History of Computing. IEEE. 19 (1): 13–15. ISSN 1058-6180.

to insert that media into the console device to play. That is no longer the only distribution means of console games, as the rise of digital distribution has greatly expanded the ways in which players and games interact, but the use of physical media is still important to the console market.

Many readers may be familiar with some of the more notable console franchises such as *Super Mario Brothers*, *Halo*, *Sonic the Hedgehog*, the *Final Fantasy* series, and more.

11.1.2.3. Mobile Games

With the introduction of the smartphone, an entirely new platform for video games was created, and in just a few short years, mobile gaming was able to overtake PC gaming in terms of overall size, with approximately $47 billion in revenues in 2016.[2] In the western markets (North America, Europe and Oceania) there are two predominant platform markets – Apple's AppStore and Google's Google Play – though others such as the Amazon App Store do exist. In Asia, however, the mobile market is much different, with a host of platform providers offering their own app marketplaces in addition to those of Apple, Google and Amazon.

Though it hardly needs to be defined, mobile gaming generally refers to any games that are built for interaction on a smartphone or tablet device. Examples of some of the more notable commercial successes on the mobile platform includes *Clash of Clans*, *Angry Birds*, and *Candy Crush*.

11.1.2.4. Social Network Games

Social network games are games designed for distribution and interaction on a particular social network – Facebook being the largest, of course. To that end, many of the first mobile games started as social network games (e.g., *FarmVille* and similar titles from Zynga). In recent years, however, the social network games market has struggled as mobile became dominant. Still, Facebook has made notable investments into various areas of video games, and the platform is not to be ignored or considered dead by any means.

---

[2] NewZoo Global Games Report 2016, available at https://newzoo.com/insights/articles/global-games-market-reaches-99-6-billion-2016-mobile-generating-37/

11.1.2.5. New Platforms

As technology evolves, so, too, do the number and types of platforms for which games are made. In the last two years, virtual reality and augmented reality have been the most frequently mentioned new platforms. Virtual reality are those technologies meant to provide the user with a virtually rendered, three-dimensional world that will track the user's eye orientation and change the visuals accordingly. Many companies are investing heavily in VR, with Facebook purchasing Oculus for $2 billion in in 2014, platform purveyors Sony and Valve both offering their own VR products, and non-traditional players such as Google and Samsung offering their own VR systems as well.

Augmented reality, on the other hand, tends to refer to technologies that are capable of layering video game worlds on top of the real world. This can be achieved through use of your smartphone's built-in technologies (the recent success of *Pokemon Go* is a great example of this) or through a dedicated wearable device (e.g., Google Glass, Microsoft Hololens, Magic Leap's yet-to-be-named device, etc.).

In addition, games that are played natively from within messaging applications such as Apple's iMessage and Facebook's Messenger are starting to gain popularity among developers. These messaging games are played from within the messaging apps themselves, as opposed to being played from within a separate application. While messaging apps are not exactly a new platform, their use as a launch pad for games is.

11.1.3. Game Types and Genres

Having established the platforms on which a game can be played, the next means of classification of games is by type or genre. This, however, is something of a fool's errand as game types and genres are constantly being invented, reinvented, combined or deconstructed to form new types and genres. Still, as this chapter is written for an audience that may not be familiar with game types (and more importantly, the acronyms that references those types), some description of these game types and genres will be useful here.

11.1.3.1. Action

Action games present players with some form of physical challenge that must be overcome to win. Action games typically require a high degree of eye-hand coordination, motor skill and timing. The player controls a single character, through whom the game is experienced. Examples include *Super Mario Bros.*, *Donkey Kong*, and some shooter-based games like *Doom*.

11.1.3.2. Adventure

Adventure games tend to be defined as games that require puzzle solving on the part of the player without the need for battle or conflict with in-game characters. Two notable examples of adventure games would be *Myst* and *Tomb Raider*.

11.1.3.3. Action-Adventure

Action-adventure games combine the tenets of both action and adventure games. They often include both puzzle solving and some form of combat against in-game characters. Examples include *Metroid, Legend of Zelda, The Last of Us* and more.

11.1.3.4. Role Playing

Role playing games historically draw their inspiration from table top games like *Dungeons & Dragons*. They ask players to take on the role of one or more characters with unique characteristics and abilities (a character may be optimized for speed, power, magic, stealth, etc.), and players success in the game by playing as that character would act. Examples of role playing games include the *Final Fantasy* series, *RuneScape, EVE Online* and others.

11.1.3.5. Simulation

Simulation games is a catch-all classification that covers a wide variety of simulation-specific game experiences. They include life simulation games like *Second Life* or *the Sims*, vehicle simulation games like *Need for Speed* or *Flight Simulator*, and many more.

Recently there have been a host of avant-garde simulator games such as *Surgeon Simulator*, *Goat Simulator* and others.

11.1.3.6. Sports

Sports games are self-defining. They include games such as *MLB: The Show* (baseball), the *Madden* series (football), *FIFA Online* (soccer) and other sports-based games.

11.1.3.7. Strategy

Strategy games emphasize strategic and tactical thinking and planning in order to achieve the win conditions the game sets forth. A classic example of a strategy game is *Civilization*, wherein the player is asked to guide a civilization from ancient times through space travel, and dominate the world in doing so. Other forms of strategy games include real-time strategy games like *Starcraft*, multiplayer online battle arenas like *League of Legends*, and tower defense games like *Plants vs. Zombies*.

11.1.3.8. Casual Games

Casual games is another catch-all category meant to define games that are intended to be played in small time segments, often less than two or three minutes per round (though players can certain play multiple rounds in a given session). *Angry Birds*, *Cut the Rope*, and *Threes* are good examples of casual games.

11.1.4. Business Models

The final means of categorizing games is by the business model the game follows. The business model a developer/publisher opts to pursue to capture consumer engagement (and allegiance) is an important distinguishing factor in video games because it dictates much about the gameplay experience from the user's perspective and the decisions a game developer or publisher makes about bringing those users to the game, and keeping them engaged with it over the game's useful life.

Historically, there were two primary business models for games – a player purchased the game for some amount of money, or received it for free. That changed with broader access to the Internet, increased Internet bandwidth, and creation of new platforms and consumer bases to support them. Today there are a variety of business models that games employ, each of which has its own strengths and weaknesses.

11.1.4.1. Premium Purchase Price

The most familiar business model to casual observers of the video game industry is that of a premium purchase game – a game that is obtained by a user for a set price. This model is still alive and well, as shown by the significant sales put up by games such as *Grand Theft Auto V*, the *Assassin's Creed* franchise, and others. It should be noted, however, that even premium priced games have recently shown a tendency to extend the purchase cycle through sales of in-game items, downloadable content ("DLC"), expansions, and more. But the important distinguishing factor is whether the user pays for and receives all or a significant amount of the game's content in an up-front purchase.

11.1.4.2. Subscription

The second business model with which many readers are likely to be familiar is that of the subscription model, where users pay a monthly (or sometimes yearly) fee for access to a game. In exchange for this fee, the developer or publisher (as the case may be, with more on this later) regularly makes available new content to enhance the game experience (and revenue opportunities). *World of Warcraft* is perhaps the most successful game that utilized the subscription model, though a host of other games also followed this path.

More recently, some games have adopted a pseudo-subscription strategy known as "game passes." The passes, which tend to be offered on a yearly basis, entitle the purchaser to a host of additional content, including free access to any DLC or new content that is made available during the course of the yearly pass term. This, however, should be considered an add-on to games of another category instead of placing those games into the subscription category, because these games do not depend on a vast number of players purchasing the yearly game pass in order to generate sufficient revenue to continue operations.

11.1.4.3. Free to Play

The third business model is that of games that are free to play. In may seem odd to categorize a game given away freely as embodying a "business" model. However, many games in the last forty plus years were created and distributed for free. In the early history of video games, this was often referred to as "freeware" or "shareware,"[3] and examples of this can be found all the way back to the BBSs (billboard services) of the 1970s and 1980s. The models for these games, of course, depended upon the kindness of strangers or on a barter-in-kind model. They did not generally lead to large commercial success, although some enjoyed huge consumer popularity.

More recently, however, "free to play" business models have risen in popularity because they have been adopted by large enterprises to great commercial success. In doing so, free to play games have transformed the industry with their popularity. There are two major subtypes of free to play games. The first, and most notable, of these variations is that of the microtransaction-supported game. A microtransaction-supported game is made available to users for free, though typically the content made available on a for-free basis constitutes a "lite" or incomplete version of the full game experience. This is where microtransactions come into play.

Microtransactions refer to small payments (usually a few dollars) that are made to obtain discrete pieces of content. For example, a player may spend one dollar on a new sword for a character, or on a vanity item such as changing the color of their character's hair. The most popular PC game in the world – Riot Games' *League of Legends* – is a microtransaction-supported game that sells a variety of items that can customize the base game (which is given away for free).

The second variation of the "free to play" business model is that of "advergames." These are games that are primarily supported through advertising that is integrated into the game, or through data collection that is aggregated and sold to advertisers.

Why do we bother classifying games by business model? Because the business model a game employs dictates much about the gameplay

---

[3] The difference between "freeware" and "shareware" is that the creators of "shareware" asked users to submit a voluntary donation if they liked the product, but one was not required in order to utilize the software. "Freeware" generally included no such ask.

experience. In the case of premium purchase games, the developer generally builds a significant amount of content prior to commercial release of the game. That content is included in the game when purchased by the user. In contrast, games that are "free to play" tend to launch with less content than is included in premium purchase games, but must plan for (and develop) consistent releases of content to support the game and attract continuing interest of players going forward. Accordingly, the deals that are cut for premium priced games can vary greatly from those for free to play games.

11.2. INDUSTRY ENTITIES AND THEIR ROLES

Having established the basics of the video game platforms, types and business models, we turn next to the various entities that work together to make games and provide them to end users, notably developers, publishers, licensors, middleware providers and service providers.

11.2.1. Developers

Developers, as their name implies, "develop" games. Their role in the industry as game-makers is not unlike that of producers in film, television, recorded music or theatre – in this case actively (or managing the work of others) undertaking everything from the writing of software code to the creation of characters, artwork, landscapes, narratives, etc. The actual work of developing games is far too broad and complex to describe in this chapter, and experts should be consulted as to what development actually entails if more information is needed. Well-known developers include Naughty Dog (*The Last of Us*), Respawn Entertainment (*Titanfall*) and Gearbox Software (*Borderlands*). Websites of these development/production companies and their competitors will provide a deeper look into the operations of these businesses and their roles in the game industry.

11.2.2. Publishers

Publishers are the entities responsible for providing games to and operating them for the end users. Historically this meant funding game development, paying for production of physical disks or cartridges, marketing the game, distributing the game to retail outlets, and being responsible for returns, customer support, and so on. With the advent of digital distribution and games that are operated as live services (instead of single distribution points for a set amount of content), the role of the publisher has taken on new dimensions.

Today, publishers provide both more and less to developers than they did 30 years ago. This is the result of the twin advents of digital distribution and live service games. Modern publishers may still fund games (though, as described in the next section of this chapter, that is not always required), may still market the game, and provide customer support. In addition to that, however, publishers can also provide technology resources such as server infrastructure, transaction processing, fraud prevention, in-game economy management, and live game execution.

What has not changed about the publisher's role, however, is the bundle of exclusive rights in and to the game that a publisher will take in order to fulfill its publishing obligations. Generally, these exclusive rights include the right to publish, market and exploit for commercial gain the game in a particular territory, the right to be the sole provider of customer support, community and public relations messaging about the game, the right to decide when and where to publish, etc. These rights are usually time limited, with the length of time varying by platform (PC and console games tend to have longer publishing periods, while mobile games have shorter periods). In addition, there are typically provisions to allow for the automatic extension of these rights depending on various factors (gross revenue, net revenue, installs, average monthly active users, etc.). Examples of major publishers include Electronic Arts, Activision, Tencent, Nexon, Scopely and others.[4]

11.2.3. Distributors and Console Manufacturers

Distributors play a role similar to publishers in that they are responsible for distributing the game to end users and processing financial transactions. That is where the similarities end, however, as distributors generally do not fund a game's development, they engage

---

[4] Of course, many of these companies will both develop and publish games. For example, Activision owns Blizzard Entertainment (both developer and publisher of *World of Warcraft*, *Diablo*, and *Hearthstone*) while also publishing games made by third parties (*e.g.*, *Call of Duty*, *Tony Hawk Pro Skater*, etc.).

in little, if any marketing, and exercise little control over the game's players or its economy. In exchange for these services, distributors will take a cut of game sales (generally a flat percentage of the sales price in the case of digital distributors, and set fees in the case of retail distribution). The best known of these distributors include Apple's App Store, Google Play, the Windows 10 Store and Steam.

Console manufacturers – namely Sony, Microsoft and Nintendo – are distributors themselves, as well as developers and publishers; but even when they are simply distributing a game, their involvement goes beyond the pure distribution role described above. That is because these companies exercise control over the systems on which games made for these platforms are played, and they promulgate rigorous requirements for such games. Any game that does not meet the console manufacturer's requirements will be refused distribution for their respective consoles.

11.2.4. Licensors and Middleware Providers

Finally, developers, publishers and distributors may work with a variety of companies in bringing the final product to market, including licensors and service providers. As to licensors, there are two types n the video game industry: those who provide intellectual property ("IP") on which a game is based, and those who provide software, hardware or other intellectual property to help the developer develop the game, the publisher operate the game, the distributor distribute the game, etc. For example, companies may provide game engines (software that drives the core functionality of a game) physics engines (software that drives the physics within a game), database software for managing the game, and software that renders lighting or shade within a game, to a developer to assist that developer in creating the overall product. Those who provide discrete software, hardware or other intellectual property are sometimes referred to as "middleware providers" in order to distinguish them from classic licensors that provide the narrative intellectual property that will form the basis of the game.

11.3. FINANCING THE CREATION OF VIDEO GAMES

Now that we have completed a survey of the terms and entities involved in the video game industry, we will turn our attention to the single most difficult hurdle to the creation of video games – finding the money to create and operate the game. There are any number of ways that a game can be funded: the developer may decide to self-fund development by putting its own money into the game, the publisher may finance the game, investors such as venture capital firms might contribute funding by investing in a game, or the game may be funded directly by the end users. Each type of funding comes with its own risks and concerns.

11.3.1 Self-Funding

When someone refers to a game being self-funded, they almost always mean that it is the developer who is paying for the development with its own money. The phrase is generally not used to denote games that are financed by publishers, even if the publisher is building the game through an in-house development arm. Therefore, the issues involved with "self-funded" games are viewed entirely from the perspective of the developer.

The biggest issue with self-funding games is financial risk. Some games can cost upwards of $60 million or more to make, and may take four or more years to complete – during which time consumer tastes, as well as supporting technology can change markedly, with significant impact (positive and negative) on a game's commercial prospects. This is a significant commitment on the part of a developer, and the developer may not have the financial capacity to make such a commitment. Moreover, if a developer self-funds a game's development, it must also consider whether it wants to fund its subsequent marketing and distribution efforts. In the case of retail distribution, this too may require a significant outlay of capital where the marketing model requires that physical disks or other media be created and distributed to retailers. And while digital distribution has somewhat alleviated the need to incur such costs, both types of distribution must still be done in conjunction with marketing for the game. Some games will have marketing budgets that far exceed the actual cost to develop the game. Thus, the financial risk to a developer that wants to "go it alone" can be significant, though many developers do opt for this strategy in order to realize their vision for the game, and some have achieved phenomenal success by doing so.

Another reason why a developer might wish to avoid self-funding their games is that publishers and distributors can provide a good deal of feedback and insight into the game's development, and thereby avoid the "group think" problem – the problem that occurs when the developer is so invested (both emotionally and financially) in a game that they cannot see when development is going wrong. Having an outside perspective can minimize this risk.

11.3.2. Publisher-Funded Games

Given the financial and developmental risks of self-funding, developers will often seek a publisher to help fund their games. To understand how publishers fund games today, however, we must start with a look at how publishers historically funded games. For much of this industry's relatively brief history, publishers were the primary source of funding game development because they controlled distribution to retail markets, they had the financial wherewithal to produce millions of cartridges, disks, CD ROMs, etc., for distribution to end users, and they were certified as publishers for the console manufacturers whose platforms offered a principal if not primary gateway to consumers (more on this below). Replicating this was a very expensive proposition for developers, and so developers more often than not turned to publishers for funding and distribution (in a manner analogous to distributor/producer relationships in the film, television and recorded music industries before and continuing into the "digital age," as noted above). Because publishers controlled so much access to end users, publishers had most, if not all, of the power in terms of dealmaking, and generally dictated terms to developers which were not entirely favorable to the developer.

This is not the situation the industry finds itself in today. Rather, developers and publishers are on a more equal footing with regard to dictating terms of funding. This is due to the rise of digital distribution for games (games being made available for nearly instantaneous global electronic download instead of requiring the purchase of physical media). Digital distribution has pushed the balance of power between publishers and developers more towards equality. As users began to flock to digital distribution services such as Steam, the Windows 10 Store, the Apple App Store, Google Play and similar services, developers were given a viable means of bringing their products to market and reaching consumers (almost) directly without the involvement of a conventional publisher.

Today, digital distribution accounts for more revenue within the video games industry than traditional retail.[5] Of course, publishers still play a valuable role, even for digitally distributed games, as the publisher generally provides marketing support, customer service, IT infrastructure, and other services. But there is no argument that digital distribution of video games did not bring publishers and developers closer to each other in terms of one's ability to dictate terms to the other.

Despite the gains in dealmaking equality that developers have enjoyed, there are still generally three major types of deals a publisher may turn to fund development: the work-for-hire arrangement, the publishing recoupment arrangement, and a prototype deal.[6]

11.3.2.1. Work-for-Hire

In a work-for-hire deal, a developer is hired by a publisher to build a game for and at the direction of the publisher. This structure may apply to a game concept independently created or acquired from other sources by the publisher (e.g., based on IP from other media), or one pitched by the developer then hired to produce the game. The publisher is responsible for funding the game, obtaining the IP license (if applicable), and providing creative and operational direction to the developer. The developer, on the other hand, is responsible for building the game to the publisher's specifications. The developer takes almost no financial risk as the publisher pays the developer's full development cost regardless of the commercial success or failure of the game. Even if the game is never brought to market, the publisher must pay the developer for its work.

As the publisher bears all financial risk, most of the terms of a work-for-hire deal -- other than as to the fees (fixed and contingent) payable to or which may ultimately be retained by the developer from production budgets for work on the game, as addressed below --are not

---

[5] According to the Electronic Software Association's annual industry survey for 2016, digitally distributed games accounted for 54% of all video game sales in the United States in 2015.

[6] As with many of the attempts to broadly categorize how the video game industry operates, there exist a number of variations upon and blends of these three pillars. For example, co-publishing deals may involve the sharing of financing between the developer and publisher, and as a result may change some of the specifics with regard to payment, earnings, etc., as are further explored in this chapter.

subject to negotiation. For example, the publisher will own the final game product, including any intellectual property created as part of its development. The developer will own any products or materials it uses as part of the game's development (i.e., software tools, resource libraries, etc.) One area that practitioners should review carefully is who owns improvements to developer-owned tools. That is, if a developer owns a particular development tool, and utilizes that tool in the development of a game under a work-for-hire deal, that developer may have cause to make improvements to that tool during the development cycle. A work-for-hire agreement that is not carefully drafted could leave unanswered the question of who owns those improvements upon completion of the game.

Important issues subject to negotiation in work-for-hire deals include how and when the publisher pays the developer, and whether the developer will receive any "back end" participation (in other words, royalties) in the game. As for payment by the publisher, there are any number of arrangements that can be used depending on the circumstances, including the parties' resources and other preferences. For example, a publisher may pay the developer's "monthly burn" (the total running costs of the company on a monthly basis, less any capital expenditures or similar costs). Another model generally seen is a milestone-based payment model. That is, the developer submits portions of the completed (or incomplete) game over time ("milestones"). When the publisher approves of the respective milestone, it pays the developer an agreed upon amount of money (in effect, a progress payment) for that milestone's deliverables. This process iterates until the development process is completed, at which point the developer will have been paid in full or may otherwise be due a final completion payment.

These two models are used at various times depending on the purpose the publisher wants to achieve. Monthly burn models are typically deployed in cases where the parties may not know upfront exactly what they want the final game product to be, and thus both parties may consequently wish to maintain optimal flexibility to change direction (including developer staffing allotments) as development progresses. This allows the publisher to control its costs in the short run and for the developer to make agile pivots to its longer-term development process, which can be useful in finding the right direction for a given game if unclear at the outset. However, it also opens the publisher to the possibility that it can waste developer time (and therefore publisher money) if the developer's progress is not carefully monitored.

Therefore, it is vitally important in a monthly deal that each side understands what rights and obligations it has with regard to staffing – how many people will the publisher pay for (whole studio versus smaller team), will the publisher pay for the entire studio rent or a prorata portion, when can the developer add or subtract people from the project, when can the publisher demand that the developer add or subtract people from the project, etc. Another critical area is payment timing, as the developer will have financial obligations to its employees, landlord(s), service providers, etc., and may consequently insist on a substantial termination notice period, or a cancellation or "kill fee" from the publisher, if the project is abandoned for reasons not due to the developer's breach or default (enabling the developer to recapture some of its set up or opportunity costs which would have been earned out over the longer contract period). As such, payment provisions tend to be stricter in terms of payment timing in monthly burn deals.

In contrast, milestone-based models are more generally seen in situations where the publisher can give detailed specifications to the developer at the outset, and can hold the developer accountable for failure to meet those specifications. This is because, in a milestone-based payment model, the publisher only pays for deliverables which satisfy the designated milestone requirements and specifications. If the milestone deliverables fail to meet the requirements, the developer does not get paid until adjustments are made and the requirements are met. Thus, the milestone model gives the publisher a bit more control and financial protection, but can also result in time wasted if the publisher's specifications do not yield good game product, which can occur in situations in which the developer meets its mark with respect to fulfillment of the milestone requirements, but the publisher decides that the technical or creative specifications for the milestone need some or substantial rethinking, in which case publisher change orders may result in.

This creates new issues for a milestone-based work-for-hire deal, the most important of which concerns setting specifications for milestones. Careful drafting of terms that dictate what constitutes failure to meet milestone specifications, what happens in the event deliverables are rejected, and what happens if a publisher wants to change a milestone's specification in the middle of development is paramount to milestone-based agreements.

Regardless of what type of work-for-hire deal is struck, one provision that is always heavily negotiated is whether the publisher will pay royalties from revenues, in addition to a production fee, to the developer. As one might imagine, developers always want this, while publishers never do (unless they can leverage back-end participation into a deep reduction of up front production fees). Generally speaking, however, work-for-hire deals will include some form of royalty for the developer, though the terms of that royalty are less generous than in a pure publishing deal in which the developer bears some or all of the costs of creating the game (with more on this issue later in the chapter). When it comes to negotiating royalty provisions in a work-for-hire deal, practitioners should pay attention to the revenue event(s) upon which royalties are calculated and how both the payment trigger and the royalty itself are defined and calculated. Typically, a developer will receive royalties based upon net revenue, but how "net revenue" is defined can vary from deal to deal, from business model to business model, and from platform to platform.

11.3.2.2. Traditional Publishing (Publisher Recoupment) Deal

Another means by which publishers will fund development of a video game is through a publishing recoupment deal (also known as a traditional publishing deal, though the "traditional" descriptor is not entirely accurate, historically-speaking). With this structure, the publisher provides funding for all (or substantially all) of the cost of development, but unlike in a work-for-hire deal, the developer, not the publisher, will own the resulting IP. To make the publisher whole, the publisher withholds some amount of the developer's royalty payment as a recoupment on development advances until such time as the publisher has recovered its negotiated recoupment entitlement in full from some or all proceeds otherwise payable the developer. Depending on the type of game being built, this recoupment may be anywhere from 25% to 100% of the developer's earned royalties from exploitation of the game, and of course the publisher bears the risk that the game may not be completed or if completed does not perform commercially at a level generating quick or full recoupment of this advance/investment.

Given this deal structure, several of its typical provisions are quite different from a work-for-hire deal. These variations will address not only the differences in financing (i.e., the recoupment structure including how much is recouped, when, how calculated, etc.) but also the relative controls ("balance of power") which the developer and the publisher will seek to respectively exercise. In a work-for-hire deal, the publisher's ownership of the IP means that they can control the game development, the marketing, everything. In a traditional publishing deal, however, the developer's ownership of the IP means that the developer has a much greater interest in controlling the course of development and marketing for the game.

When crafting a traditional publishing deal, counsel for either side – developer or publisher – must therefore anticipate how development of the game should be structured and who will have final creative control over the direction and details of the game. This can be a very difficult part of the negotiating because while the developer will own the game, the publisher is fronting all the money. This tension between the parties interests (creative and financial) in a traditional publishing deal can be notoriously bad for the process of iterating on concepts or "finding the fun" in the game during the course of development, where it is best that both sides are completely aligned as to the type of game being built, how development will proceed, and so on.

11.3.2.3. Prototype Deal

A prototype deal merges elements of the typical work-for-hire and traditional publishing deals, and generally involves a publisher paying a developer to create a prototype of a game (though what constitutes a satisfactory prototype can vary greatly from project to project). Upon delivery of the prototype, the publisher has the option to continue funding the game through principal development or to walk away, thereby limiting the publisher's downside financial risk. In addition, some prototype deals may have a mutual option for continued development (i.e., both sides have to approve), thereby giving the developer a means of ending the relationship (with some ongoing financial participation to the publisher for its initial investment if the game is subsequently completed and published elsewhere or, in some cases, renegotiating the deal based on how the prototype development goes. However, the mutual option structure is less common than a publisher-only option in a prototype deal.

In addition to offering an exit by which to limit the downside financial risk for the publisher, the prototype deal can also be especially useful if the publisher wants to determine the capabilities of the developer before making a full funding commitment. The negatives are that a prototype deal incentivizes the developer to focus on user-facing elements such as artwork, animation, combat, etc., while postponing work on "under the hood" functionality such as server and database architecture, matchmaking, AI behavior and tuning, etc. The user-facing and "under the hood" aspects of a game are equally important to the game's eventual financial success, but are not as easy to discern or evaluate in a prototype. Thus, it is not uncommon for prototype deals to result in a prototype that has to be substantially reengineered following prototype approval because the eventual backend functionality necessitates important changes to the front-end too.

In structuring prototype deals, particular attention must therefore be paid to the "walk away" provisions. At what point does the publisher get to cut off funding, and how will this impact the developer as an ongoing concern? Developers will often seek some form of termination or runway payment in the event of a prototype cancellation, but giving this eliminates many of the differences between a prototype deal and a full publishing deal (of either variety). In addition, the prototype delivery requirements should be detailed enough to give the publisher a good sense of both front- and back-end functionality of the game; a prototype that is little more than a good looking passive demonstration is generally not sufficient to allow publishers to evaluate either the ability of the developer to bring the end product to market or to find the "fun" in the game.

11.3.2.4. Equity Funding

Self-funding and publisher funding are of course not the only forms of financing for games. In recent years, many game developers have been able to finance games by selling equity in their companies to venture capital firms, hedge funds, institutional investors and high net worth individuals. Indeed, even a few publishers have gone the equity route in raising capital to fund their businesses. And while an entire chapter of this book could be written on the intricacies of equity fundraising for electronic games (and the books chapters on Motion

Picture Financing and Entertainment Industry Taxation both offer important insights to this process), as there are a myriad of issues and complications that can arise when selling equity in a company, we will focus on those issues most relevant to video game companies looking to sell equity: ownership percentage, board control and exit provisions.

The first thing a game company seeking to raise equity funds must consider is what percentage of the company's ownership will be made available for sale. This can be a delicate balancing act as too little equity in exchange for funding being sought will not excite investors, while conveying too much equity at too low a valuation can block future raises or even result in ceding control of the company to the investors and away from the founders. But the concerns go deeper than just the initial equity transfer. There are a number of investment structures, such as obtaining substantial financing through convertible notes (whereby loans may be converted to ownership interests) and/or accumulating dividends on preferred stock, that allow investors' stake in the company to increase without any action being taken and importantly without additional funds coming into the company. Of course, there are any number of ways to deal with such issues, and becoming familiar with the National Venture Capital Association's model deal documents is a good place to start for a dealmaker or lawyer not experienced in such business or project financing arrangements.[7]

The second issue, board control, is related to, though not necessarily synonymous with, ownership, and speaks to – the ability of the financiers to control the company's board. Board control will dictate all major decisions of the company – who to work with, when to staff up (or staff down), the scope of executive management authority, and more – and may be demanded by the financiers even when they do not own a majority of the company if the financial partners can control the Board.

The third major concern involves exit provisions. This concern is of particular note for video game companies because of the long cycles inherent in certain types of video game development. Specifically, PC and console development can take anywhere from 15 months to four-plus years (mobile games tend to have a shorter development cycle), and "free to play" games that involve a live service component may take years after commercial launch to hit peak revenues. Taken

---

[7] Available at www.nvca.org.

together, it is entirely possible for a video game developer or publisher to need seven to 10 years before the maximum value in the company is achieved (if not longer). However, as with investment in many other fast paced commercial sectors, many if not most financial investors will be primarily concerned with when they can get their money back at a decent return. This can lead to difficult interactions between the video game company and the investor if the investor wants to sell the company or its primary asset(s) at an early date, as this may mean an "exit" occurring before maximum value for the company, and often for its founders, has been achieved; it may also preclude pursuit of additional game projects that are important to the developer.

11.3.2.5. End-User Assisted Funding

In recent years, a new form of funding video games has emerged, as companies (both publishers and developers) are going straight to the end user to fund their games. This new form of funding takes two primary paths – crowd funding and early access sales – which can be used either alone or in combination to fund the game's development.

a. Crowdfunding

Crowdfunding is when developers or publishers ask the general public for voluntary donations towards funding the game.[8] The public may give small or large amounts of money, and usually are in return promised certain benefits or perks dependent upon the level of their donation, up to and including delivery of or access to the complete game on its publication (or sometimes in beta form). The catch is that those perks or benefits are given to the donor only upon the game's actual release; and if the game does not get released, the donors may get nothing.

Many games have used crowdfunding to raise large sums of money, but the impact this has had on development is mixed. For example, *Star Citizen* raised a record $141 million through crowdfunding, which any game developer would rate as a smashing success.[9] However, that game

---

[8] Crowdfunding has been used for a broad range of products and services, not all of which are video games. For example, the general public has successfully funded consumer electronics, books, public art displays, and many others.

[9] "Star Citizen Passes $141 Million as Dev Teases 2017 Plans;" Gamespot.com; originally posted January 7, 2017, available at http://www.gamespot.com/articles/star-citizen-passes-141-million-as-dev-teases-2017/1100-6446716/

has also been in development since 2011, and release of the full game (with all promised features) is still uncertain.

One major reason why a game funded in this manner may take so long to develop is the benefits packages fulfillment that the developer may have promised to crowdfunding donors in exchange for certain levels of donations. The developer may make promises that as it hits certain funding thresholds, it will increase the amount of content it would build into the game – from items, to missions, to game modes, to entire sub-games made part of the overall game. This means that as the public makes donations, as in the case of *Star Citizen*, the amount of work the developer must undertake on time and ostensibly on budget to fulfill the solicited support will often increase proportionately.

Star Citizen has shown that crowdfunding can be a double-edged sword if not approached strategically. Particular attention should be paid to the total funding ask, funding tiers, reward levels and promises, community engagement plans, and developer capacity. In other words, a successful crowdfunding campaign is as much art as science – a blend of optimism, psychology, structure and execution.

b. Early Access Sales

Another strategy for user-assisted funding is that of early access sales. With this strategy, developers and publishers begin selling access to games prior to their full completion. The money received from end users is then put towards completing development, analogous in many ways to a publisher advance. Early access sales can also have a positive impact on community engagement by offering users a chance to play before the general public. Being "first" can be a powerful driver of purchase behavior, and can lead to longer term engagement with the game, a more passionate fan base, and more.

Another benefit of early access sales is that it multiplies quality assurance efforts tremendously. Because developers make the game available prior to its completion, users expect there to be bugs and issues with the game. These users may then report those bugs to the developer, which can increase the effectiveness of the developer's quality assurance team.

Of course, early access sales have their own pitfalls. First and foremost, the developer or publisher (as applicable) collects revenue from the user in advance of full release, meaning that at full release the amount of revenue the developer or publisher can potentially collect could be lower than in a traditional sales model (offset of course by the additional demand early adapters may help generate for a great game). Thus, developers and publishers need to plan their cash expenditures carefully throughout the development process to ensure that they are capable of continuing operations with a potentially lower level of cash flow post-launch.

Second, users who participate in early access sales tend to expect the developer will make regular updates to the game throughout the early access period. Games that fail to do this can turn a positive community into a negative community very quickly, and see sales at full launch suffer because the early access players have all either left the game or given it negative reviews (which may be tied to customer relations and tech support issues, rather than the merits of the game itself). As such, developers should plan for regular updates to the game (sometimes as frequently as every two weeks) to show the early access backers that development continues in earnest.

c. Issues with End User-Assisted Funding

Practitioners in this space should be wary of several other unique concerns pertinent to their clients' engagement in user-assisted funding strategies. Most importantly, counsel should ensure that any communications with end users are emphatically "not" framed as solicitations to invest in the game or the company.[10] While investing in games or game companies has become somewhat more common in recent years, and there are now emerging crowdfunded securities regulations issued by the Securities and Exchange Commission for small-cap offerings of up to approximately $1 million[11], this is still an area of law best avoided by the unwary. To avoid any investment issues, counsel should ensure that there are very specific disclaimers included in the terms and conditions on the user assisted-funding strategy being employed. These terms should clearly state why the money collected from end users is an early purchase of a game, and obtaining unambiguous agreement to these terms is a necessity. Use of

---

[10] Unless, of course, this is the intention. Some services such as Fig have recently started offering the general public the ability to invest in game shares – rights to participate in the profitability of a game – or even in the game studio itself.

[11] https://www.sec.gov/info/smallbus/secg/rccomplianceguide-051316.htm

crowdfunding platforms such as Kickstarter or Indiegogo would be recommended for companies that have not already built their own payments system, although each have different policies as to how funds may be accessed if the campaign targets are not met, etc.

In addition, practitioners should include clear warnings about the process of game development, and reserve to the fullest extent possible the ability for the developer to modify rewards in the future should development so require. This is a tricky thing to accomplish, however, because being overly conservative here could result in an unfair trade practice on the part of the company. The Federal Trade Commission has long held that it is an unfair trade practice under Section 5 of the Federal Trade Commission Act that what a sales pitch promises, a disclosure cannot take away.[12] Thus, counsel cannot simply say "whatever is promised can be changed at any time for any reason, up to and including not delivering on this reward at all." A careful hand must be taken to avoid the twin pitfalls of an absolute commitment on the part of the client and an unfair trade practice.[13]

Finally, as mentioned above, end user-assisted funding should be approached strategically. A balance must be struck not only between what is promised to backers and what can be delivered in a realistic timeline, but also between the short term and long term financial prospects of the game.

11.3.2.6. Tax Credits

Tax credit funding arrangements have long been a boon to other forms of media and entertainment, but the availability of tax credit financings for video games has come somewhat late to the party. Today, however, there are dozens of government programs in the United States, Canada and Europe offering tax credits and rebates for companies producing video games. Tax credit financings tend to take the form of incentives and rebates that can lower the payroll tax costs

---

[12] 15 U.S.C. § 45.

[13] It should go without saying that counsel for a game developer or publisher should make it clear to the client that engaging in a user-assisted funding strategy is making a commitment to the purchasing public, and that commitment should be taken seriously. Negative changes to promised rewards should only be made in extreme circumstances, and therefore all funding rewards should be carefully planned. Of course, positive changes of the "I got what I expected and more" variety are always acceptable.

of the company and allow for credits to be earned based upon certain types of spending in the jurisdiction offering these benefits. These incentives and rebates may be transferrable, meaning they can be sold to an unrelated party to lower that party's tax burden, enabling the company to use the cash generated by the sale of the credit(s) to fund game development, or they can be non-transferrable and be used to lower the tax burden of the entity (which may include the developer or publisher) claiming the credit.

Of course, tax credits may not be a great solution for all projects, and care should be taken to match a possible incentive arrangement to the needs of the project. Typically there are limits on the size of the projects that can be funded, with some incentives being designed for games with huge teams and long development times, and others designed to support much smaller projects. In addition, there are complications and considerations when it comes to tax credit financings. For example, most payroll tax credits and rebates apply more generously to wages paid to residents as opposed to non-residents (and sometimes may not apply at all). There may also be restrictions on what production expenses can qualify for a rebate, and requirements to buy goods or services locally or risk losing out on the incentive. This can become a problem if the goods or services you need are not available locally, or are not of sufficient quality compared to what can be found elsewhere. Relatedly, one must also consider whether the available talent pool in the area covered by the credit will allow for successful completion of the project. The most generous incentive arrangement in the world is meaningless if you can't get your game built.

11.4. GETTING A GAME FROM CONCEPT TO THE CONSUMER

Now that you understand the landscape of the industry, its major figures, and its financing and business models, it's time to turn your game from a concept to a reality. To do this, we'll explore the process from the point of view of a game developer seeking publisher financing for a creation of a new IP, since trying to approach this from all sides would be a book unto itself. That said, we'll begin with a developer's "concepting work" at the inception of this process, and end with live game production operations. Other points of view, such as that of the publisher, licensor, or vendor, will be mentioned when illustrative of a point not yet made.

11.4.1. Concepting and Pitch Decks

All games start as an idea in the minds' of the developers. To convey that idea, however, means creating something that can be shared with others – a pitch deck. A pitch deck highlights several aspects of the game – background on the developer, the general narrative and fictional world being built, the pillars of design, the space the game will occupy in the market, the gameplay loop, and the budget. This gives the people receiving the pitch the necessary information to evaluate the opportunity at a very high level of abstraction. Developers should not expect deals to be made on pitch decks alone, as any financier (be it a publisher, equity investor or the general public) will want to know more than what is contained in the 10 or 20 pages of the deck. But it is a place to start.

When putting together pitch decks, developers should strike a balance between giving enough information for the recipient to understand the vision for the game, but not so much that the pitch becomes cumbersome or unintelligible. Opinions vary as to what is the most important part of the pitch, but many would agree that a developer should place emphasis on explaining the world narrative, design pillars, the gameplay loop, the space the game will occupy in the market, and budget.

11.4.1.1. World Narrative

The world narrative is the place where the developer gives potential financiers a vision of what the game will be. High level concepts such as player perspective, game genre, and time period should be identified, and the developer should link those choices to their design and implementation strategy. For example, if the game is set in a historical time period, how does that advance the story being told? Design choices should be made with an eye towards world coherence, and good pitches show how each choice supports, and in turn is supported by, all the other choices.

For example, a typical world narrative overview for a zombie survival roleplaying game would look something like this:

The world changed when the virus struck, and most of humanity was turned into bloodthirsty zombies. The remaining humans have banded together in colonies of relative safety –

islands, mountaintop retreats, etc. Players will start as a human survivor in one of these colonies with no skills and no money, but will quickly embark on an adventure that will lead either to the survival of humanity, or its destruction.

11.4.1.2. Design Pillars

This section of the pitch is where the developer sets forth what makes this game different from other, seemingly similar, games. Will the developer focus on player movement in three dimensions, deep character progression, constant action from start to finish, rewarding strategic play over "button mashing," and so on. There are no set number or types of design pillars, and the developer is only limited by its creativity in this area. However, these form the core of what will make the game fun and unique, and so significant attention should be paid to these in terms of building and delivering the pitch. Typically developers will focus on three or four pillars, as trying to claim every aspect of a game's development is a design pillar will be seen as naïve or disingenuous.

11.4.1.3. Gameplay Loop

The gameplay loop is an overview of the experience a player will have, and what mechanisms will encourage the player to keep playing the game after the first 10 minutes. Details about what will drive player engagement, what type of progression the player will undergo as the storyline or gameplay experience evolves, and ultimately what will drive users to return to the game, should be explained. That is, attention should be paid to two levels: how does the individual gameplay progress (matches, levels, stages, etc.) and how does the game encourage future investment of time outside of a particular match or level (this is sometimes referred to as the "meta game").

For example, the gameplay loop of a MOBA (multiplayer online battle arena) looks something like this: each match begins with two teams of five players. Every player starts at level one, with no items or skills. As the match progresses, players are able to learn new skills and purchase items to make their character stronger. At the end of the match, the winners receive more experience than the losers, and therefore rank up faster in terms of overall account level. When a new match begins, all players start the game with a level one character, even if their account level is higher. As account levels progress, players are given the opportunity to acquire with new characters, new cosmetic items, etc., and ultimately compete in a ranked ladder.

11.4.1.4. Market Analysis

This part of the pitch should be fairly self-explanatory, but financiers will want to understand what opportunity the proposed game is going after: who are the primary and secondary competitors, is this a particular market that is over- or under-saturated, and what will set the proposed game apart from the competition. Drawing parallels to past games can be useful as points of comparison for key performance indicators such as units sold through, daily and monthly active users, pay rate (if the game includes in-game monetization) and so on.

11.4.1.5. Budget

Finally, budgets form an integral part of any pitch. The proposed budgets should examine costs from several different perspectives – overall budget, monthly burn and man/month rates, and budgets for each major stage of development (prototype, alpha, closed beta, open beta, commercial launch, etc.). Budgets should also include any proposed outsourcing and necessary middleware such as game engines, database administration, etc.

Often developers can feel pressure to understate the budgetary needs for the game out of a fear that if they ask for too much, they won't get funded. This does all parties a disservice, however, because asking for more money during later development almost always results in developers giving up more than what might have been necessary had budgets been more accurately projected and conveyed at the onset. Budgets should always present an accurate picture of what the developer needs, and should highlight any areas where the numbers may vary and what those contingencies may be. In general, it is generally wise to avoid "avoidable" surprises.

11.4.1.6. Other Materials

In addition to the deck itself, a developer may create and share concept art, some preliminary technical design documents, or perhaps even a prototype for the game (as is often the case for mobile games, where the cost to develop a prototype is generally cheaper than for PC or console games). Whether such documents are included in a pitch or not depends on many factors, including the past projects the developer has completed (the more games the developer has shipped, the less the publisher will need to see up front in order to make a decision), whether the developer plans to do something radically different (*i.e.*, switching from PC development to mobile), and so on.

11.4.2. Pitching Financiers

Once the pitch materials have been put together, it is time to share it with potential financiers. This means telling others your idea, which is the core of what you hope to create (and ultimately sell). As such, you risk giving someone else the opportunity to copy your idea. But as any intellectual property lawyer will tell you, ideas are tricky things to protect. You can protect the expression of an idea (via copyright) or a useful invention of a process, machine, or article of manufacture (via patent), but ideas *qua* ideas fall somewhere in between these areas of legal protection, and so must find legal protection elsewhere.

When pitching publishers or investors, it is always advisable to execute non-disclosure agreements ("NDAs") with the recipients of the pitch. A properly drafted NDA can protect (or at least go a long way toward protecting) your idea, or at least ensure that you get paid if the recipient decides to execute on a substantially similar game concept in the future. Yet while many NDA provisions are standardized, and can be found with ease online, there are a few aspects of NDAs that are often overlooked.

A developer may want to include a provision that sets forth the expectation that if the publisher or investor executes on a substantially similar concept within some defined time frame in the future, the developer will receive some minimum defined compensation. This explicit acknowledge of expectation is be necessary to recover in a breach of implied contract suit (a suit that can allow for recovery where a copyright lawsuit would fail). This is a development of somewhat recent vintage that has found traction in the television and movie industries. However, this is not often seen in video game industry NDAs, and most publishers will be loath to accept such a provision. Several reasons for this exist, but the primary reason is that many pitches, especially at the early concept stage, look and sound alike. A publisher may get dozens of pitches that all describe the same basic idea – a first person shooter game set in a historical time period, a multiplayer dungeon crawler, etc. Any publisher worthy of the name would recognize such a provision and reject it out of hand, if for no other reason than to protect itself against unnecessary future legal liability. Therefore, practitioners in this space should be aware that, while many concepts can be borrowed from other entertainment media, not everything translates well when it comes to video games.

11.4.3. Negotiating the Publishing Deal

The next step in the process, assuming the pitch goes well, is to agree to terms with a publisher (unless self-funding, crowdfunding or other strategy is being pursued, of course). Usually this is done through the exchange of term sheets that are used as the basis for long form contracts. The term sheet won't cover all aspects of the game deal, but it will contain the most salient details – funding, development and operational responsibilities, rights and ownership, and termination.[14] The long form agreements, however, are where things start to come into focus.

11.4.3.1. Important Definitions

Just about every contract has some form of definitions section, and it would be a waste of ink to delve into detail for every defined term commonly used in a publishing agreement. However, there are several important definitions that are unique to the video games and interactive media industry that attorneys and executives should know when discussing deals of this type.

---

[14] A sample traditional publishing agreement term sheet is included in the forms accompanying this volume.

a. Gross and Net Revenue

While many definitions in a publishing agreement are important, perhaps none is as important as the definitions of gross and net revenue, because these definitions deal directly with how much money the developer will receive from the publisher and, if applicable, how much money the publisher can withhold as part of a recoupment of project financing arrangement.

Defining gross revenue tends to revolve around whether to include or exclude the costs of digital or retail distribution (as applicable). If these items are not excluded from gross, then they are excluded from net.

Net revenue, on the other hand, is where things can get complicated. There are any number of carve outs, exclusions and deductions that can be negotiated into a publishing agreement to define net revenue. At a minimum, net revenue will exclude, in the case of digital distribution, platform fees, payment gateway fees (fees incurred in processing financial transactions), taxes and returns. In retail distribution, net revenue will typically exclude cost of goods sold ("COGS"), discounts, damaged goods, advertising expenses including "co-op," rebates, refunds, credits, returns, price protection, service provider costs, shipping and taxes.

b. Developer Proprietary Technology

Generally speaking, publishing contracts contain some form of exclusivity. This may be on the game, the efforts of the developer, or some combination thereof. Yet games are rarely built entirely from the ground up; they are works that build upon efforts done previously by the developer or third parties. This can include software tools and technology, modules, libraries, engines, and other items that can be applied to many different video games, either now or in the future. As such, these items are typically excluded from the exclusivity, but negotiations may ensue over how to treat improvements to those items, as it may be that the improvements made to those tools and technologies were the result of the publisher's funding, the needs of the game being built, and so on.

c. Platform

As discussed earlier in this chapter, platforms are the system on which a game runs. A game that is made for one platform will not operate on another without substantial and generally costly reprogramming ("porting"). As such, the definition of platform provides an important limitation on a publisher's rights in a game – a publisher that has rights to all platforms has a significantly better deal than a publisher that has rights to only one platform.

Making this more complex is the fact that platforms continually evolve. A typical platform definition from twenty years ago might have said something like "Platform: Sony PlayStation." However, in the last two decades or so Sony has developed several new platforms – the PlayStation 2, PlayStation 3, PlayStation 4 and PlayStation 4 Pro – which may be excluded from the publishing deal based upon the definition of platform that is limited to just the "Sony PlayStation." Thus, executives negotiating in this area should be aware not only of existing platforms and technologies, but those that are likely to come out during the course of the publishing deal. In other words, one must consider whether and how to "future proof" the deal from a platform perspective.

d. Publisher Materials

Related to the concept of developer proprietary technology is that of publisher materials. These are items that the publisher provides to the developer so that the developer does not need to build them itself (e.g., matchmaking systems, friend systems, chat systems, etc.) or items that the publisher creates in the course of its provision of publishing services (typically, marketing materials). A well-written publishing agreement will clearly set out what is included in this defined term so that there is no confusion over who owns what, and what items are subject to the rights conveyed in the publishing deal.

e. Term

Term is the length of the publisher's rights in the game. Typically the term of a publishing deal for a premium priced game or subscription game starts at the initiation of development will run for several years following commercial launch of the game. For PC and console games, typical terms are between three and five years, with extensions available based upon some threshold (gross revenue, net revenue, and monthly and daily active users are typical thresholds for extensions). Mobile games tend to run on shorter product life cycles, so terms can be as short as two or three years post-commercialization.

Many free to play games borrow the concept of commercial launch from the premium and subscription models, but this is somewhat inaccurate as a free to play game rarely hits the point where it is "feature complete." Instead, the game is released with a limited amount of content, and new content is continually developed for the game in the hopes that it will drive purchases by the end user. Thus, deals that are tailored to free to play games tend to use terms like "worldwide launch," or "initial commercialization," instead of "commercial launch."

In addition, care should be taken if the developer or publisher wishes to explore a means of end user funding. For games that are crowdfunded or will be released via early access, the "commercialization" of the game will begin long before development is completed. As such, use of the phrase "commercial launch" may result in unintended consequences, such as the publishing term being dramatically shorter than the parties intend at the outset.

f. Territory

Territory is the geographic area in which the publisher may commercially exploit the game. Some deals are global, some are region-specific (e.g., North America, North America and Europe, etc.) and some carve out certain territories. China, Russia and Latin America are typical carve outs from non-global deals.

In retail distribution scenarios territory is more of a financial than operational concern as publishers simply refrain from distributing physical copies of the game outside of their permitted territory.[15] In digital distribution deals, however, geographic borders are a bit harder to enforce, and so the publisher must provide additional protections to ensure it complies with the terms of the deal. As these additional protections cost the publisher money, it is important to define territory early on in the negotiation process.

---

[15] Of course, grey and black market copies do leak outside of permitted territories, and retail publishers take steps to prohibit this.

11.4.3.2. Funding

Regardless of the form in which the publisher provides financing, both parties will want to know the minimum and the maximum amount of money the publisher will commit, and how and when that money will be committed and then paid. The most common ways that publishers provide money to developers is in the form of project finance funds (either recoupable or non-recoupable) and license fees and minimum guarantees. Regardless of the type of funding agreement that is pursued, all agreements should deal with the question of whether the funds advanced by the publisher are recoupable or non-recoupable, and if so, how.

a. Project Finance Funds

Project financing funds can take multiple forms, and the range of available project financing arrangements is limited only by the imagination of the parties and the realities of the given project's development. Typically, however, project financing funds are advanced on a milestone-approval basis. Also, project financing funds can be scheduled to be available both before and after principal development has been completed. Making such funds available post-commercial launch can be especially important in live service games that need regular releases of new content but where developers may not yet be receiving a royalty.

When crafting milestone payment plans, particular attention should be paid to the cash flow of the developer as failure to do this can lead to situations where a publisher needs to make a payment off-cycle (without approving a milestone) or even to giving more money to the developer than originally agreed just to protect the investment of the publisher. In addition, the contract should contemplate what happens if a publisher rejects a milestone. While the operational aspects of a milestone rejection are discussed later in this section, the publisher (and developer) must always keep in mind that if delay in fulfilling a milestone and securing associated payment threatens the developer's ability to remain in business, the entire investment by the publisher may consequently be at risk.

b. License Fees and Minimum Guarantees

License fees and minimum guarantees are usually reserved for deals where the development of the game is substantially complete by the time the publisher gets involved. As such, the publisher will typically make larger lump sum payments for license fees and minimum guarantees on projects in advanced stages of production than in a project finance deal, and will generally have fewer milestones to review and approve. Payments of license fees and minimum guarantees are also typically made on a time-dependent basis instead of an approval basis. That is, payments are made at regularly scheduled intervals (e.g., upon execution, commercial launch, and specific anniversaries of commercial launch) instead of requiring approval of a milestone submission first.

License fees and minimum guarantees are closely related concepts, and the terms are sometimes even used interchangeably (though this can lead to unnecessary confusion). Most commonly, license fees refer to non-recoupable funds paid to the developer for the publisher's rights to the game, while minimum guarantees refer to funds that are advanced to the developer but are recoupable against the royalty otherwise earned by the developer.

c. Recoupable versus Non-Recoupable Funds

One thing that all forms of publisher funding arrangements have in common is that they must deal with the question of whether the funds advanced by the publisher are recoupable or not recoupable, and if they are recoupable, what they recoup against. In a situation where the publisher is fully funding the creation of a game that the developer will own, the publisher will often recoup all funds advanced during development out of the developer's royalty stream. The recoupment can be accomplished in a variety of ways – the publisher may withhold a portion of the developer's royalty, the publisher may keep a certain portion of all revenues until full recoupment, or the publisher may require set monthly payments by the developer to the publisher once some negotiated milestone in the release of the game occurs (making the advanced funds somewhat similar to a mortgage).

However the recoupment is structured, care must be taken to ensure that the developer has enough money to make the payment and still continue operations. In a traditional "box product" deal where the end user makes a single purchase and gets all of the content that will ever be developed for the game "in the box," there can be a bit more flexibility in terms of recoupment as the developer might have moved on to other projects after release of the game. In a live service operation, however, ensuring that a recoupment arrangement does not strangle the developer's cash flow is critical to the financial success of the game, as the developer must be able to continue to develop content well after the initial commercial release of the game.

11.4.3.3. License Grants

License grants form the core of a publishing arrangement. In a traditional publishing deal, the publisher will take certain rights in and to the game in exchange for providing certain services and funding. In a work-for-hire deal, there can be developer's tools and technologies that are incorporated into the game that must be licensed. In a licensed product deal, the publisher may have multiple sets of licensing agreements with a number of parties. Thus, license terms will be important regardless of the type of deal being pursued. However, as this section is focused on the traditional publishing agreement, license terms for work-for-hire deals and licensed IP deals will not be covered.

In a traditional publishing deal, publishers will want to know exactly what rights they have in and to the game, and which of those rights are exclusive. Typically, publishers will take rights to publish, operate and commercially exploit the game and the right to market the game (though co-marketing arrangements with the publisher and developer can sometimes be useful). In addition, a publishing agreement will specify which of these rights are exclusive to the publisher, and which are not exclusive. Finally, publishers will ask for a variety of representations and warranties with regard to the game in order to protect itself against lawsuits that arise as a result of the game being published. And of course, all of this must be drafted in connection with the ownership of the game and anything created pursuant to the game.

a. Right to Operate and Commercially Exploit the Game

What constitutes operating the game is fairly clear, and generally requires little contractual definition. However, what constitutes commercially exploiting the game can be a bit more vague, and so efforts should to taken to ensure that the parties understand the breadth of the publisher's ability to commercialize the game. Common commercial-ization rights include the right to sublicense the game to sub-licensees or distributors other than the publisher,[16] to partner with third parties to exercise certain privileges related to the game such as the collection of payments,[17] and to make, sell and distribute items that are attendant to the game (*e.g.*, collector's editions of the game that include items such as collectibles, packaged in-game items, books, etc.).

Another issue that should be considered when crafting rights-related language for commercialization is how much discretion the publisher has in modifying the game's content for territories outside of the original release area. If a game is being developed with North America as the primary market, then certain design decisions will be made as a result – the game's text and spoken dialogue, if any, will be in English (for the United States and Canada, at least), and the cultural mores of that territory will be reflected in the art, character style, narrative, etc., to name but a few.[18] A publisher may want the right to modify the game's content to make the game more appealing to users in particular territories who may want a different art style, character design, etc. Whether and to what extent the right to do this falls into

---

[16] When dealing with sublicensing rights, thought must be given to how that right impacts the development plan and the term of the agreement. If the development plan calls for a launch on certain territories after primary commercial launch (as is common when launching in some Asian and European territories), the right to sublicense operations to third parties in those territories may be rendered less commercially viable if the sub-licensee's term is governed by the primary publishing agreement's term. The reason for this is that the sub-licensee will have less time to commercialize the game. As such, provisions should be considered to allow for extensions of sub-licensee terms even if the primary publishing agreement ends if the development plan calls for such a carve out.

[17] Granting a third party the exclusive right to collect payments from end users, known as "factoring," can be a useful technique for improving the speed with which the parties receive money. This is most useful for developer-distributed games and mobile games where payment cycles can be up to 60 days or longer from the date of purchase.

[18] One example of this is the well-known (though somewhat misunderstood) "rule" about showing skeletons in video games in China. The law upon which this rule is based does not prohibit the showing of skeletons in games, and in fact several Chinese-made games show skeletons. However, China has a law that prohibits the showing or distribution of content that could be seen as undermining China's law against the promotion of religion, cults or superstitions. In interpreting this law, many western game publishers and developers have chosen to remove skeletons from their games so as to steer clear of any potential issues with compliance of this law.

the right to "operate" the game in such territories is subject to negotiation between the parties.

Finally, operating and commercialization rights provisions for games that will be operated as a live service should include specific reference to management of in-game content (item availability, item pricing, in-game events, time-limited content, etc.). The publisher will want the ability to dynamically manage such aspects of the game in order to respond to changing conditions within the game environment (perhaps to balance the in-game economy, to engage the community in new and compelling ways, and so on). The reason that this right should be called out separately is because it occupies a space somewhere between pure distribution of the game and modification of the game, but it is vitally important to the success of a live service operation game that the publisher has this right. Therefore, practitioners would be well-advised to make this a separate grant of rights for games to which this would be applicable.

b. Right to Market the Game

Rights to market the game are generally separated from the rights to operate and commercialize the game, even though these two rights are inextricably intertwined. The reason for the separation is that developers have come to want more insight and control over how a game is marketed, especially in situations where the developer will own the IP. After all, it is only natural that the owner of an IP will want to control how that IP is used, and prohibit uses that do not meet with the owner's brand image. At the same time, however, publishers want to maintain as much authority over marketing decisions as possible because having to get approval from the developer for each marketing execution can be unwieldy, and can result in efficient marketing efforts as a result of time delays leading to missed opportunities or increased costs.

The most typical compromise in this situation is to have the publisher and developer decide upon a "brand book" – a set of guidelines governing how the game will be positioned in the market, and what kinds of marketing efforts are allowable – and then agree upon a regular schedule of marketing meetings where high level strategy is agreed upon between the parties. Then, based upon the brand book and the agreed upon strategy, the publisher has the authority to execute upon campaigns and executions that meets these governing conditions. This provides for flexibility and some (limited) authority on the part of the publisher while still giving the developer some measure of protection.

Another reason that the rights to market the game are set out separately from the rights to operate and publish the game is that the developer will often ask the publisher to commit to a certain amount of minimum marketing spend in the months leading up to and following commercial launch of the game.[19] If a minimum marketing guarantee is being contemplated, both sides should agree not only on the total amount of money to be spent, but also what can be included in that spend. For example, the publisher may want to include overhead costs or internally incurred costs under the marketing spend guarantee, while the developer may want to exclude these costs (depending on the capabilities of the publisher's internal marketing team). In addition, the parties may want to earmark certain amounts of that guarantee for specific marketing functions like computer generated imagery trailers, television advertising, celebrity endorsements, user acquisition, and so on.

c. Exclusive versus Non-Exclusive Rights

The most contentious of all negotiations over rights is which rights are exclusive and which are non-exclusive. While some, like the right to publish, distribute and operate the game, are usually exclusive (at least within the territory, during the term, and for the platform), other rights such as the right to market the game and the right to utilize developer tools and technologies can be either exclusive or non-exclusive, depending on the development plan and the relative bargaining power of the parties. At the same time, some rights, such as the use rights and licenses granted to the developer's tools and technologies as well as the right to utilize the developer's trademarks, are usually granted on a non-exclusive basis.

---

[19] Minimum marketing guarantees are more important in premium purchase sales strategies than in free to play sales strategies, though they have their place in both types of agreements. The reason is that free to play games generally have a longer ramp up to peak monetization, while premium priced games make most of their sales in the first three to six months following launch. This becomes doubly important in the context of a retail-distributed premium purchase product, as after the first several months on the shelves the price of the game can drop or the units can be returned to the publisher altogether.

11.4.3.4. Representations and Warranties

Any deal in which rights are being licensed from one party to another will include some number of representations and warranties, and by and large these are both familiar and templatized (such as the representation of being a valid entity capable of entering into the agreement). There are, however, a few games industry-specific representations and warranties that should be included in a publishing agreement. Most of these specific representations and warranties are for the benefit of the publisher, but some are mutual representations that benefit both parties.

a. Integration of Third Party Software, Tools and Technologies

This representation speaks both to the cost of obtaining such third party software (usually the cost is born entirely by the entity seeking to include it in the game) and to the legality of its inclusion and use in the game (from operational and intellectual property perspectives). Also, this representation is often mutual, especially in situations where the publisher is providing any form of distribution technology (i.e., a download portal), payment technology (i.e., a payment processing gateway) or anti-hack/anti-cheat technology (i.e., technology meant to prohibit unpermitted uses of the game).

b. Material Compliance with Agreed Upon Specifications

This warranty requires the developer to build the game in such a way as to meet the agreed upon specifications, at least to a material degree. This representation can be thoroughly negotiated, however, as the developer does not want to find itself in breach of this warranty in the case of minor bugs or other readily correctible errors. Nonetheless, publishers generally believe this is an important protection for their interests in a publishing agreement and will regularly seek to keep it a part of the deal.

c. Open Source Software

This warranty has become more and more important as a plethora of open source software, tools, libraries and other game elements has become widely available. "Open source" software refers to software that is distributed freely in a manner that allows modification of the source code. This can allow for customization of software to meet specific needs without having to build the entire program, tool or library from scratch, thus saving both time (for the developer) and money (for the publisher). However, open source software is also typically subject to some form of license that requires certain actions be taken if that software is used in a new work. This action may be benign (e.g., putting an attribution line in the game credits or placing a logo in the pre-roll loading screen), but others can be highly detrimental to the publishing function of the game (e.g., requiring distribution of the entire game's underlying source code for free).

The warranty on inclusion of open source software tends to strike a balance between the desire to save time and money and the desire to protect the game's future economic prospects. As such, this is often resolved by allowing open source software inclusion in the game, but only with the publisher's express consent (and generally after the publisher's legal team has had an opportunity to review the software and its underlying license to avoid future complications).

d. Viruses, Trojan Horses, and Similar Malicious Code

Many developers who see this warranty for the first time have a negative "knee jerk" reaction – "of course we would not build viruses into our games." However, the concern from which this warranty comes is broader than simple and potentially inadvertent virus inclusion; it speaks to the inclusion of code that could install executable files to copy information or otherwise manipulate an end user's computer, allowing for sharing of otherwise private things like Internet connections, personal information, websites visited, etc. This all comes from the growing importance of privacy in the digital era, and it is for this reason publishers want the warranty.

e. Easter Eggs

"Easter eggs" is a video game term for content that is included in a game but that is not readily apparent to the end user. Generally the player must take some form of specific action in order to unlock this content. In the game *Adventure*, for example, the player has to find a key that is no larger than a single pixel in one specific location in the game, take the key to another area of the game without dying, etc. in order to reach a hidden room. This is a great example of an Easter egg that caused little harm (at least to the game and its publisher), but not all examples are so benign.

In 2005, a highly controversial Easter egg was found in the game *Grand Theft Auto San Andreas*. This Easter egg allowed the player to engage in simulated sex, controlling the movements of the main character and his chosen girlfriend. Although the feature – known as "hot coffee" – was disabled for the game's release, the assets remained with various versions of the game and players were able to unlock those assets through direct manipulation of the game code. In July 2005, the "hot coffee" incident began to attract the attention of lawmakers across the globe and eventually resulted in copies of the game being removed from sale until a patch was released.

The warranty over Easter eggs stems from the desire to avoid a "hot coffee" issue in the future. Yet at the same time, publishers recognize the value in including Easter eggs as a means of rewarding diligent players. Therefore, much like the warranty on open source software, a balance is sometimes struck allowing inclusion of Easter eggs with the publisher's express consent.

11.4.3.5. Ownership

Ownership clauses in a publishing contract were once incredibly easy to negotiate (because the publisher owned everything). Today, however, ownership is infinitely more complex as there are a myriad of ways that ownership can be parsed out. The "game" may comprise of several different, distinguishable parts, each of which may be owned by the developer, the publisher or even both simultaneously. Thus, knowing how to structure ownership clauses can be one of the more interesting challenges in finalizing a publishing agreement.

a. The Game

Some elements of game ownership are inherent in the deal structure, and so there is no reason to negotiate them. For example, in a work-for-hire agreement, the publisher will own all IP created for the game – that's the nature of the deal, and the ownership clauses are simple and straightforward. Other deal structures, however, can lead to more complicated ownership provisions. Recently games are being funded by publishers who hold no ownership interest in the underlying IP; instead, publishers rely on robust publishing and commercialization rights to protect their investment. The theory behind this shift in ownership preferences is that third party development deals will result in better overall game quality if the developer is building a game that it will own, rather than simply have a royalty interest in future proceeds. Whether that theory is an accurate reflection of reality or not, however, remains to be seen.

When structuring ownership clauses for the game and its underlying IP, drafters should understand what each party to the deal hopes to accomplish, the relative bargaining power of the parties, and whether (and how) ownership moves the parties closer to accomplishing their respective goals.

b. Marketing Materials

Even in deals where a developer will own the IP of the game, ownership of certain game-related aspects such as marketing materials may be allocated to the publisher. The reason for this is that the publisher will create (or have created) those marketing materials, often taking the creative lead in doing so (e.g., creating the campaigns for which the materials are created, shaping the marketing narrative to appeal to specific user groups, etc.). In addition, the publisher will often pay for these costs out of its own pocket, at a cost to it which can be significant. For example, computer generated imagery trailers for a game can cost upwards of $500,000 or more, depending on the length, the scenes being shown, voiceover talent, etc. As such, the publisher may take the position that it should own the marketing materials even when the developer owns the underlying IP.

Resolving this can depend on a variety of factors such as length of deal, funds advanced by the publisher, and royalty shares, but most commonly the resolution achieved is one of the "mutually assured destruction" type – the publisher owns the marketing materials, while the developer owns the underlying IP. This means that neither party can use the materials after the publishing deal ends, but neither party gets a windfall either. This can be coupled with the right of the developer to buy back the materials at the publisher's cost (or some factor thereof), though many parties will find that at the end of a four or five-year publishing deal, old marketing materials no longer have much use and that the creation of new materials would be a better investment of time and resources. Therefore, the "mutually assured destruction" compromise tends to be the most common one seen in traditional publishing deals.

c. Billing and User Databases

Negotiating ownership of billing and user databases can be as contentious as the disposition of marketing materials, yet harder to resolve through compromise because they are, essentially, large compilations of data. This data, however, is critical to operating the game because it often includes usernames, passwords, real names, account information, contact information, and billing information. Without this, games – especially live service games – cannot operate, and rebuilding these databases from scratch means players losing what they've already accumulated in the game.

Thus, the desire for a developer to own the user and billing databases is clear. At the same time, however, the publisher will want to own these databases because it is the publisher who will expend time, money and resources in building those databases – acquiring players, maintaining that information, etc. As a part of this, publishers will tap into their existing player databases to bring people into the game quickly and efficiently. This means that information in the databases may span several games developed by different entities, making developer ownership of these databases impractical. Ultimately, this provision is generally resolved based upon the bargaining power of the parties and the relationship the parties want to have going forward.

d. Development and Operational Responsibilities

The next major section of a publishing deal is the breakdown of development and operational responsibilities, both on the developer side and on the publisher side.

1. **Developer Responsibilities.** While it is simple to say that developers make the game, the implications of that statement are widespread and should be carefully constructed in a publishing deal in order to avoid future issues between the developer and the publisher. The publisher will want to ensure that development goes according to plan, and the developer will want to maximize its freedom and flexibility throughout development. Thus, the key items to deal with in a developer's responsibilities section are creative control, sublicensing of development, key personnel, bug correction and ongoing content obligations.

2. **Creative Control.** Developers that will own the IP after the game is built will almost always demand final creative control over the game. This is only natural, as it will be their property upon completion, but that does not mean the publisher is willing to give up all influence over the narrative, story arc, character development, and so on. Publishers will generally allow for final creative control over many aspects of the game – mostly those that are storytelling in nature – but maintain rights to final approval over technical and functional aspects.

In addition, publishers will restrict the creative flexibility of the developers to comply with the agreed upon game specifications. This is where dealmakers need to rely on operations and development people to ensure that the specifications which get agreed upon in the deal negotiation stage speak to the publisher's concerns and provide enough coverage should the publisher (or the developer, over the publisher's possible objection) want to modify some aspects of the game's creative elements.

3. **Outsourcing and Sublicensing Development.** One way developers save time (and in some cases, money) is by outsourcing parts of the development of the game, if not the entire development. However, this can be troublesome for the publisher as it is not in direct contractual relationship with the third party sub-developer, and may have little insight into how that company functions, whether that company meets the requirements of the publisher, and how money is being spent.

Yet deals that ignore the ability to outsource development activities may result in development that is more costly in both time and money than it otherwise could have been. Thus, publishers will generally accept a developer's ability to outsource or sublicense development obligations provided that the publisher gives its prior consent and the developer remains entirely responsible for ensuring that submissions of content meet the agreed upon specifications for that milestone. Some publishers will go further and mandate that the publisher pay the outsourced firm directly, that the outsourced firm deliver materials directly to the publisher, and that the outsourced firm have regular meetings with the publisher to update the publisher on progress. These can be useful tools for situations where the publisher sees risk in a particular outsourced scenario, but may lead a potential outsourcing partner to shy away from a deal.

4. **Key Personnel.** Key personnel are staff that are integral to the vision, direction and development of the game. These are usually limited to high profile executives, particularly if part of the game pitch was made using that executive's "star" profile or significant experience. In such situations the publisher will want to protect itself should those key personnel leave or work on other projects, as this could significant alter the game's development. Thus, key personnel clauses should consider two separate scenarios: if a named person leaves the company, and if a named person begins work on a different project. In either scenario, both the publisher and developer should be clear on what will happen and what resolution can be expected. A poorly drafted key personnel clause may result in unintended consequences such as a developer being in breach of a contract because of a death or disability of a named person.

5. **Bug Correction.** Correcting bugs – errors in a game's program – is uncontroversial during principal development of a game, but correcting bugs after a game's initial release can be more difficult to resolve. A publisher will want the developer to always be responsible for bug correction, and will not want to pay the developer a "fix fee" to make the game operate as intended. On the other hand, a developer will need to spend money and resources it may not have (or want to commit) to fix the bug, especially if the bug arises from updates to computer operating systems, security patches, or other actions not in the direct control of the developer (e.g., middleware issues).

To solve this issue, publishers and developers will usually agree that the developer is responsible for fixing bugs throughout the term, but the pace at which a bug must be fixed is dependent upon the severity of the bug. Often a schedule will be agreed to which details response times for various classes of bugs, with bugs that make the game unplayable being the most severe (and thus requiring the fastest response) and bugs that are only cosmetic in nature being relatively low priority (and may be fixed only when "commercially reasonable"). Again, this is an area where a practitioner in the video games space needs to have support from development personnel to accurately classify bugs and response times, or else the obligation to continually correct bugs can be rendered meaningless or can result in obligations the developer cannot meet.

6. **Ongoing Content Creation.** Ongoing content creation is a developer responsibility that has grown in relative importance as "games as a service" games have become more popular. These games require regular releases of new content to keep players engaged. In subscription models the funding for new content development is derived from the subscription payments. But in free-to-play or hybrid game models, the reliability of funding is less secure. At the same time, however, the need for regular releases of content after launch is one of the most important factors to the commercial success of those games. To that end, publishing agreements, especially for "games as a service" titles, must deal with the creation of content, enhancements, though perhaps minor, will be introduced much more frequently.

The time period during which this obligation extends can vary based upon the type of content being contemplated. For games that intend to release significant blocks of new content, there may be several dates targeted for those releases (e.g., every four months, twice a year, etc.). For games that rely on incremental content

e. Publisher Responsibilities

Publishers' responsibilities depend largely on the developer's needs, the type of game in development, the geographic market and the platform, but most often publishers will provide milestone review and approval, quality assurance ("QA") and submission certification ("cert") services, technical infrastructure and operation, marketing for the game, customer support and management of sub-licensees and distributors, among other services.

1. **Milestone Review and Approvals.** Games are not developed in a vacuum; savvy developers will take input from many different places during a game's development in order to make sure the product is meeting the expectations of the end user. Similarly, publishers that are financing games will want to make sure that their money is being well spent. Thus, publishers and developers will agree to some form of review and approval right for milestones during a game's principal development and throughout live operations for certain types of games. The extent of that approval right, however, will depend on the underlying economics of the game's development.

In situations where publishers are financing the game, the publisher's approval right will be quite strong, though as discussed above, a balance will be struck as to the publisher's approval rights and the developer's creative control. Once that balance is determined, approval rights sections should clearly set forth the process by which the approvals happen – time taken to review, actions taken by both parties upon approval, and actions taken by both parties upon non-approval. This last part – non-approval – is perhaps the most important of the process elements that should be included in an approvals clause because non-approval can create a domino effect of consequences. Thought should be given to who bears financial responsibility in the case of individual non-approvals, how a non-approval impacts the development timeline, and at what point repeated non-approvals constitute a breach of the contract.

2. Quality Assurance and Certification. Related to, but distinct from, the milestone approval right is the performance of quality assurance ("QA") testing. This is both a right and an obligation of the publisher as it is how the publisher can confirm that the game meets the agreed-upon specifications as well as the requirements of the various platforms. As such, the publisher will perform QA testing, then submit it to the first parties in the case of consoles,[20] to a digital distributor like Value's Steam service in the case of PC,[21] or to the

---

[20] Historically, to release a game on consoles, one had first to be accepted as a publisher by the first parties. While this is still true today, the process to become an accepted publisher has become much less difficult. Today, a developer can become a registered publisher with the console first parties and effectively self-publish their games on console if they so desire. However, doing so requires the ability to perform QA and manage the game's progression through the first parties' certification process (the process by which the console manufacturer confirms that the game meets its technical and content-based requirements). If a developer does not have the desire (or capability) to do this, it will ask the publisher to do so.

[21] Releasing a game for PC can be much more simple than releasing on console because there are no first party hardware manufactures that must approve the release. Furthermore, publishing is made easier by application programming interfaces (APIs) like Valve's Steamworks, available for free, which gives statistics, piracy protection

mobile marketplaces,[22] each of which may engage in their own QA process as well.

In addition to platform certification, publishers also generally handle ratings or classifications for games. Ratings or classifications indicate the suitability of the game for particular age groups, and give purchasers of games insight into the game's content and whether that content is suitable for players of a certain age.[23] In the United States and Canada, the ratings are handled by a body called the Entertainment Software Ratings Board, or ESRB.[24] In Europe, many countries have adopted the Pan European Game Information system, known as PEGI.[25]

While not all games require a rating or classification, many (if not most) will. The rules on what games require ratings or classifications vary greatly by jurisdiction, and care should be taken to comply with all of the varying requirements as failure to do so may result in a direction to remove the game from the market in the complaining jurisdiction.[26] Failure to obtain a rating when and where required may result in the game being banned from sale to the public.[27] Additionally, a game that is changed after a rating has been issued may require re-certification, depending on the nature and scope of the changes.

---

and community options not readily available otherwise. Publishers will still play a major role in QA testing, but overall the process to get access to digital distributors such as Steam is much less rigorous than the process for console.

[22] The QA process for mobile game publishing is much more like PC publishing than console publishing in terms of simplicity and cost. Moreover, the scope of a mobile game is typically much narrower than a PC or console game, making the QA process even easier.

[23] Typically, ratings include both a numerical age designation (e.g., PEGI 16, PEGI 18, Everyone 10+, etc.) and a brief description of the content (e.g., "Game contains bad language," "content is generally suitable for ages 13 and up," etc.).

[24] www.esrb.org

[25] www.pegi.info

[26] For example, the South Korean ratings board (GRB) may review game content based upon whether the game includes any anti-societal or anti-governmental messages. Similarly, the Entertainment Software Rating Association in the Islamic Republic of Iran is responsible for classifying games according to (among other things) the existence of 'religious values violation' or 'social norms violation'.

[27] This happened to a game called *Saint's Row IV* in Australia, where the country's Classification Board refused to give it a classification because of its content. This prohibited the game from being distributed in that country. The developer cut certain content from the Australian version, and later received a MA15+ rating, which allowed it to be distributed in Australia (but prohibited the sale of the game to anyone under the age of 15). http://www.classification.gov.au/Public/Resources/Documents/2013%20media%20releases/media%20release%20Saints%20Row%204.pdf

3. Technical Infrastructure and Operation. Publishers will typically provide the technical infrastructure on which a game operates. This means operation and maintenance of the server system, peripheries and other network equipment necessary for the operation of the game, as well as the hosting and distribution of the game and all aspects related thereto. Thus, the publisher will control both the hardware on which a game operates as well as the user-facing elements such as websites, downloaders, etc.

In terms of impacting the publishing agreement, the provision of technical infrastructure has several ramifications. First, the publisher must be clear with the developer about how development needs to proceed in order to make the game work with the publisher's infrastructure. Second, developers will want to hold the publisher accountable for "uptime" and "downtime" – the availability of the game to end users – even if only to define when the publisher is in breach of the obligation to provide this service. Third, the publisher and developer should agree on a schedule, process and time requirement for regular maintenance of these systems. Finally, the publishing agreement should set forth who pays for these costs. In the case of PC and console deals, these costs are typically born by the publisher. In modern mobile publishing deals, however, this cost may be shared across both parties out of gross revenue.

Relatedly, publishers will also generally provide some form of security and fraud management for the game. This can include server and database hack monitoring and countering, fraud detection and management, and in-game hacking and macro monitoring and countering. How this gets done depends on the publisher. Some publishers will have proprietary solutions, others will utilize third party tools and technologies, and some will blend the two. Typically, these solutions are provided at the cost of the publisher, but alternative arrangements can be made.

4. Localizations. Localization refers to the process of tuning and modifying the game to appeal to the cultural and language sensibilities of particular regions. These changes and adaptations may be legally required, culturally beneficial, or commercially driven, depending on the nature of the change. As discussed above, however, the right of a publisher to make or have made localization changes may run counter to the developer's creative control. Moreover, provisions must deal with who pays for these costs, as localization changes are not free. There may be costs to make the changes, as well as costs to implement those changes into the game. This, in turn, may impact the development process by slowing things down, or making the developer assign personnel to make and implement the changes. As such, a publishing agreement should deal not only with the publisher's right to make or to have made localization changes, but also who pays for the cost of implementing them.

5. Websites and Social Media Channels. As discussed above, publishers will typically take the right to market the game (as they see fit, provided that it falls in line with the developer's overall vision for the game). In exchange for taking this right, the publisher generally pays for the marketing of the game out of its royalty share, and generally does not recoup it.[28] Included in this is the control and operation of the game's websites, social media channels and other points of contact with the end user.

Publishing agreements should contemplate not only the extent to which publishers control these channels, but also who pays for these channels during the term of the agreement, and who will own them afterwards. This should tie in to the ownership and IP provisions of the agreement so as not to cause confusion.

6. Customer Support. Customer support is the intake, processing and responding to inquiries and issues that end users have with the game. As such, it is a significant part of what a publisher provides to a game post-development, and it is common for developers to seek to include specific performance standards for the publisher's provision of customer support. For example, a developer may want to include minimum acceptable levels of average ticket queue times,

---

[28] Some recent publishing deals have been structured such that the publisher can recoup marketing expenses. This is most commonly seen in mobile game development deals because marketing, particularly paid-user acquisition costs, are directly proportionate to various success metrics like installs. Thus, in a mobile deal, the developer typically wants the publisher to spend significant amounts of money, even when such expenditures are not justified by the game's performance. The publisher, on the other hand, is incentivized to be conservative with mobile marketing spends. Thus, a new structure allowing for recoup of marketing funds has been used in recent years so that both developer and publisher can be more aligned in terms of marketing spend, strategy and risk.

overall satisfaction of the response, etc. Asking for the inclusion of such performance standards is not uncommon, but granting them is. Only in cases where the developer has sufficient bargaining power are such provisions seen in a publisher-funded development deal.

11.4.3.6. Royalties and Audits

Outside of game funding provisions, the royalties section is perhaps the most important in a publishing deal as this sets forth the underlying economics of the deal. Both parties will want to ensure that the deal is fair, that it reflects the risk allotment between the parties, and that it will provide both parties with the right incentives leading up to and following launch of the game. Generally, traditional publishing deals will provide for the developer to earn royalties off of net revenues (which we defined above), and allot some portion of that royalty to the recoupment of the development funding. To ensure that the developer gets its fair share, the deal will include some form of record keeping and reporting, audit provisions, and payment terms.

a. Royalty Terms

In a typical publisher-funded development deal,[29] developers will earn royalties of anywhere between 25% and 50% of net revenue, with 30% being the usual choice for PC and console games, and 40% to 50% being the usual choice for mobile games.[30] The royalty amount may increase based upon certain factors such as overall gross revenue or game profitability, and the developer may receive threshold balloon payments upon certain circumstance occurring (e.g., upon a certain number of installs, upon a certain level of profitability, upon the anniversary of launch, etc.). Ultimately, whatever royalties are selected should factor in the needs of the developer post-launch, which is especially important in live service games where continual development should occur after commercial release of the game.

---

[29] Work for hire deals tend to have much lower royalty rates for the developer, sometimes going as low as single digits depending on the game, the genre, the platform and the development cost.

[30] As noted above, the definitions of net revenue will generally vary between a PC or console deal and a mobile deal. These differences in definitions account for the range in royalty amounts.

b. Recoupment of Development Advances

Related to the royalty amount is how the developer will pay back the publisher for the funding it gave. The typical mechanism for this is for the publisher to withhold a portion of the royalty earned by the developer (usually 30% to 50% of the royalty). This continues until the publisher has recouped all of the funds it advanced for the game's development. This structure has both good and bad points, however. It is good in that it parlays the repayment risk into an overall bet on the game – if the game does not perform financially, the developer is not hamstrung with the need to make payments it cannot afford. On the bad side, however, it means that developers have to be very good with cash management during the initial release of the game as they may only receive half of the royalty they have otherwise earned. During negotiation of the publishing deal, attention should be paid to the recoupment provision to ensure that the developer receives enough cash to keep operating during the first few months of a game's launch.

c. Record Keeping and Audits

As it is the publisher's role to process transactions with the end user, distributor or retailer (as the case may be), publishers are required to keep detailed books and records related to those transactions, and report to the developer on those transactions on a regular basis. In retail distribution arrangements the reporting is generally done monthly or quarterly, while in digital distribution arrangements publishers may grant developers access to near real time transaction data via an online portal in addition to a formal, reconciled report on a monthly or quarterly schedule.

If near real time data is given to the developer, the publishing agreement should clarify that any data presented in the online portal is not final, and that the formal, reconciled reports are controlling for the purposes of royalty calculation, recoupment and royalty payment. The reason for this is that over the course of a month or a quarter, transactions will occur that can change sales data in material ways (returns, credit cancellations, promotions, etc.). This is especially important in territories that have a strict right of return for digital transactions (i.e., in most of Europe there is a right of return in many digital sales contracts).[31] This can in turn lead to situations in which the publisher and developer have a dispute over royalty calculations based on what the developer sees in the online portal on a day-to-day basis, versus subsequent reconciliation due to these adjustments. Clarifying that the formal reports are controlling helps avoid such disputes.

Audits in the video game industry are rarer than in other entertainment genres, but provisions for audits are nonetheless important as this is how the developer can assure it is receiving full compensation from the publisher. These provisions can be highly negotiated, but they tend to stay within a certain range of parameters. Specifically, the most common points of negotiation in an audit clause are over the minimum size and industry experience of the firm that can/must perform the audit, whether the firm can be hired on a contingency basis or not, whether there are any restrictions on how the audit is performed (time, location, must be completed by date, etc.), and what penalty gets paid if the audit discovers an under- or over-payment, with the industry standard discrepancy being between 5% and 10% of the correct amount.

d. Payment Terms

The payment terms clause details how and when the publisher will pay the development (how much is generally handed in the royalties section). Most commonly, payment of royalties to developers happens on a monthly or quarterly basis, though other structures can exist. Attention should be paid to how payment terms impact a developer's cash flow, as when a third party distributor is used (as is the case with mobile games), there can be a delay of sixty or more days before the developer receives cash from the publisher.[32] This can have a negative impact on developer cash flow unless the parties plan accordingly.

---

[31] Article 16(m) Consumer Rights Directive (2011/83/EU) allows for a 14 day right of return for digitally-purchased goods and services unless (a) the contractual performance has begun, and (b) the user has expressed their explicit consent to waive the right of return once the content has been delivered. Some game companies have run afoul of this regulation because they have not captured express user consent to this waiver in a way that complies with EU norms.

[32] For example, both Apple and Google operate on a 30 day payment cycle from the close of the calendar month. So, a publisher may not receive January revenues until the end of February. If the publisher has a 30 day payment period from receipt of cash from Apple/Google, the developer may not receive January royalties until sometime in March.

In addition, payment terms should deal with payment currencies and how to deal with foreign currency exchange (both in terms of who bears the fees and how to calculate the exchange rate) as this can account for several percentage points of profit (or cost, depending on your view).

11.4.3.7. Expiration, Termination and Wind-Down

Expiration and termination are two sides of the same coin, and represent the means by which a publishing agreement is ended. However, they are vastly different in terms of their application and focus. Expiration provisions generally focus on whether the publisher has a right to extend the deal beyond the initial term, and so can be both straightforward and simple. Termination provisions on the other hand focus on when one or the other side may kill the deal prior to its natural expiration. As such, termination provisions are generally heavily negotiated, and include a number of subsections to handle termination for cause, termination for convenience, and other termination rights. Regardless of whether a deal expires or is terminated, however, each publishing agreement should contain wind-up language that sets forth the process for taking the game out of commercial service.

a. Expiration

As mentioned in the section above discussing term, expiration of a publishing agreement will generally happen some period of years after commercial launch of the game. For PC and console deals, this is generally between three and five years after commercial launch, and for mobile deals, this is generally between two and four years after commercial launch, though of course other term provisions can be made.[33] Setting aside questions about what constitutes commercial launch (which should be dealt with in the definitions or terms sections of the agreement), expiration clauses should contemplate what extension rights, if any, a publisher has in the game.

---

[33] For example, some notable deals have been for 10 or more years, though these tend to focus on publishing rights for an entire IP, rather than one particular game, as few games make it to 10 years or more of commercial service.

Generally, if any extension rights are to be given to the publisher, they are contingent upon some factor within the reasonable control of the publisher. The most common contingencies are on gross revenue or on minimum developer royalty payments. Both are a means for ensuring that the developer is making enough money for an extension to be worthwhile, and can be used interchangeably (so long as the math reflects all deductions, carve outs and payment streams as applicable). With a gross revenue or royalties paid contingency, a publisher may have a set number of extension periods or may have unlimited extension periods as long as the contingencies keep being met.

One issue that can arise with money-based contingencies is how those contingencies are calculated over the course of a publishing agreement's term. This calculation can be done in any number of ways, but the most common structures are to calculate triggers based upon all revenues or royalties (as applicable) and over discrete periods of time. For example, in a publishing deal with a three year term, an extension right may be contingent upon total gross revenue earned or royalties paid over the life of the deal, or it may be triggered upon a more discrete period of time (i.e., the last year of the deal for the initial trigger, the prior extension period, etc.). The difference between these two is how much leeway a publisher can have for games that perform very well early in their commercial life – in deals where extensions factor in total gross revenue earned or total royalties paid, a publisher may be able to achieve extension rights long before needing them, and may even be able to trigger several extension rights during the initial term.

b. Termination for Cause

Termination for cause provisions are common among contracts of all varieties, but in publishing deals there some peculiar aspects that should be reflected in the long form agreement. Specifically, at what point in development do repeated development failures constitute a breach of the contract. After all, video game development is a creative process, and so the development cycle can be long and fraught with challenges. This is something all industry participants know and understand, but after a certain number of failures (e.g., milestones not meeting agreed upon specifications, late submissions, etc.), the publisher will have to consider whether the developer is capable of completing development.

In such cases the publisher will want to be able to terminate the agreement for cause, as a "for convenience" termination will generally involve a payment of some sort to the developer (see below for more on this) while a termination for cause will not. However, to come to an agreement on a termination for cause provision, practitioners should seek to strike a balance between allowing the developer the freedom to iterate and try new things and the publisher's desire to protect itself financially. This often means creating some definition and formula to dictate when development stumbles become failures sufficient to be a breach of the contract. For example, a publisher may set a certain number of milestone rejections, or a certain number of delivery delays, as a *per se* breach for termination for cause purposes. The number of rejections or delays will depend on the scope and financial scale of the project.

c. Termination for Convenience

Termination for convenience is, in some ways, more difficult to negotiate than termination for cause because convenience terminations are inherently subjective and (in all but a very rare number of cases) unilaterally exercised by the publisher. As such, developers want to curtail a termination for convenience right as much as possible, or in the alternative, make the termination right so expensive that the publisher is disincentivized from exercising it.

Most publishing contracts will allow the publisher to exercise a termination for convenience at any point upon providing written notice to the developer. When exercising the termination for convenience right, the publisher will pay the developer a lump sum "kill fee" of either the amounts owed for the current (in progress) milestone and the next one milestone thereafter, or the equivalent of several months of "burn" (studio operating costs). Publishers accepting a "kill fee" will often look for ways to recoup this if the developer is able to commercialize the game at a later date (e.g., by repaying the publisher if the developer self-publishes the game or if the developer agrees to terms with a different publisher).

d. Other Terminations

Some publishing contracts include other termination provisions, such as a right of termination upon acquisition of the developer by a third party (which could perhaps be a competitor or adverse party to publisher), upon failure by the developer to secure a key license needed for development, or other conditions. Such termination provisions are usually narrowly tailored to account for the concerns at hand, and are rarely (if ever) "stock" provisions.

e. Wind-Up

Regardless of the form through which a publishing deal ends, all deals must provide a path to wind up the relationship post-termination. This is because, in the case of retail, units still remain on the shelves, and in the case of digital, players will want to continue to play regardless of who publishes the game. As such, an orderly transition or wrapping up of the publishing relationship is necessary.

Wind-up periods can extend for 180 days or more after the expiration or termination of the publishing agreement. During this time, the parties will undertake certain actions such as ceasing marketing campaigns, messaging users, taking down digital storefronts, etc. In addition, the parties will need to agree on a system of cost allocation and reimbursement during this time. Most commonly, publishers will front many of these expenses (or have been throughout the term) and will include such costs as deductions in any final royalty payments owed to the development.

11.4.3.8. Downstream and Additional Rights

Downstream and additional rights can cover a broad range of rights, but generally fall into two categories: rights the publisher has in future works of the developer, and rights the publisher has in products that are ancillary to the game.

a. Rights in Future Works

Taking rights in future works are almost always for the benefit of the publisher. The reasoning is that the publisher is funding the creation of an IP as a necessary part of the game's development. As such, the publisher has an interest in being able to exploit that IP in some fashion should it find commercial success above and beyond the game at hand. Developers, of course, want to limit any future rights the publisher has to the greatest extent possible, but more often than not developers find that taking a publisher's money to develop a game also means accepting some rights to future works. While the possible permutations on rights to future works are limited only by the parties' imaginations and relative bargaining power, there are several iterations of such rights that are commonly seen in publishing agreements: rights to sequels, rights to related games, rights to ports, and rights to unrelated projects.

When negotiating sequel rights, it is important to ensure that the definition of sequel matches the expectation of the parties. "Sequel" may include prequels and follow-on games. For example, no one would argue that Valve Corporation's *Left 4 Dead* 2 was not a sequel to *Left 4 Dead*, and thus publishing rights for *Left 4 Dead* 2 could be governed by future work rights in a publishing deal for *Left 4 Dead*.[34]

However, "sequels" per se do not adequately cover expansions of the game universe in new and different ways. For example, the recent release of *Middle Earth: Shadow of War* is set in the same *Lord of the Rings* universe as *Middle Earth: Shadow of Mordor*. It may even be a "sequel" depending on how that term is drafted, but it is more likely to be seen as a follow on game or similar expansion of the game universe. As such, separate rights are often created to cover expansions of the game universe in a variety of ways, including companion applications.

One area of overlap with rights to related games is the right to port the game. "Porting" means adapting a video for one platform to another. For example, a game that is designed for PC may be "ported" to work on console, or vice versa. Publishers usually take porting rights as part of the additional rights they have in the game, though ports differ from related games in that there is usually a separate cost allocation for ports.

Finally, there are rights to unrelated games. These are game(s) that the developer intends to make that have no affiliation with the game being developed under the publishing contract being negotiated.

Regardless of which, or how many, of these rights a publisher takes, the parties should agree to the form in which these rights exist. These rights may be absolute ("the publisher has the right to publish all sequels of the game"), or may have some limitations. Most commonly, those limitations are for exclusive negotiating periods, right of first refusals, and/or last matching rights ("rights of last refusal") for the future works. These rights may end at the expiration or termination of

---

[34] This is an example only; the real history of development and publishing for the *Left 4 Dead* franchise is a bit more complex.

the publishing agreement, or they may continue for some period of time thereafter. They may also be split so that the publisher can exercise the various rights at various times, with no impact on one right should another be exercised, waived or terminated, or instead may be consecutive and dependent (i.e., failing to exercise one material option extinguishes all subsequent rights to new iterations of the IP).

b. Ancillary Products

The concept of ancillary products is seen across many entertainment media – entertainment products that are related to, but different from, the core product being built. In the case of video games, that may mean movies, television shows, comic books, and similar items. However, the term ancillary products can become an issue in the context of video game publishing agreements because of the potential overlapping jurisdiction of this term and that of platform (as discussed above) and ports and sequels (as discussed below).

Ancillary products as a defined term should be crafted so that it works with, but is not overlapping of, these other definitions. For example, would licensing of a game's IP for use in gambling-related devices, as has become popular recently with games such as *Plants vs. Zombies* and others being adapted for use in slot machines, be part of platform or be an ancillary product? A well drafted set of definitions will speak to this issue. Conversely, a poorly drafted ancillary products section may include things like marketing materials and "swag" (merchandise intended to be given away to the internal teams, to fans, etc.) which are normally carved out from ancillary products.

This becomes important in publishing deal, especially in those where development is financed by the publisher, for two reasons. First, the commercial viability of any ancillary product exists only because the publisher put up the money for development of the underlying IP and product. As such, publishers will typically want to take a part of ancillary revenues. Second, the publisher will want to make sure it can effectively market and operate the game. Poorly drafted ancillary products clauses may lead to unintended restrictions and limitations on the publisher's ability to do this.

11.4.4. Commercializing the Game and Operational Agreements

Congratulations! You've pitched your game concept, you found a publisher to fund it, and development is underway. It is now time to turn your attention to the host of operational considerations that come with commercializing a video game, and the agreements attendant thereto. Most of these concerns are applicable to publishers, but to the extent developers self-publish, these concerns will apply to them as well. The agreements covered below will only highlight the specifics applicable to video games as opposed to another form of entertainment media.

11.4.4.1. Relationships with the Console Manufacturers

While not all games are destined for play on one or more console systems, many are. For games destined for console, the most important relationships with regard to commercial success of those games are those between the developer and console manufacturer, and between the publisher and the console manufacturer. Both sides – developer and publisher – have their own agreements with console manufacturers, and both must be certified by the console manufacturer for the game to be legitimately commercialized on the platform.

a. Initial Due Diligence: Developers and Publishers

Regardless of whether a company is a developer or publisher, the first step to getting the game on a console system is to have the applicable console manufacturer perform its standard due diligence on that company. This due diligence process is meant to ensure that the party under review has the technical and financial capabilities to fulfill the requirements as per the various agreements that are needed in order to become a licensed publisher or developer. As part of the review, the console manufacturer may examine the technical expertise of a developer or publisher (as applicable), the games that the developer or publisher worked on previously, and whether the developer or publisher is certified by any other console manufacturer. The console manufacturer may also review the developer or publisher's financial stability, and seek to establish credit terms if necessary (though this is generally for physically-distributed games only).

If the developer or publisher (as applicable) passes the initial due diligence review, that entity will need to execute a series of agreements with the console manufacturer which will set the guidelines, rights, obligations, and submission procedures for games to be released on that console system.

b. Developer-Console Manufacturer Agreements

Once a developer is certified to develop games for a particular console, they will execute a tools loan agreement with the console manufacturer, which gives the developer access to the console manufacturer's development kits, programming tools, emulators and other materials needed to develop a game for that console. The tools loan agreement will cover a number of areas, including conditions of use of the tools, access to the materials, costs, ownership, representations and warranties, indemnification, a limitation of the console manufacturer's liability, and similar provisions.

In addition, there may be a separate agreement for digital distribution of a game through the console manufacturer's online storefront. This is most commonly seen as the economics for digital distribution are vastly different from those of physical distribution. However, additional issues, particularly revolving around games-as-a-service (games that are updated regularly) can be addressed in such agreements in addition to the provisions cited above.

c. Publisher-Console Manufacturer Agreement

The process for becoming a certified publisher is similar to that of becoming a certified developer, though the agreements are vastly different. The agreements to become a certified publisher generally do not convey rights to tools or similar materials, and instead convey the non-exclusive, non-transferable right to publish and distribute games on the console platform, manufacture physical disks or similar media through approved vendors, and market games for a that specific console platform. In addition, these agreements will set forth the specific procedures for submission of games that the publisher must follow.

11.4.4.2. Licenses for IP

As mentioned above, licensing IP is an important element of video game development and commercialization. Many games are based on other entertainment IP, and dealing with external licensors for IP on which a game will be based can be tricky to resolve. For example, when dealing with external IP holders, it is important to consider all play modes for the game, and ensure that brand guidelines or restrictions do not run prohibit you from building a particular game mode or style of play.

The best example of this is the somewhat recent litigation surrounding *Rock Band* and the ability to substitute members of one band into others in-game.

In the version of Rock Band released in 2008-2009, players could "unlock" the ability to have computerized representations of, for example, Gwen Stefani from No Doubt sing suggestive lyrics from the Rolling Stones' "Honky Tonk Women," or have the Kurt Cobain avatar sing any other band's songs in the game, from Bon Jovi to Bush. The band No Doubt sued publisher Activision Publishing Inc., claiming that the feature turned the bands included in the game into a "virtual karaoke circus act."[35] No Doubt sued for fraud, violation of publicity rights and breach of contract. In response, Activision claimed that there was nothing wrong with the feature and argued that the idea of "unlocking" such bonuses in a video game has been around forever in the industry.

Ultimately, Activision and No Doubt settled the suit, but the lesson remains clear: be sure to contemplate all possible game modes for your game, and ensure that any licenses of IP that you seek to include in the game cover those uses.

11.4.4.3. Marketing Support

As noted above, marketing is one of the primary functions of a publisher. However, that rarely means the publisher will do everything internally. Instead, the publisher will typically contract with several different agencies and entities to assist with paid user acquisition (UA) and brand awareness marketing.

---

[35] *No Doubt vs. Activision Publishing Inc.*, Los Angeles County Sup. Ct., case number BC425268 (2012).

a. User Acquisition

Paid user acquisition is predominantly an online-based activity, and uses the connectedness of the internet to source potential purchases and players and bring them into the game. There are various ways this gets done, from banner advertising to sponsored posts of social media, and as such there are a variety of metrics that should be known to practitioners who will negotiate user acquisition ("UA") deals. The reason for this is that these metrics are the basis on which the UA firm gets paid, and unfamiliarity with them will lead either to an ineffective campaign, or a campaign that costs more than it can expect to generate in sales revenue.

The most common acronyms used in UA deals are:

- CPM – Cost Per Thousand Impressions (used in banner ad and sponsor social media post advertising; does not depend on the viewer doing anything)
- CPC – Cost Per Click (triggered upon the viewer of the ad clicking on the banner, link, image, etc.)
- CPI – Cost Per Install (the UA cost paid to get a single player to install the game, as not everyone who sees the ad will click on it, and not everyone who clicks on the ad will install the game)
- LTV – Lifetime Value (the revenue that can be expected from a player acquired through a particular UA campaign)
- ARPU – Average Revenue Per User
- ARPDAU – Average Revenue Per Daily Active User

Knowing what these metrics mean will enable the deal negotiators to more effectively tie the UA company's incentives to those of the publisher, and can control how much the publisher is willing to spend on a particular campaign.

As these metrics are key to any UA agreement, attention should be paid to the tracking mechanisms employed by the UA firm, especially when several UA firms may be employed by a publisher simultaneously. The publisher should ensure that it only pays one UA firm for each impression, click, or install (as applicable), and the way to do this is by enforcing strict tracking standards on all UA firms.

b. Brand Awareness

Brand awareness marketing will generally encompass the classic marketing activities – television ads, game trailers, billboards, subway advertising, gamer and trade magazines, etc. Agencies, both creative and executional, can be hired by publishers to support these functions. In brand awareness agency deals, ownership and non-infringement of any IP created as part of the campaign should be primary concerns, with the publisher (or developer, as applicable under the publishing agreement) owning all IP generated for the campaign. Other considerations include how the agency accounts to the publisher for its time, what control the publisher has over the agency's team, whether the agency is acting exclusively or non-exclusively for the publisher, etc.

11.4.4.4. Customer Support

It is an inevitability of the video game business that some players will have trouble with the game – the game won't function, the player made a purchase that was not reflected in the account, etc. Players want to have these issues solved, and publishers want to solve these complaints (most of them, anyway). Thus, the vast majority of publishers offer some means by which players can have these complaints addressed, and this is the customer support function. Generally, this means having a large team of support agents available to respond to complaints as they come in. Some publishers will build their own customer support departments and hire vast numbers of agents as full time employees of the publisher, but many publishers outsource some, if not all, of the customer support function.

When looking to outsource a customer support function, there are several things that the publisher (or in the case of self-publishing, the developer) must consider. First is the number of agents that will be staffed to the account, and how the outsource partner will count those heads. Often, outsource partners may work across many games, and sometimes the partner's agents do not have enough complaints to keep them busy full time. This can result in the publisher (or developer, as applicable) overpaying for agents that are not needed. Thus, the publisher or developer should consider what mechanisms are available to dynamically ramp the number of agents up or down.

Second is the hours those agents will work on a particular game. Publishers should pay attention to the markets in which the game is available and ensure that customer support agents are available during business hours in those markets. Otherwise, the publisher will end up with severe delays in getting responses to consumers, which will likely further antagonize an already upset consumer.

Third, the publisher should consider what types of training the outsource partner's agents will receive, and have the right to visit the outsource partner to provide trainings, re-trainings and spot audit checks. Reputable outsource partners will want publishers and developers to do this (so long as the training conditions are reasonable) as it helps ensure a long term relationship between the partner and the publisher.

Finally, the publisher should consider what metrics and standards it wants to use to rate the performance of the outsource partner. Typical metrics include ticket processing volume, average ticket response time, average ticket queue and customer satisfaction survey scores. Publishers should ensure that if the outsource partner is not meeting the agreed upon metrics, the publisher has a means of rectifying this, reducing payments to the partner, or even terminating the deal.

11.4.4.5. Payment Gateways and Payment Processors

Payment gateways and processors allow the publisher or developer to take payments from the end user, generally in the form of debit cards, credit cards and stored value cards. Payment gateways tend to be third party solutions added onto your system, while payment processors tend to offer solutions that you integrate directly into your system. Regardless of whether you work with a payment gateway or a payment processor, publishers and developers who distribute games directly (that is, not through a distributor, a console manufacturer, or a retail partner) need to be aware of the requirements for doing so because without these parties, the publisher or developer would have no way to collect money from the end user.[36] Examples of common payment gateways and payment processors include PayPal, Xsolla, and others.

When contracting with payment gateways and payment processors, there are two key items to consider, both of which are actually responsibilities of the publisher. The first is fraud. Too much fraud (in the form of rejected payments, chargebacks, etc.) will lead to significant penalties for the publisher, up to and including a freezing

---

[36] Console manufacturers, distributors and retail partners already have deals in place with payment processors and payment gateways.

out of the publisher's ability to take in payments. The burden of preventing and detecting fraud falls on the publisher, and so the publisher should have a robust fraud department that is able to keep fraud to a certain "tolerable" level (generally less than 2% of all transactions, though lower levels may be desired or necessary for some situations).

The second item to consider is that of security compliance. Payment gateways and payment processors will typically require publishers and developers to adhere to some form of compliance with the Payment Card Industry's Security Standards Council requirements.[37] These requirements can be complex and may require fundamental changes to the business. As such, these requirements should not be taken lightly.

11.5. REGULATION OF VIDEO GAMES

As are all entertainment media, video games are subject to various forms of regulation. In some areas, video games are more heavily regulated, or at least, a more frequent topic of regulatory focus, than other entertainment media for two reasons: (1) it sits at the cross section of entertainment and technology in ways other entertainment media do not, and (2) video games allow players to actively engage in certain (inter)actions instead of being merely passive consumers of content. As such, a complete listing of all laws, rules, regulations, ordinances, decrees, treaties and cross-border obligations is far outside the scope of this chapter. Instead, we will focus on some of the key areas of regulation that are of significant interest to dealmakers in the video game space, and that are unique to the industry. Namely, we will focus on data privacy, consumer protection, and other regulations specific to video games.[38]

---

[37] www.pcisecuritystandards.org
[38] In no way should a legal practitioner looking to make a video game-related deal ignore other legal regimes of more general applicability, such as copyright law, trademark law, patent law, monetary regulations such as anti-money laundering, etc. These are all important areas that influence how deals get made in the video game industry, and having more than a cursory knowledge of these areas is important to properly representing your client.

11.5.1. Data Privacy

The modern video game industry is driven by the collection and exploitation of data, both because new technologies make the creation, storage and analysis of data easier, and because of the number of choices consumers have in terms of available entertainment increase the competitive challenges to launching a successful game. New and expanding technologies allow for game developers to build features into their games that collect data about user behavior, and use that data to present game experiences to users that are ever more customized to their particular desires.

Having that customization, however, comes at a cost. Namely, the user must be willing to share with the game developer and/or publisher certain information. Some of that information will be utterly benign, but other information such as email address, telephone number, credit card information, etc., may result in harm to the consumer if mishandled or misused (intentionally or unintentionally). This forms the basis of the concerns about data privacy, and even a cursory examination of legal trends over the last several years will reveal that data privacy is a hot button issue for consumers and regulatory. While the United States has aggressively expanded its protections for consumer-related data, the European Union still has (arguably) the most comprehensive and stringent data privacy regulation system.

11.5.1.1. United States Data Protection

Data protection in the United States might still in its infancy, at least by comparison to regulations in the EU. Yet the last few years have seen a significant expansion of data protection laws and regulations at both the federal and state levels, as well as seemingly ad hoc implementation of those laws and regulations through case law and decisions and guidance of the Federal Trade Commission. The starting point for any discussion of data privacy in the US is what US law and regulation deems subject to data protection laws. There are generally three classifications of data subject to various data protection laws: personally identifiable information (sometimes referred to as PII), financial data and health data. For the purposes of this chapter we will focus only on PII as it pertains to games, though one could certainly imagine a set of circumstances in which financial data or health data become relevant to games companies.

What constitutes PII will depend upon a number of factors as there is no unified definition of PII. However, there are some similarities in most definitions of PII, namely that any data that can identify an individual apart from any other individual, or any information that can be used to discretely contact a particular individual, is PII. This would include clear examples of PII such as first and last name, social security number, telephone number, etc., but it can also include individualized but anonymous data such as an account number, a unique player identifier, etc. Some individual states are more restrictive in their definition of PII, while others are more expansive. For example, Massachusetts defines PII as names, social security numbers, driver's license numbers or financial account numbers, including credit or debit card numbers,[39] while Texas defines PII as information that alone or in conjunction with other information identifies an individual, including an individual's: (A) name, social security number, date of birth, or government-issued identification number; (B) mother's maiden name; (C) unique biometric data, including the individual's fingerprint, voice print, and retina or iris image; and (D) unique electronic identification number, address, or routing code.[40]

Just as laws differ as to what constitutes PII, so too do laws regarding how PII should be handled. Some states have no regulations at all as to how PII may be handled so long as there is no breach of that data's security (that is, unauthorized access by a third party). Other states, such as California, have very specific requirements as to how PII can be treated.[41] Moreover, a majority of states and jurisdictions in the US (46 in total) have laws regarding what must be done in the event of a data breach, with some states requiring only notification to the user of the breach while other states require more proactive approaches.

---

[39] 201 CMR § 17.00
[40] Tex. Bus. And Comm. Code § 521
[41] Cal. Bus. & Prof. Code §§22575 et seq. require a website or online service operator to have a public-facing privacy policy that, at a minimum, includes: (1) a list of the categories of personally identifiable information the operator collects; (2) a list of the categories of third parties with whom the operator may share such personally identifiable information; (3) a description of the process (if any) by which the consumer can review and request changes to his or her personally identifiable information as collected by the operator; (4) a description of the process by which the operator notifies consumers of material changes to the operator's privacy policy; and (5) the effective date of the privacy policy.

In sum, US data privacy law is best described as a patchwork of intertwining laws, regulations, agency rules and court decisions, but this by no means suggests that it can be ignored. In the last decade, dozens of companies have faced millions of dollars in fines, penalties and judgements for ignoring data privacy controls. Thus, an exhaustive review of a particular game's data collection, storage and use should be undertaken before making the game available to the public.

11.5.1.2. European Union Data Protection

As mentioned above, the EU's data protection system is often seen as more robust than that of the United States. The EU system's genesis lies in the Data Protection Directive ("DPD"), passed in the 1995,[42] as amended by the E-Privacy Directive, passed in 2002.[43] At its core, the DPD and E-Privacy Directive focus on the protection and regulation of "personal data," which is defined as data that, taken on its own or in combination with other data, may be used to identify a natural person. The DPD has eight primary requirements for any individual or business which collects and/or controls personal data (such entities are known as a "data controllers"). Data controllers must:

a) Process personal data only in ways that are lawful and fair;

b) Obtain personal data only for one or more specified and lawful purposes;

c) Ensure that personal data processing is adequate, relevant and not excessive in relation to the purpose or purposes for which they are processed;

d) Keep personal data accurate and, where necessary, up to date;

---

[42] The Data Protection Directive is known officially as Directive 95/46/EC of the European Parliament and of the Council of 24 October 1995 on the protection of individuals with regard to the processing of personal data and on the free movement of such data: http://eur-lex.europa.eu/LexUriServ/LexUriServ.do?uri=CELEX:31995L0046:en:HTML

[43] The E-Privacy Directive is known officially as Directive 2002/58/EC of the European Parliament and of the Council of 12 July 2002 concerning the processing of personal data and the protection of privacy in the electronic communications sector (Directive on privacy and electronic communications): http://eur-lex.europa.eu/LexUriServ/LexUriServ.do?uri=CELEX:32002L0058:en:NOT

654 ESSENTIAL GUIDE TO ENTERTAINMENT LAW: DEALMAKING

e) Not keep personal data for longer than is necessary for that purpose or those purposes;

f) Process personal data in accordance with the rights of data subjects;

g) Have appropriate technical and organizational measures in place to ensure against unauthorized or unlawful processing of personal data and to protect against accidental loss of, destruction of, or damage to personal data; and

h) Not transfer personal data outside the European Economic Area except under certain circumstances.

While this sets the baseline for how personal data is collected, stored and processed in the European Union, the European Parliament that instituted these Directives left it up to the member states to implement these ideas in their own ways. Thus, EU data privacy law is a patchwork of laws and regulations that do not always result in a means of simple compliance across all member states.

11.5.1.3. Data Protection Best Practices

From the above it is clear that compliance with data protection requirements is a must for interactive entertainment media, but that it is also a difficult task to accomplish given the variety and nature of laws, regulations and ordinances with which compliance is required. Full legal compliance with all applicable data privacy and protection requirements requires an in-depth knowledge of each particular game's data collection, storage and maintenance needs and practices, and a tailoring of the manner in which that data is processed to the needs at hand. Thus, data privacy compliance is by nature a highly individualized effort, but certain best practices can be identified that are likely to have applicability to a wide range of data collection activities:

- Have a privacy policy that is consumer facing (this is required in several jurisdictions).

- Make sure that privacy policy accurately frames what data you will collect, for what purpose that collection will occur, and how you will treat that data. Borrowing privacy statements from other organizations is never a good idea.

- Write that privacy policy in language that is consumer friendly (avoid the temptation to use "legalese" in the drafting).
- Obtain from end consumers affirmative consent to be bound by the terms of your privacy policy (so-called "clickwrap" or "browsewrap" policies are highly disregarded today, and the enforcement thereof is prohibited in some jurisdictions).
- Revisit the privacy policy regularly to make sure the promises made to consumers therein are still being kept by your organization.
- If and when you update your privacy policy, make sure that change is clearly communicated to consumers, and obtain their affirmative consent to be bound by the terms of the new policy.
- When processing or storing data across territorial borders, know where that data originated from and what regulations apply to that data. Take special care of data that originated within the European Union, and if you are going to process European Union-originated data outside of the European Union, make sure you fall into one of the delineated purposes that allow this.

11.5.2. Consumer Protection

Another area of legal regulation which has unique application to video games and interactive media is that of consumer protection. While this is not a treatise on the full complement of consumer protection laws, rules, regulations and ordinances with which a video game company must comply, some specific issues bear noting.

11.5.2.1. COPPA

In 1998, Congress enacted the Children's Online Privacy Protection Act ("COPPA") which created special obligations on interactive or online service providers with regard to protecting the privacy of children under the age of 13.[44] Specifically, COPPA required interactive and

---

[44] 15 U.S.C. §§ 6501-6505; 16 C.F.R. Part 312.

online service operators whose content and services are "directed to children" to provide parents or guardians of children under the age of 13 with notice that the service will collect certain personally identifiable information from the child, and receive express consent from the parent or guardian to move forward with that collection prior to the collection occurring. Failure to comply with COPPA when required may result in up to $40,000 in civil penalties per violation.

Given the seriousness of compliance failures, many online and interactive services, including video games, purposefully structure their service so as to not be "directed to children." Determining whether or not a service is "directed to children," however, can be a difficult proposition because the factors that go into that determination are varied and expansive. They include subject matter, visual content, use of animated characters, music or other audio content, age of models, and the presence of celebrities who appeal to children.[45] As such, many video games may meet some or all of the above criteria which puts them at risk for being deemed to be "directed to children", even if not intentionally directed to children.

To avoid any confusion as to whether an online service is or is not "directed to children", operators of a service will often make the choice to prevent children under the age of 13 from submitting any personally identifiable information (or even using the service entirely). This is done through an "age gate," a software mechanism that checks the age of a registrant before processing the registration, that is built into the account creation process and that prohibits anyone under the age of 13 from registering for the service.

If the online service or video game at issue will be directed to children (or even if it is at risk of being deemed so and does not utilize an age gate to exclude children under 13), then there are a number of steps that the operator must take to remain in compliance with COPPA:

- Post a clear and comprehensive online privacy policy describing their information practices for personal information collected online from children;

- Provide direct notice to parents and obtain verifiable parental consent, with limited exceptions, before collecting personal information online from children;

---

[45] 16 C.F.R. § 312.2

- Give parents the choice of consenting to the operator's collection and internal use of a child's information, but prohibiting the operator from disclosing that information to third parties (unless disclosure is integral to the site or service, in which case, this must be made clear to parents);

- Provide parents access to their child's personal information to review and/or have the information deleted;

- Give parents the opportunity to prevent further use or online collection of a child's personal information;

- Maintain the confidentiality, security, and integrity of information they collect from children, including by taking reasonable steps to release such information only to parties capable of maintaining its confidentiality and security; and

- Retain personal information collected online from a child for only as long as is necessary to fulfill the purpose for which it was collected, and thereafter delete the information using reasonable measures to protect against its unauthorized access or use.

11.5.2.2. Subscription Pricing

As mentioned above, some games operate on a subscription pricing model – users pay a monthly fee in order to access the game and any new content made available therein. Such subscription plans are regulated at both the federal and state level in the United States. Federally, subscription programs are regulated by the Federal Trade Commission Act and its implementing regulations,[46] which require, among other things, that certain disclosures as to the manner, procedure and contents of the subscription be made to the consumer, and that regular written reminders be given to the consumer in advance of the renewal of their subscription contract. Under these regulations, the FTC may bring actions against companies in violation of these rules. Similarly, many states have laws that speak to the same types of harms, and their own causes of action for breach thereof.

---

[46] 15 U.S.C. §§ 41 *et seq.*

On the US state level, at least 24 states have enacted statutes regulating automatic renewals to varying degrees. While these statutes vary in strictness and scope, they generally require companies to disclose automatic renewal policies in a "clear and conspicuous" manner. Additionally, some states require companies to obtain customers' affirmative consent before charging a credit card and to disclose how to cancel the subscription to avoid future recurring payments. Games that are contemplating a subscription-based pricing model should ensure that all applicable laws and regulations are followed with regard to the subscription plan.

11.5.3. Video Games, Violent Imagery and the First Amendment

As mentioned in an earlier section of this chapter, most video games offered to the public must be rated by a ratings board (ESRB in the US/Canada, PEGI in Europe, etc.). The concern over ratings generally falls into whether the game includes content that some may find objectionable for children or young adults. Often, this means the inclusion of sexual content, questionable behavior such as drug use, and violent imagery. In fact, many jurisdictions have tried to pass laws that ban, or very strictly regulate, the sale to minors of games that include violent content.

In the United States, the landmark Supreme Court case of *Brown v. EMA* ruled on whether, and how, states can ban the sale of violent video games to minors.[47] The case concerned a California law that banned the sale of "violent" video games to anyone under age 18 and required clear labeling beyond the existing ESRB rating system.[48] In striking down the law as unconstitutional, the Supreme Court held that: (1) video games are entitled to full First Amendment protection; (2) the inclusion of violent content in a video is speech about violence, not an enactment of violence itself; and (3) while states may pass laws to block obscene material from minors as previously decided in *Ginsberg v. New York*,[49] speech about violence is not obscene, and therefore video games cannot be banned on the basis of violent content alone.

---

[47] 564 U.S. 786 (2011)
[48] California A.B. 1179 (2005)
[49] 390 U.S. 629 (1968)

This of course does not obviate the need for a game to be rated, or even give a game's developer or publisher a basis to challenge the rating. A complete ban on sale is treated very differently than the obligation to inform consumers as to the content included in the game, and there are only very few circumstances wherein the need to rate a game for age appropriateness and content would be legally questionable.

In addition, practitioners should keep in mind that the U.S. approach to violence in video games is not shared across the globe. As noted in an earlier section, other countries can and do ban games on the basis of violent content – Australia, Germany and others have banned games such as *Saints Row IV* and *Mortal Combat* because of the violent imagery included therein. Therefore, it is important to remember that content decisions can often dictate where and how a game can be distributed.

11.5.4. Right of Publicity

Rights of publicity have long been litigated in the context of entertainment media. Right of publicity lawsuits are routinely brought over books, films, songs and paintings, and video games are no exception. In the last decade, multiple lawsuits have been brought against video game publishers and developers for misappropriate of a person's right to control depictions of their name, image or likeness.[50]

What makes rights of publicity lawsuits in video games interesting is that, because of the interactivity afforded by video games, game play can lead to situations where even a generally permitted use runs afoul of a person's publicity rights. Take, for example, the No Doubt lawsuit mentioned in an earlier section. The core of that case was not that the band No Doubt hadn't licensed their respective publicity rights to have their likeness included in the game *Band Hero* (which they had); rather, it was that the band members' rights of publicity were violated through a functionality in the game that allowed players to utilize digital avatars of performers for songs they did not perform. Players could also manipulate the No Doubt characters (and others) by having

---

[50] Hart v. Electronic Arts, 717 F.3d 141 (3rd Cir. 2013); Lohan v. Take-Two Interactive Software Inc., 156443/2014, New York State Supreme Court, New York County (Manhattan); Noriega v. Activision Blizzard, Inc., et al, No. BC 551747 (Sup. Ct. Cal.) (2014). For more on this topic, the reader is directed to the chapter on Privacy and Publicity Rights found in the companion volume to this book, Essential Guide to Entertainment Law: Intellectual Property.

the band's lead female singer sound like a man and a male singer sound like a woman. This, claimed No Doubt, exceeded the scope of the likeness license they had granted to Activision, and therefore their rights of publicity were violated. Though the case settled just prior to trial, the lesson remains clear in that licenses for publicity rights should contemplate both the obvious use cases for those likenesses as well as the non-obvious use cases – those use cases that arise out of the interactivity that video games can provide.

11.6. LOOKING INTO THE FUTURE

As has been highlighted in this chapter a number of times, video games and interactive media offer unique challenges for practitioners because video games are interactive, rather than passive, forms of entertainment, and because video games sit at the intersection of entertainment and technology in ways that no other entertainment media does. Take, for example, the explosive growth in eSports, or the burgeoning worlds of virtual and augmented reality.

11.6.1. eSports

eSports is the new name for competitive video game playing by professionals, or teams of professionals, which may or may not necessarily involve electronic emulation of traditional live sports. While video game tournaments have existed for decades, the expansion of viewership opportunities through platforms like YouTube and Twitch.tv have brought competitive video game playing to the masses. In 2013, it was estimated that approximately 71.5 million people worldwide watched eSports,[51] and in 2016 that figure grew to 213 million people.[52] By 2019, that figure is projected to grow to more than 300 million viewers annually.[53]

As such, legal issues that have traditionally been seen as the province of "traditional" sports have come to the forefront of the video game industry. Teams are being formed, sometimes backed by venture

---

[51] *eSports in numbers: Five mind-blowing stats*, Phillipa Warr (April 9, 2014) available at https://www.redbull.com/ca-en/esports-in-numbers-five-mind-blowing-stats (last visited 5/10/17).

[52] eSports Market Report, Superdata Research (2016) available at https://www.superdataresearch.com/market-data/esports-market-brief/ (last visited 5/10/2017).

[53] *Id.*

capital or hedge fund investors,[54] and sometimes by "traditional" sports teams themselves.[55] Players are discussing whether unions are needed to protect their interests.[56] Publishers are finding themselves being tasked with running a sports league and dealing with issues such as franchising, and the packaging and sale of broadcasting rights.[57] As eSports continues to grow and evolve, the nature and impact of the legal challenges related thereto will only expand and take on increased importance.

11.6.2. Virtual Reality and Augmented Reality

Along with eSports, virtual reality (VR) and augmented reality (AR) technologies have received significant media (and investor) attention in recent years. In 2014, Facebook purchased VR company Oculus for $2 billion, and Magic Leap, an augmented reality-focused startup, has raised $1.6 billion from investors and is valued at more

---

[54] In October 2015, eSports organization Team 8 was purchased by an investor group led by Crosscut Ventures and included investors such as Peter Levin (president of Lionsgate) and Machine Shop Ventures (the investment arm of the band *Linkin Park*).

[55] The Phildelpha 76ers acquired eSports teams Dignitas and Apex in September 2016. Other professional sports team owners, such as the owners of the Sacramento Kings and the Washington Capitals, have also invested in eSports teams.

[56] Several attempts at forming an eSport players union have already been made, such as the World eSports Association (WESA) and the Professional eSports Association (PEA). http://www.gamerevolution.com/features/pea-controversy-its-time-for-esports-players-to-unionize While those efforts have had mixed success, the debate continues today. In addition, publishers like Wargaming have also publicly discussed whether it will form an eSport players union. http://www.gamesindustry.biz/articles/2016-04-13-wargaming-wants-an-esports-players-union

[57] For example, Riot Games, which developers and publishes *League of Legends*, often regarded as the most popular eSports title in the world, is also the operator of two *League*-based professional leagues – the North American League Championship Series (NALCS) and the European League Championship Series (EULCS) – and the semi-professional Challenger series for both of those leagues. In its role as both publisher and league operator, Riot has had to confront questions about how it handles league operations, whether and how it can implement changes to the game for the professional scene, and whether professional teams should be "franchised" or not. In addition, Riot recently agreed to a deal with BAMTech, an online streaming company that is a joint venture of Major League Baseball, the Walt Disney Company and the National Hockey League, wherein BAMTech purchase broadcasting rights to the NALCS and EULCS for $300 million over seven years. http://variety.com/2016/digital/news/bamtech-league-of-legends-mlb-disney-esports-1201944167/

than $4 billion (even without bringing a product to market). Today Google, Apple, Amazon, Microsoft, Sony and Samsung all have dedicated VR and AR groups.

So the VR and AR sectors are "hot" topics in video games right now, and are usually lumped together as if they were a single sector. Although drawing a clear line between VR and AR can be difficult as there is significant overlap between the two technologies, they are as different as they may appear similar. Both technologies fundamentally provide a new viewer experience, and usually this means providing content in three dimensions. It is how these technologies provide the 3D content to the end user that they begin to differ. VR generally means an all-encompassing visual field – the user is immersed in the content being displayed and the rest of the world is blocked out. AR, in contrast, generally tries to overlap digital or virtual content on top of real world content. Pokemon Go is a great example of AR – the game overlays digital monsters and other content on top of real world locations and items. As such, it is perhaps accurate to view VR and AR as two sides of the same coin – both seek to provide consumers with virtual, three dimensional content, with one doing so exclusively and the other doing so in combination with the real world.

What's exciting about these technologies is that games are just one type of content that can be delivered to consumers in three dimensions. Sports, concerts and other limited-time events are being delivered to VR customers, and companies are exploring the use of AR in terms of travel assistance, advertising and education. But with these new use cases come certain legal risks. For example, people utilizing AR technologies while driving can be dangerously distracted, and the makers of Pokemon Go took steps to curb its use by players while driving by taking advantage of the smartphones' accelerometers and gyroscopes to pause the game when the phone was likely to be in a moving car. This was an entirely new concern, and one that is unlikely to be contemplated by a "traditional" mobile video game deal. How the relationship between publishers and developers will evolve to deal with the new uses that these technologies will give rise to will be anyone's guess, and is more reason why practitioners should stay abreast of technological developers and user trends when dealing in this space.

11.7. CONCLUSION

Video games and interactive media are an exciting, evolving field that combines the best parts of the entertainment and technology sectors. It is an industry with both a rich history and a constant rate of change, with every year brings new developments in the space. This affords practitioners the opportunity to both continually learn new things and constantly refine their craft. Above all, though, it is a medium that is driven by passionate, dedicated people who love what they do, and lawyers who wish to practice in this space will find much more long term success if they share in that passion and dedication.

VIDEO GAMES AND INTERACTIVE MEDIA – ILLUSTRATIVE FORMS:

1. Video Game Publishing Term Sheet
2. Video Game Distribution Agreement (long form)
3. Master Services Agreement (Developer Engagement of Subcontractors)

VIDEO GAMES, INTERACTIVE MEDIA AND DEALMAKING   665

Appendix 1

ESRB Ratings

EARLY CHILDHOOD
Content is intended for young children.

EVERYONE
Content is generally suitable for all ages. May contain minimal cartoon, fantasy or mild violence and/or infrequent use of mild language.

EVERYONE 10+
Content is generally suitable for ages 10 and up. May contain more cartoon, fantasy or mild violence, mild language and/or minimal suggestive themes.

TEEN
Content is generally suitable for ages 13 and up. May contain violence, suggestive themes, crude humor, minimal blood, simulated gambling and/or infrequent use of strong language.

MATURE
Content is generally suitable for ages 17 and up. May contain intense violence, blood and gore, sexual content and/or strong language.

ADULTS ONLY
Content suitable only for adults ages 18 and up. May include prolonged scenes of intense violence, graphic sexual content and/or gambling with real currency.

RATING PENDING
Not yet assigned a final ESRB rating. Appears only in advertising, marketing and promotional materials related to a "boxed" video game that is expected to carry an ESRB rating, and should be replaced by a game's rating once it has been assigned.

Appendix 2

PEGI Ratings

PEGI 3
The content of games given this rating is considered suitable for all age groups. Some violence in a comical context (typically Bugs Bunny or Tom & Jerry cartoon-like forms of violence) is acceptable. The child should not be able to associate the character on the screen with real life characters, they should be totally fantasy. The game should not contain any sounds or pictures that are likely to scare or frighten young children. No bad language should be heard.

PEGI 7
Any game that would normally be rated at 3 but contains some possibly frightening scenes or sounds may be considered suitable in this category.

PEGI 12
Videogames that show violence of a slightly more graphic nature towards fantasy character and/or non graphic violence towards human-looking characters or recognisable animals, as well as videogames that show nudity of a slightly more graphic nature would fall in this age category. Any bad language in this category must be mild and fall short of sexual expletives.

PEGI 16
This rating is applied once the depiction of violence (or sexual activity) reaches a stage that looks the same as would be expected in real life. More extreme bad language, the concept of the use of tobacco and drugs and the depiction of criminal activities can be content of games that are rated 16.

PEGI 18
The adult classification is applied when the level of violence reaches a stage where it becomes a depiction of gross violence and/or includes elements of specific types of violence. Gross violence is the most difficult to define since it can be very subjective in many cases, but in general terms it can be classed as the depictions of violence that would make the viewer feel a sense of revulsion.

Bad Language
Game contains bad language

Discrimination
Game contains depictions of, or material which may encourage, discrimination

Drugs
Game refers to or depicts the use of drugs

Fear
Game may be frightening or scary for young children

Gambling
Games that encourage or teach gambling

Sex
Game depicts nudity and/or sexual behaviour or sexual references

Violence
Game contains depictions of violence

Online gameplay
Game can be played online

Extended Consumer Advice

This is specific information explaining why a game received its classification. A number of examples are listed below:

Contains: extreme violence, criminal techniques, glamorisation of crime, strong language

Contains: comic violence

Contains: nudity, strong language, unrealistic violence

— CHAPTER 12 —

A GUIDE TO STRUCTURING AND TAXATION IN THE ENTERTAINMENT INDUSTRY

Brad Cohen,* Shane Nix†

12.1. General Tax Principles
12.2. Considerations for Choice of Entity
12.3. Employee versus Independent Contractor
12.4. Structuring Entertainment Transactions (Formation and Operations)
12.5. Taxation of Intellectual Property in the Entertainment Industry
12.6. Estate and Tax Planning for Rights of Publicity

The purpose of this chapter is to give entertainment and business practitioners a general overview of (i) general tax principles, such as methods of accounting, tax deductions, tax credits, limitations on losses, exclusions from gross income, and taxable years, (ii) initial structuring of an entertainment business, including choice of entity, (iii) common issues that arise during operations of film/TV, music and production businesses, and (iv) tax considerations upon certain liquidity events, such as a sale of copyrights or trademarks. The discussion below is not intended to cover all potential issues and considerations that may arise, but is intended to give the non-tax practitioner an overview of various issues that may arise and that should be considered when tax planning for certain entertainers. In addition, this chapter does not address international tax or estate tax planning, and only addresses state and local taxation to a limited extent. On December 22, 2017, the Tax Cuts and Jobs Act was signed

---

* **Brad Cohen** is Partner in the Century City office of Jeffers Mangels Butler & Mitchell LLP. The author extends his gratitude to Jamie Ogden and Scott Loresch for their assistance.

† **Shane Nix** is Counsel to the law firm Venable LLP; The author proudly dedicates his work on this project to his father, Ronald Gordon Nix (1951-2016) and mother, Paula Ann Nix, and extends his gratitude to Nicholas Jacobus, for his assistance.

into law and significantly amends Internal Revenue Code of 1986, the applicable provisions of which are noted in this Chapter.[1] As of the date of this writing, however, the application of certain provisions is subject to interpretation and forthcoming Treasury Regulations.

12.1. GENERAL TAX PRINCIPLES

The primary goals of tax planning are to (i) minimize current taxation by reducing taxable income and typically converting the character of such income, known as "ordinary income" into capital gain, and (ii) defer taxation until a later taxable year (or accelerating losses and credits to the current taxable year). Income or gain that cannot be deferred until a later tax year may be minimized by generating planning opportunities to incur tax deductions and tax credits to the maximum extent possible in the tax year in which income is included in the taxpayer's gross income. In addition, if the entertainer does not operate as a sole practitioner (which is generally not recommended for tax and limited liability reasons), selecting the appropriate operating entity is a critical aspect of tax, corporate and estate planning, which is driven by the type of business in which the entertainer is engaged.

12.1.1. Income

Unless expressly excluded from gross income under the Internal Revenue Code of 1986, as amended (the "*Code*"), a taxpayer's gross income includes all income "from whatever source" derived, including (but not limited to) the following items:

(i) Compensation for services, including fees, commissions, fringe benefits, and similar items;

(ii) Gross income derived from business;

(iii) Gains derived from dealings in property;

(iv) Interest;

---

[1] P.L. 115-97 (12/22/2017). The Act initially was given the short title "The Tax Cuts and Jobs Act." However, the Senate Parliamentarian ruled that the inclusion of a short title violated the applicable procedural rules that allowed the Senate to pass the legislation with a simple majority. Therefore, the short title was stricken from the final version of the legislation.

GUIDE TO STRUCTURING AND TAXATION IN THE INDUSTRY 671

(v) Rents;
(vi) Royalties;
(vii) Dividends;
(viii) Distributive share of partnership gross income; and
(ix) Income in respect of a decedent.[2]

The definition of gross income is extremely broad and generally includes any cash or property received by the taxpayer that has value.

12.1.2. Methods of Accounting

Taxable income must be computed under the method of accounting on the basis of which a taxpayer regularly computes such taxpayer's income in keeping books and records.[3] The term "method of accounting" includes not only the overall method of accounting of the taxpayer but also the accounting treatment of any tax item.[4] Examples of such overall methods are the cash receipts and disbursements method, the accrual method, combinations of such methods, and various other methods that account for special tax items.[5]

Generally, a taxpayer can use any combination of cash, accrual, and special methods of accounting if the combination clearly reflects the taxpayer's income and such hybrid method is used consistently.[6] Certain restrictions, however, can apply to the use of hybrid methods. For example, if a taxpayer uses the cash method of accounting in computing gross income from the taxpayer's trade or business, then the taxpayer must use the cash method in computing the expenses of such trade or business.[7]

Where a taxpayer has two or more separate and distinct trade or businesses, a different method of accounting may be used for each

---

[2] IRC § 61(a).
[3] Treas. Reg. § 1.446-1(a)(1).
[4] Id.
[5] Id.
[6] Treas. Reg. § 1.446-1(c)(1)(iv)(a); IRS Publication 538.
[7] Id.; Treas. Reg. § 1.446-1(c)(2)(i); other limitations include: (i) if an inventory is necessary to account for the taxpayer's income, then the taxpayer must use an accrual method for purchases and sales, and may use the cash method in computing all other items of income and expense; and (ii) if a taxpayer uses an accrual method of accounting in computing business expenses, then the taxpayer must use an accrual method in computing items affecting gross income from his trade or business. Id.

trade or business, provided the method used for each trade or business clearly reflects the income of that particular trade or business.[8] For example, a taxpayer may account for the operations of a personal service business on the cash receipts and disbursements method, and of a merchandising business on an accrual method, provided such businesses are separate and distinct and the methods used for each clearly reflect income.[9] The method first used in accounting for business income and deductions in connection with each trade or business (as evidenced in the taxpayer's income tax return in which such income or deductions are first reported) must be consistently followed from then on.[10] Thus, a tax advisor should be consulted in the process of forming any business.

A taxpayer may adopt any permissible method of accounting in computing taxable income for the taxable year covered by such taxpayer's first tax return.[11] As noted, a taxpayer may also adopt any permissible method of accounting in connection with each separate and distinct trade or business, the income from which is reported for the first time.[12] Generally, the consent of the IRS is required to make an accounting method change, unless the taxpayer is eligible for automatic consent.[13] The IRS provides an enumerated list of automatic accounting method changes that may qualify for automatic consent if the applicable requirements are satisfied.[14] For example, a taxpayer may be able to change its overall method of accounting from the cash method to the accrual method when such taxpayer (i) is required to make such change under Section 448 (e.g., as discussed below, under certain circumstances, when a C-corporation has gross receipts of more than twenty-five million dollars), any other section of the Code or

---

[8] Treas. Reg. § 1.446-1(d)(1). No trade or business will be considered separate and distinct for purposes of Treas. Reg. § 1.446-1(d) unless a complete and separable set of books and records is kept for such trade or business. Treas. Reg. § 1.446-1(d)(2). If, by reason of maintaining different methods of accounting, there is a creation or shifting of profits or losses between the trades or businesses of the taxpayer (for example, through inventory adjustments, sales, purchases, or expenses) so that income of the taxpayer is not clearly reflected, the trades or businesses of the taxpayer will not be considered to be separate and distinct. Treas. Reg. § 1.446-1(d)(3).

[9] *See Id.*

[10] *Id.*

[11] Treas. Reg. § 1.446-1(e)(1).

[12] *Id.*

[13] *See* IRC § 446(e).

[14] *See* Rev. Proc. 2015-13 and Rev. Proc. 2015-14.

Treasury Regulations, or in other guidance published in the Internal Revenue Bulletin (collectively, "other guidance"), or (ii) wants to make such change but is not required to do so by Section 448 or any other guidance.[15] If the taxpayer is not within the scope of any automatic change request procedure for the requested year of change (or the accounting method change requested is not included in those procedures for the requested year of change), a taxpayer must seek IRS permission by filing under certain advance consent request procedures to change its overall accounting method (for example, from the accrual method to the cash method).[16]

12.1.2.1. Cash Method of Accounting

With limited exception, all individual taxpayers are cash method taxpayers. Under the cash method of accounting, and generally stated, all items of gross income are included in the taxable year in which such income is actually or constructively received, and expenditures are deducted in the taxable year in which they are actually made.[17]

Income, although not reduced to a taxpayer's actual possession, is deemed to be constructively received in the taxable year in which such amount is credited to the taxpayer's account, set apart for the taxpayer, or otherwise made available so that the taxpayer could have drawn upon it at any time (or so that the taxpayer could have drawn upon it during the taxable year if notice of intention to withdraw had been given).[18] These rules are intended, in part, to prevent taxpayers from deferring income recognition solely for tax (rather than business) reasons.

---

[15] Rev. Proc. 2015-14, Section 14.01(1)(a). Unless specifically authorized by the Commissioner or by statute, a taxpayer may not change an established method of accounting by amending its prior federal income tax return(s). Rev. Proc. 2015-13, Section 2.03(1). For a timely change in accounting method, a taxpayer required to change from the cash to accrual method under IRC § 448 must file Form 3115 no later than the due date (determined without regard to extensions) of the taxpayer's federal income tax return for the first taxable year in which the taxpayer is required to do so under IRC § 448 and the Form 3115 must be attached to that return. Treas. Reg. § 1.448-1(h)(2)(ii).

[16] See Instructions for Form 3115 (Application for Change in Accounting Method); Rev. Proc. 2015-13, superseding Rev. Proc. 97-27 as clarified and modified. Generally, the taxpayer must file Form 3115 with the IRS National Office under the advance request procedures during the tax year for which the change is requested. *Id.*

[17] Treas. Reg. § 1.446-1(c)(1)(i).

[18] Treas. Reg.

Generally, in the case of a C-corporation,[19] such as a "loanout company" (i.e., a personal service corporation), taxable income shall not be computed under the cash method of accounting unless, among other exceptions, the taxpayer (a) is a "Qualified Personal Services Corporation" ("*QPSC*"), or (b) has gross receipts of not more than five-million dollars for tax years beginning before December 31, 2017 and not more than twenty-five million dollars for tax years beginning after December 31, 2017 (the "*Gross Receipts Test*").[20] These exceptions are described in more detail immediately below.

a. Qualified Personal Services Corporation

A QPSC is any corporation with respect to which (i) substantially all of its activities for a taxable year involve the performance of services in one or more of a number of enumerated services, including performing arts (the "*Function Test*"),[21] and (ii) if at all times during the taxable year, substantially all of the corporation's stock, by value, is held, directly or indirectly, by employees performing services for such corporation in connection with the enumerated services (along with certain other permissive ownership) (the "*Ownership Test*").[22] The performance of services in the field of performing arts means the provision of services by actors, actresses, singers, musicians, entertainers, and similar artists in their capacity as such, but does not include the provision of services by (i) persons who themselves are not

---

[19] For this purpose, "C-corporation" includes any corporation that is not an S-corporation. Treas. Reg. § 1.448-1T(a)(3).

[20] IRC §§ 448(a)(1); 448(b)(3), as amended by P.L. 115-97 (12/22/2017).

[21] Treas. Reg. § 1.448-1T(e)(4). Other fields include health, law, engineering (including surveying and mapping), architecture, accounting, actuarial science and consulting. *Id.* Substantially all of the activities of a corporation are involved in the performance of services in any enumerated field, only if 95 percent or more of the time spent by employees of the corporation, serving in their capacity as such, is devoted to the performance of services in a qualifying field. *Id.*

[22] See Treas. Reg. § 1.448-1T(e)(3). The Ownership Test may also be met if the owners are (i) retired employees who had performed the enumerated services for the corporation, (ii) the estate of the current or retired employee that performs or performed the enumerated services, and (iii) any other person who acquired such stock by reason of the death of such individuals, but only for the 2-year period beginning on the date of the death of such individual. Treas. Reg. § 1.448-1T(e)(5). For purposes of the Ownership Test, "substantially all" means an amount equal to or greater than 95 percent. *Id.*

performing artists,[23] (ii) persons who broadcast or otherwise disseminate the performances of such artists to members of the public,[24] or (iii) athletes.[25] The IRS has privately ruled that only persons who perform for an audience will be considered to perform services in the field of the performing arts and, accordingly, for example, a producer or director of a film or TV show will not be considered to be involved in such services (i.e., although a director may contribute artistic skills to the production of a motion picture, the activities of a director do not involve performing before an audience).[26] Similar to a director of motion pictures, the activities of a producer, writer and other behind-the-camera talent should not involve performing before an audience. Accordingly, and provided that the C-corporation satisfies the other QPSC requirements, only the loanout of "front-of-the-camera" talent can use the cash method without limitation. Note that S-corporation loanouts generally are not subject to limitations on use of the cash method of accounting. *See* Section 12.2 below for a discussion of the distinctions between S-corporations, C-corporations, and other types of entities.

b. Gross Receipts Test

A C-corporation meets the Gross Receipts Test for any taxable year if the average annual gross receipts of such entity for the three-year taxable period (or, if shorter, the taxable years during which such corporation was in existence) ending with the immediately prior taxable year does not exceed a certain dollar threshold, which (i) is five million dollars for tax years beginning before December 31, 2017 and (ii) twenty-five million dollars for tax years beginning after December 31, 2017 (subject to certain inflation adjustments over time).[27] The

---

[23] *E.g.*, persons who may manage or promote such artists, and other persons in a trade or business that relates to the performing arts.

[24] *E.g.*, employees of a radio station that broadcasts the performance of musicians and singers.

[25] Treas. Reg. § 1.448-1T(e)(4)(iii).

[26] IRS P.L.R. 9416006 (Jan. 4, 1994). Similar to a director of motion pictures, the activities of a producer and other behind-the-camera talent should not involve performing before an audience.

[27] IRC §§ 448(c)(1); 448(c)(3)(A); Treas. Reg. § 1.448-1T(f)(2). In the case of any taxable year of less than twelve months (a short taxable year), the gross receipts shall be annualized by (i) multiplying the gross receipts for the short period by twelve,

following is an example of the application of the Gross Receipts Test drawn from the Treasury Regulations:

> Y, a calendar year C corporation that is not a qualified personal service corporation, has gross receipts of $10 million, $9 million, and $4 million for taxable years 1984, 1985, and 1986, respectively. In taxable year 1986, [Y] has average annual gross receipts for the 3-taxable-year period ending with 1986 of $7.67 million (10 million + 9 million + 4 million / 3). Thus, for taxable year 1987 ... Y [fails the gross receipts test] and must change from the cash method for such year.[28]

Accordingly, a loanout C-corporation that does not qualify as a QPSC will be required to change its method of accounting from cash to accrual in the first year in which it fails the Gross Receipts Test. Note that if the corporation in the above example was an S-corporation (in contrast with a C-corporation), then such corporation could maintain its cash method of accounting.

The twenty-five million dollar Gross Receipts Test (subject to inflation adjustments) was enacted under the Tax Cuts and Jobs Act and, as noted above, applies for taxable years beginning after December 31, 2017. Therefore, it is conceivable that a C-corporation loanout may have been forced on the accrual method of accounting in a prior taxable year as a result of failing the five million dollar Gross Receipts Test, but satisfies the twenty-five million dollar Gross Receipts Test. In such a circumstance, the entertainer should consult with his or her tax advisor to consider whether the C-corporation loanout is eligible and would benefit from a change of its overall accounting method to the cash method of accounting.

12.1.2.2. Accrual Method of Accounting

As noted above, many C-corporations are required to use the accrual method of accounting. Under the accrual method, income is included in gross income in the taxable year when all events have occurred that fix the right to receive the income and the amount of the

---

and (ii) dividing the result by the number of months in the short period. Treas. Reg. § 1.448-1 T(f)(2)(iii).

[28] Treas. Reg. 1.448-1T(f)(3), *Example* (2).

income can be determined with reasonable accuracy.[29] In the case of compensation for services, typically no determination can be made as to the right to such compensation or the amount thereof until the services are completed, and the amount of compensation is ordinarily income in the taxable year in which such determination can be made.[30] Nevertheless, a taxpayer's right to receive income is fixed upon the earliest of (i) the taxpayer's receipt of payment, (ii) the contractual due date, or (iii) the taxpayer's performance.[31]

Similarly, an expense is deductible under the accrual method when (i) all the events occur which establish the fact of the liability, (ii) the amount can be determined with reasonable accuracy (and with (i), the *"All Events Test"*), and (iii) economic performance has occurred with respect to the liability.[32] These rules (as described further below) are intended, in-part, to prevent taxpayers from accelerating deductions solely for tax (rather than business) reasons.

a. Fixed Liability

With respect to a liability, all events have occurred that determine the fact of the liability upon the earlier of (i) the event fixing the liability occurs, whether that be the required performance or other event, or (ii) the date on which the payment is due.[33]

b. Liability Determinable with Reasonable Accuracy

The second prong to the accrual method rules requires that the amounts be reasonably ascertainable before income is included or a deduction is permitted, as applicable. Generally, ascertainability is a facts and circumstances analysis based on the facts the taxpayer knows or could reasonably be expected to know at the close of the taxable year.[34] The taxpayer is expected to know information it can gain through reasonable inquiry.[35] In the case of payments calculated by

---

[29] Treas. Reg. §§ 1.446-1(c)(1)(ii); 1.451-1(a).
[30] Treas. Reg. § 1.451-1(a).
[31] *See, e.g.,* The Charles Schwab Corp., et al v. Comm'r, 107 TC 282 (1996).
[32] Treas. Reg. §§ 1.461-1(a)(2), 1.446-1(c)(2).
[33] *See, e.g.,* Rev. Rul. 80-230, 1980-2 C.B. 169.
[34] Camilla Cotton Oil Co. v. Comm'r, 31 T.C. 560, 567 (1958), *acq.,* 1959-2 C.B. 4; *see also* The Baltimore Transfer Company of Baltimore City v. Comm'r, 8 T.C. 1 (1947), *acq.,* 1947-2 C.B. 1.
[35] Schneider v. Comm'r, 65 T.C. 18, 29 (1975), *acq.,* 1976-2 C.B. 2.

reference to future events, the question is whether the taxpayer knows the facts necessary to apply the payment formula, or has reasonable access to such facts, thereby rendering the computation "a ministerial act."[36] In determining whether an amount was "reasonably ascertainable," the U.S. Supreme Court considered "whether the taxpayer had in its own books and accounts data to which it could apply the calculations required ... [to] ascertain the quantum of the award within reasonable limits."[37] A loanout company reporting under the accrual method of accounting may have a reasonable basis for the position that it should accrue amounts under its studio deals only on the date on which the relevant statements are received from the studios, as the loanout company generally will not be able to determine the amount to be received with reasonable accuracy.

c. Economic Performance

The All Events Test shall not be treated as met any earlier than when economic performance with respect to the item occurs.[38] If the liability arises as a result of another person providing services to the taxpayer, economic performance occurs as the services are provided.[39] Thus, in the entertainment industry, the All Events Test generally should be satisfied when all services required to be provided under the applicable studio contract have been completed (i.e., when economic performance has occurred).

12.1.3. Minimizing Tax Liability

12.1.3.1 Tax Deductions

A tax deduction will reduce the taxpayer's gross income and, thereby, reduce the taxpayer's ultimate tax liability for the taxable year in which the loss or expense is deductible under applicable law.[40]

---

[36] Continental Tie & Lumber Co. v. U.S., 286 U.S. 290 (1932); *see also* Camilla Cotton Oil Co., 31 TC 560 (1958) (stating that "the proprietary of an accrual must be judged by the facts which the taxpayer knew or could reasonably be expected to know at the closing of its books for the taxable year.").

[37] *Id.*

[38] IRC § 461(h)(1); Treas. Reg. § 1.461-4(a)(1).

[39] IRC § 461(h)(2)(A)(i); Treas. Reg. § 1.461-4(d)(1).

[40] A tax credit, on the other hand, will reduce a taxpayer's tax liability dollar-for-dollar (as described further below).

Generally, business expenses deductible from gross income include the "ordinary and necessary" expenditures directly connected with or pertaining to the taxpayer's trade or business.[41] Some common business expenses are summarized below.

a. Compensation for Personal Services

In the entertainment industry, entertainers often operate through a "loanout company" which generally is an S-corporation or a C-corporation formed by the entertainer and with which the entertainer will enter into an exclusive employment agreement with respect to the type of entertainment services performed through the loanout company.[42] The formation/operation of the loanout company can provide the entertainer with significant tax benefits. For example, if taxable as a C-corporation, and if structured properly, the loanout company may deduct certain medical reimbursements (and other employee benefits) paid to the entertainer. In addition, an entertainer can potentially mitigate the alternative minimum tax. If structured properly, these tax benefits, among others, can outweigh the compliance costs of creating/operating the corporation, which include corporate formation documents, annual accounting and corporate maintenance expenses, employment agreements (as discussed below), potentially increased employment tax liabilities, and annual income/franchise taxes.[43]

The loanout company then enters into contracts with the studios or other production companies. The studio will pay the loanout company compensation (fixed, deferred, and/or contingent) due for the entertainer's services pursuant to the service contract, generally without tax withholdings. The loanout company then pays all or a portion of the income generated from the studio contract to the entertainer as compensation for services, which is deductible to the loanout company to the extent that such compensation is reasonable. Reasonable salaries or other reasonable compensation for services actually rendered are deductible to the extent such payments are ordinary and necessary expenses paid or incurred in carrying on any

---

[41] IRC § 62(a)(1); Treas. Reg. § 1.162-1(a).
[42] Typically, talent should only establish a loanout company to the extent the entertainer's income sufficiently exceeds the annual operating costs of maintaining the loanout company.
[43] In California, for example, S-corporations are subject to a 1.5% entity level tax on net California source income.

trade or business.[44] The general test for deductibility is whether the amount of the payments is "reasonable" and whether in fact the payments are purely for services.[45] To determine whether the payment of purported compensation is "reasonable," the IRS generally will look to determine whether the payment is in excess of, or below, the amount that is ordinarily paid for similar services and the relationship that the payee has with the payor.[46]

For example, an amount paid by an entertainer's loanout company to the entertainer as compensation that is in excess of reasonable compensation may be recharacterized as a distribution of earnings by the corporation to the entertainer-shareholder. Such a deemed distribution may be taxable as a dividend and subject to double-tax if the loanout company is a C-corporation, since the deemed distribution will be taxable to the entertainer but not deductible by the corporation itself.[47] Provided that the IRS respects such payment as reasonable compensation, however, a C-corporation loanout company generally should have little to no corporate-level tax (and should generate little to no net operating loss ("**NOL**")) because the Company's net income will be directly offset by a corresponding reasonable compensation deduction generated from the compensation payment to the shareholder-employee.[48] In situations where the C-corporation generates a tax credit (e.g., a foreign tax credit), such credit may be unusable to the C-corporation to the extent that such corporation has no corporate-level tax liability.

Conversely, amounts paid by the entertainer's S-corporation loanout company to the entertainer as a distribution of earnings may be recharacterized as compensation to the extent compensation otherwise paid to the entertainer is below the amount considered as reasonable compensation, which may result in additional employment taxes. In cases where an S-corporation paid 100% of its net income to its shareholder as a distribution, the IRS successfully recharacterized the

---

[44] Treas. Reg. § 1.162-7(a).
[45] Id.
[46] Treas. Reg. 1.162-7(b)(1); see also Treas. Reg. § 1.162-9.
[47] See generally Id. and Treas. Reg. § 1.162-8. Note that, under the Tax Cuts and Jobs Act, the top corporate tax rate of 35% was reduced to 21%.
[48] Thus, the IRS often will attempt to characterize compensatory payments as deemed distributions (subject to double taxation). As described below in Section 12.2.2, however, the IRS will conversely attempt to characterize distributions from an S-Corporation as compensatory payments (subject to employment taxation).

full amount as compensation for services, subject to employment tax.[49] The IRS has also succeeded in recharacterizing a portion of S-corporation distributions as compensation subject to employment tax even when some compensation was paid to the shareholder-employee on the basis that the amount of compensation paid to the shareholder-employee was unreasonably low.[50] The case law and IRS authorities do not address how the foregoing rules may apply in the context of a loanout company. Legislation has been proposed, but was not enacted, that would make a shareholder's pro rata share of S-corporation income subject to self-employment tax to the extent that such shareholder provides substantial services in certain professional service businesses (including performing arts and athletics, which should pick up "front-of-the-camera" talent and athletes).[51] This rule would have applied to any "Disqualified S-corporation," which was defined as (i) any S-corporation which is a partner in a partnership that is engaged in such professional service businesses if substantially all of the S-corporation's activities are performed in connection with the partnership, and (ii) any other S-corporation which is engaged in a professional services business if the principal asset of the business is the reputation and skill of three or fewer employees.

The IRS has ruled that neither the election by the corporation as to the manner in which it will be taxed for federal income tax purposes, nor the consent to such election by the shareholder-employee has any

---

[49] *See* Rev. Rul. 74-44, 1947-1 C.B. 287.

[50] *See* Watson v. U.S., 668 F.3d 1008 (8th Cir. 2012), *aff'g* Watson v. U.S., (DC IA 05/27/2010) 105 AFTR 2d 2010-908. In *Watson*, the S-corporation paid its sole shareholder-employee approximately $203,000 (but only recorded $118,000) and $221,000 as dividend distributions in 2002 and 2003, respectively, and approximately $24,000 in each of such years as compensation for services. The IRS contended that approximately $130,000 and $175,000 of the dividend payments made in 2002 and 2003, respectively, should be recharacterized as wages subject to employment taxes. The District Court held in favor of the IRS, holding that the compensation should have been $91,000 per year, rather than $24,000 per year based on expert testimony.

[51] *See* American Jobs and Closing Tax Loopholes Act of 2010, H.R. 4213, 111th Cong. (2010); Technical Explanation of the Revenue Provisions Contained in the "American Jobs and Closing Tax Loopholes Act of 2010," For Consideration on the Floor of The House of Representatives, at https://www.jct.gov/publications.html?func=startdown&id=3684 (stating that, a "professional service business" for this purpose means a trade or business, substantially all of the activities of which involve providing services in the field of health, law, lobbying, engineering, architecture, accounting, actuarial science, performing arts, consulting, athletics, investment advice or management, or brokerage services.).

effect in determining whether such shareholder is an employee or whether payments to the shareholder are "wages" for federal employment tax purposes.[52] Ultimately, whether payments to a shareholder represent compensation for services or constitute a distribution of profits is purely a factual analysis and, given the lack of arm's length bargaining where the corporation is controlled by the employee to whom compensation is paid, courts apply special scrutiny to such determination.[53] In addressing characterization of reasonable compensation for purposes of characterizing payments as S-corporation distributions or compensation to the shareholder-employee subject to employment tax, courts generally look to the substance of the transaction based on the evidence as a whole, rather than the form of the transaction.[54] Therefore, it typically is good practice for the loanout company to maintain evidence of how and why the compensation paid to the shareholder-employee is reasonable compensation.

b. Traveling Expenses

Only traveling expenses that are "reasonable and necessary" in the conduct of the taxpayer's business and directly attributable to such business are deductible.[55] Such expenses may include travel fares, meals and lodging, and expenses incident to travel (such as telephone expenses), but not commuting expenses.[56] Any expenses that are undertaken for other than business purposes are non-deductible personal expenditures (e.g., a family vacation).[57] If the entertainer travels to a destination for both business and personal activities, the expenses to travel to and from the destination are only deductible if the trip is primarily related to the entertainer's trade or business.[58]

---

[52] Rev. Rul. 73-361.
[53] *See* Charles Schneider & Co. v. Comm'r, 500 F.2d 148 (8th Cir. 1974); Standard Asbestos Mfg. & Insulating Co. v. Comm'r, 276 F.2d 289 (8th Cir. 1960).
[54] *See* Watson v. U.S., 668 F.3d 1008 (8th Cir. 2012) (citing Joly v. Comm'r, 76 T.C.M. 633 (1998) (rejecting claim that compensation was reasonable and finding that amount did not reflect the true character of such payments); *aff'd*, 211 F.3d 1269 (6th Cir. 2000) (unpublished table decision).
[55] Treas. Reg. § 1.162-2(a).
[56] *Id.*
[57] *Id.*; IRC § 262.
[58] Treas. Reg. § 1.162-2(b)(1). If the trip is primarily personal in nature, the traveling expenses to and from the destination are not deductible even though the taxpayer engages in business activities while at such destination. *Id.* Whether a trip is

Expenses incurred while at the destination that are properly allocable to the entertainer's trade or business are deductible whether or not the travel expenses to and from the destination are deductible.[59]

If an entertainer's spouse or other family member accompanies the entertainer on a business trip, expenses attributable to such spouse or other family member are only deductible if the entertainer can adequately establish that the spouse and/or other family member's presence on the trip has a bona fide business purpose.[60] Performance of incidental services by a spouse or other family member are generally disregarded for these purposes.[61]

Under audit, the IRS generally will first establish the entertainer's "tax home."[62] Generally, a taxpayer's "home" for this purpose is the taxpayer's regular or principal place of business, without regard to the location of the taxpayer's residence.[63] If the entertainer works in more than one location in the tax year, then the taxpayer's "tax home" generally is determined by objectively analyzing the following factors: (i) the length of time that the taxpayer spent in each location, (ii) degree of the taxpayer's business activity in each place, and (iii) the relative proportion of the taxpayer's income derived from each place.[64]

If the entertainer has no principal place of business, his or her tax home will be the taxpayer's regular "place of abode." The three objective factors that are considered in determining whether the entertainer's claimed abode is his or her regular place of abode for tax purposes are:

---

related primarily to the taxpayer's trade or business or is primarily personal in nature depends on the facts and circumstances in each case. Treas. Reg. § 1.162-2(b)(2). The amount of time during the period of the trip which is spent on personal activity compared to the amount of time spent on activities directly relating to the taxpayer's trade or business is an important factor in determining whether the trip is primarily personal. *Id.*

[59] *Id.*
[60] Treas. Reg. § 1.162-2(c).
[61] *Id.*
[62] IRS, *Entertainment Audit Technique Guide*, Chapter 6 (Travel and Transportation Issues), Published October 9, 2015 (available at https://www.irs.gov/Businesses/Small-Businesses-&-Self-Employed/Entertainment-Audit-Technique-Guide).
[63] Rev. Rul. 60-189, 1960-1 C.B. 60, amplified by Rev. Rul. 83-82, 1983-1 C.B. 45; Rev. Rul. 73-529, 1973-2 C.B. 37.
[64] Markey v. Comm'r, 490 F.2d 1249, 1256 (6th Cir. 1974).

- The taxpayer performs a portion of his or her business in the vicinity of the claimed abode and at the same time uses the claimed abode for lodging.
- The taxpayer's living expenses at the claimed abode are duplicative because of business necessitated absence.
- The taxpayer either:
  o Has not abandoned the vicinity on which both his or her historical place of lodging and claimed abode are located;
  o Has family members currently residing at the claimed abode; or,
  o Uses the claimed abode frequently for lodging.[65]

If all three of the above factors are satisfied, the IRS should recognize the taxpayer's "tax home" to be at the claimed abode.[66] If two of the three objective factors are satisfied, then all the facts and circumstances must be "subjected to close scrutiny" to determine whether the taxpayer has a tax home or is an "itinerant."[67] If a taxpayer fails to satisfy at least two of the three objective factor, he will be regarded presumptively as an "itinerant" who has his or her "home" wherever he or she happens to work, as a result of which the taxpayer cannot be "away from home" for purposes of deducting travel expenses.[68]

c. Meals and Entertainment

For tax years beginning prior to December 31, 2017, 50% of the cost of meals and entertainment directly related to the active conduct of the taxpayer's trade or business were deductible by the taxpayer, unless such expenses qualified to be fully deductible.[69] While 50% of the cost of meals generally remains deductible for tax years beginning after December 31, 2017, taxpayers may no longer deduct entertainment expenses, even if such entertainment expenses are related to the active conduct of the taxpayer's trade or business.[70]

---

[65] Rev. Rul. 73-529, 1973-2 C.B. 37.
[66] *Id.*
[67] *Id.*
[68] *Id.*
[69] IRC §§ 274(a)(1), 274(n).
[70] IRC §§ 274(a)(1), as amended by P.L. 115-97 (12/22/2017).

d. Depreciation and Amortization Deductions

Certain types of costs are not permitted to be deducted currently and, instead, must be capitalized (i.e., charge the cost to a capital account or basis of property) under a permissible cost recovery method (e.g., income forecast method, discussed below). Deductions are generally more beneficial than capitalization, since deductions will reduce the taxpayer's current taxable income to a larger extent than the amortization of capitalized costs.

e. Production Costs for Certain Qualified Film, Television and Live Theatrical Productions

As discussed in more detail in Section 12.4.4.5. below, if certain requirements are satisfied, a taxpayer may be eligible to treat the cost of any qualified film or television production, and any qualified live theatrical production, as a current deductible expense in lieu of capitalizing and recovering such costs over time.

f. Pass-Through Deduction under the Tax Cuts and Jobs Act

Under the Tax Cuts and Jobs Act, sole proprietors, partners in a partnership, and shareholders of a S-corporations (but not C-corporations) may be eligible to deduct up to 20% of such taxpayer's qualified business income with respect to a qualified trade or business (the "*Qualified Business Income Deduction*").[71] For this purpose, the combined qualified business income amount that may be deductible generally is the lesser of (i) 20% of the taxpayer's qualified business income with respect to the taxpayer's qualified trade or business, or (ii) subject to exceptions, the greater of (x) 50% of the W-2 wages with respect to the qualified trade or business, or (y) the sum of 25% of the W-2 wages with respect to the qualified trade or business, plus 2.5% of the unadjusted basis immediately after acquisition of all qualified property of the trade or business (the "*W-2 Wage Limit*").[72] The W-2 wage limit does not apply if the taxpayer's taxable income for the year does not exceed a certain threshold amount (i.e., $157,500, or $315,000 if married filing jointly) and, once the taxpayer's taxable income

---

[71] IRC § 199A(b)(2). The calculation of the deduction is more complex than described here, but the calculation itself is beyond the scope of this chapter.

[72] IRC § 199A(b)(2).

exceeds such threshold amount, the W-2 Wage Limit is phased-in until the taxpayer's taxable income for the tax year is $207,500 (or $415,000 if married filing jointly).[73]

Unless the taxpayer's taxable income for the year is less than $207,500 (or $415,000 if married filing jointly), service businesses are not eligible for the Qualified Business Income Deduction, including businesses in the fields of performing arts or where the principal asset of the business is the reputation or skill of one or more of its employees or owners (a *"Reputation/Skill Service Business"*).[74] Although there is little guidance as to what is meant by "reputation or skill of one or more of its employees or owners," the IRS has issued private letter rulings that provide some insight.[75] For example, a trade or business generally should be considered a Reputation/Skill Service Business if the business offers value to its customers primarily in the form of services or individual expertise.[76] A business may not constitute a Reputation/Skill Service Business where the business activities involve deployment of manufacturing assets and intellectual property assets to create value for customers.[77]

Generally, unless the talent's taxable income for the tax year is less than the income threshold noted above, it is clear that (i) "front-of-the-camera" talent should not be eligible for the Qualified Business Income Deduction given that a business in the field of performing arts is a specified service business, and (ii) "behind-the-camera" talent also should not be eligible for the Qualified Business Income Deduction given that the principal asset of such business is the reputation or skill of the talent. Businesses that are not pure loanout companies, like management companies and production companies, should consider on a case-by-case basis whether their business may qualify for the Qualified Business Income Deduction if they can establish that the principal asset of their business is not the reputation or skill of one or more of its employees or owners.

---

[73] IRC § 199A(b)(3).

[74] IRC § 199A(d)(3). A qualified trade or business eligible for the deduction also excludes any trade or business of performing services as an employee. For a specified service business, the taxpayer is eligible for the full deduction if the taxpayer's taxable income for the tax year does not exceed $157,500 (or $315,000 if married filing jointly) and the deduction is phased out if the taxpayer's taxable income for the year is between $157,500 and $207,500 (and $315,00 and $415,000 if married filing jointly).

[75] *See generally* PLR 201436001 (9/5/14); 201717010 (4/28/17).

[76] PLR 201436001 (9/5/14); *See also* PLR 201717010 (4/28/17).

[77] *Id.*

12.1.3.2. Tax Credits

A tax credit is an amount subtracted directly from the taxpayer's tax liability, dollar-for-dollar, as opposed to a tax deduction that only reduces taxable income. When an entertainer is a U.S. person that performs services outside of the U.S., for example, and pays taxes in a foreign jurisdiction on compensation resulting from such engagement, the taxpayer may be eligible for a foreign tax credit, which is a tax credit against the taxpayer's U.S. income taxes attributable to foreign income taxes paid by the taxpayer on income earned by the taxpayer in a foreign jurisdiction. In addition, many states offer tax credits for film and television productions produced in such states, which incentivizes production companies to produce film and television in such states. A tax credit generated by an S-corporation will pass-through to its shareholder(s), which then may be used to offset such shareholder(s)' personal tax liability. In contrast, a tax credit that is generated by a C-corporation will not pass-through to its shareholder(s) and will be unusable to the extent that the C-corporation does not have any corporate level tax liability.

12.1.3.3. Loss Limitations

a. Passive Activity Losses

If a taxpayer's expenses exceed the taxpayer's gross income for a taxable year, then a loss will be generated. Whether the loss may be used will depend on many factors, including the character of the loss. An important set of loss limitation rules that often arise in the entertainment industry are the passive activity loss rules.

A taxpayer (who is either an individual, estate, trust, closely held C-corporation or a personal service corporation) is disallowed a "passive activity" loss (or credit) to the extent that passive activity deductions (or credit) exceed passive gross income for such taxable year. The disallowed loss or credit generally may be carried forward to the next taxable year, subject to the same limitations.[78] In the case of

---

[78] IRC §§ 469(a), 469(b); Treas. Reg. § 1.469-1T(a)-(b); Treas. Reg. § 1.469-2T(b)(1). For this purpose, a "closely held corporation" means a C-corporation that meets the stock ownership requirements of IRC § 542(a)(2) (taking into account the modifications in IRC § 465(a)(3)) for the taxable year and is not a personal service corporation for such year. Treas. Reg. § 1.469-1T(g)(2)(ii). Generally, a deduction is a "passive activity deduction" for a taxable year if and only if such deduction (i) arises

an S-corporation (or tax partnership), the passive loss rules apply (if at all) to owners of the S-corporation (or tax partnership), with a separate determination being made for each separate taxpayer.[79] A "passive activity" means any activity (i) which involves the conduct of any trade or business, and (ii) in which the taxpayer does not materially participate (e.g., participates in the business activity for more than 500 hours during the tax year).[80]

b. Pass-Through Loss Limitations under Tax Cuts and Jobs Act

A significant provision enacted under the Tax Cuts and Jobs Act is the imposition of certain loss limitations for taxpayers other than corporations, which applies for taxable years beginning after December 31, 2017 and before January 1, 2026 (the "*Pass-Through Loss Limitation*").[81] Under this provision, any "excess business loss" of the taxpayer for the tax year is disallowed and treated as a net operating loss.[82] *See* Section 12.1.3.3.c. for a discussion of the availability of NOLs under the Tax Cuts and Jobs Act. For S-corporations and partnerships, the Pass-Through Loss Limitation is applied at the partner or shareholder level, as applicable.[83] In addition, the application of the

---

(within the meaning of Treas. Reg. § 1.269-2T(d)(8)) in connection with the conduct of an activity that is a passive activity for the taxable year, or (ii) is treated as a deduction from an activity under Treas. Reg. § 1.469-1T(f)(4) for the taxable year. Treas. Reg. § 1.469-2T(d)(1). Generally, "passive activity gross income" for a taxable year includes an item of gross income if and only if such income is from a passive activity. Treas. Reg. § 1.469-2T(c)(1).

[79] *See, e.g.,* FSA 200035006 (passive activity loss and credit limitation of IRC § 469 applies to income, deductions, and credits at the taxpayer level, not at the pass-through entity level).

[80] IRC § 469(c).

[81] IRC § 461(l)(1).

[82] IRC §§ 461(l)(1)(B); 461(l)(2).

[83] IRC § 461(l)(4). In addition, each partner's or shareholder's allocable share of the items of income, gain, deduction, or loss of the partnership or S-corporation for any taxable year from trades or businesses attributable to the partnership or S-corporation shall be taken into account by the partner or shareholder in applying IRC § 461(l)(4) to the taxable year of such partner or shareholder with or within which the taxable year of the partnership or S-corporation ends. IRC § 461(l)(4)(B). For this purpose, in the case of an S-corporation, an allocable share shall be the shareholder's pro rata share of an item. *Id.*

Pass-Through Loss Limitation is applied after the application of the passive activity loss rules described above.[84]

For purposes of the Pass-Through Loss Limitation, an "excess business loss" is the excess, if any, of (i) the aggregate deductions of the taxpayer for the taxable year which are attributable to trades or businesses of such taxpayer (determined without regard to whether or not such deductions are disallowed for such tax year by application of the Pass-Through Loss Limitation), over (ii) the sum of (x) the aggregate gross income or gain of such taxpayer for the taxable year which is attributable to such trades or businesses, plus (y) $250,000 or $500,000 if the taxpayer files a joint return (subject to adjustments for inflation).[85]

The practical impact of the Pass-Through Loss Limitation is that an active loss that flows from an S-corporation or a partnership (e.g., loanout company or production company partnership structure) to the shareholder or partner is limited to $250,000 if such taxpayer is not filing a joint return or $500,000 if the taxpayer is filing a joint return. The disallowed portion is then characterized as an NOL and carried forward indefinitely and subject to further use limitations each year as discussed in Section 12.1.3.3.c, below.

c. Net Operating Losses

Generally, an NOL is the excess of allowable deductions (subject to certain modifications)[86] over gross income.[87] Prior to the enactment of the Tax Cuts and Jobs Act, an NOL generated during a tax year can fully offset taxable income and generally must be carried back to each of the two taxable years preceding the taxable year of such loss, and any remaining NOL must be carried over to each of the twenty taxable years following the taxable year of the loss until the NOL is fully utilized.[88] After the enactment of the Tax Cuts and Jobs Acts, (i) NOLs arising in tax years beginning after December 31, 2017 generally may only offset up to 80% of taxable income in any given tax year, and (ii) NOLs arising in tax years ending after December 31, 2017 cannot be carried back, but may be carried forward indefinitely.[89]

---

[84] IRC § 461(l)(6).
[85] IRC § 461(l)(3).
[86] See IRC § 172(d).
[87] IRC §172(c).
[88] IRC 172(b)(1)(A).
[89] IRC §§ 172(a); 172(b)(1); 172(e).

12.1.3.4. Character of Income

Depending on the circumstances, income may be characterized as either (i) ordinary income or (ii) capital gain. If income is characterized as ordinary income or short-term capital gain (gain from the sale of a capital asset held for one year or less), then such income is subject to ordinary income tax rates (the highest federal bracket is 37% as of 2018).[90] If income is characterized as long-term capital gain (gain from the sale of a capital asset held for more than one year), then (i) such gain will be subject to the long-term capital gain rate in effect at the time that the capital asset is disposed of (as of January 1, 2018, a maximum rate of 20%, plus an additional 3.8% Medicare surtax in certain circumstances).[91] A capital asset is defined as any asset other than certain assets that are enumerated in the Code, with the exclusions including inventory, certain depreciable property, accounts or notes receivable acquired in the ordinary course of business for services, and self-created copyrights, literary, musical, or artistic compositions, or similar property.[92] A taxpayer who created a musical composition or copyright may elect, however, to treat gain from the sale or exchange of such musical composition or copyrights as gain from a capital asset.[93] The method by which to make such election is discussed in Section 12.5.1. below.

12.1.3.5. Writer's Share – Musical Works

In IRS Program Manager Technical Assistance Memorandum 2007-0007, IRS counsel advised that payments made in respect of a "writer's share" interest in a musical copyright were royalty income (not compensation income) because the music publishing contract under which the songs were made (i) did not obligate the taxpayer to

---

[90] The highest federal bracket of 37% will sunset after 12/31/2025 and will revert to 39.6%.

[91] IRC §1(h); IRC §1411. C-corporations, however, are not entitled to preferential capital gain rates (i.e., income earned by a C-corporation will be subject to the applicable corporate tax rate, regardless of its character).

[92] IRC § 1221(a). Note that this rule also applies to a taxpayer in whose hands the basis of such property is determined, for purposes of determining gain from a sale or exchange, in whole or in part by reference to the basis of such property in the hands of the taxpayer-creator. IRC § 1221(a)(3)(C).

[93] IRC § 1221(a)(3).

write any music, and (ii) granted the music publisher only a limited copyright in the music – i.e., the right to use the songs in U.S. markets. In Revenue Ruling 74-555, the IRS held that amounts received by a foreign author under a contract granting a U.S. company the U.S. serial rights in his or her exclusive output of both long and short stories were royalty income because the contract "did not prescribe in any manner what the taxpayer was to write or when it was to be written.[94]

Making the determination between compensation, on one hand, and income derived from the ownership of an intangible, on the other hand, requires a careful analysis of the contract (and services being rendered) that gives rise to such income. Generally, if the income is paid under a contract to provide personal services, pursuant to which the service provider did not retain any interest in the intellectual property produced from the engagement, such income should be treated as deferred compensation. Any such deferred compensation (taxable at ordinary income rates) may be subject to the requirements of Section 409A (as described in detail below), along with the imposition of employment taxes.

In contrast, if the income relates to a "publishing" contract without any specific output requirements, the income payable to the service provider thereunder likely will be treated as royalty income (as opposed to deferred compensation) - such royalty income should not be subject to Section 409A, nor the imposition of employment taxes.[95] In this scenario, if the taxpayer anticipates selling this income stream, the taxpayer could consider undertaking a domicile shift to a lower tax jurisdiction to minimize the state income taxes owed on the gain from the sale of this "intangible."

12.1.4. Tax Deferral

Another important tax principle is tax deferral. There are a variety of tax planning strategies that may permit a taxpayer to defer taxation to a subsequent tax year when the entertainer may be subject to a lower effective tax rate based on his or her earnings or changes in the tax code. In some cases this may permit the taxpayer to receive cash in

---

[94] Rev. Rul. 74-555, 1974-2 C.B. 202 (1974).
[95] Royalty income can be subject to the federal 3.8% Medicare tax - the taxpayer can potentially mitigate the Medicare tax by actively managing the licensing of his/her intangible assets. A comprehensive discussion of these considerations is beyond the scope of this Chapter.

one year and report income in the subsequent year, enabling the entertainer to use funds that would otherwise have been withheld as taxes for other business or personal expenses before taxes are later imposed and paid.

12.1.4.1 Deferral Method for Advance Payments

For both cash and accrual method taxpayers, payments received in advance usually are income in the tax year received, provided that no restriction on use or disposition has been placed upon the use of the cash.[96] Under Revenue Procedure 2004-34, however, the IRS permits a taxpayer using or changing to an overall accrual method of accounting to defer the inclusion of advance payments until the next tax year to the extent that the recipient's performance takes place after the year of receipt (e.g., the payment is earned in whole or in part in a subsequent tax year) by making a timely "deferral method" election, hereinafter referred to as the "*Deferral Method*."[97]

The Tax Cuts and Jobs Act generally codified Revenue Procedure 2004-34 in new Section 451(c) applicable to tax years beginning after December 31, 2017. Prior to the Tax Cuts and Jobs Act, it was not entirely clear how a taxpayer should go about *adopting* the Deferral Method given Revenue Procedure 2004-34 generally provides guidance as to the procedure by which a taxpayer can *change* to the Deferral Method from another method of accounting. Procedures for making the election under new Section 451(c) are forthcoming from the IRS.[98] Once the election is made, it is irrevocable unless the IRS gives consent to revoke.[99]

Generally, a "deferral method" election to change to the Deferral Method is made under automatic consent procedures by attaching a Form 3115 to the taxpayer's timely filed (including extensions) federal income tax return for the year of change.[100] The amount deferred must

---

[96] Automobile Club v. MI v. Comm'r, 353 U.S. 180 (1957); Am. Automobile Assoc. v. U.S., 367 U.S. 687 (1961).
[97] IRS Rev. Proc. 2004-34, Sections 1, 3, and 4.01(2).
[98] *See* IRC § 451(c)(2)(A).
[99] IRC § 451(c)(2)(B).
[100] *See generally* IRS Rev. Proc. 2015-13; Instructions to Form 3115. Under certain circumstances, a taxpayer may be required to file for the Deferral Method under non-automatic consent procedures, in which case the Form 3115 is filed in the year in which the change is requested unless otherwise provided by published guidance. *Id.*

be included in income in the tax year following the tax year the payment is received, regardless of whether or not the remaining consideration for the payment is provided in that year.[101] A payment generally is an advance payment for this purpose if (i) it could be included in gross income for tax purposes immediately under the taxpayer's method of accounting, (ii) it is in whole or in part earned in a later tax year or recognized as revenue on the taxpayer's applicable financial statement[102] in a later tax year, and (iii) it is for services, the use (including by license) of intellectual property, or other enumerated items identified as permissible by the IRS.[103]

Under the Deferral Method, the amount of the advance payment recognized in revenue in the taxpayer's applicable financial statement for the year of receipt must be included in taxable income for that year.[104] If the taxpayer does not have an applicable financial statement, the amount earned in the year of receipt must be included in taxable income in that year.[105] The remainder of the advance payment is included in taxable income in the next tax year.[106]

A taxpayer may adopt any permissible method of accounting for advance payments for the first tax year in which the taxpayer receives

---

[101] IRC § 451(c)(1)(B)(ii); IRS Rev. Proc. 2004-34, Sections 1 and 5.02.

[102] The taxpayer's applicable financial statement is the first that it has of the following: (i) a financial statement to be filed with the Securities and Exchange Commission (the 10-K or the Annual Statement to Shareholders), (ii) a certified audited financial statement accompanied by the report of an independent CPA that is used for credit purposes, reporting to shareholders, or any other substantial non-tax purpose, or (iii) another financial statement (other than a tax return) required to be provided to the federal or a state government or agency other than the IRS or SEC. IRS Rev. Proc. 2004-34, Section 4.06.

[103] IRC § 451(c)(4)(A); *see also* IRS Rev. Proc. 2004-34, Section 4.01. Excluded from the definition of advance payments, and thus not deferrable under the Deferral Method, are rents, insurance premiums whose recognition is governed by subchapter L of the Code, payments with respect to financial instruments, payments with respect to warranty and guaranty contracts under which a third party is the primary obligor, payments subject to the withholding rules under Code Sections 871(a), 881, 1441, or 1442, payments in property transferred in connection with a provision of services (to which Code Section 83 applies), and any other payment specified as excluded by the IRS. IRC § 451(c)(4)(B); *see also* IRS Rev. Proc. 2004-34, Section 4.02.

[104] IRS Rev. Proc. 2004-34, Section 5.02(3)(a).

[105] IRS Rev. Proc. 2004-34, Section 5.02(3)(b).

[106] IRS Rev. Proc. 2004-34, Section 5.02(1)(a)(ii). If the next tax year is a short tax year of 92 days or less, only the amount recognized on the applicable financial statement for, or earned during, the short year is included in income, and the deferral can be extended to the following year. IRS Rev. Proc. 2004-34, Section 5.02(2).

advance payments.[107] If the taxpayer has established a different method of accounting for advance payments, a change to either the full inclusion method (i.e., including the full amount of the advance payment in the year of receipt) or the Deferral Method is a change in method of accounting.[108] A taxpayer that seeks to change its method of accounting for advance payments must use Form 3115 (Application for Change in Accounting Method).[109] A change to the deferral method qualifies for automatic consent of the IRS.[110]

Generally, the Deferral Method is a useful technique when a taxpayer, such as a production company, receives cash from a third party that is neither an owner of the production company nor a lender, and the production company is unable to fully deduct its qualified film and television production costs until the immediately subsequent year when the production is to be placed in service, as discussed below in Section 12.4.4.5. Absent the Deferral Method, such circumstance presents a timing issue because the production company generally should have taxable income upon receipt of the cash in Year 1, but is not eligible to deduct its production costs until Year 2 when the production is placed in service. This is particularly detrimental under the recently enacted NOL rules under the Tax Cuts and Jobs Act because if the deduction in Year 2 creates an NOL, the production company may not carryback the NOL to Year 1 to claim a refund. To solve this problem, if the production company is eligible for and makes the Deferral Method election, the production company may be able to successfully defer the Year 1 advance payment until Year 2 so that the income lines up with the corresponding production cost expense.

---

[107] IRS Rev. Proc. 2004-34, Section 8.01.
[108] Id.
[109] Id.
[110] See IRS Rev. Proc. 2015-14. For applications to change accounting methods that are filed on or after January 16, 2015, for a year of change ending on or after May 31, 2014, the change of accounting method procedures in Revenue Procedure 2015-13 must be followed. See IRS Rev. Proc. 2015-13 and 2015-14. Advance consent must be sought if the taxpayer wants to use the deferral method for allocated payments and the allocation is not deemed to be based on objective criteria, or if the taxpayer does not have an applicable financial statement and the amount to be deferred is to be determined on other than a straight line ratable basis. IRS Rev. Proc. 2004-34, Section 8.03.

12.1.5. Agency Theory: Exception to Gross Income

As discussed above, gross income means all income from whatever source derived, unless excluded by law.[111] Unless an exception applies, the cash method of accounting would require all taxable income – whether received in cash or property – to be included in gross income in the year that the taxpayer actually or constructively receives the income, and the accrual method of accounting would require all taxable income to be included when all events have occurred that fix the right to receive the income and the amount of the income can be determined with reasonable accuracy. IRS Revenue Ruling 59-92, however, clarifies an exception to the requirement of gross income inclusion under Code Section 61.

Specifically, where a taxpayer receives funds burdened with an obligation to be expended for a specific purpose and earmarked for such purpose (including operating costs), the funds so held do not constitute gain or income to the taxpayer, since the taxpayer does not receive beneficial ownership of the funds.[112] In Revenue Ruling 59-92, for example, the IRS adopted an *"Agency Theory"* approach when ruling that the entire amount of cash received by a taxpayer to be used for costs in a research program was not required to be included in gross income under Code Section 61 when (i) the taxpayer was obligated to expend the cash as required by the grantor, including use for operating costs such as salary for an employee, certain supplies, and equipment, (ii) any unused portion of the funds granted were to be returned to the grantor, (iii) title to any permanent equipment purchased with the granted funds remained with the grantor, and (iv) the taxpayer did not receive a salary or other economic benefit from the funds granted.[113] Under the Agency Theory, the IRS ruled that the taxpayer does not receive the funds granted to him or her as his or her own property for tax purposes when the taxpayer is obligated to use the funds for the purposes and in the manner set forth in the grant document and when any unused portion needs to be returned to the grantor.[114] The taxpayer in the ruling was a cash method taxpayer, but the Agency Theory generally should apply to both cash and accrual method taxpayers.

---

[111] California Rev. & Tax'n Code § 24271; IRC § 61.
[112] Rev. Rul. 59-92, 1959-1 C.B. 11.
[113] *Id.*
[114] *See id.*

Generally, the authority citing to and expanding upon the Agency Theory is sparse and the facts of such authorities are not specific to entertainment. The Agency Theory, however, may provide a reporting position that a production company that receives an overhead account from a studio is not required to include the receipt of such cash in gross income to the extent that the production company is required by contract to return unused funds to the studio and otherwise satisfies the requirements set forth above.

12.1.6. Taxable Years

Taxable income is computed, and a return is filed, by reference to a taxable year.[115] Generally, a new taxpayer may adopt any taxable year that satisfies the requirements of Code Section 441 and the regulations thereunder without the approval of the IRS.[116] A taxable year is adopted by the taxpayer filing its first Federal income tax return using that taxable year.[117] The filing of an application for automatic extension of time to file a Federal income tax return, the filing of an application for an employer identification number, or the payment of estimated taxes for a particular taxable year do not constitute an adoption of that taxable year.[118] Once a taxpayer has adopted a taxable year, such taxable year must be used in computing taxable income and making returns for all subsequent years unless the taxpayer obtains approval from the IRS to make a change or the taxpayer is otherwise authorized to change without the approval of the IRS under the Code and Treasury Regulations.[119] With limited exception, an individual taxpayer's tax year will be a calendar year, in contrast with a fiscal year-end available to certain eligible entities (as described below).

---

[115] Treas. Reg. § 1.441-1(a).
[116] Treas. Reg. §§ 1.441-1(c)(1); 1.441-1(c)(2)(i) (a newly-formed partnership, S-corporation, or PSC that wants to adopt a taxable year other than its required taxable year, a taxable year elected under Section 444, or a 52-53-week taxable year that ends with reference to its required taxable year or a taxable year elected under Section 444 must establish a business purpose and obtain the approval of the IRS under Section 442).
[117] Treas. Reg. § 1.441-1(c)(1).
[118] Id.
[119] Treas. Reg. § 1.441-1(e).

12.1.6.1. Fiscal Year

A fiscal year means (i) a period of 12 consecutive months ending on the last day of any month other than December, or (ii) a 52-53-week taxable year, if such period has been elected by the taxpayer.[120] A fiscal year will be recognized only if the books of the taxpayer are maintained on a fiscal year basis.[121]

With respect to a 52-53-week taxable year, an eligible taxpayer may elect to compute its taxable income on the basis of a fiscal year that (i) varies from 52 to 53 weeks, (ii) always ends on the same day of the week, and (iii) always ends on:

- whatever date this same day of the week lasts occurs in a calendar month (in this case, the year will always end within the month and may end on the last day of the month, or as many as six days before the end of the month); or

- whatever date this same day of the week falls that is the nearest to the last day of the calendar month (in this case, the year may end on the last day of the month, or as many as three days before or three days after the last day of the month).[122]

For this purpose, a taxpayer is eligible to elect a 52-53-week taxable year if such fiscal year would otherwise satisfy the requirements of Section 441 and the regulations thereunder.[123] If the taxable year of a partnership, S-corporation, or personal service corporation ("**PSC**")[124] and an employee-owner end with reference to the same calendar month, then for purposes of determining the taxable year in which an

---

[120] Treas. Reg. § 1.441-1(b)(5)(i).
[121] Treas. Reg. § 1.441-1(b)(5)(ii); books include the taxpayer's regular books of account and such other records and data as may be necessary to support the entries on the taxpayer's books and on the taxpayer's return, as for example, a reconciliation of any difference between such books and the taxpayer's return. Treas. Reg. § 1.441-1(b)(7). Records that are sufficient to reflect income adequately and clearly on the basis of an annual accounting period will be regarded as the keeping of books. *Id.*
[122] Treas. Reg. § 1.441-2(a)(1) and (2).
[123] Treas. Reg. § 1.441-2(3).
[124] Generally, a personal service corporation is a corporation that has the principal activity of performing personal services and such services are substantially performed by employee-owners (i.e., any employee who owns, on any day during the taxable year, more than 10% of the outstanding stock of the personal service corporation). IRC §§ 269A(a)(1); 269A(b); *see also* Proposed Treas. Reg. § 1.269A-1.

employee-owner takes into account items that are deductible by the entity and includible in the income of the employee-owner, the employee-owner's taxable year will be deemed to end on the last day of the entity's taxable year.[125]

A new eligible taxpayer elects a 52-53-week taxable year by adopting such year in accordance with Treasury Regulation Section 1.441(c) (e.g., by filing its first Federal income tax return using that taxable year).[126] A newly-formed partnership, S-corporation, or PSC may *adopt* a 52-53-week taxable year without the approval of the IRS if such year ends with reference to either the taxpayer's required taxable year or the taxable year elected under Section 444.[127] Generally, however, any such taxpayer must obtain approval of the IRS to *change* from an established taxable year to a 52-53-week taxable year.[128]

12.1.6.2. Required Tax Years

Generally, (i) a PSC that is wholly-owned by its employee-owner is required to use the calendar year as its taxable year,[129] (ii) an entity taxed as a partnership generally must use the same taxable year as its partners who own an aggregate interest in profits and capital of more than 50% or as determined by certain other methods if there is no such majority interest (the *"Partnership Tax Year"*),[130] (iii) an S-corporation must use

---

[125] Treas. Reg. §§ 1.441-2(e)(1); 1.441-2(e)(2). For example, X, a PSC, uses a 52-53-week taxable year that ends on the Wednesday nearest to December 31, and all of the employee-owners of X are individual calendar year taxpayers. Assume that, for its taxable year ending January 3, 2001, X pays a bonus of $10k to each employee-owner on January 2, 2001. Each employee-owner must include his or her bonus in income for the taxable year ending December 31, 2000. Treas. Reg. 1.441-3(b)(4), Example 2.

[126] Treas. Reg. § 1.441-2(b)(1).

[127] *Id.*

[128] Treas. Reg. § 1.441-2(b)(2).

[129] Calendar year means a period of 12 consecutive months ending on December 31. Treas. Reg. § 1.441-1(b)(4).

[130] IRC § 706; Treas. Reg. §§ 1.441-1(b)(2)(i)(G); 1.706-1. If there is no such majority interest, then the partnership must use the same taxable year as all the principal partners of the partnership (i.e., partners having an interest of 5% or more in partnership profits or capital.. IRC §§ 706(b)(1)(B)(ii); 706(b)(3). If there is no majority interest taxable year or principal partner taxable year, the Code and Treasury Regulations provide for other methods of determining the appropriate partnership taxable year.

the calendar year as its taxable year (the "*S-Corporation Tax Year*")[131] unless such entity:

- elects to use a taxable year other than its required taxable year under Section 444,
- elects a 52-53 week taxable year that ends with reference to its required taxable year or to a taxable year elected under Section 444, or
- establishes a business purpose to the satisfaction of the IRS.[132]

Such entity may adopt any of the foregoing taxable years without the approval of the IRS by filing its first Federal income tax return using that taxable year.[133]

A PSC that wants to change its taxable year must obtain the approval of the IRS or make an election under Section 444.[134] A PSC, however, may obtain automatic approval for certain changes, including a change to the calendar year or to a 52-53-week taxable year ending with reference to the calendar year.[135]

12.1.6.3. Section 444 Election

A partnership, S-corporation, and PSC may make or continue an election (a "*Section 444 Election*") to have a taxable year other than its required taxable year.[136] Generally, a Section 444 Election may only be made if the deferral period of the taxable year to be elected is no longer than three months (generally, a tax year ended on September 30, October 31 or November 30).[137] The term "*deferral period*" means the months between the beginning of such year and the close of the first required taxable year (i.e., in the case of a September 30 year end, the deferral period is October 1 through December 31).[138] The Section 444 Election must be filed by the

---

[131] IRC § 1378; Treas. Reg. §§ 1.441-1(b)(2)(i)(L); 1.1378-1.
[132] IRC § 441(i)(1); Treas. Reg. §§ 1.441-1(b)(2)(i)(B); 1.441-1(b)(2)(ii)(A) and (B); 1.441-3(a).
[133] Treas. Reg. § 1.441-3(b)(1).
[134] Treas. Reg. § 1.441-3(b)(2).
[135] *Id.*
[136] Treas. Reg. § 1.441-1(b)(2)(ii)(B); 1.444-1T(a)(1).
[137] Treas. Reg. § 1.444-1T(b)(1).
[138] Treas. Reg. § 1.444-1T(b)(4)(i).

earlier of (i) the 15th day of the fifth month following the month that includes the first day of the taxable year for which the election will first be effective, or (ii) the due date (without regard to extensions) of the income tax return resulting from the Section 444 Election (in the case of a new corporation, a short-period return generally must be filed by the 15th day of the third month after the short period ends).[139] However, an automatic extension of 12-months from the due date for making the Section 444 Election is granted if the taxpayer takes certain "corrective action"[140] within that 12-month extension period.[141] For this purpose, the due date for making the Section 444 Election is the extended due date of the return if (i) the due date of the election is the due date of the return, or (ii) the due date of the return including extensions and the taxpayer has obtained an extension of time to file the return.[142] The 12-month extension is available regardless of whether the taxpayer timely filed its return for the year for which the Section 444 Election should have been

---

[139] Treas. Reg. § 1.444-3T(b)(1).

[140] *"Corrective action"* means taking the steps required to file the Section 444 Election in accordance with the statute or the regulation published in the Federal Register, or the revenue ruling, revenue procedure, notice, or announcement published in the Internal Revenue Bulletin. Treas. Reg. § 301.9100-2(c). The instructions to the Form 8716 ("Election To Have a Tax Year Other Than a Required Tax Year") provide that to obtain the 12-month automatic extension, the taxpayer must type or legibly print "Filed Pursuant to Section 301.9100-2" at the top of Form 8716, and file the form within 12 months of the original due date. *See* IRS Form 8716. For those elections required to be filed with a return, corrective action includes filing an original or amended return for the year the regulatory or statutory election should have been made and attaching the appropriate form or statement for making the election. Treas. Reg. § 301.9100-2(c).

[141] Treas. Reg. §§ 301.9100-2(a)(1); 301.9100-2(a)(2)(i).

[142] Treas. Reg. § 301.9100-2(a)(1); The following Example 1 of Treas. Reg. § 301.9100-2(e) illustrates the automatic 12-month extension: Taxpayer A fails to make an election described in Treas. Reg. § 301.9100-2(a)(2) when filing A's 1997 income tax return on March 16, 1998, the due date of the return. This election does not affect the tax liability of any other taxpayer. The applicable regulations require that the election be made by attaching the appropriate form to a timely filed return including extensions. A makes the regulatory election by taking the corrective action of filing an amended return with the appropriate form by March 15, 1999 (12 months from March 16, 1998 due date of the return). If A obtained a 6-month extension to file its 1997 income tax return, A may make the regulatory election by taking the corrective action of filing an amended return with the appropriate form by September 15, 1999 (12 months from September 15, 1998 extended due date of the return).

made.[143] Taxpayers who make an election under an automatic extension (and all taxpayers whose tax liability would be affected by the election) must file their return in a manner that is consistent with the election and comply with all other requirements for making the election for the year the election should have been made and for all affected years; otherwise, the IRS may invalidate the election.[144] No request for a letter ruling is required to obtain an automatic extension.[145] Accordingly, user fees do not apply to taxpayers taking corrective action to obtain an automatic extension.[146]

A Section 444 Election is made by filing a properly prepared IRS Form 8716 ("Election to Have a Tax Year Other Than a Required Tax Year") with the IRS Service Center indicated by the instructions to Form 8716.[147] A Section 444 Election shall remain in effect until the election is terminated.[148] A Section 444 election is terminated, among other ways, when an S-corporation's S-election is terminated or when a PSC ceases to be a PSC; however, if a PSC that has a Section 444 Election in effect, elects to be an S-corporation, the S-corporation may continue the Section 444 election of the PSC and, similarly, if an S-corporation that has a Section 444 Election in effect terminates its S-election and immediately becomes a PSC, then the PSC may continue the Section 444 Election of the S corporation.[149]

A PSC that makes or continues a Section 444 Election for any taxable year (an "*applicable election year*") may limit or lose its ability to deduct compensation payments to the entertainer or his/her affiliate for the entire fiscal year if a minimum amount (determined under the Code and Treasury Regulations) is not paid to the entertainer or his/her affiliate during the deferral period as compensation.[150] This minimum

---

[143] *Id.*
[144] *Id.*
[145] Treas. Reg. § 301.9100-2(d).
[146] *Id.*
[147] Treas. Reg. § 1.444-3T(b)(1).
[148] Treas. Reg. § 1.441-1T(a)(2)(ii); *see* Treas. Reg. § 1.441-1T(a)(5) for rules governing termination of a Section 444 Election.
[149] Treas. Reg. § 1.444-1T(a)(5).
[150] Treas. Reg. §§ 1.444-1T(a)(2)(i); Treas. Reg. § 1.280H-1T(b)(1); *see also* Treas. Reg. § 1.280H-1T(b)(2) ("Any amount not allowed as a deduction in an applicable election year shall be allowed as a deduction in the succeeding taxable year."). A PSC meets the minimum pay-out requirement for an applicable election year if, during the deferral period of such taxable year, the applicable amounts (determined without regards to any amounts not allowed as a deduction carried over

pay-out requirement may entirely curtail the entertainer's ability to defer income using a fiscal year. Accordingly, the benefit to a PSC using a fiscal year should be weighed against the administrative burdens that may arise in making the minimum payment because, if the minimum pay-out requirement is not satisfied, the consequences could be disastrous if the entire deduction for compensation to the entertainer or his/her affiliate is denied as a result of an administrative error. A PSC is deemed to satisfy the minimum pay-out requirement for the first year of the corporation's existence.[151] No NOL carryback is allowed to (or from) any taxable year that a PSC has a Section 444 Election in effect.[152]

---

from prior years) for all employee-owners in the aggregate equal or exceed the lesser of (i) the amount determined under the "preceding year test", or (ii) the amount determined under the "3-year average test." Treas. Reg. § 1.280H-1T(c)(1)(i). The amount determined under the preceding year test is the product of (i) the applicable amount during the taxable year preceding the applicable election year (the "*preceding taxable year*"), divided by the number of months (but not less than one) in the preceding taxable year, multiplied by (ii) the number of months in the deferral period of the applicable election year. Treas. Reg. § 1.280H-1T(c)(2)(i). The amount determined under the 3-year average test is the applicable percentage multiplied by the PSC's adjusted taxable income that would result if the PSC filed an income tax return for the deferral period of the applicable election year under its normal method of accounting determined without regard to the applicable amounts. Treas. Reg. §§ 1.280H-1T(c)(3)(i); 1.280H-1T(c)(3)(iii)(A). For this purpose, the term "applicable percentage" means the percentage (not in excess of 95%) determined by dividing (i) the applicable amounts during the three taxable years of the corporation (or, if fewer, the taxable years the corporation has been in existence) immediately preceding the applicable election year, by (ii) the applicable income of such corporation (determined without regard to the applicable amounts) for such 3 taxable years (or, if fewer, the taxable years of existence). Treas. Reg. § 1.280H-1T(c)(3)(ii).

[151] Treas. Reg. § 1.280H-1T(e)(1). Example 2 of Treas. Reg. § 1.280H-1T(e)(5) illustrates this rule: W, a PSC, commences operations on July 1, 1990. Furthermore, for its taxable year beginning July 1, 1990, W makes a Section 444 Election to use a year ending September 30. Pursuant to Treas. Reg. § 1.280H-1T(e)(1), W satisfies the preceding year test and the 3-year average test for its first year in existence. Thus, W may deduct without limitation any applicable amounts for its taxable year beginning July 1, 1990.

[152] Treas. Reg. § 1.280H-1T(e)(3). Example 1 of Treas. Reg. § 280H-1T(e)(5) illustrates this rule: V is a PSC with a taxable year ending September 30. V makes a Section 444 Election for its taxable year beginning October 1, 1987, and incurs an NOL for such year. Because an NOL is not allowed to be carried back from an applicable election year, V may not carry back the NOL from its first applicable election year to reduce its 1985, 1986, or 1987 taxable income.

12.1.6.4. Calendar Year

A taxpayer that has not established a fiscal year must use a calendar year, which is a period of twelve consecutive months ending on December 31.[153] In certain cases, a taxpayer will be forced on the calendar year even if such taxpayer properly adopted a fiscal year. Specifically, the taxpayer's taxable year shall be the calendar year, unless consent is obtained from the IRS, if (i) the taxpayer keeps no books, (ii) the taxpayer does not have an annual accounting period, or (iii) the taxpayer has an annual accounting period, but such period does not qualify as a fiscal year.[154] Annual accounting period means the annual period (calendar year or fiscal year) on the basis of which the taxpayer regularly computes its income in keeping its books.[155] In order to mitigate potential arguments by the IRS that the company should be forced on a calendar tax year, the company should maintain books and an annual accounting period consistent with the adopted tax year from inception.

12.2. CONSIDERATIONS FOR CHOICE OF ENTITY

Generally, an entertainer should operate through a separate legal entity for limited liability purposes, or in other words, to insulate the entertainer's personal assets from potential creditors of, and liabilities arising in connection with, the entertainer's trade or business. This assumes the legal entity exclusively provides personal services, that the entity has no appreciating assets, and no other employees.

Although there are a number of entities to choose from under state law, the most common entity choice is a corporation (taxable as a C-corporation or S-corporation, each commonly identified by the "Inc." suffix in their legal names). To the extent that the studio is willing to treat the entertainer or his entity as an independent contractor, other types of entities that may be used are (i) a limited liability company ("*LLC*") wholly-owned by the entertainer, or (ii) a tax partnership ("*Partnership*"), such as general partnerships, limited partnerships or

---

[153] Treas. Reg. § 1.441-1(b)(4).
[154] IRC § 441(g); Treas. Reg. § 1.441-1(c)(2)(ii); *see also* IRC § 443 with respect to short taxable years.
[155] Treas. Reg. § 1.441-1(b)(3).

multi-member LLC.[156] Under certain circumstances, an LLC or Partnership may prove to be a more tax-efficient entity structure than a corporation (as explained in more detail below). It is often the case, however, that studios will insist on treating the entertainer as an employee of the studio subject to withholding, even if the studio contracts directly with the wholly-owned LLC or Partnership. For this reason, entertainers (especially in film/TV) may not be able to use an LLC or Partnership as their loanout company. In practice, book publishers generally tend to permit the use of an LLC loanout without withholding. In circumstances where multiple entertainers desire to share income on joint projects, to the extent the studio permits, entertainers may be the sole shareholders of their respective corporations, which in-turn, are owners of the Partnership – in this scenario, the studio can make payments in gross to the Partnership (i.e., free of employment tax withholding), which are then distributed among the owner corporations of the Partnership. Of course, the compensation paid by the corporations to the respective shareholders in the form of salary will be subject to tax withholding at that time.

12.2.1. C-corporation

A "C-corporation" is a tax term that refers to a corporation organized under state law that is taxed under Subchapter C of the Code. Absent any tax elections to the contrary, a domestic corporation will be a C-corporation by default. For tax years ending after December 31, 2017, a C-corporation generally is taxed at 21% (and prior to the enactment of the Tax Cuts and Jobs Act, C-corporations were taxed at graduated corporate tax rates with a maximum U.S. federal tax bracket of 35%).[157] A business operating as a C-corporation generally is subject to two levels of tax: (i) corporate tax at the entity level, and (ii) an additional tax at the shareholder level when earnings are distributed to the shareholder. A C-corporation, however, generally may deduct NOLs to offset its taxable income to reduce any corporate level tax at the entity level, as described in Section 12.1.3.3.c.

---

[156] In practice, the trend is to use LLCs rather than general partnerships or limited partnerships to avoid having a general partner that may be personally liable for the debts of the partnership.

[157] IRC § 11(b). As noted, C-corporations are not entitled to preferential capital gain rates for federal income tax purposes.

Liquidating and non-liquidating distributions by a C-corporation of appreciated property to the corporation's shareholders generally is treated as a deemed sale of such property by the corporation to the distributee shareholder.[158] The C-corporation is subject to corporate tax on the deemed sale gain to the extent the fair market value of the appreciated property exceeds its tax basis.[159] If the distributed property's tax basis exceeds its fair market value, the corporation is not permitted to recognize a loss.[160] The shareholder may recognize additional income in connection with the distribution and will generally have a basis in the distributed property equal to the property's fair market value.

12.2.2. S-Corporation

An S-Corporation is another tax term that refers to a corporation that is organized under state law and taxed under Subchapter S of the Code. Generally, a corporation may make an S-election if (among other things) the corporation is owned by not more than 100 shareholders who are individual U.S. citizens or residents and such corporation only has one class of stock.[161] A small business corporation makes an election to be treated as an "S-corporation" by filing a completed Form 2553 (*Election by Small Business Corporation*) (the "*S-Election*").[162] Generally, the S-Election may be made at any time during the taxable year that immediately precedes the taxable year for which the election is to be effective, or during the taxable year for which the election is to be effective provided that the election is made before the 16th day of the third month of the year (i.e., March 15th for an existing small business corporation).[163] A limited liability company

---

[158] IRC §§ 311(b)(1); 336(a); *but see* IRC §§ 332 and 337(a) (providing that no gain or loss shall be recognized by the liquidating corporation or a corporate shareholder with respect to liquidating distributions distributed to such corporate shareholder if such corporate shareholder owns eighty percent (80%) of the stock (by vote and value) of the liquidating corporation, among other requirements).

[159] *Id.*; similarly, a liquidating S-corporation recognizes gain or loss on the distribution of property in complete liquidation as if such property were sold to the distributee shareholder at its fair market value. IRC § 336(a).

[160] IRC § 311(a).

[161] IRC § 1361(b) (noting that a corporation may have shareholders that are not an individual if such shareholder is an estate, a trust described in IRC § 1361(c)(2), or an organization described in IRC § 1361(c)(6)).

[162] Treas. Reg. § 1.1362-6(a)(2).

[163] Treas. Reg. § 1.1362-6(a)(2)(ii).

that elects to be an S-corporation is treated as having made an entity classification election to be classified as a corporation simultaneously with the S-Election (provided that the limited liability company meets all of the other requirements to qualify as a small business corporation and any applicable "check-the-box" requirements).[164] The deemed election to be classified as a corporation will apply as of the effective date of the S-Election and will remain in effect until the entity makes a valid election to be classified as other than a corporation.[165]

Unlike a C-corporation, income received by an S-corporation passes through to its shareholders and is generally only subject to one level of tax at the shareholder level. Surprisingly, like a C-corporation, distributions of appreciated property from an S-corporation (whether operating or liquidation distributions) are subject to taxation as though the property was sold to the distributee shareholders, and any gain recognized on such distribution passes through to the shareholders, increasing their respective stock basis.[166] Moreover, some states impose an entity level tax (e.g., California imposes a 1.5% net income tax at the entity level) upon S-corporations.

Net loss generated by an S-corporation will pass-through to its shareholders to be used to offset each such shareholder's income, subject to certain loss limitation rules (e.g., capital loss limitations, passive activity loss limitations, and the Pass-Through Loss Limitation). Thus, an S-corporation itself does not have NOLs, since any losses are passed-through to its shareholders and any loss that may be disallowed by the Pass-Through Loss Limitation generally will be treated as an NOL at the shareholder level.

In practice, S-corporation loanout companies generally pay out at least 50-80% of gross pretax income (net of fixed overhead costs) as compensation (subject to employment tax) to the shareholder-employee for services rendered and the balance is distributed to the shareholder (not subject to employment tax, since distributions are not considered "wages"). As discussed above, however, the percentage paid as compensation must not be below what is considered to be reasonable compensation in the entertainment industry under the facts and circumstances, or else the IRS or applicable state tax authority may

---

[164] Treas. Reg. § 301.7701-3(c)(1)(v)(C).
[165] Id.
[166] IRC §§ 311(b)(1); 336(a); 1371(a) (generally providing that subchapter C applies to an S-corporation and its shareholders unless subchapter S provides otherwise).

recharacterize all or a portion of the distributions as wages subject to employment tax (along with potential penalties and interest). In recent years, it appears that the IRS has been taking the position on audit that all of an S-corporation loanout company's net income should be paid out as compensation for services given that the entity's primary business is the provision of services. There appears to be no specific authority that mandates all of the S-corporation's net income be paid as compensation if the shareholder-employee is getting reasonable compensation. As noted above, Congress has considered legislation that would impose self-employment tax on a shareholder's distributive share of income in certain circumstances, which suggests that there currently is not a legislative mandate to pay 100% of S-corporation income to the shareholder as compensation if the shareholder-employee is getting reasonable compensation. Therefore, it is important for the company to maintain records to support the determination of reasonable compensation paid to the shareholder-employee.

If a C-corporation that has built-in gain assets converts to an S-corporation, an entity level tax will be imposed (currently, a 21% corporate rate) at the federal level on the corporation if it sells such appreciated assets within five years from the first day of the first taxable year which the corporation is an S-corporation.[167] Generally, this rule also applies to any asset acquired by an S-corporation from a C-corporation with a carryover tax basis.[168] The built-in gain tax can be avoided, under certain circumstances, by eliminating the corporation's taxable income during the year in which the built-in gain is recognized. In addition, certain excess distributions from an S-corporation (that was formerly taxable as a C-corporation) may be subject to double-taxation. This problem may be avoided, where the C-corporation distributes any accumulated earnings and profits prior to the S-corporation election.

12.2.3. Tax Partnerships; LLCs

As noted, an entertainer may be unable to use a tax partnership (such as an LLC) as a loanout-company. However, a tax partnership

---

[167] IRC § 1374. This 5-year period is known as the "built-in gain period." State law may impose similar rules, but with different built-in gain periods – for example, California's current built-in gain period is 10 years.

[168] IRC § 1374(d)(8).

(most frequently, an LLC) is often used to hold intellectual property and for businesses that generate income from other than personal services (for example, film or television programming production, a band's operation, merchandising, etc.).

An LLC is taxed as (i) a partnership if it has multiple members, or (ii) as an entity disregarded from its owner if it has a single owner (a "*Disregarded Entity*").[169] An LLC may make an entity classification election by filing IRS Form 8832 to be treated as a corporation (C-corporation or, if an S-election is filed, an S-corporation).[170]

Like an S-corporation, net income or net loss of a partnership passes through to the partners of the partnership. Unlike an S-corporation, appreciated property generally may be distributed to partners in a partnership without taxation (subject to certain exceptions). Distributions of money to partners are generally not subject to taxation unless the amount of cash distributed exceeds the distributee partner's tax basis in the partner's equity interest (otherwise known as "outside basis").

If the LLC is a Disregarded Entity, then the owner of the LLC is treated as a sole proprietor of the LLC's business for income tax purposes. The single-member LLC itself, however, will typically remain responsible for withholding income and employment taxes and remitting such amounts to the IRS in connection with its employees.

12.2.4. Qualified Personal Service Company ("QPSC")

A personal service corporation is a corporation the principal activity of which is the performance of personal services and such services are substantially performed by employee-owners.[171] The term "employee-owner" means any employee who owns, on any day during the taxable year, more than 10% of the outstanding stock of the personal service corporation, taking into account certain constructive ownership rules.[172] All related persons are treated as one entity.[173] A QPSC is currently taxed at a flat federal tax rate of 21% on taxable

---

[169] Treas. Reg. § 301.7701-3(b)(1).
[170] Treas. Reg. § 301.7701-3(c); IRS Form 8832. Domestic corporations are ineligible for such "check-the-box" elections.
[171] IRC § 269A(b)(1); Treas. Reg. § 1.441-3(c).
[172] IRC § 269A(b)(2).
[173] IRC § 269A(b)(3); "related persons" has the meaning set forth in IRC 144(a)(3).

income (and prior to the enactment of the Tax Cuts and Jobs Act, a QPSC was taxed at a flat federal tax rate of 35%).[174]

A QPSC is any corporation with respect to which (i) substantially all of its activities for a taxable year involve the performance of services in one or more of a number of enumerated services, including performing arts (the *"Function Test"*),[175] and (ii) if at all times during the taxable year, substantially all of the corporation's stock, by value, is held, directly or indirectly, by employees performing services for such corporation in connection with the enumerated services, among certain other permissive ownership[176] (the *"Ownership Test"*).[177] As previously noted, the performance of services in the field of performing arts means the provision of services by actors, actresses, singers, musicians, entertainers, and similar artists in their capacity as such, but does not include the provision of services by (i) persons who themselves are not performing artists (such as directors, as described below),[178] (ii) persons who broadcast or otherwise disseminate the performances of such artists to members of the public,[179] or (iii) athletes.[180]

The QPSC exception is limited to corporations involved in the "performance of services in the fields of health, law, engineering, architecture, accounting, natural science, performing arts, or

---

[174] IRC § 11(b)(2).

[175] Treas. Reg. § 1.448-1T(e)(4). Other fields include health, law, engineering (including surveying and mapping), architecture, accounting, actuarial science and consulting. *Id.* Substantially all of the activities of a corporation are involved in the performance of services in any enumerated field, only if 95 percent or more of the time spent by employees of the corporation, serving in their capacity as such, is devoted to the performance of services in a qualifying field. *Id.*

[176] The Ownership Test may also be met if the owners are (i) retired employees who had performed the enumerated services for the corporation, (ii) the estate of the current or retired employee that performs or performed the enumerated services, and (iii) any other person who acquired such stock by reason of the death of such individuals, but only for the 2-year period beginning on the date of the death of such individual. Treas. Reg. § 1.448-1T(e)(5). For purposes of the Ownership Test, "substantially all" means an amount equal to or greater than 95 percent. *Id.*

[177] IRC § 448(d)(2); Treas. Reg. § 1.448-1T(e)(3).

[178] *E.g.*, persons who may manage or promote such artists, and other persons in a trade or business that relates to the performing arts.

[179] *E.g.*, employees of a radio station that broadcasts the performance of musicians and singers.

[180] Treas. Reg. § 1.448-1T(e)(4)(iii).

consulting."[181] Of these categories, "performing arts" could conceivably include writers of film and television shows. The Treasury Regulations, however, provide that "[t]he performance of services in the field of the performing arts does not include the provision of services by persons *who themselves are not performing artists...*" (emphasis added).[182]

This conclusion was confirmed by Private Letter Ruling 9416006 (1994) which held that a corporation that provided motion picture director services was not engaged in performing arts even though "the activities of a motion picture director are related to the performance of the services by actors and actresses" because *"the activities of a director do not involve performing before an audience"* (emphasis added). Similarly, the services of a film and television writer are related to performing artists, but do not actually involve performing before an audience.

12.2.5. Personal Holding Company

A corporation is treated as a personal holding company (**"PHC"**) if it satisfies two tests: (i) the income test, and (ii) the stock ownership test.

Under the income test, a corporation is not a PHC unless at least 60% of its "adjusted ordinary gross income" (**"AOGI"**) for the taxable year is "personal holding company income" (**"PHCI"**).[183] The gross receipts of a service business generally will be treated as its gross income for PHC purposes, without any reduction for the cost of the services provided.[184] PHCI includes amounts received pursuant to a contract under which the corporation is to furnish personal services if:

---

[181] IRC § 448(d)(2)(A).

[182] Treas. Reg. § 1.448-1T(e)(4)(iii). IRC § 448(b)(3) provides an additional exception to mandatory accrual method accounting for C corporations whose gross income averages no more than $25 million annually.

[183] IRC § 542(a)(1).

[184] Andrew Jergens Co. v. Comm'r, 40 B.T.A. 868 (1939) (Taxpayer furnishing services and facilities to its subsidiaries was permitted to include reimbursements from the subsidiaries in its gross income without any deduction for its cost for these services.); *see also* W.A. Bechtel Co. v. Comm'r, 42 B.T.A. 927 (1940) (Taxpayer contracted to remove certain pipes for a stipulated amount and then hired another to do this job for a price which would have yielded a small profit but which, when additional

- some person other than the corporation has a right to designate (by name or by description) the individual who is to perform the services, or if the individual who is to perform the services is designated (by name or by description) in the contract, and,
- at any time during the taxable year, 25% or more in value of the outstanding stock of the corporation is owned by or for the individual who has performed, is to perform, or may be designated to perform the services.[185]

The following example set forth in the Treasury Regulations illustrates that loanout company arrangements generally satisfy the above tests:[186]

> A, whose profession is that of an actor, owns all of the outstanding capital stock of the M Corporation. The M Corporation entered into a contract with A under which A was to perform personal services for the person or persons whom the M Corporation might designate, in consideration of which A was to receive $10,000 a year from the M Corporation. The M Corporation entered into a contract with the O Corporation in which A was designated to perform personal services for the O Corporation in consideration of which the O Corporation was to pay the M Corporation $500,000 per year. The $500,000 received by the M Corporation from the O Corporation constitutes PHCI.

If PHCI divided by the AOGI is equal to or greater than 60%, then the income test is satisfied. If not, then the corporation cannot be a PHC.

Under the stock ownership test, a corporation generally is not a PHC unless more than 50% in value of the corporation's outstanding stock is owned directly or indirectly (using certain attribution rules)[187] by or for not more than five individuals at any time during the last half of the corporation's taxable year.[188]

The PHC tax is imposed, in addition to the regular corporate tax, on a PHC's "undistributed personal holding company income"

---

costs were incurred, resulted in a loss. The court held that the amount the taxpayer received was includible in its gross income for PHC purposes.

[185] IRC § 543(a)(7). A shareholder's percentage of ownership is determined using the attribution rules of IRC § 544.
[186] Treas. Reg. § 1.543-1(b)(8)(iii), Example 1.
[187] For this purpose, the attribution rules of IRC § 544 are applied.
[188] IRC § 542(a)(2).

("*Undistributed PHCI*") at a rate of 20% of the undistributed personal holding company income.[189] Undistributed PHCI means the taxable income of a PHC subject to certain adjustments (e.g., reduced by federal income and excess profits taxes, etc.) minus the dividends paid deduction, which is the sum of (i) dividends paid during the taxable year, (ii) "consent dividends" for the taxable year,[190] and (iii) certain dividend carryovers.[191] The NOL deduction provided in Code Section 172 is not allowed in determining Undistributed PHCI.[192] For purposes of such computation, however, there is allowed as a deduction the amount of the NOL (subject to any use limitations set forth in Code Section 172(c)) for the preceding taxable year, except that, in computing Undistributed PHCI, the amount of such NOL shall be computed without regard to certain special deductions for corporations.[193] Accordingly, if the PHC tax applies, then the effective combined United States federal income tax rate plus the PHC tax applicable to a QPSC that is also a PHC may be up to 41%. Therefore, loanout companies generally should pay compensation and distribute any retained earnings prior to the end of such company's taxable year.

12.2.6. Accumulated Earnings Tax

An accumulated earnings tax equal to 20% is imposed on a corporation's accumulated taxable income each tax year to the extent that such corporation was formed or availed for the purpose of avoiding income tax with respect to its shareholders or the shareholders of any other corporation by permitting earnings and profits to accumulate instead of being paid out as a dividend or

---

[189] IRC § 541, as amended by the American Taxpayer Relief Act of 2012 (2012 ATRA), Pub. L. No. 112-240, § 101, § 102(c), effective for taxable years beginning after December 31, 2012.

[190] *See* IRC 565 (consent dividends are dividends).

[191] IRC s 545; *see* IRC § 564 for computation of dividend carryovers. Even if a corporation is a PHC and liable for the surtax, it may avoid the surtax by making a so-called "deficiency dividend" or special distribution to its shareholders under IRC § 547.

[192] IRC § 545(b)(4); Treas. Reg. § 1.545-2(d).

[193] *Id.* Special corporate deductions not taken into account in calculating the NOL are deductions set forth in IRC § 241 (allowance for special deductions), IRC § 243 (dividends received by corporations), IRC § 245 (dividends received from certain foreign corporations), IRC § 246 (rules applying to deductions for dividends received), IRC § 246A (dividends received deduction reduced where portfolio stock is debt financed), and IRC § 249 (limitation on deduction of bond premium on repurchase).

distributed.[194] This tax does not apply to a personal holding company and certain other exempt corporations.[195] In practice, the accumulated earnings tax should not be an issue so long as loanout companies distribute or pay as compensation all (or substantially all) of its earnings to the entertainer-shareholder.

12.2.7. State Entity Level Taxes

Although LLCs and S-corporations generally are considered pass-through entities for federal tax purposes, some states impose an entity level tax on such entities. California, as discussed below, is one such state.[196]

12.2.7.1. California Gross Receipts Tax

In addition to an entity level annual tax of $800, LLCs organized, registered to do business, or that are doing business in California are subject to a gross receipts tax.[197] The California gross receipts tax is based on the "total income from all sources derived or attributable to" the state of California for the taxable year.[198] The gross receipts tax is imposed on a graduated basis and currently does not exceed $11,790 for any taxable year.[199]

---

[194] IRC §§ 531; 532(a).

[195] IRC § 532(b) (the accumulated earnings tax also does not apply to a passive foreign investment company (as defined in IRC § 1297 or a corporation exempt from tax under subchapter F (IRC § 501 and following).

[196] For California, see https://www.ftb.ca.gov/forms/misc/3556.pdf & https://www.ftb.ca.gov/businesses/Structures/S-Corporations.shtml; also the state-by-state entity-level tax requirements, as of 2012, can be found at: http://www.taxhistory.org/www/features.nsf/Articles/229AC612C1AB1F1F852579FB00667E7B?OpenDocument. Please verify with the applicable state's tax authority for the most recent requirements, fees, and taxes.

[197] California R&TC §§ 17941(a); 17942(a).

[198] California R&TC § 17942(a).

[199] Id. The gross receipts tax is (i) $900 if gross receipts are $250k or more but less than $500k, (ii) $2,500 if gross receipts are $500k or more but less than $1m, (iii) $6,000 if gross receipts are $1m or more but less than $5m, or (iv) $11,790 if gross receipts are $5m or more.

12.2.7.2. California Net Income Tax on S-Corporations

Currently, California conforms to the Code in effect as of January 1, 2015.[200] California generally has adopted subchapter S of the Code relating to the tax treatment of S-corporations and their shareholders (with certain exceptions, such as the built-in gain period).[201] However, an S-election in California will not alleviate all corporate level taxes because California imposes a 1.5% entity-level tax on the S-corporation's net income (in addition to the pass-through tax imposed on shareholders) whether or not the income is distributed.[202] Corporations doing business in California that elect California S-corporation treatment are also subject to the minimum annual franchise tax of $800.[203]

12.3. EMPLOYEE VERSUS INDEPENDENT CONTRACTOR

If a service provider is classified as an employee, then the employer must withhold income, Social Security and Medicare taxes from the employee's wages, which is reported on the employee's IRS Form W-2.[204] For 2018, the employee-paid portion of payroll taxes withheld from the employee's compensation are (i) 6.2% for Social Security (up to the first $128,400 of taxable wages), (ii) 1.45% for Medicare, and (iii) an additional 0.9% for Medicare on wages in excess of $200,000.[205] The employer-paid portion of payroll taxes (paid by the employer and not withheld from the employee's compensation) are the same as the employee-paid portion except that the employer does not pay the 0.9% surtax.[206] The employment tax rates and thresholds (especially Social Security) are subject to change each year.

If a service provider is classified as an independent contractor, then the service provider's compensation is not subject to withholding and

---

[200] *See* https://www.ftb.ca.gov/forms/updates/conformity.shtml.
[201] California Revenue and Taxation Code § 23800 ("Subchapter S of Chapter 1 of Subtitle A of the Internal Revenue Code, relating to tax treatment of "S corporations" and their shareholders, shall apply, except as otherwise provided.").
[202] California Revenue and Taxation Code § 23802(b).
[203] A comparative table for California treatment of S-corporations and LLCs can be found at: https://www.ftb.ca.gov/Archive/Professionals/Taxnews/2013/June/Article_1.shtml.
[204] IRC §§ 3102; 3401-3403;
[205] IRC §§ 3101(a), 3111(a).
[206] *Id.*

the employer does not pay any payroll taxes.[207] Instead, the service provider is subject to self-employment taxes on compensation reflected on an IRS Form 1099 issued by the payor at the following rates as of 2018: (i) 12.4% for Social Security (up to the first $128,400 of taxable compensation), (ii) 2.9% for Medicare, and (iii) an additional 0.9% for Medicare on wages in excess of $200,000.[208] The service provider is entitled to a deduction for the portion of the self-employment taxes that would have otherwise been paid by the employer if the service provider were an employee of the payor.[209]

Generally, whether a service provider is an employee is a facts and circumstances analysis based on a number of factors, including whether the employer exercises (i) behavioral control over the service provider (e.g., whether the employer controls what the service provider does and how he/she does it), (ii) financial control over the service provider (e.g., how the service provider is paid, whether expenses are reimbursed), and (iii) the service relationship (e.g., whether it is exclusive to the employer).[210] If a service provider is misclassified as an independent contractor, the employer (or other withholding agent) may be subject to withholding tax liability and penalties for failure to withhold.[211] For this reason, film/TV studios generally will not engage talent through an LLC or directly without requiring that the talent be treated as an employee in order to mitigate potential withholding tax liability. Therefore, most film/TV talent will operate through a corporate loanout company, so that the talent is an employee of the loan out company itself.

12.4. STRUCTURING ENTERTAINMENT TRANSACTIONS (FORMATION AND OPERATIONS)

12.4.1. Loanout Companies

Generally, a "loanout company" is a company that "lends" the services of service providers (which in the entertainment context typically is the entertainer-shareholder) to a third party. In the film and television industry, a loanout company is usually a wholly-owned corporation (taxable as an S-corporation or a C-corporation) that hires

---

[207] IRC § 1402.
[208] IRC §§ 1401-1402.
[209] IRC §§ 164(f); 1402.
[210] Treas. Reg. §31.3401(c)-1.
[211] IRC §§ 3505, 6672.

it sole shareholder as an employee, and then "loans" out the services of its employee to studios. Accordingly, there are two streams of income, a compensatory payment from the studio to the loanout company pursuant to the studio contract, and a compensatory payment (and, sometimes, a distribution) to the employee-shareholder.

As noted above, in the film and television business, a corporate loanout company is commonly used as a tax planning vehicle for highly compensated entertainers; if a loanout company is not used, film and television studios generally will treat the entertainer as an employee, subject to employment tax withholding. Although, in many cases, the entertainer will satisfy the requirements to be treated as an independent contractor, the film and television studios often take a conservative approach to avoid potential withholding penalties. A loanout company structure will generally avoid these issues, since the entertainer is employed by the loanout company itself (in contrast with the studio). The loanout company can then engage in its own tax planning to defer or reduce taxes at the state and federal level that would otherwise be withheld if the employment were direct with the studio. Now, with the repeal of itemized employee business expenses under the Tax Cuts and Jobs Act, the use of loanout companies may be advisable at any income level.

In the music industry, structuring may be more complex given that the musician(s) may, directly or indirectly, own the copyright to their works, there may be multiple band members owning the loanout company, and there are liabilities unique to touring that demand a separate entity to insulate tour liabilities from other assets. Structuring for music is discussed in more detail below.

12.4.1.1. General Benefits

If a studio inappropriately mandates that the entertainer, individually, be treated as an employee, the entertainer loses a number of tax benefits that would otherwise be available to an independent contractor. Interposing a loanout company gives the studio comfort that it does not have a withholding obligation (since the studio is paying the loanout company itself) and preserves certain tax benefits and limited liability protection (as discussed above) for the entertainer. The limitations on individual-employees, and benefits of a loanout corporation (both C-corporations and S-corporations) are summarized in the table below.

GUIDE TO STRUCTURING AND TAXATION IN THE INDUSTRY 717

Issue	Individual	C-Corporation	S-Corporation
Unreimbursed Employee Expenses (e.g., agents' commissions, management fees, attorneys' fees)	No longer deductible for tax years beginning after December 31, 2017	Fully deductible,[212] including expenses that would have otherwise been disallowed by AMT	Separately stated and then subject to the individual rule
Health Insurance Premiums (Medical Expenses)	For taxable years beginning after December 31, 2016 and ending before January 1, 2019, deductible only to the extent aggregate medical expenses exceed 7.5% of AGI.[213] For taxable years thereafter, deductible only to the extent aggregate medical expenses exceed 10% (7.5% in the case of taxpayers who have attained the age of 65 before the close of the taxable year) of AGI.	Fully deductible and not income to entertainer-employee[214]	Fully deductible, but health insurance premiums are income to entertainer-employee.[215]

[212] IRC § 162(a).
[213] IRC § 213(a).
[214] IRC §§ 106(a); 162(a).
[215] IRC § 162(l) (Entertainer-employee, however, may be entitled to an above-the-line deduction as a self-employed taxpayer.).

Uninsured Medical Expenses (Medical Reimbursement Plans)	For taxable years beginning after December 31, 2016 and ending before January 1, 2019, deductible only to the extent aggregate medical expenses exceed 7.5% of AGI.[216] For taxable years thereafter, deductible only to the extent aggregate medical expenses exceed 10% (7.5% in the case of taxpayers who have attained the age of 65 before the close of the taxable year) of AGI.	May adopt medical reimbursement plans if entertainer is only employee, and reimbursement payments are deductible by loanout and are not income to entertainer-employee[217]	Deductible, but reimbursed amounts are income to entertainer-employee
Life and Disability Insurance Premiums	Not deductible	Deductible and not income to entertainer-employee[218]	Deductible, but premiums are income to entertainer-employee[219]
Home Office Expenses	Only deductible in certain circumstances, including if for the convenience of the employer[220]	Deductible even if office is in the entertainer-employee's home	Not deductible

[216] IRC § 213(a).
[217] IRC §§ 62(a); 162(a)(1); 105(b). If a loanout has more than one employee, the medical reimbursement plan will violate the Affordable Care Act (unless it is layered over a qualified ACA plan).
[218] IRC §§ 62(a); 162(a); 79(a).
[219] IRC § 162(l) (Entertainer-employee, however, may be entitled to an above-the-line deduction as a self-employed taxpayer.).
[220] IRC § 280A.

12.4.1.2. Work-for-Hire Relationship

Generally, if the work protected by copyright is made "for hire," the employer or person for whom the work was created will be deemed to be the author and granted ownership in the copyright unless the parties have otherwise agreed in writing.[221] For tax purposes, if a copyright is generated under a "work-for-hire" relationship, the person for whom the work is created is treated as the owner of the property created.

In most circumstances, the relationship between the loanout company and the studio will be a "work-for-hire" relationship and, accordingly, the loanout company will not be treated as the owner of the intellectual property. If, however, the relationship is not "work-for-hire," then the loanout company's employment agreement with the shareholder-employee should carve-out from any exclusivity provisions such arrangement so that the shareholder-employee is treated as the direct owner of the intellectual property for tax purposes. This type of carve-out is common (and should be included) in an employment agreement between a writer and his or her loanout company for any speculative screenplays, or spec scripts. By providing such carve-out, the direct ownership will allow the writer to get a "step-up" in tax basis of the intellectual property upon death, and mitigate two-levels of tax if the loanout company is a C-corporation and the copyright is sold or distributed at an appreciated fair market value.

12.4.1.3. Employment Agreement

Generally, talent that operates through a loanout company should always have an employment agreement with their loanout company. Specifically, for a loanout company to be respected by the tax authorities (as well as for limited liability protection), the employment agreement should be at arm's length terms and all corporate formalities

---

[221] 17 USC § 201(b). Under the Copyright Act, "work made for hire" is defined as (i) a work prepared by an employee within the scope of his or her employment; or (ii) a work specially ordered or commissioned for use as a contribution to a collective work, as part of a motion picture or other audiovisual work, as a translation, as a supplementary work, as a compilation, as an instructional text, as a test, as answer material for a test, or as an atlas, if the parties expressly agree in a written instrument signed by them that the work shall be considered a work made for hire.

should be followed (including annual meetings/corporate minutes).[222] A discussion of the specific terms of such an employment agreement is outside the scope of this Chapter and should be discussed with an entertainment tax lawyer.

12.4.1.4. Non-Qualified Deferred Compensation ("409A")

Section 409A potentially applies to all nonqualified deferred compensation plans, which are defined broadly to include any arrangement (including those covering only one person) that provides for the deferral of compensation.[223] For this purpose, an arrangement provides for the deferral of compensation if, under the terms of the arrangement and the relevant facts and circumstances, the service provider (in this case, both the loanout and the talent) has a legally binding right during a taxable year to compensation that, pursuant to the terms of the arrangement, is or may be payable by the service recipient (i.e., the studio) to (or on behalf of) the service provider in a later year.[224] In addition, a legally binding right may exist even where the compensation may be reduced or eliminated by operation of the objective terms of the arrangement, including a provision that creates a substantial risk of forfeiture (e.g., a vesting condition).[225]

Within the context of the loanout company structure, there generally are two deferred compensation streams that may be subject to Section 409A: (i) any deferred compensation payable by the studio to the loanout company pursuant to a studio contract, and (ii) any deferred compensation payable by the loanout company to the entertainer employee-shareholder pursuant to his or her employment agreement with the loanout company. Due to the excessive penalty that may be imposed, as well as acceleration of all deferred compensation (whether or not actually received), extreme care should be taken to ensure that any employment agreement between the employee-shareholder and the loanout company, and any studio

---

[222] *See generally* Sargent v. Comm'r, 929 F.2d 1252 (8th Cir.) (finding loanout company was created for legitimate business purposes and valid employment agreements between the talent and his loanout company established right of control over talent's services).

[223] Section 409A(d)(1) and (3).

[224] Treas. Reg. § 1.409A-1(b)(1).

[225] Treas. Reg. § 1.409A-1(b)(1).

contract between the loanout company and the studio, are compliant with (or prepared to exempt from) the requirements of Section 409A. In addition, the entertainer and/or his or her loanout company should consult with his or her tax advisors prior to entering into any transaction that may be viewed as accelerating or deferring the underlying deferred compensation stream, such as selling his or her loanout company or postponing payments to a future tax year.

12.4.2. Motion Pictures and Television

Generally, talent who are U.S. persons should consider using an S-corporation as their loanout company because an S-corporation allows tax credits (e.g., foreign tax credits) to flow through and may mitigate employment tax liability. A C-corporation, however, may be considered if the talent desires to establish a medical reimbursement plan or if the talent provides behind-the-camera service (i.e., director) and is working overseas. Non-U.S. talent must use a C-corporation (or, less frequently, an LLC) because such individuals generally may not own stock in an S-corporation. A discussion of international tax planning is beyond the scope of this Chapter.

12.4.3. Music

12.4.3.1. General Structuring Considerations

Structuring for music businesses gives rise to unique liability protection concerns. The valuable assets in a music business are (i) underlying intellectual property (i.e., copyrights and trademarks), and (ii) income streams from royalties and participation rights. Therefore, bands generally should insulate such valuable assets from potential touring liability. Accordingly, a band whose members are U.S. tax residents should consider establishing three entities: (i) an S-corporation to contract with venues for touring (the "*Touring Entity*"), (ii) an S-corporation to contract with music studios for production, which will receive royalty income (the "*Production Entity*"), and (iii) an LLC to hold the copyrights (and possibly the trademarks) to the musical productions (the "*IP Entity*"). This structure insulates touring liabilities from the production and intellectual property assets (and vice versa).

The Production Entity generally should enter into a production services agreement with the IP Entity such that the IP Entity engages the Production Entity to produce the copyrights to musical works so that the IP Entity is the owner of such copyrights for tax purposes. From then on, the IP Entity licenses the intellectual property to the Touring Entity and the Production Entity, as needed.

12.4.3.2. Tax Benefits to Separating Intellectual Property

As noted above, the intellectual property generally should be held separately in an LLC (i.e., the IP Entity, rather than the Production Entity for tax purposes). As noted, a non-liquidating or liquidating distribution of appreciated property by a corporation (including S-corporations) to the corporation's shareholders generally is treated as a deemed sale of such property by the corporation.[226] The corporation is subject to corporate tax on the deemed sale to the extent the fair market value of the appreciated property exceeds its tax basis.[227] If the distributed property's tax basis exceeds its fair market value, the corporation is not permitted to recognize a loss on a non-liquidating distribution of such property.[228] In contrast, subject to certain exceptions, distributions of appreciated property from an LLC are not subject to taxation. Therefore, as a general matter, it is more desirable for tax purposes to hold copyrights or other intellectual property in an LLC in order to eliminate (or at least mitigate) taxable gain upon a distribution of the copyrights or intellectual property to the individual owner.

From an estate planning perspective, intellectual property owned by an LLC may achieve a step-up in tax basis at the time of a band member's death (directly if it is a single member LLC, or if a "Section 754 election" is in place in the year in which the band member passes away). In contrast, if intellectual property is held by an S-corporation at the time of death, the decedent's S-corporation stock gets a step-up in tax basis, but not the underlying intellectual property held by the corporation.

---

[226] IRC §§ 311(b)(1); 336(a).

[227] Id.; similarly, a liquidating S-corporation recognizes gain or loss on the distribution of property in complete liquidation as if such property were sold to the distributee shareholder at its fair market value. IRC § 336(a).

[228] IRC § 311(a).

12.4.3.3. Shareholder Agreements

To the extent that a multi-member band forms an S-corporation, it generally is advisable to enter into a shareholder agreement to coordinate business decisions and to implement appropriate provisions governing the voluntary or forced exit of a member. From a non-tax perspective, the shareholders agreement will govern (among other things) redemption of a member if the member voluntarily or involuntarily leaves. From a tax perspective, the agreement generally should set the purchase price of such redemption to comply with the S-corporation rules governing a second class of stock and prohibit actions that might terminate the S-corporation election. For example, the redemption provision should set the redemption price at book value, fair market value, or at a price somewhere between fair market value and book value.[229] For this purpose, book value will be respected if (i) the book value is determined in accordance with Generally Accepted Accounting Principles (including permitted optional adjustments), or (ii) the book value is used for any substantial non-tax purpose.[230]

12.4.4. Production Companies

Production companies that independently finance their productions generally should be structured using an LLC because such structure (i) allows for flow-through of entity-level losses to the members (like an S-corporation) subject to the loss limitation rules discussed above, and (ii) allow for preferred equity (which is unavailable to S-corporations). Given that entertainment projects generally create front-end losses, especially to the extent that an immediate deduction for qualified production costs is available (as described in more detail below), it is critical that production companies are structured using an entity (i.e., S-corporations or LLCs) that will pass-through the benefit of such losses to the owner of the entity. Unlike an LLC, however, S-corporations cannot issue preferred equity.

12.4.4.1. Back-to-Back Loanout Structures

Given that many film/TV studios will not enter into studio contracts with LLCs, additional structuring may be necessary to

---

[229] *See* Treas. Reg. § 1.1361-1(I)(2)(iii)(A).
[230] Treas. Reg. § 1.1361-1(I)(2)(iii)(C).

maintain a production company's use of an LLC. A production company may desire to implement a back-to-back loanout structure to achieve the flexibility of an LLC while giving film/TV studios the ability to enter into a studio contract with a corporation. To facilitate such a structure, the LLC (i) forms a wholly-owned corporation, which will enter into the studio contracts with the film/TV studios, and (ii) then enters into a loanout agreement with the corporate subsidiary whereby the LLC will loan the services of its producer-members to the corporate subsidiary, which will then "loan" such services to the film/TV studios. From then on, the film/TV studios pay compensation to the corporate subsidiary pursuant to the studio contract, and the corporate subsidiary pays the LLC compensation for the producer services pursuant to the loanout agreement subject to reasonable compensation limitations. This structure generally is used in circumstances whereby the production company is engaged by a studio to develop a motion picture on a "work-for-hire" basis such that the studio retains ownership of the resulting copyright.

12.4.4.2. Structuring Collection Account Management Agreements

In the entertainment industry, a collection account management agreement ("*CAM Agreement*") governs the sharing of net proceeds from a film project. In many productions, investors and highly compensated talent with deferment or so-called "back-end" participations in the revenues of a film/TV production will require that revenues be collected and disbursed in accordance with contractual waterfall formulae agreed to in the CAM Agreement rather than the project's producers to insure greater transparency in the accounting process, with a negotiated fee paid "off the top" to the accounting firm providing such services. A CAM Agreement, however, does not necessarily create a tax partnership. Accordingly, an LLC generally should be formed to bolster the creation of a tax partnership amongst the financier and the primary producer CAM Agreement participants. The net proceeds received by the LLC generally are paid to the CAM Agreement participants (other than the financiers and the primary producers) as a deductible compensatory payment, and the balance is allocated to the financiers and primary producers and distributed thereto as partners in the partnership. The formation of the LLC in this context (such as the preparation of the Operating Agreement) is critical to bolstering the creation of a tax partnership and flow-through items of income and loss. If the LLC utilizes a subsidiary production corporation, then the LLC generally will enter into a production services agreement to engage the corporate subsidiary to provide production services on its behalf such that any funding from investors will generate a compensation expense for the LLC when paid to the corporation subsidiary, which may flow-through to the investors as a loss. If the LLC will own the resulting copyright (rather than a studio), then the production services agreement should be drafted to create a "work-for-hire" relationship such that the resulting copyright is owned by the LLC for tax purposes.

12.4.4.3. Capitalizing Production Costs

Generally, amounts paid to create an intangible asset are capitalized and added to the tax basis of the asset in accordance with the Treasury Regulations under Code Section 263(a).[231] In addition, Code Section 263A applies to taxpayers that produce property,[232] including real property or tangible personal property produced by a taxpayer for use in its trade or business or for sale to its customers.[233] Section 263A also applies to property produced for a taxpayer under a contract with another party.[234] For purposes of Section 263A, "produce" includes the following: construct, build, install, manufacture, develop, improve, create, raise, or grow.[235] Taxpayers that produce real property and tangible personal property ("*producers*") must capitalize the direct costs of producing the property and the property's properly allocable share of indirect costs, regardless of whether the property is sold or used in the taxpayer's trade or business.[236]

Generally, Section 263A applies to the costs of producing tangible personal property, and not to the costs of producing intangible

---

[231] Treas. Reg. § 1.263(a)-4(b).
[232] Treas. Reg. § 1.263A-2(a)(5).
[233] Treas. Reg. § 1.263A-2(a).
[234] *Id.*
[235] IRC § 263A(g)(1); Treas. Reg. § 1.263A-2(a)(1)(i).
[236] Treas. Reg. § 1.263A-1(a)(3)(ii). The term "capitalize" means, in the case of property that is inventory in the hands of the taxpayer, to include in inventory costs and, in the case of other property, to charge to a capital account or basis over a period of years. Treas. Reg. § 1.263A-1(c)(3).

property.[237] However, for purposes of determining whether a taxpayer producing intellectual or creative property is producing tangible personal property or intangible property, the term "tangible personal property" includes films, sound recordings, video tapes, books, and other similar property embodying words, ideas, concepts, images or sounds by the creator thereof.[238] Other similar property for this purpose generally means intellectual or creative property for which, as costs are incurred producing the property, it is intended (or is reasonably likely) that any tangible medium in which the property is embodied will be mass distributed by the creator or any one or more third parties in a form that is not substantially altered.[239] However, any intellectual or creative property that is embodied in a tangible medium that is mass distributed merely incidentally to the distribution of a principal product or good of the creator is not other "similar property" for these purposes.[240] Accordingly, without regard to characterization as tangible or intangible property under other sections of the Code, Section 263A applies to the costs of producing a motion picture or researching and writing a book even though these assets may be considered intangible for other purposes of the Code.[241] For example, the costs of producing and developing books (including teaching aids and other literary works) required to be capitalized under Code Section 263A include costs incurred by an author in researching, preparing and writing the book.[242]

Under Code Section 263A, taxpayers must capitalize their direct costs[243] and a properly allocable share of their indirect costs[244] to

---

[237] Treas. Reg. § 1.263A-2(a)(2)(i). For example, Section 263A applies to the costs manufacturers incur to produce goods, but does not apply to the costs of financial institutions to incur or originate loans.

[238] Treas. Reg. § 1.263A-2(a)(2)(ii).

[239] Id.

[240] Id.

[241] Treas. Reg. § 1.263A-2(a)(2)(ii)(A).

[242] Treas. Reg. § 1.263A-2(a)(2)(ii)(A)(*1*).

[243] Producers subject to IRC § 263A must capitalize direct material costs and direct labor costs. Treas. Reg. 1.263A-1(e)(2)(i). Direct material costs include the cost of those materials that become an integral part of specific property produced and those materials that are consumed in the ordinary course of production and that can be identified or associated with particular units or groups of units of property produced. Treas. Reg. § 1.263A-1(e)(2)(i)(A). Direct labor costs include the costs of labor that can be identified or associated with particular units or groups of units of specific property produced. Treas. Reg. § 1.263A-1(e)(2)(i)(B). For this purpose, labor

property produced or property acquired for resale.[245] In order to determine these capitalizable costs, taxpayers must allocate or apportion costs to various activities, including production or resale activities.[246] After Code Section 263A costs are allocated to the appropriate production or resale activities, these costs generally are allocated to the items of *property produced* or property acquired for resale during the taxable year and capitalized to the items *that remain on hand at the end of the taxable year*.[247] Costs that are capitalized are recovered through depreciation, amortization, cost of goods sold, or by an adjustment to basis at the time the property is used, sold, placed in service, or otherwise disposed of by the taxpayer.[248] Except for certain interest costs, producers must capitalize direct and indirect costs properly allocable to "property produced" under Section 263A, without regard to whether those costs are incurred before, during, or after the production period.[249]

---

encompasses full-time and part-time employees, as well as contract employees and independent contractors. *Id.*

[244] Indirect costs are properly allocable to property produced or property acquired for resale when the costs directly benefit or are incurred by reason of the performance of production or resale activities. Treas. Reg. § 1.263A-1(e)(3)(i). The following are examples of indirect costs that must be capitalized to the extent they are properly allocable to property produced or property acquired for resale: (i) indirect labor costs that cannot be directly identified or associated with particular units or groups of units of specific property produced or property acquired for resale (e.g., factory labor that is not direct labor), (ii) officers' compensation, rent, taxes, insurance, utilities, and capitalizable service costs. Treas. Reg. § 1.263A-1(e)(3)(ii).

[245] Treas. Reg. § 1.263A-1(c)(1).

[246] *Id.*

[247] Treas. Reg. § 1.263A-1(a)(3)(ii).

[248] Treas. Reg. § 1.263A-1(c)(4). The following indirect costs are not required to be capitalized under IRC § 263A: (i) selling and distribution costs (e.g., marketing, selling, advertising, and distribution costs), (ii) research and experimental expenditures described in IRC § 174, (iii) IRC § 179 costs for certain depreciable assets deductible at the election of the taxpayer, and (iv) losses under IRC § 165. Treas. Reg. § 1.263A-1(e)(3)(iii).

[249] Treas. Reg. § 1.263A-2(a)(3)(i). The term "production period" means, when used with respect to any property, the period (i) beginning on the date on which production of the property begins, and (ii) ending on the date on which the property is ready to be placed in service or is ready to be held for sale. IRC § 263A(f)(4)(B). With respect to pre-production costs: (i) if property is held for future production, the taxpayer must capitalize direct and indirect costs allocable to such property (e.g., purchasing, storage, handling, and other costs), even though production has not begun, or (ii) if property is not held for production, indirect costs incurred prior to the beginning of the production period must be allocated to the property and capitalized if

728 ESSENTIAL GUIDE TO ENTERTAINMENT LAW: DEALMAKING

Under the Tax Cuts and Jobs Act, any taxpayer that meets the Gross Receipts Test described in Section 12.1.2.1. is not subject to the capitalization rules under Code Section 263A,[250] but may continue to be subject to the capitalization rules under Code Section 263(a). For purposes of determining whether an individual is exempt from such capitalization rules, the Gross Receipts Test is applied in the same manner as if the individual's trade or business were a corporation or partnership.[251]

12.4.4.4. Income Forecast Method

Once production costs are capitalized, the appropriate method to recover the costs should be identified. Generally, the income forecast method may be used only for film, videotape, sound recordings, copyrights, books, patents, and other property identified by the IRS in the Treasury Regulations.[252] Under the income forecast method, the cost of an asset (less any salvage value) is multiplied by a fraction, the numerator of which is the net income from the asset for the tax year and the denominator of which is the total net income forecast to be derived from the asset before the close of the tenth tax year following the tax year in which the asset was place in service.[253] The unrecovered adjusted basis of the property as of the beginning of the tenth calendar year is claimed as a depreciation deduction in the tenth tax year following the tax year in which the asset was placed in service.[254]

If the income forecast method changes during the ten-year period, the formula is as follows: the unrecovered depreciable cost of the asset at the beginning of the tax year of revision is multiplied by a fraction, the numerator of which is the net income from the asset for the tax year of revision, and the denominator of which is the revised forecasted net income from the asset for the year of revision and the remaining years before the close of the tenth tax year following the tax year in which the asset was placed in service.[255] During the third and tenth tax years after

---

it is reasonably likely that production will occur at some future date. Treas. Reg. §1.263A-2(a)(3)(ii).
[250] IRC § 263A(i)(1).
[251] IRC § 263A(i)(2).
[252] IRC § 167(g)(6).
[253] IRC § 167(g)(1).
[254] IRC § 167(g)(1)(C).
[255] IRC § 167(g)(2).

the asset is placed in service, the taxpayer generally is required to pay or may receive interest based on the recalculation of depreciation using actual income figures.[256] This look-back rule does not apply to property that has a cost basis of $100,000 or less, or if the taxpayer's income projections were within 10% of the income actually earned.[257] Residuals and participations may be included in the adjusted basis of a property in the tax year that it is placed in service or excluded from adjusted basis and deducted in the year of payment if an election is made.[258]

Note that, in the case of property which is one or more episodes in a television series, income from syndicating the series is not required to be taken into account under the income forecast method before the earlier of (i) the fourth taxable year beginning after the date the first episode in such series is placed in service, or (ii) the earliest taxable year in which the taxpayer has an arrangement relating to the future syndication of such series.[259]

12.4.4.5. Section 181 Election / Bonus Depreciation

For qualified film and television productions commencing after December 31, 2007, and before January 1, 2018, and for qualified live theatrical productions[260] commencing after December 31, 2015 and before January 1, 2018, a taxpayer could elect to expense the first $15 million of production costs ($20 million for productions in low income communities or distressed areas) (the *"Production Cost Expense Limit"*).[261] Generally, the production must be produced in the U.S. to qualify. The Tax Cuts and Jobs Act did not extend Section 181 for

---

[256] IRC § 167(g)(1)(D).
[257] IRC § 167(g)(3)-(4).
[258] IRC § 167(g)(7); IRS Notice 2006-47.
[259] IRC § 167(g)(5)(B).
[260] Generally, a "qualified live theatrical production" is any production that (i) is a live staged production of a play (with or without music) which is derived from a written book or script and is produced or presented by a taxable entity in any venue which has an audience capacity of not more than 3,000 or a series of venues the majority of which have an audience capacity of not more than 3,000, and (ii) if 75% of the total compensation of the production is compensation (excluding participations and residuals) for services performed in the U.S. by actors, production personnel, directors, and producers (*"qualified compensation"*). IRC 181(e).
[261] IRC § 181, as amended by the Protecting Americans from Tax Hikes ("PATH") Act of 2015 (P.L. 114-113). Section 181 was expanded recently to certain live theater productions.

taxable years commencing after December 31, 2018 but, instead, qualified film and television productions and qualified live theatrical productions were included under certain "bonus depreciation" rules that apply to property that is (i) acquired after September 27, 2017, and (ii) placed in service after such date.[262]

a. Code Section 181

Under Code Section 181, an owner of any film or television production that the owner reasonably expected would be, upon completion, a qualified film or television production[263] could elect to treat production[264] costs paid or incurred by that owner as an expense that was deductible for the taxable year in which the costs were paid or incurred.[265] The term "owner" for this purpose means any person that is required to capitalize the costs of producing the production into the cost basis of the production, or that would be required to do so if Code Section 263A applied to that person.[266]

Each episode of a television series is a separate production to which the rules, limits and election requirements of the Regulations under Code Section 181 apply.[267] An owner may elect to deduct production costs under Code Section 181 only for the *first* forty-four episodes of a television series (including pilot episodes).[268] A television series may include more than one season of programming.[269]

Some states did not adopted Code Section 181. In California, for example, a California resident LLC member would not get the benefit of the Section 181 deduction in connection with calculating the member's individual California tax liability on its individual California tax return.

---

[262] For this purpose, property is not treated as acquired after the date on which a written binding contract is entered into for such acquisition.

[263] The term "qualified film or television production" means any production for which not less than 75% of the aggregate amount of compensation paid or incurred for the production is "qualified compensation." Treas. Reg. § 1.181-3(a).

[264] Except for certain sexually explicit productions, the term "production" means any motion picture film or video tape (including digital video) production that production costs of which are subject to capitalization under IRC § 263A, or that would be subject to capitalization if IRC § 263A applied to the owner of the production. Treas. Reg. § 1.181-3(b)(1).

[265] Treas. Reg. § 1.181-1(a)(1)(i).
[266] Treas. Reg. § 1.181-3(a)(2)(i).
[267] Treas. Reg. § 1.181-3(b)(2).
[268] *Id.*
[269] *Id.*

Although a Section 181 election allowed a current deduction of production costs which may generate a current year loss, such loss could still be subject to usage limitations to the extent that the loss constituted a "passive activity" loss, the Pass-Through Loss Limitation applies, or the taxpayer is subject to the "at-risk rules" (which are beyond the scope of this Chapter).

b. Bonus Depreciation

Although the Tax Cuts and Jobs Act did not extend Code Section 181, it amended Code Section 168(k) to include qualified film and television productions and live theatrical productions (in each case with the same meaning as under Code Section 181) as qualified property eligible for "bonus" depreciation. A taxpayer that owns qualified property eligible for bonus depreciation may take a depreciation deduction for the tax year in which such property is placed in service equal to such property's tax basis, multiplied by the following applicable percentage:

- 100% in the case of qualified property placed in service after September 27, 2017, and before January 1, 2023;
- 80% in the case of qualified property placed in service after December 31, 2022, and before January 1, 2024;
- 60% in the case of qualified property placed in service after December 31, 2023, and before January 1, 2025;
- 40% in the case of qualified property placed in service after December 31, 2024, and before January 1, 2026; and
- 20% in the case of property placed in service after December 31, 2025, and before January 1, 2027.[270]

Importantly, a qualified film, television, or live theatrical production for purposes of bonus depreciation have the same definitions as under Code Section 181, except that the Production Cost Expense Limit does not apply.[271] In other words, a taxpayer may now deduct the full amount of qualified production costs for productions placed in service after September 27, 2017 and before January 1, 2023

---

[270] IRC §§ 168(k)(1)(A); 168(k)(6).
[271] See IRC § 168(k)(2)(A)(i).

(followed by the phase-out summarized above), while qualified production costs could only be immediately deducted up to $15 million (or $20 million if the production was produced in certain designated low-income communities) under Code Section 181. For purposes of bonus depreciation for qualified production costs, (i) a qualified film or television production is considered to be placed in service at the time of initial release or broadcast, and (ii) a qualified live theatrical production is considered to be placed in service at the time of the initial live staged performance.[272]

To qualify as qualified property, (i) the original use of the qualified production must begin with the taxpayer, or (ii) the use of the production by the taxpayer may be by acquisition if the taxpayer never used the property at any time prior to the acquisition and generally acquired the production in a taxable transaction from an unrelated party.[273]

To the extent that a current deduction for bonus depreciation with respect to qualified productions generates a current year loss, such loss could still be subject to usage limitations to the extent that the loss constituted a "passive activity" loss, the Pass-Through Loss Limitation applies, or the taxpayer is subject to the "at-risk rules" (which are beyond the scope of this Chapter).

c. Summary of Key Distinctions between Current and Prior Law

The key differences between deducting qualified production costs under Code Section 181 and as bonus depreciation are summarized as follows:

---

[272] IRC § 168(k)(2)(H).

[273] See IRC § 168(k)(2)(A)(ii) (stating that one of the requirements to constitute qualified property for purposes of bonus depreciation is that the property's original use must begin with the taxpayer or the taxpayer must have acquired the property and met the requirements of Code Section 168(k)(2)(E)(ii)). Property satisfies the acquisition requirement under Code Section 168(k)(2)(E)(ii) if (i) the acquisition is not from a related party (within the meaning of Code Section 267 or 707(b), with modifications for family relationships to only include his spouse, ancestors, and lineal descendants), (ii) the property is not acquired by one component member of a controlled group from another component member of the same controlled group, (iii) the property does not receive a carryover basis and the basis is not determined under Code Section 1014(a) (relating to property acquired from a decedent), and (iv) the cost of property does not include so much of the basis of such property as is determined by reference to the basis of other property held at any time by the person acquiring such property.

Code Section 181	Bonus Depreciation
Deduction is in the tax year in which in which the costs are paid or incurred.	Deduction is in the tax year in which the production is placed in service.
Production Cost Expense Limit imposes limitation on amount deductible at $15 million (or $20 million in certain cases).	Production Cost Expense Limit does not apply.
An acquired production (finished or partially finished) may be eligible for deduction if the production was acquired prior to its initial release or broadcast.[274]	An acquired production may be eligible for deduction if the production was (i) never used by the acquiring taxpayer, and (ii) generally acquired in a taxable transaction from an unrelated party.[275]

12.4.4.6. Crowd Funding

Some start-up production companies may use "crowd funding" as a source of financing for its film/TV productions. Crowd funding is a relatively new method of raising funds for various purposes, whereby a person establishes a website or uses an aggregating site such as "Kickstarter" or "IndieGoGo" to launch a funding campaign, and requests that the public deposit funds for the specified cause. In most cases, the "donor" will receive something nominal in exchange, such as tickets to the premier of the movie or a t-shirt.

Additionally, under the Jumpstart Our Business Startups (JOBS) Act passed in 2012, new exemptions to longstanding federal securities law restrictions lift the ban on the public advertising ("*General Solicitation*") of private investment opportunities (Title II), and enable non-accredited investors to access investment opportunities through equity crowdfunding (Title III). Although SEC rulemaking relating to

---

[274] Treas. Reg. § 1.181-1(a)(2)(ii).
[275] Generally, any interest in a copyright, film, sound recording, video tape, book or similar property that is acquired as part of a trade or business is a Section 197 intangible and must be amortized over a 15-year period. *See* IRC §§ 197(d)(1); 197(e)(4).

the implementation of the JOBS act remains a work in progress, these developments will further impact the possibility for crowd-funding of entertainment industry productions.

The tax treatment of crowd funding in light of these distinctly different approaches to crowd-sourced project finance should be considered on a case-by-case basis.[276] Generally, to qualify as a gift (which is non-taxable to the recipient), a donor must have a gratuitous intent. Thus, to the extent that the transferor of the cash receives something of value in return, no matter how nominal, the cash transfer could potentially result in the recognition of income by the start-up production company. In all events, the transferor of the cash is unlikely to receive an income tax deduction, since: (1) gifts are not deductible and (2) the cash payment is probably not within the scope of the transferor's trade or business (or otherwise made for investment purposes). Projects may also utilize a qualified, tax-exempt "fiscal sponsor" or "fiscal agent" as the conduit for donations earmarked for project funding, which if qualified may enable the donor to obtain a tax deduction for the gift as a charitable contribution, as well.

The implications and tax treatment of crowd-sourced sales of securities is necessarily beyond the scope of this Chapter.

12.4.4.7. Overhead Accounts / Planning

Often, a film/TV studio contract may provide for an overhead account whereby the studio agrees to provide a certain amount of cash to the production company annually to cover the production company's annual overhead expenses. The production company should plan carefully to ensure that either (i) the receipt of such overhead income is fully offset with a corresponding deduction, or (ii) the overhead account is structured such that the overhead is being provided to the production company to hold as agent for the film/TV studio.

If the production company is a cash method taxpayer, then the overhead received during the taxable year should be actually spent on overhead so that the deduction is recognized in the same taxable year. If the production company is an accrual method taxpayer, then the overhead income received during the taxable year should be offset to

---

[276] *See* Department of Treasury Information Letter 2016-36.

the extent that the production company's expenses related to such overhead accrued in such year under the All Events Test.

The production company should consider structuring the studio contract such that (i) the overhead account is separate and apart from any compensation for services payable under the contract, (ii) the production company is obligated to expend the overhead funds for certain enumerated purposes and, if the overhead funds are not spent by the end of the taxable year, then the production company is obligated to return the funds to the film/TV studio, (iii) title to any permanent equipment purchased with the overhead account funds remain with the film/TV studio, and (iv) the production company does not receive a salary or other economic benefit from the overhead account funds. In this scenario, the overhead account funds may not be treated as taxable income to the production company under the Agency Theory (as described in section 12.1.5. above), although this tax position is not free from doubt.

12.4.5. State Tax Incentives

Although state and local tax is beyond the scope of this Chapter, it is important to note that the various states have different tax incentives and potential safe harbors from taxation. For example, an important safe harbor exemption in California allows a California tax resident to be absent from California for a certain period of time without being subject to California tax, although such individual retains his or her California tax residency.

California law provides currently that an individual will be considered a "resident" of California if such individual (a) is in California "for other than a temporary or transitory purpose" or (b) is domiciled in California and who is outside California "for a temporary or transitory purpose."[277] An individual who is domiciled in California and who is absent from California for an uninterrupted period of at least 546 consecutive days under an employment-related contract, is considered to be outside of California for other than a temporary or transitory purpose (the "*Safe Harbor*").[278] For this determination, if an individual returns to California for a total aggregate of 45 days or less

---

[277] Cal. Rev & Tax'n Code Section 17014(a).
[278] Cal. Rev. & Tax'n Code Section 17014(d).

during a taxable year, those days in California are disregarded.[279] The Safe Harbor is not satisfied if (i) the individual has income from stocks, bonds, notes, or other intangible personal property exceeding $200k in any taxable year during which the employment-related contract is in effect, or (ii) the principal purpose of the absence from California is to avoid personal income tax.[280] FTB Publication 1031 (Guidelines for Determining Resident Status) provides the following example:

> You and your spouse are California residents. You agreed to work overseas for 20 months under an employment contract. Your family remained in San Diego, CA. During those 20 months, you visited your family in San Diego for a month. You can be considered a nonresident during your absence under the Safe Harbor. Your month-long visit to California is considered temporary. During the year, you earned $80k on your overseas assignment and your spouse earned $30k as a teacher in San Diego. You did not have any other income. The tables below show how to report income if you filed a joint income tax return or a separate income tax return.

The following table illustrates the exemption:

---

[279] *Id.*
[280] *Id.*

GUIDE TO STRUCTURING AND TAXATION IN THE INDUSTRY 737

Joint Return
Return for Taxpayer and Spouse Form 540NR

Income	Total AGI	CA AGI (Sch CA (540NR) Col. E
Taxpayer's Wages	80,000	40,000 *
Spouse's Wages	30,000	30,000
Total Wages	110,000	70,000

Separate Returns

Income	Taxpayer's Return Form 540NR		Spouse's Return Form 540
	Total AGI	CA AGI (540NR)	Total AGI Sch CA (540) no adjustments
Taxpayer's Wages	80,000	-	40,000
Spouse's Wages	30,000	15,000	15,000
Total Wages	110,000	15,000	55,000

* Half of the taxpayer's wages are taxable to California because California is a community property state and the taxpayer's spouse or resident domestic partner is a resident of California.

12.5. TAXATION OF INTELLECTUAL PROPERTY IN THE ENTERTAINMENT INDUSTRY

Taxation of intellectual property generally varies depending on the type of asset and whether the owner is the creator of the asset. As discussed above, it is important to keep intellectual property (or other appreciable property) outside of corporate form, and hold such assets through an LLC or individually for tax planning purposes. Royalties generated from exploitation of the intellectual property through licensing should constitute ordinary income subject to applicable ordinary income tax rates. When intellectual property is transferred, it is important to structure the transfer appropriately. Depending on the structure of the deal, the transfer may constitute a sale (potentially subject to long-term capital gains rates) or a license (subject to ordinary income tax rates). Gain from the sale of an ordinary asset or a capital asset held for one year or less is subject to ordinary income tax rates. Conversely, gain from the sale of a capital asset held for more than one year is subject to a lower long-term capital gain rate.

12.5.1. Copyrights

The life of a copyright is discussed in detail in The Essential Guide to Entertainment Law: Intellectual Property (volume 2 of this series). For U.S. federal income tax purposes, a transfer of a copyright for the life of the copyright should constitute a sale, while a transfer for any lesser period should constitute a license.[281] Generally, a self-created copyright (or a copyright held by another person who received a carryover basis is treated as a non-capital asset) is treated as a non-capital asset subject to ordinary income tax rates on any gain from a sale.[282] At the election of the taxpayer, however, the sale or exchange of a self-created musical composition or copyright in a musical work may be treated as the sale of a capital asset subject to long-term capital gains rates to the extent the copyright has been held for more than one year.[283]

---

[281] See, e.g., Rev. Rul. 54-409, 1954-2 C.B. 174.

[282] IRC 1221(a)(3)(A). A taxpayer who received the copyright or musical work with a carryover basis from the creator generally will also hold the asset as a non-capital asset. IRC § 1221(a)(3)(C).

[283] See IRC 1221(b)(3).

The election is made separately for each musical composition (or copyright in a musical work) sold or exchanged during the taxable year.[284] An election must be made on or before the due date (including extensions) of the income tax return for the taxable year of the sale or exchange.[285] The election is made on Schedule D, "Capital Gains and Losses," of the appropriate income tax form (for example, Form 1040, "U.S. Individual Income Tax Return"; Form 1065, "U.S. Return of Partnership Income"; Form 1120, "U.S. Corporation Income Tax Return") by treating the sale or exchange as the sale or exchange of a capital asset, in accordance with the form and its instructions.[286]

12.5.2. Trademarks

Generally, a transfer of a trademark shall not be treated as a sale or exchange of a capital asset if the transferor retains any significant power, right, or continuing interest with respect to the subject matter of the trademark.[287] The term "significant power, right, or continuing interest" includes, but is not limited to, the following rights with respect to the interest transferred:[288]

- A right to disapprove any assignment of such interest, or any part thereof.
- A right to terminate at will.
- A right to prescribe standards of quality of products used or sold, or services furnished, and of the equipment and facilities used to promote such products or services.
- A right to require that the transferee sell or advertise only products or services of the transferor.
- A right to require that the transferee purchase substantially all of his supplies and equipment from the transferor.
- A right to payment contingent on the productivity, use, or disposition of the subject matter of the interest transferred, if

---

[284] Treas. Reg. § 1.1221-3(b).
[285] *Id.*
[286] *Id.*
[287] IRC § 1253(a).
[288] IRC § 1253(b).

such payments constitute a substantial element under the transfer agreement.

To qualify as one of the enumerated retained rights, above, the retained right must be exercisable for a period that is co-extensive with the duration of the transferred interest.[289] The above list, however, is non-exclusive. Whether a retained right that is not in the above enumerated list constitutes a "significant power, right, or continuing interest" is considered based on all the facts and circumstances.[290]

12.6. ESTATE AND TAX PLANNING FOR RIGHTS OF PUBLICITY

Moviegoers who sat down to watch the latest *Star Wars* film, *Rogue One: A Star Wars Story*, may have been surprised to see a young Peter Cushing reprising the role of Grand Moff Tarkin, the ruthless overseer of the Death Star's construction. Since Cushing passed away in 1994 at the age of 81, the posthumous performance could only be an impersonator or the work of a cutting-edge special effects studio. To those in the movie industry, the performance represents a notable achievement in special effects.[291] To trusts and estates practitioners, the posthumous performance raises a number of other questions: *Can a studio just use a celebrity's image after her death? If so, is there any way to plan ahead to avoid the misappropriation of a celebrity client's likeness after death? If a posthumous performance generates income for the performer's estate or its beneficiaries, what are the income and estate tax implications? How can the income and estate tax impact be minimized?* These questions all touch on the treatment of the right of publicity after a celebrity's death.

There is no single, clear definition of the right of publicity, but it may generally be defined as the right to use an individual's name, image, likeness, or persona.

---

[289] *Stokely USA, Inc.*, 100 T.C. 439.
[290] *Id.*
[291] To older viewers, the appearance of Cushing may bring back memories of a string of *posthumous performances in commercials in the 1990s, most notably a* Super Bowl ad in 1997 in *which* Fred *Astaire* danced with a Dirt Devil vacuum. To younger viewers, the appearance may bring to mind to the hologram of Tupac Shakur that performed at the Coachella Valley Music and Arts Festival in 2012.

The right of publicity can be distinguished from copyright in that copyright law protects the *owner* of a work, whereas the right of publicity protects the person depicted in that work. For example, a photographer may hold a copyright to a given photograph, and may bring an action under federal copyright law for a third party's unauthorized use of the photograph. In contrast, the *subject* of the photograph would not have a claim under copyright law for the unauthorized use, since he does not own a direct interest in the photograph. The subject's claim must instead be that the unauthorized use of the photograph violates a more personal right by, for example, suggesting his personal endorsement or involvement, creating unwanted associations with his likeness, or profiting from a persona that he, at least intuitively, feels should belong only to him.

Publicity rights are more analogous to federal trademark rights, which prevent one person from commercial use of words, terms, names or symbols that are likely to mislead or deceive consumers regarding association with another person, or mislead consumers regarding the quality or origin of a product or service.[292] Right of publicity and trademark may overlap, for example, where there is false endorsement, unauthorized commercial use of a celebrity's likeness, falsely suggested endorsement or likelihood of consumer confusion.[293] However, federal trademark law is concerned more with misrepresentation regarding the commercial *source* of a product (whether an individual, a corporation or otherwise), whereas the right of publicity is concerned with unauthorized commercial use of an *individual*'s name, likeness or other distinguishing characteristics.

In contrast to other intellectual property rights, such as copyrights, trademarks and patents, federal law does not provide any direct protection for an individual's right of publicity as of 2017.[294] Instead, the right of publicity developed under state common law as an outgrowth of the common law right to privacy.

---

[292] *See* 15 U.S.C. §1125(a).
[293] *See* WESTON ANSON, RIGHT OF PUBLICITY: ANALYSIS, VALUATION AND THE LAW (2015), 49.
[294] As discussed above, an individual may seek relief under federal trademark law for use of his image or likeness, for example, on the theory that the defendant's use of the individual's likeness or persona is likely to give the impression of the involvement or endorsement of the individual or his estate.

As of 2017, thirty-eight states provide a right of publicity under statute, common law, or both.[295] While each of these states protects at least the individual's name and likeness, the protection provided by states varies widely in scope, with some states explicitly extending protection to an individual's photograph, voice, signature, appearance–and even gestures and mannerisms.

After death, state laws diverge further in their protection of publicity rights. A majority of states do not extend rights of publicity after death. Of the states that do provide a right of publicity after death, fifteen states, including California, currently provide statutory protection,[296] and six states currently provide protection under common law.[297]

California's right of publicity statute was originally enacted in 1971.[298] Under the statute in its original form, rights of publicity did not extend beyond a celebrity's death. In 1979, in a case brought by the heirs of Bela Lugosi against Universal Pictures, the California Supreme Court upheld a trial court ruling concluding that Lugosi's right of publicity did not pass to Lugosi's heirs, since any rights Lugosi had in his personal image terminated at the time of his death.[299] In 1984, in part in response to the *Lugosi* case, the California legislature enacted what is now Civil Code Section 3344.1, which extended the right of publicity beyond death, and made the right inheritable by the celebrity's heirs and assignable to celebrity's beneficiaries.[300] In 1999, the California legislature further expanded the post-mortem right of publicity in California by extending the length of the right from 50 to 70 years after the celebrity's death.[301] In 2007, in response to litigation around the estate of Marilyn Monroe, California enacted a further amendment to Section 3344.1, which explicitly extends the post-mortem right of publicity to celebrities who died before January 1, 1985, and which explicitly allows for transfer of the post-mortem right

---

[295] *See* ANSON, *supra* note 293 at 72.
[296] Arizona, California, Florida, Hawaii, Illinois, Indiana, Kentucky, Nevada, Ohio, Oklahoma, Pennsylvania, Tennessee, Texas, Virginia, and Washington.
[297] Georgia, Michigan, New Jersey, Pennsylvania, South Carolina, and Tennessee. (Pennsylvania and Tennessee recognize a post-mortem right of publicity under both common law and statutory law).
[298] Stats. 1971, ch. 1595, §1.
[299] Lugosi v. Universal Pictures, 5 Cal. 3d 813 (1979).
[300] Stats. 1984, ch. 1704, §2.
[301] Stats.1999, ch. 1000, §9.5.

of publicity in contracts, trusts or other testamentary instruments executed before January 1, 1985.[302]

Perhaps unsurprisingly, California is among the states that provide the strongest protections for publicity rights after death.[303] In contrast, New York state does not provide post-mortem protection for an individual's right of publicity as of 2017. Given the disparity among state protections after death, the state in which a celebrity was domiciled at the time of her death can be the determining factor in whether the celebrity's right of publicity continues to have lasting value to her beneficiaries, as the successors to Marilyn Monroe's estate discovered. Despite the fact that Monroe was domiciled in New York state at the time of her death in 1962, a successor to Monroe's estate attempted to enforce Monroe's posthumous right of publicity in California, where Monroe was temporarily residing, against a company that was selling unauthorized merchandise bearing Monroe's likeness and photographs. As discussed above, in response to the Monroe litigation, the California legislature passed a law clarifying that even the rights of publicity of decedents who died before the January 1, 1985 effective date of California's posthumous right of publicity statute were protected under the statute.[304] However, a federal district court, affirmed by the Ninth Circuit, held that Monroe's estate was estopped from claiming California domicile, since Monroe's executor repeatedly took the position that she was domiciled in New York in probate and other proceedings.[305]

In light of the wide range of states' approaches, lack of uniformity, and increasingly national and even global scope of the use of publicity rights, some commentators have called for a federal statute addressing right of publicity.[306] Given the expanding scope of publicity rights after

---

[302] Stats. 2007 ch. 439 §2.

[303] Indiana provides even greater post-mortem protection for rights of publicity. IND. CODE §32-36-1 (protecting right of publicity for 100 years after death and extending right to gestures and mannerisms).

[304] Stats. 2007 ch. 439 §2.

[305] The Milton H. Greene Archives, Inc. v. Marilyn Monroe, LLC, 692 F.3d 983 (9th Cir. 2012), *aff'g* 568 F.Supp.2d 1152 (C.D. Cal. 2008).

[306] *See, e.g.*, J. Eugene Salamon Jr., *The Right of Publicity Run Riot: The Case for a Federal Statute*, 60 S. CAL. L. REV. 1179 (1987). More recently, in January 2017, the Uniform Law Commission announced its intention to create a committee to "study the need for and feasibility of drafting a uniform act or model law addressing the right of publicity." Uniform Law Commission, Minutes to Midyear Meeting of the Committee

death, a celebrity's estate planning advisors should plan ahead for the post-mortem management of these rights. Just as an individual's estate planning documents might name an investment advisor to assist in management of the estate's investments or a business manager to assist in oversight of a business held by the estate, a celebrity's living trust (or the irrevocable trust to which the celebrity's publicity rights are transferred) should name an individual or team responsible for management of the client's publicity rights after death. This person or team should include an experienced business manager, not necessarily the client's executor, trustee, agent or family. Not only can such an appointment help to maximize the value of the celebrity's publicity rights, but it may avoid conflict among the celebrity's beneficiaries and avoid saddling an executor or trustee with the responsibility of navigating business negotiations after the celebrity's death. If the celebrity has specific wishes regarding how his publicity rights should or should not be used after his death, his estate planning documents should provide direction to the publicity rights manager. As an example, Robin Williams' living trust reportedly provided that his right of publicity should not be exploited during the 25-year period following his death.[307]

As advances in technology expand the ways in which celebrities' likenesses are utilized after death, the tax implications of publicity rights after death will also become increasingly important. In considering a given right held by a decedent's estate, a threshold question for the estate tax practitioner is whether the right represents an asset or an income stream for income tax purposes. If the right is an asset, it may be subject to estate tax[308] and receive a "step up" in its tax basis to equal the right's fair market value.[309] If the right is instead an income stream derived from the personal efforts of the decedent during her lifetime (or "income in respect of the decedent"), it would not receive this tax basis adjustment (or "step-up").[310]

---

on Scope and Program (January 13, 2017), *available at* http://www.uniformlaws.org/NewsDetail.aspx?title=New%20ULC%20Committees%20to%20be%20Appointed.

[307] Eriq Gardner, *Robin Williams Restricted Exploitation of His Image for 25 Years after Death*, THE HOLLYWOOD REPORTER, March 30, 2015, *available at* http://www.hollywoodreporter.com/thr-esq/robin-williams-restricted-exploitation-his-785292.

[308] I.R.C. §2031(a).

[309] I.R.C. §1014(a).

[310] I.R.C. §61(a)(14); *see also* O'Daniel Est. v. Comm'r, 173 F.2d 966 (2d Cir. 1949).

Among the first cases to address directly whether a decedent's right of publicity was an asset to be included in a decedent's gross estate for federal estate tax purposes was *Estate of Andrews v. United States*.[311] V.C. Andrews was an author of young adult paperback novels in the 1970s and 1980s. When she died in 1986, Andrews' publisher sought to capitalize on the record demand for her novels by continuing to release books under her name. With the agreement of the executor of Andrews' estate and her surviving family, a ghost writer was hired to write first one and then several additional novels, which were released under Andrews's name and went on to commercial success. Andrews' estate tax return did not include the right use of Andrews' name as an asset, and on audit of the estate tax return, the IRS determined that the right of publicity was an asset with a fair market value of over $1 million, based on the anticipated revenue stream from the posthumous publication of ghostwritten novels.

More recently, the valuation of a celebrity's right of publicity arose in the estate of Michael Jackson. In reporting the value of Jackson's right of publicity on his estate tax return, the executor of Jackson's estate initially claimed the right of publicity to be worth just $2,105 at the time of his death in 2009,[312] possibly on the theory that the scandals surrounding Jackson in the years leading up to his death had significantly tarnished his brand. In an audit of Jackson's estate, the IRS claimed that his publicity rights were worth more than $400 million at the time of his death.[313] Hearings before the Tax Court regarding this issue took place in February 2017.[314]

If the decedent's right of publicity is an asset of the celebrity's estate, rather than income in respect of the decedent, estate planning practitioners must also consider whether the right of publicity constitutes a capital asset for income tax purposes in the hands of the estate and its beneficiaries. If the right of publicity is a capital asset, and the celebrity's estate later sells the right of publicity to a third party, any gain recognized by the estate on the sale would be taxed at capital gains rates, rather than ordinary income rates.

---

[311] 850 F. Supp. 1279 (E.D. Va. 1994).
[312] Jeff Gottlieb, *Michael Jackson Estate Embroiled in Tax Fight with IRS*, L.A. TIMES, February 7, 2014, *available at* http://articles.latimes.com/2014/feb/07/local/la-me-jackson-taxes-20140208
[313] *Id.*
[314] Est. of Jackson v. Comm'r, Tax Court Docket No. 017152-13. As of the date of writing, the Tax Court has not reached a conclusion on this issue.

The Internal Revenue Code defines "capital asset" negatively: if an asset is not in one of an enumerated list of excluded categories of assets, it is a capital asset subject to certain judicial exceptions. [315] Among the types of assets excluded from the definition of "capital asset" are certain self-created intangibles and certain inventory and other property used in the taxpayer's trade or business.[316]

Self-created copyrights, musical and literary works and "similar property"[317] produced by a taxpayer's personal efforts are excluded

---

[315] Although the U.S. Supreme Court has determined, and the legislative history of Section 1221 supports, that the enumerated list of non-capital assets under Section 1221 is an exhaustive (not merely illustrative) list of non-capital assets, subsequent courts view such determination as dicta and have retained the "substitute for ordinary income" doctrine, which in effect states that lump sum consideration that that seems essentially a substitute for what would otherwise be received at a future time as ordinary income may not be taxed as capital gain. *See generally*, Arkansas Best Corp. v. Comm'r, 485 U.S. 212 (1988) ("The body of [IRC] § 1221 establishes a general definition of the term 'capital asset,' and the phrase 'does not include' takes out that broad definition only the classes of property that are specifically mentioned. The legislative history of the capital asset definition supports this interpretation, see H.R. Rep. 704, 73d Cong. 2d Sess., 31 (1934) ('[T]he definition includes all property, except as specifically excluded'); H.R. Rep. 1337, 83 Cong. 2d Sess., A273 (1954) ('[A] capital asset is property held by the taxpayer with certain exceptions'), as does the applicable Treasury regulation, see 26 CFR § 1221-1(a) (1987) ('The term 'capital assets' includes all classes of property not specifically excluded by section 1221'')); U.S. v. Maginnis, 356 F.3d 1179 (9th Cir. 2004) (construing a 'capital asset' narrowly in accordance with the purpose of Congress to afford capital-gains treatment only in situations typically involving the realization of appreciation in value accrued over a substantial period of time); Lattera v. Comm'r, 437 F.3d 399 (3d Cir. 2006) (adopting a "family resemblance test" which treats property as a capital asset that is similar in nature to assets that are clearly capital assets (e.g., stock that may generate ordinary income when dividend distributions are made, but is itself a capital asset), and if the asset does not have a "family resemblance" to other such capital assets, then (i) if the transferred property is a "horizontal" carve out (one in which the transferor only disposes of part of the property interest but retains a portion), then the consideration received is ordinary income, while (ii) if the transferred property is a "vertical" carve out (a transfer of the entire interest in the property), then the consideration received is (i) ordinary income if the transferred property represents the right to "earned" income (the underlying income has already been earned and the holder only has to collect it), (ii) capital gain if the transferred property represents the right to "earn" income (the holder of the asset has to do something further to earn the income because mere ownership of the right to earn income does not entitle the owner to income)).

[316] I.R.C. §1221(a)(1)–(3).

[317] The Treasury Regulations interpreting the definition of "capital asset" clarify that the phrase "similar property" is intended to include other property eligible for copyright protection. Treas. Reg. §1.1221-1(c)(1).

from the definition of "capital asset."[318] Accordingly, if the creator of such assets sells them during his lifetime, the gain will be subject to tax at ordinary income tax rates (less favorable than capital gains rates for individual taxpayers as of 2017). Upon the death of the author, these self-created works become capital assets in the hands of the estate (since the efforts of the estate and its beneficiaries did not produce the assets). As discussed above, the right of publicity is distinct from rights under copyright law, and generally bears more resemblance to trademark rights. Accordingly, while the value of publicity rights is undoubtedly generated by the personal efforts of the celebrity, the right of publicity is probably not excluded from the definition of capital asset under the exclusion for self-created copyrights and similar works. Further, if the right of publicity is excluded from the definition of capital asset under this provision during the celebrity's lifetime, the right of publicity would become a capital asset upon his death.

Inventory and depreciable property used in a taxpayer's trade or business are generally also excluded from the definition of capital asset.[319] This raises the question of whether a celebrity's right of publicity is: (1) depreciable property in the hands of the estate or (2) used by the estate in a trade or business (rather than, for example, held for investment). The answers to these questions likely depend upon the facts and circumstances of a given case. If the estate establishes a company that licenses the celebrity's name to third parties, the right of publicity would probably constitute depreciable property used in the taxpayer's trade or business, and therefore the right of publicity would not be a capital asset. If the estate instead merely holds the right of publicity for future sale, the right of publicity probably would be a capital asset.

Regardless of whether the right of public is a capital asset in the hands of a celebrity's estate, it appears that, at least for decedents domiciled in states extending post-mortem rights of publicity, the IRS views the right of publicity as an asset of the celebrity's estate, subject to estate tax. An obvious next question for the estate tax practitioner is

---

[318] I.R.C. §1221(a)(3). However, under I.R.C. §1221(b)(3), authors of musical works may elect to treat the works as capital assets.

[319] I.R.C. §1221(a)(1)–(2). A number of interconnected provisions of the Internal Revenue Code may alter the character of gain recognized on the sale of property used in a trade or business. See, e.g., I.R.C. §§1231 & 1245. A complete discussion of these provisions is beyond the scope of this article.

whether there anything that a celebrity can do during her lifetime to remove these publicity rights from the celebrity's taxable estate, or to reduce the value of the publicity rights included in the estate.

With traditional assets, this might be accomplished by, for example, gifting or selling the assets to an irrevocable grantor trust established during the grantor's lifetime for the benefit of her children or other beneficiaries. For estate and gift tax purposes, the transfer to the irrevocable grantor trust is a completed sale or gift of the beneficial ownership of the transferred asset, meaning that the asset is removed from the grantor's estate for estate tax purposes. For income tax purposes, however, a grantor trust is disregarded,[320] meaning that the grantor would continue to be taxed on the income generated by the transferred assets. This presents an additional benefit to the grantor, since the grantor's payment of income tax: (1) is not treated as a taxable gift to the beneficiaries of the trust[321] and (2) further reduces the grantor's taxable estate.

In an estate of the magnitude of Michael Jackson's, such a transfer of publicity rights during life might save the estate from paying hundreds of millions of dollars in estate tax on an asset that may not be easily liquidated.[322] For a number of reasons, however, rights of publicity may not be so simple to remove from a celebrity's estate.

First, given the personal nature of the right of publicity, there is a threshold question as to whether the right of publicity may be transferred during the celebrity's lifetime.[323] At least in California, the answer appears to be yes. In *Timed Out, LLC v. Youabian, Inc.*,[324] a California court of appeals reversed a trial court decision holding that two models could not assign rights in their likenesses. In reaching its conclusion that the models' publicity rights were assignable during their lifetimes, the court of appeals noted that Civil Code section 3344.1(b) explicitly contemplates such a transfer:

---

[320] I.R.C. §§671-679; *see also* Rev. Rul. 85-13, 1985-1 C.B. 184 (holding that a sale between a grantor and an irrevocable grantor trust established by the grantor is disregarded for federal income tax purposes).

[321] Rev. Rul. 2004-64, 2004-2 C.B. 7.

[322] For example, if the IRS's original assertion as to the value of Jackson's publicity rights were sustained, the estate could owe in excess of $160 million in additional estate taxes (40% of $400 million).

[323] Compare, for example, rights of privacy, which are fundamentally attached to the individual and cannot be transferred or assigned in a traditional sense.

[324] 229 Cal. App. 4th 1001 (2014).

Nothing in this section shall be construed to render invalid or unenforceable any contract entered into by a deceased personality during his or her lifetime by which the deceased personality assigned the rights, in whole or in part, to use his or her name, voice, signature, photograph, or likeness [. . . .][325]

There is also precedent for celebrities selling outright interests in their rights of publicity during life. For example, in April 2016, Muhammed Ali reportedly sold an 80% interest in his name and likeness to a New York-based company for $50 million.[326]

A second issue raised by an inter-vivos transfer of a celebrity's rights of publicity is whether the celebrity's continued control over those rights following the transfer might result in the rights being included in her taxable estate, notwithstanding the transfer. Section 2036(a)(2) of the Internal Revenue Code requires that, where a decedent retained the right during his lifetime to determine the persons who may possess or enjoy the income from property, the decedent must include that property in his taxable estate upon death, notwithstanding the fact that beneficial ownership may have been formally transferred during the decedent's lifetime.

While the application of Section 2036 and related provisions of the Internal Revenue Code to rights of publicity transferred during a celebrity's lifetime remains untested, celebrities may reduce the risk of such rights being brought back into their taxable estates. First, the celebrity should not be the trustee of the irrevocable trust to which she transfers the publicity rights, and if the celebrity retains the right to replace the trustee, the terms of the trust should require that an independent trustee (rather than a related or subordinate trustee) must be chosen as the replacement. Second, the celebrity should consider selling, rather than gifting, the publicity rights to the irrevocable trust since transfers resulting from a sale "for adequate and full consideration" are outside the scope of Section 2036.[327]

A third issue is how to address the fact that if the celebrity's career is ongoing, he will no doubt need to continue to make use of his persona and likeness without, for example, first seeking the approval of

---

[325] Cited in *Timed Out*, 229 Cal. App. 4th at 1008.
[326] Greg Johnson, *Ali's Name Value Put at $50 Million*, L.A. TIMES, April 12, 2006, *available at* http://articles.latimes.com/2006/apr/12/sports/sp-ali12.
[327] I.R.C. §2036(a). The performer would need to hire an appraiser to perform an independent appraisal.

the trustee of a trust. This issue may create an opportunity, however, since the celebrity may enter into a contract with the irrevocable trust pursuant to which the celebrity is allowed to continue to use his name, likeness or other publicity rights in exchange for a series of royalty payments.[328] Since the irrevocable grantor trust is disregarded for income tax purposes, these payments will not result in taxable income to the celebrity or his beneficiaries, and since the payments will represent an arm's-length fair value price for the celebrity's use of his name or likeness,[329] the payments should not be treated as gifts to the beneficiaries of the irrevocable trust. Accordingly, the celebrity may achieve a further reduction to his taxable estate.

As technology advances and posthumous performances become more and more prevalent, post-mortem publicity rights are likely to continue to expand in scope. This will present new challenges to executors and beneficiaries, but it will also present new opportunities and responsibilities for celebrities and their advisors to plan ahead to minimize taxation, provide for their beneficiaries and manage a lasting legacy.

One final thought to ponder is whether, as technology advances to allow digital recreation of celebrities' likenesses, studios may, in an effort to reduce the cost of hiring talent, create digital amalgamations of various body parts and gestures of beloved celebrities. Such a digital Frankenstein's monster might subliminally spark feelings of recognition and goodwill in audiences, without obviously infringing on any one celebrity's rights. Another example is the rendering of Peter Cushing in *Rogue One*. Mr. Cushing died in the United Kingdom and is not afforded the post-mortem protections extended to celebrities in states such as California. The United Kingdom traditionally affords wide protection for free speech and has not yet legislated a

---

[328] Compare a grantor's payment of rent to an irrevocable trust in exchange for continued use of a personal residence that the grantor transferred to the irrevocable trust.

[329] In determining the amount of these arm's-length royalty payments, the celebrity should err on the side of overpaying the irrevocable trust, since any excess above fair value would be treated as a taxable gift. If instead the IRS determined that the celebrity was underpaying for the use of these rights, the IRS may argue that she retained an interest in the rights and that they should be brought back into the celebrity's estate for estate tax purposes.

post-mortem protection for rights of publicity.[330] Thus, Disney likely could have used Mr. Cushing's likeness without the permission of the estate. However, considering the stakes involved in a film the size of *Rogue One*, it's almost certain that Disney did their due diligence in making sure that the use of Cushing's likeness was legal; when reached for comment, a Disney representative pointed to two mentions of Cushing in the credits: "With Special Acknowledgment to Peter Cushing, OBE" and "Special Thanks to the Estate of Peter Cushing, OBE."[331] Further, *Rogue One's* visual effects coordinator, John Knoll, stated, "This was done in consultation and cooperation with his estate. So we wouldn't do this if the estate had objected or didn't feel comfortable with this idea."[332] Actors' union SAG-AFTRA, meanwhile, issued this comment: "Using a digital or virtual re-creation of a performer, deceased or living, in a film, television show, video game, or any other audio-visual work, requires, at minimum, prior consent of the performer or the performers' beneficiaries.[333] The issue for us is straightforward and clear: The use of performers' work in this manner has obvious economic value and should be treated accordingly.

---

[330] Kateryna Moskalenko, *The right of publicity in the USA, the EU, and Ukraine*, 1 Int'l Comp. Jurisprudence 113 (2013).

[331] *See*, Kevin Lincoln, *How Did Rogue One Legally Re-create the Late Peter Cushing?*, Vulture, (Dec. 16, 2016), http://www.vulture.com/2016/12/rogue-one-peter-cushing-digital-likeness.html.

[332] *See*, Andrew Pulver, *Rogue One VFX head: 'We didn't do anything Peter Cushing would've objected to'*, The Guardian, (Jan. 16, 2017), ttps://www.theguardian.com/film/2017/jan/16/rogue-one-vfx-jon-knoll-peter-cushing-ethics-of-digital-resurrections.

[333] Lincoln, *supra*.

— CHAPTER 13 —

RECURRING CONTRACT CONCERNS; SOME FURTHER THOUGHTS

Jay Shanker[*]

13.1. Billing Credit
13.2. Enforcement of Personal Performance Obligations
13.3. Arbitration
13.4. The Challenge of Defining Profits

A number of topics – for example, credits, dispute resolution, personal performance obligations, representations, warranties and indemnities, and, of course, defining how proceeds are to be accounted for – are germane to virtually every transaction in the entertainment industry. Understanding their interrelationships and relevance to a typical "deal" is imperative for the practitioner or business person in this field. The particular characteristics, needs and precedents which attach to each sector of the industry (whether film, television, music, theater, games or literary publishing), contracting party (whether large or small) and the circumstances of each transaction will impose variation on these considerations, but the similarities between the treatment of these terms across the industry generally outweigh the variances from deal to deal. Consequently, anticipating and understanding these considerations is important for anyone and everyone involved in these fields of endeavor.

Although often considered "boilerplate" to be addressed after more salient terms (e.g., scope of services/rights and financial) in an agreement are established, these topics may in many respects be as significant to the outcome of an agreement as the upfront negotiation of what might otherwise be deemed key deal points (and in fact, in many negotiations, "credit" may in fact be a key deal point).

As all of these topics will appear in agreements in every sector of the industry addressed in this volume, and although they may have

---

[*] **Jay Shanker** is a Director of Crowe & Dunlevy, P.C. and a General Editor of this volume.

been addressed in some degree of detail in preceding chapters by the numerous contributors to this volume, a brief reflection on the key components of these topics will be reprised here.

13.1. BILLING CREDIT

Billing credits are sometimes the most difficult and emotionally charged issues of a contract. This difficulty is often blamed (with some justification) on the egotism of talented (and just as often, untalented) members of the entertainment community. In fact, however, the issue of billing credit is fundamental to the careers of creative artists in commercial entertainment fields (referred to throughout this volume as the "talent" or "artist") and the marketability of entertainment industry products.

For the artist (whether actor, author/playwright/screenwriter, director, producer, singer, songwriter, composer or other contributor, including financier, production and distribution entities), credits and their position, size, prominence, and prestige have an economic value.[1] Good credits advertise the importance that is placed on the services of the contributor and can influence others who may need the services of an artist or enterprise in that capacity. They can open doors where, for example, those who engage the artist have not seen the movie (or attended the play, viewed the TV series, read the book, listened to the recording, played the electronic game, etc.) but have seen the advertisements for it or have seen the artist's name – even though they cannot remember where. That is the power of advertising and credits.

At the same time, credits are marketing tools used to sell the entertainment products. For example, when the motion picture industry first started in the United States, there were no credits for the performers. Films were initially identified by the studios that made them (i.e., Edison, Biograph, etc.).[2] It was not until the market demanded films featuring "that Biograph Girl" that Mary Pickford had her name in lights. Her name was placed there because her name sold tickets.

---

[1] This truism of the business has received judicial recognition. *See* Smithers v. Metro-Goldwyn-Mayer Studios, Inc., 189 Cal. Rptr. 20 (Cal. App. 2 Dist. 1983), *cause retransferred*, 696 P. 2nd 82 (Cal. 1985); Perin Film Enter. v. Two Prods., 400 P.T.C.J. (10-19-78) A-13 (S.D.N.Y. 1978).

[2] *See* Spectator's Comments, N.Y. Dramatic Mirror 18 (July 16, 1918) ("the Biograph Company does not make public the names of its players, holding that no good can come from it. Now comes a letter from a new independent company [identifying a former Biograph actor as a star of its upcoming film] which is ... obviously an attempt to secure free advertising").

Beyond emotion and individual egocentricities, there are two fundamental interests at stake in negotiating credit provisions. The interests of both artists and producers/presenters may, in fact, be complimentary where a "bankable star" (one whose name or reputation is a magnet for investors in anything in which the star is involved) likes what the producer is pitching, and the artist's credited attachment is presumed to assure investor interest and eventual box office. These interests may (and often do) diverge where a new, untried or relatively unknown actor (or, director, writer, musical performer, etc.) is seeking top level billing which the producer/presenter (and perhaps other more established talent also likely to be featured – and their representatives) feel to be premature or undeserved.

Credit and billing problems can be divided into three different categories: (1) title billing (on-screen, a theater marquee, DVD packaging, etc.), (2) advertising and publicity credits, and (3) merchandising and tie-in credits. Although all these issues arise in virtually all productions, there can be significant differences in the perspectives of the artist and the producer-marketer. The marketer, in addition to satisfying the artist's demands, has two overriding concerns applicable to all three categories: questions of cost (how much will the credit cost him or her?) and of how to balance the conflicting demands made by the various artists seeking credit in terms of absolute size, prominence, color, type, location (e.g., there can only be one credit in the "first position 'above the title'" location) and the relationship (size, position, etc.) of the respective credit to other credits (i.e., where other attached talent demand similar or conflicting credits on a production).

It should be noted that in addition to customary "artistic" credits, a tremendous amount of jockeying can surround producer and executive producer crediting in film, television and stage productions.[3] Although, historically, financier/packagers of film productions emerged with the "executive producer credit," and those largely responsible for the physical production aspects of a project received the "producer" credit, the rule is not a hard-and-fast one, and many whose functions fall more

---

[3] Reigning in the expanding creep of producer and executive producer credits in film and television has been a prominent goal of the Producers Guild of America, which has developed a Code of Credits designed to convey job descriptions and assure producer credits are accorded only to those actually performing the described functions in its members' productions. (http://www.producersguild.org/default.asp? page=code_of_credits).

within the "executive" responsibility range (packaging/finance) prefer to be perceived by the public as having a "hands-on" producer role in the production, and so prefer this credit. In the television industry, by contrast, the "executive producer" is generally the senior creative force – quite often the creator – on the show (in fact, originating writer-producers are commonly referred to as "show runners" because of their clout in the television industry hierarchy). The producer of television programming is typically charged with line responsibilities for day-to-day production.

13.1.1. Title Billing Credits

Title billing credits are credits given in association with the title of the work and as a part of the work. Examples of this would be credits appearing on-screen as a part of the "opening credits" of a film or television program, credits on the title page of a program, and credits appearing on the cover of a physical book or record. In the case of "A" list actors, a small group of directors and an even smaller complement of writers may appear above or before the actual title of the program in print and on-screen.

13.1.1.1. Talent's Perspective

The primary objective in seeking credit in association with the title of the work is to help build or enhance the artist's career. The advancement of that career depends, in large part, on the artist's reputation with the public and within the entertainment field. Although credit does not necessarily reflect the artistic skills of an individual, it attracts attention to the artist so that a judgment is made by the audience as to their relative prominence. It is an effort by the artist (generally abetted by agents, managers and lawyers) to say, "Hey, look at me!" This is accomplished in many ways. First, the grant of credit on the work helps to identify the artist's contributions to it. If the work is good, it may reflect positively on him or her. Conversely, if it is bad or if in the opinion of the artist or his or her representatives it is not an accurate reflection of his or her work, the artist may not want prominent credit and may even seek to have his or her credit removed.[4] Next, the position,

---

[4] See Curwood v. Affiliated Distribs., 283 F. 219 (S.D.N.Y. 1922); Geisel v. Poynter Prods., Inc., 295 F. Supp. 331 (S.D.N.Y. 1968) (reputation does not properly set the stage for viewing the work may be resisted by the marketer).

size, and location (i.e., "above the title" or "below the title") are measures of the perceived value (as judged by an employer) of the contributions made by that artist to that project in relation to others who have made contributions. Moreover, the credit that the artist received on his or her last project (movie, play, etc.) is generally a threshold on which to improve in the next negotiation. It should be noted that an above-the-title artist will also command an "above-the-title" compensation. Although it may ultimately be the audience that decides who is or is not a star, the negotiation of credit that prominently places the name of the artist before that audience not only sets the stage but influences the audience's decision.

13.1.1.2. Marketer's Perspective

The marketer's concerns with title billing consist of three elements: marketing, audience inducement, and artist inducement.

a. Marketing

The use of title billing credits as a marketing device varies according to the medium. For example, in motion pictures, television or legitimate theater, on-screen or playbill title billing has relatively little or no marketing value because in most cases the audience sees the credit after they buy the ticket or tune in, although its appearance in advertising (newspapers, billboards) may clearly induce audiences to see a program featuring a favorite "star." In contrast, on books and records the title credit to a star, author, or musician may actually help sell the work more than any other feature, including a good review. For example, on a John Grisham or Stephen King novel, the name of the author is generally as large and prominent (or larger and more prominent) than the title of the book. The use of this credit is generally balanced against concerns of graphic design (i.e., Does it "look" good as an appealing package?) and sales focus (i.e., Will the name of the author sell the book or should the title or subject of the book be what sells the book?). In the realm of digital distribution, where consumers may search a web-based menu as readily by author or star or director or musician/band as they do by title, these associations in fact become increasingly relevant.

b. Audience Inducement

Although title billing may not help in the marketing of a film, TV program, or play, the above-the-title credit of well-known artists may help to prepare an audience for the work that follows. For example, marketing a well-known comedian as the star of a program (film or play) may prepare the audience for a comedy, just as the appearance of a credit for an "action star" announces, in all likelihood, an action film. (An actor playing against "type" – i.e., a comedian in a serious role – does not serve this function quite as well.) A well-known star will always get his or her name above the title if he or she wishes (unless this conflicts with the demands of an equally prominent director or author), and may in fact withhold from the marketer the right to credit him or her above title when making a special appearance in a cameo or limited supporting role, so as not to mislead fans or convey marquee value to a film's marketer who isn't paying the artist "marquee" level fees.

A second, related element of audience inducement concerns the number of credits to which an audience will be subjected. For example, in motion pictures practically *everyone* who even vaguely has anything to do with the picture, from the star to the star's pet-sitter, may receive a credit. The marketer (distributor) does not need to worry about restricting end credits because the cost of incorporating the credits at the conclusion of the film is relatively negligible and practically nobody is paying much attention to these credits anyway (outside of the "industry" audiences in a few Los Angeles and Manhattan venues) as they leave the theatre or turn off the television (as the credits are virtually illegible on a tablet or phone, anyway). However, credits appearing during the main titles or opening credits on television are far more limited, in part due to concerns about taxing the audience's patience and the rhythm of the filmgoing experience. In these areas, the marketer does have an incentive to restrict credits to those individuals whose names are of value to the project for purposes of audience inducement or where giving such credit serves as a material inducement for the engagement of the artist.

c. Talent Inducement

The marketer often accords credit to the artist pursuant to the terms of a union agreement[5] or where such credit is demanded and is the only

---

[5] *E.g., see* Directors Guild of America Inc. Basic Agreement, *infra* Part III, §§8-101 *et seq.*

way to engage a particular artist. Because such credit satisfies the concerns of the artist with respect to billing without addressing the marketer's concerns with marketing the work or audience-inducement issues, it may be considered a form of non-monetary compensation.[6]

13.1.2. Advertising and Publicity Credits

Advertising and publicity credits are credits appearing in association with the advertising and publicity used to promote and market the work. These would include advertisements in newspapers or on television or radio, posters, marquees, in press-releases, advertising trailers, billboards and so forth.

13.1.2.1. Talent's Perspective

The objectives of seeking (or refusing) credit in the area of advertising and publicity is the same as the objectives in title billing credits. In some cases, one may require a certain number or type of display advertisements (e.g., "at least one full-page advertisement in the Sunday *New York Times* Arts and Leisure Section prior to opening") or, where the artist is particularly important, to require the credit to be made a part of the "artwork title" (a graphic-design layout of the title and other artwork that serves as a form of logo for the work).

13.1.2.2. Marketer's Perspective

The marketer's concern in advertising and publicity is first and foremost in promoting the work. This effort must, however, be offset against the cost of advertising and promotion.

---

[6] For example, where credit is accorded to a casting director, how many people in the average audience know (or *care*) what a casting director does? However, the Artist's *incentive* for seeking such credit (i.e., to build and enhance that artist's career) is magnified by the vastly greater potential of exposure afforded by such credit. As a rule, many more people will see advertisements for a motion picture (play or program), or read stories based on publicity material distributed in connection with its promotion then will actually see that picture (play or program). Thus one can become famous without being seen. Under the late Mayor Jimmy Walker's theory that "it doesn't matter what they say about you (in the press) so long as they spell your name right" such credit is all to the positive.

Because newspaper, television and online advertisements and commercials are expensive,[7] the marketer's promotion efforts center on placing before the public those elements that encourage sales of the work at the lowest possible cost. This usually translates into an effort to restrict advertising credits to only those items that will sell the work and has led to almost universal acceptance in both theater and film of "excluded" advertisements, such as ABCs (an abbreviated alphabetical listing generally consisting of only the title of the play or picture, the theater, and the schedule) or directory advertisements, teasers (a kind of "Burma Shave" periodicals-advertisement style in which a series of advertisements must be read together or in sequence in order to make sense, with each advertisement a "tease" to provoke the reader's interest in the next), critics' quotation advertisements, award and congratulatory advertisements acknowledging an industry group's recognition of a single participant's contribution in the work (e.g., a Tony or Oscar nomination or award), and other similar types of advertisements. Such excluded advertisements are generally characterized by being restricted to an inclusion of the title, the location of the work's presentation, the names of above-the-title stars, if any, and, for films, the name of the film distributor.

Although the marketer will generally seek to control the mix of exclusion and display or credit advertisements it is common practice to restrict exclusion advertisements by reference to certain sizes (e.g., "less than 1/8 of a page") or durations (e.g., "less than 10 seconds"), or to guarantee advertising credit to those who are not themselves box office draws only in certain publications (e.g., the *New York Times*, *Los Angeles Times*, *DailyVariety* and *Hollywood Reporter*).

13.1.3. Merchandising and Commercial Tie-Ins

Merchandising and commercial tie-ins are related – although frequently ill-defined – concepts that exist at the border between the promotion of a work and the marketing of products. At times, they

---

[7] For example, the Hollywood Reporter cited in 2014 that "In 1980, the average cost of marketing a studio movie in the U.S. was $4.3 million ($12.4 million in today's dollars). By 2007, it had shot up to nearly $36 million." By the summer of 2014, the print and advertising expenditures for an average studio release was $100 million, and for some films and studios the per picture cost exceeded $200 million, far more than the production cost of nearly all U.S. theatrical releases. http://www.hollywoodreporter.com/news/200-million-rising-hollywood-struggles-721818.

may be tenuously related to that work. Technically, a *merchandising use* is the marketing of a product that may be based on the work (such as posters, dolls based on characters in the work, clothing of a style inspired by the work or simply featuring its title and artwork, etc.). As previously noted, merchandising is a very significant source of income for a successful (and sometimes not so successful) entertainment production.[8] A *commercial tie-in* is a commercial arrangement between the marketer of the work and the marketer of a product in which the product marketer provides advertising for the work as a part of the advertising for its own product – the advertising of the work is "tied in" with that product (e.g., fast food merchants advertise giveaways of "collectors" cups or toys featuring a new movie and its characters).

13.1.3.1 Talent's Perspective

Commercial tie-ins and merchandising uses provide benefits to the artist, in the same manner as advertising and publicity, by getting that artist's name and features before the public. However, artists are frequently engaged to act as spokespersons for products or to endorse products at considerable fees. It is therefore appropriate that they receive some form of remuneration for the merchandising use when identifiably featured (i.e., by more than mere "name" listing in a block of credits). Also, as commercial sponsors frequently require product exclusivity (i.e., the artist may not promote a competing product), both artists and sponsors will share the concern that the artist not be overexposed in the areas of commercial endorsements (for the sponsor, because overexposure may reduce the tie-in's verisimilitude; for the artist, since audiences may perceive overexposure as "selling out", and overexposure may reduce the going price of the artist's endorsement value). It is consequently common practice to specify that the artist's name and likeness will not be used in a manner that will constitute a direct or indirect product endorsement absent express approval. Finally, in the fashion of trademark protection, the artist must be concerned that his or her name does not become associated with products or services unfavorable to the career reputation of that artist. Conversely, the advertiser will seek an "out" from merchandising and endorsement deals if a featured artist's private "conduct" crosses a line

---

[8] *See supra* §13.3.

of social acceptance for the advertiser's targeted demographic audience (e.g., highly partisan political comments by a mainstream band, or sexual misconduct allegations against an athlete or actor).

13.1.3.2. Marketer's Perspective

Commercial tie-ins and merchandising uses represent enormous benefits to the marketer. Commercial tie-ins may produce an infusion of advertising funds (supplementing the production budget or subsequent film revenues), while merchandise uses both promote the work and represent direct profit sources.[9] The marketer's concern is simply to ensure that it has acquired the rights to use the artist's name or likeness for tie-ins and merchandising, whether or not the distinction between the uses is clear, and with appropriate compensation provisions (no payments for tie-ins and the lowest possible royalty for merchandising). The marketer also wants to establish the distinction between a character's identity (which the producer/marketer will own) and the personality of the artist portraying that character (which may be subject to a separate and higher royalty).

13.1.4. Artist's Refusal of Credit

Ostensibly, an artist's refusal of credit might appear to be inconsistent with the push to seek credit. In fact, if credit is a form of currency, refusing credit is simply the other side of the coin. An artist seeks credit to build or enhance his or her reputation, while he or she refuses credit in order to defend that reputation from harm where the work with which he or she is being identified is, in the artist's opinion, of an unsatisfactory quality, or the association may otherwise diminish the artist's economic value to subsequent projects.

The right to refuse credit, unless that right is reserved absolutely by contract, cannot be exercised merely on the whim of the artist simply because the artist does not subjectively like the resulting work.[10] Such right, if it exists at all, is based on the principles of unfair competition and usually requires a showing that (1) the work does not accurately reflect the artist's contributions and (2) the work offers potential harm

---

[9] *See supra* §8.3.
[10] *Contra*: An author under the Berne Convention might be able to withdraw publication of a work or credit based on subjective feelings. *See supra* §45.3.3.

to the artist's reputation. (Taken to its extreme and depending on the severity of the potential harm and degree of culpability, these principles can be applied to restrict or prevent distribution of the work in question.[11] Lesser degrees of harm or culpability can justify the removal of the credit.)[12]

The most common refusal-of-credit controversy arises over the editing of a work after delivery by the artist or completion of the artist's performance services. It has been held that substantial cutting or alterations in a work creates a situation of misrepresentation,[13] whereas minor changes may be allowed as customary within the industry.[14] Although the former may justify preventing distribution of the work and the latter justifies no relief, those gray areas in between may justify a removal of the artists' credit.

The second most common controversy arises when the owner of works created by an artist while that artist was young and not yet successful attempts to market those works at a later time, trading on the reputation of the now "mature" and famous artist. It is not uncommon, for example, to see a previously released (or otherwise "unreleasable") film show up in online film services, television or even theatre screens following release of a breakout picture featuring the performance of the previously unknown new "star." Similarly, the early recordings of musical artists which may have failed to initially find a commercial audience may get released after the artist or band finally hits the *Billboard* Charts (sometimes years after this music was originally recorded). Although the works may properly be credited as works created by that artist (which is true),[15] the work's owner generally may not market the works in a way that suggests they are current works of the artist by – for example, by attaching a current picture of the artist to the work.[16]

---

[11] *See* Rich v. RCA Corp., 390 F. Supp 530 (S.D.N.Y. 1975); Gilliam v. American Broadcasting Cos., 538 F.2d 14 (2d Cir. 1976).

[12] *See* Curwood v. Affiliated Distribs., 283 F. 219 (S.D.N.Y. 1922).

[13] *See* Granz v. Harris, 198 F.2d 585 (2d Cir. 1952); Gilliam v. American Broadcasting Cos., 538 F.2d 14 (2nd Cir. 1976).

[14] *See* Preminger v. Columbia Pictures Corp., 267 N.Y.S.2d 594 (N.Y. Sup. Ct.), *judgment aff'd*, 269 N.Y.S.2d 913 (N.Y. App. Div.), *order aff'd*, 219 N.E. 2d 431 (N.Y. 1966).

[15] *See* Geisel v. Poynter Prods., Inc. 295 F. Supp. 331 (S.D.N.Y. 1968).

[16] *See* Rich v. RCA Corp., 390 F. Supp. 530 (S.D.N.Y. 1975).

Third, the form of the proposed credit may be significant in the resolution of a controversy. Possessory credit, that is, credit asserting that an artistic work is the creation of an identified individual (e.g., Alfred Hitchcock's *Psycho*), requires that the party being given credit for the work must have had some minimal involvement in its creation. Use of a person's name without such involvement may be enjoined.[17] In contrast, a credit indicating that a work is "based upon" another work involves both a quantitative (i.e., "how much?") and qualitative analysis of the two works in question before a determination of fair or unfair competition can be made.[18] While such "based upon" credit allows some creative liberty with the underlying material, a derivative work owner may not claim that one work (e.g., a short story) is the basis for another (e.g., a movie) unless the derivative work genuinely reflects the underlying work.[19] (And, of course, claiming this association will, for all but public domain sources, trigger the need for a rights and fees agreement for the source material.)

Finally, these controversies arise because the marketer wishes to exploit the value of that credit to the marketing of the work. In circumstances where this determination is not the subject of an upfront negotiation and contractual agreement (i.e., the right to use the artist's name or likeness in some or any manner was not obtained, and/or a credit was not approved, etc.), the marketer may be forced to remove the objectionable credit under principles of unfair competition or, if the artist is unimportant enough, may voluntarily remove the credit to avoid a controversy. In either event, the marketer usually seeks an agreement from the artist not to discuss the settlement or derogatorily discuss the work in public as a part of any agreement to remove credit.

13.2. ENFORCEMENT OF PERSONAL PERFORMANCE OBLIGATIONS

Most contracts in the entertainment industry involve the rendition of personal services, e.g., an author agreeing to write a novel, an agent agreeing to represent an artist, or an actor agreeing to appear in a film or a play. In most cases, these agreements are entered into and performed according to their terms. But what happens when one party

---

[17] King v. Innovation Books, 976 F.2d 824 (2d Cir. 1992).
[18] *Id.*
[19] Curwood v. Affiliated Distribs., 283 F. 219 (S.D.N.Y. 1922).

refuses to perform or refuses to allow the other party to perform? Courts, for many understandable reasons, are hesitant to compel specific performance of a personal services contract. Beyond the fear that such an order might violate the Constitutional prohibition against involuntary servitude,[20] judicial supervision of such an order would be extremely difficult; for example, how would the court resolve disputes over the adequacy of the efforts rendered by the performer, or the quality of the performance?

In some cases a monetary award is appropriate and reasonable. In an agreement between artist and agent, for example, where the artist seeks to withdraw from the agency relationship, the artist is generally allowed to obtain the services of a new agent subject to a continuing obligation to pay to the original agent the commission originally agreed upon without any mitigation for the balance of the period of representation in their agreement. The fact that the agent will not be required to render any additional services should be and generally is considered irrelevant to the obligation of the artist to continue paying the agreed upon commission, because in this situation the agent is being precluded from rendering services through the choice and actions of the artist. Otherwise, the contract itself would be illusory. It would effectively be a contract terminable at will based upon whether or not the artist will allow the agent to continue representing that artist for the full term of the agreement. Though rarely litigated, this approach is often taken in private settlements and/or arbitrations.

In other cases, courts have agreed that monetary damages are inadequate and have elected to enforce these agreements indirectly by issuing an injunction against a breaching party entering into a similar agreement with another party during the term of the original agreement. Though it was originally held that this remedy required a showing of irreparable harm, in practice the requirement generally is that the services of the employee are "unique and extraordinary."[21] Interestingly, the main application of this rule has been in the entertainment[22] and sports industries.[23]

---

[20] *See* Stevens, *Involuntary Servitude by Injunction*, 6 CORNELL L.Q. 235 (1921).

[21] *See* Calamari & Perillo, CONTRACTS §16-5 (2d ed. 1977).

[22] *See* Berman & Rosenthal, *Enforcement of Personal Services Contracts in the Entertainment Industry*, 7 J. BEVERLY HILLS B.A. 49 (1973); Tannenbaum, *Enforcement of Personal Service Contracts in the Entertainment Industry*, 42 CAL. L. REV. 18 (1954).

In order to insure that this indirect enforcement injunction approach is taken, if such an action becomes necessary, most producers require that a provision be inserted in the personal services agreement stating that the producer has such a right. Furthermore, because time is of the essence in situations such as where a film has commenced production, or a concert performance is scheduled, in order to avoid delays brought about by having to prove each element of the injunctive relief action, the provision is normally drafted to specify that it is agreed between the parties that the services of that employee are "special, unique, unusual, extraordinary, and of an intellectual character giving them peculiar value, the loss of which cannot be reasonably or adequately compensated in damages in an action at law." Such a provision, if accepted by the court, satisfies all the prima facie grounds for the issuance of an injunction. As additional insurance, some producers demand that the artist agree to the insertion of an additional provision that states that "in the event of any breach by Artist, the Producer will be entitled to equitable relief by way of Injunction or otherwise." Some performers may object to this latter provision on the ground that, at whatever time this provision becomes operable, there may be conditions that would justify limiting the producer's damages to monetary damages, and that such a decision should be left up to the court at that time.

Lastly, it should be noted that most producers refuse to accord artists a similar injunctive right. Indeed, it is common to provide a provision in the employment agreement that specifies that the employee will not be entitled to "enjoin or otherwise interfere with production, distribution, or exhibition of the Picture [Play, Recording, Electronic Game, etc.]" and that the employee's sole remedy will be for monetary damages only. The reason for this is that any delay in the production or distribution process costs a great deal of money, such that the threat of delay represented by an injunction becomes almost coercive in the hands of a disgruntled artist employee. Moreover, in the film and television industry most completion bond companies (companies that insure that a film or program will be completed) will not insure a producer that fails to obtain such an agreement from its employees.

Where the personal services contract is long-term and involves financial responsibilities for the performer, most notably in relation to

---

[23] *See* Brennan, *Injunctions Against Professional Athletes Breaching Their Contracts*, 34 BROOKLYN L. REV. 61 (1967).

recording contracts, some entertainers have sought to utilize the bankruptcy code to get out of these contracts, with limited and mixed results.[24] In general, it would appear that such efforts will only be successful where the contract is in fact financially onerous and probably unfair. Moreover, even if it allowed a rejection of the contract, it is an open question whether a court would issue an equitable injunction against future competitive activities by the performer. That is to say, it might reject the basic contract, but preclude the performer from entering into another agreement with a competing contractor, thus, in essence, forcing a renegotiation between the two parties.

13.3. ARBITRATION

In almost all areas of entertainment, practitioners favor the use of arbitration to resolve contract disputes. Not only is arbitration a less expensive method of dispute resolution, it avoids the long delays often encountered in conventional litigation and the risk that distribution or performance of the work will be held up by the courts. Most entertainment industry contracts in which the parties are subject to creative Guild agreements as members or signatories (e.g., WGA, DGA, SAG, AFTRA) will stipulate that disputes will automatically be subject to the respective Guild's rules and arbitration procedures in the event of a breach or default of either party. Disputes pertaining to the enforcement of agency agreements in states where agents are licensed will likely also be subject to arbitration in accordance with the state's labor statutes and adjudication procedures. For many years large entertainment companies, including the major studios and networks, preferred the threat of forcing disputes into the courts where Guild agreements did not dictate otherwise – largely because they could in this way intimidate less well-financed opponents from bringing claims or mounting a full-fledged defense. But the advantages offered by arbitration in maintaining the confidentiality of outcomes, which means adverse press from disclosures made on open court or court filings can often be avoided and that unfavorable decisions do not have power as

---

[24] Wald, *"Bankruptcy and Personal Services Contracts: What Works, What Doesn't, and Why,"* 16(1) ENTERTAINMENT & SPORTS LAWYER 3-10 (Am. Bar. Assoc.) (1998) citing such cases as: In re Noonan, 17 B.R. 793 (Bankr. S.D.N.Y. 1982); In re Carrere, 64 B.R. 156 (Bankr. CD CA 1986); In re Taylor, 92 B.R. 302 (Bankr, D.N.J. 1988), *aff'd*, 103 B.R. 511 (D.N.J. 1989), *aff'd in part, appeal dismissed in part*, 913 F.2d 102 (3d Cir. 1990).

precedent, has led even the major studios and networks to regularly opt for arbitration of disputes in their standard artist and producer agreements.

The courts support the use of arbitration. Arbitration is favored in the law.[25] Accordingly, the courts have held that parties to agreements including an arbitration clause cannot avoid them by casting their claims in tort, rather than in contract.[26] Likewise, judicial proceedings against parties and non-parties to the arbitration agreement are stayed pending the outcome of arbitration, when the action against the non-party is dependent upon interpretation of the underlying contract.[27]

However, many lawyers are concerned about the fairness of arbitration, particularly when the arbitration is set to take place in the "back yard" of a particularly powerful defendant, such as an arbitration in Los Angeles by a first time writer or director against a powerful movie studio or distributor, or in a location in which there is a paucity of arbitrators experienced in entertainment industry matters. Unfortunately, most plaintiffs who are parties to agreements calling for arbitration will be unable to avoid arbitration, even where they attempt to frame their complaint solely against a party not subject to the arbitration agreement, if the cause of action ultimately rests upon such an agreement (unless the language of the agreement expressly contemplates such an exception).[28]

Moreover, it is unlikely that the producer or distributor will be willing to remove the arbitration provision in favor of a state or federal court setting (other than with respect to *the enforcement* of an arbitrator's award). In many cases, the producer will be compelled by their agreements with completion bond insurers, financiers and/or the ultimate distributor to make sure that the production (i.e., film, recording, etc.) will not be subject to an injunction by requiring that all agreements be subject to arbitration. Consequently, the best that can be hoped for is to negotiate provisions that attempt to assure the fairness of the arbitrator selected. In some industry agreements in which the executory and/or financial stakes which may be disputed are likely to be high, this is done by empanelling three arbitrators (rather than one),

---

[25] *See* Moses H. Cone Mem'l. Hosp. v. Mercury Constr. Corp., 460 U.S. 1, 24-25 (1983).
[26] *See e.g.,* Acevedo Maldonado v. PPG Indus., Inc., 514 F.2d 614, 616 (1st Cir. 1975).
[27] *See* Subway Equip. Leasing Corp. v. Forte, 169 F.3d 324, 329 (5th Cir. 1999).
[28] Grigson v. Creative Artists Agency, L.L.C., 218 F.3d 745 (5th Cir.) *cert. denied,* 531 U.S. 1013 (2000).

with one arbitrator drawn from a panel appointed by the producers (or their representative organizations – such as the Motion Picture Association of America [MPAA]), one from a panel appointed by the union or other representative of the performer, and the third to be selected by these two approved panel arbitrators. Alternately, the parties can agree that the arbitrator can be selected from an independent source, such as the approved list of arbitrators from the American Arbitration Association (AAA), the Judicial Arbitration and Mediation Service (JAMS), or the Independent Film and Television Alliance (IFTA). There remains some risk that members of any panel may be biased towards one side or the other based upon prior professional experience or relationships, and lawyers for both sides are advised to seek as much information as possible about the reputations of proposed arbitrators at the outset of the arbitration.

Ironically, even in contractual disputes where the subject matter of disputes may be modest in terms of its financial or executory impact on the parties (e.g., a damage or payment claim of $10,000 or less), the courts may offer a more expeditious and economical alternative to arbitration. The parties may consequently agree up front that disputes involving limited claims (e.g., of less than such an amount), or where an urgent equitable remedy is required by either party, may be brought in the courts rather than before an arbitrator.

13.4. THE CHALLENGE OF DEFINING PROFITS

The risks and rewards for any project in the entertainment industry can be enormous. A film by an unheralded filmmaker, a record album produced on a shoestring budget by an unknown musician, or a novel by a previously unpublished author, could become the next blockbuster bringing in millions to the lucky artist and distributor, while the latest big-budget film production could flop, not even generating enough revenue to pay for the cost of prints and advertising. The creators of a work are anxious to share in the rewards of success while producers and distributors are anxious to limit their risks.

Traditionally, producers and distributors sought to limit their risk while maintaining their possible profits by paying creators a limited fee up front. While they faced all the risk, they also retained all the potential for high profits. As creators have gained greater power (either because they are publicly recognized – such as a star actor – or because they are otherwise in demand – such as a writer with a good reputation), they have pushed for a share of the upside as well – either in the form of royalties or through sharing in the profits earned by the venture.

This is an enormously complex area of law and practice. Terms such as gross profits, net proceeds and producer's share of profits may not always be what they appear to be, generating much litigation. Moreover, the understanding of these terms often varies from one facet of the entertainment industry (e.g., stage or music) to another (e.g., film or television) so that practitioners familiar with one area may find themselves in trouble when they try to apply their understandings to deals with which they are less familiar.[29] Consequently great care must be taken in defining all of the terms used in contracts incorporating an ongoing "profit" participation interest.

While the specifics of these deals will vary from industry to industry, there are certain common features of these deals which need to be taken into consideration. Chief among these is the nature of the distributor. Entertainment is big business and the distributors of creative works tend to be large conglomerates. Indeed, "vertical integration" has been a goal of many media enterprises. A film distributor may have several wholly-owned subsidiaries or affiliates under its substantial control who function as subdistributors in one or several media or territories. They may also own companies interested in exploiting other rights, such as merchandising, publishing or television, cable or other digital exhibition (or be a subsidiary of a larger enterprise with these interests). Consequently, creators have to be concerned that the potential profits to the titular distributor with whom they have a contract may be eaten up by the profits earned by the subsidiary before the income is passed along to the distributor. They have to make sure that the deals between such entities both conform to common practice (i.e., that rights are sold for a fair market value) and that self-dealing is limited.[30] They do this in a number of ways.

In deals involving the payment of a royalty, contracts may specify that the royalty is based upon the price intended to be or which is actually paid by the end customer (e.g., suggested retail list price appearing on a book, CD or DVD). Alternatively, where the price is

---

[29] See Mark Hamblett, *"Apollo Theater Board Sues White & Case,"* New York Law Journal (Apr. 29, 1999).

[30] See Di Mari Ricker, *"Mulder's Profits May Be The Next X-File,"* The Recorder/Cal Law (November 23, 1999).

based upon the wholesale price received by the distributor (as often occurs when the product is sold overseas or via digital delivery), or is licensed for any other exploitation, the royalty participant will seek assurance that the subdistributor or licensee is independent of the primary distributor (or if not independent, that pricing must be equivalent to that derived from an arm's length transaction). To allow the original producer to recoup expenses, the creative profit participant may also agree to a set royalty for a set number of copies sold, with the royalties increasing as additional copies are sold, less limited deductions for certain costs of sales (e.g., packaging costs) by the distributor/producer.[31] Bonuses triggered by certain box office, home video sales performance or best-seller list milestones are also frequently demanded.

In deals involving a share of income, it is useful to consider revenue and costs as levels in a metaphorical "waterfall." Participants should seek to obtain their participation at the highest level of revenue, with the fewest deductions, possible. Producers will seek to deduct as many costs as possible "off the top," or from the participant's share of proceeds (however defined) before having to make distributions to participants. Participating closer to "gross" also simplifies the audit proposition for participants, even if the relative percentage by which the participation is calculated is smaller than would be available for a "net" position further down the waterfall. And although obtaining a share of "gross" income offers greatest protection to the participant, "gross" will be achievable only by a limited number of superstar creators and performers (as it results in talent participating in project proceeds well before financiers recover their investment, if at all, and may actually prevent them from doing so).[32] Even when gross participation discussions do occur, it is common to allow some "recoupment" by the distributor and financiers by allowing the distributor to retain all income until the project has earned a set "break even" amount (usually 2 to 3 times the set costs of the production as defined in the agreement before retroactive gross participation occurs). Alternatively, "adjusted gross" definitions allow the distributor to recapture a negotiated distribution fee and/or distribution expenses, and the amount of any advances paid toward distribution rights in the program (and interest on such advances) before accounting to participants. When net proceeds participation is negotiated, efforts are made to limit financier/distributor self-dealing and

---

[31] *See*, for example, §7.3.7.2a *infra*.
[32] *See* §1.2.7.2 *infra*.

the allowable costs charged against profits. Moreover, creators with less negotiating power often attempt to require that the relevant terms (e.g., net proceeds) applied to them will be the same as those given to all others (i.e., most-favored-nations treatment) to avoid the anomalous, but not unusual, result that some people are sharing in net proceeds from a larger pool of revenue than the participant – whether for lack of leverage and/or representation by a less experienced negotiator – which has the effect of accelerating and/or enlarging the relative payout to the preferred participant(s).

In literary publishing, music, electronic game and home video distribution agreements where "profits" are typically calculated based on "units" of physical or digital product sold or shipped rather than on gross or adjusted gross licensing revenue, disputes arise over the accuracy of reporting and calculations of costs deductions which are permitted before royalties are due.

Litigation of motion picture and television "profit" definitions have led many companies to instead describe these participations as some variation of "net proceeds" or "defined proceeds" or "modified adjust gross revenues" ("MAGR") to further reduce the illusion that the participant will be entitled to any actual "profits," as the term is commonly understood in general business settings.

Negotiating provisions for the timing and detail of profit reporting and payments, along with audit rights provisions, and remedies for breach of any one or more of these agreement provisions can be no less daunting, and though beyond the scope of this chapter, should be part of every practitioner's "deal checklist."

In all cases, the actual terms of the contract will be binding on the parties. The profit definition may also require the participant to waive certain privileges or remedies which might otherwise be available and beneficial to the participant. It must be carefully drafted and the entire agreement relating to definition and calculation of such profits and their payment to a participant (which often can be as long or longer than the principal agreement for rights or services) needs to be carefully reviewed to discover if there are hidden charges that may affect the more obviously identified payment provisions. In a transaction in which the profits participation negotiation is a material aspect of the deal, the lawyer may wish to consult an accountant or auditor with experience in the field before concluding the negotiation.

— CHAPTER 14 —

FUNDAMENTALS OF ENTERTAINMENT TALENT REPRESENTATION BY AGENTS AND MANAGERS

Kirk Schroder,[*] Jay Shanker[†]

14.1. Introduction: Understanding the Roles of Agents and Managers
14.2. Agents
14.3. Personal Managers
14.4. Business Managers
14.5. Conflicts of Interest
14.6. Conclusion

14.1. INTRODUCTION: UNDERSTANDING THE ROLES OF AGENTS AND MANAGERS

Agents and managers, as well as lawyers, each play a very important role on behalf of creative artists and talent in the entertainment industry. In a business where there are limited channels for the work of creative artists to get meaningful commercial exploitation (as opposed to just public exposure), agents and managers are intermediaries to key decisionmakers who determine whether or not to take commercial economic risks on the engagements of artists. Such decisions are wide-ranging: whether involving distributing an artist's musical recordings, casting an actor in a motion picture, publishing a writer's manuscript and so forth. Simply put, agents and managers must have the ability to get the attention of such decision makers, to get them to consider their client's artistic and commercial merits and, more importantly, to convince them to make an investment in or take a commercial risk on the artist. In this sense, "good" agents and managers have the ability to identify creative artists with the potential for commercial and/or critical success, and to guide them in a

---

[*] **Kirk Schroder** is a founder and principal in Schroder Davis, Law Firm, PLC.

[†] **Jay Shanker** is a Director of Crowe & Dunlevy, P.C. Co-authors. Shanker and Schroder are also the General Editors of this volume.

manner where such success can be realized. With respect to nascent or emerging artists, agents and managers are risk-takers as well. Sometimes they see potential in an artist and sometimes they don't. Just because one agent or manager rejects the representation of an artist or an artist's specific project does not mean that another agent or manager will not agree to represent such artist or project on the path toward commercial success.

A creative artist's relationships with agents and managers are typically built around an agreement detailing the respective parties' rights and responsibilities, including fee arrangements. New artists may have little to no leverage in negotiating the relationship with an agent or a manager, especially representatives who are very experienced and have had significant prior success with other artists. As such, the engagement of professional representation (whether an agent and/or manager) may be viewed as a *"sign of arrival"* by new artists and buyers of their services, since the willingness of an agent or manager to represent them suggests the representative's endorsement of their talent and income-generating potential (the source of an agent's or manager's compensation). However, the entertainment lawyer advising the emerging artist will typically need to counsel the client's expectations in negotiations where an agent or manager is demanding more than customary rights or benefits, since the agent or manager will have more leverage in negotiating the relationship (for example, an agent who will want to broadly commission post-term revenue from agreements initiated during the term but which may be negotiated by a subsequent agent). Obviously, the emerging artist, as opposed to the established artist, may not have a substantial prior income stream from earlier deals worth fighting over.

In other situations, where the agent or manager may likewise be new to the industry or the role, with limited experience (for example, just starting in the business) or a limited track record, an artist will likely have more leverage in negotiating the terms of such a relationship, especially if the artist has enjoyed some commercial success. Sometimes the artist is well-established and is looking to move representation from an existing manager or agent. Thus, an entertainment lawyer, as discussed further in this chapter, may play an important role in helping the artist/client evaluate potential relationships with agents and managers. And no less frequently, an agent or manager may direct a client to a new manager or lawyer (particularly if the artist does not yet have such a representative as part of his or her team), or a manager, if the first "hire" in the artist's line-up of representatives, may likewise. For example, if an entertainment lawyer represents a touring band in a specific music genre and an established management company desires to also represent the band and take 15% to 20% of the band's gross revenues for its services plus expenses, it is important to ask what added value the management company will bring the band for the proposed compensation. What if the band has already saturated most or nearly all of the touring venues for its particular music genre? If a manager is a good idea for the band, is this one the best candidate?

That said, as an artist builds his or her career advisory team consisting of agent and/or manager, attorney and sometimes business manager, in one or more possible combinations and/or sequence, the effective guidance these parties can provide a creative artist or creative business can significantly enhance the client's professional opportunities, income, creative freedom and creative success, and can in many instances (particularly as regards the lawyers oversight and contributions) help insure that the artist or entity which is the beneficiary of this professional guidance is not hindered in its advancement by legal obstacles which could with foresight be readily anticipated and addressed. And when these parties can actively work together, sharing information and expertise, and sometimes playing good-cop/bad-cop in negotiations on behalf of their clients – whether at the client's urging or through the leadership of one or more of the representatives – careers and creative projects can often take flight.

Sometimes, this can be easier said than done for the entertainment lawyer, especially where an agent and/or a manager is not accustomed to a third party reviewing a deal negotiated by the agent (or manager when involved in the negotiation). Most major talent agencies and some professional managers have in-house counsel or preferred outside counsel available to review such deals and as such, may directly or indirectly downplay their clients' entertainment lawyer's role in such review on their behalf, particularly for smaller or simpler contracts that are largely boilerplate or which do not involve significant pay dates, and or exclude continuing royalty or long-term services obligations. Occasionally the agent or manager may have a separate agenda in this decision, e.g., directing the new client to a new lawyer with whom the agent or agency is more closely aligned (and in some cases it may in fact be a better fit for the client long term). Keep in mind that the talent agent's in-house counsel may first and foremost be looking out for the talent agent's interests (e.g., compensation terms) and then making sure that the client's non-compensation deal points are sufficiently covered in the agreement. An agent's legal counsel (whether a lawyer in independent practice or an in-house attorney or business affairs representative at a larger agency) is not necessarily looking out for the client's complete interest if the agent/agency is the primary "client," and there may consequently be a fundamental conflict of interest in the representation of both the agent and the client in particular transactions (a dilemma inherent in virtually any commission versus hourly or flat fee compensation arrangement, no matter what the context or industry).

As such, the independent entertainment lawyer often performs a balancing act between identifying legal issues important to the client and otherwise, addressing the client's concerns with an agent or manager, while fostering an environment where the agent or manager can succeed on behalf of the client. Admittedly, these are problems many artists might "want" to have. Many artists would "welcome" agents, as they suggest a high level of interest in his/her career and economic potential. But that potential will best be realized if and when the artist builds a team that can work efficiently and effectively together. And the artist will always be weighing the relative costs and benefits of each team member – the lawyer's hourly fees or 5% contingency; 10% to an agent; and 15% to 20% to a manager. On the other hand, at the high end of the spectrum, paying out 35% to 40% of a million-dollar plus pre-tax gross year, onto which another 5% for business/financial management may be factored, could cause the artist some pause, and this is where the artist's leverage with representatives may start to be exploited in favour of the artist in his/her "management" of his/her team.

The remainder of this chapter will discuss these specific considerations.

14.2. AGENTS

The talent agent is the most prevalent (and arguably influential) advisor and ally to the creator and performer in the entertainment industry. The primary task of the agent is to market the client's services and their works to buyers within the industry. In furtherance of this goal, they will advise and counsel the client on the best ways to develop his or her career. However, first and foremost, they are paid to sell their client's services or works. They will solicit engagements for working talent or solicit the licensing or sale of rights to the creative works of their clients. They will then negotiate some or all the terms of the agreements. For licensing or engagement agreements which are embodied in a standardized form contract, they may even issue copies of contracts for execution. Finally, an agent will follow up with the buyer of the client's services to obtain any and all agreed upon payments (and are compensated on the basis of a percentage of the payments so collected by or on the client's behalf).

The most successful agents intelligently and accurately assess and match buyers to sellers, based both on immediate opportunities and trends/prospects the agents may identify and sometimes directly help to create. They will monitor published and unpublished information about prospective buyers – old and new – and their current and prospective projects to "make a market" for their client's services and work. For a high-profile client, this may involve fielding inquiries and offers from buyers actively seeking the particular client's engagement. For less established (and frequently even well-established) artist clients, it more often means the artist's agent marketing and promoting the artist for a particular identified opportunity, alongside one or more members of the artist's team. Agents who aggressively try to sell anything and everything in their inventory will quickly lose their audience with active buyers who are looking to the agents to exercise some level of taste and intelligence as to the right talent/project "fit" they are seeking. Agents without access to active buyers will have a tough time maintaining a credible stable of desirable talent selling their services and rights.

14.2.1. Evaluating a Proposed Artist – Agent Relationship

Often a client will come to an entertainment lawyer asking for counsel on a proposed representation agreement with an agent. Whether the artist is already "sold" on the agent or is asking for the entertainment lawyer to help evaluate the pros and cons of such representation, it is important to make sure that the client considers certain basic questions even if the client has little leverage in negotiating the terms of the agent's representation agreement:

1) What is the agent's background and past track record (in other words, how qualified is this agent)?

2) What are the client's objectives with respect to the agent and do such objectives match with the agent's past track record?
3) What is the scope of the agent's representation? This is very important as some agents will insist on exclusive representation, which may include aspects of the artist's potential career in which the agent has no experience (and instead will employ co-agents or sub-agents to handle those areas)
4) What is the length of the agent's representation?
5) What goals and objectives has the agent identified (or in some cases even "promised") the client?
6) Is the agent licensed or required to be licensed under the state laws governing the agency and the proposed representation agreement? If so, what are the regulations or procedures in place to protect the client and which apply to the representation?
7) Is the agent required to be a "franchised agent" under one or more of the guilds representing creative artists?

Sometimes the client will have answers to these questions and sometimes the entertainment lawyer will need to help the client get these answers before making a final decision on whether or not the proposed relationship is a good fit for the client.

In some instances, an agent may "audition" a client by asking them to do things like revise a manuscript or a screenplay before considering offering a representation agreement, and this back and forth may go on for a while before there is a mutual decision to formalize the agent-client relationship. In other cases, an agent may "hip-pocket" a client, offering informal representation on a "per deal" basis while both agent and client assess the potential of a more formal engagement.

Typically, agents specialize in representing either one type of creator or artist and/or one area of the entertainment industry. For example, literary agents and agencies will specialize in representing writers. Some literary agents will represent only dramatists; others specialize in literary authors or screenwriters; while others will represent any or all types of authors. Some music agents will specialize in booking pop or rock musical acts, while others focus on classical music. Some agents specialize in the advertising business, representing actors or other creators in connection with the making of commercials, while others represent actors in theatre, films and/or television, and some even limit their clientele to child and juvenile actors. These "specialists" may work independently or in a small specialized boutique agency setting, or may be employed by a larger multifaceted talent agency with a much broader representational focus.

As mentioned above, it is critical to inquire about an agent's scope of expertise. It is not uncommon for agents to want to represent an artist in fields beyond the scope of the agent's expertise in order to capture a commission on other revenue streams from that artist which may later materialize, no matter how remote the likelihood may seem early in a career (e.g., actors who may want to write, writers who may eventually direct, actors appearing in commercials or musicians who may wish to act in series or film or on stage, etc.). Sometimes an agent will insist on such a broad representation with two basic arguments: 1) the agent's role in expanding the artist's fame to the point there is interest in these other fields and 2) the agent may be in a large agency that has other agents who handle these matters, or who accesses independent co-agents in these circumstances. If an artist feels compelled to agree to broad representation in such circumstances, the artist should insist on the right to approve such additional agents (at least those outside the agency) and to have such agents removed if they fail to generate any meaningful activity on the artist's behalf (whether or not such termination rights are mandated by applicable guild/agent agreements.)

There are a number of possible advantages from the artist's perspective in dealing with specialized individual agents or their specialty agencies. First, specialized agents often represent a limited number of clients, thus providing each client with a significant degree of individual attention. In dealing with such specialized agents, the agents and artist may and generally will restrict their association to activities within the agent's field of specialization. However, an agent taking on representation of an emerging artist may argue that by helping to advance the artist's career to new levels in the selected field, the artist may be primed for success in other areas as a result of the agent's initial representation and work (e.g., a novelist who becomes a screenwriter or an actress who sells a screenplay or television series pitch). In these scenarios, an agent may insist in these instances on the right to hire co-agents to assist them in other specialized areas while splitting an increased commission fee if permitted by statute and applicable Guild agreements). In these scenarios, the entertainment lawyer will still want the client, to the extent possible, to know in advance the identity of a "co-agent" and to at least have the ability to veto the attachment of a specific agent in lieu of another agent in the specialized field based perhaps on general reputation, bad chemistry or a negative prior experience, while still preserving the original agent's ability to split such revenue with the preferred co-agent. The artist may also be able to select his or her own preferred specialty agent who will simply agree to a fee split with the initial agent for a particular engagement or time period.

The difficulties with dealing with specialized agents are threefold. First, the artist loses the depth and breadth of expertise a larger and more generalized agency can provide in understanding the totality of the artist's overall career plan and its support in promoting it in all areas, including likely access to a wider and more diverse group of buyers and employers. Second, with individual agents, each agent is primarily and understandably concerned with the artist's taking every contract obtainable by the agent. Thus, even a well-intentioned individual agent may find his or her career advice influenced by his or her own interests and focus upon one area of activity, whereas an agency that participates in all aspects of the client's career will be compensated regardless of which area of activity is being stressed. Third, dealing with individual agents requires that the artist or someone she or he employs devote the time necessary to coordinate all of the activities of various agents (e.g., a "book" agent may focus on publishers but not movie producer sales; an acting agent may focus on film but not television or commercials, or filmed entertainment, but not theater). One solution to all of these problems for the prolific artist with interests and potential in multiple fields may be to engage a personal manager or attorney to provide the required expertise, unbiased advice and coordinating effort needed to complement the contributions of individual agents. Obviously, there is a "you should be so lucky" aspect to these considerations, as many emerging artists struggle to secure qualified initial representation in any area, and are thrilled to land their first agent relationship no matter how narrow or broad the representation.

14.2.2. Talent Agencies versus Independent Agent Representation

Talent agencies are in essence nothing more (or less) than a collection of individual talent agents. The individual agents of each agency will still generally concentrate in representing one type of client (e.g., writers), or may act to serve all of the agency's clients but in only one facet of the industry (e.g., the agency's actors in the field of commercials). The agency's individual agents, sometimes working as a team when targeting talent active in multiple fields, will locate and "sign" new clients for the agency, much the way individual agents locate and sign for their own practices. However, while there may be a strong relationship between an artist and an individual "signing" agent, in an agency situation the primary contractual relationship is between the talent agency as a whole and the artist, rather than being exclusively with one agent. (Although an influential artist's agents may be able to negotiate a "key-person" clause and agency contract permitting the client to follow an agent to another agency, or to leave the agency if the key agent moves on to any other outside employment or is otherwise unable to service the client's representational needs). Also, because an agency will generally employ agents in all areas of the entertainment industry, it will seek to represent (and commission) all of its clients in many if not all areas of entertainment in which it is active, and often nationally even if the agency is primarily active on one or the other coast, or only in another single major metropolitan area.

The advantage of working with a talent agency is that it will have a depth of expertise in the various areas of entertainment that will allow for the coordinated advancement of the artist's career in all areas. Moreover, particularly with the larger, more dominant agencies like William Morris/Endeavor, ICM Partners, United Talent Agency or Creative Artists Agency, representation by such agencies may bring the agency's developing clients an imprimatur of promise that a smaller agency can't as readily project (although there are great agents and agencies at all levels of the business). Because these large agencies and their agents represent so much of the important talent in the entertainment industry, they are often the first to become aware of new projects – either because producers or promoters come to them first to engage key elements of a project (such as the director, screenwriter or star performer for a movie, or show-runner writer-producers for a television series) necessary to complete a "package" for presentation to studios, networks, distributors or other financiers, or because projects may be originating with some of the agency's own important clients. Moreover, because of the depth of their representation, they can and often do "package" projects themselves, filling most or all of the available positions in a project with many of their clients.

A "packaging agent" or an agent who is "packaging" a deal is a very important distinction for entertainment lawyers to understand when advising clients. Typically, an agent who is "packaging" a deal is actually representing one party in putting together a deal involving multiple parties. However, that agent will also seek (if not be entitled) to commission the other multiple parties and will also set (or negotiate within limits) the compensation for all such parties represented by the agency. For example, an agent may represent a producer who wants to put together the key talent elements for production of a film or television series within certain budgetary and creative parameters proposed by the producer. In this scenario, the agent will likely be "packaging" the various key terms of agreements for the producer, including perhaps the writer who will adapt the story to a screenplay, along with other acting and perhaps directing talent or other essential parties necessary to put the project in development or to greenlight the project for production. The upside for the agency in these transactions is obviously both the power they attend the project, in the aggregate commissions they receive by placing multiple clients in a single project. The "packaging" agent will have each party sign an agency representation agreement with language that should disclose the "packaging" nature of the agent's representation and some provision giving consent to any conflict or to the nature of that agent's role with all of the parties in the overall deal. This language in the standard agency agreement may seem innocuous, particularly for an emerging artist who is not immediately a magnet for "packaging" attention. "Packaging" agents can often be slow to disclose their involvement in representing multiple parties in the package even when directly confronted over the nature of that agent's representation, and may be reluctant or unwilling to confirm that they are not looking out exclusively for the individual client's interests in the transaction (despite taking a commission from that client).

In these scenarios, the entertainment lawyer must generally treat the matter as if the client has no agent at all and at the very least make sure the client understands that what the agent is proposing is not necessarily the market value for the client's contribution (particularly if the client is not a centerpiece of the package.). In many instances, the agent or agency may insist the client include their outside lawyer in such negotiations. Thus, while an entertainment lawyer will not customarily debate and press an agent over the economic terms they negotiate for a client, where the agent is "packaging" the deal it is appropriate and necessary for the entertainment lawyer to make sure the client does not have a misunderstanding about the packaging agent's actual role and to address such economic terms where appropriate. Again, there is nothing wrong with a client dealing with a packaging agent (and for many artists having access to this sort of opportunity may admittedly be a big reason for their choice of agents or agencies) so long as the client understands the distinction between this type of "agent" and a customary agent that has an exclusive fiduciary duty to the client.

Besides being aware of the "packaging" function that many agencies undertake, another possible concern in dealing with a full-service agency is the risk, because of the larger client base represented, that an emerging artist might get "lost." First, this can happen simply because the agency has other (and perhaps many) clients who are competitive with that artist (for example, where the agency represents a number of "stocky, bald, British, aristocratic character actors in their early fifties"). Second, the client can be signed by one agent, who sees some special qualities in that artist that she or he thinks can be marketed, and then that agent leaves the agency or simply has trouble persuading colleagues of the artist's merits. If no other agent is similarly interested in that artist, the agency or even the signing agent may not invest much further initiative in marketing that artist, yet may be unwilling to terminate the contractual relationship with that artist "just in case" a big opportunity may arise. Third, a client active in one area may be signed for all fields with an agency by an agent specializing in that client's area of strength. What can then happen is that, since other agents in other areas of entertainment in which that client might be interested in advancing were not involved in signing that client, they may not be willing or interested in marketing that client in these other areas (often because incentives in their own compensation structure reward them more highly for work they generate for clients they've personally signed or control). For example, a reasonably successful author of science fiction novels may seek representation by a large agency, hoping to obtain employment as a screenwriter. However, unless the agents in that agency's motion picture division are interested in marketing that novelist as a screenwriter (on her books sold for development or on original projects or adaptations of other works the novelist may have independently "spec'd or [that] might be a great choice to commission a screenplay from), the author can end up not being represented by his or her agency in the motion picture screenwriting field and, at the same time, may be precluded by his or her agreement with the agency from seeking separate representation for screenwriting. Similarly, a successful commercial voice-over actor or actress may sign with a theatrical agency hoping to break into movies or the theatre, but unless agents active in these areas are interested in representing that artist, the artist may find him or herself in limbo – without committed representation in an area of prior success (i.e., commercials), with new agents coasting on the client's prior relationships and continuing demand in that field, and without recourse to seek more aggressive representation in his or her core area of the business.

While the problem of getting lost among a large roster of competing clients is largely unavoidable, it is however just as likely that a new agent can be just as effective at marshalling an artist's interest "in house" as the artist hopes the agent will be at selling his/her talents and services to outside buyers. Agents are rarely interested in signing clients simply for the sake of signing them. They seek out clients that have the potential to generate commission income, as well as to elevate the stature of the agent and the agency in success. The crucial challenge for the artist is establishing a strong relationship with the primary signing agent to insure this agent will remain truly involved and interested in that artist's career – which typically requires a combination of good work, good luck, good communication skills, patience and perseverance.

One solution to the second problem, as noted briefly above, is to condition the agency representation agreement upon the presence of the signing agent as that client's "primary or principle" agent (i.e., a so called "key person clause"). If the agent leaves the Agency, for any reason, then the client should have the right (but not necessarily the obligation) to terminate his or her agreement with the agency (whether it's to follow the agent elsewhere if she or he is still "agent-ing," or to find another agent if he/she is not).

With respect to the third problem (i.e., lack of interest in other areas of representation), this issue can be addressed in the agency representation agreements in a number of ways. First, the artist can require that "signing" (responsible) agents be identified for each of the areas of entertainment most important to his or her career. Because "signing" agents tend to be compensated both in terms of the bookings they personally negotiate with purchasers *and* for the contracts obtained by the agency as a whole for their "signed" clients, agents have twin incentives to market their signed clients and a deeper incentive to insure that other agents in the agency also promote their clients when possible (the power of multilevel marketing at work). Alternatively, artists may be able to exclude certain activities from representation (enabling them to work with another specialty agency in these particular areas), or to provide for termination of representation in these areas if the agency fails to secure suitable work for the artist (e.g., "x" number of auditions, "y" number of engagements) within a reasonable period of time (a solution embodied in several of the key guilds' agency franchise agreements to strengthen the artist's negotiation position in these circumstances). Finally, an artist may negotiate a provision in their agency agreement which provides that failure to secure a minimum level of employment (usually measured in economic terms) within any specified calendar period will entitle the artist to terminate the agency's entire representation in some or all areas in which the client is or seeks to become active (i.e., not just those covered by the artist's respective guild agreement(s)). These issues, and others to be discussed, will in almost all cases be addressed and the parties' understandings memorialized in a written Artist/Agency Representation Agreement.

14.2.3. Agent / Agency Representation Agreements

It is customary for an agent to require a client to sign a representation agreement that authorizes the agent to represent the client in a defined scope of the entertainment filed or for a specified project. Most often, these are exclusive arrangements. There are scenarios, as previously noted, where agents may consider working with an emerging or established but currently un-signed artist on a non-exclusive or so-called "hip-pocket" basis, i.e., where the agent or agency will submit that artist or his or her work to possible purchasers without an overall agreement (perhaps based on opportunities a manager or lawyer are identifying for the artist), thus allowing the artist to seek concurrent representation by other agents or agencies, and with each agent commissioning only certain contracts which they obtain on the client's behalf. The representation agreement often looks standard (small type, boilerplate-like formatting, etc.), but there is much an entertainment lawyer needs to know regarding the fact and circumstances of the proposed representation in order to properly advise the client on such matters. As mentioned previously, if the client is a member of the Actors' Equity Association (AEA), the Screen Actors Guild (SAG), the American Federation of Television and Radio Actors (AFTRA) and/or the American Federation of Musicians (AFM), the agent must be an approved "franchised agent" with the applicable guild. The guild member client is required by their guild to use only agents who are franchised by the respective guild. This requirement is meant to protect the guild member client since the applicable guild has requirements on how each franchised agent can contract and represent the guild member client. Such guild minimum terms and limitations will address issues such as when and how the client can terminate the agent relationship and how disputes between the parties are to be resolved, among many other issues. The entertainment lawyer representing talent (and of course, talent agencies) must be familiar with such regulations. In these situations, the entertainment lawyer wants to make certain that (1) the agent is in fact a franchised agent in good standing with the applicable guild/union (and will want to contact the guild/union to determine if there have been any issues or complaints against the agent) and (2) any representation agreement between their client and any franchised agent contains correct references to the applicable guild/union provisions governing the agent's representation.

Another important issue for the entertainment lawyer to address is whether or not the agent is required to be formally licensed as an agent under applicable state law. In some states, most notably in New York[1] and in California,[2] talent agents are required to be licensed and to follow certain rules of conduct set forth in state regulations. The regulations address a variety of issues relevant to the agent's conduct as an agent and the terms of representation. In some states, these

---

[1] N.Y. GEN. BUS LAW §§171(8), 172 et. seq. (McKinney 1988). See also N.Y. ARTS. AND CULTURAL AFFAIRS LAW §§171(8) pertaining to client/talent solicitation through advertising and the charging of fees as a prerequisite for representation.

[2] CAL. LABOR CODE §1700.5 (West 1986).

regulations go as far as requiring licensed agents to submit their fee schedules and representation agreements for pre-approval by the state's regulatory authority, submit to background checks of key agent personnel, and post a bond for their activities relating to processing of client funds.

In some regulated states, the consequences of someone unlicensed nonetheless acting as an agent can have serious repercussions for that person. In many instances, state laws that regulate talent agents can require the unlicensed person to return all prior commissions to the client despite being otherwise contractually entitled to these commissions for services otherwise performed. There are similar penalties for licensed agents who violate state regulations. As discussed further below, many state talent agency licensure laws distinguish between someone acting as an agent in procuring employment opportunities for the artist, and a manager who is giving advice and guidance to the artist on various aspects of the artist's career but without an agency license is prohibited from soliciting or procuring employment. These are important distinctions for the entertainment lawyer to understand because of scenarios where: (1) someone who is unlicensed, not intending to be an agent, still acts like an agent by procuring employment for the artist and (2) a manager who is procuring employment for the artist and is thus rendering agent services without a license in the applicable state. The latter scenario, in some states, is permitted under limited circumstances, in particular in the music industry or the sale of "rights" rather than services, but the distinction has been widely litigated. Otherwise successful and well-intentioned managers who are determined to have exceeded their management "advisory" roles to engage in direct solicitation of client work (even with client knowledge and approval at the time, since the infraction is statutory) have lost substantial commissions – not to mention their incurred legal fees. These issues will be more fully addressed in the "Personal Managers" discussion in Section 14.3 below.

It is very common to find artists who have signed so-called management agreements with managers who are essentially acting and fulfilling the duties of an agent in contravention of applicable state licensing requirements. These agreements are created to allow such "managers" to hold themselves out as merely advisors when in fact they are acting like agents, so that they can charge more in fees and otherwise skirt talent agent regulations. Depending on the applicable state law, these arrangements can be easily attacked by the client (who may want to exit the management relationship for a new manager, or want to avoid payment of contractual commissions (despite the possibility that the manager really was responsible for the engagement(s) and resulting income in dispute)). In some notable cases, the manager's violation of these requirements voids the entire management relationship and requires disgorgement of all fees; while in others only the transaction in which active solicitation is established will be unwound (and other prior or later commissions for sanctioned management services will remain enforceable).[3] Thus, it is very important for the entertainment lawyer to fully understand the implications of the applicable talent agent licensure laws to properly advise artistic clients of their rights with respect to an agent (or manager, as will be addressed further below) and/or to properly advise "manager" clients who are either unfamiliar with these distinctions and requirements, or who are aware of them but nonetheless do not intend to become licensed in a jurisdiction where agent licensing is required, and need to know the proper boundaries that will protect them from the consequences of improperly rendering the services of a licensed talent agent.

It is also important to note that the choice of law provisions in any talent agreement will have a significant impact on these issues, as will the methods for dispute resolution (arbitration versus a court proceeding, where the proceedings must occur, and if, an arbitration, the credentials of the eligible arbitrator candidates).

As a result of state licensure requirements, many agent representation agreements contain standard terms that do not allow for much negotiation. Further, in some states, agents who represent the

---

[3] A prominent case is *Pryor v. Franklin*, Lab. Comm'r Case No. TAC17 MP-114 (1982) where the California Labor Commissioner ordered comedian Richard Pryor's former personal manager to return all compensation he received from Pryor for his services in procuring and attempting to procure employment. In 2014, The National Conference of Personal Managers, in seeking to overturn the California's Talent Agency Act, stated in a press release, "Personal managers nationwide have forfeited an estimated $500,000,000 due to either the California Labor Commissioner voiding management contracts and ordering disgorgement of compensation or managers being forced to settle artist disputes rather than face the risks and legal costs of a TAA hearing and subsequent litigation." *Personal Managers Launch Offensive in Battle over Talent Agency Act*, Deadline Hollywood, David Robb (May 24, 2014).

literary works of authors are not considered to be acting as employment agencies to the extent they do not represent the working services of authors (i.e., they are nominally selling "manuscripts," whether of completed or prospective projects) and therefore are not required to be formally licensed. That is why most literary agents will charge a 15% commission versus the standard 10% commission established by many state talent agency regulations for employment services (and not coincidentally, it is often the pursuit of a higher commission that compels representatives to be "managers" rather than "agents" in the literary as well as other talent fields).

As previously noted, agent representation agreements are highly standardized given many of the factors discussed above (including without limitation state statutory and guild mandated requirements). But this is not to say there are no issues that may still need to be negotiated or supplemented in such standardized forms. Again, as earlier noted, the entertainment lawyer's ability to negotiate changes in agency agreements depends in large part upon the current earnings success and/or marketability of the individual client, and/or whether there is competing representation interest (the artist is leaving one agent for another, or is an emerging artist coming off a hit project and there is consequently interest of several competing agents or agencies). Most agents are willing to make reasonable adjustments in their papers to reflect the reasonable needs of their clients, and a lawyer familiar with the terms of these agreements may help his or her talent client establish what adjustments to the agreements are reasonable and customary. Some of the key terms of such an agreement are addressed below.

14.2.3.1. Duration

The first key term of the representation agreement is its duration. Most agency representation agreements tend to run between one and three years. Initial agreements are often limited to one year as a trial period, though many agencies will attempt to sign clients for a three-year term in all areas other than where the unions (such as SAG) limit the initial term to a shorter period. Renewal agreements (that is, agreements continuing the agency representation beyond its initial term), though occasionally done on a year-to-year basis, are generally entered into for a period of two to five years, with most being for three years. The artist will typically seek a shorter term to simplify an exit if the relationship is not satisfactory (or if another agency offers more aggressive services). Conversely, the agency wants as long a term as possible in recognition of the investment of time and resources that may be expended to launch a new artist and to reward itself in success (e.g., if an artist has success in the first year of the term, the agency will want to capitalize on that success in securing further agreements for the artist, each at higher levels of artist compensation benefitting both the artist and agency).

Agency Agreements subject to jurisdiction of one or more talent guilds will generally permit the artist to terminate representation in the guild in specific (if not all) areas of services if the artist fails to secure a certain minimum number of offers for months or days of employment during specified consecutive periods of the term (e.g., if no offer is secured within any four-month period). In such circumstances, the artist may wish to specify that if any guild rider covering agency representation is terminated in a particular area (e.g., writing or acting), then the artist may terminate all agreements with the agency (since otherwise the artist may find him or herself seeking new representation for their core career competency, while the initial agency continues to be involved in some or all other activities of the artist's career).

14.2.3.2. Areas of Representation

The representation agreement will then identify the areas of activity in which the agent/agency will represent the signing artist. Under the terms of this provision, the agent will have the exclusive right to negotiate on behalf of the artist within a particular (or all) area(s) of entertainment and to commission any and all agreements entered into by the client (irrespective of who may have solicited and obtained such agreements). This latter provision, i.e., the right to commission any agreement entered into whether obtained by the agent or not, is really nothing more than an enforcement mechanism for the exclusivity clause. A right is not a right, let alone an exclusive one, if the client is able to in some way avoid its application.

This provision can become problematic when applied to pre-existing agreements negotiated by a prior agent (as discussed in the following section). To avoid double commissioning, the representation agreement should identify and exclude pre-existing agreements unless the agent is called upon to "service" agreements (i.e., to renegotiate the terms of the agreement, seek to identify and collect income due under the agreement, or otherwise represent the client in respect to the agreement).

Another common scenario in literary agent agreements is where the literary agent will want to represent the motion picture and/or television rights to the literary work even though the literary agent is just that (i.e., a literary agent focused on the publishing industry, and not experienced in or likely to initiate a motion picture or television deal). In this scenario, the literary agent will seek a provision to permit him or her to co-agent or use a sub-agent who is in the motion picture and/or television field to handle that representation (which may occur before or after a publishing deal is secured or the book is actually published), and to charge the client a higher commission (typically 20%, up from the standard 15% literary agency fee) to be split equally or on some other negotiated basis between the two agents. Such scenarios may be unavoidable, but where an agent in one field has the right to partner with an agent in another field or sub-specialty and charge a higher commission for both of them to split (e.g., a literary agent's collaboration with a book-to-film specialist to pursue a sale), it is not unreasonable to want to know in advance who the co- or sub-agent is or to have approval of the agent, and more importantly to have the right to terminate the partnering agent with a substitute agent mutually agreed upon by the parties.

14.2.3.3. Commissions

The agreement will also identify the commission(s) to be retained by the agent from its collections on behalf of the artist client (or which will be paid to the agent/agency if the parties' agency agreement is negotiated to provide that payment is delivered by the employer/buyer of services to personal manager, business manager or accountant.) The amount of the commission can vary significantly, depending upon the size of the client's payday, which, in turn, will be determined by the type of work performed by the artist, the market for the work, and whether or not the representation of the client is covered (at minimum levels but by no means the maximum a client may earn) by a union agreement. As is the case in any contract in the entertainment field, the amount of the commission is subject to negotiation – though the tendency to accept the standard (10%) agency rate tends to be far higher than in other negotiations. Union negotiated agreements (such as the agency franchise agreements with SAG or AFTRA) tend to be the most favorable to the client – generally limiting commissions to 10% of the client's gross income.

While negotiated commissions can be (though rarely are) reduced in favor of the client (an agency representing a high grossing film or television star may settle for less than 10% in order to attract or retain the client), they cannot be exceeded. In contrast, non-union performer's contracts covering the same type of work, and prevalent for artists who may otherwise have limited real choice in their agent representation options, may run as high as 25% of artist earnings, which the agent justifies on the basis of their lower net earnings margins on artists with insufficient credits (and income-generating history) to be eligible for guild membership, and the fact that it may take the agency as much effort to land a new artist walk-on speaking role or entry writing assignment on a small picture (due to the competition) as it does to get a prominent actor or writer a huge pay date on a project for which there may be no or only a few competing candidates. However, as this entry-level arrangement for higher commissions tends in turn to be the admission ticket for artist access to higher paying employment opportunities (and perhaps higher profile representation at a later date) in the entertainment industry, it is not uncommonly endured if not welcomed by emerging artists.

As noted, commissions also vary by the nature of the market of use. For example, as mentioned above, authors are now typically charged a commission of 15% for domestic book publishing deals (increased from 10% by the major agencies in or around 2002 as the publishing industry began its recent cycle of revenue challenges) for trade book and other primary market (e.g., U.S.) sales and licenses. Subsidiary rights and international sales of the author's works will be commissioned at 20% to 25%. These differing amounts reflect not only increased expenses (where international sales may involve an agent's attendance at major U.S. and international markets to meet foreign publishers, the costs of which are not incidental depending on how many projects the agent is fronting in a given market cycle, and/or sharing the commission with a foreign agent), but also the declining advances, licensing fees or royalties coming to authors against which commissions are calculated.

While the standard commission rates offered by agents are rarely relaxed, certain key features or terms within the agreement concerning commissions may be negotiated, which may result in a significant savings in income for the artist under particular circumstances. In this regard, there are three key terms or concepts to be addressed: gross compensation; activities subject to the commission agreement (including exclusions and/or deductions); and duration.

First, the term "gross compensation" will generally be defined as "all the gross sums of money or other emoluments (including but not limited to salaries, earnings, royalties, fees, bonuses, securities, shares of profit, and the proceeds from the sale, lease, license or other disposition of material) received by [the client] or any person, firm or corporation on [the client's] behalf or in which [the client] has an interest." This definition is broad and the artist must evaluate if there are payments that the artist will receive that should be excluded from this definition, such a travel, lodging and per diem reimbursements or reimbursement associated with other costs of providing rights or services.

In entertainment, it is not unusual for talent to be paid by means other than a fixed up-front cash fee. While this alternative or supplemental compensation often takes the form of a profit participation interest (i.e., a payment deferred until the project reaches a certain defined economic milestone in its performance, or calculated as a percentage of the project's economic performance, however defined), it may also entail a transfer of corporate stock and/or goods, such as Arnold Schwarzenegger's receipt of a Lear jet airplane as a part of his "Terminator 3" contract, or Paramount's gift of a $100,000 Mercedes convertible to Tom Cruise for his work on "The Firm" (on top of a reported $12 Million salary and substantial profit participation).[4] Because of this broad definition of compensation, artists must be concerned whenever they receive non-cash compensation that they not be obligated to immediately compensate the agent in cash for the value of the non-monetary compensation. For example, if an artist receives corporate stock for services, the artist should have the option of fulfilling the commission obligation by either (i) compensating the agent for the commission on the value of the stock, whether upon its receipt or upon its sale, or (ii) by transferring a percentage interest in the stock to the agent representing the commission share (which may not be permitted in any event under the

---

[4] Bernard Weinrib, *"The Talk of Hollywood; Good Job! Here's Your Mercedes"* N.Y. Times (Jul. 12, 1993) §3, p.1.

terms of the stock transfer agreement to which the artist is subject)[5]. Lastly, because the exclusive representation provision is tied in with this broad compensation definition, it may at times be appropriate to specify that the formation of a personal services corporation or other entity in which the artist acquires stock will not give rise to a commission obligation or result in the agent owning a share of the artist client's own "loan out" corporation.

The second key term of the commission agreement is that the commission obligation applies to any agreement "solicited or negotiated by the agent and/or entered into by the client during the term of the agreement." But what of circumstances in which the agent solicits and negotiates an agreement, but the client fails or refuses to enter into the agreement (for what may be one or more of any number of reasons) until after the expiration of the client's representation agreement with the agent? What if the agent "pitches" a client for a project, but the deal gets delayed and an agreement is not issued to or entered into by the client until after the expiration of the agency agreement? What if the contract is concluded but the project collapses, and the employer subsequently (post-term) offers the artist and (former) client a substitute employment in order to fulfill (or avoid) its contractual obligation? To address these problems an agency agreement will provide that its commission applies to any contract that results from its efforts. In order to limit the application of this to assure that the respective engagement is the result of the agent's effort, post-term offers delivered in writing considered as arising from the efforts of the agent should be limited to offers that: arise within a limited period of time following termination (e.g., six months to a year), are directly or indirectly from the same offeror solicited by the agent, and contain terms similar to or reasonably comparable to the offer obtained by the agent. It should be added that allowing agents post-term participation does work to the benefit of the client. Absent such protection, an agent may hesitate to "pitch" a buyer on the merits of a client whose representation agreements are set to expire within a period of time that might exempt the client from a commission obligation. For example, the agent might not submit any client whose representation agreement is set to expire within two to three months, based upon the

---

[5] The artist and counsel should in any case be certain to address the tax implications of such compensation arrangements with a competent accountant or tax attorney.

reasonable assumption that the agreement(s) that might be obtained will typically not close and produce a contract for signatures within the requisite remaining time frame.

Finally, the agreement will provide that the commission obligation applies for the "life of the agreement." This will be further defined to state that it applies to "any extensions, modification, amendments, renewals, substitutions or replacements thereof including those entered into by the client and the buyer/employer (or its representatives) within a brief period (e.g., four to six months) of the expiration of a prior agreement." Such a provision is intended to assure that a client, after ending his or her representation with the agent, does not enter into a negotiation with a purchaser to create a new agreement solely to avoid his or her commission obligations to the agent. What must be stressed here is that the commission obligation potentially extends beyond the term of the agent's representation of the client (e.g., multiple television series seasons, or motion picture prequels and sequels). The agent's argument for this is that the artist would not have obtained the initial engagement without the efforts of the agent and, therefore, the agent should be entitled to participate in the income from the agreement (and its extensions/renewals/etc.) for as long as the artist does.

There are three alternate approaches which can be taken to limit or qualify post-term participation provisions. First, the agreement should provide that the agent will continue to "service" affected agreements (i.e., supervise and handle problems and collections relating thereto) throughout the time in which it is entitled to commission income from any such agreement(s). This avoids the problem of a client needing a subsequent agent to render services toward the agreement, thereby facing a second full or partial commission obligation and/or out-of-pocket legal fees for services the agent might otherwise withhold. Second, some clients will seek to limit post-term participation for a certain number of years (commonly three to five years) on an income stream that could be ongoing (e.g., compensation from a successful TV series acting role, a multi-year recording deal, or a film sequel that could arise several years after the conclusion of the agency agreement). It is argued that this is both reasonable in terms of fairly compensating the agent for his or her efforts and that the ongoing success of the agreement after such a long time may be due to the client's efforts subsequent to his or her representation by the agent. Third, the agreement may provide that the commission obligations pertain to the financial terms of the original contract, only. Thus, if an artist secures improved terms during the life of the agreement (e.g., an upward negotiation of a TV series fee in its third or fourth year, or an improvement in record royalty rates after a second or third album) which exceed those established in the original agreement, the agent does not have a right to participate in the additional income unless its services in connection with these negotiations (resulting in the improvements) were formally requested.

It is also to be noted that the principal guild/agency franchise agreements generally prevent agents from exacting commissions on prescribed guild minimum fees for artist services, and as a consequence require that employment agreements for guild members represented by a franchised agency be for fees equal to 110% or more of the applicable guild "minimum scale" for any particular services (the 10% premium representing the prescribed agency commission under the respective guild/franchise agreements). Certain guild agreements (e.g., SAG and AFTRA) restrict agents from commissioning certain artist residual payments except in circumstances where the artist's initial compensation was substantially in excess of scale, and may also restrict commissions on payments to artists intended as reimbursement for travel and other guild mandated expenses and benefits, such as employer pension, health and welfare contributions (and additionally excluding legitimate expense reimbursements from commission may be desirable for artists even when no such guild protection is mandated.)

In states where agents are not regulated nor are such agents franchised, artists need to be aware of agents "double-dipping," which may occur in two distinct scenarios: Agents (1) charge an additional commission or fee for so-called "non-agent services" and/or (2) charge a separate direct commission or fee to the producer or the party hiring the artist. The latter is similar to the fee charged by a "packaging agent" as discussed above, and addressed further in Section 14.5.3 below. Some agents in small markets will argue these fees are necessary to stay in business and each situation must be evaluated on its own merits. The key in the first scenario is to determine: if such "non-agent" services are really independent of the agent's primary and customary responsibilities; if so, whether they are indeed of benefit to the artist/client; and, if the answer is still yes, whether someone else could better provide them. In the second scenario, to the extent an artist has no choice but to permit such "double dipping," then the agreement should provide for as much transparency, restriction and accountability as possible.

14.2.3.4. Collection Rights and Payment Obligations

Representation agreements frequently provide that the agent will collect all income under agreements they negotiate, will deduct its commission and permitted expenses, and then transmit the balance to the client. This provision provides two benefits. Since one of an agent's services is monitoring and collecting income due under any agreement, it is logical that the agent should be the one receiving all payments so identified. Second, it assures the agent that she or he will receive his or her commission (lessening the risk the client will have disposed of the funds before a commission has been paid, or dispute the commission obligation once payment is received). However, in the event that a client receives direct payment, the agreement will also provide that the client must immediately remit to the agent any and all commissions due. The agent's continuing concern with even this compromise is that a performing artist (music, film, television, stage, etc.), even if generally trusted to pay the commission, may be on the road for professional projects for an extended period, and may be unable to deposit a check or in the case of a payment that is wired or directly deposited to their account may even be unable to promptly and conveniently calculate and arrange for payment to the agent on a timely basis, thus making the case for the agent or a business manager (or even a personal manager) to be the more reliable "processor" of the collection and commission payment process.

There are two possible client concerns with this provision that the agency will collect and disburse funds after deducting commissions and advanced expenses. First, in the event the agent runs into financial difficulty, the client may lose his or her income, yet still be obligated to perform under a performance contract where the purchaser has tendered proper payment to the agent. Second, the client will be concerned that the agent not unduly delay the "turnaround" on payments (i.e., the time it takes between collecting contract income and paying the client the client's share of this income). The agent, meanwhile, will argue that it is in the business of monitoring and administering these payments, and that the risk of non-payment by the client due to possible financial pressures, disorganization, etc., is of concern. To avoid the first problem, many agreements provide or require that all monies collected by the agent be held in a segregated trust account (which is a statutory or common-law obligation on agents in most jurisdictions, and is additionally addressed in the requirements of most guild/agency franchise agreements). To address the second problem the agreement may be modified to additionally require that the agent remit the client's monies in a timely manner (e.g., within ten business days of collection). Finally, some agreements may be negotiated to provide that the client or client's business manager will collect all monies and remit the commission due to the agent or alternatively that any contract negotiated by the agent will provide that the purchasing party pay the agent his or her commission directly and remit the balance to the client.

Finally, to enhance their chances to collect or claim their fees, some agency agreements will identify their commissions and rights thereto as being "coupled with an interest." This legal concept asserts that the agent has a property right in the commission owed (e.g. beyond a fee for services). When representing an artist an entertainment lawyer must be very skeptical of such language since (i) if the agent is already collecting the agent's fee at the outset it may be totally unnecessary, (ii) it tends to move the agent out of the role of a fiduciary and more into the role of a property owner and perhaps even a partner in the venture and (iii) depending on the applicable state law such a provision can give an agent a level of legal power over any decisions about the artist's works.

14.2.3.5. Performance Goals

At the outset of the relationship between a client and his or her agent, the two parties will obviously anticipate that their relationship will be mutually advantageous. They assume that the client will be creatively and commercially successful, and that the agent will make lots of money by obtaining lots of lucrative agreements or licenses on the client's behalf. Problems may arise when the client expects to make more than the agent projects as realistic. Whereas the client may expect the agent to substantially increase the client's income through increased bookings or better contract terms, the agent may be happy to commission "what comes along" based upon the present value of the artist within the marketplace. For example, a rock band may be earning $100,000 a year from a steady stream of club engagements. An agent might be happy to handle the paperwork for these club dates and commission the band's income from these engagements and merchandising sales without having to work to sell the band to new and different buyers in other markets or for bigger venues. On the other hand, the agent may take a client on at a point in his or his career when opportunities are receding for a variety of reasons possibly unrelated to the agent's passion for the client's work or the agent's general ability, and simply keeping the client's income level flat may be considered an accomplishment.

One way to resolve this problem is to put into the representation papers a set of financial goals. These provisions will provide that the agent is obligated to increase the client's gross entertainment earnings by a certain percentage annually or, more commonly, the client's gross income must meet or exceed a certain target in each year of the term or within a certain cumulative period (e.g., $200,000, using our band example from above) either for the first year of an agreement or in sequential annual steps each year of a multi-year agreement. If these goals are not met, then the client will have the right to terminate its representation agreement and to seek representation elsewhere (it being presumed if the agent cannot make money with a client despite reasonable efforts to do so, the agent will likewise be willing to let the client leave the agency, apart from the risk of possible reputational embarrassment if another agent subsequently scores an immediate hit for the client.

This type of provision is particularly popular with musical performers or stand-up comedy performers who have an ongoing career with some type of track record as to opportunities for regular touring and performances, and consequently for their earnings potential, and for whom advancement entails a relatively simple calculus of achieving a record deal with a defined scope of major record labels or a PayTV network or streaming service comedy special, or of touring with more dates, bigger venues and/or bigger appearance fees.

14.2.3.6. Documenting Adjustments to the Standard Agency Agreement

Once the artist (and/or artist's lawyer) and the agency have agreed to whatever adjustments to the agency's standard terms are appropriate, these changes may be documented in one of two principal ways.

First will be a wholesale revision to the agency agreement itself, in which the changes are incorporated in the basic agency agreement document. This solution is more common for solo agents or small agencies than large ones, where these negotiations may be relatively uncommon or infrequent, and a "redlined" comparison of the standard versus final agreement retained with a client file may be all that is required to reliably monitor the proper administration of the agreement.

For larger agencies with multiple clients and regular addition of new clients, the process is more frequently one of preparing a "sideletter" to the standard agreement(s) in which the changes are recited as "amendments" to the standard terms, and the sideletter will serve as an exhibit modifying the standard terms. The benefit of this arrangement is the changes may be relatively simpler to monitor from a contract administration standpoint. An additional benefit (and one that extends to studio and network agreements with talent from prominent talent agencies and law firms with whom the buyer companies may do a substantial volume of work) is that the agency and legal representative may be able to cut through much of these negotiations by reference to a prenegotiated "sideletter" previously established for another shared client of similar stature, in which event the lawyer and agent may agree that rather than conducting a full blown negotiation for each new artist/agency agreement, the parties will agree to impose the terms of the "Artist 'A'" or "Artist 'B'" Sideletter to the new client's agreement(s) (with the determination often made by categorizing the new client in an "A-level artist" or "B-level" tier). The benefit to the agency and lawyer involved in the negotiation is an expedited signing of value to all parties (and potentially saving the client from incurring an hourly and not insubstantial legal fee for a negotiation which is thus avoided). On the other hand, from the artist's perspective, although the resulting sideletter may improve on what the artist or the artist's representative could negotiate for him or herself on a standalone basis, it may very well not address all of his or her precise and particular needs, and the agency/lawyer relationship which may permit this (limited) favored nations treatment with respect to the sideletter may not permit the lawyer to regularly reopen the standard sideletter(s) for adjustment or improvement except in very unique circumstances or for very substantial clients.

14.3. PERSONAL MANAGERS

As discussed above, there are important legal and business distinctions between the roles of an agent and a personal manager, although at times a manager may be functioning in many respects as an agent for the artist. A personal manager is an actor's or performer's[6] principal career adviser and will render the following services on the client's behalf (most if not all of which are enumerated in this or similar form in most boilerplate management agreements):

1. Represent the artist and act as the artist's negotiator, to fix the terms governing all manner of disposition, use, employment or exploitation of the artist's talents and the products thereof;

2. Supervise the artist's professional employment and, on the artist's behalf, to consult with employers and prospective employers so as to ensure the proper and continued demand for the artist's services;

3. Be available to consult with the artist concerning all matters affecting the artist's professional career, interest, employment and publicity;

4. Exploit the artist's personality in all media;

5. Engage, discharge and direct all support personnel, including talent agents, business managers, accountants, lawyers, publicity representatives and others;

6. Represent the artist in dealings with unions; and

7. Exercise all powers necessary in performing the foregoing services, including the use of a power of attorney in order to execute agreements on the artist's behalf.

As the tasks and performances of a personal manager are very broad and often "time" intensive, most (but not all) managers will represent a smaller stable of artists at any given time than will a commercial talent agency involved with the same artists or industry activities, and managers use this fact (i.e., fewer total clients, permitting them to devote more time to the needs of individual clients)

---

[6] Non-performing artists, such as writers, composers, directors, etc., rarely require the services of personal managers, as their needs are generally served by agents (should they have them), perhaps working in tandem with lawyers. That being said, authors are increasingly pursuing the services of "literary managers" who may fulfill not only traditional personal management functions for the artist, but may provide the sort of editorial guidance and support traditionally provided by publishers and literary agencies during healthier times in the publishing industry.

to justify commissions generally in excess of those payable to agents.[7] It must be stressed, though, that the customary role of a personal manager *is not* the same as that of a talent agent. Although most personal or artist management agreements will and should stress this fact, there is a great deal of confusion on this point for a number of reasons.

First, it must be noted that in order to avoid the limitations and commission restrictions imposed on agents by unions and in certain states by the law (e.g., a 10% cap on commissions for work on behalf of SAG/AFTRA, DGA or WGA members, or in general for all entertainment and modeling talent representation in California and New York), some less scrupulous agents may call themselves personal managers and enter into personal management agreements with clients claiming that they can and will additionally act as agents and obtain employment opportunities for them, while also performing services customarily associated with a manager. These individuals will argue on their own behalf, with some justification, that as agents for clients without personal managers, they are called upon to render many personal management-type services including such tasks as advising the client on how to market himself or herself, suggesting appropriate support personnel such as other specialized agents, lawyers, publicists and accountants, coordinating travel and touring arrangements, and generally marketing the client. Moreover, and particularly when they are representing new and emerging talent, they will aver that the artist earns so little that a union-mandated 10% agency commission cap does not adequately compensate them for the amount of work required to promote the artist's career. It is axiomatic that a well-known performer is easier to sell and commands higher fees than an unknown talent, and it must be acknowledged that neither the unions nor the laws governing agents make significant allowances for this difficulty.

Some agent-managers may legitimately perform two tasks: they act both as agents (complying with all of the union and legal restrictions imposed on agents) and render additional services as managers. While this category of representatives may honestly offer the traditional

---

[7] We should note that there is a growing trend of management company expansion, in some cases rivaling the staff of mid-sized agencies in the talent and music arenas. These expanded management groups typically have an active production arm (film, TV and/or music) whereby they may obtain financing for and "employ" their clients in projects they play a direct hand in packaging and producing, whereas talent agencies are generally excluded from an active production role in, and/or ownership interest in, such undertakings.

services of both agent and manager, they will nonetheless be subject to certain regulations imposed on agents under guild agreements or statute (i.e., state laws in a number of jurisdictions with active entertainment economies which preclude anyone but a licensed talent agent from "procuring" employment for an artist/client) if a manager clearly engages in employment solicitation, and the inevitably blurred line between personal management and agency services has led to frequent arbitration and litigation in this area over the years.

Last, it must be acknowledged that inherent in the duties of a personal manager, particularly in the representation of new and emerging artists, one of the principal tasks of the manager will be in trying to develop commercial interest in the artist by bringing him or her to the attention of potential purchasers, promoters and producers who may utilize their talent. Acknowledging this duty, New York has taken the position that personal managers are excused from agent-type licensure requirements where the manager's effort "only incidentally involves the seeking of employment."[8] California has taken this one step further, in connection with the personal management of musical performers, to specifically allow managers to directly solicit and seek recording contracts for their musical performer clients.[9] But in other areas, the manager is still precluded by law (at least in New York and California) from actively soliciting employment for talent clients.

This has presented a troubling "Catch-22" for many well-intentioned managers, who may involve themselves in employment solicitation to advance a client's career with the full knowledge and encouragement of the client only to later find themselves in a lawsuit or Labor Commissioner arbitration (the common forum for such disputes in California) where the client seeks to allege such activity as the basis for voiding the management contract and commission obligations. These disputes generally arise out of three sets of circumstances involving (i) a fundamental collapse in the client/manager relationship in which the client seeks to use the technical violation of the "no-solicitation" rule to void the management contract, even though the client may have theretofore benefited from the manager's undertakings, (ii) situations in which the client, with or without guidance from new agent, legal or management representatives, seeks to void an obligation to pay commissions to a

---

[8] N.Y. GEN. BUS. LAW §§171(8) (McKinney 1988).
[9] CAL. LABOR CODE §1700.4 (West 1986).

former manager, and/or (iii) cases in which the manager may actually have acted without the knowledge or approval of the client in making commitments to an engagement for the client which may have been contrary to the client's real interests or instructions.

Managers in states in which such activities are regulated have until recently had little in the way of defense against such claims, other than arguing that their involvement in procuring client employment was under the direction of a licensed agent or attorney (in which case their involvement is generally permissible[10]). In California, courts have ruled that a single infraction of the "non-solicitation" rule of the state's Talent Agency Act could serve to void a client's commission obligations with respect to the particular engagement for which the infraction occurred, but would not automatically result in the artist obtaining the right to void the entire management agreement as to other commissions which may have been due for other projects and services for which no such violation is in evidence.[11] Moreover, while an artist might normally hope to benefit from a favorable talent bias in a Labor Commission hearing over a manager's violation of the Talent Agency Act, an express agreement to independently arbitrate manager/artist disputes, spelled out in the management agreement in a manner complying with the requirements of the Federal Arbitration Act, can "trump" the state's mandate for labor commissioner or equivalent statutory jurisdiction over some or all disputes arising under the agreement[12] – a circumstance with potentially broad implications for both management and agency agreements generally. These developments suggest an emerging shift away from nearly 40 years of "anti-manager" legal precedent in the entertainment industry.[13]

A personal management agreement is fundamentally similar to an agency agreement (and is negotiated with emphasis on many of the

---

[10] CAL. LABOR CODE §1700.4(d).
[11] Marathon Entertainment, Inc. v. Blasi, 45 Cal. Rptr. 3d 158 (Cal. App. 2 Dist.), *review granted and opinion superseded by* 143 P. 3d 656 (Cal. 2006)
[12] Preston v. Ferrer 552 U.S. 346 (2008).
[13] That said, in NCOPM v Edmund G. Brown (No. CV 12-09620 (C.D. Cal. March 5, 2013), a Federal District Court ruled against the National Conference of Personal Managers in its suit against California to end the California Talent Agency Act on constitutional grounds relating to alleged vagueness of its restrictions on manager employment solicitation. The lawsuit alleged the California Labor Commission had cancelled over $250 million in manager commissions over a 40 year period pursuant to the act.

same issues) with certain notable exceptions (in addition to the statutory restrictions discussed above).

Personal management agreements almost always cover all fields of entertainment, as the primary rationale for their existence is the necessity of coordinating and developing the artist's career in multiple areas. However, where an artist is already successful in one area of entertainment and she or he feels capable of continuing to manage that one aspect of his or her career (sometimes with another manager or agent remaining in place for this purpose), the new manager may agree to represent the client in all other areas, taking this exclusion into account via a modified commission structure.

The duration of a typical personal management contract is generally for a period of two to five years (with three years being standard), while the manager's commission normally runs from 10% to 25% of the performer's gross commission for the life of all agreements entered into during or immediately subsequent to the term of the manager's representation of the client. Established artists, and particularly with current agency representation and/or steady income pre-existing income streams, generally get commissioned at the lower end of this range, while new artists will expect to pay at the higher rates. If the manager lends a new client money to help the client get started (e.g., to help finance new publicity pictures or electronic press kits, buy costumes or underwrite travel to auditions or touring expenses), the manager may justifiably require a higher than normal percentage, or make other arrangements to recoup such expenses.

The financial terms of a manager's commission arrangements (i.e., the identification of sources and calculation) generally track those of an agent, as discussed above. However, while it is often very difficult to persuade agents to limit their post-term participation in a client's income generated from agreements entered into during the term of the agent's representation, many artists have far greater success in negotiating such limitations in their personal management agreements. Such limitations can be established simply by stating that the manager's right to commission income will continue for only a limited period of time after the term, generally one to five years (with three to five years being common), and/or that the participation will continue on a progressively decreasing basis from year to year, after which no further commissions are payable An example of the latter restriction would be for the manager to collect 100% of his or her commission for the first year following the end of the management agreement, 75% for the next year, 50% for the next, and 25% for the next (and last) year following the end of the term. Some or all of the "savings" to the artist can then be deployed to commission a new manager for prospective services, etc., as may be required to secure new representation, again if required.

Many managers will seek the right to collect all of a client's income, pre-empting the agent's right, if any, in this to conduct this activity, perhaps meriting the same concerns and considerations on the part of the client as would the agent's collection of the client's income. The one additional factor to be considered is that, while not obligated to do so, some managers will advance their clients (particularly new artist clients) sums that they may require to establish themselves professionally. Where managers have agreed to make such monetary advances, their justification for direct collection of all fee income becomes far stronger.

Additionally, as with agents, some clients will impose performance goals in their management agreements on the expectation that the manager's assistance is supposed to promote their career in a way that will result in greater income or other quantifiable benefits. This is particularly true in the case of new artists. Moreover, where the client is a new or aspiring musical recording or touring artist, in addition to or in lieu of establishing monetary goals, the artist client will often require that the manager successfully assist the artist in obtaining a commercial recording or national distribution, or alternatively a tour sponsorship contract or other defined exposure within the first year or eighteen months of the management agreement or the artist will have the right to terminate the management agreement.

Finally, artists will want to establish clear guidelines with management (as with agents) concerning which matters the manager shall have the right to obligate the artist to, with or without full consultation and/or talent's express written consent (which discussion should include any express limitations desired on a manager's power of attorney over the artist's approvals).

In recent years, managers have frequently elected to become producers themselves, frequently creating and/or attaching themselves to client-driven projects (including projects in film, television, musical recordings and theatre) for which their budgeted fees and profit participations may exceed the commissions they otherwise would be entitled to collect pursuant to their client management agreement.

Generally, these fees will be in lieu of their commissions on the respective project, but in some cases they may be "in addition" to contractual artist commissions on their client's income from the respective project. In some cases, managers have built successful production companies on the strength of the talent relationships they arguably control (and as noted above, this opportunity remains one of the significant distinctions between the "management" and "agency" businesses). The client arguably benefits from the manager's direct, personal, "hands-on" involvement in developing and insuring the success of the client's participation in such projects, and from the fact the manager's fee may be paid from the "budget" as a production or similar fee, rather than out of the talent's own fees as a commission. However, the manager doesn't always bring this value to the undertaking. A frequent compromise on this issue may entail the manager waiving commissions for artist engagements in which the manager is collecting a producer fee or other direct payment from the purchaser or employer of the talent's services. The potential for conflicts in these circumstances has consequently been the subject of recent litigation, and demands careful scrutiny by artist and management.

14.4. BUSINESS MANAGERS/ACCOUNTANTS

Once an entertainment personality has successfully established his or her career, the entertainer may find it appropriate or advantageous to engage a business manager or an accountant (often the two are the same) to help manage his or her professional and personal finances. Despite the similarity in name, a business manager is not a personal manager. A business manager is primarily concerned with the management of a client's money *after* it has been earned, not how it is earned in the first place. Moreover, while some personal managers act as business managers for their clients, most do not, as the qualifications which should be expected of the business manager are quite different from those of the personal manager (e.g., many business managers are certified public accountants). Business managers generally advise clients on tax matters, handle their financial books and records (both professional and, for successful clients, personal) and advise their clients on investment strategies, generally with the further assistance of licensed stockbrokers if the business manager is not so licensed or certified him or herself (and sometimes, regrettably, even when they are not). They will also handle routine banking matters. Some business managers will participate in structuring financial and taxation issue modelling and planning of complicated projects in which their clients may be involved, although not all may be qualified to do so.

When the business manager is involved in collection and account management for the client, as well as basic "bookkeeping," the client should seek to assure that the business manager is bonded or otherwise insured.

Compensation arrangements between business managers and their clients vary from a commission of 3% to 6% on all funds handled by the manager, to a flat monthly or yearly retainer. Where an accountant is engaged solely to act as an accountant and to handle the client's books and tax planning and preparation, the arrangement may also be based simply upon an hourly or other transaction based fee.

14.5. CONFLICTS OF INTEREST

Entertainment is an industry built on relationships. As loyalties and relationships may change, one may be well advised to avoid antagonizing important people – and in particular, on the creative side and the professionals who represent them: agents, managers and lawyers. Tough deals and negotiations – and even the occasional lawsuit – with producers and distributors are routinely taken in stride as just part of doing business. But agents and managers are always the creator's friends, *aren't they*?

Many feel this is changing as growth and consolidation of management companies and the services they may render on behalf of clients and for their own accounts continues to evolve, and a number of management companies have expanded into production and other entertainment industry pursuits the scale of which has dwarfed the business (even combined business) of their original or continuing management pursuits. Consequently, there have been headline lawsuits in the recent past by major stars against their long-time managers, agents – and even their lawyers! Some of these disputes involve the representative's conflicting interests as a producer or in some instances owner of the productions engaging their client's services. Others relate to the manager's statutory violation of New York or California statutory provisions restricting the manager's involvement in direct solicitation of artist employment in many entertainment categories (although as previously noted the New York statute contains an exception for personal managers' "procurement" of employment when merely incidental to primary management services).[14] The irony, of course, is the struggling or emerging artist may be largely dependent on zealous management support to kick-start a career, but if the manager undertakes and succeeds in soliciting engagements which contribute to the artist's substantial financial success, the manager may be ineligible, by statute, to share in some or potentially all of the rewards of their contribution to the artist's career.

As to challenges in the agent relationship, it is not uncommon for an artist to be passed over for a project in favour of another client of the agency (and sometimes even a shared agent) who the agency put up for a project (or who the buyer approached the agent to hire) and who is objectively no more right for the assignment than the client not selected (and in reality, not being selected can also be considered to be "rejected"). The "passed over" client may consult with his or her entertainment lawyer on how to motivate the agency to do better by the client without harming the agent-client relationship. In these situations, the entertainment lawyer's skills in counselling and guiding the client on how to speak to the agent and to take the appropriate incremental steps to encourage the agent is a skill beyond the mere application of legal principles. However, knowing that such situations can occur, the experienced entertainment lawyer may want to put provisions into an agency agreement where the agent will use the agent's "best" or "commercially reasonable" efforts to procure work for the client and/or require a provision where the agent will proactively update the client on the agent's efforts on the client's behalf. Such provisions are not popular with agents but if agreed upon in some form at the beginning of the agent-client relationship, they are door-openers to address these concerns should they occur down the road.

While some of the suits involving managers or agents and their clients are a product of clashing personalities or egos, there are, however, serious and legitimate concerns in many of these suits arising over real or apparent conflicts of interest between the agent or manager and his or her client. These will commonly arise in the following situations (introduced in increasing level of importance and frequency of occurrence). As discussed below many of these situations can be addressed in advance by drafting contract provisions requiring transparency in the agent's or the manager's relationship with the artist.

---

[14] N.Y. GEN. BUS. LAW §§171(8) (McKinney 1988)

14.5.1. Self-Dealing

Many representatives of creative artists may themselves be involved in a variety of entertainment activities. In addition to representing a creator, they may also operate a music publishing company, a production company or a presenting (live state or musical touring) company. While it is often the case that there may be great synergy between the creator and the companies operated by the representative (i.e., where the production company develops projects for the creator or can otherwise engage the creative client in between other "gigs"), the risk is that the representative will be perceived to make deals which may be (or appear to be) more favorable to the company than to the creative client.

As discussed earlier, there will be scenarios where an artist has set a contractual milestone or goal with an agent or a manager in order to prevent the artist from terminating an agreement. It is important that any contractual provision addressing such exclude any entities that the agent or manager may have a direct *or indirect* interest in. Consider the situation where a management agreement contains a provision stating that if the manager does not present the artist with an agreement for the artist's services with a production company within a specified period of time then the artist will have the right to terminate the agreement. What if the manager runs a production company and presents such an agreement to be in technical requirement of the agreement? This scenario can be prevented by specifying in detail the type of agreement to be presented to the artist (e.g. an agreement with a company independent of the manager) and requiring the manager's prior disclosure of the manager's interests and role in such production company, including whether or not any other clients are participating, before any such agreement is presented to the artist.

To some extent, the representative may protect against the perception that these types of deals are unfair to the client by making sure that they are reviewed by an independent party (e.g., an independent agent or lawyer). However, because the potential for conflict is so obvious, these types of deals are inherently dangerous for both the artist and representative. Thus, if such a deal is necessary for the artist an exit or termination clause, or at least an efficient mediation or arbitration mechanism, should strongly be considered. For example, an artist may permit a manager to provide additional services but have the right to terminate such function(s) if there are other third parties that later can serve that function better or less expensively. While representatives will often enter into these types of deals with new artists (for whom there may be little or no market outside of that created by the representative), they become less frequent as the artist gains marketability. And although the artist may build in written, advance approval mechanisms for engagements the agent or manager may accept for them, if information disclosing these conflicts is not available, the approval may not be a meaningful protection in every case.

These self-dealing arrangements are more common in the entertainment business than many other industries, because of the high prices paid for rights and services that are largely personal and tough to quantify by objective standards. They often stem from long-standing personal relationships between buyers and their representatives, artists and their representatives, and are often condoned if not accepted as being customary, harmless and or necessary for the artist. Sometimes, even if obvious to those with industry experience, they are hidden in whole or part to inexperienced or unsuspecting artists. As such, an entertainment lawyer should conduct due diligence on behalf of her or his artist client by asking the right questions and insisting on complete answers where self-dealing may occur, so as to guide the negotiation and contractual drafting process to shield the client from such concerns.

14.5.2. Representation of Competing Clients

A more difficult and serious problem arises in connection with an agent or manager representing multiple clients who may compete for the same jobs as other clients. It is often argued that each performer and creator is unique. However, performers are often competing for the same parts and roles.

Nonetheless, because most representatives cannot avoid representing many clients these may potentially compete for the same roles, and some clients may actually recognize a benefit from having the opportunity of being considered for projects in which the better-known star represented by the same agent may be unavailable or may have "passed" on the offer. In these circumstances, the best protection may be to articulate the concern in the representation agreement with a requirement for the representative to identify all situations in which he/she is representing multiple clients in a project or package, and for the representative to keep thorough records (e.g., submissions made, calls fielded, offers received, etc.) reflecting the efforts made on behalf of each and every client.

Another strategy is to understand how the representative will choose one client over another for submissions, or if there are multiple submissions for a single opportunity how the representative will advocate for competing clients for the same role. Such a discussion may lead to further agreed upon contractual provisions to protect the artist.

14.5.3. Leveraging

Since the demise of the studio system (i.e., the pre-1960s era in which studios staffed their films almost exclusively from a large stable of acting, writing and directing talent under long-term contracts "on the lot"), agents and managers have gained significant power in Hollywood because they have the ability to assemble creative packages of talent for buyers that no longer control such direct relationships. A major agency like William Morris/Endeavor, ICM, UTA or CAA can bring together the writer, director, stars and composers for a film or television project drawing only upon artists they represent. The studios benefit because the package comes preassembled, enabling the studio to deal with a single principal (and as we've discussed, financially motivated) talent supplier for the project. The artist benefits because the agency can put the pieces together to get a project in which they are interested off the ground and placed with a distributor. Moreover, in the absence of the studio system and given a relatively limited pool of independent producers with pre-financing for their projects available prior to attachment of key talent, these agents may be the people in the strongest position to assemble the package which can make the difference between a "green light" and a brick wall. And, of course, the agency profits from the commissions on everyone it represents and/or an overall "packaging" commission on the entire project paid by the financier, studio or network acquiring the package (generally based on a negotiated percentage of the overall project budget and not just the agency's clients' fees (no matter how substantial they may be)), with half the packaging fee typically paid on production and half as a deferment out of some portion of initial project sale or licensing proceeds.

There is the implicit risk in this situation the same the commercial value of particular star clients will be leveraged by the agency to promote the careers of less well established clients to the detriment of the star. Because of the commission received on the overall project ("package commission") or the aggregate commission on all agency represented creative talent included in the package (generally a percentage of the network license fees for the project, and an equivalent participation in the project's net proceeds) may exceed the commission to which the agency would have been entitled on their client's fees only (even when the agency is representing multiple clients in a package), the agent might be tempted to make a less favorable deal for the star to lock the "package" deal than might otherwise be obtained if fewer agency elements were attached to the movie or television series. In fairness, however, the agency will argue it is supporting its lesser artists in the star's slip stream, without prejudice to the star's interests.

The representative can also leverage the power of a star client by entering into favorable deals with a producer for the star in consideration for the producer's (or studio's) involvement with other projects or activities of the representative. For example, a manager or agent may condition a deal with a star for a project only upon the producer's agreement to finance the production of another project packaged or represented by the same agent (although understandings of this type may be confirmed by handshake and not in writing), or to involve the manager in a producer capacity for additional fees.

Where an agency takes a packaging fee or a manager accepts a producing fee in connection with a client engagement, the client's individual commission obligation is generally waived – which may placate the client when she or he learns that the agency's or manager's compensation paid directly from the project's budget may substantially exceed what the commission amount would itself have been, or in some cases the artist's own fee, and consequently diminishes the real value (and in some cases possible realization) of any back end build in to their agreements. Networks and studios regularly push back on these arrangements, as they add unwanted though sometimes unavoidable costs to the production (since the financiers are in effect paying the talent's commissions on their behalf, and all other profit participants may suffer as a consequence).

In a more extreme example, the production company which developed and licensed the hit UK television series "Who Wants to be a Millionaire" to ABC/Disney and was to have shared profits from the series 50/50 with Disney (in a deal in which the Wm. Morris Agency represented the company). The hit series, instead of generating profits, actually reported $70 million in losses for ABC/Disney according to its accountings. A jury in the District Court proceeding in the matter awarded Celador, the series' creator and UK producer, $269 million in damages, later supplemented by $50 million in interest, for ABC's violation of fiduciary obligations to Celador, which included the payment of a $16 million "packaging commission" to the Wm. Morris Agency while Celador itself, prior to the judgment, had only been paid $21 million for its half of the "profits" from the series. ABC is not the only network, and Wm. Morris is not the only agency, subjected to such scrutiny over the years in and out of the courtroom for such practices.[15]

There are unlikely contractual provisions that would be acceptable to an agency or manager to police such situations and often an artist, because of where she or he may be in their careers, must accept such scenarios. Often the agent or manager may be required by contract or by the artist's insistence (despite the representative's assertion that it is unnecessary) to consult with the artist's entertainment lawyer before such deals are closed. Then, at the very least, if the entertainment lawyer asks the right questions and gets truthful answers, the artist can decide upfront how to proceed. Such situations can be uncomfortable for the entertainment lawyer, especially if the manager or agent is prominent or is essential to the artist's career at that time. Some managers or agents will not want to disclose such information or even worse, may try to drive a wedge between the lawyer and the artist in order to avoid such scrutiny. But the lawyer may nonetheless prefer to have the conversation with other representatives upfront, rather than instead having to explain to the client when the first or fifth royalty statement arrives why the successful project is still deeply in the red.

14.5.4. Self-Promoting

Finally, the representative may be viewed by the client as using their representation relationships as a way of promoting the representative's status and launching of other projects in the industry, some of which may be perceived as competing with the client's interests.

---

[15] *See* Celador Int'l, Ltd. v. The Walt Disney Co., 347 F. Supp 2d 846 (C.D. Cal. 2004.

For example, a literary manager/agent may negotiate an executive producer credit (along with separate compensation) for herself for a movie project where she is negotiating the sale of the movie rights for her writer/client's underlying book. Instead of telling the writer/client this fact beforehand, the arrangement isn't disclosed to the client until after the fact when the terms of the deal are presented. Often the strategy is to show the client how much compensation she or he are receiving so that the fact the manager/agent is getting a producing credit in the project (perhaps accompanied by additional compensation) is acceptable to the writer/client. At that point, the writer/client is in a tricky spot in questioning the manager/agent about her executive producer role while trying to preserve the deal the manager/agent has already procured for the writer/client. This is where the entertainment lawyer will play an important role in helping the writer client determine the appropriateness of the manager/agent's side deal and at the very least, insist on seeing all agreements the manager/agent has related to the transaction *before* the writer/client is asked to finalize the deal.

Another form of self-dealing is where the agent or manager (or entertainment lawyer, for that matter) promotes the fact the she or he represents the artist in part to gain status and additional clients. Whether or not this impacts the caliber and result of the representation, this is a form of leveraging, though it often lacks the element of a direct trade off or a legal harm to the client. Much more frequently, it occurs when a creator represented by a less prominent or powerful representative suddenly becomes a star in their own right and abandons the people who worked to help him or her achieve this status, in favor of a more prominent agent, agency, manager or lawyer. While sometimes justified on the grounds that the creator is now in a position to achieve better career results through more prominent and perhaps experienced representatives, these defections may also result from the perception that the former representative is seeking to trade on the newly gained prestige of their clients to advance their own standing to comparable heights (while, no doubt, the new representative may similarly be trading on the prestige of their already successful clients in recruiting additional clients to their roster). Typically, agents and managers will have contractual provisions in their standard agreements expressly permitting them to promote the fact they represent the artist/client in their own press and PR, in ads they may take out to congratulate their clients for festival or award recognition, etc., and will have the authority to do so for as long as the relationship lasts. Thus, it will be important to address such a provision in the context of any limitations an artist may desire during the term of representation, and certainly in the event of the termination of the relationship.

14.6. CONCLUSION

Agents and managers are important – and often crucial – gatekeepers for artists' careers in the entertainment industry. The keen sensibility of an agent or manager in seeing, hearing, reading major talent in an artist's early unsung work or performance can be the essential catalyst for broader commercial industry attention in every field of entertainment endeavor. In addition to "discovering" new talent and cultivating that artist's abilities for presentation to commercial buyers, an attentive and intuitive agent or manager may help an artist move or expand a career from one artistic arena to another (film to television to theatre to recordings to literary achievement), as well as to new and expanding opportunities (each with enhancements to the artist's commercial stature) from project to project. Finally, adept (and sometimes merely lucky) agents and managers may chart a course for a new (to the agent/manager) but otherwise established artist client experiencing a career decline (perhaps linked to age, a bad review in a major project, a publicly disquieting incident, etc.) to revive an otherwise moribund career through an astute strategic change of direction or a single game-changing engagement orchestrated by the representative and his or her team.

Over decades, the power of agents and managers in the general entertainment industry may have waxed and waned, but for those representing and indirectly controlling the availability of major talent in each of the entertainment industries which are the subject of this volume, their influence may rival studio and network heads, top record label and publishing house executives, and major Broadway producers in terms of ability to both get major projects launched – or nixed before they ever leave the drawing board. In fact, it's no coincidence that top agents and managers (along with prominent entertainment lawyers) frequently and often successfully find their way mid-and late-career into the most senior executive ranks of these fields – sometimes as "toppers" – based on their networking finesse, talent relationships and dealmaking acumen, whereby the consummate sellers of creative ideas and talent become consummate buyers of the same talent and products from their former agency or management industry colleagues and competitors.

As a consequence, finding and keeping the right agent and/or manager may be the most important challenge for a new artist, and a critical asset of an established one. Lawyers in the entertainment industry can provide their clients with an invaluable service in helping them identify, navigate and sustain these relationships, and if necessary, terminate the agent or manager. Moreover, the experience and resources of agents and managers can be of immense value to new and seasoned entertainment attorneys alike who want to broaden their networks and knowledge base, and recruit new clients – interests reciprocally shared by many agents and managers who rely on their and their clients' attorney relationships as a cornerstone of successful talent representation.

For the entertainment lawyer, advising and assisting the client in managing the agent-client relationship requires the trust and respect of the client – especially if the agent attempts to convince the client that an independent lawyer is unnecessary for the client (or alternatively may try to steer the client to alternate representation with a lawyer the agent works with regularly). An entertainment lawyer can earn such trust by counselling and educating the client in advance about what to expect in the agent-client relationship. Finally, an entertainment lawyer must make the client realize the higher fiduciary standard and role that the lawyer is professionally obliged to undertake (as compared to a lesser fiduciary standard required of agents and managers) and as such, the entertainment lawyer will always provide important added-value to the client in the navigation of the client' career.

AGENTS AND MANAGERS – ILLUSTRATIVE FORMS:

- Talent Agent/ Agency Agreement
- Literary Agent Agreement
- Talent Management Agreement

— CHAPTER 15 —

DEVELOPING AN ENTERTAINMENT LAW PRACTICE

Kirk Schroder*, Jay Shanker†

15.1. Introduction
15.2. Defining Entertainment Law
15.3. Understanding the Market for Clients
15.4. Effectively Representing an Entertainment Industry Client
15.5. Conclusion

15.1. INTRODUCTION

The motivation to practice entertainment law varies among lawyers depending, as with any type of professional pursuit, on their perceptions of the benefits and demands of the practice area. For example, many lawyers view entertainment law as a way to interact with famous entertainers or to enjoy and be perceived as partaking in the glamorous lifestyle associated with the entertainment industry. This type of motivation can mislead the beginning entertainment lawyer because it is based more on misperception than reality.

As a general rule, the nature of a would-be entertainment lawyer's motivation usually indicates whether she or he has what it takes to meet the challenges of practicing entertainment law in a meaningful way. Motivation is key because very few lawyers are fortunate to jump right into an entertainment law practice that will itself provide a sustainable livelihood. Instead, most successful entertainment lawyers have worked long and hard to develop their practices in circumstances where others less motivated or resourceful opt for other pursuits (perhaps still undertaking the occasional entertainment industry representation).

---

* **Kirk Schroder** is a founder and principal in Schroder Davis, Law Firm, PLC.

† **Jay Shanker** is a Director of Crowe & Dunlevy, P.C. Co-authors Shanker and Schroder are also the General Editors of this volume.

To avoid such difficulty, lawyers interested in entertainment law – whether just out of law school or seeking to build a business in this field after actively practicing in other areas – should seek to understand the practical and ethical challenges associated with this field and consider such challenges in relation to the nature and degree of their motivation. The proper consideration of these factors can put the beginning entertainment lawyer on the path to a successful and enjoyable career.

This chapter discusses practical considerations associated with starting out in the world of entertainment law, including understanding the nature of entertainment law, assessing the market for entertainment clients, and considering ethical matters unique to this practice field. While the topics covered in this chapter are not inclusive of all issues facing budding entertainment lawyers, this chapter provides an initial framework to make effective inquiries, assessments, and plans.

15.2. DEFINING ENTERTAINMENT LAW

If you wish to become an entertainment lawyer, it stands to reason that you should be able to define the nature of entertainment law. It is crucial to recognize up front that this is not a single body of law like one might study in a first-year law school course. Entertainment law instead combines an understanding of specific economic models in the entertainment industry and specific areas of law applicable to the legal issues involved in an entertainment law-related transaction or litigation. Most entertainment law books either cover a sampling of the economic models per industry along with the applicable legal issues or they emphasize a particular area of law in relation to the entertainment industry (for example, intellectual property, labor/employment, contract drafting, taxation, etc., often from the vantage of case law study examining what went wrong in a business or legal strategy as means of defining how to get it right). Despite the lack of a single uniform body of law applicable to what most entertainment lawyers do (there are, of course, specialists whose work involves solely tax, labor/employment, intellectual property, securities, antitrust or first amendment legal issues as they apply to industry transactions), lawyers practicing in the entertainment industry operate within a realm of certain broad and often overlapping principles that distinguish their work from that in other areas of law.

As a general proposition, the scope of entertainment law contains four basic elements: (1) the case law and statutory schemes of various other legal disciplines that relate to the entertainment industry; (2) certain state statutes that regulate entertainment-related business activity; (3) collective bargaining agreements in the entertainment industry; and (4) the application of entertainment industry-related business practices and economic principles to the above three elements.

15.2.1. Drawing upon Tenets of Other Legal Disciplines

An entertainment lawyer regularly advises clients on issues involving a wide range of legal practice areas. Such areas include intellectual property law, contracts, business, labor/employment, securities, international law, taxation, immigration, and litigation. A lawyer, new or experienced, with a background in some or all of these disciplines will have some advantage in launching an entertainment law career over others who do not. The legal practice areas on which the entertainment lawyer relies most will depend on the nature of his or her clients' work within the entertainment industry. No body of case law *per se* constitutes "entertainment law." Instead, case law from various fields of law affects the entertainment industry and its accepted business practices.

One role of the entertainment lawyer is to counsel clients about their business practices in relation to such case law – whether the client is an individual or an enterprise. An example is the historic antitrust case, *U.S. v. Paramount Pictures, Inc.*,[1] the business, economic – and some would argue creative – implications of which forever reshaped the way in which motion pictures are made, distributed, and exhibited by separating production and distribution from theater ownership.

In another famous case, *Buchwald v. Paramount*,[2] writer/columnist Art Buchwald sued Paramount Pictures claiming that the Eddie Murphy film, *Coming to America,* was based upon a screen treatment of Buchwald's.[3] In that case, the court applied principles of

---

[1] 334 U.S. 131 (1948).

[2] 1990 Cal. App. LEXIS 634, 13 U.S.P.Q.2d 1497 (Supr. Ct. 1990)

[3] Art Buchwald, et. al. v. Paramount Pictures Corp., et. al., Los Angeles County Superior Court No.C 0706083 (March 16, 1992);. The Buchwald case was tried in three phases. Phase One: Breach of Contract Claim, 13 U.S. P.Q.2d (BNA) 1497 (L.A. Super. Ct. 1990), Phase Two: Unconscionability of Contract Claim, 90 L.A. Daily J. App. Rep 14482, December 26, 1990, Phase Three: Damages Claim, (March 16, 1992).

contract law and found the standard motion picture industry contract to be a "contract of adhesion."[4] Consequently, the court also found unconscionable the studio's accounting practices (specifically, net profit provisions).[5] At the time of the *Buchwald* decision, some legal experts suggested that the case also might have an adverse impact on many standardized royalty and accounting terms used in entertainment industry contracts.[6]

U.S. v. Paramount and *Buchwald* illustrate the broad application of legal principles from various fields of law to the entertainment industry. Over the years, many cases have shaped the entertainment industry. Anyone serious about practicing law in the entertainment field must know and understand those cases and their impacts on the entertainment industry.[7]

15.2.2. State Statutes and Regulations

In addition to entertainment-related case law, certain states have enacted specific statutes pertaining to the entertainment industry.[8] Such regulations cover diverse industry-related topics, such as the activities of talent agents, managers, child actors, the right of an individual to control the use of his or her name and likeness for publicity, and special state tax exemptions.

---

[4] Because the contract was drafted by Paramount, it had all of the bargaining power in the negotiations. "Except in rare instances where mega-stars with substantially more clout than Buchwald were involved, the film industry rarely negotiates any of the contractual provisions, particularly those involving accountings. Even when the industry was willing to negotiate, the [Buchwald] court labelled the resulting changes cosmetic." Leonard Marks & Robert Mulvey, *Ethical Aspects of Entertainment Law Practice*, 39 ANN. UNV. OF SO. CA. ENT. L. INST. 22. (These published papers came from a seminar titled, "Handshakes to Lawsuits: Entertainment Business Relationships," April 24, 1993.)

[5] There were no economic justifications for the net profit provisions in the standard mm industry contract (as used by Buchwald) and such provisions were designed to guarantee a profit to the film company before Buchwald would realize any net profits on his own. *See supra* note 8.

[6] L. Marks, *"Buchwald Case Has Stern Message for Labels,"* BILLBOARD, April 18, 1992, at 8.

[7] *See, e.g.*, Ron Smith, *Ten Legal Events That Shook Hollywood*, L.A. Law. 26 (California Law Business Section) March 25, 1991.

[8] *See generally* BIEDERMAN, PIERSON, SILFEN, GLASSER, AND BERRY, LAW AND BUSINESS OF ENTERTAINMENT INDUSTRIES (2nd. Ed.1992) [hereinafter Biederman, et al.].

Most entertainment-related contracts contain provisions specifying that either New York or California law should govern the interpretation of the contract. This preference is a function of both the domicile of most major entertainment companies in Los Angeles or Manhattan (which consequently insist on "home court" jurisdiction) and the concentrated development of a reliable body of entertainment case law in these jurisdictions, which makes California or New York law attractive for purposes of generally predictable outcomes in the adjudication of disputes. However, the choice of law of either state can create significantly different outcomes with respect to the interpretation and enforceability of the contract. A working knowledge of the entertainment-related regulations in those two states is essential for this practice area, even for an attorney who does not intend to practice in New York or California. Likewise, attorneys should actively identify and learn the entertainment-related statutes and regulations affecting clients in their own states. Although those statutes may not be widely known, they can have dramatic effects. For example, a little-known statute in Virginia contains a provision that exempts a foreign corporation from registering in the state if that corporation is "producing, directing, filming, crewing or acting in motion picture feature films, television series or commercials or promotional films" and does so for a period of less than ninety consecutive days.[9]

15.2.3. Collective Bargaining Agreements

Many different trade guilds and unions operate throughout the entertainment industry.[10] A beginning entertainment lawyer cannot overlook the collective bargaining agreements when dealing with client affairs. These agreements cover basic fee arrangements and working conditions for essential creative and technical personnel in the entertainment industry. They control when the client is a "signatory" to a union/guild agreement of this type and/or when the production involves union members. Even if the state has "right-to-work"[11] laws,

---

[9] Code of VA. § 13.1-757 (1993).

[10] For example, the unions just for actors/actresses alone include the Screen Actors Guild (theatrical motion picture talent), the American Federation of Television and Radio Artists (radio and television talent), and Actors Equity (live performance/theater talent).

[11] Right-to-work laws are state laws that prevent membership or nonmembership in a labor union from being a condition for employing an individual. Currently, twenty

these union rules still can have an impact on entertainment clients.[12] More importantly, the entertainment lawyer cannot assume that clients fully understand often hundreds-of-pages long collective bargaining agreements, whether they are "talent" members of creative guilds or production company signatories to guild minimum agreements for the productions they undertake. Thus, for example, an entertainment lawyer who mistakenly presumes that her or his film-producer client understands certain practices required in film industry collective bargaining agreements could find that client blaming the entertainment lawyer when the client learns those certain requirements unexpectedly and significantly raise the film project's budget, limit working hours, or require significant residuals payments from the exploitation of a film or television program in certain markets or territories that the producer failed to properly reserve from its proceeds or lay off as the responsibility of the distributor. Arguably, such business and economic structures don't cross over into the scope of legal issues typically handled by a non-labor lawyer in the general business arena, but that argument will not likely excuse an entertainment lawyer who is presumed to know how to counsel a client in such matters (even though there are employment and labor lawyers in the entertainment industry who specialize exclusively in these guild/union relation matters). Beyond understanding and learning a requisite level of how collective bargaining agreements are structured and affect producer clients, it is advisable for entertainment lawyers to contact and get to know the representatives of local (or national, if appropriate to the attorney's client activities) collective bargaining units who are likely to be dealing with their clients. In an industry where relationships are essential and in some instances, crucial, having a line of communications based on some familiarity and trust with representatives of entertainment collective bargaining units benefits the entertainment lawyer and his or her clients.

---

states have explicit right-to-work laws. See generally Thomas Haggard, COMPULSORY UNIONISM: THE NLRB AND THE COURTS: A LEGAL ANALYSIS OF UNION SECURITY AGREEMENTS (1977).

[12] For example, although a motion picture may shoot in a "right to work" state, union regulations may still apply to the production talent and crew if the production company is a signatory to the applicable collective bargaining agreements.

15.2.4. Economic Models and Business Practices

Entertainment lawyers must understand the business practices used in the entertainment industry, as well as the economic factors that guide business decisions in the entertainment marketplace. A lawyer cannot effectively counsel an entertainment client if she or he does not have a sufficient understanding of how that client does business within the entertainment industry.

Will the entertainment attorney's working knowledge of relevant cases, statutes, collective bargaining agreements, and regulations pertaining to the entertainment industry provide a sufficient basis to be a *competent* entertainment lawyer? Rule 1.1 of the ABA *Model Rules of Professional Conduct* requires a lawyer to provide competent representation to a client. In traditional legal areas, such knowledge of case law, statutes, and regulations would typically constitute sufficient competence for legal practitioners of such areas. However, the same does not hold true for entertainment lawyers. A competent and effective entertainment lawyer will generally be deeply familiar with one or more of the entertainment industry sectors explored in this volume (e.g., music, theatre, publishing, film and/or television, electronic gaming). He or she may have an additional expertise in one or more of the legal disciplines outlined above. But the lawyer will, in any event, need a familiarity with many of the industry sectors and legal disciplines outlined in this volume to enable him or her to at least "red-flag" issues of importance to the client's interest that require referral to appropriate specialists in those instances in which the lawyer recognizes the need for collaborative counsel – whether available from within or outside of the lawyer's firm or organization.

Many entertainment legal transactions can be complex and may require substantial documentation – not just in primary transactional agreements, but also in supporting of due diligence and conditions precedent to the primary transaction. That entertainment is a document-intensive business further underscores the necessity for lawyers who represent entertainment clients to not only be "good lawyers" in the sense of their general communications, drafting, negotiation and litigation skills, but also to fully comprehend the business practices of the industry. This point cannot be overemphasized. Whether a client matter involves royalty pooling arrangements for theater, the manner of manuscript delivery in a literary publishing deal, the structure of options in a recording contract, or the screen credit that original film writers receive after someone else rewrites their work, a good entertainment lawyer must have the knowledge to deal with these issues as they arise in the client's dealings, often under significant time constraints. These all are basic business issues in the entertainment industry. In fact, entertainment lawyers have found that in today's entertainment environment, it is rarely enough for them to understand the business practices of only one particular field within the industry. As one music lawyer points out, "[n]o longer is a record deal merely a record deal. Music attorneys also have to have a broad area of knowledge in motion pictures and computer industry deal-making."[13]

Not only do assets and activities within various sectors of the entertainment industry merge if not collide (music in film, television and games, adaptation of books or plays to film, or film to stage, etc.), but the structures of transactions in one sector may be either highly similar to or substantially dissimilar from those in other sectors (e.g., the rights of writers for stage and for film are substantially different). A lawyer's depth of knowledge of industry business practices almost always determines his or her degree of effectiveness.

It is fundamental for a transactional lawyer working with entertainment clients to understand how the client will earn compensation or otherwise generate revenue under contractual formulas that often are complicated and sometimes archaic. An entertainment lawyer must properly assess and counsel a client on how revenue streams will be earned under certain entertainment arrangements and the risks, associated with the formulas on how revenue is earned. In an industry full of creative people, who often are uncomfortable with the business details of their arrangements, there is a great need for the entertainment lawyer to make certain that such clients understand the business details of such arrangements.

It bears mentioning that many "creative" clients have limited business interest or acumen, their primary focus being the creative aspects of their work and careers – even in the many instances in which these people are running creative businesses employing (sometimes many) others. The entertainment attorney is often relied upon as the general "consigliere" for such clients, helping to translate complex business and legal concepts in ways that the client can comprehend and

---

[13] David Robb, *Manatt Phelps Makes Music in Legal System*, THE HOLLYWOOD REPORTER, July 28, 1994, at 20.

act upon. For many such clients, particularly those involved in new ventures to create new content and media, the lawyer is building not merely a "contract" for the client but in effect a "road map" for the client to follow to successfully build a project or business. In these cases, the lawyer needs as much of an understanding of where and how the ultimate deal being negotiated is to play out as the client does, because if the deal doesn't work out as planned, fingers will often point to the lawyer. Certainly, these same challenges are faced by lawyers in numerous other areas of law, particularly those dealing with clients in personal or small business environments. But it will not take long for the aspiring entertainment attorney to join the ranks of those who believe "left brain" / "right brain" distinctions in the pursuit of creative versus linear/business outcomes are genuinely manifested in this industry. Consequently, the entertainment lawyer may often be looked upon (and expected to provide indirect if not direct support) as the creative client's "business" as well as legal advisor, whether the lawyer seeks this broader advisory role or not.

One simple way to learn about trends and developments within the entertainment industry is to subscribe to and faithfully read the general entertainment trade papers covering all major industry sectors, such as *The Hollywood Reporter, Daily Variety* and *Weekly Variety*.[14] Also, specific fields within the industry have their own trade publications. For example, *Billboard* magazine covers the music industry and *Publisher's Weekly* caters to the literary world. The information contained in these publications is invaluable, especially for the beginning entertainment lawyer. Also, many bar and legal education organizations, such as the ABA's Forum on the Entertainment and Sports Industries, the Practising Law Institute, and the *National Law Journal*, sponsor frequent legal seminars pertaining to the entertainment industry. Such programs not only are informative on many aspects of legal and business practices, but also provide great networking opportunities for entertainment lawyers. Most, if not all, of these publications are accessible online, via subscription or otherwise, and there is a plethora of emerging web-based news services and professional blogs which can also provide valuable insight into

---

[14] These three publications are generally regarded as the newspapers covering the entertainment industry. Like traditional newspapers, they report industry news, cover industry events, and provide special features, including film reviews, paparazzi reports, and financial information about entertainment companies and industry-wide activities.

industry news and trends. These sources are in addition to the entertainment industry business coverage of the leading papers in the industry's two leading hubs, *The New York Times*, *The Wall Street Journal* (both in New York) and *The Los Angeles Times*.

15.3. UNDERSTANDING THE MARKET FOR CLIENTS

Sometimes lawyers beginning in the entertainment field improperly assess the market for available entertainment clients. This mistake can be costly in terms of time, energy, and lost opportunities. The best way to understand the market for clients in the entertainment industry is to survey the local legal market for potential entertainment clients and then compare and contrast that market to the overall level of entertainment industry activity in various geographic regions in the country. To do this properly requires research and investigation, an exercise that will help the lawyer assess whether there are enough potential clients in the local market to build and sustain a significant entertainment law practice over time.

Pick a market with reasonable prospects for building a viable client base. Geography plays a key role in the equation. The entertainment industry is primarily centered in three cities: New York, Los Angeles, and Nashville. However, Atlanta is quickly becoming a major center for film and television industry activities. The entertainment attorney who chooses to practice law in one of these cities will face a different set of challenges than someone who chooses to practice in a secondary market. For starters, entertainment lawyers in primary markets can afford to be specialized in specific fields in the entertainment industry given the high concentration of industry presence (for example, being a music attorney in Nashville or a film or television attorney in Hollywood). Large markets offer fairly "organic" opportunities for meeting and networking prospective clients (openings, industry networking and educational events, social and charitable affairs, and even at the local coffee bars in cities where every other waiter or waitress may be an aspiring actor or songwriter/musician). Entertainment lawyers in secondary markets almost have to be "general practitioners" in the various entertainment fields in order to sustain even a limited volume of business from a smaller pool of professional or pre-professional talent and projects (with invariably smaller project budgets and consequently less capacity and tolerance for large legal fees). This "general practitioner" approach has significant limits in allowing the secondary market entertainment attorney to get deep knowledge in specific areas that are required in sophisticated entertainment matters. However, this trend is changing as more and more entertainment lawyers in secondary markets are specialized in a few entertainment fields, and changing technologies make it possible for artists in smaller markets to achieve mainstream distribution and therefore wider than local audiences for their projects. College towns generate a plethora of bands to entertain students and locals, and many large colleges and universities boast film, theater, music or game programming departments that may prove a source of prospective clients from current or graduating students or even faculty. Many of these entertainment lawyers, while locating their practices in secondary markets, are also admitted to law practice in one or more of the primary entertainment market states. Thus, it is more common to find established successful entertainment lawyers in secondary markets, some of whom have entered or returned to these markets after having actively practiced in a primary market, and they should not be underestimated.

Have realistic practice development plans and expectations. Planning is important for entertainment lawyers to grow their practices. Giving serious thought and analysis to a business development plan helps manage realistic and high expectations to grow an entertainment law practice. Any such plan should address how the entertainment lawyer obtains legal and business competence. This first step is not only a qualifier to enter the world of entertainment law, but is also an important marketing tool if communicated effectively to clients. Constantly updating industry knowledge and legal education is an essential ongoing business development activity (not to mention protection against malpractice risks) – especially in an industry where new technologies and platforms result in evolving economic models and related legal issues. Handling an entertainment industry-related transactional matter once a month may lead a new lawyer to feel she or he has "arrived" in the business, but unless the clientele has some relative leverage in the transactions the lawyer undertakes, the lawyer may be learning little more than how to accept "no" gracefully from more experienced lawyers on the other side of each deal. How does a lawyer seeking to "up" his or her game do so in this circumstance? There are a number of annual entertainment law conferences and numerous entertainment industry conferences around the country (in the major markets just described, along with Miami, Chicago, Austin and Las Vegas, among other locales) taking place year-round. The successful entertainment lawyers attend select conferences on a regular basis. For the entertainment lawyer who is just starting a career, attending such conferences may be intimidating on a variety of levels and may not seem to garner much with respect to networking and other objectives. They may also require investment of expense and time seemingly out of reach of the new practitioner. However, it is important to take a long view and recognize that being consistently seen at such conferences opens many doors over time.

Network, Network, Network. The entertainment industry thrives on relationships, and that is especially true for entertainment lawyers. Simply put, an entertainment lawyer networks not only with those who work in the industry but with other entertainment lawyers. As a general rule even the most successful entertainment lawyers are "approachable" because they once had to start off doing the same thing. Moreover, for even the most successful lawyers in the business, on Monday they may be representing a "buyer" in a transaction with a "seller's" lawyer, and on Tuesday they may be representing a "seller" in a separate transaction with the same lawyer. Cordiality (as well as competence) goes a long way toward insuring that Monday's conversations will not adversely affect Tuesday's (and by extension indirectly prejudice the interests and outcomes of an entirely different client you may be representing in the second transaction). This is not unique to entertainment law, but the local entertainment bar in major industry centers – and even the national bar for the industry – is relatively small and active attorneys will not uncommonly find themselves dealing regularly with a familiar pool of attorneys in a given industry sector both across town and across the country.

One strategy to establish a relationship with more experienced entertainment lawyers is to determine their interest in working as co-counsel on matters, or to refer clients to them beyond one's own scope of expertise until the appropriate "co-counsel" opportunity in an area in which the referring attorney has greater competence of confidence (and ideally one with a large enough upside to support the involvement of both attorneys) comes along. Allowing the more experienced "co-counsel" to take the lion's share or even the entire fee may be worth it the first time around, if the "junior" attorney can then run a similar transaction "solo" when the next opportunity arises (with the same client or another).

Another strategy is to mine the potential "client" resources of your community. Attend public performances of the college music, theatre and film programs and festivals in your area, as well as in commercial clubs and theatres, as well as book store events to meet local writers. Seek out opportunities to visit with faculty, producers and club owners, all of whom are likewise on the lookout for or engaged in the support of local artists and performers, and let them know of your interest and (growing) expertise. Join boards of these organizations. You will be surprised at how quickly someone you have met through these activities – whether an artist, a principal in one of these programs (e.g., the executive director of a community theater) or someone with an artist relationship (or perhaps a prospective project financier) – may call you with an issue they are seeking to sort through, followed by the question "is this the sort of work you do?"

Be prepared to make sacrifices to build your entertainment law practice. The three biggest sacrifices that entertainment lawyers must give are time, effort and direct financial investment in the "tools" of their trade. Unless there is a steady flow of business coming from a law firm or clients with ongoing work, there is no way to avoid the reality that to be a successful entertainment lawyer a significant amount of time is almost always required to build a practice – reading, networking, traveling to related CLE and other industry events, etc. Much of this time may be unrewarded except for experience and future knowledge. Thus, determination and drive are essential, especially when it seems like not much is yet coming from one's efforts. The key is to make smart and strategic investment of available time, optimal effort and (often limited) funds.

For example, doing pro bono work for creative people who cannot afford a lawyer or for "lawyers for the arts"-type organizations is not only a way to learn certain legal issues and business customs, but to network as well. If a beginning entertainment lawyer refers work to another more experienced lawyer, she or he might reasonably insist on being a co-counsel in the matter, either identifying work in the matter that can be handled by the referring lawyer, or at least pro-bono to assist and learn in whatever way is possible if split fees cannot be justified. An entertainment lawyer's initial clients may not be able to pay legal fees at all, but they still can provide an opportunity for the lawyer to obtain valuable experience. For example, most actors and actresses struggle to make ends meet with part-time jobs. However, the types of issues they confront (talent releases, independent contractor tax issues, union affiliation) are at the core of some basic entertainment legal and business principles. Obviously, each successive actor, rights, financing or other industry deal will be easier to tackle with the prior transaction under your belt. Also, because they generally hustle for their work, they know the marketplace can share information and will possibly refer other clients if they are impressed with your work on their behalf.

Relying too heavily on forms can be disastrous in the entertainment industry practice (the unwary can easily overlook the little details that can make or break a deal) – forms are an indispensable place to start analyzing a transaction – whether at the client intake stage or after you have landed a client and start strategizing either the "buy" or "sell" side of a transaction for rights, services or other resources. The forms offered as a companion to this volume illustrate both basic and sophisticated considerations that arise in an extremely wide range of entertainment industry transactions. Other terrific resources are also available for accessing entertainment industry transactional forms and contractual analysis, including the Matthew Bender multi-volume *Entertainment Industry Contracts* series to which an editor and authors of chapters in this volume have also contributed. Studying these with some degree of serious attention *before* you actually encounter the transaction(s) you may have opportunities to work on will make you that much more comfortable in a conversation in which the opportunity of doing this work for a prospective client surfaces – not to mention giving you the ability to realistically "quote" a prospective fee for your time on planning, negotiating and/or drafting documentation for the transaction. The forms libraries of many lawyers and law firms are crucial starting points for their transactional work, but the competent lawyers in the field never succumb to over reliance on their forms, as the business is constantly changing, and no two deals are ever exactly alike.

Familiarity with the forms may also help the new entertainment attorney determine whether the lawyer for the other side is more or less competent than she or he, if that attorney's *vitae* does not indicate a deeper background in entertainment law. Deferring to a more experienced attorney in a transaction may not result in the best deal for your client in relation to the other side, but the project itself may not necessarily suffer from the imbalance. However, when two equally inexperienced attorneys attempt to tackle a modestly complicated transaction, the outcome may lead to trouble for both sides when the transaction will not consequently satisfy a financier or subsequent material party whose involvement is needed to get the project to the next level of advancement.

Finally, one of the necessary "sacrifices" in building an entertainment practice may require is a certain number of years working in another area of the law to pay the bills. If the aspiring entertainment attorney views this as a means of developing basic professional practice skills (as well as generating income to live on) that will serve the attorney well in whatever line of work she or he ultimately pursues, the transition is likely to go more smoothly. As previously noted, many different legal disciplines converge in the practice of entertainment law, and consequently an attorney dealing in corporate or securities law, intellectual property law (copyrights and trademarks), labor/employment law, general business transactions, and business litigation, among other areas of practice, may have an easier time making the transition by simultaneously engaging in work in more than one area than the lawyer in a secondary market who "bets the ranch" on building an entertainment practice in an unrealistically brief time frame. Entertainment clients will likely have that much more confidence in an attorney who has achieved some distinction in other areas of the law in addition to entertainment – and if the transition to entertainment practice does not ultimately work out, the attorney at least has the opportunity to continue working at a higher level in the "fall back" professional position and practice arena.

The Golden Rule: Competence. Investing time and energy (and yes, making sacrifices) in developing legal and business competence always pays off. If there is one important thing to remember with respect to obtaining competence as an entertainment lawyer, it is this: nearly all entertainment clients can easily tell whether a lawyer knows what she or he is doing. Thus, do not oversell yourself in the beginning as you may only have one opportunity to make a good impression on a potential entertainment client. Since it is an industry of relationships, word of mouth in such instances can either help you or hurt you depending on how you present your knowledge of this practice area. Even if one's knowledge is limited in the beginning of an entertainment law practice, there are always ways to work with a potential client. Emphasis on responsiveness, meeting deadlines and transparency in communication is always a good compass for staying on path in this regard.

15.3.1. Practicing in the Primary Markets

The vast majority of opportunities for entertainment lawyers exist in the primary entertainment industry markets mentioned earlier. Thus, the competition for clients and legal positions in corporate or other entity operations in these markets is very high, sometimes fierce. It is not uncommon to hear stories of lawyers who started off as paralegals in entertainment law departments to get a foot in the door. However, the rewards and benefits are many since practicing in a primary market not only immerses the lawyer in the entertainment industry, but also allows, over time, that lawyer to develop sophisticated knowledge in complex matters (e.g., exposure to a steady flow of entertainment transactions is preferred to only occasional transactional work in the field, in part because each transaction in some way indirectly offers a mentoring exercise through interaction with counsel on the other side of the deal). Most entertainment lawyers prefer practicing in a primary market when opportunities to do so present themselves, unless personal circumstances or a particular lifestyle choice dictates that they practice elsewhere.

15.3.2. Practicing in the Secondary Markets

Though difficult in the past, it is becoming easier for a lawyer to develop an entertainment law practice and represent entertainment clients at a sufficient level of sophistication and expertise in a secondary market. Physical, face-to-face interaction with clients and dealmakers is not demanded nearly as much as was once the case, since ubiquitous and instantaneous voice, video and data communication and transfer make it possible for attorneys to fully communicate with clients anywhere in the world at any time of the day or night. Again, success will depend on the many points already discussed in this chapter, especially, persistence and proper planning. Here are some important considerations for those who accept this challenge: The good news is local clients (and national clients looking for counsel in a particular locale can find the local entertainment attorney through the Web and social media as easily as they can identify an attorney in Los Angeles or New York; while the bad news is that the prospective local client can find an entertainment attorney in the major market by entering the same number of key strokes in a Web browser.

Assess the Market at Different Levels. What is the level of entertainment-related business activity in the local, state, and regional areas? The answers provide vital information to a lawyer starting up an entertainment law practice. Generally, if there is not significant business activity in at least two of these geographic areas, it will be difficult to succeed in entertainment law (unless the lawyer has success developing significant industry contacts as discussed above) and it may make sense to relocate. If there is significant business across the three areas, the attorney will be able to expand his or her practice from the local area to the regional area as she or he gains knowledge and experience.

Be Prepared for Doubters. Doubters ask, "Why is an entertainment lawyer living in [insert the name of city]?" And they almost always presume that the attorney does not know what she or he is doing. When confronted with a doubter, the lawyer should not take the interrogation personally. Instead, she or he should see it as an opportunity to discuss the practice development plan. Hopefully, with some local success, the calls will be new referrals from pleased clients, and the questions will more frequently be in the nature of "I have heard great things about your work – Are you taking on new clients?"

Entertainment Industry Continues to Expand into Secondary Markets. Secondary market attorneys have long had some advantages in representing emerging talent among musicians/bands and book authors who start their careers away from New York, LA and Nashville (even if these clients gravitate to big city attorneys later in their career trajectory). Advancements in technology (along with other market developments) will continue to increase the opportunities for entertainment lawyers practicing outside the primary markets in sectors such as film, television and electronic games, as the sources and production locales of content in these fields becomes more diversified. "The entertainment industry is now the driving force for new technology, as defense used to be."[15] The advent of new technologies has created many new and potential delivery systems of entertainment

---

[15] *The Entertainment Economy*, BUS. WK., March 14, 1994, at 58. According to this article, entertainment is considered by many leading industrialists as the growth industry of the 1990s, and since 1991, entertainment and recreation—not health care or automobiles—have provided the biggest boost to consumer spending.

content programming in areas such as telecommunications and computers.[16] New technology also has improved existing delivery systems.[17] Consequently, as the entertainment economy expands, more avenues for programming open, especially through nontraditional channels. As the demand for content creators increases, resulting in creators and content being sourced and recruited across the United States and the world, so will the opportunities for entertainment lawyers practicing outside New York, Los Angeles, and Nashville, because new content providers will not necessarily operate solely out of these primary markets.

All around the country, in cities such as San Francisco, Denver, Atlanta, Boston, Miami, Minneapolis, Albuquerque/Santa Fe, Chicago, New Orleans, and Washington, D.C., and in states such as Florida, Louisiana and Texas, there are established, active, and successful entertainment bars.[18]

Some people may assert that secondary market legal activity has little or minor effect on the Los Angeles and New York entertainment legal markets; however, this misses the basic point that lawyers all around the country carve out their own entertainment-related niches. This fact alone should hold promise for beginning entertainment lawyers who decide to practice in secondary markets.

As in any other area of practice, or professional disciplines generally for that matter, distinguishing yourself from the competition is critical both in finding employment and finding clients. That will always entail broadening experience and expertise in the target area of

---

[16] *See generally The Strange New World of the Internet: Battles on the Frontiers of Cyberspace*, TIME, (cover story) July 25, 1994; *Merging with Silicon Valley*, THE HOLLYWOOD REPORTER, (SPECIAL ISSUE) June 3-4, 1994; *see also Hollywood and Silicon Valley Meet in the World of Interactive Multimedia*, FILM & VIDEO, (cover story) April, 1994.

[17] For example, Silicon Graphics, Inc., a leading manufacturer of digital visual computing and data server systems has opened its own "studio," which will be dedicated to working with, among others, third party "content creators and distributors in film and video." As reported in *Briefs*, THE HOLLYWOOD REPORTER, July 22-24, 1994, at 6.

[18] For example, the Bar Association of San Francisco has an Entertainment & Sports Law Committee, even while its state counterpart does not; the Washington Area Lawyers for the Arts has a full-time staff; Washington, D.C. also has its own established entertainment and sports law section. *See also*, Karen Levine, *Big Entertainment Lawyer Says Boston's No Small Town*, 22 MASS. LAW. 43, November 29, 1993; and Nancy Holt, *Lawyer Combines Entertainment with Entertainment Law*, 14 CHICAGO LAW., October 1991.

practice. But active interests and accomplishment in other fields of endeavor, whether legal, business, political or non-profit activities, can also influence a client's or prospective employer's interest in engaging one otherwise emerging entertainment lawyer over another – or even over an experienced candidate.

15.4. EFFECTIVELY REPRESENTING AN ENTERTAINMENT INDUSTRY CLIENT

While many entertainment lawyers are called upon to offer their clients general advice as to the management of their careers and business affairs, their primary task is to identify and protect the legal interests of their clients in various relationships and activities. This entails studying and/or preparing the legal documents governing the relationship between the lawyer's client and all the foregoing support personnel (i.e., agents, personal managers, business managers, etc.) and the relationships between the client and the employers, purchasers and/or licensees of that client's works or services. The lawyer must ensure that the agreements are fairly and accurately drafted, and that they are in the best interests of the client (to the extent that she or he can affect that possibility). Most importantly, in that a lawyer cannot and should not seek to *control* his or her client, the lawyer must be sure that the client fully understands the terms of each agreement and its implications for the client's rights, generation of income, and responsibilities. The lawyers will also seek to review each agreement in relation to all the client's existing agreements to assure that there are no conflicts among them with respect to conflicting rights or obligations. An effective entertainment attorney should have a firm grasp of the business and economic structure of those aspects of the industry in which the client is currently or likely to be engaged, and will seek to ensure that the client's contracts for the acquisition and/or disposition of rights and services provide a clear and navigable road map for the client's successful transit through such activities, many of which may involve the client for years from beginning to end.

Many artists share the same "aversion" to lawyers as others in the general public, and may resist engaging lawyers just to review what may be perceived as standard contracts, most typically out of concern over expense. Many are unfamiliar with the specialized skills and insight a lawyer can contribute to the advancement of their interests in what the client may view as routine business dealings or may wish not to "antagonize" a buyer/employer with the prospect of a legal negotiation. They may also feel that their managers and/or agents are competent to negotiate and review such agreements. This is particularly true where such contracts commonly take the form of standardized, "fill-in-the-blanks" union-negotiated and prescribed form agreements (e.g., many musicians make personal appearances under AFM standard performance contracts, or actors under film or television SAG or AFTRA day-player or weekly-player agreements, where the only substantial changes likely to be made to the agreement relate to the appearance dates and the fee paid to the artist). While this situation does afford clients a reasonable degree of protection, the lawyer's position with regard to these types of agreements is that the lawyer should (i) initially review the standard union agreement with the client to ensure that the *standard* agreement conforms to the *specific* needs and expectations of that client, (ii) prepare a rider to accommodate the client's specific needs, which can be attached by the agent to each and every standard agreement issued by that agent for the particular client, and then (iii) to be available for consultation whenever it is proposed that the terms of the standard agreement (other than money terms) are to be altered.

Likewise, even in instances in which the artist and a buyer or employer of his or her rights or services may have prepared and exchanged an "original" terms sheet or so-called "deal memo" containing what are intended as the minimum essential terms of a transaction, one which on its face may seem to contain non-complicated (read "non-legal") language covering presumed terms of an understanding, what is excluded from such a document may be as critical to its performance and enforcement as the terms which do in fact appear, and only an experienced entertainment lawyer may be able to meaningfully anticipate and address such issues and concerns.

Although in some instances larger talent agencies maintain an in-house legal or business affairs staff which may participate to varying degrees with the agent in the negotiation and documentation of talent contracts, for most types of contracts it is in the interests of the client to engage an independent lawyer to also review, consider and advise the client as to the legal consequences of such agreements. The agency lawyer's client is "the agency," and (depending on agency staffing and the lawyer's level of experience) their review may sometimes be limited to top-level economic, credit and other concerns, while focusing less on subtle but complex and potentially critical administrative and boilerplate provisions where issues very much material to the client's interests and liabilities may reside. For example, talent agency lawyers do not usually conduct due diligence like an entertainment lawyer might for the artist client. So, a situation can arise in which the talent agency lawyer will only review a publishing agreement but not check with the author to make sure that all representation and warranties are being (or are capable of being) fulfilled – only to have trouble down the road where an important release or supporting document was not obtained, thus putting the author in breach of the agreement. Make no mistake, talent agents and managers do not necessarily like entertainment lawyers reviewing the agreements they negotiate and sometimes will go to significant lengths to convince an artist client that their agency lawyer can handle matters. Thus, an entertainment lawyer should communicate with talent agents and managers that she or he is there to support the process (and not to critique the talent representative's work – which usually just involves the key economic terms). Further, an entertainment lawyer should be able to explain to a prospective client how she or he can add important value (e.g. independent legal review and its advantages) to the client in such circumstances.

Many entertainment lawyers offer their services on an hourly and/or a flat fee basis (e.g., the attorney will accept a set amount in compensation for preparing all of the necessary legal paperwork for the financing and/or production of a motion picture or play, for the negotiation and review of an author's publishing or musician's recording agreement, or perhaps for the formation of a new company to serve as a vehicle for a production, or a personal services/loanout corporation for a client who will render services through that company). Hourly or flat fee representation may be accompanied by an expectation of a substantial and sometimes recurring retainer based upon the lawyer's engagement policies and projected costs of services to be performed. The retainer is sometimes refundable if a balance remains at the conclusion of services, and which may sometimes require regular replenishment for a longer transaction/engagement in which the lawyer or law firm may require the retainer balance to generally contain an amount equal to the likely charges for the next subsequent billing period as security for its efforts.

In the representation of individual creative artists, such as musical performers, actors, authors, etc., some lawyers will accept compensation on a contingent fee (i.e., a percentage/commission) basis (i.e., the lawyer participates financially in the client's success, akin to the commissions of agents or managers for their services, although usually out-of-pocket expenses incurred in connection with the legal services are borne by the client). Such percentages are generally set at 5% to 10% of a client's gross income from the transactions serviced by the lawyer, or all the client's entertainment income where the lawyer is generally available to service all of the client's personal and professional legal needs, often acting as "general counsel" to the artist client's group of professional advisors (agent, manager, business manager, publicist, etc.). The benefit to the client is that if a negotiation fails to close or even if successful does not lead to the launch of an eventual production, publication, etc., or requires significant lawyer attention long before it may generate fees to the client, the client does not get an immediate bill for services. For the lawyer whose contributions may add significant value to the client's economic upside from a particular project, this arrangement is a means for the lawyer to share in the rewards of the client's success. It also poses potential professional responsibility and ethical difficulties, where for example, an attorney who has expended a considerable amount of effort in one or more negotiations for the sale of a client's intellectual property may be inclined (whether or not consciously) to encourage the client to accept a contract that assures the lawyer his or her fees from the client's payday, even if the client's interests are not fully served by one or more material aspects of such agreement. Essentially, it is a conflict of interest that can be addressed in an engagement letter with the following type of provision:

> *Conflict Notice/Disclosure.* *The Firm's code of professional responsibility requires that whenever fees are being collected on a contingency basis or from percentage of income, to bring to your attention and consideration that such a fee arrangement can present a conflict for our Firm where the Firm is giving advice and counsel on a matter where the Firm has a stake in the financial outcome since the Firm's compensation is based on gross revenues. While the Firm certainly has no intention of advising you to ever accept any*

financial outcome because the Firm desires to receive compensation from that financial outcome, it is important for the Firm to bring this matter to your attention and for your consideration before you enter into this Agreement for services so that you may decide whether the nature of this fee arrangement, given this disclosure, is still acceptable to you. If so, by your initials below, you are representing and warranting that you understand this disclosure, have had adequate opportunity to seek the advice of other counsel regarding this Agreement and hereby waive any such conflict during the course of our representation of you under this Agreement.

Please initial your consent and waiver to the terms of paragraph (#) above:

_____
(Client's) Initials

Moreover, it must again be borne in mind that a client *always* has a right to terminate his or her attorney's legal representation at any time and no written agreement can alter or affect this right. Thus, if a lawyer is retained under a percentage retainer agreement, the agreement must provide for a right of termination.

Because of a client's ever-present right to terminate services with the lawyer, some retainer agreements will provide that if the client terminates the lawyer's services prior to a defined period of time, the lawyer otherwise engaged on a percentage-fee basis may require, or shall be compensated at, a defined hourly fee for services previously performed. Some lawyers also operate on a monthly retainer basis where the client pays a fixed fee that may or may not be periodically modified according to the amount of work actually performed by the lawyer. Additionally, creative artists may also find themselves in need of litigation counsel at one or more points in their careers. Like the medical patient who waits to visit the emergency room for treatment that might have been avoided with a routine physician check-up, often the litigator is the first entertainment lawyer the client may engage for help in enforcing or otherwise exiting a contract the client entered into without qualified independent counsel involvement or review. Some transactional entertainment attorneys are quite capable litigators, and vice versa. Often transactional entertainment attorneys are part of law firms which include or maintain affiliations with entertainment litigation specialists who may advise on contractual matters before disputes arise, and are available to prosecute or defend claims on behalf of clients when so required. And as with the myriad of specialties in the entertainment field that have been described in this work, litigation attorneys may themselves specialize in some, but not all areas of entertainment law (e.g., securities, bankruptcy, secured transactions, labor and employment, intellectual property issues such as copyright, trademark or first amendment matters, etc.). Because a lawyer is expected to exercise independent professional judgment on behalf of a client, an entertainment lawyer should not be separately engaged by the manager or agent with whom the lawyer may later be called on to negotiate or even litigate on behalf of the performer, writer or other artist. This is a very important point. In fact, if the talent agent or manager contacts the lawyer first, the lawyer should make clear that the artist will be his or her client in such matter. This can be difficult if the talent representative is a current client of the entertainment lawyer and is referring the artist (a potential source of problems any time a lawyer represents multiple parties with interests in a single transaction or business). In accepting such an arrangement, the entertainment lawyer must be very conscious that such dual representation can produce the appearance of a conflict of interest and may serve as prima facie grounds for a malpractice action, whether or not an actual conflict arises (i.e., both parties could be very happy with the eventual deal, but this alone does not negate the existence of the conflict – just the risk of claims). Nonetheless, it is not uncommon for an agent or manager to refer a new artist client to a particular attorney for personal representation, or conversely for a lawyer to assist the artist in obtaining (and sometimes replacing) agency or management representation. Such connectivity may bode well for a strong and integrated team of professional artist advisors, but the potential for conflict exists whenever problems later arise among any two or more of these parties. Obviously, these pros and cons require a lawyer to exercise good judgement in accepting such dual representation and even better judgement, to anticipate potential problems down the road and to act before they come about.

15.4.1. Lawyers Acting in Non-Lawyer Roles

Many lawyers themselves undertake to act as managers or as agents, and although receiving compensation for such services is not prohibited by any rule of law or ethics, the lawyer will continue to be held to a level of professional responsibility governed by his or her role as lawyer, and consequently percentage compensation arrangements are always of concern. As with the example of potential conflicts raised in the preceding paragraph, does the lawyer's possible short-term benefit of a percentage of immediate income (as against the possibility that the lawyer may not share in such income that is delayed or deferred into an uncertain future) produce a conflict with the lawyer's obligation to act in the best interests of the client at all times? In other words, does a commission on immediate payments, rather than on long-term benefits that may not be received until after the lawyer has been discharged, influence a lawyer's judgment?

It is a very important consideration as to whether a lawyer serving in a non-lawyer role (e.g. talent agent or manager) coinciding with legal representation is a smart move for the lawyer given the significant increase in potential conflicts since the lawyer will be assuming at least two and possibly three roles for the client, each have differing levels of fiduciary and regulatory compliance requirements. Also, malpractice insurers generally will not insure any claims against the lawyer where non-lawyer activities are mixed into the situation. So, a lawyer may find himself (or herself) the subject of a malpractice suit where the malpractice insurer declines coverage because of the non-lawyer activities involved in the matter. Thus, if a lawyer is going to engage in non-lawyer activities as part of their entertainment law practice for the same client, it is important to understand how malpractice insurance coverage is affected by such practice.

To make matters more complicated, on September 30, 2013, in the case of *Solis v Blancarte* (TAC 27089), the California Labor Commissioner ruled that an entertainment lawyer had violated the Talent Agencies Act by "procuring employment" for his client without a talent agent license. Specifically, the entertainment lawyer conducted negotiations on an employment agreement as KNBC sports reporter for his client in exchange for the "standard" 5% of the compensation received by the client. Although, the entertainment lawyer claimed he was acting as a duly licensed attorney in California, the Labor

Commissioner noted in the ruling that the Talent Agencies Act did not recognize an exemption for a licensed attorney from the Act.

Although the preceding discussion emphasizes considerations involving transactional attorneys in a general "dealmaking" entertainment practice, lawyers in the entertainment industry perform a surprisingly broad range of legal services, in numerous capacities, involving widely varied expertise. In addition to representation by private legal practitioners of individual and corporate clients, "entertainment" lawyers work "in-house" in studios, networks, production companies, publishing houses, talent agencies and management companies, record labels, guilds and unions, and in government and industry association offices involved in regulatory and policy-related work affecting the entertainment industry in the United States and abroad. Additionally, numerous legal disciplines may be drawn upon in entertainment transactions – whether simple or highly complex – including such legal specialties as copyright, trademark and patent law, taxation, bankruptcy and secured transactions, securities, employment and labor/employment, immigration, antitrust, real estate law, constitutional and first amendment law, trust and estate planning, advertising, communications, domestic and matrimonial law, and even criminal law, among others (along with specialized litigation expertise and experience which may accompany disputes involving each of these areas of law).

15.4.2. Engagement Letters

The use of engagement letters should be a standard practice for all lawyers – entertainment lawyers included. While there are many guides that discuss the basics of client engagement letters, here are some tips that are especially helpful for the entertainment lawyer/client relationship.

Scope of Representation. Entertainment lawyers need to give careful thought on how to define the scope of representation in engagement letters. Not only should the scope of representation define the areas of work the lawyer will perform, but also areas of law where the lawyer will not provide services. This is especially important in flat fee arrangements where a broad scope of representation drafted into an engagement letter could result in a client insisting that the lawyer provide services that the lawyer is unable to do and/or did not anticipate. For example, it is not uncommon for lawyers to provide flat fee arrangements to handle the legal documents during the production phase of a motion picture. To further this example, what if the scope of representation in the engagement letter is so broadly drafted to state that the lawyer will provide legal services during the production phase of the motion picture without any other qualifier? As a result, the lawyer may be expected to handle matters beyond legal paperwork, such as a labor union complaint filed during production or a claim for civil damages as a result of crew misconduct during production, etc. Since entertainment industry work typically requires varieties of legal expertise, if the scope of representation pertains to a particular phase of work or a defined project, it is important to define what specific legal tasks will be performed and to specify what types of representation will not be part of the scope of representation. An attorney competent in film or television production work may not have similar experience in private placement offerings for the financing of such productions. One common approach is to specify that legal services will not include any required tax or employment and litigation matters (as examples of excluded areas), but that should those matters be required the entertainment lawyer can enter into a separate engagement letter for such additional work or may make an appropriate referral to other lawyers, and more generally that any expansion of the services agreed upon shall require additional written acceptance of the assignment and agreement as to fees therefore.

Designated Party. On projects where there are multiple parties who will be interacting with the entertainment lawyer, it is important to designate in the engagement letter the name of parties whose authority and directions the entertainment lawyer can rely and act upon. This is a smart practice point for many obvious reasons and more importantly, provides clarity to the entertainment lawyer.

Conflicts of Interest. As discussed in other chapters in this Book, conflicts eventually arise in the practice of entertainment law. Engagement letters should address how the entertainment lawyer will address conflicts that may arise during or after the representation of the client. It is crucial that all applicable state professional codes of conflict rules are consulted and that such provisions are consistent with such rules. One area of conflict disclosure that is often overlooked is when the entertainment lawyer is to be paid on a commission or contingency basis, including to whom the underlying compensation is to be paid and when and how the attorney shall become entitled to his/her share of this compensation. A fee arrangement can present a conflict for an entertainment lawyer where that lawyer is giving advice and counsel on a matter where the lawyer has a stake in the financial outcome since compensation is based on such financial outcome. Thus, an entertainment lawyer who has worked long and hard on a matter, and has not been paid, might exert undue influence on a client to accept a deal which the client is otherwise inclined to refuse or terminate. Blended fee arrangements where some portion of the attorney's normal fees are paid irrespective of whether the deal closes or not, may address part of this concern (and keep both lawyer and client focused on getting a deal done efficiently if there's one to be made). But a provision that points out and explains this inherent conflict to a client who enters into a contingent fee arrangement with the entertainment lawyer, and more importantly, where the client acknowledges an understanding and waives this inherent conflict is important – and both sides must recognize that the final discretion over closing or passing on an agreement will always belong to the client.

Client Identification. As a general rule of professional conduct, all lawyers have a fiduciary duty to maintain client confidences, including the identity of the client. Yet, given the fame and notoriety of entertainment clients, entertainment lawyers want to promote or at least identify who they represent on their websites and in industry trade papers. But to do so requires client consent, and often obtaining formal client consent is overlooked by lawyers. However, it should not be assumed that a client will give such consent. An engagement agreement is a good place at the outset of the attorney-client relationship to address the issue of client authorization to formally identify the client as such. Such authorization language can include permission to use the client's name and/or logo, if any, on the entertainment law firm's website and in materials advertising the firm and identifying its and/or its lawyers' current and/or former clients (although some lawyers and law firms may choose to refrain from such marketing out of deference to its clients' privacy interests, whether or not the client would otherwise be inclined to consent to such identification). It is important to also permit the client to revoke such permission by agreeing to inform the law firm of such decision in writing.

15.4.3. Professional Liability Insurance

Lawyers representing their first entertainment clients should not assume that their present professional liability insurance will cover claims made against them for entertainment-related legal work. Historically, premiums for entertainment law malpractice coverage fall closely behind those for securities law work, where the malpractice risks and attendant claims lawyers might face are obviously quite high. The reasons for this are severalfold, including the fact many attorneys are tempted to practice in the field without adequate experience. The frequent lack of deep business experience of creative clients – or alternatively, the lack of entertainment industry experience of successful business people undertaking deals in the entertainment field for the first time – can make entertainment clients disproportionately litigious in comparison to clients in other legal fields. "We only accept attorneys for coverage who have ten percent or less of their law practice devoted to entertainment law," says one insurance company representative. "Even within that zero to ten percent range, the nature of the entertainment work must be viewed by us as incidental and not significant."[19] Thus, it is critically important to engage an insurance broker early on to learn what guidelines are used to provide coverage in this area.

As far back as 1986, members of the Committee on Entertainment and Sports Law of the Association of the Bar of the City of New York met with various representatives of the professional insurance industry to discuss why firms practicing entertainment law were either denied coverage or were issued unusually high premium quotes in an attempt to understand and clarify the perceived insurance risks involved in the practice of entertainment law. Although progress has been made over the years in this regard, entertainment lawyers who shop for malpractice insurance should anticipate that a number of major professional liability insurers will not insure entertainment law practices.

Nearly all of the major professional liability insurers who provide coverage for entertainment lawyers have supplemental questionnaires pertaining to the scope and nature of the applicant's entertainment representation. Careful attention should be given to these forms to

---

[19] Telephone interview with Julie Giesen, Lawyers Program Specialist with COREGIS Insurance Organizations (July 11, 1994).

provide the insurer with as much information as possible. As another insurance executive put it, "[w]e simply want to know what niche the attorneys have made for themselves and where we need to know more[,] about what exactly they're doing as attorneys."[20]

15.4.4. Determining Fees

All lawyers starting in the entertainment field (especially those starting from scratch) are, at one time or another, faced with the dilemma of how to bill clients who cannot afford to pay traditional fees. Unlike lawyers in most practice areas, lawyers in the entertainment industry can create varying fee arrangements with their clients. However, in some instances, a nontraditional fee arrangement can present professional and ethical problems.

The following is a list of fee arrangements that are typical of most entertainment lawyers:[21]

- Hourly rate charges;
- Monthly or annual retainers;
- Flat fees for specific projects or services;
- A percentage of income derived from the successful outcome of the client matter (these fees typically range from five to ten percent);
- Blended fee arrangements, in which a reduced hourly is paid "against" a success fee based upon a percentage of income resulting from a transaction or series of matters;
- Arrangements that involve partnerships with or co-ownership in the client's creative materials, rights, business ventures, or other enterprises.

Rule 1.5 of the ABA Model Rules of Professional Conduct requires that a lawyer's fee be "reasonable."[22] Many states have

---

[20] *Id.*
[21] William Krasilovsky and Robert Meloni, *Ethical Considerations for Music Industry Professionals*, 15 COLUMBIA-VLA J. OF L. AND THE ARTS 358 (1991).
[22] MODEL RULES OF PROFESSIONAL CONDUCT, Rule 1.5 (1990); *See also* Formal Opinion 93-379 of the ABA Standing Committee on Ethics and Professional Responsibility (commenting on a number of improper billing practices).

various standards for what constitutes a proper and ethical fee arrangement. For example, Rule 4-200(A) of the California Rules of Professional Conduct states that a lawyer "shall not enter into an illegal or unconscionable fee." ABA Model Rule 1.5(a) provides the following factors to determine if a fee arrangement is "reasonable":

1. The time and labor required, the novelty and difficulty of the questions involved, and the skill requisite to perform the legal service properly;

2. The likelihood, if apparent to the client, that the acceptance of the particular employment will preclude other employment by the lawyer;

3. The fee customarily charged in the locality for similar legal services;

4. The amount involved, and the results obtained;

5. The time limitations imposed by the client or by the circumstances;

6. The nature and length of the professional relationship with the client;

7. The experience, reputation, and ability of the lawyer or lawyers performing the services; and

8. Whether the fee is fixed or contingent.

A growing practice among some entertainment lawyers is to enter into percentage fee arrangements with their clients. Such practice has been common since the 1980s. As one lawyer explains, "I favor the percentage. If you put the amount received in juxtaposition to the hours expended in the abstract, you're often losing money on a particular client. In the long run, with a client who stays in the business, it evens out and no one gets hurt."[23]

Another Los Angeles entertainment lawyer warns attorneys to structure percentage fees carefully:

> Any percentage fee agreement involves an inherent potential for conflicts of interest. For example, if an attorney has a percentage agreement and is negotiating a recording contract

---

[23] *Id.*

or the sale of story rights, in which an advance is to be paid and the client is to receive some percentage of royalties or profits, the attorney faces a potential conflict situation. Should the attorney negotiate for a higher advance and lower percentage, or take the opposite approach, which makes more of the fee dependent upon the client's potential success? ... These types of potential conflicts should be disclosed to the client, and the client should consent to them at the start of the representation.[24]

Where the arrangement is primarily an accommodation to client cash flow in a long attorney/client relationship, this balancing may be worthwhile for both parties. On the other hand, a deal to provide legal services for 5% of a client's earnings when the client's reasonably anticipated earnings will generate resulting legal fees of several if not many multiples of the attorney's standard hourly legal rate for work performed, and where the lawyer's contribution is not itself "extraordinary" in relation to the deal being secured or closed, should in the normal course seem a lot less attractive to a client than paying at the hourly rate for services rendered (if the client can afford it). Although the contingent fee arrangement may lead to some significant earnings opportunities for the lawyer, an imbalance in a lawyer's or law firm's mix of hourly and contingent fee engagements, or the inconsistent timing of "payouts" for contingent fee arrangements for clients and consequently attorneys, can result in severe cash flow strain for the attorney if not carefully thought-out and managed.

Structuring fee arrangements, especially nontraditional arrangements, requires careful attention. Lawyers starting out in the entertainment field should develop acceptable fee and billing practices from an ethical and practical perspective.

15.5. CONCLUSION

As the entertainment sector of the economy grows, the field of entertainment law will likewise evolve and grow, providing many new and exciting opportunities for lawyers who wish to practice in this area (even if they do not practice in New York, Los Angeles, or Nashville). The key to a lawyer's success will depend upon how well she or he

---

[24] *Follow the Rules (Entertainment Law)*, 102 L.A. Daily J. 7, January 1, 1989.

responds to many of the practical and ethical considerations presented in this chapter. Lawyers starting out in the entertainment field should recognize that the practice of entertainment law presents challenges that are distinct from those of traditional practice areas. Among the most important are a clear understanding of the industry's business practices and a keen awareness of the rules of professional conduct. The willingness of a lawyer to address these issues will only enhance his or her efforts to develop a substantial client base and to cultivate a successful entertainment law practice.

LAW PRACTICE DEVELOPMENT – ILLUSTRATIVE FORMS:

- Attorney Engagement/Fee Agreement (hourly fees)
- Attorney Engagement/Fee Agreement (percentage fee)

— Glossary of Terms —

The terms and phrases included in this glossary appear throughout this volume and are routinely invoked in the negotiation and analysis of entertainment industry legal and business affairs transactions. For brevity, terms and expressions whose common English meanings are consistent with their meaning in these industries (e.g., "entertainment lawyers") have been omitted from the glossary.

Where a definition contains a word also included elsewhere in the Glossary, we have generally sought to **highlight** the word for the convenience of the reader's further review.

A

Above the Line: The key creative talent, such as actors, writers, directors, and producers, whose fees frequently exceed the ceiling of (or budgetary line for) guild/union wage scales.

Above-the-Line Costs: Portion of the budget covering above the line elements, including script and story development costs.

Above-Title: Credits in motion pictures and television productions (on screen and/or in advertising) placement of which precedes the regular title of the production.

Accredited Investors: Investors meeting the qualification for participation in private placement security offerings exempt from Federal Securities Regulation under various rules of Regulation D of the Securities Act, based on considerations such as net worth, investment experience, and other factors.

Active Development: The process of assembling the various creative and business aspects of an entertainment project required for financing or production greenlight.

Actors Equity Association (Equity or AEA): Stage actors and stage managers union.

Adaptation: Transformation of a work from one medium to another (e.g., book to motion picture screenplay).

Additional Insureds: Coverage for non-primary beneficiaries under production, errors and omissions, and similar production related insurance policies, usually resulting from negotiation.

Adjusted Gross Proceeds: Gross revenues from the exploitation of a production (at the distributor level) minus certain defined costs, which typically include distribution and sales agents fees, prints (in the case of motion pictures) or other duplication costs (in the case of DVDs or CDs), and advertising, but *before* recoupment of production related costs.

Administration Agreements: An alternative or supplement to certain music publishing agreements, whereby the administrator receives a fee or royalty share in exchange for the administration of licensing and collections for certain songs or catalogues.

Administration Deal: Arrangement, usually for a percentage fee, in which an individual or firm manages the copyright, business affairs and financial aspects of a music publishing rights to an individual composition or entire music catalogue.

Advance: A negotiated payment to an author, musical or other creative artist, producer, or other individual or entity, in anticipation of and recoupable from otherwise prospective fees for rights and/or services (e.g., distribution revenues, royalties or net proceeds participations).

Advance Orders: Orders placed by retailers and others in advance of a book's, CD's or DVD's street (i.e., release) date, with estimates used to determine print or manufacturing run, pricing and additional marketing/advertising considerations.

Advergames: Electronic games financed in whole or part by in-game advertising placements.

Agency Package Fee (or **Agency Packaging Commission**): Instead of receiving a commission from one client, an agent packaging a deal involving multiple clients —one or more of whom who may be the critical component for a "greenlight"—may charge the "buyer"/ employer of the clients' services a fee based on overall project budget (a "packaging fee"), in which case the individual clients may be relieved from commission obligations for the engagement.

Agent (or Agency): Representative who seeks employment and negotiates rights and services/performance contracts for artists on a commission basis. Certain activities of agents may be subject to

regulatory and licensing requirements in California, New York and elsewhere. See also **Booking Agent** and **Talent Agent.**

Album: A collection of recorded songs, originally ascribed to vinyl long play records, but still commonly used to describe CD and digital downloads of such collections.

Affiance of Motion Picture and Television Producers (AMPTP): Self-described "trade association responsible for negotiating virtually all the industry-wide guild and union contracts, including the **American Federation of Musicians (AFM); American Federation of Television and Radio Artists (AFTRA); Directors Guild of America (DGA); International Affiance of Theatrical Stage Employees (TAT SE);** International Brotherhood of Electrical Workers (IBEW); Laborers Local 724; **Screen Actors Guild (SAG);** Teamsters Local 399; and **Writers Guild of America (WGA)"**, representing over 350 motion picture and television production companies (including studios, broadcast networks, cable networks and independent producers).

All-In Royalty Rate: In recording contracts, "all-in" royalty rate is the rate paid the artist inclusive of any producer royalty, which is then paid by the artist.

American Bar Association (ABA) Rules of Professional Conduct: These Model Rules of Professional Conduct were adopted by the ABA House of Delegates in 1983. They serve as models for the ethics rules of most states.

American Booksellers Association (ABA): Trade association for independently owned retail bookstores.

American Federation of Musicians (AFofM): National association representing musicians in film, TV, music recording and traveling productions

American Federation of Television and Radio Artists (AFTRA): National labor union representing actors, journalists, radio personalities, recording artists, singers, voice actors, and other media professionals in television and radio, which merged with the Screen Actors Guild (SAG) in 2012 to form SAG-AFTRA.

American Society of Composers, Authors, and Publishers (ASCAP): The first U.S. Performance Rights Society (founded 1914), ASCAP is a membership organization for composers, songwriters,

lyricists, and music publishers that grants licenses for performances, tracks usage and collects performance royalties for a member songwriter's or publisher's music.

Ancillary Rights: Rights incidental to the core right to adapt or produce an underlying work, and which relate to the creation and exploitation of promotional and merchandising items, including toys, books, posters, CDs, T-shirts, etc., as commercial extensions of such productions.

Anonymous Work: Work by an unknown or unattributed author/creator, which may nonetheless be eligible for copyright by an identified employer or copyright proprietor.

Answer Print: The preliminary composite (i.e., including sound and images) motion picture print from the laboratory, edited, scored and mixed for further review and approval by the producer.

Approved Production Contract (APC): The form production agreement endorsed by the Dramatists Guild for stage productions based on its member playwrights works.

Arbitration: Mechanism whereby parties to contract dispute can address grievances outside formal court proceedings. Contracts not subject to arbitration provisions of guild or labor union production agreements will typically invoke statutory arbitration rules of the jurisdiction in which the contract is enforceable, or alternatively the rules of one of several private arbitration services such as American Arbitration Association (AAA), Judicial Arbitration and Mediation Service (JAMS), Independent Film and Television Alliance (IFTA), etc., which will oversee such proceedings.

Arm's Length Negotiation: Description of a good faith negotiation between unrelated third parties, often invoked as a "standard" of conduct in contracts in which buyer/licensee may be sublicensing to affiliates on a preferential basis.

A&R (Artists and Repertoire): Record label department or staff principal artist liaison, generally responsible for finding and signing artists for the label, and packaging the development of the artists' recording projects (including selection of producers, songs, etc.).

Artists: Creative contributors (individual or group) who contribute creative services or performances to a collaborative entertainment production, e.g., actor or director for film, television or stage productions, musical talent in recording or live performance productions, etc.

Assigned Material: Work or other intellectual property assigned from one party to another.

Assignment: The transfer of some or all rights in an intellectual property from one owner or licensee of copyright interests to another buyer or licensee. See also **License**.

Auction: A submissions process, often used for the sale of a literary property or screenplay, in which a select group of buyers (studios, production companies, publishers, etc.) are given a limited period of time to review and bid on the purchase of a Work, with the process culminating in a sale (or if unsuccessful, a withdrawal of the Work from the market).

Audiovisual Work: A work combining sound and image, presented in a sequence or series, intended to be shown through the use of a machine, and which is eligible for copyright.

Audit Rights: In the entertainment industry, the negotiated contractual right of a royalty participant or a participant in the defined proceeds of a project or production to examine the books of the financier or distributor to determine whether revenues, costs and distributable proceeds are being properly accounted for.

Auteur: A perception arising from French film criticism in the 1950s that "authorship" of a motion picture is derived primarily from a strong director's vision, rather than via the collaboration of writer, cinematographer, actors, producers and others.

Author: The creator of a work eligible for copyright, whether artistic, literary, dramatic, musical, etc., and which under copyright law may be one or more collaborating individuals, or entity commissioning one or more such individuals to create the intended work. *See also* **Work Made for Hire.**

Author's Discount: The reduction in list or wholesale price offered to an author for the purchase of his or her book(s), typically ranging between 20% and 40% and determined by negotiation.

Author's Rights: The Copyright Act of 1976 provides that the author of a copyrighted work (which may include an entity which owns the intellectual property under the doctrine of "work for hire") has the right to: 1) reproduce the work; 2) us the work as the basis for derivative works; 3) publicly distribute the work; 4) perform the work publicly; and 5) publicly display the work. As a "bundle of rights", these rights may be licensed or assigned under contract in whole or in part.

B

Back End: Participation in the profit of an entertainment property (e.g., film, television production, game or recording), usually after costs of production and distribution have been recouped.

Below-the-Line: That portion of the budget devoted to the actual physical production of the film including stages and locations, set construction, crew, and the photographic unit and film/digital processing, but excluding **above-the-line** elements such as producer, director, on-screen talent or literary rights fees.

Below Title: The placement of talent or other credits *after* the appearance of the production's title on screen (in the case of film or television projects) and/or in programs, posters and advertising in the so called "billing block", where "below" can mean either literally below the production's title, or to the right of the title when read from left to right. See also **Above Title.**

Berne Convention: The first significant multilateral copyright treaty, dating to 1886 in Berne, Switzerland, covering treatment of copyrights among participating nations. The Berne Union (as the member states are called), which now numbers over 175 countries (including the U.S.), is administered by the World International Property Organization (WIPO).

Bible: The creative outline for one or multiple seasons of a television series, suggesting the arc of plot/story dynamics over multiple episodes, and to which subsequent episodic teleplays are intended to conform.

Billing: The order/placement of an artist's name in the credits for a production. *See* also **Credits**.

Blanket License: An omnibus license granted by a public performing rights society to a broadcaster, network, radio station or other "volume" licensee authorizing public performance of the society's complete catalogue in a particular medium, location and/or time period.

Boilerplate: Standard legal language or provisions that are commonly part of many agreements and that are commonly referred to as "boilerplate."

Book: A publishable literary work (novel or non-fiction publication). This also denotes a script for a stage musical (as distinguished from music and lyrics for the production).

Book Packager: In publishing, a person or entity acting in a role similar to that of a motion picture or record producer in their industries, who assembles elements of a book (one or more of which may include author, illustrator, editor, printer) leading to a finished (or *packaged*) book for sale to a publisher, and often credited as a "co-publisher" for its contributions.

Booking Agent: An individual or entity who acts to secure engagements for a creative artist or musical artist or act, typically on a commission basis for fees ranging from 10 to 15 percent of the artist's earnings. See also **Talent Agent**.

Box Office Bonus: A fixed payment due when the reported amount of box office receipts on a theatrical motion picture release reaches a specified level.

Box Office Receipts: Gross revenue from ticket sales at the box office, split between the theater owner and the producer of the featured film, musical or stage performance. (In the motion picture industry, the portion then owed to the film's studio/distributor is called **"rental payments"**).

Breakage: A supplemental contribution to production budgets agreed to by the network in excess of its initial negotiated license fee meant to subsidize and incentivize the producer to enhance the production value and marketability of the series (typically tied to high-level talent attachments).

Breakeven: The stage in the accounting calculations for an entertainment venture (film, television, stage production, recording, book, etc.), when revenues from all sources equal the costs associated with producing and distributing the respective production. See also **Cash Break Point.**

Bridge Financing: Intermediate financing provided by a pre-production loan enabling the production to "keep the lights on" during the period after the project has been greenlit, but before the completion bond is effective and the full production loans are funded.

Broadcast Music Incorporated (BMI): A non-profit rights organization, formed in the 1930's, that licenses performance rights to musical compositions and handles collections and distribution of license fees to member songwriter/composers and music publishers.

Broadway: The central midtown New York City theatre district, named for the street which runs through it, populated by America's principal concentration of large commercial theaters.

Bus-and-Truck Tour: A low-budget production of a play or musical, which travels to smaller cities for limited runs.

Business Manager: A representative, often an accountant, who supervises an artist's personal and professional financial life, including income, expenses and investments, either for an hourly fee or a fee calculated as a percentage (usually 5 percent) of the artist client's income.

C

Cash Break Point (or Cash Breakeven): The stage in the accounting calculations for a motion picture when revenues from all sources on a "cash" basis equal the sum of defined **Distribution Fees** and **Distribution Expenses,** the **Negative Cost** (including **Gross Participations** and **Deferments,** if any, paid up to the point of Cash Breakeven, contractual Studio **Overhead Charges** on **Negative Cost,** contractual Interest on Negative Cost and Overhead, Depending on the leverage of the proceeds participant in defining these terms (e.g., reductions in standard distribution fees, caps on certain expenditures), participations upon Cash Breakeven will be more favorable than participations based upon a "standard" Net Proceeds definition (i.e., as a result of the more favorable break point, the participation payments will commence sooner). Nonetheless, a Cash Breakeven definition will be less favorable than a participation based upon defined **Gross Proceeds** or **Adjusted Gross Proceeds**.

Cast: The group of actors performing in a film or stage production (i.e., *the* "cast"), or the process of auditioning and engaging such actors for the production (i.e., *to* "cast").

CD (or Compact Disc): A plastic optical disc used to store digital data for retrieval through portable or component playback devices or computers, originally developed for storing digital audio files as a replacement for vinyl recordings.

Certificate of Authorship (or Certificate of Engagement): A document utilized in establishing "chain of title" for copyright purposes in which an "author" attests to a work's origin as his or her own work, or as "work-for-hire".

Chain of Title: The documentary evidence of the transfer of ownership in a work from the author/creator to the party(s) claiming current title to some or all rights in the work, established by, among other records, writer/author employment (work-for-hire) agreements and/or certificates of authorship, option agreements, purchase agreements, copyright registration certificates, title searches, copyright assignments and legal opinions.

Clearances: Licenses or releases permitting exploitation of third party intellectual property or other rights in a motion picture, television, stage or recorded music production, or literary publication.

Clickwrap: A mechanism enabling electronic game publishers to obtain an affirmative end-consumer consent to be bound by terms of a privacy policy before a game can be fully accessed.

Clip License: Contractual permission for use of a short film, television program or commercial scene or sequence in a specific and limited manner in another production in the same or another medium, usually for a negotiated fee.

Collection Account: Segregated account designated for the collection on revenues and proceeds related to a single entertainment project.

Collection Account Manager: An agent entity appointed to collect and administer all gross receipts payable to the production special purpose or other licensing vehicle/entity. Also, manages and controls the collection account, by holding the proceeds in trust for the beneficiaries of the funds to be dispersed as per the collection account management agreement.

Collective Work: A collection or assemblage (e.g., an anthology or a motion picture) of individual works by one or more authors, each of which may or may not be separately copyrightable.

Commercial Tie-In: A relationship between the producer of a film or television production or game and an advertiser by which a commercial product is featured in a production in exchange for a payment, exchange of goods or other promotional benefit.

Commission: Compensation to agents or managers calculated as a percentage of a client's earnings (both fixed and/or contingent [i.e., based on some performance measurement from project revenues). Also refers to a contractual engagement to create an original work or component of a work, ownership (including copyright) to which will be owned by the employer (as in *specially commissioned work* under copyright law).

Common-Law Copyright: Form of protection of a work based on state common laws, superseded by a single national system effective January 1, 1978.

Compilation: A collection of individual works which may or may not be individually subject to copyright. See also **Collective Work.**

Completion Bond (also **Completion Guaranty**): An insurance policy, often required as a condition of production financing, guarantying that so long as certain criteria in the production of a film are complied with, the film will be completed so as to satisfy financing and/or distribution obligations (i.e., by the guarantor assuming such additional supervisory responsibilities and expenditures as may be required to effect completion); failing which the bonding company, acting as guarantor, is obliged to repay certain loan or investment obligations incurred in the production of the film.

Composer: The *author* of a musical work.

Composer's Share (also **Writer's** or **Songwriter's Share**): That portion of the royalties from the performance or exploitation of a musical composition paid to the songwriter(s), as distinguished from the

Publisher's Share, and established by the Publishing Rights societies as 50% of 100% of the gross royalties paid for such exploitation (with the remaining 50% representing the Publisher's Share).

Compulsory (Mechanical) License: A license established by Section 115 of the Copyright Act permitting a musical artist to "cover" for purposes of a phono-record a previously recorded and commercially released, non-dramatic musical composition, in consideration of payment of a statutory license fee, representing an exception to the exclusive rights of the author under copyright.

Concert Promoter (or **Tour Promoter**): An individual or entity who produces live concert events, booking performers directly or through their agents, and then orchestrating the logistics of securing venue(s), ticket sales, marketing and overall execution of the event(s), which may be a single venue production or a tour.

Conflicts of Interest: Circumstances in which two or more parties' rights or obligations in a transaction in which they may seek to partner, collaborate or utilize joint representation may not coincide by virtue of contingent circumstances, whether known or unknown but predictable, and which under professional responsibility codes preclude a single attorney from representing such parties jointly in the absence of an express waiver (in some but which may not extend to all circumstances) of the conflicts and their possible consequences.

Consideration: A fundamental element in a binding contract, representing the compensation (usually reflecting the exchange of a monetary interest for the transfer of a right or forbearance of a right, or services) agreed upon for the fulfillment of the contract.

Contingency Reserve: a portion of a film's production budget (typically 10%) established to cover cost overruns. Typically required as condition of a completion guarantor or financiers to insure the project can be completed with reduced risk of additional unexpected capital infusions being required in late stages.

Contingent Compensation: Compensation only payable if a film, music or stage or other production is completed and is successful by some negotiated measure, and which may take the form of deferred fees, royalties based on sales or box office performance, and/or participations in profitability.

Controlled Composition Clause: A negotiated provision in a recording contract requiring that an artist/songwriter who owns or controls copyright to his or her compositions license the **mechanical rights** to record them on a reduced or no fee basis in relations to normal industry practices for compositions not similarly "controlled" by the artist.

Cooperative (or Co-op) Advertising: A contractual arrangement between book publisher, film distributor or record label and the "retail" seller of its products (bookstore, movie theatre, record retailer) to share in the advertising expenses of promoting a work in the retailer's (usually local) market(s).

Co-Production: A theatrical, concert, motion picture/television, game, or other production (including a motion picture or television production) undertaken as the joint enterprise of two or more production companies.

Co-Publishing: The joint publication of one or more copyrighted works (e.g., books or songs) by two publishers.

Copy: For purposes of copyright, a reproduction of a protectable work containing images, text and/or audiovisual information, not necessarily in the original medium (e.g., paper to digital file, or film to DVD). Where the reproduction is unauthorized, the "copying" may constitute an infringement of an underlying copyright in the work (as opposed to the coincidental independent development of a substantially similar work without resort to copying). (Note that in the realm of trademark, infringement is based merely on the similarity, whether or not copying occurs *per se.*)

Copyright: The exclusive right granted authors, composers and other creators of intellectual property for protection of their works from unauthorized copying or exploitation. Under U.S. copyright law, the copyright owner is exclusively entitled to exploit a so-called "bundle of rights" including the right to reproduce the copyrighted work; to prepare derivative works based on the copyrighted works; to distribute copies of the work; to perform the works publicly; to display the works publicly; and in the case of sound recordings, to perform the copyrighted works publicly by means of a digital audio transmission. To "copyright" a work also describes the process of securing protection for the work through proper registration with the Copyright Office.

Copyright Infringement: Unauthorized exploitation of a right or rights in a work protected by copyright. See also **Infringement.**

Copyright Mortgage: Collateral in a copyright provided as security for a financial obligation.

Copyright Notice: A statutory prerequisite for copyright enforcement under U.S. Law requiring affixation of a "possessory statement" to the Work consisting of (i) either the © symbol, the word "copyright" or the abbreviation "Copr.", followed by (ii) the year the Work has been registered for copyright or the year of its first Publication, and (iii) the copyright owner's name.

Copyright Royalty Tribunal: A panel created by Public Law 94-553, to establish and then periodically adjust the compulsory license royalty rates for music performance applicable to educational television, cable television, jukeboxes, and sound recordings from January 1, 1978 onward.

Copyright Search: An investigation of ownership of some or all copyrights to a particular work, which may be conducted directly through Copyright Office records or by a specialized research firm.

Copyright Term: See **Term of Copyright.**

Cover Price: The publisher's recommended retail price of a book printed on the cover or dust jacket.

Cover Record: A second or subsequent recording of a previously recorded song, usually by a performer other than the originating artist.

Creative Control: The power to make decisions as to the content and direction of a project.

Credits: The list of names and titles of contributors to a production which appears in a film (at the beginning or end), in a theatre playbill, or on a musical recording's cover or inner sleeve, as well as in the advertising for all such media.

Cross-Collateralization: An accounting practice, established by contract, which permits a financier or distributor to charge costs incurred or revenue received from one project in which a particular financial or profit participant may have an interest, against the costs or revenues of another project in which the party may or may not also have an interest. Often applied to record agreements, whereby the label's losses from one project may be recouped from revenues from another more successful project by the same artist.

Crowdfunding: For an entertainment or other project obtained online in the form of voluntary donations (or more recently micro-investment) from the general public, sometimes incentivized by gift perks depending on donation level.

Cutouts: Product titles discontinued by the record label or home video distributor, usually due to lack of sales, which are often liquidated at deep discounts via wholesalers or specialty distributors, generally at an even more steeply reduced royalty to profit participants. See also **Remainders.**

Compilation: A Work consisting of a collection of preexisting material, assembled in a new and original manner or sequence (but with the individual components unchanged).

Cybersquatting: A form of unfair competition in which a party knowingly reserves, registers and utilizes a domain name consisting of or incorporating an existing trademark or variation on the trademark of another party for purposes of capturing unwitting consumer traffic and/or selling the right to the domain name back to the party originating the mark in other media or territories.

D

Day and Date: Variously, the simultaneous release of a film in multiple cities, in multiple territories (e.g., U.S. and Europe), or in multiple media (e.g., theatres and home video).

Day Player: An actor contracted on a day to day basis for a film or television production (usually for small roles).

Deal Memo: An abbreviated contract which contains the principal financial and executory terms pertaining to a contemplated transaction, and which usually contemplates execution of a more formal agreement containing these terms and customary applicable boilerplate provisions.

Debt Financing: The financing of entertainment productions through borrowing from banks, institutional lenders or individuals, often secured by presale agreements or other distribution contracts anticipating completion and delivery of the respective production, and/or additional recourse considerations against producer assets.

Defamation: A false statement causing damage to the reputation of an individual or entity.

Deferment: A portion of contractual compensation delayed until the occurrence of a predetermined and often conditional event (e.g., the release of a production in a particular medium) or financial performance point (e.g., recoupment of production costs by investors). A practice usually employed to reduce or control upfront cash budgets of productions.

Deliverables: The list of specific technical and documentary items that need to be assembled in an entertainment project in order for a contractual or other obligations of the financier (usually in the form of documents and attachments pre-production) or distributor (usually in the form of documents and technical elements post-distribution) to be triggered.

Delivery Date: The contractually stipulated date for delivery of completed film or television production, musical master recording or manuscript to its respective distributor (e.g., respectively, studio or network, record label or publisher).

Delivery Requirements: The contractually stipulated documentary and technical requirements constituting delivery of a motion picture or television (e.g., chain of title documents, negative, print and digital

master materials, music soundtracks, cue sheets, still photography, credit requirements, etc.).

Demo: A recording made by a songwriter or publisher to demonstrate (thus the phrase "demo") a song to a potential recording artist, by a producer or recording artist to demonstrate their work or abilities to a label, or by a novice film or television director to demonstrate their style to a prospective producer or studio.

Deposit Copy: A "best version" of an entire work the submission of which is required by the Copyright Office concurrently with a copyright registration. Traditional physical filing requirements have been superseded by electronic filing protocols for some categories of works.

Derivative Work: A new work based on or derived from one or more preexisting works that is changed, condensed, transformed or otherwise adapted (e.g., a translation, musical arrangement, dramatization, motion picture adaptation or abridgement.

Descriptive Mark: A trademark or service mark consisting of a word, picture, or other symbol that *describes* an aspect of the goods or services to which it is applied (e.g., size, color, product category, or some characteristic of its use or the result of its use), and which is not eligible for registration until the mark acquires a distinctive **secondary meaning** in association with the respective product or service.

Development: The process in the film and television industries of creating or acquiring and then expanding an idea, **pitch** or **treatment** into a finished **screenplay.**

Development Deal: An agreement between a writer, producer or director of film or television programming and a studio, network or substantial production company in which the latter picks up costs of development for one or more of the creative's projects, in exchange for a pre-negotiated position to acquire the project for production, distribution or exhibition if certain of its creative and commercial prerequisites are satisfied at the conclusion of the development process.

Directors Guild of America (DGA): The union representing film and TV directors, assistant directors and unit production managers, which sets minimum terms for salary, work conditions, benefits and amenities for its members working for signatory production companies.

Digital Download: The digitally encoded embodiment of a musical or audiovisual recording which may be required via a file transfer between a digital provider (whether an individual or entity) and a consumer via wired or wireless internet or mobile telecommunications channels.

Digital Millennium Copyright Act (DMCA): Amendments to the U.S. copyright laws, codified in 1998, that modernized the treatment of works with regard to new digital technologies and served to bring U.S. law into conformity with foreign treaty developments that had preceded the Act.

Dilution: A use of a trademark by a licensee or infringer which diminishes the value of the mark by undermining its distinctiveness or the perception of the product/service with which it is associated, whether or not the dilution actually gives rise to confusion as to the source of goods or services to which the mark is applied.

Director: The person principally charged with the creative staging of actors' performances in a work for the stage, or during principal photography of a film or television production, and who in the motion picture industry will also typically be called on to provide creative supervision over the editorial process during the postproduction of the program, culminating in its delivery to the distributor.

Director's Cut: The version of the film edited and delivered by the director, which in some instances, including those in which the director's stature is sufficient to make it a point of contractual negotiation and agreement, may be or may become the final version accepted by the producer and distributor for release.

Direct-to-Video: A film released into the video market before distribution in any other medium, either intentionally or because the production was unable to secure the theatrical or network television exhibition in a market for which it was intended.

Digital Rights Management (DRM): Technologies used to restrict or manage the conversion and thus portability of digital media content among various consumer devices.

Distribution Agreement: The agreement between a producer of entertainment programming (e.g., film, television series, or recording) and a distributor which deals with the terms governing distribution of the product. When secured prior to production of the product, this agreement may be referred to as a **"pre-sale"** or **"bankable"** distribution agreement, which may be used as collateral to secure **debt** or **equity** financing for the production.

Distribution Expenses: The direct and certain indirect costs borne by a distributor in the distribution and marketing of a musical recording, film, television production or book, which costs are usually deducted from the distributor's revenues, after deduction of distribution fees, and before funds (usually defined as **adjusted gross proceeds**) are remitted to the copyright proprietor.

Distribution Fee: The fee charged by a distributor for distributing a film, television production, book or recording.

Distribution Rights: An exclusive right (one of six) of a copyright owner to distribute copies of a work to the public via sale, lease or rental. The right is infringed by the unauthorized transfer of even a single copy of the work, whether or not lawfully manufactured, except under the **first sale doctrine** which permits a purchaser to resell a copy of a purchased work.

Distributor: A company responsible for disseminating creative works from their "manufacturers" to consumers around the world, generally through one or more additional intermediaries. In publishing, distributors get books and magazines to retailers and specialized wholesalers. In the music industry, distributors get CDs to large retail music outlets and other specialty distributors and jobbers that reach independent stores and sales outlets. In film and television, distributors (which include the major studios) deliver completed productions to theatres, television networks or stations for exhibition, and (in the form of home video devices or electronic files) to consumers as DVDs in retail outlets or as streaming or VOD media via the internet and other emerging digital delivery channels. Distributors usually charge a **distribution fee** for their services calculated as a percentage of gross revenues from their sales efforts, and will recoup some or all of their expenses from remaining revenue before remitting proceeds to the copyright proprietors whose works they service.

Domain Name: Also referred to as a **"URL"**, the words (which may include the preexisting name of a corporation, product or service) that designate a registered Internet website address.

Domestic Rights: Generally, the rights to a work for the territories of the U.S. and (English-speaking) Canada.

Dramatic Rights: The right to adapt a literary work or motion picture for the stage.

Dramatists Guild: The premiere association of professional playwrights, and the source of the Approved Production Code ("APC") guidelines for commercial stage production of dramatic works.

Droit de Suite: French for "right to follow", a right grated to artists or their heirs in some jurisdictions to participate in the proceeds of a buyer's resale of their artwork, following its initial sale by the artist.

Droit Moral: French for **"Moral Rights."** A doctrine that gives artists protections beyond those available under copyright law, generally to prevent their works from being altered without express permission (e.g., from having a film edited or colorized, from having a sculpture painted, etc.), but also from having credit removed, another artist's or author's credit added, and/or to withdraw the work from publication if the author feels it is no longer representative of his or her views or creative expression.

Drop and Pick-up: When an actor is not scheduled for continuous days during a scheduled shoot (usually marked by a gap of 10 or more days) his or her engagement may be structured as a "drop and pick up" whereby no compensation is required for the inactive hold period.

Dubbing: The process of recording additional music or dialogue to a filmed or taped production (not captured in the initial filming, etc.) to complete a soundtrack to be synchronized with the production.

DVD (Digital Versatile Disc): An optical storage device encoded with digital information that can be processed through an electronic component player to reproduce high quality audio and video signals for consumer entertainment.

E

Election to Proceed: In the motion picture and television industries, a contractual date by which a studio, network or financier must commit to further development or production of a project, failing which obligations relating to rights may revert or talent may be released.

Electronic Book (or **E-Book**): A book published in electronic formats that can be downloaded via network or wireless connectivity and read on computers or handheld digital devices such as the Kindle or iPhone.

Electronic Download: Digital, non-physical delivery of entertainment content or software via the internet or mobile media.

Electronic Sell-Through: Permanent digital downloads of television episodes or movies through online retailers.

Edition: All copies of a work (usually referencing a book, but also applicable to the reproduction of photographs or fine art) published in one or more impressions in a single format. An edition may be subsequently revised and updated, and if the revisions are substantial may be republished in a subsequent (e.g., second, third, etc.) new edition.

End Date: A negotiated date upon which a production (e.g., stage or film/television) must conclude due to conflicting commitments of a key member of the creative team, a booking of a theatre by another production, etc.

End Titles (or **End Credits**): The **credits** accorded to above and below the line personnel, technical contributors, music, etc., appearing at the end of a motion picture or television production.

Engineer: The individual in a recording studio setting primarily responsible for overseeing the technical aspects of a recording.

Enhanced E-Books: An electronic book that contains additional audio, video, and interactive content that goes beyond printed words of the electronic version of the book augmenting the traditional physical/ text only reader experience.

Entertainment Software Rating Board: The Entertainment Software Rating Board (ESRB) ratings provide concise and objective information about the content in video games and apps so consumers, especially parents, can make informed choices.

EP (for **Extended Play**): A record containing three or more compositions, but usually less than the ten or more typically found on a full recorded (long play or **LP**) album. The term originated with vinyl recordings, but continues into the digital age.

Equitable Relief: See **Injunctive Relief.**

Equity: See **Actors Equity Association.**

Equity Financing: Funding obtained from private investors (individual and/or institutional) for production or business operations through sale of stock in a corporation or membership interests in a limited liability company, whereby investors assume the risk of profit or loss (and which investment is usually subordinate to **debt financing).**

Errors and Omissions Insurance: Insurance covering claims against producers, distributors and related parties (including costs of defense as well as of adverse judgments) in intellectual property matters, including such causes of action as copyright infringement, defamation, invasion of privacy, etc.

Escalation Clause: A contractual provision that establishes an increase in a rights holder's or creative artist's compensation terms (whether fixed or royalty based) in the event that certain contingencies occur (e.g., an award acknowledgement for a book or production, box office performance for a film or stage production, units sold for a book or musical recording, length of run for a stage production, etc.).

Exclusive Rights: Under §106 of the Copyright Act, each of six activities reserved to a copyright proprietor, including (i) the right to reproduce copies or phono-records, (ii) to prepare derivative works, (iii) to distribute copies of works or phono-records to the public by sale, rental or loan, (iv) to perform the work (excluding sound recordings), (v) to display the work publicly, and (vi) in the case of sound recordings, to perform the work publicly by means of digital audio transmission.

Exclusive Songwriting Contract: An agreement restricting a songwriter for a defined period of time from writing for more than a single publisher, typically agreed to by the writer in exchange for one or more advance payments for the proceeds of such writing.

Exclusivity Clause: A contractual provision prohibiting a party from entering into a conflicting or competing relationship with a third party (e.g., an acting contract that prohibits a television series actor from appearing in any other television series, or a musical artist from recording for another label, etc.).

Executive Producer: A stage, film or recording credit typically given the individual responsible for coordinating the financing or other packaging of a production. In the television arena, the credit is commonly accorded the writer/producer responsible for creating and executing the production.

Exploit: The process of seeking and administering the commercialization of a creative work.

F

Fair Use: Under copyright law, a defense to a charge of infringement when a portion of a work is included without permission in a new work. Often but not always in the context of a critical or academic review or commentary, but such use may also appear in a new commercial work (e.g., music sampling). Analysis by the courts generally hinges on the balancing of four criteria: the purpose and character of the disputed use (e.g., is it "transformative"); the nature of the copyrighted work; the importance (quality and/or quantity) of the portion used in relation to the underlying work as a whole; and the potential impact of the purported "fair use" on demand for and value of the appropriated work.

False Light: The portrayal of a person or circumstances in a negative or untrue manner that is misleading or false.

Favored Nations (also **Most Favored Nations** or **MFN**): A negotiated accommodation by which one contracting party (typically a produce or distributor) assures the other (e.g., artist's such as an actor, author or musical artist) that no other third party contracts for a particular production or endeavor will contain terms more favorable to another party than those contained in the artist's own agreement. In a motion picture production, favored nations assurances to an actor might for example extend to salary, credit characteristics, bonuses and profit participations or the size of and amenities placed in dressing rooms.

Feature Film: A narrative motion picture, typically 90 to 120 minutes in length, generally intended for release in movie theatres but which may be intended for television or direct to home video exploitation.

Federal Communications Commission (FCC): The independent United States government agency charged with overseeing and regulating telecommunications involving telephone, radio, broadcast, cable and satellite television and other forms of wired and wireless electronic media.

Federal Trade Commission (FTC): is an independent agency of the United States government, established in 1914 by the Federal Trade Commission Act. Its principal mission is the promotion of consumer protection and the elimination and prevention of anticompetitive business practices, such as coercive monopoly.

File-sharing: The exchange of digital information via transfer and downloads over the Internet and private networks, whether using peer-to-peer (P2P) or other protocols, and through which frequently unauthorized exchange of copyrighted video or musical materials occurs.

Film Rental: That portion (with fifty percent being standard) of movie theatre box office ticket sale receipts the theatre owner pays a motion picture distributor for the right to exhibit the film.

Final Cut: The final edited and mixed (i.e., sound and visuals) version of a motion picture.

Final Draft: The complete version of a manuscript for a book/article, or motion picture or television production, accepted for publication/production.

First Amendment: The First Amendment to the United States Constitution grants the rights of free speech and freedom of the press relevant to limitations on expression and censorship in each of the entertainment industries.

First-Dollar Gross: A negotiated form of contingent participation in Gross Proceeds before deduction of distribution fees, expenses, or investor/production cost recoupment (but usually permitting expenditures for checking and collection costs, residuals and taxes, and some deferments.

First-look: A contractual arrangement whereby a publisher (in the case of a writer) or studio, network or distributor (in the case of a screenwriter, producer or director) requires that artist to furnish the company with the right to review that artist's prospective project(s) for acquisition before their submission to any other entity for such purpose.

First Monies: Generally describes the adjusted gross revenues available to producers from the distributors of a film or television production (or in the case of a sound recording a label or distributor) from which deferred contractual fee obligations (**"deferments"**) to talent or contributors to the production and investor repayment occurs (not necessarily in that order, subject to contract) prior to the calculation of "profit" on the respective production.

First Negotiation Right: The contractual right to make or receive the first offer to be entertained by a party offering defined rights or services, within a negotiated time frame, and typically linked to another related transaction between the parties for rights or services which could be affected by the unrestricted disposition of such rights or services.

First Refusal Right: A mechanism supplementing a first negotiation right which may not have resulted in an agreement between a party offering rights or services and a prospective buyer of such rights/services, which gives the buyer the right to match the first bona fide third party offer that the seller is otherwise willing to accept in connection with the subject matter of the right. See also **Last Refusal Right.**

First Run: The initial exhibition cycle (domestic and/or foreign) of a new motion picture, before its release to television or home video markets, and in some cases, return to theatres. In the television arena, the term denotes the initial network exhibition of a production (or its initial airing via "first run" syndication on independent stations) before the production or series enters cable or syndicated television markets for a second cycle of exhibition. See also **Syndication.**

First Sale Doctrine: An exception to the exclusive right of a copyright owner to distribute copies of a protected work, permitting a purchaser to control subsequent (re)sale of a single purchased copy,

Fiscal Sponsor / Fiscal Agent: A qualified, tax-exempt entity used as the conduit for donations earmarked for project funding, which if qualified may enable the donor to obtain a same-year tax deduction for the gift as a charitable contribution (rather than as an investment in an otherwise worthwhile project with little chance of profit and a longer "write off" trajectory as to potential tax losses).

Fixed in a Tangible Medium of Expression: As defined under the Copyright Act, **copyright** attaches to an original literary, artistic or intellectual work as soon as it is "fixed in a tangible medium of expression", i.e., written down or recorded with sufficient permanence to enable it to be perceived, reproduced or communicated for a period of more than transitory duration.

Flat Fee: A pricing structure that establishes a single fixed fee for a service, regardless of usage, time involved or other pricing variables.

Floor: A contractual "minimum" fee a buyer offers the seller of rights or services over which certain contingent fees or payments may be earned based on, in the case of motion picture productions, such factors as budget or commercial performance, or in the case of publishing, the minimum royalty guaranty irrespective of sales. The term may also be used to express the minimum sale or purchase price that will be accepted by an author or offered by a publisher in an **auction** of book rights. It is further used to describe certain minimum percentage levels to which distributors will accede in their fees or cost recoupments under various negotiated **breakeven** scenarios in accounting for net proceeds of a motion picture or television series revenue.

Force Majeure: Literally "greater force", the occurrence of a force majeure clause in a contract may suspend a parties' performance obligations or liability while unavoidable circumstances beyond their control interrupt a production or prevent fulfillment of an executory obligation (e.g., hurricane at a film location, fire or labor strike at a theatre).

Foreign Rights: The right to produce and exploit a work outside the territory of its creation or initial intended exploitation, such as the right to translate and/or publish and manufacture a book abroad, and/or to distribute a motion picture or television production or musical recording in a foreign territory.

Foreign Sales Agent: A person or entity representing the licensing and sale of distribution rights to motion pictures, television programs and/or publishing rights to books (including **translation** rights) in foreign territories.

Format: A plan for the organization of a television series production (e.g., half hour sitcom, one-hour drama, game show, reality show, etc.). In publishing, a work's material form or layout of a publication. In film, television and music, the technical characteristics of the recording or distribution medium (e.g., CD, DVD-Audio; iTunes or MP3; standard or Blu-Ray DVD; etc.).

Four-Walling: A method of promoting a concert or distributing a film involving the rental of a theatre by a promoter or the distributor. who in turn assumes responsibility for production (in the case of a live performance) and/or promotion, and where the theatre owner typically derives only a flat fee for the rental rather than a participation in ticket sales.

Free Goods: Copies of books, games, CDs or DVDs distributed as promotional items to stimulate sales, and/or as a means of providing an indirect discount to wholesale and retail resellers based on the volume of units purchased (thus reducing the marginal costs of an entire order). Manufacturing costs are generally deducted in royalty accounting statements for such items, even though no income is generated.

Free Television: The advertiser (or in the case of public television, underwriter) supported transmission of television programming over the air to viewers, including in the U.S. via national broadcast networks such as ABC, CBS, Fox, and NBC through transmissions by their local owned and operated and/or affiliated stations, and/or via unaffiliated independent stations.

Free to Play: Games available to consumers for free, which monetize the game through optional in-game micro-transaction purchases, or through advertising. See **Advergames**.

Free Video on Demand: Access to digital content without a direct charge, subscription (SVOD) fee, or requirement of viewing ads.

G

General Partners (or **General Managers**): The individuals or entities charged with day to day operating and principal business decision responsibilities of a **partnership** or **limited liability company**, respectively. In the financing and production of motion pictures and stage plays, these entitles are generally run by the producers or executive producers of the respective production, who use these entities as vehicles for securing investment and producing the production, and who will serve in these capacities on behalf of the entity (as well as the respective production) while the investors participate as **limited partners** (or members of the **limited liability company**).

Generic: A common descriptive name for a class or category of products or services (e.g., "portable music player") that may consequently not (without attachment to additional distinguishing words, logos, etc.) be claimed as a trademark or service mark due to its lack of distinctiveness.

Good WM: The value which emerges over time from the commercial reputation of a business, service or product, and which by attachment to a trademark is used as a reference point in determining the damages which may be suffered from an **infringement** of a **trademark**.

Grand Rights: The dramatic performance rights to use a musical composition (usually song and lyrics) as the basis for telling a story on the stage or in film (e.g., as the basis for an opera or musical theatre production, more particularly illustrated by the use of the Who's *"Tommy"* as the basis for a stage musical).

Green Light: The formal, executive decision by studio, distributor, network or otherwise ultimately responsible financier to actively produce a film or television program following its successful development and packaging.

Gross after Break-Even: Revenues from the exploitation of an entertainment property (usually a film, stage or musical production) available for distribution to participants at this accounting level after a certain level of costs or revenue (defined by negotiation) is surpassed.

Gross Margin: In book publishing, musical recording and home video distribution, the difference between revenue from sales and the cost of goods sold. Note the publisher's/distributor's calculation may include certain operating and overhead expenses of manufacture and warehousing, while the wholesaler or retail reseller will use a calculation concerned with a product's retail pricing less costs of goods (adjusted for discounts and returns).

Gross Participation (or **Gross Deal**)**:** A royalty calculated at the highest available level of revenue for an entertainment production, before deduction or recapture of the material costs of producing or distributing/monetizing the production (including without limitation investor recoupment), and which is available, if at all, only to the super star echelon of creative talent participating in such transactions.

Gross Proceeds (or **Gross Receipts**)**:** All moneys actually received by a distributor from exploitation of an entertainment property, from all contemplated media in the territory(s) for which exploitation is authorized, before deductions for distribution fees, distribution and sales expenses, costs of product manufacturing and/or the cost of producing the underlying creative property.

Guaranty: A formal promise or assurance that certain conditions will be fulfilled and such assurance will be guaranteed by specific performance and/or by payment of funds by a guarantor (often a financier, producer or distributor, or a bonding company on their behalf).

H

Hardcover (or **Hardback**) **Book:** An edition of a book with a cloth or finished cardboard cover which is the general format of first edition trade and text book publishing, (as distinguished from and usually preceding the publication of a paperback edition of the same work), generally commanding a higher price and consequently royalty to authors than their paperback (whether trade or mass-market) counterparts.

Hard Floor: A negotiated minimum below which a producer's or contributing artist's percentage of the backend revenues from a project is contractual shielded from reduction below a certain negotiated percentage.

Holdback: A contractual covenant whereby a party holding rights or offering services agrees with another party not to do so, usually to enable that party to successfully launch another production in which the party agreeing to the holdback has contributed other (and often related) rights or services. For example, the author of a book on which a film is to be based may agree to a holdback for a set number of years before the rights to a sequel novel (whether or not already written) may be offered as the basis for a subsequent sequel motion picture).

House: The seating area in a theatre or concert venue, with the house capacity determining the economics of productions at a particular location.

House Nut: The weekly operating expenses of a live performance or movie theater (as distinguished from the costs of mounting a production in the venue),

Hyphenate Personnel: Persons who fulfill two or more major roles in a motion picture or television production, such as writer-director, writer-producer or actor-director.

I

Idea-Expression Dichotomy: The fundamental concept of intellectual law that copyright protects only a specific, fixed expression of an idea — and not the idea itself.

Indemnity: A contractual obligation by which one party agrees to assume the costs of another's defense from certain claims or risks established by negotiation, and/or to make that party whole from any losses or damages that may be suffered as a consequence of the specified circumstances (which usually relate to the breach or default of the obligations, representations and/or warranties of the party providing the indemnity).

Indie (or Independent): A common reference to a company in the business of publishing and distributing books, or producing and/or distributing records, film and/or television programming, which is not directly affiliated with a substantial (or so-called "major") corporate enterprise in that or a related industry. See also, **Major Studio.**

Inducement Letter: A letter of personal assurance and guarantee by an individual artist or person that she or he will perform all of the contractual promises that their personal business "loan out" entity (such as a corporation or limited liability company) is committing them to deliver in an entertainment related agreement.

Infringement: A misappropriation or other violation of an exclusive right under copyright or trademark law. In the case of copyright, infringement may include reproduction, adaptation, distribution, public performance, or pubic display of a protected work without the authorization of the author or owner. In the case of trademarks, infringement involves the unauthorized use of another's mark to deceive, confuse, or mislead others as to identify or source of goods or services.

Injunctive Relief (or Equitable Relief): A court-ordered act, or prohibition against an act or condition, that is provided in order to protect a party's status quo interest from damages should an agreement be breached, often sought or imposed where payments alone cannot adequately compensate a party for prospective damages (or the party in anticipated or actual breach may be unlikely to compensate the injured party for such damages).

In Perpetuity: Used in contracts to define unlimited duration (e.g., for the survival of an agreement or the grant of rights.).

Intellectual Property: The tangible expression of an intellectual or creative idea which may be eligible for legal protection under laws of copyright, trademark, patent, trade secrets, unfair competition the right of publicity, so called moral rights, etc.

Intent to Use Application: A preliminary filing option for federal trademark and service mark protection, available in the U.S. since 1989, which enables the applicant to in effect "reserve" the intended mark based upon a declaration of good faith intention to use the mark on defined goods or services, and requiring a subsequent supplemental filing to confirm the actual use of the mark in interstate commerce within a defined period of time.

Intercreditor Agreement: A document setting forth the respective rights of all secured parties in the common film collateral which will regulate the provision of loans by other lenders to the production and the grant of liens to secure them.

International Affiance of Theatrical Stage Employees Union (TATSE): Union representing a large group of motion picture and television "below-the-line" personnel categories.

International Film and Television Affiance (IFTA): A trade association of independent (i.e., non-studio affiliated) motion picture distributors, and successor organization to the American Film Marketing Association (AFMA).

International Standard Book Number (ISBN): The universal unique ten-digit identifier for each commercially published book, appearing in both numeric and bar code form in virtually all contemporary publications, and which identifies country of origin, publisher and each unique title for tracking purposes through the entire chain of distribution, sales (and returns).

International Standard Serials Number (ISSN): The ISBN equivalent for journal and magazine publishing.

Internegative: A color negative made from a color positive.

Interparty Agreement: Financing documents among the key parties to a project (financier, distributor, production company, bonding company) that affect the payments of minimum guarantees by: (a) assigning payment from the owner to a financier; (b) waiving any conditions to payment other than delivery; and (c) limiting the number of items that must be delivered to those that a completion guarantor will guarantee.

Interpositives: A positive duplicate of a film used for manufacturing additional film prints for theatrical exhibition.

Invasion of Privacy: A tort that encompasses a range of wrongful conduct violating the rights of an individual, including unjustified appropriation of person's name, image or likeness; publicizing of private facts pertaining to another person absent justification; placing a person in a false and derogatory light without adequate consideration (or via intentional abuse) of pertinent facts; and/or intrusion into another's reasonable expectation of privacy in a private setting by eavesdropping or other forms of surveillance.

J

Jobber: A distributor of books and recorded media (CDs; DVDs) who acts as a middle man between wholesalers and smaller retail vendors in the delivery of mass market product for sale.

Joint Authors: A category of authorship under copyright law describing two or more collaborating creators who intend to merge their respective contributions into a single, jointly owned work and copyright, resulting in each having the non-exclusive right to license and exploit the work, subject to a duty to account to the co-author for profits, as "tenants in common."

K

Key Art: Artwork used in creating motion picture posters and advertising.

Key Man Provision (or Key Person Provision): A contractual provision that permits a party to modify or terminate an agreement if an individual deemed material to the other party's performance becomes unavailable to render services by virtue of death, disability or the termination of his relationship with the other party to the contract (e.g., an artist may insist on the right to terminate an agreement with a management company or an agency, if the principal individual agent or manager responsible for servicing the artist leaves that company's employ).

Kill Fee: A negotiated "cancellation" payment made to an artist if the artist's services are not used or are cancelled (for reasons other than the artist's breach or default) during or following a specified time frame.

L

Laboratory Pledgeholder Agreement: Agreement among a project's producer, financiers and distributor establishing where and how the physical elements of the film or video materials may be stored, acknowledging the lenders' priority interests in the physical elements of the materials, establishing that the controlling lender has the right to give instructions to the laboratory on the release of the materials, and confirming who may otherwise have access to the physical elements of the production held by the lab.

Lanham Act: The Lanham Act (also known as the Trademark Act of 1946) is the federal statute that governs trademarks, service marks, and unfair competition. It was passed by Congress on July 5, 1946 and signed into law by President Harry Truman.

Last Refusal Right: An agreement granting a prospective buyer the right to pre-empt any otherwise final third party offer to acquire rights, engage services, etc., within a negotiated time frame, by matching the financial and/or other terms of the offer otherwise acceptable to the party subject to the last refusal right. This right is typically invoked after the parties have failed to reach agreement in the course of the exercise of a **First Negotiation Right,** and where the Buyer elected not to exercise a **First Refusal Right** which the Seller in turn failed to conclude on the terms originally proposed, or which has attracted new terms or an additional offer. See also **First Negotiation Right** and **First Refusal Right.**

Letter of Intent: A letter from one party to another confirming interest (which may or may not be binding, depending on intent and drafting) in participating in a specified transaction, which may include an actor or director's confirmation to a producer of interest in a motion picture production (which will usually recite conditions relating to later agreement as to scheduling, compensation or other conditions), and/or a financier's expression of interest in underwriting of a production (likewise subject to certain conditions, which may include the concurrent talent and director attachment or satisfaction of other conditions).

Libel: Defamation appearing in a published writing (as distinguished from an oral communication, which instead constitutes **slander**).

Library of Congress: The national library of the United States, located in Washington D.C., which acts as the country's primary repository of works registered for copyright.

License: A limited grant of rights (e.g., as to usage, term or territory) to a work protected by copyright, which may be exclusive or non-exclusive depending on negotiation and context (and when exclusive the "licensee" of the exclusive right will be entitled to enforce the copyright against infringers of the licensed right(s).

Life Rights Agreement: An agreement for purchase of rights to portray someone's personal life story (or portions thereof) in a film, television production or on stage. The rights may be obtained independently, or in association with the acquisition of rights to the subject's autobiography, or an independently written biographical work on the subject.

Limited Liability Company (LLC): A form of doing business, established by statute, which combines the limited liability of a corporation with the flow through tax structure of a partnership.

Limited Partnership (LP): A form of doing business in which general partners initiate and control the partnership's business, which is, in turn, financed by investors who participate as limited partners with no control over the day-to-day conduct of partnership business, and who consequently can enjoy limited liabilities beyond their investment. Commonly used as the vehicle for financing and producing motion picture and live stage productions prior to the more recent advent of the **limited liability company (LLC),** which offers additional protection against participant liability from certain third party claims.

Line Producer: The personnel in a film or television project who supervise the day-to-day **below the line** aspects of preproduction, production and post-production (a position subject to DGA jurisdiction on projects produced by that guild's signatory producers).

List Price: The publisher's or distributor's recommended list sales price for a book, CD or DVD, often printed or affixed to the product itself.

Literary Agent: a person or entity acting on behalf of the author to seek publication and other subsidiary rights exploitation (e.g., film, television and/or stage adaptation) of their client's literary work,

including negotiation of contracts and management of collections, usually for a commission equal to fifteen percent (for domestic rights) to twenty percent (for foreign rights) of the author's revenues from such undertakings.

Literary Work: A work generally consisting of prose or poetry in written form, generally intended for initial publication in print.

Live Stage Rights: The right to adapt a creative work or life story for performance perform on a stage in front of a live audience.

Loan-Out Company (also, **Personal Services Corporation**): A company, usually a Subchapter-S entity, through which highly paid creative artists provide their services to productions (as "employees" of the "lending" company, which then "loan" services to the producing entity), which provides both tax benefits and certain limited liability protection to the artist.

Location Agreement: Agreement obtained by producers of audiovisual works (motion pictures, television programs and/or commercials) to utilize (and feature) a physical location in the respective production.

Logo Credit / Company Credit: A valuable billing accorded to high level production companies (or the Loanout companies of producers or important creative talent such as directors) in the form of a logo which appears in the opening and/or end credits in a film, television or other audio-visual production, or if text-rendered may take the form of "in association with", "an X-company production", etc.

Long Form Agreement: A comprehensive written agreement, commonly generated by legal counsel, that is intended to "dot the T s' and cross the 'T's'" of a shorter document which may initiate a transaction (e.g., a "term sheet", "heads of agreement" or "deal memo"), through the addition of substantive supplemental terms and conditions (often referred to as **"boilerplate terms"**).

Long-form TV: Broadcast productions exceeding half hour or hour--long series formats, such as made for television movies and/or so called miniseries.

Lyricist: The writer of the words to a song.

M

Main Titles: Reference to the placement of credits in the opening sequences of a motion picture, as distinguished from credits appearing at the conclusion of the picture (i.e., the **end titles**).

Major Studio: Traditionally, any one of the prominent Hollywood motion picture production and distribution companies which controlled their own production facilities, now generally regarded as including only The Walt Disney Company, Paramount, Sony, 20th Century Fox, Universal, and Warner Bros.

Manager: An individual or company which acts as a creative artist's general representative in career planning and coordination, and who for successful clients will often coordinate or oversee the work of agents, lawyers, accountants and other professional and personal services providers. See also **Personal Manager; Tour Manager, Road Manager.**

Mass Market Paperback: A small format book with a soft paper (as opposed to a hard bound) cover, which may represent an original publication or a new edition of a work previously issued in hardback or trade paperback formats, and which is distributed through traditional newsstand channels (e.g., airports, grocery stores and drug stores), in addition to bookstores outlets).

Master: The final physical embodiment of an edited and complete film, video or sound recording (or their digital equivalents) from which subsequent copies are duplicated or manufactured.

Master Use: In the music industry, the use of a preexisting actual sound recording or "master" as a sample incorporated in another recording or performance. In film and television, "master use" represents the inclusion of a preexisting recording in an independent audio-visual work. Each typically requires a license under copyright law.

Mechanical License: Authorization from a music publisher or songwriter controlling copyright in a musical composition for its use in sound recordings (i.e., most notably records and compact discs). The term originated in the "mechanical" process of manufacturing records.

Mechanical Rights Organization: A company (e.g., the Harry Fox Agency or the American Mechanical Rights Agency) which represents music publishers and songwriters in the licensing and collection of royalties from the mechanical reproduction of their catalogues.

Mechanical Royalties: Fees paid by a record company in consideration of a **mechanical license.**

Merchandising Rights: The right to license, manufacture and distribute products (e.g., clothing, toys, posters, etc.) featuring the names and likeness of entertainers and/or characters, titles or events appearing in a motion picture, television production, stage play and/or book.

Mezzanine / Gap Financing: In motion pictures, a form of intermediate financing structured either as debt (typically an unsecured and subordinated note or the right to convert the debt to equity or preferred stock) whereby a producer completes the film finance package by procuring a **loan** secured by the film's then unsold territories and rights.

Middleware Providers: Providers of a certain type of software used to connect two other software and/or hardware applications by passing data between them.

Minimum Basic Agreement (MBA): The production agreements established (and periodically renegotiated) between the major Hollywood talent unions (e.g., SAG, DGA and WGA) and the studios and producers of motion picture and television productions and commercials, which contain the "minimum" terms of engagement for the respective union's personnel on the producer's productions.

Minimum Guarantees: An agreed upon fee or payment that will serve as the minimum amount payable for a certain transaction (a **"floor"**) for rights or services, even if the otherwise negotiated calculation of such payment (a percentage of certain revenues, for example) would result in a lesser payment than the minimum guarantee.

Minimum Release Commitment: A negotiated and agreed upon contractual obligation of a distributor of an entertainment production to distribute to or exhibit in a minimum number of venues, territories or media, usually for a minimum amount of time and within a certain allotted time period (e.g., to 500 screens in 50 markets within six months of theatrical release), with repercussions to the distributor for failure to do so.

Modified Adjusted Gross Receipts (MAGR): The monies if any, remaining after deducting from gross revenues certain defined expenses, usually in a particular order of priority. For example, a film or television agreement may provide for modified adjusted gross receipts that reflect deduction from gross revenues of expenses such as distribution fees, distribution expenses, production costs and interest, following which MAGR is available for distribution to contractual profit participants.

Moral Rights: See **Droit Moral.**

Motion Picture Association of America (MPAA): Lobbying, advocacy and administrative alliance of the major motion picture studios.

Music Publisher: An individual or entity that undertakes the commercial exploitation of songs by soliciting, issuing licenses for, and then collecting resulting revenue from **mechanical, synchronization, performing, print** and other authorized uses of songs, typically in exchange for an assigned percentage of the songwriter's copyright interest in and royalties from such exploitation.

Musical Work (also referred to as a **Musical Composition** or **Song**): Work eligible for copyright protection, expressed in musical notation or sounds (which may include lyrics), and which may be embodied and fixed in physical objects constituting either "copies" (e.g., sheet music) eligible for a music work copyright or "phono-records" (e.g., records, tapes and compact discs) eligible for a sound recording copyright.

N

National Academy of Recording Arts and Sciences (NARAS): A recording industry professional society representing business, technical and creative persons, and which producers the annual Grammy Awards.

National Association of Music Merchants (NAMM): Musical equipment manufacturers trade association, which has been formally renamed the International Music Products Association.

National Association of Record Merchandisers (NARM): The trade association for music retailers.

Negative Cost: The direct and sometimes by contract indirect (i.e., overhead and interest) cost of producing a motion picture, including its development, pre-production, production, and post production (but excluding costs associated with distribution), and which is a reference to a film "negative" from which prints will be made, rather than to a mathematical "negative" number.

Negative Pickup: An agreement between a film producer and a distributor in which the distributor agrees to acquire the motion picture on its completion and delivery (in compliance with a negotiated set of delivery elements) as of an agreed upon deadline, in exchange for a pre-fixed payment (the contract for which the producer will generally seek to use as collateral for production financing prior to production of the subject motion picture). Late delivery or delivery of a picture which fails to comply with contractual specifications (whether creative or technical) will result in the distributor being freed from the obligation to accept and pay for distribution rights to the picture.

Net Pricing: A method of determining a wholesale price for books, CDs or DVDs after all discounts and allowances to the wholesaler or reseller are calculated, without reference to a suggested retail price (which may be omitted from the product enabling the wholesaler or retailer to set its own price to the consumer).

Net Profits (or **Net Proceeds**): That portion of the financial proceeds from exploitation of an entertainment property (whether a film, television program, stage production, book game or musical recording, which remain after all expenses allowable under the parties' contract (which may include fees and expenses for distribution, advertising and marketing, production and manufacturing, other preferentially paid royalties or participations calculated as deferments or payments from gross or adjusted gross proceeds, etc. are calculated and deducted, and which is usually expressed as a numerical percentage of one hundred percent (e.g., 5% of 100%) of the net profit or net proceeds of the respective project or production.

New Edition: The republication of an existing title incorporating substantial new material (generally ten percent or more), or republication of an out-of-print title.

Notice: For purposes of copyright and trademark law, indication affixed to (i) a work subject to copyright protection (i.e., the symbol "0" or the abbreviation "Copr" or the word "Copyright followed by the year of first publication and the name of the author or copyright proprietor), (ii) an object for which trademark protection (identified by the mark "TM") or (iii) materials identifying a service mark (identified by the mark ("℠") or the word "Service mark") (or the symbol ® following successful registration of such a mark).

Novelization: The adaptation of a motion picture screenplay into narrative prose for publication as a "novel."

O

Off-Broadway: A New York City metropolitan area theatre located outside the Broadway theatre district and seating from 100 to 500.

Off-Network (or **Off-Net**): Television programming exhibited via syndicated station groups, whether in its initial television exhibition or following initial exhibition via a national broadcast or cable network. See also **Syndication.**

On-Demand: Digital services which permit a consumer to circumvent a viewing schedule and access selected content at any time.

On-Demand Book (or **On-Demand Printing**): The manufacture of a single copy of a book in response to customer order (i.e., "just in time"), now available from publishers of certain scientific and technical works for which demand is limited, but anticipated to become increasingly common for trade and other general publications to reduce the risk and costs of overprinting and unsold publisher inventories.

On-or-About: Used to describe a start date for principal photography of a film or television production which entitles the producer to give an actor 24 hours advance notice to for an actual start on, one day before or one day after the "on or about" date.

On Spec (or Speculative) Screenplay: An original screenplay written by a writer for his or her own account absent a producer's commission for the work, or for a producer for no upfront fee, with the expectation of compensation if the project is later financed and produced.

One-Sheet: A standard (usually 27" by 40") promotional movie poster, displayed in lobbies or showcases on a theatre's exterior. It also describes a promotional one-page summary of the film or recording (including information pertaining to commercial release) included in press kits and marketing materials.

Option: A limited right, exercisable within a defined time period, to acquire certain additional negotiated rights to a creative work, life story, etc., for further exploitation, which is dependent on the occurrence of one or more contingencies (which may be nothing more than the party holding the option providing notice of its election to complete the full acquisition of contemplated rights, accompanied by a negotiated payment or fulfillment of other executory contingencies.

Option/Purchase Agreement: An agreement outlining the terms of an option and its exercise, and which usually provides the prospective buyer with the exclusive right to further develop the underlying rights/property during the pendency of the option.

Option Fee: The fee paid to acquire an option a literary or other creative property, which may be structured in sequential steps over an extended option term, and which based on negotiation may or may not be treated as applicable against the exercise price or other subsequent payment obligations.

Out of Print: When a book is "sold out" from a publisher's physical inventory or catalogue, and is no longer available to buyers, it is "out of print", and in many contracts the author can terminate the agreement if the book is not put back in print promptly after notice to the publisher of this circumstance and demand for a further printing (a certain to be challenged by the digital distribution of books and similar materials).

Output Deal: An agreement between a distributor and a supplier (typically a producer or production company) of film, video, musical or other entertainment programming that entitles the distributor to exclusive access to supplier's prospective productions, generally in exchange for some advance or other financial consideration, and usually for a defined time period and defined category(s) of productions.

Out Takes: Scenes filmed during production that are not utilized in the final edited production of a motion picture or television program. (In pre-tape and pre-digital times, these described lengths of negative film literally "left on the cutting room floor.")

Over Budget: A reference to those costs which exceed projected expenses in the production of an entertainment product or program.

Overhead Charges: The indirect costs of studio and/or distributor business operations, including offices, general personnel, and other G&A expenditures, which they (seek to) charge, on the basis of a negotiated accounting definition, against proceeds of productions, usually as an override equal to a percentage of production budgets but which may be claimed against total revenues.

P

Package: A term used to describe the basic creative building blocks assembled for a film or television production (which may include screenplay, talent, director, and producer, among others), or for a book (author, artwork, editor, marketing strategy), on which the election to finance, produce and distribute or publish the work prior to its production may be based.

Packager: An individual or company which assembles a viable creative package for a film or television production, or a book for publication.

Packaging Agent: An agency that initiates (or may otherwise hold substantial control over) a film or television project which must rely primarily on writers, directors and/or actors the agency represents (one or more of whom will be of the essence to the project), enabling the agency to control additional placements (and leverage agency **packaging fees**) from the production's financiers or buyer.

Packaging Fee: See Agency Packaging Fee.

Paperback (Softcover) Rights: The rights to publish a book in a softcover edition, whether as its initial printing in a language or territory, or following a prior hardcover publication, and which may be extend to trade paperback (higher quality), mass market, or both.

Pari Passu: An accounting term describing equal, concurrent payments to two or more participants entitled to compensation under a net proceeds, royalty or other definition (as distinguished from possible payment to each in sequence).

Parody: A literary or artistic work that mimics the style or character of another work or its author for comic or satirical effect.

Participation: The negotiated contingent payments to a person or entity (each, a **"Participant"**) entitled to compensation calculated on the basis of variously the gross, adjusted gross, or net profit or proceeds of an entertainment production.

Patent & Trademark Office: Organization within the U.S. Department of Commerce charged with administering and processing Trademark and Service mark registrations.

Payola: A bribe encouraging a radio station manager, program director or on air host to favor a particular artist, label or more commonly song in play rotation, intended to drive sales of the recording.

Pay-or-Play: An offer to a creative or performing artist (film, concert, recording project, etc.) that guarantees payment of negotiated compensation irrespective of whether the artist's services are actually utilized in a production which may or may not be staged or produced.

Pay-Per-View: Transmission of film or television programming via satellite or cable television to viewers who use a decoder box or other interface to select the program to be viewed and are charged on a program by program basis. See also **Video on Demand.**

Pay (Subscription) Television: Television programming channels (e.g., HBO, Showtime), delivered by cable or satellite, access to which is restricted to paying subscribers via decoder boxes that control signal access.

Pension, Health & Welfare (PH&W): Contractual fringe benefits payable to members of certain entertainment industry unions and guilds based upon their engagement for services in productions falling under the jurisdiction of their membership organization's collective bargaining agreements with producers, typically calculated on the basis of wages paid.

Per Diem: A guild mandated or otherwise contractually established allowance for food and incidentals provided to performers and crew working on a film, television or touring production (music or theatre), usually calculated on a daily (i.e., per diem) basis.

Performance: Copyright conveys to a creator or subsequent owner of a work the exclusive right to "perform the copyrighted work publicly", which may take the form of reciting or rendering the work through live presentation by actors, dancers, or musicians before a live audience, or the projection, broadcast or other transmission of recorded versions of such presentations (excluding for purposes of copyright, the pictorial representation of sculptural or pictorial work, or transmission of **sound recordings**).

Performance Royalties: Monies earned by a song's copyright owner (composer and/or publisher) from its license for radio, film, television and other forms of public performance.

Performing Rights Society (or **Performing Rights Organization**): The associations or companies, including **ASCAP**, BMI and SESAC in the U.S., that issue performing rights licenses for radio, TV, and public commercial establishments like clubs, restaurants and bars, track public performances, collect performing license revenues, and distribute those revenues to the compositions copyright owners (i.e., songwriters and music publishers).

Permanent Digital Downloads: Entertainment content (such as a sound recording or a motion picture or television episode) downloaded electronically by the consumer and which may be retained and played by the consumer on his/her/their own devices on a permanent basis.

Permissions: An expression describing the granting of limited special use rights to a limited excerpt of a quotation from a book, and/or clips from a musical recording or film/television program, for inclusion in another book or production (and which may require payment to the owner/licensor of a negotiated fee). See, also **Clip License.**

Personal Manager: A person engaged to guide the career of an artist or performer, often for the successful artist in a "chief of staff" capacity coordinating the efforts of agent, lawyer, accountant or business manager/accountant, personnel staff and more, generally in exchange for a fee based on the artist's gross revenue for a negotiated term of years (and then typically at a 15% to 20% of gross income rate).

Personal Services Corporation: See **Loan-Out Company.**

Phono-records: As defined under U.S., copyright law, the physical objects (e.g., audiotapes, vinyl records, CDs and/or silicon chips) embodying sound recordings of copyrighted songs. (Note: Recordings of audio-visual works are not considered phono-records.)

Pilot: A (usually) full length episode of a prospective television series produced to test the viability of the concept and its execution (story, writing, casting, etc.) before commitments are given for a more substantial production order.

Pilot Commitment: A commitment by a television network to order, and pay its share, for the production of a pilot or a very limited number

of series episodes to test viewers' interest in the project before the network commits to a full season or larger number of episodes.

Piracy: The unauthorized and illegal duplication and distribution of copyrighted works or trademarked goods.

Pitch: The presentation of the core concept(s) of a creative work to a prospective collaborator or buyer, orally or in writing, and/or the core concepts of such a presentation, themselves, usually expressed in a highly abbreviated, summary form.

Platforming: A release strategy for a motion picture in which a limited number of prints are initially distributed in a small number of theaters in a particular locale or region, with the intention of an expanded rollout to more theaters and regions as the film gains critical or commercial acclaim.

Player: Common reference to an Actor in the theatre industry.

Playwright: The writer of a work for theater, whose rights and influence over the production of the work extends to production (unlike the typical role of writers in motion pictures or television).

Podcast: Digital delivery of sound and/or video file representing a produced radio or television program or its equivalent which can be accessed, downloaded, and recorded to portable digital music device (including an iPod — hence the name) or computer for immediate or delayed listening or viewing.

Points: The percentage participation an artist or other profit or royalty participant is entitled to receive from the proceeds of a production, whether records, games, books, film/TV or stage.

Point of Sale Merchandising: Display material provided by distributors or books, games, CDs or DVDs to retailers for display in the vicinity of check-out counters supporting sale of selected titles.

Possessory Credit: A film or television credit, usually to an author or director with substantial creative or commercial signature, which signifies the person's marked influence over the production (e.g., "Orson Welles' *Citizen Kane*" or "Stephen King's *"The Shining")*.

Positive Film or Print: See **Print**.

Post-production (or simply **"Post"**): That portion of a film or television production which takes place after completion of **principal photography** with actors, including editing, musical scoring, addition of sound and visual effects and mixing.

Power of Attorney: A written authorization to represent or act on another's behalf in private affairs, business, or some other legal matter. The person authorizing the other to act is the principal, grantor, or donor (of the power).

Pre-production: The planning period (for script development, location scouting, budgeting, casting, etc.) which precedes production and photography on a film or television project.

Pre-production (aka Development) Finance: Financing occurring in the early phase(s) of a motion picture's creative life that allows the film to move through development to production.

Prequel: A film or television production or book based on a prior production or book, which explores the original story or its characters in a time period anticipating that of the previous work. See also **Sequel**.

Presales Commitment: Film or television distributors may seek contracts for end-use rights to their productions from buyers for a particular territory or territories prior to commencement of productions guarantying future payments on delivery of the production and thereafter, contracts for which (assuming the buyers are credit worthy) may in turn be used as security with banks or other financiers for the production of the respective undertaking.

Press Kit (also Promo Package): A professional package containing print (e.g., biographies, release or appearance schedules, reviews, etc.) photographs and often CD or DVD materials intended as a sales or marketing tool for an author, artist or a production to the media and others.

(Pressing and) Distribution Deal: In the music industry, an arrangement whereby one record label's recordings may be distributed through another label's distribution channels, with the distributor taking a negotiated share of gross sales as a distribution fee for access to its capacity to move product into wholesale and retail channels.

Principal Photography: That phase of a motion picture production in which actors appear before the cameras.

Print (or Positive Print): A positive image, produced from a film negative, capable of being projected in a theatre (and which will eventually be replaced in the motion picture industry by digital delivery and projection capabilities).

Print License: In the music industry, a publisher's or songwriter's authorization for a song to be published in printed form as sheet music.

Print Run: The units of a book, prints of a motion picture, and/or CD or DVD (also called a "pressing") manufactured at a particular time for commercial release.

Prints and Advertising (P&A): The prints of a motion picture delivered to theaters in connection with film's theatrical run, and the advertising associated with the film's initial and subsequent release, the costs of which are usually recouped from proceeds by a distributor after deduction of its percentage distribution fee, and before the recoupment of the costs of production of the film (whether financed by the distributor or an independent financier).

Producer: In any complex entertainment industry productions, the person(s) or entity(s) which shapes and constructs the project from inception to completion — functions which may be likened to those of both the developer and general contractor in the construction industry. Through its packaging and management role, the producer may have a profound influence on the creative shape and success of such a production. In music, the producer (either as the initiator of a project or employee of an artist or label) assembles the musicians (including the featured artist(s)), the repertoire, the recording studio, the engineer and mixers and manages the creative and business processes of producing a recording. In film and television, the producer (likewise as a financier or studio employee, or as an independent creative entrepreneur or company) may find the underlying creative idea or property that will ultimately reach the screen, select and supervise writers, assemble financing, then director, cast and crew, manage physical production of the undertaking, secure distribution and supervise the project's marketing (processes often involving multiple producers, with varying titles of producer, executive producer, line producer and variations thereon depending on their function. Producer's for theatre and live concert events perform like functions.

Producers Guild of America: The Producers Guild of America is a trade association representing television producers, film producers and New Media producers in the United States.

Producer's Share: The sum of money or revenues due to be paid to (or retained by) a producer or production company from 100% of the defined contingent proceeds of a production, either after financiers are paid their negotiated return on investment and contingent participations and/or after both financiers and other contractual talent participants are paid distributions they are due from 100% of such proceeds, depending on how the term is defined from case to case.

Product Placement: A contractual arrangement whereby some fee or other consideration flows between a producer of an entertainment property (typically film or television, but which may include a video game, or even a book) and the source (or agent for the source) of goods or services incorporated in such work or production. The prominence and characteristics of the placement and the expected size of the audience for the work will determine the consideration exchanged, and its timing. See also **Commercial Tie-In**.

Production: The process of creating an entertainment property, or the resulting property itself, created through the interplay of live, interacting contributors. In motion pictures, "production" is more particularly that phase of the process involving the undertaking of the film's **principal photography**.

Production-Financing/Distribution (P/F/D) Agreement: An agreement in which the producer acquires financing for a motion picture production, in exchange for a grant of distribution rights to a studio or distributor acting as or with the financier.

Production Insurance: Insurance coverage for physical liability arising in the course of a motion picture, television, stage or other production.

Production Rebates: Payments a government authority directly reimburses a producer based on some percentage of the producer's direct (or occasionally indirect) expenditures within the jurisdiction, offered as an incentive to locate production activities in the jurisdiction.

Production Services Agreement: An agreement whereby a third party entity is engaged to render substantial or complete services as "general contractor" for production of a film or television production on behalf of a financier, network, studio or "packaging" production entity not engaged in physical production (whether for practical reasons based on resources, location or expertise, and/or for financing and tax purposes).

Profit Participation: Contingent compensation to a creative, executive, financier or other contributor to a production, calculated on the basis of a percentage of the revenue of a film, television, recorded music, concert or stage production, with the definition of the revenue stream and calculation of the participation subject to (generally detailed) contractual negotiation as to the revenue stream(s) from which the participation will be derived, and the costs which may be deducted before the participant realizes any contingent income.

Promoter: A person or entity which producers and promotes a concert or other live entertainment event or series of events. In the record business, Promoter also refers to an individual or company hired by a label or the artist to get records played on radio or in clubs.

Pro Rata: An accounting term indicating that payments will be made to participants in contingent proceeds or royalties in proportion to their relative entitlements from proceeds to be distributed.

Public Domain: A creative work not protected by intellectual property law (whether never eligible, or for which eligibility has for any reason expired), which works are consequently available for unrestricted use, including copying or other adaptation, by anyone without restriction. The limitation on the duration of **statutory copyright** is intended to deliver all creative works, eventually to the public domain.

Public Performance: The exhibition of a work (whether by live performers or by transmission/projection of prerecorded media) to the general public (which may occur in theaters, over television, radio or online, etc.).

Publication: The dissemination of copies of a creative work to the public, whether or not for commercial sale.

Publication Date: The projected date (sometimes included in a contract) for a book's commercial availability to the public via bookstores (which will have generally received delivery of the work by the intended date), as distinguished from the "release date", which is when the book is shipped to wholesalers and retailers. The publication date will determine the rollout of publicity and promotional undertakings supporting the sale of the book, including advance delivery to various publications for review, etc.

Publicity Rights: The right, obtained through contract or license, to exploit an individual's **"right of publicity"**; frequently granted in the context of an entertainment industry negotiation to aid the promotion of an artist and/or artist's work (e.g., a film or television production, book, record or play).

Publisher: In the book industry, the individual or entity that acquires or develops (including editing and design), and then manufactures and markets a completed book, typically paying a royalty to authors from resulting sales of books or their equivalent, and from the licensing of **subsidiary rights.** In the music industry, the publisher is the individual or entity which acquires and exploits rights in a musical composition, including the marketing, licensing and administration of the composition for placement in recordings, film and television programming, commercials, etc., typically splitting resulting revenues with the composer/songwriter for its exercise of such publishing and administration rights. In the electronic games industry, the **distributor** is often referred to as the publisher.

Publisher's Representative / Sales Representative: In the book publishing industry, a salesperson who presents a publisher's catalogue (forthcoming and current) to and solicits orders from current and prospective customers of a publisher (retail bookstores, libraries, university visits prospective customers of a publisher (booksellers, wholesalers, librarians, university and school officials responsible for textbook selection, etc.).

Publisher's Share: The portion of revenue derived by the publisher from the licensing of compositions under its control, retained after payment of the **Composer's Share** (and usually representing 50% of respective income).

Publishing Agreement: A written contract allowing a book publisher to exploit the primary and subsidiary rights to a literary work in a defined territory for a defined term, or a music publisher to exploit the works of a composer or songwriter during a negotiated time frame. See **Publisher.**

Q

Quality Paperback. See **Trade Paperback.**

Quitclaim: A release of a claim to a particular work or right, which may be utilized to "quiet" title to a property, but is accompanied by limited representations and warranties as to the transfer of good title. "Quitclaim" also implies the act of furnishing such a release.

R

Reality Television: Unscripted television programming constituting an integration and portrayal of "real" life on television, which may document real-life, real-time events, events and relationships that convey real or "choreographed" spontaneous interaction, and/or which may be edited from such recorded "real" events to create the impression of dramatic or comedic tension otherwise associated with scripted, narrative productions.

Recommended Retail Price: See **List Price.**

Record Label: A company engaged in the production and generally distribution of records.

The Recording Academy (formerly known as the **National Association of Recording Arts & Sciences** or **NARAS**): This music industry trade group recognizes and promotes music industry achievements, and presents the annual Grammy Awards.

Recording Industry Association of America (RIAA): A music industry trade group historically associated with the major record labels, engaged in advancing member commercial rights and recently at the forefront of anti-piracy initiatives in the U.S. and abroad. Also certifies U.S. music sales through recognition of recordings as gold, platinum, and diamond.

Recoupment: The contractually defined point at which a project's or production's revenues equal expenses. See also **Breakeven,** or **Cash Breakeven.**

Release Print: The composite print(s) made for general distribution to theatres after the final **answer print** has been approved.

Remainder: A book publisher's overstock of a discontinued edition or title, liquidated at a steeply reduced price through jobbers and booksellers, generally at a reduced (or no) royalty to the author. See also **Cutouts.**

Remake: A new production of a previously produced motion picture (which may include a U.S./English adaptation of a foreign language film, or a new version of an earlier English language title).

Renewal: The extension of the term of an existing trademark or copyright registration.

Rental Payments: That portion of a motion picture's box office receipts payable to the studio/distributor.

Repackage: Collection of songs, films and television programs, and/or articles or books that is assembled ("repackaged") and sold as a new album (e.g., under a new title, such as a single artist's greatest hits CD or a multi-artist collection), a boxed set of DVD's (e.g., the original and all sequel films, a season of TV episodes, or several films by a particular director or featuring a particular actor), or a book (e.g., anthology) or boxed set of books by a single author or in a series (e.g., "The Complete Harry Potter" or "The Complete Shakespeare").

Reprint: A second or subsequent printing of a book.

Rerun: The second and subsequent exhibition(s) of an original television movie, special or series, following the initial exhibition via network, cable, **first run syndication,** etc.

Reserved Rights: Copyright extends to a *bundle of rights* in a creative work, which can be separated and distinguished through varying levels of refinement. Reserved rights are those elements of the bundle of rights not expressly granted (i.e., when the grant or license is specific) or expressly held back (i.e., when the grant or license is otherwise broad) by the creator or owner of the work or rights in question.

Reserves: Portion of revenue from entertainment project exploitation set aside to cover prospective expenses, which may be certain or contingent (e.g., expenses incurred by not yet invoiced by vendor in a production, or revenue from sales of CD or DVD units, or of books shipped to wholesalers/retailers, which may be subject to return and thus a refund or credit of sales revenue).

Residuals: Guild mandated royalties to actors, writers, directors or musicians from revenues derived for exploitation of their productions in media/territories other than for which the production was primarily intended (e.g., television exhibition of a theatrical motion picture, foreign television exhibition of a U.S. television series, DVD release of a made-for-television movie, etc.).

Returns: Unsold books, games, DVDs or CDs returned for cash or credit to the publisher/distributor, in accordance with a distributor's contractual "return policy" as to timing and permitted quantities (e.g., some or all units purchased) for such returns.

Reversion: Negotiated contractual mechanism providing for restoration of rights to author or licensor upon failure of purchaser or licensee to achieve specified milestones (e.g., without limitation, relating to publication, production, distribution, revenue, etc.).

Review Copy: Advance copy of a new book or musical recording furnished by publisher or label to the media for purposes of promotion or review.

Right of Privacy: The right "to be left alone" and not to be subjected to unjustified expropriation of one's name, image or likeness; or the publication (via print, film or other forms of commercial speech) of private details of one's life.

Right of Publicity: The right to control the commercial use of one's own identity, including name and likeness.

Rights: The legal (statutory, common law and/or contractual) privileges of a creator/author or owner of intellectual property. Under U.S. copyright law and as negotiated by buyer/seller or licensor/licensee, a transfer of rights may be complete as to the subject work, or may be limited to one or several aspects of the work's potential for exploitation. See also **Copyright.**

Road Manager: See **Tour Manager.**

Rolling Right: A right or privilege (equivalent to a periodic option) to continue to engage an artist's services or exploit a licensed right in some intellectual property contingent on the ongoing, sequential fulfillment of certain conditions precedent to that exploitation (which may be triggered by the satisfaction of certain preset and repeating milestones, the payment of some additional periodic fee or advance, etc.).

Rough Cut: A preliminary assemblage of film footage after completion of a motion picture production which is sequentially refined (by producers, director, editor and studio and/or distribution executives) into a **director's cut** and **final cut.**

Royalty: A contingent payment made to authors or creative artists by publishers, distributors, labels or producers, based on revenue from the exploitation of the works created by the artist or to which the artist has contributed. Royalties may be calculated as a percentage of sales revenue (e.g., on a gross basis from the retail or wholesale price for each unit sold), or of net revenues after recoupment of certain production, manufacturing or marketing costs.

Royalty Pool: A profit-sharing structure frequently found in the theater industry which repays certain parties (such as investors or creative talent) at the same time it pays other contractual percentage royalty participants, by dividing the weekly operating profit between the investors and the royalty participants.

S

Sales Agent: An individual or entity engaged to sell rights to a film or television production to exhibitors and other distributors, usually in foreign territories, for a sales commission calculated on the basis of gross revenue from the resulting sale or license.

Sampling: The process of duplicating audio passages from one musical work (which may be limited to a vocal or instrumental phrase, melodic or rhythmic segment, or more substantial musical passage), and incorporating it into another recorded musical work.

Scale: The minimum salary permitted by a union or guild for the services of its members, which will generally vary based on type, intended medium, budget, duration and location of employment for a respective production.

Score: The extended sheet music for a musical, film soundtrack, symphony, or other extended musical work.

S-Corporation: A closely-held corporation which falls under subchapter S of chapter 1 of the Internal Revenue Code for taxation purposes. The primary feature of this tax recognition is to allow the corporation to avoid paying a corporate tax and instead to have each shareholder report and pay their tax liability on their share of distributions from the S-corporation directly on their personal income tax return.

Screen Actors Guild (SAG): The union representing actors on productions (primarily those filmed before single cameras) in the motion picture and television industries.

Screen Actors Guild (SAG) Producers Agreement: The agreement between SAG and producers of film or television productions who seek to employ SAG members, covering the rules of employment, compensation and other terms prescribed under the guilds then current industry collective bargaining agreement. See also **Minimum Basic Agreement.**

Screenplay: The written scenario on which a motion picture production is based, which may be identified as a sequence of "drafts" (e.g., first, second, "final"), "rewrites" and/or "polishes", and generally consisting of 100 to 120 formatted pages for a feature length motion picture.

Secondary Meaning: General public recognition, through extended exposure, that an otherwise descriptive word, name or symbol is associated with and identifies a particular brand of products or services (constituting a trademark or service mark).

Security Agreement: An agreement which provides a creditor with an enforceable interest in a specified asset or property pledged as collateral for a loan, investment or other obligation. In the event that the borrower defaults, the pledged collateral can be seized and sold, potentially mitigating the default risk the creditor faces.

Sequel: A book or film that expands upon or chronologically continues a story, or further develops a set of characters, from a prior work.

Serial Rights: The right to reproduce all or a portion of a book in one or more parts either before or after the book's official publication.

Series: A group of works (books or articles, television programs or motion pictures) with a common theme and/or titles. In television, a weekly serialization of such a work or group of programs.

Service Mark: A word, slogan, design, picture or symbol, alone or in combination, which identifies and distinguishes a distinct service or service provider from another. See also **Trademark,** which services to identify a *product* as opposed to a *service.*

SESAC (originally, **Society of European Stage Authors and Composers):** Performing rights organization representing songwriters and publishers in collection of public performance royalties for music (e.g., from film, television, live performance, juke boxes, etc.). Provides services similar to those of, and competes with, ASCAP and BMI.

Settlement: The final daily accounting at the conclusion of a live stage production for music or theatre (or nightly for a concert engagement) in which income and expenses are calculated and the producer or performer who is compensated on the basis of box office revenue gets paid.

Seven Years Rule: A California law which renders unenforceable personal service contracts with terms longer than seven years.

Shopping Agreement: An agreement that allows a producer or third party to "shop" an entertainment project (almost always on an exclusive basis for a defined period of time) to potential financiers such as studios, networks and production companies, typically providing that if the producer is successful in obtaining financing he/she/they/it will be "attached" to the project as producer, while the proprietor of the rights or services being shopped will have the right to enter into direct negotiation with the financier for the disposition of its rights and services (without the broader preconditions that typically characterize a formal option agreement, and without necessitating the parties' negotiation and entry into a more formal option agreement before there's assurance of buyer interest).

Showrunner: An experienced television series executive producer deemed by a network to be capable of delivering a project to the networks creative, technical and budgetary specifications. In the scripted television arena, showrunners are often writers with prior experience on similar successful series.

Sideletter: A usually abbreviated document which serves to amend the terms of an already negotiated agreement, or may modify certain "fine print" standard terms of long form **boilerplate** "agreements."

Signatory: A company obliged by an agreement with a union or guild to comply with the rules of that union (e.g., SAG, AFTRA, DGA, WGA, Equity, etc.) with respect to the employment of its members.

Single Card Credit: In motion pictures, a screen credit that appears in a distinct frame rather than in a scrolling list (such as end credits), and is usually shared by no more than several names. Derived from practice in early days of industry in which credits were literally placed on "cards" which were photographed and incorporated in the film.

Single Song Agreement: An agreement whereby a songwriter will assign either one hundred percent or fifty percent of his/her/their copyright in a composition (i.e., the "publishing rights") plus full worldwide administration rights to a record company or (its) publisher, in exchange for payment and/or a recording/distribution commitment.

Slander: An oral (as opposed to written) defamatory statement, for which the victim may seek legal redress for damages to reputation.

Soft Floor: A negotiated minimum below which any further reductions to a producer's or other profit participant's **backend** return must be made in lockstep (point for point or in some negotiated proportion) with reduction in the financier's backend return.

Songwriter: A person who contributes the words and/or music to a song.

Sound Recording: A recorded performance of a song, musical composition or other work eligible for copyright when embodied on a phono-record.

Sound Recording Copyright Symbol: The letter "P" enclosed in a circle and affixed to a sound recording, which when it appears adjacent to the year of first publication of the sound recording, and the name of the owner of copyright in the sound recording, constitutes notice satisfying the requirements of statutory copyright on publication (consistent with the use of © in connection with literary and other copyrightable textual or visual works).

Soundtrack: A commercial recording containing the musical content of a motion picture or television production, which may include either or both the original score for the production and/or songs produced for or licensed to be included in the production. "Soundtrack" is also the technical term given the magnetic strip on the edge of actual motion picture film on which the sound (e.g., voices, atmospheric sound and music) are embedded in the product.

Source Material: The underlying material or work (which may or may not itself be subject to copyright protection) on which a separate copyrighted work may be based (e.g., a novel or stage play as the basis of a film).

Spec: Short for "speculative", and used to describe a manuscript, screenplay or teleplay initiated independently by a writer on a non-commissioned basis (and not commissioned by a third party), which the author or writer intends to shop and license or sell on its completion.

Special Purpose Vehicle (SPV): An entity (in the U.S., a corporation or limited liability company) formed for the express purpose of financing of financing, developing, producing and/or exploiting a single entertainment property, permitting both protections to and from assets created or obtained by the entity (limitations on liability) and isolation of accounting and contracting issues from those of unrelated projects.

Specialized Distributors: Distributors which specialize in delivering product to niche buyers or audiences, including for example independent bookstores (publishing), record stores (music), or art house cinemas (film), most often relying on publicity, reviews and word of mouth rather than substantial marketing budgets to drive sales.

Spin Off: A television series based on characters derived from another series, or from a motion picture.

Split Publishing: Arrangement by which two or more music publishers jointly control publishing rights to a composition.

Stage Manager: Staff person at a theatre or live performance venue responsible for coordinating physical aspects of performance or presentation.

Start Date: In a film or television production, the date set for commencement of talent services in connection with principal photography.

Statutory Copyright: Status acquired by a work upon registration with the Copyright Office or upon publication with proper copyright notice.

Statutory Damages: A relief granted whereby the total amount of damages awarded are prescribed by the statute (e.g., copyright or trademark law) regulating the violating conduct.

Statutory Royalty Rate: The rate established by the Copyright Royalty Tribunal under §115 of the Copyright Act for a musical recording "covering" a previously recorded and released composition, currently 9.1 cents per recording or 1.75 cents per minute of playing time or fraction thereof, whichever is greater. See also **Compulsory License.**

Story: In motion pictures and television productions, the basic creative outline on which any subsequent **treatment and screenplays/ teleplays** are based, and which may convey certain rights and royalties to the creator under **WGA** rules.

Streaming: A method through which live or recorded audio or visual content may be accessed on a continuous basis by a consumer over the internet, mobile or other similar digital transmission.

Strip-Series: A television series produced for daily (i.e., five-days a week) rather than weekly exhibition. (Term derived from five-panel comic *strip* appearing in daily newspapers.)

Sub-Distributor: An agent contracted by a primary distributor (for example in film, television or the record industry) to handle distribution in a particular territory or medium, usually in conformity with marketing guidelines established by the primary distributor.

Sub-Publisher: An agent engaged by the primary music publisher of a composition or song to exploit and administer the song in one or more foreign territories.

Subscription Video on Demand (SVOD): Authenticated access for paying subscribers to a library of on-demand streaming content.

Subsidiary Rights: In an extensive grant of rights or license, those rights which supplement the primary rights which are the subject of the agreement, e.g., in publishing, rights other than those to the primary publication of the work (e.g., foreign editions, including translations, audio books, film and television rights, etc.) and/or in film and television, rights other than those to produce the primary film or television production (e.g., sequels and remakes, merchandising, audio soundtrack rights, the novelization rights to an original screenplay, etc.).

Substantial Similarity: That level of similarity between a copyrighted work and another work (whether based on verbatim copying or other substantive resemblance) that will, together with proof of copying, constitute copyright infringement under U.S. law.

Suggested Retail Price: The price at which a distributor or a manufacturer "suggests" the sale of its product.

Synchronization Rights (Synchronization License): Right to use music in timed relation (i.e., *"synchronization"*) with visual images (as in a motion picture or television program or commercial), which under copyright law must be obtained from both composer/lyricist and music publisher.

Synchronization Royalty: Fee or royalty paid for granting of synchronization license.

Syndication: In publishing, the license of publishing rights to all or a portion of an original work to multiple publications, most frequently newspapers in multiple markets, that will in turn publish the material for their readers (usually, concurrently). In television, the practice of licensing exhibition to a television series or special to local stations or station groups, rather than through a single national network, usually (as in publishing) for concurrent national exhibition.

T

Taft-Hartley Law: Federal law permitting non-union members to work under a union contract for their first production, subsequent to which they must join the union to be employed on further union projects, if otherwise eligible.

Talent: Persons contributing artistic/creative services to entertainment productions (e.g., writers, actors, directors, musicians), as distinguished from those involved in the business and technical aspects of such productions.

Talent Agent: Individual or entity who acts as an Artist's representative in procuring bookings and employment, typically for a commission equal to ten to fifteen percent of the Artist's earnings. See also **Agent** or **Booking Agent.**

Tax Credits: Government issued incentives and rebates used to lure productions to operate on location in the governmental jurisdiction by

lowering the net costs of production and/or otherwise reducing investor risks through direct or assignable (and thus saleable) tax offsets.

Technical Rider: Addendum to a performer's contract, most frequently in concert, touring musical or stage productions, that specifies technical aspects of the artist's production requirements, including on stage and off-stage equipment, staffing and amenities.

Teleplay: A **Screenplay** written for a television series or motion picture for television.

Term of Copyright (also, **Duration of Copyright**): The effective period of a copyright, during which the copyright owner may sell or license some or all of its rights in the protected work. Duration will vary depending on certain variables such as the date of the work's creation (e.g., pre- or post-1978), and whether the work is one of individual authorship or is a "work-for-hire."

Theatrical: Generally refers to a feature-length motion picture intended for initial exhibition in theatres (rather than via television or home video). My also be used to refer to a dramatic production intended for the live stage.

Theatrical Distribution Fees: The fees charges by a motion picture studio or distributor for placing a motion picture in theaters — generally between 20% and 40% of gross film rentals (i.e., box office receipts remitted to distributor by theatre owner), with variation depending on assessment of commercial strength of film, territory (e.g., domestic or foreign, and if foreign which particular countries), and whether or not the distributor has advanced funds for production of the picture, or against prospective profits of the picture.

360 Deal: Recording agreements in which the label seeks to participate in musical artist touring/performance and merchandising revenues, in addition to traditional recorded music revenue (with name reflecting total "360 degree" involvement in the artist's economic life, and which is largely a response to tectonic shifts in record industry economics in the "on-line" and "digital" age).

Title: The name of a book, recording, motion picture or television property, by which it is known. May also refer to a generic product, such as a book, recording or film. May also be used (**"Titles"**) to refer to the opening credits in a motion picture or television production in which the name of the production also appears.

Tour: A series of a live concerts or special event performances taking place in a defined geographical area over a limited or extended period.

Tour Manager: The person who oversees the day to day business of a touring musical artist or theatre production while "on the road" — a responsibility which may include a combination of creative, technical, administrative and general artist management functions depending on size and scale of tour.

Trade Books (Trade Edition): Books intended for the general public or general circulation through libraries, as distinct from textbooks, reference books, professional treatises, etc.

Trade Discounts: A markdown of from 30 to 45 percent off of publisher recommended list price *(see* **Cover Price**), established for selling general books to retailers. A trade discount schedule may vary by volume ordered (i.e., the discount will be deeper for a title acquired in large quantities by a major retail chain, versus more limited order by a small independent bookseller.

Trade Paperback (also **Quality Paperback**): A premium quality (and priced) paperbound book to be sold through normal bookstore channels, which may follow publication of a hardbound version of the work, or represent a more limited edition of a mass market paperback (but generally of superior paper/design quality). Generally follows hardback publication, but may be concurrent with publication of mass market paperback.

Trademark and Service Mark: A word, symbol or phrase used to identify and distinguish an individual's or company's goods and services, particularly as to *source* and *quality,* from those of another. "Trademark" refers to products, while "Service mark" refers to services. One *"trademarks"* one's brand or services by registering the intended trademark or service mark with the U.S. Patent and Trademark Office.

Trade Name: A word, symbol or logo used to identify and distinguish a company per se, as opposed to marks used to identify and distinguish goods or services. See also **Trademark** and **Service mark.**

Trades: The specialized daily or weekly business periodicals servicing entertainment industry professionals, including *Billboard* (music industry), *Publishers Weekly* (publishing), *Dramalogue* (theatre) and *Variety* or *Hollywood Reporter* (motion pictures and television).

Transactional Video on Demand: Paid access to content online, with purchase and/or rental fees paid on a specific product-by-product basis.

Translation: The reproduction and/or adaptation of a book, movie, play or other work from one language into another.

Treatment: A prose summary of a motion picture storyline, typically 20 to 30 pages in length and without elaborate dialogue or directorial commentary. A treatment is a more detailed elaboration of story, plot and characters than an outline, and generally precedes the writing of a full draft screenplay.

Turnaround: A contractual arrangement whereby a music, film or television project, once abandoned by a purchaser or licensee, becomes available to the originating producer or artist for a specified period of time (a "Turnaround Period") during which it may be "shopped" to and acquired by other financiers, distributors, etc., usually subject to a buyout clause in favor of the party relinquishing rights. Also, for cast and crew of a stage, film or television production, the period between the end of one days rehearsal of production and the call time for the next day's work.

U

Underlying Work: Work from which an adaptation is created (e.g., short story to novel, novel to motion picture, motion picture to stage musical, etc.).

Unfair Competition: Conduct, including trademark infringement, false advertising, product disparagement, trade secret infringement, and expropriation of the right of publicity which the law considers unfair and which give rise to relieve in civil action by the injured party against the party responsible for such activity.

Uniform Commercial Code (UCC): First published in 1952, the Uniform Commercial Code is one of a number of uniform acts that have been put into law with the goal of harmonizing the law of sales and other commercial transactions across the United States of America (U.S.) through UCC adoption by all 50 states, the District of Columbia, and U.S. territories.

Union Scale: Minimum wage scale earned in employment by members of a guild or union, including entertainment industry organizations such as SAG, AFTRA, DGA, WGA, AFofM, Equity, etc.

V

Vanity Press: A publishing arrangement (also called a "subsidy press") where the author pays costs of printing and of some or all marketing, while retaining copyright. Usually connotes a book for which there is little or no commercial interest.

Venue: Location for a live musical or dramatic production.

Video On Demand (VOD): Describes process by which consumer's access film, television or other video programming on an a la carte basis via cable or satellite television, the internet or wireless devices at times of their choice (i.e., not scheduled by distributors or programmers).

W

Warranty: An assurance by one party as to a fact or set of facts upon which the other party is intended or entitled to rely.

Weekly Player: Actor for stage, screen or television under a week to week contract.

Wholesaler: A party acting as an intermediary between a publisher or distributor of entertainment products (e.g., books, CDs and/or DVDs) and individual retailers or libraries, whether involving single or multiple copies, consolidating the supply side responsibilities of large and small publishers, labels and distributors. For mass-market products (as distinguished from trade books) the function may also be performed by **"jobbers."**

Wide Release: Concurrent release of a motion picture nationally to a large number of theaters (usually in excess of 1,000, and up to 3,500 or more).

Window: Time frame projected for exhibition of a project in a given market or medium (e.g., for a motion picture, there are sequential

"windows" for initial theatrical release, home video release, pay television, free television and syndication).

World Intellectual Property Organization (WIPO): A United Nations specialized agency formed in 1967 to promote cooperation in the creation and enforcement of international copyright standards and treaties.

Work: Any result of creative effort that may be subject to copyright, including without limitation musical, dramatic (i.e., stage), visual or literary creations.

Work Made for Hire (or **Work for Hire**): Refers to any type of copyrightable work (e.g., lyric, song or other musical composition, news article, screenplay, etc.), which is (i) prepared by an employee within the scope of employment, or is (ii) specially ordered or commissioned as a contribution to a collective work (e.g., a motion picture or a magazine), provided there is a written agreement or other acknowledgement between "employer" and "employee" (hiring party and contributor) that it is a work made for hire, and that the employer is the intended owner of copyright under Copyright Law, thereby becoming the "author" for copyright purposes.

World Rights: Rights to distribute or exploit a particular Work throughout the entire world, as distinguished from distribution rights to a particular individual country or geographic or linguistic region.

Writers Guild of America (WGA): Union representing professional writers for motion pictures, television and radio, establishing minimum fee schedules *("scale")* for various forms of productions based on media, budgets and patterns of exploitation, as well as other conditions relating to use of work, credit, etc.

— ILLUSTRATIVE FORMS LIST —

ABOUT THE FORMS AND HOW TO ACCESS THEM

A series of 84 illustrative forms have been assembled to accompany *The Essential Guide to Entertainment Law: Dealmaking*.

The forms illustrate issues encountered in the structuring of the wide range of entertainment law transactions identified in the volume's chapters. Although an understanding of the forms is intended to assist lawyers and others in structuring their own transactions in the various entertainment industry sectors covered by EG2EL, these forms are intended for **educational and illustration purposes** only. Although some of these forms may appear generic and suitable for certain transactions without significant modification, they are nonetheless intended solely for reference purposes and as negotiation checklists rather than as transactional templates.

The editors and contributing authors therefore urge our readers to utilize these forms with care, and no professional advice is implied or should be assumed via the inclusion of these forms for educational review.

These illustrative Dealmaking Volume forms are available via PDF download free of further charge to qualified purchasers of *EG2EL: DEALMAKING*.

For readers who have purchased this book online through either www.jurispub.com or www.EG2EL.com, instructions for obtaining the Illustrative Forms download were included in your purchase.

If you have purchased the book through another source, please send an email containing your contact information (name, organization, address, phone and email, along with a scan or photo or your receipt for purchase) to info@EG2EL.com, and we will provide qualified purchasers (those who have acquired the book new through an authorized reseller) with download instructions.

DISCLAIMER

OUR PROVISION OF THESE FORMS DOES NOT CONSTITUTE LEGAL ADVICE.

THE PUBLIC DISSEMINATION/RE-PUBLICATION OF THE FORMS IN ANY MANNER WITHOUT THE EXPRESS PRIOR WRITTEN PERMISSION OF JURIS PUBLISHING IS EXPRESSLY PROHIBITED.

***

Chapter 1 – Motion Picture Development and Production – Illustrative Forms:

- 1-1 Literary Rights Option-Purchase Actor Agreement
- 1-2 Motion Picture Screenwriter Agreement
- 1-3 Director Agreement
- 1-4 Actor Agreement
- 1-5 Producer Agreement
- 1-6 Head of Department / Crew Agreement
- 1-7 Services/Rights Agreements – Standard Terms and Conditions

Chapter 2 – Motion Picture Distribution – Illustrative Forms:

- 2-1 Acquisition Agreement
- 2-2 Negative Pickup Distribution Agreement
- 2-3 IFTA Form Sales Agency Agreement
- 2-4 IFTA Multiple Rights Distribution Agreement

Chapter 3 – Motion Picture Finance – Illustrative Forms:

- 3-1 Gap-Senior Lender Loan and Security Agreement
- 3-2 Mezzanine Financing Term Sheet Agreement (Early Stage)
- 3-3 Notice of Assignment

Chapter 5 – Unscripted Television – Illustrative Forms:

- 5-1 Acquired Footage Still Photograph Form
- 5-2 Authorization to Use Name, Product, Logo Release
- 5-3 Composer Agreement Form
- 5-4 Co-Production Option Agreement Form
- 5-5 Distribution Agreement Form
- 5-6 Independent Contractor Agreement Form
- 5-7 Joint Venture Agreement Form
- 5-8 Location Agreement
- 5-9 Merchandise and Product Placement License Agreement
- 5-10 Minor Release
- 5-11 Master Recording and Music Synchronization License Agreement
- 5-12 Public Filming Notice
- 5-13 Release of Liability and Assumption of Risk Form
- 5-14 Release for Ultrahazardous Activity
- 5-15 Standard Appearance Release
- 5-16 Talent Agreement (long form)
- 5-17 Talent Attachment Agreement (short form)

Chapter 6 – Scripted Television – Illustrative Forms:

- 6-1 Book Rights Agreement
- 6-2 Writing/Writer-Producer Agreement
- 6-3 Pilot Director Agreement
- 6-4 Series Regular Actor Agreement

Chapter 7 – Music Industry Law: A 360° View – Illustrative Forms:

- 7-1 360 Collateral Entertainment Agreement – Merchandising
- 7-2 Administration Agreement
- 7-3 Artist Management Agreement
- 7-4 Band Partnership Agreement
- 7-5 Booking Agreement and Rider
- 7-6 Distribution Agreement
- 7-7 Exclusive Songwriter Agreement
- 7-8 Label Services Agreement

7-9 Master (Sampling) Agreement
7-10 Master Use License (Television)
7-11 Merchandise Agreement
7-12 Musician Session Release
7-13 Net Profits Definition
7-14 Publishing / Sample Interpolation Agreement
7-15 Recording Agreement
7-16 Single Song Recording Agreement
7-17 Songwriter Split Agreement
7-18 Sponsorship Agreement (Events)
7-19 Sponsorship Agreement (Products)
7-20 Tour Promoter Agreement
7-21 Touring (Band) Member Agreement

Chapter 8 – Music Publishing Law – Illustrative Forms:

8-1 Music Composition Interpolation (Sample) License
8-2 Music Publishing Catalog Administration Agreement (short form)
8-3 Songwriter Co-Publishing Agreement (short form)
8-4 Synchronization License

Chapter 9 – Theater Law – Illustrative Agreements:

9-1 Dramatists Guild Music Collaboration Agreement
9-2 Theatrical Play Commission Agreement
9-3 Underlying Rights Agreement for Dramatico-Musical Work (Movie Studio Form for adaptation from screenplay)
9-4 Dramatico-Musical Production contract – Off Broadway
9-5 Rider for Approved Production Contract for Musical Plays (Specimen)
9-6 Professional Production Agreement between Agent for Dramatist and Producer of (straight) Play
9-7 Director's Agreement (Broadway)
9-8 Choreographer's Agreement (Broadway)
9-9 General Management Agreement for Musical
9-10 Agreement to a Single Engagement by a Presenter
9-11 Underlying Rights Agreement (Broadway Revival)

Chapter 10 - Literary Publishing – Illustrative Forms:

- 10-1 Literary Publishing Agreement
- 10-2 Foreign Rights Publishing Agreement
- 10-3 Self-Publishing Agreement
- 10-4 Collaboration (Co-Writer) Agreement
- 10-5 Collaboration (Ghost Writer) Agreement

Chapter 11 - Video Games, Interactive Media and Dealmaking – Illustrative Forms:

- 11-1 Video Game Publishing Term Sheet
- 11-2 Video Game Distribution Agreement (long form)
- 11-3 Master Services Agreement (Developer Engagement of Subcontractors)

Chapter 14 – Fundamentals of Entertainment Talent Representation by Agents and Managers – Illustrative Forms:

- 14-1 Talent Agent/Agency Agreement
- 14-2 Literary Agent Agreement
- 14-3 Talent Management Agreement

Chapter 15 - Developing an Entertainment Law Practice – Illustrative Forms:

- 15-1 Attorney Engagement/Fee Agreement (hourly fees)
- 15-2 Attorney Engagement/Fee Agreement (percentage fee)

— INDEX —

A

ACCOUNTING(S)
Music royalties. *See* **MUSIC ROYALTIES**
Taxation. *See* **TAXATION**

ADVANCES
Music publishing. *See* **MUSIC PUBLISHING**
Music recording agreements, 7.4.7.1
Tax deferral method for advance payments, 12.1.4.1
Video-game development advances, recoupment of, 11.4.3.6.b

ADVERTISERS
Television, 4.2.6

ADVERTISING CREDIT(S)
Generally, 13.1.2
Marketer's perspective, 13.1.2.2
Talent's perspective, 13.1.2.1

ADVERTISING RIGHTS
Motion picture distribution agreements, 2.3.3, 2.5.2.2

ADVERTISING-SUPPORTED VIDEO ON DEMAND (AVOD)
Television, 4.3.1.2

AGENT/AGENCY REPRESENTATION
Generally, 14.1, 14.2, 14.6
Agency relationship, 14.2.1
Agreements. *See* **AGENT/AGENCY REPRESENTATION AGREEMENTS**
Competing clients, representation of, 14.5.2
Conflicts of interest
  Generally, 14.5
  Competing clients, representation of, 14.5.2
  Leveraging, 14.5.3
Self-dealing, 14.5.1
Self-promoting, 14.5.4
Evaluation of proposed artist, 14.2.1
Independent agent representation *versus* talent agencies, 14.2.2
Role of agents, 14.1
Self-dealing, 14.5.1
Self-promoting, 14.5.4

AGENT/AGENCY REPRESENTATION AGREEMENTS
Generally, 14.2.3
Adjustments to standard agreements, 14.2.3.6
Areas of representation, 14.2.3.2
Collection rights, 14.2.3.4
Commissions, 14.2.3.3
Duration of, 14.2.3.1
Literary publishing
  Generally, 10.6
  Author agreements, 10.2.2.14
Payment obligations, 14.2.3.4
Performance goals, 14.2.3.5

AGREEMENTS
Agent/agency representation. *See* **AGENT/AGENCY REPRESENTATION AGREEMENTS**
Collective bargaining agreements, 15.2.3
Employment agreements (loanout companies), 12.4.1.3
Literary publishing. *See* **LITERARY PUBLISHING; TRADE BOOKS**
Motion picture(s). *See* **MOTION PICTURE DEVELOPMENT; MOTION PICTURE DISTRIBUTION AGREEMENTS; MOTION PICTURE FINANCE; MOTION PICTURE PRODUCTION**
Music/music industry
  Personal appearance(s). *See* **MUSIC PERFORMANCE(S)**

923

Publishing agreements. *See*
  MUSIC PUBLISHING
Recording agreements. *See*
  MUSIC RECORDING
  AGREEMENTS
Periodicals. *See* **PERIODICALS**
Television. *See* **SCRIPTED**
  TELEVISION; UNSCRIPTED
  TELEVISION
Theater(s). *See* **THEATER(S)**
Video games. *See* **VIDEO GAMES**

ARBITRATION OF DISPUTES
Generally, 13.3
Unscripted television, talent agreements, 5.3.2.3.h

ASSIGNMENT(S)
Notices of. *See* **NOTICES OF**
  ASSIGNMENT (NOAS)
Unscripted television
  Independent contractor agreements, 5.5.7
  Talent agreements, 5.3.2.3.f

ASSUMPTION OF RISK
Unscripted television, 5.6.3

ATTORNEYS. *See*
  ENTERTAINMENT LAW
  PRACTICE

AUDIT(S)
Music royalties, 7.4.8.5
Video game royalties, 11.4.3.6.c

AUGMENTED REALITY
Interactive media, 11.6.2

B

BANKRUPTCY ISSUES
Music recording agreements, 7.4.9

BILLING CREDIT(S). *See*
  CREDIT(S)

BONUSES
Box office. *See* **BOX OFFICE**
  BONUSES
Scripted television. *See* **SCRIPTED**
  TELEVISION

BOOK PUBLISHING. *See*
  LITERARY PUBLISHING

BORROWERS
Motion picture financing, 3.2.3

BOX OFFICE BONUSES
Motion picture development, 1.3.7.1
Motion picture distribution agreements, 2.8.5

BROADCAST STATIONS
Television, 4.2.5

BUSINESS MANAGERS
Generally, 14.4

BUSINESS PRACTICES
Entertainment law, 15.2.4

C

C-CORPORATIONS
Choice-of-entity tax considerations, 12.2.1

CHAIN OF TITLE
Motion pictures, underlying rights to, 1.2.1

CHILDREN'S ONLINE PRIVACY
  PROTECTION ACT (COPPA)
Video games, 11.5.2.1

CHOICE-OF-ENTITY TAX
  CONSIDERATIONS
Generally, 12.2
Accumulated earnings tax, 12.2.6
California gross receipts tax, 12.2.7.1
California net income tax on S-corporations, 12.2.7.1
C-corporations, 12.2.1

Limited liability companies (LLCs), 12.2.3
Personal holding companies, 12.2.5
Qualified personal service companies (QPSCs), 12.2.4
S-corporations, 12.2.2, 12.2.7.1
State-entity level taxes, 12.2.7
Tax partnerships, 12.2.3

CHOREOGRAPHER CONTRACTS
Theater(s), 9.8.1

CLEARANCES
Motion picture production, 1.4.4

COLLECTION ACCOUNT MANAGEMENT AGREEMENTS
Motion picture finance, 3.4.10
Structuring entertainment production company transactions for tax purposes, 12.4.4.2

COLLECTION AGENT(S)
Motion picture financing, 3.2.8

COLLECTIVE BARGAINING AGREEMENTS
Entertainment law practice, 15.2.3

COMMERCIAL TIE-INS
Generally, 13.1.3
Marketer's perspective, 13.1.3.2
Talent's perspective, 13.1.3.1

COMPLETION GUARANTOR(S)
Motion picture financing, 3.2.5

COMPLETION GUARANTY
Motion picture financing, 3.4.8

CONCERT PERFORMERS/ PERFORMANCES. *See* **MUSIC PERFORMANCE(S)**

CONFIDENTIALITY
Music publishing, non-disclosure agreements in, 8.2.9.1

Unscripted television. *See* **UNSCRIPTED TELEVISION**

CONSENT DECREES
Music licensing, 8.3.6

CONSENTS. *See* **UNSCRIPTED TELEVISION**

CONSUMER PROTECTION. *See* **VIDEO GAMES**

COPYRIGHT(S)
Motion picture distribution agreements, 2.5.1
Music/music industry. *See* **MUSIC PUBLISHING**
Taxation of intellectual property in, 12.5.1
Trade books, 10.2.2.11

COPYRIGHT MORTGAGES
Motion picture(s), 2.10.2, 3.4.5

CREDIT(S)
Generally, 13.1
Advertising/publicity credits
 Generally, 13.1.2
 Marketer's perspective, 13.1.2.2
 Talent's perspective, 13.1.2.1
Artist's refusal of, 13.1.4
Commercial/merchandising tie-ins
 Generally, 13.1.3
 Marketer's perspective, 13.1.3.2
 Talent's perspective, 13.1.3.1
Television. *See* **SCRIPTED TELEVISION; UNSCRIPTED TELEVISION**
Theater. *See* **THEATER(S)**
Title billing credit
 Generally, 13.1.1
 Marketer's perspective, 13.1.1.2
 Talent's perspective, 13.1.1.1

"CROSS-BORDER PORTABILITY"
Motion picture distribution agreements, 2.4.4

CROSS-BORDER SECURITY ISSUES
Motion picture financing, 3.4.2

CROWDFUNDING
Motion picture production, 3.3.4.5.c
Structuring entertainment production company transactions for tax purposes, 12.4.4.6
Video games, 11.3.2.5.a

D

DATA PRIVACY. *See* **VIDEO GAMES**

DAT HOME RECORDINGS
Music recording agreements, 7.4.3.1.b

DEFERMENTS
Motion picture development, 1.3.7.3

DERIVATIVE RIGHTS
Motion picture distribution agreements, 2.5.2.4

DESIGNER CONTRACTS
Theater(s), 9.8.2.3

DEVELOPMENT
Motion picture(s). *See* **MOTION PICTURE DEVELOPMENT**
Theater(s). *See* **THEATER(S)**

DIGITAL BROADCASTING
Music recording agreements, 7.4.3.1.c
Television
 Digital content companies, roles of, 4.3.3
 Network license agreements, 6.5.1.6.b, 6.5.1.6.c
 Scripted television, 6.5.1.6.b, 6.5.1.6.c

DIGITAL PHONOGRAM DISTRIBUTION
Artist's royalties, 7.4.7.2.a.2.4

DISTRIBUTION
Motion picture(s). *See* **MOTION PICTURE DISTRIBUTION**
Television. *See* **TELEVISION**
Video game distributors, 11.2.3

DISTRIBUTORS
Motion picture distribution agreements, 2.2
Motion picture financing, 3.2.1
Television multichannel video primary distributors (MVPDs), 4.2.4
Video games, 11.2.3

E

ECONOMIC MODELS
Entertainment law, 15.2.4

EDUCATIONAL PUBLICATIONS
Literary publishing, 10.1.1.2

EMPLOYMENT AGREEMENTS
Loanout companies, 12.4.1.3

ENGAGEMENT LETTERS
Entertainment law practice, 15.4.2

ENTERTAINMENT LAW PRACTICE
Generally, 15.5
Client-market
 Generally, 15.3
 Primary markets, 15.3.1
 Secondary markets, 15.3.2
 Understanding, 15.3
Client-representation
 Generally, 15.4
 Effective representation, 15.4
 Engagement letters, 15.4.2
 Fees, determination of, 15.4.4
 Non-lawyer roles, lawyers acting in, 15.4.1
 Professional liability insurance, 15.4.3
Collective bargaining agreements, 15.2.3

INDEX 927

Defining "entertainment law," 15.2
Developing, 15.1
Engagement letters, 15.4.2
Fees, determination of, 15.4.4
Non-lawyer roles, lawyers acting in, 15.4.1
Other legal disciplines, drawing on tenets of, 15.2.1
Professional liability insurance, 15.4.3
State statutes/regulations, 15.2.2

EQUITY FUNDING/INVESTMENTS
Mezzanine loans. *See* **MEZZANINE LOANS**
Video games, 11.3.2.4

eSPORTS
Interactive media, 11.6.1

ESTATE PLANNING
Publicity rights, for, 12.6

EUROPEAN UNION
Motion picture distribution, 2.4.4

EXPLOITATION RIGHTS
Motion picture distribution agreements, 2.5.2.1

F

FILM. *See* **MOTION PICTURE(S)**

FINANCIERS
Motion picture financing, 3.2.4

FINANCING/FUNDING
Crowdfunding. *See* **CROWDFUNDING**
Motion picture(s). *See* **MOTION PICTURE FINANCE**
Theater productions, 9.7
Video games. *See* **VIDEO GAMES**

FIRST AMENDMENT ISSUES
Video games, 11.5.3

FREE VIDEO ON DEMAND (FVOD)
Television, 4.3.1.4

G

GROSS PARTICIPATIONS
Motion picture development, 1.3.7.2

GUARANTEES
Motion picture distribution agreements. *See* **MOTION PICTURE DISTRIBUTION AGREEMENTS**
Scripted television
 Actor agreements, series guarantees in, 6.3.4.5
 Staffing writer agreements, 6.3.5.4
Video game, minimum guarantees, 11.4.3.2.b

GUILDS
Motion picture financing, 3.2.7
Unscripted television, talent agreements, 5.3.2.3.d

H

HOLDBACKS
Motion picture distribution agreements, 2.6

I

INDEMNITY AND INDEMNIFICATION
Author agreements, 10.2.2.7
Unscripted television
 Music licensing agreements, 5.8.3.3
 Product and service placement agreements, 5.7.5

INDEPENDENT CONTRACTORS
Tax issues, 12.3
Unscripted television agreements. *See* **UNSCRIPTED TELEVISION**

INSURANCE
Motion picture production, 1.4.5
Professional liability insurance, 15.4.3

INTELLECTUAL PROPERTY
Copyright(s). *See* **COPYRIGHT(S)**
Musical entertainment transactions, tax considerations in structuring, 12.4.3.2
Taxation
  Generally, 12.5
  Copyrights, 12.5.1
  Music transactions, tax benefits for separating IP in, 12.4.3.2
  Trademarks, 12.5.2
Trademarks. *See* **TRADEMARKS**
Video game license(s), 11.4.4.2

INTERACTIVE MEDIA
Augmented reality, 11.6.2
ESports, 11.6.1
Future of, 11.6
Video games. *See* **VIDEO GAMES**
Virtual reality, 11.6.2

INTERCREDITOR AGREEMENTS
Motion picture financing, 3.4.7, 3.4.7.3

INTERPARTY AGREEMENTS
Motion picture distribution, 2.7.2
Motion picture financing, 3.4.7, 3.4.7.2

J

JOURNALS
General circulation, 10.1.1.4
Literary publishing
  General circulation journals, 10.1.1.4
  Professional journal publications, 10.5
Professional publications, 10.5

L

LABORATORY
Motion picture financing, 3.2.6

LABORATORY PLEDGEHOLDER AGREEMENTS
Motion picture financing, 3.4.9

LAW PRACTICE. *See* **ENTERTAINMENT LAW PRACTICE**

LIABILITY INSURANCE
Entertainment law practice, 15.4.3

LICENSE(S)/LICENSE AGREEMENT(S)
Motion picture distribution payment terms, 2.7.1.3
Music/music industry. *See* **MUSIC LICENSING**
Scripted television. *See* **SCRIPTED TELEVISION**
Theater(s), 9.10
Unscripted television. *See* **UNSCRIPTED TELEVISION**
Video games. *See* **VIDEO GAMES**

LICENSORS
Motion picture financing, 3.2.3
Video games, 11.2.4

LIKENESS. *See* **NAME AND LIKENESS**

LIMITED LIABILITY COMPANIES (LLCS)
Choice-of-entity tax considerations, 12.2.3
Membership pledge agreements (motion picture financing), 3.4.6

LINE PRODUCERS
Motion picture development, 1.3.2

LITERARY PUBLISHING
Generally, 10.1
Agency agreements/provisions
  Generally, 10.6
  Author agreements, 10.2.2.14

INDEX

Agreements
  Agency. *See* subhead: Agency agreements/provisions
  Author agreements. *See* **TRADE BOOKS**
  Freelance periodical agreements. *See* subhead: Freelance periodical agreements
Author agreements. *See* **TRADE BOOKS**
Categories of publications, 10.1.1
Copyright(s). *See* **COPYRIGHT(S)**
Educational publications, 10.1.1.2
Freelance periodical agreements
  Generally, 10.4
  Expenses, 10.4.4
  Grant of rights, 10.4.2
  Payments, 10.4.4
  Representations and warranties, 10.4.3
  Subject of the work, 10.4.1
Grant of rights
  Freelance periodical agreements, 10.4.2
  Trade books, 10.2.2.3
Journals
  General circulation journals, 10.1.1.4
  Professional journal publications, 10.5
Nature of industry, 10.1
Newspapers, 10.1.1.3
Periodicals
  Freelance periodical agreements. *See* subhead: Freelance periodical agreements
  General circulation periodicals, 10.1.1.3
Professional publications, 10.1.1.5, 10.5
Reference books, 10.1.1.2
Representations and warranties
  Freelance periodical agreements, 10.4.3
  Trade books, 10.2.2.7
Royalties. *See* **TRADE BOOKS**
Scholarly publications, 10.5
Self-publishing, 10.3
Trade books. *See* **TRADE BOOKS**

LLCS. *See* **LIMITED LIABILITY COMPANIES (LLCS)**

LOANOUT COMPANIES
  Generally, 12.4.1
  Employment agreements, 12.4.1.3
  Non-qualified deferred compensation ("409A"), 12.4.1.4
  Overall tax benefits of, 12.4.1.1
  Work-for-hire relationship(s), 12.4.1.2

LOCATION AGREEMENTS. *See* **UNSCRIPTED TELEVISION**

LOGOS, AUTHORIZATION TO USE
  Unscripted television, 5.6.6

M

MANAGERS
  Generally, 14.1, 14.6
  Business, 14.4
  Competing clients, representation of, 14.5.2
  Conflicts of interest
    Generally, 14.5
    Competing clients, representation of, 14.5.2
    Leveraging, 14.5.3
    Self-dealing, 14.5.1
    Self-promoting, 14.5.4
  Personal, 14.3
  Role of, 14.1
  Self-dealing, 14.5.1
  Self-promoting, 14.5.4

MARKETING
  Billing credit(s) from marketer's perspective
    Generally, 13.1.1.2, 13.1.1.2.a
    Audience inducement, 13.1.1.2.b
    Talent inducement, 13.1.1.2.c
  Video games. *See* **VIDEO GAMES**

MEDIATION OF DISPUTES
  Unscripted television, talent agreements, 5.3.2.1.h

MERCHANDISING INCOME
Music performance(s), 7.3.4.4
Music royalties, 7.4.7.3

MERCHANDISING RIGHTS
Music recording agreements, 7.4.3.4
Scripted television, actor agreements, 6.3.4.9

MERCHANDISING TIE-INS
Generally, 13.1.3
Marketer's perspective, 13.1.3.2
Talent's perspective, 13.1.3.1

MEZZANINE LOANS
Generally, 3.3.4
Equity, 3.3.4.4
Equity investments. *See* subhead: Securities laws and equity investments
Loan agreement, 3.3.4.2
Securities laws and equity investments
  Generally, 3.3.4.5
  Crowdfunding, 3.3.4.5.c
  Regulation D, 3.3.4.5.a
  Regulation S, 3.3.4.5.b
Senior loan documents, 3.3.4.3
Term sheet, 3.3.4.1

MINORS
Unscripted television, appearance releases, 5.6.4

MOTION PICTURE(S)
Agreements. *See* MOTION PICTURE DEVELOPMENT; MOTION PICTURE DISTRIBUTION AGREEMENTS; MOTION PICTURE FINANCE; MOTION PICTURE PRODUCTION
Copyright mortgages, 2.10.2, 3.4.5
Development. *See* MOTION PICTURE DEVELOPMENT
Distribution. *See* MOTION PICTURE DISTRIBUTION
Financing. *See* MOTION PICTURE FINANCE
Music synchronization licenses, 8.3.7.1
Piracy, 2.12
Production. *See* MOTION PICTURE PRODUCTION
Security interests
  Distribution agreements. *See* MOTION PICTURE DISTRIBUTION AGREEMENTS
  Finance agreements. *See* MOTION PICTURE FINANCE
Taxation
  Structuring entertainment transactions, 12.4.2
  Tax deduction for production costs, 12.1.3.1.e
UCC financing statements, 2.10.1
Underlying rights
  Generally, 1.2
  Chain of title, 1.2.1
  Securing, 1.2.2

MOTION PICTURE DEVELOPMENT
Generally, 1.1, 1.3
Actor agreements, 1.3.5
Agreements
  Actor agreements, 1.3.5
  Director agreements, 1.3.4
  Producer agreements, 1.3.3
  Writer agreements, 1.3.1
Box office bonuses, 1.3.7.1
Contingent compensation
  Generally, 1.3.7
  Box office bonuses, 1.3.7.1
  Deferments, 1.3.7.3
  Gross participations, 1.3.7.2
  Net participations, 1.3.7.4
Deferments, 1.3.7.3
Director agreements, 1.3.4
Finance agreements, 3.3.1
Gross participations, 1.3.7.2
Line producers, 1.3.2
Net participations, 1.3.7.4
"Pay or play," 1.3.6
Producer agreements, 1.3.3

INDEX 931

Underlying rights
  Generally, 1.2
  Chain of title, 1.2.1
  Securing, 1.2.2
  Writer agreements, 1.3.1

MOTION PICTURE DISTRIBUTION AGREEMENTS
Generally, 2.1
Advertising rights, 2.3.3, 2.5.2.2
Ancillary rights, 2.5.2.3
Approvals, 2.3.5
Box office bonuses, 2.8.5
Budget, 2.3.1
Cast, 2.3.1
Copyright(s), 2.5.1
"Cross-border portability," 2.4.4
Delivery of pictures, 2.9
Derivative rights, 2.5.2.4
Director, 2.3.1
Distribution expenses, 2.8.3
Distribution fees, 2.8.2
"Distributor," definition of, 2.2
Duration of, 2.4.1
Essential elements of, 2.3.2
Exploitation rights, 2.5.2.1
Forms, 2.1
Gross receipts
  Generally, 2.8.1
  Application of, 2.8
Guarantees. *See* subhead: Minimum guarantees
Holdbacks, 2.6
Interparty agreements, 2.7.2
Minimum guarantees
  Generally, 2.7
  Interparty agreements, 2.7.2
  Payment terms. *See* subhead: Payment terms
  Recoupment of, 2.8.4
  Sales agents/intermediaries, 2.7.3
Miscellaneous provisions, 2.14
Notices of assignment (NOAs), 2.7.2
Parties
  "Distributor," 2.2
  Owner, 2.2
Payment terms
  Generally, 2.7.1

Domestic distribution, 2.7.1.1
Foreign distribution, 2.7.1.2
License agreements, 2.7.1.3
Picture specifications
  Generally, 2.3
  Advertising rights, 2.3.3
  Budget, 2.3.1
  Cast, 2.3.1
  Director, 2.3.1
  Essential elements of, 2.3.2
  Miscellaneous specifications, 2.3.6
  Production cost, 2.3.4
  Screenplay, 2.3.1
Production cost, 2.3.4
Remedy provisions, 2.13
Rights
  Advertising rights, 2.3.3, 2.5.2.2
  Ancillary rights, 2.5.2.3
  Copyright(s), 2.5.1
  Definition of, 2.5.2
  Derivative rights, 2.5.2.4
  Exploitation rights, 2.5.2.1
Sales agents/intermediaries, 2.7.3
Screenplay, 2.3.1
Security interests
  Generally, 2.10
  Copyright mortgages, 2.10.2
  State-federal law conflicts, 2.10.3
  UCC financing statement, 2.10.1
Territory/territorial definitions, 2.4.2, 2.4.3
Theatrical release commitments, 2.11
Video on demand (VOD) bonuses, 2.8.5
Windows, 2.6

MOTION PICTURE FINANCE
Generally, 3.1, 3.5
Agreements
  Generally, 3.3
  Collection account management agreements, 3.4.10
  Development finance, 3.3.1
  Intercreditor agreements, 3.4.7, 3.4.7.3
  Laboratory pledgeholder agreements, 3.4.9

LLC membership pledge
   agreements, 3.4.6
Pre-production finance. *See*
   subhead: Pre-production
   finance
Production finance. *See* **MOTION
   PICTURE PRODUCTION**
Sales agent interparty agreements,
   3.4.7, 3.4.7.2
Security agreements, 3.4.1
Stock agreements, 3.4.6
Borrowers, 3.2.3
Collection account management
   agreements, 3.4.10
Collection agent(s), 3.2.8
Completion guarantor(s), 3.2.5
Completion guaranty, 3.4.8
Copyright mortgages, 3.4.5
Cross-border security issues, 3.4.2
Distributors, 3.2.1
Financiers, 3.2.4
Guilds, 3.2.7
Intercreditor agreements, 3.4.7, 3.4.7.3
Interparty agreements, 3.4.7, 3.4.7.2
Laboratory, 3.2.6
Laboratory pledgeholder agreements,
   3.4.9
Licensors, 3.2.3
LLC membership pledge agreements,
   3.4.6
Miscellaneous parties, 3.2.9
Notices of assignment (NOAs), 3.4.7,
   3.4.7.1
Parties
   Generally, 3.2
   Borrowers, 3.2.3
   Collection agent(s), 3.2.8
   Completion guarantor(s), 3.2.5
   Distributors, 3.2.1
   Financiers, 3.2.4
   Guilds, 3.2.7
   Laboratory, 3.2.6
   Licensors, 3.2.3
   Miscellaneous parties, 3.2.9
   Production special purpose vehicle
      (SPV), 3.2.3
   Sales agent(s), 3.2.2
Pre-production finance
   Budget, 3.3.2
   Finance plan, 3.3.2
   Pre-production facility, 3.3.3
   Strike price, 3.3.2
Production special purpose vehicle
   (SPV), 3.2.3
Sales agent(s)
   Generally, 3.2.2
   Interparty agreements, 3.4.7,
      3.4.7.2
Security interests
   Generally, 3.4
   Copyright mortgages, 3.4.5
   Creation in the U.S., 3.4.3
   Cross-border security issues, 3.4.2
   Perfection under UCC, Article 9,
      3.4.4
   Security agreements, 3.4.1
Stock agreements, 3.4.6

MOTION PICTURE PRODUCTION
Generally, 1.1, 1.4
Above-the-line personnel, 1.4.1
Agreements
   "Boilerplate" provisions, 1.4.2
   Forms, 1.5
   Production service and effects
      agreements, 1.4.7
Below-the-line personnel, 1.4.1
"Boilerplate" contract provisions,
   1.4.2
Clearances, 1.4.4
Crowdfunding, 3.3.4.5c
Finance agreements
   Pre-production finance. *See*
      subhead: Pre-production
      finance
   Production finance. *See* subhead:
      Mezzanine loans
Insurance, 1.4.5
Locations, 1.4.6
Mezzanine loans
   Generally, 3.3.4
   Equity, 3.3.4.4
   Loan agreement, 3.3.4.2
   Securities laws, 3.3.4.5
   Senior loan documents, 3.3.4.3

INDEX

Term sheet, 3.3.4.1
Music, 1.4.3
Pre-production finance
  Budget, 3.3.2
  Finance plan, 3.3.2
  Pre-production facility, 3.3.3
  Strike price, 3.3.2
Production service and effects agreements, 1.4.7
Underlying rights
  Generally, 1.2
  Chain of title, 1.2.1
  Securing, 1.2.2

MOVIES. *See* **MOTION PICTURE(S)**

MULTICHANNEL VIDEO PRIMARY DISTRIBUTORS (MVPDS)
Television, 4.2.4

MUSIC/MUSIC INDUSTRY
Generally, 7.1
Agreements
  Personal appearance(s). *See* **MUSIC PERFORMANCE(S)**
  Publishing agreements. *See* **MUSIC PUBLISHING**
  Recording agreements. *See* **MUSIC RECORDING AGREEMENTS**
Copyright(s). *See* **MUSIC PUBLISHING**
Licensing. *See* **MUSIC LICENSING**
Motion picture production, 1.4.3
Performance(s). *See* **MUSIC PERFORMANCE(S)**
Publishing. *See* **MUSIC PUBLISHING**
Royalties. *See* **MUSIC ROYALTIES**
Tax considerations in structuring entertainment transactions
  Intellectual property, tax benefits for separating, 12.4.3.2
  Shareholder agreements, 12.4.3.3
  Structuring considerations, 12.4.3.1

Theater(s). *See* **MUSICAL THEATRE; THEATER(S)**
Unscripted television. *See* **UNSCRIPTED TELEVISION**

MUSIC LICENSING
Generally, 8.3, 8.3.3
Basic principles of, 8.3.8
Consent decrees, 8.3.6
Master license, 7.4.5
Mechanical licenses, 8.3.1
Performance right(s), 8.3.2
Revenue, 8.3.4
Synchronization licenses
  Generally, 8.3.7
  Motion pictures, 8.3.7.1
  Television, 8.3.7.2
Theater. *See* **THEATER**
Types of licenses/license agreements, 8.3.1, 8.3.5, 8.3.11
Video games, 8.3.9

MUSIC PERFORMANCE(S)
Generally, 7.2
Concert performers
  Generally, 7.2
  "Businesses," as, 7.2.1
  Business form, selection of, 7.2.1.2
  Names, 7.2.1.1
  Personal appearance contracts. *See* subhead: Personal appearance contract(s)
Merchandising income, 7.3.4.4
Music licensing, 8.3.2. *See also* **MUSIC LICENSING**
Personal appearance contract(s)
  Generally, 7.3
  Ancillary market income, 7.3.4.3
  Compensation derived from performance(s), 7.3.4
  Conditions of performance, 7.3.1
  Dressing room(s), 7.3.1.4
  Electricity, 7.3.2.3
  Equipment, 7.3.2.4
  Fan clubs, 7.3.4.5
  Food, 7.3.1.5
  Ground transportation, 7.3.1.2
  Hotel(s), 7.3.1.1

Merchandising income, 7.3.4.4
Performance fees, 7.3.4.1
Performance personnel, 7.3.2.5
Presentation conditions, 7.3.3
Safety requirements, 7.3.2.6
Security, 7.3.1.3
Sponsorship fees, 7.3.4.2
Stage crew, 7.3.2.1
Stage requirement, 7.3.2.2
Technical conditions, 7.3.2
Tour support, 7.3.4.2
Underwriting fees, 7.3.4.2
Venue licensing, 7.3.2.7
VIP ticket packages, 7.3.4.5
Repertoires, 7.2.2
Touring
  Generally, 7.2, 7.2.3
  Tour support, 7.3.4.2
Trademarks, 7.2.1.1

MUSIC PUBLISHING
Acquisition agreements
  Generally, 8.2.9
  Acquisition proposal, 8.2.9.3
  Due diligence, 8.2.9.5
  Financial due diligence, 8.2.9.5.b
  Legal due diligence, 8.2.9.5.a
  Letter of intent, 8.2.9.4
  Long-form, 8.2.9.7
  Non-disclosure agreements, 8.2.9.1
  Prospectus, 8.2.9.2
  Purchase price, 8.2.9.6
Administration agreements
  Generally, 8.2.5
  Accrued royalties, right to, 8.2.5.6
  Administrator's role, 8.2.5.1
  Advances, 8.2.5.5
  Co-administration agreements, 8.2.6
  Controlled compositions, 8.2.5.3
  Fees, 8.2.5.4
  Retention of rights, 8.2.5.7
  Reversion of rights, 8.2.5.6
  Royalties, 8.2.5.4, 8.2.5.6
  Songwriters, payment of, 8.2.5.8
  Term of, 8.2.5.2
Advances
  Administration agreements, 8.2.5.5
  Co-publishing agreements, 8.2.3.4
  Exclusive songwriter agreements, 8.2.2.5
  Foreign subpublishing agreements, 8.2.7.5
  Joint venture agreements, 8.2.8.4, 8.2.8.6
Agreements
  Generally, 8.2
  Acquisition. *See* subhead: Acquisition agreements
  Administration. *See* subhead: Administration agreements
  Co-administration, 8.2.6
  Common, 8.2
  Co-publishing. *See* subhead: Co-publishing agreements
  Exclusive songwriter. *See* subhead: Exclusive songwriter agreements
  Foreign subpublishing. *See* subhead: Foreign subpublishing agreements
  Joint venture. *See* subhead: Joint venture agreements
  License. *See* **MUSIC LICENSING**
  Participation, 8.2.4
  Recording. *See* subhead: Recording agreements
  Single-song, 8.2.1
Approvals
  Co-publishing agreements, 8.2.3.5
  Exclusive songwriter agreements, 8.2.2.6
Co-administration agreements, 8.2.6
Controlled compositions
  Administration agreements, 8.2.5.3
  Foreign subpublishing agreements, 8.2.7.2
  Recording agreement clause(s), 7.4.3.2.b
Co-publishing agreements
  Generally, 8.2.3
  Administration, 8.2.3.2
  Advances, 8.2.3.4
  Approvals, 8.2.3.5
  Copyright ownership of composition, 8.2.3.1

First negotiation and matching
 rights, 8.2.3.7
Income-sharing, 8.2.3.3
Retention of rights, 8.2.3.6
Reversion of rights, 8.2.3.6
Copyright(s)
 Generally, 8.1
 Co-publishing agreements, 8.2.3.1
 Exclusive rights, 8.1.1
 Income sources, 8.1.3
 Music publisher's role, 8.1.2
Exclusive songwriter agreements
 Generally, 8.2.2
 Advances, 8.2.2.5
 Album-per-contract-period
   commitments, 8.2.2.2
 Approvals, 8.2.2.6
 Minimum delivery commitments,
   8.2.2.1
 Option pickups, 8.2.2.3
 Retention of rights, 8.2.2.7
 Reversion of rights, 8.2.2.7
 Royalties, 8.2.2.4
Foreign subpublishing agreements
 Generally, 8.2.7
 Advances, 8.2.7.5
 Controlled compositions, 8.2.7.2
 Retention of rights, 8.2.7.6
 Rights granted, 8.2.7.3
 Royalties, 8.2.7.4
 Term of, 8.2.7.1
Income-sharing
 Co-publishing agreements, 8.2.3.3
 Joint venture agreements, 8.2.8.10
Joint venture agreements
 Generally, 8.2.8
 Additional advances to joint
   venture party, 8.2.8.8
 Advance payments to signed
   writers, 8.2.8.4
 Advance payments to writers in
   option years, 8.2.8.6
 Exclusivity as to potential
   signings, 8.2.8.2
 Income-percentages, sharing of,
   8.2.8.11
 Income-sharing, 8.2.8.10
 Options, exercise of, 8.2.8.7

Overhead, 8.2.8.9
Reversion of administration rights,
 8.2.8.13
Signing fund, 8.2.8.5
Songwriter agreements,
 preparation of, 8.2.8.3
Term of, 8.2.8.12
Writers to be signed, 8.2.8.1
License agreements. *See* **MUSIC
 LICENSING**
Non-disclosure agreements, 8.2.9.1
Participation agreements, 8.2.4
Recording agreements
 Generally, 7.4.3.2.a
 Controlled compositions clause,
   7.4.3.2.b
 Rerecording restriction, 7.4.3.2.c
Retention of rights
 Administration agreements, 8.2.5.7
 Co-publishing agreements, 8.2.3.6
 Exclusive songwriter agreements,
   8.2.2.7
 Foreign subpublishing agreements,
   8.2.7.6
Reversion of rights
 Administration agreements, 8.2.5.6
 Co-publishing agreements, 8.2.3.6
 Exclusive songwriter agreements,
   8.2.2.7
 Joint venture agreements, 8.2.8.13
Royalties
 Administration agreements,
   8.2.5.4, 8.2.5.5
 Exclusive songwriter agreements,
   8.2.2.4
 Foreign subpublishing agreements,
   8.2.7.4
Single-song agreements, 8.2.1
Songwriter agreements
 Exclusive. *See* subhead: Exclusive
   songwriter agreements
 Preparation of, 8.2.8.3

MUSIC RECORDING AGREEMENTS
Generally, 7.4
Bankruptcy issues, 7.4.9
Control issues, 7.4.6, 7.4.6.1
DAT home recordings, 7.4.3.1.b

Delivery issues, 7.4.6, 7.4.6.2
Digital broadcasting, 7.4.3.1.c
Exclusive artist's agreements, 7.4.1.1
Master purchase agreements, 7.4.1.3, 7.4.5
Merchandising rights, 7.4.3.4
Production agreements
   Generally, 7.4.1.2, 7.4.4
   Performer's services, 7.4.4.2
   Production company's services, 7.4.4.1
   Rights granted, 7.4.4.3
Publicity rights, 7.4.3.3
Publishing rights. *See* MUSIC PUBLISHING
Recording commitment, 7.4.2.1
Royalties. *See* MUSIC ROYALTIES
Scope of rights granted
   Composition, rights granted in the, 7.4.3.2
   Merchandising rights, 7.4.3.4
   Publicity rights, 7.4.3.3
   Recording, rights granted in the, 7.4.3.1
   Web site rights, 7.4.3.5
Scope of services
   Generally, 7.4.2
   Exclusive services, 7.4.2.3
   Recording commitment, 7.4.2.1
   Services to be delivered, 7.4.2.2
Types of, 7.4.1
Web site rights, 7.4.3.5

MUSIC ROYALTIES
Accounting(s)
   Generally, 7.4.8
   Audit rights, 7.4.8.5
   Cross-collateralization, 7.4.8.4
   Periods, 7.4.8.1
   Recoupment, 7.4.8.3
   Reserves against returns, 7.4.8.2
Advances, 7.4.7.1
Artist's royalties
   Generally, 7.4.7.2.a
   Adjustments, 7.4.7.2.a.2
   Alternate royalties, 7.4.7.5
   Ancillary distribution, adjustment for, 7.4.7.2.a.2.B

Basic rate, 7.4.7.2.a.1
Digital phonogram distribution, 7.4.7.2.a.2.4
Free goods, adjustment for, 7.4.7.2.a.2.A
New "media" formats, adjustment for, 7.4.7.2.a.2.C
Packaging deduction, 7.4.7.2.a.2.D
Statutory royalties, 7.4.7.3
Audit rights, 7.4.8.5
Calculation
   Generally, 7.4.7.2
   Artist's royalties, 7.4.7.2.a
   Mechanical royalties, 7.4.7.2.b
Collateral entertainment activities, 7.4.7.6
Mechanical royalties, 7.4.7.2.b
Merchandising income, 7.4.7.3
Musical theatre license, royalty pools, 8.3.10.2
Music videos, 7.4.7.5
Publishing royalties
   Administration agreements, 8.2.5.4, 8.2.5.6
   Exclusive songwriter agreements, 8.2.2.4
   Foreign subpublishing agreements, 8.2.7.4
   Recording agreements, 7.4.7.4
Recording agreements
   Generally, 7.4.7
   Advances, 7.4.7.1
   Calculation of royalties. *See* subhead: Calculation
   Collateral entertainment activities, 7.4.7.6
   Merchandising income, 7.4.7.3
   Music videos, 7.4.7.5
   Publishing royalties. *See* subhead: Publishing royalties
   Recording costs, 7.4.7.1
   Videograms, 7.4.7.5
Recording costs, 7.4.7.1
Videograms, 7.4.7.5

MUSICAL THEATRE
Licenses
   Generally, 8.3.10

Dramatists Guild of America
approved-production contract,
8.3.10.1
Fixed dollar shows, 8.3.10.3
Royalty pools, 8.3.10.2
Production rights, 9.2.1

MUSIC VIDEOS
Music royalties, 7.4.7.5

N

NAME AND LIKENESS
Concert performers, 7.2.1.1
Scripted television, actor agreements,
6.3.4.8
Unscripted television
Authorization to use names, 5.6.6
Independent contractor agreements,
5.5.6

NET PARTICIPATIONS
Motion picture development, 1.3.7.4

NETWORKS
Television, 4.2.3

NEWSPAPERS
Literary publishing, 10.1.1.3

NON-DISCLOSURE AGREEMENTS
Music publishing, 8.2.9.1

NOTICES OF ASSIGNMENT (NOAS)
Motion picture distribution
agreements, 2.7.2
Motion picture financing, 3.4.7, 3.4.7.1

O

ONLINE VIDEO DISTRIBUTION.
See **TELEVISION**

OUT-OF-PRINT BOOKS
Trade books, 10.2.2.9

P

PARTNERSHIPS
Tax partnerships, 12.2.3

"PAY OR PLAY"
Motion picture development, 1.3.6

PERFORMANCE OBLIGATIONS
Enforcement of, 13.2

PERIODICALS
Agreements. *See* subhead: Freelance
periodical agreements
Freelance periodical agreements
Generally, 10.4
Expenses, 10.4.4
Grant of rights, 10.4.2
Payments, 10.4.4
Representations and warranties,
10.4.3
Subject of the work, 10.4.1
General circulation, 10.1.1.3
Literary publishing
Freelance periodical agreements.
See subhead: Freelance
periodical agreements
General circulation periodicals,
10.1.1.3

PERSONAL HOLDING COMPANIES
Choice-of-entity tax considerations,
12.2.5

PERSONAL MANAGERS
Generally, 14.3

PERSONAL PERFORMANCE OBLIGATIONS
Enforcement of, 13.2

PILOTS
Scripted television, 6.1.3.1.d

PIRACY
Motion picture(s), 2.12

PITCHING
Scripted television, 6.1.3.1.b

PRIVACY. *See* **VIDEO GAMES**

PRODUCER AGREEMENTS
Motion picture development, 1.3.3

PRODUCTION
Companies. *See* **PRODUCTION COMPANIES**
Costs
   Capitalizing, 12.4.4.3
   Motion picture distribution agreements, 2.3.4
   Scripted television, backend, 6.4.6
   Tax deduction for, 12.1.3.1.e
Motion picture(s). *See* **MOTION PICTURE PRODUCTION**
Television programs
   Scripted television. *See* **SCRIPTED TELEVISION**
   Tax deduction for production costs, 12.1.3.1.e
   Unscripted television. *See* **UNSCRIPTED TELEVISION**
Theater(s)
   Production rights. *See* **THEATER(S)**
   Tax deduction for production costs, 12.1.3.1.e

PRODUCTION COMPANIES
Collection account management agreements, 12.4.4.2
Music recording agreements, 7.4.4.1
Structuring entertainment transactions for tax purposes
   Generally, 12.4.4
   Back-to-back loanout structures, 12.4.4.1
   Capitalizing production costs, 12.4.4.3
   Collection account management agreements, 12.4.4.2
   Crowdfunding, 12.4.4.6
   Income forecast method, 12.4.4.4
   Overhead accounts/planning, 12.4.4.7

Section 181 election/bonus depreciation, 12.4.4.5

PRODUCTION SPECIAL PURPOSE VEHICLE (SPV)
Motion picture financing, 3.2.3

PROFESSIONAL LIABILITY INSURANCE
Entertainment law practice, 15.4.3

PROFESSIONAL PUBLICATIONS
Literary publishing, 10.1.1.5, 10.5

PROFITS
Challenge of defining, 13.4

PUBLIC FILMING NOTICE
Unscripted television, 5.6.7

PUBLICITY CREDIT(S)
Generally, 13.1.2
Marketer's perspective, 13.1.2.2
Talent's perspective, 13.1.2.1

PUBLICITY/PUBLICITY RIGHTS
Estate planning, 12.6
Music recording agreements, 7.4.3.3
Scripted television, actor agreements, 6.3.4.13
Tax planning, 12.6
Video games, 11.5.4

PUBLISHING
Literary. *See* **LITERARY PUBLISHING; TRADE BOOKS**
Music/music industry. *See* **MUSIC PUBLISHING**
Video game publishers, 11.2.2. *See also* **VIDEO GAMES**

Q

QUALIFIED PERSONAL SERVICE COMPANIES (QPSCS)
Cash method of accounting, 12.1.2.1.a
Choice-of-entity tax considerations, 12.2.4

INDEX

R

REALITY-TV SHOWS. *See* **UNSCRIPTED TELEVISION**

REFERENCE BOOKS
Literary publishing, 10.1.1.2

RELEASES AND CONSENTS
Theatrical release commitments, in motion picture distribution agreements, 2.11
Unscripted television releases. *See* **UNSCRIPTED TELEVISION**

REPERTOIRES
Music performance(s), 7.2.2

REPRESENTATIONS AND WARRANTIES
Author agreements, 10.2.2.7
Freelance periodical agreements, 10.4.3
Literary publishing
  Freelance periodical agreements, 10.4.3
  Trade books, 10.2.2.7
Unscripted television
  Music licensing agreements, 5.8.3.3
  Product and service placement agreements, 5.7.5
  Talent agreements, 5.3.2.3.g
Video games. *See* **VIDEO GAMES**

RETENTION OF RIGHTS. *See* **MUSIC PUBLISHING**

REVERSION OF RIGHTS
Books and articles, underlying rights agreements for, 6.2.1.11
Music publishing. *See* **MUSIC PUBLISHING**

REVISIONS
Trade books, 10.2.2.10

REVIVALS
Theater(s), 9.11

ROYALTIES
Music/music industry. *See* **MUSIC ROYALTIES**
Scripted television. *See* **SCRIPTED TELEVISION**
Theater(s)
  Dramatists Guild approved-production contracts, 9.5.2
  Underlying rights agreements, 9.3.3.4
Trade books
  Generally, 10.2.2.6.a
  Advances against royalties, 10.2.2.6.b
  Author agreements, 10.2.2.6.a, 10.2.2.6.b
Video games. *See* **VIDEO GAMES**

S

SALES AGENTS/INTERMEDIARIES
Motion picture distribution agreements, 2.7.3
Motion picture financing
  Generally, 3.2.2
  Interparty agreements, 3.4.7, 3.4.7.2

SCHOLARLY PUBLICATIONS
Literary publishing, 10.5

S-CORPORATIONS
Choice-of-entity tax considerations, 12.2.2, 12.2.7.1

SCREENPLAYS
Motion picture distribution agreements, 2.3.1

SCRIPT DEVELOPMENT
Scripted television, 6.1.3.1.c

SCRIPTED TELEVISION
Generally, 6.1.1, 6.6
Actor agreements
  Generally, 6.3.4
  Biography approvals, 6.3.4.8

Credit/billing, 6.3.4.6
Dressing room(s), 6.3.4.7
Exclusivity, 6.3.4.12
Likeness, 6.3.4.8
Merchandising rights, 6.3.4.9
Miscellaneous approvals, 6.3.4.10
Miscellaneous consultations, 6.3.4.10
Photos, 6.3.4.8
Pilot fees, 6.3.4.3
Pilot services, 6.3.4.2
Promotion, 6.3.4.13
Publicity, 6.3.4.13
Relocation, 6.3.4.11
Series fees, 6.3.4.3
Series guarantees, 6.3.4.5
Series options, 6.3.4.4
Test options, 6.3.4.1
Travel, 6.3.4.11
Agency package commissions, 6.3.6
Agreements
  Actor. *See* subhead: Actor agreements
  Agency package commissions, 6.3.6
  Co-production. *See* subhead: Co-production agreements
  Miscellaneous, key talent agreements, 6.3.7
  Network license. *See* subhead: Network license agreements
  Non-writing-producer(s). *See* subhead: Non-writing-producer agreements
  Pilot director(s). *See* subhead: Pilot director agreements
  Staffing writer(s). *See* subhead: Staffing writer agreements
  Underlying rights. *See* subhead: Underlying rights agreements
  Writer/writing-producer(s). *See* subhead: Writer/writing-producer agreements
Backend
  Generally, 6.4
  Books and articles, underlying rights agreements for, 6.2.1.4
  Cost of production, 6.4.6
Distribution expenses, 6.4.3
Distribution fees, 6.4.2
Gross receipts, 6.4.1
Interest, 6.4.5
Non-writing-producer agreements, 6.3.2.8
Overhead, 6.4.4
Pilot director agreements, 6.3.3.6
Tax incentives, treatment of, 6.4.8
Third-party participations, 6.4.7
Writer/writing-producer agreements, 6.3.1.9
Bonuses
  Books and articles, underlying rights agreements for, 6.2.1.5
  Non-writing-producer agreements, 6.3.2.6
  Pilot director agreements, 6.3.3.5
  Writer/writing-producer agreements, 6.3.1.8
Books and articles, underlying rights agreements for
  Backend, 6.2.1.4
  Bonuses, 6.2.1.5
  Consulting services, 6.2.1.8
  Credit(s), 6.2.1.9
  "Frozen rights," 6.2.1.7
  Granted rights, 6.2.1.6
  Non-fiction pieces, 6.2.1.12
  Option fees/terms, 6.2.1.1
  Purchase price, 6.2.1.2
  Reserved rights, 6.2.1.7
  Reversions, 6.2.1.11
  Royalties, 6.2.1.3
  Subsequent productions, 6.2.1.10
Consulting services
  Books and articles, underlying rights agreements for, 6.2.1.8
  Non-writing-producer agreements, 6.3.2.7
  Writer/writing-producer agreements, 6.3.1.6
Co-production agreements
  Generally, 6.5, 6.5.2
  Deficit(s), 6.5.2.3.d
  Distribution expenses, 6.5.2.3.c
  Distribution fees, 6.5.2.3.b
  Distribution rights, 6.5.2.2

Gross receipts, 6.5.2.3.a
Lead studio, 6.5.2.1
Lead studio overhead, 6.5.2.3.f
Revenues, allocation of, 6.5.2.3
Studio net proceeds, 6.5.2.3.h
Third-party participations, 6.5.2.3.g
Unapproved overages, 6.5.2.3.e
Credit(s)
  Actor agreements, 6.3.4.6
  Books and articles, underlying rights agreements for, 6.2.1.9
  Non-writing-producer agreements, 6.3.2.9
  Pilot director agreements, 6.3.3.7
  Staffing writer agreements, 6.3.5.2
  Writer/writing-producer agreements, 6.3.1.10
Distribution
  Generally, 6.1.3.3
  Co-production agreements, distribution rights under, 6.5.2.2
  Expenses, 6.4.3, 6.5.2.3.c
  Fees, 6.4.2, 6.5.2.3.b
  Media, 6.1.3.3.a
  Territory, 6.1.3.3.b
  Time, 6.1.3.3.c
Exclusivity. *See* subhead: Services and exclusivity
Guarantees
  Actor agreements, series guarantees in, 6.3.4.5
  Staffing writer agreements, 6.3.5.4
Idea to production, from
  Generally, 6.1.3.1
  Packaging, 6.1.3.1.a
  Pilots, 6.1.3.1.d
  Pitching, 6.1.3.1.b
  Script development, 6.1.3.1.c
  Set-up, 6.1.3.1.b
  Staffing, 6.1.3.1.f
  Studio rights acquisition, 6.1.3.1.a
  Upfronts, 6.1.3.1.e
  Writing, 6.1.3.1.f
License agreements. *See* subhead: Network license agreements
Life cycle of a TV series
  Distribution, 6.1.3.3
  Idea to production, from, 6.1.3.1

Production, 6.1.3.2
Locks
  Non-writing-producer agreements, 6.3.2.3
  Writer/writing-producer agreements, 6.3.1.3
Medium, as a, 6.1.2
Merchandising rights, 6.3.4.9
Network license agreements
  Generally, 6.5, 6.5.1
  Breakage, 6.5.1.4.b
  Contingent compensation, 6.5.1.13
  Derivative productions, 6.5.1.10
  Development contributions, 6.5.1.1
  Digital rights (digital platforms), 6.5.1.6.c
  Digital rights (traditional licensees), 6.5.1.6.b
  Initial pilot/series license fees, 6.5.1.4.a
  Later season pilot/series license fees, 6.5.1.4.c
  Minimum orders, 6.5.1.5
  Network approvals, 6.5.1.11
  Network exclusivity, 6.5.1.8
  Network exhibition and runs, 6.5.1.6.a
  Network promotional rights, 6.5.1.12
  Pilot license fees, 6.5.1.4
  Pilot options, 6.5.1.2
  Revenue backstops, 6.5.1.9
  Rights licensed, 6.5.1.6
  Series license fees, 6.5.1.4
  Series options, 6.5.1.2
  Series term, 6.5.1.3
  Subsequent seasons, 6.5.1.10
  Success bonuses, 6.5.1.4.d
  Term of license, 6.5.1.7
  Territory covered, 6.5.1.7
Non-writing-producer agreements
  Generally, 6.3.2
  Backend, 6.3.2.8
  Bonuses, 6.3.2.6
  Consulting services, 6.3.2.7
  Credit(s), 6.3.2.9
  Development fees, 6.3.2.1
  Locks, 6.3.2.3

Perks, 6.3.2.10
Producing fees, 6.3.2.2
Royalties, 6.3.2.5
Services and exclusivity, 6.3.2.4
Subsequent productions, 6.3.2.11
Packaging, 6.1.3.1.a
Perks
   Non-writing-producer agreements, 6.3.2.10
   Pilot director agreements, 6.3.3.8
Pilot director agreements
   Generally, 6.3.3
   Backend, 6.3.3.6
   Bonuses, 6.3.3.5
   Credit(s), 6.3.3.7
   Directing fees, 6.3.3.2
   Executive producing, 6.3.3.3
   Perks, 6.3.3.8
   Royalties, 6.3.3.4
   Services, 6.3.3.1
   Subsequent productions, 6.3.3.9
Pilots, 6.1.3.1.d
Pitching, 6.1.3.1.b
Producing fees
   Non-writing-producer agreements, 6.3.2.2
   Writer/writing-producer agreements, 6.3.1.2
Production of program(s)
   Generally, 6.1.3.2
   Co-production agreements. *See* subhead: Co-production agreements
   Idea to. *See* subhead: Idea to production, from
Royalties
   Books and articles, underlying rights agreements for, 6.2.1.3
   Non-writing-producer agreements, 6.3.2.5
   Pilot director agreements, 6.3.3.4
   Writer/writing-producer agreements, 6.3.1.7
Script development, 6.1.3.1.c
Services and exclusivity
   Actor agreements, 6.3.4.12
   Network license agreements, 6.5.1.8

Non-writing-producer agreements, 6.3.2.4
Pilot director agreements, 6.3.3.1
Staffing writer agreements, 6.3.5.6
Writer/writing-producer agreements, 6.3.1.4
Set-up, 6.1.3.1.b
Staffing, 6.1.3.1.f
Staffing writer agreements
   Generally, 6.3.5
   Credit(s), 6.3.5.2
   Episodic scripts, 6.3.5.5
   Exclusivity, 6.3.5.6
   Fees, 6.3.5.3
   Guarantees, 6.3.5.4
   Options, 6.3.5.1
   Showrunners, 6.3.5.7
   Term, 6.3.5.1
Studio business affairs perspective, 6.1.1
Studio rights acquisition, 6.1.3.1.a
Subsequent productions
   Books and articles, underlying rights agreements for, 6.2.1.10
   Network license agreements, 6.5.1.10
   Non-writing-producer agreements, 6.3.2.11
   Pilot director agreements, 6.3.3.9
   Writer/writing-producer agreements, 6.3.1.12
Talent agreements
   Actor(s). *See* subhead: Actor agreements
   Agency package commissions, 6.3.6
   Miscellaneous, key agreements, 6.3.7
   Non-writing-producer(s). *See* subhead: Non-writing-producer agreements
   Pilot director(s). *See* subhead: Pilot director agreements
   Staffing writer(s). *See* subhead: Staffing writer agreements
   Writer/writing-producer(s). *See* subhead: Writer/writing-producer agreements

INDEX

Tax incentives, 6.1.4, 6.4.8
Underlying rights agreements
  Books and articles. *See* subhead:
    Books and articles, underlying
    rights agreements for
  Format rights, 6.2.3
  Life rights, 6.2.2
Upfronts, 6.1.3.1.c
Writer/writing-producer agreements
  Generally, 6.3.1
  Backend, 6.3.1.9
  Bonuses, 6.3.1.8
  Consulting services, 6.3.1.6
  Credit(s), 6.3.1.10
  Perks, 6.3.1.11
  Preexisting commitments, 6.3.1.5
  Producing fees, 6.3.1.2
  Royalties, 6.3.1.7
  Services and exclusivity, 6.3.1.4
  Subsequent productions, 6.3.1.12
  Writing and spec acquisition, 6.3.1.1
  Years/locks, 6.3.1.3
Writing, 6.1.3.1.f

SECURITIES LAWS. *See*
MEZZANINE LOANS

SECURITY INTERESTS. *See*
MOTION PICTURE
DISTRIBUTION AGREEMENTS;
MOTION PICTURE FINANCE

SELF-PUBLISHING
Literary publishing, 10.3

SHAREHOLDER AGREEMENTS
Musical entertainment transactions, tax considerations in structuring, 12.4.3.3

SOCIAL MEDIA CHANNELS
Video games, 11.4.3.5.e.5

SPORTS
eSports, 11.6.1
Video games, 11.1.3.6

STOCK AGREEMENTS
Motion picture financing, 3.4.6

STUDIOS
Television, 4.2.2

SUBSCRIPTION VIDEO ON
DEMAND (SVOD)
Television, 4.3.1.1

SUBSIDIARY RIGHTS
Trade books, 10.2.2.6.c

T

TALENT REPRESENTATION. *See*
AGENT/AGENCY
REPRESENTATION;
MANAGERS

TAXATION
Generally, 12.1
Accounting method(s)
  Generally, 12.1.2
  Accrual method, 12.1.2.2
  Cash method, 12.1.2.1
Accrual method of accounting
  Generally, 12.1.2.2
  Determinations of liability, 12.1.2.2.b
  Economic performance, 12.1.2.2.c
  Fixed liability, 12.1.2.2.a
Accumulated earnings tax, 12.2.6
Amortization deductions, 12.1.3.1.d
Calendar year, 12.1.6.4
Cash method of accounting
  Generally, 12.1.2.1
  Gross receipts test, 12.1.2.1.b
  Qualified personal service corporations, 12.1.2.1.a
Choice-of-entity considerations
  Generally, 12.2
  Accumulated earnings tax, 12.2.6
  California gross receipts tax, 12.2.7.1
  California net income tax on S-corporations, 12.2.7.1
  C-corporations, 12.2.1

Limited liability companies
  (LLCs), 12.2.3
Personal holding companies,
  12.2.5
Qualified personal service
  companies (QPSCs), 12.2.4
S-corporations, 12.2.2, 12.2.7.1
State-entity level taxes, 12.2.7
Tax partnerships, 12.2.3
Credits
  Generally, 12.1.3.2
  Publisher-funded video games,
    11.3.2.6
Deductions
  Generally, 12.1.3.1
  Amortization, 12.1.3.1.d
  Depreciation, 12.1.3.1.d
  Entertainment expenses, 12.1.3.1.c
  Film production costs, 12.1.3.1.e
  Meal(s) expenses, 12.1.3.1.c
  Pass-through deduction (Tax Act
    and Jobs Act), 12.1.3.1.f
  Personal services compensation,
    12.1.3.1.a
  Television production costs,
    12.1.3.1.e
  Theater production costs, 12.1.3.1.e
  Traveling expenses, 12.1.3.1.b
Deferral(s)
  Generally, 12.1.4
  Advance payments, deferral
    method for, 12.1.4.1
Depreciation deductions, 12.1.3.1.d
Entertainment expenses, 12.1.3.1.c
Film production costs, 12.1.3.1.e
Fiscal year, 12.1.6.1
Gross income exception (agency
  theory), 12.1.5
Income
  Generally, 12.1.1
  Accumulated earnings tax, 12.2.6
  Character of, 12.1.3.4
  Gross income exception (agency
    theory), 12.1.5
  Personal services compensation,
    12.1.3.1.a
Independent contractors *versus*
  employees, 12.3

Intellectual property
  Generally, 12.5
  Copyrights, 12.5.1
  Music transactions, tax benefits for
    separating IP in, 12.4.3.2
  Trademarks, 12.5.2
Loanout companies
  Generally, 12.4.1
  Employment agreements, 12.4.1.3
  Non-qualified deferred
    compensation ("409A"),
    12.4.1.4
  Overall benefits of, 12.4.1.1
  Work-for-hire relationship(s),
    12.4.1.2
Loss limitations
  Net operating losses, 12.1.3.3.c
  Passive activity losses, 12.1.3.3.a
  Pass-through loss limitations (Tax
    Act and Jobs Act), 12.1.3.3.b
Meal(s) expenses, 12.1.3.1.c
Minimizing tax liability
  Character of income, 12.1.3.4
  Loss limitations. *See* subhead:
    Loss limitations
  Tax credits. *See* subhead: Credits
  Tax deductions. *See* subhead:
    Deductions
  Writer's share (musical works),
    12.1.3.5
Motion pictures
  Structuring entertainment
    transactions, 12.4.2
  Tax deduction for production
    costs, 12.1.3.1.e
Musical works (writer's share),
  12.1.3.5
Music transactions, structuring
  Intellectual property, tax benefits
    for separating, 12.4.3.2
  Shareholder agreements, 12.4.3.3
  Structuring considerations, 12.4.3.1
Net operating losses, 12.1.3.3.c
Passive activity losses, 12.1.3.3.a
Pass-through deduction (Tax Act and
  Jobs Act), 12.1.3.1.f
Pass-through loss limitations (Tax
  Act and Jobs Act), 12.1.3.3.b

INDEX

Personal services compensation, 12.1.3.1.a
Production companies
  Generally, 12.4.4
  Back-to-back loanout structures, 12.4.4.1
  Capitalizing production costs, 12.4.4.3
  Collection account management agreements, 12.4.4.2
  Crowdfunding, 12.4.4.6
  Income forecast method, 12.4.4.4
  Overhead accounts/planning, 12.4.4.7
  Section 181 election/bonus depreciation, 12.4.4.5
Publicity rights, tax planning for, 12.6
Qualified personal service companies (QPSCs)
  Cash method of accounting, 12.1.2.1.a
  Choice-of-entity considerations, 12.2.4
  Section 444 election, 12.1.6.3
Structuring entertainment transactions
  Loanout companies. *See* subhead: Loanout companies
  Motion pictures, 12.4.2
  Music. *See* subhead: Music transactions, structuring
  Production companies. *See* subhead: Production companies
  State tax incentives, 12.4.5
  Television, 12.4.2
Taxable years(s)
  Generally, 12.1.6
  Calendar year, 12.1.6.4
  Fiscal year, 12.1.6.1
  Required years, 12.1.6.2
  Section 444 election, 12.1.6.3
Tax Act and Jobs Act
  Pass-through deduction, 12.1.3.1.f
  Pass-through loss limitations, 12.1.3.3.b
Television
  Scripted television, tax incentives for, 6.1.4, 6.4.8

Structuring entertainment transactions, 12.4.2
Tax deduction for production costs, 12.1.3.1.e
Television production costs, 12.1.3.1.e
Theater production costs, 12.1.3.1.e
Traveling expenses, 12.1.3.1.b

TELEVISION
Generally, 4.1
Advertisers, 4.2.6
Advertising-Supported Video on Demand (AVOD), 4.3.1.2
Agreements. *See* **SCRIPTED TELEVISION; UNSCRIPTED TELEVISION**
Broadcast stations, 4.2.5
Credit(s). *See* **SCRIPTED TELEVISION; UNSCRIPTED TELEVISION**
Digital broadcasting
  Digital content companies, roles of, 4.3.3
  Network license agreements, 6.5.1.6.b, 6.5.1.6.c
  Scripted television, 6.5.1.6.b, 6.5.1.6.c
Distribution
  Agreements. *See* **UNSCRIPTED TELEVISION**
  Online video. *See* subhead: Online video distribution
  Scripted television. *See* **SCRIPTED TELEVISION**
Free Video on Demand (FVOD), 4.3.1.4
Multichannel video primary distributors (MVPDs), 4.2.4
Music synchronization licenses, 8.3.7.2
Networks, 4.2.3
Online video distribution
  Generally, 4.3
  Advertising-Supported Video on Demand (AVOD), 4.3.1.2
  Digital content companies, roles of, 4.3.3

Free Video on Demand (FVOD), 4.3.1.4
Miscellaneous key distinctions, 4.3.2
Subscription Video on Demand (SVOD), 4.3.1.1
Transactional Video on Demand (TVOD), 4.3.1.3
Types of, 4.3.1
Video on Demand (VOD), 4.3.1.5
"Players" involved, 4.2
Production costs, tax deduction for, 12.1.3.1.e
Production of program(s)
  Scripted television. See SCRIPTED TELEVISION
  Unscripted television. See UNSCRIPTED TELEVISION
Scripted. See SCRIPTED TELEVISION
Studios, 4.2.2
Subscription Video on Demand (SVOD), 4.3.1.1
Talent (service providers), 4.2.1
Taxation
  Structuring entertainment transactions, 12.4.2
  Tax deduction for production costs, 12.1.3.1.e
Transactional Video on Demand (TVOD), 4.3.1.3
Unscripted. See UNSCRIPTED TELEVISION
Video on Demand (VOD), 4.3.1.5

THEATER(S)
Generally, 9.1
Actor's agreements
  Designer contracts, 9.8.2.3
  Minimum, basic agreements, 9.8.2.1
  Musical arranger contracts, 9.8.2.4
  Orchestrator contracts, 9.8.2.4
  Star contract, 9.8.2.2
Agreements
  Actor's. See subhead: Actor's agreements
  Choreographer contracts, 9.8.1
  Collaboration, 9.4
  Designer contracts, 9.8.2.3
  Development enhancement, 9.6.1
  Director contracts, 9.8.1
  Dramatists Guild approved-production contracts. See subhead: Dramatists Guild approved-production contracts
  Musical arranger contracts, 9.8.2.4
  Orchestrator contracts, 9.8.2.4
  Star contract, 9.8.2.2
  Underlying rights. See subhead: Underlying rights agreements
Choreographer contracts, 9.8.1
Collaboration agreements, 9.4
Credit(s)
  Development, 9.6.5
  Underlying rights agreements, 9.3.3.5
Designer contracts, 9.8.2.3
Development
  Generally, 9.6
  Control issues, 9.6.3
  Credit(s), 9.6.5
  Enhancement agreements, 9.6.1
  Enhancement funds, 9.6.2
  Financial participations, 9.6.4
  Physical production, 9.6.6
Director contracts, 9.8.1
Dramatic personae, 9.1
Dramatists Guild approved-production contracts
  Generally, 9.5
  Advance payments, 9.5.1
  Billing, 9.5.6
  Cast albums, 9.5.8
  Commercial use products, 9.5.7
  Musical theatre licenses, 8.3.10.1
  Option payments, 9.5.1
  Option periods, 9.5.1
  Production rights, additional, 9.5.4
  Royalties, 9.5.2
  Subsidiary rights, 9.5.3
  Travel expenses, 9.5.5
Financing, 9.7
License agreements, 9.10
Motion picture distribution agreements, 2.11

INDEX 947

Music/music industry
  Arranger contracts, 9.8.2.4
  Musical theatre. *See* subhead"
    Musical theatre
  Orchestrator contracts, 9.8.2.4
  Pre-existing musical compositions,
    right to use, 9.3.3.7
Musical theatre
  Licenses. *See* subhead: Musical
    theater licenses
  Production rights, 9.2.1
Musical theatre licenses
  Generally, 8.3.10
  Dramatists Guild approved-
    production contracts, 8.3.10.1
  Fixed dollar shows, 8.3.10.3
  Royalty pools, 8.3.10.2
Orchestrator contracts, 9.8.2.4
Physical production, 9.6.6
Pre-existing musical compositions,
  right to use, 9.3.3.7
Production
  Rights. *See* subhead: Production
    rights
  Tax deduction for costs of,
    12.1.3.1.e
Production rights
  Dramatists Guild approved-
    production contracts, 9.5.4
  First-class productions, 9.2.2
  For-profit theatre, 9.2.3
  Miscellaneous productions, 9.2.2
  Musicals, 9.2.1
  Non-profit theatre, 9.2.3
  Plays, 9.2.1
Release commitments, 2.11
Revivals, 9.11
Royalties
  Dramatists Guild approved-
    production contracts, 9.5.2
  Underlying rights agreements,
    9.3.3.4
Star contract(s), 9.8.2.2
Touring, 9.9
Underlying rights
  Agreements. *See* subhead:
    Underlying rights agreements
  Kinds of underlying material, 9.3.1
  Rights that need to be acquired,
    9.3.2
Underlying rights agreements
  Credit(s), 9.3.3.5
  Merger, 9.3.3.3
  Net profits, 9.3.3.4
  Option exercise, 9.3.3.2
  Option payments, 9.3.3.4
  Option periods, 9.3.3.1
  Pre-existing musical compositions,
    right to use, 9.3.3.7
  Royalties, 9.3.3.4
  Special studio-issues, 9.3.3.6
  Terms of, 9.3.3

TITLE BILLING CREDIT(S)
Generally, 13.1.1
Marketer's perspective
  Generally, 13.1.1.2, 13.1.1.2.a
  Audience inducement, 13.1.1.2.b
  Talent inducement, 13.1.1.2.c
Talent's perspective, 13.1.1.1

TOURING
Music performance(s)
  Generally, 7.2, 7.2.3
  Tour support, 7.3.4.2
Theater(s), 9.9

TRADE BOOKS
Generally, 10.1.1.1
Author agreements
  Accounting statement and
    inspections, 10.2.2.12
  Advances against royalties,
    10.2.2.6.a
  Agency provision, 10.2.2.14
  Analyzing the terms of, 10.2.2
  Compensation, 10.2.2.6
  Competing works, 10.2.2.13
  Copyright, 10.2.2.11
  Delivery of work, 10.2.2.4
  Description of the work, 10.2.2.2
  Grant of rights, 10.2.2.3
  Indemnification provisions, 10.2.2.7
  Manuscript, acceptance of, 10.2.2.5
  Next works, 10.2.2.8
  Opening provisions, 10.2.2.1

Out-of-print books, 10.2.2.9
Representations and warranties, 10.2.2.7
Revisions, 10.2.2.10
Royalties, 10.2.2.6.a, 10.2.2.6.b
Subsidiary rights, 10.2.2.6.c
Work, the, 10.2.2.2
Copyright, 10.2.2.11. *See also* **COPYRIGHT(S)**
Getting the deal, 10.2.1
Out-of-print books, 10.2.2.9
Revisions, 10.2.2.10
Royalties
  Generally, 10.2.2.6.a
  Advances against royalties, 10.2.2.6.b
  Author agreements, 10.2.2.6.a, 10.2.2.6.b
  Subsidiary rights, 10.2.2.6.c

TRADEMARKS
Music performance(s), 7.2.1.1
Taxation of intellectual property in, 12.5.2
Unscripted television, talent agreements, 5.3.2.3.a

TRANSACTIONAL VIDEO ON DEMAND (TVOD)
Television, 4.3.1.3

TRAVEL
See also **TOURING**
Expenses
  Dramatists Guild approved-production contracts, 9.5.5
  Tax deduction for, 12.1.3.1.b
  Scripted television, actor agreements, 6.3.4.11

U

UCC FINANCING STATEMENTS
Motion picture(s), 2.10.1

ULTRA-HAZARDOUS ACTIVITIES
Unscripted television releases, 5.6.3

UNIONS
Collective bargaining agreements, 15.2.3
Unscripted television, talent agreements, 5.3.2.3.d

UNSCRIPTED TELEVISION
Generally, 5.1, 5.9
Acquired footage license, 5.6.5
Agreements
  Composer agreements. *See* subhead: Composer agreements
  Co-production agreements. *See* subhead: Option, co-production, and joint venture agreements
  Distribution. *See* subhead: Distribution agreements
  Independent contractors. *See* subhead: Independent contractor agreements
  Joint venture agreements. *See* subhead: Option, co-production, and joint venture agreements
  Location agreements. *See* subhead: Location agreements
  Music licensing. *See* subhead: Music licensing agreements
  Option agreements. *See* subhead: Option, co-production, and joint venture agreements
  Product placement agreements. *See* subhead: Product and service placement agreements
  Service placement agreements. *See* subhead: Product and service placement agreements
  Talent agreements. *See* subheads: Talent agreements; Talent attachment agreements
Appearance releases
  Minors, 5.6.4
  Standard appearance. *See* subhead: Standard appearance release
Assignment(s)
  Independent contractor agreements, 5.5.7
  Talent agreements, 5.3.2.3.f
Assumption of risk, 5.6.3

INDEX

Composer agreements
  Generally, 5.8.1
  Credits, 5.8.2.3
  Fees, 5.8.2.1
  Ownership rights, 5.8.2.2
Confidentiality
  Independent contractor agreements, 5.5.8
  Location agreements, 5.6.1.4
  Standard appearance release, 5.6.2.3
Consents. *See* subhead: Releases and consents
Co-production agreements. *See* subhead: Option, co-production, and joint venture agreements
Credits
  Composer agreements, 5.8.2.3
  Independent contractor agreements, 5.5.3
  Option, co-production, and joint venture agreements, 5.2.4
Distribution agreements
  Generally, 5.4
  Approvals, 5.4.4
  Delivery of programs, 5.4.5
  Editing of programs, 5.4.5
  Granted rights, 5.4.1
  Guidelines, 5.4.4
  License fees, 5.4.3
  Payments, 5.4.3
  Production budgets, 5.4.3
  Promotion of series, 5.4.6
  Territory, 5.4.2
Indemnity and indemnification
  Music licensing agreements, 5.8.3.3
  Product and service placement agreements, 5.7.5
Independent contractor agreements
  Generally, 5.5.1
  Assignment(s), 5.5.7
  Benefits, 5.5.3
  Confidentiality, 5.5.8
  Consideration, 5.5.3
  Credits, 5.5.3
  Duration of, 5.5.2
  Expenses, 5.5.3
  Name and likeness, 5.5.6

Services to be provided, 5.5.2
Status of contractor, 5.5.4
"Work for hire," 5.5.5
Joint venture agreements. *See* subhead: Option, co-production, and joint venture agreements
Licenses/license agreements
  Acquired footage license, 5.6.5
  Music licenses. *See* subhead: Music licensing agreements
  Still photograph license, 5.6.5
Location agreements
  Generally, 5.6
  Compensation, 5.6.1.3
  Confidentiality, 5.6.1.4
  Duration of, 5.6.1.2
  Grant of rights, 5.6.1.1
Logos, authorization to use, 5.6.6
Minors, appearance releases for, 5.6.4
Music
  Composer agreements. *See* subhead: Composer agreements
  Licensing agreements. *See* subhead: Music licensing agreements
Music licensing agreements
  Generally, 5.8.1
  Compensation, 5.8.3.2
  Grant of rights, 5.8.3.1
  Indemnification provisions, 5.8.3.3
  Warranties, 5.8.3.3
Name and likeness
  Authorization to use names, 5.6.6
  Independent contractor agreements, 5.5.6
Option, co-production, and joint venture agreements
  Generally, 5.2
  "Control" terms, 5.2.3
  Credits, 5.2.4
  Duration of, 5.2.1
  Fees and payments, 5.2.2
  "Freeze period," 5.2.1
  Post-term obligations/rights, 5.2.5
  "Tail period," 5.2.1
Product and service placement agreements
  Generally, 5.7.1
  Failure to place product, 5.7.2

Fees and payments, 5.7.4
Indemnity provisions, 5.7.5
Manner of display, 5.7.3
Placement of product, 5.7.2
Representations and warranties, 5.7.5
Production of program(s)
  Co-production agreements. *See* subhead: Option, co-production, and joint venture agreements
  Distribution agreements and production budgets, 5.4.3
  Talent agreements, 5.3.2.1.c
Products
  Authorization to use, 5.6.6
  Placement agreements. *See* subhead: Product and service placement agreements
Public filming notice, 5.6.7
Releases and consents
  Generally, 5.6
  Acquired footage license, 5.6.5
  Logos, authorization to use, 5.6.6
  Minors' appearance releases, 5.6.4
  Names, authorization to use, 5.6.6
  Products, authorization to use, 5.6.6
  Public filming notice, 5.6.7
  Standard appearance. *See* subhead: Standard appearance release
  Still photograph license, 5.6.5
  Ultra-hazardous activities, 5.6.3
Representations and warranties
  Music licensing agreements, 5.8.3.3
  Product and service placement agreements, 5.7.5
  Talent agreements, 5.3.2.3.g
Service placement agreements. *See* subhead: Product and service placement agreements
Standard appearance release
  Compensation, 5.6.2.2
  Confidentiality, 5.6.2.3
  Grant of rights, 5.6.2.1
  Medical information, authorization for release of, 5.6.2.5
  Third-party releases, 5.6.2.4
Still photograph license, 5.6.5

Talent agreements
  Generally, 5.3.2
  "Access" provisions, 5.3.2.1.d
  Additional participation, 5.3.2.1.h
  Arbitration of disputes, 5.3.2.3.h
  Assignments, 5.3.2.3.f
  Contingent compensation, 5.3.2.1.b
  "Employment relationship," 5.3.2.3.e
  Fixed compensation, 5.3.2.1.a
  Grant of rights, 5.3.2.2
  Guilds, 5.3.2.3.d
  Locations, 5.3.2.1.e
  Mediation of disputes, 5.3.2.3.h
  On-camera services, 5.3.2.1.f
  Participation provision(s), 5.3.2.1
  Post-production participation, 5.3.2.1.g
  Pre-production of program, 5.3.2.1.c
  Production of program, 5.3.2.1.c
  Promotional appearances, 5.3.2.1.i
  "Remedy" provisions, 5.3.2.3.c
  Representations, 5.3.2.3.g
  Termination rights, 5.3.2.3.b
  Trademark restrictions, 5.3.2.3.a
  Unions, 5.3.2.3.d
Talent attachment agreements
  Generally, 5.3
  Compensation, 5.3.1.4
  Development services, 5.3.1.3
  Length of attachment, 5.3.1.1
  Non-compete provision(s), 5.3.1.2
Ultra-hazardous activities, 5.6.3

V

VIDEO GAMES
Generally, 11.1, 11.7
Action-adventure games, 11.1.3.3
Action games, 11.1.3.1
Adventure games, 11.1.3.2
Agreements
  Developer-console manufacturer agreements, 11.4.4.1.b
  Operational, 11.4.4
  Publisher-console manufacturer agreements, 11.4.4.1.c

INDEX 951

Publishing. *See* subhead:
  Publishing agreement(s)
Ancillary products, rights in,
  11.4.3.8.b
Approvals, 11.4.3.5.e.1
Business models for
  Generally, 11.1.4
  Free-to-play model, 11.1.4.3
  Premium purchase price, 11.1.4.1
  Subscriptions, 11.1.4.2
Casual games, 11.1.3.8
Certification(s), 11.4.3.5.e.2
Children's Online Privacy Protection
  Act (COPPA), 11.5.2.1
Commercializing, 11.4.4
Concepting and pitch decks
  Generally, 11.4.1
  Budget(s), 11.4.1.5
  Design pillars, 11.4.1.2
  Gameplay loop, 11.4.1.3
  Market analysis, 11.4.1.4
  Miscellaneous materials, 11.4.1.6
  World narrative(s), 11.4.1.1
Console games, 11.1.2.2
Console manufacturers
  Generally, 11.2.3
  Developer-console manufacturer
    agreements, 11.4.4.1.b
  Initial due diligence, 11.4.4.1.a
  Publisher-console manufacturer
    agreements, 11.4.4.1.c
  Relationships with, 11.4.4.1
Consumer protection
  Generally, 11.5.2
  Children's Online Privacy
    Protection Act (COPPA),
    11.5.2.1
  Subscription pricing, 11.5.2.2
Creation
  Budget(s), 11.4.1.5
  Financing/funding. *See* subhead:
    Financing/funding
  Pitch decks. *See* subhead:
    Concepting and pitch decks
  Pitching financiers, 11.4.2
Crowdfunding, 11.3.2.5.a
Customer support, 11.4.3.5.e.6,
  11.4.4.4

Data privacy/protection
  Generally, 11.5.1
  Best practices, 11.5.1.3
  Children's Online Privacy
    Protection Act (COPPA),
    11.5.2.1
  European data protection, 11.5.1.2
  U.S. data protection, 11.5.1.1
Definitions, 11.4.3.1
Design pillars, 11.4.1.2
Developer(s)
  Generally, 11.2.1
  Advances, recoupment of, 11.4.3.6.b
  Console manufacturers,
    relationships with, 11.4.4.1
  Developer-console manufacturer
    agreements, 11.4.4.1.b
  Development responsibilities. *See*
    subhead: Development and
    operational responsibilities
  Initial due diligence, 11.4.4.1.a
  Proprietary technology of, 11.4.3.1.b
Development and operational
  responsibilities
  Generally, 11.4.3.5.d
  "Bug" correction, 11.4.3.5.d.5
  Creative control, 11.4.3.5.d.2
  Developer responsibilities,
    11.4.3.5.d.1
  Key personnel, 11.4.3.5.d.4
  Ongoing content creation,
    11.4.3.5.d.6
  Outsourcing development,
    11.4.3.5.d.3
  Sublicensing development,
    11.4.3.5.d.3
Distributors, 11.2.3
Downstream and additional rights,
  11.4.3.8
End-user assisted funding
  Generally, 11.3.2.5
  Crowdfunding, 11.3.2.5.a
  Early access sales, 11.3.2.5.b
  Issues with, 11.3.2.5.c
Equity funding, 11.3.2.4
European data protection, 11.5.1.2
Financing/funding
  Creation of games, 11.3

INDEX

End-user. *See* subhead: End-user assisted funding
Minimum guarantees, 11.4.3.2.b
Negotiating the publishing deal, 11.4.3.2
Pitching financiers, 11.4.2
Project finance funds, 11.4.3.2.a
Publishers. *See* subhead: Publisher-funded games
Recoupable/non-recoupable funds, 11.4.3.2.c
Self-funding, 11.3.1
First Amendment issues, 11.5.3
Free-to-play business model, 11.1.4.3
Future works, rights in, 11.4.3.8.a
Gameplay loop, 11.4.1.3
Genres, 11.1.3
Industry entities, 11.2
License(s)/license grant(s)
   Generally, 11.4.3.3
   Exclusive *versus* non-exclusive rights, 11.4.3.3.c
   Intellectual property, 11.4.4.2
   License fees, 11.4.3.2.b
   Representations/warranties. *See* subhead: Representations and warranties
   Right to commercially exploit game, 11.4.3.3.a
   Right to market the game, 11.4.3.3.b
   Right to operate game, 11.4.3.3.a
   Sublicensing development, 11.4.3.5.d.3
Licensors, 11.2.4
Localization(s), 11.4.3.5.e.4
Marketing of games
   Generally, 11.4.3.3.b
   Brand awareness, 11.4.4.3.b
   Market analysis, 11.4.1.4
   Marketing materials, ownership of, 11.4.3.5.b
   Marketing support, 11.4.4.3
   User acquisition, 11.4.4.3.a
Meaning of term "video game," 11.1.1
Middleware providers, 11.2.4
Milestone review, 11.4.3.5.e.1
Mobile games, 11.1.2.3
Music licensing, 8.3.9

Negotiating the publishing deal
   Generally, 11.4.3
   Definitions, 11.4.3.1
   Downstream and additional rights, 11.4.3.8
   Expiration of agreement, 11.4.3.7.a
   Funding, 11.4.3.2
   License grants, 11.4.3.3
   Ownership terms, 11.4.3.5
   Representations and warranties, 11.4.3.4
   Royalties and audits, 11.4.3.6
   Termination of agreement, 11.4.3.7.b–d
   Winding-up, 11.4.3.7.e
New platforms, 11.1.2.5
Nomenclature, 11.1
Operational agreements, 11.4.4
Operational responsibilities. *See* subhead: Development and operational responsibilities
Outsourcing development, 11.4.3.5.d.3
Ownership clauses in publishing agreements
   Generally, 11.4.3.5
   Billing databases, 11.4.3.5.c
   Development responsibilities. *See* subhead: Development and operational responsibilities
   Game, 11.4.3.5.a
   Marketing materials, 11.4.3.5.b
   Operational responsibilities. *See* subhead: Development and operational responsibilities
   Publisher responsibilities. *See* subhead: Publisher reponsibilities
   User databases, 11.4.3.5.c
Payment gateways, 11.4.4.5
Payment processors, 11.4.4.5
PC games, 11.1.2.1
Pitch decks. *See* subhead: Concepting and pitch decks
Pitching financiers, 11.4.2
Platform(s)
   Generally, 11.1.2
   Definition of, 11.4.3.1.c
Premium-purchase-price business model, 11.1.4.1

INDEX

Prototype deals, 11.3.2.3
Publicity right(s), 11.5.4
Publisher(s)/publishing
   Generally, 11.2.2
   Agreements. *See* subhead:
      Publishing agreement(s)
   Console manufacturers,
      relationships with, 11.4.4.1
   Funding games. *See* subhead:
      Publisher-funded games
   Initial due diligence, 11.4.4.1.a
   Negotiating the deal. *See* subhead:
      Negotiating the publishing deal
   Publisher-console manufacturer
      agreements, 11.4.4.1.c
   Publisher materials, definition of,
      11.4.3.1.d
   Publisher responsibilities. *See*
      subhead: Publisher responsibilities
Publisher-funded games
   Generally, 11.3.2
   End-user assisted funding, 11.3.2.5
   Equity funding, 11.3.2.4
   Prototype deal, 11.3.2.3
   Recoupment deal, 11.3.2.2
   Tax credits, 11.3.2.6
   Traditional publishing deal,
      11.3.2.2
   Work for hire, 11.3.2.1
Publisher responsibilities
   Generally, 11.4.3.5.e
   Approvals, 11.4.3.5.e.1
   Certification(s), 11.4.3.5.e.2
   Customer support, 11.4.3.5.e.6
   Localization(s), 11.4.3.5.e.4
   Milestone review, 11.4.3.5.e.1
   Quality assurance, 11.4.3.5.e.2
   Social media channels, 11.4.3.5.e.5
   Technical infrastructure/
      operation(s), 11.4.3.5.e.3
   Web sites, 11.4.3.5.e.5
Publishing agreement(s)
   Ancillary products, rights in,
      11.4.3.8.b
   Definitions, 11.4.3.1
   Development responsibilities. *See*
      subhead: Development and
      operational responsibilities

Downstream and additional rights,
      11.4.3.8
Expiration of, 11.4.3.7, 11.4.3.7.a
Future works, rights in, 11.4.3.8.a
License grants. *See* subhead:
   License(s)/license grant(s)
Minimum guarantees, 11.4.3.2.b
Negotiating. *See* subhead:
   Negotiating the publishing deal
Operational responsibilities. *See*
   subhead: Development and
   operational responsibilities
Ownership terms. *See* subhead:
   Ownership clauses in
   publishing agreements
Publisher responsibilities. *See*
   subhead: Publisher
   responsibilities
Representations/warranties. *See*
   subhead: Representations and
   warranties
Royalties. *See* subhead: Royalties
Termination of, 11.4.3.7,
   11.4.3.7.b–d
Term of, 11.4.3.1.e
Territory, 11.4.3.1.e
Winding-up, 11.4.3.7.e
Quality assurance, 11.4.3.5.e.2
Recoupable/non-recoupable funds,
   11.4.3.2.c
Recoupment deals, 11.3.2.2
Regulation of, 11.5
Representations and warranties
   Generally, 11.4.3.4
   Agreed union specifications,
      material compliance with,
      11.4.3.4.b
   "Easter eggs," 11.4.3.4.e
   Malicious code, 11.4.3.4.d
   Open source software, 11.4.3.4.c
   Third-party
      software/technology/tools,
      integration of, 11.4.3.4.a
   Trojan horses, 11.4.3.4.d
   Viruses, 11.4.3.4.d
Revenue from
   Gross revenue, 11.4.3.1.a
   Net revenue, 11.4.3.1.a

954   INDEX

Role-playing games, 11.1.3.4
Royalties
   Generally, 11.4.3.6
   Audits, 11.4.3.6.c
   Development advances,
      recoupment of, 11.4.3.6.b
   Payment terms, 11.4.3.6.d
   Recordkeeping, 11.4.3.6.c
   Royalty terms, 11.4.3.6.a
Self-funding of, 11.3.1
Simulation games, 11.1.3.5
Social media channels, 11.4.3.5.e.5
Social network games, 11.1.2.4
Sports games, 11.1.3.6
Strategy games, 11.1.3.7
Sublicensing development,
   11.4.3.5.d.3
Subscription(s)
   Generally, 11.1.4.2
   Pricing, 11.5.2.2
Technical infrastructure/operation(s),
   11.4.3.5.e.3
Types of, 11.1.3
Violent imagery, 11.5.3
Web sites, 11.4.3.5.e.5
Works for hire, 11.3.2.1
World narrative(s), 11.4.1.1

VIDEOGRAMS
Music royalties, 7.4.7.5

VIDEO ON DEMAND (VOD)
Motion picture distribution
   agreements, 2.8.5
Television, 4.3.1.5

VIRTUAL REALITY
Interactive media, 11.6.2

W

WARRANTIES. *See*
REPRESENTATIONS AND
WARRANTIES

WEB SITES
Music recording agreements, 7.4.3.5
Video games, 11.4.3.5.e.5

WINDOWS
Motion picture distribution
   agreements, 2.6

WORK(S) FOR HIRE
Loanout companies, 12.4.1.2
Publisher-funded video games,
   11.3.2.1
Unscripted television, independent
   contractor agreements, 5.5.5

WRITER AGREEMENTS
Motion picture development, 1.3.1

WRITING
Scripted television, 6.1.3.1.f